T0399305

THE OXFORD HANDBOOK OF

THE LATIN AMERICAN NOVEL

THE OXFORD HANDBOOK OF

THE LATIN AMERICAN NOVEL

Edited by

JUAN E. DE CASTRO

and

IGNACIO LÓPEZ-CALVO

OXFORD

UNIVERSITY PRESS

OXFORD
UNIVERSITY PRESS

Oxford University Press is a department of the University of Oxford. It furthers
the University's objective of excellence in research, scholarship, and education
by publishing worldwide. Oxford is a registered trade mark of Oxford University
Press in the UK and certain other countries.

Published in the United States of America by Oxford University Press
198 Madison Avenue, New York, NY 10016, United States of America.

CIP data is on file at the Library of Congress

ISBN 978–0–19–754185–2

DOI: 10.1093/oxfordhb/9780197541852.001.0001

Printed by Integrated Books International, United States of America

For Magdalena De Castro

For Gonzalo Alfonso López Calvo and Inés Sánchez Almagro

CONTENTS

PART IV: GENDER AND SEXUALITY

PART V: NARRATIVE TRENDS

PART VI: AUTHORS

PART VII: RECEPTION

Acknowledgments

The co-editors of *The Oxford Handbook of the Latin American Novel* would like to thank Holly Mitchell and especially Elda Granata, from Oxford University Press, for their confidence and for their unflagging help in bringing this project to fruition. We also want to extend our thanks to our contributors; if this *Handbook* is, as we believe, a major contribution to the understanding of the Latin American novel, it is due to their insight and brilliance. Finally, we also need to thank the many writers, from Carlos de Sigüenza y Góngora, in the seventeenth century, to Rita Indiana, in our time, whose works constitute the brilliant narrative tradition that this volume studies and celebrates.

CONTRIBUTORS

Gene H. Bell-Villada is the Harry C. Payne Professor of Romance Languages at Williams College. He has authored books on Borges and García Márquez. His wide-ranging history *Art for Art's Sake and Literary Life* was a finalist for the 1997 National Book Critics Circle Award. He has also published a memoir titled *Overseas American: Growing up Gringo in the Tropics* (2005).

Anadeli Bencomo is Professor of Latin American Literature and Cultural Studies at the University of Houston. She has published two books on Mexican narrative journalism and coedited two volumes on the Latin American short novel. Her current projects are on Mexican tropicalism (Acapulco) and on the audiobook format.

Nicholas Birns teaches at New York University and is the author of *The Hyperlocal in Eighteenth and Nineteenth-Century Literary Space* (2019). He is also co-editor of *Vargas Llosa and Latin American Politics* (2010), *Roberto Bolaño as World Literature* (2017), and editor of the forthcoming *Cambridge Companion to the Australian Novel*.

Mariana Bolívar Rubín holds a Ph.D. in Hispanic American literatures and cultures from the University of Colorado. Her interdisciplinary research approaches topics within race, gender, and trans-nationality in the context of Latin America and its diasporas in the United States. Currently, she examines Caribbean religions imaginaries in Latinx literature and film.

Persephone Braham (Ph.D., University of Pennsylvania) is Professor of Latin American and Caribbean Literature at the University of Delaware. She is the author of *From Amazons to Zombies: Monsters in Latin America* (2015) and *Crimes Against the State, Crimes Against Persons: Detective Fiction in Cuba and Mexico* (2004), and has published numerous articles on the Gothic, science fiction, detective literature, and the fantastic in Latin America.

Nanci Buiza is Associate Professor of Spanish at Swarthmore College, where she is also faculty in Peace and Conflict Studies, as well as Latin American and Latino Studies. Her work focuses on Mexican and Central American studies, particularly on issues of migration, violence, human rights, ethics, and postwar trauma.

Martín Camps is a poet and Professor of Spanish at the University of the Pacific. He is the author of *Cruces fronterizos: hacia una narrativa del desierto* (2008) and editor of *Dialogues on the Delta: Approaches to the City of Stockton* (2018), *La sonrisa afilada:*

Enrique Serna ante la crítica (2018), and *Transpacific Literary and Cultural Connections: Latin American Influence in Asia* (2020).

Alexis Candia-Cáceres is currently a researcher at the Center for Advanced Studies at the University of Playa Ancha, Chile. His research focuses on contemporary Latin American narrative: comparative studies of Roberto Bolaño's literature, representations of eroticism in Latin American narrative, and the construction of urban imaginaries in the city of Valparaíso, Chile.

Luiz Carlos Simon teaches Brazilian Literature at Londrina State University. He is the author of *Duas ou três páginas despretensiosas* (2011), on Rubem Braga and the *crônica*. His most recent projects focus on masculinities in Brazilian narratives and on a history of Brazilian novels from the late nineteenth century to the 1960s.

Amaryll Chanady is Professor of Comparative Literature at the University of Montreal, Canada. Among her publications are *Magical Realism and the Fantastic: Resolved versus Unresolved Antinomy* (2020), *Entre inclusion and exclusion: la symbolisation de l'autre dans les Amériques* (1999), and, as editor, *Latin American Identity and Constructions of Difference* (1993).

Raquel Chang-Rodríguez (Ph.D., New York University) is a Distinguished Professor of Hispanic literature and culture at the City College and the Graduate Center of the City University of New York. She is the author of *Cartografía garcilasista* (2013) and co-editor of *Talking Books with Mario Vargas Llosa. A Retrospective* (2020).

Christina E. Civantos teaches Hispanic and Arabic literary and cultural studies. Her research focuses on Arabic-speaking immigrants in Hispano-America and Spain, South-South relations between Latin America and the Arab world, empire and coloniality, nationalisms, language ideologies, memory studies, and tolerance. She is the author of three books and numerous essays.

Jorgelina Corbatta is Emerita Professor of Latin American Literature/Director of Women Studies at Wayne State University, and Academic Analyst and Associate Faculty at the Michigan Psychoanalytic Institute. She has taught at universities all around the world, published six books on literary criticism, and more than a hundred articles in peer-reviewed journals. She received a Fulbright Award, among several others.

Juan E. De Castro is Professor of Literary Studies at Eugene Lang College, The New School. He is the author of six books on Latin American culture, including *Writing Revolution in Latin America: From Martí to García Márquez to Bolaño* (2019) and *Bread and Beauty: The Cultural Politics of José Carlos Mariátegui* (2020).

Rita De Maeseneer is Professor Emeritus of Latin American Literature at the University of Antwerp, Belgium. She is an internationally renowned specialist in Spanish Caribbean literature and, particularly, Dominican literature. Some of her areas of interest are food studies, sensory studies, reception studies, intertextuality, formation of canon, and popular culture.

Francesca Denegri is Professor of Hispanic American Literature at the Pontifical Catholic University of Peru. She is the author of *El abanico y la cigarrera. La primera generación de ilustradas en el Perú* (1996, 2001, 2018) and *Soy señora. Testimonio de Irene Jara* (2000, 2021). She has also edited several books.

Fernando de Sousa Rocha is Associate Professor in the Department of Luso-Hispanic Studies at Middlebury College, Vermont. His main areas of research are in food studies and in Afro-Brazilian cultures, particularly in the areas of Afro-Brazilian religions and a reassessment of representations of slavery in Brazilian literature and culture.

Roberto Ignacio Díaz is Associate Professor of Spanish and Comparative Literature at the University of Southern California. He is the author of *Unhomely Rooms: Foreign Tongues and Spanish American Literature* (2002) and is presently writing a monograph on the historical and textual convergences of opera and Latin America.

Paul Dixon has taught Latin American Literature in Portuguese and Spanish at Purdue University since receiving his Ph.D. from the University of North Carolina in 1981. He has published five books and numerous articles, mostly about Machado de Assis.

Cecilia Esparza received her doctorate from New York University and is a professor in the Department of Humanities at the Pontifical Catholic University of Peru. She researches contemporary Spanish-American narratives, specializing in autobiographical writings.

Melissa A. Fitch is University Distinguished Professor at the University of Arizona. Since 2010, she has been researching the mutual cultural influences between the Americas and Asia, particularly China and India, found within popular culture, mass media, social media, and digital culture.

Ana Gallego Cuiñas is Professor of Latin American Literature and Dean of the Faculty of Philosophy and Letters at the University of Granada. Her most recent books are *Las novelas argentinas del siglo 21: Nuevos modos de producción, circulación y recepción* (2019), *Otros. Ricardo Piglia y la literatura mundial* (2019), and *Cultura literaria y políticas de mercado. Editoriales, ferias y festivales* (2022).

Javier García Liendo is Associate Professor of Hispanic Studies at Washington University in St. Louis. He specializes in Andean and Latin American cultural history and literature. His publications include *El intelectual y la cultura de masas: Argumentos latinoamericanos en torno a Ángel Rama y José María Arguedas* (2017).

José Eduardo González is Associate Professor of Spanish at the University of Nebraska-Lincoln. His current research employs a quantitative approach to study narrative form. His publications include *Appropriating Theory: Ángel Rama's Critical Work* (2017) and *Borges and the Politics of Form* (1998).

Sabine Köllmann is an independent scholar based in London. She is the author of *A Companion to Mario Vargas Llosa* (2014; paperback edition 2020) and *Vargas Llosa's Fiction and the Demons of Politics* (2002).

Andreas Kurz has a Ph.D. in Comparative Literature from the University of Vienna and is Professor of Hispanic Literature at the University of Guanajuato. He is the author of several books about nineteenth- and twentieth-century Latin American literature. He has published more than 150 articles in peer-reviewed journals, magazines, and cultural supplements.

Darrell B. Lockhart is Professor of Spanish and Vice-Provost at the University of Nevada, Reno. He is a specialist in Jewish-Latin American literature and cultural production, with numerous publications in this field. He is also a literary translator. Lockhart is currently co-president of the Latin American Jewish Studies Association.

Ignacio López-Calvo is Presidential Chair in the Humanities and Professor of Literature at the University of California, Merced. He is the author of nine books, including *The Mexican Transpacific: Nikkei Writing, Visual Arts, Performance* (2022) and *Saudades of Japan and Brazil: Contested Modernities in Lusophone Nikkei Cultural Production* (2019).

Benjamin Loy is a Lecturer of Romance Studies at the University of Vienna. His research areas include Modern and Contemporary Hispanic and French literature, theories and practices of translation, World Literature and global book markets, and the history of conservative and reactionary thinking and literature in France, Spain, and Latin America.

William Luis is the Gertrude Conaway Vanderbilt Professor of Spanish at Vanderbilt University, where he edits the *Afro-Hispanic Review*. He has authored, edited, and co-edited fourteen books and more than one hundred scholarly articles. Luis is regarded as a leading authority on Latin American, Caribbean, Afro-Hispanic, and Latino U.S. literatures.

Tracey Maher teaches Arabic literature at the University of South Florida. She has a Ph.D. in Middle Eastern Languages and Cultures (University of Texas at Austin, 2019), with a dissertation titled "Imagining Diaspora: Arabic Novels from Early 20th-Century Latin America." Her interests include Arabic literature and culture; migration, diaspora, and exile; and teaching Arabic as a foreign language.

Gorica Majstorovic is Professor of Spanish and Latin American Studies at Stockton University. She is the author of *Global South Modernities: Modernist Literature and the Avant-Garde in Latin America* (2020) and co-editor (with Axel Gasquet) of *Cultural and Literary Dialogues Between Asia and Latin America* (2021).

José Manuel Medrano is Assistant Professor of Spanish in the Department of World Languages and Cultures at St. Bonaventure University. He is the co-author of the book *90 años de la novela moderna en Colombia (1927–2017): de Fuenmayor a Potdevin* (2018).

Tamara L. Mitchell is Assistant Professor of Spanish at the University of British Columbia, Vancouver, where she specializes in twentieth- and twenty-first-century Latin American literatures and cultures. Her research examines the relationship among aesthetics, politics, and the literary tradition, with a focus on Mexican and Central American narrative fiction.

Jonathan B. Monroe is Professor of Comparative Literature and a member of the graduate fields of Comparative Literature, English, and Romance Studies at Cornell University. He is the author of *Framing Roberto Bolaño. Poetry, Fiction, Literary History, Politics* (2019) and editor of *Roberto Bolaño in Context* (forthcoming).

María Rosa Olivera-Williams is Professor of Latin American literature at the University of Notre Dame. Her research focuses on modern and contemporary Latin American literature and culture; women's literature and feminisms; memory studies; militant movements, dictatorships, and transitions to democracy in the Southern Cone; and popular culture, music, dance, and film.

Carolina Orloff is a translator and researcher in Latin American literature. In 2016, after obtaining her Ph.D. from the University of Edinburgh, she co-founded Charco Press, where she acts as publishing director. She is also the co-translator of Ariana Harwicz's *Die, My Love*, longlisted for the Booker International Prize (2018).

María Begoña Pulido Herráez is a member of the Research Center on Latin America and the Caribbean at the National Autonomous University of Mexico. She is the author of *Carlos Fuentes: imaginación y memoria* (2000), *Poéticas de la novela histórica contemporánea: La campaña, El general en su laberinto y El mundo alucinante* (2006), and *El Boletín Titikaka y la vanguardia andina* (2017).

Miguel Rocha Vivas is Associate Professor at the Pontifical Xavierian University, where he is the Director of the Center of Ecocriticism and Intercultural Studies. He won the National Prize for Research in Literature in 2009 and is the author of four anthologies of multilingual indigenous literatures. His *Mingas de la palabra* (2016) won the Casa de las Americas Award in Cuba in 2016.

Michael K. Schuessler is Professor of Humanities at the Universidad Autónoma Metropolitana, Cuajimalpa, in Mexico City. He is the author of several books, including *Elena Poniatowska: An Intimate Portrait* (2007) and *Foundational Arts: Mural Painting and Missionary Theater in New Spain* (2013).

Amanda M. Smith is Assistant Professor of Literature at the University of California, Santa Cruz, where she specializes in twentieth- and twenty-first-century Latin America. Her book *Mapping the Amazon: Literary Geography after the Rubber Boom* (2021) analyzes the political and ecological consequences of charting Amazonia in narrative fiction.

Doris Sommer is Professor of Romance Languages and Literatures, as well as African and African American Studies at Harvard University. She founded the "Cultural Agents

Initiative," to revive Humanism's civic mission. Sommer promotes www.pre-texts. org, an arts-based pedagogy for literacy, creativity, and citizenship. Her books include *Foundational Fictions* (1991) and *The Work of Art in the World* (2013).

Philip Swanson is Hughes Professor of Spanish at the University of Sheffield, United Kingdom. His many publications on Latin American literature include *José Donoso: The Boom and Beyond* (1988), *Cómo leer a Gabriel García Márquez* (1991), *The New Novel in Latin America: Politics and Popular Culture after the Boom* (1995); and the edited volumes *Landmarks in Modern Latin American Fiction* (1990), *The Companion to Latin American Studies* (2003) and *The Cambridge Companion to Gabriel García Márquez* (2010).

Maarten van Delden is Professor of Latin American Literature and Chair of the Department of Spanish and Portuguese at UCLA. He is the author of *Carlos Fuentes, Mexico, and Modernity* (1998), *Gunshots at the Fiesta* (with Yvon Grenier, 2009), and *Reality in Movement: Octavio Paz as Essayist and Public Intellectual* (2021), all published by Vanderbilt UP.

Vinodh Venkatesh is Professor of Spanish at Virginia Tech. He is the author of *Capitán Latinoamérica: Superheroes in Cinema, Television, and Web Series* (2020), *New Maricón Cinema: Outing Latin American Film* (2016), and *The Body as Capital: Masculinities in Contemporary Latin American Fiction* (2015).

Núria Vilanova is Associate Professor of World Languages and Cultures and Associate Dean of Undergraduate Studies at American University. Her research focuses on the literature of the Andean region and the Mexican-US border. She is the author of *The Impact of Social Change upon Peruvian Literature* (1970–1990) (1998) and *Border Texts: Writing Fiction from Northern Mexico* (2007).

Helene C. Weldt-Basson holds a Ph.D. from Columbia University and is Professor of Latin American literature at the University of North Dakota. She is a noted specialist on the Paraguayan writer Augusto Roa Bastos. She has published four single-authored books and three edited collections, as well as more than thirty peer-reviewed articles.

Claire Williams is Associate Professor in Brazilian Literature and Culture at the University of Oxford. Her research interests lie in women's writing and life-writing from the Portuguese-speaking world, and in contemporary Brazilian literature. She has published widely on Clarice Lispector, including a monograph and two co-edited collections of critical essays.

Raymond L. Williams is the author of nineteen single-authored books and holds the title of Distinguished Professor Emeritus. He specializes in modern Latin American narrative with an emphasis on Colombia and Mexico. His most recent book is *Novela y poder en Colombia y el Gran Tolima* (2019).

INTRODUCTION

JUAN E. DE CASTRO AND IGNACIO LÓPEZ-CALVO

IN English-language discussions about the history of Latin American literature, it is customary to note that, at one point, some of the most eminent Anglophone critics expressed their disdain for the region's cultural production. For instance, Edmund Wilson and Lionel Trilling, two of the arbiters of US culture during the first half of the twentieth century, found little of interest in the novel—or any other literary or cultural expression—of Latin America: the former, though a polyglot, proudly proclaimed his Hispanophobia, not having learned Spanish or read any Spanish-language works; the latter, finding the region's narrative only of "anthropological value."[1] This negative evaluation of the region's literature and, in particular, of narrative would temporarily be replaced by a euphoric reception in the 1960s and early 1970s, when the region's modern narrative started to be more widely translated. The works of Jorge Luis Borges (1899–1986) began to influence writers in the English-speaking world and beyond, particularly after 1961, when he, jointly with Samuel Beckett, was awarded the Formentor Prix International, a once-in-a-lifetime award given to the then-greatest living writer. The rise of the so-called Boom novelists—Julio Cortázar (Argentina, 1914–1984), Carlos Fuentes (Mexico, 1928–2012), Mario Vargas Llosa (Peru, 1936–), and Gabriel García Márquez (Colombia, 1927–2014)—solidified this interest. In particular, the English-language translation of García Márquez's masterwork *Cien años de soledad* (*One Hundred Years of Solitude*, 1967) in 1970 caused a stir not only in North America and Europe, but also throughout the rest of the world, including the Global South.

However, this interest in the Latin American novel would be shown to be ultimately superficial. In addition to the intrinsic quality of the works being translated, it reflected the stir caused by the Cuban Revolution, which had come to power in 1959. As interest in the Cuban Revolution waned—not only due to the revolution's political hardening, but also because of the limits of North American and European attention spans—so did interest in the region's literature. While (some) Latin American writers continued to be translated and celebrated—one can mention Manuel Puig (Argentina, 1932–1990), especially his *El beso de la mujer araña* (*Kiss of the Spider Woman*, 1976), which was adapted into a successful English-language film by Argentine-Brazilian Héctor Babenco in 1985, and the more commercially minded Isabel Allende (Chile, 1942–) and Paulo Coelho (1947–),[2] the latter perhaps the most widely read Brazilian writer—it would only be until the English-language publication of *Los detectives salvajes* (*The Savage Detectives*, 1998) by Roberto Bolaño (Chile, 1953–2003), in 2007, that curiosity about the region's novel was rekindled. (However, not even the popularity of Bolaño, or, for that matter, any other non-Anglophone writer has been able to stem the ever-decreasing number of literary translations in the United States). Therefore, from European and US perspectives, in addition to being a relatively new phenomenon—since it is seen as having only reached maturity in the 1960s—Latin American literature and, especially, the novel, is of only intermittent interest.

However, as will be seen in the chapter on the Boom, Vargas Llosa, García Márquez, Cortázar, and García Márquez actually held similar views about the history of the Latin American novel. García Márquez, in his memoirs *Vivir para contarla* (*Living to Tell the Tale*, 2002), recalls having discovered, already in his youth, what he considered defects in the writings of Rómulo Gallegos (Venezuela, 1884–1969), the then-preeminent Venezuelan and, arguably, Latin American novelist: "I was beginning to see the seams in our native novel" (29).[3] If the "native," *vernácula* (vernacular) novel in García Márquez's Spanish original *Vivir para contarla* was technically flawed, for García Márquez, it was in the European and North American modernists that the true craft of novel-writing could be learned.

Needless to say, the Boom writers' dismissal of their predecessors is nothing but a generational attempt at opening a space for their works within the international literary circles. Instead of rejecting the view of the region's literature as inferior held by the center, as exemplified by Wilson or Trilling, the Boom novelists embraced it while insisting on their difference from previous generations of Latin American authors. After all, Vargas Llosa, García Márquez, Fuentes, and Cortázar, among other writers, could now place themselves in a genealogy that included no less than the modernist masters of the novel: James Joyce, Franz Kafka, Marcel Proust, and Virginia Woolf, among others. For instance, in 1950, a young García Márquez wrote:

> The novel, undoubtedly and fortunately influenced by Joyce, Faulkner or Virginia Woolf has not yet been written in Colombia. I say fortunately, because I don't believe that Colombians can now be an exception to the flow of influences. In her Prologue to *Orlando*, Virginia Woolf confesses her influences. Faulkner himself could not deny the influence that Joyce has had on him. . . . Franz Kafka and Proust roam free over the literature of the modern world. If we Colombians were to make the right decision, we would need to irremediably join this current.
>
> ("¿Problemas de la novela?" 213)[4]

One Hundred Years of Solitude, as well as other key works of the Boom, such as Fuentes's *La muerte de Artemio Cruz* (*The Death of Artemio Cruz*, 1962), Vargas Llosa's *La ciudad y los perros* (*The Time of the Hero*, 1963), and Cortázar's *Rayuela* (*Hopscotch*, 1963), would be an example of the novel demanded by García Márquez more than a decade before the Boom hit its stride.

A Long Tradition

However, as the essays in this *Handbook*, obviously written long after the Boom's parricidal gesture, point out, the novels of the Boom, as well as those of later writers, can be seen as instances in a long tradition. Instead of intermittency, the region's narrative and, specifically, the novel, has a continuous history. In fact, as, in different manners, Vargas Llosa and Rodríguez Monegal noted, there was an important modernist tradition in Latin America that was roughly contemporary and in dialogue with that of Europe. Limiting ourselves to narrative, authors such as Mário de Andrade (Brazil, 1893–1945), Martín Adán (born Ramón Rafael de la Fuente, Peru, 1908–1985), and Pablo Palacio (Ecuador, 1906–1947) wrote major modernist narratives—*Macunaíma* (1928), *La casa de cartón* (*The Cardboard House*, 1928), and *Un hombre muerto a puntapiés* (A Man Kicked to Death, 1927), respectively—during the heyday of modernism and the avant-garde.

But the Latin American narrative tradition goes much further back. According to Raquel Chang-Rodríguez's chapter in this volume, "novels were . . . written and published in viceregal Spanish America. Some circulated in manuscript form among the cultural elite, while others were printed and enjoyed a wider readership." As she also notes, "the most representative works of the genre written by Peninsular authors also were disseminated in colonial Spanish America." Colonial writers were thus inheritors of arguably the richest novelistic tradition in the Western world during the sixteenth and seventeenth centuries, producing masterpieces such as Fernando de Rojas's *La Celestina* (*Celestina*, 1499), *El Lazarillo de Tormes* (anonymous, *The Life of Lazarillo de Tormes*, 1554) and *Don Quijote de La Mancha* (*Don Quixote* 1605, 1615), by Miguel de Cervantes. Additionally, the region's narrators were inheritors of the seventeenth-century Spanish *crónicas de conquista* (chronicles of conquest) and *cartas de relación* (letters or dispatches with a personal account of the conquest or exploration), which, blending historical discourse and fiction, attempted to depict the New World brutally conquered and created by the conquistadors and the first colonists. These include such major historical and literary masterworks as Bernal Díaz del Castillo's (1495/1496–1584) *Historia verdadera de la conquista de la Nueva España* (*The Conquest of the New Spain*, 1575, published in 1632). Other colonial texts were written by mestizos born in the Americas, such as the monumental *Comentarios Reales de los Incas* (*Royal Commentaries of the Incas*, 1609), written by Inca Garcilaso de la Vega (1539–1616), the son of a conquistador and an Inca princess.

Of course, before the arrival of the conquistadors, there were distinct indigenous literary traditions, whether these be oral, written on codices, in glyphs and/or pictographs, or in alternative writing systems, such as the Andean quipu. It is true that, in addition to a handful of surviving codices, some of these writings were partially archived after the incoming of the Europeans, such as Nahuatl poetry, or creation and other myths, such as the Mayan *Popol Vuh* or the Andean *Manuscrito de Huarochirí* (*Huarochirí Manuscript*). One can also mention the indigenous chronicles of the conquest, such as *El primer nueva corónica y buen gobierno* (*The First New Chronicle and Good Government*, c. 1615), by Guamán Poma de Ayala. However, while these texts serve as proof of the literary vitality of pre-conquest and early post-conquest indigenous cultures, given that they were only rediscovered in the late nineteenth and twentieth centuries, they did not exert influence on the region's novelists and narrators, until more recent times, with the novels of writers such as the Guatemalan Miguel Ángel Asturias (1899–1974) or the Peruvian José María Arguedas (1911–1969).

It is, therefore, not surprising that the work often seen as the first fully formed Spanish-language Latin American novel, the multivolume *El Periquillo Sarniento* (*The Mangy Parrot*, 1816–1831) written by José Joaquín Fernández de Lizardi (1776–1827) and published in Mexico, can be loosely classified as a picaresque novel.[5] Even if by 1816, other narrative trends were dominant in the international novel, the fact is that Lizardi was able to continue this Hispanic narrative tradition, adapting it to a new location and new cultural and political trends.

Doris Sommer writes, in her chapter in this *Handbook*, "Mexico is the hero of his book, in all its registers of language and racial variety. Mexico could become, for Lizardi, a cosmopolitan member of an Enlightened family of nations." Sommer also notes that, after *El Periquillo Sarniento*, many of the region's nineteenth-century novels, such *O Guarani* (*The Guarany* 1857) by Brazilian José de Alencar (1829–1877), *María* (1867) by Colombian Jorge Isaacs (1837–1895), or *Enriquillo* (*The Cross and the Sword* 1882) by Dominican Manuel Jesús de Galván (1834–1910), were "national romances" that allegorized in their plots the kind of multicultural and multiracial alliances that were necessary for the creation of the new Latin American nations: "Stability and prosperity depended on making deals and learning to live together. The literary training project to foster alliances took advantage of the irresistible language of love." Moreover, even if in dialogue with works from other regions, such as North America, represented by James Fenimore Cooper's (1789–1851) *The Last of the Mohicans* (1826), these novels fulfilled a "foundational function" in the new Latin American republics, as Sommer notes.

Even those works that Trilling described as being only of "anthropological" value—the realist, often socially conscious, narrative that was often produced in the region until the rise of the new modernist novels—are being reread from post-modernist and post-colonial perspectives. Thus, according to Begoña Pulido, in this *Handbook*, "social realism's incorporation of both literary and non-literary styles, its setting up of a dialogue among these, is certainly literary and innovative, regardless of the quality achieved. In this sense, it would be interesting to reconsider the place of social realism in current redefinitions of hybrid genres, such as testimony, non-fiction novel, and literary chronicle." In other words, as the values that informed modernist writing, such as privileging originality and difficulty over communication, become themselves old-fashioned, the "pre-modernist" narrative of the region has begun to undergo a process of revaluation. And, though obviously, with enormous differences, including the important influence of the Boom, contemporary authors, such as Alfredo Bryce Echenique (Peru, 1939–) or Ricardo Piglia (Argentina, 1941–2017), and the much younger Samantha Schweblin (Argentina, 1978–), are also indebted to such pre-Boom authors as José Diez Canseco (Peru, 1904–1949), Roberto Arlt (Argentina, 1900–1942), and María Luisa Bombal (Chile, 1910–1980), respectively.

The fact that this *Handbook* includes individual chapters based on a chronological vision of the Latin American novel, as well as others responding to schools and styles, including regionalism, the Boom, and the Post-Boom and postmodern narrative—does not imply a belief, as was the case with the Boom writers, in the history of the Latin American novel as composed of discrete and ultimately disconnected periods and trends. Without necessarily denying the critical validity of these stylistic and chronological divisions, the structure of this volume should be seen as representing a didactic purpose, as well as the actual existence of these periods and styles. However, this stress on tradition is not incompatible with a similar emphasis on its masterworks and its authors. The *Handbook*, therefore, also includes chapters on such major figures, as the four Boom authors, Juan Rulfo (Mexico, 1917–1986), Clarice Lispector (Brazil, 1920–1977), as well as more recent writers, such as Puig, Mexican Elena Poniatowska (1932–), and Rita Indiana (Dominican Republic, 1977–).

Is There Such a Thing as Latin America?

As singer and public intellectual Caetano Veloso once noted, Brazil is often presented in his country's schools and media "as an independent continent, a huge island in the middle of the South Atlantic" discovered on its own by Pedro Cabral,[6] the Portuguese explorer (3). The belief in the cultural distance between Brazil and Spanish America here expressed by Veloso is far from idiosyncratic or limited to the Portuguese-speaking nation. Walter Mignolo, for instance, reminds us that "Brazil was marginal to the idea of 'Latin' America" as developed in the Hispanophone countries (159). Therefore, when reading this *Handbook*, one must keep in mind that the novelistic traditions of Spanish-speaking countries of Latin America and Portuguese-speaking Brazil mostly developed separately. However, based on the frequent similarities and analogies in the development of the country's literature with that of the Spanish-speaking countries of the region, on critical custom, as well as for heuristic purposes, several of the chapters in the *Handbook* include Brazilian authors together with those of what used to be called Spanish America. Despite its putative insularity, the development of Brazilian literature followed similar patterns to those of the region's Spanish-speaking countries. As we have seen, one can classify Alencar's *O Guarany*, as well as his *Iracema* (1865), among the Latin American national romances. Also, *O Cortiço* (*The Slum* 1890) by Brazilian Aluísio Azevedo (1857–1913) was, together with *En la sangre* (In the Blood, 1887) by Argentinian Eugenio Cambaceres (1843–1888) and *Santa* (1903) by Mexican Federico Gamboa (1864–1939), among the major realist/naturalist novels written in the late nineteenth century. The same parallel development characterizes Portuguese and Spanish language modernism and the avant-garde—confusingly (for Spanish speakers) known in Brazil as *modernismo*, thus sharing the name of the earlier Hispanic poetic movement led by the Nicaraguan Rubén Darío (1867–1916). As noted above, Brazilian *modernismo* produced such major works as Mario de Andrade's *Macunaíma*, as well as *Memórias sentimentais de João Miramar* (João Miramar's Sentimental Memoirs 1924) by Oswald de Andrade (1890–1954). Likewise, the early works of Jorge Amado (1912–2001), such as *Capitães de areia* (*Captains of the Sand*, 1937), exemplify the social-realist vein characteristic of much Latin American narrative during the first half of the twentieth century. Moreover, the "new novel" and the "Boom" writers can be seen as having such major Brazilian analogues in João Guimarães Rosa (1908–1967) and Clarice Lispector (1920–1977).

The similarity between the literary traditions in these two linguistic regions can, however, obfuscate significant differences. After all, while the nineteenth-century Spanish American novel found its conclusion in the realist narratives of Chilean Alberto Blest Gana (1830–1920) or the early *indigenismo* of Peruvian Clorinda Matto de Turner (1852–1909), in Brazil it led to the works of the author often considered the master not only of his country's narrative but of its literary tradition: Joaquim Machado de Assis (1839–1908). As Vargas Llosa states, precisely as he dismisses his Spanish-language predecessors, "the work of Machado de Assis endowed prose fiction with a dimension which would not be attained in Spanish America until the twentieth century" (7). Machado de Assis's early novels can be classified within romantic parameters exemplified, for instance, by Alencar, especially in the latter's novels set in urban settings, such as *Senhora* (*Senhora: Profile of a Woman*, 1875). However, with *Memórias póstumas de Brás Cubas* (*Posthumous Memoirs of Brás Cubas*, 1881), Machado broke with all romantic, realist, and naturalist narrative frames. What Paul Dixon notes about *Dom Casmurro* (1899), in his essay for our volume, is applicable to all of Machado's mature work: "the novel transcends that realistic project, universalizing its themes, couching them within overarching literary traditions, and above all, enthroning subjective relativity as a more realistic kind of realism." The fact that Machado de Assis is relatively little known in the Spanish-speaking world, despite the fact that *Memórias póstumas* was first translated into Spanish in 1902, while Borges, García Márquez, and Bolaño are widely read in Brazil, shows that the borders between both linguistic regions have also been built with Hispanic hands. One must note, however, that, in addition to Coelho's bestsellers, Lispector's narrative is widely read in the Spanish-speaking countries of Latin America. In addition to her work's enormous intrinsic value, Lispector's popularity may have been also caused by her work being championed by such well-known critics as the French feminist Hélène Cixous, as well as by the success of the Spanish-language version of Benjamin Moser's biography. Nevertheless, Machado, despite his centrality to the Brazilian literary tradition, "remains a famous writer only known by a few" in Brazil's Hispanic neighbors (Espinosa Domínguez 68).[7]

But additionally, there have been moments when the Spanish-speaking mainstream, on occasion even the region as a whole, has attempted to imagine itself as constituting some kind of unity. Among these, one can mention the following: the period of the struggles for independence (1810–1824); the late nineteenth century as a response to the Spanish-American war (1898); the 1920s, when the Mexican and Russian

Revolutions, as well as the reaction against the rising wave of US imperialism (for instance, in Nicaragua), led to a growing sense of continental identity; or the 1960s, when, in addition to the enthusiasm generated by the Cuban Revolution, economic growth and the concomitant rise of literacy and higher education created a continental market for the Boom authors. These periods represent moments when a shared sense of Latin Americanness was culturally celebrated and stressed. But the relative fragility of this pan-Latin American identity, or at least, the fragility of its material basis, is evidenced by the fact that by the early 1990s, when Chilean novelists Sergio Gómez (1962–) and Alberto Fuguet (1963–) began compiling their influential short-story anthology *McOndo*, they discovered to their chagrin that "Despite the marvels of communication . . . communication with foreign countries was . . . difficult, backwards, scarce, and developed at a slower rhythm than expected" (12).[8] Underlying their sense of isolation from anything resembling a Latin American community of writers is the fact that the 1980s had been a decade in which the region suffered one of its worst economic setbacks. The pan-Latin American ethos characteristic of the 1960s, which one must remember was of greater importance among Spanish-language writers than among Portuguese-language ones, had been undermined by the breakdown of the region's markets.

However, by 1996, the year of publication of *McOndo*, a process of social and economic change was firmly in place, and not only when it came to communication media. As Ana Gallego Cuiñas points out in her chapter included in this *Handbook*, "Latin American narrative of the twenty-first century has its roots in the 1990s, when three global phenomena fully impacted the book market: post-Fordist capitalism, neoliberal globalization, and the development of new technologies." Ironically, it is global publishing corporations that have reconstituted the Latin American, often pan-Hispanic, market, even if one can question whether any putative Latin American identity has also been fully reconstituted.[9]

Given the fragility of the notion of Latin America—a statement that should not be taken as a denial of its existence as a cultural idea, of the concept's usefulness in understanding the region's literature, or of its importance in the literary production of specific authors, and, therefore, of the interpretation of their works—it is also necessary to study the region's novelistic output from the perspective of its (sub)regions. Thus, one can see close commonalities not only among novelists working within national traditions, such as Mexico or Brazil—but also among those writing in Central America, the Caribbean, the Andean regions, and the Southern Cone, to mention the geographical groupings used in this book. But while geographic and cultural considerations help explain certain (sub)regional developments, such as *indigenismo* in the Andean region, or the novel of the "Mexican Revolution" in, naturally, Mexico, there are other traditions that are investigated in the *Handbook*.

For instance, while, at least until recently, there has not been much communication among indigenous authors, to a great degree due to the unfortunate cultural and social marginalization experienced by their communities, there have often been recurrent developments in their narrative and, often, shared attitudes. As Miguel Rocha points out in his article on the indigenous novel and, in particular, Antonio Joaquín López Epieyuu's foundational indigenous novel *Los dolores de una raza* (A Race's Sorrows, 1956/1957), one of the key characteristics of a text written by an indigenous author is that their "perspective . . . originates from a community 'we.'" Obviously, this communal perspective differs significantly from the individualist authorial position characteristic of Western writers, including those from Latin America. More recently, novels written in indigenous languages in Abya Yala, as indigenous activists often prefer to call the Western Hemisphere, have entered the book markets, even if these texts have often been published together with a Spanish or Portuguese translation. Therefore, given the variety in cultures and languages among the diverse indigenous communities, indigenous narrative is clearly differentiated from Hispanophone and Lusophone novelistic traditions. But, of course, indigenous authors do not constitute the only tradition within Latin American literature. The *Handbook*, therefore, includes chapters on the Afro-Latin American novel, the Asian-Latin American novel, as well as articles on novels written by Women, LBGTQ+ authors, and more.

DIASPORAS

One must, however, remember that while indigenous people, Europeans, both Spaniards and Portuguese, and people of African ancestry, mostly enslaved, but on occasion as conquistadors, participated in what once was called the "encounter of two worlds," but is more rightly described as an invasion, many other ethnic and cultural groups have also contributed to Latin American culture. Already during colonial days, the Manilla Galleon, which connected the Philippines with the rest of the vice-royalty of New Spain, brought what would become Latin America in contact with Asia. This material and cultural commerce between Asia and Latin America would increase after independence. Many East Asian immigrants were tricked into emigrating to Latin America as indentured servants brought to progressively replace enslaved people (many worked along with enslaved Africans), as a result of British pressure against the Atlantic slave trade. Arabs, mostly Christian ones from the Levant (Syria, Lebanon, and Palestine) in what then was the Ottoman Empire, came in search of greater freedoms. But Asia, including the near East as well as North Africa, were not the only continents from which migrants came to Latin America. While Jewish migrants came to Latin America from the beginnings of its colonization, often escaping from the ever-growing restrictions experienced in the Iberian Peninsula—one must remember that in 1492 Spanish Jews were forced to choose between living in Spain and their religion—in the twentieth century many Jews emigrated to the region escaping from pogroms, discrimination, and death in Europe. This *Handbook*, therefore, includes chapters analyzing the writing of East Asian, Arab, and Jewish immigrants and their descendants in Latin America, which brings new concerns and outlooks to the region's novel.

STRUCTURE OF THE BOOK

Written by over forty experts from Latin America, the United States, and Europe, and from diverse critical perspectives, *The Oxford Handbook of the Latin American Novel* attempts to provide as complete a survey of the region's novelistic production as possible. The first group of articles in the *Handbook* attempts to provide a chronological survey of the region's novelistic production. The opening chapter, "The Novel in the Colonial Period," by Raquel Chang-Rodríguez, looks at how novels developed and circulated in colonial Spanish America. Discussing both well-known and rediscovered novels, it discloses the main obstacles to their production, including censorship, a limited reading public, emphasis on publishing religious books, and competition from Spanish authors. According to Chang-Rodríguez, although initially embedded in European literary traditions, New World novels eventually developed a new literary sensibility.

Doris Sommer's "A Picaresque Parrot and Decent Domesticity: Novel Nations in Latin America" analyzes the genre's contribution to the creation of new national imaginaries. After the revolutions of independence, we learn, a canon of national romances, typically written by founding fathers, appeared roughly between the 1850s and 1880s. Through the language of love, these novels projected a path toward national reconciliation and economic growth. José Joaquín Fernández de Lizardi's *El Periquillo Sarniento* (*The Mangy Parrot: The Life and Times of Periquillo Sarniento Written by himself for his Children*; written in 1816) opened the way to this new type of novel with an irreverent, baroque adventure story that foreshadowed the upcoming anti-colonial resistance.

Paul Dixon's "The Nineteenth-century Brazilian Novel and the Transcendence of Machado de Assis" provides a survey of the first century of Brazil's narrative, as well as of the author whose novels serve as its capstone. Beyond any other Brazilian novelist, Dixon explains, Machado de Assis transcended the influence of European romanticism, realism, and naturalism to create a personal aesthetic that incorporated the local flora, fauna, and human geography. He also adopted a digressive, associative style, engaged in metafictional discourse, described the dynamics of his own narrative and of literature in general, and resorted to narrators who encouraged their readers to find more independent ways of reading.

The study of the twentieth-century Latin American novel is begun by Tamara Mitchell and Amanda M. Smith, whose "The Regional Novel and the Novel of the Mexican Revolution on Common Ground" investigates the most characteristic early-twentieth-century genres. In particular, Mitchell and Smith offer an alternative reading of the telluric novel or novel of the land by José Eustasio Rivera, Rómulo Gallegos, Ricardo Güiraldes, and Horacio Quiroga, and of the novels of the Mexican Revolution, including Rulfo's *Pedro Páramo* (1955) and recent novels by Laia Jufresa and Juan Villoro, by exploring their contributions to the current ecological turn in Latin American literature. In "Social realism, *indigenismo*, and the vindication of the other," Begoña Pulido Herráez continues the study of the socially minded novel of the first half of the twentieth century, showing its complex, heterogeneous, and varied nature. Pulido Herráez places these social-realist and *indigenista* novels in their specific historical, social, and political contexts, a process that, in her view, explains their artistic form and even their hybridity with myth or sociological essays.

For his part, Philip Swanson's "The New Novel in Latin America (1920–1950)" studies the first generation of avant-garde and modernist novelists in the region, whose works were often overlooked in favor of the later Boom novels. Swanson explores the dialogue between these works—which respond to a quest for Latin American identity and for rupturing literature's link to reality while still seeking to comment on it—and the Novel of the Land, French surrealism, and modernism. In "The Latin American Novel in the 1960s and Early 1970s: The Boom and Beyond," Juan E. De Castro looks at the novels that brought the region's narrative to the world, focusing in particular on the Boom authors' relationship with Latin American modernist narrative, which began in the 1920s. He also reveals the connections between this literary Boom with the economic, commercial, and political realities that made it possible, all the while exploring the reasons underlying the exclusion from the Boom of authors such as José María Arguedas. Elena Garro, and Rosario Castellanos.

In "The Postmodern Novel and the Post-Boom in Latin America," José Manuel Medrano and Raymond L. Williams analyze the novels written during the last decades of the twentieth century. After providing a review of the avant-gardes and revisiting the terms "modern," "postmodern," and "Post-Boom," they focus on authors they consider postmodern and those who are part of the Post-Boom. As they explain, while the postmodern novel questions dominant discourses and is characterized by disruption, discontinuity, decentering, dislocation, indeterminacy, and antilocalization, the Post-Boom, which insisted on storytelling, constitutes a reaction against the hyperexperimentation of the modern novel of the 1960s Boom. The chronological study is concluded by Ana Gallego Cuiñas who, in "Latin American Narrative in the Late Twentieth and Early Twenty-First Century," not only analyzes some of the most influential current writers in the region, but also stresses the changes in global book publishing that impact today's novelistic practice, including the consolidation of the large Spanish publishing conglomerates and the growth of independent publishing, fairs, and festivals. After 2001, adds Gallego Cuiñas, there was a proliferation of new aesthetic and narrative styles that reflected both national and global identities.

The second set of articles studies the region's novel from geographical and cultural perspectives. It begins with "From the Center to the Margins: Itineraries of Modernity in the Mexican Novel," a survey of the country's novel written by Martín Camps. From Fernández de Lizardi's *El Periquillo Sarniento* it moves to the Mexican reception of realism and naturalism, the "Ateneo de la juventud" (Mexican Youth Athenaeum) movement, and the novel of the Mexican Revolution. Camps then focuses on the 1920s and 1930s, the rise of avant-garde movements, and the start of the modern novel. He then analyzes the literature of the 1960s, the novels of La Onda (The Wave), the generation of the "Crack" during the 1990s, writers from northern Mexico, and younger generations women writers.

For her part, Nanci Buiza provides a survey of the novel in Central America from the early twentieth century (the *modernista* and *costumbrista* traditions) to the present. Along the way, she explores the documentary realism that engaged the region's agro-export dependency and military regimes, the rise of the testimonial novel, the reflection of the wave of state terror and left-wing insurrections from the 1960s to the 1980s, the post-war Central American novel, the various narrative modes through which novelists responded to the depredations of neoliberalism and urban violence, and the Central American novel's most recent developments, dealing with questions of gender, race, indigeneity, environmentalism, diaspora, and migration.

In "Imagined Multitudes in The Spanish-Language Caribbean Novel," Mariana Bolívar surveys the literary movements that have shaped the novel in the region, emphasizing the interruptions that the multitude causes in the national imaginaries created in these novels. Drawing from Hardt and Negri's notion of "multitude" and Giorgio Agamben's "coming community," she addresses the configurations of the multitude as unfinished imagined communities unveiling forms of political organization beyond the confines of the modern nation-state, and as political actors disaffected by the failure of modern capitalism. Nuria Vilanova studies how the novel constructs the imaginary of the Andes in "The Andean Novel: The (De)Construction of a Written Territory." From its beginnings in the nineteenth century, Vilanova examines the paternalistic approach of the *indigenista* novel, and then, still within the framework of the Andean novel, the literary reflection of the confrontation between the terrorist group Shining Path and the Peruvian state by the end of the twentieth century. She also analyzes how Vargas Llosa depicts the Andes as a trope of desolation, hostility, and violence. The chapter also points out how and why Colombia did not develop an *indigenista* novel akin to that of the other Andean countries.

Goriça Majstorovic offers a chronological survey of "The Southern Cone Novel (Argentina, Chile, Uruguay, and Paraguay)," beginning with the critical role that the novel played in nation formation throughout the nineteenth century, going through the Argentine *Novelas de la Bolsa* (Novels of the Stock Exchange), the realist novel, and ending with Roberto Bolaño, the digital revolution, the electronic literature of today, and the contemporary "boom" of women writers. Majstorovic also surveys the regionalist novel, the modern urban novel, the novel focusing on urban alienation, and women novelists who, writing under a pseudonym, challenged patriarchal impositions.

In the concluding chapter of this section, "The Brazilian Novel: An Outline from the Nineteenth to the Twenty-first Century," Fernando de Sousa Rocha and Luiz Carlos Simon provide an overview from the early 1840s to the present. Following a chronological organization, the chapter is divided into five sections: 1840s to the 1870s, centered on romanticism; 1880s to the 1910s, focusing on realism and naturalism; 1920s to 1940s, devoted to different forms of modernisms; 1950s to 1980s, foregrounding the novels' reengagement with new forms of literary language; finally, the last section is dedicated to contemporary fiction.

The *Handbook* continues with a group of articles that examine the novelistic practice of minority groups. As mentioned earlier, in "The Indigenous Novel: *Los dolores de una raza*, a Forerunner work," Miguel Rocha uses López Epieyuu's presentation of the Wayuu community's internal conflicts and intercultural challenges as a starting point to study other related issues, including internalized colonialism and historical and auto-ethnographic discourses, as well as the dialectical tensions between civilization and barbarism, and the Ladino-Mestizo and the Indian.

William Luis, in "The Afro-Latin American Novel and the Novel about Afro-Latin Americans," provides a review of the novelistic production by Afro–Latin American authors, as well as a survey of some of the main attempts at representing Black characters by the region's mainstream. Luis analyzes works by Juan Francisco Manzano, Cirilo Villaverde, and others, all the way to the newest voices, including the authors of Caribbean descent Junot Díaz, Dahlma Yanos-Figueroa, and Veronica Chambers.

Darrell Lockhart's "The Jewish-Latin American Novel" reviews some of the key works by writers of that ethnic group, primarily throughout the twentieth and twenty-first centuries. Structured as a thematical survey of the Jewish novel (not only novels written by Jewish authors, but also those in which Jews, Jewishness, and Judaism are central to the theme), the essay focuses on topics such as the novel of immigration and assimilation, the (new) historical novel, novels of the Holocaust, the (neo)Sephardic novel, family narratives, the gay/lesbian/queer novel, and the auto/biographical novel. In "The Arab Novel of Latin America," Christina Civantos and Tracey Maher examine novels written by Arabic-speaking immigrants to Latin America and their descendants, addressing how they were concerned with problems in both the home country and the *mahjar* or place of emigration. The chapter points out that the Arab Latin American novel includes works written in Arabic, Spanish, and Portuguese, and engages multiple languages, dialects, and registers, as well as the literary heritage of both the Arab world and Latin America.

In "The Asian-Latin American Novel," Ignacio López-Calvo studies Nikkei novels and authors from Brazil, Peru, Argentina, and Chile, as well as the main novels by authors of Chinese ancestry in Peru, Panama, and Costa Rica. He claims that the increasing cultural production by Latin American and Caribbean authors of Chinese and Japanese ancestries in recent decades reflects the emergence of two diasporic, minority discourses that are redefining national cultures by making them more transnational and by calling into question the White-indigenous and White-Black dichotomies of the discourses of *mestizaje* and *mulataje*, respectively.

The novels written by women are explored in two chapters. The first, "Nineteenth-Century Women Writers and the Nation," by Francesca Denegri, not only reviews a significant nineteenth-century body of work that was unfairly marginalized in the official histories of Latin American literature, but also looks at the complex relationship between national and gender ideology in these novels, as well as between the literary field and the consolidation of the new republics, especially in the second half of the century. Denegri also examines the strategies used by these women authors against the dominant patriarchal discourse. "Twentieth-Century Women Writers and the Feminist Novel," Mario Rosa Olivera-Williams continues the study of novels written after 1950, when women ventured into a genre they had barely published in the past. The chapter traces, through the evolution of the novel, the multiple positions taken by Latin American feminism until the end of the twentieth century. "Form and Difference in the Latin American LGBTQ Novel" by Vinodh Venkatesh reveals the connection between literary form and content in non-heteronormative novels beginning with Adolfo Caminha in Brazil during the nineteenth century, until the early twenty-first century, with authors such as Mayra Santos-Febres and Pedro Lemebel. He also offers an overview of the state of Latin American LGBTQ literary studies, identifying key theorists and concepts, and touchstone novels, which are then grouped according to criteria such as confessional monologue, musical novel, historical fiction, and the fantastical novel.

The next group of articles studies diverse sub-genres of the region's novel. In "The Latin American Historical Novel Through the Lens of the Dictator(ship) Novel," Helene Weldt-Basson explores the nature and evolution of historical fiction in Latin America from the nineteenth century to the present through the lens of the dictator (and dictatorship) novel. Among its main characteristics, she underscores the exploration of national identity as well as the use of magical realism, historical symbolism, and historical intertextuality. As to its evolution, Weldt-Basson highlights the turn toward feminism and postcolonialism, and the transition from the portrayal of concrete dictatorships directly experienced to the memory of dictatorship by second-generation writers. Amaryll Chanady's "Magical Realism and the Marvelous Real in the Novel" analyzes two literary modes that have inaccurately become synonymous with the region's narrative. She defines both terms, highlights parallels and distinctions, and analyzes key novels. Chanady also discusses controversies surrounding them and explores the connections between these modes and ethnographic fiction, primitivism, hybridity, cultural heterogeneity, transculturation, postcolonial theory, postmodernism, discourses of identity, the pluriverse, and the ecology of others.

Cecilia Esparza's "The Testimonial Novel and Autofiction" begins studying the period when *testimonio* seemed to bring non-lettered voices into the canon and concludes by analyzing, all the way to today's autofiction, which, blurring the boundaries between autobiography and the novel, has become the most widely used mode of writing by young writers. Esparza examines the most influential testimonial novels as well as the critical and theoretical discussion about these works, which appeared in the 1960s with the political intention of denouncing the violence and historical experiences of discrimination faced by marginalized communities. She also analyzes autofiction as a strategy or authorial figuration, beginning with those narratives that are close to the autobiographical novel and the literature of memory, and concluding with those characterized by metafictional play. Persephone Braham studies, in "Popular Fictions and Artistic Narrative: Detective Fiction, Science Fiction, and Fantasy in Latin America," how these genres have been practiced by several major authors, including Borges, Fuentes, and Vargas Llosa. Braham divides her chapter into four sections: detective and crime fiction; speculative and science fiction; fantasy, horror, and the gothic; and genre reading. The final section demonstrates how genre criticism applied to canonical "artistic" literature can produce revealing interpretations, and how more celebrated literary modes and genres such as magical realism and romance actually share the same attributes of accessibility and market success that define genre fiction.

In "Experimental Novel in Latin America," Andreas Kurz discusses the concept "experimental" in literature, describes the development of the experimental novel in Latin America, and stresses the role it plays in the narrative of Cortázar and, in particular, in Mexican Salvador Elizondo's (1932–2006) *Farabeuf.* As he explains, experimental literature appeared as a reaction to predominating realism, but it was only at the beginning of the twentieth century that it gained visibility as a counterpart to more traditional movements. Interestingly, Kurz adds, authors like Severo Sarduy and Fernando del Paso rejected magic realism and *lo real maravilloso* as a type of literature for a non–Latin American readership and viewed, instead, experimental literature as a vehicle to reach literary independence and to construct a Latin American reader.

The following group of articles considers the impact of the Latin American novel on the region's thinking about literature, as well as the impact of popular culture and technology on the narrative. The first topic is studied in "The historical, critical, and theoretical work on the Latin American novel," where José E. González argues that the reading of the novel in Latin American criticism has traditionally been viewed in connection to the concept of the nation, thus embracing the type of novels that could lend themselves to this kind of allegorical interpretation. This tendency has also led to ignoring periods or styles (*modernism*, avant-garde), in which narrations took more of an individually oriented form. González also points out the critical changes that came about when the Boom authors moved the novel away from representation through national content to an originality expressed through innovative writing techniques.

In turn, Melissa Fitch's "The Latin American Novels and New Technology" explores the impact of digital media on the writing of the novel from Colombia, Venezuela, Brazil, Argentina, and Chile. She delves into what constitutes a "novel" or even an "author" within such a radically different format. In her opinion, fluidity is one of the characteristics of digital literature. It also requires a change of focus on the part of scholars, which departs from the interpretation of a literary work and focuses instead on insights into the text derived in part from the multisensorial experience of accessing it.

The next section analyzes the works and lives of some of the best-known, as well as most representative, modern and postmodern Latin American novelists. It begins with Alexis Candia's "The new frontiers in the narrative of María Luisa Bombal," which studies the writer's biographical journey, questioning of official religion, representation of women and eroticism, and break with naturalism, one of the main literary movements of the time. Anadeli Bencomo's "Mapping Rulfo" addresses the Mexican author's texts as objects to be mapped. Her use of the term "mapping" also refers to the notion that narratives function as cartographies for the real and imagined spaces of human experiences (Geocriticism). Bencomo first refers to the maps traced by literary studies in which Rulfo is defined as one of the epicenters of narrative modernism in Latin America, and then analyzes *Pedro Páramo* as a cultural cartography of modernization in Mexico.

Javier García Liendo's "José María Arguedas's Poetics of the Novel" analyzes the Peruvian *indigenista's* "poetics of the novel" focusing on *Yawar Fiesta* (1941), *Los ríos profundos* (1958), and *El zorro de arriba y el zorro de abajo* (1971). The chapter examines Arguedas's response to the challenge of narrating Peru's historical transformation during the twentieth century, particularly the clash between indigeneity, traditional social relations, and capitalist modernization. In turn, in "One Hundred Years of Clarice Lispector: The Star of the Hour," Claire Williams describes how the Brazilian author is celebrated for her idiosyncratic prose, which challenges conventions of genre, form, and content. The chapter describes how Lispector's centenary was commemorated in 2020 and outlines her life and career, focusing on the narrative strategies that make her novels so strange and compelling. It then presents her literary afterlives: homages to her literary originality, her beauty and aloofness, and the intimacy and bravery she inspires in her readers.

The study of the Boom authors begins with Carolina Orloff's chapter on the trajectory of Julio Cortázar (1914–1984). According to Orloff, from *Divertimento* (written in 1949; published posthumously in 1986) to *El libro de Manuel* (*A Manuel for Manuel*), the last novel he published in life in 1973, Cortázar experimented with the novel's form, in a manner unmatched by any other of his contemporaries. In particular, his masterpiece *Rayuela* (*Hospcotch*, 1963) became a watershed in Latin American narrative. His support of Latin American revolutionary movements during the 1960s reflects the fact that, for him, literary experimentation was a political endeavor linked to a necessity of questioning thought and behavior outside the realm of the fictional text.

"García Márquez as Local and Universalist, Traditional cum Modernist Storyteller" by Gene H. Bell-Villada briefly recounts García Márquez's life and development as a writer, surveys his body of work in the light of the above traits, and describes his overall legacy and place in world literary culture. For his part, Maarten van Delden, in "Carlos Fuentes's Narrative Universe," explores Fuentes's approach to the relationship between the individual and the community, and how he emphasized our obligations to our fellow human beings. He also looks at the representation of geographic space in his works and points out the influence of Octavio Paz and Pablo Neruda on Fuentes's writing. Closing this section, Sabine Köllman's "Mario Vargas Llosa: Between Literature and Politics" discusses critical attempts to divide the Peruvian author's body of work into different phases. She also analyzes the author's aesthetic exploration of the nature of fiction and the role of literature in society; his treatment of themes such as authoritarianism, fanaticism, and the search for the truth; and his use of narrative features such as multiperspectivism and dual structures.

The following articles study some of the writers who came of age after the Boom and whose writings can be seen as responding, as well as attempting to go beyond, the Boom. Thus, Jorgelina Corbatta, in "Manuel Puig: Between Pop Art and Psychoanalysis," pays attention to Puig's use of psychoanalysis for his socio-political investigation of Argentina's social evils and as a tool to create his characters. She also explains his exploration of the "collective myths" permeating the collective unconscious, which are present in popular culture and mass media.

Michael K. Schuessler's "Reportage, Testimony, and Biography in the Novels of Elena Poniatowska" looks at the writings of the Paris-born Mexican novelist, who is best known for the journalistic genres she reinvented in Mexico, such as the chronicle and the group testimonial evoking comparison with the New Journalism of the 1960s.

Jonathan B. Monroe's "Transnational, Intermedial Pressures in Roberto Bolaño's Prose Poem Novels" studies the narrative of the best-known of all novelists who came after the Boom, through the prism of his interest in poetry. As Monroe elucidates, central to the development of his "prose poem novels," from *Amberes* (*Antwerp*) to *2666*, is the history and legacy of the prose poem, from Poe, Baudelaire, and Rimbaud forward, and of the novel's increasing competition with other genres, discourses, and media. Finally, Rita de Maeseneer looks at the works of a relatively young Dominican novelist in "Rita Indiana's Tentacled Novels." Rita Indiana epitomizes, in her view, the precarious and constantly shifting position that contemporary glocal writers, originating from a Latin American peripheral area, adopt in the twenty-first century. As de Maeseneer explains, Indiana's literary texts deal with topics that are considered contentious in the Dominican Republic, such as anti-haitianism and non-heteronormativity. She has also published coming-of-age novels, eco-futurist time-travel narratives, and radiographies of the revolutionary disenchantment in Cuba and the Dominican Republic.

The final section of the *Handbook* provides a glimpse of the relationship between the Latin American novel and that of the world. Roberto Ignacio Díaz's "The Latin American Novel in French and English" focuses mainly is on works by Eduarda Mansilla de García, W.H. Hudson, María Amparo Ruiz de Burton, and Jules Supervielle, but also considers various English-language novels by Latinx and Latin American authors working in the United States, as well as French-language novels by Latin American authors living in France. According to Díaz, this is not just a matter of taxonomy or literary history, but of reading new meanings often hidden by narrow notions of linguistic determinism and monolingual national literatures. In "The worldwide influence of the Latin American Novel," Nicholas Birns provides a review of the presence of the region's narrative in Europe and the United States. According to Birns, it was after 1950 that Latin American literature was widely recognized outside the region. The anomalous case of Borges, a writer evaluated almost totally in aesthetic and philosophical terms, helped keep the world resonance of the later Boom writers away from a strictly referential or political treatment. In the twenty-first century, adds Birns, Latin American literature became seen as already global. Brazilian literature was the object of even more intermittent notice, even as classics such as Machado de Assis and Lispector finally began to receive more metropolitan notice.

The *Handbook* concludes with Benjamin Loy's "The Latin American Novel as World Literature," which discusses the changing locations of the Latin American novel in World Literature from modernity to the present, focusing in particular on the material and aesthetic conditions of production and reception. Loy first zeroes in on modernist writers' cosmopolitanism and early forms of international circulation (1880–1960) and then examines the material conditions of Boom and Post-Boom novels as world literature between 1960 and 1990. Finally, he looks at the changes in the Latin American and global book markets since 1990, and at how new material conditions around the selection, translation, and circulation of literature have shaped the contemporary global Latin American novel.

As should be clear, in its chronological, cultural, and geographical scope, *The Oxford Handbook of the Latin American Novel* constitutes a ground-breaking survey of the region's novel.

NOTES

1. According to Emir Rodríguez Monegal, "We all know that Edmund Wilson, the brilliant critic and indefatigable polyglot, has steadfastly refused to learn Spanish, because he was convinced that nothing has been written in the language that would justify his exertions. Lionel Trilling, a most perceptive mind, once told one of his students that he had read Latin American literature and that in his judgment it had only an anthropological value" ("The New Latin American Literature in the USA" 3).

2. One must note that there is an ongoing process of revaluation of Isabel Allende's narrative as exemplified by María Rosa Olivera-Williams's "Twentieth Century Women Writers and the Feminist Novel," and Amaryll Chanady's "Magical Realism and the Marvelous Real in the Novel," included in this *Handbook*.

3. "Empezaba a verle costuras a la novela vernácula" (García Márquez, *Vivir para contarla* 34).

4. "Todavía no se ha escrito en Colombia la novela que esté indudable y afortunadamente influida por los Joyce, por Faulkner o por Virginia Woolf. Y he dicho 'afortunadamente', porque no creo que podríamos los colombianos ser, por el momento, una excepción al juego de las influencias. En su prólogo a *Orlando*, Virginia confiesa sus influencias. Faulkner mismo no podría negar la que ha ejercido sobre él el mismo Joyce. Algo hay— sobre todo en el manejo del tiempo—entre Huxley y otra vez Virginia Woolf. Franz Kafka y Proust andan sueltos por la literatura del mundo moderno. Si los colombianos hemos de decidirnos acertadamente, tendríamos que caer irremediablemente en esta corriente" (García Márquez, "Problemas de la novela" 213).

5. As Raquel Chang-Rodríguez notes in her article in this *Handbook*, there were other less well-known novels published before Lizardi's *Periquillo*. Among these one can mention Gonzalo Fernández de Oviedo's novel of chivalry *Libro del muy esforçado e invencible Cavallero de la Fortuna propiamente llamado don Claribalte* (Book of the Very Brave and Invincible Knight of Fortune Properly Named Don Claribalte, 1519), which though written in the Americas, was first published in Spain; and *El Evangelio en Triunfo, o historia de un filósofo desengañado* (The Gospel of Triumph, or the Story of a Disenchanted Philosopher, 1797), an epistolary novel, also published in Spain, which details the disillusionment with enlightenment ideas of the Peruvian Pablo de Olavide (1725–1803).

6. uma ilha descomunal no meio do Atlântico Sul" (Veloso 13).

7. "Machado de Assis, quien sigue siendo un famoso escritor que sólo unos cuantos conocen" (Espinosa Domínguez 68).

8. A pesar de las maravillas de la comunicación . . . La comunicación con el exterior, por lo tanto, fue difícil, atrasada, escasa, y surgió a un ritmo más lento del que esperábamos" (Gómez and Fuguet 12).

9. In fact, Cuban critic Rafael Rojas noted recently (2021) that "Latin America is going though one the lowest moments regarding pan-Latin American identity, given that there is multiple

ideological polarization between right and left, that has led to conflicts between Colombia and Venezuela, Brazil and Venezuela, Argentina and Brazil, or Chile and Bolivia" ("América Latina vive uno de los momentos más bajos del latinoamericanismo, ya que hay una polarización ideológica múltiple, entre derechas e izquierdas, que se traduce en conflictos entre Colombia y Venezuela, Brasil y Venezuela, Argentina y Brasil o Chile y Bolivia," n.p.).

WORKS CITED

Espinosa Domínguez, Carlos. "Andanzas póstumas de Machado de Assis en español." *Caracol*, no. 1, 2010, pp. 65–85.

Fuguet, Alberto, and Sergio Gómez, "Presentación del país McOndo." *McOndo*, edited by Fuguet and Gómez. Mondadori, 1996, pp. 9–20

García Márquez, Gabriel. *Living to Tell the Tale*. Vintage, 2004.

García Márquez, Gabriel. "¿Problemas de la novela?" *Obra periodística* I, edited by Jacques Girard, vol. 2, Oveja Negra, 1983, pp. 212–13.

García Márquez, Gabriel. *Vivir para contarla*. Vintage Español, 2002.

Mignolo, Walter. *The Idea of Latin America*. Blackwell, 2005.

Rodríguez Monegal, Emir. "The New Latin American Literature in the US." *Review: Literature and Arts in the Americas*, vol. 1, no. 1, 1968, pp. 3–13.

Rojas, Rafael. "América Latina vive uno de los momentos más bajos del latinoamericanismo." Interview by Emilio Rivaud Delgado. *Letras Libres*, no. 27, July 2021, https://letraslibres.com/historia/america-latina-vive-uno-de-los-momentos-mas-bajos-del-latinoamericanismo-entrevista-a-rafael-rojas/.

Vargas Llosa, Mario. "The Latin American Novel Today: An Introduction." Translated by Nick Mills. *Books Abroad*, vol. 44, no. 1, 1970, pp. 7–16.

Veloso, Caetano. *Tropical Truth: A Story of Music and Revolution in Brazil*. Translated by Isabel de Sena. Knopf, 2002.

Veloso, Caetano. *Verdade Tropical*. Companhia das Letras, 1997.

PART I

HISTORY

CHAPTER 1

....

THE NOVEL IN THE COLONIAL PERIOD

....

RAQUEL CHANG-RODRÍGUEZ

CONTRARY to what often has been alleged, novels were indeed written and published in viceregal Spanish America. Some circulated in manuscript form among the cultural elite, while others were printed and enjoyed a wider readership. They were molded by styles forged in three, often intertwined, literary periods: the Renaissance, the Baroque, and the Enlightenment. The most representative works of the genre written by peninsular authors also were disseminated in colonial Spanish America. The universally acclaimed novel of Spanish literature, *Don Quixote* (Madrid, 1605), arrived in Lima in 1606 (Leonard 386–95). Therefore, it is not surprising that, as recorded in the account of the Pausa festivities in the Andean highlands, Don Quixote and his squire Sancho Panza paraded at a celebration held there in October or November 1607 (Rodríguez Marín 129–37).[1] However, for decades there was a widespread myth that novels were not written in the New World and that novels published in Spain did not circulate there. This misconception was based on early decrees issued by Ferdinand and Isabella, the Catholic kings who, worried about the harmful impact on the indigenous population of "libros de entretenimiento" (books of entertainment), banned their exportation (Leonard 81–85). The sovereigns feared that the natives would prefer novels over religious treatises and would mold their conduct on the "vices" and falsehoods represented there. The pioneering research of Irving A. Leonard on book commerce between Spain and the Americas collected in his *Books of the Brave* published in 1949 demonstrated this falsehood, which continues to be repeated even today.

When we think of novels during the colonial period, different modalities of the genre as practiced in Spain come to mind: sentimental, pastoral, picaresque, allegorical, chivalric. While epic poetry was the favorite genre, —Alonso de Ercilla's *La Araucana* (1st part, 1569) was a bestseller—the novels of chivalry were read by an educated minority and well liked by the general population. The chronicler Gonzalo Fernández de Oviedo completed in America the *Libro del muy esforçado e invencible Cavallero de la Fortuna propiamente llamado don Claribalte* (Book of the Very Brave and Invincible Knight of

Fortune Properly Named Don Claribalte) (Valencia, 1519), which is considered by some critics the first novel written in the Spanish colonies. While Oviedo promised to continue the saga telling the exploits of Liporento, the son of Claribalte, he devoted himself to his major work, *Historia general y natural de las Indias, Islas y Tierra Firme del Mar Océano* (*General and Natural History of the Indies, Islands and Continent of the Ocean Sea*, 1st part, 1535). The essays by the Peruvian writer Mario Vargas Llosa, collected in his book *Carta de batalla por "Tirant lo Blanc"* (*A Defense of Tirant lo Blanc*, 1991) about this 1490 novel of chivalry written by the Valencian Joanot Martorell, show the enduring interest in this narrative modality.

In order to write and publish in the viceregal period, an author required a sponsor. The other alternative was to cover the cost of paper and fees to publish the manuscript, which, in addition, had to pass civil and ecclesiastical censorship. Authors had to be daring enough to compete with major Spanish writers such as Jorge de Montemayor, Miguel de Cervantes, Francisco de Quevedo, and Diego de Torres Villarroel, whose works traveled quickly to America and were sought after by readers. After complying with all requirements, there was yet another obstacle: printing presses in Lima and Mexico gave preference to the publication of religious books aimed at catechizing neophytes. Any manuscript sent to Spain for publication ran the risk of being lost or misplaced during the transatlantic crossing and experienced delays on its way to the printing press unless its author had an influential patron. The literate public was restricted to small groups in the main cities; therefore, poems, treatises, and novels circulated in reduced runs or in manuscript form in *tertulias* (literary salons) and academies sponsored by viceroys and other personalities. As was to be expected, manuscript circulation resulted in many lost works. Later, printed books and manuscripts often were transferred to libraries, museums, and archives, where they waited to be discovered. This is the case of five novels rescued, published, and discussed in this essay. These difficulties, together with the increasing prestige of poetry, which was regularly promoted in literary contests, contributed to restricting the production of novels.

Fictional narratives, however, circulated in other venues. Indigenous legends, passages from travel books, and accounts of shipwrecks and fantastic adventures were incorporated into epic poems, letters, and chronicles first written by European soldiers, sailors, and officers, and later by literate criollos, Indians, mestizos, and Afrodescendants. In his 1982 speech on receiving the Nobel Prize, Gabriel García Márquez recalls the "strictly accurate account" of Antonio Pigafetta—who circumnavigated the globe with Magellan—and labels it a "venture into fantasy." The Colombian writer highlights the wonders—from legless birds to pigs with their navel in their spine—described by that Florentine sailor. For García Márquez, this book contains "the seeds of our contemporary novels." In fact, it has often been pointed out how the spectacular and the marvelous appear in early texts from colonial Spanish America. Although today we study these documents from various disciplinary perspectives, they belong in the realm of historical, rather than literary, writing.

I will restrict my comments to a selection of works from the literary series conceived as fiction and marked by a diverse set of influences. Their authors are criollos and

Spaniards; both groups belong to privileged social sectors, and some are ecclesiastics. Each one is anxious to earn literary fame in the New and the Old World, and fame is obtained by showing mastery of peninsular models and following them through *imitatio*. Thus, American geography slowly penetrated these writings because the representation of the landscape was governed by the Renaissance rhetoric of the *locus amoenus*. Words that originated in America entered as needed to describe new situations, objects, flora, and fauna. Typical social subjects began to be depicted in roughly the second half of the eighteenth century. The presence of women writers is more common in poetry than in narrative. The novelists concentrated on the vice-regal capitals where, with uneven success, they tried to circulate and publish their manuscripts. The genre begins in New Spain (Mexico) in the first decade of the seventeenth century with a pastoral novel, *Siglo de oro en las selvas de Erífile* (Golden Century in the Forests of Erífile [1608]) by Bernardo de Balbuena. This category was on the wane if we take into account the realistic marks of works like *La vida de Lazarillo de Tormes* (*The Life and Adventures of Lazarillo de Tormes*, 1554) and the turning toward a Baroque and satiric sensibility as evidenced in Quevedo's *El Buscón* (*The Life and Adventures of Buscon the Witty Spaniard*, 1626). However, this could be challenged if we take into consideration the recent classification as a novel of a Peruvian historical account, *Relación de las guerras de los Pizarros y Almagros* (Account of the Wars between the Pizarros and Almagros) by fray Vicente de Valverde, now attributed to the Spanish poet Diego de Silva y Guzmán (?–1629) and retitled *La toma del Cuzco* (The Siege of Cuzco, 1539) (Coello 2008).

THE MEADOWS AND SHEPHERDS
OF NEW SPAIN

Bernardo de Balbuena (1561–1627), *Siglo de Oro en las selvas de Erífile* (Golden Century in the Forests of Erífile, 1608)

While we lack documentation about Balbuena's life and literary formation, we know he was born in Valdepeñas, a town in the Spanish province of Ciudad Real, from an illegitimate relationship. His mother remained in the peninsula while his father brought the child (ca. 1564) to be reared in New Spain. He spent his childhood and early youth with the Balbuena family in Guadalajara and later moved to Mexico City (ca. 1580), where he enrolled in the university, participated in the cultural life of the city, received awards in literary contests, and began his ecclesiastical career. During this time, he composed an epic poem, *El Bernardo o Victoria de Roncesvalles* (Bernardo or Roncesvalles's Victory, 1624), and a pastoral novel, *Siglo de Oro en las selvas de Erífile*. His most admired work is *Grandeza mexicana* (Mexican Grandeur, 1604), an epistolary poem in hendecasyllabic tercets published in Mexico. Young, ambitious, and well positioned among the upper echelons of the viceregal church, Balbuena traveled to Madrid in 1606, where he published his pastoral novel with a dedication to the powerful Pedro Fernández de Castro y Andrada, count of Lemos (1608). Balbuena achieved his objective and was appointed abbot of Jamaica (1608) and bishop of Puerto Rico (1619), where he lost his library in a pirate attack (1623) and later died (Rabasa 53–54; Avalle Arce, "Balbuena" 1: 461–62).

The sources of *Siglo de Oro* have been well established by modern critics. Both Fucilla (101–19) and Avalle Arce (*Novela pastoril* 209–14) have explained how the bishop of Puerto Rico's novel diverges from the Spanish pastoral tradition established by writers such as the Portuguese-born Jorge Montemayor, whose *Diana* (ca. 1559) is considered the founding work of the genre in the peninsula. Balbuena follows, instead, an Italian model: Sannazaro's *Arcadia* (1504). In the twelve eclogues of *Siglo de Oro*, poetry and prose freely alternate. Each eclogue can be read independently because neither action nor characters link the various scenes. Through Balbuena's artistic imagination, the novel creates a beautiful and evocative fresco of a lost time (González Boixo 294–95).

As Sannazaro's *Arcadia* does with respect to Naples, in eclogue six of *Siglo de Oro*, a nymph guides the pastor narrator through a dark cavern, where he explains:

> suddenly I was under a deep and wide lagoon, whose incredible grandeur made me believe that at that point the famous Ocean with all its regions of water, had passed over my head. But then sitting on top of its delicate waves, I saw a proud and populous city, and not without much amazement, I thought: this no doubt is that Grandeza Mexicana, whose many wonders the world recounts.[2]

This is followed by comments praising the architecture of Mexico and the character and good looks of its inhabitants of European descent, themes elaborated by the author in his well-known poem (Balbuena 133). These are the only references to Balbuena's adopted "patria" in the novel. The pastoral genre has another important follower in the criollo Francisco Bramón, whose novel introduces Mexican details into the Spanish bucolic tradition.

Francisco Bramón (?–1664), *Los sirgueros de la Virgen sin original pecado* (The Goldfinches of the Virgin without Original Sin, 1620)

We have few facts on the life of clergyman Francisco Bramón. The information about him emerges mostly from the study of the front matter of his only known work, *Los sirgueros de la Virgen sin original pecado*, and from the novel itself. He competed unsuccessfully for the chair of rhetoric at the Royal and Pontifical University of Mexico (1618) and later became "counselor" of this institution (1619). Bramón participated in at least two literary competitions (1618 and 1654) with the theme of the Immaculate Conception of Mary. As *Los sirgueros* is dedicated to another criollo, the bishop of Michoacán, Fray Baltasar de Covarrubias, and his coat of arms appears on the cover of the book published in Mexico, it has been speculated as to whether he received the endorsement of such an important personage (Martínez Barac 6–7). The Mexican novelist Agustín Yáñez first published *Los sirgueros*—the title refers to goldfinches, and in the novel the shepherds who sing in praise of the Virgin—in 1944 in an abbreviated edition from which he omitted almost all the poems and gave preference to the religious drama[3] with which the novel closes. Until the publication in 2013 of the complete, annotated edition by Trinidad Barrera, Yáñez's was the only available modern edition, and it led to limited appreciation of the novel. Thanks to Giulia de Sarlo's research, two significant facts can be added to our understanding of this novel: (1) its author borrowed from the *Letanías peruanas* (Peruvian Litanies) of Toribio de Mogrovejo, bishop of Lima canonized in 1726, to highlight the attributes of the Virgin; (2) Bramón requested and received permission on July 14, 1620, to send seventy copies of *Los sirgueros* to Lima (199–218). We do not know what Bramón's links to Peru were, but these findings offer a tenuous glimpse into the cultural connections between the two viceregal capitals.

The novel treats the topic, then in intense debate, of original sin and the Immaculate Conception. Thus, it is a bucolic novel "a lo divino" (in the divine way), a variety popular in Spain, where it was cultivated by, among others, Lope de Vega in his *Pastores de Belén* (Shepherds of Bethlehem, 1612). Divided into scenes, its three books are linked by the Marian theme: in the first, the shepherds talk about how to celebrate the feast of the Immaculate Conception; in the second, they prepare the festivities and travel to the place where they will be held; the third book describes the celebration itself and includes the religious comedy, *Auto del triunfo de la Virgen y gozo mexicano* (Auto of the Triumph of the Virgin and Mexican Joy).

There are several unique details in *Los sirgueros*. Frequently, the real world is introduced through comments by Anfriso, the protagonist-narrator also identified with the author, and other characters who converse with him. The allusions to the Royal and Pontifical University of Mexico ground the work in New Spain, as when Anfriso explains why he is in this bucolic environment—to rest from a contest in which he participated with distinction in the "Academia Mexicana" (Bramón 122). The motif of the "play within the play" (Bravo vol. 3, 4494) is evident when the shepherds in the narrative become spectators of the religious comedy written by Anfriso. The praise of Mexico, minimal but grand in Balbuena's novel, is frequent and precise in *Los sirgueros*, as indicated by Anfriso's comment: "in these Mexican gardens and plentiful lagoons we see every day so many talented persons that the world is amazed by them; . . . they are justly appreciated as famous men in all endeavors, sciences and art."[4] As we know, praise of the architectural beauty of Mexico, of the talents of its citizens, of its climate and the surrounding landscape, including fruits and plants, constitutes a central theme in the development of local identity. Their presence helps to forge a sentiment of difference and gradually builds into the so called "criollismo colonial," which begins to develop in seventeenth-century viceregal poetry and narrative. Indeed, *Los sirgueros* is unique: a sacred pastoral novel consistently marked by Mexico's presence.

The novel closes with the *Auto del triunfo de la Virgen y gozo mexicano*, a religious comedy in which Original Sin appears not in the abstract but rather as a highway robber

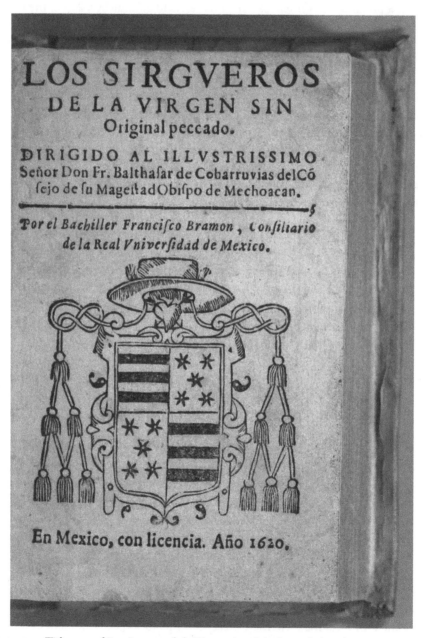

FIGURE 1.1: Title page of *Los sirgueros de la Virgen sin original pecado* (1620).

Source: Hispanic Society Museum and Library, NYC

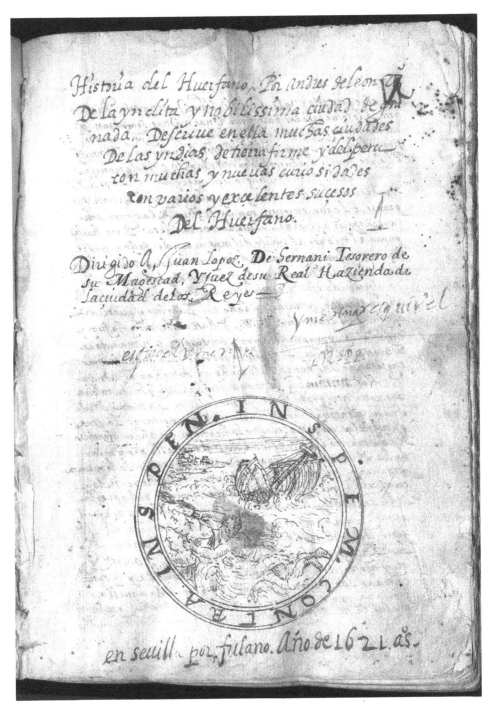

FIGURE 1.2: Title page of *Historia del Huérfano* (1621).

who imprisons travelers. Characters such as Cain, Jeremías, and their servant, the "gracioso" (comical figure) Edonio, are victims of his treachery. Saint Joseph anticipates the appearance of the Virgin as a young woman, and her presence ends the reign of Original Sin. All celebrate the apotheosis of Mary, including the Nación Mexicana (Mexican Nation), cloaked in feathers and gold, carrying a shield with its symbols—the eagle on the cactus—and accompanied by six caciques dressed in robes embroidered in gold. They dance a "mitote or tocotín" while these couplets were sung: "Dance, Mexicans; / play the *tocotín*, / because Mary has won / with joyful happiness."[5] With its references to Mexico and its symbols, one can well understand why Yáñez acknowledged the importance of this religious comedy.

Despite their stylistic beauty and references to the culture of New Spain, the novels discussed did not reach the popularity—multiple editions and several translations in Europe—of the religious treatise *El pastor de Nochebuena. Práctica breve de las virtudes, conocimiento fácil de los vicios* (The Christmas Shepherd. Brief Practice of Virtues, Easy Recognition of Vices, 1644) by Juan de Palafox y Mendoza (1600–1659), bishop of Puebla and a leading figure in the ecclesiastical culture of New Spain. It shows how well liked the presentation of mystical topics within a bucolic framework was. Two seventeenth-century novels both published contemporarily—one from Lima and the other from Bogota—develop the topic of asceticism through their protagonists.

ADVENTUROUS LIVES AND ASCETIC DEATHS

Andrés de León (pseudonym of Martín de León, 1584–1655), *Historia del huérfano* (The Orphan's Story, 1621)

The only manuscript known of this long novel that also includes important poetry selections is located at the Hispanic Society Museum and Library in New York. It was discovered by Antonio Rodríguez Moñino (*Catálogo*; "Poetas" 164–88) and was finally published in 2017, carefully edited by Belinda Palacios. Initially described as the biography of its author (Martín de León) written under a pen name (Andrés de León), thanks to Palacios's research we can reconsider that attribution and place *Historia del Huérfano* in the category of fictional biographies because "neither the author nor the protagonist share the same life trajectory, nor is the hero of the text a real person."[6] It is worth asking then who Martín de León was, and why he created such a peripatetic protagonist and placed him in so many adventures and geographies.

Martín de León y Cárdenas was born in Archidona, Málaga, in 1584. At the age of sixteen (1600), he was admitted as a novice into the Order of Saint Augustine in Seville and ordained in 1611. After a brief stay in Salamanca, he traveled to the Viceroyalty of Peru and settled in Lima. He was there in 1612 when he witnessed the funeral procession honoring Queen Margarita Teresa (1584–1611) sponsored by Viceroy Mendoza y

Luna, marquess of Montesclaros. The author belonged to the literary circle supported by this ruler and likely participated in the deliberations of the famous Academia Antártica described in *El discurso en loor de la poesía* (Discourse in Praise of Poetry, 1608) by Clarinda, the poet's pen name. It is known that Martín de León was in Spain by 1616, a year after the return of the marquess of Montesclaros. León's ecclesiastical career prospered, and he was appointed to occupy the bishopric of Trivento (1630) and other important posts in Spanish Italy. In 1651 he was president and captain general of the Viceroyalty of Sicily and died in Palermo in 1655 (Palacios, Introducción xiii–xx).

There are two extant examples of León's literary interests: *Relación de las exequias que . . . don Juan de Mendoza y Luna . . . hizo en la muerte de la reina nuestra señora doña Margarita* (Account of the Obsequies . . . that don Juan de Mendoza y Luna . . . Sponsored on the Death of the Queen our Lady Doña Margarita, 1613) and the *Historia del Huérfano* (1621). After witnessing the funeral ceremony, he composed and published its description in Lima; the latter was completed a few years after departing the vice-regal capital (Palacios, Introducción xiii–xviii). As León continued his friendship with former viceroy Mendoza, one may surmise he wrote *El Huérfano* hoping to please him and thus continue in the favor and protection of such a powerful personage. And León was successful because, shortly before his death (1628), Juan de Mendoza y Luna named him his executor (Palacios, Introducción xvi).

Written in the third person, the novel by Martín de León tells the adventures of the Orphan, a teenager from a modest family in Granada who, at the age of fourteen, travels to the New World in search of a better life. After some misdeeds in Lima, he ends up taking refuge in an Augustinian convent and is ordained. However, on a trip to Spain to attend to family matters, he stops at Santa Fe de Bogota where a superior—we do not know the reason why because there are missing folios in the manuscript—forbids him to wear the monastic habit of the Augustinian Order. Orphan escapes, plies several trades, and travels to Spain and then to Italy, where he requests and receives papal forgiveness for his misdeed. During the long journey, he participates by land and sea in historical events, such as the attack by Francis Drake on San Juan de Puerto Rico and the sacking of Cádiz by the British navy. His adventurous life takes him back to America and to the Augustinian convent in Lima. There, he rejects important positions and reaffirms his dedication to an ascetic life.

To create the character, León turns, as Palacios has verified, to the treatises of princes, to the "accounts" written by anonymous soldiers and conquerors, to his own experiences, and to those told by adventurers he must have met in Peru and elsewhere (Introducción xxvii–xxviii). Orphan's life is seasoned with episodes that remind us of Byzantine and picaresque novels, with precise portraits of historical characters (e.g., the governor Pedro Ozores de Ulloa [León 260–61]), with detailed descriptions of cities, as well as including historical facts—such as the account of his visit to Guayaquil (León 382–83) and of the lavish celebrations of the arrival of future queen Margarita in Ferrara (León 193–99). It also includes horrifying deeds—how can one forget the episode in which Orphan bites off the nose of his rival (León 188) or of the gentleman from Extremadura who in Potosí stabs an opponent and then drinks his blood (León 289).

Together with the wanderings of such a contradictory character, the narrator does not hesitate to include digressions on very disparate topics—morals, climate, geography, history, fashion, and manners. He also presents the contribution of other writers to support his arguments. In chapter 33, for example, he tries to explain the lack of rain on the coast of Peru, basing his assertions on Miguel Cabello Valboa's *Miscelánea antártica* (Antartic Miscellany, 1591), whose manuscript León surely was familiar with because it circulated among Lima's palace literati (Palacios, Introducción xxxii–iii).[7] As for the digressions included in novels of the period—as in Mateo Alemán's *Guzmán de Alfarache* (1599)—they abound in *Historia del Huérfano*. Among them, I highlight the comments about an unknown animal in Europe: the llama—called "carnero de la tierra" (ram of the earth) by the Spaniards—from the Andean highlands. The narrator's observations about these camelids promote pejorative ideas about the temperament of the indigenous population, judged to be similar to that of these animals (León 285). One major concern in the novel is the extinction of the natives and the consequences that this would have on mining and the reception in Spain of the needed gold and silver from the Indies (León 274).

In other digressions, the narrator shares with the protagonist a feeling of admiration towards the criollos (León 271).[8] Both the third-person narrator as well as the embattled hero take turns in criticizing corrupt officials and plundering the royal treasury in the vast territories traveled by Orphan. It is very likely that to freely express these criticisms, the author used a pseudonym, and, as we can well imagine, with so many negative comments, the manuscript was unlikely to pass censorship and go on to publication. In addition to the adventures of its protagonist, *Historia del Huérfano* offers a rich and complex portrait of the empire, both in America and in Spanish Italy. The novel shows the literary culture of Martín de León while underscoring manuscript circulation of "obras de entretenimiento" whose hybrid nature corresponds to the taste of the period. This is also evident in a novel written in seventeenth-century Bogota, discovered and published in the twentieth century.

Pedro Solís y Valenzuela (1624–1711), *El desierto prodigioso y prodigio del desierto* (The Prodigious Desert and the Prodigy in the Desert, ca. 1650)

The earliest information about this novel was reported by Spanish priest Baltasar Cuartero Huerta in 1963, when he discovered one of two extant manuscripts, containing twenty-two "mansiones" or chapters, in the library of the Fundación Lázaro Galdiano (Madrid). The second and briefer manuscript, with three "mansiones," is currently at the Instituto Caro y Cuervo (Bogota), which sponsored the first publication of the novel under the editorship of Rubén Páez Patiño (1977–1985).[9] Its title, *El desierto prodigioso y prodigio del desierto*, refers to the Augustinian convent of Nuestra Señora de La Candelaria, which came to be known as the Desert of La Candelaria (south of

Ráquira), due to the frugal and solitary life of the friars who resided there. The wonders of this place are revealed as the narrative unfolds. In addition to its fictional component, the novel contains religious poems—some in Latin—by Solís and various authors, including his brother Fernando (also known as Bruno). In addition, there are meditations, a biography of San Bruno, a religious comedy now lost,[10] and short accounts attributed to different pens.

Pedro Solís y Valenzuela, the author of the novel, was born in Santa Fe de Bogota—where *El desierto* also develops—one of seven children of a well-to-do family. He entered the priesthood and held different ecclesiastical posts, including notary of the Holy Office of the Inquisition. A cultured and generous individual, he donated numerous books of religious content to the Shrine of Monserrate, a chapel that he had helped build with some friends. He wrote religious works such as *Panegírico sagrado, en alabanza del serafín de las soledades, San Bruno* (Sacred Panegyric in Praise of the Seraph of the Solitudes, Saint Bruno) (Lima, 1646). Some were attributed to his brother Fernando, while others are known to us only by their title (Orjuela 297–300).

The plot of *El desierto prodigioso* is very complex. It offers several overlapping stories told by different narrators and, like *Historia del Huérfano*, is interspersed with religious, philosophical, and moral digressions. The novel commences in La Candelaria desert, where the brothers Pedro and Fernando, their cousin Andrés, and friend Antonio go hunting. Chasing a deer, Andrés comes to a cave, where he finds religious objects and a folder with poems and meditations on death. He is very moved when reading the poetry and develops a strong desire to enter a religious order (Solís, Mansión 1). The following day, the friends meet again in a place resembling the *locus amoenus* of bucolic novels. All want to meet the inhabitant of the cave and thus return to find the hermit Arsenio (Solís, Mansión 4). During the meeting, Arsenio gives an account of his sinful life and tells other stories. Touched by what he has heard, Andrés decides to become a priest and with the anchorite's help enters the Augustinian convent. The movement of Andrés and his friends toward a pious life alternates with the story of the licentious existence of the hermit, thus revealing the binary structure of the novel where religiosity and debauchery, present and past, history and fiction, the field and the convent, appear as opposites (Robledo I, 1439). When Arsenio narrates his dissipated past, he includes a variety of episodes, some of which can be read and understood independently, such as the story of his love affair with his cousin Casimira or Pedro Porter's journey to hell.[11]

When discussing tales of travel and adventure, it is impossible to ignore *Infortunios de Alonso Ramírez* (*Misfortunes of Alonso Ramírez*, 1690), a work often studied from a literary perspective and classified by some as a novel. However, it belongs to the historical series, as has been confirmed by Fabio López Lázaro's research (87–104). It was written by the Mexican savant Carlos de Sigüenza y Góngora (1645–1700) based on the account told by Alonso, a carpenter turned pirate originally from San Juan de Puerto Rico. That the cosmographer Sigüenza inserts detailed nautical information, or that Alonso enhances his story as he tells it, does not alter the historical nature of the work and the fact that Alonso was a real person describing what happened to him. His devotion to the Virgin of Guadalupe is noteworthy as it grounds the tale in Mexico and offers a link in the development of criollo consciousness. Reshaped by the Enlightenment, religiosity will become a guiding light in the behavior of characters in eighteenth-century narratives, as we will see when discussing Pablo de Olavide's novel.

VIRTUOUS LIVES AND FANTASTIC JOURNEYS IN ENLIGHTENMENT NARRATIVES

Pablo de Olavide (1725–1803), *El Evangelio en triunfo o historia de un filósofo desengañado* (The Gospel in Triumph or History of a Disillusioned Philosopher, 1797–1798)

Among colonial authors who espoused Enlightenment ideas, the best known is Pablo Antonio de Olavide y Jáuregui. This distinguished alumnus of the University of San Marcos became *oidor* (judge) of the Royal Court and auditor general of the Viceroyalty of Peru when he was very young. After the earthquake that devastated Lima in 1746, he was summoned to Madrid to answer allegations about his mismanagement of funds in public commissions. He arrived in Spain in 1752 and never returned to the Viceroyalty of Peru. Very soon thereafter, the Council of the Indies tried him for embezzling funds in Lima and sentenced him to prison for three years in 1754. Although Fernando VI forgave him, Olavide was prohibited from holding public office for the next ten years. His marriage in Spain to a wealthy widow allowed him to travel through Europe and to hold large gatherings in his Madrid home, where influential figures met and new ideas were discussed. Fond of comedy, Olavide built a theater in his residence where French plays were performed. The "limeño" stood out among intellectuals influenced by Enlightenment ideas and was noticed by the powerful count of Aranda, Pedro Pablo Abarca de Bolea (1718–1798), who called on him to occupy important positions. It was an intense time when Olavide participated in agrarian and university reform projects—particularly remembered is his idea of implementing a more just rural society in the Sierra Morena— damaging powerful interests and creating many enemies (Défourneaux).[12]

The fall of his protector as well as Olavide's Francophilia contributed to the Inquisition, initiating a secret trial against Olavide and eventually accusing and condemning him as a heretic in 1778. During his exile in the Sahagún monastery he devoted himself to writing religious poetry. However, Olavide could not endure the solitude of the cloister and in 1780 fled to France where he resided for several years and was awarded the title of "Adopted Citizen of the French Republic." Although prosecuted and imprisoned during the Reign of Terror, soon a movement in his favor began in Spain. Regretful of his actions and doubting his enlightened ideas, Olavide returned to Madrid in 1798 with the support of King Carlos IV.

As for his novelistic prose, Olavide's best known work is *El Evangelio en triunfo o historia de un filósofo desengañado* (The Gospel in Triumph or the Story of a Disappointed Philosopher). Very popular in its time, it reached fourteen editions in Spain between 1797 and 1848; it was later translated into French. *El Evangelio* uses an epistolary format to describe the "conversion" of a philosopher, champion of the enlightened ideology and later a fierce detractor. The Peruvian critic Estuardo Núñez called attention to another aspect of Olavide's narrative by introducing him as the author of sentimental novels and publishing six of them (*Obras narrativas desconocidas*; *Obras selectas* xi–ciii).[13] Subsequent investigations by María José Alonso Seoane ("Los autores" 1–22) have confirmed that the "limeño" translated and adapted several of these novels from French authors.[14] A novel whose authorship was attributed to Olavide, *Teresa o el terremoto de Lima* (Teresa or the Lima Earthquake, 1818, translation 1823), was actually written after his death (Alonso Seoane, "*Thérèse*" 1017). Future research will undoubtedly shed light on this aspect of Olavide's intellectual life.

El Evangelio en triunfo presents forty-one letters written by the Philosopher to his friend Theodore (I–XXXV) and by Mariano to Antonio (XXXVI–XLI). The first thirty-five letters deal with the conversion of the Philosopher from a libertine to a traditionally decent individual; the remaining six tell how a town and the standard of living of its inhabitants improve thanks to the efforts of the Philosopher. The correspondence goes in only one direction, and therefore the comments by the recipients are summarized in the letters written by Mariano or the Philosopher. Frequently, digressions and episodes, as is often seen in novels of this period, stand on their own, such as the description of the Philosopher's duel. In the prologue, Olavide uses the "lost manuscript" theme, popularized by Cervantes in *Don Quixote*, when he attributes the letters to a well-known philosopher and explains the importance of publishing them in Spain, the bastion of Christianity. The model for the work, as Olavide confesses, is the not very extensive *Les Délices de la religion, ou le Pouvoir de l'Évangile pour nous rendre heureux* (The Delights of Religion, or the Power of the Gospel to Make Us Happy, 1788) by Abbé Lamourette (Olavide, Prologue vol.1, viii–x).

In an assessment of *El Evangelio*, Gérard Dufour reiterates its hybrid character and confirms its division into two parts: the first thirty-five letters can be read as a novel about the life of the Philosopher, while the remaining six missives constitute a "utopian tale." The French critic recognizes that the letters are the unifying thread of the story. However, he questions whether *El Evangelio* can be classified within the epistolary genre because the letters flow in only one direction and thus do not allow for the presentation of different perspectives (109–10). While Dufour points to other novelistic traits such as the presence of secondary characters whose sudden appearance and reappearance give unity to the different sections of the narrative, he also wonders why the novel was so popular and proposes that perhaps the sanctimoniousness of the times contributed to its success (114–15).

When we turn to Olavide's "Prologue," it quickly becomes apparent that he presents his novel as edifying and useful. Following one of the neoclassical tenets, he aims to teach and to entertain. In this regard, it is important to note that religious ideas imbued by Enlightenment thought promoted the exercise of civil virtues by the Philosopher. The trajectory of the Philosopher proposes the return to nature, to a simpler life in which helping family and neighbors is an integral part of the "hombre benéfico's" (charitable man's) behavior (Goić 396). In an important shift, the ascetic life proposed in Baroque fictions is refashioned into a way of life that combines both religious and civil virtues as evidenced in *El Evangelio*.

Novels written during the mid-eighteenth century and the beginning of the nine-teenth century predominantly in the Viceroyalty of New Spain still show a prefer-ence for Baroque style, while timidly introducing Enlightenment ideas. The contact between the old and new models reveals the tensions that eventually led to a dif-ferent literary and cultural sensibility. Three novels from this period,[15] are: *Sizigias y cuadraturas lunares* (Lunar Syzygies and Quadratures, ca. 1772) by Manuel Antonio de Rivas, a Franciscan friar living in Mérida;[16] *Segunda parte de los soñados regocijos de la Puebla* (Second Part of the Dreamed Joys of Puebla),[17] of unknown author and dated about the middle of the eighteenth century; and *La heroína mexicana* (The Mexican Heroine, ca. 1809),[18] a brief work also anonymous. The manuscript of the second novel can be found at the National Library in Madrid and is a continuation of a work written three years earlier, though apparently not well received in Puebla, according to José Pascual Buxó, its modern editor (28). In the novel, an impoverished student from Puebla (Francisco Poderoso Alcatraz) visits Mexico City and strikes up a conversation with a beggar (Tejocote) who repeatedly asks his interlocutor to translate into Spanish the Latin words he utters. During the exchange, they defend the theater, criticize in-struction in religious schools, and exhibit their anticlericalism (Pascual Buxó 28–32). As pointed out by Nancy Vogeley, the discussion between the two characters can be placed within a larger context: does entertainment lead to vice or virtue (230).

Discovered in the Archivo General de la Nación (National General Archive) in Mexico, the third novel narrates the abduction of Matilde and her mother by English pirates in Veracruz and how the protagonist, during the two years of captivity, acquires navigational skills as well as independence of criteria. After many incidents, mother and daughter return to the port city. Trinidad Barrera has proposed Francisco de Paula Urbizu as author—he requested and was denied permission to publish the novel ("Heroína" 18)—while María Isabel Terán, the modern editor of *La heroína*, suggests a female author (*La heroína* 421). The protagonist and her travails have been interpreted as an allegory of the difficult political situation faced by New Spain at the time—navigating Spanish, British, and criollo ambitions (Barrera, "Heroína" 22–23). Since the novel was announced as *Primera parte de la novela titulada, La heroína mexicana* (The First Part of the Novel Entitled, The Mexican Heroine), it leads us to think that it was conceived as a serialized publication, a format popularized in the second half of the eighteenth century as a way to circumvent censorship and maintain the interest of readers.

I now return to *Sizigias*, the first novel mentioned, and will dwell on it because it serves as a bridge between the old traditions and the new ideas. Marked by a satir-ical bent, this short text alternates between astrology and astronomy, fantasy and science, and reality and myth, and it therefore exemplifies the friction between baroque and enlightened knowledges in New Spain. The story was discovered by Pablo González Casanova in 1958 in the files of the inquisitorial trial against Rivas. Almost four decades later (1994), Ana María Morales published it for the first time. In *Sizigias*, "antíctonas" or inhabitants of the Moon describe, in two letters to an amateur earthling who observes the movements of the Moon, the arrival there on his spaceship—"A flying car or vessel with two wings and a rudder"—[19]of Onésimo Dutalón, a French astronomer with whom they had maintained scientific correspondence and now are discussing Isaac Newton's theories and René Descartes's philosophy. The gathering is interrupted by demons on their way to the Sun, where new theories have relocated Hell. The theme of space travel is not new. Texts such as *The Journey to the Moon* (1657) by Cyrano de Bergerac, the *Fantastic Voyage of the Great Piscátor of Salamanca* (1724) by Diego de Torres Villarroel—an author well known in Mexico—and Voltaire's *Micromégas* (1752) awakened the interest in topics marked by the fantastic as well as in presenting recent scientific or pseudo-scientific theories, welcomed by readers eager for novelties. The fiction of José Mariano Acosta Enríquez, a writer familiar with the new ideas but unwilling to abandon the Baroque path, can also be situated at this juncture.

José Mariano Acosta Enríquez (ca. 1751–1818), *Sueño de sueños* (Dream of Dreams, ca. 1801)

Thanks to Marco A. Guillén's research (53–78), we have more information about Acosta Enríquez's biography and about the approximate date when his novel was completed. The author lived in Querétaro, where he was an active participant in literary circles. As a poet, he favored religious themes and was also known for his generosity when praising his peers. His short novel, *Sueño de sueños*, was first published by Julio Jiménez Rueda in 1945. As its title announces, it is structurally framed by the well-known literary device of the dream and the journey to hell made famous by Dante's *Divine Comedy*. However, in *Sueño de sueños* the author completes the journey guided by Quevedo, Cervantes, and Torres Villarroel, his favorite writers. While its tone is satirical, it lacks the pungency of the main influence in the novel, Quevedo's *Sueños*. Author and narrator are differentiated through the discourse of the awake (the former) and sleeping man (the latter) (Guillén 60). In fact, while reading works by Quevedo and remembering those by Cervantes and Torres Villarroel, the author falls sleep and begins "to dream ... With so much clarity, that all I dreamed in all my life compared to what I dreamed that night is like comparing what I dreamed with what actually happens when awake."[20] In *Sueños*, the presence of the Enlightenment is evident in a lengthy list of novels by Spanish, French, and English authors that circulated in New Spain and were known or read in translation by Acosta Enríquez and his contemporaries.[21] With a majority of French titles, as Vogeley noted, the list indicates a predominance of "Bourbon taste" in Spain and its American dependencies as well as a moralizing tendency (226–28).

From a linguistic perspective, it is important to underscore the appearance in *Sueños* of popular sayings and words characteristically from New Spain. The presence of Mexico and its people is shown in comments on costumes and types (Guillén 64–65). Among the "tipos" worth highlighting are the "currutaco" (Acosta 128–29)[22] and the "lépero." The narrator describes the former to Cervantes, one of his partners on the trip to Hell, as being "cheerful, young and conceited," often characterized as a dandy.[23] Quevedo, another travel companion of the narrator, comments on the social role of the latter, indicating that they are carefree and lazy because "the world praises idleness, laziness, doing nothing"[24] (Acosta 186). As Guillén has indicated in his assessment of *Sueño de sueños*, "it reflects the cultural transition from the 18th to the 19th century," the "transformation in process"[25] of fictional prose in New Spain (76).

As we have discussed, in colonial Spanish America, novels were written and circulated in printed and manuscript form among a limited number of readers. Following Spanish literary taste, several varieties of the genre were cultivated in the New World. Its origins can be traced to New Spain and the pastoral novel nuanced by the American milieu. For example, in *Los sirgueros de la Virgen sin original pecado*, the Mexican context disrupts the traditional bucolic atmosphere by offering a unique counterpoint. In later novels religiosity manifests itself in transformations by which the protagonist leaves a life of debauchery for an ascetic life, as evidenced in *Historia del Huérfano* and *El desierto prodigioso y prodigio del desierto*. Following Baroque preferences, both works intersperse moral and philosophical digressions then so well liked by readers.

Influenced by Enlightenment ideas, the virtues associated with a pious life are linked to those associated with civil life. Together, they give rise to the representation of a behavior marked by the interest in the public good and the personal practice of correct conduct. Sometimes, as we have observed in *El Evangelio en triunfo*, and in the two previously mentioned novels, the protagonist is totally changed. The path to such transformations allows for the inclusion of trips to hell, encounters with pirates, adventures in exotic places, and even romances that keep the reader's interest. Slowly, local concerns are presented in the various novels that correspond to the eighteenth century. Particularly in the *Segunda parte de los soñados regocijos de Puebla*, the interlocutors criticize the clergy, and one of the characters mockingly demands plain language and not the Latin quotes that one of the speakers abuses. Tenuously, as we have seen in *Sueño de sueños*, social subjects unique to Mexico begin to appear. Weaving together criticisms of the civil and ecclesiastical authorities, the evolution from a pious life to a conduct linked to religious and civil virtues, the desire for an accessible language, and the presence of American types and landscape, a new sensibility begins to develop. Coupled with the arrival of Romanticism and its emphasis on emotions, it will eventually forge the modern Latin American novel.

ACKNOWLEDGMENTS

My thanks to Gabriella de Beer and Fred Luciani for reading and commenting earlier versions of this essay. Their suggestions were extremely valuable.

NOTES

1. From Rodríguez Marín's research, we know that Cervantes characters paraded in New Spain festivals, at least since 1621. For a summary of the early presence of Cervantes' masterpiece and its influence in the Spanish Indies, see González Cañal.

2. "Súbitamente me vi debajo de una profunda y ancha laguna, cuya increíble grandeza me hizo creer que en aquel punto el famoso Océano con todas sus regiones de agua hubiese pasado sobre mi cabeza. Mas luego que sentada encima de sus delicadas ondas vi una soberbia y populosa ciudad, no sin mucha admiración dije en mi pensamiento: esta sin duda es aquella Grandeza Mejicana, de quien tantos milagros cuenta el mundo" (Balbuena 132). All translations in this essay are mine.

3. I follow Hopkins Rodríguez's reclassification (77–94).

4. "En estos mexicanos jardines y abundosas lagunas vemos cada día ingenios tan floridos que al mundo admiran, ... pues los estima, como es justo, por hombres en todas facultades, sciencias [sic] y artes famosísimos" (Bramón 72).

5. "Bailad, mexicanos; / suene el tocotín, / pues triunfa María / con dicha feliz" (Bramón 212).

6. Porque "ni el autor ni el protagonista comparten la misma trayectoria vital, ni es el héroe del texto una persona real" (Palacios, Introduction xxii).

7. See the edition by Isaías Lerner.

8. Palacios develops this theme in "Criollismo" (505–16).

9. The narrative part was published separately by Orjuela (1983).

10. In Mansion 10, sixty-five folios including a play are missing (Orjuela 300).

11. Journeys to and from hell are often described in novels of the period. *La endiablada* (ca. 1624) (A Devilish Tale), a narrative by the chronicler Juan Mogrovejo de la Cerda (?–1664) published contemporaneously (Chang-Rodríguez 43–76), describes a conversation between two demons in a Lima street.

12. All biographical information from Deforneaux.

13. The collection *Lecturas útiles y entretenidas* (*Useful and Entertaining Readings*) by Olavide under the pseudonym Atanasio de Céspedes y Monroy included novels translated and adapted from the French. Some of the original models have been identified (See Alonso Seoane, "Adaptador" 1157–66).

14. Some of his translations circulated in New Spain (Vogeley 236).

15. *La portentosa vida de la Muerte* (The Portentous Life of Death, 1792), by brother Joaquín Bolaños, is better studied as a moral treatise.

16. My thanks to Carmen Boullosa for this reference.

17. Discovered and published by José Pascual Buxó in a facsimile edition in 1998.

18. María Isabel Terán discovered it in 1999 and published the novel in 2008.

19. "Un carro o vajel [sic] volante instruido de dos alas y un timón" (Rivas 40).

20. "A soñar . . . Con tanta vivacidad, que cuanto he soñado en toda mi vida comparado con lo que soñé esta noche es como comparar lo soñado con lo que realmente le pasa a uno despierto" (Acosta 116).

21. Among the English, Henry Fielding, Sarah Fielding, Zaccharia Seriman; among the French, the Marchioness of Sillers, François Guillaume Ducray-Duminil (Vogeley 227).

22. Esteban de Terralla y Landa wrote about this social type in "Vida de muchos o una semana bien empleada por un currutaco de Lima," in *Diario de Lima* (1791).

23. "Esa clase de gente alegre, moza y presumida . . . " (Acosta 128–29).

24. "Se hace gala de la ociosidad, zanganería y leperuscada en el mundo." (Acosta 186).

25. "Refleja el paso cultural del siglo XVIII al XIX" . . . la "transformación en proceso." (Guillén 76).

WORKS CITED

Acosta Enríquez, J. M. *Sueño de sueños*. Edited by Julio Jiménez Rueda. Universidad Nacional Autónoma de México, [1945] 1995.

Alonso Seoane, María José. "Los autores de tres novelas de Olavide." *Andalucía y América en el siglo XVIII*, edited by Bibiano Torres Ramírez and José J. Hernández Palomo, vol. 2, Escuela de Estudios Hispano-Americanos, 1985, pp. 1–22.

Alonso Seoane, María José. "Olavide, adaptador de novelas: una versión desconocida de *Germeuil*, de Baculard d'Arnaud." *Actas del X Congreso de la Asociación Internacional de Hispanistas*, edited by Alonso Vilanova Andreu, vol. 2. PPU, 1992, pp. 1157–66.

Alonso Seoane, María José. "La obra de René-Jean Durdent *Thérèsa, ou la Péruvienne* (París, 1818) y su traducción al castellano, *Teresa, o El terremoto de Lima* (París, 1829)." *Rumbos del hispanismo en el umbral del Cincuentenario de la AIH*, edited by Patrizia Bota, vol. 5 in *Moderna y Contemporánea*, edited by Laura Silvestri, Loretta Frattale and Matteo Lefèvre, Bagatto Libri, 2012, pp. 10–17.

Avalle Arce, Juan Bautista. *La novela pastoril española*. Istmo, 1974.

Avalle Arce, Juan Bautista. "Bernardo de Balbuena." *Diccionario enciclopédico de las letras de América Latina*, edited by Nelson Osorio Tejeda, vol. 1, Biblioteca Ayacucho, 1995, pp. 461–62.

Balbuena, Bernardo de. *Siglo de Oro en las selvas de Erífile*. Edited by José Carlos González Boixo. Universidad Veracruzana, 1989.

Barrera, Trinidad, editor. *Por lagunas y acequias. La hibridez de la ficción novohispana*. Peter Lang, 2013.

Barrera, Trinidad. "*La heroína mexicana*, una alegoría de la patria." In Barrera, ed., *Por lagunas y acequias. La hibridez de la ficción novohispana*. Peter Lang, 2013, pp. 13–23.

Bramón, Francisco. *Los sirgueros de la Virgen sin original pecado*. Edited by Trinidad Barrera. U de Navarra and Iberoamericana-Vervuert, 2013.

Bravo, María Dolores. "Los sirgueros de la Virgen." *Diccionario enciclopédico de las letras de América Latina*, edited by Nelson Osorio Tejeda, vol. 3 Biblioteca Ayacucho, 1995, pp. 4493–94.

Cabello Valboa, Miguel. *Miscelánea antártica*. Edited by Isaías Lerner. Fundación José Manuel Lara, 2011.

Chang-Rodríguez, Raquel. "*La endiablada*, relato peruano inédito del siglo XVII." *Prosa hispanoamericana virrienal*, edited by Raquel Chang-Rodríguez, Borrás, 1978, pp. 43–76.

Coello, Óscar, *Los orígenes de la novela castellana en el Perú. "La toma del Cuzco" (1539)*. Academia Peruana de la Lengua-UNMSM, 2008.

Défourneaux, Marcelin. *Pablo de Olavide, el afrancesado*. Translated by Manuel Martínez Camaró. Padilla Libros, 1990.

Dufour, Gérard. "Elementos novelescos de *El Evangelio en triunfo* de Olavide." *Anales de Literatura Española*, no. 11, 1995, pp. 107–15. Biblioteca Virtual Miguel de Cervantes, http://www.cervantesvirtual.com/nd/ark:/59851/bmc2b9b9.

Fernández de Oviedo, Gonzalo. *Libro del muy esforzado e invencible caballero don Claribalte*. Real Academia Española, 1956.

Fucilla, J. G. "Bernardo de Balbuena's *Siglo de Oro* and its Sources." *Hispanic Review*, vol. 15, 1947, pp. 101–19.

García Márquez, Gabriel. "La soledad de América Latina." Nobel Lecture, December 8, 1982. https://www.nobelprize.org/prizes/literature/1982/marquez/25603.

Goić, Cedomil. "La novela hispanoamericana colonial." *Historia de la literatura hispanoamericana. Época colonial*, edited by Luis Íñigo Madrigal, vol. 1, Cátedra, 1982, pp. 369–406.

González Boixo, José Carlos. "La prosa novelística." *Historia de la literatura mexicana. La cultura letrada en la Nueva España del siglo XVII*, edited by Raquel Chang-Rodríguez, vol. 2, Siglo XXI, 2002, pp. 288–322.

González Cañal, Rafael. "Don Quijote de la Mancha en tierras americanas." *Memoria del Nuevo Mundo. Castilla-La Mancha y América en el Quinto Centenario*, edited by Pedro Miguel Ibáñez, U de Castilla-La Mancha, 1992, pp. 205–23.

González Casanova, Pablo. *La literatura perseguida en la crisis de la colonia*. Colegio de México, 1958.

Guillén, Marco J. "José Mariano Acosta Enríquez, epígono novohispano de Francisco de Quevedo." *La Perinola*, no. 13, 2009. *Gale OneFile: Informe Académico,* https://link.gale.com/apps/doc/A426654972/IFME?u=nysl_ca_nyempire&sid=IFME&xid=8a122147.

Hopkins Rodríguez, Eduardo. "Fiesta religiosa y virtuosismo artístico en *Los sirgueros de la Virgen sin original pecado*, de Francisco Bramón." *Atalanta*, vol. 1, no. 2, 2013, pp. 77–94.

La heroína mexicana. Edited by María Isabel Terán. Terracota, 2008.

León, Andrés de [pseudonym of Martín de León]. *Historia del Huérfano*. Edited by Belinda Palacios. Fundación José Antonio Castro, 2017.

Leonard, Irving A. *Books of the Brave*. With a new introduction by Rolena Adorno. U of California P, [1949] 1992.

López Lázaro, Fabio. "La mentira histórica de un pirata caribeño: el descubrimiento del trasfondo histórico de los *Infortunios de Alonso Ramírez* (1690)." *Anuario de Estudios Americanos*, vol. 64, no. 2, 2007, pp. 87–104.

Martínez Barac, Rodrigo. "*Triunfo de la Virgen y gozo mexicano*." *Literatura Mexicana*, vol. 18, no. 2, 2007, pp. 5–37.

Núñez, Estuardo. Estudio preliminar. In Olavide. *Obras selectas*, Lima: Banco de Crédito del Perú, 1987, pp. xi–ciii.

Olavide, Pablo de. *El Evangelio en triunfo o historia de un filósofo desengañado*, Madrid: Don Joseph Doblado, 1799. https://books.google.com/books.

Olavide, Pablo de. *Obras narrativas desconocidas*. Prólogo y compilación de Estuardo Núñez, Biblioteca Nacional del Perú, 1971.

Olavide, Pablo de. *Obras selectas*. Preliminary Study, Compilation and Bibliography by Estuardo Núñez. Lima: Banco de Crédito del Perú, 1987.

Orjuela, Héctor H. "*El desierto prodigioso y prodigio del desierto*, primera novela hispanoamericana." *Thesaurus*, vol. 38, no. 2, 1983, pp. 261–324.

Palacios, Belinda. Introducción. In León [pseudónimo de Martín de León], *Historia del Huérfano*. Edited by Belinda Palacios. Fundación José Antonio Castro, 2017, pp. xi–l.

Palacios, Belinda. "Algunas claves para el análisis de la posición criollista de Martín de León y Cárdenas en la *Historia del Huérfano* (1621)." *Hipogrifo*, vol. 8, 2020, pp. 505–16.

Pascual Buxó, José. "Ficción novelesca y defensa del teatro en la *Segunda parte de los soñados regocijos de la Puebla* (manuscrito novohispano del siglo XVIII)." In Barrera, ed. *Por lagunas y acequias. La hibridez de la ficción novohispana*. Peter Lang, 2013, pp. 25–44.

Rabasa, José. "Bernardo de Balbuena." *Latin American Writers*, edited by Carlos A. Solé and Maria Isabel Abreu, vol. 1, Scribner's, 1989, pp. 53–57.

Rivas, Manuel Antonio de. *Sizigias y cuadraturas lunares*. Edited by Carolina Depetris, Introductory Studies by Adrián Curiel Rivera and Carolina Depetris. Universidad Nacional Autónoma de México, 2009. https://www.cephcis.unam.mx/wp-content/uploads/2020/04/01-sizigias_baja.pdf.

Robledo, Ana. "*El desierto prodigioso y el prodigio del desierto*." In *Diccionario enciclopédico de las letras de América Latina*, edited by Nelson Osorio Tejeda, vol. 1, Biblioteca Ayacucho, 1995, pp. 1438–39.

Rodríguez Marín, Francisco. "Don Quijote en América;" "Don Quijote en América en 1607." *Estudios cervantinos*, Atlas, 1947, pp. 107–37; 573–96.

Rodríguez Moñino, Antonio "Sobre poetas hispanoamericanos de la época virreinal." *La transmisión de la poesía española en los Siglos de Oro*, edited by Edward M. Wilson, Ariel, 1976, pp. 164–88.

Rodríguez Moñino, Antonio, and María Brey Mariño. *Catálogo de los manuscritos poéticos castellanos (siglos xv, xvi y xvii)*. Hispanic Society of America, 1965.

Sarlo, Giulia de. "Alejándonos de la metrópoli: *Los sirgueros de la Virgen*, una obra americana." Barrera, ed. *Por lagunas y acequias. La hibridez de la ficción novohispana*. Peter Lang, pp. 199–218.

Segunda parte de los soñados regocijos de la Puebla. Introduction by J. Pascual Buxó. Secretaría de Cultura del Estado de Puebla, 1998 (ed. facsimilar).

Sigüenza y Góngora, Carlos de. *Infortunios de Alonso Ramírez. Seis obras*, edited by William C. Bryant. Prologue by Irving A. Leonard. Biblioteca Ayacucho, 1984, pp. 3–47.

Sigüenza y Góngora, Carlos de. "The Misfortunes of Alonso Ramírez." *The True Adventures of a Spanish American with 17th Century Pirates*. Introduction and critical translation by Fabio López Lázaro. U of Texas P, 2011.

Solís Valenzuela, Pedro. *El desierto prodigioso y prodigio del desierto*. Edited by Rubén Páez Patiño. Introduction, Study and Notes by Jorge Páramo Pomareda, Manuel Briceño Jáuregui, Rubén Páez Patiño. 3 Vols. Instituto Caro y Cuervo, 1984.

Solís Valenzuela, Pedro. *El desierto prodigioso y prodigio del desierto*. Edited by Héctor H. Orjuela. Instituto Caro y Cuervo, 1984.

Vargas Llosa, Mario. *Carta de batalla por "Tirant lo Blanc."* Seix Barral, 1991.

Vogeley, Nancy. "La novela." *Historia de la literatura mexicana. Cambios de reglas, mentalidades y recursos retóricos en la Nueva España del siglo XVIII*, coords. Nancy Vogeley and Manuel Ramos Medina, vol. 3, Siglo XXI, 2011, pp. 221–42.

CHAPTER 2

A PICARESQUE PARROT AND DECENT DOMESTICITY

Novel Nations in Latin America

DORIS SOMMER

TURN THE PAGE

BEFORE Latin America fell in love with itself, before the Revolutions of Independence broke some bad habits of colonial corruption and abandoned Spain's obstacle course of economic and political underdevelopment, José Joaquín Fernández de Lizardi published the restless, iconoclast, irreverent but affectionately multi-voiced *El Periquillo Sarniento* (*The Mangy Parrot: The Life and Times of Periquillo Sarniento Written by Himself for His Children*). Written in 1816, the last four volumes would not be published until 1831, as a result of government censorship. A bit later, after liberators rallied a class of Creole decision-makers to make deals with the multi-layered societies of enslaved people, artisans, peasants, and other various victims of the Spanish crown, Latin Americans would spin stories of love affairs between competing regions and races of their new countries. The self-styled political orphans decided to become "bereft" of old authority, once France deposed the Spanish king in 1808. The aggression against the legitimate crown "obliged" Creoles to form self-governing *cabildos* (city councils). That was the turning point. Subjects had become citizens and would refuse to submit to the Spanish monarchy once it had been restored. They were committed to keeping their freedom, which allowed them to court each other as new fellow citizens to make romantic alliances in novel families.

Lizardi's enlightened itch is different from the later romantic urge for political courtship to consolidate new nations during and after the civil wars that typically followed independence. The energy in his book is not sexual but ethical. It is an effervescent inconformity with the colonized country that he loved. Mexico is the hero of his book, in all its registers of language and racial variety. Mexico could become, for Lizardi, a cosmopolitan member of an enlightened family of nations. He was wary of the passionate patriotism that had already inflamed people to zealous and destructive armed conflict. In his ideal country, citizens could opt for perpetual peace.[1] The villain is clear in both versions of future history, the enlightened cosmopolitanism and romantic patriotism. The enemy is a crusty colonial culture that values useless Latin phrases, that venerates worthless nobility and shuns honest work. Spain brought to America the trappings of Old World elegance as if these were marks of distinction. Periquillo uncovers the lie in one episode after another. The elitist colonial culture supported an irrational state. It cost people a sense of purpose and dignity in honest productive labor.

El Periquillo Sarniento is a picaresque novel, a late iteration of a Spanish literary genre that flourished in the sixteenth and seventeenth centuries.[2] The adventures of Lizardi's anti-hero fill more than seven hundred pages of first-person testimony about his life from birth to death in episodes about education, odd jobs, and encounters throughout Mexico and during a side trip to Manila, practically a colony of Mexico at the time. Nevertheless, according to Nancy Vogley, Lizardi was at pains to distinguish his book—offered in newspaper installments—from European genres.[3] Colonial readers would have been trained to appreciate Baroque artifice and edifying literature, she writes; Lizardi gives them neither. What he does deliver is a revival of the popular Iberian literary genre narrated in the voice of some clever but not distinguished survivor of its author's own life. *Lazarillo de Tormes* (*The Life of Lazarillo de Tormes and his Fortunes and Adversities*, 1554) is the standard reference. But an "American" variant such as Catalina de Erauso's *La monja alferez* (*The Lieutenant Nun: Memoir of a Basque Transvestite in the New World*, 1829; probably written in 1624) became a successful scandal on both continents. Erauso is a cross-dressed butch adventurer who stunned her readers with exploits of military violence and sexual conquest. "Obliged" by her confessor to luxuriate in the details of a lurid life, Erauso spent her last years in Mexico, New Spain. Quite possibly, Lizardi knew her book.

In any case, it is worth considering that the Spanish picaresque itself was practically made in America. Picaresque novels are fictions that follow a form that was generated from the self-writing of adventurers who recruited themselves for the conquest and hoped to win rewards by narrating their contributions.[4] Add to this innovation of a first-person contemporary and popular tone, the literary virtuosity of Miguel de Cervantes, who multiplies voices through local language variants and combinations of high and low registers, and you will appreciate the liberating range of literary resources available to Lizardi. Crippling, on the other hand, was the everyday colonial life that Lizardi and his contemporaries lived by the time he wrote his novel. Society had hardened into a brittle bureaucracy with trappings of elegance, empty ethics, and a cold soul. The Renaissance spirit of exploration, the Baroque exuberance and overload, the ethical Enlightenment had all been flattened into a showcase of elite paraphernalia. The colony felt to Lizardi like a cage controlled by powerful peninsular administrators: ecclesiastical, educational, military, economic. All these fronts were targets for Lizardi, low-hanging rotten fruit, ripe for ridicule.

If Miguel de Cervantes began his *Don Quixote* (1605) with charming banter between the author and a friend—to imagine how to dedicate the book and which fictional characters might offer fictional blurbs to endorse it—Lizardi begins similarly, at a loss to conjure a generous patron or ideal readers. The difference is that two centuries later and an ocean of colonial subordination apart, the humor darkens. The American prologue is all about money and failure. Money mattered in Cervantes's day too—"Poderoso caballero es don Dinero" ("Powerful gentleman is Mr. Money) quipped his contemporary Francisco de Quevedo[5]—but now money is a complicated capitalist trap. The author calculates with precision, as cost and benefit line up fruitlessly, until the poor writer is left with no hope for a patron. Lizardi will have to rely on clients, local ones:

> Because once my little work is printed and bound, it will certainly cost eight or ten pesos at the least; so even if it was a worthy book, how would I dare to send a boxful to Spain knowing that as expensive as it is here, it will necessarily be far too expensive over there? Because, if you start with ten pesos of printing costs, and add another two or three in shipping, rights and commissions, it would have to go for thirteen pesos or more; to make any money in this business, you would have to sell it for fifteen or sixteen pesos a copy, and then who would buy it there? (4)[6]

In other words, *El Periquillo Sarniento* begins by leaving Spain behind and selling himself nearby, for money. There is a word for this business in moralizing literature about sexuality. Prostitution is the fate of colonial subjects caught inside schemes of exploitation. What's more, the only real clients will be cut-rate readers including "descendants of Cain and Dalilah, traitors, and riff raff of every color."[7] Sophisticated readers trained in Baroque literary artifice also knew the charms of rough-and-tumble picaresque style. Evidently, this charm has staying power. Even today, the American roots of picaresque narrative have contemporary expressions, as writers cast themselves as roguish literary vagrants.[8] Vogeley is right to say that this novel is more than a potboiler; in fact, it resists stirring the erotic passions. That comes a generation later. Lizardi is still an enlightened moralist, hoping that reason will come to the rescue before romanticism makes passion pass for progress. Pedro Sarmiento confesses at the end of his life. He reflects with authority on theft, corruption, abuses, and so on, as someone who knows first-hand what he denounces as colonial snares.

Lizardi belongs to the generation of whistle blowers. Though he is sometimes identified with the beginning of romanticism in Latin America, it is better to locate him at the end of the Enlightenment. He is rational and ironic, critical, and clear headed. Though he lavishes affectionate attention on unsung popular subjects, Lizardi writes a cold coda to the colony, not a romantic beginning for republics. He witnessed the first phase of violent rebellion and worried about politics inflamed by passions.

LOVE THY NEIGHBOR *AND* THYSELF

Armed revolution was soon unstoppable throughout Spanish America. It broke oppressive political shackles, and this presaged the work of new constructions. With populations that had been subject to absolutist authority for centuries, how would the emotional and psychological shackles of servitude loosen? Lizardi's criticisms of colonial rule, after all, included people's personal preferences for unproductive habits of heart and mind. It is one thing to achieve political freedom and another to *feel* free, to turn subjects of authoritarian rule into autonomous citizens of new republics. War and warlike rhetoric target an enemy. Once the targets are gone and the campaigns end, what motivates people to construct a new country? Survivors of the change may even feel bereft of a ruling structure, even if the structure was oppressive. In response to this anxiety and to the dangers of regional revolts by still armed caudillos who vied for power, several new states considered establishing constitutional monarchies as an alternative to republics. The republican option was riskier than choosing political continuity through an enlightened ruler. Republics require participants who develop a modern sense of self that combines self-interest with dedication to the public good, like a loving parent who derives personal pleasure from a family that flourishes.

Overwhelmingly, Latin Americans chose republican citizenship. After very real military victories, militants put down their weapons and were ready to love themselves and each other. Self-liberated heroes decided to become mutually authorizing citizens as new countries took shape and constructed institutions. This period of intense engagement and optimism is when national romances were written. Authors of national novels were typically also political founding fathers who helped to consolidate their new republics by means of the creation of democratic institutions, roughly between the 1850s and 1880s. Legislators, or generals, or diplomats by day, they were creative writers by night. The novels projected a path toward harmony and growth through the language of love. Old World tyranny had ended, and people were free to husband the land. Husbands needed wives to produce new generations of citizens.

The vocabulary of marriage is more than a metaphor; it is a synecdoche for the national family. Coupling was a way to understand alliances. It was also a practice among different sectors of society who launched productive collaborations. *Laissez-faire* was the slogan for the times. Desire for love-marriages and for free enterprise went together, even if romantic French and English novels kept them tragically apart. Duty and desire pointed in different directions, for Flaubert, Stendhal, Dickens, Brontë, and others, though Jane Austin dared to pair them up. Sliding from sentimental to economically rational referents, the tangle of modern desire for family and nation channeled practically all activities through the natural language of sex, as Foucault argued.[9] In fact, this modern desire to be free and productive can be understood as *the* fundamental desire to be modern, period.

Nineteenth-century readers and writers in Latin America would take for granted this slippage between *eros* and *polis*. Love doubled its registers as both intensely personal and broadly political. Love is not new to novels; in fact, mothers would forbid their daughters to read the sexually exciting books. But the otherwise salacious theme of love is here refreshingly virtuous. Foundational romances take advantage of literary habits that assume readers will identify with heroes—as in elite classic tragedies. But Latin American national novels smuggle in new lovers, handsome youths of color from politically marginal groups. Their love affairs with elite partners generate for readers an intensely personal and shared public desire for marriage and political consolidation across racial and class barriers. By the end of the century, enthusiasm for mixed marriages subsides because alliances had broken down and the pessimism of naturalist literature set in. The short-lived dream of democracy and prosperity had already dimmed.

But the novels that nations consecrated as foundational fictions were written during the glorious generation of optimism for Latin American republics. Citizens felt an intuitive overlap between erotics and economics, and they embraced them together as a double-barreled engine for progress. Even if the engine was designed earlier, in Europe, it was the New World that built the prototypes. Hannah Arendt even speculated that John Locke learned how to theorize liberal government by observing North American economic practices.[10]

"The French always say . . . *l'amour fait rage, et l'argent fait marriage*; but here, love makes both madness and *marriage*!" (Blest Gana 257).[11] This quip from a comic character in *Martín Rivas* (Chile 1862) gets the moral of his and other mid-century stories admirably right. The speaker is the spoiled son of a banker who had married a rich wife. Recently returned from Paris, the young heir to the family fortune is outraged by the news that his brilliant and beautiful sister plans to marry beneath their social rank. Leonor chose a humble but industrious fiancé, even though her combined personal and economic worth made her the center of attention for many attractive suitors. She preferred the hard-working provincial law student, in part because his administrative talents made the family business thrive. This is not what should happen, the brother protests, having been trained in French taste, so that he was caught by surprise in a plot that is obviously modeled after Stendahl's tragic *Le rouge et le noir* (*The Red and the Black*, 1830). The French novel ends with the provincial hero's refusal to be saved by love, preferring instead to become a martyr to aristocratic ideals. The American Julien preferred to live and to prosper. Other Latin Americans also knew the difference between elitist Europe and practical America. Though they admired French and English models, Latin Americans did not simply imitate them; they used Europe. Imported novel styles were adjusted to flatter local figures. So, the disoriented fop who comes back home to Santiago actually manages—with this *bon mot*—to theorize the main ideological alteration of European novels to fit Latin Americans of the period. It was the same difference between American development and European dissolution that made José Martí warn readers against foreign fictions. There, love is destructive, a threat to harmony and to prosperity. Desire versus duty. Tragic heroes had to choose. But "here" in the New World, the unsettled brother protests, desire coincides with duty and becomes the single double agent of all happiness.

His surprise at the streamlined formula is understandable. European conventions could not have prepared him for love as economically rational. Nor could he have expected the corollaries of that enabling convergence between love and money. One corollary is the even-handed treatment of men and women in Latin American foundational novels. Another is the assertiveness of heroines while heroes can be coy and even delicate. These are unanticipated and still exhilarating moves that come from the purposeful confusion of reason with rapture. Surprising too is the fact that the formula is repeated from country to country. The very fact that we can identify an international genre that is driven by productive desire was news for literary historians. For political historians too. And feminists who expected to see women subordinated, as usual in literature and in life, will have to admit that here the portrayals of partners are surprisingly equitable.

National novels that governments required as reading in public schools and that by now blend into patriotic histories read like local variations on one theme. This had been hard to notice because the books did not travel far at first. And then, with the 1960s "boom" of experimental narrative, they seemed too simple for sophisticated tastes. So hardly anyone read them together or bothered to make general observations. But the overlaps are astounding. To begin with, all of these books are love stories.

Why should national, state-promoted, novels all be about romantic love? An easy an-swer, of course, is that nineteenth-century novels were all love stories in Latin America. But the answer raises a question about what novels have to do with requirements for civic education. The novels were not immediately taught in public schools, except per-haps in the Dominican Republic, where *Enriquillo* (1882) appeared rather late and where the small number of students probably meant that there were enough copies available.[12] In other cases, serialized sentimental novels were hardly academic or even proper lit-erature at first, to judge by their exclusion from the first national literary histories that hoped to consolidate a "progressive-conservative" tradition through poetry.[13] The oxy-moron of "progressive-conservative" in official histories is a sign that young and precar-ious republics learned to coordinate differences. But the official histories omit the most useful renderings of oxymoronic consolidations. These are the romances that celebrated or predicted an identification between hearts and minds, the sentimental nation and its institutionalized state.[14] The novel as the meeting ground for passion and patriotism is not a fantasy or a wishful reading. It is the accomplishment of foundational fictions when democracy seemed within reach.

Until the 1990s, historians had supposed that popular movements in the nineteenth century were almost by definition opposed to the state, just as feminist literary critics supposed that nineteenth-century national novels were patriarchal and dismissive of women. But fresh literary readings bring women into focus as protagonists, often drivers of the novels. Similarly, fresh historical readings rescue the creativity and mo-bility of subaltern groups that were assumed always to be oppositional, either silenced or driven to rebellion. Groups that represented marginalized subjects of the Spanish colonies—indigenous peoples, Afro-Latin Americans, artisans, campesinos, women— were energized by independence. They were challenged to carve out new roles in the new republics. Their undefined social status and political identities allowed some wiggle room to develop strategies and enhance opportunities. Subaltern colonial subjects be-came active citizens of Latin American republics. Though the nineteenth century did witness heroic rebellions of marginalized groups against the Creole elites, other popular movements participated in national life. They allied with elites, as if acting out the plots of romantic novels. They demanded resources, voted, and bargained with powerful sectors to win more rights and resources. While there is no simple synthetic narrative for these popular participatory movements because historical accounts require detail, the general tendencies offer a stunning parallel and validation for the pattern of foundational fictions in the region. Partnerships across races, classes, and regions of new countries were as real as they were romantic.[15]

Required reading came generations after the first—often serialized—publications; precisely when and under which particular circumstances in each country are questions that merit a different study.[16] But in general, one can surmise that after renewed internal oppositions pulled the image of an ideal nation away from the existing state, like a mask from a masquerader, after nationalism could be understood as a political movement against the state,[17] nineteenth-century novels offered a way for states to cover over the chasm between power and desire. The books that were so immediately seductive for elite readers, whose private desires overlapped with public institutions, became portals to induct new citizens into the (natural and irresistible) desires for/of the government in power.

Erotics and politics go together almost everywhere in Latin America. The combination is shared in the cultural DNA of the region. A particular novel may be celebrated in its national tradition as autochthonous, characteristic, and somehow inimitable, yet each romance shares much more than its institutional status with the others. The resemblances may be symptomatic of nationalism's general paradox: cultural features that seem unique and worthy of patriotic (self)-celebration are often typical of other nations too and even patterned after foreign models.[18] Almost like sexual intimacy, whatever seems most private turns out to be embarrassingly public knowledge.[19] A range of divergent partisan programs in particular settings might seem to overload any common structure to the point of crushing it. Read individually, the foundational fictions are very different ones from the others, accepting racism here, advocating abolition there, sometimes defending free trade, other times arguing for protectionism. A few examples can illustrate the range.

Argentina's *Amalia* (José Mármol, 1851) sets European civilization against American barbarism as the backdrop to a love affair between antagonistic regions of the country. A hot-headed Buenos Aires boy recuperates—*Ivanhoe* style—from a wound inflicted by the enemy in the home of a dignified provincial young widow. Chile's *Martín Rivas* (Alberto Blest Gana, 1862) amplifies the historical alliance between the dynamic bourgeoisie of northern miners and the "aristocratic" class of southern bankers. In Cuba, mitigation of conflict has to be imagined rather than acknowledged. Abolitionist novels condemn slavery in tragic Cuban novels written before independence. They make interracial love an incentive for achieving a new social order. The mixed-race hero *Sab* (Gertrudis Gómez de Avellaneda, 1841) sacrifices himself for the love of his white mistress. After he dies, she recognizes and reciprocates his passion. Four decades later, racism seems inextricable in *Cecilia Valdés* (*Cecilia Valdés or El Angel Hill*) (Cirilo Villaverde, Cuba, 1882); the privilege of Creole elites is now a goal for free people of color who are nevertheless stuck behind an indelible color line. Race relations are tragic too in *Aves sin nido* (*Torn from the Nest*) (Clorinda Matto de Turner, 1889), this time between Peru's Indians and whites, while *El Zarco* (*El Zarco: The Bandit*)

(Manuel Altamirano, 1888) promises national regeneration through the partnership of an Indian leader who learns to love his mestiza admirer during the same years that Mexicans were learning to admire their Indian president Benito Juárez. And though color hardly seems an issue in *María* (Jorge Isaacs, 1867), Latin America's most popular nineteenth-century novel, racial disturbance erupts in the Colombian planters' paradise through the trembling body of originally Jewish María, doubly damned for representing the incestuous plantocracy and the racially inassimilable blacks. In Brazil's *O guaraní* (*The Guarany: Brazilian Novel*) (José de Alencar, 1857), enslaved blacks do not appear. Instead, the country's racial tensions are represented by an amorous Indian whose mistress finally escapes with him, while in *Iracema* (1865) the Tupí maiden's passion for a Portuguese soldier produces the first Brazilian, both Tupí and not Tupí. Santo Domingo's *Enriquillo* (*The Cross and the Sword*) (Manuel de Jesús Galván, 1882) similarly replaces rebellious blacks for peace-loving native Americans. A lasting cultural consequence has been that some people of color in the country still identify as indigenous "indios."

As a rhetorical solution to the various crises in these novels/nations, cross-racial love is often the figure for subsuming the "primitive" or "barbarous" sector of the Creole elite in color-coded flirtations between liberals and conservatives. The real alliances often are between white antagonists with conflicting agendas; the conservatives are cast as Creoles and the liberals as indigenous nobility. Brazil's romances are examples, as are Ecuador's *Cumandá* (*Cumandá: The Novel of the Ecuadorian Jungle*) (Juan León Mera, 1887), where the Indian heroine is revealed as the missionary's lost daughter, and Uruguay's *Tabaré* (*Tabaré: An Indian Legend of Uruguay*) (Juan Zorrilla de San Martín, 1888), which sacrifices the heroic mestizo (possibly associated with imperializing Brazil) so that Hispanic civilization can prevail. With a late iteration in Venezuela's *Doña Bárbara* (Rómulo Gallegos, 1929), the authoritarian father—who had stepped aside during nineteenth century to allow youth to court freely—takes control again. Venezuela seemed neither ready for conciliation nor desperate enough to defer sovereignty to an indigenous Enriquillo-type figure. Instead, this anti-imperialist novel makes its hero an apprentice to the domineering mestiza vamp whom he will replace once he marries her daughter.

Is there common ground for Chile's vertical integration, Cuba's racial integration, Argentina's color-coded campaigns, Colombia's retrograde idyll, Ecuador's Jesuitical paternalism, Venezuela's vamp-raiding? The common grounding, as I have said, is productive erotic passion. The recognizable genre of national novel varies, in particular regarding political goals and cultural assumptions. Nevertheless, a core element of the genre is clear: it is an erotic energy that hopes to reconcile antagonistic sectors cast as lovers who desire each other. Whether the plots end happily or not, the romances are invariably about love. Passionate, heterosexual romance is what moved the imaginary protagonists along with their flesh-and-blood readers. Their countries claimed legitimacy through nature and rebelled against the unnatural powers of Spain and Portugal. The new nations continued to fight internally, often between centralists and federalists, throughout the mid-nineteenth century. Stability and prosperity depended on making deals and learning to live together. The literary training project to foster alliances took advantage of the irresistible language of love.

Long novels came out in newspaper installments over enough time to rehearse readers in the novel feelings of bonding and citizenship. Written by nation-builders themselves during lulls in the civil wars or once peace promised to recover some damages, the novels appealed to citizens-in-the-making. The appeal was to stop fighting and to become real citizens by founding national families. Make love not war, was the implied slogan of legislation as well as literature. The author of Argentina's 1853 constitution, Juan Bautista Alberdi, turned the slogan into a practical campaign. His foundational points for the constitution actually took erotic attraction into account. He famously promoted a strategy to increase the population because "gobernar es poblar" ("to govern is to populate"). And his tactics included generous immigration policies, for which he is remembered. But he also encouraged marriages between industrious Anglo-Saxons and Argentina's "army" of beautiful women, eminently equipped for the eugenics campaign to "improve" local and "inefficient" Spanish stock. Without women who could conquer industrious European men, Argentine Creoles risked just giving up the country's resources to the hard-working foreigners. During the twenty years of Alberdi's matchmaking, luring the sword-wielding Joshuas of independence to reform their tools into Isaiah's ploughs, novelists were also reforming one thing into another: valor into sentimentalism, epic into romance, hero into husband. This helped to solve the problem of establishing the white man's legitimacy in the New World, now that the illegitimate conquerors had been ousted. Without a proper genealogy to root them in the land, Creoles had at least to establish conjugal and then paternity rights, making a generative rather than genealogical claim. They had to win America's heart and body so that the founders could husband her and reproduce themselves in cultivated children. To be legitimate, their love had to be mutual; even if the fathers set the tone, the mothers had to reciprocate.[20]

The novels worked like training manuals, paced over long periods of time to wean the public away from fruitless passions gradually, and then to quicken the pulse of productive desire. A typical plot begins with an easy erotic hook for conventional readers. Cuban Carlota falls in love with a dazzling Englishman, for example, and Indian Nicolás lusts after white Manuela who loves the blue-eyed bandit El Zarco. But then the narratives undo aristocratic traps to follow a lifeline of new and liberal passions, beyond the murderous differences of class, region, and race. A wholesome object of desire displaces a corrupt fantasy. For example, the Indian hero of *El Zarco* suffers heartbreak because of the ruthless blond before the mestiza heroine turns his head; *Amalia*'s intransigent boyfriend learns some flexibility from a double agent in order to survive in Argentina; Cuban Carlota realizes too late that she wasted her passion on the Englishman when mulatto Sab was her ideal lover; and Chile's haughty heiress dismissed poor Martín Rivas so often that she almost loses him.

All over Latin America, the "active citizenry" was coming to understand personal desire as the motor for both passionate and patriotic projects. Desire mobilized modernity, as the goad for capitalist accumulation *and* as the unaffected, natural, name for love (between opposite sexes, and opposing national sectors). Desire is the intensely personal feeling that takes risks on intimate unions among dissimilar citizens. There was no shame in celebrating risk in the new republics.

Latin Americans who read Hegel may have felt flattered or confirmed in their mission to promote modernity as the natural destiny of the Americas. Like him, they knew that love was the grounding for ethics, which begin in the family unit where members subordinate their own interests to other members through feelings of love.[21] But they would have winced to see how quickly Hegel moved from democratizing lateral bonds to patriarchal hierarchy, where women willingly submit to their men. The novelists were more patient; they took time to play out the tensions of mutual desire, even if they agreed that families should be mini-polities naturally headed by fathers, like hegemonies of active citizens and willing supporters. In fact, *Martín Rivas* ends happily when the strong-willed heroine marries Martín and becomes his "angel of submission." But this happens at the end of five-hundred pages, while readers strain to get the lovers together and confirm that Leonor is the decision maker. It is the gambit of reciprocal desire—developed between equally ideal and coy lovers during long pages and many months of newspaper installments—not the endgame of submission, which was so promising for patriots. What it promised was a remedy for the rifts of civil war. Without representing both established money and risky businesses as equally powerful opponents who need each other (the popular classes only support the entrepreneurial hero, it is true), Chile's national romance cannot work. Desire is the name of the energy that pulls the heroes toward each other, and then holds them together through contracts, including marriage contracts. Thanks to their ardor, lovers strive to overcome the obstacles to modernity and, thereby, simultaneously consolidate their new country. Subjective personal feelings can bring objective national results, in the fantasies that fueled patriotic purpose. When citizens are allowed to do as they will, in liberal fiction and philosophy, they will combine in productive associations.

Evidently, liberalism in Latin America (and elsewhere) went deeper than economic reasoning. From John Locke, Adam Smith, Immanuel Kant, and others, we know that liberalism includes a dimension of sociability and sympathy. Latin American romantics took unorthodox liberties to stretch that dimension toward passionate love. Asking for permission to stretch did not concern them. Philosophical rigor was one nuisance they could simply wish away, unlike the material nuisances of war debts, and wasted fields and mines, all of which fanned regional and racial rage. The will to repair the damage was certainly reasonable, and agents of modernity could appreciate that. But the energy required seemed beyond reasonable hope in countries where elites were used to demanding submission rather than winning it through hegemonic arrangements. Love was that energy, irrational and benevolent.

Turn a Phrase

How did the novels manage to enlist eroticism in campaigns for national consolidation? It was, after all, a significant literary accomplishment to interpolate readers of romance and to reform their feelings in ways that prepared them to become active citizens. Rhetorically, the accomplishment was achieved by sleight-of-the-invisible-hand of nature. Nature is the ubiquitous bridge between passion and productivity. Invisible and unspoken, a culture's most basic assumptions need no defense or articulation. Silences are the giveaway to understand fundamental social conventions, Pierre Macherey points out (95). In this collective Latin American case, one basic assumption is that heterosexual love is natural and therefore unstoppable. Another assumption is that sex and other natural practices are productive. With these cultural anchors, authors could substitute one assumption for another and could count on the analogy between erotics and alliance to jump-start a desire for national consolidation. Consolidation was the novel challenge that new nations faced. Otherwise, countries risked falling into cycles of continuing conflict that cost lives and capital. Instability threatened independence, as became dramatic in the Dominican Republic when the Creole state invited Spain back to recolonize the country. Where politics looked precarious, personal passion looked constant. Literarily, at least, erotic love could tether the conflicting parties and link them to a deeper, more natural, level of feelings. On the one hand, sexual desire legitimated political alliances as natural; and on the other hand, the political purpose of desire heightened the passion and consecrated the sexual union of partners with a public purpose.[22] Briefly put, eros and polis take each other as the legitimating ground of their respective stories. One dynamic represents the other and fuels it. The unrequited passion of the love story produces a surplus of energy, just as Rousseau suggested it would,[23] a surplus that can hope to overcome the political interference between the lovers. And the enormity of social abuse invests the love story with an almost sublime sense of purpose. As the plots progress, the intensity of feeling grows in tandem with the dedication to patriotism until the tangle of desires make personal and political goals indistinguishable from each other.

One libidinal investment ups the ante for the other. The obstacles that lovers face increase our desires and tighten the tangle between passion and patriotism. The two levels of desire are different, but they are not discrete.[24] Desire weaves between the individual and the public family in a way that shows the terms to be contiguous, coextensive as opposed to merely analogous. And desire keeps weaving, or doubling, at personal and political levels, because the obstacles it encounters threaten both levels of happiness.

From our historical distance, both romantic love and patriotism can seem natural because we are all beneficiaries or victims of the training process associated with foundational fictions. Feelings can remain even when we know that the desires are produced artificially, perhaps, by the very novels that (re)present them. To acknowledge this possibility is also to ask whether what may have passed for effects of the greater culture in the novel (romantic love or conciliatory nationalism) may be artificial construct of that culture. If heroes and heroines in Latin American novels were passionately desiring each other by trespassing traditional lines and desiring the new state that would join them, they were not repeating timeless or essential affections. Those passions would not have prospered a generation earlier. *El Periquillo Sarniento* would not have fallen for the sentimental strategy. But modernizing lovers by mid-century were learning how to dream their erotic fantasies by reading the frustrating European romances they hoped to improve.

The broad work that national novels do to consolidate patriotism and encourage productivity in Latin America is a window onto modernity in general. Other regions of the world produced varieties of the same modernizing genre that conjugated sexuality with nationalism. Examples extend to China and Africa, and surely elsewhere.[25] The reading lesson that Latin America can teach about the reliance of modernity on heterosexual love cum patriotism derives from the consistency of the pattern despite the particularities of national projects. Novels conjugate insights from Michel Foucault's *The History of Sexuality* and from Benedict Anderson's *Imagined Communities* to create a combustion system for progress in the framework of capitalist development. Novels represent an alliance between these two books. The assumed and therefore silent drive of heterosexual love, to follow Foucault, and the taken-for-granted enthusiasm for republican patriotism, in Anderson's view, support each other as mutual anchors for feelings that might have remained mono-dimensional had they not implied public commitments in private courtships and private flourishing in public policies. Neither Foucault's brilliant book nor Anderson's acknowledges the other's contributions or discovers this dynamic allegory. Dialectical, dynamic, allegory is a literary structure that Walter Benjamin rescued from Baroque drama to defend the importance of time and process in history. His essay on "Allegory and Trauerspiel" (1928),[26] is a polemic against Nazi contemporaries who were beguiled by eternal truths and who refused to consider the effects of time. Latin American novels are dynamic, as they establish allegorical relationships between love and country. They enact a movement that shuttles between public and private levels of romance to pick up enough steam to launch campaigns on both levels of development.

In the nineteenth century everyone was reading romances, which is the reason that Mexican Ignacio Altamirano, among many others, was using them for patriotic projects. "Novels are undoubtedly the genre that the public likes best," he wrote in 1868; "they are the artifice through which today's best thinkers are reaching the masses with doctrines and ideas that would otherwise be difficult to impart" (17).[27] Sexual love was *the* trope for associative behavior, unfettered market relationships, and for nature in general. And the state evidently derived some of its power from its positive attractions as the guarantor (or promisor) of rights, services, and national pride. While nations were being embodied, their borders meticulously drawn and their resources territorialized, so too were the sexual bodies that attract Foucault's attention. He understands his project to be a "history of bodies" (Foucault, 152), much as Anderson's is a study of national bodies.

Anderson valued the novel, like the newspaper, for its synchronicity, its *horizontal* and democratizing commonality of time, rather than for the desire that drives time in diachronic movement forward. Print communities were being consolidated because everyone read the same news, but Latin America's serialized novels are evidence that the print communities were also anticipating next installments of novels to pant or cry together as they read the paper. Had Anderson read his own featured example of homogeneous time through more than one lens, the opening "Social Gathering" chapter of

José Rizal's Filipino national novel, *Noli me tangere*, he would have identified sex as the forward-directed motor of erotic sociability. At the party, the bored protagonist turns into a dynamic hero when he leaves the room full of men and crosses over to where the women are: "The room is almost full, the men separated from the women like in Catholic churches and in the synagogues" (7).[28] And:

> The young man found himself alone in the center of the room. The owner of the house had disappeared, and there was no one to introduce him to the young ladies, many of whom were looking at him with great interest. After vacillating for a few seconds, he went towards with a simple, natural grace.
> "If you will allow me," he said, "I hope we can leap over the rules of strict etiquette. I have not been in my country for seven years, and now that I am back, I cannot refrain from greeting its most beautiful attribute, its women." (17)[29]

Nature was no longer the classical space of predictable law but the scene of flux where energy could meet obstacles and turn frustration into more fuel for change. The allegories of sentimental lovers who double as patriotic heroes create echo systems in which one role legitimates the other. Both, as I have been saying, are grounded in the legitimating language of nature. Since enlightened independence, nature had been conveniently redefined as interactive rather than hierarchical. Modern nature produced angels and monsters, not clockwork. The allegories strain at points; it is true. For one thing, the writing elite was loathe to give up its hierarchical privilege to conciliatory projects, and for another thing, characters can exceed or somehow miss an ideally assigned meaning. Novels have a way of allowing discord and surprise, as Bakhtin taught us under the safer term "dialogue."[30]

My point is more general than particular. Beyond examples of anomalies and partial failures, we should register the remarkable measure of the allegory's success. In many cases, the double-dealing romance actually helped to give cognitive expression and emotional mooring to the social and political formations that the romances desired. Historical novels became national icons in their respective countries. The term "national novel" refers less to their market popularity, although some of these novels were immediately popular, than to their usefulness as required reading in school curricula. By the first decades of the twentieth century, young citizens were falling in love with each other and with their countries through the guided connections between the two objects of desire thanks to consecrated national novels. The romantic promise of a nationalizing embrace was particularly appealing for countries that had stimulated massive immigration at the end of the nineteenth century and worried that they would forfeit their cultural core. Later, after turn-of-the-century mass migrations, a new incentive for sharing the same patriotic dream was the Great Depression, which had spawned "foreign" ideologies (of socialism and communism) that competed with patriotic programs for economic and civic development. These states, in other words, took advantage of the nineteenth-century pot-boilers to reinforce national families that had, by then, established authoritative governments.

FUEL FOR THE FUTURE

Romance works whether or not it ends well. In fact, the tragedies and frustrations of heroes and heroines destined to love each other fire readers up to dismantle the obstacles that amount to cruel and unnatural constraints. National histories in Latin America hardly ever take a triumphalist tone because the nineteenth century and much of what followed stayed mired in the obstacles of colonialist culture and personalist competitions for power. Racism and *caudillismo* are chronic ailments. Even when the national novels identify available remedies, the obstacles continue to plague new and precarious countries. The very language of disease and disorder that merits the description of "naturalism" in the following generation of novels is a sign of fatigue and discouragement. Nature is no longer a platform for growth but a process of decay. Benjamin understood historical allegories in this downward spiraling movement. At the cusp of this downturn, and at opposite ends of political options, consider the difference between two almost contemporary Ecuadorian novels. One is patriotic *Cumandá* (finally published in 1887), Juan León Mera's endorsement of Garcia Moreno's heavy-handed authority that nevertheless revived a Jesuitical commitment to integrate indigenous communities, and Miguel Riofrío's *La emancipada* (The Free Woman, 1863). Written in exile, at a safe distance from García Moreno's dictatorship, Riofrío tells the tragic story of an educated and liberated young woman who refuses colonial and patriarchal constraints. She ends badly, in a brothel, consumed by syphilis.

Is it any wonder that *Cumandá* is Ecuador's national novel and not *La emancipada*? *Cumandá* displays real literary value and its attention to geography, and ethnography merited the attention of the Royal Spanish Academy that elected Mera as an offshore member. But other detailed and powerfully written novels in Latin America were sidelined in national curricula by more programmatic options. Manuel Payno's *Los bandidos de Río Frío* (*The Bandits from Río Frío: A Naturalistic and Humorous Novel of Customs, Crimes, and Horrors*, 1889–1891) was probably more popular than *El Zarco*, for example, but the adventures of bandits could not compete for educational value with the story of bringing bandits to justice through an alliance between an Indian hero and a mestiza heroine. Endorsements of productive love and civic commitment prevail in national curricula over conclusions that modernity is not worth the risk. National novels capture the moments and the movements of possible progress to fire up the optimism that sustains hard work, for the glory of the "gran familia nacional" (great national family).

NOTES

1. Turpin, Kristen Meylor, "Slippery Solidarity: Performative Complements to the National Allegory" (2016). Publicly Accessible Penn Dissertations. 2066. https://repository.upenn.edu/edissertations/2066

2. Claudio Guillén. (1987). The anatomies of roguery. Garland Pub.

3. Vogeley, Nancy. "Defining the 'Colonial Reader': El Periquillo Sarniento." *PMLA*, vol. 102, no. 5, Modern Language Association, 1987, pp. 784–800, https://doi.org/10.2307/462308.

4. On the connections between the self-writing of the conquistadors and the picaresque, see Erik Camayd-Freixas. (1998). Realismo mágico y primitivismo : relecturas de Carpentier, Asturias, Rulfo y García Márquez. University Press of America.

5. "Poderoso caballero es don Dinero" is the title of a poem by Francisco de Quevedo (1580–1645). https://www.poemas-del-alma.com/poderoso-caballero-es-don-dinero.htm

6. "Porque haz de cuenta que mi obrita, ya impresa y encuadernada, tiene de costo por lo menos ocho o diez pesos; pues aunque fuera una obra de mérito, ¿cómo había yo de mandar a España un cajón de ejemplares, cuando si aquí es cara, allí lo sería excesivamente? Porque si a diez pesos de costos se agregaban otros dos o tres de fletes, derechos y comisión, ya debería valer sobre trece pesos; para ganar algo en este comercio, era preciso vender los ejemplares a quince o dieciséis pesos, y entonces, ¿quién la compraría allá?" (Lizardi, *El Periquillo Sarniento* vii).

7. "You are related by kinship with the fratricidal Cains, the idolatrous Nebuchadnezzars, the prostituting Delilahs, the sacrilegious Balthasars, the accursed Hams, the traitorous Judases, the perfidious Sinons, the thieving Cacuses, the heretical Ariuses, and a host of roguish ladies and gents who have lived, past and present, in the same world as ourselves" (6) ("Tenéis relaciones de parentesco con los Caínes fratricidas, con los idólatras Nabucos, con las prostitutas Dalilas, con los sacrílegos Baltazares, con los malditos Canes, con los traidores Judas, con los pérfidos Sinones, con los herejes Arrios, y con una multitude de pícaros y pícaras que han vivido y aún viven en el mismo mundo que nosotros" (x)).

8. On contemporary revisions of the picaresque, see Jorge Tellez. (2021). The Picaresque and the Writing Life in Mexico. University of Notre Dame Press. https://doi.org/10.2307/j.ctv 19m64ht

9. For Foucault, sex is the language for everything: see *The History of Sexuality*, vol. 1. Michel Foucault, & Hurley, R. (1988). The history of sexuality (1st Vintage Books ed.). Vintage Books.

10. "On the contrary, if Locke in a famous passage states, 'That which begins and actually constitutes any political society is nothing but the consent of any number of freemen capable of majority, to unite and incorporate into such society,' and then calls this act the 'beginning to any lawful government in the world,' it rather looks as though he was more influenced by the *facts and events in American*, and perhaps in a more decisive manner, than the founders were influenced by his *Treatises of Civil Government* . . . the way Locke construed this 'original' original compact,' in line with the current social-contract theory, as a surrender of rights and powers to either the government or the community, that is, not at all as a 'mutual' contract but as an agreement in which an individual person resigns his power to some higher authority and consents to be ruled in exchange for a reasonable protection of his life and property" Hannah Arendt. (1963). On revolution. Viking Press. pm 168).

11. "Los franceses . . . dicen: '*l'amour fait rage et l'argent fait mariage*' pero aquí el amor hace los dos *rage* et *marriage*" Alberto Blest Gana, Martín Rivas (Novela de costumbres político-sociales) Prólogo, Notas, and Cronología by Jaime Concha (Caracas: Biblioteca Ayacucho, 1977): 249. (Blest Gana 249).

12. Franklin J. Franco tells us that *Enriquillo* was ""elevated since the past century to the level of required reading in the public school system" (67). But other national novels became required reading later, after governments had resources for massive publication of anything but textbooks (often of natural law, philosophy, literature, through selections of

Latin classics, and later history). As in the United States, American literature did not have immediate academic legitimacy. The first documented ""Programa de literatura española y de los estados hispano-americanos" in Argentina is the 1884 course by Professor Calixto Oyuela for the fourth year at the Colegio Nacional de la Capital: *Amalia* figures along with *La Cautiva* and *Gauchesca* poetry (16). But literature as part of patriotic education was still being argued for by Ricardo Rojas in *La restauración nacionalista* (1922). In Mexico the first university courses in literature were instituted in 1912, with the beginning of the (antipositivist) revolution. See Alfonso Reyes (214). By 1933, required readings had for some time included Altamirano along with Fernández Lizardi, Payno, Sierra, and others; see Programas detallados para las escuelas secundarias (54).

The example of Chile has a documented analog in teaching national history. It is the delayed cult of Arturo Prat, the 1879 hero of the War of the Pacific. Iván Jaksic speculated for me that *Martín Rivas* was probably required by the same nationalist leaders and educators who responded to civic demands during the depression—and in the "face" of alien ideologies—by institutionalizing Prat's heroism, turning it into a model of hard work and national reconciliation. On Prat, see Sater.

13. Written at the same mid-century moment as the novels and with largely the same legitimizing impulse, their authors had considerable political credentials but more classical criteria than the novelists. Literary historians selected a kind of elite prehistory for the "progressive-conservative" consolidations that were stabilizing the new states; see Beatriz González Stephan (2012). Fundaciones: canon, historia y cultura nacional: La historiografía literaria del liberalismo hispanoamericano del siglo XIX. Vervuert Verlagsgesellschaft., esp.pp. 159 and 193. Most of the literary historians had rigorous religious training, and some studied to be priests. They borrowed aesthetic criteria from Aristotle, Boileau, and Luzán, and they worked in party politics as lawyers, university professors, or deans; most were senators, deputies, ministers, and diplomats. Often the project was more a desideratum than a record, since new countries, so resistant to their colonial past, had little literature to report on, Brazil being an exception.

14. Also excluded from first literary histories were indigenous literatures, oral Hispanic literature, many chronicles, and various hybrid forms, see González Stephan (191–92).

15. Mallón's 1995 pioneering study is the best, but compares only Mexico and Peru. Mallón's study shares many theoretical preoccupations with Joseph and Nugent (1994), an edited volume to which the author contributed; both of these studies have informed many subsequent works. Florencia Mallon. (1995). Peasant and nation. University of California Press.

George Reid Andrews (2004) Afro-Latin America, 1800-2000. Oxford University Press, offers a magisterial overview of the Afro-Latin American experience post-independence, with a much broader purview than popular movements, but does cover such actions in the nineteenth century. For those interested in Afro-Latin American experience after slavery, Rebecca Scott and Michael Zeuskeprovide an exhaustive bibliography in which to look for popular movements. Rebecca Scott, & Michael Zeuske, M. (2002). Property in Writing, Property on the Ground: Pigs, Horses, Land, and Citizenship in the Aftermath of Slavery, Cuba, 1880–1909. *Comparative Studies in Society and History*, 44(4), 669–699. https://doi.org/10.1017/S0010417502000324

16. In anticipation of such a sociology of literature, one way to read the history of institutionalization is symptomatically, from the record of publications. I am grateful to Antonio Cornejo Polar for this suggestion, and to Ludwig Lauerhaus of the library at UCLA for assenting. That record is often thin until the 1920s or 1930s, when large editions would follow one

another almost yearly. In the admittedly spotty entries of *The National Union Catalog Pre-1956 Imprints*, several editions of *Amalia* appear before the 1930s (more in Europe than in Buenos Aires, and two editions for American students, with notes and exercises). But from 1930, Sopena—first in Barcelona then in Buenos Aires—begins to repeat printings every two or three years even in this incomplete list. Simultaneous publishers of *Amalia* are Espasa-Calpe in Madrid and Buenos Aires, and also in Buenos Aires, Editorial Estrada. Altamirano's *El Zarco* (another favorite of American Spanish teachers, as indeed were almost all of these national novels) appeared in 1901 and shows three printings in this list until 1940. In the following decade, Espasa-Calpe of Buenos Aires and Mexico reissued it four times, joined by Mexico's Editora Nacional in 1951. *Tabaré*, by Zorrilla de San Martín, to give just one last example from the *Catalog*, has had a remarkable number of printings and editions over time especially since the 1920s (two full pages of the catalog for this one work). And Blest Gana's *Martín Rivas* seems to have been standard reading early (for Chileans as well as for American students through the D. C. Heath edition). Jorge Román-Lagunas's "Bibliografía anotada de y sobre Alberto Blest Gana," informs that during the last century the novel had five printings; in this one, by 1980, it has already had thirty. [This long note was lifted from an MLA essay I did in 200, called "FOR LOVE AND MONEY: OF POTBOILERS AND PRECAUTIONS."]

17. This is John Breully's general definition in *Nationalism and the State*.

18. "The demand for a nation-state with many of the features of other nation-states seems hard to reconcile with the justification that a unique nation needs its own special form of independence" (Breully 342).

19. González Stephan repeatedly notes (e.g., 184) that this was one of the contradictions faced by elite nation-builders in the nineteenth century. Because they were elite they imitated Europe; and because they were American nation-builders they celebrated their pre-modern surroundings.

20. The uncompromising and heroic militarism that expelled Spain from most of America was now a threat to her development. What America needed now were civilizers, founding fathers of commerce and industry, not fighters. Juan Bautista Alberdi, whose notes for Argentina's 1853 constitution became a standard of political philosophy throughout Latin America wrote that "glory has ceded its place to utility and comfort, and military heroism is not the most competent medium for the prosaic needs of commerce and industry" ("a la necesidad de gloria, ha sucedido la necesidad de provecho y de comodidad, y el heroísmo guerrero no es el organo más competente de las necesidades prosaicas del comercio y de la industria") (as if to say the prose of domestic fiction should now replace grandiloquent epic verse) (Alberdi 92). Alberdi and Domingo F. Sarmiento agreed, if on little else, on the need to fill up the desert, to make it disappear. What sense was there in heroically reducing warm bodies to dead ones, when Alberdi pronounced that in America, "to govern is to populate" ("governar es poblar") (Alberdi 108)) Few slogans have caught on and held on so well as this one. Husband the land and father your countries, he was saying. They have already yielded and now they must be loved and worked.

 Juan Bautista Alberdi, "Las Bases y Puntos de Partida para la Organización Política de la República Argentina" (1852). See also Tulio Halperín Donghi, *Proyecto y construcción de una nación (Argentina, 1846-1880)* (Caracas: Biblioteca Ayacucho, 1980): 84-111; 92

21. "Love, however, is feeling, i.e. ethical life in the form of something natural. . . . Love therefore, is the most tremendous contradiction; the Understanding cannot resolve it since there is nothing more stubborn than this point of self-consciousness which is negated and which nevertheless I ought to possess as affirmative. Love is at once the propounding and

the resolving of this contradiction. As the resolving of it, love is unity of an ethical type"
G.W.F. Hegel, Philosophy of right, trans. T.M. Knox (London: oxford university press,
1967) pp. 261-262.

22. See Sommer, "Allegory and Dialectics: A Match Made in Romance." Doris Sommer. (1991).
Allegory and Dialectics: A Match Made in Romance. *Boundary 2, 18*(1), 60–82. https://doi.
org/10.2307/303382

23. I owe this provocative comment to Jean Bethke Elshtain.

24. Catherine Gallagher, in *Industrial Transformations in the English Novel*, develops a sim-
ilar double reading. I am grateful to Marshall Brown for pointing out the book. Catherine
Gallagher, *The Industrial Reformation of English Fiction: Social Discourse and Narrative
Form, 1832-1867*

25. See, for example, Kenny Kwok-kwan Ng (2004). Monumental fictions: geopoetics, Li
Jieren, and historical imagination in twentieth-century China. (18); Dodgson-Katiyo,
who draws on the work of Doris Sommer (1991) on the romance as foundational fiction
in nineteenth-century Latin American writing, argues that Seretse and Ruth presents the
story of the Khamas as a foundational fiction in which star-crossed lovers from different
races and regions eventually unite the new nation of Botswana. See Pauline Dodgson-
Katiyo The Story of Seretse and Ruth: A Southern African Foundational Fiction Journal of
Literary Studies 25(1) March 2009 pp. :64–79 DOI:10.1080/02564710802261790

26. Published originally as *Ursprung des deutschen Trauerspiels*. I will refer to the English
translation in *The Origin of German Tragic Drama* by John Osborne in parenthetical page
references in the text. *Walter Benjamin; John Osborne (2003). The origin of German tragic
drama. Verso. ISBN 978-1-85984-413-7. Retrieved 20 August 2011.*

27. "La novela es indudablemente la producción literaria que se ve ccn más gusto por el
público . . . Pudiérase decir que es el genéro de literatura más cultivado en el siglo XIX y el
artificio con que los hombres pensadores de nuestra época han logrado hacer descender á
las masas doctrinas y opiniones que de otro modo habría sido difícil hacer que aceptasen"
(Altamirano 17).

28. "La sala está casi llena de gente: los hombres separados de las mujeres, como en las iglesias
católicas y en las sinagogas" (Rizal 9).

29. "Vióse el joven solo en medio de la sala: el dueño de la casa había desaparecido, y no
encontraba quién le presentase á las señoritas, muchas de las cuales le miraban con interés.
Después de vacilar algunos segundos, con una gracia sencilla y natural se dirigió á ellas:
"—Permítanme ustedes,—dijo,—que salte por encima de las reglas de una rigorosa
etiqueta. Hace siete años que falto en mi país, y al volver á él, no puedo contener mi
admiración y dejar de saludar á su más precioso adorno, á sus mujeres" (18).

30. See Bakhtin's "Discourse and the Novel.", the last essay in Mikhail Bakhtin, The Dialogic
Imagination, Texas University Press, 1982.

Works Cited

Alberdi, Juan Bautista Alberdi. "Las bases y puntos de partida para la organización Popítica de
la República Argentina." 1852. *Proyecto y construcción de una nación (Argentina 1846–1880)*,
edited by Tulio Halperin Donghi, Biblioteca Ayacucho, 1980, pp. 84–111.

Altamirano, Ignacio M. "La literatura nacional." 1868. *La literatura nacional*, edited by José Luis
Martínez, Porrúa, 1949, pp. 9–40.

Arendt, Hannah. *On Revolution*. The Viking Press, 1963.

Bakhtin, M. M. "Discourse in the Novel." *The Dialogic Imagination: Four Essays*. Translated by Caryl Emerson and Michael Holquist. U of Texas P, 1981, pp. 259–422.

Benjamin, Walter. *The Origin of German Tragic Drama*. Translated by John Osborne. New Left Books, 1977.

Blest Gana, Alberto. *Martín Rivas. Novela de costumbres politico-sociales*. Biblioteca Ayacucho, 1977.

Blest Gana, Alberto. *Martín Rivas*. Translated by Tess O'Dwyer. Oxford UP, 2000.

Breuilly, John. *Nationalism and the State*. U of Chicago P, 1985.

Camayd-Freixas, Erik. "From Epic to Picaresque: The Colonial Origins of the Latin American Novel." *The Picaresque Novel in Western Literature: From the Sixteenth Century to the Neopicaresque*, edited by J. A. Garrido Ardila, Cambridge UP, 2015, pp. 224–46. https://doi.org/10.1017/CBO9781139382687.012

Colegio Nacional de la Capital. 4to año de estudios. Programa de literatura preceptiva. Profesor D. Calixto Oyuela. Imprenta Biedma, 1884.

Dodgson-Katiyo, Pauline. "The Story of Seretse and Ruth: A Southern African Foundational Fiction." *Journal of Literary Studies/TLW* no. 25, 2009, pp. 64–79. 10.1080/0256471080226179o

Fernández de Lizardi, José Joaquín. *El Periquillo Sarniento*. Vol. 1. Imprenta de V. G. Torres, 1842.

Fernández de Lizardi, José Joaquín. *The Mangy Parrot: The Life and Times of Periquillo Sarniento Written by Himself for his Children*. Translated by David Frye. Hackett, 2004.

Foucault, Michel. *History of Sexuality*, vol. 1: *An Introduction*. Translated by Robert Hurley. Pantheon Books, 1978.

Franco, Franklin. *Trujillismo: Génesis y rehabilitación*. Editora Cultural Dominicana, 1971.

González Stephan, Beatriz. *La historiografía literaria del liberalismo hispanoamericano del siglo XIX*. Casa de las Américas, 1987.

Guillén, Claudio. "Toward a Definition of the Picaresque." *Literature as System: Essays Toward the Theory of Literary History*. Princeton UP, 1977, pp. 71–106.

Hegel, Georg Wilhelm Friedrich. *Philosophy of Right*. Translated by T. M. Knox. Oxford UP, 1967.

Macherey, Pierre. *A Theory of Literary Production*. Translated from the French by Geoffrey Wall. Routledge, 2006.

Ng, Kenny Kwok-kwan. *The Lost Geopoetic Horizon of Li Jieren: The Crisis of Writing Chengdu in Revolutionary China*. Brill, 2015.

Programas detallados para las escuelas secundarias. Secretaría de Educación Pública, 1933.

Reyes, Alfonso. "Pasado inmediato." 1939. *Obras completas*. Fondo de Cultura Económica, 1960, vol. 12, pp. 173–271.

Rizal, José. *Noli me tangere*. Biblioteca Ayacucho, 1982.

Rizal, José. *Noli Me Tangere: (Touch Me Not)*. Translated by Harold Augenbraum, Penguin, 2006.

Rojas, Ricardo. *La restauración nacionalista*. 1909. Librería de la Facultad, 1922.

Román-Lagunas, Jorge. "Bibliografía anotada de y sobre Alberto Blest Gana." *Revista Iberoamericana*, nos. 112–13, July–December 1980, pp. 605–47.

Sater, William. *The Heroic Image in Chile: Arturo Prat, Secular Saint*. U of California P, 2003.

Scott, Rebecca, and Michael Zeuske. "Property in Writing, Property on the Ground: Pigs, Horses, Land, and Citizenship in the Aftermath of Slavery, Cuba, 1880–1909." *Comparative*

Studies in Society and History, vol. 44, no. 4, 2002, pp. 669–699. https://doi.org/10.1017/
S0010417502000324

Sommer, Doris. *Foundational Fictions: The National Romances of Latin America*. U of
California P, 1991.

Sommer, Doris. "Allegory and Dialectics: A Match Made in Romance." *Boundary 2*, vol. 18, no.
1, 1991, pp. 60–82.

Téllez, Jorge. "Valuing Literature: The Picaresque and the Writing Life in Mexico," *Latin
American Research Review*, vol. 55 no. 1, 2020, pp. 110–21. http://doi.org/10.25222/larr.358

Turpin, Kristen M. "Lessons Abroad: Cosmopolitanism in *El Periquillo Sarniento*." *Hispanófila*,
no. 176, January 2016, pp. 117–35.

Vogeley, Nancy. "Defining the 'Colonial Reader': *El Periquillo Sarniento*." *PMLA*, vol. 102, no. 5,
October 1987, pp. 784–800.

CHAPTER 3

THE NINETEENTH-CENTURY BRAZILIAN NOVEL AND THE TRANSCENDENCE OF MACHADO DE ASSIS

PAUL DIXON

As a former Portuguese colony, Brazil experienced the usual importation of European models in establishing its own literary traditions. The adoption of the established schools of romanticism, realism, and naturalism in Brazil's fiction of the nineteenth century, however, was tempered by a strong desire to lay the foundations of a national literature with a uniquely American aspect. For most of the major novelists, the European schools were absorbed primarily through the reading of Portuguese and French writers, and the movements' values were simply transplanted into the flora and fauna of the Brazilian landscape, simply superimposed upon the recognized customs and demography of its people. A few exceptions to this rather passive absorption of continental modes do exist, and although Machado de Assis (1839–1908) was not the only example of this more independent spirit, he was surely the most important. Machado's early novels are usually associated with romanticism, but in significant ways, they conform only reluctantly to many norms of the movement. A second phase of his novelistic output, product more of a creative explosion than a mere evolution, has been labeled as his realistic stage, though Machado himself was highly critical of European realism. The characterization of the mature Machado as a realist cannot really be made without substantial qualifications.

Undisputedly, the center of intellectual life in nineteenth-century Brazil was Rio de Janeiro, which had become the nation's capital in 1763. When in response to Napoleon's invasion of the peninsula, more than 15,000 members of the Portuguese court took up residence there between 1808 and 1821, the city became the capital of the entire Portuguese empire. Upon King João VI's return to Portugal, he left behind libraries, printing presses, and theaters that guaranteed Rio's preeminence as a cultural axis. Many of the important novelists were born in outlying areas, most notably in northeastern

Brazil, but nearly all eventually made their way to Rio, where their talents could be more fully developed.

This essay will discuss several of Brazil's most important novels in chronological phases, without initially including the works of Machado de Assis. After showing how these canonical novels establish a norm or esthetic background, the essay will bring in Machado's novels and show how they respond to and often subvert these characteristics.

ROMANTICISM

Romanticism in Brazil was primarily about individual subjectivity with a strong emphasis on emotions. In the rest of Latin America, the movement often had strident notes of political activism, reflecting the fact that the Spanish-speaking countries had to go to battle to win their independence and, after establishing fledgling republics, often had to struggle with authoritarian movements. Because Brazil's independence was essentially bloodless, the product of an agreement within the Portuguese royal family, and because its transition was to a relatively stable monarchy, one finds very little of that kind of political struggle. Anxieties exist, to be sure, but they are typically of a more personal, affective, or moral nature.

A moreninha (*Moreninha*, 1844), by Joaquim Manuel Macedo (1820–1882), is an excellent example of the intimate and emotional emphasis of Brazilian romanticism. The novel is a love story involving young adults Augusto and Carolina. Augusto is invited with a group of male friends to spend the Sant'Ana holidays at a house on the island of Paquetá, located in Rio's Guanabara Bay. The well-chaperoned celebration is also attended by a group of young women, including, of course, Carolina. Augusto has the reputation of being capricious and uncommitted in his relationships with ladies, and even confesses to those faults at dinner. This information turns away all the young women except Carolina. Later, in a sincere conversation with the matron of the house, Augusto confesses that he has never gotten over a passionate alliance from his early boyhood. On a family visit to a beach, he had met a young dark-haired girl, swearing his love to her after a charitable collaboration in which the two saved a destitute man. Eventually the novel reveals that Carolina remembers him; she is the very girl from that early encounter on the beach. Their affective commitment is renewed and promises an inspiring future. One respect in which the novel transcends its rather conventional plot is in its metafictional genesis. August and his friend Felipe have made a bet that if the former falls in love during the holiday getaway, he will have to write a novel; if not, the latter will be obliged to write one. The book we are reading, then, is the product of its own narrated bet.

Manuel Antônio de Almeida's *Memorias de um sargento de milícias* (*Memoirs of a Militia Sargeant*, 1852), while belonging chronologically to the romantic movement in Brazil, is really more indebted to the picaresque tradition from the Iberian Peninsula, as well as to the norms of the novel of customs. Since a famous essay by

Antônio Cândido in 1970, a great deal of discussion has centered around the novel's portrayal of "malandragem" (roguishness), which is Brazil's own version of the picaresque, including perhaps a little more personal charisma in its depiction of the rascal type. In the essay, Cândido declared that the novel's protagonist, Leandro, is the first great "malandro" of Brazilian fiction (71). He claims that the character embodies a very Brazilian dialectic, where individuals must negotiate between the desire for legitimacy or respect for the rules, and the temptation to circumvent those rules through sideways, sometimes illegal, maneuvers and personal favors. Further, Cândido asserts that there is a direct line from Leandro to Macunaíma, the hero of Mário de Andrade's novel by the same name (88), which is universally regarded as an allegorical representation of the prototypical Brazilian. Leandro is a rascal whose shenanigans continually get him in trouble with his family and other members of his community. But at the same time, he is open and loveable, a trait that puts him in a position to obtain advantages from influential people.

The novel *Úrsula* (1859, untranslated), by Maria Firmina dos Reis (1825–1917), returns to the norms of European romanticism, with melodramatic tones. The work has great historical importance in that it is perhaps the first novel published by a Brazilian woman and, even more remarkably, by an Afro-Brazilian woman (the author was the illegitimate daughter of white and black parents). *Úrsula* is often labeled as an abolitionist novel, which is true in an indirect way. The main characters—Úrsula and Tancredo—are both white. They fall in love, but their happiness is ruined by a villain who demands the beautiful young woman for himself. An important element in the novel is the presence of black characters who are not mere accessories, but who in fact contribute to the plot and whose subjective lives are integral to the work. Túlio is a slave who saves Tancredo's life, and who receives his freedom from the rich protagonist, out of gratitude. Two significant values communicated by Túlio are a strong desire for liberty, and an undying loyalty, which could even be called a friendship, with a white man. Old Man Antero is a slave who shows the long-term effects of oppression, having become an alcoholic so as to escape from the depression of his servitude. The most significant display of a slave's subjectivity belongs to Susana, a servant in Úrsula's household, born in Africa, who in a lyrical and extended interior monologue remembers her life before captivity, her separation from beloved family members, and her passage over the ocean in a slave ship. Early histories of Brazilian literature do not mention this novel, and its discovery in the 1960s was an important literary event.

The most successful novelist of Brazilian romanticism was José de Alencar (1829–1877), who undertook the project of dedicating works to many of Brazil's recognizable character types, such as gaúchos from the south, backwoodsmen from the central plains, and miners of precious metals and gems from the central mountains. He is most remembered for his indigenist novels, cultivating the notion of the "noble savage." Along with the poet Antônio Gonçalves Dias (1823–1864), he deserves credit for assuring that the literary image of Brazilian nationality was inextricably tied to its natives (in spite of the fact that, culturally speaking, Brazil has nothing like the indigenous presence of a Mexico or a Peru).

O guarani (*The Guarani*, 1857, translated in serial form 1893) is a good example of Alencar's real strength as a novelist, which is the elaboration of highly intriguing plots. The main character, Peri, shows how early characterizations of natives were essentially projections of European values: he is the embodiment of courtly love in his chaste devotion to the young white woman, Cecília (whom he calls Ceci). Peri saves her life several times and indeed protects her entire family from numerous dangers, including natural disasters, Indian attacks, and the treachery of disloyal servants. He is more than willing to give his own life for the benefit of Ceci and her family. For example, he proposes to eat poison and to allow himself to be captured by an enemy tribe about to attack. Knowing of their cannibalistic practices, he plans to kill numerous warriors when they consume his tainted flesh. The novel has a curious and poignant ending, where Peri again saves (or at least tries to save) Ceci, this time from a devastating flood. The closing paragraphs show Peri grasping Cecília and climbing with her to the top of a palm tree. Alencar's description of the still-rising waters suggests a sublime romantic contemplation of the awesome powers of nature. While perched in that precarious position, Peri recounts to the maiden a tribal tale reminiscent of the biblical account of Noah's ark. The implacable waters continue their ascent, and with all the force he can muster, Peri uproots the palm tree. The book closes with the image of the native and the young woman, still clinging to the tree and floating off together into the horizon. On the one hand, this inconclusive ending points to an ecstatic, romantic way to die. But on the other, it suggests the possibility of survival. If that is so, it also suggests an allegorical future for the Brazilian people, recalling the emblematic status of the palm tree as a national symbol. The two races go forth embracing, riding together into the future.

If Alencar's *O guarani* closes with a subtle suggestion that Brazil's future identity lies in the mixture of its races, his *Iracema* (*Iracema*, 1865) takes the question of miscegenation beyond a mere suggestion and leaves it firmly established as a defining characteristic of the country's founding narrative. Here, rather than creating a highly developed plot, Alencar chooses to indulge poetic expression, full of botanical and zoological vocabulary derived from indigenous languages, in building a vision of mythic origins in a Brazilian Eden. The novel idealizes the primordial encounter between the arriving white man (the soldier Martim), and the receptive native (Iracema), who come together in idyllic fashion to give life to Moacir, a child described as first member of a new nation. Importantly, the novel inverts the historical reality where European males so often forced themselves on defenseless native females. Here, it is Iracema who takes the initiative, for while Martim loves Iracema, he resists upsetting the stability of the indigenous community. The union is consummated only because Iracema makes him unable to refuse by giving him a hallucinogenic potion.

Both *O guarani* and *Iracema* have famously been studied by Doris Sommer as "foundational fictions," that is, as narratives using allegories of heterosexual love to suggest mythologies of national origins, in accordance with idealized values. Alencar's romantic novels are widely noted for their contribution to a narrative of racial mixture as a positive phenomenon in the constitution of the Brazilian people. What is not so widely recognized, but what is also pointed out by Sommer (151–53), is the significant erasure of the African from Alencar's mythic world. He glorifies the comingling of Europeans and natives but seems unable to touch upon a similar union involving blacks.

As an imported esthetic, romanticism arrived relatively late in Brazil, and it lingered rather a long time. Although published in 1872, *Inocência* (*Inocência*), by Alfredo Escragnolle Taunay (1843–1899), still clearly belongs to the norms of the movement. The novel glorifies the landscapes of Brazil's interior and provides a story of impossible love involving emphatically emotional characters. One might also call the novel a portrayal of customs and local color, primarily for its representation of the stubborn and suspicious sertanejo (rustic backlander) in the form of the father of the beautiful Inocência, whose purity concurs with her name. An interesting contrast to the sertanejos in their obsession with personal honor appears in the form of the German scientist, Dr. Meyer, a hunter of rare butterflies, who with his own kind of cultural innocence unwittingly sets in motion a tragedy of jealousy. *A escrava Isaura* (*The Slave Isaura*, 1875), by Bernardo Guimarães (1825–1884), still belongs clearly within the norms of romanticism. It has exaggerated characters (both bad and good), strong emotions, and the usual exaltation of nature. Isaura is an abolitionist novel, even though it makes many concessions to racial biases of the time. Instead of choosing to portray the injustices suffered by a slave of more usual appearance and status, the novel creates a beautiful and cultured female protagonist, light enough to pass as a white person, who has been raised with all the protections and privileges of a prosperous girl from a plantation mansion. The sexual predation she must fight from the novel's villain is the sort of treatment that millions of real female slaves quietly had to endure, but the novel invites the reader's indignation, at least in part, because Isaura is almost white.

MACHADO'S "ROMANTIC" NOVELS

Machado de Assis's first four novels appear toward the later end of the time frame established by these other Brazilian romantic novels, and in a limited sense they do indeed appear to belong to that movement. They are all love stories, therefore having an essentially emotional basis. Characters can be impulsively controlled by their emotions. However, the novels show a significant reluctance to embrace romanticism in any but a limited, moderate, way. There is barely a hint of melodrama, and it is hard to identify anyone as a villain. Female characters, rather than being exaggeratedly pure and virtuous, are righteous, self-conscious, and sometimes calculating persons who try to achieve a degree of agency in their limited social circumstances. The novels are unusually psychological for the period, often examining thoughtful characters in moral dilemmas. The books have a keen eye for characters' hypocrisies and obsessions with social status. And descriptions of nature are much more limited in Machado's novels, which are usually more centered in urban settings than in the countryside.

Machado's first novel, *Ressurreição* (*Resurrection*, 1872), examines the psychological factors that can interfere with love. Félix becomes enamored with the young widow,

Lívia, who returns his affection. They become engaged. But his suspicious and paranoid nature causes him to give too much credence to false rumors and treacherous letters. He decides he cannot go forward with the marriage.

A mão e a luva (*The Hand and the Glove*, 1874) explores the fragile equilibrium in courtship between social ambition and love. Guiomar, the goddaughter of a baroness, is ready to choose a husband and is pursued by three attractive young men. In different degrees, the men combine disinterested affection, lust, and ambitions for social advancement. Guiomar receives proposals from all three and, in the end, chooses not the man who is most devoted to her, but the one who combines affection with social ambition. The novel shows that those qualities conform to Guiomar's own perspective, fitting like a hand in a glove.

Of all Machado's novels, *Helena* (*Helena*, 1876) comes closest to being a truly romantic work, flirting with incestuous passion. Estácio's wealthy father dies and in his will reveals the existence of an illegitimate daughter, Helena. He asks that she be taken into the family. Although Estácio is engaged to be married, he decides he must put off the wedding, sensing but not fully allowing himself to recognize his growing attraction to his recently discovered half-sister. Helena is clever and beautiful, but at certain moments seems evasive and troubled. The novel reveals that she is secretly visiting an older man, and much later reveals him to be her real father. Estácio's father did in fact have a relationship with the young woman's mother, but it was after Helena was born. He made a false claim in his will to benefit Helena, whom he loved like a daughter, trying to lift her out of poverty. The truth eventually is revealed, allowing Estácio to countenance his passion for Helena. But their love must remain unrealized; she is so emotionally distraught by the dishonor of her ruse that she sickens and dies.

Iaiá Garcia (*Iaiá Garcia*, 1882) addresses a theme that was initiated in the previous novel, that of love between persons of differing social classes. Secondarily, it also continues to examine what happens when an intelligent and attractive young person from a poor background is informally adopted by a wealthier family (a circumstance that really happened in the life of the author, apparently). A truly romantic action involves the hero's volunteering to fight in the Paraguayan War (1864–1870), wishing to die because his mother will not allow him to marry a poorer woman. He survives and returns home to find that his mother has taken the lively but poorer young woman, Iaiá, under her wing. Iaiá falls in love with Jorge but comes to realize that he has been in love with the woman who is now her stepmother. With time, things are straightened out, and Jorge falls for Iaiá, who by now has assimilated most of the habits and values of a more privileged woman, at the same time preserving her humility and sense of compassion.

Realism/Naturalism

As esthetic movements (or complementary aspects of a single movement), realism and naturalism did not become fully established in Brazil until the last two decades of the nineteenth century, but novels in those veins continued to be published well into the twentieth century. While romanticism tended to gravitate toward the countryside, realism and naturalism were more inclined toward urban settings.

O ateneu (*The Athenaeum*, 1988), by Raul Pompeia (1863–1895), is a blistering portrayal of a flawed educational system, centering on an all-male boarding school. This Bildungsroman follows Sérgio as he enters the school at age eleven and begins to learn the how physical abuse, psychological intimidation, and affective manipulation function within the realm of social interactions. When they are not maneuvering for advantage one over the other, students are obsessed with Ema—the wife of the headmaster, the school nurse, and the only female at the school. The novel boldly introduces the theme of homosexual behavior, which in this context seems more an expression of frustration within a closed-off environment than a question of gender identity. The novel ends with a student burning down the entire school, an occurrence that suggests the completion of young Sérgio's instruction into the ways of the world.

Another early novel that explores homosexuality is *Bom crioulo* (*The Black Man and the Cabin Boy*, 1895), written by Adolfo Caminha (1867–1897). This is clearly a work about sexual identity; it is considered the first gay-themed novel in Brazil, and indeed one of the first in the world. Also, it is one of the first novels where the main character is black. Amaro, the protagonist, is an escaped slave admired for his physical strength and his skill as a sailor. He is dependably homosexual in his passions and tends toward uncontrollable violence when he drinks. The sailor develops a relationship with a white, adolescent cabin boy. When the young man abandons Amaro in favor of an older Portuguese woman, there are disastrous results.

O cortiço (*The Slum*, 1890), by Aluisio Azevedo (1857–1913), is Brazil's best example of a naturalist novel. The work quite clearly shows the influence of evolutionary ideas on literature, for the novel's figurative language describes the growth of the housing complex in very organic terms, as if it were an amoeba on its way to becoming a species of higher complexity. The book also explores adaptation as a means of survival, particularly in the lives of three Portuguese males who have come to Rio de Janeiro, and who must now try to thrive in their new tropical environment. Miranda is a prosperous, proper store owner who has been able to establish his commercial success through the inherited fortune of his wife. Though his spouse is serially unfaithful, he must remain married to her because he needs her money. Just over the backyard wall from Miranda's tidy residence is the improvised tenement of João Romão, a brute whose companion, a slave named Bertoleza, works hard in the kitchen of the tavern on the premises. João Romão steals building materials and cheats workers, using every possible trick to expand his business. Jerônimo is a disciplined quarry worker who arrives with his wife and young daughter to live in the tenement. Over time, the sturdy immigrant becomes captivated by Brazilian food, music, and women, leaving his wife and child and moving in with Rita Baiana, a sensuous dark-skinned beauty.

In a sense, the true protagonist of the novel is collective—the entire, varied cast of characters who inhabit the sprawling tenement. Azevedo's novel skillfully gives glimpses of the personal dramas of many characters, who as a group represent the entire Brazilian nation in its unruly development. It is significant that one of the definitions of the word "cortiço" is "beehive." Most of the functions of a beehive, or indeed of an organism—alimentation, reproduction, removal of useless material, growth, protection, and so on—are shown to play out in the organization of João Romão's tenement.

In its depiction of social evolution, the novel transmits some of the racist paradigms of the time, referring to whites and blacks as "superior" and "inferior" races. It also deserves some of the blame for a prejudicial idealization of the "mulata" woman (here Rita Baiana) as a paradigm of erotic attraction, a stereotype that endures to this day.

O cortiço conforms to the naturalist practice of attempting to correct the ills of society through an objective, distanced approach of merely identifying problems, and generally refraining from positing solutions. The novel is especially strong in its depiction of unscrupulous ambition, and the collateral damage that devolves to weaker participants. The pitiful outcome for Jerônimo's abandoned wife and child is notable; what happens to João Romão's companion, Bertoleza, when he no longer needs her services, is an unforgettably shocking moment at the end of the book.

A major voice in the Brazilian novel, who divided his production between the nineteenth and twentieth centuries, was Henrique Coelho Neto (1864–1934). Neto is known for his vivid imagination and for his impressive verbosity, a spontaneous and fluent eloquence that manifests itself in brilliant dialogs and eloquent descriptions. His A conquista (The Conquest, 1899) treats the abolition of slavery, which occurred in Brazil in 1888 and which was one of the main intellectual and social movements of the last part of the century. Although the author himself appears to have been highly committed to the abolitionist cause, in the novel the topic receives a rather ironic treatment. A conquista explores the loves, festivities, intellectual projects, and general shenanigans of a group of young bohemians in Rio de Janeiro. The work is usually considered to be a roman à clef, and it is thought that the main character, Anselmo, was based on the author himself. Although the young men in the novel do contribute their efforts to the abolition of slavery, they act almost as if it were a game among their other diversions, and there is little attention given to the genuine suffering of the captives. Crebillon, the character repeatedly referred to as "the abolitionist," is a capricious bon vivant who lives in a mansion equipped with all the latest luxuries, and who has numerous Afro-Brazilian servants.

MACHADO DE ASSIS, REALIST?

One of the most influential philosophies in Brazil during the latter nineteenth century was positivism, the cult of science and method primarily associated with the French philosopher Auguste Comte (1798–1857). That fact that the Brazilian flag immortalizes the positivist motto, "Ordem e Progresso" (order and progress), attests to the centrality of the philosophy in the thinking of Brazil's elite. In many ways, the biography of Machado de Assis (at least what the limited documentary data allow) can be viewed as a demonstration of positivistic principles. Born into a poor family, the descendent of slaves on the side of his father, Machado nevertheless rose to the pinnacle of Brazilian society by continual productive effort, thorough professionalism and profitable social interactions. He rose to become the founding president of the Brazilian Academy of Letters and was eulogized by the most important men of the country when he died in 1908. Nevertheless, some reversals in his life belie what otherwise might seem like an unbroken trajectory of ascension.

Machado had a socially advantageous marriage to a Portuguese woman, which by nearly all accounts was stable and happy. However, the couple never had any children. At several moments in his fiction, characters show powerful paternal or maternal feelings, and it can be assumed that Machado must have felt some of those longings himself. Another area of disappointment must have been Machado's health. His usually uninterrupted work schedule was forced into a hiatus for several weeks in 1878–1879 because of a physical crisis. Documented later events where he suffered seizures suggest that Machado experienced either the onset or the aggravation of epilepsy. The general tenor of Machado's later work seems contrary to positivism; the enthusiasm for science and the goal of solving problems through systematic method must have seemed too simplistic to the author, either on a purely theoretical basis or because it did not square with his personal experiences in life.

Soon after his health crisis, Machado published a novel so radically different from his previous works, so brashly contrary to the general trends of his contemporaries, that most readers did not know what to make of it. *Memórias póstumas de Brás Cubas* (*Posthumous Memoirs of Brás Cubas*) appeared in installments in the *Revista Brasileira* in 1880, and the next year in book form. The noted critic Capistrano de Abreu seemed to have spoken for a good share of the reading public when he asked, "Are the Posthumous Memoirs of Brás Cubas a novel?" Machado must have delighted in the question, without being inclined to give an answer. He included it in the preface to the book's third edition and answered with the words of his narrator, that for some it would seem to be a novel, while for others it would seem not to be. The prologues to the first and third editions are also important for clearly identifying the authors who had inspired the narrator's method of telling his story—Laurence Sterne (1713–1768), Xavier de Maistre (1763–1852), and Almeida Garrett (1799–1854). Here we see a major difference between Machado and his Brazilian contemporaries. The primary influences upon realistic novelists in Brazil were French authors such as Gustave Flaubert (1821–1880), Honoré de Balzac (1799–1850), and Emile Zola (1840–1902), and, somewhat more directly, the Portuguese novelist Eça de Queirós (1845–1900). In contrast, the prologues cite the influences of three novelists from an earlier period, all known for their meandering, digressive style of narration.

Indeed, *Memórias póstumas*, with its 160 very short chapters, insists on ranging all over the map, defying any sense of chronological, causal, or spatial order. It could not have been more different from the earlier novels, whose third-person narrators were conventional and well behaved. Cubas's memoir is a capricious and even belligerent improvisation that deliberately challenges the reader to discover an underlying coherence beneath a rhapsodic and apparently chaotic surface.

In some ways, the novel conforms to realistic expectations, for it satirizes the injustices and social obsessions of Rio's privileged classes during the first part of the nineteenth century. But in other important ways, it defies those conventional norms. First, it builds its entire foundation on a blatantly unrealistic conceit. These memoirs are not "posthumous" in the expected way, that is, a narration penned by an author during his life, and then published after his death. They are written not by "author now dead," but rather by a "dead man now an author." Cubas never imagined an autobiography while he was on earth. Only after settling into his afterlife and finding himself either bored or dissatisfied with the legacy he has left behind does he decide to narrate his adventures. From the very beginning, the reader is required to make a gigantic concession to impossibility.

Another way in which the novel goes against the typical practices of realism is in its lack of detail (and this is a quality that will characterize all the later novels). The usual practice of creating a sense of trueness to life through descriptions with abundant detail is simply not a part of the esthetic picture. Nature is only incidentally present. Streets, gardens, plazas, and buildings are named but not described. Characters are given vivid life not through their physical presentation, but only through their words and actions. In short, the novel shows little of the objective orientation one normally attributes to realism and naturalism. It is all about subjectivity; its famous seventh chapter, the delirium that precedes Cubas's death and that takes him, straddling a hippopotamus, backward through the centuries to the beginning of time for an interview with a gigantic female who seems simultaneously to embody Nature, Mother, and Pandora, emphatically demonstrates that the true world of the novel is the world of the mind.

Memórias póstumas signals a new world for readers, where the text no longer expects us passively to accept how it tells us the world is. Readers must exercise their own judgment, primarily through the evaluation of problematic narrators. The delirium just mentioned seems to carry a pessimistic message about humanity, but its validity must be questioned because the narrator admits it was a moment of insanity. Brás Cubas tells us in his last chapter that the fact that he never had any offspring was a positive thing, because he "never transmitted to another being the legacy of our misery" ("não transmiti a nenhuma criatura o legado da nossa miséria") (ch. 160).[1] But earlier in the account, the same narrator has shared his thrill in learning that his lover is pregnant, and his sincere disappointment when she miscarries. The book's extended conversation with a "philosopher" named Quincas Borba seems to reinforce a pessimistic message, by claiming that individual lives are only significant insofar as they contribute to the continuance of collective viability. But the thinker Quincas Borba is described as mentally imbalanced. Cubas's postmortem memoir as a whole is an account of a series of personal failures, which in the end are justified by the narrator's sour-grapes claim that life was not worth the effort, anyway. Such suspicious assertions will characterize all the later novels; each one has a narrator who is problematic on one way or another. The characterization of these narrators as unreliable seems insufficient because with an unreliable narrator, readers can still decide what the true, stable message should be. Machado's narrators, exemplified by Brás Cubas, are more like ungrounded narrators, for they tend to destroy the logical basis for deciding one way or the other.

In 1891 Machado published *Quincas Borba*, which carries forward the semi-deranged philosopher from *Memórias póstumas*. The eccentric thinker has inherited a fortune, and when he dies, he will give it all to his ingenuous caretaker Rubião, but not before exposing the young man to his philosophy claiming that individual lives are as insignificant as single bubbles in the boiling cauldron of universal life, and before putting him in charge of the well-being of his beloved dog, who is also named Quincas Borba. Rubião decides that his new social importance requires that he relocate to the capital. In Rio he befriends numerous parasitic "friends," who gradually lay claim to his every penny. The protagonist dies a starving, insane man, convinced that he is the emperor of France.

Some readers of *Quincas Borba* expressed disappointment that after the pugnacious first-person narrator of the previous novel, Machado decided to return to the third person, the narrative paradigm of earlier novels. There is a degree of misunderstanding in that disappointment. For one thing, it is not the first-person perspective that makes a narrator brash and bristly. The latter novel's narrator is still strident, harshly opinionated, literate, and clever, much like the voice of the former one. And Rubião, the main character of the novel, just would not have done as a first-person narrator, because he is too ignorant, too naïve, too unworthy of Machado's pen. The author's project seems to have been to write a kind of complement to *Memórias postúmas*. Both novels, in a general sense, are intensely social works, exploring how it is that when people interact, there are going to be winners and losers. Brás Cubas, in the former work, declares himself to be a "winner" (if only a "small" one), and most would agree, because in an objective sense, the protagonist and his immediate circle are wealthy and at least superficially successful. In that same very general sense, Quincas Borba is about losers—not only Rubião, but also other acquaintances in his group, including, of course, his dog. We see what it feels like to be a loser through the device of interior monologue, provided by an omniscient, third-person narrator. Readers get to see those characters' thoughts, without having to hear them in their less incisive words.

If *Memórias póstumas* is Machado's most virtuosic novel, *Dom Casmurro*, published in 1899, is his most profound. Here, Machado returns to a first-person narrator, who, as the name "casmurro" implies, is rather a crank or a sourpuss. The novel is a memoir told by an older man, Bento Santiago, about falling in love as an adolescent with Capitu, the girl next door, about overcoming the obstacle of the narrator's mother having promised God to have him become a priest, about their marriage, about their long wait for a first and only child, and about the husband's eventual conclusion that the child is not really his, but rather his best friend's, because Capitu has been unfaithful to him.

Dom Casmurro continues Machado's trend, in the later novels, of providing more agency to the reader by creating a problematic narrative voice. Santiago himself admits that as a youth, he was insecure in his masculinity, prone to jealousy and suspicion, and possessed of a very active imagination. On that basis alone, the reader can begin to doubt the veracity of his accusations. But additionally, Santiago's story gives us facts that in themselves are doubly directed. For example, Ezequiel, the couple's son, has gestures and even facial traits that call to mind Escobar, the narrator's closest friend. Capitu herself has remarked about this. But the boy is also recognized by all the household for his skill at imitating other people—a quality that suggests a non-physical explanation for any perceived similarity.

The reception of Machado's novel has a fascinating history, insofar as it is recorded in published reviews and analyses (Dixon 217–21). For two or three generations, readers took Bento Santiago's word at face value, ascribing infidelity to Capitu. But in the middle of the 1900s, around the time the novel began to appear in translation in other countries, readers started sympathizing with the female character, seeing her as the innocent victim of her husband's patriarchal obsessions. The novel's allusions to Shakespeare's *Othello* would seem to harmonize with this other mode of reception. The reading favoring Capitu's victimhood has a dominance in Brazil to this day, partly because it provides a convenient opening for ideological readings that see Santiago as a representative of the domineering prejudices of Brazil's ruling elites. However, during the last quarter of the twentieth century, a more literarily sophisticated group of readers emerged, including several non-Brazilians, which claimed that both readings—Capitu guilty or Capitu innocent—are merely partial accounts of the richness of the novel, and that a full appreciation for the book requires an acknowledgment of a meticulously constructed ambiguity, where the entire question of the woman's culpability is undecidable.

The problem of adultery was one of the great themes of nineteenth-century fiction. The fact that there is little doubt about the facts in nearly all the novels on the topic says something about the self-assured mentality of the time. It could well be, however, that Machado's *Dom Casmurro* is the first of these novels to put the adulterous facts into question.

It would be a mistake to put too much weight on the protagonists' marital problems. Were *Dom Casmurro* just about a domestic misunderstanding, it would carry little of the philosophical weight that makes it a literary classic. The narrator not only desires to condemn a contrary and unfaithful companion; he wants to condemn the entire universe. A network of poetic figures equates Bento's life with a cosmic opera, of which the devil is the composer and God is the librettist. Mr. Casmurro's disappointing life, therefore, was written that way by destiny itself.

Besides portraying the story as a contention of universals, the novel embeds itself within a rich tradition of heroic voyages, paying special attention to the great epic poem *Os lusíadas*, by Portugal's Luís de Camões (1524–1580). Capitu has "undertow eyes" that, siren-like, call adventurers toward an isle of love, in the end revealing their destructive horrors. The narrator enthusiastically indulges such epic metaphors, in the processing inviting an ironic reaction from more independent readers.

The narrator sees himself as the conservator of a waning mindset. He claims to write his memoir to restore a sense of authenticity that has been lost. He was a warrior for sincerity and truth as a young lover, and now, in a world where such truth seems absent, he sets about trying to recuperate some share of that verity. If heroes of old battled dragons, Dom Casmurro tries to battle time.

As if there were already not enough going on in the novel, *Dom Casmurro* also takes on literature itself. A metaliterary tendency—a discourse about writing and reading—characterizes all the later novels but is probably most pronounced in this one. One chapter consults book worms to learn their opinions about the accessibility of the pages they consume. Another informs us that the narrator prefers to read books with omissions, so that he can imagine things that were never actually stated. The narrator then invites the reader to apply that approach to his own book.

Dom Casmurro can be seen as the summit of nineteenth-century Brazilian literature, and also as the culmination of Machado's fictional project. Two more novels would be published in the first decade thereafter,[2] but they are more of a dénouement than a climax. In a sense, *Dom Casmurro* belongs within the contours of the realism of Machado's contemporaries, exposing the failings, obsessions, contradictions, and hypocrisies of an important segment of Brazilian society. But in another sense, the novel transcends that realistic project, universalizing its themes, couching them within overarching literary traditions, and above all, enthroning subjective relativity as a more realistic kind of realism.

NOTES

1. Gregory Rabassa's translation reads, "I haven't transmitted the legacy of our misery to any creature" (*The Posthumous Memoirs* 203).
2. *Esaú e Jacó* (*Esau and Jacob*, 1904) is a blatantly dialectical novel about twin brothers with opposing personalities, living at the time of Brazil's transition from monarchy to republic. *Memorial de Aires* (*Counselor Ayres' Memorial*, 1908) is a nostalgic novel exploring the ambiguous relationship between a young widow, Fidélia, and an older couple that has informally adopted her as their child.

WORKS CITED

Alencar, José de. *Iracema*. Melhoramentos, 1948.

Alencar, José de. *Iracema*. Translated by Clifford Landers. Oxford UP, 2000.

Alencar, José de. *O guarani*. Melhoramentos, 1966.

Alencar, José de. "*The Guarany*." Translated by James W. Hawes. *Overland Monthly and Out West Magazine*, vols. 21–22, series 2, January–December 1893, pp. 121–32.

Almeida, Manuel Antônio de. *Memórias de um sargento de milícias*. Saraiva, 1962.

Almeida, Manuel Antônio de. *Memoirs of a Militia Sergeant: A Novel*. Translated by Ronald Sousa. Oxford UP, 1999.

Assis, Machado de. *Obra completa*. 3 vols. Aguilar, 1985.

Assis, Machado de. *Counselor Ayres' Memorial: A Novel*. Translated by Helen Caldwell. U of California P, 1972.

Assis, Machado de. *Dom Casmurro*. Translated by John Gledson. Oxford UP, 1998.

Assis, Machado de. *Esau and Jacob: A Novel*. Translated by Elizabeth Lowe. Oxford UP, 2000.

Assis, Machado de. *The Hand and the Glove*. Translated by Albert I. Bagby, Jr. U of Kentucky P, 1970.

Assis, Machado de. *Helena: a Novel*. Translated by Helen Caldwell. U of California P, 1984.

Assis, Machado de. *Iaiá Garcia*. Translated by Albert I. Bagby, Jr. U of Kentucky P, 1977.

Assis, Machado de. *The Posthumous Memoirs of Brás Cubas*. Translated by Gregory Rabassa. Oxford UP, 1997.

Assis, Machado de. *Quincas Borba*. Translated by Gregory Rabassa. Oxford UP, 1999.

Assis, Machado de. *Resurrection*. Translated by Karen Sherwood Satelino. Latin American Literary Review, 2013.

Azevedo, Aluísio. *O cortiço*. Briguiet, 1939.

Azevedo, Aluísio. *The Slum: A Novel*. Translated by David H. Rosenthal. Oxford UP, 2000.

Caminha, Adolfo. *Bom crioulo*. Todavia, 2019.

Caminha, Adolfo. *The Black Man and the Cabin Boy*. Translated by E. A. Lacey. Gay Sunshine, 1982.

Camões, Luís de. *Os lusíadas*. Edited by Frank Pierce. Oxford UP, 1973.

Cândido, Antônio. "Dialética da malandragem: caracterização das Memórias de um sargento de milícias." *Revista do Instituto de Estudos Brasileiros*, vol. 8, 1970, pp. 67–89.

Coelho Neto, Henrique. *A conquista*. Lello & Irmãos, 1913.

Dixon, Paul. "Dom Casmurro e o leitor." *Nos laberintos de Dom Casmurro: ensaios críticos*, edited by Juracy Assmann Saraiva, Editora da Pontifícia Universidade Católica do Rio Grande do Sul, 2005, pp. 211–23.

Guimarães, Bernardo. *A escrava Isaura*. Ática, 2012.

Macedo, Joaquim Manuel de. *A moreninha*. Francisco Alves, 1975.

Macedo, Joaquim Manuel de. *Moreninha*. Atlantico, 2012.

Pompeia, Raul. *O ateneu: crônica de saudade*. Ática, 1984.

Pompeia, Raul. *The Athenaeum: A Novel*. Translated by Renata Wasserman. Northwestern UP, 2015.

Reis, Maria Firmina dos. *Úrsula*. Olímpico, 1975.

Sommer, Doris. *Foundational Fictions: The National Romances of Latin America*. U of California P, 1991.

Taunay, Alfredo d'Escragnolle. *Inocência*. Melhoramentos, 1944.

Taunay, Alfredo d'Escragnolle. *Inocência*. Translated by Henriqueta Chamberlain. Macmillan, 1945.

CHAPTER 4

··

THE REGIONAL NOVEL
AND THE NOVEL OF THE
MEXICAN REVOLUTION ON
COMMON GROUND

··

TAMARA L. MITCHELL AND AMANDA M. SMITH

THE culmination of the regional novel—a primarily South American phenomenon—and the novel of the Mexican Revolution coincide temporally, and though they are sometimes interpreted as separate trends (Rutherford; González Echevarría, *Modern Latin American*), they are generally considered as part of the same literary movement (Franco; Gollnick). Cases for grouping them together are loosely rooted in periodization—they appear in the early decades of the twentieth century, primarily between 1920 and 1950—and in a shared set of topics or aesthetic concerns, namely their perceived provincialism (Vargas Llosa 7), the predominance of landscape over characters (Rodríguez Monegal 45), and a conservativism toward literary innovation (Rama 25–26). In general, regional novels narrate the particularities of rural realities as a literary response to questions of "Latin America's cultural specificity" with regard to Europe and the United States (Alonso 37). The novel of the Mexican Revolution, on the other hand, reflects critically on the armed phase of the revolution from approximately 1910 to 1920, with particular attention to the ways in which the peasant class demanded political recognition through the conflict (Williams, The Mexican Exception 50). Both tend toward national allegory set in the "interior" provincial regions of their respective nations beyond the infrastructural reach and cultural influence of the capital cities. These early twentieth-century novels are generally written by urban intellectuals, most often men, from a locus of cultural exteriority. In terms of genre, each mode's literary realism frequently draws on naturalism, romanticism, *costumbrismo*, and *modernismo* to convey a sense of rural life through the use of regional vernacular, popular forms, representations of character types and local customs, and landscape descriptions.

This article's point of departure is an unexplored commonality across these narrative modes, namely, their close relationship with changing configurations of Latin American *tierra*. Regional novels—also known as *novelas de la tierra* or telluric novels—bring undeveloped land into high relief, almost as a protagonist of the story.[1] Likewise, in Mexico the revolutionary slogan "Tierra y libertad" (Land and Liberty) situates land rights as a central motive force at the heart of the Mexican Revolution. In light of the importance of land in the novel of the Mexican Revolution, it has recently been reassessed for its proto-ecocritical discourse (Anderson; Oloff; Fornoff). Regional novels, likewise, now form part of the Latin American environmental canon. Despite these commonalities, a rigorous comparative study of the function of land in the two modes has yet to be undertaken. Indeed, when Raymond L. Williams, focusing on early twentieth-century novels, argues that "land" is "the key word for an initial approach to the Latin American novel," he omits the novel of the Mexican Revolution from his consideration (67).

To till the common ground of the regional novel and the novel of the Mexican Revolution, we focus on the meaning of land in both literary phenomena as a response to the systemic codification of Latin American terrain as capital in the first half of the twentieth century. To this end, we explore how these two literary modes may be read alongside and against each other in order to open up as yet unplumbed comparative analyses. Concretely, we examine both traditions as literary explorations of land's significance in light of its reconfiguration as the economic base of "commodity-driven republics" (Beckman ix). From 1870 to 1930, Latin American countries focused on the production of raw materials for manufacture and sale abroad as the only viable pathway to economic liberalization (Beckman ix). Whether the commodity was rubber in the Amazon, crude oil in Mexico and Venezuela, or agriculture and livestock in Argentina, the large-scale exportation of Latin American resources indelibly bound the region's lands to global supply chains. Predictably, a shift occurs in the popular imaginary and political rhetoric surrounding land, and that rhetoric permeates novels that, in the ensuing decades, thematize and critique emerging relationships with land.

We examine the novelistic tropes and discourses that represent, romanticize, and denounce changing relationships to land across several novels, focusing on two emblematic works from each tradition: José Eustasio Rivera's *La vorágine* (*The Vortex* 1924) and Martín Luis Guzmán's *El águila y la serpiente* (*The Eagle and the Serpent* 1928). In each case, we argue that land is deployed symbolically to ground or deracinate national projects, as authors contend with neocolonial powers to define land's its cultural, economic, and political significance. In proposing both kinds of novels as telluric literature, we do not negate the specific geohistorical circumstances out of which each text emerges and to which each responds. Instead, we propose that disparate sociopolitical contexts arose in reaction to the broader insertion of the Latin American republics into a neocolonial order. By excavating each tradition's relationship to land, we identify literary landscapes from Mexico to Argentina that portray the ruins of ill-devised paths to modernization. Those landscapes suggest that, intent on modernizing the nation, the intellectual and political class often overlooked the voracious expansiveness of the neocolonial gaze.

THE REGIONAL NOVEL

Though regional novels were immensely popular at the time of their publication, in the 1960s, authors of the Latin American Boom would characterize regionalism's deliberate focus on rural cultures as literary provincialism. Despite the fact that authors like Carlos Fuentes, Mario Vargas Llosa, Gabriel García Márquez, and Julio Cortázar were heavily indebted to the tropes and themes developed by regional authors, they nonetheless took the nomenclature *novela de la tierra* literally, famously construing such novels as "the coarse, unfinished foundation of the structure [of the new Latin American novel], whose principal function is to give support to the building erected on them" (Alonso 38).[2] This rhetorical campaign to distance the cosmopolitan aspirations of the Boom novels from the supposed provincial conservativism of their predecessors proved successful, and for many years regionalism lay "lost or disregarded between the great literary achievements of the twentieth century: *modernismo* and *vanguardismo*" (French 8).

Several important studies by Roberto González Echevarría, Carlos Alonso, Jennifer French, Charlotte Rogers, and Lesley Wylie have since reassessed regionalism's contributions to the literary tradition. Each author insists that regional literature is in fact self-consciously critical of its seemingly unsophisticated qualities as a response to Latin American modernity. If regionalist writers foregrounded the natural world to "the detriment of their characters and plot" (French 28), González Echevarría suggests that they did so in order to question nature's centrality in constructing the geopolitical identity of the region since the time of the conquest (*The Voice* 44). Alonso also focuses on regionalism's engagement with cultural specificity, recasting its provincialism as a fraught discursive project to assess Latin American literary autochthony in the face of the globalization of European and US discourses of modernity. French's study, through a historical materialist lens, reads regionalism's depiction of nature as a response to "neo-colonial pressures on the production of agricultural and extractive goods" (36). Furthermore, her emphasis on *The Vortex*'s development of a "radical environmentalism" has been influential in the ecocritical reappraisal of regionalist discourse mentioned above (153).[3]

The ecocritical moments in the telluric novel undoubtedly relate to its preoccupation with Latin America's rapid incursion into the global market by way of resource extraction. Latin America's commodity-driven economic liberalization, as detailed by Ericka Beckman, meant that land was the motor of economic and technological modernization. Additionally, as Scott DeVries has highlighted, the resulting political ecology had lasting environmental consequences. Industrialized monoculture caused "various tree infestations, fungal epidemics, and other crop blights" leading to "land exhaustion, desertification, and the widespread use of harmful pesticides" (162). This geopolitical reality explains why Alonso stresses the rhetorical quality of Latin American modernity: everywhere foreign capital was surveying and destroying Latin American lands in service of a globalized economy. The region's pampas, plains, and jungles, therefore, did not belong to Latin American elites any more than they had prior to independence. By considering the regional novel as a drama about the challenges of locating national character in such expropriated lands, we expand the approaches to reassessing regionalism and reconfigure regional novels—against the grain—as discouraging portents of a baseless Latin American modernity. Such cynicism, in turn, brings regionalism's concerns in line with those of the novel of the Mexican Revolution.

The three most discussed regional novels are the Colombian poet Rivera's only novel *The Vortex* (1924), Ricardo Güiraldes's Argentine bildungsroman *Don Segundo Sombra* (1926), and the Venezuelan author Rómulo Gallegos's *Doña Bárbara* (1929).[4] Of these, *The Vortex* has been deemed exceptional for refusing the opportunistic synthesis so typical of the genre. The narrative possesses all of the formal qualities of a regional novel, including elaborate geographic details, local vocabulary glossed at the back of the text, phonetic depictions of regional speech, and Eurocentric ethnographic descriptions of Indigenous and Afro-descendant peoples. Additionally, the first-person account of Arturo Cova's journey from Bogotá to the Colombian plains and into the transnational Amazonian region is thematically recognizable as the regionalist quest of an elite urban *criollo* male into the national frontier. But whereas *Doña Bárbara* and *Don Segundo Sombra* feature protagonists who ultimately imagine themselves and their countries— however imperfectly—through the plains and pampas, respectively, *The Vortex* closes tragically with "The jungle devoured them!" (219),[5] referring to Cova, his love interest, and their new baby. Furthermore, everywhere Cova turns in the antagonistic forest, he encounters foreigners: Peruvians, Venezuelans, Turks, Syrians, Italians, and Lebanese. Some of the last words frantically penned by Cova censure the deplorable deficiencies in Colombia's cartographic record, which Cova blames for the foreign nightmare of the Colombian hinterlands. In some ways, Rivera's irreparably fragmented Colombian national geography resonates more closely with the disillusion of the novel of the Mexican Revolution than the regional novel. By focusing on this seeming outlier, though, we reveal how even some of the more idiosyncratic elements of the novel respond to the neocolonial land appropriation that inflects all of the regional novels, and thus the work serves as a sort of bridge between the regional novel and the novel of the Mexican Revolution.

The Vortex's skepticism toward the possibility of national integration begins as a tale about a criollo elite's desire to root himself in an idealized rural countryside. Cova flees with his love interest Alicia for the eastward-lying plains of Casanare after having offended Bogotá's high society with their affair. In an epigraph to the diary left behind by Cova—the novel itself—he explains, "Ruthless fate *uprooted me* from incipient prosperity" (our emphasis).[6] Because *The Vortex* entered the canon as a social realist *novela de la tierra* about the crimes of the Amazon rubber boom (1850–1920), most criticism has focused on the second and third parts of the text, which unfold in the jungle. However, before Cova takes up the cause of those enslaved by rubber production, he spends time in the plains obsessed with the selfish pursuit of re-rooting himself in Colombian soil in order to cultivate a new path to prosperity. With the possibility of a cattle-rounding business venture, he daydreams about returning to Bogotá with his accumulated wealth, buying a house, recounting his adventures in the plains, and gathering friends in his garden to recite poetry (125). The image is rife with critical irony. The elite urban poet, whose verses, as one character indicates, "bind to the heart of the fatherland his dispersed children and create national subjects even in foreign lands" (our translation),[7] lacks the requisite skills for success in cattle rounding. He is neither Gallegos's protagonist Santos Luzardo, who seems to have retained muscle memory for breaking horses from his youth in the Venezuelan plains, nor is he a humble child, like Güiraldes's narrator, poised to learn. Nonetheless, Cova bullheadedly dreams of comfortably reaping riches from the national periphery to attain property ownership in the city, where he can appreciate a highly manicured version of "nature" in his domestic space. Eventually, Cova romanticizes a future life in the plains, too, settling in a house built with his own hands (161), but these daydreams are as much a fiction as his poetry's intimacy with the land. Beckman characterizes the novel's engagement with exaggerated *modernista* tropes and aesthetics as a critique of the "empty signifiers of a 'civilization' that does not recognize the exploitation on which it is built" (180). Cova's fantasies develop a similar critique of Colombian intellectuals as detached opportunists who literally and metaphorically claim ownership over other peoples' land.

The presence of the British empire interrupts Cova's delusions. The city dandy cannot claim Casanare for himself or, by extension, for Colombian criollo society at large, because the British already have. French examines the absence of the Peruvian Amazon Company, a part-British rubber conglomerate, in the later jungle scenes as a deliberate omission that "severs the ties between the criollo aristocracy to which Cova belongs and the British capitalists" (154). But the British empire appears overtly in the first section of the novel in Casanare. There, the local currency is the pound sterling, and the man who brings British notes to the plains is the rubber baron Narciso Barrera, the personification of rubber profit seeking. Cova and his companions ultimately leave for the jungle because Barrera has monopolized the sale of commodities locally, cutting Cova's friend Franco off from his usual source of revenue. When the men resort to cattle rounding for income, an angry bull pierces one of Barrera's men through the ear and severs his head (176). In response, Barrera hangs another man in Franco's barn and frames Cova and his companions as the murderers, forcing them to flee the law. Rivera depicts British capital in collusion with local legal institutions and as responsible for gruesome deaths and economic downfall well beyond the sites of rubber extraction. In the wake of the 1903 US annexation of Panama, this depiction of frayed national sovereignty outside of the capital city constituted a goading critique of Colombian nationhood. Thus, as Cova's fantasies eclipse his awareness of local realities, *The Vortex* implicates criollos' pursuit of individual wealth—via land ownership—as causal in the destruction of both rural ways of life and the national economy by foreign entities.

The jungle awakens Cova's class consciousness, altogether dormant in Casanare. Once in "the vortex," he confronts more of the rubber economy's corporeal waste, a poignant metaphor for extractivism's annihilation of the Colombian body politic. Two Maipurean guides drown in whirlpools like so many nameless Indigenous bodies lost to the rubber trade.[8] Clemente Silva, a key character, exposes his disfigured back scarred by the whip of rubber overseers as a sort of carnal echo of the tapped rubber trees. He arrives on the scene with maggot-infested leech wounds that present his body as an undead corpse in service of rubber extraction: "Maggots in me, while I'm still alive!" (118).[9] Silva tells stories of workers fleeing the debt peonage that bound them to rubber camps only to be devoured down to the bone by carnivorous ants. Cova's proximity to these human casualties of extractivism compels a shift in his interests from personal wealth to retribution for abused and enslaved rubber tappers within Colombia's national borders. Whereas neocolonialism presented a threat only to his aspired social status in the plains, once closer to rubber's economic base, he discovers a vital threat to the country's most disenfranchised, though it is worth noting that even in this awakening, Indigenous peoples are only marginally included in the poet's concerns.

Cova's privilege limits the scope of his understanding. Furthermore, because he remains temperamental, volatile, and immature throughout the text, readers are led to dislike him and distrust not only the story he tells but also his strategies to resolve the crisis. The grandiose role he assumes in reporting rubber crimes and informing Colombian officials about what is really happening in the country's jungles—especially in light of the earlier highly publicized international outcry over rubber abuses—resembles white saviorism more than disinterested altruism.[10] Until the very end, Cova remains caught between trying to save his sense of self as part of the criollo elite and ending the exploitation of other Colombian bodies. He never understands that his unskilled urbanite fantasies of comfortable wealth would necessarily hinge on a colonial labor hierarchy resembling, to a certain degree, the structure of the rubber economy. Indeed, Antonio Gómez Restrepo (46) and Alfonso González (196) have compared Cova and friends to conquistadors romping through the jungle. On an allegorical level, the elite subject can neither perceive nor resolve the contradiction between his advocacy and his positionality; he cannot save both himself and the country as a collective because his version of prosperity depends on the exploitation of others. Therefore, the novel's closing scene indicates that the self-important, internally colonizing subject must disappear in order for the country to forge a path away from the kind of colonial violence initiated with the conquest, but even in his absence, neocolonial economic interests remain.

Felipe Martínez-Pinzón has characterized *The Vortex*'s hopelessness as a "party pooper" during a time of "capitalist euphoria" and "optimism" in Bogotá (167). A cursory reading of the novel as part of the regionalist corpus may also suggest that among regional novels, *The Vortex* is a downer. However, when considering *Don Segundo Sombra* and *Doña Bárbara* through the lens of criollo relationships to the land, a parallel pessimism emerges. In Güiraldes's bildungsroman, *a guacho* (regional Quechua term for a young orphan) finds a mother in the Argentine plains and a father in a gaucho, but they constantly run into Englishmen and their property lines, signaling both British investment in the cattle industry and the anachronism of gaucho life: "There was by now no need for the gaucho rodeos to separate, sell, and trade livestock whose owners were identified by branded cattle; the fences took care of that" (DeVries 162). The narrator will be conveniently called away from the pampa by an unexpected inheritance at the end of the novel, a foreshadowed plot twist that allows him to remain a gaucho at heart without having to constantly trip over the barbed wires of neocolonial geopolitics.

Though *Doña Bárbara* is a more triumphant tale of an acculturated *llanero* (a man from the Venezuelan plains) who returns "home" from Caracas and successfully recovers his property and sense of belonging, the protagonist, Santos Luzardo, initially intends to assess the property for sale to fund his studies in Europe. His plans of profiting from his family's parcel and embracing European modernity are thwarted by two inconvenient factors: the traumatized Indigenous woman, doña Bárbara, symbol of Venezuelan barbarism, and the caricature of US imperialism, the American usurper Míster Danger.[11] Though *Doña Bárbara* takes place prior to President Juan Vicente Gómez's opening of oil fields to Royal Dutch Shell and Rockefeller's Standard Oil—well underway at the time of writing—Gallegos's "not-so-veiled indictment of [Gómez's] dictatorial regime" implicates the nefarious American as a symbol of the selling off of the Venezuelan subsoil (Alonso 109). Both characters must disappear: doña Bárbara, because, "like the native she is . . . she belongs to the past, and her kind has no future in the new Venezuela," and Míster Danger, because corrupt American interests threaten the just and rational exploitation of natural resources that Luzardo proposes with the oft-referenced metaphor of property divisions (Barrueto 192). As in *The Vortex*, the elite subject's victory depends on exclusion: only by literally fencing out both neocolonial land-grabbing and Indigenous peoples can the elite maintain their connection to the land.

In each case, regional novels depict criollos' imagined relationships to their nations' lands as mere fairytale. These novels focus on characters who envision their countries and themselves as national subjects through a relationship of entitlement to lands far from the cities and towns from which they come. Thus, the regional novel—disguised as provincial costumbrismo—takes aim at the hypocrisy of the urban elite, whose attachment to anachronistic fantasies of land tenure makes them complicit in selling the very source of their inspiration and subjugating the peoples living there in the process.

THE NOVEL OF THE MEXICAN REVOLUTION

In Mexico, land is both setting and catalyst for the politicized struggle of the people. The motto of the Mexican Revolution, "Tierra y libertad," underscores two of the central conflicts of the civil war: the longstanding grievances of peasants and tenant farmers who worked for wealthy landowners in near slave-like conditions, and the opposition to the thirty-year dictatorship of Porfirio Díaz, who ruled without regard for democratic elections or presidential term limits. Thus, following Díaz's fraudulent 1910 election to a seventh term, a broad coalition coalesced to demand a return to constitutional governance. Among the revolutionaries were nationalists and progressives, as well as Indigenous people and landless peasants who fought to implement long-sought agrarian reform, including the expropriation of land from the elite for redistribution, the nationalization of land, and the reestablishment of *ejidos* (common lands). General Emiliano Zapata best articulated this demand in his "Plan de Ayala" (1911), which displayed dissatisfaction with the incrementalism of Díaz's successor, President Francisco Madero,[12] particularly in terms of property rights and land reform. Fittingly, Zapata was the first to brandish the maxim "Tierra y libertad," and his troops were chiefly comprised of the disenfranchised individuals who would benefit most from an agrarian agenda.

Despite the centrality of land reform to the revolutionary struggle, the second term of the revolutionary motto—libertad—has received more critical attention due to the ways in which canonical novels foreground political and popular struggles and the aspirations of the revolution and its leaders. This thematic focus is likely because, as Carlos Monsiváis makes clear, one of the core unifying elements of the novel of the Mexican Revolution is the sustained meditation on the failures and violence of the time period (375).[13] Notwithstanding the populist motives detailed above, the revolution turned into a power grab for its military cadre, and the demands of the masses that made up the bulk of the revolutionary armies were left unfulfilled. Horacio Legrás underscores how early critical assessments of literature of the revolution home in on this disillusion, which is related to the fact that, in many ways, the Mexican Revolution "was not *really* a revolution. It lacked programs and did not alter the form of the state in favor of those who carried on the fights" (*Literature* 113, original emphasis).

As has been widely discussed, the novel of the Mexican Revolution is not defined in terms of formal characteristics or genre, but rather in regard to thematic concerns (Monsiváis 375; Glantz 870; Castro Leal 17; Olea Franco 481). In general, these works treat the events and milieu during the decade of military activity beginning in 1910; however, some texts, such as Agustín Yáñez's *Al filo del agua* (*The Edge of the Storm* 1947) and José Vasconcelos's *Ulises criollo* (*A Mexican Ulysses* 1935), also focalize the buildup to the armed conflict. Despite the wide-ranging formal characteristics of the texts, some dominant stylistic traits emerge. Works frequently contain autobiographical elements that reflect the lives and experiences of their authors, such as Martín Luis Guzmán's *The Eagle and the Serpent*, Nellie Campobello's *Cartucho. Relatos de la lucha en el Norte de México* (*Cartucho: Tales of the Struggle in Northern Mexico* 1931), José Rubén Romero's *Apuntes de un lugareño* (*Notes of a Villager* 1932), and José Vasconcelos's *A Mexican Ulysses* and *La tormenta* (*The Storm* 1936). Many of the novels of the revolution—following Mariano Azuela's *Los de abajo* (*The Underdogs* 1916) as a sort of urtext of the genre—have an episodic structure, chronicling battles and confrontations, as well as political and popular tensions, in vignettes and through encounters with myriad characters, both historical and fictional. As John Rutherford details, in 1925, at a moment when Mexico was seeking to define its national culture, Francisco Monterde recuperated Azuela's novel for the national literary scene by praising it in the national press as an example of "modern Mexican literature" (217). Following the delayed canonization of Azuela's novel, other authors began reflecting on the armed conflict, and dozens of novels of the Mexican Revolution appeared in the ensuing decades, which accounts for why most works are penned well after the military conflict has ended.

We now turn to Guzmán's *The Eagle and the Serpent*, which underscores how geopolitical and economic anxieties are made manifest in the treatment of land in the novel of the Mexican Revolution. In particular, the relationship between economic class and land is of fundamental concern to the revolutionary struggle and literary depictions of the conflict period. In Guzmán's novel, anxieties about land take the form of encounters between the lettered class and the often illiterate masses of the rural lower class, the disruptive effects of burgeoning technological modernity, and the onset of neocolonial extractive capitalism—the latter of which unveils apprehensions about the eminence of the United States and this northern neighbor's influence on Mexican cultural, political, and economic development and autonomy. Thus, despite the overtly political nature of the novel of the Mexican Revolution, the works' preoccupation with land and land rights reveals an unaddressed connection to the telluric novel of South America.

Guzmán's semi-autobiographical novel proffers a self-aware critique of the ways in which the ideals and objectives of the Mexican Revolution were nearly universally betrayed by the political ambitions and character faults of its leaders. The text chronicles the years 1913–1915, as the narrator-protagonist Luis Guzmán flits from revolutionist camp to revolutionist camp, meeting generals, attending dances, wooing women, and dining on fare to which regular soldiers in the armies do not have access.[14] Many of these trivial episodes are described in terms of battle,[15] thus emphasizing the absurd nature of the military and political elite who often determine the direction of the war safely distant from the front lines. With few exceptions, the revolutionary leaders that Luis meets are a great disappointment—inept, selfish, or dangerously ambitious. In *The Eagle and the Serpent*, the lofty goals of the revolution are betrayed by its cynical and power-hungry leadership, and Guzmán's writings have been dubbed a sort of *mea culpa* by an author complicit in the decadence of the revolutionary elite (Bruce-Novoa 137).

The depiction of General Pancho Villa stands out in this critique. Whereas the narrator views most revolutionary generals as opportunistic cynics, Villa is represented as a reactive leader of pure animal instinct. Sophie Esch writes of the profound chasm that exists between Luis as cultured intellectual and Villa as a violent man guided by a "politics of the firearm" (76). Esch's reading unveils how each is "disarmed" in his confrontation with the Other: the narrator by Villa's raw emotion and affection, and Villa is literally disarmed—the narrator takes his pistol away—by Luis's eloquence and reasoning (74–76). The novel underscores the difference between the narrator as urban intellectual and Villa as rural outlaw. Upon seeing Villa one morning, the narrator remarks: "The glitter in his eyes made me realize suddenly that mankind is not of one species, but of many, and that these species are separated by limitless space, have no common denominator. An abyss cleaves them, and it may cause vertigo to look from one of these worlds to the other, which lies opposite" (292).[16] The depiction of Villa has been read under the rubric of "civilization and barbarism" (Parra; Abeyta)—a trope also typical of the regional novel.[17] Similar tendencies of cultural elitism populate other novels of the Mexican revolution, such as Azuela's *The Underdogs*, in which narrator Luis Cervantes (Cervantes, of course, alluding to the author of *Don Quijote*) is a "curro," or middle- or upper-class intellectual from the city who looks down on Indigenous and mestizo peasants (Waisman 137).

The contradistinction between Luis and Villa indexes a fundamental disconnect between the lettered elite and the rural peasant classes, and this gulf becomes visible in each figure's differential relationship to land. Villa's unparalleled genius as a strategist and combatant is linked to his connection to nature. In one episode, the narrator is mesmerized when Villa attempts the seemingly impossible task of shooting a casing from twenty paces away with a bullet of the same caliber: "[his] pastime, in spite of the sanguinary memories his pistol evoked, was strangely in keeping with the smile of the light and the profound peace of the countryside" (281).[18] In contrast to the bond that Villa, the former "outlaw in the hills" (282),[19] maintains with the land, Luis and his upper echelon peers have a more utilitarian view of the earth. Whereas Villa lives in an almost symbiotic relationship to land, the military and political elite conceive of it as a way to enrich themselves and their cause and to bring Mexico into the modern present. Their extractive relationship to land is particularly salient in regard to the technologies of industrial modernity.

The figure of the train—the literal and figurative engine of technological modernity and the earlier Industrial Revolution—becomes the charged symbol of Mexico's incompetence and stunted development in Guzmán's novel. Whereas railways are often associated with economic mobility, in *The Eagle and the Serpent*, the train becomes a chaotic space of unrealized potential and apocalyptic foreboding. The cars are dilapidated, with worn out and missing seats, torn curtains, and broken windows. The narrator observes that the "state of things was eloquently reflected in the passengers . . . At every point life on the train showed clearly a return to the primitive" (126).[20] People become confused with bundles of cargo and shed any remnant of civilized humanity, eating on the floor "among dirt and rubbish" (126).[21] Later, the military convoys take over the passenger and cargo lines for their machinations, transporting generals and their officers back and forth across Mexican terrain (309). Rails are no longer used for passenger and freight transport, but rather for military strategy, and thus are not monetarily or materially productive. The narrator observes that the trains "transport[ed] with lightning speed the armies and the ideas of the revolutionary tempest" (309).[22] However, these ideas go nowhere, merely zipping back and forth along the rails. In this light, the revolution institutes a sort of limbo, an ahistorical no-man's land between the Porfirian past and a future modern Mexico, symbolized by the senseless monopoly of land routes by revolutionary leadership.

A related anxiety is manifested in Campobello's *Cartucho*. In one vignette, a half-crazed man rants about the growing influence of mechanized technology—"'Machines, land, plows, nothing but machinery and more machinery!' . . . 'The government doesn't understand. It doesn't see'" (36).[23] He is then strung up by a group of men on horseback and hung from a telegraph pole, and the child narrator watches him die as her train pulls away from the station. Whereas technology unveils the untapped potential of Mexican modernity in *The Eagle and the Serpent*, in *Cartucho*, the violence of the revolution is sutured to the trains and telegraph lines that scar the land.

The ambiguous nature of technological modernity reaches its apotheosis in Guzmán's novel in an episode entitled "La carrera en las sombras" (163) ("Night Flight" 134). Luis travels to Hermosillo with General Rafael Buelna, an orderly, two officers, and a driver in Buelna's slapdash motorized handcar. They set out at night, passing through dangerous, unfamiliar terrain, with only a lantern hastily affixed to the motor to light their way (136–37). The narrator observes that the journey is both rash and ill-advised and that the passengers are risking their lives (138). Hours into the journey, Luis stares sleepily ahead, attempting to make out the rails and landscape in the dark night. Suddenly, shapes come into focus, and he witnesses a somnolent vision of the harmonious fusion of the Mexican landscape with the technological accoutrements of burgeoning modernity:

> My efforts to penetrate the darkness were finally rewarded. I could see as clearly as though the sun were shining: a perfect road, lined with trees on either side, tele-graph poles, carefully laid ties; villages below, mountains against the horizon, silver-rimmed clouds in the sky. The track with all its ups and downs, its curves, its swerves, its crossings did not represent the least danger. It was a smooth, clear track on which one could not imagine the slightest obstacle. There was nothing to worry about; one could sleep... sleep... (139–40)[24]

As the narrator nods off, the handcar collides with something and is derailed, injuring some of its passengers and halting on the track. Legrás reads this dangerous journey and stumbling block as symbolic of the entire revolutionary endeavor, concluding that the unknown obstacle in the track is representative of the emergent political agency of the peasant masses, which is inconceivable to the Mexican elite, symbolized by Luis (*Literature* 127).

We would add to Legrás's reading, noting that the dreamlike vision comprises a harmonious mingling of two incommensurable actors: the urban elite and rural masses. The track, road, and telegraph poles symbolize the political-economic modernity sought by the elite, which, in his dream, Luis views as in sync with the natural world of the peasantry, figured by mountains, trees, and peaceful sky. Significantly, this vision violently dissipates when the narrator is jolted awake by the handcar crash, which is caused by what turns out to be a mule in the tracks (140). The tidy synthesis of these two bands of the Mexican revolutionary forces is thrown off course by the sterile mule, revealing an anxiety about the barrenness of the revolution and Mexico's nascent national project. Much like Rivera's critique of British profiteering during the rubber boom in *The Vortex*, the problematic figure of the train in *The Eagle and the Serpent* subtly points to the contradiction at the heart of Mexico's national project. As a commodity republic, Mexico sought to modernize and improve its economic lot via trains, agriculture, and mining, yet these natural resources and technologies were often expropriated by international interests, thus limiting the profits reaped by Mexican nationals.[25]

Ironically, considering that much of the Mexican rail was foreign owned, the chaos and deficiency of the Mexican rail systems stand in stark contrast to the representation of the United States in the novel. At various junctures Luis must cross over into

US territory, which is depicted as clean and organized and as a space of abundant commodities. During one such trip, he travels from Nogales, Mexico, to Nogales, Arizona, and the juxtaposition of these two Nogales produces a conspicuous critique of US imperialism's hand in the disordered state of Mexican affairs. The United States appears as an extractive parasite, lapping up "remnants of the country's wealth which the Revolution sold for whatever it could get because it was in dire need of money" (142).[26] Even more pernicious, US entities acquire Mexican wealth—cattle, minerals, and other "national patrimony" (143)[27]—at depreciated prices, then use these riches to produce arms and supplies that are sold back to Mexicans so that they may purchase all the necessary supplies to continue killing one another (142).

The narrative distrust of the United States reflects historical resentment. In the century preceding the revolution, the United States made its imperial aspirations in Mexico painfully known through the battles of the Mexican-American War (1846–1848), which resulted in a loss of nearly one-third of Mexico's territory. Prior to the outbreak of the revolution, the United States bought up Mexican land for mining and oil drilling, and this international appropriation of land was one of the central motivations behind resistance to Porfirio Díaz. Moreover, US companies were infamous for underpaying Mexican laborers, strikebreaking, compensating workers in company scrip, and maintaining dangerous working conditions, which are the impetus behind the deadly 1906 Cananea and 1907 Río Blanco worker strikes. Likewise, the United States intervened in the Mexican Revolution, supporting those factions that it deemed most sympathetic to its geopolitical and economic interests. Just as in the clash between the rural peasantry and urban intellectual classes in Mexico, in literature, land becomes the fulcrum upon which the anxieties surrounding technological modernity and the ongoing threat of US imperialism emerge.

THE LEGACY OF LAND IN THE REGIONAL NOVEL AND THE NOVEL OF THE MEXICAN REVOLUTION

Our analysis brings to the fore how neocolonial incursions by foreign capital on Latin American soil permeated the aesthetic concerns of both the telluric novel and the novel of the Mexican Revolution, thus broadening the scope of their similarities. In Mexico, revolutionary forces waged a scattered and disorganized revolt against a conservative system deemed culpable for the inequities arising from land's new signification under accelerated modernization. By contrast, regarding the economic situation in Colombia, the center of rubber production shifted to Southeast Asia and concerns over illicit activities in the tropical lowlands temporarily abated. In Venezuela the caudillo stronghold of Juan Vicente Gómez continued to influence the petrostate's economic policies long after the end of his third presidential term, and in Argentina the British hold on industry would mark politics through Peronism and into the Falklands War. The paths worn by each country's confrontation with neocolonial powers diverged, but the novels we have examined here reveal that those paths were seeded with similar anxieties and aspirations.

Mexican authors and South American regionalists exhume land's distressed relationship to technologies of modernization, political representation, human violence and environmental devastation, socioeconomic status, and regional belonging. Our readings highlight how both literary modes either suffer from or critique—and in some cases both—a sort of lettered myopia regarding who has a hand in charting the future of land and politics. As we have demonstrated, the elite's willingness to pillage land and natural resources in the name of modernization fragments cultural projects of national integration, and authors of both regional novels and the novel of the Mexican Revolution write self-consciously against their own class interests, exposing the avarice and ignorance of Latin American elites before the question of land (dis)possession. They represent the effects of top-down impositions of modernizing processes as infrastructure—labor camps, railways, fences, telegraph poles, barbed wire—that pierce the land and disorder peoples' relationship to communal and open space. In turn, displaced workers, Indigenous peoples, campesinos, llaneros, and gauchos threaten the new partitioning of the land.

Future studies might engage comparatively with both kinds of novels to trace their shared legacy in contemporary narrative and other forms of cultural production that take up twenty-first-century iterations of land struggles, including extractivism, hydroelectric modernization, Indigenous sovereignty, and migration. The disenchantment affectively sown by the novels we have analyzed persistently registers the plundering of land and the systematic refusal to recognize the land rights and belonging of disenfranchised peoples—particularly Indigenous and rural mestizo citizens. This abuse and neglect became the political rallying cry behind organized revolts as diverse as Zapatismo in Mexico and the Fuerzas Armadas Revolucionarias de Colombia (FARC, Revolutionary Armed Forces of Colombia). Today, not only do such vastly different forms of popular resistance generate political pressure, but they also disrupt literary history, fracturing the monologic quality of the land stories outlined here, in which "the underdogs" are stock characters in criollo stories. Both the regional novel and the novel of the Mexican Revolution criticize the kinds of injustices that will galvanize later generations to demand rights and restitution for decades of deterritorialization, displacement, and despoliation.

NOTES

1. Regional novels are variously called by other names, including *criollista* or *costumbrista* novels, or sometimes by subcategories of novela de la tierra such as *novela campesina, novela de la selva*, or *novela gauchesca*.
2. Though the Boom authors strived to distinguish themselves from the regionalist writers, their continuity with their literary forebearers is indisputable: "The Boom novel would not have been possible without advances made in the preceding decades" (Gollnick 44).
3. Camps, DeVries, and Flores, among others, evaluate the regional novel ecocritically.

4. In Brazil regionalism is closely associated with the *romance do Nordeste* (Northeastern novel) such as Rachel de Queiroz's *O quince* (1930), Graciliano Ramos's *Vidas secas* (1938), and José Lins do Rego's *Fogo morto* (1943). Antônio Cândido (159) makes a distinction between the Spanish American phenomenon of regionalism, which is temporally limited, and what he proposes as the longue durée of Brazilian regionalism, though in this respect, Cândido is not unlike Ángel Rama or José Miguel Oviedo, who likewise trace a long trajectory of regionalism in Spanish American literature beginning with independence.

5. "¡Los devoró la selva!" (Rivera 385). English translations of *The Vortex*, unless otherwise indicated, are taken from John Charles Chasteen.

6. "El destino implacable me desarraigó de la prosperidad incipiente" (Rivera 77, English translation ours).

7. "Encadenar al corazón de la patria los hijos dispersos y crearle súbditos en tierras extrañas" (114, English translation ours).

8. Recent estimates indicate that the infamous rubber company Casa Arana, which operated in Putumayo, Colombia, was responsible for 100,000 deaths (Velez-Ocampo et al.).

9. "¡Engusanado, engusanado y estando vivo!" (Rivera 246).

10. Cova's arrogance becomes even more ridiculous when we consider that Benjamín Saldaña Rocca's denunciations in the Iquitos newspaper *La felpa* circulate in the novel. Additionally, Roger Casement's and Walter Hardenburg's public outcry had already drawn national and international attention before Cova supposedly begins his manuscript.

11. Alonso first notes the caricaturesque quality of *Doña Barbara*'s characters as key to the novel's allegorical function (117).

12. Madero came from a wealthy landowning family in northern Coahuila. An advocate of single term limits, he came to power in 1911 after Díaz was ousted by revolutionary forces. In 1913, he was assassinated after a military coup and replaced by conservative General Victoriano Huerta, who had participated in Madero's ouster. Huerta was in power until revolutionary forces defeated the federal army in the Battle of Zacatecas in July 1914.

13. In the section "En lo moral" ("In terms of morality"), Monsiváis explains that the novel of the Mexican Revolution is characterized by: "disenchanted testimony, the demythification and deglamorization of an epic (because the corollary of bloodshed and military feats is uselessness and ascension of scoundrels to power)" ("el testimonio desencantado, la desmitificación y desglamorización de una épica [ya que el corolario de la sangre vertida y de las hazañas bélicas es la inutilidad, el encumbramiento de los bribones])" as well as "the frequent affirmation—even in the best moments of its prose—of cruelty and *physical* violence as the meaning of the revolution, which is exemplified by the chapter 'The Carnival of Bullets' of *The Eagle and the Serpent*" ("la consignación frecuente—incluso en algunos de los mejores momentos prosísticos—de la crueldad y de la violencia *físicas* como el sentido de la revolución. Ejemplo óptimo: el capítulo 'La fiesta de las balas' de *El águila y la serpiente*"; original emphasis, 375).

14. For clarity, to distinguish between the author and the narrator, we refer to the author as Guzmán and the narrator as Luis, as the protagonist is called both Luis Guzmán and Luisito in the novel.

15. See episode, "A Revolutionary Dance" (104–10; "Un baile revolucionario" 127–33) for a concrete example in which Luis and his friends "battle" (107; "combate" 130) the newly conquered Culiacán society, who did not want to send their daughters to a dance with the revolutionaries.

16. "A mí los fulgores de sus ojos me revelaron de súbito que los hombres no pertenecemos a una sola especie, sino a muchas, y que de especie a especie hay, dentro del género humano, distancias infranqueables, mundos irreductibles a común término capaces de producir, si desde uno de ellos se mira al fondo del que se le opone, el vértigo de *lo otro*" (344–45). All English translations of *The Eagle and the Serpent* cited in the body of the article are drawn from Harriet de Onís's 1965 translation.

17. The perhaps overused rubric of civilization and barbarism has organized a number of studies on the regional novel, and critics have also applied it to interpreting Guzmán's novel. However, recent criticism has challenged the appropriateness of this model for the novel of the Mexican Revolution (Legrás, "Martín Luis Guzmán"; Esch).

18. "[Su] entretenimiento, pese a las sanguinarias evocaciones de la pistola, concordaba de extraña manera con la sonrisa de la luz y la profunda paz del campo" (332).

19. "De huida por la sierra" (333).

20. "Ese estado de cosas se reflejaba con enérgica elocuencia en los viajeros mismos . . . El tono de la vida a bordo del tren significaba por dondequiera un retorno a lo primitivo" (152).

21. "Con la mugre del suelo y su inmundicia" (153).

22. "Viajaban, con la rapidez del rayo, los ejércitos y las ideas animadoras del huracán revolucionario" (364).

23. "'Máquinas, la tierra, arados, nada más que maquinarias y más maquinarias' . . . 'El gobierno no sabe, el gobierno no ve'" (89). Above English translation drawn from Doris Meyer and Irene Matthews's 1988 translation.

24. "En fuerza de querer penetrar las sombras, acabé por ver. Vi como si el sol alumbrara: un camino perfecto, arboledas laterales, postes del telégrafo, durmientes cuidadosamente balastados; pueblos en el fondo, montañas en el horizonte, nubes orladas de plata en el cielo. La vía, con todos sus altibajos, con sus curvas, sus desviaciones, sus cambios, sus cruzamientos, no ofrecía el menor peligro. Era una vía limpia y despejada donde no se concebiría el obstáculo más leve. Se podía confiar, se podía dormir . . . dormir . . ." (169).

25. Michael Matthews notes that much of the rail laid during the Porfiriato was backed by US capital and that foreign companies were often granted the contracts to build and operate the lines (27–30). Moreover, two of the main railroad lines, the Interoceanic and the Mexican Central, were owned by British and US entities, respectively (280).

26. "Los restos de la riqueza que la Revolución malbarataba por razones imperativas" (173).

27. "Patrimonio nacional" (143).

Works Cited

Abeyta, Michael. "The 'Man-Beast' and the Jaguar: Mariano Azuela and Martín Luis Guzmán on Pancho Villa as the Sovereign Beast in *El águila y la serpiente*." *Equestrian Rebels: Critical Perspectives on Mariano Azuela and the Novel of the Mexican Revolution*, edited by Roberto Cantú, Cambridge Scholars Publishing, 2016, pp. 100–24.

Alonso, Carlos J. *The Spanish American Regional Novel: Modernity and Autochthony.* Cambridge UP, 1990.

Anderson, Mark Daniel. "Was the Mexican Revolution a Revolt of Nature? Agustín Yañez's Ecological Perspective." *Revista de Estudios Hispánicos*, vol. 40, no. 3, 2006, pp. 447–67.

Azuela, Mariano. *Los de abajo.* Imprenta de El Paso del Norte, 1916.

Barrueto, Jorge J. "The Othering of Women in the Twentieth-Century Latin American Canon: Misogyny in Rómulo Gallegos' *Doña Bárbara*." *Misogynism in Literature: Any Place, Any Time*, edited by Britta Zangen, Peter Lang, 2004, pp. 181–97.

Beckman, Ericka. *Capital Fictions: The Literature of Latin America's Export Age*. U of Minnesota P, 2012.

Bruce-Novoa, Juan. "Recharting the Heartland: Art-As-In-Autobiography in Ignacio E. Lozano, Martín Luis Guzmán and Frances Toor." *Nuevo Texto Crítico*, vol. 15–16, no. 29–32, 2002–2004, pp. 131–50.

Campobello, Nellie. *Cartucho. Relatos de la lucha en el Norte de México*. 1931. 2nd ed., Biblioteca Era, 2018.

Campobello, Nellie. *Cartucho: Tales of the Struggle in Northern Mexico*. Translated by Doris Meyer and Irene Matthews. U of Texas P Austin, 1988.

Camps, Martín. "Barbarian Civilization: Travel and Landscape in *Don Segundo Sombra* and the Contemporary Argentinean Novel." *The Natural World in Latin American Literatures: Ecocritical Essays on Twentieth Century Writings*, edited by Adrian Taylor Kane, MacFarland, 2010, pp. 154–74.

Cândido, Antonio. *A educação pela noite & outros ensaios*. Ática, 1989.

Castro Leal, Antonio. *La novela de la Revolución Mexicana*. 9th ed., Aguilar, 1991.

DeVries, Scott M. *A History of Ecology and Environmentalism in Spanish American Literature*. Rowman & Littlefield, 2013.

Esch, Sophie. *Modernity at Gunpoint: Firearms, Politics, and Culture in Mexico and Central America*. U of Pittsburgh P, 2018.

Flores, William. *Ecocrítica poscolonial y literatura moderna latinoamericana*. Fondo Editorial de la UNMSM, 2015.

Fornoff, Carolyn. "The Nature of Revolution in Rafael F. Muñoz's *Se llevaron el cañón para Bachimba*." *Mexican Literature in Theory*, edited by Ignacio Sánchez Prado, Bloomsbury Academic, 2018, pp. 93–110.

Franco, Jean. *An Introduction to Spanish-American Literature*. Cambridge UP, 1994.

French, Jennifer. *Nature, Neo-Colonialism, and the Spanish American Regional Writers*. Dartmouth College P, 2005.

Gallegos, Rómulo. *Doña Bárbara*, edited by Domingo Miliani. Cátedra, 2001.

Glantz, Margo. "La novela de la revolución mexicana y *La sombra del caudillo*." *Revista Iberoamericana*, vol. 59, July-December 1989, pp. 869–78.

Gollnick, Brian. "The Regional Novel and Beyond." *The Cambridge Companion to the Latin American Novel*, edited by Efraín Kristal, Cambridge UP, 2005, pp. 44–58.

Gómez Restrepo, Antonio. "*La vorágine*." *La vorágine: textos críticos*, edited by Montserrat Ordóñez, Alianza Editorial Colombiana, 1987, pp. 45–48.

González, Alfonso. "Elementos hispánicos y clásicos en la caracterización de *La vorágine*." *La vorágine: textos críticos*, edited by Montserrat Ordóñez, Alianza Editorial Colombiana, 1987, pp. 191–98.

Gonzalez Echevarría, Roberto. *Modern Latin American Literature: A Very Short Introduction*. Oxford UP, 2011.

Gonzalez Echevarría, Roberto. *The Voice of the Masters: Writing and Authority in Modern Latin American Literature*. U of Texas P, 1985.

Güiraldes, Ricardo. *Don Segundo Sombra*, edited by Sara Parkinson de Saz, Cátedra, 2009.

Guzmán, Martín Luis. *El águila y la serpiente*. 1928. 6th ed., Compañía General de Ediciones, S.A., 1956.

Guzmán, Martín Luis. *The Eagle and the Serpent*. Translated by Harriet de Onis. Dolphin Books, 1965.

Legrás, Horacio. *Literature and Subjection: The Economy of Writing and Marginality in Latin America*. U of Pittsburgh P, 2008.

Legrás, Horacio. "Martín Luis Guzmán: el viaje de la revolución." *MLN*, vol. 118, no. 2, 2003, pp. 427–54.

Martínez-Pinzón, Felipe. "La voz de los árboles: fiebre, higiene y poesía en *La vorágine*." *Bulletin of Hispanic Studies*, vol. 91, no. 2, 2014, pp. 163–81.

Matthews, Michael. *The Civilizing Machine: A Cultural History of Mexican Railroads, 1876–1910*. U of Nebraska P, 2014.

Monsiváis, Carlos. "Notas sobre la cultura mexicana en el siglo XX." *Historia general de México: Volumen IV*, edited by Berta Ulloa, Lorenzo Meyer, Jorge Alberto Manrique, and Carlos Monsiváis, Colegio De Mexico, 1976, pp. 303–476.

Oloff, Kerstin. "The 'Monstrous Head' and the 'Mouth of Hell': The Gothic Ecologies of the 'Mexican Miracle.'" *Ecological Crisis and Cultural Representation in Latin America*, edited by Mark Anderson and Zelia Bora, Lexington, 2016, pp. 79–98.

Olea Franco, Rafael. "La novela de la Revolución Mexicana: una propuesta de relectura." *Nueva revista de filología hispánica*, vol. 60, no. 2, 2012, pp. 479–514.

Oviedo, José Miguel. *Historia de la literatura hispanoamericana*. Alianza, 2012.

Parra, Max. *Writing Pancho Villa's Revolution: Rebels in the Literary Imagination of Mexico*. U of Texas P, 2005.

Rama, Angel. *Transculturación narrativa en América Latina*. El Andariego, 1989.

Rivera, José Eustasio. *La vorágine*, edited by Montserrat Ordóñez. Cátedra, 2006.

Rivera, José Eustasio. *The Vortex*. Translated by John Charles Chasteen. Duke UP, 2018.

Rodríguez Monegal, Emir. "The New Latin American Novel." *Books Abroad*, vol. 44, no. 1, 1970, pp. 45–50.

Rogers, Charlotte. *Jungle Fever: Exploring Madness and Medicine in Twentieth-Century Tropical Narratives*. Vanderbilt UP, 2012.

Romero, José Rubén. *Apuntes de un lugareño*. Imprenta Núñez, 1932.

Rutherford, John. "The Novel of the Mexican Revolution." *The Cambridge History of Latin American Literature*, vol. 2: *The Twentieth Century*, edited by Enrique Pupo-Walker and Roberto Gonzalez Echevarría, Cambridge UP, 1996, pp. 213–25.

Vargas Llosa, Mario. "The Latin American Novel Today: Introduction." *Books Abroad*, vol. 44, no. 1, 1970, pp. 7–16.

Vasconcelos, José. *La tormenta*. Ediciones Botas, 1936.

Vasconcelos, José. *Ulises criollo: la vida del autor escrita por él mismo*. 3rd ed., Botas, 1935.

Velez-Ocampo, Juan, Carolina Herrera-Cano, and María Alejandra González Pérez. "The Peruvian Amazon Company's Death: The Jungle Devoured Them." *Dead Firms: Causes and Effects of Cross-Border Corporate Insolvency*, vol. 15, Emerald, 2016, pp. 35–46.

Waisman, Sergio, translator. *The Underdogs: A Novel of the Mexican Revolution*. By Mariano Azuela, Penguin, 2008.

Williams, Gareth. *The Mexican Exception: Sovereignty, Police, and Democracy*. Palgrave Macmillan, 2011.

Williams, Raymond L. "Nature in the Twentieth-Century Latin American Novel (1900–1967) and in *Cien años de soledad* of García Márquez." *The Natural World in Latin American Literatures: Ecocritical Essays on Twentieth Century Writings*, edited by Adrian Taylor Kane, McFarland, 2014, pp. 66–88.

Wylie, Lesley. *Colonial Tropes and Postcolonial Tricks: Rewriting the Tropics in the Novela de la Selva*. Liverpool UP, 2009.

Yáñez, Agustín. *Al filo del agua*. Porrúa, 1947.

CHAPTER 5

SOCIAL REALISM, *INDIGENISMO*, AND THE VINDICATION OF THE OTHER

MARÍA BEGOÑA PULIDO HERRÁEZ

SOCIAL REALISM

THE heyday of the social realist novel spans from the 1920s to the 1950s and responds to the Latin American social transformations of the time. In very broad terms, the social novel is concerned with sociological issues; is oriented toward the experiences of displaced, exploited, discriminated, and marginalized sectors (almost always popular); frequently seeks to denounce and protest their condition; and participates in the political analysis of the time, as well as in the social sciences that were developing (Perus, *El realismo* 169). The social novel is characterized by the presence of both ideological and aesthetic projects: it is conceived as an artistic practice with a social role. Despite not all authors having an explicit political affiliation, the social novel is inscribed within leftist political projects, and the struggles of workers, peasants, and other popular and *indigenista* movements. Moreover, the social novel participated in this period's anti-imperialism, which rejected the intervention of foreign capital, as well as the dependent development of Latin American capitalism. In *El realismo social en perspectiva*,[1] Françoise Perus describes the social structures and processes defining the conditions that produced this social narrative and explains why the novel was the prevailing genre and realism its most widely used form:

> The choice of a dominant narrative genre responds to the need to reconstruct processes –one could say, grasp the present reality as a result of a historical inheritance that can be transformed in one way or another–, while the emphasis on the realist purpose stems from the search for the objectivity that characterizes intellectual work. However, in this same sense, it is worth mentioning that as the physical and

intellectual division between political, literary, and scientific fields had not yet taken place (we are obviously referring to the field of social science that was still being developed at that time and had no institutional existence), literature, and more concretely social narrative, took part in these three fields.

(Perus, *El realismo social* 168–69)[2]

Realism thus responds to a mimetic purpose of "truth" and "objectivity," as well as to the intention of reflecting the historically concrete nature of the reality to be represented. Instead of copying a specific realist poetics, for example that cultivated in France by Balzac and Stendhal—where description and narration, the historical narrator, and the belief that language can serve as a transparent representation of reality are the prevalent features—in Latin America, realism stems from a mimetic conception of narrative that attempts to give an objective and truthful account of reality. Therefore, what is understood as realism is not restricted to a group of established procedures. There are numerous and less conventional forms of realism than those suggested by the dichotomy that posits an opposition between realism and the avant-garde.

Defending what they called the "creative," "new," or "language" novel, which corresponded to their defense of the narrative of the Latin American Boom, critics such as Emir Rodríguez Monegal, Mario Vargas Llosa, and Carlos Fuentes dismiss the social novel as primitive, devoid of form, and lacking conflict or characters (the protagonist always being Nature): "A picturesque and rural novel . . . The technique is rudimentary, pre-Flaubertian: the author interferes and gives her opinion together with the characters, ignores the notion of objectivity in fiction and disregards points of view; it seeks not to show, but to tell" (Vargas Llosa 30).[3] Moreover, Rodríguez Monegal points out that the nature of this literature is more testimonial and documentary than strictly literary (13).

As can be seen in the previous comments, these questions affect our understanding of the novelistic genre—in particular, how it has been appropriated, what forms have been used, and its development in Latin America. In this so-called primitive novel, the protagonist is not at the center of the story and lacks an individual psychology; there is a presence of elements related to folklore, legend, and myth; it includes epic and archetypal features, generally seen as outside the order of the Western novel; and it exhibits a precarious awareness of historical time (conceived as sequence and change) that reverts to compositional forms where independent tableaux predominate and hence problematize its sequential organization. These are all considered non-literary and anti-novelistic traits. However, this evaluation is based on a formalist conception of language in general and of literature in particular, since, in actuality, there is no novel without artistic form. The efforts to find narrative forms capable of expressing phenomena, processes, and transformations characteristic of Latin American societies are seen as primitive and with scant literary value. Ultimately, the distance between this ideal model of what the novel should be and the social realist novel could be evaluated in a completely different way that sees social realism as an unconventional, even avant-garde, narrative exercise. The study of specific social realist novels enables us to discover the various forms of dealing with particular Latin American problems and social experiences, which are hidden under the generic denomination of social realism.

A relevant aspect of this social realist literary trend is that it redefined the boundaries between the literary and the non-literary (Perus, *Transculturaciones* 274). Rodríguez Monegal and Vargas Llosa define the literary according to the degree or absence of a testimonial or documentary character. Hence, social realism, with its predominance of testimony and documentary material (a novel such as *Metal del diablo* [The Devil's Metal, 1946] by Augusto Céspedes introduces fragments of chronicles and journalistic news) would be a style that is little or not at all artistic. Nonetheless, social realism's incorporation of both literary and non-literary styles, its setting up of a dialogue among these, is certainly literary and innovative, regardless of the quality achieved. In this sense, it would be interesting to reconsider the place of social realism in current redefinitions of hybrid genres, such as testimony, non-fiction novel, and literary chronicle. Another aspect to consider is that this genre broke with the linear causality of narration, as can clearly be seen César Vallejo's *El tungsteno* (*Tungsten*, 1930). Moreover, social realism sought to organize narrative differently: for example, through the confrontation between space and time, or between myth and history (Perus, *Transculturaciones*; Cornejo Polar, *Escribir*).

Social realism developed throughout Latin America from 1920 to 1950 in an intimate relation with the political and social processes of each region: popular struggles, impact of imperialism, development of a dependent capitalism, and the emergence of socialist and communist parties. However, Ecuador is, perhaps, the one country where the national literary historiography grants social realism the central position.[4] The common aim of these Ecuadorian writers was to incorporate the speech of the middle and popular classes into literary language (until then characterized by its *aristocratizing* bent); to include characters from marginalized groups, such as Indians, blacks, *cholos* (halfbreeds), *montubios* (peasants from the coast), and proletarians, inserted in social and historical conflicts of exploitation; and, in general, to contribute to the creation of a national popular culture. For Agustín Cueva, the subject of these novels is always the same, "a savage capitalism . . . that advances with blood and fire over all previous economic, social and cultural forms, with an implacable logic of plunder and subjugation" (*Literatura* 639),[5] and the novels aim to denounce and protest this harsh reality.

Argentinean social realism was studied by David W. Foster in *Social Realism in the Argentine Narrative* (1988), where he vindicates a group of writers who wrote social realist narrative between 1930 and 1950 but were omitted from the canon.[6] Elías Castelnuovo (1893–1982), Álvaro Yunque (1889–1982), and Leónidas Barletta (1902–1975) formed part of the Boedo group in the 1920s. These writers aimed at creating a social literature that promoted social and political awareness by describing, with the greatest accuracy possible, the world of the poor, marginalized, and unemployed, as well as that of the workers (Saítta 91). Their realist writing has also been called the literature of poverty.

Chilean social realism, cultivated by the generation of '38, focused on urban popular subjects. Nicomedes Guzmán (1914–1964) (*Los hombres oscuros* [The Dark Men,

1939], *La sangre y la esperanza* [Blood and Hope, 1943]) and Juan Godoy (1911–1981) (*Angurrientos* [Greedy 1940]) are two of its representative authors. In Bolivian literature, Augusto Céspedes's (1904–1997) novel *Metal del diablo* (1946), about the figure of Simón Patiño and the mining industry, is one of the most important works of social realism. In Costa Rica, social realism has its most important exponent in *Mamita Yunai* (Mother US, 1941), by Carlos Luis Fallas (1909–1966). In Mexico, social realism is fused with the novel of the revolution, as is the case with the *indigenista* novel.

Within the vast panorama of social realism, I wish to examine El *tungsteno*[7] by César Vallejo (1892–1938), one of the first novels of this movement (published in the collection *La novela proletaria* [The Proletarian Novel], by Editorial Cénit in Spain). For Vallejo, revolutionary literature is that which gives back to words their social content: "The word is empty. It suffers from a sharp and incurable social consumption . . . truncated and crushed in the individual mouth . . . drowning in individualism. The word–the most human of all forms of social relations–has thus lost all its essence and collective attributes" (*El arte* 95).[8] *El tungsteno* is related to his interest in returning social content to words. Hence, it does not narrate the life or experience of a specific character but instead aims to depict a concrete historical process: the social decomposition caused by the presence of a transnational company, the Mining Society, which acts in alliance with the local authorities and bourgeoisie, characterized by their lack a sense of national identity.

The novel shows three moments of this historical process: in the first part, it focuses on the exploitation of the local indigenous population and workers in an isolated area of the Andes (supposedly near Cuzco, the once-capital of the Inca empire, perhaps in order to fulfil a symbolic function) inhabited by Sora Indians. The characters are prototypes of the different forces involved in this process of exploitation, dispossession, and destruction of social relations; certain events are narrated allegorically in order to show that the conflict is of national proportions. This is the case with the rape of Graciela (called La Rosada), which becomes an allegory of power and sexuality. Graciela symbolizes Peru, sold, played in a crap game by the merchant José Merino, who gives her away as if she were a commodity he owns. She is raped in an order that illustrates the hierarchy of power: first by the managers, then by the commissioner, cashier, engineer, and teacher: "Out of modesty, gallantry or delicacy, José Merino went last" (*Tungsten* 41).[9]

The second part takes place in Colca, the district capital, where the tungsten mines are located, and describes the rise of a petite bourgeoisie made up of unscrupulous, individualistic merchants who work in alliance with local authorities so that they can haul workers for the mines (in practice forced labor) among the Yanacona Indians.[10] Again, one finds the same prototypical characters, representing the forces in conflict, of individual and not collective interests, the power of money, but now confirming national disintegration and the exclusion of the Indians.

The third part includes three characters: the surveyor Leónidas Benítez, expelled from the Mining Society; the timekeeper who had been Graciela's partner; and Servando Huanca, a man of the people (a pure Indian in racial terms but a worker in class terms, a blacksmith who had previously been a mechanic and worked in different industrial centers). This character represents class-conscious workers. Huanca becomes a guide who encourages the uprising in the mines for justice and "citizen rights," though his goal is yet greater: a revolution "to overthrow all the gringos and exploiters in the world and free the Indians everywhere" (*Tungsten* 113).[11] Huanca is not individualist: he is a member of the people who is acquiring social conscience; he studies, reads, and joins associations and unions because the only way to fight for and protest injustice is to do so collectively.

El tungsteno is not organized around a character or a space; neither does it follow specific causal or chronological organizations, because such structures do not represent the density of social transformations, disintegration of human relationships, or the lack of nationality that Vallejo wants to highlight in the novel. Therefore, in order to better represent the different dimensions of these problems, there are shifts in topics and space in the three parts of the novel, and characters are presented as prototypes, representing forces rather than psychological individuality (which, in fact, is irrelevant to this story). Hence, the novel allows a reading beyond the mimetic account of the Mining Society's imperialism and exploitation. Instead, it becomes an allegory of Peru and of the fractures and conflicts it faces. The fragmented composition and the absence of individual characters lead the narrator to establish links between the parts of the novel and to explain the origins, consequences, scope of the actions and the characters' thoughts. It is the most important voice (in a sense, the only one as the other characters are images rather than voices), the one who guides the readers, perhaps workers with a social conscience who are unaware of Peruvian reality.

The action of *El tungsteno* takes place in 1917, when the United States enters World War I and the Bolshevik Revolution is triumphing in Russia. The opposing forces in Peru, capital at the service of imperialism and a working class that is developing its consciousness, are the same forces that are in the midst of a confrontation throughout the world. Rather than considering the narrative structure of *El tungsteno* a failure, it should be interpreted according to the author's ethical and aesthetic objectives: the need to promote values other than those consistent with the economic needs of imperialism: in other words, social justice. It is through the mediation of the narrator, who questions, speculates, interprets, and proposes answers, that forms of social organization promoting exploitation are unmasked, and that the need to fight for justice is proposed, both in Peru and in the rest of the world.

INDIGENISMO

The *indigenista* novel, as an ethical-aesthetic project, is characterized by contradictions and paradoxes. The main one is rooted in the fracture and tension implicit in a narration created outside the indigenous reality it seeks to represent. This exteriority stems from the fact that the story is told and written by a narrator and author, who is usually an urban *mestizo* or white. The author/narrator is ignorant of indigenous language and culture, and addresses his text to his own socio-cultural sector. Indigenous "reality" and characters are figured as a homogenous, *other*, and *alien* world, clearly distinct from those of whites or *mestizos* (Cornejo Polar, *Escribir, Literatura, La novela indigenista: un género*). The narrative form reproduces the sociocultural heterogeneity, that is, the fracture, foreignness, and incomprehension, observed in the social and national reality. Moreover, the different artistic solutions of the indigenist novel can register the "impact of the referent" (Cornejo Polar, *Literatura y sociedad* 56). In fact, the indigenous world, the object of representation, is not something inert, objectivized, and distant; instead, it struggles to intervene, make itself visible in the complexities of its uses and customs, myths, religious beliefs, songs, and language. The impact of the referent on the novelesque form, through the presence of genres and discursive forms such as songs, legends, and myths, which are transmitted orally, and not written and learned like the novel, lead to other forms of heterogeneity: this time, not in the production circuit or consumption of the work of art but in the heart of the work itself. It is the dynamics internal to the text itself that make the artistic solutions of the *indigenista* novel more complex and diverse.

This fundamental and foundational aporia of origin, that is, its heterogeneity, is in fact what originates the particularity of the *indigenista* novel. This particularity concerns the poetic narrative and transcends all definitions of *indigenismo* based on its content: representation of the "Indian," vindication of the indigenous world, condemnation of the state of misery in which they live, and social conflicts in which they become involved due to the exploitation and servitude they suffer. Moreover, it is what enables a glimpse of the diversity of artistic solutions; that is, the variety and complexity of a genre that cannot be explained merely by its insertion within realism or based on its object of representation.

Henri Favre distinguishes between an *indigenista* trend and current. The current of opinion in favor of Indians dates back to the conquest and the first debates that question not only the "humanity" of the inhabitants of the New World but also the "right" or "legitimacy" of Spanish dominance over territories and people. In this sense, Dominican friar Bartolomé de las Casas would become one the first and most decisive protectors of the Indians. Rooted in the reaction against the conquest, the indigenist current spans Latin American modern history and is related not only to humanist movements, but also to those of resistance, revolution, independence, and modernization.

Indigenismo is also an *ideological movement* that dates back to the early 1900s. Hence, *indigenismo* is "not the manifestation of indigenous thinking, but a *criollo* [Spaniards born in the New World] and *mestizo* reflection on Indians" (Favre 11).[12] It stems from and expands in the historical conjuncture of the 1920s and 1930s,[13] where at times it is assimilated into the official national ideology. Later, the movement is diluted, without fully disappearing, within the vindications proposed by indigenous groups[14] (often in their own languages) beginning in the 1970s. The underlying issues are the division and separation between Indians and non-Indians at the heart of the nation;[15] the view that ethic and cultural differences were blocking the success of a nation imagined in homogenous terms; and, above all, the condemnation of the exploitation, margination, and exclusion that indigenous populations suffer in the national projects. These must be understood as framed by national socio-economic structures in which oligarchic social or semi-feudal formations coexist with the incipient implantation of a dependent capitalism accompanied by foreign capital. *Indigenismo* is a vindicative movement. The so-called Indian problem becomes a paradox in that Indians are beginning to be considered as the necessary foundation for the precarious or incomplete nations after one hundred years of independence, while they are, at the same time, seen as a liability that hinders the process of modernization. The proposed solution, in this context, is the acculturation and incorporation of indigenous populations into Western culture. On the one hand, the problem can be the source of Latin American authenticity; on the other, it is what halts and even hinders progress. This contradiction is relevant to *indigenista* novels, since the subject of change or permanence of the indigenous world is at their heart.

The *indigenista* novel, a particularly Latin American genre, is unexplainable if one does not ultimately take into account the conquest of America. The genre experiences its moment of greatest creativity and importance during the 1930s and 1940s, when its most emblematic novels were published. Unlike the earlier romantic Indianism,[16] during this later period, novels take the social and economic reality of the indigenous experience as their starting point; hence, for these authors, realism is the necessary style for the object represented. Moreover, these novels frequently consider Indigenous cultural components, which ultimately remit to the construction of "Indian communities," such as Rumi, in El *mundo es ancho y ajeno* (Broad and Alien is the World, 1941), by Peruvian Ciro Alegría (1909–1967). Even when the stories introduce, to a greater or lesser extent, aspects of identity or culture (such as a form of communal life, which implies a respectful relationship with nature, collective decision-making, respect for figures of leadership, characterized by wisdom, knowledge and respect for traditions, but also by superstitions, forms of pantheistic religiousness, myths), at the end these are subordinated to the criticism and denunciation of the social and political order. Thus, in addition to the traits previously mentioned, the *indigenista* novel is characterized by social criticism, and the presentation of conflicts on the basis of class differences and relationships of dominance and exploitation, which dilute cultural and ethnic problems of culture. This also explains why the *indigenista* novel can be read as testimony of an era, as an act of social conscience, and as an artistic achievement that sought to recount very particular socio-cultural processes and issues related to national identity.

José Carlos Mariátegui (1894–1930) was the first to identify one of the main features of *indigenismo* as an artistic form when he distinguished, in "El proceso de la literatura" ("The Process of Literature," 1927), between *Indian* and *indigenista* literatures. The latter is the work of someone who does not belong to the indigenous universe he describes but seeks to, exhibiting an inextricable paradox, represent it "authentically." Several traits characterize *indigenismo*, such as exteriority and aim for authenticity and representativity. Moreover, Mariátegui points out: "Indigenist literature cannot give us a strictly authentic version of the Indian, for it must idealize and stylize him. Nor can it give us his soul. It is still a mestizo literature and as such is called indigenist rather than indigenous" (*Seven Interpretive Essays* 274).[17] Along with this exteriority regarding the world of the narrator, Mariátegui adds another aspect to the paradox of *indigenista* literature: even when the author and narrator claim authenticity and fidelity to a referent, indigenous characters appear idealized and stylized.

While Mariátegui alluded to idealization and stylization, Cornejo Polar discusses the brusque and unjustified switch from the code of realism to an allegorical idealism in the narrative solution of the conflicts presented in *indigenista* novels. After an unremitting history of opprobrium and massacres in both reality and fiction, for which realism is the most suitable code, the genre seems unable to end its narrative by cancelling indigenous future as reality suggests. While this genre presents a treatment of historical time that advocates for change, these novels seem unable to imagine future for indigenous people different from the repeated reality of exploitation and massacre, be it by means of the triumph of indigenous rebellions or by the achievement of justice, such as in the Mexican Revolution. The narrator, therefore, replaces the code of realism (based on history and truth) for one that is ideal and focused on nature, with which she aims develop a "premonitory allegory of future justice" (Cornejo Polar, *Writing in the Air* 138).[18] The end of *Huasipungo*, after the massacre of the indigenous people, focuses on the barley ears that emerge between the bodies, as "their skinny arms like some grim harvest," murmuring "*¡Ñucanchic huasipungo!*" (Icaza, *Huasipungo* 171).[19]

Regarding this ending, which cannot be deduced from the events narrated, there is another important aspect that Cornejo Polar proposes in the poetics of *indigenista* novels: the difficulty of writing the indigenous world's history. Plots begin with the irruption of an element foreign to the indigenous environment that will incite, alter, and set in historical motion a community that, until then, seemed to live beyond history, in a social order of repetitions related to agricultural and human cycles, or as the repetitive experience of injustice and abuse.

Outside the Andean area, I believe that the novel *El resplandor* (*Sunburst,* 1937), by Mauricio Magdaleno (1906–1986), is representative of the *indigenista* novel as described above. Indigenous life is made suitable for representation in a novel by presenting an exceptional situation in which Saturnino Herrero, a mestizo of Otomi ancestry, running for governor, returns to his home in San Andrés de la Cal. The announcement revives indigenous hopes of overcoming poverty through the construction of a dam and by means of the implementation of the land distribution proposed by the agrarian reform carried out in Mexico in the 1930s. The conclusion is no different to that seen in other historical periods prior to the Mexican Revolution: not only is there no redemption of the Indian people but rather the insult is yet greater, as now injustice, abuse, and exploitation are perpetrated in the name of social revolution and by the son of a member of the community. Once again, the novel ends with a massacre of the indigenous community. Since the novel implies that indigenous reality will never change, not even with a revolution, one cannot envisage a future for the Otomi people of the Mezquital Valley. In this case, the novel does not end with an idealized image of daybreak, or a foreboding allegory (as pointed out by Cornejo Polar). Instead, it concludes with a scene of childbirth, which, even if it is an allegory, it is one of unending pain: "She lay crying like a condemned creature. Another cry answered, a puny imperious cry. The bundle had plunged from Lorenza's womb, it was a being now, implacably clamped to the breast of the girl" (288).[20]

Another characteristic of the *indigenista* novel is the imbrication of contradictory and sometimes opposing historical and ideological points of view. In this novelistic genre, the denunciation of the exploitation of indigenous groups, and of "the latter's irreversible dehumanization and the incapacity to manage their own lives individually and socially" (Cornejo Polar, *Writing in the Air* 140),[21] together with the defense of indigenous rights (human rights, rights to land, education, food, and life), coexist with hopelessness regarding the possibility that indigenous peoples can defend themselves, since they are presented as damaged "individually and socially," and as capable of violent and savage acts. From this viewpoint, indigenous people cannot assume the reins of their own history. They cannot become subjects of history.

Having analyzed the characteristics of the *indigenista* novel in terms of content and artistic form, I will now link these and outline the specificity of *indigenista* narrative poetics in three emblematic works from the 1930s and 1940s: *El indio* (*El Indio*, 1935),[22] by Mexican Gregorio López y Fuentes; *Huasipungo* (*Huasipungo* 1934), by Ecuadorian Jorge Icaza; and *El mundo es ancho y ajeno*, by Peruvian Ciro Alegría.

El indio and Magdaleno's *El resplandor*, written after the Mexican Revolution, strongly criticize the failed revolution. They also exhibit a profound pessimism toward the possibilities of Indian *integration* into the new nation. They were both published during the government of Lázaro Cárdenas (1934–1940), a time in which indigenist policies were part of government programs. (These included an agrarian reform and the distribution of lands among indigenous communities). However, both novels show that the state of exploitation, misery, isolation, and mistrust had not substantially changed despite laws and policies granting indigenous rights. They had not been incorporated into the Mexican nation.

Nevertheless, the portrayal of indigenous groups in these novels—the Otomi of the Mezquital Valley in *El resplandor* and Nahuas in *El indio*—reproduces certain stereotypes: sorrow, lack of intelligence, alcoholism, superstition, fear, propensity for violence, and ignorance, which make them easy prey to deceit and manipulation. Such stereotyped representation does not consider them a community with valuable beliefs, way of life, and traditions. Although, in López y Fuentes's novel, these practices are recognized in an ethnographic and journalistic sense, they are observed from a distance, without investigating their meaning. For instance, there are three chapters devoted to presenting, always in a distant, descriptive, even anthropologic manner, such cultural practices as the dance of the flyers (*voladores*), the belief in guardian spirits (*nahuales*), the council of elders, and the legend of *yoloxóchitl* (flower of the heart). However, the belief in *nahuales* or shamans is presented as superstition that hinders insertion into the Western cultural system (one chapter is significantly called "Superstición," another "Música, danza y alcohol"),[23] and the festivity ends in alcohol, violence, and death.

The disparity between the two universes leaves open only the possibility of acculturation, that is, the "redemption" of the Indian by means of her insertion (through education) into the Western cultural system, which in Mexico is of a *mestizo* nature. In both works, however, continuity in the chain of injustices makes it impossible to imagine a future that is not repetition.

In this sense, I do not believe the narrator in López y Fuentes's novel is exactly the Indians' representative and "spokesperson." Instead, the narrator always places herself at such a distance as to be able to describe the social situation, but without putting herself in the place of the other's perception and feelings. It is clear in this novel that the narrator is foreign to indigenous reality, despite her show of solidarity and her desire for their "redemption." This novel's realism aims to *portray* ("a spectacle seen from outside," according to Pilar Bellido [85[24]]) the reality of an Indian community during the post-revolution period (probably during Plutarco Elías Calles's government): the persistent abuse experienced by members of the community, the causes for their mistrust and fear, and the impossibility of eliminating this social and cultural duality and of doing away with the distrust of the indigenous population and the corruption and manipulativeness of the Westernized *mestizos*. All of this is framed by theories that insisted on the importance of the incorporation of the indigenous people into the national mestizo society.

In his novel, López y Fuentes treats the Indian as a collective character, to such a degree that there are no personal names nor any expression of individual spirit. The narrator identifies the characters by their roles: the guide, the interpreter, the mayor. Neither is a story built around any particular Indian character. The novel exemplifies Cornejo Polar's idea that it is the presence of something foreign that sets the story in motion (until then, the community had existed enclosed in itself, conceived as a homogenous whole, and lived the cyclical repetition of everyday chores). The presence of outsiders repeats the secular history of abuse, exploitation, and violence. For Indians, the arrival of "white people" is always a cause for disaster, and they are once again defeated.

Among the non-indigenous characters, there are similar recurrent prototypes: the exploitative landlord, the priest uninterested in those who do not provide economic benefits for him, corrupt authorities who do not promote justice for the Indians, and the teacher, a new figure that is understood in the context of the Cárdenas government's educational policies. However, as is the case with the other prototypical characters, the teacher seeks her own interest instead of that of the Indians. In this manner, the novel questions the scope of these policies. In *El indio*, it is through a teacher that López y Fuentes voices the causes that hinder the incorporation of Indians into the Mexican nation. Mistrust (justified, as is proved once again with the arrival of the gold-seekers) toward everything that comes from *civilization* and *people of reason* is what makes a change in the indigenous people's situation impossible. The novel ends with this mistrust—indeed, the title of the final chapter.

A persistent feature in *indigenista* novels is that the story or plot is elaborated in a fragmented fashion, as if it were impossible or too difficult to organize the story in a linear manner, with identifiable actions and transformations from beginning to the end. The fact that these novels do not present clearly defined characters ranked according to their functions and importance distorts the traits associated with the novel. The *indigenista* novel is constituted by juxtaposed thematic threads that open, expand, go in diverse directions, migrate from genre to genre, and make use of discursive forms other than those belonging only to fiction and the novel. These novels incorporate journalistic and ethnographic descriptions, inserting legends or songs. Therefore, the narration seems fragmented. The brief chapters of *El indio* act as tableaux connecting events that are not clearly entwined, without a clear time sequence. In fact, the treatment of time and the frequent use of the present tense seem to signify the atemporality of events and the cyclic repetition of the same abuses. These brief vignettes are brought together by the reader, who weaves relationships among them, thus building the portrayal of a world affected by revolutionary and post-revolutionary processes, but which, however, still continues the exploitation of the indigenous population by *people of reason* (*gente de razón*) and their civilization.

Huasipungo, Jorge Icaza's novel published in Ecuador during the same period (1934), has been characterized as an example of social *indigenista* realism. Its discourse has been classified as a non-style (Cueva 38) due to its use of short phrases, direct everyday language, interposed by Quechua syntax and phonetics (when uttered by Indians). Nevertheless, *Huasipungo* exhibits a complex work with these languages, because the narrator (once again, the main voice) appropriates different languages and switches between them. In this manner, the reader becomes involved with a story that is being told in different ways. Some of these languages are descriptive, with scarce stylistic marks, but in others the narrator takes pleasure in using an avant-garde language full of metaphors or images,[25] in what would constitute the flip side of the novel's putative non-style. The literary language in its vanguardist aspect coexists with crude descriptions of indigenous misery, but also with irony and caricatures, which imply another means of relating to the characters. The language that focuses on the misery and exploitation experienced by the Indians seeks to arouse the reader's lethargic conscience and stimulate criticism and action. The language used to approach the authorities, the landlord, priest and also minor politicians is full of irony and promotes the reader's distance, implying a criticism of these authorities, who act in collusion with American imperialism and, more generally, with capital.

This heterogeneity of languages used to narrate reality allows the reader to glimpse the ambiguity present in this ideological-aesthetic project. The ambiguous location of enunciation is characterized by the paradox that criticism of the authorities is carried out by describing the degradation to which the Indians have been led. Their lives are characterized by exploitation, misery, impotence and fear, thus making it impossible for them to be subjects of their own liberation. The novelistic form reproduces the tensions and ambiguities of the social context.

El mundo es ancho y ajeno was published in 1941 (the same year as José María Arguedas's *Yawar fiesta*) by Ciro Alegría, author of other *indigenista* novels, such as *La serpiente de oro* (The Golden Serpent, 1935) and *Los perros hambrientos* (The Hungry Dogs, 1939), which are considered by critics (Escajadillo, Cornejo Polar) as belonging to a different phase of *indigenista* narrative. On one hand, although the narrator is foreign to indigenous worlds, his proximity to the community and his esteem for its culture and values are much greater. The language used, at times close to poetry, contributes to this rapprochement with the community's forms of perception. In fact, the novel begins by presenting the *ayllu* (the indigenous commune) as a social organization characterized by wisdom and justice. It is a place where nature is respected and where one can live with dignity. The characters of *El mundo es ancho y ajeno* have a greater psychological depth than those from other *indigenista* novels. As readers, we enter the conscience of Rosendo Maqui or Benito Castro and understand the way they see the world. However, the conflict is not between the individual and the society to which she belongs, as in the European bourgeois novel, but between whole communities, in this case the traditional indigenous community, and capital, represented here by the land-owning oligarchy. These conflicts cause dispossession and disintegration, with an evident risk for the traditional community's disappearance.

Both social realism and *indigenismo* are thus understood in relation to the pressing social and cultural realities of the historical moments they seek to account for. However, the breadth and complexity of their meanings, as well as the variety of cognitive and evaluative attitudes they propose with respect to these realities, which are expressed in the narrative poetics, prevent their flattening and reduction to a mere denunciation of injustice. Likewise, the richness of social realist and *indigenista* texts precludes seeing them as being merely of sociological or anthropological interest. It is, therefore, necessary to return to the specific artistic form of each of the novels in order to understand these texts and appreciate their formal innovations.

NOTES

1. The only study that analyzes the social realism of this period and points out its importance is *Historia y crítica literaria: el realismo social y la crisis de la dominación oligárquica*, by Françoise Perus (Casa de las Américas, 1982). There is a second edition: *El realismo social en perspectiva* (UNAM, 1995). On Argentinian social realism a relevant work is David W. Foster's *Social Realism in the Argentine Narrative*.

2. "La selección del género narrativo como forma predominante obedece a la necesidad de reconstituir procesos –vale decir, de aprehender la realidad presente como el resultado de una herencia histórica que puede ser transformada en uno y otro sentido–, mientras el hincapié en el propósito realista responde a la voluntad de objetividad que caracteriza al quehacer intelectual en su conjunto. Sin embargo, en este mismo sentido, conviene señalar también que, al no haberse producido todavía en esa época la posterior división física e intelectual entre las actividades políticas, literarias y científicas (nos referimos, obviamente, al campo de la ciencia social entonces todavía en formación, y sin existencia institucional), la literatura, y más concretamente la narrativa social, participan de estas tres esferas conjuntamente" (Perus, *El realismo social* 168–69).

3. "Novela pintoresca y rural . . . La técnica es rudimentaria, pre-flaubertiana: el autor se entromete y opina en medio de los personajes, ignora la noción de objetividad en la ficción y atropella los puntos de vista; no pretende mostrar, sino demostrar" (Vargas Llosa 30). John Beverly, on the other hand, considers that the dichotomy between the social novel and the avant-garde novel is not legitimate (Beverly 173).

4. Realism in Ecuador begins with the publication, in 1930, of *Los que se van* ("*cuentos del cholo y del montubio*") (Those Who Leave) by Joaquín Gallegos Lara (1911–1947), Enrique

Gil Gilbert (1912–1975) and Demetrio Aguilera Malta (1909–1981). The three formed the Guayaquil Group, together with José de la Cuadra and Alfredo Pareja Diezcanseco. José de la Cuadra's book *Horno* (Oven), was published in 1932, and in 1933, *Barro de la sierra* (Highland Mud), by Jorge Icaza, *Yunga*, by Enrique Gil Albert, *El muelle* (The Dock), by Alfredo Pareja Diezcanseco, *Don Goyo*, by Demetrio Aguilera Malta [Don Goyo. Translated by John and Carolyn Brushwood. Humana Press, 1980], *Camarada* (Comrade), by Humberto Salvador. Books published in 1934 were *Huasipungo*, by Jorge Icaza, and *Las sangurimas*, by José de la Cuadra. The publications continued during this decade and the 40s; in 1946, *Las cruces sobre el agua* (Crosses On the Water), by Joaquín Gallegos Lara.

5. "Un capitalismo salvaje, aun realizando tareas de acumulación originaria, que avanza a sangre y fuego sobre todas las formas económicas, sociales y culturales previas, con una lógica implacable de despojo y avasallamiento" (Cueva, "Literatura y sociedad" 639).

6. Foster studies *Reina del Plata* (Queen of the River Plate, by Bernardo Kordon (1915–2002); *La ciudad de un hombre* (A Man's City) by Leónidas Barletta (1902–1975); *Puerto América* (Port America), by Luis María Albamonte (1911–1982); *Tercera clase* (Third Class), by José Rabinovich (1903–1978); *En esos años* (During those Years) by Bernardo Verbitsky (1907–1979); *Madre América* (Mother America) by Max Dickmann (1902–1991); *El pueblo* (The People) by Carlos Ruiz Daudet (1900–1974); *Larvas* (Larvae), by Elías Castelnuovo (1893–1982); *No hay vacaciones* (There Are No Vacations) by Alvaro Yunke (1889–1982); *El río oscuro* (Dark River) by Alfredo Varela (1912–1986); *44 horas semanales* (44 Hours Per Week) by Josefina Marpons (1910–1979), and *Lago argentino* (Argentine Lake) by Juan Gonayarte (1900–1967).

7. *El tungsteno* has been analyzed as an *indigenista* novel as well, and not only as a social realist one. Even when he denounces the abuses committed against the Sora Indians, this happens especially in the first part. The whole of the novel points to a problem of exploitation and collusion of economic imperialism of broader proportions, since it affects the nation as a whole. Likewise, the problems arise as a result of class conflicts and economic forces, and less from the ethnic or cultural base (see for this the character and the speech of Servando Huanca in the last part).

8. "El verbo está vacío. Sufre de una aguda e incurable consunción social . . . trunco y aplastado en la boca individual . . . se ahoga de individualismo. La palabra –forma de relación social la más humana entre todas– ha perdido así toda su esencia y atributos colectivos." (Vallejo, *El arte y la revolución* 30).

9. "José Marino, por modestia, galantería o refinamiento, fue el último." (Vallejo, *El tungsteno* 250).

10. The narrator interrupts the action to explain how this system of forced labor works in Peru, suggesting that Vallejo had an implicit reader in mind who was unfamiliar with Peruvian reality, probably a Spanish audience, perhaps working class, ideologically committed to socialism or communism: "For in Peru, particularly in the sierra, the patrones use the police to force the workers to honor their civil contracts. The worker's obligation can be compelled by armed force, handled as it were a crime . . . It is, in short, a system of forced labor" (Vallejo, Tungsten 67). ("Porque en el Perú, y particularmente en la sierra, a los obreros les hacen cumplir los patrones sus contratos civiles, valiéndose de la Policía. . . . Es, en pocas palabras, el sistema de los trabajos forzados" [Vallejo, *El tungsteno* 273]).

11. Spanish original: "que eche abajo a todos los gringos y explotadores del mundo, para liberar a los indios y trabajadores de todas partes" (Vallejo, *El tungsteno* 313).

12. "El movimiento indigenista no es la manifestación de un pensamiento indígena, sino una reflexión criolla y mestiza sobre el indio" (Favre 11). The Indianista movement which emerged in the 1960s, and which in the case of Mexico received a strong impulse as of the Zapatista uprising in 1994, seeks to be, unlike *indigenismo*, the expression of authentic Indian vindications, created within de Indian world. This Indianismo of the end of the twentieth century must not be confused with that which took place in the literary sphere during the nineteenth century, where an idealized and romantized defense of the Indians resulted. Such is the case of *Aves sin nido* (Birds without a Nest), 1889, by Clorinda Matto de Turner; this is the Indianismo Concha Meléndez analyzed in her classic study of 1934, *La novela indianista en Hispanoamérica (1832–1889)*.

13. In Peru, José Carlos Mariátegui is a decisive figure in the conformation of *indigenismo* as a movement of vindication; his thesis alludes to the fundamentally economic character of the indigenous problem.

14. Despite experiencing very different and political processes, one can identify, during the 1920s, a common concern in Mexico and the Andean national with rethinking the position of the Indian with the nation. In the case of Manuel Gamio's *Forjando patria* (Mexico, Creating the Nation1916), it was the impact of anthropology that led to this concern. Moreover, it was undeniably connected to Mexican Revolution, which began in 1910 and made Indians visible. President Lazaro Cárdenas's agrarian reform of the 1930s and his incorporation of *indigenismo* as part of his government's political agenda, led the "indigenous problem" to become a central issue. Two of the most emblematic *indigenista* novels are published at the time: *El indio* (El Indio) by Gregorio López y Fuentes, and *El resplandor* [Sunburst], by Mauricio Magdaleno, which can be classified as both *indigenista* novels and novels of the Mexican Revolution. In the Andean region, since the beginning of the twentieth century there have been significant and generalized indigenous uprisings. Moreover, since the 1920s, and even earlier if we consider Manuel González Prada's famous "Discurso en el Politeama" ("Speech at the Politeama" [1888] and the article "Nuestros indios ["Our Indians," 1904], where he alluded to the "brutalising trinity": of the priest, the governor, and the judge), the "indigenous problem" is present in all the studies on nationality. During this decade José Carlos Mariátegui writes fundamental works on the subject, including "El problema del indio" (The Problem of the Indian) (in *Siete Ensayos de interpretación de la realidad peruana* [Seven Interpretive Essays on Peruvian Reality]), and is involved in a polemic with Luis Alberto Sánchez, on literary *indigenismo*. In Ecuador, Agustín Cueva (1978), writes about the semi-feudal context of the country during the 1920s, when the first manifestations of literary *indigenismo* emerge. For Cuevas, Ecuador, at the time, is a society in which the transition from feudalism to capitalism has not even been completed. In fact, in the highlands, this transition had only just begun. This explains the "simplicity," "schematism," and lack of complexity of the social literature, including the indigenista novel, of that period.

15. J. C. Mariátegui speaks of the duality of Peruvian history and soul. During the 1920s works of ample repercussion emerge such as *Tempestad en los Andes* (Tempest in the Andes, 1927), by Luis E. Valcárcel, where the indigenous system is considered superior to the Western one, a view that can also be perceived in the essays, poetry and stories created by Grupo Orkopata (specifically those by Gamaliel Churata) from the city of Puno. In Ecuador, *El indio ecuatoriano* (The Ecuadorian Indian), by Pío Jaramillo Alvarado, is published in 1922.

16. It is convenient to demarcate the *indigenismo*, the object of this work, which begins during the 1920s and which Tomás Escajadillo calls orthodox *indigenismo*, from that other cultivated during the nineteenth century in works such as *Aves sin nido* (*Torn from the Nest* 1889), by Clorinda Matto de Turner, sometimes classified as Indianismo due to its exotic nature, its paternalistic vindication (closer to piety), and absence or incomprehension of the socio-economic basis of the issue. Cornejo Polar links the term Indianism to the aesthetic and ideological system of romanticism, thus "Indianism would be romantic indigenismo" ("el indianismo sería el indigenismo romántico," Cornejo Polar, *Literatura y Sociedad en el Perú* 39). The three conditions Escajadillo mentions for a work to be called indigenist are: sentiment of social vindication, the overcoming of certain social burdens such as a romantic vision of the Andean world, and "sufficient proximity" regarding the world portrayed, Indians and the Andes (Escajadillo 118). He classifies the previous works as romantic-realist-idealist Indianismo or modernist Indianismo; and he presupposes a second phase of evolution regarding orthodox *indigenismo*, which he calls neo-*indigenismo*.

17. "La literatura indigenista no puede darnos una versión rigurosamente verista del indio. Tiene que idealizarlo y estilizarlo. Tampoco puede darnos su propia ánima. Es todavía una literatura de mestizos. Por eso se llama indigenista y no indígena" (Mariátegui, 7 ensayos 283).

18. "Una alegoría premonitoria de la justicia que se avecina" (Cornejo Polar, *Escribir* 179).

19. "Sementera de brazos flacos;" "Ñucanchic huasipungo" (Icaza, *Huasipungo* 250).

20. "Miró el bulto que se agitaba en el vientre de Lorenza, la pequeña masa tumultuosa que acabó prendiéndose a un pecho de la muchacha, y dejó manar, en las piernas de la parturienta, todo el dolor que le hervía, el sordo y ominoso dolor de los hijos de San Andrés de la Cal" (Magdaleno, *El resplandor* 1023). In the original Spanish there is a link between the pain and San Andrés de la Cal, which the translation eliminates.

21. "La insalvable e irreversible deshumanización de los indios y su incapacidad para gestionar individual y socialmente sus propias vidas" (Cornejo Polar, Escribir en el aire 182).

22. Published by Ediciones Botas, this novel won the National Literature Prize in 1935. Its success led to an English edition illustrated by Diego Rivera (Bobbs-Merrill Company, Indianapolis, 1937, translated by Anita Brenner, and with a preface by Lyn Carrick).

23. The English translation by Anita Brenner diminishes the chapter titles' pejorative character by calling "Fiesta," the chapter "Música, danza y alcohol" and as "Fear," the one titled "Superstición" (López y Fuentes 1979, 116, 133; in Spanish, López y Fuentes 2008, 52, 61). One must also consider the way in which this novel deals with Nahuatl, the indigenous language supposedly spoken by the characters. It is the narrator who provides the Nahuatl original in italics, then provides the translation, or this can be deduced from the context. But he never shows the language in use by the indigenous people, who seldom express themselves throughout the work. The narrator is both mediator and translator.

24. "El mundo indigenista en la novela de López y Fuentes es un espectáculo contemplado desde fuera, sin que la mirada signifique comprensión y aceptación de las diferencias" (Bellido 85).

25. One of such images describes the square on a sunny day as: "blowfly attached to an enormous quilt of a thousand patches of colour" ("moscardón prendido en una enorme colcha de mil retazos de colores") (Huasipungo 139; my translation. The text is not included in the English version).

Works Cited

Alegría, Ciro. *Broad and Alien Is the World*. Translated by Harriet de Onís. Farrar & Rinehart, 1941.

Alegría, Ciro. *The Golden Serpent*. Translated by Harriet de Onís. The New American World Library, 1963.

Alegría, Ciro. *El mundo es ancho y ajeno*. Edited by Antonio Cornejo Polar. Biblioteca Ayacucho, 1978.

Alegría, Ciro. *Los perros hambrientos*. Cátedra, 2018.

Alegría, Ciro. *La serpiente de oro*. Academia Peruana de la Lengua, 2017.

Arguedas, José María. *Yawar Fiesta*. Compañía de Impresiones y Publicidad, 1941.

Arguedas, José María. *Yawar Fiesta*. Translated by Francis Horning Barraclough. U of Texas P, 1985.

Bellido Navarro, Pilar. "La visión indigenista en la novela de la Revolución Mexicana." *Narrativa de la Revolución Mexicana. La Revolución en las artes y en la prensa*. Fundación el Monte/Universidad de Sevilla, vol. 1, 1996, pp. 81–91.

Beverley, John. "*El Tungsteno*. Hacia una reivindicación de la novela social." *Revista de Crítica Literaria Latinoamericana*, vol. 15, no. 29, 1988, pp. 167–77.

Céspedes, Augusto. *Metal del diablo*. Casa de las Américas, 1965.

Cornejo Polar, Antonio. *Escribir en el aire. Ensayo sobre la heterogeneidad sociocultural en las literaturas andinas*. Latinoamericana, 2003.

Cornejo Polar, Antonio. "La novela indigenista: una desgarrada conciencia de la historia." *Lexis*, vol 4, no. 1, 1980, pp. 77–89.

Cornejo Polar, Antonio. "La novela indigenista: un género contradictorio." *Texto Crítico*, vol. 14, 1979, pp. 58–70.

Cornejo Polar, Antonio. *Literatura y sociedad en el Perú: la novela indigenista. Clorinda Matto de Turner, novelista. Estudios sobre* Aves sin nido. Índole *y* Herencia. Latinoamericana, 2005.

Cornejo Polar, Antonio. *Writing in the Air: Heterogeneity and the Persistence o Oral Tradition in Andean Literature*. Translated by Lynda J. Jentsch. Duke University Press Books, 2013.

Cueva, Agustín. "En pos de la historicidad perdida (contribución al debate sobre la literatura indigenista del Ecuador)." *Revista de Crítica Literaria Latinoamericana*. vol. IV, nos. 7–8, 1978, pp. 23–38.

Cueva, Agustín. "Literatura y sociedad en el Ecuador: 1920–1960." *Revista Iberoamericana*, vol. 54, nos. 144–45, 1988, pp. 629–47.

Escajadillo, Tomás. "El indigenismo narrativo peruano." *Philologia Hispalensis*, vol. 4, no. 1, 1989, pp. 117–36.

Favre, Henri. *El indigenismo*. Fondo de Cultura Económica, 1998.

Foster, David W. *Social Realism in the Argentine Narrative*. North Caroline Studies in the Romance Languages and Literatures, 1986.

Icaza, Jorge. *Huasipungo*. Edited by Teodosio Fernández. Cátedra, 2002.

Icaza, Jorge. *Huasipungo*. Translated by Mervyn Savill. Dobson Books, 1962.

López y Fuentes, Gregorio. *El indio. Novela mexicana*. Prologue by Antonio Magaña Esquivel. Porrúa, 2008.

López y Fuentes, Gregorio. *El Indio*. Translated by Anita Brenner. Frederick Ungar Publishing Co., 1979.

Magdaleno, Mauricio. "El resplandor." In *La novela de la Revolución Mexicana*, vol. 2, edited by Antonio Castro Leal, Aguilar, 1971, pp. 864–1023.

Magdaleno, Mauricio. *Sunburst*. Translated by Anita Brenner. The Viking Press, 1944.

Mariátegui, José Carlos. *Siete ensayos de interpretación de la realidad peruana*. Prologue by Aníbal Quijano. Notes, chronology, and bibliography by Elisabeth Garrels. Biblioteca Ayacucho, 1995.

Mariátegui, José Carlos. *Seven Interpretive Essays on Peruvian Reality*. Translated by Marjorie Urquidi. U of Texas P, 1971.

Matto de Turner, Clorinda. *Aves sin nido*. Alfaguara, 2006.

Matto de Turner, Clorinda. *Torn from the Nest*. Translated by John Polt. Oxford UP, 2003.

Meléndez, Concha. *La novela indianista en Hispanoamérica (1832–1889)*. Ediciones de la Universidad de Puerto Rico, 1961.

Perus, Françoise. *El realismo social en perspectiva*. UNAM, 1995.

Perus, Françoise. *Transculturaciones en el aire (en torno a la cuestión de la forma artística en la crítica de la narrativa hispanoamericana)*. CIALC-UNAM, 2019.

Rodríguez Monegal, Emir. *Narradores de esta América*. Alfa, 1969.

Saítta, Sylvia. "La narración de la pobreza en la literatura argentina del siglo XX." *Revista Nuestra América*, no. 2, 2006, pp. 89–102.

Valcárcel, Luis E. *Tempestad en los Andes*. Populibros Peruanos, 1963.

Vallejo, César. *El arte y la revolución*. Mosca Azul, 1973.

Vallejo, César. *El tungsteno. Novelas y cuentos completos*. Edited by Ricardo González Vigil. COPÉ, Petróleos del Perú, 2005, pp. 213–324.

Vallejo, César. *Tungsten: A Novel*. Translated by Robert Mezey. Syracuse UP, 1988.

Vargas Llosa, Mario. "Novela primitiva y novela de creación en América Latina." *Revista de la Universidad de México*, vol. 23, no. 10, 1969, pp. 29–35.

CHAPTER 6

THE NEW NOVEL IN LATIN AMERICA (1920–1950)

PHILIP SWANSON

ODDLY enough, the most crucial figure in the development of the Latin American new novel in the period covered in this chapter is someone who never published a novel at all. Jorge Luis Borges (Argentina, 1899–1986), arguably the greatest writer never to win a Nobel Prize for Literature and, for many, the most important figure in Spanish American or, indeed, Spanish letters, was a writer of short stories (as well as poetry and essays) whose volume *Ficciones* (*Fictions*) of 1944 (incorporating *El jardín de senderos que se bifurcan* [*The Garden of Forking Paths*] from two years earlier and *Artificios* [*Artifices*], and subsequently expanded in 1956) became the single most influential work in modern Latin American narrative. Although Borges obviously did not emerge from some kind of cultural vacuum, his position is unique, and the new novel as we now understand it might never have developed in the same way without the sheer magnetism of his production and persona, and of the phenomenon that he came to be. In one sense, Borges's ludic and cerebral stories, often set in far-off or invented lands, freed the literature of the subcontinent from the obsessive need to replicate slavishly the supposed reality of its own regions, and from the burden of realism more broadly. This movement away from a limited notion of social realism and, more pertinently, the challenging of the knowability of reality and of literature's ability to capture it in writing would become the hallmarks of the new novel proper in the 1950s and 1960s. It is unsurprising, for example, that Borges would later publish the first major story by Julio Cortázar (Argentina, 1914–1984), the author of the quintessential new novel of the Latin American Boom, *Rayuela* (*Hopscotch*, 1963).

Cortázar, like Borges, was often initially considered a Europeanist writer (Boldy 119). Many of the fiercest critics of Borges and the new novel would frequently dismiss both as elitist and Eurocentric, as this new writing was perceived as a rejection of autochthony and regionalism, as well as of socio-political commitment, and as overly concerned instead with existential and philosophical rumination, willful ambiguity, fantasy, experimentation, and modernist aesthetics. There is a degree of truth in this. While much of the excitement of the new narrative stems from authors' newfound freedom from the obligation of social commentary on so-called reality, there can be a sense of modernity in Latin American letters being seen as playing a game of catch-up with European or North American models of literary modernism. However, the criticism is also fundamentally flawed. There is a regional, national, and continental sensibility in Borges and Cortázar. The undercurrent of virulent anti-Peronism in their work is very political (albeit with possible elitist overtones), and, of course, Cortázar would later revise his position on Peronism, embrace socialism, and write in an almost propagandistic vein on Argentina under dictatorship and the Cuban and Nicaraguan Revolutions. *Hopscotch* itself is structurally divided in such a way (between Paris and Buenos Aires) as to constitute a reflection on what it means to be an Argentinean, and all the major novels of the most celebrated writers of the Boom deal openly with identity, society, and politics in Latin America.

The story "El Sur" ("The South") from Borges's *Fictions* illustrates this duality. Unlike his more obviously metaphysical tales like, say, "Tlön, Uqbar, Orbis Tertius" or "La biblioteca de Babel" ("The Library of Babel"), it is very much set in contemporary Argentina and concerns the journey of a lettered resident of Buenos Aires to the rural south and, by implication, into the past and into Argentine cultural tradition. In one sense, the story is a classic example of the intellectually playful New Narrative that would have such an impact on the likes of Cortázar. In an alert, active or second reading, what Cortázar would call the "lector cómplice" (or reader-accomplice) realizes that the carefully described journey of the sickly protagonist Juan Dahlmann may never have actually happened at all and may be little more than the projected fantasy of a sedentary city man on his delirium-fueled death bed, who imagines a rather more heroic and quintessentially Argentine destiny in which he meets his end in a kind of gauchesque knife-fight. However, this cerebral game about the subjectivity of time and perception is obviously also a powerful reflection on the seminal "Civilization and Barbarism" debate first prompted by the Argentine Domingo Faustino Sarmiento (1811–1888) in his 1845 work *Facundo*,[1] an enactment of the ongoing frustrated quest for identity and authenticity in Argentina and a warning about the shadow of violence that the cult of the gaucho, machismo, populism, and nationalism continue to cast over the nation.

These national considerations ought to remind us that Borges, despite his astounding stand-alone influence, did not come from nowhere and was very much part of a specific cultural tradition. Apart from the lingering legacy of Spanish American *modernismo*[2] (sometimes embraced, often rejected), the emergence of a *vanguardia* or avant-garde in the 1920s would begin to change the nature of Spanish American literary production. One important if unusual figure, and a great friend of Borges, was Macedonio Fernández (1874–1952). A speaker and influencer, rather than a mere writer, his major work, *Museo de la novela de la Eterna* (*The Museum of Eterna's Novel*), was only published posthumously in 1967, though versions and drafts or sketches for it were being produced from the 1920s. His ideas and practice did, however, seem to have some influence in Buenos Aires literary circles between the 1920s and 1940s, as well as later. He coined the not immediately translatable term "belarte" in order to articulate a seeming desire to shake readers' complacency, even their "sureness of existing"[3] (Fernández, "Doctrina" 417), and to promote a kind of active reader who would edit or rewrite the text they were reading. More specifically, the Buenos Aires avant-garde coalesced around two circles or groups, Florida and Boedo. Borges is sometimes associated with the snooty criollismo[4] of the Florida group (and, in his youth, he did share some of their views), while the Boedo group is more linked to an identification with the popular and immigrant classes. In practice, the groups were in some ways loosely constituted and often very similar in their thought; and both ignited a culture of literary change that soon extended from poetry to prose. The apprehension of a sense of newness or modernity is key here and it precipitated developments in both form and content in literature. Borges, his friend Adolfo Bioy Casares (1914–1999) and Victoria Ocampo (1890–1979) were of particular importance, especially later, via the hugely influential literary magazine *Sur* ("South"), founded by Ocampo in 1931, and to which Borges and Bioy contributed regularly. Meantime, writers like Roberto Arlt (1900–1942), commonly identified with Boedo, turned their hand to a new kind of urban fiction that combined a sort of gritty social realism with stylistic and formal experimentation, ambiguity, and existential angst.

Bioy's most famous work is probably still the short novel *La invención de Morel* (*The Invention of Morel*), published in 1940 with an introduction by Borges, who heralds it as a new genre (science fiction in Spanish). In reality rather reminiscent of H. G. Wells's (1866–1946) *The Island of Doctor Moreau* (1896), the book is about a fugitive stranded on an uninhabited Polynesian island who starts having visions of visitors to the island. The question of whether this is about the protagonist's madness or a tale of fantasy is resolved when it is revealed that the scientist Morel has fabricated a machine that is capable of recording the actions of people and reproducing reality (a species of hologram technology *avant la lettre*, though there is talk of capturing souls, resurrection, and the creation of a better, alternative reality). Despite the pseudo-scientific explanation of the phantasmagoric phenomenon at the heart of the story, Bioy's use of unreliable narrators and his toying with the interplay of fiction and reality hint at the new narrative to come. Arlt's vision of the machine age, on the other hand, is much grimmer. Though little known outside of his native Argentina, Arlt also became something of a cult figure for writers like Cortázar. His *Los siete locos* (*The Seven Madmen*, 1929) and its sequel *Los lanzallamas* (The Flamethrowers, 1931) explore the dehumanizing effects of a mechanical society, yet the crazed attempt by the two protagonists, Erdosain and the Astrologer, to overthrow capitalism using underground sects, deadly rays, and poisonous gases is as parodic as it is political. The esperpentic[5] characters and the distorted structure herald a modernist vision of an inhuman industrial society, but this ultimately collapses into a more generalized existential malaise about the human condition. Arlt's more popular *El juguete rabioso* (*Mad Toy*, 1926) (literally The Rabid Toy) also combines social realist elements with existential ones. Its relentlessly hyperbolic emphasis on filth and degradation, in which the main character Silvio (a forerunner of Erdosain) is reduced to feeling like a dog (Arlt, *El juguete rabioso* 95; *Mad Toy* 110), implies a perverted reality devoid of meaning. Yet, this "dog" is a rabid one who bites back. His penchant for arson illustrates this resistance, but also its inevitable failure. Silvio's attempt to torch a bookshop may be taken as a swipe at a certain sector of a smugly satisfied society, but his later effort to set alight a tramp is not much more than an absurd act of futile rage. The latter is echoed by his gratuitous betrayal of his acquaintance Rengo and Erdosain's bungled scheme to murder Barsut. These attempts at self-affirmation or fulfillment through self-degradation will recur again and again in authors of the New Narrative, most especially in Uruguay's Juan Carlos Onetti (1909–1994) and Cortázar—the famously grotesque descent into dirt during Horacio Oliveira's sexual encounter with the Parisian *clocharde* Emmanuèle in *Hopscotch* epitomizing this trend, and teaching the lesson of learning to look at the world through the lens of the asshole ("ojo del culo" translating literally as "eye of the ass" [Cortázar, *Rayuela* 253]).[6]

The darkness of Arlt's perspective is, in many ways, intimately connected to the centrality of Buenos Aires in the development of the modern novel in Latin America. For example, Leopoldo Marechal's (1900–1970) *Adán Buenosayres* (*Adam Buenosayres*, 1948), another of Cortázar's favorite novels, is very much about the city that gives the book its title and its cultural scene, but is also deeply metaphysical, charting (albeit with some satirical humor) the existential crisis of a 1920s vanguard writer. The point is that Buenos Aires is at the heart of the economic and literary transformation that was driving Latin American modernity, but this very modernity, with its accompanying urbanization, social dislocation, immigration, overcrowding and poverty, advancing technology, and so forth generated widespread anxiety and alienation. The excitement of literary modernity was matched by a sense of loss and malaise, and, not surprisingly, there was something of an accompanying shift away from pure localism to a wider sense of universal existential crisis. One could think perhaps of the prolific psychological novelist Eduardo Mallea (1903–1982), who combines regenerationist thinking about national renewal in Argentina with an overwhelming mood of solitude and emptiness. Agata, the protagonist of *Todo verdor perecerá* (*All Green Shall Perish*, 1943), embodies a decline into destructive isolation and madness, in her specific case following the collapse of her marriage and the death of her husband. At the same time, Mallea conceives the text as explicitly modern, claiming that he was attempting to "burst the seams" of the traditional, well-made novel (Shaw 104). A more enduring manifestation of the modern existential novel from Argentina would appear five years later in the form of *El túnel* (*The Tunnel*, 1948) by Ernesto Sabato (1911–2011). This is a prototype new novel, and Sabato would go on to be seen in the 1960s and 1970s as an essential name in the evolution of the new narrative in and around the Boom. Though set largely in contemporary Buenos Aires, there is not that much in the way of contextualizing temporal and spatial referents, and the anonymous big city is largely a backdrop for an exploration of the psychology of subjectivity, as everything is presented through the unreliable lens of the mind of the disturbed artist Juan Pablo Castel, who attempts to furnish an account and justification of the murder of his lover María Iribarne. This is the new novel's challenge to conventional social observation and its emphasis on subjective rather than objective reality, the move away from the consciously social also leading to a universalizing expression of the absurdity of human existence and the meaninglessness of the universe—the painter's madness ultimately coming across as less of a specific affliction than a manifestation of the chaos of human experience in general. We also see the beginnings of an effort to tally form with content, as the novel seeks, for instance, to match pace and structure to the workings of inner time, rather than time as externally measured, by following the meanderings of Castel's internal thought processes. Finally, the image of the tunnel anticipates the theme of solitude, which would become one of the great foci of the new novel, as in Gabriel García Márquez's (Colombia, 1927–2014) monumental *Cien años de soledad* (*One Hundred Years of Solitude* 1967). Castel feels that he lives isolated in a kind of tunnel. His hopes that the parallel tunnels that he and María inhabit will merge are dashed, and he comes to see the world as divided between those who live in tunnels and those who do not: the existential awareness of those who recognize the painful reality of the absurdity of life brings inevitable isolation, as those outside the tunnel remain oblivious, preferring to ignore the truth and depending on frivolous evasion to survive. As Castel plunges his knife into María's chest and stomach, he comments: "I have to kill you, María. You left me alone" (Sabato, *The Tunnel* 135).[7]

Buenos Aires, in this broader existential context, is beginning to lose some of its specificity. And, of course, despite its cultural significance, this city was by no means the only locus of the emerging New Narrative. The country of Mexico remained for some time (even after the Boom, to some extent) in the thrall of the so-called Novel of the Mexican Revolution, though some, like Mariano Azuela (1873–1952), did try to bring nuance to the genre to a degree in the 1930s and 1940s. A good example of such innovation in the novel of the Mexican Revolution is *El filo del agua* (*The Edge of the Storm* 1947) by Agustín Yáñez (1904–1980). The "modern" qualities of this novel have probably come to be more appreciated by other writers and critics with the benefit of hindsight, particularly with regard to its possible anticipation of the so-called "total novel" later touted by the likes of Mario Vargas Llosa (Peru, 1936–). Set in a small, isolated town in Jalisco in 1910, before the impact of the revolution has been felt and when only very distant rumblings of change can be discerned (a foretaste here of the great new novel of 1955 by Juan Rulfo [Mexico, 1917–1986], *Pedro Páramo*), the text offers a rather unedifying portrait of the tedious and limited existence of an uncultured provincial people, whose lives are overshadowed by the church and the power of landowners and oligarchs. What is interesting is the sometimes impressionistic style, the indirect take on the revolution, the emphasis on individual and communal psychology, the drift away from mainstream linear narration, and, above all, the presentation of multiple points of view. There are obvious shades of William Faulkner (USA, 1897–1962) and John Dos Passos (USA, 1896–1970) here, and of the totalizing drive to expand the frontiers of traditional realism by offering a richly wide and complex canvas of human perceptions of reality rather than a conventionally omniscient perspective. This certainly chimes with the aims of later Boom writers like the younger Vargas Llosa, who drew inspiration from the narrative techniques of the North American novelists just mentioned. In a more obviously vanguardist vein, the group associated with the Mexican magazine *Contemporáneos* (The Contemporaries) embraced modernist aesthetics in the late 1920s and early 1930s, while the followers of *estridentismo* (stridentism, founded in Puebla in 1921 by Manuel Maples

Arce [1900–1981]) promoted a more action-based political avant-garde (vague echoes here of Florida and Boedo).

Elsewhere, novelists popped up across the subcontinent in fragmentary form rather than as part of a coherent scene, producing books with varying degrees of a new viewpoint or new aesthetic in the wake of what one might dub social realism. An interesting example is the troubled Chilean (though she did move to Buenos Aires and worked on *Sur*) María Luisa Bombal (1910–1980), whose *House of Mist* (1947) and *La amortajada* (*The Shrouded Woman* 1938)[8] depart from conventional realism, use symbolic language, re-create the inner perspective of the female mind (the latter novel is daringly written from the viewpoint of a dead woman in her coffin), and offer a melancholy outlook on life.[9] However, probably the most important non-Argentine link with the new novel and the Boom is another River Plate novelist, the Uruguayan Juan Carlos Onetti. His early short novel *El pozo* (*The Pit*, 1939) features another protagonist who presents reality from an internal perspective; he uses fantasy (a soon-to-be major feature of the new novel) to avoid hopelessness, and his social alienation in a bourgeois environment also takes on the quality of a metaphysical unease. This character, Linacero, is an embryonic precursor of Onetti's later Brausen, the antihero of 1950's *La vida breve* (*A Brief Life*), a work that Donald Shaw has evaluated as the first novel of the Latin American Boom (Shaw 110–12). The novel includes some remarkable breaks with traditional realism. It has a strong self-referential element, alluding to its own writing and introducing at one stage into the fiction the figure of the author himself. Brausen, an echo of the frustrated Arltian protagonist pursuing self-degradation, flees Montevideo following an abusive relationship with a prostitute in whose murder he becomes complicit. Astonishingly, the place he runs away to is actually the imaginary town of his daydreams, Santa María (which will become the setting of many of Onetti's subsequent novels). This place is clearly a forerunner of Juan Rulfo's Comala (in *Pedro Páramo*) or Gabriel García Márquez's Macondo. A cult figure among many of the new novelists, Onetti sets a tone in *A Brief Life* that would be repeated throughout the 1950s and 1960s and beyond, inaugurating a type of fiction that would play with the roles of reader and author, problematize radically the relationship between literature and reality, and mercilessly probe the lack of order and meaning in human experience.[10]

One other vitally important location outside Argentina for the evolution of a modernist consciousness is São Paulo, Brazil. The Semana de Arte Moderna or Modern Art Week, which took place there in February 1922, is a watershed moment in the development of Brazilian Modernism. Offering art, poetry, concerts, and lectures, this provocative and controversial festival established São Paulo as a new cultural center in the face of the more conservative Rio de Janeiro. It fostered a new kind of modernism, based on an attempt to cultivate a uniquely Brazilian aesthetic. This did have the unfortunate effect of leading to a nationalist branch of the new modernist movement, but it also prompted the much more dynamic and ultimately influential trend of cultural "cannibalism" whose values came to be encapsulated in Oswald de Andrade's (1890–1954) "Manifesto antropófago" ("Anthropophagic *Manifesto*") published in 1928. This Paulista poet's line was not to reject outright European or Anglo-American Modernism, but to absorb it, to gobble it up, to make use of it by ingesting and then regurgitating it in a form now fused with intrinsically Brazilian values and experiences. This cheeky cannibalization manages to celebrate both primitivism and modernity, and offers a sort of national modernism that is also an implicit gesture of resistance to and a quasi-accommodation with what would later be termed the postcolonial experience. In novelistic terms, one influential offshoot of the Modern Art Week was Mário de Andrade's (1893–1945) *Macunaíma* (1928). This novel plays out the modernist anthropophagic aesthetic in its creation of a magical Amazonian tribal figure, Macunaíma, who becomes a sort of metaphor for Brazil. There is, however, as always in these modern narratives, some degree of ambiguity. Macunaíma may well represent a vibrant multiracial multiculturalism, but he is somewhat tainted by a sojourn in the city—hinting at the dangers of sacrificing national identity to foreign notions of progress.

The term "modernist" has actually tended to be used rather widely in Brazil, often referring to a variety of styles of novelistic writing, ranging sometimes from the seemingly social realist to the willfully hermetic. The fact that the lands that make up Brazil did not fragment into different viceroyalties and then nations as in Spanish-speaking Latin America means that there is perhaps a little less of a national emphasis in Brazilian literature and more of a regional flavor. For example, two of the authors often badged as "modernist" who emerged in the 1930s, Graciliano Ramos (1892–1953) and Jorge Amado (1912–2001) are strongly associated with two respective regions: the poor northeastern *sertão* or outback; and Bahia, a state marked by the legacy of slavery and Afro-Brazilian culture. Graciliano's *Vidas secas* (*Barren Lives*, 1938) portrays the cyclical misery of a family suffering in the drought-devastated hinterlands, as seen from the various perspectives of the different family members, including, unusually, that of the dog Baleia. The extraordinarily prolific Jorge Amado, who would become hugely popular in the second half of the twentieth century with his colorful folk novels that inspired a series of films and soap operas, began in much more of a social realist or protest mode. His most famous early work (actually his ninth) was the seminal *Terras do sem fim* (*The Violent Land*, 1943): it is about the cocoa wars between Bahian landowners and is still considered a classic of Brazilian literature. Very different was the woman writer Clarice Lispector (1920–1977), who would go on in the later decades of the century to be a sort of literary heroine for high-brow artists and intellectuals, notably embraced, for instance, by standard-bearer for French post-structuralist feminism Hélène Cixous (1937–). Lispector's writing was more urban, in a sense, but with a deeply interiorizing style. Her most substantial works would not come until the 1960s and 1970s, but her first novel, *Perto do coração selvagem* (*Near to the Wild Heart*), appeared in 1943 and seemed dramatically new in that it imitated the stream-of-consciousness techniques typical of many Anglo-American Modernists. Her much less successful 1949 book, *A cidade sitiada* (*The Besieged City*), was characterized by the near impenetrability of a certain strand of high modernism, though the very level of difficulty displayed represents the qualities that would actually go on in the future to make her so fashionable in certain circles.

Novels like *Barren Lives, The Violent Land*, and, above all, *Macunaíma* return us to the question of the relationship between the rural and the urban in the new narrative, as hinted at in the opening discussion of Borges's "The South." It is sometimes thought that the rise of the new novel is connected to a switch of emphasis from the rural to the urban. City culture was a significant factor in the growth of a new mentality, but it is plainly not the case that the new novel is necessarily urban. Indeed, some of the great novels of the Boom of the 1960s, such as Vargas Llosa's *La casa verde* (*The Green House* 1966) and García Márquez's *One Hundred Years of Solitude*, are set almost exclusively in peripheral jungle or rural areas. Nonetheless, the sort of interior-based novels that in many ways dominated Latin American fiction in the early twentieth century are normally seen as the very type of literature against which the new novel was a reaction, an idea popularized amongst intellectuals and by Vargas Llosa in particular (see Swanson 2005, 42). This type of narrative is variously referred to as the regionalist novel, the criollista novel, the novel of the land, the telluric novel, or the autochthonous novel. These texts, elaborated in relatively new and only relatively recently independent nation-states, attempted to explore Latin American reality by focusing on the regions (that which were thought to be somehow exclusively Latin American and less tainted by European or North American influence). They represented a project of challenging established versions of the civilization-and-barbarism debate and forging a sense of identity around myths of belonging to a tradition rooted in the essence of the countryside. In a variation on this sensibility, some novels, like the Peruvian Ciro Alegría's (1909–1967) 1941 saga *El mundo es ancho y ajeno* (*Broad and Alien is the World*), deal with the indigenous experience in the Andes from a sympathetic outsider's perspective. Other writers, often classified as neo-indigenists, attempted to build on the new awareness of the subjectivity of reality to try and imagine or present indigenous experience from within (something that would foreshadow in some ways what later became popularly known as magical realism, often seen as an effort to express reality via a rural, indigenous, black, mixed-race, or fundamentally Latin American apprehension of it). *Macunaíma* tries to do this to some extent, and the Guatemalan Miguel Ángel Asturias's (1899–1974) *Hombres de maíz* (*Men of Maize*, 1949) goes even further, mimicking the syntax and mythical worldview of indigenous people. The most important exponent of what is called neo-indigenism was, though, the native Quechua-speaking Peruvian Jose María Arguedas (1911–1969). His best novels were written in the 1950s and 1960s, though the first version of his early work *Yawar Fiesta* (or "Blood Festival") appeared in 1941. Indigenism and neo-indigenism are not the focus here, however.

The three most renowned Novels of the Land proper were *La vorágine* (*The Vortex* 1924) by José Eustasio Rivera (Colombia, 1889–1928), *Don Segundo Sombra* (1926) by Ricardo Güiraldes (Argentina, 1886–1927), and *Doña Bárbara* (1929) by Rómulo Gallegos (Venezuela, 1884–1969). *The Vortex*, though the earliest, is probably closest to the kind of new narrative that would come to prominence mid-century. The city man Arturo Cova escapes stifling conservatism by heading to the jungle, but rather than finding an idyllic sense of authenticity or identity, he is forced to witness the horrific exploitation of rubber workers in the Amazon and, in what becomes a rather delirious psychological narrative, gets sucked into near madness in the nightmarish vortex of the jungle, almost swallowed up by a monstrously devouring nature. Gallegos's novel is the most traditional of the trio, though its mainstream civilization-versus-barbarism thrust, in which sophisticated city dweller Santos Luzardo brings enlightenment to the barbaric Venezuelan plains, is tempered by a good deal of ambiguity as Santos succumbs to some extent to the terrible allure of the flatlands and eventually adopts the violent methods of his enemies in order to defeat them. Most interesting, perhaps, and certainly the most ambiguous is Güiraldes's gaucho novel of the pampa *Don Segundo Sombra*. Ostensibly a re-working and idealization of the gaucho figure once vilified under the civilization-and-barbarism ethic, the novel appears to project gaucho values as the essence of Argentine identity and as a model for the future of the nation. Of course, by 1926, the traditional, free, nomadic gaucho has, in the real world, more or less disappeared from a pampa now parceled off into farms, staffed by former cowboys subsumed into the new labor system, criss-crossed by roads and railways, and peppered with refrigeration units and storage facilities to facilitate the export of meat products and hides. Thus, despite the novel's association with traditional forms, consciousness of (or anxiety about) modernity underlies it, as the land-owning elite of which Güiraldes was representative struggles to cope with changing economic and social realities. The cult of the gaucho as national model (nebulous as a notion, in any case) therefore reveals itself as an unsustainable illusion. Indeed, in one crucial scene, the model gaucho, Don Segundo, effectively provokes a young man, Antenor Barragán, into an unwanted knife-fight that results in death and destruction: this episode shows how a barely repressed fear of the dangerous shadow of gaucho barbarism inadvertently seeps out to unsettle the narrative. In the end, it is perhaps necessary that Don Segundo should trot off into the sunset as he does, while his youthful urchin disciple, Fabio, suddenly revealed to be the inheritor of a large estate, is left behind to manage the symbolic future of the nation by accommodating the gaucho ways he has learned with the responsibilities of economic status and social leadership. The entire tension underlying this apprenticeship is underscored by the often highly poeticized and even at times Frenchified language (Güiraldes was Paris-educated and a leading light of the Florida circle) that overlays the attempted rendering of snatches of agrestic patois, in which modernist or *modernista* aesthetics rub against the realist gesturing. The question is whether this is all mere uncertainty and confusion, or self-aware ambiguity. One cannot help but suspect a strong element of the former, but it is notable that what is sometimes dismissed as inconsistency and mess in regionalist fictions is precisely what is praised to the hilt as productive ambiguity in the more consecrated examples of the later new novel. There is a case, then, for seeing the type of fiction that the new novel is usually alleged to be reacting against as actually comprising the opening stages in the very development of that new narrative.

The regional or continental dimension, focused on the specificity of supposedly marginal experience and the quest for a sense of Latin American identity, links also to the development of what would become one of the most commented on aspects of the new novel, the genre of so-called magical realism. Two authors are pivotal in this respect: Cuba's Alejo Carpentier (1904–1980) and Guatemala's Miguel Ángel Asturias.

Ironically, another city is fundamental here, and, doubly ironically, it is a European one: Paris. Both men lived in temporary exile in Paris, respectively between 1928 and 1939, and 1924 and 1933. Here they came under the influence of French surrealism, gained an interest in Freud's notion of the unconscious, and were exposed to new disciplines such as ethnology and anthropology. When Carpentier returned home from Paris and following a spell in Haiti in 1943, he began to see the realm of the surreal that he had discovered in Europe as part of the quotidian existence of Latin American life. Building on his earlier interest in Afro-Cuban music and culture, and on his celebration of a notion of primitivism, he elaborated the seminal concept of the "marvelous real" (or "lo real maravilloso"). He first used the phrase in the prologue to his 1949 novel *El reino de este mundo* (*The Kingdom of this World*), which follows the eighteenth- and nineteenth-century revolutionary movement in Haiti (led by Touissant Louverture [1743–1803]), from slave rebellions to black rule, and culminating in the ascension of the black leader Henri Christophe (1767–1820) to the position of first and only king of Haiti. What is dramatically new here is the way in which reality is presented and transformed through the perspective of a former slave, Ti Noel, who has been immersed in ancient oral traditions and magical beliefs. This was the beginning of a kind of magical realist aesthetic in which Eurocentrism is reversed and the world is presented through the lens of the subaltern, a radically different way of perceiving reality to that privileged in the hitherto dominant literary canon based on conventional versions of rational discourse. Though massively influential, the "marvelous real" was always going to be a problematic concept, however. The expression of a purportedly authentic Latin American consciousness through the filter of an inherited European cultural precedent that sees the subcontinent's reality as a kind of marvel inadvertently echoes certain strands of colonial thinking. It is unsurprising that a subsequent generation of writers and critics, particularly after the artistic triumphs of Gabriel García Márquez, would eventually reject magical realism as a pernicious exotification and commodification of Latin American culture.

Asturias, meantime, would use his Parisian experience and ethnological training to develop a kind of magical form of neo-indigenism that would revive a world view rooted in Mayan legend, most notably in his great work *Men of Maize*. His most influential novel, however, was set in a nightmarish anonymous city (echoing Guatemala City under the dictatorship of Manuel Estrada Cabrera [1857–1924] between 1898 and 1920). This was *El Señor Presidente* (*The President*), written in 1933 but not published, because of political concerns, until 1946. This is arguably the first true example of the Latin American New Novel. While some, as suggested earlier, have attributed this status to Onetii's *A Brief Life*, the opening of *The President* has been famously described as the first seven pages of the Boom (Gass 1987). The novel represented a radical rupture. Despite the assumed Guatemalan setting, this novel actually takes place in no particular time nor place, and chronological and spatial referents become increasingly hazy. There is little plot to speak of, and characterization is often reduced to sketch or caricature. The structure amounts to not much more than a series of loosely linked episodes or repeated motifs, and language is frequently fragmented and expressionistic rather than descriptive. Reality is actually often presented in what might be called a magical realist style, with subjective perceptions often projected on to external reality in a literal way. So, for instance: a distressed wife, following the news of her husband's death sentence, collapses on to a bench that is said to disappear into the darkness of the night; a terrified and mentally disturbed beggar on the run raises his hands to protect himself from the nails of rain that are being fired at him. Here, emotion and delirium are expressionistically transformed into actual fictional reality, and the opposition between the subjective and the objective is dissolved. In fact, virtually none of the elements traditionally associated with realistic writing are really present at all in this novel. The work offers itself primarily as a work of fiction, to be judged as an autonomous world in its own right, and not as a reflection of reality. This break with realism would become the defining feature of the new novel in its most productive decades.

Yet, this story of the evil and cruelty of dictatorship in Latin America clearly is about reality in some sense. However, the only political rebellion in the novel, that planned by General Canales, is barely touched upon and fizzles out as soon as it starts. The only real rebellion is one of emotion and love, that is, the slight dealt to the President by his favorite henchman, Angel Face, by falling for Camila, the daughter of Canales, the enemy the unnamed President is seeking to have framed and killed. And even this rebellion fails—with Camila persuaded of her lover's infidelity and Angel Face banished to rot in the deepest and darkest dungeon (though the birth of a son and Camila's flight to a bucolic countryside may hint at resilience and future potential redemption). What *The President* actually inaugurates is the great ambiguity, tension, or contradiction that would dog the new novel up to, during, and after the Boom. There is an attempt to comment on Latin American social and political reality, while simultaneously seeming to assert that life makes no sense and that literature is incapable of grasping or therefore offering any meaningful perspective on reality. The exhilarating thrill of the new would transform Latin American literature, but ultimately lead to accusations of self-indulgent elitism and evasion. The problem with the "new" is its unavoidably finite quality, that it inevitably contains the seeds of its own unbecoming or demise. From the start, the new novel initiated the beginnings of its own end.

NOTES

1. For more on civilization and barbarism, see, for example, Swanson 2003.
2. *Modernismo* was a specifically Spanish American (and also Spanish) finesecular movement, associated with aestheticism, exoticism, and escapism, though it did gradually take on more Americanist themes. It is largely associated with poetry, but there were also significant *modernista* novels and short stories. Different to modernism in the Anglo-American sense, it could nonetheless be regarded as marking the first inconsistent steps towards embracing what would eventually come to look like modernism in Latin America.
3. "Certidumbre de ser" (Fernández 417).
4. The term criollismo is used rather loosely to refer to a cultural elite of largely European descent whose family and forebears are often seen as having a noble place in national history. It is also used to refer to a specifically regionalist type of writing, as in the criollista

novel (to be considered later). Confusingly, the term comes from the word "creole," which, though frequently used to refer to those of mixed European and black descent, is, in this context, connected to notions of purity of descent in a new national context.

5. "Esperpentic" refers to grotesque people or things. The Spanish term "esperpento" was used by Ramón del Valle Inclán (Spain, 1866–1936) to describe a literary technique of systematic distortion.

6. Gregory Rabassa translated this phrase as "eye of the asshole" (*Hopscotch* 215).

7. "Tengo que matarte, María. Me has dejado solo" (Sabato, *El tunel* 134).

8. *La última niebla*; *La amortajada*. Bombal reworked these into English versions in 1947 and 1948, respectively.

9. Shaw places another Chilean alongside Bombal in terms of importance, Eduardo Barrios (1884–1963) (Shaw 71–74). Barrios's 1922 novel *Brother Ass* (*El hermano asno*) certainly has much of the ambiguity of the new novel and something of an emphasis on emotion rather than rationality as such, though its style is still very much indebted to *modernismo* (see note 7).

10. One other Uruguayan author worth mentioning is Felisberto Hernández (1902–1964). Little known outside of Latin America, he nonetheless is sometimes seen as seen as another precursor of the New Narrative and had something of a cult following amongst some new novelists. A rather eccentric short-story writer rather than a novelist, he played with fantasy and the subconscious, and had a tendency to imbue inanimate objects with a somewhat magical inner life of their own.

WORKS CITED

Alegría, Ciro. *Broad and Alien Is the World*. Translated by Harriet de Onis. Farrar & Rinehart, 1941.

Alegría, Ciro. *El mundo es ancho y ajeno*. Alianza, 1994.

Amado, Jorge. *Terras do sem fim*. Companhia das letras, 2008.

Amado, Jorge. *The Violent Land*. Translated by Samuel Putnam. Penguin, 2013.

Andrade, Mario. *Macunaíma: o herói sem nenhum caráter*. Martins, 1969.

Andrade, Mario. *Macunaíma*. Translated by E. A. Goodland. Random House, 1984.

Andrade, Oswald. "Manifesto Antropófago." *Nuevo Texto Crítico*, vol. 12, nos. 23/24, 1999, pp. 25–31.

Arguedas, José María. *Yawar Fiesta*. Editorial Universitaria, 1968.

Arguedas, José María. *Yawar Fiesta*. Translated by Frances Horning Barraclough. U of Texas P, 1985.

Arlt, Roberto. *El juguete rabioso*. Losada, 1973.

Arlt, Roberto. *Los lanzallamas*. Losada, 1977.

Arlt, Roberto. *Mad Toy*. Translated by Michele McKay Aynesworth. Duke UP, 2002.

Arlt, Roberto. *Los siete locos*. Losada, 1973.

Arlt, Roberto. *The Seven Madmen*. Translated by Nick Caistor. New York Review of Books, 2015.

Asturias, Miguel Ángel. *Hombres de maíz*. Alianza, 2005.

Asturias, Miguel Ángel. *Men of Maize*. Translated by Gerald Martin. U of Pittsburgh P, 1995.

Asturias, Miguel Ángel. *El señor presidente*. Vintage, 2020.

Asturias, Miguel Ángel. *The President*. Translated by Frances Partridge. Waveland, 1997.

Bioy Casares, Adolfo. *La invención de Morel*. Losada, 1940.

Bioy Casares, Adolfo. *Morel's Invention*. Translated by Ruth L. C. Simms. New York Review of Books, 2003.

Boldy, Steven. "Julio Cortázar: *Rayuela*." *Landmarks in Modern Latin American Fiction*, edited by Philip Swanson, Routledge, 1990, pp. 118–40.

Bombal, María Luisa. *La amortajada*. Nascimento, 1941.

Bombal, María Luisa. *House of Mist*. Farrar, Straus & Giroux, 1947.

Bombal, María Luisa. *The Shrouded Woman*. Farrar, Straus & Giroux, 1948.

Bombal, María Luisa. *La última niebla*. Nascimento, 1941.

Borges, Jorge Luis. "El sur." *Ficciones*, Random House Mondadori, 2011, pp. 209–19.

Borges, Jorge Luis. "The South." *Fictions*. In *Collected Fictions*, translated by Andrew Hurley, Penguin, 1999, pp. 174–79.

Carpentier, Alejo. *El reino de este mundo*. Austral, 2015.

Carpentier, Alejo. *The Kingdom of This World*. Translated by Pablo Medina. Farrar Straus & Giroux, 2017.

Cortázar, Julio. *Hopscotch*. Translated by Gregory Rabassa. Random House, 1966.

Cortázar, Julio. *Rayuela*. Sudamericana, 1969.

Fernández, Macedonio. "Doctrina estética de la novela." *Revista de las Indias*, no. 19, July 1940, pp. 412–17.

Fernández, Macedonio. *El museo de la novela de la eterna*. Archivos, 1993.

Fernández, Macedonio. *The Museum of Eterna's Novel (The First Good Novel)*. Translated by Margaret Schwartz. Open Letter/University of Rochester, 2010.

Gallegos, Rómulo. *Doña Bárbara*. Cátedra, 2005.

Gallegos, Rómulo. *Doña Bárbara*. Translated by Robert Malloy. U of Chicago P, 2012.

García Márquez, Gabriel. *Cien años de soledad*. Sudamericana, 1967.

García Márquez, Gabriel. *One Hundred Years of Solitude*. Translated by Gregory Rabassa. Harper & Row, 1970.

Gass, W. H. "The First Seven Pages of the Boom." *Latin American Literary Review*, no. 29, 1987, pp. 33–56.

Güiraldes, Ricardo. *Don Segundo Sombra*. Plaza, 2016.

Güiraldes, Ricardo. *Don Segundo Sombra*. Translated by Patricia Owen Steiner. U of Pittsburgh P, 1994.

Lispector, Clarice. *The Besieged City*. Translated by Johnny Lorenz. New Directions, 2019.

Lispector, Clarice. *A Cidade Sitiada*. Rocco, 1998.

Lispector, Clarice. *Near to the Wild Heart*. Translated by Alison Entrekin. New Directions, 2012.

Lispector, Clarice. *Perto do coração selvagem*. Rocco, 2019.

Mallea, Eduardo. *All Green Shall Perish: And Other Novellas and Stories*. Knopf, 1966.

Mallea, Eduardo. *Todo verdor perecerá*. Cátedra, 2000.

Marechal, Leopoldo. *Adam Buenosayres*. Translated by Norman Cheadle and Sheila Ethier. McGill-Queen's UP, 2014.

Marechal, Leopoldo. *Adán Buenosayres*. Archivos, 1997.

Onetti, Juan Carlos. *A Brief Life*. Translated by Hortense Carpentier. Serpents Tail, 1993.

Onetti, Juan Carlos. "The Pit" and "Tonight". Translated by Peter Bush. Quartet, 1991.

Onetti, Juan Carlos. *El pozo*. Punto de Lectura, 2007.

Onetti, Juan Carlos. *La vida breve*. Sudamericana, 1968.

Ramos, Graciliano. *Barren Lives*. Translated by Ralph Edward Dimmick. U of Texas P, 1965.

Ramos, Graciliano. *Vidas secas*. Record, 2020.

Rivera, José Eustasio. *La vorágine*. Diana, 1958.

Rivera, José Eustasio. *The Vortex*. Translated by John Charles Chasteen. Duke UP, 2018.

Rulfo, Juan. *Pedro Páramo*. Fondo de Cultura Económica, 1955.

Rulfo, Juan. *Pedro Páramo*. Translated by Margaret Sayer Pedens. Northwestern UP, 1994.

Sabato, Ernesto. *El túnel*. Seix Barral, 1983.

Sabato, Ernesto. *The Tunnel*. Translated by Margaret Sayers Peden. Random House, 1988.

Sarmiento, Domingo Faustino. *Facundo: Civilization or Barbarism*. Translated by Kathleen Ross. U of California P, 2003.

Sarmiento, Domingo Faustino. *Facundo o civilización y barbarie*. Biblioteca Ayacucho, 1993.

Shaw, Donald L. *A Companion to Modern Spanish American Fiction*. Tamesis, 2002.

Swanson, Philip. "Civilization and Barbarism." *The Companion to Latin American Studies*, edited by Philip Swanson, pp. 69–85. Arnold, 2003.

Swanson, Philip. *Latin American Fiction*. Blackwell, 2005.

Vargas Llosa, Mario. *La casa verde*. Seix Barral, 1966.

Vargas Llosa, Mario. *The Green House*. Translated by Gregory Rabassa. Harper & Row, 1968.

Yáñez, Agustín. *Al filo del agua*. Archivos, 1996.

Yáñez, Agustín. *The Edge of the Storm*. Translated by Ethel Brinton. U of Texas P, 1963.

CHAPTER 7

THE LATIN AMERICAN NOVEL IN THE 1960S AND EARLY 1970S

The Boom and Beyond

JUAN E. DE CASTRO

IN 1970, future Nobel Prize winner Mario Vargas Llosa published an article clearly intended as a celebration of the Latin American novel in one of the main venues for the dissemination of this then (apparently) new and exciting narrative: *Books Abroad*. This essay, titled "The Latin American Novel Today" was part of a volume of the journal devoted to the region's narrative. In it, the Peruvian novelist concludes triumphantly: "Edmund Wilson boasted several years ago of never having been interested in the Latin American novel. I wonder if he would repeat today with the same conviction this somewhat abrupt remark" (16). Leaving aside the rather peculiar appeal to Wilson as a cultural arbiter—a comparable article written in the twenty-first-century would, at least until October 2019, probably have assigned Harold Bloom a similar role—the text presents a triumphalist story. It depicts the region's novel as going from "imitative" (nineteenth century) to "primitive" (first decades of the twentieth century) "to creative" (last twenty years) (7–8). In fact, Vargas Llosa clearly sees the Latin American novel as having superseded that of the Global North, or First World, as was the terminology of the time: "the qualitative changes experienced by Latin American fiction during the postwar period parallels a certain stagnation of the European and North American novel which, after a period of notable splendor–culminating in the works of Joyce, Proust, Kafka, Faulkner—lost its impetus" (8). Underlying the development of this "creative" (as Vargas Llosa calls it), in other words, modern, even modernist, novel, was the rise of a number of major writers beginning with Jorge Luis Borges (1899–1986), who ironically was not a novelist, and ending, obviously, with Vargas Llosa (1936–) himself.[1]

THE CREATIVE NOVEL AND THE BOOM

In fact, the year of publication of this article, 1970, is precisely when the English version of *Cien años de soledad* (*One Hundred Years of Solitude*, 1967), Gabriel García Márquez's masterpiece, was published and, through its translation, began to impact the literatures of the Global South and North. One could even say that this year marked the high point of the Boom. This term coined by Luis Harss in 1966, before the publication of García Márquez's best-known novel, responded to the popularity of Vargas Llosa's *La ciudad y los perros* (*The Time of the Hero*) and Julio Cortázar's *Rayuela* (*Hopscotch*), both published in 1963, as well as the growing media presence of these and other writers, in particular Carlos Fuentes. In other words, the Boom was as much a commercial and media event, as an aesthetic one. As Vargas Llosa, who does not use the word Boom, notes, "Not only are the novels circulating in greater numbers (previously an Argentine, Chilean, or Colombian novelist could expect to sell only 1,000 copies if his work were a success; now an edition of 20,000 is not exceptional); but also the novelist has become a popular figure whose picture appears in newspapers and who is met in the street by autograph seekers" (15). In fact, the economic growth of the 1950s and 1960s made possible greater investment in tertiary education that helped create a larger number of potential sophisticated readers[2] and led to the development of a continental, even pan-Hispanic, market for these new novels. It also established he conditions that led to the rise of new book publishers, such as the Mexican Ediciones Era and Joaquín Mortiz, founded in 1960 and 1961, respectively, and the renewed Catalan Seix Barral, which aimed to satisfy this growing demand. The literary Boom would have been impossible without these concomitant economic, commercial, and educational booms.

But as the interest of *Books Abroad* proves, the impact of the Latin American Boom, again understood as this conjunction of artistic and commercial success, was not limited to the region but had an equally important international dimension.[3] Clearly referring to the Boom, Pascale Casanova claims: "The emergence of an aesthetically coherent body of writing in Latin America in the late 1960s forced critics in the center to confront the fact of a genuine literary unity on a continental scale that until then they had failed to notice" (234). While the "unity" of Latin American literature is surely debatable, the fact is that the simultaneous rise in popularity of a group of (relatively) young novelists, and the fact that these often presented themselves as a group, gave the appearance of a greater homogeneity than the literary reality justified. Be that as it may, one way of defining the Boom, as distinct from the "creative novel," would be to see it as constituted by those creative novelists who achieved recognition in the "center," as well as commercial success in Latin America and beyond. Because of the conjunction of quality, visibility, and commercial success of these modernist writers—those who followed alternative aesthetics were excluded from the group—not only in Latin America and Spain, but also throughout the Western world, Vargas Llosa could assume that the notably Eurocentric and United States–centric (if such a word exists) Edmund Wilson would have had to acknowledge the importance of the literary tradition to which the Peruvian novelist belonged.[4]

Throughout "the Latin American Novel Today," Vargas Llosa defines the "creative novel" as characterized by: the "shift from nature to man" (8), the incorporation "into fiction of other dimensions of human existence, such as imagination and dreams" (9), the use of urban settings ("the city is the permanent setting of the creative novel") (10), and the exploration of language and narrative structure ("likewise invents new narrative techniques") (10). As should be clear, this raises the question of whether this "creative" novel is itself imitative of European and North American tendencies represented, for instance, by such modernist writers as Joyce, Proust, Kafka, Faulkner, Sartre, and Camus, whose works can also be generally defined by these traits, just to limit ourselves to those authors mentioned by Vargas Llosa. In fact, the "creative novel," including his own work, is described by Peruvian novelist as delinked from the writings of his "primitive" or "imitative" predecessors. That said, a similar embrace of European and North American modernist masters was acknowledged by most of the major Boom writers. Thus, in 1950, a very young García Márquez complained: "The novel undoubtedly and fortunately influenced by Joyce, Faulkner, or Virginia Woolf has not been written in Colombia. I have said 'fortunately,' because I don't believe we Colombians just by being Colombians can be an exception to the play of influences" (213).[5] Even if García Márquez would, for many, become the paradigm of non-Western modes of narrativization, he saw himself as working under the influence of Joyce, Faulkner, and Virginia Woolf. That said, as any reader knows, and as exemplified by García Márquez, Vargas Llosa, and the other Boom authors, being influenced is often a necessary first step toward originality.

However, a more important question is raised by the chronological tensions between Vargas Llosa's history of the "creative novel" and the (in his article) absent but unavoidable idea of the Boom. After all, according to most critics, such as Lucille Kerr, the Boom was a "phenomenon of the 1960s" (597); therefore, it clearly becomes a subset of the "creative novel," dated by Vargas Llosa back to circa 1950 ("the last twenty years") in 1970. Limiting oneself to the authors mentioned by Vargas Llosa, one could easily come up with a longer trajectory for the creative novel. Thus, Borges, who, obviously, wrote short stories but given his influence was assimilated into the history of the "creative" novel, published his first collection *El jardín de senderos que se bifurcan* (The Garden of Forking Paths) in 1941, later incorporated into *Ficciones* (1944), while Juan Carlos Onetti, also mentioned in the text, published his first novel *El Pozo* (*The Pit*) in 1939.

While Onetti's *the Pit*—to mention the first work of a writer that was often singled out by Vargas Llosa as the most important early instance of the "creative novel"—would only be translated into English in 1991,[6] the writers of the Boom generation (relatively) rapidly became celebrities in Latin America and, more importantly, within the specific boundaries of what has been called the World Republic of Letters. According to Kerr: "*Labyrinths* (1961), published just after Borges shared the International Publisher's (or Formentor) Prize with Samuel Beckett, was among the first of the translated tides to gain recognition for the Latin American literary tradition" (599). Even if not a novelist, the critical success of Borges whetted the appetite of the Anglophone world for

Latin American literature. Thus, the Boom, unlike the "creative novel" or "new novel," the term used by both Emir Rodríguez Monegal, in "The New Latin American Novel" (1970), published in the same *Books Abroad* issue, and Fuentes, in *La nueva novela hispanoamericana* (1969), was a moment not only in the region's novel, but also within the world prestige book circles and market. However, as Ángel Rama noted about the international reception of the Boom: "The knowledge of Mario Vargas Llosa preceded that of Julio Cortázar, and the latter's came before that of Jorge Luis Borges. This contributed to the synchronic flattening of the history of [Spanish] American narrative" (52).[7] While Rama was writing about the reception of the Boom in Barcelona, this flattening of the history of Spanish American narrative where the Borges of *Ficciones* becomes (nearly) a contemporary of the García Márquez of *One Hundred Years of Solitude* was characteristic of the reception of the region's narrative in other European countries and the United States.[8]

THE FAB FOUR

After the dust settled, for most, the Boom—as distinct from the "creative novel" or "new novel"—was primarily comprised of only four authors. Parodying, as well as expanding on, the market logic that, to a great degree informed the Boom, Gerald Martin notes:

> There was in fact an explosion of interest in the Latin American novel from the early 1960s, which did indeed lead to an increased demand for the product, a demand which in its turn led to an expanded supply and a further spiral of interest. Moreover, four product leaders emerged to dominate the new market: Carlos Fuentes, Julio Cortázar, Mario Vargas Llosa and Gabriel García Márquez. (74)

While some have proposed additional names—Kerr, for one adds José Donoso to this list (597)—these four are generally seen as the founding members of "the most exclusive club in the cultural history of Latin America . . . that holds the immutable principle of having only five seats and not one more . . . Out of these four . . . those corresponding to Julio Cortázar, Carlos Fuentes, Mario Vargas Llosa, and Gabriel García Márquez, are in perpetual 'property' . . . The fifth . . . has been assigned to [writers] from Carpentier to Donoso, from Lezama Lima to Guimarães Rosa" (Rama 83).[9] Making explicit what has surely been thought by many a reader of Latin American literature, Martin—Gerald not George—argues that "A comparison with their contemporaries the Beatles—another four-man group—proves to be more illuminating than would seem likely at first" (75). As was the case with the Fab Four, "the writers of the Boom who, as well as being colleagues, were close friends during the 1960s, found themselves drifting apart during the 1970s" (75). In fact, the search for the fifth member of the Boom resembles the idea of the Fifth Beatle.[10] The question then remains about what, if anything, in addition to being celebrity "product leaders" in the Latin American and international markets, differentiates the writings of these literary "Fab Four" from the larger group of Latin American "creative" or new novelists.[11]

Boom Politics

At first glance, it could seem that the Boom authors shared little beyond a common commitment to modernism and to modernizing the region's novel. After all, Cortázar, born in 1914, who in Rodríguez Monegal's "The New Latin American Novel," is placed in an earlier generation together with the Brazilian João Guimarães Rosa and José Lezama Lima (46–47), was indebted to Joyce and the surrealists. Fuentes borrowed, for instance, in his *La región más transparente* (*Where the Air is Clear* 1958), from such diverse sources as Alejo Carpentier's Real Marvelous and Sartrean existentialism, to construct a fresco of Mexican society and history. Vargas Llosa, the youngest of the group, further developed the narrative innovations of Faulkner to update the realist tradition in his three masterpieces of the 1960s: *The Time of the Hero*, *La Casa Verde* (*The Green House* 1966), and *Conversación en La Catedral* (*Conversation in the Cathedral* 1969). Finally, García Márquez, also an admirer of the sage of Yoknapatawpha, borrowed the latter's creation of distinct imaginary literary territories (Macondo)—a lesson previously learned by Onetti—in his early *La hojarasca* (*Leafstorm* 1955) and his classic *One Hundred Years of Solitude*; while, in the latter, continuing and developing the fusion of the fantastic and the real earlier proposed by Carpentier and Miguel Ángel Asturias. Nevertheless, the Boom writers, especially Fuentes, Vargas Llosa, and García Márquez, can be seen, in Martin's words, as writing, during the period, novels that "are about the historical formation of Latin America, the relation between that history and other mythical versions, and the contribution of both to contemporary Latin American identity" (74). In fact, from slightly different perspectives, both Vargas Llosa and Fuentes will stress the importance of representing national and cultural totality in their narratives. According to Fuentes, "only the given word can strip off that which passes for 'reality' in order to show us the real; what accepted reality hides: the totality hidden or mutilated by conventional logic" (*La nueva novela hispanoamericana* 85).[12] For Fuentes, as for Vargas Llosa, and, in a different way, for García Márquez, modernism and true realism are imbricated. For the Boom writers, only by bypassing the documentary realism of the "primitive novel" is it possible to truly portray Latin America.

The reason why these writers and this type of writing achieved world-wide recognition can also be seen as directly connected to one of the key events of the twentieth century in Latin America: the Cuban Revolution. Cuba, seen as a burgeoning tropical utopia, created enormous interest worldwide in a region that, to many, had seemed until then at the margins of history. Even if they did not deal with Cuban history, the Boom novels were seen as presenting insight into the region. Fuentes's *La muerte de Artemio Cruz* (*The Death of Artemio Cruz* 1962), which through the life of the titular character passes review to the history of Mexico from the revolution to then-present; Vargas

Llosa's *The Time of the Hero*, which by narrating the violence that girds the life of a group of young cadets in a military school presents "a powerful depiction of the structures of power that have governed the social and political order in Peru" (Kerr 602); and García Márquez's *One Hundred Years of Solitude*, which was often read as encapsulating behind its magic the history of Colombia and the region—these books satisfied this interest. Even Cortázar's *Hopscotch*, which as an experimental text can be seen as distant from the sociological and historical concerns of his confreres' novels, has been described as "also an inquiry into the cultural values that characterize Argentine, if not Latin American, society around mid-century" (Kerr 602).

The representativeness of these writers and their novels was further enhanced by their common and vociferous support of the Cuban Revolution. As Donoso, who, beyond his possible status as the Fifth Boomer, embraced the role of historian of this literary moment, writes about the Boom writers' common "support for the Cuban cause" (49):

> I think this faith and political unanimity—or near unanimity—was then, and continued be until the Padilla case exploded in 1971,[13] one of the major factors in the internationalization of the Latin American novel, unifying outlooks and goals, providing an ideological structure . . . and for a time giving the feeling of a continental cohesion. (49)

However, this cohesion went beyond the support of Cuban autonomy against US opposition and interference, but also informed the hope, as Vargas Llosa famously noted, "for Latin America to enter, once and for all, a world of dignity and modernity, and for socialism to free us from our anachronism and our horror" ("Literature is Fire" 73). In fact, the Cuban Revolution as a prediction of a future modern Latin America, served to create a regional ethos in these writers, even if their actual novels were generally set in their home countries. Nevertheless, although their narrative often dealt with social topics, the Boom writers did so by borrowing and developing the high modernist arsenal of Joyce, Woolf, Faulkner, Kafka, and Proust.

Magical Realism

Although these four main Boom writers and their best-known novels were, beyond their common embrace of modernism, significantly different, they have often been categorized as magical realists, even by some of the most important contemporary critical voices. Mariano Siskind notes about this mode of writing, "the world of magical realist texts is one where the ordinary and extraordinary coexist without conflict, without even calling attention to each other's Otherness" (62). If one looks briefly at the most characteristic novels written by our Fab Four during the 1960s: *Hopscotch* and its metafictional experimentation, *The Death of Artemio Cruz*'s historical exploration of the Mexican revolution through the psychology of the titular character, *The Time of the*

Hero and its exploration of *machismo* and violence in a Peruvian military academy—only *One Hundred Years of Solitude* can be considered as magical realist. In fact, García Márquez previous novels of the decade—*El coronel no tiene quien le escribe* (*No One Writes to the Colonel* 1961) and *La mala hora* (*In Evil Hour* 1962)—were not written in the style. However, such was the worldwide success of García Márquez's masterpiece that it overshadowed these other masterpieces. Regarding *One Hundred Years of Solitude*, for some in the United States and European literary establishments, no hyperbole was hyperbolic enough. Thus, for US novelist William Kennedy, "*One Hundred Years of Solitude* is the first piece of literature since the Book of Genesis that should be required reading for the entire human race" (*One Hundred Years of Solitude* 11).

Given the impact of *One Hundred Years of Solitude*, it rapidly became a cliché to describe all Latin American literature of the 1960s as magic realist. Even as celebrated a critic as Casanova, has described the "aesthetically coherent body of writing in Latin America in the late 1960s" as " 'Magical realism' (a term coined only once the new style had already blossomed)" (234). But the French critic is not alone in lumping all of the Boom novels under the magical realist umbrella. As no less an authority than Homi Bhabha, whose theories of hybridity have often served as the interpretational paradigm with which to read writings from Asia, Africa, and even Latin America, stated in 1990, " 'Magical Realism' after the Latin American Boom becomes the literary language of the emergent post-colonial world" (7). While Bhabha's statement does justice to the enormous impact of García Márquez's writings on such major novelists as fellow Nobel Prize winner Toni Morrison or Salman Rushdie, it is a grotesque simplification of the Boom and the creative/new novel. Perhaps partly as a reaction against this simplification, few later Latin American writers will embrace magical realism. In fact, those who do, such as the Chilean Isabel Allende (1942–) with *La casa de los espíritus* (*The House of the Spirits* 1982) and the Mexican Laura Esquivel (1950–) with *Como agua para chocolate* (*Like Water for Chocolate* 1989), who have written magical realist family sagas from a female perspective, or the Peruvian Manuel Scorza (1928–1983), whose cycle of novels *La guerra silenciosa* (*The Silent War* 1970–1979) detail the struggles of an Andean indigenous commune against a foreign mining company and the government, have often been seen as commercial rather than "serious" writers.[14]

Women Novelists, Rural Writers, and Political Authors

As with any literary concept, that of the Boom—understood as a group of narrators and narratives that are modernist, international, as well as Latin American—is as much based on the exclusion of specific authors, novels, as well as literary practices, as it is on an accumulation of common traits. We have already seen that writers who practiced an older, realist, pre-modernist, narrative were, by definition, excluded from the Boom.

Even some authors widely acknowledged as major—for instance, Juan Rulfo, whose *Pedro Páramo* (1955) is declared by Fuentes as "the greatest expression achieved till now by the Mexican novel" (16)—[15] did not ultimately make it into the Boom. After all, while admired in Mexico and more generally Latin America, as an absolute masterpiece, Rulfo's novel did not generate the kind of international critical and commercial interest that the books of the four major Boom writers did. And, of course, Rulfo is just one of the most obvious examples of the way in which pan-Hispanic and, even more importantly, international critical and commercial reception were central to the constitution of the Boom.

The case of José María Arguedas, Peru's other great novelist, is of particular interest. Unmentioned by Vargas Llosa, in his "Latin American Novel Today," in Rodríguez Monegal's "The New Latin American Novel," or Fuentes's *La nueva novela hispanoamericana*, Arguedas's novels, often depicting indigenous life, would seem to be completely outside the Boom's urban and modernist writing. However, in Vargas Llosa's "Novela primitiva y novela de creación" (1969), an early draft of "The Latin American Novel Today," Arguedas is mentioned together with Rulfo and João Guimarães Rosa, who will remain in the latter essay, as exemplars of how creative novelists can deal with rural topics.[16]

More importantly, as the above discussion of the Boom's four major writers, as well as potential fifth members, should have already insinuated, women writers were relegated from all discussions of this literary group. While given the central role book sales played in determining who were the actual members of the Boom, one could, perhaps argue that it was rather the (supposedly) impersonal forces of the market that determined the exclusion of women writers. However, as we have seen, critical reputation also played a major role in this determination, and here bias surely played a role. The analogy to the Cuban Revolution, that transformed Fidel Castro and Ernesto "Che" Guevara into icons, or, for that matter, the Beatles, shows how agents of social, political, or cultural change were expected to be male during the 1960s.

But even if this commercial and critical context were seen as determining the actual catalog of writers belonging to the Boom, the fact is that a number of important women writers were excluded from the larger listings of "creative" or "new writers." While Donoso briefly mentions a group of Argentine women writers, such as Beatriz Guido (1922–1988), Elvira Orphée (1922–2018), Norah Lange (1905–1992), Victoria Ocampo (1890–1979), and Silvina Bullrich (1915–1990), the context is more that of friendly acquaintances than literary influences (30–31). Fuentes, on his part, briefly mentions Mexican writer Elena Garro (1916–1998), a major contemporary, whose *Recuerdos del porvenir* (*Recollections of Things to Come* 1963) shows numerous points of contact with the major Boom novels (51). However, to limit ourselves to the two essays included in the same *Books Abroad* issue, neither Vargas Llosa's "The Latin American Novel Today," which lists fifteen writers, nor Rodríguez Monegal's "The New Latin American Novel," which refers to thirteen, includes any women writers. What makes Vargas Llosa's and Rodríguez Monegal's omissions particularly problematic is that they are basically listing a history of the modernist novel in the region from the 1940s to 1970.

In addition to the writers (briefly) mentioned by Donoso and Fuentes, one could add to the list of women writers marginalized in critical evaluations written during the 1960s and early 1970s such notable novelists as the Chilean María Luisa Bombal (1910–1980), whose *La última niebla* (*House of Mist* 1934) and *La amortajada* (*The Shrouded Woman* 1937) were among the first fully achieved modernist novels published in Spanish America. But as the case of Garro, whose major novel was published the same year as Vargas Llosa's *The Time of the Hero* and Cortázar's *Hopscotch* shows, the writers omitted were often close contemporaries of the major Boom writers. In Mexico, Rosario Castellanos (1925–1974), the author of *Balún Canán* (*The Nine Guardians* 1957), *Oficio de tinieblas* (*The Book of Lamentations* 1962), and the posthumously published *Rito de iniciación* (Rite of Initiation, 1996), was a full-fledged woman of letters—novelist, playwright, poet, essayist, and major second-wave feminist. Likewise, Elena Poniatowska (1932–) published *Hasta no verte Jesús mío* (*Here's to You, Jesusa*, 1969), precisely before the publications of both Vargas Llosa's and Rodríguez Monegal's articles, but merited no mention in either text. The fact that *Here's to You, Jesusa* is an early testimonial novel that told the story of Jesusa Palancares, a poor Mexican washerwoman, and did not share in the Boom's high modernist ethos may explain its omission. However, Manuel Puig's different though equally radical rejection of high modernist techniques did not lead to his exclusion from Rodríguez Monegal's "new Latin American novel." In fact, the Uruguayan critic saw him, together with the poststructuralist Severo Sarduy (1937–1993), as one of the two high points in which the new novel culminated.[17]

Another group excluded from both the Boom and the creative/new novel were those whose writings were seen as being too tilted toward political description and analysis. Paradoxically, given the Boom's explicit radical politics, authors such as the Mexican José Revueltas (1914–1976) or the Argentine David Viñas (1927–2011), whose novels explored the lives and ideas of Mexican Marxist activists, in the case of the former, and the social structures of Argentina, in the case of the latter, were absent from most considerations of the new novel.

THE END OF THE BOOM

As we have seen, like the Fab Four, the Boom writers began to break apart in the early 1970s. If their common support for the Cuban Revolution (and revolution tout court) brought them together, it was their divergent responses to the Revolution's hardening—as exemplified by the censoring and brief jailing of Cuban poet Heberto Padilla (1971)—that led to their progressive distancing. The last hurrah of the group was the attempt to create an independent radical magazine, *Libre* (Free), that only published four volumes between 1971 and 1972.[18] After the "Padilla Affair" and *Libre*, García Márquez and Cortázar would continue supporting the Cuban Revolution, while Fuentes and Vargas Llosa became ever harder critics.

However, the personal loss of faith, in particular by Vargas Llosa and Fuentes, in the Cuban Revolution and, in the case of the former, in the possibility of revolution, was more than just part of these authors' biographies. It was instead a generational change in Latin America and the world. The 1970s saw the progressive loss of the utopian expectations that had surrounded the Cuban Revolution. In fact, one can see in the 1973 coup in Chile against Salvador Allende's attempt at reconciling democracy and socialism not only the final nail on the revolutionary coffin—reaffirmed by the coups in Uruguay (1973) and Argentina (1976)—but as signaling the breakdown of the association between Latin America and utopia. These political changes help explain the lessened international interest in the region's narrative after the early 1970s. This weakening of the world market for the region's narrative did not directly affect the four major Boom writers—in fact, García Márquez would win the Nobel Prize in 1982, while Vargas Llosa, would receive his in 2010—but it did limit the reception of the novelists who came of age after the 1960s.

Moreover, "The stable environment upon which Latin America's growth was predicated in the three previous decades disappeared with the quadrupling of oil prices in 1973–74" (Goddard). The impact of the world crisis led to a breakdown in the import substitution models that had guided Latin America's economic policy, a significant loss in disposable income on the part of the majorities, a defunding of public education, and ultimately to a crisis in the book market, all of them factors that had made the early success of the Boom possible.

AFTER THE BOOM

As mentioned above, there were several writers who, precisely at the height of the Boom, were developing alternative types of narrative to the total novel, that attempted to fully represent Latin American societies and history, or even magical realism, in the case of García Márquez. One must mention as first among these the Argentine Puig, whose novels embraced popular culture—Hollywood films, tangoes, and boleros, as well as depicting queer lives and topics. In fact, his first major novel, *La traición de Rita Hayworth* (*Betrayed by Rita Hayworth* 1968), had begun as a screenplay, before the author decided to turn it into a novel. His narrative reached its greatest international success with *El beso de la mujer araña* (*Kiss of the Spider Woman*, 1976), the story of the developing relationship between two prisoners: a gay window dresser and a Marxist activist. The novel was adapted into a play (1983), Oscar nominated English-language film (1985), and, posthumously, a Tony Award winning Broadway musical (1993). Given that Puig's concern with queerness and popular culture dovetailed perfectly with the evolution of international culture after 1968, he is clearly the writer who generated the most interest throughout the world republic of letters during the late 1970s. Puerto Rican Luis Rafael Sánchez's *La guaracha del Macho Camacho* (*Macho Camacho's Beat* 1976) incorporates the discourses of popular music and radio programming, as well as numerous references to television, into its investigation into the island's politics—one of the main characters is a senator—and mores. A similar concern with popular culture, though now brought up to date to include rock and the youth counterculture of the 1960s, characterized the Onda (wave) writers in Mexico, such as José Agustín (1944–) (*La tumba* [The Tomb 1964], *De perfil* [In Profile 1966] and Gustavo Sainz (1940–2015) (*Gazapo* [Young Rabbit 1965], *La princesa del Palacio de Hierro* [The Princess of the Palacio de Hierro 1974]). While it is true that authors such as the Cuban Guillermo Cabrera Infante and Fuentes had thematically incorporated popular music, in the case of the former's linguistically playful exploration of Havana's pre-revolutionary nightlife *Tres tristes tigres* (*Three Trapped Tigers* [1967]), and film, in the latter, exploration of the impact of movie stardom on a mother-and-son relationship in *La zona sagrada* (*Holy Place* 1967), these novels could still be seen primarily as high modern explorations of form and structure. Puig, Sánchez, and La Onda, on the other hand, without losing rigor, explored popular culture as part of narrative modes that were much more accessible to readers and, in the case of La Onda, perhaps even addressed, to young readers. As Kerr notes, "the diversification and proliferation of narrative forms in the 1970s and 1980s signal perhaps a democratization of the tradition" (602).

While García Márquez's *El otoño del patriarca* (*Autumn of the Patriarch* 1975) represents a high modernist moment in the Colombian master's oeuvre, the three other (former) Boom masters would evolve in the directions indicated in different ways by Puig and La Onda—that is, toward the "democratization of the tradition," which one must note is perfectly compatible, and often a consequence, of a growing concern with the market. Even Cortázar, whose *Hopscotch*, despite its playfulness and references to jazz, has been seen as the major Latin American experimental novel, published his *Fantomas contra los vampiros multinacionales. Una utopia realizable* (*Fantomas Versus the Multinational Vampires: An Attainable Utopia* 1975), a text that makes incorporates the comic book character and makes use of comic strips. However, the clearest instance of this embrace of popular culture by the major Boom writers can be found in Vargas Llosa. During the 1960s, the author of searing total novels, his works of the 1970s—*Pantaleón y las visitadoras* (*Captain Pantoja and the Special Service* [1973]), about the setting up of a prostitution service for the military in the Peruvian Jungle, and *La tía Julia y el escribidor* (*Aunt Julia and the Scriptwriter* [1977]), a fictionalized version of the author's romance with his aunt by marriage—were characterized by what has been called the "discovery of humor" (Williams 93). Moreover, both novels embraced melodrama and were written in an accessible style. Furthermore, as a very early example of autofiction, *Aunt Julia and the Scriptwriter* can be seen not only as participating in the democratizing tendencies of the 1970s, but also as predicting the autobiographical turn of much contemporary Latin American narrative.

There were, however, other writers who followed more individual paths. Donoso, for instance, published *El obsceno pájaro de la noche* (*The Obscene Bird of Night* 1970), the story of a patrician Chilean family that ends in corruption and monstrosity, as well as *Casa de campo* (*House in the Country* 1978), described by Idelber Avelar, "one of the most ambitious Latin American allegorical novels of the past few decades" (71). (According to

Avelar, allegories became the favored mode for Latin American writers to deal with the political defeat of the revolutionary hopes of the 1960s and early 1970s.) *Un mundo para Julius* (*A World for Julius* 1970) by Alfredo Bryce Echenique (1939–f) is a loosely auto-biographical bildungsroman of an upper-class Peruvian boy, tinged with social criticism and nostalgia. It has on occasion been considered the best Peruvian novel.[19] One can also mention the Cuban Reinaldo Arenas, whose *El mundo alucinante* (*Hallucinations: Being an Account of the Life and Adventures of Friar Servando Teresa de Mier* 1969), in addition to representing a fusion of metafiction and magical realism, also prefigured the turn to history that characterized the region's novels during the early 1980s. Another important precedent for these later historical novels is *Yo el supremo* (*I the Supreme* 1974) by the Paraguayan Augusto Roa Bastos (1917–2005). The novel is as much a fictionalization of the life of nineteenth century Paraguayan dictator José Gaspar Francia, as its deconstruction.

CONCLUSION

As one would expect, after their heyday during the 1960s and early 1970s, writers and scholars have not been shy about criticizing the Boom. For instance, the sexism that characterized their novels, as well as their views on the history of Spanish American narrative, has often been pointed out. In particular, Cortázar has been taken on many an occasion to task for his overt sexism: most famously in the dichotomy between the passive "female reader," as he characterized those incapable of creative analysis, and the "accomplice reader" proposed in *Hopscotch*, but also in his descriptions of male/female relationships.[20] Moreover, Fuentes's novels after *Terra nostra* (1975)—his attempt at fictionalizing the whole of Hispanic history, culture, and literature from the 16th century to the present—if not after *The Death Artemio Cruz* have rarely been considered complete successes.[21] García Márquez's novels, including *One Hundred Years of Solitude*, have been accused of exoticizing Latin America.[22] Moreover, Vargas Llosa's continuous political rightward drift has been resisted by many a reader and critic.[23] Though the obvious weaknesses of his recent novels has also contributed to this rise in negative criticisms.

However, in 2012, when Juan Gabriel Vásquez, the contemporary Colombian writer then riding high on the international success of his *El ruido de las cosas al caer* (*The Sound of Things Falling* 2011), was giving a presentation at the Cervantes Institute at Dublin, he was asked about the relevance—or lack thereof—of the "literary Boom" to contemporary writers. He responded that he saw them:

> as the real founders of my tradition, the tradition I try to write in began with them . . . Vargas Llosa, García Márquez, Carlos Fuentes, Julio Cortázar . . . Vargas Llosa, García Márquez are still living; at the same time, they are classics, they are living classics . . . sharing the same world with them is almost as if a 21st century Irish writer could pick up the phone and call James Joyce.

Vásquez is not alone. For most major contemporary writers, despite the changes in the region's novel, despite the weaknesses of much of their post 1970s writings, the Boom authors and their contemporaries, such as Donoso, Cabrera Infante, Puig, and Garro, represent one of the pillars, if not the actual keystone, on which contemporary Spanish American narrative is founded.

NOTES

1. In chronological order, the "creative" novelists mentioned by Vargas Llosa in the article are the following: Jorge Luis Borges (Argentina, 1899–1986), Miguel Ángel Asturias (Guatemala, 1899–1974), Alejo Carpentier (Cuba, 1904–1980), João Guimarães Rosa (Brazil, 1909–1967), Juan Carlos Onetti (Uruguay, 1909–1994), José Lezama Lima (Cuba, 1910–1976), Ernesto Sábato (Argentina, 1911–2011), Julio Cortázar (Argentina, 1914–1984), Juan Rulfo (Mexico, 1917–1986); José Donoso (Chile, 1924–1996), Gabriel García Márquez (Colombia, 1927–2014), Carlos Fuentes (Mexico, 1928–2012), Salvador Garmendia (Venezuela, 1928–2001), Guillermo Cabrera Infante (Cuba, 1929–2005), Severo Sarduy (1937–1993). Needless to say, Borges was in actuality not a novelist but a short-story writer.

2. Economist C. Roe Goddard writes about "the region's spectacular growth of the 1960s." He adds: "In the period from 1950 until the quadrupling of oil prices in 1973, Latin America was able to achieve a relatively high level of growth. . . By the time of the 1973–1974 oil crisis, Latin America's growth rate was higher than that of the industrialized world."

3. In addition to Vargas Llosa's article, the *Books Abroad* Winter 1970 issue includes an important overview by Emir Rodríguez Monegal, as well as articles on Borges, Cortázar, García Márquez, Guimarães Rosa, Lezama Lima, Vargas Llosa, and, somewhat surprisingly, a bibliography of works on Lezama Lima.

4. According to Kerr, "However, what is important about this moment is perhaps not so much that many Spanish American critics saw it, correctly or not, as inaugurating a revolutionary writing that successfully moved away from the era's dominant models of narrative fiction (i.e., realism, regionalism, criollismo) . . . Perhaps more important is that, because of the widespread attention brought to Spanish American literature by the Boom novels during this period, there was also a burgeoning, parallel boom of writing about Spanish American fiction, and about Spanish American literature more generally both inside and outside the academy" (597–98).

5. "Todavía no se ha escrito en Colombia la novela que esté indudable y afortunadamente influida por los Joyce, por Faulkner o por Virginia Woolf. Y he dicho 'afortunadamente', porque no creo que podríamos los colombianos ser, por el momento, una excepción al juego de las influencias" (García Márquez 213).

6. In his widely read "Literature is Fire," a speech given during the ceremony for the first Rómulo Gallegos Award granted to *La casa verde* (*The Green House* 1966), Vargas Llosa went out of his way to mention "other Latin American writers with more books and merit than me should have received [the Award] instead—I'm thinking of the great Onetti" (74).

7. "El conocimiento de Mario Vargas Llosa fue anterior al de Julio Cortázar y el de éste anterior al de Jorge Luis Borges lo que contribuyó a un aplanamiento sincrónico de la historia de la narrativa americana" (Rama 52).

8. The flattening of the history of Latin American literature also responded to the fact that many older writers were still active during the 1960s. For instance, *El hacedor* (1960), a

compilation of diverse texts by Borges, including short narratives, was published in English as *Dreamtigers* in 1964, and toward the end of the Boom period, his collection of new short stories, *El informe de Brodie* (1970), translated as *Doctor Brodie's Report* (1972), came out. Miguel Ángel Asturias not only continued writing novels, but five of his earlier works, including his masterpiece *El señor presidente* (*The President*, 1946), were translated during the 1960s. Carpentier, on his part, wrote one of the most important novels of the period, *El siglo de las luces* (1962), translated as *Explosion in the Cathedral*, in 1963.

9. "El club más exclusivista que haya conocido la historia cultural de América Latina ... que tiende a aferrarse al principio intangible de solo cinco sillones y ni uno más ... De ellos cuatro son ... 'en propiedad' los correpondientes a Julio Cortázar, Carlos Fuentes, Mario Vargas Llosa y Gabriel García Márquez ... El quinto ... lo han recibido desde Carpentier a Donoso, desde Lezama Lima a Guimaraes Rosa [sic]" (Rama 83).

One must note that the presence of Guimarães Rosa, a Brazilian author among these candidates for the position of "Fifth Boomer." While Guimarães Rosa was one of the key innovators of his country's narrative, his inclusion can be seen as expressing the desire of critics and novelists for subcontinental cultural unity, rather than actual influence or, for that matter, a mass readership in Spanish America. It is true that Guimarães Rosa is included in Luis Harss's and Doehmann's foundational book of interviews with Latin American writers *Los nuestros Into the Mainstream*. However, that book includes other older authors such as Borges, an honorary "creative" and "new" novelist for Vargas Llosa and Rodríguez Monegal, Asturias, and Carpentier in the Boom. Moreover, Donoso does not mention Guimarães Rosa in his *The Boom in Spanish American Literature*. As David William Foster notes: "What has come to be called the Spanish American literary Boom . . . had scant intersection with Brazilian literature" (137). However, *Grande Sertão: Veredas* (1956) had been published in Spanish in 1967 by Seix Barral.

10. According to *The Rough Guide to the Beatles*, "The phrase 'The Fifth Beatle' was coined early in the band's history to describe satellite members of The Beatles' organization. These days the phrase has practically entered the language of the wider world as shorthand for anyone involved in a project outside of the limelight but in a notable way" (Ingham, 287).

11. The centrality of the pan-Hispanic, as well as, more generally, international, dimension of the Boom is evidenced by the fact that these four writers—as well as many of the other creative and new novelists—have additionally been linked to local literary groups and movements. For instance, Cortázar could be seen as one of the youngest members of the Sur group formed around Borges and Victoria Ocampo; while García Márquez was a key member of the Barranquilla group that included both older writers—the Catalan modernist Ramón Vinyes (1882–1952), Alfonso Fuenmayor (1885–1966)—as well as (then) more experienced contemporaries, such as Germán Vargas (1919–1991) and Álvaro Cepeda Samudio (1926–1972); Fuentes, for his part, was often seen as a central member of the so-called Mafia, a group of Mexican writers that included poet Octavio Paz (1914–1998), Salvador Elizondo (1932–2006), who published the experimental novel *Farrabeuf* in 1965, and critic, and occasional narrator, Carlos Monsiváis (1938–2010), among others; while Vargas Llosa has often been seen as a tardy member of the Peruvian generation of the 1950s, that also included important novelists such as Sebastián Salazar Bondy (1924–1965), Enrique Congrains (1932–2009), and Julio Ramón Ribeyro (1929–1994), among others.

12. "Sólo la palabra vertida puede descolorar eso que pasa 'por realidad' para mostrarnos lo real: lo que la 'realidad' consagrada oculta: la totalidad escondida o mutilada por la lógica convencional" (Fuentes, *La nueva novela hispanoamericana* 85).

13. The "Padilla affair" is briefly studied below.

14. The novels by Scorza that constitute *La guerra silenciosa* (*The Silent War*) are the following: *Redoble por Rancas* (*Drums for Rancas* 1970), *Historia de Garabombo, el Invisible* (*Garabombo, the Invisible* 1972), *El jinete insomne* (*The Sleepless Rider* 1977), *Cantar de Agapito Robles* (*The Ballad of Agapito Robles* 1977), and *La tumba del relámpago* (*Requiem for a Lightning Bolt* 1979).

15. "La máxima expresión que ha logrado hasta ahora la novela mexicana" (Fuentes 16).

16. In "Novela primitiva y novela de creación," Vargas Llosa argues about Arguedas: "Although the one closest among the new writers to the patterns of the primitive novel, Arugedas does not fall into its most obvious traps because he does not attempt to photograph the Indian world (that he knows intimately): he wants to install the reader inside it" (Aunque el más apegado, entre los nuevos, a los patrones de la novela primitiva, Arguedas no incluye en sus defectos más obvios porque no intenta fotografíar al mundoindio (que él conoce profundamente): quiere instalar al lector en su intimidad) (32). While a study of the relationship between Arguedas and the Boom is beyond the scope of this essay, one must note that after his suicide in 1969 and his controversy with Cortázar regarding the putative opposition between local and cosmopolitan writers, he became Vargas Llosa's aesthetic bête noir. On the problematic relationship between Arguedas and Vargas Llosa, see Moraña and Castro-Klarén.

17. Writing about Puig and Sarduy, Rodríguez Monegal states: "With this novel by Sarduy [*De donde son los cantantes* [*From Cuba with a Song* 1967], as with *La traición de Rita Hayworth* [*Betrayed by Rita Hayworth* Puig, 1967], the theme of the Latin American novel which had been brilliantly developed by at least three groups of novelists, achieves a veritable fusion of poetic and narrative forms" (50).

18. The four major Boom writers would collaborate in *Libre*, together with many of the major Spanish American (such as Octavio Paz) and Spanish (Juan Goytisolo, Manuel Vásquez Montalban) of the time. The magazine would ultimately propose the possibility of the conjunction between socialism and, as its title indicates, intellectual freedom. As Claudia Gilman notes, if in the wager of *Libre* there was something pragmatic and not suicidal, it was its alliance, even if symbolic, with the Chile of the Unidad Popular ("si en la apuesta de *Libre* había algo de pragmático o no del todo suicida, era su alianza, cierto que simbólica, con el Chile de la Unidad Popular") (286).

19. See "Encuesta sobre la major novela peruana."

20. To his credit, Cortázar himself accepted these criticisms: "In *Hopscotch* I designated passive readers as female, which has gained me a storm of criticism during my recent trips to Latin America. I stopped thinking in this manner a long time ago, but in those days [of *Hopscotch*], I fell into this trap, the same into which today so many *machistas* fall" ("En *Rayuela* yo califiqué a los lectores pasivos de lectores hembras, lo cual me ha valido una lluvia de palos en mis últimos viajes por América Latina. Hace mucho que dejé de pensar así, pero en aquella época caí en la trampa, como siguen cayendo hoy tantos machistas") ("El camino de damasco").

21. Contemporary Mexican novelist Julián Herbert makes this point: "The Carlos Fuentes of his/my youth was a real star. Whoever doesn't see this is because she's blind. Whoever has seen it cannot forgive him for growing old" ("el Carlos Fuentes de (su/mi) juventud era un maldito lucero. Quien no lo ve es porque fue enceguecido. Quien lo vio no le pudo perdonar la vejez").

22. According to Reinaldo Arenas: "On the path of exoticism, which Europeans and North Americans paternally appreciate, one can easily achieve fame and often even the Nobel Prize. It is enough to mention the examples of Miguel Ángel Asturias and García Márquez" ("Por el camino del exotismo, que es el que con paternal agradecimiento y comprensión acepta el europeo y el norteamericano, se llega con facilidad a la fama y a muchas veces hasta el premio Nobel. Baste con citar los casos de Miguel Ángel Asturias y de García Márquez") (18).

23. On Vargas Llosa's political evolution, see my *Mario Vargas Llosa: Public Intellectual in Neoliberal Latin America*.

WORKS CITED

Agustín, José. *De perfil*. Mortiz, 1966.

Agustín, José. *La tumba*. Mester, 1964.

Allende, Isabel. *La casa de los espíritus*. Plaza y Janes, 1982.

Allende, Isabel. *The House of the Spirits*. Translated by Magda Bovin. Knopf, 1985.

Arenas, Reinaldo. *Hallucinations: Being an Account of the Life and Adventures of Friar Servando Teresa de Mier*. Translated by Gordon Brotherston. Harper and Row, 1971.

Arenas, Reinaldo. *El mundo alucinante. Una novela de aventuras*. Diógenes, 1969.

Arenas, Reinaldo. "Subdesarrollo y exotismo." *Memoriales*, edited by Jorge Camacho, El Fantasma de la Glorieta, 1991, pp. 15–22.

Asturias, Miguel Ángel. *The President*. Translated by Frances Partridge. Victor Gollancz, 1963.

Asturias, Miguel Ángel. *El señor president*. Costa-Amic, 1946.

Avelar, Idelber. *The Untimely Present: Postdictatorial Latin American Fiction and the Task of Mourning*. Duke UP, 1999.

Bhabha, Homi. "Introduction: Narrating the Nation." *Nation and Narration*, edited by Homi Bhabha, Routledge, 1990, pp. 1–7.

Bombal, María Luisa. *La amortajada*. Sur, 1938.

Bombal, María Luisa. *House of Mist*. Translated by the author. Farrar, Straus, and Co., 1947

.Bombal, María Luisa. *The Shrouded Novel*. Translated by the author. Farrar, Straus, and Co., 1948.

Bombal, María Luisa. *La última niebla*. Nascimento, 1931.Borges, Jorge Luis. *Doctor Brodie's Report*. Translated by Norman Thomas Di Giovanni. E. P. Dutton, 1972.

Borges, Jorge Luis. *Dreamtigers*. Translated by Mildred Boyer and Harold Morland. U of Texas P, 1964.

Borges, Jorge Luis. *Ficciones*. Sur, 1944.

Borges, Jorge Luis. *Ficciones*. Translated by Anthony Kerrigan, et. al. Grove Press, 1962.

Borges, Jorge Luis. *El hacedor*. Emecé, 1960.Borges, Jorge Luis. *El informe de Brodie*. Emecé, 1970.Borges, Jorge Luis. *Labyrinths: Selected Stories and Other Writings*. Translated by James E. Irby et al. Grove P, 1962.

Bryce Echenique, Alfredo. *Un mundo para Julius*. Barral, 1970.

Bryce Echenique, Alfredo. *A World for Julius*. Translated by Dick Gerdes. U of Texas P, 1992.

Cabrera Infante, Guillermo. *Three Trapped Tigers*. Translated by Donald Gardner and Suzanne Jill Levine. Harper and Row, 1971.

Cabrera Infante, Guillermo. *Tres tristes tigres*. Seix Barral, 1967.

Carpentier, Alejo. *Explosion in a Cathedral: A Novel.* Translated by John Sturrock. Little, Brown, 1963.

Carpentier, Alejo. *El siglo de las luces.* Compañía General, 1962.Casanova, Pascale. *The World Republic of Letters.* Translated by M. B. DeBevoise. Harvard UP, 2004.

Castellanos, Rosario. *Balún Canán.* Fondo de Cultura Económica, 1957.

Castellanos, Rosario. *Book of Lamentations.* Translation by Esther Allen. Penguin, 1998.

Castellanos, Rosario. *The Nine Guardians.* Translated by Irene Nicholson. Readers International, 1993.

Castellanos, Rosario. *Oficio de tinieblas.* Mortiz, 1972.

Castellanos, Rosario. *Rito de iniciación.* Alfaguara, 1996.

Castro-Klarén, Sara. "Disentangling the Knots: Vargas Llosa and José María Arguedas in *La utopia arcaica.*" *Critical Insights: Mario Vargas Llosa,* edited by Juan E De Castro, Salem Press, 2014, pp. 71–88.

Cortázar, Julio. "El camino de Damasco de Julio Cortázar." Interview with Rosa Montero. *El País Semanal,* March 13, 1982, https://elpais.com/elpais/2015/07/22/eps/1437562493_886 614.html

Cortázar, Julio. *Fantomas contra los vampiros multinacionales. Una utopia realizable.* Excelsion, 1975.

Cortázar, Julio. *Fantomas Versus the Multinational Vampires, An Attainable Utopia.* Translated by David Kurnick. Semiotexte, 2015.

Cortázar, Julio. *Hopscotch: A Novel.* Translated by Gregory Barrasa. Random House, 1966.

Cortázar, Julio. *Rayuela.* Sudamericana, 1963.

De Castro, Juan E. *Mario Vargas Llosa: Public Intellectual in Neoliberal Latin America.* U of Arizona P, 2011.

Donoso, José. *The Boom in Spanish American Literature: A Personal History.* Translated by Gregory Kolovakos. Columbia UP, 1977.

Donoso, José. *Casa de campo.* Seix Barral, 1978.

Donoso, José. *A House in the Country.* Translated by David Pritchard and Suzanne Jill Levine. Knopf, 1984.

Donoso, José. *The Obscene Bird of Night.* Translated by Hardie St. Martin and Leonard Mades. Knopf, 1973.

Donoso, José. *El obsceno pájaro de la noche.* Seix Barral, 1970.

Elizondo, Salvador. *Farabeuf, o, la crónica de un instante.* Mortiz, 1965.

Elizondo, Salvador. *Farabeuf: The Chronicle of an Instant.* Translated by John Incledon. Garland, 1992.

"Encuesta sobre la major novela peruana de todos los tiempos." *Revista Debate,* Vol. 82, 1995, pp. 48–60.

Esquivel, Laura. *Como agua para chocolate: novela de entregas mensuales, amores y remedios caseros.* Planeta, 1989.

Esquivel, Laura. *Like Water for Chocolate: A Novel in Monthly Installments, with Recipes, Romances, and Home Remedies.* Translated by Carol and Thomas Christensen. Doubleday, 1992.

Foster, David William. "Teaching Brazil and the Boom." *Teaching the Latin American Boom,* edited by Lucille Kerr and Alejandro Herrero-Olaizola, MLA, 2015, pp. 137–46.

Fuentes, Carlos. *The Death of Artemio Cruz.* Translated by Alfred MacAdam. Farrar, Straus and Giroux 1991.

Fuentes, Carlos. *Holy Place.* Translated by Suzanne Jill Levine. Dutton, 1972.

Fuentes, Carlos. *La muerte de Artemio Cruz*. Fondo de Cultura Económica, 1962.

Fuentes, Carlos. *La nueva novela hispanoamericana*. Mortiz, 1969.

Fuentes, Carlos. *La región más transparente*. Fondo de Cultura Económica, 1958.

Fuentes, Carlos. *Terra Nostra*. Mortiz, 1975.

Fuentes, Carlos. *Terra Nostra*. Translated by Margaret Sayers Peden. Farrar, Straus, and Giroux, 1976.

Fuentes, Carlos. *Where the Air Is Clear*. Translated by Sam Hileman. I. Obolensky, 1960.

Fuentes, Carlos. *Zona sagrada*. Siglo XXI, 1967.

García Márquez, Gabriel. *The Autumn of the Patriarch*. Translated by Gregory Rabassa. Harper and Row, 1976.

García Márquez, Gabriel. *Cien años de soledad*. Sudamericana, 1967.

García Márquez, Gabriel. *El coronel no tiene quien le escriba*. Aguirre Editor, 1961.

García Márquez, Gabriel. *La hojarasca*. Ediciones S.L.B, 1955.

García Márquez, Gabriel. *In Evil Hour*. Translated by Gregory Rabassa. Harper and Row, 1979.

García Márquez, Gabriel. *Leafstorm*. Translated by Gregory Rabassa. Penguin, 1996.

García Márquez, Gabriel. *La mala hora*. Era, 1966.García Márquez, Gabriel. *No One Writes to the Colonel*. Translated by J. S. Bernstein. Harper and Row, 1968.

García Márquez, Gabriel. *One Hundred Years of Solitude*. Translated by Gregory Rabassa, Harper Perennial, 2006.

García Márquez, Gabriel. *El otoño del patriarca*. Bruguera, 1975.

García Márquez, Gabriel. "¿Problemas de la novela?" *Obra periodística I*, edited by Jacques Girard, Oveja Negra, 1983, pp. 212–13.

Garro, Elena. *Recollections of Things to Come*. Translated by Ruth L. C. Simms. U of Texas P, 1969.

Garro, Elena. *Recuerdos del porvenir*. Mortiz, 1963.

Gilman, Claudia. *Entre la pluma y el fusil. Debates y dilemas del escritor revolucionario en América Latina*. Siglo XXI, 2003.

Goddard, C. Roe. *U.S. Foreign Economic Policy and the Latin American Debt Issue*. Kindle ed., Routledge, 1993.

Harss, Luis, and Barbara Dohmann. *Into the Mainstream: Conversations with Latin American Authors*. Harper and Row, 1967.

Herbert, Julián. "Mi nombre es Ixca Cienfuegos." *Letras Libres*, July 4, 2012. https://www.letraslibres.com/mexico/mi-nombre-es-ixca-cienfuegos

Ingham, Chris. *The Rough Guide to The Beatles*. 3rd ed. Rough Guides, 2009.

Kennedy, William. "The Great Novel of the Americas." *One Hundred Years of Solitude* by Gabriel García Márquez, Harper Perennial, 2006, pp. 8–12.

Kerr, Lucille. "Imagining Narrative Territories." *Literary Cultures of Latin America: A Comparative History*, edited by Mario J. Valdés and Djelal Kadir, Oxford UP, 2004, pp. 594–610.

Martin, Gerald. "Boom." *Encyclopedia of Latin American and Caribbean Literature 1900–2003*, edited by Daniel Balderston and Mike González, Routledge, 2004, pp. 74–77.

Moraña, Mabel. *Arguedas/Vargas Llosa: Dilemmas and Assemblages*. Translated by Andrew Ascherl. Palgrave Macmillan, 2016.

Onetti, Juan Carlos. *The Pit and Tonight*. Translated by Peter Bush. Quartet Books, 1991.

Onetti, Juan Carlos. *El pozo*. Arca, 1939.

Poniatowska, Elena. *Hasta no verte Jesús mío*. Era, 1969.

Poniatowska, Elena. *Here's to You, Jesusa!* Translated by Deanna Heikkinen. Penguin, 2002.

Puig, Manuel. *El beso de la mujer araña*. Seix Barral, 1976.

Puig, Manuel. *Betrayed by Rita Hayworth*. Translated by Suzanne Jill Levine. Dutton, 1971.

Puig, Manuel. *Kiss of the Spider Woman*. Translated by Thomas Colchie. Vintage, 1980.

Puig, Manuel. *La traición de Rita Hayworth*. Centro Editor de América Latina, 1967.

Rama, Ángel. "El 'boom' en perspectiva." *Más allá del boom: literatura y mercado*. Edited by Ángel Rama. Folios ediciones, 1984, pp. 51–110.

Roa Bastos, Augusto. *I the Supreme*. Translated by Helen R. Lane. Knopf, 1986.

Roa Bastos, Augusto. *Yo el supremo*. Siglo XXI, 1974.

Rodríguez Monegal, Emir. "The New Latin American Novel." *Books Abroad*, vol. 40, no. 1, 1971, pp. 45–50.

Rulfo, Juan. *Pedro Páramo*. Fondo de Cultura Económica, 1955.

Rulfo, Juan. *Pedro Páramo*. Translated by Lysander Kemp. Grove Press, 1969.

Sainz, Gustavo. *Gazapo*. Mortiz, 1965.

Sainz, Gustavo. *La princesa del Palacio de Hierro*. Oceano, 1974.

Sánchez, Luis Rafael. *La guaracha del Macho Camacho*. Ediciones de la Flor, 1976.

Sánchez, Luis Rafael. *Macho Camacho's Beat*. Translated by Gregory Rabassa. Pantheon, 1980.

Sarduy, Severo. *De dónde son los cantantes*. Mortiz, 1967.

Sarduy, Severo. *From Cuba with a Song*. Translated by Suzanne Jill Levine. Sun and Moon, 1994.

Scorza, Manuel. *The Ballad of Agapito Robles*. Translated by Anna-Marie Aldaz. Peter Lang, 1996.

Scorza, Manuel. *Cantar de Agapito Robles*. Monte Ávila, 1977.

Scorza, Manuel. *Drums for Rancas*. Translated by Edith Grossman. Harper and Row, 1977.

Scorza, Manuel. *Garabombo, the Invisible*. Translated by Anna-Marie Aldaz. Peter Lang, 1994.

Scorza, Manuel. *Historia de Garabombo el invisible*. Planeta, 1972.

Scorza, Manuel. *El jinete insomne*. Monte Ávila, 1977.

Scorza, Manuel. *Redoble por Rancas*. Planeta, 1970.

Scorza, Manuel. *Requiem for a Lightning Bolt*. Translated by Translated by Anna-Marie Aldaz. Peter Lang, 2000.

Scorza, Manuel. *The Sleepless Rider*. Translated by Anna-Marie Aldaz. Peter Lang, 1996.

Scorza, Manuel. *La tumba del relámpago*. Siglo XXI, 1979.

Siskind, Mariano. *Cosmopolitan Desires: Global Modernity and World Literature in Latin America*. Northwestern UP, 2014.

Vargas Llosa, Mario. *Aunt Julia and the Scriptwriter*. Translated by Helen R. Lane. Faber, 1983.

Vargas Llosa, Mario. *La casa verde*. Seix Barral, 1966.

Vargas Llosa, Mario. *Captain Pantoja and the Special Service*. Translated by Gregory Kolavakos and Ronald Christ. Noonday P, 1990.

Vargas Llosa, Mario. *La ciudad y los perros*. Seix Barral, 1963.

Vargas Llosa, Mario. *Conversación en La Catedral*. Seix Barral, 1969.

Vargas Llosa, Mario. *Conversation in the Cathedral*. Translated by Gregory Rabassa. Harper and Row, 1975.

Vargas Llosa, Mario. *The Green House*. Translated by Gregory Rabassa. Avon, 1968.

Vargas Llosa, Mario. "The Latin American Novel Today." Translated by Nick Mills, *Books Abroad*, vol. 44, no. 1, 1971, pp. 7–16.

Vargas Llosa, Mario. "Literature Is Fire." *Making Waves: Essays*. Translated by John King. Penguin, 1998, pp. 70–74.

Vargas Llosa, Mario. "Novela primitiva y novela de creación." *Revista de la Universidad de México*, vol. 10, June 10, 1969, pp. 29–36.

Vargas Llosa, Mario. *Pantaleón y las visitadoras*. Seix Barral, 1973.

Vargas Llosa, Mario. *La tía Julia y el escribidor*. Seix Barral, 1977.

Vargas Llosa, Mario. *The Time of the Hero*. Translated by Lysander Kemp. Grove P, 1966.

Vásquez, Juan Gabriel. "Juan Gabriel Vásquez en el Instituto Cervantes de Dublin." *Youtube*, December 10, 2012. https://www.youtube.com/watch?v=xufZ6xYwkyI&t=494s

Vásquez, Juan Gabriel. *El ruido de las cosas al caer*. Alfaguara, 2011.Vásquez, Juan Gabriel. *The Sound of Things Falling*. Translated by Anne McLean. Bloomsbury, 2012.

William, Raymond L. *Mario Vargas Llosa*. Ungar, 1986.

CHAPTER 8

THE POSTMODERN NOVEL AND THE POST-BOOM IN LATIN AMERICA

JOSÉ MANUEL MEDRANO
AND RAYMOND L. WILLIAMS

THE roots of modern, postmodern, and post-Boom narrative are to be found in various manifestations of avant-garde Latin American fiction in the 1920s and 1930s. More specifically, scholars have pointed to the *Semana de Arte Moderna* in Brazil, as well as the fiction of Gilberto Owen (1904–1952) and Jaime Torres Bodet (1902–1974) in Mexico and Vicente Huidobro (1893–1948) in Chile, in addition to a host of others who were the forerunners to the modern and postmodern novel in Latin America, which was produced from 1945 to 2015. The key connectors between the *vanguardias* and the rise of the modern novel were Jorge Luis Borges's (1899–1986) short-story collection *Ficciones* (1944) and Miguel Ángel Asturias's (1899–1974) novel *El señor presidente* (*The President,* 1946). After briefly reviewing the avant-gardes, as well as the terms "modern," "postmodern," and "post-Boom," this essay covers Latin American fiction from Asturias and Agustín Yáñez (1904–1980) in the 1940s, to Roberto Bolaño (1953–2003), to Isabel Allende (1942–), and Cristina Rivera Garza (1964–) in the twentieth century, as well as their respective contemporaries. Among the post-Boom novelists still writing today, Allende, Carmen Boullosa (1954–), Carlos Orlando Pardo (1947–), and César Aira (1949–) are among the most prominent.

The modern, postmodern, and post-Boom novel in Latin America follow patterns comparable to the modernism of Marcel Proust, James Joyce, T. S. Elliot, Franz Kafka, and William Faulkner, as well and the postmodernism of Italo Calvino, John Barth, William H. Gass, and Thomas Pynchon. The commonly accepted tenets of literary modernism, such as the formal innovations of using multiple points of view, fragmentation, and neologisms, involved a breakdown in the nineteenth-century insistence on causality, and an incumbent search for order in a chaotic world. Although some critics have pointed to the uncritical stances of European and North American literary modernism, this is not necessarily the case with the modern novel in Latin America.

Literary modernism in Europe and the United States has been often associated with a subjectivist relativism, as Steven Conner pointed out in his 1989 book *Postmodernist Culture, An Introduction to the Theories of the Contemporary*. This modernism had relatively little to do with the world of "ideas or substances" that may be objectively known in themselves. A first generation of modernists in Latin America, consisting of relatively ignored writers such as the Brazilian Mário de Andrade (1893–1945), the Mexican Jaime Torres Bodet (1902–1974), Huidobro, and the Peruvian Martín Adan (1908–1985), among others, unabashedly subscribed to this credo. Novels such as Mário de Andrade's *Macunaíma: el héroe sin ningún carácter* (*Macunaíma: The Hero with no Character*, 1928) and Torres Bodet's *Primero de enero* (*January First*, 1934), for example, were prominent celebrations of this subjectivist relativism. In the early examples of Latin American modernism (not to be confused with *modernismo*), truth became nothing more than the subjective experience of individuals. Later on, beyond this period of the avant-garde, Asturias, in *El señor presidente*, filters the image of an authoritarian dictator through several characters' consciousness, employing well-known narrative strategies in Anglo-American modernism. Similarly, Gabriel García Márquez (1927–2014) used Faulknerian strategies in this early work, most prominently *La hojarasca* (*Leaf Storm*, 1955), *El coronel no tiene quién le escriba* (*No One Writes to the Coronel*, 1961), and *La mala hora* (*In Evil Hour*, 1962), all three of which privilege individual consciousness.

The modernist novel in Latin America has spanned from the 1920s to the present, but its most noteworthy production was from the 1940s (with Borges, Asturias, Yáñez, and the Cuban Alejo Carpentier [1904–1980]) to the 1960s, culminating in such complex products of reconstructing individual consciousness as Juan Rulfo's *Pedro Páramo* (*Pedro Páramo*, 1955), Carlos Fuentes's (1928–2012) *La muerte de Artemio Cruz* (*The Death of Artemio Cruz*, 1962), Álvaro Cepeda Samudio's *La casa grande* (*La Casa Grande: A Novel*, 1962), Mario Vargas Llosa's (1936–) *La ciudad y los perros* (*The Time of the Hero*, 1963), and Julio Cortázar's (1914–1984) *Rayuela* (*Hopscotch*, 1963). In Anglo-American and European modernism, this subjectivism was accompanied by several important monuments about the end of individual subjectivity, including Joyce's and T. S. Eliot's respective defenses of impersonality. Fuentes made a similar statement in his novel *La muerte de Artemio Cruz*, employing the protagonist's subjective (first-person and second-person narrative perspective) passages and the passages with the detachment of the third person. Similarly, the Colombians Eduardo Santa (1927–2020) and Eutiquio Leal (1928–1997), with their novels *El girasol* (*The Sunflower*, 1956) and *Después de la noche* (*After the Night*, 1962), respectively, demonstrated that individual consciousness could be developed along with impersonal distance in the same novel.

Before the 1960s Boom, the 1940s novels that were indicators of a general movement toward modernism in the Latin American novel were *El señor presidente* (1945) by Asturias, *Al filo del agua* (*The Edge of the Storm*, 1947) by Yáñez, *Adán Buenosayres* (1948) by Argentine Leopoldo Marechal (1900–1970), and *El reino de este mundo* (*The Kingdom of this World*, 1949) by Carpentier. These four novels, seen together, represented a handbook of the stratagems and aesthetics of the high modernism of North America and Europe, and, at the same time, of stories based on local history and cultural traditions.

A strong current of modernist narrative influenced by Faulkner arose in several regions of Latin America, and most prominently in Colombia. It was represented by the following novels: García Márquez's *La hojarasca*, Santa's novel *El girasol*, Héctor Rojas Herazo's (1921–2002) *Respirando el verano* (Breathing the Summer, 1962), Cepeda Samudio's (1926–1972) *La casa grande* (1962), and Eutiquio Leal's *Después de la noche*. With these five novels appearing over a period of seven years, the Colombian novel, written under the sign of Faulkner and modernism, became unequivocally "modern."

The culminating moment of Latin American modernism was the Boom. However, it can hardly be viewed (as Fredric Jameson would have it in the case of First World modernism), simply as a product of capitalism that employs containment strategies to deny the truth of history. Thus, in his novel *La muerte de Artemio Cruz*, Fuentes does not utilize the strategies of containment that Jameson found in certain modernist novels, which, in Latin America, would only be associated with 1920s *vanguardia* novels, such as Brazilian Mário de Andrade's *Macunaíma: el héroe sin ningún carácter* and the novels of the Chilean Vicente Huidobro, such as *Mío Cid Campeador: Hazaña* (The Cid: Feat, 1930). In fact, Fuentes's early novels are a critique of Mexico's version of modern capitalism. All in all, the Latin American novelists of the 1960s Boom were fully committed to social criticism.

Regarding the Latin American postmodern novel, it follows the patterns associated with 1970s and 1980s North Atlantic postmodernism: disruption, discontinuity, decentering, dislocation, indeterminacy, and antilocalization. Postmodernism is inherently contradictory: it tends to install and then subvert the very concepts it challenges, as seen in the 1970s writing of the Cuban Severo Sarduy (1937–1993) and in the twenty-first-century fiction of the Colombian Carlos Pardo Viña (1970–). Postmodernism often questions dominant discourses more explicitly than modernism, as evidenced in the Chilean Diamela Eltit's (1949–) writing. Ihab Hassan contrasted modern and postmodern fiction in *The Dismemberment of Orpheus: Toward a Postmodern Literature* (1971). Yet, there are still unresolvable contradictions within postmodernism. Severo Sarduy, Ricardo Piglia (1941–2017), and Alberto Duque López (1943–2010) are among the best-known Latin American postmodern writers.

According to Umberto Eco, the postmodern was born when we realized that the world had no fixed center. Michel Foucault, for his part, argued convincingly that power was not something unitary that existed outside of us. In Latin American literature, the postmodern moment began with the rise of Borges, who became a significant influence on many European theorists and an even more groundbreaking writer for the postmodern Latin American novelists of the 1960s and 1970s. The two key books were *Ficciones* (1944) and *El Aleph* (The Aleph, 1949). One of the constant images in Borges's fiction was that of the universe as a centerless labyrinth; he developed this figure most famously in the stories "El jardín de los senderos que se bifurcan" ("The Garden of Forking Paths") and "La biblioteca de Babel" ("The Library of Babel"). Along these lines, language functions as a priority over empirical reality in another short story, "Las ruinas circulares" ("The Circular Ruins"), where the protagonist has the power to dream a person into existence. At the end of this story, he realizes that he, too, is nothing more than someone else's dream. Thus, the imagined reality of dreams and language are both more powerful than empirical reality.

Borges's short stories "The Library of Babel" and "Pierre Menard, autor del Quijote" ("Pierre Menard, Author of the Quixote") are also key texts for postmodern fiction in Latin America, as they blur the line between fiction and essay, opening the way for the fictionalized, theoretical prose of Argentine Piglia, Venezuelan José Balza (1939–), Mexican José Emilio Pacheco (1939–2014), and Colombian Darío Jaramillo (1947–), among others. A new generation of this kind of postmodern writers, born since 1960, would include Mexican Rivera Garza and Colombian Carlos Pardo Viña.

The discourse and concepts of First World postmodernism were circulating in Latin America in the 1980s and 1990s—*lo indeterminado* (the indeterminate), *la problematización del centro* (the problematization of the center), *la marginalidad* (marginality) *la discontinuidad* (discontinuity), *la simulación* (simulation), and the like. One of Diamela Eltit's favorite terms, *precariedad* (precariousness), is similar to "the provisional," which many North Atlantic postmodern writers and thinkers emphasized. In the 1990s and twenty-first century, Rivera Garza has continued with the elaboration of the provisional. Arguably, the most influential postmodern author in European, North American, as well as Latin American, postmodernism is Borges. Borges has been cited by the European poststructuralist theorists Roland Barthes and Foucault. He has influenced both Rivera Garza and North American Rikki Ducornet, both of whom are contemporary postmodern writers.

After Borges, the most notable contributors to the later development of a Latin American postmodern fiction were João Guimarães Rosa (1908–1967) with *Grande Sertão: Veredas* (*The Devil to Pay in the Backlands*, 1956) and Cortázar with *Rayuela*. These two novels were not postmodern works in themselves, but they implied a radical proposal for experimental and postmodern fiction. Following Cortázar's and Guimarães Rosa's leads, writers of the late 1960s and 1970s began publishing postmodern novels usually inspired by either one or more of these novels. *Tres tristes tigres* (*Three Trapped Tigers*, 1967) by Cuban Guillermo Cabrera Infante (1929–2005), *Siberia Blues* (*Siberia Blues*, 1967) by Argentine Néstor Sánchez (1935–2003), and *La traición de Rita Hayworth* (*Betrayed by Rita Hayworth*, 1968) by Argentine Manuel Puig (1932–1990), are the key examples. Two key works followed these early novels for the Latin American postmodern—Sarduy's *Cobra* (*Cobra*, 1972) and Brazilian Osman Lins's (1924–1978) *Avalovara* (*Avalovara*, 1973).

Soon several other radically experimental novelists began appearing on the Latin American scene, including Argentines Reina Roffe (1951–) and Héctor Libertella (1945–2006); the Mexicans Salvador Elizondo (1932–2006), Boullosa and José Emilio Pacheco; the Colombians Rafael Humberto MorenoDurán (1945–2005), Darío Jaramillo (1947–), and Albalucía Ángel (1939–); the José Emilio Pacheco, the Venezuelan José Balza (1939–); and the Chilean Eltit. Eltit continued the linguistic experimentation explored by Sarduy, although she openly rejected parody. These writers pursued radically different kinds of postmodernisms—perhaps a postmodern phenomenon in itself: if Culture (with a capital C and in the singular) becomes cultures in postmodernity, as Linda Hutcheon has suggested in *A Poetics of Postmodern ism, History, Theory, Fiction* (1988) and in *The Politics of Postmodernism* (1989), then the provisional character and heterogeneity of postmodern cultures in Latin America have been even more extreme than in the global North. Frequently, Latin American postmodern writers, like their North American counterparts, have been interested in heterogeneous discourses of theory and literature. Sarduy's essays read like fiction and vice versa; Eltit's fiction appropriated the theoretical discourse of Derrida, Baudrillard, Deleuze, and others. Balza preferred not to distinguish between essays and the fiction he called his "ejercicios" (exercises).

Latin American postmodern fiction shared in several of the trends of North American postmodernism of the 1980s and 1990s, as noted by Hassan, Brian McHale, Hutcheon, and Steven Conner. A broad range of scholars share the consensus that the postmodern as a cultural phenomenon arose in the 1960s, a noteworthy parallel with Gadamer's *Truth and Method*, which was published in 1960 and that places emphasis on the truth, above all, of language. This privileging of language in itself became doctrine for postmodern writers. Many Latin American women writers share what Hutcheon calls the postmodern valuing of the margins with their First World counterparts. Women postmodern novelists in Latin America frequently write with a self-conscious awareness of feminist and poststructuralist theory. This is the case with Albalucía Ángel, whose novels incorporate the language of feminist theory, as do the writings of the Brazilian Helena Parente Cunha (1929–), Argentine Sylvia Molloy (1938–), Diamela Eltit, and others.

Several North Atlantic scholars observed the postmodern bridging of the gap between elite and popular art. Since the 1960s, the Latin American writers who have been the object of intense academic study have, at the same time, frequently been bestsellers, particularly García Márquez, Vargas Llosa, Allende, Luis Rafael Sánchez (1936–), and Puig. Three of the works that have sold particularly well to both the general public and to academe (and seemingly bridged the gap between elite and popular art) are Vargas Llosa's *La tía Julia y el escribidor* (*Aunt Julia and the Script Writer*, 1977), Allende's *La casa de los espíritus* (*The House of the Spirits*, 1982), and García Márquez's *Crónica de una muerte anunciada* (*Chronicle of a Death Foretold*, 1981)—three novels that could arguably be called, for a variety of reasons, postmodern. For Hutcheon, postmodernism's relationship with contemporary mass culture is not just one of implication, but also one of critique.

Eltit's postmodern novelistic project was born in the 1980s, after she began participating in the underground resistance in Pinochet's Chile during the 1970s and early 1980s. Her first two novels can most obviously be associated with the postmodernism of First World writers and Latin Americans such as Sarduy and Piglia. *Lumpérica* (*L. Iluminata*, 1983) takes place in a public square in Santiago de Chile, has no real plot, and has as protagonist a character named L. Iluminada. This public square is Baudrillard's postmodern world, where human beings have the same exchange value as merchandise. Eltit's second novel, *Por la patria* (*For the Country*, 1986), is even more markedly experimental. She alludes to Pinochet regime's political repression, always returning to the historical origins of language, oppression, and resistance. In this novel, she associates Medieval wars with the contemporary situation. Consequently, Eltit's postmodernist novel is patently historical and political, and could be identified as an allegorical fiction of resistance. Her third novel, *El cuarto mundo* (*The Fourth World*, 1988), deals with family relationships and is related by two narrators: the first half of the work is narrated by a young boy, María Chipia, the son of the family, and his twin sister tells the second half. *El cuarto mundo* does not attempt to present broad historical truths as is the case with *Cien años de soledad* (*One Hundred Years of Solitude*, 1967) or *La muerte de Artemio Cruz*. The generation of García Márquez and Fuentes remained not only overtly historical, but also engaged in a project of social emancipation based on the uncovering of truth. However, *El cuarto mundo* is about other kinds of truths—the truths of private and public space, the truths of relationships, the truths of the body, and the questioning of the possibilities that language holds for articulating these truths.

El cuarto mundo and a few other Latin American postmodern novels question the truth industry of modernism. In the Latin American case, the novel of the 1970s and 1980s moved from utopia to what Foucault calls heterotopia—from the centered and historical universe of the utopian Carpentier and García Márquez to the centerless universe of the postmodern Severo Sarduy, Chico Buarque (1944–) and Diamela Eltit. What is at stake for the Latin American postmodern authors who have appeared since the late 1960s—Pacheco, Sarduy, Buarque, Eltit, and others—is not truth. Jean-François Lyotard in *The Postmodern Condition, A Report on Knowledge. Theory and History of Literature* (1989) claims that the question is no longer "Is it true?" but "What use is it?" and "How much is it worth?" The latter are the questions posed in *El cuarto mundo* and in much of what might be called Latin American postmodern fiction.

The juxtaposition of García Márquez's modern literary project, which includes *Cien años de soledad* (and his other fiction set in Macondo and published from 1955 to 1967), and Eltit's postmodern writing suggests the transitional state of truth in Latin American fiction and the particular conditions—difficult ones under which truth claims can be considered. *Cien años de soledad* plays on images of center, with the ultimate centers being the Buendía family and Macondo. In contrast, Eltit's figures represent marginality, just as the art of her generation in Chile, *la avanzada* (avant-garde), uses imagery of the marginalized.

In the twenty-first century, some writers have successfully drawn from both the modern and postmodern trends, most prominently Rivera Garza, the Chilean Bolaño, and the Colombian Evelio Rosero (1958–). Rivera Garza and Rosero have published several postmodern novels in the twenty-first century, and Bolaño reaffirmed the vitality of both kinds of fiction in 2004 with his novel *2666*, an encyclopedia of postmodern strategies and motifs. One of the most experimental postmodern novels to appear in Mexico in the twenty-first century was *La torre y el jardín* (*The Tower and the Garden*, 2012) by Alberto Chimal (1970–). The postmodern novel in Mexico, Colombia, and Argentina offers a representative sample of trends throughout Latin America.

On the other hand, the novel of the post-Boom was a reaction specifically against the modern novel in Latin American associated with the 1960s Boom. As Donald Shaw argued, early post-Boom writers, such as Antonio Skármeta (1940–), Mempo Gardinelli

(1947–), and Luisa Valenzuela (1938–), generally rejected the aesthetic and political agenda of the writers of the 1960s Boom. Unlike the writers of the Boom in the late 1960s and the postmodern writers of the 1970s and 1980s, post-Boom writers rejected these novelists' hyper-experimentation. The Puerto Rican Rosario Ferré (1938–2016) and the Chilean Allende became leading writers of the post-Boom while insisting on storytelling as opposed to technical experimentation. Thus, Allende in particular and the post-Boom writers in general were more commercially successful than the postmodern writers. Allende's novel *La casa de los espíritus* has been as widely read in English as any novel of the Boom. Boullosa and Aira have also been widely read.

Much of Mexico's literary culture has been postmodernized, commercialized, and sometimes trivialized from the 1960s to today. The Mexican middle class read and heard the names of poet Octavio Paz (1914–1998) and Fuentes regularly, and the novelists of the Boom remained in vogue in the 1980s and 1990s, above all, García Márquez and Vargas Llosa. They also read Stephen King, Irving Wallace, Michael Crichton, Tom Robbins, and James Michener in both Spanish and English. Bookstores were replete with their novels in both languages; the same bookstores were also filled with self-help paperbacks in both languages.

However, Fuentes and the other Boom writers were not the only novelists to penetrate mass consciousness in postmodern Mexico. The 1980s and 1990s witnessed the popularity of women writers, a phenomenon that began in Mexico with the mass marketing of the fiction of the Allende throughout Latin America by the Plaza y Janes publishing company, a Hispanic branch of the German multinational Bertelsmann. Two Mexicans, Ángeles Mastretta (1949–) and Laura Esquivel (1950–), followed in Allende's footsteps. Mastretta's *Arráncame la vida* (*Mexican Bolero*, 1988) was a bestseller in Mexico for a full two years in the late 1980s, followed by Esquivel's *Como agua para chocolate* (*Like Water for Chocolate*, 1990). The latter, the most commercially successful novel in Mexico during the early 1990s, became a movie distributed in Mexico, and soon thereafter became a commercially successful as both movie and novel in the United States. *Like Water for Chocolate* appeared on the *New York Times* bestseller list in 1993. Thus, Mastretta and Esquivel can be associated with some understandings of both the postmodern and modern.

An early literary manifestation of this crisis of modernism in Mexico was the fiction of the La Onda movement. Postmodern fiction in Mexico became a viable cultural expression by 1967, when José Emilio Pacheco published *Morirás lejos* (*You Will Die in a Distant Land*) and Fuentes, *Zona sagrada* (*Holy Place*) and *Cambio de piel* (*A Change of Skin*), followed in 1968 by *Inventando que sueño* (*Inventing that I'm Dreaming*) by José Agustín (1944–)—all works with some postmodern qualities. In addition to Pacheco, Fuentes, and Agustín, writers of Mexico's first wave of transitional postmodern fiction included Salvador Elizondo (1932–2006) and Gustavo Sainz (1940–2015). After 1968, a second wave of more patently postmodern fiction included some of the work of Fuentes, Agustín, Elizondo, and Sainz, as well as the postmodern work of Boullosa, Luis Arturo Ramos (1947–), María Luisa Puga (1944–2004), Brianda Domecq (1942–), Sergio Pitol (1933–2018), Federico Patán (1937–), Daniel Leyva (1949–2019), and Héctor

Manjarrez (1945–). With the publication of Fuentes's *Terra Nostra* (*Terra Nostra*) in 1975, the Mexican postmodern became clearly a dominant cultural force. Brian McHale has appropriately described *Terra Nostra* as one of the paradigmatic texts of postmodern writing, literally an anthology of postmodern themes and devices.

The first wave of Mexican transitional postmodern writing emanated directly from Borges and Cortázar, writers whom Pacheco and Fuentes popularized among Mexican intellectuals in the early 1960s. Fuentes already dominated the literary scene with his modernist works *La región más transparente* (*Where the Air is Clear*, 1958) and the previously mentioned *La muerte de Artemio Cruz*. They were totalizing novels that questioned the state project of modernizing Mexico initiated in the 1940s and soon to be internationally known as the "Mexican miracle." In these two novels, major narrative works of the century, Fuentes used many of the narrative strategies of the First World modernists, as did the modernists Yáñez, Juan Rulfo, Vicente Leñero (1933–2014), Juan García Ponce (1932–2003), and Fernando del Paso (1935–2018). The early reaction against this modernism came in the form of the irreverent young writers of La Onda, Gustavo Sainz, and José Agustín.

The early novels of Gustavo Sainz and José Agustín question the traditional boundaries between high and low culture, a common strategy of postmodern writers. Like Elizondo's *Farabeuf* (1965), Sainz's *Gazapo* (*Errata*, 1965) offers the reader a sense of both fiction and empirical reality as versions and possibilities, but shares little else with Elizondo's fiction. An early and key text of the Onda, *Gazapo* was a postmodern experiment: it brought the language of adolescents into the Mexican novel and the then new communication technologies, such as tape recorders and other media. Above all, Sainz's early fiction was an irreverent antidote to the dominant modernist practices in early 1960s Mexico. A story of relationships among teenagers and trivial actions, it seems apparently distant from Fuentes's and Pacheco's more evidently historical and political fiction. However, the history of *Gazapo* is that of a continual present in which the narrative transpires, for *Gazapo* privileges social reality by literally transcribing the events as they occur in Mexico City. *Gazapo* also privileges memory: what human memory might forget is recorded in precise detail on tapes. *Gazapo*, like much postmodern fiction, insists that we, as readers, remember as active participants; forgetting is an option. After *Gazapo*, Sainz rejected the experimentation of his early work and wrote more accessible and commercial novels that have led some critics to associate him with the post-Boom.

By 1967, signs of this early postmodernism were evident with the publication of three experimental and historical novels that year: Pacheco's *Morirás lejos* and Fuentes's *Zona sagrada* and *Cambio de piel* (*A Change of Skin*). The three works have some of the epistemological qualities of modernist fiction and some of the ontological qualities typical of postmodernist writing. Pacheco and Fuentes ask epistemological questions in these novels, such as: How can I interpret this world of which I am part? What is there to be known? Who knows it? How do they know it and with what degree of certainty? More specifically, they explore what the limits of the knowable are. These three texts also pose postmodernist ontological questions: What happens when different kinds of worlds are placed in confrontation? When are boundaries between the worlds violated? What is the mode of existence of a text, and what is the mode of existence of the world it projects?

In *Morirás lejos*, as in Fuentes's *Zona sagrada* and *Cambio de piel*, Pacheco questions how we know the world and the degree of certainty of our knowledge. *Morirás lejos* includes historical references to such historical events as the experience of the Jews under attack by the Romans in Israel in the first century CE, and the Holocaust in Poland during the Second World War. Pachecothe-modernist questions how the reader knows this world of human atrocity by rewriting and reinventing Jewish history in a fragmented form that invites analysis. The degree of certainty with which the reader believes Pacheco's text varies as the novel progresses: all the narrative segments become questionable. In the end, little certainty is possible.

Morirás lejos consists of 101 narrative segments that develop, on one level, as a modernist novel that moves from chaos to unity. The apparent chaos lies in the fact that the narration moves from one narrative segment to another in time and space, across centuries and nations, from the first century CE to the twentieth, from Israel and Europe to Mexico. Adding to this initial impression of chaos is the presence of a series of necessarily ambiguous narrative segments ("Salónica") that systematically negate much of what they affirm. These "Salónica" sections initially portray a character named Erne (Em in English) who, from the window of an apartment building in Mexico City, observes a character named Alguien (Someone) sitting on a park bench below, reading a newspaper. Once this situation is clarified, however, the narrator begins subverting most of the operating premises about this starting premise or situation. Consequently, the reader necessarily questions whether Erne and Alguien really exist and whether the situation ever took place. Finally, in the early stages of the novel, the reader questions what relationships might exist between the destruction of the Jews in Israel and the novel's setting in Mexico City, between the Holocaust in Warsaw and Mexico City.

Pacheco's generation of Mexican intellectuals had read Cortázar's *Rayuela* with interest. *Morirás lejos* is one of the most challenging post-*Rayuela* novels to effect that novel's Morelli's proposal for a "lector macho" or (stated in less sexist terms) an "active reader." *Morirás lejos* contains a series of strategies that oblige the postmodern reader to engage in a more active role than required by the modernist complexities of Rulfo's *Pedro Paramo* and Fuentes's *La muerte de Artemio Cruz*. At several points, Pacheco offers affirmative readings and invites the reader to choose his or her own reading. The difference between the active involvement of the reader of much modernist fiction and the choices the reader must make in *Morirás lejos* represents Pacheco's postmodern turn in Mexico.

Fuentes's *Zona sagrada* and *Cambio de piel* share many postmodern qualities with *Morirás lejos*. The title of Pacheco's novel refers to an "other" space: a woman in Leipzig reads Eme's palm and tells him "You will die in a distant land." In this novel, as in the two works by Fuentes, the space of the novel is the territory of the other. The "holy place" of *Zona sagrada* is a sacred and personal space that, initially, is "far from my mother's territory, at the other end of the city" (28).[1] Time after, the narrator-protagonist, who occupies various urban spaces from Mexico City to Rome and from Paris to Orvieto, asks "Is there another place?" (125).[2] This is the postmodern question par excellence with respect to space. In another instance, he expresses the desire to be, as he says in English in the Spanish original, "out of bounds" (77, 96). Space in *Zona sagrada*, like the characters, is in constant transformation—a constant rearranging of boundaries. The narrator states at one point: "Nothing unfolds, all is transfigured" (55).[3] Indeed, like space, characters are in a constant state of transformation, emphasizing their indeterminate and unfixed quality. The protagonist himself, the twenty-nine-year-old Guillermo Nervo, suffers an identity crisis under the shadow of a dominant mother, a film celebrity. He finds no resolution to this crisis but, rather, speaks of his "other being" (123).[4]

The transitional postmodern period in Mexico closes with the Tlatelolco massacre and two experimental novels of 1968, Agustín's *Inventando que sueño* and Elizondo's *El hipogeo secreto* (*The Secret Crypt*, 1968). Both are so experimental, in fact, that many readers in the late 1960s were unsure if they should even be identified as "novels." *Inventando que sueño* consists of a set of stories that can be read separately or as a novel. As one critic has pointed out, it functions like a rock concept album, while, at the same time, rock music is a major presence in this book. Like Fuentes's *Gringo viejo* (*The Old Gringo*, 1985), *Inventando que sueño* is metafiction but not historiographical metafiction. In the cases of Agustín and Elizondo, history is now, told as in the present moment. Like much postmodern fiction, the structure of *Inventando que sueño* is metonymic, developing on the basis of associations. It provides different versions of the world represented, and like Elizondo's *El hipogeo secreto*, its main interests are more ontological than epistemological. In Elizondo's experimental metafiction, creating a character does not imply creating a "real" character.

After the hyper-experimentation of the late 1960s, which culminated in the fiction of Pacheco, Fuentes, Agustín, and Elizondo, post-1968 postmodern fiction in Mexico became progressively less hermetic and more accessible. Nevertheless, postmodern attitudes of the 1960s became more acute, leading to a metafictional literature of exhaustion by the late 1980s. In addition to the work of such internationally recognized writers as Fuentes, the later postmodern in Mexico included novelists such as Ramos, Boullosa, Puga, and Domecq who were widely read in Mexico and relatively unknown beyond, although Boullosa has been translated into English. Since the 1980s, it has been possible to associate Boullosa and Mastretta's more commercial storytelling with the post-Boom. These writers, as well as Allende, are arguably more optimistic in general about the future of Latin American society than were the writers of the 1960s Boom. They also tended to incorporate popular culture in their novels more than had been the case with the writers of the 1960s Boom or the earlier postmoderns.

Terra Nostra is Fuentes's rewriting of the architecture of "El Escorial," his major and culminating rereading of Latin American culture and history. In addition, it is the major project of Mexican postmodernity on identity, knowledge, and the novel itself. Vargas Llosa had asked the historical question "At what precise moment had Peru fucked itself up?" (3),[5] and, in an attempt to respond to this question, wrote a lengthy historical and political novel, *Conversación en La Catedral* (*Conversation in The Cathedral*). Near the end of *Terra Nostra*, Fuentes poses a similar question, but in broader terms:

"At what moment had Spanish America fucked everything up" (761).[6] In addition to the particulars of Latin American history, Fuentes is concerned with how history, culture, and identity are constructed and then understood. As a reader of José Ortega y Gasset and Foucault, Fuentes has understood history not as a compilation of immutable truths, but as a living world in transformation. Once again, displacement is one of the major actions in the novel.

Although *Terra Nostra* has some modernist, totalizing impulses, it exhibits closer proximity to the postmodern, justifying McHale's description of it as an anthology of postmodern themes and devices. As a postmodern text, *Terra Nostra* articulates the twelfth-century proclamation that "Nothing is true, everything is permitted." Attributed to Hasa-i-Sabbah in the year 1164, this statement is particularly appropriate because Fuentes, too, frequently returns to the Middle Ages in his quest to recover history and knowledge.

In the twenty-first century, the most significant additions to late-twentieth-century Mexican postmodern fiction have been the novels of Rivera Garza, Luis Felipe Lomelí (1975–), and Chimal. Authors of several books of fiction, they are among the most experimental writers in Mexico today. Future studies of twenty-first-century Mexican postmodern fiction will include novels such as Rivera Garza's *La cresta de Ilión* (*The Iliac Crest*, 2003) and Chimal's *La torre y el jardín*, two of the most radical Mexican fiction experiments thus far in the century.

Colombian postmodern fiction has its roots in the 1960s and can be most clearly identified in the novel *Mateo el flautista* (*Mateo the Flute Player*, 1968) by Alberto Duque López. Innovative precedents to postmodern fiction, hardly noticed in Colombia's tradition-bound literary culture, were the still ignored novels *Después de la noche* by Leal, *Los días más felices del año* (*The Happiest Days of the Year*, 1966) by Humberto Navarro, and *El terremoto* (*The Earthquake*, 1966) by Germán Pinzón. After the freedom of imagination inaugurated by the Borges and Cortázar (who were widely read by Colombia's young intellectuals in the 1960s), as well as García Márquez's *Cien años de soledad* and López's *Mateo el flautista* in Colombia, the postmodern innovators who appeared on the scene during the 1970s were Andrés Caicedo (1951–1977), Umberto Valverde (1947–), Albalucía Ángel, Rodrigo Parra Sandoval, and R. H. Moreno-Durán. Moreno-Durán authored a substantive body of innovative fiction during the 1980s and 1990s; other postmodern fiction writers who published their initial books in this period were Darío Jaramillo Agudelo (1947–), Boris Salazar (1955–), Hugo Chaparro Valderrama (1961–), Héctor Abad Faciolince (1958–), and Orietta Lozano (1956–).

Moreno-Durán published a hermetic trilogy titled *Femina Suite* (*Feminine Suite*, 1997) during the late 1970s and early 1980s, and then *Los felinos del Canciller* (*The Chancellor's Cats*, 1985) and *El caballero de la invicta* (*The Undefeated Gentleman*, 1993). He considered himself a postmodernist first, a Colombian second. His literary masters were Cervantes, the European moderns (particularly Robert Musil and Pierre Klossosky), Borges, Cortázar, and the Mexican Juan García Ponce. He also knew the American experimental writers well, from Ron Sukenick to William Gass and Robert Coover, all of whom he admired. The roots of Moreno-Durán's *Femina Suite* are found not in the empirical reality of Colombia but rather, as in the case of much postmodern fiction, in modernist literature. He has explained how poems by T. S. Eliot and Paul Valéry generated the first novel of the trilogy, *Juego de damas* (*Ladies' Game*, 1977). The reader's most immediate literary association with *Juego de damas* is the work that announced the postmodern project in Latin America, Cortázar's *Rayuela*: elements of the former (such as the split columns on the page) and its content (such as youths listening to jazz) recall Cortázar's proposal for a new, open novel. *Juego de damas* deals with a group of female intellectuals, beginning with their radicalized student life in the 1960s and continuing through three stages of social climbing and power acquisition, stages in which the narrator identifies them as *Meninas* (young princesses), *Mandarinas* (middle-aged social climbers), and *Matriarcas* (matriarchs). Moreno-Durán presents elaborate relationships between language and power in most of his fiction: he employs a series of strategies, including parody and euphemism, to subvert language. This subversive activity is supported in the text by Monsalve, a character who serves as an author figure. The two main characters of the trilogy's second book, *El toque de Diana* (*Diana's Touch*, 1981), Augusto Jota and Catalina Arevalo, are also intellectuals who engage in the linguistic and sexual exercises found in *Juego de damas*. Augusto is a military man who fails both in the military and in his sexual relationship with Catalina; in the lovemaking of these two devotees of Latin, she "conjugated" while he "declined." In the third and most hermetic novel of the trilogy, *Finale capriccioso con Madonna* (*Whimsical Ending with Madonna*, 1983), Moreno-Durán explores to their limits both the eroticism of language and the language of eroticism. He poses the question, for example, of the relationship between "semantics" and "semen" and, in the process, creates a lengthy, playful, and dense description of a *ménage à trois*. From the introduction of Laura, the main character, who finds herself caught between two men, this novel explores a series of triangular relationships. It is a playful novel of erotic and linguistic excesses with intertextual allusions ranging from Marcel Proust to Elizondo. Other Colombian postmodern novelists—Albalucía Ángel, Darío Jaramillo Agudelo, Alberto Duque Lopez, Rodrigo Parra Sandoval, and Andrés Caicedo—are generally as demanding of their readers as Moreno-Durán.

Ángel's novels, particularly *Misiá Señora* (*Ms. Lady*, 1982) and *Las andariegas* (*The Travellers*, 1984), are part of a literary project that emanates directly from feminist theory and fiction. She had already published two early experimental novels, *Los girasoles en invierno* (*Sunflowers in the Winter*, 1970) and *Dos veces Alicia* (*Twice Alicia*, 1972), in addition to one on Colombia's La Violencia period, *Estaba la pájara pinta sentada en el verde limón* (*The Colored Bird Was Sitting on the Green Lemon Tree*, 1975). *Misiá señora* and *Las andariegas* are her most hermetic and feminist works. *Misiá señora* deals with different aspects of female sexuality and gender issues. The fictional world of this novel creates a tenuous line between empirical reality and pure imagination. An essential aspect of this richly imaginative experience is the creation of a new, feminist discourse as part of Ángel's feminist project. *Las andariegas* is a radical experiment that can be read, on the one hand, as a search for a "écriture féminine," on the other, as an evocation of a feminine identity. As in Moreno-Durán's fiction and in that of many postmodern writers of her generation, language is the principal subject in *Las andariegas*. Much of the narrative consists of brief phrases with unconventional punctuation often functioning as images. The use of verbal imagery in the novel is supported by visual images—a set of twelve drawings of a female body. Ángel also experiments with the physical space of language in the text, often in a manner similar to concrete poetry. In fact, four pages in the novel, composed of circular and semicircuilar arrangements of the names of famous women, can be read as concrete poetry.

Darío Jaramillo Agudelo's most characteristically postmodern novel, *La muerte de Alec* (*Alec's Death*, 1983), is also metafiction—in this case, a self-conscious meditation on the function of literature. It is an epistolary work directed to an unidentified "you," one of the characters implicated with Alec. This "you" and the letter writer are friends of Alec, who dies under the waters of a turbulent river. The characters are Colombian, but the novel is set in the United States; the letter writer is a novelist at the University of Iowa Writers' Program. Jaramillo Agudelo inverts the commonly accepted relationship between empirical reality and fiction: according to the narrator, it is not literature but life that is artificial, baroque, and twisted. Similarly, the acts of storytelling (placing order to a story) and interpretation (giving meaning to a story) become the main concern of the narrative, taking precedence over other forms of understanding reality.

Andrés Caicedo, Rodrigo Parra Sandoval (1938–), and Alberto Duque López have conceived different kinds of postmodern projects. Caicedo's *¡Que viva la música!* (*Liveforever*, 1977), like the fiction of the Mexico's first-generation postmodern writers of La Onda, involves a fictional world of 1960s rock music and drugs. Beyond this superficial comparison, however, Caicedo has little in common with the young Mexican writers. *¡Que viva la música!* is an experimental confrontation with a particular generation's cultural crisis in 1960s Colombia. Caicedo deals with this crisis with sobriety rather than with the humor and play of the Mexicans Sainz and Agustín. Parra Sandoval's *El álbum secreto del Sagrado Corazón* (*The Secret Album of the Sacred Heart*, 1978) is a collage of passages from diverse texts-books, newspapers, letters, documents, voices—representing an assault on the novel as a genre. The implied author suggests that the novelistic genre suffers limitations similar to those experienced by the protagonist, who lives in a very limiting and repressive religious seminary. As seen in Caicedo, Colombia's postmodern cultural crisis is depicted in Parra Sandoval's novel as a questioning of the nation's official and institutional images. *El álbum secreto del Sagrado Corazón* contains two main characters so ambiguously portrayed that they could well be the same person; Alberto Duque López proceeds similarly in *Mateo el flautista*, which in two parts offers two versions of the protagonist, Mateo. There is no authoritative voice in this narrative nor any authoritative version of Mateo's life. Consequently, *Mateo el flautista* is a quintessential postmodern text that explicitly emanates from *Rayuela*, as indicated by the novel's dedication to one of its characters, Rocamadour.

As noted by Raymond L. Williams and José Manuel Medrano in *90 años de la novela moderna en Colombia (1927-2017): De Fuenmayor a Potdevin* (2018), the most recent postmodern fiction in Colombia has been produced by Héctor Abad Faciolince, Hugo Chaparro Valderrama, Evelio Rosero, Philip Potdevin (1958–), Jorge Franco (1962–), and Carlos Pardo Viña, who have published a substantive body of works since the 1990s. Abad Faciolince's first novel, *Asuntos de un hidalgo disoluto* (*The Joy of Being Awake*, 1994), shares some of the narrative techniques found in Moreno-Durán's and Jaramillo Agudelo's novels, while functioning on the same uncertain narrative ambiguity of Balza and Ribeyro. Like Moreno-Durán and Severo Sarduy, Abad Faciolince cultivates the art of digression. *Asunto de un hidalgo disoluto* is the self-conscious and narcissistic story of a seventy-two-year old man who narrates the vicissitudes of his life from his adolescence, using the model of the Spanish picaresque novel. Like several postmodern writers, such as Jaramillo Agudelo and the Mexican Ramos, Abad Faciolince's novel presents a character who searches for signs and believes in a world of chance that is not limited by modern systems of rational thought.

Novelists associated with the post-Boom in Colombia have included Gustavo Álvarez Gardeazábal (1945–), Jorge Eliécer Pardo (1950–), Laura Restrepo (1950–), and Carlos Pardo Viña. Writing in a style influenced by García Márquez, Álvarez Gardeazábal was the most widely read post-Boom writer in Colombia in the 1970s. In the twenty-first century, the most widely read post-Boom storytellers have been Restrepo and Eliécer Pardo. The first wave to write radically experimental and self-conscious works in Argentina included the young writer Néstor Sánchez, whose novel *Siberia Blues* (1968) has intrigued many critics. With *Siberia Blues*, Cortázar's *62: Modelo para armar* (*62: a Model Kit*, 1968), Héctor Libertella's *El camino de las hiperbóreos* (*The Road of Southern Nations*, 1968), and Puig's fiction, in addition to Humberto Costantini's *Háblenme de Funes* (*Speak to Me about Funes*, 1970), it was evident that Argentine fiction was undergoing a revolution, clearly a break from the modernist tradition that had dominated in Argentina since the 1940s. One of the most experimental postmodern works published in Argentina, Sánchez's *Siberia Blues* is primarily concerned with language, even on the structure of its sentences.

After the publication of *Rayuela*, several Argentine and Latin American postmodern writers of the next generation accepted Morelli's invitation to create a novel more by the principles of chance than by reasoned logic (Morelli, a writer and literary theorist, is a character in Cortázar's novel). In *Rayuela's* chapter 62, Morelli suggests the possibility of creating a novel on the basis of random notes and observations. Cortázar himself pursued this idea in *62: modelo para armar*, a work in which even the very concepts of character and plot are questioned, and where the "entities" (who often appear more as abstractions than characters who represent human beings) are caught up in a pattern of events that seem to occur at random in four places: London, Paris, Vienna, and the City. Libertella, however, creates a protagonist in *El camino de las hiperbóreos*, but there is no traditional plot, other than the protagonist's vague search for something undefined. In addition, Libertella subverts any concept of individual identity by creating a character with multiple identities. In *Háblenme de Funes*, Costantini constructs a three-part structure consisting of three vaguely related stories, the third of which is metafiction dealing with a writer's creative process. This writer's protagonist, in turn, invents even more characters. Costantini uses entirely different styles in the three parts of this book, which are related in a variety of ways.

Manuel Puig's postmodern fiction, which he initiated with the (then) daringly experimental *La traición de Rita Hayworth* in 1968, consists of eight novels that had a major impact on Argentine and Latin American postmodern fiction since the 1970s and 1980s. *La traición de Rita Hayworth* required a postmodern reader who necessarily had an implied and unstable role to play. There is no controlling omniscient narrator to organize anecdotal material related by a multiplicity of voices that appear in the text in monologues or dialogues.

A second wave of Argentine postmodern fiction has been produced by writers well aware of their debts to Borges, Cortázar, and North Atlantic postmodern culture in general. Among the most prominent writers of this second wave of postmodern writers in Argentina are Piglia, Libertella, Molloy, and Pizarnik. As a group, these Argentine postmodern creators were, for the most part, politically progressive and among the most experimental fiction writers in Latin America. Piglia's fiction was arguably one of the most aesthetically innovative and politically significant since the writings of Cortázar. It posited a forceful response to Jameson's categorization of the postmodern as politically conservative. Noteworthy among Piglia's early books of fiction are *Nombre falso* (*Assumed Name*, 1975) and *Respiración artificial* (*Artificial Respiration*, 1980).

Rivera Garza and Bolaño are two of the most prominent novelists writing postmodern fiction in Latin America in the twenty-first century. Among the Brazilians, Nelson de Oliveira (1966–) has been among the more experimental Brazilian postmodern novelists. Other prominent postmodern writers are Bernardo Carvalho (1960–), Luiz Ruffato (1961–), and Marcelo Mirisola (1966–). The most recognized Brazilian writer to be associated with the post-Boom was Jorge Amado (1912–2001). Amado, whose career preceded Vargas Llosa, is easily associated with both the modern and the post-Boom in Latin America, even though critics in Brazil would not make such associations, primarily because Basilian literary history has focused far more on Modernism since the 1920s. In Colombia, Evelio Rosero, Jorge Franco, Facciolince, Potdevin, and Carlos Pardo Viña are among the most noteworthy postmodern novelists in the first two decades of the twenty-first century. At the same, the tradition of the modern novel has continued with the ongoing post-Boom writing of Restrepo, Jorge Eliécer Pardo, and a host of others. Of the survivors of the twentieth-century post-Boom, Allende has been the mostly widely read and successful in the world, with novels that have been read in over forty languages worldwide. Of the writing projects emanating from the modern novel in Latin America, the postmodern fiction of Bolaño and Rivera Garza, as well as the post-Boom writing of Allende, Boullosa, Mastretta, Pardo, and Aira, all speak to the viability of the modern novel in Latin America.

NOTES

1. "Lejos del espacio de mi madre, en el otro extremo de la ciudad" (Fuentes, *Zona sagrada* 29).
2. "¿Hay otro lugar?" (Fuentes, *Zona sagrada* 164).
3. "Nada se desarrolla. Todo se transfigura" (Fuentes, *Zona sagrada* 65).

4. "El otro ser" (Fuentes, *Zona sagrada* 162).
5. "¿En qué momento se había jodido el Perú?" (Vargas Llosa, *Conversación en La Catedral* 17).
6. "¿A qué hora se jodió la América Española?" (Fuentes, *Terra Nostra* 765).

Works Cited

Abad, Faciolince H. *Asuntos de un hidalgo disoluto*. Penguin Random House Grupo Editorial S.A.S, 2017.

Abad, Faciolince H. *The Joy of Being Awake*. Translated by Nathan Budoff. Brookline Books, 1996.

Ángel, Albalucía. *Dos veces Alicia*. Barral, 1972.

Ángel, Albalucía. *Estaba la pájara pinta sentada en el verde limón*. Argos Vergara, 1984.

Ángel, Albalucía. *Las andariegas*. Argos Vergara, 1984.

Ángel, Albalucía. *Los girasoles en invierno*. Linotopia Bolivar, 1970.

Ángel, Albalucía. *Misiá señora*. Argos Vergara, 1982.

Allende, Isabel. *La casa de los espíritus*. Plaza & Janes, 1995.

Allende, Isabel. *The House of the Spirits*. Translated by Magda Bogin. Knopf, 1985.

Andrade, Mário, and Telê P. A. Lopez. *Macunaíma: O Herói Sem Nenhum Caráter*. ALLCA XX, 1996.

Andrade, Mário, and Telê P. A. Lopez. *Macunaíma: The Hero with no Character*. Translated by Katrina Dodson. New Directions, forthcoming.

Asturias, Miguel Ángel. *El señor presidente*. Alianza, 1986.

Asturias, Miguel Ángel. *The President*. Translated by Frances Partridge. Waveland P, 1993.

Agustín, José. *Inventando que sueño*. Mortiz, 1974.

Baudrillard, Jean. *Simulations*. Semiotext(e), 1983.

Bolaño, Roberto. *2666*. Anagrama, 2011.

Bolaño, Roberto. *2666*. Translated by Natasha Wimmer. Farrar, Straus & Giroux, 1008.

Borges, Jorge Luis. *El Aleph*. Planeta, 1969.

Borges, Jorge Luis. *Ficciones*. Sur, 1944.

Borges, Jorge Luis. *Ficciones*. Translated by Anthony Kerrigan. Everyman's Library, 1993.

Cabrera, Infante Guillermo. *Tres tristes tigres*. Seix Barral, 1995.

Cabrera, Infante Guillermo. *Three Trapped Tigers*. Translated by Donald Gardner and Suzanne Jill Levine. Dalkey Archive Press, 2004.

Caicedo Estela, Andrés. *Liveforever*. Translated by Frank Wynne. Penguin, 2014.

Caicedo Estela, Andrés. *¡Que viva la música!* Editorial Planeta Colombiana, 2019.

Carpentier, Alejo. *The Kingdom of this World*. Translated by Harriet de Onís. Farrar, Straus & Giroux, 1957.

Carpentier, Alejo. *El reino de este mundo*. Seix Barral, 2019.

Cepeda Samudio, Álvaro. *La casa grande*. La Navaja Suiza, 2017.

Cepeda Samudio, Álvaro. *La casa grande: A Novel*. Translated by Seymour Menton. U of Texas P, 1991.

Chimal, Alberto. *La torre y el jardín*. Oceano exprés, 2015.

Conner, Steven. *Postmodernist Culture, An Introduction to the Theories of the Contemporary*. Blackwell, 1989.

Cortázar, Julio. *62: A Model Kit*. Translated by Gregory Rabassa. Random House, 1972.

Cortázar, Julio. *62, Modelo para armar*. Debolsillo, 2016.

Cortázar, Julio. *Hopscotch*. Translated by Gregory Rabassa. Colin and Harvell Press, 1967.

Cortázar, Julio. *Rayuela*. Penguin Random House. 2019.

Costantini, Humberto. *Háblenme de Funes*. Centro Editor de América Latina, 1983.

Duque López, Alberto. *Mateo el flautista*. Pijao, 2008.

Elizondo, Salvador. *El hipogeo secreto*. Fondo de Cultura Económica, 2000.

Elizondo, Salvador. *Farabeuf o la crónica de un instante*. Cátedra, 2016.

Eltit, Diamela. *El cuarto mundo*. Planeta Chilena, 2011.

Eltit, Diamela. *The Fourth World*. Translated by Dick Gerdes. U of Nebraska P, 1995.

Eltit, Diamela. *E. Iluminata*. Translated by Ronald Christ. Lumen 1997.

Eltit, Diamela. *Lumpérica*. Casa de las Americas, 2008.

Eltit, Diamela. *Por la patria*. Planeta Chilena, 2014.

Esquivel, Laura. *Como agua para chocolate*. Debolsillo, 2018.

Esquivel, Laura. *Like Water for Chocolate: A Novel in Monthly Installments with Recipes, Romances, and Home Remedies*. Translated by Carol Christensen and Thomas Christensen. Anchor, 1995.

Fuentes, Carlos. *Cambio de piel*. Seix Barral, 1991.

Fuentes, Carlos. *A Change of Skin*. Translated by Sam Hileman. Farrar Straus & Giroux, 1968.

Fuentes, Carlos. *The Death of Artemio Cruz*. Translated by Alfred McAdam. Farrar, Straus & Giroux, 1991.

Fuentes, Carlos. *Gringo viejo*. Santillana, 2013.

Fuentes, Carlos. *Holy Place*. Translated by Suzanne Jill Levine. E. P. Dutton, 1978.

Fuentes, Carlos. *La muerte de Artemio Cruz*. Punto de Lectura, 2010.

Fuentes, Carlos. *The Old Gringo*. Translated by Margaret Sayers Peden. Farrar, Straus & Giroux, 1985.

Fuentes, Carlos. *La región más transparente*. Alfaguara, 2000.

Fuentes, Carlos. *Terra nostra*. Fondo de Cultura Económica, 2016.

Fuentes, Carlos. *Where the Air is Clear*. Translated by Sam Hileman. Farrar, Straus & Giroux, 1988.

Fuentes, Carlos. *Zona sagrada*. Siglo XXI, 2009.

Foucault, Michel. *The Order of Things, An Archeology of the Human Sciences*. Translation of *Les Mots et les Choses*. Vintage Books, 1973.

Gadamer, Hans-Georg. *Truth and Method*. Second Revised Edition. Translated and revised by Joel Weinsheimer and Donald G. Marshall. Crossroad, 1990.

García Márquez, Gabriel. *Chronicle of a Death Foretold*. Translated by Gregory Rabassa. Harper & Row, 1982.

García Márquez, Gabriel. *Cien años de soledad*. Debolsillo, 2013.

García Márquez, Gabriel. *Crónica de una muerte anunciada*. Oveja Negra, 1981.

García Márquez, Gabriel. *El coronel no tiene quien le escriba*. Anagrama, 1993.

García Márquez, Gabriel. *In Evil Hour*. Translated by Gregory Rabassa. Harper & Row, 1979.

García Márquez, Gabriel. *La hojarasca*. Literatura Random House, 2015.

García Márquez, Gabriel. *La mala hora*. Plaza & Janés, 2002.

García Márquez, Gabriel. *No One Writes to the Colonel and Other Stories*. Translated by J. S. Bernstein. Harper & Row, 1967.

García Márquez, Gabriel. *One Hundred Years of Solitude*. Translated by Gregory Rabassa. Harper Collins, 1970.

Hassan, lhab. *The Dismemberment of Orpheus, Toward a Postmodern Literature*. Second ed. U of Wisconsin P, 1982.

Hutcheon, Linda. *A Poetics of Postmodern ism, History, Theory, Fiction*. Routledge, 1988.

Hutcheon, Linda. *The Politics of Postmodernism*. Routledge, 1989.

Jameson, Fredric. *Postmodernism or the Cultural Logic of Late Capitalism*. Duke University Press, 1991.

Jaramillo, Darío. *La muerte de Alec*. Alfaguara, 1999.

Leal, Eutiquio. *Después de la noche*. Casa de Libros, 2008.

Libertella, Hector. *El camino de las hiperbóreos*. Paidos, 1968.

Lins, Osman. *Avalovara: Romance*. Companhia das Letras, 2005.

Lins, Osman. *Avalovara*. Translated by Gregory Rabassa. Knopf, 1979.

Lyotard, Jean-François. *The Postmodern Condition, A Report on Knowledge. Theory and History of Literature*, vol. 10. U of Minnesota P, 1989.

Mastretta, Ángeles. *Arráncame la vida*. Seix Barral, 2019.

Mastretta, Ángeles. *Mexican Bolero*. Translated by Ann Wright. Viking, 1990.

McHale, Brian. *Postmodernist Fiction*. Methuen, 1987.

Moreno-Durán, Rafael H. *El caballero de la invicta*. Montesinos, 1994.

Moreno-Durán, Rafael H. *Finale capriccioso con Madonna*. Tercer mundo, 1990.

Moreno-Durán, Rafael H. *Juego de damas*. Tercer Mundo, 1988.

Moreno-Durán, Rafael H. *Los felinos del Canciller*. Planeta, 1998.

Moreno-Durán, Rafael H. *El toque de Diana*. Montesinos, 1990.

Navarro Lince, Humberto. *Los días más felices del año*. Tercer Mundo, 1966.

Pacheco, José E. *Morirás Lejos*. Era, 2016.

Pacheco, José E. *You Will Die in a Distant Land*. Translated by Elizabeth Umlas. U of Miami P, 1991.

Parra Sandoval, Rodrigo. *El álbum secreto del Sagrado Corazón*. Oveja Negra, 1985.

Piglia, Ricardo. *Artificial Respiration*. Translated by Daniel Balderston. Duke UP, 1994.

Piglia, Ricardo. *Assumed Name*. Translated by Sergio Waisman. Latin American Literary Review P, 1995.

Piglia, Ricardo. *Nombre falso*. Siglo XXI, 1975.

Piglia, Ricardo. *Respiración artificial*. Debolsillo, 2020.

Pinzón, Germán. *El terremoto*. Tercer Mundo, 1966.

Puig, Manuel. *Betrayed by Rita Hayworth*. Translated by Suzanne Jill Levine. E. P. Dutton, 1971.

Puig, Manuel. *La traición de Rita Hayworth*. Seix Barral, 2009.

Rivera Garza, Cristina. *La cresta de Ilión*. Literatura Random House, 2018.

Rivera Garza, Cristina. *The Iliac Crest*. Translated by Sarah Booker. The Feminist Crest, 2017.

Rulfo, Juan. *Pedro Páramo*. Planeta, 2008.

Rulfo, Juan. *Pedro Páramo*. Translated by Margaret Sayers Peden. Grove Press, 1994.

Rojas Herazo Hector. *Respirando el verano*. El Tiempo, 2003.

Rosa, Jõao G. *Grande Sertao Veredas*. Feltrinelli, 1995.

Rosa, Jõao G. *The Devil to Pay in the Backlands*. Translated by Harriet de Onís. 1963.

Sáinz, Gustavo. *Gazapo*. Ediciones del Ermitaño, 2009.

Sánchez, Néstor. *Siberia blues*. Seix Barral, 1972.

Santa, Eduardo. *El girasol*. Iqueima, 1957.

Sarduy, Severo. *Cobra*. Edhasa, 1981.

Sarduy, Severo. *Cobra*. Translated by Suzanne Jill Levine. E. P. Dutton, 1975.

Torres Bodet, J. *Primero de enero*. Espasa-Calpe, 1935.

Vargas Llosa, Mario. *Aunt Julia and the Scriptwriter*. Translated by Helen Lane. Farrar Straus & Giroux, 1982.

Vargas Llosa, Mario. *Conversación en La Catedral*. Punto de lectura, 2001.

Vargas Llosa, Mario. *Conversation in the Cathedral*. Translated by Gregory Rabassa. Harper & Row, 1974.

Vargas Llosa, Mario. *La tía Julia y el escribidor*. Alfaguara, 2016.

Vargas Llosa, Mario. *La ciudad y los perros*. Cátedra, 2020.

Vargas Llosa, Mario. *The Time of the Hero*. Translated by Lysander Kemp. Farrar, Straus & Giroux, 1966.

Williams, Raymond L., and José Manuel Medrano. *90 años de la novela moderna en Colombia (1927–2017): De Fuenmayor a Potdevin*. Ediciones desde abajo, 2018.

Yáñez, Agustín. *Al filo del agua*. Porrúa, 1997.

Yáñez, Agustín. *The Edge of the Storm*. Translated by Ethel Brinton. U of Texas P, 2011.

CHAPTER 9

LATIN AMERICAN NARRATIVE IN THE LATE TWENTIETH AND EARLY TWENTY-FIRST CENTURIES

ANA GALLEGO CUIÑAS

LATIN American narrative of the twenty-first century has its roots in the 1990s, when three global phenomena fully impacted the book market: post-Fordist capitalism, neoliberal globalization, and the development of new technologies. To these we must add three other events that specifically concern Hispanic culture: (i) the Spanish celebration of the quincentenary of the "Discovery" of America in 1992, which promoted a pan-Hispanist ideology based on language and shared tradition; (ii) the demand for a transatlantic publishing market, due to the need of the large Spanish conglomerates (such as Planeta and Alfaguara) to expand economically; and (iii) the 1996 publication of the *McOndo* anthology, edited by the Chileans Alberto Fuguet and Sergio Gómez, and the appearance in that same year of the *Crack* manifesto, signed by the Mexicans Jorge Volpi, Ignacio Padilla, Pedro Ángel Palou, Eloy Urroz, and Ricardo Chávez.

The McOndists, on the one hand, defended a (Latin American) individual and urban identity expressed through the global influence of mass media, of a local language and fragmented narrative, with little interest in politics. On the other hand, for the Crack signatories, (Latin American) literary identity was based on formal and aesthetic risk, on the cultivation of high culture, on the use of irony, on theoretical and philosophical reflection, and on the historical story. Nevertheless, both groups shared the same literary—and commercial—strategy of opposition to the Eurocentric association of Latin American fiction with the land, violence, political history, magical realism, and exoticism, which had been a burden since the Boom period. Of course, this aesthetic standpoint is not new, as cosmopolitism and universalism had been seeded during the twentieth century in Latin America, although they did not enjoy much visibility—that is to say, in terms of marketing interest—beyond national borders. However, what does entail novelty in the Latin American literary system (aside from Borges's early proposals in "The Argentine Writer and Tradition") is the unravelling of the idea of a narrative identity tied to national or regional geography, along with the expansion of literary areas beyond the borders of each country. This is mainly the consequence of the new logic of the global market and the neoliberal ideology that underpins it, crystallized in the gradual process of "Alfaguarization" of Latin American literature at the end of the twentieth century, which the members of McOndo and Crack were perfectly adept at gauging. What is this "Alfaguarization"? You may well ask.

In 1993, the publisher Juan Cruz launched the "Alfaguara Global" initiative as part of a cultural and economic project of Hispanist kinship that was driven by Spain through the inauguration of the Casa de América (1990), the Instituto Cervantes (1991), and the numerous celebratory events of the Quincentenary of the "Discovery" of America (1992). The goal of the director of the Alfaguara publishing house at that time was to achieve the simultaneous publication of certain works in the entire geographical area of the Spanish language (Latin America, Spain, and the United States). With this publishing policy, they would be able to form the long-desired common market in Spanish where Spain would act as the mediator between Latin America and Europe, which obviously implied the commercial and (neo-)colonial control of production. Moreover, this market was to challenge the English-speaking market, although this did not entail an equal interchange between Spain and Latin America either—in fact, quite the opposite, since the latter's share of all books published did not surpass 2.5% of the total (Pohl). This percentage has barely changed today.

Similarly, some Latin American writers began to claim the Spanish language as one homeland or identity, rejecting the existence of a "Latin American literature." This was argued by those who made up McOndo and Crack, but also other well-known authors, including Rodrigo Fresán, Edmundo Paz Soldán, Roberto Bolaño, Jorge Eduardo Benavides, Fernando Iwasaki, and Andrés Neuman. The fashion was "to define themselves as stateless, perpetual wanderers, citizens of a global world, free from signs or traces of their own identity, nation, or culture . . . To substitute an ontology of identity for another of not-belonging" (Becerra 287).[1] Strictly speaking, the fiction of these authors is deterritorialized in virtue of a "sensorium" (Ránciere) that is reasserted in the globalization of culture, in global mobility (most of the writers mentioned live in Spain or the United States) or in what Tim Parks calls the "New Global Novel."

This concurs with the policy regarding the transnational circulation of book adopted by Alfaguara, and by Planeta, the other great Spanish conglomerate—these publishing houses endeavored to publish and promote these aesthetics and writers now that the Boom was no longer a gold mine for them. Thus, the "global" mode of production has a correlate in Latin American literary creation—which gives rise to the representation of themes and settings that are international, dystopian, gothic, fantasy, and so on—and in the construction of "cosmopolitan" author figures, as well as in the space where the texts are received, both in the mass media and in academia. It is no triviality that in the same period, literary criticism began to coin certain terms and reading frameworks such as "world," "glocal," "transnational," and "transatlantic" literature, which were borrowed from the English-speaking sphere. However, in national spaces of criticism in Latin America, local readings outlined by tradition continued to be completely relevant (e.g., Rodrigo Rey Rosa, Fernando Vallejo, Mario Bellatin, Horacio Castellanos Moya, Cristina Rivera Garza, Martín Kohan), in contrast to the proposals of McOndo and Crack, which hardly caused a ripple.

Likewise, also in the 1990s, a further twist to the problem of Latin American identity occurs with the emergence of Latinx writers from the United States who write in English, such as Julia Álvarez, Junot Díaz, and Daniel Alarcón, which also jeopardized the ontological and epistemological configuration of the Latin American literary object, based on the common use of the Spanish language. This entails a resignification of the literary field as an ambiguous (political) dimension, articulating other forms of belonging linked neither to the land nor to the language, which are increasingly more travelled and widespread.

Few studies with an overview of Latin American narrative published after 2001 can be found to date (Fornet; Montoya and Esteban; Ludmer; Quesada; Gallego Cuiñas; Hoyos; Brescia and Estrada; Premat; González; Guerrero; Valero and Estrada; Corral). In all of these, the names of the writers born in the period from the 1970s to the 1990s are repeated or exchanged, because what is visible for some spaces and schools is not so for others. Furthermore, the overproduction of books makes it very difficult to transcend the case study, which contributes greatly to the difficulty of choosing some authors rather than others and of setting an aesthetic and ideological value that brings together a corpus of texts as a cultural model. Nevertheless, I believe that it may prove advantageous to make a heuristic effort—despite its reductionist and partial nature—to name the most noteworthy aesthetic "directions" or "turns" taken in the first two decades of the twenty-first century, which affect forms, procedures, and topics of contemporary Latin American narrative. To clarify, I use the concept of aesthetics here not through an idealist approach but in the sense that Rancière gives it: in its "speaking of the real," in its ethical and political dimension. This is not rendered into new literary techniques, but rather into a new mode of "visibility" or stance "in the face of time" (63). The effectiveness of the following ten representative aesthetic turns comes, therefore, from their adherence to a "community of feeling" (Rancière 37), which means the Latin American social, political, and literary structures of this new century:

1. *The subjective turn*, or autobiographical turn, expressed from the end of the twentieth century through the processes of autofiction, the diary, or epistolary writing, which have been revitalized, exhibiting a new type of subjectivity marked by affect and vulnerability. In this area we can include authors such as Mike Wilson, Jeremías Gamboa, Guadalupe Nettel, Valeria Luiselli, Rodrigo Hasbún, Romina Paula, María Gainza, Mauro Libertella, Margarita García Robayo, Carolina Sanín, Roberto Martínez Bachrich, Alan Mills, and Janette Becerra.

2. *The documentary turn*, which champions the factual story through the use of articles/accounts, opening the door to so-called docu-fiction to show the porosity of the division between documentation and fiction (Eduardo Halfon, Marta Dillon,

Selva Almada, Carlos Busqued, Renzo Rosello, Gabriela Wiener, Felipe Restrepo Pombo, Diego Zúñiga, Carlos Manuel Álvarez, Frank Báez, etc.).

3. *The (post)memory turn*, which cultivates the imaginary of the (post)dictatorship, where the "literature of the children" of the Southern Cone is included: Julián López, Laura Alcoba, Patricio Pron, Félix Bruzzone, Raquel Robles, Mariana Eva Pérez, Nona Fernández, Andrea Jeftanovic, Álvaro Bisama, Alejandro Zambra, Alia Trabucco, and Carlos Wynter, et cetera.

4. *The neorealist turn*, in which the following converge: the detective or noir genre (Leonardo Oyola, Mercedes Giuffré, Wilmer Urrelo, Melba Escobar, Juan Manuel Robles), the historical novel, narco-literature, narratives of violence (Yuri Herrera, Daniel Alarcón, Daniel Ferreira, and Mónica Ojeda), and the literature of the poor (Julián Herbert, Verónica Gerber Bicecci, Pedro Mairal, Matías Celedón, Sergio Gutiérrez Negrón). In this area, we can also place the notable progress of that "realismo raro" ("weird realism") (Harman) that has been likened to Lovecraft (Federico Falco, Hernán Ronsino, Juan Cárdenas, Katya Adaui, etc.) and that could also be linked to the "speculative realism" that philosophers such as Graham Harman or Quentin Meillassoux have developed, in which no pre-existing reality is represented, but, rather, new forms of social logic are invented.

5. *The neofantasy turn*, which encompasses the notable development of science fiction (currently considered an outstanding variant of realism), dystopia, gothic, and the horror genre (Mariana Enríquez, Samanta Schweblin, Luciano Lamberti, Nicolás Mavrakis, Martín Felipe Castagnet, Damián González Bertolino, Gabriela Jauregui, Daniela Tarazona, Giovanna Rivero, Liliana Colanzi, Fedosy Santaella, Karina Sainz Borgo, Erick J. Mota, etc.).

6. *The feminist turn*, which reveals new assemblages and deconstructions of the heteropatriarchal norm through the disruptive imagining of motherhood, family, romantic love, incest, filicide, or violence against women (Mariana Dimópulos, Ariana Harwicz, Inés Acevedo, Fernanda Trías, Fernanda Melchor, Daniela Tarazona, Ena Lucía Portela, Claudia Salazar Jiménez, María José Cano, Lina Meruane, Sol Linares, etc.).

7. *The queer turn*, which sets out non-normative sexualities and dissident LGBTTIQ + processes of subjectivation, with particular development of trans/transvestite narratives over the last decade (Fernanda Laguna, Lucía Puenzo, Gabriela Cabezón Cámara, Camila Sosa Villada, Dani Umpi, Rita Indiana, Giuseppe Campuzano, Giuseppe Caputo, Natalia Berbelagua, Manuel Gerardo Sánchez, Luis Negrón, etc.).

8. *The nomadic turn*, or wandering or diasporic turn, which follows the trail of travel, exile, nomadic or transitory narratives, which were extremely prolific in the nineties and gave rise to the aforementioned debate on the multi- or trans-territorialization of Latin American literature. In this area, the most noteworthy authors are Junot Díaz, Andrés Neuman, Alejandra Costamagna, Nataly Villena, Raquel Abend, and Juan Pablo Villalobos, among others. We could also include here another aesthetic that has been expanding and gaining more and

more notoriety, which is the *border turn*, embodied in stories from the Mexico-US border, as found in texts by Antonio Ortuño, Heriberto Yépez, and Emiliano Monge, among others.

9. *The digital turn*, or technological or electronic turn, which occupies the transmedial and hypertextual, as exemplified by Pola Oloixarac, Carlos Labbé, Ramiro Sanchiz, Doménico Chiappe, and so on.

10. *The neo-ruralist turn*, which returns the countryside to the literary scene, at the mercy of the economic crises that made urban life unsustainable, with the new environmental awareness, care for health and well-being, and even the recent emergence of the coronavirus pandemic, which is also bringing about a return to rural settings. Some examples of writers in this theme are Iosi Havilio, Oliverio Coelho, Magela Baudoin, and Carlos Fonseca, among others.

As we can see, these turns are not new and neither do they occur in a pure state; rather, they appear in the mix not only of aesthetics but also of temporalities (modern, postmodern, metamodern), disciplines, genres, and, of course, politics of literature. Of all these, I argue that the feminist and queer turns are especially relevant, given that writing by women, feminized bodies, and dissident subjectivities have acquired an unprecedented protagonism in the Latin American literary field over the last decade. Never before have so many women writers, nor so many gender-neutral and/or trans/transvestite individuals, been published, and neither have they attained such a degree of legitimacy before, in the academy and in the market, nationally and transnationally. Of course, this is not something that has happened spontaneously. Rather, it is the consequence of the articulation of a literary discourse, transfeminist and dissident in origin, that has been developing in Latin America since the 1970s and 1980s (Rosario Castellanos, Elena Poniatowska, Manuel Puig, Copi, Sylvia Molloy, Luisa Valenzuela, Angélica Gorodischer, María Moreno, Pedro Lemebel, Laura Restrepo, Gioconda Belli), but it has begun to flourish the most over the last decade or so.

This is due, on the one hand, to the fact that in Latin America the latest Western trans-feminist (Valencia) movements have had a great effect: queer theory (Butler), post-feminism (Haraway), new materialisms (Jane Bennett and Elizabeth Gross), and post-pornography (Paul B. Preciado). At the same time, a spectacular development of Latin American feminist thought has taken place, embodied by international names such as Marcela Lagarde, Rita Segato, Silvia Rivera Cusicanqui, and Verónica Gago, who focus their criticism on capitalist violence, neo-colonialism, and the (subordinating) processes of subjectivation of Latin American women.

On the other hand, the institutional politics that promote gender equality and feminism as its own area of knowledge have had an impact, as has the fact that women have been occupying public spaces of legitimacy in Latin America (Michelle Bachelet, Cristina Fernández, Dilma Rousseff, Laura Chinchilla, Mireya Moscoso). This is a social factor that has contributed to expanding their presence in literary discourse as well. This panorama has fostered the growth of Latin American feminist activism, which has had unprecedented global impact, led by women who are mostly related to the sphere of literature and art, as has occurred with the Argentinian movement Ni Una Menos. If the year 1959 and the Cuban Revolution brought about the start of the boom in Latin American, Pan-American, and anticolonial literature, then the year 2015 and Ni Una Menos ("Not One [Woman] Less") crystallized the boom of (trans-)feminist, pan-Hispanic, and anti-patriarchal literature. From the organic epic nature of the fiction of the 1960s, their reconstruction of national/continental history, and their struggle against authoritarianism and American imperialism, there is a shift in the twenty-first century to an inorganic narrative of local/communal stories and disobedient subjectivities. These narratives reproduce politics of the common and modes of resistance to represent the crisis of cisgender subjectivities, of the model of the heteropatriarchal family and of normative affective relationships. Thus the dissidence of sex and gender finds, in literature, a path for enunciation and making itself visible, as occurred with the subjectivities of the Latin American left half a century before.

The international impact of the wholly new Latin American feminist narrative is projected onto this emancipatory horizon, which "shatters the old cliché of what women's writing should be" (Drucaroff 462). In what way? At least two clear mechanisms can be distinguished: first, the reappropriation of resources such as dark humor and violence, which were intrinsic to male writing and to the social role of men; second, the deconstruction and reconstruction of the processes of female subjectivation. It is no longer a question of narrating what women say, but what they do not say. The aim is not only to have access to the word but to draw back the ideological veil that the hegemonic patriarchal discourse has spread over the female body and its functions: as mother, as lover, as victim of structural violence. Thus, this narrative shows, in a political act, the limits, the gaps, the shadows of femininity (Ludmer 98). With this, they challenge both patriarchal ideology and *feminine* literature, undermining the institution of marriage, the roles of wife and mother, the family, the materiality of the body and identity, in transformation and performance, of women.

However, if we undertake a materialist reading of this extremely novel feminist narrative, it is easy to see that the growth of its importance in the Latin American literary sphere is also accompanied by the expansion of the publishing industry. The ease of access to publication has undoubtedly favored women writers: more is published, and, as a result, more women are published. For the publishing houses, both large and small, backing such valued market sectors as women and emerging authors is currently fundamental for the make-up of their catalogues. However, when we put the spotlight on a larger scale, on what is called "world literature," women's writing continues to be invisible. Therefore, if women occupy a lesser place in the transnational circulation of Latin American literature, their condition is doubly subordinate in the space of world literature: because they are Latin American *and* because they are women. The explanation can be found in the fact that the most acclaimed and renowned women writers in the global system have been, up until the end of the twentieth century, those who did not display any great difference in gender terms—in other words, their literature resembled the canon, of patriarchal nature. Otherwise, they were renowned because the gender difference was a product in itself, whether as the story of "feminine" matters or as openly feminist struggle, conveyed as the telling of situations of abuse, violence, and oppression, such as in Margaret Atwood's bestseller *The Handmaid's Tale* (1985). This assertion can be demonstrated if we look at the themes that have given prominence to the last few female winners of the Nobel Prize for Literature: Svetlana Alexiévich (military conflict), Herta Müller (totalitarianism), Doris Lessing (racial conflict), Wislawa Szymborska (memory), Nadine Gordimer (economy and corruption), and Olga Tokarczuk (crime novel and historical novel). Since the 1990s, only three feminist writers have won the award: Toni Morrison, Elfriede Jelinek, and Alice Munro.

The last decade has also seen an authentic boom in Latin American queer/trans/transvestite literature, which has become one of the most prominent in the Spanish language due to the significance that certain trans artists, intellectuals, and activists have attained by presenting politics and aesthetics with immense dissident potential (Batato Barea, Lohana Berkins, Marlene Wayar, Mauro Cabral, Effy Beth, Claudia Rodríguez, and Frau Diamanda). One of their literary precursors was Severo Sarduy, who was a forerunner to the appearance in Latin America of a neo-baroque transvestite narrative (parodic, hyperbolic, fragmented, experimental), transnational, transsexual, and transcultural in nature, which would confront the binarism and univocality of the sex/nation/high-culture triad that defined the boom. His work as a translator, critic, and publisher made him the consummate mediator—he lived in Paris—of Latin American literature on sexual disobedience, which from the eighties and nineties expanded with the emergence of the likes of Néstor Perlongher, Luis Zapata, Reinaldo Arenas, Joaquín Hurtado, Cristina Peri Rossi, and Diamela Eltit. In the twenty-first century, they have been joined by Mayra Santos-Febres, Mario Bellatin, Dani Umpi, Giuseppe Campuzano, Ena Lucía Portela, Gabriela Cabezón Cámara, Naty Menstrual, and Camila Sosa Villada, among others. In the works of these authors, three traits recur that denote the articulation of politics of the common—of an alternative social trans-community—and of aesthetic dissidence: the queer use of the literary chronicle and of the neo-baroque, the presence of the body, the monstrous and the animal, and the literary enunciation of a "precarious" subjectivity (Butler).

However, the greatest transformation that Latin American narrative has undergone between the 1990s and the second decade of the twenty-first century does not involve the formulation of new aesthetics or the emergence of women writers of queer, trans, or transvestite subjectivities; rather, it concerns the changes that have occurred in the book market on a global scale. Latin American literature is not the combination of a language and a cultural way of thinking in abstract; it is a commodity, which in the twenty-first century is subordinated to a neoliberal logic intersected by two variables: the already mentioned globalization, which accelerated the modes of production and circulation of cultural assets (Bourdieu), and the economic crises of the new millennium that have affected the methods of publishing access and distribution. Both circumstances have, in turn, given rise to two material changes that cannot be omitted from this analysis because they have a clear symbolic effect: first, the expansion, rationalization, concentration, and hyper-segmentation of the Latin American publishing sector; second, the multiplication of "gatekeepers" (Marling) who have an influence on the processes of creation and circulation of Latin American literature in the global system—that is, on perception, the formation of taste and on the processes of recognition and canonization established. Traditionally, the crucial role—both positive and negative—that these mediators play in the literary scene has been ignored. Today, however, we cannot disregard the function of this "new breed of managers, agents of market forces" (Bauman 109), in the filtering process and in the deterritorialization of the symbolic capital of Latin American writers. Good examples of this are the Frankfurt Book Fair; the Hay Festival and its Bogotá39 list (2007/2017); the "The Best of Young Spanish-Language Novelists" in *Granta* (2010/2021); literary agents (most of whom are located in Barcelona and Madrid); translators, scholarships, and residencies (e.g., The International Writing Program at the University of Iowa); the expansion of creative teaching spaces; creative writing workshops and MAs such as that at NYU; and so on. All of these are builders of "world literature," and they take place far from Latin America, in the United States, the United Kingdom, Germany, and Spain.

However, local "gatekeepers" do exist, who act in and out of Latin America, such as certain independent publishers in Mexico and the Southern Cone (e.g., Eterna Cadencia, Sexto Piso, Hueders); book fairs in Argentina, Colombia, Mexico, and Brazil; and prizes such as the Premio García Márquez, Premio Bienal de Novela Mario Vargas Llosa, Premio Roberto Bolaño a la Creación Literaria Joven, Premio Iberoamericano de Letras José Donoso, and Concurso Literario Juan Carlos Onetti, among others. These awards on occasion give more visibility and symbolic and financial return than the sale of books, which implies a hidden mode of acting that affects the (re)production and reception of recent Latin American narrative. Thus we can identify four material "events" (Agamben) that mark the consumption of Latin American literary culture in the twenty-first century: (i) independent publishing, book fairs, and festivals; (ii) the "spectacularization" of the writer and the increasing precariousness of the literary occupation; (iii) the professionalization, growth and increasing visibility of the mediators of literature, who now act as assessors of literary worth; and (iv) the "Randomization" of Latin American literature. I will briefly explain each of these below.

Independent publishers, fairs and festivals. Firstly, in the twenty-first century there has been a notable increase in small and medium-sized publishers—called "independent" (Gallego Cuiñas, "La editoriales independientes" ["Independent Publishers"]). On the one hand, they promote bibliodiversity with the publication of "minor" genres (Deleuze and Guattari) (e.g., poetry, short stories, essays, drama) that are neglected by the large corporations. On the other hand, they revive a kind of "material counterculture" (Gallego Cuiñas, *Novísimas*) through alternative means of production to standardized industrial goods—that is, artisan or handcraft such as the *cartonera* publishers, *cordel* books (chapbooks), and so on. This material dissent also has its symbolic correlate in certain imprints (e.g., Mansalva, Rosa Iceberg, Laurel, Almadía, Libros del Pez Espiral) that have become true drivers of experimental methods of production and commercialization. They are deeply anchored in local/national tradition, to the extent of being "anachronistic" (Didi-Huberman), and tend to be subsequently swallowed up by large publishing houses such as Anagrama or Literatura Random House. They thus act as laboratories of literary value, which reveals them as gatekeepers of world (Latin American) literature (Gallego Cuiñas, "Las narrativas del siglo XXI").

The role that "independent" publishers play in the current Latin American literary space is similar to the pioneering artistic actions typical of the most pugnacious avant-garde of the early twentieth century. Then it was magazines and journals that published manifestos; now this is done—out of activism—by the small publishers, which have been the great revitalizers of an alternative literary culture (Vanoli 84–85), out of which systems of association and collaboration have arisen for the creation and distribution of books (e.g., the independent and alternative/self-organized book fairs). These have brought about the formation of subcontinental and transatlantic networks of publishing sociality networks, because contemporary Latin American narrative is also published by "independent" imprints in (Western) non-Spanish-speaking countries, such as La Nuova Frontiera (Italy), Métailié (France), Klaus Wagenbach (Germany), and Sudaquia (USA). All of this marks out a counter-hegemonic circuit of the Latin American book, an alternative to the Spanish and German publishing industries that control the majority of its literary market. Hence we can even talk of "decolonial materialism" (Gallego Cuiñas "Las editoriales independientes" ["Independent Publishers"]) to characterize the work that the small and medium-sized Latin American publishers carry out today.

However, at the same time that the production and commercialization of books is being digitalized, the live experiences of literary fairs and festivals are increasing in Latin America, in which "communities" (Nancy) of writers and readers participate that make a literary use of life. They are defined by the "communitization" of the symbolic and material experience of literature as a "residual sociolect" (Brouillette 288) that is shared in spaces of the "non-state public sphere" (Virno 14). They may, however, be state spaces, because the most important literary festivals are, in part, sponsored by state institutions and/or corporate foundations (e.g., HAY, FILBA), which invest in cultural events as a policy of self-promotion and even as an investment in tourism. In general, they function as "systems of patronage" (Vanoli 46), but also as political dispositifs in which, paradoxically, reflection on the literary comes before the consumption of books (even in the fairs, which have also been "festivalized" in recent years). In these spaces, there is an intellectual atmosphere that gives rise to the continuous and self-legitimating (re-)view of the contemporary meanings and future possibilities of literature, under the premise and acceptance of its social functionality—of its use value. Paradoxically, in both festivals and fairs, we witness a return to the sublime, to the utopia of an "autonomous" literary world, full of hope, that shares one same "structure of feeling," as Raymond Williams would say. In the shared experience of the "learned community" of the twenty-first century (Gallego Cuiñas, Novísimas), new subjectivities are produced, "forms of life" (Agamben) and sociabilities that create needs both in the production and in the consumption of "literary culture" (the socialized experience of the *performance* of the literary), which is displacing "literature" (the solitary experience of reading) more and more.

Therefore, what it is ultimately about is keeping alive that faith or literary credit, not to gain more readers but to generate more producers/consumers of literature. This brings about the proliferation of versatile figures who are simultaneously readers-writers-publishers (Washington Cucurto, Félix Bruzzone, Diego Zúñiga, Daniel Tabarovsky, Tamara Tenembaun, among others). In these cases, which are burgeoning above all in the Southern Cone, intellect (theory), work (poiesis or production), and action (political praxis) (Virno 104) are interwoven in pursuit of a collective project (Belleza y Felicidad [Beauty and Happiness], Furia del Libro [Book Fury], etc.) of bibliodiverse, egalitarian, sustainable, and inclusive intellectual life—in other words, committed.

The spectacularization of the writer and increasing precariousness of the literary occupation. Writers have gone from being the producers of literary objects to becoming products themselves, based on the notable "spectacularization" (Sibilia) and commercialization of the "public image" (Groys) that the market demands. With this exercise in self-exhibition, the "aura" (Benjamin) shifts from the book to the author, the guarantee of the authenticity of the creative work, to be judged, in a neoromantic drive, as a kind of tragic hero, bearer of aesthetic transcendence and politics of art, who despises neoliberal capitalism. In this way, writers assemble their biography according to a particular literary identity (Arfuch): as the epic/anti-expression of a creative genius, whose mediatic paradigm in the Iberian-American space is Jorge Luis Borges. Thus, the three basic manifestations of learned Latin American culture of the twentieth century (publishing houses, fairs, and festivals) are articulated around the body and the writer's discourse, which is the true literary work. These spaces undeniably fetishize the author and live off their "festivalization," but also off the image or public performance of the rest of the mediators (publishers, translators, agents), who had hitherto remained unseen but who increasingly participate in fairs and festivals, because the consumers of "literary culture," as I noted above, are also increasingly producers: writers, publishers, translators, and so on. The same happens in the sphere of criticism, where the author—once they have overcome their Barthesian death—is once again at the center of certain methodological movements whose main tool for analysis is the archive (papers, manuscripts, etc.) of the writer and/or of the agents of literature.

Finally, one cannot omit mention of the increasing precariousness of the literary occupation. In the twenty-first century, writing is still an elite profession (Brouillette 288), although it has become more precarious—if we understand from the perspective of book sales—and more diversified: writers also publish; make music; perform; write plays, screenplays, television scripts, and subtitles for series and films; participate in commercial advertising; give workshops and classes; and so on. Hernán Vanoli has called this working with all types of cultural materials "aesthetic bioprofessionalization" (41), which also occurs in other creative occupations (artists, designers, web programmers, etc.), based on self-exploitation, flexibility, the breakdown of the differentiation between amateur and professional and with non-existent safety net.

If in the mid-twentieth century, the financial mainstay of the writer was principally journalism (e.g., Arlt, Onetti, Borges, García Márquez, Vargas Llosa), and later, after the boom, it was university teaching (e.g., Piglia, Saer, Rivera Garza, Eltit, Paz Soldán, Kohan, Herrera, Meruane), in the twenty-first century the writer lives off the public construction of their image (including their digital identity, their participation in cultural events, and so on)—they are "entrepreneurs of the self" (Vanoli 42). Similarly, other occupations of literary culture are more precarious (festival workers, publishers, translators, teachers, cultural critics, etc.) and attain neither a living wage nor a stable position. The economy of culture does not manage to integrate itself on a more ideological plane than a material one, in the real economy. This lack of integration also reinforces—in a deceptive way—the idea of art's autonomy, its irreducibility to a marketing status, or its ability to function inside and outside market-technical logic, hence the belief that literature is a category of artistic expression that needs to be protected by the state and other patrons, which in turn acquire symbolic capital through their protective attitude. This is due to literature's evident loss of power and influence in the cultural sphere, and the development of the business of the professionalization of the writer and other mediators of the field, which restores part of the profit lost in book sales and expands what the creative industry has to offer. This occurs, for example, with MA writing courses and festivals, many of which are promoted—not by chance—by large and medium-sized publishing companies (e.g., Planeta, Alfaguara, Eterna Cadencia). Both are sides of the same coin, because without the presumption of literature's autonomy, there is no protection (patronage/sponsorship), and without protection there is no (sufficient) business: no professionalization or mediation. Literature has become a spectacle and, as we know, the show must go on.

Professionalization, proliferation of mediators and new ways of legitimization. The professionalization of the writer's occupation through workshops and creative writing courses, and the rest of the agents who intervene in the mediation and dissemination of the literary object, is an effect of the neoliberal restructuring of society. There is a need to regulate, in the global market, the creative work in order to make the most of the meagre financial return provided by both book publishing and literary studies in universities. This has had the evident consequence of deterritorialization, an increased and greater professionalization of the mediators who partake in the business of literature, which has expanded its field of action beyond the publication of the book-object (what I have been calling "literary culture"): there are more agents, scouts, translators, and, as we have already seen, many more fairs and festivals. These last two have, in the twenty-first century, become privileged dispositifs for creating and appraising the worth of what is new, an activity that was formerly carried out by cultural and academic criticism, (national) prizes and anthologies. Today, *Granta* magazine, the Hay Festival Bogotá39 list, or "The 25 best kept secrets of Latin America" of the Guadalajara FIL (Book Fair) act as the authentic canonizers of "Latin American world literature." In these, a jury—usually consisting of established writers—gives legitimacy to a group of writers chosen by virtue of youth, novelty, and lack of visibility, as well as for the (aesthetic) quality of their work by means of anthologies and awards. The international coverage of these lists of writers and their high impact within cultural media and social networks confers value on them, since they are sponsored by extremely popular magazines, fairs, and festivals that are driven by the urge to have an influence on the tastes of local and global reader-consumers. This approach reproduces the symbolic capital that the reviews in literary supplements used to have but which have lost credibility. Additionally, anthologies, such as Diego Trelles Paz's *El futuro no es nuestro: nueva narrativa latinoamericana* (2009) (*The Future Is Not Ours: New Latin American Fiction*, 2012), Salvador Luis's *Asamblea portátil* (Portable Assembly, 2009), and Claudia Apablaza's *Voces 30. Nueva narrative latinoamericana* (Voices 30: New Latin American Narrativa, 2014), have lost the ability to mediate between authors and consumers. They have been reduced to serving, at best, as business cards for writers who wish to become known beyond their native countries (Mesa Gancedo).

The Randomization of Latin American Literature. The internationalization of an author continues to be the main variable for measuring literary success, since it is an indispensable requirement for their circulation/globalization (Sapiro). This is attained through publication with large corporations that tend to be the gateway to transnational visibility and translation into hegemonic languages such as English. If in the 1990s Alfaguara, along with Planeta, was the brand that represented contemporary Latin American and global literature, in the second decade of the twenty-first century it is Literatura Random House. This is the great publisher of up-and-coming Latin Americans on the way to recognition and entry into world literature. It was founded in 2014, following the purchase of Santillana by Penguin Random House, part of the German conglomerate Berltesmann. They have had three publishing policies up until now: 1) recruitment of young talent with certain previous symbolic capital (Monge, Cabezón Cámara, and Fernanda Melchor); 2) giving priority to Latin American writing over that of Spain, since it is a huge market that needed to be given an outlet; and 3) committing to women writers and those with dissident subjectivities (Gabriela Wiener, Selva Almada, Giuseppe Caputo, among others) as representing a fresh and barely tapped market source. Moreover, the publishing house is noteworthy for its use of social media in its promotion targeted at young people ("Me gusta leer"–"I like to read"). This is a commercial approach more frequently used by the "independents" than by the large publishers. Also worthy of mention is the *Mapa de las Lenguas* (Map of Languages) initiative that Literature Random House and Alfaguara launched in 2015 to promote the transnational circulation of specific books from their catalogues. If the strategy of "global Alfaguara" in 1996 did not fully succeed in making the Ibero-American transatlantic market of books a reality, the *Mapa de las Lenguas* series (note that the nomenclature refers to territories in the plural, as opposed to the homogenizing idea of globalization of the nineties) has done so by relaunching outside their areas of origin works by authors who are already established or on the way to becoming so (Osvaldo Lamborghini, María Moreno, Julián Herbert, etc.). Furthermore, if we look at Literatura Random House's Spanish-language catalogue from the last five years, we can see how, for example, more Argentinian authors have been published in Spain than Spanish authors. Therefore, although there is still a degree of retreat in Latin American national markets, the initiative has enabled some transnational dialogue that was unthinkable a decade ago. Thus, the progressive "Randomization" of literature in the Spanish language has, to date, opened up a significant access route to Spain—and Europe—to Latin American books and narratives by contemporary authors, with Argentinian and Mexican women occupying a prominent position, due to their intense activist work (Moreno, Almada, Enríquez,

Cabezón Cámara, and Melchor, among others). It is clear that the large conglomerates absorb any aesthetic effort with certain symbolic capital to convert it not only into a commodity but also into a political marketing act for the brand itself; thus, projecting an image of itself as open, politically committed, and cosmopolitan. This does not invalidate the necessary work of giving visibility to female, queer and gender-fluid authors, feminized bodies and dissident subjectivities carried out by the large publishing groups, which are likewise indispensable to guaranteeing a plural and balanced book ecosystem.

Lastly, I would like to refer briefly to the place Latin American narrative occupies in twenty-first-century world literature. To do so, we need to bear in mind two variables: first, that Latin American literature has a "minor" (in the Deleuzian sense) condition as opposed to that of hegemonic languages such as English, French, and German. Second, its publishing industry, on the whole, is subordinated to the monopoly of the large groups of Spanish and/or German capital that do not allow it to compete autonomously. In most cases, the first step a Latin American writer has to take to be translated or to break into the international circuit is, still, to be published in Spain. Hence the global reception of Latin American narrative in Europe or the United States has barely changed since the 1970s, when, fueled by the Boom, and its exotic and violent stereotypes, a framework of reading and consumption was constructed. This framework is still in place despite the criticism made by groups such as McOndo and the Crack in the 1990s. The processes of appraising the canonical value of "Latin American literature" in world literature is still based on the dominant logic of the Western tradition through which the culture of Latin America is read. A better way of saying this would be that this occurs through a set of universal values that privilege high literature (Casanova) and the most commercial genre, the novel. However, as I have argued throughout this article, twenty-first-century Latin American narrative and its "literary culture" are extremely diverse in their aesthetics, materialities, and subjectivities. It is not difficult, therefore, to conclude that the narrative of the region will continue to expand and mutate until it conquers new forms, both local and global, to express one of the richest and most fertile of literatures in the world.

Translated from the Spanish by James Hayes

NOTE

1. "ahora se lleva definirse como apátridas, errantes perpetuos, ciudadanos de un mundo globalizado, sin señas ni rastros de identidad, raza, nación o cultura propias [. . .] Para sustituir una ontología de la identidad por otra de la no-pertenencia" (Becerra 287).

WORKS CITED

Agamben, Giorgio. *Homo Sacer. Sovereign Power and Bare Life.* Translated by Daniel Heller-Roazen. Stanford UP, 1998.

Apablaza, Claudia. *Voces 30. Nueva narrative latinoamericana.* Patagonia, 2014.

Arfuch, Leonor. *El espacio biográfico. Dilemas de la subjetividad contemporánea.* Fondo de Cultura Económica, 2010.

Bauman, Zygmunt. *Culture in a Liquid Modern World.* Translated by Lydia Bauan. Polity Press, 2011.

Becerra, Eduardo. "El interminable final de lo latinoamericano: políticas editoriales españolas y narrativa de entresiglos." *Pasavento*, no. 2, 2014, pp. 285–96.

Benjamin, Walter. *Work of Art in the Age of Mechanical Reproduction.* Translated by J. A. Underwood. Penguin, 2008.

Borges, Jorge Luis. *Obras completas II.* Emecé, 2009.

Brescia, Pablo, and Oswaldo Estrada, editors. *McCrack: McOndo, el Crack y los destinos de la literatura latinoamericana.* Albatros, 2018.

Bourdieu, Pierre. *The Field of Cultural Production: Essays on Art and Literature.* Edited by Randal Johnson. Columbia UP, 1993.

Brouillette, Sarah. "Neoliberalism and the Demise of the Literary." *Neoliberalism and Contemporary Literary Culture*, edited by Mitchum Huehls and Rachel Greenwald, John Hopkins UP, 2017, pp. 277–90.

Butler, Judith. *Precarious Life: The Powers of Mourning and Violence.* Verso Books, 2020.

Casanova, Pascale. *The World Republic of Letters.* Translated by Malcolm DeBevoise. Harvard UP, 2007.

Corral, Wilfrido H. *Discípulos y maestros 2.0. Novela hispanoamericana hoy.* Iberoamericana, 2019.

Deleuze, Gilles, and Félix Guattari. *Kafka. Toward a Minor Literature.* Translated by Dana Polan. U of Minnesota P, 1986.

Didi-Huberman, Georges. *Ante el tiempo.* Adriana Hidalgo, 2006.

Drucaroff, Elsa. *Los prisioneros de la torre. Política, relatos y jóvenes en la postdictadura.* Emecé, 2011.

Fornet, Jorge. *Nuevos paradigmas en la narrativa latinoamericana.* Latin American Studies Center-University of Maryland, 2005.

Fuguet, Alberto, and Sergio Gómez, editors. *McOndo.* Mondadori, 1996.

Gallego Cuiñas, Ana. "El boom en la actualidad: las literaturas latinoamericanas del siglo XXI." *Cuadernos Hispanoamericanos*, no. 803, 2017, pp. 50–62.

Gallego Cuiñas, Ana. "Las editoriales independientes en el punto de mira literario: balance y perspectivas teóricas." *Caravelle*, no. 113, 2019, pp. 61–76.

Gallego Cuiñas, Ana. "Las narrativas del siglo XXI en el Cono Sur: estéticas alternativas, mediadores independientes." *Ínsula*, nos. 859–60, 2018, pp. 8–12.

Gallego Cuiñas, Ana, editor. *Novísimas. Las narrativas latinoamericanas y españolas del siglo XXI.* Iberoamericana, 2021.

González, Aníbal. "Nuevísimos: Truth and Authenticity in Latin America's New Twenty-First-Century Literature." *Review. Literature and Arts of the Americas*, no. 51, 2018, pp. 3–6.

Groys, Boris. *Going Public.* Sternberg Press, 2010.

Guerrero, Gustavo. *Paisajes en movimiento. Literatura y cambio cultural entre dos siglos.* Eterna Cadencia, 2018.

Harman, Graham. *Towards Speculative Realism: Essays and Lectures.* Zero Books, 2010.

Ludmer, Josefina. *Aquí América Latina.* Eterna Cadencia, 2010.

Luis, Salvador. *Asamblea portátil. Muestrario de narradores iberoamericanos.* Casatomada, 2009.

Marling, William. *Gatekeepers. The Emergence of World Literature & the 1960s.* Oxford UP, 2016.

Meillassoux, Quentin. *After Finitude: An Essay on the Necessity of Contingency*. Translated by Ray Brassier. Continuum, 2009.

Mesa Gancedo, Daniel. "Crisis y proyección de la narrativa hispanoamericana en la España actual. Una lectura a distancia." *Revista Letral*, no. 23, 2020, pp. 192–232.

Montoya, Jesús, and Ángel Esteban, editors. *Entre lo local y lo global: la narrativa latinoamericana en el cambio de siglo (1990–2006)*. Iberoamericana, 2008.

Nancy, Jean-Luc. *The Inoperative Community*. Translated by Peter Connor and Lisa Garbur. U of Minnesota P, 1991.

Parks, Tim. *Where I'm Reading: The Changing World of Books*. Harvill Secker, 2014.

Pohl, Burkhard. "¿Un nuevo *boom*? Editoriales españolas y literatura latinoamericana en los años 90." *Entre el ocio y el negocio: Industria editorial y literatura en la España de los 90*, edited by José Manuel López de Abiada, Hans-Jörg Neuschäfer, and Augusta López Vernasocchi, Verbum, 2001, pp. 261–92.

Premat, Julio. *Non nova sed nove. Inactualidades, anacronismos, resistencias en la literatura contemporánea*. Quodlibet, 2018.

Rancière, Jacques. *Aesthetics and Its Discontents*. Translated by Steven Corcoran. Polity, 2009.

Quesada, Catalina. *Literatura y globalización: la narrativa hispanoamericana en el siglo XXI (espacio, tiempo, géneros)*. Universidad de Antioquia, 2014.

Sapiro, Gisèle, editor. *Les contradictions de la globalisation éditoriale*. Nouveau Monde, 2009.

Sibilia, Paula. *La intimidad como espectáculo*. Fondo de Cultura Económica, 2008.

Trelles Paz, Diego. *El futuro no es nuestro: nueva narrativa latinoamericana*. Fondo de Cultura Económica, 2009.

Valencia, Sayak. *Capitalismo gore*. Melusina, 2010.

Valero Juan, Eva, and Oswaldo Estrada, editors. *Literatura y globalización. Latinoamérica en el nuevo mileno*. Anthropos, 2019.

Vanoli, Hernán. *El amor por la literatura en tiempos de algoritmos. 11 hipótesis para discutir con escritores, editores, gestores y demás militantes*. Siglo XXI, 2019.

Virno, Paolo. *La idea de mundo. Intelecto público y uso de la vida*. La marca editora, 2017.

Volpi, Jorge, Ignacio Padilla, Pedro Ángel Palou, Eloy Urroz, and Ricardo Chávez Castañeda. *Manifiesto del Crack (1996) Postmanifiesto del Crack (1996–2006)*. CreateSpace Independent Publishing Platform, 2017.

Williams, Raymond. *Culture and Society, 1780–1950*. Columbia UP, 1983.

PART II

SPACE

CHAPTER 10

FROM THE CENTER TO THE MARGINS

Itineraries of Modernity in the Mexican Novel

MARTÍN CAMPS

THE FIRST NOVEL: END OF THE SPANISH COLONY

IN this essay, I map the development of the novel in Mexico and, arguably, the country's history, through the study of this literary genre. Early examples of what could be considered proto-novels include such works as *Infortunios de Alonso Ramírez* (The Misfortunes of Alonso Ramírez, 1690) by Carlos de Sigüenza y Góngora (1645–1700), which narrates the dynamics of colonization using a hybrid of the picaresque, a style that describes the adventures of a deceitful and ingenious hero, and the travel narrative. This text is indebted to the chronicles that recounted the conquest during the previous century, such as the *Cartas de relación de Hernán Cortés* (Hernán Cortés: Letters from Mexico, 1519–1526) by Hernán Cortés (1485–1547) and *Naufragios* (Chronicle of the Narváez Expedition, 1542) by Álvar Núñez Cabeza de Vaca (1490–1559). However, *El Periquillo Sarniento* (The Mangy Parrot, 1816) by Joaquín Fernández de Lizardi (1776–1827) is often recognized as the first novel of Mexico and Latin America. It depicts the end of Spanish colonization as it becomes unable to effectively govern a new social order, as well as the birth of a national identity that led to Father Miguel Hidalgo's revolt against Spanish rule. The novel also belongs to the picaresque genre. Its main character, Pedro Sarmiento, is a jack of all trades with a will to survive in an adverse and corrupt society, which he also criticizes. For Benedict Anderson, in *El Periquillo Sarniento* "we see the 'national imagination' at work in the movement of a solitary hero through a sociological landscape of a fixity that fuses the world inside the novel with the world outside" (46). In his novel *La Quijotita y su prima* (The Little Female Quixote and her Cousin,

1818–1819), Lizardi's moralizing intentions are more apparent. In turn, in *Don Catrín de la fachenda* (*Life and Deeds of the Famous Gentleman Don Catrín de la Fachenda*, 1820), the author delves further into the picaresque style, this time setting aside his didactic editorial comments.

THE MEXICAN-AMERICAN WAR: SANTA ANNA AND NOVELS OF MANNERS

By the middle of the nineteenth century, Mexico had lost half of its territory as a result of the Mexican-American War that ended in 1847 with the Treaty of Guadalupe-Hidalgo. This war defined Mexico's relationship with the United States, the expansionist imperial power to the north. General Antonio López de Santa Anna (1794–1876), who was president eleven non-consecutive times, is mostly remembered for losing the war with the United States and selling Mexico's territory.[1] Ten years later, Mexico experienced the War of Reform (1858–1861) between liberals and conservatives that ended with the victory for Benito Juárez, but the impasse opened the door to foreign interventions, principally that of France.

The first major novel of this period is *El diablo en México* (The Devil in Mexico, 1859) by Juan Díaz Covarrubias (1837–1859). This is a romantic *novela de costumbres* (novel of manners) depicting the hypocrisy of the ruling elites of the time. A member of the liberal party, Covarrubias was executed at age twenty-two, after the battle of Tacubaya between conservatives and liberals. His characters fluctuate between positivism and spiritualism, reality, and fantasy. Another important novel from this time is *Monja y casada, virgen y mártir* (Nun and Married, Virgin and Martyr, 1868) by Vicente Riva Palacio (1832–1896), the grandson of President Vicente Guerrero. *Monja y casada, vigen y mártir* describes the cruelties of the Inquisition and defends the liberal project. After the restoration of the republic, Riva Palacio also edited newspapers, such as *El Ahuizote* (The Water Dog, in Aztec Mythology). He also wrote numerous plays, poetry, essays, and novels influenced by Alexander Dumas. *Monja y casada, virgen y mártir* (Nun and Married, Virgin and Martyr, 1868) and its sequel, *Martín Garatuza* (1868), narrate the adventures of Garatuza, who, following the model of the "capa y espada" (cloak-and-dagger) narrative, faces both the inquisition and his friends' betrayals to defend his love. This work is a precursor to the historical novel in its use of the archives of the Inquisition as inspiration for the stories.

Another novelist of this period is José Tomás de Cuéllar (1830–1894), who participated in the defense of the Castle of Chapultepec during the American invasion. He published the historical novel *El pecado del siglo* (The Sin of the Century, 1869), which narrates the real-life assassination of merchant Joaquín Dongo Marker in 1789 by a former assistant. He also wrote *La linterna mágica: Baile y cochino y La noche buena* (*The Magic Lantern: Having a Ball and Christmas Eve*, 1889–1892), in *costrumbrista* style. *Having a Ball* examines the influence of foreign values in fashion, and *Christmas Eve* gives snapshots of the moral decadence of the middle class at the end of the nineteenth century.

SECOND FRENCH INTERVENTION: JUÁREZ, AND THE ASCENT OF DÍAZ

The Second French Intervention from 1862 to 1867, which put into power Archduke Maximilian as emperor of Mexico in 1864, occurred when President Juárez decided to suspend foreign debt payments.[2] The empire lasted until 1867, when the restored republican government, led by President Benito Juárez, reclaimed power and executed Maximilian. The return of Juárez and the end of the French Empire ushered in a period known as the Restored Republic. Some of the following novels were written by journalists and politicians relating to the customs and conditions of the time. Novelist Manuel Payno (1810–1894), who had fought in the Mexican-American War and was persecuted during the Second French Intervention, published his masterpiece *Los bandidos de Río Frío* (*The Bandits from Río Frío*, 1891). This novel includes an array of rocambolesque incidents and misdeeds but also includes characters (Lamparilla and Reulmbrón, among many others) from all walks of life, professions, and social classes. Payno describes this work in the subtitle as "naturalistic, humorous, of crimes and horrors." The protagonist, Juan Robreño, falls in love with Mariana, and they later have a child who is kidnapped by healers for a ritual to Tonantzin, the Aztec mother goddess. The child is abandoned in the trash, rescued by a dog, then raised by indigenous women. When he is older, he meets his father. Margo Glantz, in her reading of the novel, sees the character as a "protagonist of a myth of origin, of a new Mexican social conscience, conceived after independence" (223).[3]

El Zarco (*El Zarco: The Blue-Eyed Bandit*, 1901) was written between 1884 and 1886 by Ignacio Manuel Altamirano (1834–1893), a critic of Benito Juárez particularly for incorporating gangs of bandits into his forces. The novel, an example of Mexican romanticism, is characterized by its nationalist sentiment and interest in popular voices and customs. It narrates the adventures of El Zarco, the leader of "Los plateados" (the silver-plated gang), in Yautepec. A woman named Manuela is courted by Nicolás, whom she despises for being of indigenous descent. She is interested, instead, in El Zarco, who is blond and blue-eyed, and she runs away with him, but, after discovering that he is an outlaw, she wants to return to Nicolás. El Zarco is eventually detained by Martín Sánchez de Chagollán, the hero of the story, who hangs him for his crimes. As a result, Manuela loses her mind.

Tomochic (1899) by Heriberto Frías (1870–1925) relates the story of the confrontation between rural villagers and the Mexican Army from 1891 to 1892 in the state of Chihuahua. This revolt became a symbol of resistance against Porfirio Díaz's government, which had begun a process of centralization of power. This movement was led by Cruz Chávez, under the influence of Teresa Urrea, "la santa de Cabora" (saint from Cabora). Miguel Mercado, a military man who has fallen in love with the daughter of the leader of the rebellion, narrates, from his perspective, the abuses of *porfirismo* in northern Mexico. The conflict ends with the death of three hundred townsfolk. This revolt was a precursor to the Mexican Revolution. This novel provides a good bridge to the political movements that impact the following century of novels.

The Athenaeum, the Novel of the Mexican Revolution, and the First Avant-Garde Novels

The twentieth century, characterized by political and social unrest, began in the Mexican novel with *Santa* (1903) by Federico Gamboa (1864–1939). A realist and naturalist narrative, *Santa* became the first Mexican bestseller. *Santa* takes place in a brothel in an era characterized by the hypocritical Porfirian "moral values." Santa had been abandoned by the soldier who got her pregnant. After getting an abortion, she was then rejected by her family. Santa is forced to work in a brothel. A man named Hipólito falls in love with her, but, as is customary in naturalistic novels, the protagonist is unable to escape her destiny and dies of cancer. This figure of the fallen woman tricked by a Don Juan (seducer) is one of the great tropes of Spanish-language literature (as exemplified by José Zorrilla's *Don Juan Tenorio*) that still strikes a chord in the Mexican imaginary.

In 1909, the "Ateneo de la juventud" (Youth Athenaeum) was founded with the mission of promoting culture through debates, lectures, and public meetings. It was characterized by its opposition to Auguste Comte's positivism, which had become the ideology of President Díaz's regime and his technocratic advisors, known as the "científicos" (scientists).[4] The Mexican Athenaeum, composed of such important scholars as Dominican-born literary critic Pedro Henriquez Ureña, writer and philologist Alfonso Reyes, philosopher José Vasconcelos, and the philosopher Antonio Caso, championed a humanistic education and promoted academic freedom. That made it possible to leave behind the positivist ideology of the Díaz regime, which has been used to justify social inequality and its privileging of foreign ideas. The Athenaeum looked to the nation's past and to its present realities to build a national identity.

The Mexican Revolution (1910–1920) was inspired by the ideals of "tierra y libertad" (land and liberty) and cost the lives of a million citizens in a country of fifteen million. Francisco I. Madero launched an anti-reelection campaign against Díaz, resulting in the subsequent rise of military campaigns in the north with Pascual Orozco and Pancho Villa, and Emiliano Zapata in the south. Eventually, Díaz resigned and went into exile in 1911. In 1917, the Mexican Constitution was promulgated with nationalistic social goals. These goals were reflected in the novels of the revolution that depict the realities of the war and were often written by eyewitnesses of the conflict.

Mariano Azuela's (1873–1952) masterpiece was *Los de abajo* (*The Underdogs*, 1915), which narrates some of his experiences as a field doctor for Julián Medina, a follower of Villa. The novel depicts a failing revolution that has betrayed its ideals and become merely another opportunity for new demagogues who are as corrupt as the ones overthrown, leaving the poor in the same situation as before the conflict. In the novel, Demetrio Macías, hunted by Mexican government troops, seeks refuge in the mountains, where he forms a guerrilla group. Referring to the unstoppable impulse of the uprising, after tossing a rock down a canyon, he states: "Look at that stone, how it never stops" (222).[5] The narrator concisely relates the struggle for "the cause" and the displacement of the "underdogs," the outcasts who fight for the revolution.

If Mariano Azuela wrote about the "underdogs," Martín Luis Guzmán (1867–1976) depicted, instead, the ones above, the politicians who benefitted from the revolution. Guzmán served under Villa during the revolution and used these experiences in his novel. In *El águila y la serpiente* (*The Eagle and the Serpent*, 1928), the author uses his real-life experiences in the revolution to compose a hybrid text that combines historical fact and fiction. The novel describes events that took place between 1913 and 1915. The chapter "La fiesta de las balas" ("The Festival of Bullets"), one of its most telling episodes, relates the viciousness of Rodolfo Fierro (an actual general of Villa), who fires his gun against his rivals until his finger becomes swollen from pulling the trigger. Guzmán describes the sound as a horrific symphony and the piles of bodies as ghastly hills. A year after the publication of this novel, he published *La sombra del caudillo* (*The Shadow of the Strongman*, 1929), which describes the presidency of Alvaro Obregón, who favored the candidacy of Plutarco Elías Calles during the presidential elections of 1924. The novel shows that the institutionalization of the revolution was built on political cruelty and assassinations. As Enrique Serna has Carlos Denegri state in his novel *El vendedor del silencio* (*The Merchant of Silence*, 2019), "In the forties, the Revolution exchanged the horse for the Cadillac" (312).[6]

Rafael F. Muñoz (1899–1972) wrote in a cinematographic style that was easily transferred to the big screen by director Fernando de Fuentes in his 1936 adaptation of the novel, *¡Vámonos con Pancho Villa!* (Let's Go with Pancho Villa! 1931). One of the masterpieces of the literature of the revolution, it shows, through the story of Tiburcio Maya, the cruelties and ferocity of a revolution that was in actuality a civil war among many factions. The figure of Villa appears again in *Se llevaron el cañón para Bachimba* (They Took the Cannon to Bachimba, 1941) also by Muñoz, who resorts to his biography as a source of inspiration. The novel is an example of a regionalist novel that interprets life in the provinces.

Published in the same year as the previous novel by Muñoz, the semi-autobiographical novella *Cartucho* (*Cartucho: Tales of the Struggles in Northern Mexico*, 1937) by Nellie Campobello stands out amid the works of these mostly male novelists. The originality of Campobello's work resides in the facts that show the horrors of the revolution from the perspective of a child and that it also narrates intimate spaces where women and children become spectators of this devastation. For example, in a part in her novel, the child describes a body that she sees from the window as if it were a doll. Campobello presents the effects on the daily life of the conflagration, highlighting the fortitude of the "soldaderas" (female companions of the male soldiers and sometimes also fighters themselves).

The 1920s and 1930s saw the appearance of the *estridentistas*, largely a movement of avant-garde poets who tried to capture in their works the emerging communication technologies. Mexican avant-garde literary movements and their eccentric manifestos were in synchrony with other movements in Europe, such as "futurism" and "dadaism." The *estridentistas* were also influenced by Marcel Proust's *À la recherche du temps perdu* (*In Search of Lost Time*, 1913–1927). In this vein, *La señorita etcétera* (Miss Etcetera, 1922) by Arqueles Vela (1899–1977) is composed of visual poems—cinematic descriptions and disquieting metaphors in his quest to find an original metaphor. "Miss Etcétera" represents all women in the form of a collage. Gilberto Owen (1904–1952), in *Novela como nube* (Novel like a Cloud, 1923), follows this same style. He uses the Greek myth of Ixion, who seduces Hera, Zeus's wife. Zeus then makes a false Hera (Nephele) from a cloud (hence the title) to trick and punish Ixion.

Members of the *Contemporáneos* (Contemporaries) group, named after the magazine of the same name, which first appeared in 1928, published several important novels. José Martínez Sotomayor (1895–1980) published *La rueca de aire* (Spinning Wheel of Air, 1930), a novel written in poetic prose. Other short novels by members of the Contemporáneos group are *Dama de corazones* (Lady of Hearts, 1928) by Xavier Villaurrutia (1903–1950), *Margarita de niebla* (Foggy Margarita, 1927) by Jaime Torres Bodet (1902–1974), and *El joven* (The Youngster, 1923) and *Return Ticket* (1928) by Salvador Novo (1904–1974).

AFTER THE REVOLUTION: THE MODERN NOVEL, FROM YÁÑEZ TO RULFO

Al filo del agua (*The Edge of the Storm*, 1947) by Agustín Yáñez signals the beginning of the modern novel in Mexico. It describes the start of the revolution in Jalisco and shows the disruption of life caused by the violence about to be unleashed. According to John S. Brushwood, the novel "embodies the characteristics of a new direction. It incorporates and surpasses the anecdote, the costumbrismo, the social protest" (8). It is a breakthrough in Mexico's cultural production as it reflects the influence of John Dos Passos and James Joyce, thus becoming, according to Joseph Sommers, "a decisive moment in Mexican fiction" (91).[7]

Mauricio Magdaleno (1906–1986) studied in Spain, where he worked for the newspaper *El Sol* (The Sun), directed by Martín Luis Guzmán during his exile in Europe. His novel *El resplandor* (*Sunburst*, 1937) addresses the plight of the indigenous populations that suffered during the revolution but do not reap the benefits of the rebellion, as they continue to confront racism from mestizos. The protagonist, Saturnino Herrera, represents the political hopes of an impoverished town in Hidalgo. The novel is considered an example of the *novela indigenista* (indigenist novel), which was a movement that depicted and condemned the terrible living and working conditions endured by the native populations in the Americas.

The novels of José Mancisidor (1894–1956), who participated in the defense of the port of Veracruz against the US military intervention in 1914, are characterized by their socialist ideology. For example, in *La ciudad roja: novela proletaria* (Red City: A Proletarian Novel, 1932) he re-creates the renters' strike in Veracruz and, in *Nuestro petróleo* (Our Oil, 1953), the pressures that President Lázaro Cárdenas receives from foreign countries during the nationalization of Mexican oil. Xavier Icaza (1892–1969), who worked as a lawyer for the oil company "El Águila" (The Eagle), also published an important novel, *Panchito Chapopote* (Little Francisco Black Tar, 1928), about the abundance of oil in Mexico and the perils associated with its extraction and production.

José Revueltas (1914–1976), one of the major Mexican novelists of the twentieth century, was part of a talented family of artists that included his siblings Silvestre, one of Mexico's greatest classical composers; Rosaura, an actress; and Fermín, a painter. He was jailed for his communist ideas and labor activism. In *Los muros del agua* (Walls of Water, 1941), he relates his experiences on the Islas Marías, where he was confined as a political prisoner. He was imprisoned again in the Palacio de Lecumberri penitentiary (he humorously described it as the best institution of higher learning) under the false accusation of masterminding the 1968 pro-democracy student movement. Based on his experiences in prison, his novel *El apando* (The Hole, 1969) deals with the plan of a group of prisoners to introduce drugs into the penitentiary using their girlfriends and the mother of one of the prisoners. For Christopher Domínguez Michael, author of the two-volume anthology of twentieth-century Mexican literature *Antología de la narrativa mexicana del siglo XX* (Anthology of the Mexican Narrative of the Twentieth Century, 1991), the novel is written: "in a tense prose that makes it difficult for the reader to breathe" (Domínguez 417).[8] Other novels by Revueltas include *El luto humano* (The Human Mourning, 1943), about the Cristero War; *Los días terrenales* (Earthly Days, 1949), a critique of Mexican communism; and *Los motivos de Caín* (Cain's Motives, 1958), about a Mexican American soldier returning home after defecting from the Korean War.

1950s Mexico witnessed President Miguel Alemán's (1946–1952) project of modernization, known as the "Mexican miracle," which led to a significant increase in migration to the city. In 1953, Juan Rulfo published his masterful short-story collection *El llano en llamas* (The Burning Plain, 1953) and, two years later, his novel, *Pedro Páramo*, considered the masterpiece of the Mexican novel. Both works reflected the devastation caused by the revolution (1910–1920) and then the Cristero War (1926–1929), which was a revolt that originated when President Plutarco Elías Calles decided to implement the anticlerical articles of the constitution. Employing an economical style, we hear the voices of peasants, devastated by the crossfire between poverty and pillage, who were promised land in exchange for their participation in the revolution but, instead, are only given barren land. In the novel, Pedro Páramo is a local *cacique* (chieftain and landowner) who inhabits a town tormented by ghosts and sorrows. With only these two books, Rulfo was able to capture the poetics of the landscape—a talented photographer, his stories seem to dialogue with the black-and-white photographs that he took of small towns, indigenous people, and the surrounding nature.

THE URBAN NOVEL: MID-CENTURY GENERATION

The generation of "Medio siglo" (Mid-century) or Generación de la ruptura (Rupture Generation) was composed of novelists born in the 1920s and 1930s who began publishing in the 1940s or 1950s and elaborated on the different realities and spaces of the country. Their novels ranged from describing life in the gargantuan city of Mexico to describing the peculiarities of life in the provinces, to re-creating Mexican history during the Second Empire of Maximilian, experimenting with the form of the novel, to analyzing Mexican customs through the lens of parody.

Reminiscent of John Dos Passos's polyphonic representation of New York in *Manhattan Transfer* (1925), Carlos Fuentes's (1928–2012) *La región más transparente* (*Where the Air Is Clear* 1958) is an urban novel set in Mexico City, characterized by its diversity of voices, social classes, and neighborhoods. Fuentes was a member of the Latin American Boom, a group of modernist novelists that included Colombian Gabriel García Márquez, Peruvian Mario Vargas Llosa, and Argentinian Julio Cortázar. Fuentes later authored other novels often dealing with Mexico's history. Among these, one can single out *La muerte de Artemio Cruz* (*The Death of Artemio Cruz*, 1962), which by means of the deathbed ruminations of the titular character presents a fresco of life in Mexico, from the Mexican Revolution to the establishment of the ruling party that dictated the life of Mexico for close to a century. This same concern with Mexican history is also found in *Terra Nostra* (1975) and *Gringo Viejo* (*The Old Gringo*, 1985). An example of how Fuentes's narrative presents a reflection on Mexican history and culture is found in his novella Aura (*Aura*, 1962). In it, a young historian named Felipe Montero is hired to translate a memoir, and he slowly participates in a magical ritual led by a sorceress named Aura to transform himself (or remember) that he is General Llorente, who participated in the Second French Intervention in Mexico in 1861. In his novels, Fuentes uncovers the buried mirror of Mexico's historical past to explore the possible future of Mexico.

Salvador Elizondo's (1932–2006) novel *Farabeuf* (1965) deals with a nineteenth-century French surgeon who wrote a "chronicle of an instant" narrating the torture of a Chinese person slowly dismembered in a series of photographs. Inspired by film techniques, Elizondo's collage renders a puzzling experimental text, the shattered mirror of a disjointed memory. "Do you remember?" is one of the phrases repeated in a blend of tortuous and gratifying reading. Another experimental novel is Juan García Ponce's (1932–2003) gargantuan *Crónica de la intervención* (Chronicle of the Intervention, 1982). Ponce's novel mixes eroticism and philosophy, influenced by Austrian writer Robert Musil (1880–1942). In it, the protagonists, identical twins Mariana and María

Inés, propel the sexual imaginary of a novel that has the student movement of 1968 in the background, as it makes the private sphere (the house where the sexual encounters happen) coincide with the public space of a country in conflict.

In a different manner from the experimental novels by Elizondo and García Ponce, Sergio Pitol's cosmopolitan novels present a distinctive vision of Mexico. Pitol (1933–2018), in his novel *El tañido de una flauta* (The Twang of the Flute, 1972), depicts a filmmaker who, while watching a Japanese movie at the Vienna Film Festival, deems that he is watching the life of his friend, the writer Carlos Ibarra. The novel uses cinematic conventions to experiment with narrative. His novels include: *Juegos florales* (Floral Games, 1982) about a decayed writer describing the failure of a couple's relationship; *El desfile del amor* (*The Love Parade*, 1984) about an investigation of a murder in the Mexico of the 1940s, and *La vida conyugal* (Married Life, 1991), about the decay of a marriage. Pitol's writing is marked by his incessant travel throughout Europe, his work as a translator of Joseph Conrad and Henry James, and his connection to his birthplace, the city of Xalapa.

Another distinctive vision of Mexico, this time based on humor, is found in the novels of Jorge Jorge Ibargüengoitia (1928–1983). Ibargüengoitia was a master satirist whose life was cut short in the plane crash that also took the life of noted Uruguayan literary critic Ángel Rama, Argentinean art critic and novelist Marta Traba, and Peruvian novelist Manuel Scorza. In his novels *Maten al león* (*Kill the Lion!*, 1969), *Estas ruinas que ves* (These Ruins Here, 1974), *Las muertas* (*The Dead Girls*, 1977), and *Dos crímenes* (*Two Crimes*, 1979), he uses humor as an analytical tool to write a political satire on the corruption of contemporary Mexico. In *Los relámpagos de agosto* (*The Lightning of August*, 1964), he lampoons the myths of the Mexican Revolution. In the latter, the protagonist, General Arroyo, after being confronted with the news that the elected president of Mexico has died from a stroke, must scramble to protect his interests.

Fernando del Paso's (1935–2018) *Noticias del Imperio* (*News from the Empire*, 1986) is a masterful historical novel based on Maximilian, the emperor of Mexico, and his wife Carlota. Following the execution of Maximilian after the French Intervention in Mexico, she is secluded in the Bouchout castle for many years. Resorting to stream-of-consciousness techniques, the novel focuses on Carlota's monologues, which alternate with letters from other members of the nobility, and historical figures such as Benito Juárez and Napoleon III. Influenced by James Joyce and William Faulkner, he also wrote *José Trigo* (1966) and *Palinuro de México* (*Palinuro of Mexico*, 1977). In his *Latin America's New Historical Novel*, Seymour Menton describes this latter novel as a "Bakhtinian symphony" (81).

POWERFUL WOMEN'S VOICES

Mexican women novelists had to overcome the invisibility imposed by a cultural patriarchal establishment. The following authors paved the way for authors like Carmen

Boullosa (1954) and Mónica Lavín (1955), among many others, who are currently leading a boom in literature written by women not only in Mexico but also in the rest of Latin America.

Elena Garro (1916–1998), with her novel *Los recuerdos del porvenir* (*Recollections of Things to Come*, 1963), deserves a place among the Boom writers and is often considered a precursor of magical realism. She was born in Puebla but moved to the state of Guerrero to escape the Cristero War. Her book, set during this war, is told from the perspective of the Moncada brothers, who live in Ixtepec, a small town controlled by the brutal general Rosas and his reign of blood. The poet Felipe Hurtado arrives in town to read poetry and stage plays. Eventually, Hurtado runs away with Julia, the general's partner. Rosas, in revenge, starts a campaign of terror and orders to kill the sacristan and close the town's church.

Rosario Castellanos (1925–1974) published the Chiapas trilogy *Balún Canán* (1957), *Oficio de tinieblas* (*Book of Lamentations*, 1962), and her short-story collection *Ciudad Real* (*City of Kings*, 1974). These novels depict the exploitative working conditions experienced by the indigenous population in the large haciendas of Chiapas. Castellanos was raised in Comitán, Chiapas, where she witnessed first-hand both the discrimination toward indigenous peoples and the mistreatment of women in a patriarchal society. In her novels, she depicts the indigenous uprising of the Tzotzil people, who were being exploited by the mestizos or "ladinos" (non-indigenous).

Elena Poniatowska (1932–) has dedicated her oeuvre to addressing social problems and to giving voice to the disenfranchised. Among her many novels, the following stand out: *Hasta no verte Jesús mío* (*Here's to You Jesusa!*, 1969), the testimony of Jesusa Palancares (based on the interviews of Josefina Bohórquez), a humble woman from Oaxaca who participated in the Mexican Revolution; *Tinísima* (1991), about American photographer Tina Modotti; *La piel del cielo* (*The Sky's Skin*, 2001), based on the life of her late astronomer husband, Guillermo Haro; *El tren pasa primero* (*The Train Passes First*, 2006), about the Railway Workers Movement; and *Leonora* (2011), about surrealist painter Leonora Carrington.

THE PERFECT DICTATORSHIP: *LA ONDA* AND THE TLATELOLCO MASSACRE

In the 1960s, the novels of "La onda" ("The Wave" or "The Vibe") captured the Mexican young people's world of sex, drugs, and rebellion against parents and authority. This generation of writers experienced the social earthquake of the 1968 Tlatelolco Massacre, a few days before the start of the Olympic Games when Mexico was expected to take over the world's center stage. To present an image of peace and unity, the Díaz Ordaz regime decided to quell the pro-democracy student-led movement and all criticism. More than 300 demonstrators were killed at the Plaza de las Tres Culturas at Tlatelolco, and many more were jailed. This tragedy awoke the country to the repressive reality of the Institutional Revolutionary Party (PRI), described by Mario Vargas Llosa as "the perfect dictatorship." Poniatowska depicts the movement in the testimonial *La noche de Tlatelolco* (*Massacre in Mexico*, 1971).

The novels of *La onda*—including José Agustín's (1944–) *La tumba* (The Grave, 1964) and *De perfil* (Profile, 1966); Parménides García Saldaña's (1944–1982) *Pasto verde* (Green Grass, 1968), whose title was going to be "la onda" (the wave); and Gustavo Sáinz's (1940–2015) *Gazapo* (Blunder, 1965)—depict slang, humor, troubles, and music, providing "a pop music rhythm to the language" (Glantz, 13).[9] The 1960s youth counter-culture movement criticized Mexico's government and created the conditions to defy the authoritarian one-party system. The "wave" was a slang colloquial expression, similar to "what's up" that was used in the novels, but it referenced the times of change of the Mexican "beat" literature.

Most of the authors born in the 1940s, who were in their twenties during the events of Tlatelolco, published novels that have been (or should be) the subject of study and translations; they are "protagonists of Mexican literature" (1965), to use the title of Emanuel Carballo's book of interviews. Among the events that influenced them are the 1970 World Cup hosted by Mexico, which required investments in infrastructure, as well as the "Mexican Miracle," fueled by economic programs that began in the 1940s and lasted until the 1970s. Moreover, in 1971 Mexico saw another episode of repression known as "the massacre of Corpus Day." The rebellious movement of the 1960s opened the door to the expression of marginalized groups living in the impoverished areas of Mexico City, as well as to previously marginalized sexual identities, for instance in the works of Luis Zapata (1951–2020).

Armando Ramírez's (1952–2019) *Chin Chin el Teporocho* (Chin Chin the Drunkard, 1971) talks about marginalized characters trying to escape their social environments, in this case, the lower-class barrio of Tepito. Ramírez captures the world of drugs and prostitution using slang-filled language. Luis Zapata's *El vampiro de la colonia Roma* (*Adonis García: a Picaresque Novel*, 1979) is a milestone in Mexican queer literature, being the first mainstream novel celebrating same-sex desire. The protagonist, Adonis García, narrates his erotic adventures set in the Roma neighborhood. There were calls for banning the novel due to its content.

TOWARD A NEW CENTURY: THE "CRACK" OF THE PRI AND THE CRACK NOVELS

If the massacre of students in Tlatelolco can be described as one of the first "cracks" of the regime of the ruling party, the rebellion of the Ejército Zapatista de Liberación Nacional (EZLN) in 1994, led by the charismatic Sub-Comandante Marcos, was another. In 1993, Mexico had signed the North American Free Trade Agreement, and, in response, the

Zapatista National Liberation Army started an armed insurrection on January 1, 1994. This group contested the incorporation of Mexico into the global economy market led by neoliberal president Carlos Salinas de Gortari, while also exposing unresolved social problems that affected the country's indigenous population in the state of Chiapas and elsewhere. Moreover, Salinas's neoliberal policies led to a significant increase in undocumented and documented migration to the United States. However, Salinas's presidency also launched the National Endowment for Culture and Arts, which supported and promoted literature in the form of monetary grants and scholarships that led to an increase in the number of novels published.

In the mid-1990s, the literature of the "Crack" movement appeared as a reaction to the overarching shadow of the Latin American Boom, particularly the post-Boom commercialization. These authors set their narratives in other countries and historical times. While Jorge Volpi's *En busca de Klingsor* (*In Search of Klingsor*, 1999) depicts the Manhattan Project and its nuclear scientists, in Ignacio Padilla's (1968–2016) *Amphitryon* (*Shadow Without a Name*, 2000), a novel that is mostly set inside European trains during World War I, World War II, and the Cold War, major world conflicts are resolved through chess games with life-or-death consequences. By being granted the Biblioteca Breve Prize (Seix Barral Publisher's Prize) in 1999, *En busca de Klingsor* reestablished a prize that had not been awarded since 1972. Earlier Mexican recipients of the award included Vicente Leñero for *Los albañiles* (The Masons) in 1963 and Carlos Fuentes for *Cambio de piel* (*A Change of Skin*) in 1967. Likewise, Padilla's *Amphytrion* was awarded the Premio Primavera de Novela (Spring Novel Prize) in 2000. Another member of the Crack group, Pedro Ángel Palou (1966–) is a prolific writer with more than twenty-six novels, among them *Con la muerte en los puños* (Fists of Death, 2003). Other authors of the group include Eloy Urroz (1966–), author of *Fricción* (Friction, 2008), a campus novel; and Ricardo Chávez Castañeda (1961–), with *El día del hurón* (The Day of the Ferret, 1997), a dark novel about a hitman in a chaotic city ravaged by disease.

The 1990s also saw the rise of border literature, regions that had been seen as cultural deserts, too close to the United States. Border cities had grown during Prohibition and by receiving migrants that had not been able to cross to the United States. The literature of the "north" includes a notable group of writers, characterized by topics, as well as a language that is different from that of the capital. A representative work is Daniel Sada's (1953–2011) *Porque parece mentira la verdad nunca se sabe* (Because it Seems Like a Lie the Truth is Never Known, 1999), an exuberant but also poetic novel about political violence in a small northern desert town, which captures a multiplicity of voices of the Mexican border.

At the same time that the imaginary of the north was built by writers born in the northern provinces, writers born or settled in Mexico continued to produce powerful novels. Juan Villoro (1956) is a versatile public intellectual who covers many genres and themes. In *El testigo* (The Witness, 2004), he narrates the story of Julio Valdivieso, who returns to Mexico after a stay in Europe to research poet Ramón López Velarde, and finds a country with a new ruling party and engulfed in violence.

Enrique Serna (1959–) has made dark humor one of the characteristic traits of his novels. His novel *El seductor de la patria* (The Seductor of the Nation, 1999) deals with Antonio López de Santa Anna, the Mexican strongman who was blamed for losing the war against the United States and for the loss of half of the national territory. The novel is built around testimonies of historical figures and letters, decrees, and diaries. Serna has a particular fascination with complex historical characters. For example, in his latest novel, *El vendedor de silencio* (The Merchant of Silence, 2019), he narrates the life of corrupt journalist Carlos Denegri, an influential political columnist who received bribes to keep quiet about corruption scandals. Serna has also been a fearless voice even satirizing Mexico's intelligentsia, as in his novel *El miedo a los animales* (Fear of Animals, 1995), where, with characteristic humor, he exposes the corruption in the literary world. In this same strain of historical novels, Rosa Beltrán's (1960) *La corte de los ilusos* (The Court of Dreamers, 1995) narrates the rise and fall of Agustín de Iturbide, the first Mexican Emperor. Beltrán's sardonic tone highlights the absurdity of the historical characters and the theatrics of power. Ignacio Solares's (1945–) *Madero, el otro* (Madero's Judgment, 1989) narrates the spiritist side of Madero, the politician who opposed Porfirio Díaz and started the Mexican Revolution. Solares presents Madero's belief in spiritism and his communications with his deceased brother, giving another view of the crucial events of the Mexican Revolution but from a psychological and emotional perspective. Born in the state of Tamaulipas, Cristina Rivera Garza's (1964) *Nadie me verá llorar* (No One Will See Me Cry, 1999) narrates the story of Matilda Burgos, a patient in Mexico City's La Castañeda Asylum, and of the photographer Joaquín Buitrago, who takes snapshots of her and tries to find out more about her. The novel focuses on the humanization of illness, on the bodies that have been institutionalized.

Narcoliterature on the Border and the New Century of Women

The title of Mexican critic Juan Carlos Ramírez Pimienta's book *Del Periquillo al Pericazo* (2006) refers first to *El Periquillo Sarniento* and then to the "pericazo," a slang term for "a line of cocaine," and, therefore, a reference to the rise of the drug trade in late twentieth-century Mexico. Short-story writer Carlos Velázquez was equally explicit in his non-fiction book *El Pericazo Sarniento. Selfie con cocaína* (2017). The title and subtitle reflect the fact that many novels of the last fifteen years have dealt with the development of a drug war, among the cartels and the government, and its effects on Mexican society, in terms of violence, murder, and disappearances.

With the victory of Vicente Fox, candidate for the Partido Acción Nacional (National Action Party; PAN), in the presidential elections of 2000, the start of the twenty-first century saw the end of the long rule by the Institutional Revolutionary Party (PRI). However, the new president, who had been a chief executive officer of Coca-Cola

Mexico, did not live up to the expectations of change and reforms needed to move the country forward. His presidency was followed by that of Felipe Calderón, another member of the PAN, who in 2006 started a war against the drug cartels. This launched a dark period of bloodshed and disappearances, as the country was under the cross-fire between heavily armed cartels and the military deployed in the cities. The violence was first evident in border towns like Tijuana, Ciudad Juárez, and Nuevo Laredo, but it quickly became widespread throughout the country, and the repercussions of that violence are still felt today. The narrative produced during these years is abundant. The characteristics of this narcoliterature are similar to those of crime, *noir*, and detective novels.

Precursors of the detective fiction genre are María Elvira Bermúdez (1916–1988), author of *Diferentes razones tiene la muerte* (Death has Different Reasons, 1953), and Rafael Bernal (1915–1972), author of *El complot Mongol* (*The Mongolian Conspiracy*, 1969). In Francisco José Amparán's (1957–2010) *Otras caras del paraíso* (The Other Side of Paradise, 1995), the protagonist, a professor at a university in Torreón, solves crimes in his spare time. Due to the nature of violence in the stories related to the drug war, narcoliterature continued the vein of detective fiction or Mexican *noir*. Narcoliterature described the collusion of politicians and police with organized crime.

Born in the northern state of Sinaloa, Elmer Mendoza (1949–), the best-known name in the genre of "narcoliterature" (literature about drug trafficking), created the detective saga of "El zurdo Mendieta" (Lefty Mendieta). Among his novels are *Un asesino solitario* (A Lone Murderer, 1999) and *El amante de Janis Joplin* (Janis Joplin's Lover, 2019). Yuri Herrera's (1970–) *Los trabajos del reino* (*Kingdom Cons*, 2004) deals with a composer of "narcocorridos" (folk songs about drug lords) that describes the violent reality in Mexico. Lobo, the protagonist, composes stories inside and out of the court to popularize the cartel. The novel's refined language offers something different from what one reads in the news about *narcos*. *Fiesta en la madriguera* (*Down the Rabbit Hole*, 2010) by Juan Pablo Villalobos (1973–) relates the exotic whim of Tochtli, the son of a drug lord, who wants a midget hippopotamus for his private zoo. Orfa Alarcón's (1979–) *Perra brava* (*Bitch Doll*, 2010) narrates the horrors of narcoviolence from the perspective of a female writer and protagonist. Julián Herbert's (1971–) masterpiece *Canción de tumba* (*Tomb Song*, 2011) narrates the life of the author's mother, a former prostitute, who is dying from leukemia. The novel reflects the mother-son relationship, memory, and violence in northern Mexico.

Despite the importance of Mexico's border literature, an even more significant development is the publication of numerous major novels by women authors. Today, there is a significant group of talented female writers who refuse to be ignored or erased historically or culturally. Indeed, these women have created their own "boom femenino." The main works by these talented contemporary authors are Guadalupe Nettel's (1973–) *La hija única* (Only Child, 2020), an exploration of motherhood in the story of three women; Brenda Navarro's (1982–) *Casas vacías* (*Empty Houses*, 2019), which deals also with motherhood but from the perspective of a stolen child; Fernanda Melchor's (1982–) *Temporada de huracanes* (Hurricane Season, 2017), about the murder of the Witch of La

Matosa; Valeria Luiselli's (1983–) *Desierto sonoro* (*Lost Children Archive*, 2019), about the children separated from their migrant parents at the border; and Laia Jufresa's (1983–) *Umami* (2019), a novel about grief in a neighborhood in Mexico City.

CONCLUSION

The novel continues to be the most effective vehicle for representing the reality of Mexican life. It seems that every hundred years we are immersed in violence—from the struggle for Mexican independence in 1810 to the revolution of 1910, to the narco violence that since 2006 has left thousands of victims. From Lizardi's *Periquillo sarniento* to contemporary fiction, novels have depicted these violent episodes, but they have also helped to heal and define our national identity. In these traumatic national episodes, we have a robust number of novelists who captured the process of nation building and the price of modernization.

The complexities of contemporary Mexican reality—from the tragedy of children separated from their parents at the border, depicted in Luiselli's *Desierto sonoro*, to the storm of violence and machismo in Fernanda Melchor's novel, which takes as its starting point, the real-life murder of a real-life witch—are fictionalized and explained, this time by a "boom femenino" that will not be marginalized. The new century in Mexico looks challenging in terms of economic disparities and the unstoppable narco-violence that has spread beyond the north to different parts of the country. Novels will continue to reflect on these problems by documenting or presenting these stories.

NOTES

1. Santa Anna was president from May 16, 1833, to June 3, 1833, from June 18, 1833, to July 3, 1833; October 27, 1833, to December 15, 1833; April 24, 1843, to January 28, 1835; March 18, 1839, to July 10, 1839; October 10, 1841, to October 25, 1842; May 5, 1843, to September 6, 1843; June 4, 1844, to September 12, 1844; March 21, 1847, to April 2, 1847; May 20, 1847, to September 16, 1843; April 21, 1853, to August 12, 1855.
2. The First French Intervention was also known as the "Pastry War" from 1838 to 1839.
3. "Protagonista de un mito de origen, el de la nueva conciencia social mexicana, gestada a partir de la independencia" (Glantz 223).
4. The "científicos," a group of positivist intellectuals supportive of the Díaz regime, included physician and philosopher Gabino Barreda, historian, and writer Justo Sierra, and economist José Yves Limantour.
5. "Mira esa piedra como ya no se para" (130).
6. "En los años cuarenta, la Revolución se bajó del caballo y se subió al Cadillac" (Serna, *El vendedor de silencio* 312).
7. "Un momento decisivo de la ficción mexicana" (91).
8. "En una prosa tensa, texto que dificulta la respiración del lector" (417).
9. "Un ritmo de música pop al idioma" (Glantz 13).

WORKS CITED

Agustín, José. *De perfil.* Joaquín Mortiz, 1966.

Agustín, José. *La Tumba.* Mester, 1964.

Alarcón, Orfa. *Perra brava.* Planeta, 2010.

Alarcón, Orfa. *Bitch Doll.* Ediciones B, 2013.

Altamirano, Ignacio Manuel. *El Zarco: episodio de la vida mexicana en 1861–63.* Espasa-Calpe, 1972.

Altamirano, Ignacio Manuel. *El Zarco: The Blue-Eyed Bandit.* Lumen Books, 2007.

Amparán, Francisco José. *Otras caras del paraíso.* Almadía, 2017.

Anderson, Benedict. *Imagined Communities: Reflections on the Origin and Spread of Nationalism.* Verso, 1983.

Azuela, Mariano. *Los de abajo.* FCE, 2014.

Azuela, Mariano. *Azuela and the Mexican Underdogs.* Translated by Stanley L. Robe. UC Press, 1979.

Azuela, Mariano. *Los de abajo,* FCE, 1960.

Beltrán, Rosa. *La corte de los ilusos.* Planeta, 1995.

Bermúdez, María Elvira. *Diferentes razones tiene la muerte.* UNAM, 2021.

Bernal, Rafael. *El complot mongol.* J. Mortiz, 1969.

Bernal, Rafael. *The Mongolian Conspiracy.* Translated by Katherine Silver. New Directions, 2013.

Brushwood, John S. *Mexico in Its Novel: A Nation's Search for Identity.* U of Texas P, 2014.

Campobello, Nellie. *Cartucho.* Cátedra, 2019.

Campobello, Nellie. *Cartucho and My Mother's Hands.* Translated by Doris Meyer and Irene Matthews. UT Press, 1988.

Carballo, Emmanuel. *Protagonistas de la literatura mexicana.* Ermitaño, 1986.

Castellanos, Rosario. *Balún Canán.* FCE, 2014.

Castellanos, Rosario. *Book of Lamentations.* Translated by Ester Allen. Penguin Classics, 1998.

Castellanos, Rosario. *City of Kings.* Translated by Robert S. Rudder. LALRP, 1992.

Castellanos, Rosario. *Ciudad Real.* Veracruzana, 1982.

Castellanos, Rosario. *Oficio de tinieblas.* J. Mortiz, 1962.

Chávez Castañeda, Ricardo. *El día del hurón.* Nueva Imagen, 1997.

Cortés, Hernán. *Cartas de relación de Hernán Cortés.* Porrúa, 2007.

Cortés, Hernán. *Hernán Cortés: Letters from Mexico.* Yale UP, 2001.

Covarrubias, Juan Díaz. *El diablo en México: novela de costumbres.* CONACULTA, 2000.

Cuéllar, José Tomás de. *El pecado del siglo: novela histórica (Época de Revillagigedo–1789).* UNAM, 2007.

Cuéllar, José Tomás de. *La linterna mágica.* UNAM, 1941.

Cuéllar, José Tomás de. *The Magic Lantern: Having a Ball and Christmas Eve.* Translated by Margaret Carson. Oxford UP, 2000.

Del Paso, Fernando. *José Trigo.* FCE, 2015.

Del Paso, Fernando. *News from the Empire.* Translated by Alfonso González. Dalkey Archive Press, 2009.

Del Paso, Fernando. *Noticias del imperio.* Plaza & Janés, 1998.

Del Paso, Fernando. *Palinuro de México.* Plaza & Janés, 1993.

Domínguez Michael, Christopher. *Antología de la narrativa mexicana del siglo XX,* vols. 1–2. FCE, 1997.

Elizondo, Salvador. *Farabeuf.* El Colegio Nacional, 2015.

Fernández de Lizardi, Joaquín. *Don Catrín de la fachenda: Noches tristes y día alegre.* Cátedra, 2001.

Fernández de Lizardi, Joaquín. *El Periquillo Sarniento.* UNAM, 2017.

Fernández de Lizardi, Joaquín. *La Quijotita y su prima.* Porrúa, 2009.

Fernández de Lizardi, Joaquín. *Life and Deeds of the Famous Gentleman Don Catrín de la Fachenda.* Translated by Bonnie Loder. MLA, 2022.

Fernández de Lizardi, Joaquín. *The Mangy Parrot: The Life and Times of Periquillo Sarniento.* Translated by David Frye. Hackett, 2004.

Fuentes, Carlos. *Aura.* Bilingual Edition. Translated by Lysander Kemp. Farrar, Straus and Giroux, 1975.

Fuentes, Carlos. *A Change of Skin.* Translated by Sam Hileman. Farrar, Straus and Giroux, 1968.

Fuentes, Carlos. *Cambio de piel.* Alfaguara, 2016.

Fuentes, Carlos. *Gringo viejo.* FCE, 2012.

Fuentes, Carlos. *La región más transparente.* Cátedra, 1991.

Fuentes, Carlos. *Old Gringo.* Translated by Margaret Sayers Peden and Carlos Fuentes. Farrar, Straus and Giroux, 1985.

Fuentes, Carlos. *Terra Nostra.* FCE, 2014.

Fuentes, Carlos. *Where the Air is Clear.* Translated by Sam Hilman. Dalkey Archive, 2004.

Frías, Heriberto. *Tomochic,* Porrúa, 1968.

Gamboa, Federico. *Santa.* Cátedra, 2018.

García Ponce, Juan. *Crónica de la intervención.* CNCA, 1992.

García Saldaña, Parménides. *Pasto verde.* Jus, 2011.

Garro, Elena. *Los recuerdos del porvenir.* J. Mortiz, 1963.

Garro, Elena. *Recollections of Things to Come.* Translated by Ruth L. C. Simms. UT Press, 1991.

Glantz, Margo. "Huérfanos y bandidos: *Los bandidos del Río Frío.*" *Del fistol a la linterna. Homenaje a José Tomás de Cuéllar y Manuel Payno en el centenario de su muerte,* edited by Margo Glantz, UNAM, 1997, pp. 221–39.

Glantz, Margo. *Onda y escritura en México.* Siglo XXI, 1971.

Guzmán, Martín Luis. *El águila y la serpiente.* Porrúa, 2001.

Guzmán, Martín Luis. *La sombra del caudillo.* FCE, 2020.

Guzmán, Martín Luis. *The Eagle and the Serpent.* Translated by Harriet de Onís. Knopf, 1930.

Guzmán, Martín Luis. *The Shadow of the Strongman.* Translated by Gustavo Pellón. Hackett, 2017.

Herbert, Julián. *Canción de tumba.* Penguin, 2014.

Herbert, Julián. *Tomb Song.* Translated by Christina MacSweeney. Graywolf Press, 2018.

Herrera, Yuri. *Los trabajos del reino.* Periférica, 2020.

Herrera, Yuri. *Three Novels: Kingdom Cons.* Translated by Lisa Dillman. And Other Stories, 2021.

Ibargüengoitia, Jorge. *Dos crímenes.* Plaza & Janés, 1994.

Ibargüengoitia, Jorge. *Estas ruinas que ves.* Novaro, 1976.

Ibargüengoitia, Jorge. *Kill the Lion!* Translated by Helen R. Lane and Ronald J. Christ. FCE, 2018.

Ibargüengoitia, Jorge. *Las muertas.* J. Mortiz, 2018.

Ibargüengoitia, Jorge. *Los relámpagos de agosto.* J. Mortiz, 2015.

Ibargüengoitia, Jorge. *Maten al león.* J. Mortiz, 2015.

Ibargüengoitia, Jorge. *The Dead Girls.* Translated by Asa Zatz. Picador, 2020.

Ibargüengoitia, Jorge. *The Lightning of August.* Translated by Irene del Corral. Avon Books, 1986.

Ibargüengoitia, Jorge. *Two Crimes: A Novel.* Translated by Asa Zatz. Godine, 1984.

Icaza, Xavier. *Panchito Chapopote.* Veracruzana, 1986.

Jufresa, Laia. *Umami.* Random House, 2019.

Leñero, Vicente. *Los albañiles.* Seix Barral, 2015.

Luiselli, Valeria. *Desierto sonoro.* Traducción de Daniel Saldaña y la autora. Sexto Piso, 2020.

Luiselli, Valeria. *Lost Children's Archive.* Penguin, 2019.

Magdaleno, Mauricio. *El resplandor.* Espasa Calpe, 1950.

Magdaleno, Mauricio. *Sunburst.* Translated by Anita Brenner. Viking Press, 1944.

Mancisidor, José. *La ciudad roja: novela proletaria.* Veracruzana, 1995.

Mancisidor, José. *Nuestro petróleo.* Platina, 1956.

Martínez Sotomayor, José. *La rueca del aire.* Mundial, 1930.

Melchor, Fernanda. *Temporada de huracanes.* Random House, 2021.

Mendoza, Elmer. *El amante de Janis Joplin.* Tusquets, 2019.

Mendoza, Elmer. *Un asesino solitario.* Tusquets, 2014.

Menton, Seymour. *Latin America's New Historical Novel.* U of Texas P, 1993.

Muñoz, Rafael F. *Se llevaron el cañón para Bachimba.* Era, 2016.

Muñoz, Rafael F. *¡Vámonos con Pancho Villa!* Espasa-Calpe, 1935.

Navarro, Brenda. *Casas vacías.* Sexto Piso, 2020.

Navarro, Brenda. *Empty Houses.* Translated by Sophie Hughes. Daunt Books, 2021.

Nettel, Guadalupe. *La hija única.* Anagrama, 2020.

Novo, Salvador. El joven. Mundial, 1933.

Novo, Salvador. *Return Ticket.* Cultura, 1928.

Núñez Cabeza de Vaca, Álvar. *Chronicle of the Narváez Expedition.* Translated by Fannie Bandelier. Penguin, 2002.

Núñez Cabeza de Vaca, Álvar. *Naufragios.* Cátedra, 2011.

Owen, Gilberto. *Novela como nube.* Ulises, 1928.

Padilla, Ignacio. *Amphitryon.* Espasa-Calpe, 2000.

Padilla, Ignacio. *Shadow Without a Name.* Translated by Peter Bush. Picador, 2004.

Palou, Pedro Angel. *Con la muerte en los puños.* Alfaguara, 2005.

Payno, Manuel. *Los bandidos de Río Frío.* Trillas, 2005.

Payno, Manuel. *The Bandits from Río Frío.* Translated by Alan Fluckey. Wheatmark, 2007.

Poniatowska, Elena. *El tren pasa primero.* Planeta, 2017.

Poniatowska, Elena. *Hasta no verte Jesús mío.* Alianza, 2020.

Poniatowska, Elena. *Here's to You Jesusa!* Translated by Deanna Heikkinen. Penguin, 2002.

Poniatowska, Elena. *La noche de Tlatelolco.* Era, 1991.

Poniatowska, Elena. *La piel del cielo.* Alfaguara, 2018.

Poniatowska, Elena. *Leonora.* Seix Barral, 2011.

Poniatowska, Elena. *Massacre in Mexico.* Translated by Helen R. Lane. U of Missouri P, 1991.

Poniatowska, Elena. *Tinísima.* Planeta, 2016.

Poniatowska, Elena. *Tinisima.* Translated by Katherine Silver. U of New Mexico Press, 2006.

Proust, Marcel. *À la recherche du temps perdu.* Laffont, 1987.

Pitol, Sergio. *El desfile del amor.* Anagrama, 1984.

Pitol, Sergio. *El tañido de una flauta.* Era, 1972.

Pitol, Sergio. *Juegos florales.* Siglo XXI, 1982.

Pitol, Sergio. *La vida conyugal.* Era, 1991.

Pitol, Sergio. *The Love Parade.* Translated by George Henson. La Vergne: Deep Vellum Publishing, 2022.

Ramírez, Armando. *Chin Chin el Teporocho*. Grijalbo, 2001.

Ramírez Pimienta, Juan Carlos. *De El periquillo al pericazo: ensayos sobre literatura y cultura mexicana*. UACJ, 2006.

Revueltas, José. *El apando*. Era, 2016.

Revueltas, José. *El luto humano*. Era, 2016.

Revueltas, José. *Los días terrenales*. Era, 2015.

Revueltas, José. *Los motivos de Caín*. Era, 2014.

Revueltas, José. *Los muros de agua*. Era, 2015.

Revueltas, José. *The Human Mourning*. U of Minnesota P, 1990.

Riva Palacio, Vicente. *Martín Garatuza*. Porrúa, 2005.

Riva Palacio, Vicente. *Monja y casada, virgen y mártir*. Porrúa, 2002.

Rivera Garza, Cristina. *Nadie me verá llorar*. Tusquets, 2008.

Rulfo, Juan. *El llano en llamas*. Cátedra, 2020.

Rulfo, Juan. *Pedro Páramo*. Cátedra, 2020.

Rulfo, Juan. *Pedro Páramo*. Translated by Margaret Seyers Peden, et al. Grove Press, 1994.

Rulfo, Juan. *The Burning Plain and Other Stories*. Translated by George D. Shade. UT Press, 1967.

Sada, Daniel. *Porque parece mentira la verdad nunca se sabe*. Tusquets, 2016.

Sáinz, Gustavo. *Gazapo*. J. Mortiz, 1965.

Serna, Enrique. *El miedo a los animales*. Debolsillo, 2019.

Serna, Enrique. *El seductor de la patria*. J. Mortiz, 1999.

Serna, Enrique. *El vendedor de silencio*. Alfaguara, 2019.

Sigüenza y Góngora, Carlos. *Infortunios de Alonso Ramírez / The Misfortunes of Alonso Ramírez (1690)*. Bilingual Edition. Translated by José F. Buscaglia Salgado. Rutgers UP, 2019.

Solares, Ignacio. *Madero el otro*. Debolsillo, 2016.

Solares, Ignacio. *Madero's Judgement*. York, 1999.

Sommers, Joseph. *Yáñez, Rulfo, Fuentes: La novela mexicana moderna*. Monte Ávila, 1969.

Torres Bodet, Jaime. *Margarita de niebla*. Cultura, 1927.

Urroz, Eloy. *Fricción*. Alfaguara, 2008.

Urroz, Eloy. *Friction*. Translated by Ezra E. Fitz. Dalkey Archive Press, 2010.

Vela, Arqueles. *La señorita etcétera*. FCE, 2012.

Velázquez, Carlos. *El Pericazo Sarniento: Selfi con cocaína*. Cal y Arena, 2017.

Villalobos, Juan Pablo. *Down the Rabbit Hole*. Translated by Rosalind Harvey. Farrar, Straus and Giroux, 2012.

Villalobos, Juan Pablo. *Fiesta en la madriguera*. Anagrama, 2010.

Villaurrutia, Xavier. *Dama de corazones*. UNAM, 2014.

Villoro, Juan. *El testigo*. Anagrama, 2018.

Volpi, Jorge. *En busca de Klingsor*. Alfaguara, 2018.

Volpi, Jorge. *In Search of Klingsor*. Translated by Kristina Cordero. Scribner, 2002.

Yáñez, Agustín. *Al filo del agua*, SEP, 2014.

Yáñez, Agustín. *The Edge of the Storm*. Translated by Ethel Brinton. UT Press, 2021.

Zapata, Luis. *Adonis García: A Picaresque Novel*. Gay Sunshine Press, 1981.

Zapata, Luis. *El vampiro de la colonia Roma*. Mondadori, 2004.

Zorrilla, José. *Don Juan Tenorio*. Castalia, 1994.

CHAPTER 11

···

THE CENTRAL
AMERICAN NOVEL

···

NANCI BUIZA

THE Central American novel has always been dogged by obscurity and isolation. Lacking cosmopolitan centers of the stature of Mexico City or Buenos Aires, or even of Bogotá or Lima, Central America often figures as a cultural and economic backwater. Lying between two continents and geopolitical spheres, it has been conceptualized as an in-between space, as merely something to be traversed or exploited for the benefit of remote hegemonic centers of cultural production and consumption (Rodríguez 9–13). This has been so since the earliest of colonial times, when the isthmus was known as the Real Audiencia de los Confines (Royal Court of the Confines). If ever there was a title that suggested remoteness and even irrelevance, this was it. Since then, a sense of marginality has plagued Central American writers. The Honduran-Salvadoran writer Horacio Castellanos Moya put it well when he explained that Central America "lacks resonance in the concert of world literature" and that its writers often experience what he calls "the provincial lament" (*La metamorfosis* 42).[1]

And yet, as "one of the Cold War's last killing fields," as historian Greg Grandin put it (5), and as the site of utopian projects and movements, Central America has held a powerful allure for the literary imagination. The Guatemalan writer Rodrigo Rey Rosa noted as much when he remarked: "I don't know why I've stayed in Guatemala. Sometimes I think it's because there's so much material. . . the cases you hear about seem like fiction. In these countries of anarchy and contrast between great wealth and extreme poverty, human relations of all types are possible. You don't have to do much to build a story— just drawing from your own memory, or even writing automatically, is enough" (qtd. in Rodríguez Marcos).[2] To find inspiration, Central American writers need not look far. Central America may be small and marginal, but its history offers plenty to fascinate— and at times horrify.

NINETEENTH-CENTURY ORIGINS

The origin of the Central American novel can be traced back to the second half of the nineteenth century, when Central America came into its own as a culture distinct from that imposed by the Spanish colonial order. This was a moment marked not by the 1821 proclamations of independence but by global capitalism's absorption of Central America as a producer and exporter of coffee (Ramírez, *Balcanes* 17–18). As would be expected of a marginal region lacking cosmopolitan centers, the novel in Central America developed haphazardly, with virtually no literary public sphere of its own. Its existence was precarious and largely reliant on the literary trends in the rest of Latin America and Europe, which often arrived late and out of chronological order due to the remoteness of the region. Consequently, from the mid-nineteenth century to well into the 1920s, the historical novel, the sentimental romance, the *modernista* novel, and the *costumbrista* novel all coexisted with one another.

Guatemala's highly revered writer José Milla (pseudonym Salomé Gil; 1822–1882) is often cited as Central America's first novelist. Famous for his costumbrista articles, Milla wrote a series of historical novels set in colonial Guatemala: *La hija del adelantado* (The Governor's Daughter, 1866), *Los nazarenos* (The Nazarenes, 1867), and *El visitador* (The Inspector, 1868), as well as the novelistic semi-autobiographical travel memoir *Un viaje al otro mundo pasando por otras partes* (A Voyage to the Other World and Other Destinations, 1875), where the popular stock character Juan Chapín, an embodiment of Guatemalan stereotypes, first appeared. Also in the costumbrista vein are Milla's sentimental novel *Historia de un pepe* (The Story of an Orphan, 1882), his satirical *Memorias de un abogado* (Memoirs of a Lawyer, 1876), and his picaresque *El esclavo de don Dinero* (The Slave to Mr. Money, 1881).

Another key figure in the development of the novel in Guatemala was Ramón A. Salazar (1852–1914), who published three novels focusing on the theme of love: *Alma enferma* (Distressed Soul, 1896), *Stella* (1896), and *Conflictos* (Conflicts, 1898). Of these, the most accomplished is *Conflictos*, which centers on a marriage that is torn apart by the conflict between science-oriented liberalism and religious conservatism, leading ultimately to tragedy.

In Costa Rica, a writer whose work has gained recognition in recent years is Manuel Argüello Mora (1834–1902), who published a trilogy of short historical novels set during the invasion of Nicaragua by William Walker: *Elisa Delmar* (1899), *Margarita* (1899), and *La trinchera* (The Trench, 1899). These novels portray Juan Rafael Mora, the nineteenth-century Costa Rican president who fought against Walker, as a foundational figure of the Costa Rican nation. A classic of Costa Rican literature is Joaquín García Monge's (1881–1958) *El Moto* (The Orphan, 1900), which depicts life in the countryside with stories of love and betrayal and offers a critical view of Costa Rican society.

One of the earliest novels by a Nicaraguan author is José Dolores Gámez's (1851–1923) *Amor y constancia* (Love and Loyalty, 1878), a historical-sentimental novel about a youthful love affair disrupted by the turmoil surrounding the creation of the Central American Federal Republic. The earliest Honduran novels were also in a romantic-sentimental vein, these being Carlos F. Gutiérrez's (1861–1899) grisly and erotically charged *Angelina* (1898) and Lucila Gamero de Medina's (1873–1964) *Blanca Olmedo* (1908), which depicts the religious hypocrisy and political corruption of Honduran society through the trials and tribulations of its eponymous free-thinking protagonist. In El Salvador, Salvador Salazar Arrué (Salarrué; 1899–1975) published *El Cristo Negro* (The Black Christ, 1926), a short novel set in colonial Guatemala and inspired by the religious figure of the Black Christ of Esquipulas, the patron of Central America. Here, Salarrué explores the nature of good and evil through a dark-skinned friar crucified by the Inquisition.

The most important modernista novelist to come out of Central America, though he spent his career in France, was Guatemala's Enrique Gómez Carrillo (1873–1927), who wrote three novels early in his career: *Del amor, del dolor y del vicio* (Of Love, Pain, and Vice, 1898), *Bohemia sentimental* (Sentimental Bohemia, 1899), and *Maravillas* (Marvels, 1899), the last of which was retitled *Pobre clown* (Poor Clown) in later editions. Collected in revised form under the title *Tres novelas inmorales* (Three Immoral Novels, 1919), these novels deal with love, sex, and bohemian life in Paris. A more accomplished novel by Gómez Carrillo is *El evangelio del amor* (The Gospel of Love, 1925), which thematizes the struggle between sensuality and divine love in fourteenth-century Byzantium.

The Honduran modernista Froylán Turcios (1875–1943) published *El vampiro* (The Vampire, 1910), a novel which is set in Antigua, Guatemala, and brings together the supernatural and the Gothic. The vampire is a Catholic priest who preys upon a young woman, the embodiment of purity and love, and ultimately murders her. Echoing this anticlerical theme and also set in Antigua is *Alba Emérita* (1920) by Guatemala's César Brañas (1899–1976). Written in the decadentist style, *Alba* is about a young writer who aspires to literary triumph while his beloved falls victim to the ravenous lust of a priest. *Corazón joven* (Young Heart, 1904) by Costa Rica's Rafael Ángel Troyo (1870–1910) is another decadentist novel. Filled with sumptuous settings and bucolic scenes, *Corazón joven* is, seemingly, about a Parisian libertine who falls in love with a young woman while visiting his aunt in the countryside. The novel's focus, however, is not the couple's love affair but the jealousy and resentment of the elderly aunt.

BANANA AND COFFEE REPUBLICS

Whether through the escapist opulence of modernismo or the romanticized view of costumbrismo, the early Central American novel was largely unconcerned with the realities of social exploitation, injustice, and underdevelopment. A series of historical events would change this. Both the Mexican and Russian Revolutions would throw into relief the possibilities of popular resistance and of literature as a means of representing social conflict. The US intervention in Panama's independence (1903), the construction of the Panama Canal (1904–1914), and the invasion of Nicaragua by US Marines (1912–1933) made clear the imperialist ambitions of the United States in Central America. In Guatemala, under the dictatorships of Manuel Estrada Cabrera (1898–1920) and Jorge Ubico (1931–1944), political repression took on a new brutality. In El Salvador, that brutality became particularly vicious with La Matanza, where over 30,000 peasants were massacred after an ill-coordinated revolt against the dictatorship of Maximiliano Hernández Martínez (1931–1944). All the while, the United Fruit Company was consolidating itself as the region's largest landowner, driving the region's exploitative export economy and becoming a symbol of US imperialist power.

Anti-imperialism became one of the distinctive features of the Central American novel. *El problema* (The Problem, 1899) by Guatemala's Máximo Soto-Hall (1871–1944) is, in this sense, foundational. This dystopian novel imagines a Central America thirty years into the future, where the isthmus has been annexed to the United States, English has become the dominant language, and Catholicism has been replaced by Protestantism. Several years before the actual construction of the Panama Canal, Soto-Hall imagines a canal built through Nicaragua as a key to the United States's imperialist enterprise, which the novel suggests owes much to the indifference and neglect of Central Americans themselves. Parallel to this is a story of love involving Julio, who personifies the Latin race, and Emma, who is married off to a North American industrialist. Demoralized by the annexation of his homeland and the marriage of Emma, Julio commits suicide by throwing himself into an oncoming train, a symbol of technological progress shaped by North American interests. In Soto-Hall's *La sombra de la Casa Blanca* (The Shadow of the White House, 1927), the action takes place primarily in the United States, where politicians, bankers, and leaders of the "Tropical Fruit Company" conspire to take control of Nicaragua. The conspiracy is organized not in the halls of the White House, but in its shadow—Wall Street. The protagonist is a Nicaraguan exile, Alberto Urzúa, who conspires to liberate Nicaragua through armed insurrection.

El árbol enfermo (Redemptions, 1918) by Costa Rica's Carlos Gagini (1865–1925) depicts North America's influence in Costa Rica and the destruction of local customs and national identities. It tells the story of Mr. Ward, a banker and entrepreneur buying up land in Costa Rica, and of Margarita, the young Costa Rican heiress of a wealthy coffee grower. A symbol of Costa Rica's predicament, Margarita must either succumb to the North American's advances or stand by the colonial Hispanic heritage of her father. Ultimately, Mr. Ward seduces Margarita, and her father is killed when an ailing fig tree—the symbol of a weak and degraded Costa Rica—falls on him.

The exploitation of loggers in the jungles of Belize is the subject of *Hombres contra la muerte* (Men Against Death, 1942) by El Salvador's Miguel Ángel Espino (1902–1967). *Hombres* portrays the tensions between mestizo, black, and indigenous workers and narrates the events leading to their insurrection against the English colonial authorities over the brutality of their working conditions. Two leading conspirators of the insurrection are a former schoolteacher from El Salvador and a former combatant of Sandino's army. Their extensive discussions address the conflict between violent insurrection and nonviolent resistance.

Sandino's anti-imperialist struggles are depicted in *Sangre en el trópico* (Blood in the Tropics, 1930) by Nicaragua's Hernán Robleto (1895–1968). Based on Robleto's own experience fighting alongside Sandino, *Sangre* narrates the exploits of a group of students from Mexico who travel to Nicaragua to join Sandino and heroically confront the hardships of guerrilla warfare. The novel stands out for its raw descriptions of the violence of the struggle.

The banana production industry and the destructive imperialist powers driving it inspired several novels. Prime examples are *Mamita Yunai* (Mommy United, 1941) by Costa Rica's Carlos Luis Fallas (1909–1966), which depicts the clash between workers and the United Fruit Company; *Puerto Limón* (1950) by Costa Rica's Joaquín Gutiérrez (1918–2000), which describes the social implications of the Great Banana Strike of 1934 in Costa Rica; and *Prisión verde* (Green Prison, 1950) by Honduras's Ramón Amaya Amador (1916–1966), which depicts the brutality of life in the banana plantations in Honduras and the corruption and violence that sustains United Fruit's dominance.

Guatemala's Miguel Ángel Asturias (1899–1974), winner of the Nobel Prize in Literature in 1967, published a trilogy on the banana production industry. The first installment, *Viento fuerte* (Strong Wind, 1950), is about a workers' revolt against the monopoly of a banana company. The second, *El papa verde* (The Green Pope, 1954), narrates the economic and political maneuverings of a North American who sets out to exploit Guatemala's fruit industry and the consequences this has on Guatemalan workers. The third, *Los ojos de los enterrados* (The Eyes of the Interred, 1960), centers on the 1944 general strike by banana plantation workers that helped to topple the rule of the Guatemalan dictator Jorge Ubico.

The tyrannical rule of Central America's military dictatorships is the subject of Asturias's acclaimed *El señor presidente* (The President, published in 1946; written in 1923). Without naming a precise time or location, the novel lodges a protest against Guatemalan dictator Manuel Estrada Cabrera. Using surrealist and experimental narrative forms, *El señor presidente* depicts a society ruled by a cruel and terroristic regime, where every aspect of life is controlled by a nightmarish bureaucracy, and where citizens must exploit each other to survive. Here, the technologies of progress and civilization, such as trains and telephones, become instruments of surveillance and control.

Also centering on the figure of the dictator is *Amanecer* (Dawn, 1953) by Ramón Amaya Amador, author of the aforementioned *Prisión verde*. *Amanecer* portrays the social and political consequences of the 1944 general strike in Guatemala that brought down the Ubico dictatorship and inaugurated the democratic presidency of Juan José Arévalo (1945–1951). The network of corruption and inhumanity that had sustained the dictatorship is contrasted with the utopian possibilities of democratic and agrarian reform. Although Manichean in its political vision, *Amanecer* captures in detail the atmosphere of that transformative time.

The social devastation suffered under military rule in Central America is brought to light in *Andanzas y malandanzas* (Adventures and Misadventures, 1936) by El Salvador's

Alberto Rivas Bonilla (1891–1985). *Andanzas* depicts the roguish adventures of a hungry and sickly dog named Nerón, whose story stands as an allegory of the miseries of rural life and of the dehumanizing conditions to which the poor are subjected.

The theme of rural misery also informs *Pedro Arnáez* (1942) by Costa Rica's José Marín Cañas (1904–1980). The novel is narrated by a doctor from Costa Rica who, during a medical mission in the countryside, meets a peasant laborer named Pedro Arnáez. Over the course of several encounters, the doctor hears Arnáez tell of his life in the highlands, jungles, and coasts of El Salvador and Costa Rica, and of the injustices suffered by the rural poor. Eventually, the two men find themselves in the middle of the 1932 insurrection in El Salvador, with Arnáez fighting alongside the peasants, and the doctor healing the wounded.

REVOLUTION, TESTIMONIO, AND THE BOOM

The Central American novel underwent significant changes in the 1960s and 1970s. Of profound influence was the Latin American Boom, whose stylistic innovations and diglossic, pluralistic aesthetic opened up possibilities for Central American writers, enabling them not just to experiment formally but also to redefine the national-popular as something heterogeneous, as consisting of a multiplicity of discourses and perspectives. The revolutionary movements that emerged during these decades also played a significant role. Prior to the 1960s, Central America's oligarchy had been able to maintain a stable social order through its concentrated ownership of land. That order, however, began to break down as the region shifted from an agro-export economy to an industrialized commodities market. The rapid growth of urbanization, the proliferation of mass media, and the growing influence and shifting alliances of intellectuals meant that the popular masses could no longer be controlled without a more repressive apparatus. In response, landowners and business leaders—particularly in Guatemala, El Salvador, and Nicaragua—escalated their use of the police and the military as instruments of repression and control.

Compounding all this was the widespread frustration over the policies of the Central American Common Market (1960) and Alliance for Progress (1961), which had promised to bring economic development and democracy to the region but largely failed. Disillusioned, the middle sector merged its interests with those of the popular classes, which in turn polarized national politics even further. Inspired in part by the Cuban Revolution, liberation movements and leftist political parties began to mobilize throughout the isthmus. As members of that disillusioned middle sector, many intellectuals sympathized with these movements and began viewing literature as an instrument of revolution through which a new social and political imaginary could be forged. These intellectuals, however, faced a predicament. Though they were committed to advancing the interests of the popular classes—peasants, the rural and urban poor, the indigenous—they themselves were not quite of those classes. In representing or speaking for them, these writers could easily deviate from the "correct" revolutionary path and end up establishing yet another form of cultural elitism. Therefore, to legitimate their literature as an instrument of revolution, they had to give voice to the subaltern Other, not as an act of charity but as an exercise in solidarity. Doing so would enable their literature to reveal the popular ideologies and forms of resistance that had hitherto been misunderstood or neglected by traditional intellectual elites.

One way to achieve this was through *testimonio*, a narrative mode that involves the recording or transcription of a witness's account of her experience of poverty, struggle, and political repression. The individual is often an illiterate or marginalized member of the popular sector, or if she is literate or semi-literate, she is not a professional writer. In either case, there is usually an interlocutor—a journalist, writer, or social activist—who records the witness' account and disseminates it in the hopes that solidarity might be established across class lines. As a narrative mode grounded in truthfulness and ethical commitment, testimonio was believed to possess a unique aesthetic-ideological power not offered by traditional literary genres. As revolutionary movements ramped up their operations, testimonio gained prestige as a way of conveying the urgency of the political crisis. Writers experimented with its factual and poetic capabilities. Some fused the testimonial function with Boom-style narrative techniques, others distilled assemblages of testimonies into novelized form, and others refrained from any narrative elaboration and let the testimonios stand on their own, in "pure" form. Whatever mode it took, testimonio yielded a new type of narrative discourse that was reflective of its time.

Central America's most celebrated testimonio is *Me llamo Rigoberta Menchú y así me nació la conciencia* (*I, Rigoberta Menchú: An Indian Woman in Guatemala*, 1983), a masterwork that fuses the story of Menchú's (1959–) personal transformation as a Maya-Quiché activist with that of her indigenous community in Guatemala. Menchú's testimonio was recorded and transcribed by Elizabeth Burgos (1941–) and was immediately translated into multiple languages. Based on oral tradition and memory, Menchú offers an epic of survival, resistance, and transformation, where indigenous cosmology, political resistance, and Guatemalan history merge together. Her account highlights not just the oppression suffered by her community but also how the entire political, economic, and social system of Guatemala institutionalizes that oppression and threatens to destroy her ancient culture. Despite the bleakness of her story, Menchú also offers moments of joy and playfulness in the life of her community and in its practices of resistance.

The guerrilla insurrection that spread throughout Central America was a precarious one, driven at times by an idealism that could easily devolve into disillusionment and frustration. This is reflected in the testimonios of Mario Payeras (1940–1995). In *Los días de la selva* (*Days of the Jungle*, 1980), Payeras offers an account of the early days of guerrilla mobilization in Guatemala's northern highlands. At times humorous and poetic, Payeras's testimonio describes how the realities of surviving in the jungle amid indigenous communities suspicious of outsiders reshaped the guerrilla's *foco*-based revolutionary theory, which had assumed an easy fusion between urban Ladino groups and indigenous rural ones. In a subsequent testimonio, *El trueno en la ciudad: episodios de la lucha armada urbana de 1981 en Guatemala* (Thunder in the City: Episodes of the Urban Armed Struggle in 1981, 1987), Payeras follows the guerrilla's urban activities and describes how disillusionment set in after it became clear that the movement had underestimated the strength of the counterinsurgency offensive.

La montaña es algo más que una inmensa estepa verde (*Fire from the Mountain: The Making of a Sandinista*, 1982) by Nicaragua's Omar Cabezas (1950–) is a coming-of-age novel about a young, middle-class college student who, after learning about social injustice and political repression, joins the guerrillas operating in the mountains. *La montaña* inspired many guerrilla fighters, for whom the mountain came to symbolize the possibility of a moral ascent toward historical "responsibility" and commitment toward others. As an autobiographical text describing the author's rebirth into an identity rooted in the national collective, *La montaña* became an emblematic text of the Nicaraguan Revolution. If it has the feel of an oral monologue, it is because Cabezas originally tape-recorded himself and then transcribed the text.

A foundational narrative of left-wing activism is *Miguel Mármol: los sucesos de 1932 en El Salvador* (*Miguel Mármol*, 1972) by El Salvador's Roque Dalton (1935–1975). Fusing testimonio, political commentary, history, and autobiography, *Miguel Mármol* is revolutionary in both form and content. It is Dalton's account of the life of Miguel Mármol, a founding member of El Salvador's Communist Party, a survivor of La Matanza, and a quasi-legendary figure of militancy whose life reflects the history of working-class struggles in El Salvador. Dalton's text stems from his interviews with Mármol, whom he met in 1966 in Prague, where both were living in exile. *Miguel Mármol* plays out as a kind of dialogue between a militant of the old generation and a militant of the new one, between the "folk" historian Mármol and the academically trained writer Dalton. At its center is the question of armed insurrection and the relationship between intellectuals and the popular classes.

Another key work of Dalton's is *Pobrecito poeta que era yo* (The Poor Little Poet I Was, 1976). Set in the 1960s and partly autobiographical, *Pobrecito poeta* is a testimonial novel about the lives of young left-wing writers who revel in alcohol, sex, and politics but whose trajectories lead them in different directions: militancy, conformism, selfish opportunism, and despair. Dalton's novel is a collage of various documentary fragments and narrative modes: dialogues, monologues, streams of consciousness, diary entries, literary criticism, and journalism. With humor and sarcasm, the novel evokes the sorry state of culture and education in El Salvador and dramatizes the tension between revolutionary consciousness and bourgeois individualism. Ultimately, the novel harbors a skepticism toward the role of the writer in political revolution.

In *Los compañeros* (*Comrades*, 1976), Guatemala's Marco Antonio Flores (1937–2013) satirizes the foibles of urban revolutionaries, whose discipline and commitment is undercut by their selfishness and hedonism. A product of disenchantment with the revolutionary ideal, the novel depicts the frustration in the ranks of the guerrilla and the excesses of its militant leaders, as well as the oppression and violence perpetrated by the Guatemalan government. It blends together testimonial narrative with the playful elements typical of the Boom novel, such as wordplay, sexual imagery, pop culture, free association, temporal fragmentation, and a plurality of narrative voices and perspectives.

El Salvador's Manlio Argueta (1935–) uses the testimonial novel to capture not just the turmoil of his time but the epical history of his country. Although his work may be polit-ically tendentious, it is always suffused with the lyricism of a poet and the experimental techniques of a Boom novelist. His *Un día en la vida* (*One Day of Life*, 1980) reconstructs the history of El Salvador through the memories of a peasant woman whose life has been tragically shaped by La Matanza and the political forces that in 1979 culminated in civil war. In *Cuzcatlán, donde bate la mar del sur* (*Cuzcatlán: Where the Southern Sea Beats*, 1986), Argueta expands his epic vision of El Salvador by framing the novel as the story of a peasant family that stems back six generations and has been torn apart by historical-political forces. The family serves as an allegory of ideologies in conflict, where a her-itage of struggle rooted in an ancient precolonial culture collides with a modern state apparatus of exploitation and repression.

An antecedent to this expansive vision of El Salvador is *Cenizas de Izalco* (*Ashes of Izalco*, 1966) by Salvadoran-Nicaraguan writer Claribel Alegría (1924–2018) and North American co-author Darwin Flakoll (1923–1995). Merging the historical novel with testimonio of a more intimate type, *Cenizas* narrates the story of a Salvadoran upper-class woman who returns to El Salvador for her mother's funeral and is entrusted with the letters and diaries left behind by her mother. Through these personal documents, the novel re-creates the violent and repressive history of El Salvador and interweaves it with the intimate life of the mother. In *No me agarran viva: la mujer salvadoreña en la lucha* (*They Won't Take Me Alive: Salvadorean Women in Struggle for National Liberation*, 1983), Alegría and Flakoll address the role of women and motherhood in the revolu-tionary process. *No me agarran* evokes the life of an upper-class woman who becomes a heroic guerrilla leader and is killed in action. Her story is reconstructed through a series of testimonies from friends and comrades whose accounts shed light on the dynamics of gender, machismo, and political repression in El Salvador.

Nicaragua's Sergio Ramírez (1942–) stands as one of Central America's most re-nowned novelists. His highly acclaimed *¿Te dio miedo la sangre?* (*To Bury Our Fathers*, 1977) consists of a multiplicity of voices that give testimony of everyday life under the Somoza regime. These voices—of guerrillas, national guardsmen, street vendors, musicians, prostitutes, bartenders, politicians, and peasants—express a collective con-sciousness whose motley and unruly character subverts the authoritarian discourse of the Somoza regime. In *Castigo divino* (*Divine Punishment*, 1988), Ramírez builds a who-dunit mystery about a man on trial accused of poisoning his wife in León, Nicaragua, in the 1930s. The novel plays with testimonial discourse by satirizing the officialism of the trial and the contradictory accounts of witnesses, suggesting the corruption of truth in a degenerate society.

Considered one of Central America's most experimental and accomplished novels, *Diario de una multitud* (Diary of a Multitude, 1974) by Costa Rica's Carmen Naranjo (1928–2012) re-creates the experience of social fragmentation in modern San José. It weaves together an eclectic array of voices engaged in ordinary daily activities—among these voices, a university student, an elderly woman, a bureaucrat, a schoolchild, a sales-clerk, a hair salon customer. In this collage of voices there is no sense of solidarity or collective identity, nor even the possibility of individuation; there is only discontent and disorder. Though pessimistic about the possibility of collective ethical action, the novel's polyphony also enacts a carnivalesque liberation from monolithic notions of Costa Rican identity (Arias, *Gestos* 107–29).

El tiempo principia en Xibalbá (*Time Commences in Xibalbá*, written in 1972, published in 1985) by Guatemala's Luis de Lión (1939–1984) also involves a collectivity of voices but takes place in an indigenous village. Narrated through a cyclical chronology of flashforwards and flashbacks, Lión's novel depicts an indigenous world filled with eroticism, violence, and Maya symbology. It tells the story of a promiscuous indigenous woman named Concha, whom the local men idolize as the village's new Virgen de Concepción. Both an object of lust and an agent of female sexuality, Concha symbolizes the complex dynamics between race and gender, and between religion and colonialism.

The themes of gender and sexuality play out rather differently in *La mujer habitada* (*The Inhabited Woman*, 1988) by Nicaragua's Gioconda Belli (1948–). Written amid the triumphs of the Sandinista revolution, Belli's novel is shaped by a spirit of feminine resistance and sexual liberation. Through a conventional third-person narration with elements of magical realism, *La mujer habitada* is about an upper-class woman named Lavinia who, driven by the spirit of an indigenous warrior princess, joins the guerrilla and dies a heroic death. A composite of autobiography, history, and allegory, Lavinia represents the indigenous and mestizo heritage of Nicaragua and the possibilities of feminine solidarity across ethnic divides.

Also partly autobiographical is *Después de las bombas* (*After the Bombs*, 1979) by Guatemala's Arturo Arias (1950–), which centers on Máximo Sánchez and his development as a writer amid the turmoil unleashed by the CIA's 1954 overthrow of the Árbenz government in Guatemala. In his search for liberation, Máximo confronts the dilemma of "armas o letras" (arms or letters) faced by Central American intellectuals in the 1970s. Through its rapid alternation of voices and discourses, and by fusing playfulness and humor with dread and terror, the novel mimics the chaos and contradictions of that historical moment.

THE AFTERMATH OF WAR

With the signing of the peace accords in El Salvador in 1992 and in Guatemala in 1996, and with the defusing of Nicaragua's Contras War in the early 1990s, Central America entered a new phase in its history. The armed conflicts that had devastated the region for decades finally gave way to a broad peace-building process, inspiring a great deal of optimism. The Cold War had ended, and it was time to bring Central America into neoliberal modernity. To this end, military forces were demobilized, political structures were reformed, and structural adjustment programs promising to build the region up as a modern economy were implemented. Although the transition to peace was officially hailed as a success, the reality on the ground was always less bright. Shaped more by a free-market ideology than by a socially responsive politics, the postwar period deepened rather than alleviated people's sense of risk and precarity. It offered, on one hand, an economic system that reinforced the structures of poverty and inequality, and, on the other, a culture of violence and corruption that ordinary citizens often deemed to be "worse than the war." Crime rates in peacetime skyrocketed to alarming levels—particularly in Guatemala, Honduras, and El Salvador—so much that by 1995 El Salvador's murder rates had matched, and perhaps even surpassed, those of wartime (Moodie 46). The wave of postwar violence has been such that one journalist remarked: "Outside the contemporary killing grounds of Syria and Iraq . . . few regions are as consistently murderous as is 'peacetime' Central America" (Anderson xii). Inevitably, the optimism that the peace process had inspired quickly devolved into disillusionment.

Still, for Central American writers, the arrival of peace granted liberties that had not been available to them during the decades of political turmoil. With the threat of political repression no longer looming so ominously, and the demands of political commitment no longer imposing themselves so urgently, writers were free to explore themes that in previous decades would have been deemed dangerous or impolitic. The circumstances for the production of literature, however, remained challenging. With the exception of those few who have enjoyed the backing of major international publishers, the majority of Central American writers find themselves working in a context that lacks the infrastructure for promoting and disseminating their work. With few local publishers, bookstores, and literary magazines to count on, and with meager support from public and private organizations, Central American writers are at the mercy of multinational media conglomerates whose roster of international best-selling authors leaves little room for them. The challenge they face has also been existential. If during wartime Central American writers had enjoyed a certain prestige as the critical consciousness of their society, as a vanguard of historical change, now, with the ending of the revolutionary projects, they find themselves disinherited from any sense of historical or political purpose. Nevertheless, Central American writers have persisted and have produced a robust number of novels that engage with the traumas and transformations of the Central American experience.

Two of the most acclaimed novels of the postwar period are Sergio Ramírez's *Margarita, está linda la mar* (*Margarita, How Beautiful the Sea*, 1998) and *Sombras nada más* (Only Shadows Remain, 2002). In *Margarita*, Ramírez reconstructs Nicaraguan history from 1907, when Ruben Darío returns triumphally to Nicaragua, to 1956, when the country's dictator Anastasio Somoza García is assassinated by a group of poets. In narrating the poets' assassination plot and discussions of Darío's life, the novel establishes parallels and distinctions between Darío and Somoza and presents them not as legendary figures but as individuals of flesh and blood. *Sombras nada más* dramatizes the story of a hapless functionary of the Somoza regime who is captured by power-hungry Sandinista guerrillas. The novel depicts the Sandinista revolution not as a righteous struggle against tyranny but as a pageant of hubris and folly. It reflects a disenchanted vision of postwar Nicaragua, where Sandinista ideals have devolved into political chauvinism.

The Honduran-Salvadoran writer Horacio Castellanos Moya (1957–) has become one of the leading figures of Central American literature. His novels depict psychologically damaged characters who must navigate a violent and hostile society still reeling from the traumas of war. His dark but hilarious novel *El asco: Thomas Bernhard en San Salvador* (*Revulsion: Thomas Bernhard in San Salvador*, 1997) consists of a long-winded rant by a Salvadoran exile who has returned to San Salvador and is overwhelmed by the hostility and corruption he encounters there. Through an upper-class housewife driven to madness in *La diabla en el espejo* (*The She-Devil in the Mirror*, 2000) and a contract killer named Robocop in *El arma en el hombre* (The Weapon in Man, 2001), Castellanos Moya explores the web of corruption, violence, and impunity that sustains the elite sector of Salvadoran society. His highly regarded novel *Insensatez* (*Senselessness*, 2004) narrates the story of a racist protagonist who undergoes a radical psychological transformation as he copyedits a human rights report on the testimonies of witnesses and survivors of the Guatemalan genocide. Here, the testimonio form that had so concerned the previous generation of writers is given new potency when its affective truth content breaks through the racist ideological carapace of the protagonist.

Managua, Salsa City (¡Devórame otra vez!) (Managua, Salsa City: Devour Me Again!, 2000) by Guatemalan-Nicaraguan writer Franz Galich (1951–2007) presents a Managua where the utopian revolution of the Sandinistas has degenerated into an inferno of social decay and corruption. A thriller filled with the street slang of Managua's underworld, *Managua, Salsa City* centers on a former Sandinista army officer who, having been discarded by the state, must resort to criminal activity to survive. The novel culminates in a dramatic shootout with a rival gang that triggers flashbacks to the Contras war, a scene that suggests that if violence was once driven by political ideology, now it is driven by sheer self-interest.

Cruz de olvido (Cross of Oblivion, 1999) by Costa Rica's Carlos Cortés (1962–) centers on another disillusioned Sandinista, but this time a Costa Rican named Martín Amador, who returns to his country to investigate the disappearance of his son, believed to be one of the victims of the infamous La Cruz de Alajuelita massacre in San José. In the process, Martín reunites with old friends who have become powerful political figures and are implicated in a network of corruption and crime with possible ties to the massacre. Disillusioned not just by the Sandinista revolution but also by the sordidness he finds in San José and the disarray in his family, Martín must reckon with his own existential conflicts and identity as a Costa Rican.

Existential anguish is also at the heart of *A-B-Sudario* (A-B-Shroud, 2003) by El Salvador's Jacinta Escudos (1961–). *A-B-Sudario* is cast as a collection of writings, letters, and fragments from the memoir and diary of Cayetana, a writer who, amid the postwar devastation of an unnamed Central American country, contends with drug abuse, self-destruction, and a deep sense of malaise as she attempts to write a novel, that novel being *A-B-Sudario* itself. A product of Cayetana's fanciful imagination, the text moves playfully from one narrative mode to another—from descriptions of fantasy worlds, to streams of consciousness, to lyrics of popular music—and eschews all stylistic decorum. For Cayetana, writing provides refuge from a world of spiritual desolation and ruin, but it also awakens the agonies and traumas that torment her. By giving expression to Cayetana's repressed psychic turmoil, *A-B-Sudario* becomes a kind of allegory that calls into question the neoliberal rhetoric of peace and reconciliation that looks cheerily to the future while giving short shrift to the ugly, simmering realities of postwar life. *A-B-Sudario* was republished in 2019 under the title *Memorias del año de la Cayetana* (Memoirs of the Year of Cayetana). Escudos's grim yet playful narrative vision also informs *El asesino melancólico* (The Melancholic Murderer, 2015), which centers on the unlikely friendship between a woman intent on committing suicide and the man she hires to murder her, as she lacks the courage to do so herself. She, an upper-middle class housewife, and he, a lowly parking lot attendant, inhabit a world without hope or meaning, where both their lives are defined by solitude and the frustration of failing to achieve the consumer capitalist ideal of happiness.

Guatemala's Rodrigo Rey Rosa (1958–) has become one of Central America's most celebrated writers. His novels examine the violent history of Guatemala and the clashes between the country's indigenous heritage and the depredations of neoliberal modernity. His most popular novel, *El material humano* (Human Matter, 2009), centers on the secret archive of the Guatemalan National Police that was discovered in 2005 in a compound that had served as a torture and detention center during the Guatemalan civil war. The novel consists of a series of notes through which the narrator-protagonist documents his visits to the archive in search of material for a book project. Gradually, he finds that the traumas and conflicts of the past are not mere historical data but are such a part of the present that not even he, a cool-headed intellectual, can escape their reach. Rey Rosa's *El país de Toó* (The Land of Toó, 2018) narrates the conflict between a rural Maya community and an international mining corporation that intends to exploit indigenous lands. The novel ties this conflict to the mass anti-corruption protests of 2015 that led to the downfall of high-level government officials in Guatemala. The destinies of the characters involved, and the intrigues and conspiracies that move them, are framed within a Maya cosmology.

The plight of Maya communities is the focus of *El retorno de los mayas* (Return of the Maya, 1998) by Guatemala's Gaspar Pedro González (1945–). *El retorno* narrates the military's destruction of a Maya village and the exodus of the survivors, who must suffer the indignities of life in a refugee camp in Mexico. The protagonist is an orphan survivor who, years later, as an adult, returns to the site of destruction. González's earlier novel, *La otra cara* (A Mayan Life, 1992), is a bildungsroman of a Maya man named Lwin, whose life is shaped by the anti-Maya racism and violence that pervades Guatemalan society. The narrative traces Lwin's struggles with his indigenous identity, his re-immersion in his ancestral tradition, and his development as a Maya community leader.

The violence that has plagued Guatemala City is the subject of *Diccionario esotérico* (Esoteric Dictionary, 2006) by Guatemala's Maurice Echeverría (1976–). *Diccionario* tells the story of a violent and sadistic gang leader who is obsessed with the occult arts and launches a dirty war against the evangelical churches that have transformed

Guatemalan society. The novel explores the demented mind of its protagonist and depicts Guatemala City as a place where violence and hysteria reign. Echeverría's *Labios* (Lips, 2004) explores the theme of lesbian sexuality and the changing role of women in postwar Guatemala. Throughout the novel, tension plays out between the male narrator and the female protagonists.

The experience of women is also the subject of *Ana sonríe* (Ana Smiles, 2015) by Guatemala's Denise Phé-Funchal (1977–). The story of a family is told through the fragmentary and traumatic memories of three sisters whose lives have been shaped by the gendered violence and patriarchal structures that persist in Guatemalan society. Through parallel stories and cinematic time shifts, the novel portrays the conflicts between traditional gender roles and women's ambitions and desire for freedom.

In *Roza, tumba, quema* (Slash and Burn, 2017), El Salvador's Claudia Hernández (1975–) situates the experience of women in the context of civil war and its aftermath. Through the story of a female ex-guerrilla fighter and mother of four daughters, *Roza* depicts the numerous struggles faced by women in a country plagued by gendered violence and poverty. The novel shuttles between the civil war and the postwar, suggesting a continuity not just of the traumas of women but of their tenacity for survival. The themes of gendered violence and machismo are also developed in *El verbo J* (The Verb J, 2018), whose protagonist is a trans woman. Seeking to live true to her identity, the protagonist flees her impoverished hometown in El Salvador and migrates to the United States. Along the journey through Guatemala and Mexico, she falls victim to violence and abuse but ultimately reaches the US, where she finds freedom and support but not yet acceptance from her family in El Salvador.

Queer identity is also taken up in *Días del Olimpo* (The Days of El Olimpo, 2019) by El Salvador's Miguel Huezo Mixco (1954–). During the brief years of optimism that followed the signing of the Salvadoran peace accords, the gay nightclub El Olimpo opened its doors and offered new possibilities for liberation, possibilities that were ultimately extinguished by the war's residual violence. Huezo Mixco's *La casa de Moravia* (The Moravia House, 2017) weaves together El Salvador's postwar present and its insurgent past through the memories of a former guerrilla. The novel conjures the sense of wonder and adventure that drove the insurgency and contrasts that visionary spirit with the imaginative sterility of the postwar present.

The theme of memory is central to *Mañana nunca lo hablamos* (Tomorrow We Never Did Talk About It, 2011) by Guatemala's Eduardo Halfon (1971–). Blurring the line between novel, memoir, and short story, *Mañana* revisits the Guatemalan civil war through the perspective of a Jewish child in the late 1970s and early 1980s. Framed as a series of remembrances by the now adult protagonist, the novel evokes the oblique ways in which Guatemala's political turmoil shaped the protagonist's life, as well as the omissions and silences that shaped his memory. At its heart lies the question of Jewish identity in a country whose political conflicts fall along racial and ethnic categories defined by indigenous and mestizo identities.

Asalto al paraíso (Assault on Paradise, 1992) by Costa Rica's Tatiana Lobo (1939–) addresses the question of national identity. Set in the early eighteenth century, when present-day Costa Rica was part of the Real Audiencia de Guatemala, *Asalto* weaves together two narrative strands: one, on the Indian rebellion led by Pabru Presbere against the Spanish colonizers, and another, on the love affair between a fugitive from the Inquisition in Seville named Pedro Albarán and an indigenous woman known as La Muda. The novel depicts a violent and corrupt colonial world sustained by the exploitation of Indians and the African slave trade, and confers on Pedro and La Muda's relationship both the utopian possibilities of mestizaje and the racial hierarchies of colonialism. *Asalto* undercuts the myth of Costa Rica as being a terrestrial paradise and a white and ethnically homogeneous nation.

Costa Rica's Anacristina Rossi (1952–) also takes up the question of Costa Rican identity by probing the history of the Afro-Caribbean people of Puerto Limón. In *Limón Blues* (2002), Rossi re-creates the experience of the Afro-Caribbean immigrants employed by the United Fruit Company. The protagonist is a black Jamaican immigrant with ties to Marcus Garvey and the Universal Negro Improvement Association. In *Limón Reggae* (2007), Rossi examines a period spanning from the 1970s to the novel's present. The protagonist is named Laura, a woman of mulatto and Lebanese background with family ties to Limón. Her struggles to identify with Costa Rican society and with Limón's black emancipation activists lead her to join the Salvadoran guerrilla movement. Both these novels tie Costa Rica to the larger history of Central American revolutions and pan-African liberation movements.

A precursor to the work of Lobo and Rossi is Quince Duncan (1940–), considered to be Costa Rica's first novelist of African descent. In novels such as *Hombres curtidos* (*Weathered Men*, 1971), *Los cuatro espejos* (*The Four Mirrors*, 1973), and *Kimbo* (1989), Duncan (2018) recovers the contributions of the Afro-Caribbean laborers who arrived in Costa Rica's Caribbean coast at the end of the nineteenth century. These novels explore the themes of cultural hybridization and the loss of ancestral homelands. His most popular novel, *Final de la calle* (Dead-End Street, 1979), centers on a different matter: namely, the question of democracy and political power after the 1948 civil war in Costa Rica. A story of disillusionment and frustration, the novel depicts a country where political ideals are forgotten, corruption persists, and the oligarchy still holds power.

In recent years, the Central American novel has gained increased attention. This despite the fact that conditions in the isthmus have been anything but kind to the novelistic craft. Heirs to a culture of hardship, Central American writers have had to make a virtue of their situation. In doing so, they have produced an extraordinary array of narrative styles whose complexity and vision reveal the depth of Central American reality.

Notes

1. "Carece de resonancia en el concierto de la literatura mundial" . . . "el lamento provinciano" (Castellanos Moya, *La metamorfosis* 42; my translation).
2. "No sé por qué sigo en Guatemala. A veces pienso que es porque hay tanto material. . . Casos que oyes y que parecen ficción. En estos países de anarquía y de contraste entre gran riqueza y pobreza extrema cabe cualquier relación humana. No hay que armar mucho el relato,

sirve con recordar, vale casi con aplicar la escritura automática" (qtd. in Rodríguez Marcos; my translation).

Works Cited

Alegría, Claribel, and Darwin J. Flakoll. *Ashes of Izalco.* Translated by Darwin J. Flakoll. Curbstone, 1989.

Alegría, Claribel, and Darwin J. Flakoll. *Cenizas de Izalco.* Seix Barral, 1966.

Alegría, Claribel, and Darwin J. Flakoll. *No me agarran viva: la mujer salvadoreña en la lucha.* Era, 1983.

Alegría, Claribel, and Darwin J. Flakoll. *They Won't Take Me Alive: Salvadorean Women in Struggle for National Liberation.* Translated by Amanda Hopkinson. Women's Press, 1987.

Amaya Amador, Ramón. *Amanecer.* Tipografía Nacional, 1953.

Amaya Amador, Ramón. *Prisión verde.* Latina, 1950.

Anderson, Jon Lee. Foreword. *A History of Violence: Living and Dying in Central America,* by Oscar Martínez, translated by John B. Washington and Daniela Ugaz, Verso, 2016, pp. xi–xv.

Argüello Mora, Manuel. *Elisa Delmar, Margarita, La trinchera. Costa Rica pintoresca: sus leyendas y tradiciones. Colección de novelas, cuentos, historias y paisajes,* by Manuel Argüello Mora, Lines, 1899.

Argueta, Manlio. *Cuzcatlán, donde bate la mar del sur.* Editorial Universitaria, 1986.

Argueta, Manlio. *Cuzcatlán: Where the Southern Sea Beats.* Translated by Clark Hansen. Vintage, 1987.

Argueta, Manlio. *One Day of Life.* Translated by Bill Brow. Vintage, 1991.

Argueta, Manlio. *Un día en la vida.* UCA, 1980.

Arias, Arturo. *After the Bombs.* Translated by Asa Zatz. Curbstone, 1990.

Arias, Arturo. *Después de las bombas.* Mortiz, 1979.

Arias, Arturo. *Gestos ceremoniales: narrativa centroamericana, 1960–1990.* Artemis-Edinter, 1998.

Asturias, Miguel Ángel. *The Eyes of the Interred.* Translated by Gregory Rabassa. Delacorte, 1973.

Asturias, Miguel Ángel. *The Green Pope.* Translated by Gregory Rabassa. Delacorte, 1971.

Asturias, Miguel Ángel. *Los ojos de los enterrados.* Losada, 1960.

Asturias, Miguel Ángel. *The President.* Translated by Francis Partridge. Waveland, 1997.

Asturias, Miguel Ángel. *El papa verde.* Losada, 1954.

Asturias, Miguel Ángel. *El señor presidente.* Costa-Amic, 1946.

Asturias, Miguel Ángel. *Strong Wind.* Translated by Gregory Rabassa. Delacorte, 1968.

Asturias, Miguel Ángel. *Viento fuerte.* Losada, 1950.

Belli, Gioconda. *La mujer habitada.* Vanguardia, 1988.

Belli, Gioconda. *The Inhabited Woman.* Translated by Kathleen March. Curbstone, 1994.

Brañas, César. *Alba Emérita.* Alsina, 1920.

Burgos, Elizabeth, and Rigoberta Menchú. *I, Rigoberta Menchú: An Indian Woman in Guatemala.* Translated by Ann Wright. Verso, 1984.

Burgos, Elizabeth, and Rigoberta Menchú. *Me llamo Rigoberta Menchú y así me nació la conciencia.* Casa de las Américas, 1983.

Cabezas, Omar. *Fire from the Mountain: The Making of a Sandinista.* Translated by Kathleen Weaver. Crown, 1985.

Cabezas, Omar. *La montaña es algo más que una inmensa estepa verde*. Casa de las Américas, 1982.

Castellanos Moya, Horacio. *El arma en el hombre*. Tusquets, 2001.

Castellanos Moya, Horacio. *El asco. Thomas Bernhard en San Salvador*. Arcoiris, 1997.

Castellanos Moya, Horacio. *La diabla en el espejo*. Linteo, 2000.

Castellanos Moya, Horacio. *Insensatez*. Tusquets, 2004.

Castellanos Moya, Horacio. *La metamorfosis del sabueso: ensayos personales y otros textos*. Universidad Diego Portales, 2011.

Castellanos Moya, Horacio. *Revulsion: Thomas Bernhard in San Salvador*. Translated by Lee Klein. New Directions, 2016.

Castellanos Moya, Horacio. *Senselessness*. Translated by Katherine Silver. New Directions, 2008.

Castellanos Moya, Horacio. *The She-Devil in the Mirror*. Translated by Katherine Silver. New Directions, 2009.

Cortés, Carlos. *Cruz de olvido*. Alfaguara, 1999.

Dalton, Roque. *Miguel Mármol: los sucesos de 1932 en El Salvador*. Editorial Universitaria Centroamericana, 1972.

Dalton, Roque. *Miguel Mármol*. Translated by Kathleen Ross and Richard Schaaf. Curbstone, 1987.

Dalton, Roque. *Pobrecito poeta que era yo*. Editorial Universitaria Centroamericana, 1976.

Duncan, Quince. *Los cuatro espejos*. Editorial Costa Rica, 1973.

Duncan, Quince. *Final de la calle*. Editorial Costa Rica, 1979.

Duncan, Quince. *Hombres curtidos*. Cuadernos de Arte Popular, 1971.

Duncan, Quince. *Kimbo*. Editorial Costa Rica, 1989.

Duncan, Quince. *Quince Duncan's Weathered Men and The Four Mirrors: Two Novels of Afro-Costa Rican Identity*. Translated by Dorothy E. Mosby. Palgrave Macmillan, 2018.

Echeverría, Maurice. *Diccionario esotérico*. Norma, 2006.

Echeverría, Maurice. *Labios*. Magna Terra, 2004.

Escudos, Jacinta. *A-B-Sudario*. Alfaguara, 2003.

Escudos, Jacinta. *El asesino melancólico*. Alfaguara, 2015.

Escudos, Jacinta. *Memorias del año de la Cayetana*. Catafixia, 2019.

Espino, Miguel Ángel. *Hombres contra la muerte*. Tipografía Nacional, 1942.

Fallas, Carlos Luis. *Mamita Yunai*. Soley y Valverde, 1941.

Flores, Marco Antonio. *Los compañeros*. Mortiz, 1976.

Flores, Marco Antonio. *Comrades*. Translated by Leona Nickless. Aflame, 2008.

Gagini, Carlos. *El árbol enfermo. Esbozo de novela costarricense*. Trejos Hermanos, 1918.

Gagini, Carlos. *Redemptions*. Translated by E. Bradford Burns. San Diego State UP, 1985.

Galich, Franz. *Managua, Salsa City (¡Devórame otra vez!)*. Géminis, 2000.

Gámez, José Dolores. *Amor y constancia*. Biblioteca Nacional Rubén Darío, 1997.

Gamero de Medina, Lucila. *Blanca Olmedo*. Guaymuras, 2008.

García Monge. Joaquín. *El Moto: costumbres costarricenses*. Gran Imprenta de Vapor de Alfredo Greñas, 1900.

Gómez Carrillo, Enrique. *El evangelio del amor*. Renacimiento, 1925.

Gómez Carrillo, Enrique. *Tres novelas inmorales*. Mundo Latino, 1919.

González, Gaspar Pedro. *A Mayan Life*. Translated by Elaine Elliott. Yax Te' Foundation, 1995.

González, Gaspar Pedro. *La otra cara*. Ministerio de Cultura y Deportes, 1992.

González, Gaspar Pedro. *El retorno de los mayas*. Fundación Myrna Mack, 1998.

González, Gaspar Pedro. *Return of the Maya*. Translated by Susan G. Rascón with Fernando Peñalosa and Janet Sawyer. Yax Te' Foundation, 1998.

Grandin, Greg. *The Last Colonial Massacre: Latin America in the Cold War*. Updated ed. U of Chicago P, 2011.

Gutiérrez, Carlos F. *Angelina*. Guaymuras, 1989.

Gutiérrez, Joaquín. *Puerto Limón*. Nascimento, 1950.

Halfon, Eduardo. *Mañana nunca lo hablamos*. Pre-Textos, 2011.

Halfon, Eduardo. *Tomorrow We Never Did Talk About It*. Translated by Anne McLean. Massachusetts Review, 2016.

Hernández, Claudia. *Roza, tumba, quema*. Laguna, 2017.

Hernández, Claudia. *Slash and Burn*. Translated by Julia Sanches. And Other Stories, 2020.

Hernández, Claudia. *El verbo J*. Laguna, 2018.

Huezo Mixco, Miguel. *Días del Olimpo*. Alfaguara, 2019.

Huezo Mixco, Miguel. *La casa de Moravia*. Alfaguara, 2017.

Lión, Luis de. *El tiempo principia en Xibalbá*. Serviprensa Centroamericana, 1985.

Lión, Luis de. *Time Commences in Xibalbá*. Translated by Nathan C. Henne. U of Arizona P, 2012.

Lobo, Tatiana. *Asalto al paraíso*. Universidad de Costa Rica, 1992.

Lobo, Tatiana. *Assault on Paradise*. Translated by Asa Zatz. Curbstone, 1998.

Marín Cañas, José. *Pedro Arnáez*. Letras Nacionales, 1942.

Milla, José. *El esclavo de don Dinero*. In *Canasto del sastre: cuadros de costumbres*. Montealegre, 1924.

Milla, José. *La hija del adelantado*. Imprenta de la Paz, 1866.

Milla, José. *Historia de un pepe*. El Modelo, 1890.

Milla, José. *Memorias de un abogado*. Taracena, 1867.

Milla, José. *Los nazarenos*. Imprenta de la Paz, 1867.

Milla, José. *Un viaje al otro mundo pasando por otras partes, 1871–1874*. Impr. del Comercio, 1875.

Milla, José. *El Visitador*. Imprenta de la Paz, 1868.

Moodie, Ellen. *El Salvador in the Aftermath of Peace: Crime, Uncertainty, and the Transition to Democracy*. U of Pennsylvania P, 2010.

Naranjo, Carmen. *Diario de una multitud*. Editorial Universitaria Centroamericana, 1974.

Payeras, Mario. *Days of the Jungle: The Testimony of a Guatemalan Guerrillero, 1972–1976*. Translated by Lita Paniagua. Monthly Review, 1983.

Payeras, Mario. *Los días de la selva*. Casa de las Américas, 1980.

Payeras, Mario. *El trueno en la ciudad: episodios de la lucha armada urbana de 1981 en Guatemala*. Pablos, 1987.

Phé-Funchal, Denise. *Ana sonríe*. F&G, 2015.

Ramírez, Sergio. *Balcanes y volcanes y otros ensayos y trabajos*. Nueva Nicaragua, 1983.

Ramírez, Sergio. *Castigo divino*. Mondadori, 1988.

Ramírez, Sergio. *Divine Punishment*. Translated by Nick Caistor with Hebe Powell. McPherson, 2015.

Ramírez, Sergio. *Margarita, está linda la mar*. Alfaguara, 1998.

Ramírez, Sergio. *Margarita, How Beautiful the Sea*. Translated by Michael B. Miller. Curbstone, 2008.

Ramírez, Sergio. *Sombras nada más*. Alfaguara, 2002.

Ramírez, Sergio. *¿Te dio miedo la sangre?* Monte Ávila, 1977.

Ramírez, Sergio. *To Bury our Fathers*. Translated by Nick Caistor. Readers International, 1984.

Rey Rosa, Rodrigo. *Human Matter*. Translated by Eduardo Aparicio. U of Texas P, 2019.

Rey Rosa, Rodrigo. *El material humano*. Anagrama, 2009.

Rey Rosa, Rodrigo. *El país de Toó*. Alfaguara, 2018.

Rivas Bonilla, Alberto. *Andanzas y malandanzas: apuntes para la historia de un pobre chucho*. Talleres Gráficos Cisneros, 1936.

Robleto, Hernán. *Sangre en el trópico: la novela de la intervención yanqui en Nicaragua*. Cenit, 1930.

Rodríguez, Ana Patricia. *Dividing the Isthmus: Central American Transnational Histories, Literatures, and Cultures*. U of Texas P, 2009.

Rodríguez Marcos, Javier. "Violencia y redención." *El País* September 14, 2012.

Rossi, Anacristina. *Limón Blues*. Alfaguara, 2002.

Rossi, Anacristina. *Limón Reggae*. Legado, 2007.

Salazar, Ramón A. *Alma enferma*. Tipografía Nacional, 1896.

Salazar, Ramón A. *Conflictos*. Guatemala, Tipografía Nacional, 1898.

Salazar, Ramón A. *Stella*. Tipografía Nacional, 1896.

Salazar Arrue, Salvador (Salarrué). *El Cristo Negro: leyenda de San Uraco*. Imprenta Cuscatlania, 1926.

Soto-Hall, Máximo. *El problema*. Lines, 1899.

Soto-Hall, Máximo. *La sombra de la Casa Blanca: libro de emoción, de pasión, de verdad y de justicia*. El Ateneo, 1927.

Troyo, Rafael Ángel. *Corazón joven*. Alsina, 1904.

Turcios, Froylán. *El vampiro*. Tip. Nacional, 1910.

CHAPTER 12

IMAGINED MULTITUDES IN THE SPANISH-LANGUAGE CARIBBEAN NOVEL

MARIANA BOLÍVAR RUBÍN

IN modern languages, the terms *Caribe* and *Caribbean* are relatively neutral referents for geography and cultures, but origins of the term account for processes of linguistic "creolization."[1] Originally the name *Carib* or *Canib* was an autonym for the Kalinago and Kalina indigenous people of the southern and western Caribbean basin, which meant "brave, fierce," reflecting the one—time Kalinago dominance in the region. However, the neighboring Arawak used *Carib* pejoratively, meaning "cannibal" or one who "ate roasted human flesh," connotations reflected in early colonial writings. Since Columbus's *Carta a Luis de Santángel* (Letter to Luis de Santángel, 1493) and *Diario de abordo* (*The Journal of Christopher Columbus*, 1491–1506), the Spanish imagination has accounted for indigenous Caribbean cultures through the silencing, disavowal, and demonization of indigenous epistemologies and lifeways.

Inevitably, Spanish-Caribbean culture is the product of colonial difference[2] rooted on two conflicting impulses: one, the colonial and imperial drive to claim authority over the "new world" by arranging and renaming social space by territorial, linguistic, racial/ethnic, and sexual categories; the other, the drive of Spanish-American intellectuals for self-representation and the configuration of a collective identity. Since the nineteenth century, the Spanish-language Caribbean novel has played prominently in the articulation of imagined communities[3] grounded in totalizing narratives, such as foundational romances, scientific narratives, political fictions, and historic-mythical worlds. Moreover, these totalizing fictions tend to employ hegemonic cultural paradigms of *mestizaje*, transculturation, hybridity, and even heterogeneity as tropes to imagine the nation-state across colonial difference. While the Spanish Caribbean novel has functioned as an ontological discourse in Latin America by privileging discourses of cultural and national/regional identities (Legras 7), it also functions as a textual space where discursive elements (multiple archives, textual registers, narrative temporalities) and non-discursive elements (rhythm, myth performance, orality) coexist, paradoxically interrupting imagined communities.

The dual aims of this chapter are the following: first, to provide a holistic account of the literary traditions and movements that have shaped the genre through the drive for self-representation and configuration of collective (national, regional, cultural) identities; and second, to demonstrate that the Spanish Caribbean novel can also interrupt community fictions. Deviating from the canonical representation of the *multitude* within Latin American literary criticism—peasant mobs or politicized urban masses—I examine the representation of the multitude as a rhetorical device, a metaphorical axis, and emphasize non-discursive elements of Afro-Caribbean histories and ontologies. The representative novels—Gertrudis Gómez de Avellaneda's *Sab* (1841), Arturo Úslar Pietri's *Las lanzas coloradas* (*The Red Lances*, 1931), Alejo Carpentier's *El reino de este mundo* (*The Kingdom of this World*, 1959), Manuel Zapata Olivella's *Changó, el gran putas* (*Changó, the Biggest Badass*, 1983), and Mayra Santos-Febres's *Fe en disfraz* (Faith in Disguise, 2006)—can be read as fictional configurations of interrupted communities centered around the notion of "becoming," rather than being. These impossible imagined communities rearrange colonial/imperial differences beyond the confines of hegemonic politico-cultural paradigms rooted in mestizaje, thus configuring forms of cultural practice and political organization beyond totalizing community myths.

SPANISH CARIBBEAN MULTITUDE: THE MESTIZO MYTH INTERRUPTED

The discourse of mestizaje—conciliating synthesis of racial and ethnic miscegenation—has long functioned as a paradigm for political legitimacy and cultural authenticity in Latin America. As politico-cultural paradigm, mestizaje flourished in the eighteenth-century Spanish Caribbean, and was central to early emancipation movements, emerging discourses of national consolidation, and cultural identity. During the late nineteenth-century and the early twentieth-century, mestizaje became a highly ideological notion rooted in the idea of race framed by the Eurocentric logic of positivism. As the emerging social sciences of the mid-nineteenth century questioned the emancipatory capacity of mestizaje, other paradigms surfaced—including transculturation, hybridity, and heterogeneity, which were nonetheless concerned with how the displacement of colonial difference continued to define social space. Antonio Cornejo Polar questions the validity of the paradigm of mestizaje, as well as discourses like transculturation and hybridity that appeal to impossible syncretic conciliations, claiming that mestizaje "falsifies the condition of our cultures and literatures, as it offers a harmonious image of what is obviously disjointed and confrontational opposing representations" ("Mestizaje and Hybridity" 761). Of course, Cornejo Polar's own revised mestizaje, known as "cultural heterogeneity"—the copresence of Hispanic and Amerindian (Quechua, Aymara) cultural systems—fails to account for the presence of African cultural system within the Caribbean. Problematically, mestizaje and related paradigms still shape aesthetic models, production, and critique of the Spanish Caribbean novel, perpetuating issues associated with the displacement of difference and the hegemonic locus of cultural and literary production.

Addressing the inadequacies of mestizaje-based paradigms with concern for how the creole text re-signifies the Caribbean nation, Édouard Glissant examines oral, literary, and non-literary Caribbean texts for resistance strategies that challenge the logic imposed by the plantation system. For Glissant, the Caribbean text is opaque—unreadable—since its legitimacy and authenticity are always disputed by non-discursive elements silenced or excluded from the narrative itself. To account for excluded voices, Glissant proposes the deconstruction of the historical archive, and the "re-semantization" of the category of "The Other" by looking at subaltern loci of enunciation (Glissant 13). Like Glissant's opaque text, the multitude embodies the refusal to be othered by defying fixed representation. For Hardt and Negri, the multitude is not a concept of population, but as a model of resistance against global systems of power (2014). Hence, the concept itself disputes the iconic representation of the "masses" and the "People" in the political iconography of the nineteenth and twentieth centuries—as a part of the body of the sovereign, a social class, or a mass of disempowered victims. "A multitude is an irreducible multiplicity; the singular social differences that constitute the multitude must always be expressed and can never be flattened into sameness, unity, identity, or indifference" (105).

The irreducibility of the multitude functions as a metaphoric axis linking the reader to trans-historic, and non-linear elements of African ontology present throughout the narrative, thus unsettling arrangement of the social imposed by politico-cultural paradigms rooted in mestizaje. That is to say, the configuration of multitude in the novels renders colonial/imperial difference as an "insurmountable" struggle to define the prescriptive statements of the human and non-human.

The multitude cannot be reduced to totalizing national narratives. Yet, the novels here examined imagined the multitude as a becoming community constituted by "singularities" rather than individuals acing in common, even if momentarily, to disarrange/rearrange the national space. Like Agamben's *coming community*, the multitude is not mediated by the condition of belonging to a nation, region, or culture, but by belonging itself, that is the "insurmountable disjunction," resulting from "a struggle between the State and non-State (humanity)" (Agamben 86).

Writers since Columbus sought to incorporate Amerindian non-discursive elements like mythical traditions, oral histories, religious practices, and so on, into textual representations of the "New World." Early chronicles of the Indies—documents from Spain's Golden Age narrating different aspects of the "discovery," conquest, and colonization of the Americas—merged testimony and historiography into a proto-literary world view centered on the harmonious coexistence of languages, ethnicities, and races.

Notable chronicles are Spanish Friar Ramón Pané's *Relación acerca de las antigüedades de los indios* (*An Account of the Antiquities of the Indians*, 1571), which draws from

Arawak oral tradition to describe Taino lost cultural traditions, and Friar Bartolomé de las Casas's *Brevísima relación de la destrucción de las Indias* (*A Short Account of the Destruction of the Indies*, 1522), which denounces the many atrocities committed by the Spanish conquerors against the indigenous population. Generally, the chronicles are descriptive and historical, but sometimes they are also philosophical and political. In las Casas, the multitude—rendered through the performance of indigenous and African religious practices—frames colonial difference as human and non-human. While Christian European males became icons of modernity and thus humanity, the Amerindians and Black Africans were seen as "barbarians," to be subjected to "humanization" by means of conversion to Christianity. Humanity, at this time, was not yet ranked by racial classifications based on skin color, but these were nonetheless racial "because it ranked human beings in a top-down scale assuming the ideals of Western Christians" as the ideal model of humanity (Mignolo 16). Spanish Caribbean literary expression in seventeenth- and early eighteenth-century colonial society was dominated by plays and poetry, with prose being used mostly in descriptions and histories. One notable incursion into creative writing is José de Oviedo y Baños's *Historia de la conquista y población de la Venezuela* (*The Conquest and Settlement of Venezuela*, 1723). In a Baroque style, Oviedo y Baños chronicles the foundation of provincial Caracas by realistically describing episodes, places, and characters from the conciliatory perspective of a *criollo* writer. Most interesting is Juan Rodríguez Freyle's *El Carnero* (*The Conquest of New Granada*, 1859), a colonial chronicle of the Spanish conquest of Muisca (present day Colombia), written in 1636–1638, but not published until nearly two hundred years later.

THE ANTI-SLAVERY NOVEL: THE ROMANTIC HERO AMIDST INVISIBLE CROWDS

The early nineteenth-century Caribbean was rife with conflicts, and Hispanic Caribbean islands participated in the first insurrections against Spain. Venezuela and Colombia obtained independence from Spain in 1811 and 1810 respectively, but fought over political control of the emergent Republic of Gran Colombia. The Spanish Caribbean novel flourished soon after early movements for emancipation with *Cecilia Valdés o la Loma del Angel* (*Cecilia Valdes or El Angel Hill*, 1839) by Cuban Cirilo Villaverde, *Los Mártires* (*The Martyrs*, 1842) by Venezuelan Fermín Toro, *Ingermina* (1844) by Colombian Juan José Nieto, *El Gíbaro* (*The Gíbaro*, 1849) by Puerto Rican Manuel Alonso, and *El Montero* (*The Hunter*, 1856) by Dominican Pedro Francisco Bonó. The ease with which history lends itself to fictionalization accounts largely for the novelistic genre's success. In particular, the historical novel enabled interpretations of the past that reinforced narratives of national consolidation.

While black slavery was yet to be abolished throughout the Spanish Caribbean, Indian slavery was prohibited in Spanish colonies by 1542. It took Toussaint Louverture's 1801

Haitian invasion of Santo Domingo to temporarily abolish slavery and emancipate in the Spanish territories. Several events emboldened the abolitionist spirit in the Caribbean: Antillian slave revolts, "Black Jacobin" leadership inspired by the French Revolution; the Declaration of the Rights of Man and of the Citizen in 1789. Nevertheless, Spanish Caribbean colonies and new nations did not abolish slavery until the second half of the nineteenth century: Colombia in 1852, Venezuela in 1854, Puerto Rico in 1873, and Cuba in 1880. This period was marked by marronage,[4] and uprisings of enslaved blacks, people of mixed Indian and African ancestry against colonial institutions. Throughout the century, both slavery and post-abolition exploitation of black labor became the focus of intellectual debate and literary production throughout the Spanish Caribbean, particularly Cuba. Influenced by European and Latin American literary trends of realism, *costumbrismo*, and romanticism, the anti-slavery novel narrates impossible love stories while rendering the socio-political tensions and the ideological struggle around slavery. Romantic rhetoric in the nineteenth-century Latin American novel articulated allegorical fictions around marital/familial unions across differences—races, class, territory—to promote hegemonic projects of national consolidation.[5] Hence, the questions of race and gender were generally suppressed in order to put forth an image of national unity coexistent with colonial hierarchies. In this way, the novels' subversive abolitionist arguments and denunciations imbued with pathos and melodrama failed to accurately portray colonial difference as the foundation of slavery as an economic and social institution.

Novels like Puerto Rican Alejandro Tapia y Rivera's *La cuarentona* (*Juliet of the Tropics* 1867), Venezuelan Fermín Toro's *La Síbila de Los Andes* (The Sybill of the Andes, 1840), Díaz Castro, Eugenio. *Manuela*. Bogotá: Casa Editorial El Tiempo (2003), Colombian José Eugenio Díaz Castro's *Manuela* (1856), and also Colombian Jorge Isaacs's *María* (1867) present idealized, if tragic, love affairs across racial boundaries, set in romanticized landscapes and amidst exoticized non-white characters. In particular, Cuban anti-slavery novels of this period explore romanticized themes of race, class, and slavery, including *Cecilia Valdés* (1838) by Cirilo Villaverde, *Francisco* (1839) by Anselmo Suárez y Romero, *Sab* (1841) by Gertrudis Gómez de Avellaneda, and *El negro Francisco* (Francisco, the Black, 1873) by Antonio Zambrana y Vázquez. Juan Francisco Manzano's *Autobiografía de un esclavo* (*Autobiography of a Slave*, 1838) is the only surviving slave narrative in Spanish. While Manzano is influenced by his close association with the colonial ruling class and its ambiguous abolitionist aspirations, his narrative illustrates the Afro-Cuban struggle for self-representation and writerly inclusion in the Cuban cultural imagination.

Gómez de Avellaneda's *Sab*, sometimes compared to Harriet Beecher Stowe's *Uncle Tom's Cabin*, is an impossible romance involving a mixed-race individual in love with his owner, Carlota, who is the criolla heiress of the Bellavista family. The novel's frustrated romantic union has been read as an interruption of national unity due to the repudiation of inter-racial marriage with Afro-descendants among the Cuban Creole elite (Sommer 255). *Sab* portrays very little of the plantation economy and the conditions of the enslaved, but despite Afro-descendants being left outside the representation of the body of the nation, the multitude is always present in the narrative, not least as potential for slave insurgency. The multitude occupies the characters' minds, reminding the reader of the impossibility of an imagined mestizo community.

The novel incorporates non-discursive elements of the oral tradition when Sab retells the local legend of the *Cacique de Camagüey*. When the Bellavista family and Sab visit a cave that holds pre-Columbian indigenous cave paintings, they see a "brilliant, pale light that flickered far away on the summit of a steep hill" (*Sab and Autobiography* 71).[6] Having heard the story from Martina, Sab's adoptive Indian mother, Sab explains that the lights were the soul of a Camagüey chief thrown from the top of the hill by Spaniards. The chieftain had appeared to Martina to convey the prophecy of slave insurgency: "The earth which once was drenched in blood will be so again: the descendants of the oppressors will themselves be oppressed, and black men will be the terrible avengers of those of copper color" (73).[7] Martina's mourning ritual for the disappearance of the Ameridian peoples race bleeds into the narrative, unsettling colonial arrangement of difference. Fearing Sab's story would conjure the revenge of the "copper men" and materialize as rebellion of black slaves in Cuba, Don Carlos demands him to stop his tale: "Cubans, always in a state of alarm after the frightful and recent example of a neighboring island, could never hear without fear any words in the mouth of a man of that unfortunate color which made patent the feeling of his abused rights and the possibility of recapturing them" (73).[8]

Martina's prophecy draws attention to an invisible multitude—an elusive political subject—rising from ancestral indigenous resistance and slave revolts in a nameless neighboring island, capable of destroying the plantation system and the republican social hierarchies. Like the Camaguey chieftain, insurgent slaves haunt the imagination of the Cuban creole aristocracy, seeking to settle accounts with the past by rearranging the colonial social space. Yet, Avellaneda makes sure that the menace of the invisible multitude is subsumed by the protagonist; Sab condemns slavery as a crime against the rights of men, but he refuses to partake in any sort of uprising: "The slaves patiently drag their chains: in order to break them they might only need to hear one voice which cries out to them 'You are men!,' but I assure you that voice will not be mine" (97).[9]

THE CREOLE NOVEL: INDISTINGUISHABLE HORDES WITHIN THE NATION-STATES

Most Caribbean nations achieved independence from Spain by the end of the nineteenth century, but the Spanish-American War of 1898 left Cuba as a US protectorate, and Puerto Rico, Guam, and the Philippines as *de facto* US colonies. During this time the discourse of mestizaje emerged as the prominent paradigm for Latin American political legitimacy and cultural authenticity in the face of European and/or Anglo-American values. Predominantly, the Caribbean novels of the late nineteenth and early twentieth centuries functioned as platforms to denounce social injustices or as pedagogical tools for building a national character, promoting regional autonomy from North American and European cultural influences. While drawing from European literary influences of costumbrismo, romanticism, naturalism, realism, and the avant-garde, Spanish Caribbean Creole literature experimented with regional literary movements such as Indianismo, criollismo, *modernismo*, and *novela de la tierra* to explore the environment, history, and political realities of the region.

The Indianist novel is concerned with an idealistic return to the Amerindian past, particularly indigenous rebellions, in order to build its national identity. Continuing the romantic tradition of *Sab*, Gómez de Avellaneda's novels *Guatimozín, último emperador de México* (Guatimozín, The Last Emperor of Mexico, 1846) and *El cacique de Turmeque* (The Cacique of Turmeque, 1860) romanticize indigenous leaders of the conquest and pre-colonial periods, as do Puerto Rican Eugenio María de Hostos's criollista novel *La peregrinación de Bayoán* (Pilgrimage to Bayoán, 1863), and Alejandro Tapia y Rivera's *La Palma del Cacique* (The Cacique's Palm, 1862).

Enriquillo, leyenda histórica dominicana (1503–1533) (*The Cross and the Sword*, 1882) by Manuel de Jesús Galván is based on the chronicles' accounts of Enriquillo's revolt, and is considered the mayor Indianist novel that deals with national identity. By relocating Taino experience to a mythological past and erasing altogether the African colonial experience, Galván reshapes Dominican racial identity by erasing its African history and cultural past.

Criollismo, a regionalist tendency among Spanish American writers in the first decades of the twentieth century, sought to create an autochthonous and homogenous portrayal of the nation amid the processes of modernization and urbanization. The criollista novel depicts local landscapes and popular customs of sugar cane laborers, landless peasants, urban poor, and destitute women facing exploitation and indifference of the state. Some representative works are Puerto Rican Manuel Alonzo's *El Gíbaro* (1849), Venezuelan Manuel Vicente Romero García's *Peonía* (1890), Venezuelan Eduardo Blanco's *Zárate* (1882), and Colombian José María Samper Agudelo's Costumbrista *Florencio Conde* (1875).

In the late nineteenth century, Spanish Caribbean criollismo merged with naturalism. Like realism, naturalism rejected the literary tenets of romanticism and sought to depict the world as an objective reality. Unlike realism, naturalism embraced the experimental notions of Émile Zola that argued for representing reality with documentary objectivity and according to social Darwininst ideas (Paravisini-Gebert 691). The Cuban Manuel Morúo Delgado, known as the "Caribbean Black Zola," wrote novels dealing with slavery and the racial issues, such as *Sofía* (1891) and *La familia Unzúazu* (The Unzúazu Family, 1901). In Puerto Rico, Salvador Brau y Asencio drew from local customs and legends to present an objective image of the country's social problems *Un tesoro escondido* (A Hidden Treasure, 1883), and *La Campesina* (The Peasant, 1887), and *La pecadora* (The Sinner, 1890). Puerto Rico's experiments with naturalism explored women's role in Spanish Caribbean societies, including Carmela Eulate Sanjurjo's *La muñeca* (The Doll, 1895) and Ana Roque's *Luz y sombra* (Light and Shadow, 1903). Manuel Zeno Gandia's

La Charca or *Crónicas de un mundo enfermo* (*The Pond*, 1894), as well as *Garduña* (1896), *El Negocios* (The Business, 1922). and *Redentores* (Redeemers, 1925) explore illness and corruption as metaphors for conditions in Puerto Rico. The works of the Venezuelan Manuel Díaz Rodríguez's *Ídolos Rotos* (Broken Idols 1901) and *Sangre Patria* (Noble Blood, 1902) and later in the Colombian José Asunción Silva's *Sobremesa* (*After-Dinner Conversation: The Diary of a Decadent*, 1925) are representative of modernista narrative in the Spanish-Caribbean. Aside from the highly stylized language, these novels center on the psychological world of the decadent hero, a cultured and refined individual with a pessimistic and negative attitude toward American reality. By the late 1920s, some writers began to combine new aesthetic forms with social realism rooted in regional landscapes and the rural experience. The *novelas de la tierra*, also known as regionalist novels, were set in rural settings to depict regional autochthonous values and man's struggle to tame an often violent and chaotic nature. Rómulo Gallegos, the first freely elected president in Venezuela, was also an acclaimed writer who successfully portrayed his social, economic, and political ideology in his best-known novel, *Doña Bárbara* (*Doña Barbara*, 1929). In the tradition of Argentine intellectual Domingo Faustino Sarmiento's (1811–1888) positivist dichotomy of civilization and barbarism, *Doña Bárbara*, set in the Venezuelan plains, emphasizes the struggle between European ideas and values versus Latin American socio-cultural realities to reflect on the anxieties roused within the Venezuelan middle and upper classes around themes of race and culture amid the country's democratic aperture. His other novels, *Reinaldo Solar* (1920), *Cantaclaro* (1934), *Canaima* (1935), *Pobre negro* (Poor Black,1937), and *Sobre la misma tierra* (On the Same Land, 1943), are set in different regions of Venezuela. Another well-known *novela de la tierra* is *La Vorágine* (*The Vortex*, 1924) by Colombian José Eustasio Rivera, who experiments with avant-garde trends to describing living and working conditions for Guahibo Indians and others exploited by the rubber boom in Colombia.

The avant-garde movement began in visual arts and poetry, combining varied aesthetic tendencies during the First World War, 1914–1918. Responding to the absurdity of the war and the emergence of existentialism, psychoanalysis, and Marxism, the avant-garde embraces literature as a mean to expose and combat social alienation produced by modern capitalism. In the Spanish Caribbean, the avant-garde engages with the history and cosmovision of the African diaspora in the context of modernization (technology, race and class upheaval, mass urbanization) and neo-colonialism at the hand of the United States. For many, the late nineteenth- to early twentieth-century national discourses based on the dichotomy between civilization and barbarism hampered not only the process of modernization (and democratization) but also the production of culture and knowledge, in that they failed to account for a new public sphere: the popular masses.

Venezuelan Enrique Bernardo Núñez's *Cubagua* (1931), a key work of the avant-garde movement in Venezuela, plays with parallel temporalities. Venezuelan Arturo Uslar Pietri's *Las lanzas coloradas* (*The Red Lances*, 1931) is a source of national pride as both a remarkable historical novel and as an exemplary narrative experiment. The novel traces the trajectory of the Acerdo Fonta family, members of the Venezuelan white creole elite, during the Civil War (1813–1820). During the chaos, Presentación Campos, the mulatto foreman of the Acerdo Fonta state, rapes Fernando's sister and burns the property. Motivated by republican ideals, Fernando Fonta joins the patriotic troops, while Presentación joins the royalist insurgency in search of recognition and glory.

The narrative scheme allows a metonymic representation of Simón Bolívar.[10] The Liberator is never explicitly represented, yet his spectral image emerges as a synthesis of voices echoing the historical accounts of creole intellectuals and popular tales from slave brotherhoods. The novel opens with an assembly of slaves listening in wonder to Espíritu Santo's tales of Bolívar's legendary feats. Likewise, the novel ends with voices reverberating in the cobblestone streets of the city, "Long live the Liberator! He is coming. That man who has become his obsession. Who has become the obsession of all the land of Venezuela. He is coming" (233).[11] Bolívar's spectral representation allows for an indeterminate image; each of the opposing protagonists conjures an image of the Liberator. For Fernando, Bolívar conveys the emancipatory promise of the creole intellectual class, for Presentación, Bolívar embodies the egalitarian impulse of the *llaneros*.[12] Bolívar's specter configures a paradigm of the American creole soul, a synthesis of two essences: the barbaric violence of the regional caudillos and their speared *llaneros* (peoples from the grasslands) and the civilizing promise of the lettered city (Parra 58).

However, the multitude appears as an indeterminate space, where "war has intermingle and mixed" the "sinewy plainmen, rounded-headed Corianos, and talkative easterners, men from Guayana"(160),[13] eventually converge on the final battle:

> The ground disappears from sight to become a confused, heaving mass. Lances and hose's hoofs cleaved the air from every side. . . Blood drips from lance point, runs down the shaft, coagulates on the handle, flows down the tendoned arms, staining haft the horse. A bay horse with a dark right side, a roan with a brown right side, a white horse with a red right side. (213–14)[14]

Men of different territories, races, and classes fuse together during the battle as if a spontaneous political event where the emergent masses underscoring the (im)possibility of the modern nation grounded on racial democracy.

THE GRAN NARRATIVE NOVEL: MYTHICAL MASSES AS A RADICAL AFFIRMATIONS OF DIFFERENCE

Afrocriollismo was not only an aesthetic and literary movement, which flourished from the 1920s to the 1940s in response to socio-political context that brought about the visibility of Afro-Caribbean experience. In the wake of the Négritude movement,[15] many Afro-Caribbean artist and intellectuals, formulated their identity around the "creolization process" where cultures merge and converge in constant flux (Gilroy 209). Responding to the inadequacies of the paradigm of mestizaje to explain the conflicting process of creolization, Fernando Ortiz, in *Contrapunteo cubano del tabaco y el azúcar* (*Cuban Counterpoint: Tobacco and Sugar*, 1940), claims that the conjunction of races, cultures, languages, and historical temporalities in the Spanish Caribbean results in the phenomenon of *transculturation*, or a singular cultural identity tainted with the homogenizing discourses of capitalist modernity (Ortiz 257). Transculturation is the creation of new cultural material as a result of combining different cultural elements.

On the Spanish-speaking Caribbean islands, Afrocriollism expressed itself mostly in *negrista* poetry of Dominican Manuel del Cabral's *Trópico negro* (Black Tropic 1941), Luis Palés Mato's Afro-Antillian poetry and the Afro-Cubanism of Nicolás Guillén and Emilio Ballagas y Cubeñas. Early afrocriollista novels include Cuban Alejo Carpentier's *Ecue-Yamba-O* (1927), Cuban Linás Calvo's *El negrero* (The Slaver, 1933), Venezuelan Juan Pablo Sojo's *Nochebuena negra* (Black Christmas Eve, 1943), Venezuelan Ramón Díaz Sánchez's *Mene* (1935) and *Cumboto* (1950), Colombian Amoldo Palacios's *Las estrellas son Negras* (Stars Are Black, 1948), and Colombian Manuel Zapata Olivella's *Pasión vagabunda* (Vagabond Passion, 1949) and *He visto la noche* (I Have Seen the Night, 1953). These novels deal with the social, economic, and working conditions experienced by Afro-Caribbean workers, and explore elements of Afro-Caribbean identity and national character.

In the prologue of *El reino de este mundo*, Carpentier's concept of "lo real maravilloso" ("the marvelous real") puts forward an aesthetic and a literary strategy to account for America's natural and cultural realities, not yet captured by European literary schemes, resulting from the profound *mestizages* emerging from the colonial experience (Carpentier 24–25). The novel reframes mestizaje and transculturation by means of the parallels between Haitian Vodou spirituality and Western historiography. Relying on official historical archives, the novel portrays the rise and fall of representative black leaders of the Haitian Revolution: François Mackandal, Dutty Boukman, and Henri Christophe through the eyes Ti Noel, a slave and Vodou devotee. *El reino de este mundo* presents a syncretic vision of the Haitian Revolution: the French colonists see black slaves as idolatrous sorcerers practicing savage rituals; while the slaves dismiss the whites' ignorance of the revolution: "What did whites know of Negro matters? In his cycles of metamorphosis, Mackandal had often entered the mysterious world of the insects, making up for the lack of his human arm with the possession of several feet, four wings, or long antennae" (44).[16]

Mackandal's metamorphoses are a radical affirmation of difference. Mackandal was believed to be an houngan or vodou priest, who led the maroons to rebel against the colonists in Saint Domingue and initiated a series of "slave revolts" culminating with the Hattian declaration of independence from the French in 1801. When representing the multitude—Vodou devotees and insurgent slaves—Vodou ritualism is a valid non-discursive cultural mechanism to understand conflicting realities, histories, violence, and sexualities resulting from racial and class differences. After Mackandal spreads terror among the slave owners, French colonial authorities capture him and sentence him to be burnt alive. However, at the stake, while the houngan thrashing and "howling unknown spells" Mackandal's restraints fell off and "the body of the Negro rose in the air, flying overhead, until it plunged into the black waves of the sea of slaves" (45).[17]

Thus begins the Haitian Revolution, amid confusion, the noise of the guards, and the "howling black mass" knowing that Macandal's prophecy of liberation would be fulfilled. Similarly, the Slave Revolt of 1791 begins with a religious ceremony at Bois Caiman, when Boukman, also a *great houngan*, evokes the African *loas* or deities, ritually sealing the pact of war against the colonists. The horde departs for the Cape, leaving fire, rape, and death in its wake, until deterred by Boukman's decapitation. Even after the insurgency was defeated, the colonial authorities couldn't undermine the *loas* call to arms, and they must acknowledge the meaning of the black drums, "a drum might be more than just a goatskin stretched across a hollow log. The slaves evidently had a secret religion that upheld and united them in their revolts" (72).[18]

Carpentier represents the Haitian Revolution as a Homeric epic or a biblical myth, thus re-signifying universal history and the Caribbean as a mythical community. Nonetheless, the non-discursive elements of Afro-Caribbean spirituality rearrange colonial difference into a radical reaffirmation of racial difference, allowing for new modes of black self- representation. As an aged, free-man, Ti Noel hears anew the chains of slavery as forced labor is implemented by Henri Christophe to build his Citadelle Laferrière. From the ruins of his former master's hacienda, Ti Noel declares war. Whether by senility, or ecstasy, Ti Noel eventually metamorphosed into a vulture and sitting with his open wings, awaits for death to come, until he "finally folded itself up and flew off into the thick shade of Bois Cayman" (180),[19] as Mackandal once did. With *El reino de este mundo*, Carpentier inaugurates a Baroque style by blending history and fiction, and using repetition to emphasize the cyclical nature of events.

Carpentier's interest in using concepts of the seventeenth-century Spanish Baroque to reflect on Spanish Caribbean culture and identity was as also shared by Cubans José Lezama Lima and Severo Sarduy. These authors theorized and developed the neo-Baroque style, or *Barroco Americano*, that posits the playful display of the riches of language in order to explore the American reality in mythical and metaphorical ways.

Lezama Lima's Neobaroque o barroco americano masterpiece *Paradiso* (1966) challenges social realism with the poetic and mythic imaginary of the bildungsroman of a young Creole man, José Cemí. *Paradiso* relies heavily on allegory, Christian symbolism, and esoteric allusions to Taino and African belief systems, creating an immensely complex conception not only of the protagonist's cultural heritage, but also of his sexual, artistic and national identity. Severo Sarduy's erotic novel *De donde son los cantantes (From Cuba with a Song*, 1967) explores in a parodic manner Cuban ethnic elements (African, Asian and Spanish) through a series of linguistic puzzles, gender reversals, and religious spectacles, all culminating in a carnivalesque display of the Cuban identity. Also Cuban Guillermo Cabrera Infante's *Tres tristes tigres (Three Trapped Tigers*, 1967) uses urban slang to depict the chaotic, almost schizophrenic life during pre-revolutionary Havana, presenting a linguistic revolution against Fulgencio Batista's military dictatorship (Wilson and King 99). Cuban Reinaldo Arenas's *Mundo Alucinante*

(*Hallucinations: or the Ill-Fated Peregrinations of Fray Servando*, 1966) is an experimental, burlesque memoir of the Dominican friar and hero of independence. The Boom of the Latin American novel was not entirely an aesthetic movement, but rather a collection of textual products from the decade of the 1960, coinciding with development of urbanscapes, the rise of a large middle class, the increasing communication and the rise of mass media (Poblete 195). Mario Vargas Llosa embraces the notion of the *novela total*, or grand narrative, as a hybrid narrative that, on one hand, accounts for a "universality" of perspectives on life, and on the other, portrays the limitations of literary expression to represent any reality (26). Colombian Gabriel García Márquez's international bestseller and the masterpiece of the Boom, *Cien años de soledad* (*One Hundred Years of Solitude*, 1967), exemplified these grand narratives' reliance on mythical structure to illustrate the hybridity of Latin American cultural identity. Drawing on popular beliefs and oral histories of coastal Colombia, the tragicomic novel narrates the lives of several generations of the Buendía family. Their rise and fall unfold in a dreamlike atmosphere woven into a factual historical account. This literary technique, magical realism, exposes the fictionality of the official record by recounting history as ancestral myth, adding a sense of temporal circularity to the otherwise linear history of Spanish America.

THE POST-BOOM NOVEL: THE CONTRADICTORY TOTALITY OF MULTITUDE

By the mid-1970s, the Boom novel's promise of a new political and literary totality of was shattered by the growing disappointment with the Cuban Revolution, the rise of right-wing dictatorships in South America, and economic recession due to the oil crisis. The Post-Boom generation and emerging writers faced the new socio-cultural realities of the time, focusing on everyday culture, mass media, and pop culture genres, while integrating traits characteristic of post-modernist narrative, such as the use of unreliable narrators, intertextuality, and metafiction. Post-Boom writers rejected the Boom's overall aesthetics and socio-historical perspective, by taking distance from the technical virtuosity of the neo-baroque style, the ambition of the *novela total*, and the mystification of Spanish American reality (Pellón 280). Hence the Post-Boom novel becomes more reader-accessible as it returns to more conventional narratives forms that characterized popular genres, and deals with the impact of mass culture, complex issues of gender and sexuality, and subaltern histories (Pellón 281).

The *testimonio* gained popularity with Miguel Barnet's 1966 ethnographic study/documentary novel *Biografía de un cimarrón* (*Biography of a Runaway Slave*), a first-person account of 104-year-old ex-slave Esteban Montejo. The new historical novel questioned official histories through intertextuality with alternative registers (myth, oral histories, and testimony), acting as a counter-history by acknowledging plural histories and the complexities of the human character. García Márquez's historical novel *El general en su laberinto* (*The General in his Labyrinth*, 1989) confronts the role of the dictator in Latin American official historiography and demystifies the figure of the Liberator, Simón Bolívar. Puerto Rican Edgardo Rodríguez Juliá's *La renuncia del héroe Baltazar* (*The Renunciation*, 1974) returns to the eighteenth century to ponder the possibility of black political power in Puerto Rico. Dominican Marcio Veloz Maggiolo's *De abril en adelante: protonovela* (From April On: Proto-Novel, 1975), a stylistically complex satire, juxtaposes several revolutionary feats before and during the *Trujillato*. Venezuelan Denzil Romero's *La esposa del Doctor Thorne* (Doctor Thorne's Spouse, 1988) is a new historical novel with a pornographic twist. In a neo-Baroque style and with the linguistic complexity of the Boom novels, Romero contraposes the hyperbolic erotic adventures of the Ecuadorian Manuelita Sáenz, Simón Bolívar's lover, to the European enlightenment.

Cornejo Polar's rereading of Andean discourses, worldviews, and literary systems confronted the "destabilizing hybridity" fundamental to Latin American cultural heterogeneity (*Writing in the Air* 4). Cultural heterogeneity is understood as a "contradictory totality" ("Mestizaje, Transculturation, Heterogeneity" 118) that highlights the copresence of "dissonant, and sometimes incompatible cultural systems" of languages, discourses and worldviews ("Writing in the Air" 5). The Post-Boom novel captures the "contradictory totality" of Latin American popular discourses, subaltern worldviews, silenced histories, and undermined literary systems, paying special attention to the dismantling of a culturally privileged focus of enunciation.

Changó, el gran putas (1983) by the Colombian Manuel Zapata Olivella is an ambitious attempt to vindicate blackness in the Americas through the recovery of African histories and ontologies. The novel has been read as a historic metafiction that "decenters, disrupts and de-mystifies Eurocentric accounts of the literary representations presented in the work while focusing attention in the fictionalization of actual social, political, and historical realities in an 'Africanized context'" (Tillis 96). The novel narrates an imaginary world guided by Yoruban deities and cosmovision. Omniscient Ngafúa narrates and transits between the living and the dead, inhabiting the past, present, and future. Ngafúa traverses five hundred years of collective memories, recovering diverse moments and scenarios from the arrival of the first slave ships to the Caribbean coasts to the United States' Civil Rights movement.

Changó's narrative scheme relies on non-discursive elements of traditional African literature, and Yoruba notions of time. In poetic free verse, the author/creator "speaks" into existence the textual universe, deconstructing creationist and evolutionary origin myths. In the remaining text, a straightforward discourse focuses on the endless pursuit for liberation from racial oppression (Tillis 97). The Yoruba notion of time yields to a historical sense of continuity. In traditional Yoruba society three-dimensional time encompasses past, present, and future, which is experienced in relation to events. *Changó's* juxtaposition of time disrupts Western concepts and dislodges the linear narrative by bringing historical dates and figures into the narrative present. Unlike the cyclical nature of mythical time in Carpentier's *El reino de este mundo* (*The Kingdom of this World*), *Changó's* mythical time is a continuum. This conception of time orders the historical plot of the novel and the fates of both fictional and historical characters, who arrived in America on slave ships according to the mythical curse of Changó: after having fallen from grace for fighting his brothers, he instigated the wrath of *Orula*, the lord of life and death. The promised destiny of the sons of Changó in the new continent is their freedom from Orula's curse: "The rebellious slaves, / Runaway slaves, / Sons of avenging Orichas, / In America born, / Will wash away the horrible, / The blind / Curse of Changó!" (24).[20] It is Changó who will give the "American *Mantu*" the spiritual strength to be reborn in the New World and to drive freedom, equality, and equity in the Americas (5).

The novel deals with racial/ethnic difference in innovative ways. The protagonist is a collective of fictional and historical voices: Benkos Biojo, Toussaint l'Overture, Simón Bolivar, Martin Luther King Jr., and Malcolm X; and fictional voices from the African universe, such as *orishas*, slaves, *maroons*, and activists. Characters, author, and reader become part of an evasive, yet potent political collectivity; they become a multitude. In "To the fellow Traveler," the author invites the reader to embark on a slave ship, while leaving Western cultural preconceptions behind:

> Whatever your race, culture, or class, don't forget that the land where you tread is America, the New World, humanity's new dawn. So become a child.... Forget about the academics, verb tenses, the boundaries between life and death, because in this saga there is no more trace than the one you leave behind: you are the prisoner, the discoverer, the founder, the liberator. (xxxv)[21]

The individual stories of historical and fictional characters are bound through time, in life and death, creating a sense of continuity, rather than fusion. The multitude is a continuous sequence of particularities under the shadow of African gods.

THE INTRAHISTORIC NOVEL: MULTITUDE AS THE *COMING COMMUNITY*

Women authors became more visible in the early 1990s, many concerned with revising official historiography from which they had been excluded. The intrahistoric novel, or *novela intrahistórica*, is a subgenre of the historic novel that fictionalizes the past from the marginalized spaces, and confronts official historiography with meta-historical reflections that show the complexity of the elaboration of alternative historiographic discourses from the perspective of women authors (Rivas 20). In Venezuela, the novels of Milagros Gil Mata's *La casa en llamas* (The House on Fire, 1989), Ana Teresa Torres's *Doña Inés contra el olvido* (*Doña Inés Against Oblivion*, 1990), and Laura Antillano's *Solitaria, Solidaria* (Solitary, Solidary, 1990) reflect on the construction of memory from the domestic space. Colombia's Laura Restrepo merges a journalistic style and Magical Realism in her novels. *La multitud errante* (*A Tale of the Dispossessed*, 2001) narrates (female) forced displacement and homelessness amid cyclic violence that devastated late twentieth-century Colombian society. Internationally recognized expatriate Cuban authors include Zoé Valdes (France), Daína Chaviano (Miami), and Mayra Montero (Puerto Rico). Montero's novels *La trenza de la hermosa luna* (The Braid of the Beautiful Moon, 1987), *Del rojo de tu sombra* (*The Red of your Shadow*, 1992), *Tú, la oscuridad* (*In the Palm of Darkness*, 1995), and *Purpura Profunda* (*Deep Purple*, 2000) draw on gothic and horror conventions to narrate erotic tales tangled with Afro-Caribbean spirituality, and Dominican and Haitian national histories.

Dominican Ángela Hernández's novel *La mudanza de los sentidos* (The Evolution of the Senses, 2001) are erotic evocations of disharmony between a lost internal world and quotidian existence. Feminist Puerto Rican poet Ana Lydia Vega's detective novel *Pasión de la historia* (Pasion for History, 1991) parodies a disappearance story. Also Puerto Rican Rosario Ferré's novel *Maldito amor* (*Sweet Diamond Dust*, 1995) explores political and cultural struggle in Puerto Rico through a family saga.

Puerto Rican Mayra Santo-Febres's body of work concerns Afro-Puerto Rican heritages, Afro-Caribbean immigration, and US cultural imperialism. Her novel *Fe en disfraz* (Faith in Disguise, 2009) summons slave women's voices and perspectives kept outside official history to examine the roles of memory and sexuality in the articulation of trans-Caribbean identities. Characters such as Martín Tirado, a white Puerto Rican, and Fe Verdejo, a black Venezuelan woman, are professional historians who engage in an erotic relationship while working in a digital repository containing manuscripts, historical archives, and other artifacts of enslaved seventeenth-century black women in Latin America.

During her research, Fe discovers a dress at a convent in Brazil that becomes central to the sexual rituals she creates with Martín. Purportedly, the dress belonged to Xica da Silva, a famous enslaved woman who became rich and powerful in the eighteenth century. The dress carries a powerful curse: all who wear it will struggle with the stereotype of black women as sexual objects of white desire, including becoming objects of rape. Against the advice of the nuns, Fe wears the cursed dress, fusing her skin with that of her ancestors. Wearing the dress becomes a ritual, inseparable from her sexual pleasure with her lover Martín. The physical and spiritual pain she experiences wearing the dress links her to the horrors of the slavery suffered by her ancestors during the colonial times, and its modern permutations of imperial desire. First-person narrator Martín reads the legal records describing the atrocities committed against slave women by their masters, and then must navigate the oversexualization and stereotyping of black women's bodies that he's inherited from the privileged condition of his ancestors.

Unlike the Latin American foundational romantic fictions that allegorically deal with sociopolitical tensions around sexual and racial difference as a mean for national consolidation, *Fe en disfraz* does not resort to an inter-ethnic erotic union to reaffirm the colonial/imperial difference grounded on the "othering" of the colonial subject through sexual violence. Nonetheless, sexuality is central to the rearrangement of difference around new forms of relation with the "other," rooted on vulnerability rather than rape. The novel explores and challenges colonial hierarchical classifications grounded on racial and sexual difference by including the voices of silenced enslaved women within the social space, but most significantly through sexual rituals.

The multitude does not appear at the level of representation, but through multifarious forms of desire. Even though the novel challenges historical colonial representations of black subjectivities, *Fe en disfraz* does not privilege identity as the main category for political organization. Fe and Martin's relationship is not based on affiliations of class, gender, or race, but on sexual submission and emotional vulnerability. The erotic surrender developed through the sexual ritual opens the possibility of mutually fulfilling flows of desires that may at least transform, the subject positions determined by colonial histories (Figueroa).

This transformation is portrayed as progression through three sexual rituals. At the beginning, Martin submits only hesitantly to Fe's demands for the infliction of physical pain. Later, he accepts Fe's suffering and suffers with her. In the last ritual, both cut themselves, mixing their blood during the erotic act, without being able to distinguish whose blood was flowing. Martín's participation in the Other's suffering requires vulnerability—surrendering white male privilege—and redefines power structures that initially defined them. However, in an attempt to liberate Fe from her curse (the dress), Martin visualizes his desire to become a white savior: "Fe will scream, I will cover her mouth . . . I must undo the barrier that stops our final, lasting union" (106).[22] The violence of the language resembles a potential struggle for equilibrium, a romantic union, yet their colonial/imperial inscription of desire interrupts the myth of community. Their capacity to be *affected*, to be touched by each other's histories, bodies, and terrors, is what bonds then in the search for new paths for their desire (Figueroa).

Since its emergence in the nineteenth century, the Spanish Caribbean novel has functioned as an ontological discourse in Latin America, privileging cultural paradigms around national and regional identity. Cultural paradigms around mestizaje, such as transculturation, hybridity, and heterogeneity, confirm intellectuals' efforts to synthetize Latin America and the Caribbean ethnic and racial elements and ontologies as a cohesive cultural collectivity. The analysis above demonstrates the impossible configuration of totalizing community myths rooted in national or regional cultural paradigms by examining the multitude as an irreducible multiplicity that brings forward the non-discursive elements rooted Afro-Caribbean histories and ontologies. The novels here examined imagined the multitude as a *coming* community that renders the insurmountable struggle to arrange/disarrange colonial/imperial difference.

Notes

1. Even though the concept of creolization emerges from linguistics, it has become a key paradigm within the social sciences and humanities concerned with the configuration of difference in multicultural contexts.

2. In *Local Histories/Global Designs, Coloniality, Subaltern Knowledges and Border Thinking*, Walter Mignolo explains the double implication in colonial difference. On the one hand, it recognizes the power dynamics behind the way Europeans have represented their Others rooted on the normative and teleological project of modernity. On the other, it brings to

the foreground a dimension of human history silenced by discourses of modernity, post-modernity, and Western civilization.

3. See Benedict Anderson's relevant analysis of nationalism, *Imagined Communities: Reflections on the Origin and Spread of Nationalism.*

4. *Marronage* was a form of slave resistance where many escaped from plantations toward the mountains and other secluded places where they would form settlements known as *cumbes, quilombos,* or *palenques.*

5. See Doris Sommer's seminal work, *Foundational Fictions: The National Romances of Latin America.*

6. "Una luz vacilante y pálida que oscilaba a lo lejos en lo más alto de una empanada loma" (Gómez de Avellaneda, *Sab* 166).

7. "La tierra que fue regada con sangre una vez lo será aún otra: los descendientes de los opresores serán oprimidos, y los hombres negros serán los terribles vengadores de los hombres cobrizos" (Gómez de Avellaneda, *Sab* 168)

8. "Porque siempre alarmados los cubanos, después del espantoso y reciente ejemplo de una isla vecina, no oían sin terror en la boca de un hombre del desgraciado color cualquiera palabra que manifestase el sentimiento de sus degradados derechos y la posibilidad de reconquistarlos" (Gómez de Avellaneda, *Sab* 168–69).

9. "Los esclavos arrastran pacientemente su cadena: acaso sólo necesitan para romperla, oír una voz que les grite: ¡sois hombres! Pero esa voz no será la mía, podéis creerlo" (Goméz de Avellaneda, *Sab* 206–7)

10. Simón Bolívar (1783–1830), also known as the Liberator, was a Venezuelan military and political leader who led the countries of Venezuela, Bolivia, Colombia, Panama, Ecuador, and Peru to independence from Spain.

11. "¡¡¡Viva el Libertador!!! Viene. Aquel hombre que lo ha obsesionado. Que ha obsesionado toda la tierra de Venezuela. Está llegando" (Uslar Pietri, *Las lanzas coloradas* 301).

12. *Llanero* refers to the peoples from the grasslands of Venezuela and Colombia. During the wars of independence, and civil wars, the llaneros served in both the republican and royalist calvaries.

13. "Hay hombres flacos del Llano, corianos de cabeza redonda, orientales parlanchines, hombres de Guayana" (Uslar Pietri, *Las lanzas coloradas* 219).

14. " . . . la tierra se borra y viene a formar una turba convulsa y revuelta . . . . La sangre chorrea de las lanzas, corre por las astas, se coagula en el labrado de las manos, trepa por los brazos tensos, alcanza los cuerpos y baña la mitad del caballo. Caballo alazano con el lado derecho oscuro, caballo zaino con el lado derecho negro, caballo bayo con el lado derecho marrón, caballo blanco con el lado derecho rojo" (Uslar Pietri, *Las lanzas* 286).

15. Originating among francophone intellectuals and political activists of the African diaspora during the 1930s, Négritude refers to a framework for social critique (also a literary theory) concerned with the empowerment of "black consciousness." The movement drew on Marxist political philosophy.

16. "¿Qué sabían los blancos de cosas de negros? En sus ciclos de metamorfosis, Mackandal se había adentrado muchas veces en el mundo arcano de los insectos, desquitándose de la falta de un brazo humano con la posesión de varias patas, de cuatro élitros o de largas antenna" (Carpentier, *El reino de este mundo* 48–49).

17. "Aullidos de hechizos desconocidos"; "su cuerpo negro saltó en el aire, volando por encima, antes de hundirse en las olas negras de la masa de esclavos" (Carpentier, *El reino de este mundo* 49).

18. "Un tambor podría significar, en ciertos casos, también más que una piel de cabra tensa sobre un tronco hueco. Los esclavos tenían, debido a una religión secreta que los aleteaba y los apoyaba en sus rebeliones" (Carpentier, *el reino de este mundo* 63).

19. "Dobla y hunde el vuelo en los matorrales de Bois Cayman" (Carpentier, *El reino de este mundo* 121).

20. "Los esclavos rebeldes / esclavos fugitivos / hijos de los vengadores de Orichas / nacidos en América / lavarán la terrible / ciega / maldición de Changó" (Zapata, *Changó* 26).

21. "Cualquiera que sea tu raza, cultura o clase, no olvides que pisas la tierra de América . . . la aurora de la nueva humanidad . . . Olvidate de la academia, de los tiempos verbales, de las fronteras que separan la vida y la muerte, porque en esta saga no hay más huella que la que tú dejes: eres el prisionero, el descubridor, el fundador, el libertador" (Zapata, *Changó* 35).

22. This is my translation from Spanish the original text, "Fe gritará, le cubriré la boca . . . Debo deshacer la barrera que detiene nuestra unión final y duradera" (Santos-Febres, *Fe en Disfraz* 106).

WORKS CITED

Agamben, Giorgio. *The Coming Community*. Translated by Michael Hardt. U of Minnesota P, 2013.

Alonso, Manuel A. *El Gibaro*. Instituto de Cultura Puertorriqueña, 1974.

Antillano, Laura. *Solitaria solidaria*, edited by Tabatha Lisette Rojas Marín. Monte Ávila Editores Latinoamericana, 2007.

Blanco, Eduardo. *Zárate*. Monte Avila Editores, 1997.

Bonó, Pedro F. *El montero*. Editorial Santuario, 2007. http://www.digitaliapublishing.com/a/8821/

Brau, Salvador. *La campesina (disquisiciones sociológicas)*. [S.l.]: [s.n.]. Imp. de José González Font, 1886. http://www.iberoamericadigital.net/BDPI/Search.do;jsessionid=0D1B9C9E4 FD2F4957E8926D5FAA48C56?numfields=1&field1=docId&field1val=bdh0000084 715&field1Op=AND&advanced=true&hq=true&important=T%C3%ADtulo%3A+La+ campesina++%3A++(disquisiciones+sociológicas)

Brau, Salvador. *Episodios puertorriqueños: un tesoro escondido (estudio del natural)*. Imprenta de José González Font, 1886. Published on Feb 16, 2018. https://issuu.com/coleccionpuertor riquena/docs/un_tesoro_escondido__estudio_del_na/1

Brau, Salvador. *Pecadora*. Alexander Street Press, 2007.

Anderson, Benedict R. O. G. *Imagined Communities: Reflections on the Origin and Spread of Nationalism*. Verso, 2016.

Cabral, Manuel del. *Trópico negro*. Editorial Sopena argentina, s. r. l., 1941.

Cabrera Infante. *Guillermo, Tres tristes tigres*, edited by G. Nivia Montenegro and Enrico Mario Santi. Catedra, 2017.

Carpentier, Alejo. *Écue-Yamba-Ó*. Alianza, 2002.

Carpentier, Alejo. *The Kingdom of This World*. Translated by Harriet De Onis. Collier Books, 1970.

Carpentier, Alejo. *El reino de este mundo*. Lectorum, 2013.

Cornejo Polar, Antonio. *Writing in the Air: Heterogeneity and the Persistence of Oral Tradition in Andean Literatures*. Translated by Lynda J. Jentsch. Duke UP, 2013. JSTOR, www.jstor.org/stable/j.ctv11cw3hc

Cornejo, Polar. "Mestizaje, Transculturation, Heterogeneity." *The Latin American Cultural Studies Reader*, edited by Ana Del Sarto et al., Duke UP, 2004, pp. 116–119.

Cornejo, Polar. "Mestizaje and Hybridity: The Risks of Metaphors—Notes." *The Latin American Cultural Studies Reader*, edited by Ana Del Sarto et al., Duke UP, 2004, pp. 760–764.

Díaz Castro, Eugenio. *Manuela*. Casa Editorial El Tiempo, 2003.

Díaz Rodríguez, Manuel. *Idolos Rotos*. Editorial America, 1901. https://ia803203.us.archive.org/5/items/idolos-rotos/Idolos%20rotos.pdf

Díaz Rodríguez, Manuel. *Sangre patricia*. Monte Avila Editores, 1972.

Díaz Sánchez, Ramón. *Cumboto*. Editorial Panapo, 1986.

Díaz Sánchez, Ramón. *Mene*. Editorial Panapo, 1993.

Eulate Sanjurjo, Carmela. *La muñeca*, edited by Angel M. Aguirre. Editorial del Instituto de Cultura Puertorrigueña, 1987.

Ferre, Rosario. *Maldito amor y ostros cuentos*. Vintage Español, 1998.

Figueroa, Víctor. *Desiring Colonial Bodies in Mayra Santos-Febres's Fe en disfraz*, v. 38, Wayne State UP, n.p. https://www.lehman.edu/faculty/guinazu/ciberletras/v38/figueroav.htm

Gallegos, Rómulo. *Cantaclaro*. Monte Avila Editores, 1972.

Gallegos, Rómulo. *Canaima*, edited by Eduardo Liendo Zurita. Editorial Panapo, 1999.

Gallegos, Rómulo. *Doña Barbara*. Chicago, IL: Bristol, 2012.

Gallegos, Rómulo. *Pobre negro*. Monte Avila, 1973.

Gallegos, Rómulo. *Reinaldo Solar*. Espasa-Calpe, 1982.

Gallegos, Rómulo. *Sobre la misma tierra*. Organización Continental de los Festivales del Libro (1943), 1960.

Galván, Manuel de J. *Enriquillo: leyenda histórica dominicana (1503–1533)*. J. Cunill, 1909. http://catalog.hathitrust.org/api/volumes/oclc/21418138.html

García Márquez, Gabriel. *Cien años de soledad*, edited by Jacques Joset. Cátedra, 1999.

Gilroy, Paul. *Small Acts: Thoughts on the Politics of Black Cultures*. Serpent's Tail, 1994.

Glissant, Édouard, and J. M. Dash. *Caribbean Discourse: Selected Essays*. UP of Virginia, 1999.

Gomez de Avellaneda, Gertrudis. *El cacique de Turmeque*, edited by Luis T. González del Valle. Biblioteca Castro, 2015.

Gomez de Avellaneda, Gertrudis. *Guatimozin, último emperador de México*, edited by Luis T. González del Valle and José Manuel Pereiro Otero. Cátedra, 2020.

Gómez de Avellaneda, Gertrudis. *Sab*. Cátedra, 1997.

Gómez de Avellaneda, Gertrudis. *Sab*, edited by José Servera Baño. Catedra, 2013.

Gómez de Avellaneda, Gertrudis. *Sab and Autobiography*. Translated by Nina M. Scott. U of Texas P, 1993.

Hernández, Angela. *Mudanza de los sentidos*. Editorial Santuario, 2017.

Hostos, Eugenio María. *La peregrinación de Bayoán*. Biblioteca Virtual Miguel de Cervantes, 2011. http://www.cervantesvirtual.com/nd/ark:/59851/bmc5d9b8

Isaacs, Jorge. *María*, edited by Donald McGrady. Cátedra, 2006.

Las Casas, Bartolomé de. *Brevísima relación de la destruición de las Indias*, edited by André Saint-Lu. Cátedra, 2001.

Legras, Horacio. *Literature and Subjection: The Economy of Writing and Marginality in Latin America*. University of Pittsburgh Press, 2008.

Lezama Lima, José. *Paradiso*, edited by Eloísa Lezama Lima. Cátedra, 2019.

Manzano, Juan Francisco. *Autobiografia del esclavo poeta y otros escritos*. Iberoamericana, 2016.

Mata Gil, Milagros. *La casa en llamas*. Fundarte, 1989.

Mignolo, Walter D. *Local Histories/global Designs: Coloniality, Subaltern Knowledges, and Border Thinking*. Princeton UP, 2012.

Mignolo, Walter D. *The Idea of Latin America*. Blackwell Publishers, 2012.

Montero, Mayra. *Tú, la oscuridad*. Barcelona: Tusquets Editores, 1995

Montero, Mayra. *Del rojo de su sombra*. Barcelona: Tusquets. 1998.

Montero, Mayra. *La trenza de la hermosa Luna*. Barcelona: Anagrama, 1987

Montero, Mayra. *Púrpura profundo*. Barcelona: Tusquets Editores S.A. 2014.

Morua Delgado, Martín. *Obras completas*. Publicaciónes de la Comisión Nacional del Centenario de Don Martín Morúa Delgado, 1957.

Morúa Delgado, Martín. *Sofía*. Linkgua Ediciones, 2008.

Ortiz, Fernando. *Contrapunteo cubano del tabaco y el azúcar: advertencia de sus contrastes agrarios, económicos, históricos y sociales, su etnografía y su transculturación*, edited by Enrico M. Santí. Cátedra, 2002.

Negri, Antonio, and Michael Hardt. *Multitude: War and Democracy in the Age of Empire*. Penguin, 2014.

Nieto, Juan José. *Ingermina o la hija de Calamar*. EAFIT, 2001.

Novás Calvo, Lino, and Abilio Estévez. *El negrero: vida novelada de Pedro Blanco Fernández de Trava*. Tusquets Editores, 2011.

Oviedo y Baños, José de. *Historia de la conquista y población de la provincia de Venezuela*, edited by Tomás Eloy Martínez. Bloque Editorial Latinoamericano de Armas, 1992.

Palacios, Arnoldo. *Las estrellas son negras*. Ministerio de Cultura, 2010. http://babel.banrepcultural.org/cdm/ref/collection/p17054coll7/id/1

Pané, Ramón. *Relación acerca de las antigüedades de los indios las cuales, con diligencia, como hombre que sabe la lengua de ellos, las ha recogido por mandato del almirante*. Red Ediciones S.L., 2012. http://libroselectronicos.cervantes.es/?id=00005052

Paravisini-Gebert, Lizabeth. "Caribbean Literature in Spanish." *The Cambridge History of African and Caribbean Literature*, edited by F. Abiola Irele and Simon Gikandi, Cambridge UP, 2012, pp. 670–710.

Parra, Teresita J. *Visión histórica en la obra de Arturo Uslar Pietri*. Pliegos, 1993.

Pellón, Gustavo. "The Spanish American Novel: Recent Developments." *The Cambridge History of Latin American Literature*, vol. 2, edited by Roberto González Echevarria and Enrique Pupo-Walker, Cambridge UP, 2006, pp. 279–302.

Poblete, Juan. "The Boom, the Literary, and Cultural Critique." *Journal of Latin American Cultural Studies*, vol 28, no. 2, January 2019, pp. 195–213. https://doi.org/10.1080/13569325.2018.1528440

Núñez, Enrique Bernardo. *Cubagua*. Monte Ávila, 1996.

Restrepo, Laura. *La multitud errante*. University Readers, 2017.

Rivas, Luz M. *La Novela Intrahistórica: Tres Miradas Femeninas De La Historia Venezolana*. El otro el mismo, 2004.

Rodríguez Freyle, Juan. *El carnero*. El tiempo, 2003.

Rodríguez Juliá, Edgardo. *La renuncia del héroe Baltasar: conferencias pronunciadas por Alejandro Cadalso en el ateneo puertorriqueño, del 4 al 10 de enero de 1938*, edited by Benjamín Torres Caballero. Fondo de cultura económica, 2008.

Roqué, Ana, and Lizabeth Paravisini-Gebert. *Luz y sombra*. Inst. de Cultura Puertorriqueña [u.a.], 1991.

Samper, José María. *Florencio Conde, escenas de la vida Columbiana novela original*. Imp. de Echeverría hnos, 1875. http://catalog.hathitrust.org/api/volumes/oclc/78227500.html

Santos Febres, Mayra. *Fe en disfraz*. Santillana/Alfaguara, 2009.

Sarduy, Severo. *De donde son los cantantes*, edited by Roberto González Echevarría. Cátedra, 2010.

Silva, José Asunción. *Poesía; De sobremesa*, edited by Remedios Mataix. Cátedra, 2006.

Sojo, Juan Pablo. *Nochebuena negra novela*. Empresa El Cojo. 1968.

Sommer, Doris. *Foundational Fictions: The National Romances of Latin America*. U of California P, 1991.

Suárez y Romero, Anselmo. *Francisco, el ingenio, o, Las delicias del campo*, edited by Mario Cabrera Saqui. www.linkgua-digital.com, 2019. http://www.digitaliapublishing.com/a/62420/

Tapia y Rivera, Alejandro. *Juliet of the Tropics: A Bilingual Edition of Alejandro Tapia y Rivera's*, edited by John Thomas Maddox La cuarterona. Cambria Press, 2016.

Tapia y Rivera, Alejandro. *La palma del cacique : leyenda histórica de Puerto Rico*. Imprenta del Tiempo, 1862. https://www.cervantesvirtual.com/buscador/?q=+La+Palma+del+Cacique

Tillis, Antonio. "Changó, El Gran Putas: A Postmodern Historiographic Metafictional Text." *Afro-Hispanic Review*, vol. 21, nos. 1/2, 2002, pp. 171–78. *JSTOR*, www.jstor.org/stable/23054497

Toro, Fermin. *Los mártires novela*, edited by Gustavo Luis Carrera and Amaya Llebot de Perez. Universidad Central de Venezuela, 1966.

Toro, Fermín, and Virgilio Tosta. *Tres relatos y una novela*. Universidad Central de Venezuela, 1971.

Torres, Ana Teresa. *Doña Inés contra el olvido*. Monte Avila Editores, 1992.

Uslar, Pietri A. *Las lanzas coloradas*, edited by Domingo Miliani. Cátedra, 2014.

Uslar, Pietri A. *The Red Lances*. Translated by Harriet Onís and Federico Onís. Alfred A. Knopf, 1963.

Vargas, Llosa M. *Carta de batalla por* Tirant Lo Blanc. Alfaguara, 2016.

Vega, Ana Lydia. *Pasión de historia y otras historias de pasión*. Ediciones de la Flor, 2015.

Veloz Maggiolo, Marcio. *De abril en adelante: protonovela*. Archivo General de la Nación, 2018.

Villaverde, Cirilo. *Cecilia Valdés o La loma del ángel*, edited by Jean Lamore. Cátedra, 2016.

Wilson, Jason, and John King. "Spanish American Narrative, 1920–1970." *The Cambridge Companion to Modern Latin American Culture*, edited by John King, Cambridge UP, 2006, pp. 84–104.

Zambrana y Vázquez, Antonio. *El negro Francisco novela orijinal de costumbres cubanas*. Imprenta de la Libreria del Mercurio, 1875. http://catalog.hathitrust.org/api/volumes/oclc/237627750.html.

Zapata, Olivella M. *Changó, the Biggest Badass*. Translated by Jonathan Tittler. Texas Tech UP, 2010.

Zapata, Olivella M. *Changó, el gran putas*. Oveja Negra, 1983.

Zapata Olivella, Manuel. *He visto la noche*. Bedout, 1982.

Zapata Olivella, Manuel. *Pasión vagabunda*. Ministerio de Cultura, 2000.

Zeno Gandía. *Garduña*, edited by Manuel and Lilliana Ramos Collado. La Editorial, Universidad de Puerto Rico, 2010.

Zeno Gandía, Manuel. *La charca*. Caracas, Venezuela: Biblioteca Ayacucho, 1978. http://biblioteca.clacso.edu.ar/gsdl/collect/clacso/index/assoc/D14560.dir/La_charca_Manuel_Zeno_Gandia.pdf

Zeno Gandía, Manuel. *El negocio: crónicas de un mundo enfermo*. Edil, 1973.

Zeno Gandía, Manuel. *Redentores*, edited by Aníbal González. La Editorial, Universidad de Puerto Rico, 2010.

CHAPTER 13

THE ANDEAN NOVEL

The (De)construction of a Written Territory

NÚRIA VILANOVA

THE Andes as a cultural and territorial entity has historically been articulated through artistic practices. With the Spanish colonization in the sixteenth century, writing not only became an instrument of exploitation and subordination but also a tool of communication and negotiation. Oral literary forms of expression in Quechua and Aymara—the two main original languages of the Andes—were transferred into writing using the Latin alphabet,[1] while new genres emerged in Spanish in a region with profound oral traditions. This chapter focuses on the impact of the Andes on a genre that more solidly belonged to a written European tradition: the novel. It addresses the tension between literacy and orality and delves into the discussion on *indigenismo,* as a characteristic artistic, political, and social movement related to Andean indigeneity, going back to the nineteenth century, emphasizing the work of intellectuals at the turn of the twentieth century, such as Manuel González Prada and José Carlos Mariátegui. This text presents an historical outlook into the genre of the novel by exploring those elements that have contributed to determine the Andeanness of novels associated with the region.

Many questions arise when attempting to identify a corpus for the Andean novel. Thus, the following pages examine works in which the Andes are the driving force that constructs their aesthetics and narrative discourses, like *Aves sin nido* (*Torn from the Nest*, 1889), by Clorinda Matto de Turner. It also explores those in which the Andes are the force that structurally disrupts and reformulates the very genre of the novel, as is the case with Gamaliel Churata's (Arequipa 1897–Lima 1969) *El pez de oro* (The Golden Fish, 1957) and José María Arguedas's (Andahuaylas 1911–Lima 1969) *El zorro de arriba y el zorro de abajo* (*The Fox From Up Above and the Fox From Down Below*, 1971). It also looks at novels in which the Andes are used as a reference or a setting but do not impact their literary construction, as in Nobel Laureate Mario Vargas Llosa's (Arequipa 1938–) *Lituma en los Andes* (*Death in the Andes*, 1993). These different literary interventions of the Andes capture the narrative dynamics and tensions identifiable in most novels associated with the region. In this sense, this article aims at reflecting on the elements that construct the literary imaginary of the Andes, while seeking to explore how novels related to the Andes have generated their own imaginary of the region. In summary, rather than a classification of the different literary trends within the broad categorization of the Andean novel, or an exhaustive list of novels from the region, this article addresses works predominately from the three countries at the core of the Andes, Bolivia, Ecuador, and Peru, in order to enquire about the imaginary construction of the written Andes. These countries share cultural and demographic features characterized by the presence of a large indigenous population, mainly Aymara and Quechua. In Colombia, the exploration of indigeneity through written works has developed within different dynamics and parameters, and thus the literary presence of the Andes has evolved through other avenues, as seen later in the chapter.

The traumatic impact of the Spanish occupation was profoundly felt throughout the Andean region, running across one of the longest mountain ranges of the world from what is today Colombia and Venezuela all the way to southern Chile. The implementation of an extractionist economic system, the enforcement of slave labor practices, the imposition of an alien religion and foreign cultural customs, and the irruption of an unknown language were the main determining components in the shaping of the region, following the disruptive arrival of the colonizers. While these streams are all intertwined, the imposition not only of a new language but even more importantly of an unfamiliar system of communication is at the core of this chapter. Andean writing needs to be addressed vis-à-vis orality as the predominant modality of linguistic communication in the region. Among others, Antonio Cornejo Polar and Martin Lienhard shed light on the decisive role played by the tension between orality and literacy to understand cultural processes in the Andean area since colonial times.[2] As noted by both, from early on, writing became an instrument of oppression and domination and subsequentially—and conditioned to survival—one of communication and negotiation. Economic rule as well as religious imposition took the form of the written word. Both the Bible, presented as the uncontestable, sacred expression of the only conceivable God, and the *encomienda*, the Spanish Crown decree that granted colonizers the right to the land and indigenous labor, were imprinted and enforced in writing. Thus, since the early colonial times, the written word became associated with the imposition of power and the oppression of the indigenous people under colonial rule.

Writing soon evolved to be also the instrument enabling communication and negotiation with the Spanish colonial administration. Whereas many missionaries learned indigenous languages to interact with individuals and communities and to accomplish their evangelical mission, and even transferred the oral tongues into writing using the Latin alphabet,[3] written documents prove that one of the means for the indigenous people to resist and eventually negotiate their abusive circumstances was the use of the same language and the same mode of communication that had erupted into their world: writing. The prominent epistolary work of Quechua intellectual Felipe Guamán Poma de Ayala, *El Primer Nueva Corónica y Buen Gobierno* (*The First New Chronicle and Good Government*), written in 1615 in Spanish with a Quechua substratum, is unique in its broad dimension and extent, and in the blatant way in which Guamán Poma challenges the corrupt Spanish administration and the abusive clergy. However, this exceptional text is not the only testimonial work of the sort. While restricted to those individuals, predominantly men, who could learn how to write and become acquainted with Spanish, a written form of denunciation and resistance by individuals with diverse background within the indigenous hierarchy, usually from the upper ranks, became practice from mid-sixteenth century onward.[4] Testimonials, manifestos, letters and other documents that constitute this important corpus that runs parallel to the chronicles written by the Spaniards present a revolutionary approach to writing. This is due not only to the contesting nature of these texts, but also to their rupture with Spanish conventional forms of writing in the day. In other words, the Aymara and Quechua oral bedrock permeated indigenous Spanish texts. While the first novels in Spanish emerging in the Andes in the nineteenth century tend to follow a standardized Hispanic narrative tradition, groundbreaking works connecting with an Andean unconventional form of writing emerged afterward, foremost by writers such as Gamaliel Churata and José María Arguedas, as seen later in this chapter. As part of a broader movement addressing the colonial heritage of oppression and exploitation of indigenous peoples, the first novels identified as Andean because of their thematic universe and its referential world are the so-called *indigenista* novels. These are characterized by their heterogeneous approaches, similarly to the *indigenista* political, social, and artistic movement at large.[5] Mostly, the *indigenista* works shed light on the abuse exercised by the ruling civil and religious authorities on indigenous individuals and communities. The Latin American *indigenista* novel thrived in the Andean countries studied in this article and Mexico. By and large, the writers who embraced *indigenismo* were generally white criollos (of European ascendence) from the middle-upper classes, who had become aware of the injustices and marginalization endured by the indigenous population under the structures of power inherited from the colonial administration and the society that resulted from that experience.[6] Nonetheless, their perspective and hence that of their novels, while compassionate and sympathetic, tends to also be external, paternalistic, and predominantly tinted by their criollo, Western outlook. As reflected in their work, most *indigenista* writers believed that the indigenous population should be educated following European-inherited standards to become assimilated into a mainstream culture that would enable a better life under a Western episteme and a fuller integration into a national economic system. A main precursor of this prolific current in the Andes is the Peruvian female writer Clorinda Matto de Turner (Cusco 1852–Buenos Aires 1909) and her paradigmatic novel *Aves sin nido*.[7] The novel captures the long and disturbing history of abuse in the persona of a priest who has fathered the two protagonists who, unaware of their blood ties, fall deeply in love. While Matto de Turner openly uses her narrative to denounce the longstanding mistreatment and marginality undergone by Andean indigenous people, *Aves sin nido* depicts indigenous characters and their communities as a defenseless collective who need to be saved by the intervention of urban, educated characters, who are portrayed as their saviors and guides to a more prosperous life; hence the external, compassionate, yet also condescending approach of the novel in tune with the predominant *indigenista* outlook.

Another outstanding woman author of the time is the Bolivian writer Adela Zamudio (Cochabamba 1854–1928), who pioneered the feminist movement with her multifarious and committed writing. Although most prolific as a poet, her novel *Íntimas* (Close Friends, 1913) deserves special mention insofar as it is considered the first Bolivian feminist novel.[8] Far more conservative, Alcides Arguedas (La Paz 1879–Chulumani 1946) was one of the first writers to depict the indigenous population of the Bolivian Andes in his narrative. As the titles of his better-known works reveal, the Bolivian writer approaches indigeneity as a problem, as a national dilemma that has not been sufficiently addressed. As Omar Rocha notes, in Arguedas's essay *Pueblo enfermo* (Sick People, 1909) and in his novel *Raza de bronce* (Bronce Race, 1919), Arguedas presents his country from the perspective of its deficiencies (Rocha 103), its unresolved political, social, economic, and cultural divides—a situation he clearly attributes to the country's large indigenous population. Thus, as Elizabeth Monasterios and Rosario Rodríguez point out, Alcides Arguedas's works straddle between compassion and condemnation of the indigenous population, whom he ultimately perceives as the origin of Bolivia's ills (Monasterios and Rodríguez 107). The two scholars go a step further by asserting that *Raza de bronce* hints at the preoccupation with a potential revolution led by the Aymara people if the white liberal oligarchy fails to act together to defend their interests, identified by the Bolivian writer as the interest of the country as a whole (Monasterios and Rodríguez 118).

Also from Bolivia, Jesús Lara (Cochabamba 1898–1980), provides a very different perspective in his approach to indigeneity. With left-wing convictions, Lara was an active militant in the Communist Party. He also fought in the Bolivian-Paraguayan Chaco War (1932–1935). Both events had a profound impact on his essays and fiction writing. His activism impacts his narrative, and thus his style and literary discourse evolve around his main mission as an activist writer. The main characters of his fictional work, which includes several novels, such as *Surumi* (1943), *Yanakuna* (1952), *Yawarninchij* (1959), *Sinchicay* (1962), *Llalliypacha* (1965), *Inkallajta* (1967), and *Paqarin* (1974) are the Quechua population of his native Cochabamba, in the Andean valley in central Bolivia, with whom he identifies and sees as main victims of prevalent political, social, and economic injustice and oppression. Estelle Tarica has associated Lara's work with Antonio Cornejo Polar's concept of the *heteróclita pluralidad* (heteroclite plurality), which captures the literary outcome of the tension between orality and literacy at the core of Andean writing, and the cultural contradictions between indigeneity and the European heritage, addressed in Cornejo Polar's influential article "Heterogeneidad y contradicción en la literatura andina." Furthermore, echoing Bolivian thinker René Zavaleta's idea of *realidad abigarrada*, translated into English as "motley reality" (Freeland), Tarica approaches Lara's fictional work from the internal frictions revealed in his writings, foremost the struggle to reconcile the tensions described in his characters and in the plot of his novels. Additionally, his works unveil the author's eagerness to identify as Quechua even though his fiction was written in Spanish and evolved within the parameters established by Ángel Rama in his transcendental conceptualization of the *ciudad letrada* (lettered city), to capture the impact of writing in the urban milieu as the symbolic and real site where state power has been exercised since colonial times.[9] Very significant is also the work of Néstor Taboada Terán (La Paz 1929–Cochabamba 1985), particularly his novel *Manchay Puytu. El amor que quiso ocultar Dios* (Manchay Puytu: The Love that Wanted to Hide God, 1977) located in the Andean city of Potosí.

In Peru, several writers left a significant exploratory trail of approaches toward Andean indigeneity and its artistic—foremost literary—representation. In different ways, all shared a political stance closely connected to their literary expression. It is important to mention María Wiesse (Lima 1894–1964), who actively contributed to Mariátegui's cultural and political magazine *Amauta* (1926–1930), and wrote two novels, poetry, essays, and short stories such as "El forastero" ("The Stranger," 1928) and "El veneno" ("Poison," 1929), where she denounces the abuse and oppression undergone by indigenous people; Gamaliel Churata, who has had a long-lasting impact on Andean letters; Jorge Icaza (Quito 1906–1978); Ciro Alegría (La Libertad 1909–Chaclacayo 1967); and José María Arguedas, whose transcendent work is at the heart of the embedded contradictions in Andean letters. In Peru, the support for indigenous people and their political and social struggle has a main precursor in Luis E. Valcárcel's non-fictional account of the Peruvian Andean world *Tempestad en los Andes* (Tempest in the Andes, 1927). With a prologue by José Carlos Mariátegui, the book evokes pre-colonial Andean civilizations to conclude that the time has arrived to confront and defy the long-lasting oligarchical powers that had suppressed indigeneity since colonization. Valcárcel's thesis of a "storm" approaching the Andes is in tune with Mariátegui´s belief in a future socialist Peruvian nation led by the values embedded in Andean indigenous societies. Enrique López Albújar and his *Cuentos andinos* (Andean Stories, 1920) are also influential insofar as he attempts to provide a view into Andean indigeneity that escapes a simplistic, folklorized view on indigenous individuals and communities. Nonetheless, his views are still shaped by his external positionality. In 1932, he published *Nuevos cuentos andinos* (New Andean Stories), where he tried to convey more social awareness toward his indigenous characters and their struggles. Albújar has also rightly been identified as the pioneer of Andean fiction on brigandage (Dawe and Lewis 247).

The writer's political stance is the driving force of Manuel Scorza's novels. Born in Lima in 1928,[10] Scorza, similarly to Lara in Bolivia, was a committed poet when he published his first novel *Redoble por Rancas* (*Drums for Rancas*, 1970), which, along with his other novels,[11] "marks a significant contribution to *indigenista* fiction" (Higgins 316). In this sense, Scorza reproduces in his fiction the long-standing history of exploitation suffered by indigenous communities, but he identifies their struggle within a political framework rather than within a social context, as most *indigenista* writers would do.

Indigenista literature was also produced in Ecuador. A main figure in that respect is Jorge Icaza, whose first novel, *Huasipungo* (*The Villagers*, 1934), is his most transcendental. In his masterwork, Icaza addresses the degrading conditions of Ecuadorian indigenous peoples in the first half of the twentieth century, their lives practically submitted to slavery with the complicity of the economic and political powers and the

Catholic Church. *Huasipungo*'s social denunciation transcends traditional *indigenismo* due to its focus on the economic injustice and inequality impacting the subaltern classes, including the working class. Similarly to that of Bolivian Jesús Lara, Icaza's *indigenista* literary work is closely related to the political critique and denunciation of social and economic injustices prevailing in Ecuador and in the Andes, more generally. Another Ecuadorean writer, Alicia Yáñez-Cossio (Quito, 1929) delves into the condition of women in an alienating world. Her first novel, the award-winning *Bruna, soroche y los tíos* (*Bruna and her Sisters in the Sleeping City*, 1973), was followed by *Más allá de las islas* (Beyond the Islands, 1980). In Colombia, with the important precedent of José Eustasio Rivera's acclaimed novel *La vorágine* (*The Vortex*, 1924), in which the exploitation of indigenous peasants during the rubber boom comes to light, several novels in the 1940s and 1950s denounce the hardship undergone by indigenous communities and individuals throughout the diverse Colombian topography. Set in the Andes, Juan Álvarez Garzón's *Los Clavijos* (1943) and Guillermo Edmundo Cháves's *Chambú* (1947) encourage indigenous uprisings in response to appalling economic conditions.

Back in Peru, Ciro Alegría personifies the *indigenista* writer. A member of the APRA party,[12] Alegría wrote a book that, to many, embodied the *indigenista* novel (Higgins 129). *El mundo es ancho y ajeno* (*Broad and Alien is the World*, 1941; hereafter *El mundo*) is also his most insightful novel. At its core is the deeply entrenched struggle between the indigenous community and the alien hegemonic power of the rural oligarchy. Unlike his previous novels,[13] Alegría's most influential work presents indigenous lives responding to the oppressive actions of the local landowners and the dominant structures supporting them. Similarly to other *indigenista* works,[14] *El mundo* implicitly sustains the thesis that *mestizaje* is the path forward to indigenous emancipation.[15] Like many other characters in *indigenista* novels, such as Wáskar Puma, in Lara's *Surumi*, Benito Castro in *El mundo* is a young man who has gained an education outside his community that enables him to lead his people to a perceived brighter future while preserving their indigenous identity. More complex and thus more representative of Andean reality, Arguedas's *Yawar Fiesta* presents Escobar, a student from Puquio living in Lima, who also represents, to a certain extent, the character who comes back to their community to become a mediator between the two worlds perceived as irreconcilable. The implication of this recurrent character is that prosperity and "integration" are to be mediated by those who, emerging from indigenous communities, are able to learn and understand the practices and values of Westernized white society and thus lead their people to a more successful future by incorporating such views into their own culture. In late nineteenth-century *Aves sin nido*, the two characters who are equipped to "save" the indigenous people of Killac from the oppression exercised by the abusive local authorities—the priest, the governor, the judge—are the Marín couple from Lima. They represent the liberal modernizing urban spirit whose impact on the community is to lead the mistreated inhabitants of Killac to a better future through their assimilation into the urban modern capitalist civilizational project they symbolize. Written in the early 1940s, *El mundo es ancho y ajeno*, as well as *Surumi* and *Yawar Fiesta*, are a step forward in their representation of the agency of indigenous individuals to lead their own lives according to their values and their ethos. Benito and Wáskar are indigenous themselves, and Escobar is a *mestizo* with a profound connection with the indigenous community.[16] However, the ability of these characters to play the role their literary creators ascribed to them is still subject to a process of Westernization. This controversial approach is aligned with the concept of *mestizaje*, hence invalidating any option by indigenous individuals and communities to conduct their lives and evolve in different ways other than the Western-criollo paradigm imposed by the white ruling classes upon the Andes since colonial times.[17] It also assumes that indigenous people live immersed in a backward, stagnant world from which they can only escape by being integrated into mainstream white/mestizo ethos.

Repeatedly reproduced in mainstream *indigenista* narrative, this perspective on indigeneity is at the heart of *indigenista* thinking. Two writers notably challenged this view at the time of its greatest influence: Churata and José María Arguedas. Born at the end of the nineteenth century, Arturo Peralta, known as Gamaliel Churata, is an extraordinary case when we address the Andean novel and the writers behind its most emblematic and significant works. Only fully recognized in recent years,[18] his writing departs from the traditional Hispanic influence in its search for a genuine Andean aesthetic form. Churata's innovative and disruptive views found written expression in the journal *Boletín Titikaka* (1926–1930), founded with his brother Alejandro Peralta (1899–1973).[19] Capturing such innovative views and spirit in what the writer himself defined as the "Vanguardia Plebeya del Titikaka" (Titikaka Plebeian Avant-garde), Churata's very concept of the avant-garde as compatible with indigeneity challenges conventional views by which the avant-garde is associated with urban groundbreaking modernity, hence viewed as removed from indigenous cultures, intimately connected at that time with the rural milieu. In this respect, it is relevant to recall the polemic exchange between Argentinian writer Julio Cortázar and José María Arguedas in the late 1960s, by which two forms of understanding fiction writing and its context became a confrontation between what Cortázar understood as "regionalism" represented by Arguedas, versus "cosmopolitanism" as Cortázar's writing would be described. Underlying this dialectical conflict is the embedded friction between misleading dualistic conceptualizations of Latin America and its realities and symbolic representations. This polemic reveals the deeply entrenched idea that modernity cannot be associated with indigeneity, that modernity by default pertains to a westernized concept of progress. Both José María Arguedas and Gamaliel Churata challenge this long-standing view with their own writing.

A pioneer of a decolonizing approach to the Andes and its cultures and symbolic representations, in its over five hundred pages, Churata's main novel, *El pez de oro* (The Golden Fish, 1957), subverts conventional literary forms, undermines the hegemony of the Hispanic civilizational project, and questions the very concept of the novel (Monasterios, *La vanguardia*, 232). With his challenging artistic stance and his endless intellectual and artistic inquiry, Churata's revolutionary views disrupted the core of the former parameters of conceiving the Andes.

A similar spirit permeates Arguedas's fictional writing, foremost in his last text, *El zorro de arriba y el zorro de abajo*. As previously mentioned, Arguedas's work is emblematic of the tensions present in the indigenista approach, as his novels evolve into a total rupture with the *indigenista* project.[20] His ambitious novel *Todas las sangres* (All Bloods, 1964) captures the complexity of representing a social, political, and economic indigenous project in the conflicted character Demetrio Rendón Willka.[21] His *Los ríos profundos* (*Deep Rivers*, 1958) lyrically immerses the reader into the real and symbolic journey of its adolescent protagonist Ernesto through the Andes.[22] Later, published posthumously in 1971, *El zorro de arriba y el zorro de abajo* becomes a testament to the conflictual tension found in the attempt to reconcile Andean indigeneity with Andean *misti* (white) culture. This tension is a reflection of a wider-ranging friction impacting all areas of economic, social, political, and cultural dynamics since the times of the colony. The indigenous cultural universe Arguedas addresses in his last and most intricate novel is tightly intertwined with the text's political, social, and economic referents, but it also is intimately interwoven with its linguistic dimension, hence the rupture of the text with any identifiable literary (European) genre and discourse.[23] This disruptive narrative speaks to Arguedas's struggle to find a genuine and inclusive written Andean literary form; it also reveals his most intimate, personal, and psychological battles transmitted to a cultural and linguistic terrain.

The site of Andean literary indigeneity is also approached from outside the *indigenista* episteme in the work of Jaime Sáenz (La Paz 1921–1986). Characterized by its sharp and anguished reflection on the Bolivian national subject, a poet, and a novelist, Sáenz depicts the Andean indigenous individual as representing a counter-hegemonic logic that challenges standardized preconceptions of modernity (Monasterios, "La provocación" 334). Sáenz´s self-reflective novel *Felipe Delgado* (1979) delves into issues of nation and identity. As throughout most of his writing, in his novel, the indigenous subject is integrated into the very concept of the nation. Indigeneity is approached as an intrinsic, organic component of the nation, rejecting other approaches by which indigenous individuals and communities were always singled out and treated as a differentiating factor.[24] In more recent years, La Paz has also been a main setting as a site of reflection of the Andean reality in *Periférica Blvd.* (2004) by Adolfo Cárdenas (La Paz 1950) and *Cuando Sara Chura despierte* (When Sara Chura Wakes Up, 2003) by Juan Pablo Piñeiro (La Paz 1979).

Scholars and intellectuals such as Enrique Dussel, Walter Mignolo, Aníbal Quijano, and Silvia Rivera Cusicanqui, among others, have extensively argued for the dismantlement of the long-standing belief that development and progress could only be achieved through a modernity unescapably associated with Western thinking. Moreover, in 2006, with the first government led by an indigenous president, Evo Morales, Bolivia's official discourse and government's actions recognized indigenous agency and the historical cost of centuries of colonialism. By the first decade of the 2000s, Andean countries like Bolivia and Ecuador engaged in an alternative model of development grounded in Andean indigenous values, primordially the ecologically balanced harmony between human lives and nature. In Quechua, *Sumak Kawsay*—*Buen Vivir* in Spanish, *Well Living* in English—breaks away from extended, capitalist economic practices to promote, instead, local knowledge and a more equitable distribution of resources. In our globalized world, the challenges encountered by *Sumak Kawsay* cannot be underestimated, but it is nevertheless significant to understand how long-standing conceptions involving the indigenous peoples of the Andes have evolved not only in their symbolic representations, but also in their more tangible experiences.[25]

Colombia, a country with a very rich novelistic tradition, and with its capital city in the Andes, has not substantially developed a literary production inscribed in the Andean trends described through this article. However, the Andes is both the tangible and intangible space within which some of its most important narrative is set. The traces of the Andes can be followed in canonical novels such as Gabriel García Márquez's *El general en su laberinto* (*The General in his Labyrinth*, 1989), which describes a prematurely old and exhausted Simón Bolívar and his journey from Santa Fe de Bogotá through the Magdalena river to the Caribbean coast. Moreover, one of the most important Latin American novelists today, Juan Gabriel Vásquez, who was born in Bogotá (1973), captures his natal country in masterpieces such as *El ruido de las cosas al caer* (*The Sound of Things Falling*, 2011) and *La forma de las ruinas* (*The Shapes of the Ruins*, 2018), both exploring the violence that has characterized Colombia throughout most of the twentieth century. Also born in Bogotá, Laura Restrepo (1950), like Vásquez, lived in several countries as reflected in her novels. Nonetheless, like him, Colombia, its political turmoil and drug-trafficking brutality impacts her works, foremost *Historia de un entusiasmo* (Story of a Fascination, 1986) and *Leopardo al sol* (*Leopard in the Sun*, 1993). Born in the Andean city of Pereira in 1939, Albalucía Ángel's writings are impacted by her political activism and feminist approach to life and literature. The prize-winning novel *Estaba la pájara pinta sentada en el verde limón* (The Colorful Bird Sat On the Green Lemon Tree, 1975) is one of her most celebrated novels.

An interesting case is that of Evelio Rosero's novels. Born in Bogotá in 1958 and raised in another Andean city, Pasto, the space of the writer's childhood seamlessly permeates his narrative. In his first works—*Mateo solo* (Mateo Alone, 1984) and *Juliana los mira* (Juliana Looks at Them, 1986)—the presence of childhood and adolescence is most powerful, and the narrative space penetrates the oppressive ambience evoked. In *En el lejero* (In the Distant Place, 2003), the isolated and remote space where the protagonist arrives is physically located in a village surrounded by the Andean mountains that acquires a significant role in the novel.[26] It is also relevant to emphasize that Colombian literary critics have generally paid little attention to the impact of indigeneity on their country's novels. While the work of some writers such as Soledad Acosta de Samper (Bogotá 1833–1913), Daniel Sámper Ortega (Bogotá 1895–1943), Diego Castrillón Arboleda (Popayán 1917–2009), Juan Álvarez Garzón (Tuquerres 1898–1974), and Jesús Botero Restrepo (Jardín, Antioquia 1921–Medellín 2008) is identified with Andean-indigenous elements, there is a tendency to underestimate the impact of indigenous individuals and communities upon national life and hence on its arts and literature.

Since the mid-twentieth century, the conventional but misleading dualist approach to Andean society has been shaken and a more complex, multi-faceted reality emerged.

This new outlook has broken with binary notions associated with rural/urban, indigenous/*misti* (white ruling class with *mestizos* caught in-between), traditional/modern and has given way to new forms of narrating the Andes. In them, the experience of migration and the trauma of violence are at the forefront. As discussed, toward the late 1950s, Churata and Arguedas had already transformed the outside gaze into an increasingly inner view of indigeneity. This inner perspective on indigenous life also characterizes the writing of other writers such as Eleodoro Vargas Vicuña (Cerro de Pasco 1924–Lima 1997) and Edgardo Rivera Martínez (Jauja 1933–Lima 2018). Even though Vargas Vicuña's narrative work is composed of short stories compiled in his two main books–*Ñahuín* (1953) and *Taita Cristo* (Father Christ, 1963)—his narrative presents such a powerful insight into the Andean indigenous subject from within that it is necessary to consider it when addressing Andean fiction-writing. Closely connected to Vargas Vicuña's work, Rivera Martínez is the author of the acclaimed novel *País de Jauja* (Country of Jauja, 1993). Set in his native Jauja in the middle of the twentieth century, the coming of age of the novel's protagonist, Claudio Ayala, reveals the coexistence of the two worlds—broadly Andean and European—influencing his upbringing.

More recently, literary exploration from within indigeneity comes from Quechua and Aymara writers such as Óscar Colchado (Huallanca 1947) and Enrique Rosas Paravicino (Ocongate 1948). They both have a significant body of fiction, predominantly short stories addressing the space of the Andes and its people from inner indigenous perspectives.[27] Similarly to Arguedas, both Colchado and Rosas Paravicino incorporate Quechua words and linguistic structures in their narrative, disrupting the Spanish text. In recent years, some novelists have written in their native language, as is the case of Federico Tórrez Márquez (La Paz 1965), whose award-winning Aymara novel *Jach'a tuntachawita-pachakutiwi* (From the Great Assembly to the Great Return, 2010) takes a historical perspective in order to understand Aymara resistance and the condition of Aymara people in present-day Bolivia. Written in Quechua, the Bolivian novellas *Sumaq Urqu* (2012)—name of the Potosí hill known in Spanish as Cerro Rico—by Zulena Pary Montesinos, and *Saqapa-El Cascabel* (2013), published in a bilingual Quechua and Spanish edition by Jinés Cornejo Endara, should be mentioned. While not constituting novels, because of their length and the scope of the stories, both novellas make an important contribution to contemporary indigenous narrative, considering the disproportionally richer production of short stories and poetry in Quechua and Aymara when compared with novels. In Peru, Pablo Landeo Muñoz (Huancavelica, 1959) published his first novel in Quechua—*Aqupampa*— in 2016, awarded Peru's national prize for literature in an indigenous language.[28] As in the case of Tórrez Márquez's prize-winning novel in Aymara, the recognition of *Aqupampa* as an indigenous novel, and not just as a national Peruvian one, implicitly assigns the novel a subaltern category. Landeo Muñoz, who has extensively worked to promote the production of Quechua writing, sets his novel in the outskirts of Lima, recounting the experience of Margarita who was born in Huancavelica department in the Andes and, like many Quechuas, migrated to the city during the violent days of the armed conflict.[29] The urban impact of migration from the interior of Peru, foremost the Andes had been addressed since mid-twentieth century in the works of novelists such as Julio Ramón Ribeyro (Lima 1929–1994) and Enrique Congrains (Lima 1932–Cochabamba, Bolivia 2009). Ribeyro's "Los gallinazos sin plumas" ("The Featherless Buzzards," 1955) and "Al pie del acantilado" ("At the Bottom of the Cliff," 1959) and Congrains ' "El niño de Junto al Cielo" ("The Boy Next to Heaven") anticipated the massive rural migration that transformed Lima and Peru at large.[30] The hardship undergone by the protagonists of these short stories is dramatically captured in Congrains's novel *No una sino muchas muertes* (Not one but Many Deaths, 1957). Years later, the voice of migrants was articulated in literature, and a novella like *Montacerdos* (1980) or a novel like *Patíbulo para un caballo* (Gallows for a Horse, 1989) both written by Cronwell Jara (Piura, 1949) and whose protagonists bears the same name as that of Congrains's novel—Maruja—provided a unique internal gaze that produced an innovative narrative discourse and aesthetics emerging from inside the migrant experience.[31]

The last two decades have seen a rich narrative production, mainly in Spanish, following the most violent conflict in the Andes in contemporary days: the armed struggle in the southern Peruvian Andes that confronted the revolutionary communist party and armed organization Sendero Luminoso (Shining Path) and the state, catching thousands of Peruvians, mainly Quechuas, in the crossfire. Claudia Salazar Jiménez's *La sangre de la aurora* (*Blood of the Dawn*, 2013) is a testament to the quality of some of these works. Born in Lima in 1976, Salazar Jiménez recounts the terror experienced during the brutal armed conflict in the 1980s and 1990s through the perspective of three women. The armed conflict crosses Peruvian literature in many different ways; Salazar's novel explores the conflict in a subtle and suggestive manner. Others have exposed the fear and the terror in more blatant and sometimes less convincing ways, like Santiago Roncagliolo's (Lima, 1975) in *Abril rojo* (*Red April*, 2006). The novel nevertheless became a bestseller and won the Spanish Alfaguara Prize the year of its publication.

While the political and social context still occupy an important space in Andean fiction-writing, recent novelistic production in the region has also seen a proliferation of works that address multiple themes and present a myriad of characters, revealing a broad range of questions and aesthetic explorations underlying the text. Katya Adaui (Lima 1977) has written *Nunca sabré lo que entiendo* (I Will Never Know What I Understand, 2014), a novel that explores the existential questions raised by their protagonist involving family relations, maternity, and self-questioning. Powerfully speaking to the diversity of approaches, scenarios, themes and characters is the work of the Brazilian-born Ecuadorean writer Gabriela Alemán (Río de Janeiro 1968). A major voice in Ecuadorian contemporary letters, Alemán has developed a prolific and acclaimed literary career. She has written three novels—*Body Time* (2003), *Poso Wells* (2005), and *Humo* (Smoke, 2017)—and other narrative works such her book of chronicles *Álbum de familia* (Family Album, 2011). Alemán's novels explore different themes and characters in which the space and challenges of women play a prominent role. While she does not directly address Andean indigeneity in her writings, most of her works are created from the Andes, and thus in their multiply facets, the Andes are absorbed in her texts.

Finally, this chapter should acknowledge that, among the many novelistic expressions of the Andes, canonical Latin American writers such as Vargas Llosa have constructed the Andes as a trope of desolation, hostility, and violence. Vargas Llosa's *Historia de Mayta* (*The Real Life of Alejandro Mayta*, 1984), *¿Quién mató a Palomino Molero?* (*Who Killed Palomino Molero*, 1986), and *Lituma en los Andes* were written at the peak of the Peruvian armed conflict, the first two, and toward its end the third one, coinciding with Vargas Llosa defeat in the 1990 Peruvian presidential election, won by Alberto Fujimori. The three novels can be studied together as they all develop around a detective plot, exploring acts of extreme violence in the Andean region. In 1983, Vargas Llosa led the investigation of the murder of eight journalists at the hands of indigenous peasants, mistaken as members of the Shining Path, according to the *Informe sobre Uchuraccay* (1983), published by this commission. The impact of the novelist's participation on this critical investigation can be traced in these novels, particularly in *Historia de Mayta* (hereafter *Historia*) and *Quién mato a Palomino Montero?*, written in the aftermath of the tragic event (Sheriff 106–29). In different ways, the three novels are immersed in a violent world impacted by the civil war, though thematically *Historia* goes back to a revolutionary insurrection in the early 1960s in the Andean town of Jauja led by Alejandro Mayta, who comes from the Peruvian coast but travels to the Andes to lead a revolution, where he believes are the seeds of success. The three novels depict an irrational and telluric universe in which, according to their perspectives, indigenous communities are immersed. This rather apocalyptic image of the Andes is reinforced in *Lituma en los Andes* with a resentful view toward a world that had clearly rejected its author as presidential candidate. Contributing little to Vargas Llosa's outstanding novelistic corpus, which includes masterpieces such as *La ciudad y los perros* (*The Time of the Hero*, 1963), *Conversación en La Catedral* (*Conversation in the Cathedral*, 1969), and *La casa verde* (*The Green House*, 1966), these three novels provide a fictional platform to demonize a universe that echoes degrading views on Andean life found in some *indigenista* narrative such as Alcides Arguedas's novels in the 1920s, as seen above. Nonetheless, the Andes are also home of remarkable characters found in urban novels, as is the case of Julius's nanny Vilma in the beautiful novel *Un mundo para Julius* (*A World For Julius*, 1970) by Vargas Llosa's contemporary novelist Alfredo Bryce Echenique (Lima, 1939).

A journey through novels that have captured the Andes in their narrative discourse, in their aesthetics, in their souls, or in their more intimate essence reveals a vigorous region producing an innovative and rich literature. Since its violent arrival in the area with the Spanish colonization, writing has proven to be both a convenient and effective tool as well as a dangerous and oppressive instrument. Nonetheless, the novels emanating from the region celebrate the power of literature to interpret, reinterpret, construct, and deconstruct social, cultural, and aesthetic norms and structures. The Andes are multidimensional, heterogenous, and in constant evolution; they are a physical space as well as a symbolic intangible one. Largely, literary depictions of the region and its people have been external and condescending. Increasingly, though, more internal, organic perspectives have emerged. This literary journey is long and rich and bound to progressively add innovative novels written in the original Andean languages, mainly Aymara and Quechua.

To James Higgins. In Memoriam

NOTES

1. There are many other languages in the Andes, including Kichwa in Ecuador and parts of Colombia, a variant of Quechua sufficiently differentiated to be considered a different language. However, this article focuses on the two languages that have had a major impact on both oral and written literary works.

2. See their two foundational works: Antonio Cornejo Polar, *Escribir en el aire. Ensayos sobre la heterogeneidad socio-cultural en las literaturas andinas*, and Martin Lienhard, *La voz y su huella*.

3. This is a common practice throughout the Americas, particularly where the missionaries found well-established societies such as the Maya and the Nahuatl. Outstanding examples are the *Popol Vuh* and the *Florentine Codex*. In the Andes, this is also the case of the untitled Quechua manuscript from the late sixteenth century describing religious beliefs and cultural practices of the Quechua people, compiled by Father Francisco de Ávila. The volume was edited and translated into Spanish by José María Arguedas in 1966 under the title *Dioses y hombres de Huarochirí* (*Huarochiri Manuscript*). Previously, the text had been translated into German (1939) and Latin (1942).

4. See Martin Lienhard, *Testimonios, cartas y manifiestos indígenas. Desde la conquista hasta comienzos del siglo XX*.

5. Throughout the twentieth century and until today, many intellectuals have elucidated the meaning and scope of this complex concept. Among others, Luis Alberto Sánchez, Washington Delgado, Antonio Cornejo Polar, Tomás Escajadillo, Mirko Lauer, Sara Castro-Klaren, José Antonio Mazzotti, Juan Ulises Zevallos, Mabel Moraña, Elizabeth Monasterios, Andrew Canessa, Javier García Liendo, and Jorge Coronado.

6. The continuity of these structures was captured by Peruvian sociologist Aníbal Quijano with the concept of coloniality of power used to describe the prevalence of colonial power structures and its impact on today's society. See "Coloniality of Power, Eurocentrism, and Latin America."

7. Interestingly, the *indigenista* novel, like the abolitionist, was embraced by women. Some of the most representative writers of the literary movement are women, as is the case of the Mexican writer Rosario Castellanos (1925–1974).

8. Thanks to the works of Dora Cajías, *Adela Zamudio transgresora de su tiempo* (1996) and Leonardo García-Pabón's second edition of *Íntimas* in 1999, a fresh reading of the Bolivian female writer enhanced her groundbreaking work.

9. See Estelle Tarica, "El indigenismo de Jesús Lara: entre el campo y la ciudad letrada" and *The Inner Life of Mestizo Nationalism*, pp. 30–79.

10. Scorza died in 1983 in a plane crash near Barajas airport in Madrid along with Mexican writer Jorge Ibargüengoitia, Uruguayan literary critic Ángel Rama, and Argentinean art critic Marta Traba. They were all going to the same conference in Madrid.

11. *Garabombo el invisible* (1972), *El jinete insomne* (1977), *Cantar de Agapito Robles* (1977), and *La tumba del relámpago* (1979).

12. *Alianza Popular Revolucionaria Americana* (American Popular Revolutionary Alliance), Peru's populist, nationalist party, was founded in 1924 by Víctor Raúl Haya de la Torre and came to power in 1985, when Alán García was elected president. In 2006, García won a second term.

13. *La serpiente de oro* (*The Golden Serpent*) (1935) and *Los perros hambrientos* (*The Hungry Dogs*) (1938).

14. Jesús Lara´s *Surumi*, and José María Arguedas's early novel *Yawar Fiesta*, also published in 1941, came to parallel conclusions.

15. The controversial concept of *mestizaje* refers not only to mixed blood but to the cultural transformation of indigenous individuals under the influence of their white-Western inherited background.

16. As has been noted, Escobar embodies Mariátegui´s ideal in that he represents the driving force of a future political project led by socialist ideals in tune with indigenous collective values. Cornejo, *Los universos narrativos de José María Arguedas*.

17. Many scholars and critics have discussed the implications and controversies surrounding the idea of *mestizaje*. Among others, see Antonio Cornejo Polar, Jorge Coronado, and Aníbal Quijano.

18. Amongst others José Luis Ayala, Marco Thomas Bosshard, Meritxell Hernando, Mauro Mamani, Elizabeth Monasterios, Mabel Moraña, Helena Usandizaga, Riccardo Badini, and Paola Mancosu have substantially published on Churata´s work.

19. Thanks to the outstanding edition of the *Boletín Titikaka* by Mauro Mamani and Helena Usandizaga, this was published in 2016 by the Centro de Estudios Literarios Antonio Cornejo Polar and Lluvia Editores. Elizabeth Monasterios, Cynthia Vich, and Juan Zevallos have also published on Churata´s *Boletín Titikaka*.

20. It is important to recognize that Arguedas is approached by some scholars and intellectuals as *indigenista*. Among those, see Mario Vargas Llosa's *La utopía arcaica. Jose María Arguedas y las ficciones del indigenismo*, a book that expresses an opposite view from that embraced in this chapter.

21. See Antonio Cornejo Polar, *Los universos narrativos de José María Arguedas*, pp. 230–47.

22. For an insightful study of *Los ríos profundos* and its musicality connected to the Andean world, see William Rowe, *Ensayos arguedianos*, pp. 35–58.

23. Although written in Spanish, the incorporation of Quechua subverts its use. José María Arguedas committed suicide himself, leaving the manuscript of *El zorro* unfinished. The complex and anguish narrative of his last book speaks to the author's conflicting days. To what extent Arguedas's mental health was impacted by his struggle to reconcile the Andean worlds fighting in himself has been questioned by many scholars and critics who have addressed his work, among others: Martin Lienhard, Antonio Cornejo Polar, William Rowe, and Javier García Liendo.

24. For further insight, see Elizabeth Monasterios, "La provocación de Sáenz"; and Leonardo García-Pabón, *La Patría íntima*, pp. 213–48.

25. For further reading on *Sumak Kawsay*, see Alberto Acosta, Xavier Albó, Eduardo Gudynas, Nancy Postero, and Raúl Prada, among others.

26. Juliana Martínez has described such space and its narrative and aesthetic impact as spectral. See *Haunting Without Ghosts: Spectral Realism in Colombian Literature, Film and Art*, pp. 38–76.

27. It is important to highlight the editorial work carried out by Enrique Quiroz's *Lluvia Editores* since early 1980 in disseminating Peruvian writers. The proliferation of poetry and fiction writing in Peru by authors emerging from traditionally marginalized social sectors since the 1970s owes to *Lluvia Editores* the platform to see many of these works published. For further insight see Núria Vilanova. "The Emerging Literature of the Peruvian Underclass."

28. Landeo Muñoz has made a point of not translating the novel into Spanish, alluding that the novel discourse is closely attached to Quechua and a translation in Spanish would alter the novel's perspective. See interview in *American Quarterly*, October 6, 2016.

29. See César Itier. *Aqupampa*, de Pablo Landeo Muñoz, la primera novela escrita en quechua. https://hawansuyo.files.wordpress.com/2016/07/itier-aqupampa-1.pdf

30. Lima grew exponentially in the second half of the twentieth century. The massive arrival of migrants was described as "el desborde popular" (popular overflow) by Peruvian anthropologist José Matos Mar. See his book *El desborde popular y crisis de estado.*

31. See Núria Vilanova, *Social Change and Literature in Peru 1970–1990*, pp. 99–136.

WORKS CITED

Adaui, Katya. *Nunca sabré lo que entiendo.* Planeta, 2018.

Alegría, Ciro. *Broad and Alien Is the World.* Translated by Harriet de Onís. Farrar &Rhinehart, 1941.

Alegría, Ciro. *El mundo es ancho y ajeno.* Alianza, 1982.

Alegría, Ciro. *La serpiente de oro.* Alianza Editorial, 2001.

Alegría, Ciro. *Los perros hambrientos.* Alianza Editorial, 1997.

Alegría, Ciro. *The Golden Serpent.* Translated by Harriet de Onis. Farrar & Rhinehart, 1943.

Alemán, Gabriela. *Álbum de familia.* Panamericana Editorial, 2011.

Alemán, Gabriela. *Body Time.* Planeta, 2003.

Alemán, Gabriela. *Humo.* Penguin Random House/Grupo Colombia, 2017.

Alemán, Gabriela. *Poso Wells.* Eskéletra, 2007.

Alemán, Gabriela. *Poso Wells.* Translated by Dick Cluster. City Lights, 2018.

Álvarez Garzón, Juan. *Los clavijos.* Cromos, 1943.

Ángel, Albalucía. *Estaba la pájara pinta sentada en el verde limón.* Oveja Negra, 1985.

Arguedas, Alcides. *Raza de bronce.* Alba, 2010.

Arguedas, Alcides. *Pueblo enfermo.* Anthropos, 2000.

Arguedas, José María. *Deep Rivers.* Translated by Frances Horning Barraclough. U of Texas P, 1983.

Arguedas, José María. *Dioses y hombres de Huarochirí.* Siglo XXI, 1975.

Arguedas, José María. *The Fox from Up Above and the Fox from Down Below.* Translated by Frances Horning Barraclough. Pittsburgh UP, 2000.

Arguedas, José María. *Los ríos profundos.* Planeta, 1984.

Arguedas, José María. *Todas las sangres.* Horizonte, 1987.

Arguedas, José María. *Yawar Fiesta.* Horizonte, 1988.

Arguedas, José María. *Yawar Fiesta.* Translated by Frances Horning Barraclough. U of Texas P, 1985.

Arguedas, José María. *El zorro de arriba y el zorro de abajo.* Consejo Nacional para la Cultura y las Artes. Colección Archivos, 1992.

Bryce Echenique, Alfredo. *A World for Julius.* Editorial Laia, 1979.

Bryce Echenique, Alfredo. *Un mundo para Julius.* Translated by Dick Gerdes. U of Wisconsin P, 2004.

Cajías, Dora. *Adela Zamudio transgresora de su tiempo.* Ministerio de Desarrollo Humano, 1996.

Cárdenas, Adolfo, *Periférica Blvd.* Carrera de Literatura, UMSA, 2004.

Cháves, Guillermo Edmundo. *Chambú*. Bedout, 1960.

Congrains, Enrique. *No una sino muchas muertes*. Planeta, 1975.

Cornejo Endara, Jinés. *Saqapa-El Cascabel*. Plural, 2013.

Cornejo Polar, Antonio. *Escribir en el aire. Ensayo sobre la heterogeneidad socio-cultural en las literaturas andinas*. Horizonte, 1994.

Cornejo Polar, Antonio. "Heterogeneidad y contradicción en la literatura andina: (Tres incidentes en la contienda entre oralidad y escritura)." *Nuevo Texto Crítico*, Año V no. 9, 10, 1992, pp. 103–11.

Cornejo Polar, Antonio. *Los universos narrativos de José María Arguedas*. Losada, 1974.

Churata, Gamaliel. *El pez de oro*. Edited by Helena Usandizaga. Cátedra. Letras Hispánicas, 2012.

Dawe, John and Lewis Taylor. "Enrique López Albújar and the Study of Peruvian Brigandage." *Bulletin of Latin American Research*, vol. 13, no. 3, 1994, pp. 247–80.

Freeland, Anne. "Motley Society, Plurinationalism, and the Integral State Álvaro García Linera's Use of Gramsci and Zavaleta." *Historical Materialism*, vol. 27, no. 3, 2019, pp. 1–28.

García Liendo, Javier. *El intelectual y la cultura de masas. Argumentos latinoamericanos en torno a Ángel Rama y José María Arguedas*. Purdue UP, 2017.

García Márquez, Gabriel. *El general en su laberinto*. Mondadori, 1989.

García Márquez, Gabriel. *The General in His Labyrinth*. Translated by Edith Grossman. Vintage, 2003.

García Pavón, Leonardo. *La patria íntima. Alegorías nacionales en la literatura y el cine de Bolivia*. Plural, 1998.

Guamán Poma de Ayala, Felipe. *El Primer Nueva Corónica y Buen Gobierno*. Siglo XX1, 1992.

Guamán Poma de Ayala, Felipe. *The First New Chronicle and Good Government: On the History of the World and the Incas up to 1615*. Translated by Roland Hamilton. U of Texas P, 2021.

Higgins, James. *A History of Peruvian Literature*. Francis Cairns Publications, 1987.

Icaza, Jorge. *Huasipungo*. Losada, 1960.

Icaza, Jorge. *The Villagers*. Translated by John Charles Casteen. Arcturus Books, 1964.

Jara, Cronwell. *Monatcerdos*. Lluvia, 1981.

Jara, Cronwell. *Patíbulo para un caballo*. Mosca Azul, 1989.

Landeo Muñoz, Pablo. *Aqupampa*. Instituto Francés de Estudios Andinos, 2016.

Lara, Jesús. *Inkallajta*. Los Amigos del Libro, 1967.

Lara, Jesús. *Llalliypacha*. Platina, 1965.

Lara, Jesús. *Paqarin*. Los Amigos del Libro, 1974.

Lara, Jesús. *Sinchicay*. Platina, 1962.

Lara, Jesús. *Surumi*. Los Amigos del Libro, 1988.

Lara, Jesús. *Yanakuna*. Juventud, 1958.

Lara, Jesús. *Yawarninchij*. Platina, 1959.

Lienhard, Martin. *Cultura andina y forma novelesca: zorros y danzantes en la última novela de Arguedas*. Latinoamericana, 1981.

Lienhard, Martin. *Testimonios, cartas y manifiestos indígenas. Desde la conquista hasta comienzos del siglo XX*. Biblioteca Ayacucho, 1992.

Lienhard, Martin. *La voz y su huella*. Casa de las Américas, 1990.

López Albújar, Enrique. *Cuentos andinos*. Juan Mejía Baca, 1977.

Martínez, Juliana. *Haunting Without Ghosts: Spectral Realism in Colombian Literature, Film and Art*. U of Texas P, 2020.

Matos Mar, José. *Desborde popular y crisis del Estado*. Instituto de Estudios Peruanos, 1984.

Matto de Turner, Clorinda. *Aves sin nido*. Universidad Jaume I, 2006.

Matto de Turner, Clorinda. *Torn from the Nest*. Translated by John Polt. Oxford UP, 1999.

Monasterios, Elizabeth. *La vanguardia plebeya del Titikaka. Gamaliel Churata y otras beligerancias estéticas de los Andes*. Plural/ Instituto francés de estudios andinos, 2015.

Monasterios, Elizabeth. "La provocación de Sáenz." *Hacia una historia crítica de la literatura en Bolivia*, vol. 1, edited by Alba María Paz Soldán, Programa de Investigación Estratégica en Bolivia, 2002a, pp. 327–403.

Monasterios, Elizabeth, and Rosario Rodríguez. "Indiscreciones de un narrador: *Raza de bronce*." *Hacia una historia crítica de la literatura en Bolivia*, vol. 2, edited by Alba María Paz Soldán, Programa de Investigación Estratégica en Bolivia, 2002, pp. 106–18.

Orrego Arismendi, Juan Carlos. "La crítica de la novela indigenista colombiana: objetos y problemas." *Estudios de Literatura Colombiana*, vol. 30, January–June 2012, pp. 31–54.

Pary Montesinos, Zulema. *Sumaq Urqu*. Santillana, 2012.

Piñeiro, Juan Pablo. *Cuando Sara Chura despierte*. Portaculturas, 2014.

Quijano, Aníbal. "Coloniality of Power, Eurocentrism, and Latin America." *Nepantla: Views from the South*, vol. 1, no. 3, 2000, pp. 533–80.

Rama, Ángel. *La ciudad letrada*. Arca, 1998.

Restrepo, Laura. *Historia de un entusiasmo*. Punto de Lectura, 2010.

Restrepo, Laura. *Leopard in the Sun*. Translated by Stephen Lytle. Vintage, 2000.

Restrepo, Laura. *Leopardo al sol*. Rayo, 2005.

Rivera, José Eustasio. *La vorágine*. Planeta, 1984.

Rivera, José Eustasio. *The Vortex*. Duke UP, 2018.

Rivera Martínez, Edgardo. *El país de Jauja*. Peisa, 1996.

Ribeyro, Julio Ramón. *Cuentos Completos*. Alfaguara, 1994.

Ribeyro, Julio Ramón. *Marginal Voices. Selected Stories*. Translated by Dianne Douglas. Texas UP, 1993.

Rocha, Omar. "Las dolencias de Alcides Arguedas." *Hacia una historia crítica de la literatura en Bolivia*, edited by Alba María Paz Soldán, vol. 2, Programa de Investigación Estratégica en Bolivia, 2002, pp. 103–6.

Roncagliolo, Santiago. *Abril rojo*. Alfaguara, 2002.

Roncagliolo, Santiago. *Red April*. Translated by Edith Grossman. Vintage, 2010.

Rosero, Evelio. *En el lejero*. Planeta, 2013.

Rosero, Evelio. *Juliana los mira*. Tusquets Editores, 2014.

Rosero, Evelio. *Mateo solo*. Cooperativa Editorial Magisterio, 1995.

Rowe, William. *Ensayos arguedianos*. Universidad Nacional Mayor de San Marcos/Sur, 1996.

Sáenz, Jaime. *Felipe Delgado*. Plural, 2007.

Salazar Jiménez, Claudia. *Blood of the Dawn*. Translated by Elizabeth Bryer. Deep Vellum, 2016.

Salazar Jiménez, Claudia. *La sangre de la aurora*. Animal de Invierno, 2013.

Scorza, Manuel. *Cantar de Agapito*, De la Campana, 1977.

Scorza, Manuel. *Drums for Rancas*. Translated by Edith Grossman. Harper & Row, 1977.

Scorza, Manuel. *Garabombo el invisible*, Planeta, 1972.

Scorza, Manuel. *La tumba del relámpago*. Siglo XXI Editores, 1979.

Scorza. Manuel. *Redoble por Rancas*. Peisa, 1987.

Taboada Terán, Néstor. *Manchay Puytu. El amor que quiso ocultar Dios*. Los Amigos del Libro, 1988.

Tarica, Estelle. "El indigenismo de Jesús Lara: entre el campo y la ciudad letrada." *Revista de crítica literaria latinoamericana*, vol. 34, no. 67, 1st semester 2008, pp. 237–54.

Tarica, Estelle. "*The Inner LIfe of Mestizo Nationalism.* U of Minnesota P, 2008.

Tórrez Márquez, Federico. *Jach'a tuntachawita-pachakutiwi.* Santillana, 2011.

Varcárcel, Luis E. *Tempestad en los Andes.* Universo, 1972.

Vargas Llosa, Mario. *Conversación en La Catedral.* Seix Barral, 1969.

Vargas Llosa, Mario. *Conversation in the Cathedral.* Translated by Gregory Rebassa. Harper & Row Publishers Inc., 1974.

Vargas Llosa, Mario. *Death in the Andes.* Translated by Edith Grossman. Picador, 2007.

Vargas Llosa, Mario. *Historia de Mayta.* Seix Barral, 1984.

Vargas Llosa, Mario. *La casa verde.* Seix Barral, 1966.

Vargas Llosa, Mario. *La ciudad y los perros.* Seix Barral, 1963.

Vargas Llosa, Mario. *Lituma en los Andes.* Planeta, 1993.

Vargas Llosa, Mario. *¿Quién mató a Palomino Molero?* Seix Barral, 1986.

Vargas Llosa, Mario. *The Green House.* Harper Collins, 1968.

Vargas Llosa, Mario. *The Real Life of Alejandro Mayta.* Translated by Alfred MacAdam. Farrar, Straus & Giroux, 1998.

Vargas Llosa, Mario. *The Time of the Hero.* Translated by Lysander Kemp. Farrar, Straus & Giroux, 1966.

Vargas Llosa, Mario. *Who Killed Palomino Molero.* Translated by Alfred MacAdam. Noonday Press, 1998.

Vargas Llosa, Mario, Abraham Guzmán Figueroa, and Mario Castro Arenas. *Informe sobre Uchuraccay.* https://www.verdadyreconciliacionperu.com/admin/files/libros/376_digital izacion.pdf (accessed 02/20/2022).

Vargas Vicuña, Eleodoro. *Ñahuín.* Milla Batres, 1975.

Vargas Vicuña, Eleodoro. *Taita Cristo.* San Marcos, 1999.

Vásquez, Juan Gabriel. *El ruido de las cosas al caer.* Alfaguara, 2011.

Vásquez, Juan Gabriel. *La forma de las ruinas.* Alfaguara, 2016.

Vásquez, Juan Gabriel. *The Shapes of the Ruins.* Translated by Anne McLean. Riverhead, 2018.

Vásquez, Juan Gabriel. *The Sound of Things Falling.* Translated by Anne MacLean. Riverhead, 2014.

Vilanova, Núria. "The Emerging Literature of the Peruvian Underclass." *Bulletin of Latin American Research,* vol. 17, no. 1, 1998, pp. 1–15.

Vilanova, Núria. *Social Change and Literature in Peru 1970–1990.* The Edwin Mellen Press, 1999.

Yáñez-Cossio, Alicia. *Bruna and her Sisters in the Sleeping City.* Northwestern UP, 1999.

Yáñez-Cossio, Alicia. *Bruna, soroche y los tíos.* Editorial Oveja Negra, 1997.

Yáñez-Cossio, Alicia. *Más allá de las islas.* Colegio Técnico Juan Bosco, 1980.

Zamudio, Adela. *Íntimas.* Edited by Leonardo García-Pabón. Plural, 1999.

Zavaleta Mercado, René. *Lo nacional-popular en Bolivia.* Plural, 2008.

CHAPTER 14

THE SOUTHERN CONE NOVEL (ARGENTINA, CHILE, URUGUAY, AND PARAGUAY)

GORICA MAJSTOROVIC

THE emergence of the novel in the nineteenth century is associated with the rise of the idea of nation formation. In *Imagined Communities*, Benedict Anderson traces the novel's beginnings to the early Industrial Revolution and the emergence of print capitalism. Although Anderson's claim has been scrutinized by feminist scholars such as Francine Masiello, when seen through this lens, the novel is a literary form that simultaneously constructs the social imaginary of a homogenous community within set borders while reflecting human life, be it collectively or individually. In the context of the Southern Cone countries after independence (Argentina, Uruguay, Chile, and Paraguay), the novel served as the principal means for imagining the new nations.

Romanticism encouraged Latin American writers to celebrate individual freedom and to break with Spanish tradition in order to form what Doris Sommer has called "foundational fictions." These fictions were primarily nation-building projects that "invested private passions with public purpose" (Sommer 7). The determination to carry this out and create original national literature in Argentina is manifest in Esteban Echeverría's (1805–1851) short story "El matadero" ("The Slaughterhouse," 1871) and Domingo Faustino Sarmiento's (1811–1888) work of creative non-fiction *Facundo: civilización y barbarie* (*Facundo: Civilization and Barbarism*, 1845), both hybrid texts with novelistic elements, and especially in the first Argentine novel, *Amalia* (1851). Written during José Mármol's (1817–1871) exile from the Rosas dictatorship, this political novel was deemed a "true best-seller of its time."[1] With historical figures included in the novel and depicting the rift between unitarian and federalist camps, *Amalia* was written when the tragic events of Rosas's tyrannical rule were still fresh in the author's mind. Jean Franco notes that at one dramatic moment in the novel, "Rosas is seen bathed in the reflection of a red curtain as if he were covered in blood" (57). While Rosas is associated with political violence and seen as the embodiment of "barbarism," Mármol and especially Sarmiento are seen as civilizing writers and public figures who advanced a program for modernizing Argentina. Writing about the dictator in this political context "served as a forum for envisioning alternative political futures for the emerging nation" (Armillas-Tiseyra 37). As Julio Ramos suggests, "writing in Sarmiento is defined along the lines of a modern utopia, as a kind of machine that will transform American 'barbarity' into the sense and order of 'civilization'" (164).

The historical novel conceived of literature as a definition of the national spirit. Cultivated throughout the Southern Cone, it was propelled by an intense confrontation with the colonial past and coupled with the simultaneous imagining of an entirely different future. Argentine writer Fidel Vicente López wrote *La novia del hereje* (The Heretic's Bride, 1870), a novel about the Spanish Inquisition whose protagonist is a Protestant sea captain working for the pirate Francis Drake. In Uruguay, Alejandro Magariños Cervantes's *Caramurú* appeared in 1848, while Eduardo Acevedo Díaz (1851–1921), the political leader of the nationalist, rurally oriented Blanco party, wrote novels such as *Ismael* (1888), portraying an outcast hero who joins the gaucho guerillas fighting the Spaniards. His novels *Nativa* (Native, 1890) and *Grito de gloria* (Cry of Glory, 1893) narrate the uprising of the Uruguayans against the Brazilian occupation.[2] While fostering nation-building and national pride, most of Acevedo Díaz's novels were written during his exile in Argentina.

The Argentine Juana Manuela Gorriti (1818–1892) is one of the most prominent woman writers of the nineteenth century. In 1869, she wrote a ghost story novella entitled *El Pozo de Yocci* (translated as *The Yocci Well* in 2020), a romance filled with elements of fantasy and gothic horror, and *Oasis en la vida* (Life's Oasis) in 1888. The central themes in Gorriti's narratives are violence against women, the supernatural, and popular culture. The Argentine Eduarda Mansilla de García (1834–1892) covered topics ranging from the *cautiva* legends during the early conquest depicted in *Lucía Miranda* (1882), to the nation's intense political debates in *Pablo ou la vie dans les pampas* (Pablo or Life on the Pampas, 1869). This novel humanizes the gaucho Pablo, who is forced to leave the pampas and recruited into the border war against Paraguay. Originally written in French, a language whose culture exerted deep influence on the Southern Cone region, the novel was then translated into German and Spanish.

Rosario Orrego (1834–1879) is considered the first woman novelist in Chile. Her debut novel was *Alberto el jugador* (Alberto the Player, 1860), a romantic novel published in installments. It depicts the daily life of the bourgeoisie and confronts the moral and social codes of the time. Although left unfinished, Orrego's second novel, titled *Los busca-vidas* (The Hustlers), was also published in serial form, in 1862, in *Revista del Pacífico*, the journal she co-founded with her husband. Published in the magazine *Valparaíso* (which she also founded), *Teresa* (1873) completes Orrego's romantic trilogy. Representing *costumbrismo*, a literary current that emphasized the description of local customs and everyday life, Teresa Lamas Carísimo (1887–1976) wrote *Tradiciones del hogar* (Traditions of the Home, 1921), the first novel published by a woman in Paraguay.

Alberto Blest Gana (1830–1920) is the author of the first realist novels in the Spanish language. He also wrote historical novels such as *Durante la Reconquista* (During the

Reconquest), which he began in 1864 and published in 1897. It is set during the struggles for Chilean independence from Spain. In his adaptation of realism as cultivated by Balzac, Flaubert, and Stendhal in France, Blest Gana still relies on pervasive elements of romanticism, especially those pertaining to the historical novels by Sir Walter Scott. Thus, his novel *Martín Rivas* (1862) reflects social change and a new Chilean society in which self-made worth means more than family status given by birth. Overall, the realistic ambition of Blest Gana cannot be separated from the patriotic conscience from which the novelist tried to contribute to the emerging Chilean national identity.

La gran aldea (The Great Village, 1884), by the Argentine Lucio Vicente López (1848–1894), is profoundly shaped by the social change that the nation was experiencing at the time. It is the first novel that shows how modernization laid the foundation for a transformed urban space in Buenos Aires. And nowhere in Latin America had society changed more drastically than in Argentina at the turn of the century. Its rapid economic development and influx of immigrants are reflected on the pages of a new genre, *La novela de la bolsa* (The Stock Market Novel). This genre was influenced by the French writer Emile Zola whose naturalist novels were popular at the time. Written through the lens of naturalism, a literary current informed by determinism, seen as the inability of human beings to resist the biological, social, and economic forces that dictated their behavior, this genre was preoccupied with an objective scientific observation of human life.

The stock market novel appeared at a time when the Argentine reformulations of individual and national identity were faced with what it perceived as a threatening irruption of "Otherness." Multiple formulations of these strategies in late nineteenth- and early twentieth-century Argentine literature include narratives of gender and immigrant displacement, among other forms of relating "self" to "Other." The subsequent constructions of the demarcation of borders, between both individual and communal identities, were prominently at stake in the social discourses and literary cultures of the time.

In the Southern Cone society at large, the arrival of thousands of immigrants at the turn of the twentieth century triggered the production of a complex set of regulative discourses. The reasons for this abundant discursive production with regulative purposes can be found in the dramatic demographic and socio-economic changes that the region experienced at that time, a claim that had been scrutinized in José Enrique Rodó's *Ariel* (1900): "Our democracies grow rapidly by the continual addition of a vast cosmopolitan multitude, by a stream of immigration . . . This rapid growth exposes our future to the dangers of a democratic degeneration that smothers under the blind force of the mass all idea of quality" (1922, 65–66).[3]

In Rodó's text, immigrants are viewed not only as the "cosmopolitan multitude" (65) but also as a blind force of numbers that, in their quantities and quantitative interests, are compelled to pursue material progress. They are also viewed as a potential cause of the "degeneration of democracy" (66). As carriers of material progress, immigrant subjects can thus be thought of as the antipode to the Latin American spiritual unity that Rodó's *Ariel* fervently advocates. *Novelas de la bolsa* and other naturalist novels were written in a socio-political context where miscegenation was discouraged and sustained national efforts were channeled toward the preservation of social and gender purity. The stock market novel gave central importance to the processes of regulation and "border control" around the definitions of masculinity, femininity, social class, and national identity.

A large corpus of Argentine novels of the time expresses a similar disdain for immigrants' economic pursuits. However, as some of these novels also promote an explicit agenda of "*acriollamiento*" (creolization) and the subsequent assimilation of immigrants into the preexisting national model, immigrants' economic success is also viewed as a potentially useful asset to this model. Adolfo Saldías's *Bianchetto: La patria del trabajo* (Bianchetto: The Country of Work, 1896), Francisco Grandmontagne's *Los inmigrantes prósperos* (The Prosperous Immigrants, 1896), and Francisco Sicardi's *Libro extraño* (The Strange Book, 1894–1902), where a contagious prostitute infects other characters, are only a few examples from the large body of texts that address immigrant themes and subjects in late nineteenth-century Argentina.

A stark division may be noted between the writings of the late nineteenth and early twentieth centuries in Argentina, a division being formulated around two main groups. The first group, belonging to the *Hispano-criollo* discourse, advocates for the homogenization of immigrants into the Argentine national agenda. Among such novels are those written by Eugenio Cambaceres (1843–1888), Antonio Argerich (1855–1940), Julián Martel (1867–1896), Francisco Sicardi (1856–1927), Lucio Mansilla (1831–1913), Santiago Calzadilla (1806–1896), Miguel Cané (1851–1905), and Eduardo Wilde (1844–1913). Cambaceres's novel *Sin rumbo* (Without Direction, 1885) is considered the first naturalist novel in Latin America. *La bolsa* (The Stock Exchange, 1890), the novel that gave name to this subgenre, was written by Julián Martel (pseudonym of the journalist José María Miró) and deals with the downfall of a successful businessman who gambles recklessly on the stock market.

In the other group, Roberto Payró (1867–1928), Fray Mocho (1858–1903), Adolfo Saldías (1849–1914), and Francisco Grandmontagne (1866–1936) wrote with a favorable view of immigration, and thus promoted possibilities of heterogeneity in the composition of Argentine society. Roberto Payró, for example, denounced the corruption of Argentine society in his novels *El casamiento de Laucha* (Laucha's Marriage, 1906) and the *Divertidas aventuras del nieto de Juan Moreira* (The Amusing Adventures of the Grandson of Juan Moreira, 1910), where he narrates the rise of a corrupt politician. José S. Álvarez (who wrote under the pseudonym Fray Mocho, 1858–1903) worked as the director of the Argentine illustrated magazine *Caras y caretas* and is the author of short stories and a novel titled *Memorias de un vigilante* (Memoirs of a Policeman, 1897). Fray Mocho is the first author to introduce *lunfardo*, the linguistic expression of the lower classes, into Argentine literature. He portrays *la picaresca porteña* and "widens the linguistic arc with the register of speech from the underworld of crime" (Morillas Ventura 271).[4] Alberto Gerchunoff (1883–1950) published *Los gauchos judíos* (*The Jewish Gauchos*) in 1910, the year that marked the centenary of Argentine independence. The novel is composed of a series of narrative sketches that describe the community of Russian Jews who fled the Russian tsarist pogroms and settled in rural Argentina.

The novel of the time depicts the complex ways in which economic, political, and cultural relations manifest themselves in representations of the social dynamics, but also of nature and the non-human world. One of the most emblematic novels of this period, Cambaceres's *En la sangre* (In the Blood, 1887), depicts in the opening chapter an Italian immigrant beating his wife, while the closing chapter describes this immigrant's son attacking his wife. Such scenes of domestic violence appear in the novelistic production of a time when xenophobia and antisemitism were being propagated by Julián Martel, Manuel Gálvez, and other writers and public figures. The social climate of turn-of-the-century Argentina included other highly troublesome and controversial issues arising from the growing national anxiety about the changing nature of the country's national identity. R. W. Connell's work, however, reminds us that masculinities are not about the "essence" of gender, but rather about socially constructed gender relations. The arrival of immigrants (mostly single men) and the subsequent changes in Argentina's demographic structure significantly affected the preexisting gender definitions. A slow but increasingly more visible process of the formation of a *femme nouvelle* and large numbers of single, immigrant men were major social phenomena perceived as a threatening "Otherness" *vis-à-vis* the hegemonic national masculine "self." This threatening situation for the "purity" of the national "self" resulted in a proliferation of regulative texts— medical, hygienist, and legal—and in the dissemination of a homophobic ideology which Jorge Salessi calls "the homosexual panic" (337).

When women novelists attempted to challenge patriarchy, they often had to resort to writing under a male pseudonym. Such is the case of *Stella: una novela de costumbres argentinas* (Stella: A Novel of Argentine Customs, 1905) written by César Duayen, pseudonym for the Argentine writer Emma de la Barra de Llanos (1861–1947), who founded the first professional school for women in Argentina and the National Red Cross. Set against the backdrop of the rapidly changing Argentine society, she also published five extraordinarily successful novels defined by a key element: "self-constitution of women in fiction" (Masiello 35). The central character of *Stella* is a young woman who engages in an uphill battle to educate and transform not only her own upper-class family, but also society as a whole. Salvadora Medina Onrubia (1894–1972) was the wife of Natalio Botana, the celebrated publisher of the newspaper *Crítica*, but also a writer in her own right. She wrote *Akasha* (1924) following theosophical ideas in vogue at the time, but also actively participated in the anarchist movement and wrote for the newspaper *La Protesta*. Fights for the equal participation of women in the political realm and the suffragist movement grew over the next decades and Argentine women finally won the right to vote in 1947.

The realist novel was often written with the purpose of exposing social injustice, a tendency that continued in the regional novels of the 1920s and 1930s. Ángel Rama has written about the novels of this period as largely belonging to the literary current he calls *realismo crítico urbano* (urban critical realism), while other critics have focused more on its counterpart, *La novela de la tierra* (the novel of the land), a genre that encompasses an autochthonous regional Latin American experience. A case in point, Ricardo Güiraldes's (1886–1927) *Raucho* (1917) is a novel whose protagonist, disillusioned with Europe and cosmopolitan urban life, returns to rural Argentina. The setting of Güiraldes's *Don Segundo Sombra* (1926) is the Argentine pampa and the novel's protagonist a *gaucho*, the rural cowhand who had become a national emblem. Benito Lynch (1885–1951) is another writer who focused on life in the Argentine provinces, most notably in his best-known novel *El romance de un gaucho* (The Romance of a Gaucho, 1930). Here the tension between Westernized lifestyles and rural ways informs the lives of the novel's protagonists, a city woman and a local gaucho.

In contrast to the regional novelists, Eduardo Mallea (1903–1982) wrote about inner struggles often independent of the surrounding reality, but still intensely focused on Argentina's geography and national identity. Existentialist thought, particularly the writings of Kierkegaard and Kafka, influenced his anguished analysis of modern urban society. Mallea sets *Todo verdor perecerá* (All Green Shall Perish, 1941) in the Argentine interior, portraying a farmer's wife who detests life in the countryside and is surrounded by crops that fail to produce. His novelistic production was particularly large in the 1950s, when he published *Los enemigos del alma* (The Enemies of the Soul, 1950), *Chaves* (1953), *La sala de espera* (The Waiting Room, 1953), and *Simbad* (1957).

In Uruguay, Enrique Amorim (1900–1960) depicted the Uruguayan countryside as politically divided and transformed by industrialization and immigrant labor. His novels *El paisano Aguilar* (The Compatriot, Aguilar, 1934) and *El caballo y su sombra* (The Horse and Its Shadow, 1941) attest to the social change Uruguay was undergoing in the 1930s and 1940s. In Paraguay, this complex social dynamic is reflected in Gabriel Casaccia's novelistic production. In Argentina, the profound societal change is also exemplified through the novels *Los burgueses* (The Bourgeois, 1964) by Silvina Bullrich (1915–1990) and *Memorias de un hombre de bien* (Memories of a Good Man, 1964) by Pedro Orgambide (1929–2003).

In Chile, Pedro Prado (1886–1952) published *El juez rural* (The Rural Judge, 1924); Eduardo Barrios (1884–1963), *Gran señor y rajadiablos* (Gentleman and Hellraiser, 1948); and Manuel Rojas (1896–1973) wrote social realist novels such as *Lanchas en la bahía* (Boats in the Bay, 1931) and *Hijo de ladrón* (Thief's Son, 1951). Although not regarded as a regionalist writer *per se*, Leopoldo Marechal (1900–1970), an Argentine novelist often associated with the avant-garde but also the ideologies of Peronism, wrote *Adán Buenosayres* (*Adam Buenosayres*) in 1948. The Dantesque circles of hell that are depicted in this novel include prominent members of society, especially businessmen and traders.

The years between 1900 and 1940 were a time of great stress and structural change in Southern Cone societies. They led to a sharpening of what has come to be called "the crisis of identity," which is manifest not only in the novels of Roberto Arlt, but also in the essays by Raúl Scalabrini Ortiz and Julio Mafud, among others. For Argentine intellectuals of this period, the city, as a topic and a problem, played a crucial role in the different ways of approaching this crisis. The "desire for the city" (viewed as a blessing and a curse, often at the same time), Beatriz Sarlo observes, "is as strong, in the Argentine tradition, as the rural utopias" (166).

Roberto Arlt (1900–1942) is regarded as the founder of the Latin American urban novel and is considered the continent's first modern novelist. *El juguete rabioso* (*The Mad Toy*, 1926), his first novel, continued the theme of the pursuit of material progress within an urban modernity that the Argentine novel had been portraying since the late nineteenth century. Arlt situates *El juguete rabioso*'s narrative development within the *barrios* of Buenos Aires and their bustling city crowds. However, unlike writers from more privileged backgrounds who read the latest novels in their original French or English versions, Arlt was a reader of Russian novels in translation and serialized dime novels.

These novels appeared weekly and also included the translations of the British crime writer Edgar Wallace, published in the immensely popular *Colección Misterio* by the editor J. C. Rovira. This and other penny press productions were widely circulated in Argentine cities, where they were often read on trains, streetcars, and other means of public transportation. Rocambole, the bandit protagonist of a group of enormously popular nineteenth-century serialized novels written by Pierre Alexis Ponson du Terrail, *Les Chevaliers du Clair de Lune* (*Los caballeros del claro de luna*, or *Moonlight Knights*), is used by Arlt as the favorite literary character of Silvio Astier, the protagonist of *El juguete rabioso*. If salons were exclusive spaces that the select few of the generation of the 1880s, the *Centenario*, and subsequent elites occupied, the spaces of Arlt's urban narratives are those of the street and the multitudes. These spaces are the setting for the stories of anguished and tormented individuals, such as Remo Erdosain, the protagonist of *Los siete locos* (*The Seven Madmen*, 1929).

Los siete locos and its sequel *Los lanzallamas* (*The Flamethrowers*, 1931) depict ways in which technological advances can bring about a revolution to be carried out by a secret society: El Buscador de Oro (The Gold Prospector) will organize the revolutionary cells and also gold extraction in the mines of the Argentine Chaco. El Rufián Melancólico (Melancholy Ruffian) will organize the network of brothels that will provide society with the money necessary for the realization of its dystopian plans. The Mayor will be responsible for the infiltration of revolutionary plans in the Argentine army. This whole vision, however, is just a plan, a simulacrum of power. Arlt visualized a technological dystopia in *Los siete locos* and repeatedly warned in his newspaper columns against the fascist war machinery in the making and the horrific advent of World War II.

The only Argentine novelist of the "Boom"—an "explosion" of interest in Latin American literature that developed in an international cultural arena traversed by global publishing markets—is Julio Cortázar (1914–1984). He is one of the most translated and widely disseminated novelists from the Southern Cone. Cortázar's *Rayuela* (*Hopscotch*, 1963) is a formally experimental novel whose chapters can be read in numerical sequence, in an alternate order suggested by the author, or in any order chosen by the reader. The reader is likely to attempt to follow both ways of reading at once: if the reader chooses to follow the alternate sequence, s/he will encounter multiple simultaneous events. Characters in this novel are marginal to society, and their behavior, unconventional.

"For Cortázar as for Sábato," Jean Franco suggests, "the novel is concerned with the crisis of modern man, and it must make the reader exercise the creativity which is one way of overcoming alienation" (329). Juan Carlos Onetti (1909–1994) and Ernesto Sábato (1911–2011) followed Arlt's and Cortázar's focus on urban alienation. In *Sobre héroes y tumbas* (*On Heroes and Tombs*, 1961), Sábato attempts a total novel, one that would encompass all alienating Argentine forces, including those of the past and the present. *La vida breve* (*The Short Life*, 1950), *El astillero* (*The Shipyard*, 1961), and *Juntacadáveres* (*Body Snatcher*, 1965) by Juan Carlos Onetti are existential novels set in Santa María, a mythical space invented by the author.

The Chilean novelist José Donoso (1924–1996) is the author of *El lugar sin límites* (*Hell Has No Limits*, 1966) and *El obsceno pájaro de la noche* (*The Obscene Bird of the Night*, 1970), among other novels, as well as the literary memoir, *Historia personal del boom* (*The Boom in Spanish American Literature: A Personal History*, 1972). Donoso's *La desesperanza* (*Curfew*, 1986) offers a detailed look at the suffocating Chilean military dictatorship in 1985 and employs a narrative style that Ángel Rama has called "*realismo de la decrepitud*" (191). The story unfolds over the course of just twenty-four hours, starting immediately after the death of Matilde Neruda, the widow of celebrated Chilean poet and Nobel prize winner Pablo Neruda.

The effects of totalitarian regimes are visually engaged by the Argentine novelist Manuel Puig. Deeply influenced by cinema and popular culture, Puig wrote *La traición de Rita Hayworth* (*The Betrayal of Rita Hayworth*, 1967), where the narrative is delivered by several characters, and also by documents and dialogue in which no single character occupies the position of narrator. The novel by Puig that, according to Juan E. De Castro, "most thoroughly explores the political options of the 1970s" (8) is *El beso de la mujer araña* (*Kiss of the Spider Woman*, 1976). It involves vivid dialogue by two cellmates, a gay man named Molina and a Marxist militant named Valentín. The novel is largely composed of their interactions, in which Molina recounts to Valentín various films, both real and invented.

The explosion of global interest in Latin American literature (its critics saw it in terms of marketing, as a "promotional" explosion) happened via New York, Barcelona, and Paris, while also including an influential writer from Paraguay, Augusto Roa Bastos. The first issue of the literary magazine *Mundo Nuevo*, edited by the Uruguayan critic Emir Rodríguez Monegal in Paris, in July 1966, contained a story by Roa Bastos. In "Writing: A Metaphor for Exile," Roa Bastos notes that the writer is compelled "to invent stories that are the transgression of official history" (291). Exiled from General Alfredo Stroessner's dictatorship, Roa Bastos wrote *Yo, el supremo* (*I, the Supreme*, 1974) while living in Buenos Aires. Rama has described it as "an unclassifiable book: history, novel, sociological essay, moral philosophy, fictionalized biography, autobiographical confession, revolutionary pamphlet, supporting document, prose poem, debate on the limits of literature, questioning of the verbal system" (210).[5] By blurring the distinction between history and fiction, the novel incorporates a polyphonic account of the life of José Gaspar Rodríguez de Francia, known as "El Supremo," a dictator who ruled Paraguay from 1814 to 1840.

Dictators and military juntas ruled over the region in the 1970s and 1980s: in Argentina from 1976 to 1983, in Uruguay from 1973 to 1985, in Chile from 1973 to 1990, and in Paraguay from 1954 to 1989. Cristina Peri Rossi (1941–) was exiled in Spain during the Uruguayan dictatorship. She published *La nave de los locos* (*The Ship of Fools*, 1984) in Spain, where she still lives. Peri Rossi was the 2020 recipient of the José Donoso Award. Luisa Valenzuela (1938–) also went into exile, to New York, before returning to Argentina, where she published *Novela negra con argentinos* (*Black Novel with Argentines*, 1990), and other well-known texts. Her novels most closely dealing with the dictatorship are *Como en la guerra* (As in War, 1977) and *Cola de lagartija* (*The Lizard's Tail*, 1983). In *La máscara sarda, el profundo secreto de Perón* (The Sardinian Mask, the Deep Secret of Perón, 2012), Valenzuela returned to the topic of Peronism, which is also that of *La novela de Perón* (*The Perón Novel*, 1985) and *Santa Evita* (1995) by Tomás Eloy Martínez (1934–2010).

Clara Obligado (1950–) moved to Spain from Argentina in 1976, as a political exile, and wrote *La hija de Marx* (*Marx's Daughter*) in 1996. Ariel Dorfman (1942–) worked as a cultural adviser to Chilean president Salvador Allende and was exiled in France, Holland, and the United States after General Pinochet's coup in 1973. He is the author of *La última canción de Manuel Sendero* (*The Last Song of Manuel Sendero*, 1982) and *Máscaras* (*Mascara*, 1988), among other texts. The Chilean Antonio Skármeta (1940–), the author of *Ardiente paciencia* (*The Postman*, 1985) and other novels, was exiled first in Buenos Aires, and then in Berlin, from 1975 to 1988. Before moving to Spain, where he published *Un viejo que leía novelas de amor* (*The Old Man Who Read Love Novels*, 1989), Luis Sepúlveda (1949–2020) was imprisoned and tortured by the Pinochet regime.

La invención de los soles (*Sun Inventions*, 1982) is a novella first published in Stockholm, Sweden, where its author, Teresa Porzecanski (1945–), was exiled from the Uruguayan dictatorship. Her *Perfumes de Cartago* (*Perfumes of Carthage*, 1994) describes the life of a family of Sephardic Jews in the River Plate in the 1930s, and that of their servant Ángela, a descendant of African slaves. *Barrio Palestina* (Palestine Neighborhood, 1998) by the Paraguayan author Susana Gertopan (1956–) follows the arrival of a Jewish Polish family to Paraguay right before World War II. In Chile, Sonia Guralnik, Marjorie Agosín, and Andrea Jeftanovic, among others, engage with complex themes and histories of Jewish identity.

Since Sarmiento, hegemonic national narratives in Argentina have promoted the idea of homogeneous whiteness. In such a cultural context, where racial differences have been obliterated, a growing corpus of texts has been formed representing Asian-Argentines and Arab-Argentines, including novels such as *Gaijin* (2002) by Maximiliano Matayoshi, *Flores de un solo día* (Single Day Flowers, 2002) by Ana Kazumi Stahl, *Un chino en bicicleta* (A Chinese on a Bicycle, 2007) by Ariel Magnus, *Tacos altos* (High Heels, 2016) by Federico Jeanmaire, and *Don Abdel Zalim: el burlador de Dominico* (Don Abdel Zalim: the Trickster of Dominico, 1972), by Jorge Asís.

César Aira (1949–), admired by Roberto Bolaño and increasingly more translated, is the author of *El congreso de literatura* (*The Literary Conference*, 1997), *Un episodio en la vida del pintor viajero* (*An Episode in the Life of a Landscape Painter*, 2000), *Como me hice monja* (*How I Became a Nun*, 1993), *El mármol* (The Marble, 2011), and other novels. *Ema, la cautiva* (*Ema, the Captive*, 1981) is a spoof of a nineteenth-century captive narrative, while one of his most recent novels, published in 2020 under the title *Lugones*, is focused on the last day of the Argentine poet. A prolific author of over one hundred *novellas* that span a wide range of themes, Aira wrote *Fulgentius*, also in 2020. Its narrative is set during the time of the Roman Empire.

The best known of the exiled writers and the most widely read Latin American writer today is Roberto Bolaño (1953–2003). He left Chile first for Mexico, and later settled in Catalonia, Spain, achieving global fame only posthumously. Ignacio López-Calvo notes that both successful and marginal writers populate Bolaño's fiction, "which often deals with the role of literature in life and of literary culture/writers in society and under repressive governments" (3). Bolaño's most translated and analyzed novels are *Los detectives salvajes* (*The Savage Detectives*, 1998), *2666* (2004), *Estrella distante* (*Distant Star*, 1996), and *Nocturno de Chile* (*By Night in Chile*) (2000).

Juan José Saer (1937–2005) is another exiled, largely influential writer of the Southern Cone region. He left Argentina and moved to Paris in 1968, fleeing the repression of military dictator Juan Carlos Onganía. The best-known of Saer's novels is *El entenado* (*The Witness*, 1983), a narrative of a discovery voyage and faux-historical expedition filled with enactments of "cannibal gore" and shades of Melville and Conrad (as announced in promotional materials accompanying the English translation). Antonio di Benedetto's *Zama* (1956), recently turned into an award-winning film by Lucrecia Martel, is set during the last decade of the eighteenth century, in a remote colonial outpost.

A reader of Borges and Arlt, Ricardo Piglia is considered one of the most influential Argentine literary critics of the twentieth century. He is also the author of acclaimed novels such as *La ciudad ausente* (*The Absent City*, 1992), which denounces the silence with which Argentine society treated the dictatorship. Los *diarios de Emilio Renzi: Años de formación* (*The Diaries of Emilio Renzi: Formative Years*, 2015) is a first of three volumes that Piglia wrote as novelistic autofiction, a genre that plays a significant role in the cultural production of the region, as exemplified by *Lenta biografía* (*Slow Biography*, 1990) by Sergio Chejfec, *El Libro de los recuerdos* (*The Book of Memories*, 1994) by Ana María Shua, *Katrilef, hija de un ülmen williche. Relato de su vida* (Katrilef, daughter of an ülmen williche. Account of her life, 2015) by Graciela Huinao, *Vivir entre lenguas* (*Living Between Languages*, 2016) by Sylvia Molloy, *El hijo judío* (*The Jewish Son*, 2018) by Daniel Guebel, *Mona* (*Mona*, 2019) by Pola Oloixarac, and *El sistema del tacto* (*The Touch System*, 2019) by Alejandra Costamagna, among other texts.

Alejandro Zambra (1975–), the author of *Poeta chileno* (*Chilean Poet*, 2020), follows the style of the experimental novels enacted first by the avant-garde writers Juan Emar in Chile and Macedonio Fernández in Argentina, and later continued by Cortázar, Saer, and Bolaño. His *Facsímil: libro de ejercicios* (*Multiple Choice*, 2014), for example, pushes the boundaries of fiction even further (as a novel written through the format of a multiple-choice aptitude test) and allows Zambra to reinvent literary form as an act of political protest. By sharpening the critique of magical realism, a critique of the pressure to represent the region through an exotic lens that was first articulated in the Southern Cone context by the Chilean writers Alberto Fuguet and Sergio Gómez of the McOndo group, contemporary Southern Cone novelists and those writing from abroad—Guillermo Martínez, Rodrigo Fresán, Pedro Mairal, Amir Hamed, Mario Levrero, Carlos Franz, Jorge Edwards, Martín Cohan, Leopoldo Brizuela, Jorge Marchant Lazcano, Andrés Newman, Patricio Pron, Martín Caparrós, Alan Pauls, Hernán Ronsino, Antonio Díaz Oliva, and Luciano Lamberti, among others—continue to grapple with issues of literary representation and other themes.

Women are arguably the most exciting new voices in Southern Cone literature from the past two decades. Social activism and feminist movements such as *Ni una menos*, *Mayo feminista*, *Marea Verde*, the Chilean feminist collective *Las tesis*, *El colectivo autoras chilenas (Auch)*, and *Por una constitución feminista* have influenced contemporary literature in ways that have shaped it as an instrument of social critique. Despite notable mid-century exceptions, such as Chilean novelists María Luisa Bombal (*La última niebla*, The Final Mist, 1934, and *House of Mist*, written in English, 1947) and Marta Brunet (*María Nadie*, Maria Nobody, 1957), as well as the Uruguayan Armonía Somers (*La mujer desnuda*, *The Naked Woman*, 1950), women writers were largely ignored or sidestepped by the Boom. This final section attempts to do them justice by highlighting the Southern Cone novelists that are particularly prominent in the contemporary resurgence of Latin American literature written by women.

Contemporary novels encompass a wide array of themes: gender inequality and emancipation, urban infrastructure, the home and dictatorship, political narrative and memory, the environment, and virtual space. Subgenres include *literatura fantástica*, such as horror, sci-fi, fantasy, and dystopian novel, crime novel and detective fiction, historical novel, novel/essay, autofiction and bildungsroman, hybrid, electronic, and other forms of experimental novel.

Narratives of crime and investigation are constructed as a composite of many subgenres, including detective fiction, investigative thriller, noir, spy, and crime novel. Such multiplicity of subgenres enables its authors to lay bare the historical and contemporary contradictions, both social and political, that characterize the Southern Cone societies. They write about ways in which crime writing simultaneously reflects societal dynamics and influences popular conceptions of politics, the law, and the self in the Argentine crime genre.

Mariana Dimópulos's *Cada despedida* (*All My Goodbyes*, 2010), for example, is a thriller about a murder in Patagonia and the subsequent quest for answers that focuses on fictional representations of displacement as well as legal and forensic practices. Claudia Piñeiro writes detective novels with strong female protagonists, such as *Las viudas de los jueves* (*Thursday Night Widows*, 2005), and *Tuya* (*All Yours*, 2006), while Ariana Harwicz writes crime fiction and feminist critiques of motherhood in *Matate, Amor* (*Dye, My Love*, 2012), and other novels. Selva Almada, in her investigative thriller novels that follow the "documentary fiction" format, reflects on the ways in which our understanding of reality has been constructed over the past few decades. Her novel *Chicas muertas* (*Dead Girls*, 2014) investigates three femicides that occurred in her Argentine hometown while she was growing up in the 1980s.

Argentine writers that foreshadow the contemporary speculative turn in literature written by women are Vlady Kociancich, the author of *La octava maravilla* (The Eighth Wonder, 1982), and Angélica Gorodischer (*Kalpa Imperial*, a collection of short stories originally published in 1983 and translated into English by Ursula Le Guin in 2003). *Cadáver exquisito* (*Tender Is the Flesh*, 2017) by Agustina Bazterrica has elements of science fiction, dystopian novel, and horror.

The classic sci-fi precursor novel is Adolfo Bioy Casares's *La invención de Morel* (*The Invention of Morel*, 1940). Dealing with a condemned man who invents a means of mechanically reproducing people, it is considered a touchstone of the genre. The Uruguayan Fernanda Trías is the winner of the Sor Juana Prize in 2021 for *Mugre Rosa* (Filthy Rose), a dystopian novel set in a port city reminiscent of Montevideo that is ravaged by a mysterious plague.

Mariana Enríquez (1973–) is the most highly acclaimed novelist of the Latin American gothic fiction genre. Drawing on southern gothic literature from the United States, but also the locally produced tradition of fantastic literature, cultivated in short stories written by Jorge Luis Borges and Adolfo Bioy Casares, Enríquez is a journalist and prolific author of novels, short stories, and essays, such as *Ese verano a oscuras* (That Summer in the Dark, 2019), a bildungsroman with elements of crime fiction and horror novel, and *La hermana menor: un retrato de Silvina Ocampo* (The Little Sister: A Portrait of Silvina Ocampo, 2014). Ocampo's own merit as a writer has been overshadowed by her associations with her husband Adolfo Bioy Casares and her older sister, Victoria Ocampo, the founder and editor of the journal *Sur* (1931–1979). Silvina Ocampo's *La promesa* (The Promise, 2010) and her short stories, such as those comprising the collection *Viaje olvidado* (The Forgotten Journey, 1937), have been re-printed and newly translated into English, exerting a deep influence on Enríquez and other contemporary women writers.

In her seven-hundred-page novel *Nuestra parte de noche* (*Our Part of the Night*, 2019), Enríquez includes eclectic elements ranging from a peculiar supernatural inheritance to the ability to summon the Dark, a capricious and primitive deity. This narrative strategy allows the author not only to draw from Anglophone gothic while engaging with horror, sci-fi, and fantasy, but also to illuminate different episodes of Argentine history, from the disappearances during the years of the military junta to the crisis of democracy during the 1990s. The novel speaks of violence to bodies: they are tortured, raped, disappeared, examined or violated by doctors and medicine, radiographed, possessed by black souls, severed, moistened by heat or burning, kidnapped, and killed.

Corpses figure prominently at the beginning and throughout the novel *La resta* (*The Remainders*, 2014) by the Chilean writer Alia Trabucco Zerán (1983–). Her work belongs to a growing corpus of narrative texts that assemble political discourse and memory studies. The Chilean dictatorship is also visually represented in Nona Fernández's *La dimensión desconocida* (The Unknown Dimension, 2016) and *Space Invaders* (Space Invaders, the original title is in English, 2013), a novella whose opening scene depicts a ten-year old schoolgirl at the celebration of the 1980 constitution. Chiefly authored by the Pinochet adviser Jaime Guzmán, the constitution is compromised by its links to

Chilean dictatorship. While a large social mobilization has successfully been calling for a new constitution in Chile, these texts are written against the historical background in which sites of memory have been at the center of negotiations with the region's traumatic past. *Museo Sitio de Memoria ESMA* in Buenos Aires and *El Museo de la Memoria y los Derechos Humanos* in Santiago honor the victims of human rights violations during the civic-military regimes by military juntas in the region. Considered more broadly, sites of memory include not only museums and monuments but also novels that critically examine necropolitics in the post-dictatorship societies of the Southern Cone. The question often being asked is the following: how can a novel be strategically harnessed to not only remember and denounce but also to rebuild and configure new spaces after conflict and atrocity?

The *novela de iniciación* or bildungsroman continues to seek answers to these difficult questions. Alejandro Zambra, in *Formas de volver a casa* (*Ways of Going Home*, 2011), remarks that dictatorship is "the novel of the parents" in which children are marginalized (56–57).[6] What happens when children become protagonists is the topic of two Chilean novels published in 2020: *La gente como uno* (People Like Us) by Bernardita García and *La ideología de los perros* (The Ideology of the Dogs) by Mauricio Embry. By mixing the personal and the political, both novels take the capture of Augusto Pinochet, in London, in 1998, as their starting point. This is a decisive political moment that allows them to reflect on Chile's recent past. The child protagonists in both novels challenge the official account and the silences in which they are being raised. They reject the dictatorship's inheritance but nevertheless are left to engage with deep self-reflection and questioning of the political discourses on the right and the left that define contemporary Chile.

Hybrid novels involve a transmedia approach mixing *crónica*, movie or video script, fiction, and non-fiction. Using this type of hybrid narrative, Diamela Eltit composed *El padre mío* (My Father, 1989) about a schizophrenic vagabond in post-dictatorship Chile, while Lila Larra wrote *Sprinters* (2016) about the horrific abuses during Pinochet's regime in Colonia Dignidad. Argentine writer María Moreno, known for writing *crónicas* as a literary instead of a journalistic genre, published her first novel, *El affair Skeffington* (The Skeffington Affair), in 1992. It is a fictional biography of an apocryphal North American author. Other acclaimed writers who cultivate a hybrid genre that fuses fiction and essay are Leila Guerriero and María Gainza. Gainza's *El nervio óptico* (*Optic Nerve*, 2014) evokes Sara Gallardo's novel *Enero* (January, 1958), as well as Argentine novelist Norah Lange's *Personas en la sala* (*People in the Room*, 1950). Chilean novelist Eugenia Prado, "perhaps Chile's greatest digital literature female creator" (Meza 191), wrote the novel *El cofre* (The Chest), which was published in 1987 (with a reprint in 2013), while her current project, a "blog-novel," appears under the title *Hembros: asedios a lo Post Humano* (Fe/males: Sieges of the Posthuman, 2006–). The Paraguayan author Damián Cabrera wrote two multilingual lyric novels by mixing Spanish, Guaraní, and Portuguese.

If the Boom first helped to promote the internationalization of the publishing markets, the growing English-language readership of the novels from the Southern Cone has been further consolidating this global trend. However, while translated writers of the Boom generation were male, most of the contemporary literary stars are female. Translation has certainly played a major role in shaping the circulation patterns of Southern Cone novels across transnational markets and cultural spaces. Many women writers whose work appears in translation reside abroad: Ariana Horwicz lives in France, Samantha Schweblin in Germany, Isabel Allende, Lina Meruane, and Diamela Eltit in the United States, to name only a few. *Talleres de escritura* or writing workshops played another important role in increasing accessibility to novel production: Hebe Uhart held a well-attended *taller* in Buenos Aires, while Samantha Schweblin attended Liliana Heker's *taller*, and she herself held a writing workshop in Berlin.

Schweblin's novella *Kentukis* (2018) is about virtual reality, while her novel *Distancia de rescate* (*Fever Dream*, 2014) inaugurates Argentine eco-noir and is considered a cornerstone of Latin America's emergent environmental canon. Feminist critique of patriarchy, among other issues, guides the narrative of the Chilean writer Lina Meruane in *Contra los hijos* (Against Children, 2014), *Sistema nervioso* (*Nervous System*, 2019), and *Sangre en el ojo* (*Seeing Red*, 2012). Argentine transgender writer Camila Sosa Villada published her novel *Malas* (The Bad Ones) in 2015, for which she won the Sor Juana Prize in 2020. Pedro Lemebel, in Chile, first tested the new ground by making sense of social change through the representation of gay, lesbian, and queer characters. *Tengo miedo torero* (*My Tender Matador*, 2015) is set in a Santiago working-class neighborhood, where the gay and aging Queen of the Corner offers up his home to the young Carlos to use as a gathering space for the resistance.

In the novel *Las aventuras de China Iron* (*The Adventures of China Iron*, 2017) by the Argentine writer Gabriela Cabezón Cámara, China is the abandoned wife of Martín Fierro who embarks on life adventures of her own. By following her life story, the reader actually follows a compelling counter-narrative, one that encompasses a critique of the myth of national origins and a feminist rewriting of the nineteenth-century foundational fictions. In a literary canon long dominated by men, these works represent not only the questioning of the nineteenth-century foundational narratives but also the invigorating opening up of the Southern Cone novel to other perspectives, particularly those of women and other underrepresented groups. This opening and the new literary maps have been enabled by the enormous talent of authors discussed here as well as the increased presence of independent publishing houses, literary and translation workshops, electronic literature, digital media, and other channels shaping contemporary (trans)national networks.

NOTES

1. "Verdadero best-seller de su tiempo" (Berenguer Carisomo 57).
2. Unless otherwise indicated, I use translations of novel titles from Jean Franco's *An Introduction to Spanish American Literature* (1975). Only for the first part of the essay.
3. "El presuroso crecimiento de nuestras democracias por la incesante agregación de una enorme multitud cosmopolita; por la afluencia inmigratoria . . . nos expone en el porvenir a los peligros de la degeneración democrática, que ahoga bajo la fuerza ciega del número toda noción de calidad" (Rodó, 1991, 25).

4. "Amplia el arco lingüístico con el registro del habla del submundo de la delincuencia" (Morillas Ventura 271).

5. "Un libro inclasificable: historia, novela, ensayo sociológico, filosofía moral, biografía novelada, confesión autobiográfica, panfleto revolucionario, documento justificativo, poema en prosa, debate sobre los limites de la literatura, cuestionamiento del sistema verbal" (210).

6. "La novela de los padres" (Zambra 56–57).

WORKS CITED

Acevedo Díaz, Eduardo. *Grito de gloria*. Barreiro y Ramos, 1894.

Acevedo Díaz, Eduardo. *Nativa*. Barreiro y Ramos, 1894.

Aira, César. *Como me hice monja*. Ediciones Era, 2006.

Aira, César. *El congreso de literatura*. Ediciones Era, 2006.

Aira, César. *El mármol*. La Bestia Equilatera, 2011.

Aira, César. *Ema, la cautiva*. Literatura Random House, 2015.

Aira, César. *Un episodio en la vida del pintor viajero*. Ediciones Era, 2018.

Almada, Selva. *Chicas muertas*. Literatura Random House, 2015.

Amorim, Enrique. *El caballo y su sombra*. Club del Libro, 1941.

Amorim, Enrique. *El paisano Aguilar*. Losada, 1958.

Arlt, Roberto. *El juguete rabioso*. Cátedra, 1985.

Arlt, Roberto. *Los siete locos. Los lanzallamas*. Biblioteca Ayacucho, 1978.

Armillas-Tiseyra, Magalí. *The Dictator Novel: Writers and Politics in the Global South*. Northwestern UP, 2019.

Asís, Jorge. *Don Abdel Zalim: el burlador de Dominico*. Corregidor, 1972.

Barrios, Eduardo. *Gran señor y rajadiablos*. Nascimento, 1948.

Bazterrica, Agustina. *Cadáver exquisito*. Alfaguara, 2018.

Berenguer Carisomo, Arturo. *Literatura argentina*. Labor, 1970.

Blest Gana, Alberto. *Martín Rivas*. Orbe, 1974.

Bolaño, Roberto. *2666*. Anagrama, 2005.

Bolaño, Roberto. *Estrella distante*. Anagrama, 1996.

Bolaño, Roberto. *Los detectives salvajes*. Anagrama, 1998.

Bolaño, Roberto. *Nocturno de Chile*. Anagrama, 2000.

Bombal, María Luisa. *La última niebla*. Editorial Andina, 1969.

Brunet, Marta. *María Nadie*. Zig Zag, 1957.

Bullrich, Silvina. *Los burgueses*. Sudamericana, 1966.

Cabezón Cámara, Gabriela. *Las aventuras de China Iron*. Literatura Random House, 2019.

Cambaceres, Eugenio. *En la sangre*. Colihue/Hachette, 1980.

Cambaceres, Eugenio. *Sin rumbo*. Cátedra, 1999.

Chejfec, Sergio. *Lenta biografía*. Alfaguara, 2007.

Cortázar, Julio. *Rayuela*. Cátedra, 2008.

Costamagna, Alejandra. *El sistema del tacto*. Anagrama, 2018.

De Castro, Juan E. *Writing Revolution in Latin America: From Martí to García Márquez to Bolaño*. Vanderbilt UP, 2019.

Di Benedetto, Antonio. *Zama*. Alianza, 1984.

Dimópulos, Mariana. *Cada despedida*. Adriana Hidalgo Editora, 2010.

Donoso, José. *El lugar sin límites. El obsceno pájaro de la noche.* Biblioteca Ayacucho, 1990.

Donoso, José. *Historia personal del boom.* Anagrama, 1972.

Donoso, José. *La desesperanza.* Seix Barral, 1986.

Dorfman, Ariel. *La última canción de Manuel Sendero.* Siglo XXI, 1982.

Dorfman, Ariel. *Máscaras.* Editorial Sudamericana, 1988.

Duayen, César. *Stella: una novela de costumbres argentinas.* Maucci, 1909.

Eloy Martínez, Tomás. *La novela de Perón.* Legasa Literaria, 1985.

Eloy Martínez, Tomás. *Santa Evita.* Planeta, 1995.

Eltit, Diamela. *El padre mío.* Francisco Zegers, 1989.

Enríquez, Mariana. *Ese verano a oscuras.* Editorial Página de Espumas, 2019.

Enríquez, Mariana. *La hermana menor: un retrato de Silvina Ocampo.* Anagrama, 2018.

Embry, Mauricio. *La ideología de los perros.* Libros del Amanecer, 2020.

Enríquez, Mariana. *Nuestra parte de noche.* Anagrama, 2019.

Fernández, Nona. *La dimensión desconocida.* Literatura Random House, 2016.

Fernández, Nona. *Space Invaders.* Alquimia, 2013.

Franco, Jean. *An Introduction to Spanish American Literature.* Cambridge UP, 1975.

Gainza, María. *El nervio óptico.* Anagrama, 2017.

Gallardo, Sara. *Enero.* Fiordo Editorial, 2019.

García, Bernardita. *La gente como uno.* Libros del Amanecer, 2020.

Gerchunoff, Alberto. *Los gauchos judíos.* Aguilar, 1984.

Gertopan, Susana. *Barrio Palestina.* Arandura Editorial, 1998.

Gorriti, Juana Manuela. *El Pozo de Yocci.* Cátedra, 2010.

Gorriti, Juana Manuela. *Oasis en la vida.* Félix Lajouane, 1888.

Grandmontagne, Francisco. *Los inmigrantes prósperos.* Aguilar, 1933.

Guebel, Daniel. *El hijo judío.* Literatura Random House, 2021.

Güiraldes, Ricardo. *Don Segundo Sombra.* Losada, 1982.

Harwicz, Ariana. *Matate, Amor.* Paradiso, 2012.

Huinao, Graciela. *Katrilef, hija de un ülmen williche. Relato de su vida.* ICIIS, 2015.

Jeanmaire, Federico. *Tacos altos.* Anagrama, 2016.

Kazumi Stahl, Ana. *Flores de un solo día.* Seix Barral, 2002.

Kociancich, Vlady. *La octava maravilla.* Seix Barral, 1999.

Lamas Carísimo, Teresa. *Tradiciones del hogar.* La Mundial, 1928.

Lange, Norah. *Personas en la sala.* Barataria, 2011.

Lemebel, Pedro. *Tengo miedo torero.* Anagrama, 2001.

López, Fidel Vicente. *La novia del hereje o la Inquisicón de Lima.* Editorial Doble, 2008.

López-Calvo, Ignacio. Introduction. *Roberto Bolaño, a Less Distant Star: Critical Essays,* edited
    by Ignacio López-Calvo, Palgrave Macmillan, 2015, pp. 1–17.

Lynch, Benito. *El romance de un gaucho.* Librerías Anaconda, 1933.

Magnus, Ariel. *Un chino en Bicicleta.* Editorial Norma, 2000.

Mallea, Eduardo. *Chaves.* Losada, 1953.

Mallea, Eduardo. *La sala de espera.* Sudamericana, 1953.

Mallea, Eduardo. *Los enemigos del alma.* Editorial Sudamericana, 1950.

Mallea, Eduardo. *Simbad.* Sudamericana, 1957.

Mansilla de García, Eduarda. *Lucía Miranda.* Iberoamericana-Vervuert, 2007.

Mansilla de García, Eduarda. *Pablo ou la vie dans les pampas.* E. Lachaud, 1869.

Masiello, Francine. *Between Civilization and Barbarism: Women, Nation, and Literary Culture
    in Modern Argentina.* U of Nebraska P, 1992.

Matayoshi, Maximiliano. *Gaijin*. Alfaguara, 2004.

Meruane, Lina. *Contra los hijos*. Literatura Random House, 2018.

Meruane, Lina. *Sangre en el ojo*. Literatura Random House, 2017.

Meruane, Lina. *Sistema nervioso*. Literatura Random House, 2019.

Meza, Nohelia. "Women Creators of Latin American Electronic Literature: a Geographical Overview." *Texto Digital*, vol. 16, no. 1, 2020, pp. 183–216.

Mocho, Fray. *Memorias de un vigilante*. Vaccaro, 1920.

Molloy, Sylvia. *Vivir entre lenguas*. Eterna Cadencia, 2016.

Moreno, María. *El affair Skeffington*. Bajo la Luna, 1992.

Morillas Ventura, Enriqueta. "Fray Mocho." *Historia de la Literatura Hispanoamericana*, vol. 2, edited by Luis Iñigo Madrigal, Cátedra, 1987, pp. 267–73.

Obligado, Clara. *La hija de Marx*. Lumen, 1996.

Ocampo, Silvina. *Viaje olvidado*. Emecé Editores, 1998.

Oloixarac, Pola. *Mona*. Literatura Random House, 2019.

Onetti, Juan Carlos. *El astillero*. Cátedra, 1983.

Onetti, Juan Carlos. *Juntacadáveres*. Alianza Editorial, 1981.

Onetti, Juan Carlos. *La vida breve*. Biblioteca Artigas, 2009.

Orgambide, Pedro. *Memorias de un hombre de bien*. Falbo, 1964.

Orrego, Rosario. *Alberto el jugador*. Revista del Pacífico, 1860.

Payró, Roberto. *El casamiento de Laucha*. Losada, 1971.

Peri Rossi, Cristina. *La nave de los locos*. Seix Barral, 1984.

Piglia, Ricardo. *La ciudad ausente*. Editorial Sudamericana, 1992.

Piglia, Ricardo. *Los diarios de Emilio Renzi: Años de formación*. Anagrama, 2015.

Piñeiro, Claudia. *Las viudas de los jueves*. Alfaguara, 2007.

Piñeiro, Claudia. *Tuya*. Alfaguara, 2012.

Porzecanski, Teresa. *La invención de los soles*. Arca, 1994.

Porzecanski, Teresa. *Perfumes de Cartago*. Trilce, 1994.

Prado, Pedro. *El juez rural*. Andrés Bello, 1980.

Prado, Eugenia. *Hembros: asedios de lo post humano*, 2006. http://hembros-eugeniaprado.blogspot.com/.

Puig, Manuel. *El beso de la mujer araña*. Seix Barral, 1976.

Puig, Manuel. *La traición de Rita Hayworth*. Seix Barral, 1976.

Rama, Ángel. *La novela en América Latina. Panoramas 1920–1980*. Ediciones Universidad Alberto Hurtado, 1982.

Ramos, Julio. *Divergent Modernities: Culture and Politics in Nineteenth-Century Latin America*. Translated by John D. Blanco. Duke UP, 2001.

Roa Bastos, Augusto. "Writing: A Metaphor for Exile." *The Oxford Book of Latin American Essays*, edited by Ilan Stavans, Oxford UP, 1997, pp. 288–93.

Roa Bastos, Augusto. *Yo, el supremo*. Alfaguara, 1985.

Rodó, José Enrique. *Ariel*. Porrúa, 1991.

Rodó, José Enrique. *Ariel*. Translated by F. J. Stimson. Houghton Mifflin Company, 1922.

Rojas, Manuel. *Hijo de ladrón*. Cátedra, 2001.

Rojas, Manuel. *Lanchas en la bahía*. Zig Zag, 1932.

Sábato, Ernesto. *Sobre héroes y tumbas*. Biblioteca Ayacucho 1986.

Saldías, Adolfo. *Bianchetto: La patria del trabajo*. F. Lajouane, 1896.

Salessi, Jorge. *Médicos, maleantes y maricas. Higiene, criminología y homosexualidad: Argentina 1870–1914*. Beatriz Viterbo, 1995.

Sarlo, Beatriz. "Modernity and Cultural Mixture: The Case of Buenos Aires." *Mediating Two Worlds: Cinematic Encounters in the Americas*, edited by John King, Ana M. López, and Manuel Alvarado, British Film Institute, 1993, pp. 164–75.

Sarmiento, Domingo Faustino. *Facundo*. Ediciones Culturales Argentinas, 1962.

Sepúlveda, Luis. *Un viejo que leía novelas de amor*. Tusquets Editores, 1993.

Shua, Ana María. *El Libro de los recuerdos*. Editorial Sudamericana, 1994.

Sicardi, Francisco. *Libro extraño*. Granada, 1910.

Skármeta, Antonio. *Ardiente paciencia*. Ediciones del Norte, 1985.

Somers, Armonía. *La mujer desnuda*. Trampa Ediciones, 2020.

Sommer, Doris. *Foundational Fictions: The National Romances of Latin America*. U of California P, 1984.

Trabucco Zerán, Alia. *La resta*. Demipage, 2014.

Trías, Fernanda. *Mugre Rosa*. Literatura Random House, 2020.

Valenzuela, Luisa. *Cola de lagartija*. Bruguera, 1983.

Valenzuela, Luisa. *Como en la guerra*. Sudamericana, 1977.

Valenzuela, Luisa. *La máscara sarda, el profundo secreto de Perón*. Seix Barral, 2012.

Valenzuela, Luisa. *Novela negra con argentinos*. Plaza & Janés, 1990.

Vicente López, Lucio. *La gran aldea*. Centro Editor de América Latina, 1967.

Zambra, Alejandro. *Facsímil: libro de ejercicios*. Sexto Piso, 2015.

Zambra, Alejandro. *Formas de volver a casa*. Anagrama, 2011.

Zambra, Alejandro. *Poeta chileno*. Anagrama, 2020.

....

CHAPTER 15

THE BRAZILIAN NOVEL

*An Outline from the Nineteenth to
the Twenty-First Century*

....

FERNANDO DE SOUSA ROCHA
AND LUIZ CARLOS SIMON

NOT many critics have undertaken the task of reconstructing a history of the novel in Brazil, which spans almost two hundred years. However, many of their works have assigned a fundamental space for the novel in the history of Brazilian literature. Chapters from Antonio Candido's *Formação da literatura brasileira* (Formation of Brazilian Literature), for instance, are essential for composing a portrait of the romantic novel in Brazil, Luís Bueno has done research that is fundamental to our study of the genre in the prolific 1930s, Alcmeno Bastos has focused on political novels of the 1970s and 1980s, and the volume *Livro do Seminário* (Book of the Seminar) includes several analyses of modernist novels. Broader perspectives are adopted in literary-history volumes that encompass all genres, such as Coutinho (1986), Bosi (1994), and Stegagno-Picchio (2004), as well as in other works whose circulation is now rather precarious: Montenegro (1953) and Linhares (1987) are a couple of these in which a panoramic view is drawn, more specifically, around the novel. All these studies employ, as one may notice, a chronological framework, which we have also adopted in this chapter, dividing it into sections dealing with different decades: from the 1840s to 1870s, 1880s to 1910s, 1920s to 1940s, 1950s to 1980s, and 1990s to present day. We hope that this chronological division will help readers find the required information without much difficulty. However, recurring to chronology as the main point of reference may lead to the expectation of precision regarding writers' trajectories. To give one example, although this is certainly not the only case, we might cite one of the most internationally renowned names in the Brazilian novel: Jorge Amado. This author, who was born in 1912 and died in 2001, began writing at an early age, published his first novel in 1931, and continued to publish novels up to the 1990s. He, therefore, might have been included in three different sections of this chapter. Cases such as Amado's require an evaluation of the affinities between novels and the periods in which they are housed. One must also mention here authors, such as Manuel de Oliveira Paiva (1861–1892) and Nelson Rodrigues (1912–1980), whose works were first published in newspapers and only later republished in their book form.

The selection of authors cited in this chapter, to a varying degree, needed to be rigorous, given its length requirements, and do not include authors prior to 1844, who are sometimes mentioned as novel writers in histories of Brazilian literature. Important novels and authors may not even be cited, given that an exhaustive inclusion of works and/or authors might render our text a mere list of names and titles. It is fundamental, nonetheless, to acknowledge certain developments in the field of literary studies that, over the last twenty or thirty years, have been affecting historiographic perspectives and calling for certain reevaluations. Moreover, since at least the 1970s, Brazilian TV has found, in many Brazilian novels from the nineteenth and early twentieth centuries, raw material for soap operas. This practice, together with other trends in Brazilian cinema, has led to a circuit between literature and cinema/TV, thereby generating re-readings of classic Brazilian novels. From the 1980s onward, literary studies have been adding elements to this breakdown of medial borders. In Brazil, the development of new areas of inquiry, such as women and literature—in relation to representations of women as well as women as authors—LGBTQ, and Afro-Brazilian literatures, as well as analyses of the configurations of social peripheries in literature, promote the need to revise and reconstruct the literary canon. Thus, authors such as Maria Firmina dos Reis (1822–1917) and Júlia Lopes de Almeida (1862–1934), previously absent from literary histories, started to gain during the last decades a certain projection, and others, such as Afonso Henriques de Lima Barreto (1881–1922) and Adolfo Caminha (1867–1897), were pulled out of the forgotten corners of history and obtained more visibility.

Our brief mapping of the Brazilian novel intends, therefore, to be a recognition of the plurality, in time, of the focalized geographical spaces and the narrated contexts. We hope that the reader will obtain the necessary information to discover, from the mid-nineteenth century to the present day, readings of novels that respond to various personal and academic interests.

1840S TO 1870S

The novel becomes highly relevant for Brazilian literature from the 1840s onward. If poems are still written and circulate in cultured society's salons, short stories are not as attractive yet to prose writers, and the theater remains as the main source of popular entertainment for society, displaying an unassuming comedic vein. Therefore, the new trend, in terms of literary genre, would be the novel, which benefited from the printed media, above all newspapers, as a space for their circulation. One must acknowledge that some works on the history of Brazilian literature go back to the seventeenth, eighteenth, or the first half of the nineteenth century, to cite certain texts that might be considered novels. Such procedure is justified, in part, because the authors themselves claim the classification of novel for their publications, even though at times they did not exceed thirty pages. Authors such as Teresa Margarida da Silva e Orta (1711–1793) and Antônio Gonçalves Teixeira e Sousa (1812–1861) are cited as precursors to the genre. Access to their works is, however, quite difficult, and the historiographic evaluation of their works is, at times, negative. Moreover, publishing houses have refrained from republishing them, underscoring the idea that the Brazilian novel only gains more consistency from the 1840s onward, as romanticism finally takes root in the country's cultural scene.

More than twenty years, therefore, go by after Brazil's political independence from Portugal until the publication of the first novel that would be considered a milestone in Brazilian literary history. We are referring here to *A moreninha* (Moreninha, 1844), by Joaquim Manuel de Macedo. This novel, which has gained prestige among critics and, above all, readers from several generations, belongs to a lineage of texts that focus on contemporary issues while adopting urban spaces as their settings. Such lineage is common among Brazilian romantics, following the example set up by European writers such as Victor Hugo, Alexandre Dumas in France, and Camilo Castelo Branco in Portugal. In Brazil, besides Macedo's prolific output, which is associated with urban social life, also noteworthy are José de Alencar's *Lucíola* (1862) and *Senhora* (*Senhora: Profile of a Woman*, 1875), as well as early novels by Machado de Assis, such as *A mão e a luva* (*The Hand and the Glove*, 1874) and *Iaiá Garcia* (*Iaiá Garcia*, 1878).

The urban setting in Macedo's *A moreninha* affords his novel certain particularities that have led to its permanence and recognition in Brazilian literary histories. Based on a well-balanced set of twists and turns surrounding the romantic couple Augusto and Carolina, the narrative is devoid of the tragic element often present in many European novels of the time. In this sense, it differs from Alencar's novels, such as *Lucíola* and *Senhora*, which are much more bent on a critical portrayal of society. At the same time, Macedo's light-handed and humorous text is a precedent to Manuel Antônio de Almeida's (1831–1861) *Memórias de um sargento de milícias* (*Memoirs of a Militia Sergeant: A Novel*, 1852), which brings to the forefront convincing popular types from contemporary urban Brazilian society. In Macedo's novel, the configuration of physical space is also important. If the city is the space where the young characters live their lives, the island where they meet for festive celebrations turns out to be a refuge for realizing their aspirations, becoming thus a counterpoint to frivolous urban customs. On the island, love relationships and the unfolding of the narrative will gradually favor authenticity over inconstance. Carolina's irreverence and vivaciousness become tonalities that will function as a reference for a good number of expressive feminine characters in Brazilian novels of subsequent decades.

Besides this urban setting to contemporary issues, present in romantic Brazilian novels and well represented by *A moreninha*, one must highlight the Indianist and historical trends, which are particularly associated with Alencar's *O Guarani* (The Guarani, 1857) and *Iracema* (*Iracema: A Novel*, 1867). Although this trend would be strongly influenced by European romantic ideals, one may detect in these types of novels the national component that was so fundamental to Brazilian literature at the time. Abundant references to nature stand out as indicators of a valorization of Brazil's territory, its fauna and flora, all of which constitute important and local aspects that had not yet found their portrayal in literature. Brazilian life was admired as part of a process in the construction of national pride, triggered by the experience of freedom befitting the post-independence period. Alencar thus pursued, in the figure of the indigenous person, seen at a remote time in the past, a representative of the qualities desired for the Brazilian character. Alencar created emblematic characters. Peri, in *O Guarani*, and Iracema, in the homonymous novel, reflect the author's idealization of the Brazilian character and his intent on safeguarding a mythical standing for his heroes.

Peri's abnegation and altruism, underscored by his unconditional defense of Cecília, the young white woman whom Peri protects, ensures that the aristocrat D. Antônio would admire him and recognize his noble character. D. Antônio sees in Peri "a Portuguese nobleman in the body of a savage!" (102).[1] In another passage, the narrator does not refrain from using a laudatory tone. A portrayal of Peri is thus introduced with the observation that the recounted story is robed in "his very poetic and rich language" (*O Guarani* 186).[2] Furthermore, the indigenous man's physical strength is lauded as incomparable. An episode at the beginning of the novel exposes the confrontation between the protagonist and a jaguar—"two savages from Brazil's jungles" (*O Guarani* 74)[3]—foreshadowing Peri's bravery in subsequent combats. Throughout *O Guarani*, the text's epic dimension is associated with lyrical refinement. This lyricism is also characteristic of Alencar's later *Iracema*, particularly in the construction of female characters and in the description of love relationships.

The valorization of the country's geographic space is not limited to Indianist novels. Some authors decided to use Brazil's hinterland as the setting for their novels. In this manner, these works are both distant from the temporal displacement that constituted historical novels such as *O Guarani* and *Iracema* and from the real urban life that was only timidly organizing itself, but that already possessed its own moral codes. Visconde de Taunay (1843–1899) depicts in *Inocência* (*Inocência*, 1872) a rural life that wishes to remain immune to urban influences. From the same year is *O seminarista* (The Seminarian), by Bernardo Guimarães (1825–1884), with a young protagonist who is tormented by the adversities that compromise his relationship with his beloved Margarida: the friction among offspring, parents, and families is tied to social differences typical of life in the hinterland. Guimarães also wrote *A escrava Isaura* (The Slave Girl Isaura, 1875), a novel in which the transit between rural and urban spaces, together with the debate on slavery and abolition, creates great dramatic tension. *O sertanejo* (The Backcountry Man 1875), by José de Alencar, and *O Cabeleira* (Cabeleira 1876), by Franklin Távora (1842–1888), contribute to the gallery of romantic characters with heroes—at times, as in Távora's novel, no longer virtuous—who belonged to this hostile terrain which is the *sertão*, Brazil's northeastern hinterland. One already notices in this group of novels, all of which published in the 1870s, a transition to realism in the Brazilian novel.

1880S TO 1910S

The period comprehended in this section consists of Brazilian novels published between the 1880s and the 1910s. These last two decades in the nineteenth century and the first two in the twentieth might be considered an interlude, precisely because they represent a transition between one century and the other. The first years of this period correspond to the end of a century that was marked by romanticism, whereas the last ones antecede modernism, a key movement in Brazilian literature. The lack of a shared style raises difficulties when readers and critics attempt to engage with novels written during this period. However, these novels are of enormous relevance to our understanding of Brazilian fiction.

The first year in this period is already quite representative of what was to come. In 1881, both Aluísio Azevedo's (1857–1913) *O mulato* (*Mulatto*) and Machado de Assis's *Memórias póstumas de Brás Cubas* (*The Posthumous Memoirs of Brás Cubas*) would come to print. One must emphasize that both writers had already published novels in the previous decade. Assis, for example, began publishing novels in 1872. Azevedo has his debut in the genre in 1879, with *Uma lágrima de mulher* (Tear of a Woman). However, only in 1881 would they reach full literary maturity as they rid their writings of romantic stylistic patterns. Both writers would gain a central position in the latter part of the nineteenth century and in relation to subsequent literature.

Machado de Assis occupies a place apart from the bulk of Brazilian literary production. Histories of Brazilian literature stress the author's incomparable talent and award him the position of most cited writer of all times, even after more than a hundred years after his death. His prestige goes beyond the realm of the novel, encompassing his poetry, plays, chronicles, and short stories. With *Memórias póstumas de Brás Cubas*, the novelist revolutionizes the form of narrative techniques, creating the role of the deceased first-person narrator and bringing to the fore irony, skepticism, cynicism, and the loss of illusions as forces that compose his worldview. In *Dom Casmurro* (*Dom Casmurro: A Novel*, 1899), his memorialistic tone also becomes a fictional recourse to recount the long and controversial relationship between the two main characters, the couple Bentinho and Capitu, not to mention Escobar, the character/narrator's friend, whom Bentinho suspects of having had an affair with his wife. Bentinho wishes to recuperate his own past and, to do so, he reconstructs the home where he had spent his childhood and youth. During this process of revision, materialized in a refined prose, several issues come up: the disturbing relations between time and memory, the art of narration and the mechanisms for selecting the facts to be remembered, and the dynamics for social ascension. Machado de Assis also wrote *Quincas Borba* (*Quincas Borba*, 1892), *Esaú e Jacó* (*Esau and Jacob: A Novel*, 1904), and in 1908 (the year of his death) *Memorial de Aires* (*Counsellor Ayres' Memorial*).

Azevedo, on the other hand, was a central figure in establishing naturalism as an influential literary movement in Brazil. After the publication of *O mulato*, Azevedo achieves a rather irregular success with his other novels published before 1895. The ones that stand out are *Casa de pensão* (The Boarding House, 1884) and *O cortiço* (*The Slum: A Novel*, 1890). If, in the former, the physical space of the boarding house where the young middle-class student lives was already perceived at the time as somewhat odd, in the latter the setting of an impoverished space of collective dwelling redefines the relationships among characters and their relevance to the narrative. It is often argued that the protagonist in *O cortiço* is the slum itself. Mainly during the last two decades of the nineteenth century, Azevedo was an inspiration of sorts to other Brazilian novelists who saw new novelistic possibilities opened by naturalistic models of writing.

Adolfo Caminha, for instance, dared focus on male homosexuality between sailors in *Bom-Crioulo* (*Bom-Crioulo: The Black Man and the Cabin Boy*, 1895). The novel, which for a long time had been received with reservations or even repugnance, has been more widely read recently and the object of more regular studies in the last forty years, most likely due to its treatment of a once-taboo topic. This new trend has also led to a new edition of *Um homem gasto* (A Wasted Man, 1885), by Ferreira Leal (1850–1914), in which the author analyzes how the protagonist, after suffering sexual abuse in a religious boarding school and leading a promiscuous life in Paris, becomes impotent (hence the novel's title). Analyses of the most unacceptable aspects of social life are constitutive of many of the naturalistic novels. In *O marido da adúltera* (The Husband of the Adulteress, 1882), by Lúcio de Mendonça (1854–1909), the writer revisits the topic of adultery, so frequent in late nineteenth-century novels, but emphasizing masculine actions and investigating to what extent the husband, protagonist of the novel, was guilty. João Carlos de Medeiros Pardal Mallet (1864–1895), in *Hóspede* (Guest, 1887), focuses on intriguing characters, such as a Brazilian dandy and a housewife who is torn between abiding by social conventions or following her affective and sexual desire.

Novelists Manuel de Oliveira Paiva and Domingos Olímpio (1850–1906), in *Dona Guidinha do Poço* (1892) and *Luzia-Homem* (Luzia-Man, 1903), respectively, create expressive feminine characters, like the powerful woman in a rural setting—as in Paiva's novel—and the poor, masculine young woman, in *Luzia-Homem*, who is at the same time physically strong and beautiful. Finally, Inglês de Sousa (1853–1918) sets his novel *O missionário* (The Missionary, 1888) in the Amazon region, which, more than a background, becomes one more element fostering the protagonist's anguished perception of an antagonism between religious precepts and the manifestations of vanity and sexual impulses.

Other novels of the period are also noteworthy, albeit not being greatly influenced by naturalistic trends. Raul Pompeia's (1863–1895) *O ateneu* (*The Aethenaeum: A Novel*, 1888) paints the daily life in a boarding school, its principal's despotism, and the protagonist's sociality with schoolmates, reviewed from the perspective of his present adulthood. Pompeia's narrative has impressionist traces, constituting a work outside of the Machadian or naturalistic axes that dominated the period. In *A viúva Simões* (The Widow Simões, 1897) and *A falência* (Bankrupcy, 1901), among other novels, Júlia Lopes de Almeida emerges as a significant woman writer of the period. Rarely mentioned in volumes of literary history, her works have been reassessed in studies on women and gained renewed attention by publishers, with recent editions of her novels being published. Almeida presents less stereotyped constructions of feminine characters, furthering the debate on women's position in Brazilian society. Her narrative has recently generated more interest than the novels written by other women writers of her time, such as Emília Freitas (1855–1908), Francisca Clotilde (1862–1932), Andradina de Oliveira (1864–1935), Albertina Bertha (1880–1953), and Carmen Dolores (1852–1910).

At the end of this period, one finds literary practices that one may already identify as being pre-modernist. Among the novelists publishing during the first two decades of the twentieth century, Henrique Maximiano Coelho Neto (1864–1934), João do Rio (João Paulo Emílio Cristóvão dos Santos Coelho Barreto, 1881–1921), and Lima Barreto are the most notable ones. Author of a vast number of novels, Coelho Neto portrays, in *Turbilhão* (Bewilderment, 1906), modern life's dilemmas while recounting the protagonist's desperate search for his sister. Better known for his chronicles and short stories, João do Rio is attuned to the contemporary time in *A profissão de Jacques Pedreira* (Jacques Pedreira's Profession, 1911) by creating a frivolous protagonist. However, Lima Barreto would be the one to achieve the most significant oeuvre, with novels such as *Recordações do escrivão Isaías Caminha* (Memories of the Scrivener Isaías Caminha, 1909) and *Triste fim de Policarpo Quaresma* (*The Sad End of Policarpo Quaresma*, 1916). Focusing on the incessant struggle between ordinary individuals and structures of power, Lima Barreto widens the spectrum of social relations represented, with a vigor and style that would require several years, after the publication of his novels, to be fully recognized.

1920S TO 1940S

In the early twentieth century, an event would have long-term ripple effects in the Brazilian cultural field: the *Semana de Arte Moderna* (Modern Art Week), which took place in São Paulo in 1922. It consisted of a week-long exhibition of visual arts and a series of literary and musical performances involving artists who would become very influential in Brazil, such as writers Mário de Andrade (1893–1945), Oswald de Andrade (1890–1954), and Manuel Bandeira (1886–1968). Coinciding with the hundredth anniversary of the country's independence from Portugal, the *Semana* aimed at introducing a new era in Brazilian culture, based on the various modernist aesthetics that had been refashioning the European artistic landscape. Transposed to Brazilian soil, these novel aesthetic movements led to a renewed interest in popular as well as indigenous cultural creations and their modes of perceiving the world. From such bases, Brazilian modernist intellectuals would attempt to fashion a Brazilian language and to redefine the national identity. As a result of his own research in these areas, Mário de Andrade published, in 1928, his novel *Macunaíma: o herói sem nenhum caráter* (*Macunaíma*). In this narrative, we follow Macunaíma's adventures from his birth in the Amazon region until his death. From an early age, Macunaíma's character is marred by negative traits, justifying the book's subtitle: the hero with no character. This might be understood, in very simple terms, as someone who lacks the moral fiber constitutive of heroism, as described in Western literature. However, that is clearly a simplification of the novel's protagonist. Functioning as a trickster, Macunaíma does not operate according to an either/or, a good/evil logic. Instead, he calls into question any dichotomic delimitation. He is capable of the most ingenious acts, solving problems that others are unable to solve, thereby guaranteeing the survival of his immediate group. But he can also be violent, destructive, and vindictive. In the end, Macunaíma becomes a mythical hero whose ambiguity in character points to a vital openness in the process of reconfiguring Brazilian national identity. Macunaíma ends up distant and belonging to a vanished ethnic group, but his stories, storytelling, and speech are saved by a parrot, and later by the writer himself, who learns them from the parrot. Thus, a "talk in a gentle tongue, something new, completely new!" (168)[4] is presented to Brazilian readers.

This new style of writing that incorporates Brazilian popular language would soon take new forms, often unrelated to the idea of foundational myths, as had been the case of Andrade's novel. In the 1930s, a group of new novelists would emerge, refocusing their attention to social analyses of issues pertaining to local or regional spaces and societies. Such a shift had already been set in motion by José Américo de Almeida's (1887–1980) *A bagaceira* (*Trash*), a novel that, published the same year as *Macunaíma*, portrayed the vicissitudes of a family who suffers from both the droughts that force them to migrate and the despotic power exerted by big landowners. Like Almeida, many of these emerging writers were from Brazil's northeastern region, the most renowned ones being Rachel de Queiroz (1910–2003), Jorge Amado (1912–2001), José Lins do Rego (1901–1957), and Graciliano Ramos (1892–1953), all of whom at times wrote on topics such as droughts and forced migrations, as in Queiroz's first novel *O Quinze* (The Nineteen-fifteen Drought, 1930) and Ramos's *Vidas secas* (*Barren Lives*, 1938); the power of big landowners and the exploitation of workers, as in Amado's *Cacau* (Cocoa, 1933) and Ramos's *São Bernardo* (*São Bernardo: A Novel*, 1934); or the decline of rural oligarchic families, as in Rego's sugar cane cycle and Ramos's *Angústia* (*Anguish*, 1936).[5] In his prefatory note to *Cacau*, Amado asks his readers if his was a proletarian novel, given his attempt at minimizing the text's literariness in favor of an honest account of the workers' lives in cocoa plantations. Informed by leftist ideas and socialist realism, Amado's questioning points not only to a new form of storytelling, but also to the emergence of collective protagonism and the possible recognition of new literary heroes, as we see in his later novel *Capitães da Areia* (*Captains of the Sands*).

Published in 1937, this urban novel focuses on a group of street kids who live in an old warehouse located on a beach in Salvador, Bahia. The title of the novel itself already indicates that there is not one individual protagonist, although the gang requires a leader, Pedro Bala, to function effectively. Akin to other novels focusing on marginalized groups, such as *O cortiço*, by Aluísio Azevedo, *Capitães da Areia* depicts the network of lives and relationships within the group and, to a certain extent, between the group and broader society. More than types, what we see in the novel's multitude of characters is a wide spectrum of beings who are in pain, struggling with their own personal trauma while creating ways to cope with a life-threatening reality. Morally am-bivalent, the street boys are shown as respecting and protecting their female members of the gang and, at the same time, as being sexual predators when it comes to girls out-side their group. However, rather than morally judging these "captains of the sands," the novel presents their behavior as a consequence of their marginalized social conditions. In novels where heroism occurs in the extreme setting of a completely inhospitable land, as we see in Ramos's *Vidas secas*, it is reduced to minimal acts of survival, and, rather than witnessing the greater social movement of migrants, implied at the end of Ramos's novel, we are immersed in one family's misery.

One might argue that social criticism is one current within the 1930s novels and, furthermore, that regionalist novels did not necessarily preclude more psychological analyses, as we see in *São Bernardo*'s protagonist's delving into his own psyche. In fact, narratives that were more bent on psychological realism were also quite significant, represented by writers such as Cornélio Penna (1896–1958), but also adopted at times by regionalist novelists, as noted in Rachel de Queiroz's *As três Marias* (*The Three Marias*, 1939). The latter is a *bildungsroman* of a bourgeois girl named Guta, who lives within the ideological framework of a romanticized male-centered world, which she desires as much as she rejects. No doubt Queiroz's immense contribution lies in her acute psycho-logical description of her protagonist's inner life, which is in contradiction with a patri-archal world. In this sense, one might say that *As três Marias* is representative of other novels published by women writers in the 1930s and 1940s, such as Clarice Lispector's (1920–1977) first novel, *Perto do coração selvagem* (*Near to the Wild Heart*, 1943).[6] At the end of Queiroz's novel, the protagonist confesses that she does not know how much longer she will be "lonely and forsaken, shining in the dark," like a star, "until [her] light goes out" (178).[7]

Guta is a distant lonely protagonist but devoid of any recuperative mythical, heroic standing. National identity cannot be organized around her story and storytelling. Her solitude is thus similar to that of other literary characters marked by failure, like Luís da Silva in Ramos's *Angústia* or the bureaucrat in Cyro dos Anjos's (1906–1994) *O amanuense Belmiro* (*Diary of a Civil Servant*, 1937), or by an ambiguous sense of accom-plishment, like Leniza in Marques Rebelo's (1907–1973) *A estrela sobe* (*The Star Rises*, 1939) or Naziazeno in Dyonélio Machado's (1895–1985) *Os ratos* (The Rats, 1937). Guta's distant brilliance indicates that, contrary to Amado's belief in collective power, to live in society is often an act of isolation, as we see in *O resto é silêncio* (*The Rest is Silence*, 1943), by Erico Verissimo (1905–1975). Like his contemporaries from the northeast (Verissimo was from Rio Grande do Sul, the southernmost state in Brazil), he also wrote about small-town life and the decline of rural oligarchic families, but, in his 1943 novel, he focuses on how one event, a young girl's suicide, impacts the lives of many different characters. His use of a counterpoint narrative technique, also employed in *Caminhos cruzados* (Crossroads, 1935),[8] allows for the development of parallel narratives. From mythical heroism, collective action, and inner scrutiny, Brazilian readers would be invited to consider societal isolation and individualism.[9]

1950S TO 1980S

In the 1950s and 1960s, some writers that had begun their careers in previous decades would continue to publish and consolidate their recognition, both on the part of critics and wide-audience readers, and new ones would emerge who would further transform the novel form. Herberto Sales (1917–1999), for instance, who first published a novel in 1944, titled *Cascalho* (Gravel), would later publish *Além dos marimbus* (Beyond the Swamp, 1961) and *Dados Biográficos do Finado Marcelino* (Biographical Information on the Late Marcelino, 1965). Like Jorge Amado, Sales sets his first two novels in specific regions in the state of Bahia and the latter in its capital, Salvador. As far as Amado is concerned, he published some of his most acclaimed novels in the period—*Gabriela, cravo e canela* (*Gabriela, Clove and Cinnamon*), for instance, appeared in 1958, and *Dona Flor e seus dois maridos* (*Dona Flor and Her Two Husbands*) in 1966—as did Erico Verissimo. The publication of his trilogy *O tempo e o vento* (*Time and the Wind*) spanned from late 1940s to early 1960s.[10] Lúcio Cardoso (1912–1968), whose psychological, introspective novel *A luz no subsolo* (Light in the Underground) appeared in 1936, also published his most important work, *Crônica da casa assassinada* (*Chronicle of the Murdered House*, 1959), in this period. In the latter, Cardoso chronicles the decadence of a family, a topic that would also be the focus in a cycle of novels by an author who began publishing in the 1950s, Maria Alice Barroso (1926–2012), and whose use of multiple narrators in some of her novels is associated with the French *nouveau roman*.[11]

Another novelist who began publishing in the previous decades but reached her maturity during this period is Clarice Lispector, whose first novel, as mentioned, appeared in 1943. In the 1960s, both *A paixão segundo G.H.* (*The Passion According to G.H.*, 1964) and *Uma aprendizagem, ou o livro dos prazeres* (*An Apprenticeship or the Book of Pleasures*, 1969) were published. In the former, Lispector deepens her use of stream of consciousness to work on the character's self-analysis, reducing social indicators to a minimal when constructing the character, about whom we know very little: her name's initials (G. H.), that her maid has quit work, or that she most likely belongs to the upper class. Lispector's undoing of the genre would find its culmination in *Água viva* (1973). What is left is, nonetheless, a constant inquiry into the nature of language (a few of her novels are, at least in part, metalinguistic) and a search for existential meanings.

Both existentialism and an inquiry into language had already given new life to well-established literary currents, such as regionalism, as we see in João Guimarães Rosa's *Grande sertão: veredas* (*The Devil to Pay in the Backlands*, 1956). His only novel, *Grande sertão*, on the one hand, returns to a topic that had been examined by northeastern regionalist novelists: the underdog's heroism or banditry (depending on one's perspective) in the face of local power, originating, in many instances, in his defense of a man's honor.[12] On the other, Guimarães Rosa explores how popular language and storytelling techniques may be used to create a literary work, procedures with which Mário de Andrade had also engaged. In Rosa's case, however, it led to an intensified use of neologisms and to a first-person narrative, strengthening the underdog's voice in the novel. Both Lispector's and Guimarães Rosa's works have lent themselves to renewed readings, opening critical perspectives unforeseen to the authors themselves. Guimarães Rosa's protagonist Diadorim, a woman who cross-dresses, has invited the discussion of transgenderism in recent analyses of the novel.

Lispector's works, which often portray women protagonists, may be seen as examples, at times, of *écriture feminine* and taken as points of reference for other women writers, such as Adélia Prado (1935–).[13] In the 1970s, novels authored by women would continue to investigate women's place in Brazilian society. Lygia Fagundes Telles's (1923–2022) *As meninas* (*The Girl in the Photograph*, 1973) focuses on the lives of three women during the military dictatorship (1964–1985). Coming from different backgrounds, the three protagonists must deal with questions pertinent to their time, such as drug use or the value of revolutionary acts to counter totalitarianism, as well as the issue of women's sexual liberation. Like Lispector, Telles makes use of stream of consciousness techniques to delve into her characters' psyche but also adopts a multi-focal perspective for the novel, which is narrated at times in the third person and, at others, in the first.

As the military dictatorship became more repressive after the 1968 Institutional Act No. 5, which suspended constitutional rights, other novels would, in different manners, examine the impact of the lack of freedom and of institutionalized violence on Brazilian society. Ignácio de Loyola Brandão's (1936–) *Zero* (*Zero*, 1975), for example, is an experimental narrative resembling, to a certain extent, those by modernist authors such as Oswald de Andrade. By means of a fragmented narrative, Brandão's novel juxtaposes the violence of totalitarianism to that practiced within domestic spaces and personal relationships. The protagonist, José, both discovers a pleasure in killing, as he robs to support his wife's lifestyle (later joining a guerrilla group), and maintains a marital relationship that disgusts him, but in which sexual pleasure is associated with abuse and contempt. The intermingling of sex and violence is also present in Rubem Fonseca's (1925–2020) fiction, as we see in his very first novel, *O caso Morel* (The Morel Case, 1973). Fonseca often elaborates on violence as a trigger for pleasure as the Brazilian bourgeoisie develops a phantasmatic fixation on being assaulted by criminals coming from the lower class, and he does so by creating (and parodying) detective or police novels. His *A grande arte* (*High Art*, 1983) begins with the assassination of a female prostitute by an unknown man, exposing both an extreme misogyny and the fear that violence is no longer exclusively attributable to oppressive dictatorial authorities. As the narrator states, reflecting the murderer's mind, "[i]t was a waste of time to speculate why particular things give us pleasure" (3).[14]

However, Fonseca is also making metaliterary commentaries in his novel by subtly establishing an analogy between detective investigations and hermeneutical practices. Metafiction is already present in his first novel and will be taken up again in *Bufo & Spallanzani* (1986), thus situating some of his works within a current of novels that question fictional writing itself, as we later see, for example, in Chico Buarque's *Budapeste* (*Budapest: A Novel*, 2003). Social analysis may therefore also entail literature's folding onto itself.

1990S TO 2010S

The narrative trends of the 1990s continue those characteristic of the 1980s. In fact, many of the principal writers of the 1990s began publishing during the previous decade. Such is the case of Fonseca, whose *Agosto* (*Crimes of August: A Novel*) and *O selvagem da ópera* (The Savage of the Opera) appeared in 1990 and 1994, respectively. Similarly, Milton Hatoum (1962–), who first published the novel *Relato de um certo oriente* (*The Tree of the Seventh Heaven*) in 1989, returns to the genre in 2000 with *Dois irmãos* (*The Brothers: A Novel*), and João Gilberto Noll (1946–2017), whose *A fúria do corpo* (The Body's Fury) appears in 1981, would be quite active in the 1990s, with *Harmada* (1993) and *A céu aberto* (The Open Sky, 1996). Cristovão Tezza (1952–), who had achieved success with *Trapo* (Rag, 1988), continues in his literary trajectory with *A suavidade do vento* (The Softness of the Wind, 1991) and *Uma noite em Curitiba* (A Night in Curitiba 1995), among other works. One should also mention here Carlos Heitor Cony (1926–2018), a novelist whose career started in the 1950s and, after over twenty years without writing a novel, would publish in 1995 *Quase memória* (Almost a Memoir), among other publications that would win him several prizes.

One must also note that the last decade of the twentieth century is marked by the emergence of novelists who would soon be acclaimed by critics, winning several national prizes, and maintaining solid careers up to the present time. That is the case of Chico Buarque (1944–), author of *Estorvo* (*Turbulence*, 1991), and Bernardo Carvalho (1960–), with *Os bêbados e os sonâmbulos* (The Drunks and the Sleepwalkers, 1996), among others. Furthermore, in the century's last years, certain novels stand out, such as *Cidade de Deus* (*City of God*) by Paulo Lins (1958–), and *Capão Pecado* (2000), by Ferréz (Reginaldo Ferreira da Silva, 1975–), both of which focus on marginalized communities that lend their names to the titles of their novels, as well as Miguel Sanches Neto's (1965–) experience in autofiction, *Chove sobre minha infância* (It Rains on my Childhood, 2000). Lastly, it is important to cite here Roberto Drummond (1939–2002), an author who makes recourse to both politics, either contemporary or of the recent past, and media elements to construct his fictional world, as we attest in the relevant novel *Hilda Furacão* (*Hilda Hurricane: A Novel*, 1991).

The new century ushered in the debut of Michel Laub (1973–), one of the most talented novelists in contemporary Brazilian literature. After his first novel, *Música anterior* (Earlier Music, 2001), many others have been published, such as *O gato diz adeus* (The Cat Says Goodbye, 2009) and *Diário da queda* (*Diary of the Fall*, 2011). His novels are loaded with conflicts raised by memory and intimacy, being in syntony with contemporary life. Also worthy of mention here is Rubens Figueiredo's (1956–) *O passageiro do fim do dia* (The Passenger of the Day's End, 2010), which narrates a long trip on a city bus, allowing for the most unexpected episodes and sensations. Two of the most acclaimed authors of these initial decades of the twenty-first century were born in the 1970s: Ana Paula Maia (1977–) and Itamar Vieira Junior (1979–). Maia, whose novels include titles such as *De gados e homens* (Of Cattle and Men, 2013), *Assim na terra como embaixo da terra* (As It Is on Earth, It is Below Earth, 2017), and *Enterre seus mortos* (Bury your Dead, 2018), has gained great recognition, attested by her winning the Prêmio São Paulo de Literatura two years in a row for the last two above-mentioned novels. In her novels, we see devastated scenarios, such as the slaughterhouse close to the polluted river in *De gados e homens*, and the isolated penal colony in *Assim na terra como embaixo da terra*. It is a tense relation with the land that is also portrayed in Vieira Junior's *Torto arado* (Crooked Plow, 2018), which won the Jabuti and Oceanos awards. The novel, which focuses on a family that is scarred by their own traditions and economic misery, revitalizes the debate on Brazil's social reality, without losing sight of the dramatic intimate issues experienced by its protagonists, the sisters Bibiana and Belonísia.

The last years of our brief survey of the Brazilian novel witness the vigor of topics that give us a glimpse into both recent and continued evolutions in Brazilian society. The place of women in society is represented in Martha Batalha's (1973–) *A vida invisível de Eurídice Gusmão* (The Invisible Life of Euridice Gusmao, 2016) and Tatiana Salem Levy's (1979–) recent *Vista Chinesa* (2021). Novels such as Victor Heringer's (1988–2018) *O amor dos homens avulsos* (The Love of Loose Men, 2016), Alexandre Vidal Porto's (1965–) *Cloro* (Chlorine, 2018), and Luísa Geisler's (1991–) *Luzes de emergência se acenderão automaticamente* (Emergency Lights Will Turn on Automatically, 2014) tackle diverse sexualities and affective relationships. Violence marks the protagonist's wanderings in Maria Valéria Rezende's (1942–) *Quarenta dias* (Forty Days, 2014) and is present in novels we have already mentioned, such as *Cidade de Deus* or *O passageiro do fim do dia*. Other writers who use violence as a major element in their narratives are Marçal Aquino, as in *Cabeça a prêmio* (Head for a Prize, 2003), and Patrícia Melo (1962–), in *Elogio da mentira* (In Praise of Lies, 1998). A few authors have also explored different ethnic communities in Brazil, as Hatoum does in *Dois irmãos*, focusing on Lebanese Brazilians, and Oscar Nakasato (1963–), in *Nihonjin* (2011), on Japanese Brazilians. Finally, several authors have been publishing novels both on issues related to black lives in Brazilian society, as in Paulo Scott's (1966–) *Marrom e amarelo* (Phenotypes, 2019), and on Afro-Brazilian history and cultures, as we see in Nei Lopes's (1942–) *Mandingas da Mulata Velha na Cidade Nova* (The Spell of the Old Mulatta in Cidade Nova, 2009), leading critics to develop the new field of study of Afro-Brazilian literature.

One of the most acclaimed Afro-Brazilian writers is Conceição Evaristo (1946–), who published *Ponciá Vicêncio* (Ponciá Vicencio) in 2003 and *Becos da memória* (Alleys of Memory) in 2006. In her novels, Evaristo recovers nearly forgotten stories and voices, and so does Miriam Alves in (1952–) *Bará—na trilha do vento* (Bará—On the Wind's Trail 2015). Eliana Alves Cruz (1966–), in her last two novels *O crime do Cais do Valongo* (The Crime at the Valongo Wharf, 2018) and *Nada digo de ti, que em ti não veja* (I Don't Say Anything About You, I Don't See in You, 2020), recedes further back in time, examining and re-creating historical periods. A similar procedure is used by Ana Maria Gonçalves (1970–) in *Um defeito de cor* (A Defect in Color, 2006). Finally, we should mention here Joel Rufino dos Santos's (1941–2015) *Claros sussurros de celestes ventos* (The Clear Whispers of the Celestial Winds, 2012), a creative literary homage paid to two great Afro-Brazilian writers, poet João da Cruz e Sousa (1861–1898) and novelist Lima Barreto.

CONCLUSION

Brazilian novels give evidence of the country's sociohistorical constitution, since their first significant manifestations in the nineteenth century to present times. To read a great number of these novels, while recognizing the relevance of different historical times and the need to be exposed to a variety of geographical settings, is a fundamental step in understanding Brazil's plurality. If there are nowadays many critical studies on women writers and the representation of women, on Afro-Brazilian authors and how people of African descent have their experiences represented, or on LGBTQs and their uses of focalization and expression, all this academic mobilization tends to foment a network in which novelists are effectively engaged. These questions, essential in narrating contemporary life and for our development as present-day readers, already have a secure place in part of contemporary authors' works. It is nonetheless indispensable to understand the Brazilian novel within a history that we are constantly reconstructing. It would be a mistake to either reduce our readings and studies to twenty-first-century narratives or to forget the plentiful material produced throughout almost two hundred years. In the trunk where all this material is stored, one may find treasures to be reclaimed and revised by the new perspectives we have pointed out—how have women, blacks, or LGBTQs been inserting themselves (and been represented) in literature—or by other frameworks that may be of interest to research, knowledge, or an ample understanding of cultural practices, not to mention entertainment. The body of works that constitute the Brazilian novel includes both canonical authors and those whose production is no longer as read or studied as before, or never gained a significant readership. This chapter concludes, therefore, by indicating a long reading path to be trodden.

NOTES

1. All translations to Alencar's *O Guarani* are ours. Original text: "é um cavalheiro português no corpo de um selvagem!" (102).
2. Original text: "sua linguagem tão rica e poética" (186).
3. Original text: "dois selvagens das matas do Brasil" (74).
4. Original text: "falando numa fala mansa, muito nova, muito!" (222).
5. Rego's sugar cane cycle is composed of five novels, starting with *Menino de engenho* (*Plantation Boy*, 1932).
6. We might also cite here Lúcia Miguel Pereira's (1901–1959) *Em surdina* (Surreptitiously, 1933) and *Amanhecer* (Sunrise, 1938); Ondina Ferreira's (1909–2000) *Vento da esperança* (Wind of Hope, 1947) and *Navio ancorado* (Anchored Ship, 1948); and Carolina Nabuco's (1890–1981) *A sucessora* (The Successor, 1934) and *Chama e cinzas* (Fire and Ashes, 1947).

7. Original text: "sozinha e desamparada, brilhando na escuridão, até que [sua] luz se apague" (160).

8. Verissimo translated Aldous Huxley's *Point Counter Point*, whose counterpoint technique he adapted to his own novels. Verissimo's translation of Huxley's novel was published in Brazil in 1934.

9. One must also note here that a more conservative assessment of Brazilian society's ills would be elaborated by Otávio de Faria in his long cycle *Tragédia Burguesa*, which encompassed thirteen novels whose publication years span from 1937 to 1979.

10. Verissimo's trilogy is composed of *O continente* (The Continent, 1949), *O retrato* (The Portrait, 1951), and *O arquipélago* (The Archipelago, 1962).

11. *História de um casamento* (Story of a Marriage, 1960) and *Um simples afeto recíproco* (A Simple Reciprocal Affection, 1963) are two of her novels that can be rather stimulating for a present-day reader.

12. We are referring here to what is known in Brazil as *cangaço* and the world of the *jagunços*. It also appears, for instance, in Adonias Filho's *Corpo vivo* (Living Body, 1962) and João Ubaldo Ribeiro's *Sargento Getúlio* (Sergeant Getúlio, 1971).

13. Two of Prado's novels are *Solte os cachorros* (Free the Dogs, 1979) and *Cacos para um vitral* (Shards for a Stained Glass Window, 1980).

14. "Era uma perda de tempo especular por que determinadas coisas dão prazer" (Fonseca, *A grande arte* 9).

WORKS CITED

Alencar, José de. *O Guarani*. Ateliê, 1999.

Alencar, José de. *Iracema*. L&PM, 2019.

Alencar, José de. *Iracema: A Novel*. Translated by Clifford E. Landers. Oxford UP, 2000.

Alencar, José de. *Lucíola*. Nova Fronteira, 2016.

Alencar, José de. *Senhora*. Ática, 2003.

Alencar, José de. *Senhora: Profile of a Woman*. Translated by Catarina Feldmann Edinger. U of Texas P, 2010.

Alencar, José de. *O sertanejo*. Ática, 2003.

Almeida, José Américo de. *A bagaceira*. José Olympio, 2017.

Almeida, José Américo de. *Trash: A Novel*. Translated by R. L. Scott-Buccleuch. Peter Owen, 1978.

Almeida, Júlia Lopes de. *A falência*. Companhia das Letras, 2019.

Almeida, Júlia Lopes de. *A viúva Simões*. Mulheres, 1999.

Alves, Miriam. *Bará—na trilha do vento*. Ogum's Toques Negros, 2015.

Amado, Jorge. *Cacau*. Companhia das Letras, 2010.

Amado, Jorge. *Capitães da areia*. Companhia das Letras, 2008.

Amado, Jorge. *Captains of the Sands*. Translated by Gregory Rabassa. Penguin, 2013.

Amado, Jorge. *Dona Flor and Her Two Husbands*. Translated by Harriet de Onís. Vintage, 2006.

Amado, Jorge. *Dona Flor e seus dois maridos*. Companhia das Letras, 2008.

Amado, Jorge. *Gabriela, Clove, and Cinnamon*. Translated by James L. Taylor and William L. Grossman. Vintage, 2006.

Amado, Jorge. *Gabriela, cravo e canela*. Companhia das Letras, 2012.

Andrade, Mário de. *Macunaíma*. Translated by E. A. Goodland. Random House, 1984.

Andrade, Mário de. *Macunaíma: o herói sem nenhum caráter*. Martins, 1979.

Anjos, Cyro dos. *O amanuense Belmiro*. Biblioteca Azul-Globo, 2006.

Anjos, Cyro dos. *Diary of a Civil Servant*. Translated by Arthur Brakel. Associated UP, 1988.

Aquino, Marçal. *Cabeça a prêmio*. Cosac & Naify, 2003.

Assis, Joaquim Maria Machado de. *Counsellor Ayres' Memorial*. Translated by Helen Caldwell. U of California P, 1982.

Assis, Joaquim Maria Machado de. *Dom Casmurro*. Penguin Companhia, 2016.

Assis, Joaquim Maria Machado de. *Dom Casmurro*. Translated by John Gledson. Oxford UP, 1997.

Assis, Joaquim Maria Machado de. *Esau and Jacob*. Translated by Helen Caldwell. U of California P, 1965.

Assis, Joaquim Maria Machado de. *Esaú e Jacó*. Penguin Companhia, 2012.

Assis, Joaquim Maria Machado de. *The Hand and the Glove*. Translated by Albert I Bagby Jr. UP of Kentucky, 2014.

Assis, Joaquim Maria Machado de. *Iaiá Garcia*. Ática, 1995.

Assis, Joaquim Maria Machado de. *Iaiá Garcia*. Translated by Albert I. Bagby Jr. UP of Kentucky, 1977.

Assis, Joaquim Maria Machado de. *A mão e a luva*. Ática, 1995.

Assis, Joaquim Maria Machado de. *Memorial de Aires*. Ática, 2000.

Assis, Joaquim Maria Machado de. *Memórias póstumas de Brás Cubas*. Penguin Companhia, 2014.

Assis, Joaquim Maria Machado de. *The Posthumous Memoirs of Brás Cubas*. Translated by Flora Thomson-DeVeaux. Penguin, 2020.

Assis, Joaquim Maria Machado de. *Quincas Borba*. Penguin Companhia, 2012.

Assis, Joaquim Maria Machado de. *Quincas Borba*. Translated by Gregory Rabassa. Oxford UP, 1998.

Azevedo, Aluísio. *Casa de pensão*. Ática, 1981.

Azevedo, Aluísio. *O cortiço*. Penguin Companhia, 2016.

Azevedo, Aluísio. *Uma lágrima de mulher*. Martins, 1966.

Azevedo, Aluísio. *O mulato*. Ática, 2010.

Azevedo, Aluísio. *The Slum*. Translated by David Rosenthal. Oxford UP, 2000.

Barreto, Afonso Henriques de Lima. *Recordações do escrivão Isaías Caminha*. Penguin Companhia, 2010.

Barreto, Afonso Henriques de Lima. *The Sad End of Policarpo Quaresma*. Translated by Mark Carlyon. Penguin, 2014.

Barreto, Afonso Henriques de Lima. *Triste fim de Policarpo Quaresma*. Penguin Companhia, 2011.

Bastos, Alcmeno. *A história foi assim: o romance político brasileiro nos anos 70/80*. Caetés, 2000.

Batalha, Martha. *The Invisible Life of Euridice Gusmao*. Translated by Eric M. B. Becker. One World Publications, 2018.

Batalha, Martha. *A vida invisível de Eurídice Gusmão*. Companhia das Letras, 2016.

Bosi, Alfredo. *História concisa da literatura brasileira*. 39th ed. Cultrix, 1994.

Brandão, Ignácio de Loyola. *Zero*. Global, 2019.

Brandão, Ignácio de Loyola. *Zero*. Translated by Ellen Watson. Dalkey Archive, 2004.

Buarque de Hollanda, Francisco (Chico). *Budapest: A Novel*. Translated by Alison Entrekin. Grove Press, 2005.

Buarque de Hollanda, Francisco (Chico). *Budapeste*. Companhia das Letras, 2005.

Buarque de Hollanda, Francisco (Chico). *Estorvo*. Companhia das Letras, 2004.

Buarque de Hollanda, Francisco (Chico). *Turbulence*. Translated by Peter Bush. Pantheon, 1993.

Bueno, Luís. *Uma história do romance de 30*. Unicamp, 2006.

Caminha, Adolfo. *Bom-Crioulo*. Guerra & Paz, 2018.

Caminha, Adolfo. *Bom-Crioulo: The Black Man and the Cabin Boy*. Translated by E.A. Lacey. Gay Sunshine P, 1982.

Candido, Antonio. *Formação da literatura brasileira*. 2 vols. 6th ed. Itatiaia, 1981.

Cardoso, Lúcio. *Chronicle of a Murdered House*. Translated by Margaret Jull Costa and Robin Patterson. Open Letter, 2016.

Cardoso, Lúcio. *Crônica da casa assassinada*. Civilização Brasileira, 1999.

Cardoso, Lúcio. *A luz no subsolo*. Civilização Brasileira, 2003.

Carvalho, Bernardo. *Os bêbados e os sonâmbulos*. Companhia das Letras, 1996.

Coelho Neto, Henrique. *Turbilhão*. Edições de Ouro, 1966.

Cony, Carlos Heitor. *Quase memória*. Nova Fronteira, 2014.

Coutinho, Afrânio, ed. *A literatura no Brasil*. 6 vols. 3rd ed. EdUFF, 1986.

Cruz, Eliana Alves. *O crime do Cais do Valongo*. Malê, 2018.

Cruz, Eliana Alves. *Nada digo de ti, que em ti não veja*. Pallas, 2020.

Drummond, Roberto. *Hilda Furacão*. Buobooks, 2020.

Drummond, Roberto. *Hilda Hurricane: A Novel*. Translated by Peter Vaudry-Brown. U of Texas P, 2010.

Evaristo, Conceição. *Becos da memória*. Geral, 2019.

Evaristo, Conceição. *Ponciá Vicêncio*. Pallas, 2017.

Evaristo, Conceição. *Ponciá Vicencio*. Translated by Paloma Martínez-Cruz. Host Publications, 2007.

Ferréz (Reginaldo Ferreira da Silva). *Capão Pecado*. Planeta, 2013.

Figueiredo, Rubens. *Passageiro do fim do dia*. Companhia das Letras, 2010.

Fonseca, Rubem. *Agosto*. Companhia das Letras, 2000.

Fonseca, Rubem. *A grande arte*. 12th ed. Companhia das Letras, 1991.

Fonseca, Rubem. *O caso Morel*. Companhia das Letras, 1995.

Fonseca, Rubem. *Crimes of August: A Novel*. Translated by Clifford. E. Landers. Tagus Press at U MassDarmouth, 2014.

Fonseca, Rubem. *High Art*. Translated by Ellen Watson. Carrol and Graf, 1986.

Fonseca, Rubem. *O selvagem da ópera*. Companhia das Letras, 1991.

Geisler, Luisa. *Luzes de emergência se acenderão automaticamente*. Alfaguara, 2014.

Gonçalves, Ana Maria. *Um defeito de cor*. Record, 2006.

Hatoum, Milton. *Dois irmãos*. Companhia de Bolso, 2006.

Hatoum, Milton. *The Brothers*. Translated by John Gledson. Farrar, Straus & Giroux, 2002.

Hatoum, Milton. *Relato de um certo oriente*. Companhia de Bolso, 2008.

Hatoum, Milton. *The Tree of the Seventh Heaven*. Translated by Ellen Watson. Atheneum, 1994.

Heringer, Victor. *O amor dos homens avulsos*. Companhia das Letras, 2016.

Laub, Michel. *Diário da queda*. Tinta da China, 2013.

Laub, Michel. *Diary of the Fall*. Translated by Margaret Jull Costa. Other Press, 2014.

Laub, Michel. *O gato diz adeus*. Companhia das Letras, 2009.

Laub, Michel. *Música anterior*. Companhia das Letras, 2001.

Leal, Lourenço Ferreira da Silva. *Um homem gasto*. O Sexo da Palavra, 2019.

Levy, Tatiana Salem. *Vista Chinesa*. Todavia, 2021.

Linhares, Temístocles. *História crítica do romance brasileiro: 1728–1981*. EDUSP, 1987.

Lins, Paulo. *Cidade de Deus. Romance*. Companhia das Letras, 1997.

Lins, Paulo. *City of God: A Novel*. Translated by Alison Entrekin. Grove Atlantic, 2007.

Lispector, Clarice. *Água viva*. Rocco, 1998.

Lispector, Clarice. *Água viva*. Translated by Stefan Tobler. New Directions, 2012.

Lispector, Clarice. *Uma Aprendizagem Ou O Livro Dos Prazeres*. Rocco, 2020.

Lispector, Clarice. *An Apprenticeship or the Book of Pleasures*. Translated by Stefan Tobler. New Directions, 2022.

Lispector, Clarice. *Near to the Wild Heart*. Translated by Alison Entrekin. New Directions, 2012.

Lispector, Clarice. *A paixão segundo G.H*. Rocco, 2020.

Lispector, Clarice. *The Passion According to G.H*. Translated by Idra Novey. New Directions, 2012.

Lispector, Clarice. *Perto do coração selvagem*. Rocco, 2019.

Lopes, Nei. *Mandingas da Mulata Velha na Cidade Nova*. Língua Geral, 2009.

Machado, Dyonélio. *Os ratos*. Editora Ática, 1986.

Macedo, Joaquim Manuel de. *A moreninha*. Atlantico Press, 2013.

Maia, Ana Paula. *Assim na terra como embaixo da terra*. Record, 2017.

Maia, Ana Paula. *De gados e homens*. Record, 2013.

Maia, Ana Paula. *Enterre seus mortos*. Companhia das Letras, 2018.

Mallet, João Carlos de Medeiros Pardal. *Hóspede*. Tres, 1974.

Melo, Patrícia. *Elogio da mentira*. Rocco, 2010.

Melo, Patrícia. *In Praise of Lies*. Translated by Clifford E. Landers. Bloomsbury, 1999.

Mendonça, Lúcio de. *O marido da adúltera*. Vermelho Amarilho, 2019.

Montenegro, Olívio. *O romance brasileiro*. José Olympio, 1953.

Nakasato, Oscar. *Nihonjin*. Benvira, 2011.

Noll, João Gilberto. *A céu aberto*. Record, 2008.

Noll, João Gilberto. *A fúria do corpo*. Record, 1981.

Noll, João Gilberto. *Harmada*. Francis, 2003.

Noll, João Gilberto. *Harmada*. Translated by Edgar Garbelotto. Two Lines Press, 2020.

Olímpio, Domingos. *Luzia-homem*. Melhoramentos, 1977.

Paiva, Manoel de Oliveira. *Dona Guidinha do Poço*. Ática, 1995.

Pompeia, Raul. *O ateneu*. Penguin, 2013.

Pompeia, Raul. *The Atheneum: A Novel*. Translated by Renata M. Wasserman. Northwestern UP, 2015.

Porto, Alexandre Vidal. *Cloro*. Companhia das Letras, 2018.

Proença Filho, Domício, ed. *O livro do seminário*. L. R., 1983.

Queiroz, Rachel de. *O quinze*. J. Olympio, 2006.

Queiroz, Rachel de. *The Three Marias*. Translated by Fred P. Ellison. University of Texas Press, 1985.

Queiroz, Rachel de. *As três Marias*. 21st ed. Siciliano, 1992.

Ramos, Graciliano. *Anguish*. Translated by L. C. Kaplan. Greenwood, 1976.

Ramos, Graciliano. *Angústia*. Record, 2019.

Ramos, Graciliano. *Barren Lives*. Translated by Ralph Edward Dimmick. U of Texas P, 1965.

Ramos, Graciliano. *São Bernardo*. Record, 2019.

Ramos, Graciliano. *São Bernardo*. Translated by Padma Viswanathan. NYRB Classics, 2020.

Ramos, Graciliano. *Vidas secas*. Record, 2019.

Rebelo, Marques. *A estrela sobe*. José Olympio, 2009.

Rego, José Lins do. *Menino de engenho*. José Olympio, 2010.

Rego, José Lins do. *Plantation Boy*. Translated by Emmi Baum. Knopf, 1966.

Rezende, Maria Valéria. *Quarenta dias*. Objetiva, 2014.

Rio, João do. *A profissão de Jacques Pedreira*. Scipione, 1992.

Rosa, João Guimarães. *The Devil to Pay in the Backlands*. Translated by Harriet de Onís and James Lumpkin Taylor. Knopf, 1963.

Rosa, João Guimarães. *Grande Sertão: Veredas*. Companhia das Letras, 2019.

Sales, Herberto. *Além dos marimbus*. Ediouro, 1990.

Sales, Herberto. *Cascalho*. É Realizações, 2011.

Sales, Herberto. *Dados biográficos do finado Marcelino*. É Realizações, 2009.

Sanches Neto, Miguel. *Chove sobre minha infância*. Record, 2000.

Santos, Joel Rufino dos. *Claros sussurros de celestes ventos*. Bertrand, 2012.

Scott, Paulo. *Marrom e amarelo*. Companhia das Letras, 2019.

Scott, Paulo. *Phenotypes*. Translated by Daniel Hahn. And Other Stories, 2022.

Sousa, Inglês de. *O missionário*. Ática, 2001.

Stegagno-Picchio, Luciana. *História da literatura brasileira*. 2nd ed. Nova Aguilar, 2004.

Telles, Lygia Fagundes. *The Girl in the Photograph*. Translated by Margaret A. Neves. Dalkey Archive, 2012.

Telles, Lygia Fagundes. *As meninas*. Companhia das Letras, 2009.

Tezza, Cristovão. *Uma noite em Curitiba*. Record, 2014.

Tezza, Cristovão. *A suavidade do vento*. Record, 2015.

Tezza, Cristovão. *Trapo*. Record, 2007.

Verissimo, Erico. *Caminhos cruzados*. Globo, 2002.

Verissimo, Erico. *The Rest Is Silence*. Translated by L. C. Kaplan. Macmillan, 1946.

Verissimo, Erico. *O resto é silêncio*. Companhia das Letras, 2008.

Verissimo, Erico. *O tempo e o vento. Parte I. O continente*. Companhia das Letras, 2019.

Verissimo, Erico. *O tempo e o vento. Parte II. O retrato*. Companhia das Letras, 2017.

Verissimo, Erico. *O tempo e o vento. Parte III. O arquipélago*. Companhia das Letras, 2018.

Verissimo, Erico. *Time and the Wind*. Translated by L. D. Barrett. Greenwood P, 1951.

Vieira Junior, Itamar. *Torto arado*. Todavia, 2019.

PART III

RACE AND
ETHNICITY

CHAPTER 16

THE INDIGENOUS NOVEL

Los dolores de una raza,
a Forerunner Work

MIGUEL ROCHA VIVAS

WRITING under the pen name Briscol, in the mid-1950s, Antonio Joaquín López (1897–1989) published what is likely the first novel by a Wayuu writer: *Los dolores de una raza: novela histórica de la vida real contemporánea del indio guajiro* (The Suffering of a Race: A Historical Novel on the Real Life of the Present-Day Guajiro Indian; hereafter *Los dolores*). *Los dolores* is also one of the first novels written by a self-described indigenous person from Central or South America, with López, a member of the Epieyuu clan, also having the kind of multi-faceted identity that tends to characterize Wayuu authors from the border region between Colombia and Venezuela. The precise date when López Epieyuu published the novel is unclear. According to the Guajiro researcher Víctor Bravo Mendoza, the novel first appeared in 1956, serialized in the journal *La Columna de Maracaibo*. Others claim that it first was published in 1957, while the poet Vito Apüshana claims it was published in 1958 (10).

Many non-Wayuu authors had written previously about La Guajira and the Wayuu homeland. For example, in 1879 Priscila Herrera, sister-in-law of one of Colombia's future presidents, Rafael Núñez, finished writing her novel *Un asilo en la Goajira* (A Refuge in the Guajira), and several decades later Eduardo Zalamea Borda published his *Cuatro años a bordo de mí mismo* (*Four Years Aboard Myself*, 1934). The protagonists of these two novels are displaced and move to La Guajira region, coming into contact with the Wayuu in a space that this indigenous community refer to as Woumain (Our Land). In other words, both protagonists travel to the periphery of the colonial Western world, the eccentric and marginal Caribbean of the Wayuu (Duchesne 2015), where they find themselves simultaneously attracted to and repelled by experiences and images of racialization, indigenous erasure, and "othering." Herrera de Núñez's novel is marked by the romanticized exile of a white woman among the Indians, while Zalamea Borda's explores the interior monologue of an urban traveler. Despite these stylistic differences, the characters in both novels use their outsider's gaze to describe an indigenous territory that temporarily relieves them of their boredom with Eurocentric civilization.

By contrast, López Epieyuu's *Los dolores* presents the reader with images of a Wayuu world—in his own words "a race"—that he feels is capable of making great contributions to the so-called "civilized world." Although nowadays the Wayuu use the traditional name Woumain instead of La Guajira, as still seen in *Los dolores*. López Epieyuu's Guajira is fraught with the contradictions, dreams, and tensions of a heterogeneous society in the midst of a transformation, as the Wayuu nation was increasingly impacted by the laws of the two states that control it: Colombia and Venezuela. The Wayuu in the novel are a "race" or ethnic group internally shaken by the crude violence of the blood debts that have historically unleashed wars between entire families and clans, and led to the extermination of entire *rancherías* (communitarian settlements), as well as to the enslavement of the survivors of such conflicts and their subsequent sale, via Wayuu intermediaries, to *Arijuna* (non-Wayuu) smugglers in exchange for firearms. The Wayuu worlds of *Los dolores* bleed, fall apart, and contradict one another, as the novel contemplates possible futures in which the author envisions possible "redención" (redemption), while acknowledging the terrible consequences of using blood and fire to defend the honor of those impacted by violence among clans or *eirüku*, "flesh."[1]

The novel is structured around movements of displacement and return, phenomena that Cherokee critic Christopher Teuton has described in the context of symbolic geographies in his study on indigenous narratives and novels in North America (248–67). *Los dolores* has a semicircular structure insofar as its final return is implied but not recounted in the novel itself. 1) The novel begins in the Valley of Irotsima, on the ranchería of the cacique Talhua. 2) A war mostly between the Epieyuu and Pushaina clans is unleashed after an interclan murder. 3) Members of Talhua's Pushaina clan migrate to the southern Guajira, and more specifically to the savannahs of Maicao. They establish themselves there with the goal of finding better economic conditions and in hopes that Colombian law is able to settle disputes and impart justice amidst worsening conflicts among the Wayuu. 4) Talhua's clan is partially wiped out through murders and conflicts in which the military and non-Wayuu civil authorities, among others, are implicated. 5) Disillusioned, Talhua dies in the Savannahs of Maicao. While he lies dying, he tells the survivors to take his land and go back to the Irotsima Valley. In essence, Talhua's travels between Irotsima and Maicao provide the frame for the novel. At the end, Talhua concludes: "no matter the government, we are lost, we can only live within our own environment and under the rule of our own traditions. Take all of my land and go back to Irotsima"[2] (López Epieyuu 150).[3] In sum, the movements between displacement and return that structure the novel are the following: 1) the presentation of the Epieyuu clan's roots and life in the north in the Irotsima Valley, 2) interclan conflicts, 3) the clan's exile and migration from the north to the south and the Maicao Savannah, 4) external conflicts and the failure to reestablish themselves, and 5) extermination, failure, and a call to return to the north from the south, moving from the savannah to the valley.

Wayuu Complicity in Slavery: Self-critical Insights by an Indigenous Novelist

Los dolores de una raza describes the moment when Wayuu law, which sanctioned blood feuds, starts giving way to Colombian national law, which prohibits them: "—Today things are different, replied Talhua, because we can appeal to the law of the local Police, the National Army, and the federal Police, when we are confronted by violence, and so there will no longer be a need to go to such extremes" (López Epieyuu 86).[4] In the novel's last page, however, Talhua insists on blood revenge as a way to recover his honor once he has passed away. It is a decision born of deep pain, given that at the end of his life he declares to his people: "Now we have the Special Police and the Army, we can no longer do the things we did in Irotsima and Mastua; in the name of the Law of the Republic, the government is in charge of giving us justice and avenging the spilling of innocent blood" (López Epieyuu 148).[5] Nonetheless, López Epieyuu's story is based on historical events, such as the human trafficking of Wayuu who survive interclan conflicts. Ferrer and Cadena state that "he wrote important essays on mestizaje and Wayuu enslavement," and that "He was in Aracataca, Magdalena, where more than two-hundred Wayuu had been taken to work before being driven back again to the Guajira two days before the banana massacre, which he foresaw (as a premonition) in 1928" (Ferrer and Cadena 125).[6]

According to Vito Apüshana, *Los dolores* is a novel that tells the story of the interclan wars "from 1920 to 1935" (10). In an archival document that was only published in the 2017 edition of *Los dolores*, López Epieyuu speaks about the imminent publication of an unnamed book that may well have been the novel itself:

> Being a representative intellectual from La Guajira and sincerely interested in the fate and redemption of his race, over the past few years the author has dedicated himself to studying the culture and customs, traditions, laws, language, idiosyncrasies, and the social environment in which the Guajiros live, with the goal of writing a book that will soon reveal these details to the public, and provide further information about the diverse economic, administrative, and social problems that confront the beautiful Peninsula on whose soil the author had the fortune to be born. These facts will be of universal interest. (2017, 251)[7]

What is certain is that in 1943 the Venezuelan writer Rómulo Gallegos published *Sobre la misma tierra* (On the Same Land, 1943), a novel that tells the story of Demetrio Montiel, a smuggler from the Colombia-Venezuela border who sold Wayuu to landowners on the Venezuelan side. In a sense, Gallegos's novel is thus a possible predecessor to López Epieyuu's.

Compared to other novels from South America that were written during the same period, however, *Los dolores* is an indigenous literary work, as opposed to earlier *indigenista* works. The first key difference between the novel and the works of *indigenistas* is that the author of *Los dolores* describes himself as a writer, a *cacique* (communal leader), and a representative of an indigenous community; his perspective thus originates from a community "we" that shifts due to his status as a mestizo Wayuu or Guajiro. The second difference is that the novel is an historical and self-critical exercise on the heterogeneity of Wayuu society, during a period in which Mexican *indigenismo* and muralism resorted to stereotypes of victimization in their idealized image of the Indian. As in *indigenismo*, in López Epieyuu the Wayuu, or Guajiro Indian, is the victim of social marginalization, but he is also the victim of self-inflicted problems caused by the excessive use of alcohol and weapons, reflecting what outsiders in the novel would refer to as the guajiro's "savage," "obstinate," and "indomitable" nature. As made clear by the novel's subtitle, part of López Epieyuu's project lies in establishing a multifaceted narrative about the lived reality of the Guajira's indigenous people.

In *Los dolores*, the heartbreaking image of the Wayuu warrior contrasts with the wisdom of those *Alaülayu* (elders), like Talhua himself, who maintain their peaceful, sound judgment amid an unending chain of terrible events that generate more and more tragedy. Even when the Arijunas, "those who throw pain" in the literal translation of many Wayuu speakers, are not the perpetrators of such acts, these are local tragedies frequently brought about by the bloody fury that comes in the wake of losing one's honor. For example, this is what happens in the case of Catalina and Echeto, lovers who flee Wayuu territory in an attempt to avoid being torn apart by social stratification, internalized racism, and traditional Wayuu law.

Catalina Woulhiu was the daughter of Petnat, a well-regarded cacique, and Antonio Echeto was the son of Wotconot, a young Wayuu woman who traveled to Maracaibo, where she was then deceived and raped by an arijuna or non-Wayuu. When he was a child, Echeto's father used him as a domestic servant or "chinito."[8] Having grown up and been educated as an Arijuna, Echeto "remembers his mother," returns to the Woumain (Wayuu territory), and falls in love with Catalina Woulhiu. Combined with his inability to pay her dowry, being a mestizo precludes Echeto's making any kind of marital arrangement with Catalina's proud father. As a result, Catalina writes a letter renouncing her position in Wayuu society and takes off with Echeto for Maracaibo, the big city, where Wayuu racial social stratification tends to be erased. After receiving his daughter's letter, the cacique Petnat calls his family together and says: "The man with whom she has left is the impure product of his mother's adventures, his father is unknown, he has neither material goods nor wealth. What will the reputation of my caste be compared to others? . . . This cannot go unpunished. It is an unheard-of insult that can only be cleansed with blood" (López Epieyuu 78).[9] The narrator states that this was how the Jitnu caste almost completely disappeared. After a war of extermination, "[Petnat's clan] imprisoned forty women and children and five men" (López Epieyuu 79),[10] whom they then sold in Castilletes like broken merchandise. After learning what happened, Wotconot, feeling responsible for both the intergenerational tragedy of her son's birth and this more recent blood feud, hangs herself. The daughter of the cacique Petnat, Catalina, also hangs herself. When Echeto finds his lover's dead body, he decides to kill himself by ingesting drugs. These three individual tragedies are thus added to the collective drama that the novelist calls the race's "sufferings."

Along these lines, readers of *Los dolores* encounter a never-ending chain of violent and terrible events that turn in a "tragic circularity" and comprise a collective destiny that drives the author to seek redemption from outside the community itself, whether this outside entity be the government, the church, the school, and so on. Even so, these possibilities are momentarily foreclosed for the Epieyuu caste in the novel as, upon the death of the protagonist, Talhua, the few remaining survivors of the migration to the southern La Guajira return to the warmer north.

As previously stated, the novel begins in 1920 on a *ranchería* in the high Guajira's Irotsima Valley, and ends on the savannahs of Maicao, a transitional area between the lower Guajira and Venezuela. Hunger, disease, drought, and internal conflicts are not the only reasons that Talhua and his people migrate to the spring-like southern part of the peninsula. In essence, these Wayuu migrants reenact the histories of other Wayuu caciques such as José Dolores who, according to López Epieyuu, migrated to the southern Guajira in 1860, waging wars, and being met with an unleashing violence in ways that are characteristic of military expansion or internal colonialism. Upon finalizing the decision to migrate, when Talhua hears the story of José Dolores, he tells his people: "we have to emigrate, because if we don't we'll be ruined here, whereas there we'll see if the dog's bite matches his bark" (López Epieyuu 86).[11]

In turn, the novel's final page responds to questions Talhua asked in previous passages some years earlier: "The devouring savannah of Maicao finished off Talhua and his heirs; the haciendas of Pishimana and Mainyatuy returned to what they were before: virgin wilderness. Jimay, Jiwwolhua, Alhayat, and Joúner gathered their flocks and left for Irotsima" (López Epieyuu 151).[12] However, López Epieyuu interprets the hate that causes these conflicts as a collective force that is tied to another hidden force: destiny. The Wayuu murderers in *Los dolores* would seem to be by López Epieyuu as subjects of the impulsive forces of "a race" and "a destiny" that is simultaneously hopeful and blind: "the criminal act was not a common homicide committed by a man, but the crime of an entire RACE" (López Epieyuu 42).[13] Referring to when Joúmuna murders Warralhlamatn of the epieyú clan, the initial crime that sets the novel's plot into motion, the main narrator asks and answers several questions, giving different perspectives on multiple characters, before concluding that, indeed, "Joúmuna, beyond being guilty, was the miserable toy of that dark force we call DESTINY" (López Epieyuu 43).[14]

When Talhua is confronted with another homicide, Joúner tells him a bit more reflexively that, "alcohol is what killed [your] nephew" (43),[15] with alcohol being something that unleashes a person's so-called inner beast, the violence and pride that, according to the narrator, frequently result in fatalities. For López Epieyuu the civilizing process is akin to domesticating one's inner animal: "That is how I wanted to see you, son, responded Talhua, proving your manhood in public, because you conquer the savage the same way that you defeat the man" (López Epieyuu 19).[16] Further on, Talhua alludes to the "terrible bucking of the Wild Colt that every Guajiro has buried deep in his human flesh" (López Epieyuu 103)[17] and to the "fierce instinct of an outraged human beast"

(103).[18] According to the novelist, in their original cultural context these irrational and animalistic tendencies are expressed through an eagerness for retaliation, unmeasured ambition, impassioned pride, and the very social stratification that rejects the people it calls "injertos" (literally "grafts," meaning roughly mixed-breeds or strange people) or "advenedizos" (newcomers), and those Wayuu who are seen as being from lower castes. As the Wayuu warrior Luis Fernández tells the slaver intermediary, coronel Troncoso,

> An Indian from this Ulhlewana family killed one of my nephews and fled for Venezuela. They are from a lower class than we are and one of our dead is worth a thousand of theirs. We were obligated to ruin their haciendas and kill them all, but since you all think they have an economic value, we commuted their death sentence and are selling them to you for money. So tell me, colonel, are we on the right track or not?
>
> (López Epieyuu 53)[19]

Wayuu and the Arijuna (non-Wayuu) interpolate each other in conversations like this throughout the novel. In the passage above, Fernández tries to soothe his conscience after selling the survivors of a clan war to Arijuna traffickers. In *Los dolores* this can be read as the dark side of smuggling with *far-off Arijunas* and, as demonstrated in the testimonial documents that the author recorded and that were published as an epilogue to the novel's first digital edition in 2017, it speaks to some Wayuus complicity in these acts. Indeed, "when the ships dropped anchor in the port of Maracaibo, the owners of the human merchandise had everything ready" (López Epieyuu 61).[20]

LOS DOLORES DE UNA RAZA AND THE INDIGENOUS CONTEMPORARY NOVEL

Los dolores de una raza is a precursor to both Wayuu literature and contemporary indigenous literatures insofar as it is one of the first works whose author self-identifies as indigenous. Moreover, it is an indigenous work insofar as its locus of enunciation, the problems it sheds light on, and the histories it narrates are related to the main challenges faced by indigenous peoples (land, self-determination, traditional laws, self-representation, etc.).

Los dolores is a precursor to contemporary Wayuu literature insofar as it anticipates authors who would be active in the sixties, seventies, and eighties, such as the short-story writers Glicerio Pana Uriana (1899–1989), Ramón Paz Ipuana (1937–1992), and Miguel Ángel Jusayú (1933–2009). López Epieyuu also anticipates Ramiro Larreal (1957–1986) and his novel *Hermano mestizo* (Mestizo brother. 1983), where the mestizo condition is at the core of the narrative, since one of the main characters of the Wayuu contemporary narrative is a mixed heritage person between worlds, law systems, and racial exclusions.

The Wayuu writers only began to acquire greater visibility during the nineties, when their texts began to describe the problems of the Wayuu people and to appeal to the sensibilities of the general public. This is the case, for example, with texts by Miguelángel López (Vito Apüshana) (1965), who received the Casa de las Américas Prize in 2000 for his poetry collection *Encuentros en los senderos de Abya Yala* (Encounters along the Roads of Abya Yala, 2009).

Latin American *indigenismo* was slowly discredited during the second half of the twentieth century, as the voices of self-identified indigenous peoples began to acquire greater prominence. Today, some indigenous peoples prefer to say that they are part of the continent called Abya Yala, a term for the Western Hemisphere borrowed from the Gunadule people, an indigenous nation located on both sides of the Colombia-Panama border in the Caribbean, whose language belongs to the Chibcha family.

Abya Yala is a Chibcha word that translates as "bleeding earth." First, the Gunadule say that the land bleeds because it gives life as a mother constantly giving birth. Second, they say it also bleeds because of violent conflicts with the colonizer. In fact, in the sung narratives of *Babigala*, Abya Yala is the fourth land, having been saved after a cataclysm and after other disasters put an end to the different ways of life in the three previous lands. Abya Yala would have ended with tidal waves and floods, but its land was spared. Politically speaking, however, Abya Yala now translates as "Land in a state of full maturity," and recently tends to be written Abiayala in order to differentiate it from its more specifically Gunadule etymology and cultural dimensions. First proposed as a way to talk about the continent in the 1980s by the Aymara Takir Mamani, Abya Yala is an image, concept, and symbol that opposes the colonial idea of *terra nullius*, the new world, or unknown land. In short, Abya Yala is a Native American, pan-indigenous name for the whole continent, which is neither limited to the area of Latin America, nor synonymous with it.

While we can still read *Los dolores* in the context of the Latin American novel, readers and critics must also be attuned to the independent interruption of contemporary indigenous textualities and verbalities in the text. As critics like Paul M. Worley and Rita M. Palacios (2019) affirm, when speaking of many indigenous works and books, we can only make provisional use of the term "literature," as we are actually describing heterogeneous and varied forms of verbal communication that either come from or are in dialogue with verbal arts and genres like *arutam* among the Shuar, *rafue* among the Murui, *haylli* among the Quechua, the *jayeechi* among the Wayuu, and innumerable others.

Los dolores was first published in the 1950s around the same time as the narratives and novels of the Peruvian José María Arguedas, a Quechua speaker who is considered one of the precursors of contemporary Quechua literature, although many critics classify him only as a Peruvian writer. *Los dolores* is contemporary of *Los ríos profundos* (*Deep Rivers*, 1958), in which Arguedas combines the use of Quechua and Spanish, and novelistic writing with musicality, images, and voices from Quechua orality. Both López and Arguedas can be situated at a moment of transition from *indigenismo* to the contemporary indigenous literary movements that emerged during the following decades. Both authors, however, speak from an indigenous locus of enunciation and not only about indigenous peoples, and both find themselves implicated in and look for ways to overcome their respective societies' political and cultural marginalization. In terms of themes, concerns, and characterization, in their novels indigenous peoples take center stage, more so than in *indigenismo* and its politics. That said, since Arguedas and López Epieyuu are narrators who are implicated in and/or self-identify as Quechua or Wayuu-Guajiro, respectively, there is a greater degree of veracity in their ethical intention to establish a locus of enunciation from within these collectives, or at the very least a locus that is closer to their cultural experiences of those voices. At the beginning of the novel, Ernesto, the young Andean character in *Los ríos profundos*, states about the Inca remains: "Wherever I go the Inca Roca's stones will go with me. I should like to swear to it right here" (8).[21] This oath can be understood as Ernesto's commitment to his Andean Quechua roots and perspectives.

Los dolores de una raza and *Los ríos profundos* anticipate more recent novels that have been written by writers who self-identify as indigenous in a continent that tends to see itself as Latin and Hispanic. Some of these novels come from the Wallmapu, or the Mapuche territory of present-day Chile and Argentina, as in the case of *Cherrufe, la bola de fuego* (Cherrufe, Ball of Fire, 2008) by Ruth Fuentealba Millaguir and *Desde el fogón de una casa de putas Huillche* (From the Hearth of a Huilliche Whorehouse, 2010) by Graciela Huinao (1956–). Maya authors have written novels such as *El tiempo principia en Xibalbá* (*Time Commences in Xibalbá*, 1985) by the Kaqchikel writer Luis de Lión (Guatemala 1939–1984); *X-Teya, u puksikal koolel* (X-Teya, the Heart of a Woman, 2008), *T'ambilák men tunk'uliloob* (Call of the Tunkules, 2011), *Sujuy k'iin/ Día sin mancha* (Day Without Stain, 2011), and *Chen tumeen x ch'úupen/Solo por ser mujer* (Just for Being a Woman, 2015) by the Yucatec Maya writer Marisol Ceh Moo (1968–); and *U yóok otiloob áak'ab/Danzas de la noche* (Night Dances, 2010) by the Yucatec Maya writer Isaac Esau Carrillo Can (1983–2017). Also in Mexico, *Nu pama pama nzhogú/ El eterno retorno* (The Eternal Return, 2019) by the Mazahua author Francisco Antonio León Cuervo (1987–).

In the current field of indigenous literary studies, we understand as indigenous novel a long narrative innovative genre, written in native or Romance languages, by authors self-defined as indigenous. Many indigenous novels have been written partially or completely in Spanish. For some indigenous writers Spanish is their only or predominant maternal language, due to colonial processes, but also because they consider Spanish as their native language after centuries of appropriation of colonizers languages. Moreover, in some indigenous contexts where orality is still the predominant form of communication, there are not enough readers of creative writing in indigenous languages in comparison with Spanish. In fact, some indigenous novelist (Ceh Moo, León Cuervo, Carrillo Can) originated in their communities the practice of writing novels, as well as the reading of novels, in indigenous languages. However, in the twentieth century the first contemporary indigenous novels in the region were written in Spanish (*Los dolores de una raza* and *El tiempo principia en Xibalbá*), or in Spanish with vocabulary and grammar structures from the indigenous languages (*Los ríos profundos*).

U yóok otiloób áakʼab/Danzas de la noche (Dances of the Night, 2011) is written in Yucatan, which is, like Woumain/Guajira, another Caribbean peninsula with multiple indigenous legacies and traditions. In this bilingual novel, Flor shares her visions and feelings about family, tradition, and the modern world. In contrast to the masculine perspective of *Los dolores*, where the female characters are permanently exposed and subjugated, in Carrillo Canʼs novel the protagonist reconciles with the masculine presence and emerges as an integral Maya woman. Night appears as a loving spirit mother who guides the young Flor to her father and also to a town where the Maya dance legacy is alive. Carrillo Can places literary emphasis on the wisdom of dreams, where internal and animal voices advise the dreamer, takes a radical narrative path, different from the historical approach of López Epieyuu. If the cruelty of war and human trafficking happens in *Los dolores* under inhospitable sunlight in *U yóok otiloób áakʼab/Danzas de la noche*, the Night is a symbolic presence and space for the psychological development of the protagonist and the setting for her spiritual encounter with her dead mother. While Flor ascends as a realistic Maya realistic hero, Talhua descends and falls from his place as an epic Wayuu patriarch.

A female indigenous perspective is also present in *Cherrufe, la bola de fuego* (Cherrufe, the Fire Ball, 2008), in which Charito, a Mapuche girl, discovers her communityʼs past through the grandfatherʼs stories. The author, Ruth Fuentealba Millaguir, declares that she wrote the novel to let her daughter know her family history. *Cherrufe* is considered the first novel written by a Mapuche.

Similarly, *X-Teya, u puksikal koolel* (X-Teya, the Heart of a Woman, 2008) is the first novel written in Maya by Marisol Ceh Moo. While Cej Moo writes in both Maya and Spanish, Fuentealba Millaguir and López Epieyuu write only in Spanish but using vocabulary coming from Mapudungun and Wayuunaiki languages, respectively. Another novel by Ceh Moo, *Sujuy kʼii/Día sin mancha* (Day Without Stain, 2011), presents many female voices. Socorro, the older daughter of a Yucatec Maya family, decides to leave school to help her mother with domestic duties. Talking to her worried teacher, she states: "I will do what the women do in this town: I will get married and have children" (Ceh Moo 113).[22] Socorro is a sixteen-year-old girl who seems to know that women do not have many opportunities, so she does not find it practical to continue with her studies or even to dream about working in the city. Indeed, some of the stories in *Sujuy kʼiin/Día sin mancha* reflect her communityʼs point of view about Maya migrants who fail in their new locations, as it happens with the Talhua clan in *Los dolores*. This is the specific case of San and Tides in *Sujuy kʼiin/Día sin mancha*. They went to work at Playa del Carmen and were killed by drug traffickers. In regard to the process of migration as a path to economic success, Mila, Socorroʼs mother and protagonist of the novel, avers: "Maybe if San and Tides had settled for what there is, they would be alive . . . but ambition is a bad counselor" (Ceh Moo 166).[23] In *Sujuy kʼiin/Día sin mancha*, the oral tradition guarded traditionally by women warns about the dangers outside the community, while it believes in and preserves local customs: marriage as an alliance between families, the *janal pixan* or rituals of the dead, the town celebration of the Virgin of Inmaculada Concepción, and also the story about the night spirits who kill Agapito, the youngest boy of Mila and Tacho.

Marisol Ceh Moo's and, similarly, Isaac Esau Carrillo's writings in Yucatec Maya have been fundamental in the modernization of indigenous narratives, languages, and modes of transmission and reception. But where both Yucatec novelists articulate a female perspective, another Maya novelist, the Kakchiquel Luis de Lión, communicates a contradiction regarding female models. In *El tiempo empieza en Xibalbá*, one of the male characters steals the town's image of the Virgen de la Concepción and attempts to have sexual intercourse with it, thus expressing the simultaneous desire and hatred for the Ladina (non-indigenous) body and the religious icon that represents it.

A similar criticism of the Catholic tradition is at the core of *Nu Pama Nzhogú/El eterno retorno* (The Eternal Return, 2020), a novel in Mazatec and Spanish by Francisco León Cuervo. Xuba, the main Mazatec character, loses his name after a confession with a Catholic priest, who told him that he needed a new Christian name: Francisco. In fact, Xuba goes to town, as Flor does in Carrillo Can's novel, looking for redemption, but for opposite reasons and with opposite results. Don Jacinto, the landlord and patron, sent Xuba to the priest to confess to the murder of a blonde woman he killed thinking she was the incarnation of a mermaid. So Xuba has to wait until the priest arrives for the town's celebration of Santa Ana. From the standpoint of the priests, Xuba needs a new name because his indigenous name, the result of never having been christened, explains why he experienced an awful encounter with the devil in the guise of a mermaid.

As in León Cuervo novel, *Nu Pama Pama Nzhogú/El eterno retorno*, the desire for the foreign white woman expresses the contradiction between oppressors and oppressed. Although the story about the mermaid comes from an indigenous character who warns about places at night and about the dangers of drunkenness—as in the stories of the Wayuu Pulowi (natural female entities)—the blonde mermaid represents at the same time the presence of the colonizer and a danger for the Mazatec men. For the priest, the mermaid is the devil, while for a Mazatec medicine woman, the blonde is a mermaid who steals Xuba's soul. Therefore, the only option for him is to follow the advice for the medicine woman, face his fear, and kill her.

Not knowing how to pronounce his Christian name, Francisco, Xuba calls himself Pancho, instead. In the following years he will forget his indigenous name. But when he dies, he is incapable of going to heaven, because the Catholic angel calls for Francisco and he does not answer to that name. At the same time, when the dead start to ascend through nine stages of the afterlife, according to Mazatec beliefs, they call in their language, "Mojodya, Xuba (let's go right now, Xuba)" (León Cuervo 172),[24] but he is not able to answer to that name, either. The same happens with his dead dog, who waits to help him to cross the river of the dead. The dog only understands Mazatec. When Xuba ask him whom he waits, the black dog says: "Mi tenk'ue Xuba, me'edya: (I had been waiting for you, Xuba, let's go right now)" (León Cuervo 172).[25] But Xuba states that his name is Pancho. Indeed, Xuba loses the opportunity of meeting his parents at the other side of the river. In sum, because he has forgotten his indigenous name, Xuba is rejected from the Mazatec afterlife, as well as from the Christian heaven and hell. He cannot find a place in either the Mazatec or in the Catholic worlds of the dead. Finally, he is transformed into a ghost who never finds rest on earth and is always looking for the mermaid to kill her. This kind of postmortem return is a personal and collective failure, as happens with the historical return of the Talhua descendants to the upper Guajira in the final pages of *Los dolores*.

In conclusion, as seen in López Epieyuu's novel, the Wayuu have been historically decentralized, semi-nomadic, and heterogeneous. Their strategies for survival and their accommodation to colonial contact, as well as their slow absorption into the social and judicial systems of Colombia and Venezuela, have taken place concurrently with wars, alliances, and cross-border smuggling. Since the second half of the twentieth century, they have incorporated and adapted alphabetic literary resources as an extension of their own verbal arts and for their own ends. In his poem "Culturas" (1992), Vito Apüshana, pen name of the Wayuu writer Miguelángel López, gives us the image of contemporary Wayuu writing as being the smuggling of dreams with Arijuna friends. In the first digital edition of *Los dolores*, which was coincidentally the first edition of the novel to be widely available to the public, Vito
Apüshana writes that:

> Told from within the community, *Los dolores de una raza* is the story of a fate of a people marked by social drama; of a people who face life dancing on the edge of their own abyss, . . . In light of current debates on interculturality in Colombia, reading this sixty-year-old novel represents an important approximation to the aesthetics of indigenous thought, and an act recognizing the other that shapes us in the image of a plural and inclusive Nation. (12–13)[26]

Apüshana's confidence in the creation of a horizontal interculturality is not found in López Epieyuu. The novelist's own political bets and personal call for civilizing redemption is complicated and contradicted by the voices of his characters who express tremendous mistrust in the state and its armed forces: "Caramba! What is happening! So then you must believe that the government has sent those people to get rid of us" (López Epieyuu 129).[27] At the same time, he is also self-critical of the Wayuu: "The practice of condemning an entire caste for the isolated crime of an individual or a small group of individuals should be consigned to the past—said various people in the gathered multitude" (López Epieyuu 147).[28]

Disgusted by the never-ending death, loss of goods, and the difficulty of fulfilling blood debts, toward the end of the novel Talhua and Santanawa are the main protagonists in a chapter that discusses the continent's earlier military invasion: "like Moctezuma confronted by the loss of the Aztec empire, they were condemned to death, shut up in their rooms, there was no one who could force them to take nourishment" (López Epieyuu 148).[29] As the story comes to a close, the aged Talhua's impotence and desperation are all-encompassing. He declares, "My beloved children, I'm dying from the pain of leaving you all alone in this corrupt world! I cannot live with the dishonor of my caste and the pain of my impotence!" (López Epieyuu 150).[30] He then gives a final order that reflects his complete mistrust of the state, and ends his attempt to move to the warm south and thus closer to the benefits of "civilization": "remove yourselves from the sight of the government, and do not forget to go after the murderer . . . " (López Epieyuu 150).[31]

Antonio Joaquín López Epieyuu narrates Talhua's frustration but not his descendants' return to the high Guajira. The novel reaches its climax with words that resound like prophecy, and that are, in reality, a patriotic call not to abandon the Wayuu and, paradoxically, the seeds of Wayuu political and judicial sovereignty: "Flattering PAMPA[32] of the Guajira, promising plains! Fertile for crime, prodigious in drama and tragedy, until today you have only lived for PAIN, tomorrow or in the past, sooner or later, eventually the hour of your anxiously awaited redemption must resound!" (López Epieyuu 151, emphasis in the original).[33]

In the epilogue found in the latest electronic book edition of *Los dolores de una raza* (2017), López Epieyuu cites a written testimony of a Wayuu enslaved in Venezuela who lost his name during the kidnapping process. The enslaved person said that his real name in Wayuunaiki is Aypiakí, instead of the Spanish name. Many contemporary indigenous narratives are part of personal and collective processes of recovering and reinventing native names, stories, family ties and perspectives. While in *Los dolores* the Wayuu migrants fail to adapt and survive in the lower Guajira Peninsula, overrun by Colombian laws and social corruption, in *U yóok otiloob áakab/Danzas de la noche*, Flor strengthens her Yucatec Maya identity through the reencounter with her culture's dance rituals, the Maya people, and her father. Socorro, the Maya girl in *Sujuy K'iin*, validates the conservative and regenerative female roles within the family and the Yucatec Maya community, although this process occurs as a reaction to the scarcity of opportunities for women in society. While in *Los dolores* Catalina Woulhiu is unable to marry outside the community, which was a direct challenge to Wayuu law, in *Sujuy k'ii/Día sin mancha* (Day Without Stain), Socorro accepts a traditional marriage and her parents' will to decide her future.

The acceptance of the Catholic tradition and colonial rule transforms Xuba, the main character of *Nu Pama Pama Nzhogú/El eterno retorno*, into a confused ghost who cannot find his place after death. Indeed, by losing his indigenous name and taking up a Christian one, he simultaneously loses any spiritual direction, sense of place, and cultural belonging. However, León Cuervo and López Epieyuu locate their dramas in clear historical contexts: the nineteenth and twentieth centuries, respectively. The historical frames provided in the novels studied in this chapter offer indigenous perspectives where the official narratives avoid it. In fact, Ernesto, in Arguedas's *Los ríos profundos*, found in the Inca's stones in Cusco, the basis for a personal and collective Andean way of feeling, thinking, and self-determination. If Xuba lost his soul by accepting a Christian name, and forgetting his people, Ernesto find his soul by taking part in the chichera women's demonstration and with the constant ritual repetition of the Quechua songs and names: zumbayllu, yawar mayu, Pachachaca, and so on.

In *Los dolores*, the savannahs of Maicao, like the Amazonian jungle in the novel *La Vorágine*, finally devour most of the novel's characters. As a precursor to contemporary Wayuu and indigenous literatures, however, several questions are left unanswered. Will the characters be redeemed by returning to their original homelands? Will they be able to reestablish their original condition of autonomy? Can the traumatic experiences of contact and intercultural conflict be resolved? All these questions remain relevant for the Wayuu and the indigenous migrants who continue to move, either seasonally or permanently, to the cities and fields of this continent.

Translated by Miguel Rocha Vivas, Universidad Javeriana, and Paul M Worley, Western Carolina University.

NOTES

1. Clan membership is determined by one's maternal lineage.
2. "Con uno u otro gobierno estamos perdidos, no podemos vivir sino dentro de nuestro peculiar ambiente y bajo el imperio de las leyes de nuestra tradición. Tomen posesión de todas mis haciendas y márchense para Irotsima" (López Epieyuu 150).
3. Unless otherwise indicated, all citations from the novel come from the original undated edition (1956, 1957, or 1958), that was published in Maracaibo. It is listed first in the references.
4. "Hoy son distintas las cosas —replicó Talhua— porque tenemos una autoridad Comisarial, el Ejército Nacional y la Policía ante quien quejarnos en casos de violencias como aquellas, que trataren de molestarnos en alguna forma y por lo mismo no habrá necesidad de que apelemos a medios extremos" (López Epieyuu 86).
5. "Hoy no podemos hacer lo que hicimos en Irotsima y Mastau en otros tiempos, ya tenemos una Comisaría Especial y un Ejército; ellos están encargados de impartirnos justicia y vengar la sangre inocente en nombre de la Ley de la República" (López Epieyuu 148).
6. "Estuvo en Aracataca, Magdalena, donde había llevado a trabajar a más de 200 wayuu conduciéndolos nuevamente a La Guajira, dos días antes de la matanza de las bananeras, ya que a través de un sueño había sabido de la masacre de 1928" (Ferrer and Cadena 125).
7. "El suscrito, representante intelectual de La Guajira, sinceramente interesado por la suerte y la redención de su raza, se ha dedicado, desde algunos años para acá, a estudiar los usos y las costumbres, las tradiciones, las leyes, el idioma, la idiosincrasia y el medio ambiente social en que el Guajiro vive y, con tal fin, ha llegado a formar un volumen, que próximamente dará a conocer a la luz pública todos esos detalles, así como los diversos problemas de carácter económico, administrativo y social que confronta la hermosa Península, en cuyo suelo ha tenido la dicha de nacer, detalles que necesariamente han de ser universal utilidad" (López Epieyuu 2017).
8. Wayuu domestic servitude has been a recurrent theme in Wayuu literature down to the contemporary stories of Vicenta María Siosi (2002) and Estercilia Simanca (2005, 2006).
9. "El hombre con quien se ha ido es el producto impuro de las aventuras de su madre, no se le conoce padre, ni bienes de fortuna. ¿Cómo queda la reputación de mi casta ante los demás? . . . El precedente no puede quedar impune, vejamen tan inaudito solo debe lavarse con sangre" (López Epieyuu 78).
10. "Aprisionaron cuarenta mujeres y niños y cinco hombres" (López Epieyuu 79).
11. "Nuestra emigración es imperiosa, porque si no aquí nos arruinaremos, allá adelante veremos si el tigre es en verdad tan feo como lo pintan" (López Epieyuu 86).
12. "La devoradora sabana de Maicao acabó con el cacique Talhua y sus herederos; las haciendas de Pishimana y Mainyatu y volvieron de nuevo a lo que fueron antes: montañas

vírgenes. Jimay, Jiwwolhua, Alhayat y Joúner recogieron sus rebaños y se fueron para Irotsima" (López Epieyuu 151).

13. "El hecho criminal no fue el homicidio común perpetrado por un hombre, fue el crimen de la RAZA" (López Epieyuu 42).

14. "Joúmuna, más que culpable, fue el juguete miserable de esa fuerza oculta que se llama DESTINO" (López Epieyuu 43).

15. "Es el alcohol quien ha matado a su sobrino (López Epieyuu 43).

16. "Así quería verte hijo —le respondió Talhlua—, probar tu hombría ante el público, por qué conforme dominas al salvaje, así mismo vencerás al hombre" (López Epieyuu 19).

17. "Arranques terribles del Potro Cerril que todo guajiro lleva escondido dentro de su envoltura humana" (López Epieyuu 103).

18. "Fiero instinto de la bestia humana sublevada" (López Epieyuu 103).

19. "Un indio de esta familia Ulhlewana asesinó a uno de mis sobrinos y se fugó para Venezuela; ellos son de baja clase y nosotros somos de alta categoría; un muerto nuestro vale por un millar de los de ellos. Nuestro deber era arruinarles sus haciendas y darles muerte a todos, pero ya que ustedes le dan un valor económico, le conmutamos la pena capital vendiéndoselos por dineros. Dígame ahora, coronel, ¿si procedemos bien o mal?" (López Epieyuu 53).

20. "Cuando los barcos fondearon en el puerto de Maracaibo, los dueños de la mercancía humana lo tenían todo preparado" (López Epieyuu 61).

21. "Donde quiera que vaya, las piedras que mandó formar Inca Roca me acompañarán. Quisiera hacer aquí un juramento" (Arguedas 147).

22. "Voy a hacer lo que hacen las mujeres en este pueblo: voy a casarme y a tener hijos" (Ceh Moo 113).

23. "Quizás si San y Tides se hubieran conformado con lo que hay, estuvieran vivos (. . .) pero la ambición es mala consejera" (Ceh Moo 166).

24. "Vámonos ya, Xuba" (León Cuervo 172).

25. "Te estaba esperando Xuba, vámonos ya" (León Cuervo 172).

26. "Los dolores de una raza es el relato, desde adentro, de un destino signado por el drama social de un pueblo que asume la vida danzando sobre el filo de su propio abismo (. . .) Leer esta novela, de casi sesenta años de publicada, en los actuales debates de la interculturalidad colombiana, representa una aproximación a la estética del pensamiento indígena y un acto de reconocimiento al otro que nos reconstruye en la imagen de una Nación plural e incluyente" (Apüshana 12–13).

27. "¡Caramba! ¡Qué es lo que está pasando! Entonces hay que creer que el gobierno ha mandado esa gente para acabar con nosotros" (López Epieyuu 129).

28. "—Eso de recriminar una casta entera por el delito aislado de un individuo o de un grupo reducido debe ya pasar a la historia —decían varios individuos de la multitud" (López Epieyuu 147).

29. "Como Moctezuma ante la pérdida del imperio azteca, se condenaron al hambre, encerrados en sus estancias no hubo poder humano que los obligara a ingerir alimentos" (López Epieyuu 148).

30. "Hijos amados, ¡me muero con el dolor de dejaros solos en este mundo corrompido! ¡No puedo sobrevivir a la deshonra de mi casta y al dolor de la impotencia!" (López Epieyuu 150).

31. "Aléjense de la vista del gobierno, pero no olviden perseguir al asesino . . . " (López Epieyuu 150).

32. Emphasis in the original.
33. "¡Lisonjeras PAMPAS guajiras, llanuras promisorias! Fecundas para el crimen, pródigas para el drama y la tragedia, que hasta hoy sólo han vivido para el DOLOR, mañana o pasado, tarde o temprano, al fin ha de sonarles en el reloj del tiempo la hora de su ansiada redención!" (López Epieyuu 151).

WORKS CITED

Apüshana, Vito. "Prólogo." *Los dolores de una raza, novela histórica de la vida real contemporánea del indio guajiro, Maracaibo*. Ministerio de Cultura. Biblioteca Nacional de Colombia, 2017. Books bbcc. Web. June 1, 2020, pp. 9–13.

Arguedas, José María. *Deep Rivers*. Translated by Frances Horning Barraclough. Waveland Press, 2002.

Arguedas, José María. *Los ríos profundos*. Cátedra, 2019.

Carrillo Can, Isaac Esau. *Danzas de la noche / U yóok' otilo'ob áak'ab*. Consejo Nacional para la Cultura y las Artes, Dirección General de Culturas Populares, 2011.

Ceh Moo, Marisol. *X-Teya, u puksi'ik' al koolel / Teya, un corazón de mujer*. Consejo Nacional para la Cultura y las Artes. Dirección General de Culturas Populares, 2008.

Ceh Moo, Marisol. *Sujuy k'iin / Día sin mancha*. Instituto de Cultura de Yucatán, 2011.

Ceh Moo, Marisol. *T'ambilák men tunk'ulilo'ob / El llamado de los tunk'ules*. Consejo Nacional para la Cultura y las Artes, Dirección General de Culturas Populares, 2011.

Ceh Moo, Marisol. *Chen tumeen chu'úpen / Sólo por ser mujer . . .* Consejo Nacional para la Cultura y las Artes, 2015.

De Lión, Luis. *El tiempo principia en Xibalbá*. Artemis-Edinter, 1997.

De Lión, Luis. *Time Commences in Xibalbá*. Translated by Nathan C. Henne. U of Arizona P, 2012.

Duchesne, Juan. *Caribe, Caribana: cosmografías literarias*. Callejón, 2015.

Duchesne, Juan. *Hermosos invisibles que nos protegen, antología de la literatura wayuu*. IILI, 2016.

Ferrer, Gabriel Alberto, and Yolanda Rodríguez Cadena. *Etno-literatura wayuu, estudios críticos y selección de textos*. Fondo de Publicaciones de la Universidad del Atlántico, 1998.

Fuentealba Millaguir, Ruth. *Cherrufe, la bola de fuego*. CONADI, 2008.

Gallegos, Rómulo. *Sobre la misma tierra*. Élite, 1943.

Herrera, Priscila. "Un asilo en la Goajira." *Varias cuentistas colombianas*, edited by Daniel Samper Ortega, Minerva, 1935, pp. 109–50.

Huinao, Graciela. *Desde el fogón de una casa de putas williche*. CONADI, 2010.

Jusayú, Miguel Ángel. *Ni era vaca ni era caballo . . .* Ekare, 2004.

Larreal, Ramiro *Hermano mestizo*. Los Teques, 1983.

León Cuervo, Francisco Antonio. *Nu pama pama nzhogú/El eterno retorno*. Plia, 2019.

López Epieyuu, Antonio Joaquín. *Los dolores de una raza, novela histórica de la vida real contemporánea del indio guajiro*. La Columna, 1956–1958.

López Epieyuu, Antonio Joaquín. *Los dolores de una raza, novela histórica de la vida real contemporánea del indio guajiro, Maracaibo*. Ministerio de Cultura, Biblioteca Nacional de Colombia, 2017. Bbcc books. Web. June 5, 2020.

López, Miguel Ángel (Vito Apüshana). *Contrabandeo sueños con alijunas cercanos en Woummainpa*. Secretaría de Asuntos Indígenas, Universidad de La Guajira, 1992.

López, Miguel Ángel (Vito Apüshana). *Encuentros en los senderos de Abya Yala*. Abya-Yala (Malohe), 2000.

López, Miguel Ángel (Vito Apüshana). *Encuentros en los senderos de Abya Yala*. Travesías (Malohe), 2009.

Paz Ipuana, Ramón. *Mitos, leyendas y cuentos guajiros*, Instituto Agrario Nacional, Programa de Desarrollo Indígena, 1972.

Siosi Pino, Vicenta María. *El dulce corazón de los piel cobriza*. Fondo Mixto para la Promoción de la Cultura y las Artes de La Guajira, 2002.

Simanca Pushaina, Estercilia. *Manifiesta no saber firmar, nacido: 31 de diciembre*. Antillas, 2005.

Simanca Pushaina, Estercilia. *El encierro de una pequeña doncella*. Lama Producciones, 2006.

Teuton, Christopher. "El ciclo de remoción y retorno: una geografía simbólica de la literatura indígena." *Cuadernos de Literatura*, vol. 19, no. 38, 2015, pp. 246–58.

Worley, Paul M., and Rita M. Palacios. *Unwriting Maya Literature: Ts'íib as Recorded Knowledge*. U of Arizona P, 2019.

Zalamea Borda, Eduardo. *Cuatro años a bordo de mí mismo, diario de los cinco sentidos*. Compañía Grancolombiana de Ediciones, 1950.

....

CHAPTER 17

THE AFRO-LATIN AMERICAN NOVEL AND THE NOVEL ABOUT AFRO-LATIN AMERICANS

....

WILLIAM LUIS

THIS chapter discusses authors who write about Afro-Latin Americans and Afro-Latin American authors who write about people of African ancestry. While there is a current predisposition in some Latin American countries to give voice to writers of African descent, the norm has been to group all writers, regardless of race or color, under a national category. For Benedict Anderson, the national is a social construct the elites promote for their best interest (*Imagined Communities*). Revisiting the historical events of Latin American countries with significant African heritage highlights the contribution of blacks to the nation's literature, music, dance, religion, art, and other cultural manifestations. Literary movements such as Cuba's antislavery novel of the first half of the nineteenth century, *negrismo* poetry of 1920s and 1930s, and Negritude in the Francophone Caribbean of the 1930s and 1940s and its many manifestations throughout Latin America contribute to a black awareness. Events outside of the region, namely the US Civil Rights and Black Power movements and their impact in countries south of the border, provide a necessary counter-discourse to the discourse of power, especially in regions that have become fertile ground for US interventions, another pressing concern of Latin American writers.

Since the second half of the twentieth century, an increasing number of US critics have joined pioneering Latin American scholars and writers by providing another understanding of authors who write about blacks and blacks who write about their experiences. Some of these scholars include Richard Jackson, Miriam DeCosta-Willis, Marvin Lewis, Ian Smart, and William Luis but also others like Clementine Rabassa and Vera Kutzinski have helped to set the groundwork for a critical approach to a literature of and about people of African descent.[1] Most recently, the UN Declaration of the International Decade of People of African Descent (2015–2024) has given additional impetus for many Latin American countries to revisit their turbulent past and bring visibility to a population that continues to be neglected, marginalized, and silenced.[2]

The focus of this essay is the novel, but other genres, and in particular poetry, have contributed to disseminating the black experience in Latin America, even when promoted by non-blacks, whose problematic representation often became more acceptable to a wider audience than those fostered by blacks themselves. However, blacks continue to take ownership of their own voice and experiences.

As a novelistic or narrative movement, black characters and their enslaved condition appear in Cuba of the first half of the nineteenth century, when the Spanish colony became the world's largest sugar producer and imported high numbers of enslaved Africans to fuel the industry. During this period enslaved and free blacks outnumbered whites and those in power promoted the fear that Cuba would become another Haiti. During this tense period, Domingo del Monte founded his literary circle (1834–1843) and encouraged writers to document the Cuban landscape, and the presence of the enslaved. From Del Monte's salon emerged the Cuban antislavery narrative that includes the enslaved poet Juan Francisco Manzano's *Autobiografía* (*Life of the Negro Poet*, written in 1835, translated by Richard Madden in 1840), Anselmo Suárez y Romero's *Francisco* (written in 1839) and his rewriting of Manzano's *Autobiografía*, Félix Tanco y Bosmeniel's collection of stories *Escenas de la vida privada en la isla de Cuba* (Scenes from Private Life in the Island of Cuba, written in 1838), and Cirilo Villaverde's short story "Cecilia Valdés," the first volume of the namesake novel (published in 1839), whose final version he completed in exile in New York in 1882.[3]

Critics acknowledge that Del Monte showcased the poet Manzano and encouraged him to write his autobiography. In this unpublished until 1937 work, which describes how he taught himself to read and write, Manzano highlights the happy and tragic episodes of his life. When the injustices increased, Manzano had no other recourse but to escape and seek protection provided by slavery laws. However, Manzano was a well-known poet many years before meeting his benefactor in 1830, as he had published *Poesías líricas* (Lyric Poetry) in 1821 and *Flores pasageras* ([sic]; Passing Flowers) in 1830. After studying Manzano's early poetry, I argue that Del Monte used the ideas contained in the early poetry to configure a vision of Cuba's foundational literature and that Manzano was its center pillar.[4]

Manzano authored the first and only autobiography written by an enslaved person in Latin America, but *Cecilia Valdés* (*Cecilia Valdés or El Ángel Hill*) is the most important novel of the nineteenth century. Villaverde narrates the incestuous relationship between half brother and sister, Leonardo Gamboa, the son of a Spanish father and a wealthy Cuban mother, and Cecilia, the daughter of the same father and a Mulatto mother. The first volume introduces the reader to a heterogeneous society made up of Spaniards, white Cubans, mulattos, free blacks, and enslaved blacks; the second one denounces the iniquities of the sugar economy and supports the benevolence of the coffee plantation, one represented by Cándido Gamboa and the other by Isabel Ilincheta, Leonardo's wife to be, respectively.[5]

Gertrudis Gómez de Avellaneda's *Sab* (1841) is the other important novel of the first half of the nineteenth century. Though Avellaneda did not belong to the Del Monte group, she wrote from Spain about slavery in her beloved homeland. The compassionate enslaved Sab falls in love with his mistress, Carlota, who is engaged to the Englishman Enrique Otway. When she comes upon hard times, Sab wins the lottery and gives the prize to Carlota to marry Enrique. The white but poor Teresa loves Sab, but the romantic enslaved man stays true to his feelings. Years later after Sab's passing, Carlota finds a letter outlining his love for her. As in *Cecilia Valdés*, the unsuspecting Sab and Carlota were cousins, thus continuing to insist on an incestuous reading of Cuban culture.[6]

Unlike other countries in Spanish America that obtained independence from the Spanish colonial power in the first half of the nineteenth century, Cuba did not become a republic until 1902. However, the structures of Cuban literature and culture were present at the same time they developed in the other sister republics. Of the countries in Hispanic America, Cuba has produced the most consistent literature of and about blacks.

Other significant novels in nineteenth-century Cuba include Francisco Calcagno's *Romualdo, uno de tantos* (Romualdo, One of Many, 1891) and *Aponte* (1901), whose title is associated with the black leader of the Aponte Conspiracy of 1812. During this period blacks and some whites attempted to overthrow the colonial government and to end slavery. *Romualdo* condemns slavery and the plantation system. Influenced by Suárez y Romero's *Francisco*, Calcagno's mulatto protagonist falls in love with an enslaved woman named Dorotea, and the jealous overseer punishes both lovers. However, Romualdo's father, Castaneiro, unintentionally participates in his son's death. If the historical Aponte was decapitated and his head displayed in a cage for everyone to see, in the novel, Aponte's master, Juan Pérez, educates his enslaved man, Hipólito, and transforms him into the Marqués de Represalia (revenge). His mission is to court the beautiful countess, who rejected Pérez, and to embarrass her and her husband by exposing her suitor's race. Hipólito accepts his role and considers himself to be superior to all of them, accomplishing in two years what whites, including his master, could never achieve in a lifetime. The successful education of a black man had already been addressed in Manzano's *Autobiografía*.

The black writer Martín Morúa Delgado wrote two significant novels, *Sofía* (1901) and *La familia Unzúazu* (The Family Unzuazu, 1901). Both works were published the same year, the former written between 1888–1890 and the latter completed by 1896, and they share the same narrative period, between 1878 and 1880, the conclusion of the Ten Years' War and the years of the Guerra Chiquita (Little War). Morúa's first novel, *Sofía*, rewrites *Cecilia Valdés* and subjects the unsuspecting white protagonist to the inequalities enslaved people experienced on a daily basis. Morúa's second novel refers to the life of the mulatto Fidelio, who is arrested for helping the anticolonial opposition.

Morúa Delgado is best remembered not for his novels but for his politics. He was the first black president of the Cuban Senate under the presidency of his friend, José Miguel Gómez. He penned the Morúa Amendment, outlawing the creation of political parties on the basis of color and used it to suppress the Partido de los Independientes de Color (the Black Independents Party), who demanded the rights promised to blacks for fighting in Cuba's War of Independence (1895–1898), and whose members were massacred one hundred years after the Aponte rebellion, in 1912.[7]

While Manzano and Morúa Delgado are exceptional black writers, Manzano is a main pillar of the foundation of Cuban literature and culture. Not only did he teach himself to read and write when enslaved people were denied a formal education, but he did so undeterred by the terror of the Aponte Conspiracy. Manzano may have known that he was risking his life when writing against the slavery system. However, I consider Aponte to be the first black cultural promoter in Cuba. He was a sculptor, woodcarver, and painter, and he compiled a notebook of drawings about notable blacks, including his father and himself, that was later lost. The fate of the missing notebook has become the concern of recent scholars.[8] The failure of the Aponte Conspiracy, the Ladder Conspiracy of 1844, and the massacre of Los Independientes de Color discouraged other black writers from narrating their stories.

In the twentieth century, Alejo Carpentier emerges as one of the greatest Latin American novelists. His interest in blacks was first explored in ¡Ecué-Yamba-O! (Lord Be Praised, 1933), about marginal African descendants who live in Havana's ghetto and practice Abakuá, an African religion. But he is better known for authoring *El reino de este mundo* (*The Kingdom of This World*, 1949), concerning the historical transition of the first black republic, from the French colony of Saint Domingue to Haiti, from the uprising of enslaved people in 1791 and the founding of Haiti in 1804, to the reign of Henri Christophe, who ruled the northern part of Haiti as a monarch (1811), to the arrival of the mulattos and the unification of the island under the Jean-Pierre Boyer government (1818–1843). Carpentier structures the novel around cycles of repression and rebellion to accentuate the historical changes first represented by the French planters and the enslaved workers. The two cycles are repeated by Henri Christophe, who accepted European culture and the blacks who remained loyal to their African religions, and by the mulatto republicans and the followers of Vodun. There are three historical moments associated with exploitation, represented by whites, blacks, and mulattos. However, each cycle of oppression is followed by one of rebellion, which continues well into the end of the novel and into the twenty-first century.

A few years after Carpentier wrote about marvelous realism, a precursor of magical realism,[9] in the preface to *The Kingdom of this World*, Lino Novás Calvo authored *El negrero, vida novelada de Pedro Blanco Fernández de Traba* (The Slave Trader: A Novel about the Life of Pedro Blanco Fernández de Traba, 1933), about the infamous but influential Pedro Blanco, whose slave factory in the Gulf of Gallinas was known throughout the Western world. Novás Calvo's rendition draws on the biography of another slave trafficker, Theodore Canot and his *Adventures of an African Slaver* (1928).

Though not considered a novel in the traditional sense, Miguel Barnet and Esteban Montejo's *Biografía de un cimarron* (*Biography of a Runaway Slave*, 1966) is one of the most successful works written after Fidel Castro's 1959 revolution. A foundational work that defined the parameters of the testimonial novel, *Biografía* is based on a series of interviews the ethnographer recorded with the 104-year-old former fugitive maroon, which outline the island's historical changes: slavery, emancipation, the War of Independence, and the start of the Republic of Cuba. The interviews continued into the present time of the revolution, but these were edited from the final version, perhaps because of Montejo's independent nature and anti-government perspective, or because showed the lack showed the lack of true political change not only in the republic but also during the revolution. The book's coherence, chronology, language, and some of Montejo's ideas belong to Barnet, who organized, edited, and restructured the interviews that conformed more to the oral tradition than to written memory. Regardless, *Biografía* allows those once silenced to speak, including Barnet himself, and it has led to the creation of the testimonial genre. Today, it figures prominently in subaltern and postcolonial studies.[10]

Castro's revolution came to power to end inequality, but, in In so doing, the government did not support black racial identity. Ironically, this lack of support continued the policies of the previous governments. Writing about the historical past was encouraged, and this may also explain why Barnet did not incorporate the last section of interviews about the current government. There are also a few historical novels written during the revolutionary period: Reinaldo Arenas's *La loma del Ángel* (*Graveyard of the Angels*, 1995) is a fanciful rendition of Villaverde's *Cecilia Valdés*, also written in New York. In Cuba, Marta Roja, known for her journalistic work and books about the Cuban revolution, authored two historical novels. *Santa lujuria o papeles de blanco* (Holy Lust, 1998) uncovers the racial complexities of the colonial period: the beautiful Lucila Mendes accepts her racial identity and helps those discriminated by society; but her son Filomeno, product of her relationship with the Marqués de Aguas Claras, strives to whiten himself, racially and culturally. *El harén de Oviedo* (Oviedo's Harem, 2003) narrates the life of a nineteenth-century slaver who kept a harem of enslaved women.

Cuba counts with a long tradition of authors writing about slavery and the post-slavery periods, but other authors in Hispanic America also have narrated black experiences. In Colombia, Jorge Isaac's romantic novel, *María* (1867), offers an early depiction of blacks of the period. Chapters 40–46 highlight the story of Nay and Sinar in Africa and the New World. Back home she was the daughter of an Ashanti warrior and he, the son of a captured enemy chief. The history of slavery becomes the reason for separation in this version of *Romeo and Juliet*. Uprooted from their native land, Nay is purchased by Efrain's father, and the son recounts the story Nay shared: her capture, Christianization, and manumission in New Granada, thus unveiling another and more benevolent side of slavery. Recalling some early works in Cuban literature, not all masters are cruel and some even sympathize with the enslaved people. The emphasis on Feliciana is as Nay is known by Efraín meant to draw the white reader to accept the docile female figure, a strategy used in the Cuban antislavery narrative that may not have been successful by concentrating on Sinar's warrior aggressivity.

Racism and discrimination are dealt more explicitly in later works represented primarily by Afro-Colombian writers like Arnaldo Palacios and Manuel Zapata Olivella, from the Pacific coast of El Chocó and Lorica, near the Caribbean Sea, respectively. Palacios's *Las estrellas son negras* (The Stars are Black, 1949) describes the human suffering of its black characters in a way that the reader feels what they experience. By leaving El Chocó for Cartagena, Irra (Israel), who is searching for his "promised land," shows that there is no real difference for blacks to live on one coast or on the other, for there is no escaping the racism they experience. The first two of four chapters, "Hambre" (Hunger) and "Ira" (Anger), describe how one situation leads to another, and the third, "Niva," takes the title from the name of Irra's girlfriend, whom he seduces. In the end, in the fourth chapter, there is "Luz interior" (Interior Light), an awareness that includes the government's complicity and an acceptance of his own black identity. There is a fall, but there is also determination and a glimmer of hope.

Zapata Olivella has been tenacious and prolific in his writings about African descendants in his native Colombia. A medical doctor, anthropologist, folklorist, and essayist, he has authored noteworthy novels like *Tierra mojada* (Wet Land, 1947), *En Chimá nace un santo* (*A Saint is Born in Chimá*, 1963), and *Chambacú, corral de negros* (Chambacu, Barracks for Blacks, 1965), but *Changó, el gran putas* (*Changó: The Biggest Badass*, 1983) is his most important work. In fact, there is no other comparable novel, irrespective of language. *Changó* is the novel of the African diaspora. Told from a Bantu perspective, the reader is invited to abandon Western culture and board the slave vessel as another enslaved person making the transatlantic journey, cramped in the bow of the ship, like an animal, pressed against others, with little food, water, or fresh air. *Changó* begins with an epic poem that tells the story of how the ruler of Oyo exiled the *muntu*, a Bantu concept that refers to the living and the dead, humans and non-humans, animate and inanimate objects, and ancestors and Orishas. In seventeenth-century Cartagena, Father Pedro Claver fails to Christianize Benkos Biojo, the founder of the runaway enslaved community Palenque de San Basilio. In the Saint Domingue of the eighteenth and nineteenth centuries, we hear the voices of Mackandal, Tousaint Louverture, Jacques Dessalines, and other notable figures of the Haitian Revolution. In eighteenth-century Brazil, the mulatto Alejadrinho suffers leprosy and is reared by white parents; with his amputated hands and feet, he sculpts with instruments tied to his wrists and learns about the past from the spirit of his deceased uncle. In nineteenth-century Venezuela, Simón Bolívar betrays his Mulatto general, José Prudencio Padilla, who supports the emancipation of the enslaved. In nineteenth-century Mexico, Afro-indigenous Father José María Morelos fights for the independence of his country. In twentieth-century United States, in the longest chapter, the novel describes the life of Agne Brown (a fictional rendition of Angela Davis) and that of countless characters from Booker T. Washington, Sojourner Truth, John Brown, to the two prophets Marcus Garvey and Malcolm X. In the end, Changó is disappointed with the *muntu* for not liberating itself, complying with his wishes, and returning to Africa.

In Venezuela Guillermo Meneses's *Canción de negros* (Black Song, 1934) describes the unfortunate life of blacks who must better themselves to improve their condition. The protagonist Julián Ponce is imprisoned and has time to think about his future. Rómulo Gallegos's *Pobre negro* (Poor Black, 1937) outlines the life of African descendants from emancipation in 1854 to the end of the Guerra Federal in 1863, during which the black *conuqueros* (farmers) of Barlovento work under deplorable conditions.

Black speech, religious belief systems, and other cultural traits were discouraged, the descendants of Africans descendants had to distance themselves from their past and move into the present. The novel argues for the integration of blacks and mulattos of mixed heritage, as represented by Pedro Miguel, the son of a forbidden relationship between the well-to-do Ana Julia Alcorta and the enslaved Negro Malo. Pedro Miguel fights in the Guerra Federal and commands black troops against the colonial forces and the racist society.

More in line with black experiences, Juan Pablo Sojo's *Nochebuena negra* (Black Christmas Eve, 1943) takes place on the cocoa plantation of Pozo Frío, after emancipation and between 1884 to 1928. The novel narrates the racial oppression of black workers, who continue to suffer at the hands of whites. Regana and Cristanto, who constitute a repository of cultural knowledge, work for the Sanabria family. After Crisanto's death, Regana tells his story, which is continued by Crisanto's son, Pedro, who represents the future. Their situation has not changed, and nature is the ultimate witness. Other characters include the black Tereso, who desires to live in the capital with a white lover; and Pedro, who returns to his roots and does not compromise his values. In Ramón Díaz Sánchez's *Cumboto, cuento de siete leguas* (*Cumboto*, 1950) the black servant, Natividad, narrates his search for identity within his African past and the present of white culture, which his childhood friend, Federico, represents.

In Ecuador, Adalberto Ortiz's *Juyungo, historia de una isla, unos negros y otros negros* (*Juyungo: A Novel*, 1943) describes the lives of blacks in a South American country comprised by white, blacks, indigenous, mulatto, and mestizo groups. Asunción Lastre's rejection to be baptized forces him to flee and undergo a personal development typical of the picaresque genre, but in his case away from his blackness or "savage" nature. He joins the Colombian smuggler Cástulo Canchingre and after his assassination, Lastre lives with the Cayapa Indians, who name him Juyungo, the devil, then works with other blacks in a farm on the Pepepán island. Unfortunately, Mr. Hans buys the farm from Don Clemente Ayoví and provokes the resistance of the owner and workers, the death of Juyungo's son, and the mental breakdown of his mulatto wife, María de los Ángeles. Juyungo develops a national identity, joins the army and other ethnic groups, and dies in the war against Peru. Ortiz draws a distinction between the black Nelson Días and the mulatto Asunción Lastre, whom Richard Jackson criticizes for desiring a white woman and placing social upheaval and class over race (Jackson, *Black Writers*). The glossary at the end of the novel is reminiscent of those that accompany *negrista* poems for the benefit of white readers.

Nelson Estupiñán Bass narrates life in his native black province of Esmeralda. His most celebrated novel, *Cuanto los guayacanes florecían* (The Guaiacums Flowered So Much, 1954), describes Captain Concha Torres's fight to liberate Alberto Morcú, Juan Cagua, and Pedro Tamayo, who join the struggle to avenge the assassination of Eloy Alfaro against the will of Doña Jacinta. They fight against the Ecuadorian army and are forced to participate in atrocities they despise. The cycle is repeated after Concha's defeat and the workers return to Doña Jacinta's ownership. The day before their return, Juan and Alberto escape and the soldiers track and assassinate them.

The uprising of African descendants against the government is a theme the prolific Estupiñán Bass returns to in *El paraíso* (Paradise, 1958) and *El último río* (The Last River, 1966), two novels about the pressures of "blanqueamiento" or whitening. *Senderos brillantes* (Shinny Paths, 1974), about Calamares (the Galapagos), is more in line with a national discourse against US imperialism and the moral decay of society that foreigners bring along with them. Workers are inspired to take up arms against the foreign invaders. This experimental novel conforms to the characteristics of the Latin American Boom novel of the 1960s. His other works include *Las puertas del verano* (The Doors of the Summer, 1978), *Toque de queda* (*Curfew*, 1978), *Bajo el cielo nublado* (Under the Cloudy Sky, 1981), and *Al norte de Dios* (*The Other Son of God*, 1994).

In Peru, black writers demonstrated their narrative talents. Enrique López Albújar's groundbreaking *Matalaché* (1928) takes place in 1816, a few years before the abolition of the slave trade in 1821 and the same year Peru and its sister nations gained independence from Spain, but years before slavery was abolished in 1854. The enslaved people work for Juan Francisco de los Ríos in the manufacturing of soap and leather in Piura, and his daughter falls in love with the learned mulatto José Manuel Sojo (Matalaché), who is rumored to be the son of the previous owner, de Sojo. She is attracted to his body, humanity, and musical talents, among other qualities. María Luz discovers that before her arrival from Lima, Matalaché was used to breed with enslaved servants. Both fall in love. Her father discovers the affair and her pregnancy, and he has Matalaché thrown in with the boiling soap. Though the novel is about a forbidden love, it takes a peculiar stance against slavery. It does so, not by celebrating blacks but mulattos, who are educated, talented, and the product of relationships with enslaved women. However, the novel associates the privileged María Luz with the same sexual actions experienced by the black female servants. She and Matalaché meet for the first time in the breeding house. The dark room where they consummate their relationship recalls that same dim space. Regardless of the love they feel for each other, Matalaché is reduced to his sexuality. His death refers to the intolerance that whites have for mulattos, even those who are talented.

Contemporary Afro-Peruvian writers include Antonio Gálvez Ronceros's *Monólogo desde las tinieblas* (Monologue from the Darkness, 1975), Gregorio Martínez's *Canto de Sirena* (Siren's Song, 2012), and Lucía Charún-Illescas's *Malambo* (2001).

Central American writers include authors who write about their own complex racial identity. In the post-slavery period, emancipated blacks were integrated in varying degrees into the country's national identity. There were others hired from the Caribbean islands to work on the Panama Canal and to build the railroads in Costa Rica. However, their French or English language and culture were not accepted, and they were subjected to racial, cultural, and linguistic discrimination.

In Panama writers like Joaquín Beleño Carrillo, in *Luna verde* (Green Moon, 1951), *Gamboa Road Gang* (1960), and *Curundú* (1963) are sympathetic to those West Indian blacks who work in the Canal and the railroads, and who contribute to the Panamanian economy. In Costa Rica, Carlos Luis Fallas's *Mamita Yunai* (1941) refers to the strike of 1934. As a result, President León Cortez prohibited black laborers from working for the

United Fruit Company on the Pacific coast of the country. Joaquín Gutiérrez's *Puerto Limón* (1950) narrates the story of Tom Winkelman and his sister Azucena and their arrival from Jamaica to work on the railroad.

African descendant Costa Rican Quince Duncan's *Los cuatro espejos* (*The Four Mirrors*, 1973) takes place in his native Puerto Limón, a city that also welcomed Marcus Garvey and still maintains an office of his United Negro Improvement Association. Here Duncan addresses racial discrimination by whites against blacks of Jamaican ancestry, who speak English and Spanish with a West-Indian accent. Charles McForbes, a light-skinned black from a prominent Jamaican family, abandons his identity, marries the white Esther, and seeks salvation in her white world. In reality, the acceptance of his black identity becomes his salvation as he journeys back home on the train. But true salvation is embracing all people, regardless of color. In *La paz del pueblo* (*The Town's Peace*, 1978), blacks have no other option but to leave Puerto Limón for Panama for the same reasons outlined in *Mamita Yunai*, but this time the episode is told from the perspective of West Indians who directly suffered discrimination. Duncan also writes about African religions practiced by West Indians in his collection of stories *La rebelión Pocomía y otros relatos* (*The Pocomía Rebellion and Other Stories* 1976).

Carlos Guillermo Wilson (Cubena) also provides a compassionate view of West Indians. His three novels, *Chombo* (1981), *Los nietos de Felicidad Dolores* (The Grandchildren of Felicidad Dolores, 1991), and *La misión secreta* (The Secret Mission, 2005), span key moments in the history of West Indians and their contribution to building the Panama Canal. In *Chombo*, a derogatory word that refers to someone from the Anglophone Caribbean, Litó returns home from the United States to witness the signing of the Torrijos-Carter Treaty of 1977. He narrates the history of his grandparents, Papá James and Nenén, who journeyed from Barbados and Jamaica to help build the Panama Canal.

Los nietos de Felicidad Dolores takes place at the JFK Airport where Dolores awaits the arrival of her grandchildren to make the trip back to Panama after the United States relinquished control of the Canal in 2000 and guaranteed its neutrality. For the reasons stated in the novel, their return implies racial discrimination and conflicts of identity that had continued in Panama after the family emigrated to the United States, where life was more hospitable than back home. During the construction of the railroad in 1850, two Panamanian families, that of the Afro-Hispanic Juan Moreno and that of the West Indian John Brown, provide insights into the tension between these two groups. Almost a century later, in 1941, West Indians were forced to accept the Spanish language and culture or to return to their parents' country of origin. Felicidad Dolores is the center of this novel, which incorporates African-based religions. In *La misión secreta*, Papamambí, a descendant of Felicidad Dolores, returns to Panama to be present at the one-hundred-year anniversary of the completion of the canal in 2014. He revisits the past through dreams that underscore the experiences of two families, those of Juan Garido and Felicidad Dolores, and their contributions to the African diaspora.

In Puerto Rico important writers like José Luis González, Rosario Ferré, Luis Rafael Sánchez, and José Ramos Otero and others focus on the US impact the once Spanish colony. However, Isabelo Zenón Cruz's *Narciso descubre su trasero* (Narciso Discovers His Behind, 1974) became the first work to underscore a racial problem most Puerto Ricans preferred not to discuss. In recent years, Mayra Santos-Febres has emerged as a talented and prolific narrator, poet, and essayist, and all of her novels merit attention: *Sirena Selena vestida de pena* (*Sirena Selena*, 2000), *Cualquier miércoles soy tuya* (*Any Wednesday I'm Yours*, 2002), *Nuestra señora de las noches* (*Our Lady of the Night*, 2006), *Fe en disfraz* (Fe in Costume, 2009), *Yo misma fui mi ruta: la maravillosa vida de Julia de Burgos* (I Myself Was the Route: The Wonderful Life of Julia de Burgos, 2014), and *La amante de Gardel* (Gardel's Lover, 2015). *Fe en disfraz* deals with the Afro-Venezuelan historian Fe Verdejo, who, working at the University of Chicago, uncovers early petitions of enslaved women. She hires another historian, the Puerto Rican Martín Tirado, to assist her and digitize the documents "reproduced" in the novel. Martin, the narrator, becomes sexually aroused when reading the documents Fe sends him. Then, she weaves an intricate plan to make Martín part of her sexual pleasure.

There is no question that enslaved women were victims of their masters, but the archives reveal another possible interpretation: that the victims also enjoyed the sexual encounter and used it to their advantage. As part of her research, Fe visits the convent of Recogimiento de las Macaúbas in Brazil, where sexual abuse and rape were rampant. The nun's mother and grandmother were also sisters of the convent and so was Fe's mother, who was expelled because she became pregnant. A cousin also rapes Fe, an experience she enjoyed. The nun gives Fe a dress with a harness used by Xica da Silva, an enslaved woman who had children with her master and accumulated great wealth. Xica's dress created intense pain but also immense pleasure. Santos-Febres questions the passivity or victimization of enslaved women and their traditional sexual roles, and explores their complexities.

Black literature in the Dominican Republic is difficult to classify, since Dominicans do not consider themselves to be black. Blacks, as Other, are the Haitians. The Dominicans tend to consider themselves *Indios* or indigenous people. However, race comes into perspective in Freddy Prestol Castillo's *El Masacre se pasa a pie* (*You Can Cross the Massacre on Foot, 1973*), a testimonial account of the dictator Trujillo's 1937 order to kill Haitians and Haitian Dominicans living near the border between the two countries. For obvious political reasons, this novel could not be published during the time of writing.

Hispanics and Latinx living in the United States contribute to making this country after Mexico, the second-largest Spanish-speaking population in the world. While Latinx literature has come under the purview of English departments, I contend that Latinx writers occupy an in-between space, between Latin American and US (English) literatures, that is also discussed in this essay. Blackness and Afro-Latino identity helps to negotiate culturally different spaces and occupies central stage in the post-modern discourse. It should be clear that Afro-Latino (Afro Latinx) is not interchangeable with Afro-Latin American, just as there is no correlation between Latino or Latinx and Latin American as some critics tend to believe.[11]

As previously mentioned, in the nineteenth century Cirilo Villaverde completed his *Cecilia Valdés* in his adopted country, where Andrés de Avelino Orihuela also wrote *El sol de Jesús del Monte* (*The Sun of Jesús del Monte*, 1852), an antislavery novel he drafted at the same time he translated into Spanish Harriet Beecher Stove's *Uncle Tom's Cabin*. These and other works associated with the literature and language of the author's country of origin are also impacted by the history and culture of his/her country of residence. Evelio Grillo's *Black Cuban, Black American: A Memoir* (2000) is one of the few works that provides a first-hand account of the lives of black Cubans in the United States at the turn of the twentieth century. Grillo narrates race relations in Cuba and in Tampa, the "Cigar-Making Capital of the World." He offers an archeology of the city, in particular of the area inhabited by whites and those settled by black Cubans, African Americans, and some poor whites. Whites and blacks worked together in the cigar industry, but they lived in segregated neighborhoods. Race became a stronger marker of identity than language; it was a force that brought all people of color together, and Grillo found comfort in the African American community.

The first and most important work about black Hispanics in the United States is Piri Thomas's bestseller *Down these Mean Streets* (1967). A dark-skinned Puerto Rican living in El Barrio (Spanish Harlem), Piri struggled with his "national" and racial identities. He believed that his lighter-skinned siblings were treated differently in and outside of the home. For this reason, Piri identified with his African American buddy, Bru. To experience race relations, they undergo a journey through the South, where Piri sees the world from Bru's perspective. In the end, race becomes less important when Piri joins two white acquaintances, and they rob an establishment frequented by gays, an event covered widely by New York newspapers. The attempted robbery fails and Piri is shot, goes to prison, and serves a seven-year sentence, the topic of his third book *Seven Long Times* (1974). He also authored *Savior, Savior Hold My Hand* (1972) about his religious conversion, and *Stories from El Barrio* (1978).

Latinx writers of Cuban descent have incorporated African traditions into their writings. Cristina García uses Santería to frame her first two novels, *Dreaming in Cuban* (1993) and *The Agüero Sisters* (1998), and highlights the transnationality of Caribbean culture. In *Dreaming in Cuban*, Pilar returns to the island and learns about her family past. However, the structures of Cuban culture that she finds on the island are mirrored in the adopted country: Santería, anti-Castro sentiments, and pro-Castro support, to name the most obvious ones. The journey to visit her grandmother, Celia, recover her letters, and access her family history is also a way of understanding how the past of her family in Cuba intersects with her presence in the United States. And Pilar's curiosity about Santería in New York points to Felicia's rituals on the island and Herminia's narration.

In *The Agüero Sisters*, Santería is more prominent and determines the course of the novel, which takes place in Cuba and the United States. Reina, who works as an electrician in the region of El Cobre, the city of Cuba's patron saint (Oshún in Santería), is struck by lighting and undergoes a transformation in which the skins of others are grafted onto hers. She prays to the Virgen de la Caridad del Cobre, her spiritual mother, but her father, the deity of lighting, is Changó (Saint Barbara). The reader is charged with the task of understanding why Ignacio killed his wife Blanca, conceivably because she returned pregnant with someone else's child, whom she names Reina. The narration opens and closes with Blanca's death, on September 8, 1948, the day of Cuba's patron saint, and Blanca's lover is a black man; the mother represents Oshún and her father, Changó.[12]

Other Latinx writers like Esmeralda Santiago, Judith Ortiz Cofer, García, and Julia Álvarez are Latinas and also Afro-Latinx; they draw on what they perceive to be the strengths of blackness that includes the African component of Caribbean identity. Álvarez's US experience inspired her to understand the linguistic, cultural, and racial isolation experienced by Dominicans of African descent in her parents' country of origin. These writers are treated as if they were "black," and they too begin to negotiate a racial identity unimaginable in their parents' homeland. In *How the Garcia Girls Lost Their Accent* (1991), the protagonist, Yolanda, searches for a childhood past in the Dominican Republic that also includes the black maids. Under different circumstances, prosperous Dominicans, regardless of race, are oblivious to them. She embraces the "invisible" black Dominicans who also influenced her life.

Álvarez has continued to explore the concept of race in *In the Name of Salomé* (2000), where she interlaces two narrations about the mother, real-life poet Salomé Ureña, in the Dominican Republic of the nineteenth century, and her daughter, Camila Henríquez Ureña, a professor at Vassar College. Race and gender are considered when highlighting the life of the country's first national poet, and how she was mistreated by her white Dominican husband, who had another family, and her compatriots. In the end, the mother wants her daughter to learn from her mistakes. The daughter does not marry and has an affair with another woman. The stories Álvarez narrates have given great visibility to Dominican history and culture and could not have been told on the island, where other writers deny Dominican blackness.

In Loida Maritza Pérez's *Geographies of Home* (1999), a university student calls the protagonist "nigger" and targets the main character for her dark skin. She seeks shelter in her home environment, which, ironically, exposes her to the family trauma: she becomes a victim of incestuous rape in the presumed sanctity of the household.

Afro-Latinx images will continue to challenge national and transnational discourses on identity as more Dominican American writers explore the racial tensions they see and experience on the mainland, looking for ways of interpreting their parents' culture. One of the more successful writers to do this is Junot Díaz, whose collection of short stories *Drown* (1996) became an instant success. His stories are concerned with issues of race, as evidenced in the title "How to Date a Browngirl, Blackgirl, Whitegirl, or Halfie." Though gender is an issue, race also becomes a concern when dating women. In his Pulitzer-winning novel, the *Brief Wondrous Life of Oscar Wao* (2007), Díaz intertwines two geographical spaces and cultural identities where race becomes all too noticeable. Oscar is a dark-skinned Dominican American, who is mistaken for a Puerto Rican, and struggles with his identity. Oscar's mother, Belicia, is a black Dominican, an adjective in the Dominican Republic more aptly reserved for Haitians, and her own daughter, Lola, identifies her as a Haitian.

New voices continue to emerge and women of African descent are leading the way. Afro-Puerto Rican Dahlma Yanos-Figueroa's *Daughters of the Stone* (2009) narrates the story of five generations of women, from Africa to Puerto Rico to the US mainland, and the evolution of their lives in the new and changing environments. Marta Moreno Vega's *When the Spirits Dance Mambo* (2002) narrates life in East Harlem where Afro-Caribbean religion, dance, music, and identity persist. Afro-Panamanian Verónica Chambers' *Mama's Girl: A Memoir* (1997) reflects on her mother-daughter relationship. Without a doubt, Latin American writers of African descent in general and Afro-Latinx in particular are setting the foundation for the literature of the twenty-first century.

NOTES

1. For a list of their works see Works Cited: Jackson (*The Black Image in Latin America Literature* and *Black Writers in Latin America*); Miriam DeCosta-Willis (*Blacks in Hispanic Literature* and *Daughters of the Diaspora: Afra-Hispanic Writers*); Marvin Lewis (*Afro-Uruguayan Literature: Postcolonial Perspectives* and *Ethnicity and Identity in Contemporary Afro-Venezuelan Literature*); Ian Smart (*Central American Writers of West Indian Origin* and *Religious Elements in the Narrative of Quince Duncan*); William Luis (*Literary Bondage: Slavery in Cuban Narrative* and *Voices from Under: Black Narrative in Latin America and the Caribbean*); Clementine Rabassa (*Demetrio Aguilera Malta and Social Justice*); and Vera Kutzinski (*Afro-Hispanic American Literature* and *Sugar's Secrets*).
2. (https://www.un.org/en/observances/decade-people-african-descent).
3. All references to the Cuban antislavery novel of the nineteenth and twentieth centuries come from my *Literary Bondage: Slavery in Cuban Narrative*.
4. See my "The Life and Works of the Cuban Enslaved Poet Juan Francisco Manzano." (Unpublished book manuscript).
5. Also see my "Cuban Counterpoint, Coffee and Sugar."
6. See my "How to Read *Sab*."
7. See my interview: "Los independientes de color: Entrevista a Gloria Rolando" and Gloria Rolando's three documentaries on *Los independientes de color, 1912: Voces para un silencio, Breaking the Silence*. DVD, 2013.
8. See: Special Section: José Antonio Aponte of the *Afro-Hispanic Review*, vol. 38, no.1, spring 2019, 134–223.
9. Magical realism, associated with Gabriel García Márquez's *One Hundred Years of Solitude*, translated by Gregory Rabassa, and other writers, is based on Carpentier's marvelous realism, which is the coming together of African magic and European history or reality in the Americas.
10. See my "Memory and Politics in Writing in the *Biography of a Runaway Slave*."
11. This all-to-common mistake is not historical; rather, it is based on linguistic similarities and not recognizing that Hispanic and Latino mean different things in Spanish and English. See my *Dance Between Two Cultures* and my introduction to *Looking Out, Looking In: Anthology of Latino Poetry*, Arte Público Press, 2013.
12. See my "Hurricanes, Magic, Science, and Politics in Cristina García's *The Agüero Sisters*."

WORKS CITED

Álvarez, Julia. *How the Garcia Girls Lost Their Accent*. Penguin Group, 1992.

Álvarez, Julia. *In the Name of Salomé*. Penguin Putnam, 2001.

Anderson, Benedict. *Imagined Communities*. Verso, 2010.

Arenas, Reinaldo. *Graveyard of the Angels*. Translated by Alfred MacAdam. Avon Books, 1987.

Avelino de Orihuela, Andrés. *El sol de Jesús del Monte*. Ideal, 2007.

Barnet, Miguel. *Biography of a Runaway Slave*. Translated by Nick Hill, introduction by William Luis. Curbstone, 2016.

Beleño Cedeño, Joaquín. *Curundú*. Ediciones del Ministerio de Educación, 1963.

Beleño Cedeño, Joaquín. *Gamboa Road Gang*. Librería Cultural Panameña, 1970.

Beleño Cedeño, Joaquín. *Luna verde*. Librería Cultural Panameña, 1970.

Calcagno, Francisco. *Aponte*. Tipografía de Francisco Costa, 1901.

Calcagno, Francisco. *Romualdo, uno de tantos*. El Pilar de Manuel de Armas, 1891.

Canot, Theodore. *Adventures of an African Slaver; Being a True Account of the Life of Captain Theodore Canot, Trader in Gold, Ivory and Slaves on the Coast of Guinea: His Own Story As Told in the Year of 1854 to Brantz Mayer and Now Edited with an Introduction by Malcom Cowley*. A. & C. Boni, 1928.

Carpentier, Alejo. *¡Ecué-Yamba-O!* Xanandú, 1968.

Carpentier, Alejo. The *Kingdom of this World*. Translated by Harriet de Onís. Knopf, 1957.

Chambers, Veronica. *Mama's Girl: A Memoir*. Riverhead Books, 1997.

Charún-Illescas, Lucía. *Malambo*. Universidad Nacional Federico Villareal, 2001.

DeCosta-Willis, Miriam. *Blacks in Hispanic Literature*. Kennikat P, 1977.

DeCosta-Willis, *Daughters of the Diaspora: Afra-Hispanic Writers*. Ian Randle Publishers, 2003.

Díaz, Junot. *The Brief Wonderous Life of Oscar Wao*. Riverhead Books, 2008.

Díaz, Junot. *Drown*. Riverhead Books, 2008.

Díaz Sánchez, Ramón. *Cumboto*. Translated by John Upton. U of Texas P, 2012.

Duncan, Quince, *Los cuatro espejos*. Editorial Costa Rica, 1973.

Duncan, Quince, *La paz del pueblo*, Editorial Costa Rica, 1978.

Duncan, Quince, La rebelión Pocomía y otros relatos. Editorial Costa Rica, 1976.

Estupiñán Bass, Nélson. *Bajo el cielo nublado*. Sistema Nacional de Bibliotecas, 1997.

Estupiñán Bass, Nélson. *Cuanto los guayacanes florecían*. Libresia, 2008.

Estupiñán Bass, Nélson. *Al norte de Dios*. Casa de la Cultura Ecuatoriana, 1994.

Estupiñán Bass, Nélson. *El paraíso*. Casa de la Cultura Ecuatoriana, 2014.

Estupiñán Bass, Nélson. *Las puertas del verano*. Casa de la Cultura Ecuatoriana, 1978.

Estupiñán Bass, Nélson. *Senderos brillantes*. Casa de la Cultura Ecuatoriana, 2002.

Estupiñán Bass, Nélson. *Toque de queda*. Casa de la Cultura Ecuatoriana, 1978.

Estupiñán Bass, Nélson. *El último río*. Libresca, 1992.

Fallas, Carlos. *Mamita Yunai*. Imprenta Nacional de Cuba, 1961.

Gallegos, Rómulo. *Pobre negro*. Aguilar, 1971.

Gálvez Ronceros, Antonio. *Monólogo desde las tinieblas*. Inti Sol, 1975.

García, Cristina. *The Agüero Sisters*. Ballentine Books, 2011.

García, Cristina. *Dreaming in Cuban*. Ballentine Books, 1992.

García Márquez, Gabriel. *One Hundred Years of Solitude*. Translated by Gregory Rabassa. London: Jonathan Cape, 1970.

Gertrudis Gómez de Avellaneda. Sab. Translated by Nina Scott. U of Texas P, 1993.

Gutiérrez, Joaquín. *Puerto Limón*. Editorial Legado, 1977.

Grillo, Evelio. *Black Cuban, Black American: A Memoir*. Arte Público Press, 2000.

Jackson, Richard L. *The Black Image in Latin American Literature*. U of New Mexico P, 1976.

Jackson, Richard L. *Black Writers and the Hispanic Canon*. Twayne Publishers, 1997.

Jackson, Richard L. *Black Writers in Latin America*. U of New Mexico P, 1979.

Isaacs, Jorge. *María*. Mint Editions, 2021. "José Antonio Aponte." *Afro-Hispanic Review*, vol. 38, no. 1, spring 2019, pp. 134–223.

Kutzinski, Vera. "Afro-Hispanic American Literature." *The Cambridge History of Latin American Literature*, vol. 2, edited by Roberto González Echevarría and Enrique Pupo Walker, Cambridge UP, 1996, 164–94.

Kutzinski, Vera. *Sugar's Secrets: Race and the Erotics of Cuban Nationalism*. U of Virginia P, 1993.

Lewis, Marvin. *Afro-Uruguayan Literature: Postcolonial Perspectives*. Bucknell UP, 2003.

Lewis, Marvin. *Ethnicity and Identity in Contemporary Afro-Venezuelan Literature: A Culturalist Approach*. U of Missouri P, 1992.

López Albújar, Enrique. *Matalaché*. Casa de las Américas, 1978.

Luis, William. "Cuban Counterpoint, Coffee and Sugar: The Emergence of a National Culture in Fernando Ortiz's *Cuban Counterpoint: Tobacco and Sugar* and Cirilo Villaverde's *Cecilia Valdés*." *PALARA*, no. 2, 1998, pp. 5–16.

Luis, William. *Dance Between Two Cultures: Latino Caribbean Literature Written in the United States*. Vanderbilt UP, 1997.

Luis, William. "How to Read Sab." *Revista de Estudios Hispánicos*, no. 32, 1998, pp. 175–86.

Luis, William. "Hurricanes, Magic, Science, and Politics in Cristina García's The Agüero Sisters." *Contemporary U.S. Latino/a Literary Criticism*, edited by Lyn Di Iorio Sandín and Richard Pérez, Palgrave, 2007, pp. 144–64.

Luis, William. "The Life and Works of the Cuban Enslaved Poet Juan Francisco Manzano." (Unpublished book manuscript).

Luis, William. *Literary Bondage: Slavery in Cuban Narrative*. U of Texas P, 1991.

Luis, William. "Los independientes de color: Entrevista a Gloria Rolando." *Afro-Hispanic Review*, vol. 33, no.1, 2014, pp. 273–86.

Luis, William. "Memory and Politics in Writing in the *Biography of a Runaway Slave*." *Biography of a Runaway Slave* by Miguel Barnet, translated by Nick Hill, Curbstone Press, 2016, pp. xi–xlvi.

Luis, William, ed. *Looking Out, Looking In: Anthology of Latino Poetry*. Arte Público P, 2013.

Luis, William, ed. *Voices from Under: Black Narrative in Latin America and the Caribbean*. Greenwood, 1984.

Manzano, Juan Francisco. *Autobiografía del esclavo poeta y otros escritos*. Edited by William Luis. Iberoamericana, 2007.

Manzano, Juan Francisco. *Flores pasageras*. 1830

Manzano, Juan Francisco. *Poesías líricas*. 1821

Madden, Richard Robert. *Poems by a Slave in the Island of Cuba*. Ward, 1840.

Martínez, Gregorio. *Canto de Sirena*. Peisa, 2012.

Meneses, Guillermo. *Canción de negros*. Editorial "La Nación," 1932.

Moreno Vega, Marta. *When the Spirits Dance Mambo*. Crown Publishing, 2004.

Morúa Delgado, Martín. *La familia Unzúazu*. Forgotten Books, 2015.

Morúa Delgado, Martín. *Sofía*. Verbum, 2018.

Novás Calvo, Lino. *El negrero, vida novelada de Pedro Blanco Fernández de Traba*. Espasa-Calpe, 1955.

Ortiz, Adalberto. *Juyungo: A Classic Afro-Hipsanic Novel*. Translated by Susan F. Hill and Jonathan Tittler. Lynne Reiner, 1991.

Palacios, Arnoldo. *Las estrellas son negras*. Editorial Revista Colombiana, 1971.

Pérez, Loida Maritza. *Geographies of Home*. Penguin, 2000.

Prestol Castillo, Freddy. *You Can Cross the Massacre on Foot*. Translated by Margaret Randall. Duke UP, 2019.

Rabassa, Clementine. *Demetrio Aguilera-Malta and Social Justice: The Tertiary Phase of Epic Tradition in Latin American Literature*. Fairleigh Dickinson UP, 1980.

Roja, Marta. *El harén de Oviedo*. Letras Cubanas, 2003.

Roja, Marta. *Santa lujuria o papeles de blanco*. Letra Viva, 2013.

Rolando, Gloria. *1912: Voces para un silencio, Breaking the Silence*. DVD, 2013.

Santos-Febres, Mayra. *La amante de Gardel*. Planeta, 2015.

Santos-Febres, Mayra. *Cualquier miércoles soy tuya*. Planeta, 2002.

Santos-Febres, Mayra. *Fe en disfraz*. Alfaguara, 2009.

Santos-Febres, Mayra. *Nuestra señora de las noches*. Rayo, 2006.

Santos-Febres, Mayra. *Yo misma fui mi ruta: la maravillosa vida de Julia de Burgos*. Municipio Autónomo de Carolina, 2014.

Santos-Febres, Mayra. *Sirena Selena vestida de pena*. Planeta, 2000.

Smart, Ian. *Central American Writers of West Indian Origin: A New Hispanic Literature*. Passeggiata P, 1984.

Smart, Ian. "Religious Elements in the Narrative of Quince Duncan." *Afro-Hispanic Review*, vol. 1, no. 2, May 1982, pp. 27–31.

Sojo, Juan Pablo. *Nochebuena negra*. Monte Ávila Editores Latinoamericana, 2017.

Stove, Harriet Beecher. *La cabaña del tío Tom*. Translated by Andrés Avelino de Orihuela. Bogotá, 1853.

Suárez y Romero, Anselmo. *Francisco, el ingenio o las delicias del campo*. Editorial de Arte y Literatura, 1974.

Tanco y Bosmeniel, Félix. *Escenas de la vida privada en la isla de Cuba* (1838). Adriana Lewis Galanes, "'El hombre misterioso'/'el cura': el texto del segundo relato en las *Escenas de la vida privada en la isla de Cuba* por Félix Manuel Tanco Bosmeniel." *Anuario de Estudios Americanos*, vol. 51, no. 1, January 1994, pp. 185–211.

Thomas, Piri. *Down These Mean Streets*. Vintage, 2010.

Thomas, Piri. *Savior, Savior Hold My Hand*. Doubleday, 1972.

Thomas, Piri. *Seven Long Times*. Arte Público P, 1994.

Thomas, Piri. *Stories from El Barrio*. Avon Books, 1978.

Wilson, Carlos Guillermo (Cubena). *Chombo*. Universal, 1981.

Wilson, Carlos Guillermo (Cubena). *La misión secreta*. Alexander Street P, 2005.

Wilson, Carlos Guillermo (Cubena). *Los nietos de Felicidad Dolores*. Universal, 1991.

Villaverde, Cirilo. *Cecilia Valdés or El Ángel Hill*. Translated by Helen Lane. Oxford UP, 2005.

Yanos-Figueroa, Dahlma. *Daughters of the Stone*. St. Martin's, 2009.

Zapata Olivella, Manuel. *Changó: The Biggest Badass*. Translated by Jonathan Tittler. Introduction by William Luis. Texas Tech UP, 2010.

Zapata Olivella, Manuel. *Chambacú, Black Slum*. Translated by Jonathan Tittler. Latin American Literary Review P, 1989.

Zapata Olivella, Manuel. *A Saint is Born in Chimá*. Translated by Thomas E. Kooreman and John Stubbs Brushwook. U of Texas P, 1991

Zapata Olivella, Manuel. *Tierra mojada*. Espiral, 1947

Zenón, Cruz, Isabelo. *Narciso descubre su trasero*. Furidi, 1979.

CHAPTER 18

....

THE JEWISH-LATIN
AMERICAN NOVEL

....

DARRELL B. LOCKHART

It is a significant advancement that a volume such as this one, which purports to provide a thorough assessment of the Latin American novel, should include a chapter dedicated to the Jewish novel. As a rule, Jewish authors and literature have been excluded from histories of Latin American literature. This is not to say that there have not been occasional inroads of inclusion. However, for the most part, these include examples of Jewish literature considered more as marginal curiosities than integral components of Latin American literary history. Indeed, the struggle for legitimacy has been something with which Jewish Latin Americans, and by inclusion writers, have had to persistently contend. Jewish-Latin American writing is positioned in an awkward and often invisible place, not fully recognized within Latin America and not acknowledged or even known about outside of Latin America, as a branch of Jewish Studies, for example.

Because Jewishness is often perceived as being exotic, strange, and foreign to Latin America, especially in societies that value homogeneity over cultural pluralism, Jewish-Latin American writing in the main is positioned as a marginalized literary discourse that is shaped by otherness and difference vis-à-vis the dominant Luso- and Hispano-Catholic societies from which it arises. As such, Jewish writing exists very much at the periphery of national literatures. Nevertheless, some Jewish writers have indeed attained a status of national prominence as authors. Salient examples might include Margo Glantz (1930– Mexico), Isaac Chocrón (1930–2011 Venezuela), Clarice Lispector (1925–1977 Brazil), Mauricio Rosencof (1933– Uruguay), and Bernardo Verbitsky (1907–1979 Argentina).

The aim of this article is to present a summary overview of the Jewish novel as it has developed. As we shall see, there are early manifestations of Jewish narrative in Latin America that may be viewed as precursory texts, but the story of the Jewish novel (and literature in general) is one that primarily evolved over the course of the twentieth century and now thrives in the twenty-first century. This panoramic view of the Jewish-Latin American novel will take into account key foundational authors and texts, major themes, and new trends. While the intent is to be as comprehensive as possible, it is inevitable that an endeavor such as this one will necessarily be fraught with omissions. Argentina, by far, is home to the largest number of Jewish writers by virtue of the history of Jewish immigration to that country in the late nineteenth and early twentieth centuries, when thousands of Ashkenazic Jews from Russia and Eastern Europe settled on the agricultural colonies established by the philanthropist Baron Maurice de Hirsch. At the peak of immigration, Argentina was home to the fifth-largest Jewish population in the world. While Mexico and Brazil do not have Jewish populations as large as Argentina, both have significant numbers of Jewish authors who have reached national and international standing. It is the literature of these three countries that has received the lion's share of attention. However, authors from Uruguay, Chile, Colombia, Venezuela, and to a lesser extent Peru, Paraguay, Cuba, and Costa Rica also have made substantial contributions to Jewish-Latin American literature.

FOUNDATIONAL NOVELS

The earliest example of Jewish narrative in the Americas was penned by Luis Rodríguez de Carvajal, more commonly known as Luis de Carvajal, el Mozo (1567–1596). The story of Carvajal is well documented in the archives of the Spanish Inquisition in Mexico and preserved and recounted by multiple historians. He was placed on trial on two occasions for Judaizing, and on December 8, 1596, he was burned at the stake in an *auto-da-fé* along with his mother and three of his sisters. Prior to his death he had changed his name to José/Iosef Lumbroso as a testament to his enlightenment and return to Judaism. While he left a number of writings, his most famous is the testimonial and autobiographical text titled simply *Vida* (Life), which was written between 1592 and the time of his death.

It is not until the nineteenth century that there emerges a specifically Jewish novel: the romantic foundational fiction *María* (1867) by Jorge Isaacs (1837–1895). Many critics may question the Jewish identity of Isaacs, the extent to which he identified as a Jew, or, for that matter, the "Jewishness" of the novel beyond its symbolic function. Doris Sommer has been instrumental in analyzing Jewishness as the central "problem" in *María*, which was banned by the Vatican in 1905, presumably because it was about a Jewess (Sommer 270). Sommer likewise has unequivocally demonstrated that "As the son of a converso, Isaacs would gradually assume and then embrace his Jewish identity, almost as a rebellious response to those who called him Jew as an intended offense" (269). While Sommer has been the most outspoken critic to address the "Jewish" elements in *María*, she is by no means the only one. Naomi Lindstrom has traced the history of critical inquiry as regards the Jewish identity of Isaacs and Jewishness in his novel in detail (Lindstrom "Shifting Critical Approaches"). *María* is not only a foundational fiction within the Latin American nineteenth-century narrative project of nation building, but it is a cornerstone of Jewish narrative as well.

Notwithstanding these early examples, the Jewish-Latin American novel did not begin to emerge as an identifiable narrative corpus until the early twentieth century. There can be little doubt that the genesis of the Jewish novel in Latin America is Alberto Gerchunoff's (1884–1950) *Los gauchos judíos* (*The Jewish Gauchos of the Pampas*, 1910). Born in Russia, Gerchunoff arrived in Argentina as a boy in 1890, where the family settled in Moisés Ville (province of Santa Fe), the most famous and iconic of the agricultural colonies established by the Jewish Colonization Association (hereafter, JCA). Following the murder of his father by a gaucho, his family moved to the colony of Rajil in Entre Ríos, and finally to Buenos Aires in 1895. His early experiences in the agricultural colonies would become the subject of his most enduring text. In 1908 Roberto Payró sponsored his entry to the journalistic staff of *La Nación*, where he had a long and productive career and where he became integrated into the inner circles of *Porteño* intelligentsia. It was also in 1908 that he published his first narrative vignettes about Jewish life in the agricultural colonies in the pages of *La Nación*. In 1910, Leopoldo Lugones (1874–1938) commissioned Gerchunoff to write a text that would be incorporated as part of the literary commemorations of the Argentine centennial. Thus was born the 1910 version of *Los gauchos judíos*, which is not *stricto sensu* a novel, but a series of loosely connected episodic stories that narrate different aspects of life in Moisés Ville. The definitive version of *Los gauchos judíos* was published in 1936 and contains two additional chapters as well as substantial revisions. For some, the early version of *Los gauchos judíos* was too eagerly assimilationist and painted an exaggeratedly idyllic view of Jewish life on the pampas in which Gerchunoff imagined Argentina as a New Zion and a "promised land" for Jews escaping persecution. However, one may also view Gerchunoff's appropriation of the gaucho—the most ideologically charged symbol of the nation—as a clever, and even daring, way of advancing the cause of Jewish integration at an opportune point in history. *Los gauchos judíos* was first published in English translation in 1955 (above title), but it is Aizenberg's translation that should be considered the definitive English version, as she worked with both original versions in her rendering of Gerchunoff's classic tale (*The Jewish Gauchos* in her *Parricide on the Pampa*). Notwithstanding the varying ideological positions that have been taken up by critics and subsequent authors alike, *Los gauchos judíos* has stood the test of time as a foundational text in Jewish-Latin American letters, as well a classic text of Argentine literature.

Another representative of the group of pioneer authors is Mordejai (Marcos) Alperson (1860–1947), who is commonly known as the dean of Yiddish literature in Argentina. He was born in Russia in 1860, emigrated to Argentina in 1891 and settled in Colonia Mauricio in the province of Buenos Aires, where he remained for forty-three years. In contrast to Gerchunoff, he was an outspoken critic of the JCA and often wrote scathing accounts of its disorganization, corruption, and general failings. He authored numerous volumes of memoirs, plays, and short stories, in addition to the novels *Af Argentiner Erd* (In the Land of Argentina, 1931) and *Der Lindzshero* (1937). The latter has been translated into Spanish as *El linyera* (2012). The title is taken from the Argentine *lunfardo* (slang) term that refers to an itinerant worker or drifter who takes on odd jobs and is indicative of the way in which Yiddish writers incorporated Argentine words into their vocabularies. *El linyera*, a *costumbrista* novel, is an excellent example of *criollismo ídish* (Yiddish Creolism) that provides detailed portrayals of daily life in the farming communities of the JCA and of the colonists' efforts to engage in Jewish life in a new geographical and social environment.

The majority of agricultural colonies established by the JCA were located in Argentina. However, the project also extended to Brazil, primarily in the southern state of Rio Grande do Sul. A key novel from this region is *Numa clara manhã de abril* (*On a Clear April Morning*) by Marcos Iolovitch. Originally published in 1940, a second edition appeared in 1987 with an enthusiastic preface by Moacyr Scliar, who acknowledges his debt to Iolovitch, calling *Numa clara manhã de abril* an "inspirational book" (*On a Clear April Morning* xiv). It is an autobiographical novel that traces the protagonist's path from Russia to settle on the agricultural colony of Quatro Irmãos. Like many such works, it is critical of the JCA. The family left the colony for Porto Alegre, where their economic situation did not improve by much. Iolovitch describes in detail the poverty and hardship endured as an immigrant.

The circumstances of Jewish colonization in Argentina and Brazil naturally meant that early literary manifestations reflected the rural beginnings of immigrant Jews. However, Jewish literature soon became a primarily urban expression, when the second generation of Latin American-born Jews began to migrate to major cities. In countries such as Uruguay, Chile, and Mexico, where Jewish immigration did not go through the rural to urban population shift, early novels are from the beginning set in urban spaces. This is the case of the novels by Efraín Szmulewicz (1911–1991), who emigrated from Poland to Chile as a young man in the early 1930s. He quickly became active in Chilean literary circles as a writer and literary critic. He also served as a cultural attaché with the Chilean embassy in Argentina. Szmulewicz published a collection of short stories in 1937, but his first novel, *Un niño nació judío* (*A Boy Was Born a Jew*), was published in 1940 with a prologue by the Peruvian author Ciro Alegría (1909–1967). It is an autobiographical *bildungsroman* that narrates, in two stages, the life of Josef Grinberg, a young Polish Jew: his boyhood and his entrance into manhood after his bar mitzvah at the age of thirteen until the time that he leaves Poland to start a new life in a new country. The novel describes how the boy is cognizant from a very early age that having been born a Jew will forever mark his life. The ever-present threat of antisemitism looms large over the young boy. The psychological development of Grinberg traces his gradual shift from religiosity to secular political activism. Josef Grinberg's story continues in the second novel, *El hombre busca la tristeza* (*Man Searches for Sadness*, 1950), with the character struggling to make a new life for himself in Chile. At the same time that the plot follows the progress of Grinberg as an immigrant (he establishes a bookstore, gains his independence and a sense of belonging in Chile), it also describes the changing sociopolitical and cultural climate of Chile over the course of time. While he manages to derive satisfaction as a new Chilean citizen, Grinberg is tormented by the Nazi invasion of Poland, the events in Europe, and the certain loss of his family that remained behind.

The difficulties associated with assimilation coupled with the psychological development of the young character, Pablo Levinson, are also central to Bernardo Verbitsky's first novel *Es difícil empezar a vivir* (It's Hard to Start Living, 1941). Levinson struggles over the course of the lengthy novel with both his integration into Argentine society and his participation in Jewish life and culture. Verbitsky masterfully interweaves these two narrative tensions into a novel that integrates Jewish concerns into a larger social picture by means of juxtaposing symmetrical narrative constructions that alternately address Jewish issues and social concerns affecting Argentine society at large. As Naomi Lindstrom states, "These parallel constructions make the point that Jewish issues are, in many cases, aspects of difficulties affecting the entire social structure" (*Jewish Issues* 80). Indeed, what Verbitsky achieves in this first novel will become a guiding principle throughout his career as a writer. His work, especially his early novels, are models of the social realism that prevailed in Argentine narrative in the 1930s and 1940s. One cannot overestimate Verbitsky's place and influence in the literary landscape of mid-twentieth-century Argentina. In his analysis of Verbitsky's extensive 1947 novel *En esos años* (In Those Years), David William Foster elucidates just how the author creates a vast narrative mosaic that presents Argentina's preoccupation with the war through different discursive techniques and across a spectrum of Argentine society, one component of which, naturally, is the Jewish response to and concern with the events that ravaged Europe and the effects of such as felt at home. Verbitsky wrote over a dozen novels, the majority of which do not have any specific thematic ties to Jewish identity other than to incorporate Jews—overtly or by default—into his overall portrayal of Argentine, middle-class social reality. Certainly, one of his most successful, in that it reached readers across Latin America and not just in Argentina, is his *Villa miseria también es América* (The Slum Too Is America, 1957). While the setting is a large slum and revolves around the social conditions and lives of its inhabitants, it is clearly directed to the sector of society that ignores the existence of such marginal spaces and citizens or shows little concern for the lives of the poor. If *Villa miseria* speaks in overarching terms about poverty within society, Verbitsky's last novel, *Hermana y sombra* (Sister and Shadow, 1977), brings the topic to a very personal level in this his most autobiographical novel. The title is taken from the protagonist's mother in the novel, who describes their penury as always being accompanied by Sister Poverty, who, like a shadow, follows them and is part of the family (19–20). In *Hermana y sombra* Verbitsky describes the poverty in which he was raised, the struggles of his immigrant parents to eke out a living, and the insistence on providing their children with an education and upbringing steeped in culture, despite the privations they endured and defined by the competing forces of tradition (Judaism) and progress (assimilation).

Much of the novelistic enterprise of Jewish authors entails defining, questioning, and interpreting the hybrid nature of Jewish-Latin American identity. A useful trope in this regard has been the concept of *mestizaje*, which has been traditionally understood as the racial enmeshing of Spanish and indigenous ethnicities and cultures to create a separate and unique identity. In the Jewish-Latin American imaginary, this notion was first taken up by the Argentine poet Carlos Grünberg (1903–1968) in an effort to establish compatibility between both aspects of his identity. His poem "Mestizo," from the poetry collection *Mester de judería* (Minstrelsy of the Jews, 1940) comingles Jewish and Argentine references to create a single, new identity such that "Grünberg's conceptualization of the Jewish Argentine *mestizo* subverts a familiar term in Latin American culture in order to introduce the Jewish component if a less threatening manner" (Lockhart, "Grünberg" 245). Novelist Ricardo Feierstein (1942–) more extensively develops this ideological posture in his novel *Mestizo* (*Mestizo: A Novel*, 1988), which was reissued in a revised and expanded edition in 1994. The complex novel is ostensibly structured around a family mystery that the protagonist, Julio Schnaiderman, attempts to unravel. In doing so he peels back several generations of family history and questions national history at the same time. In the end, the Jewish-Argentine amalgamation results in a new type of *mestizo*.

Moacyr Scliar (1937–2011), a physician and undeniably the most prolific and well-known Jewish author from Brazil, creates a different type of *mestizo* in one of his most iconic novels, *O centauro no jardim* (*The Centaur in the Garden*, 1980). The main character, Guedali Tartakovsky, is a centaur born to Russian immigrants in Brazil who clearly stands as an allegory for the dual identity of Jewish-Brazilians. Guedali ultimately undergoes a surgery that transforms him wholly into a man. As much as he tries to hide his true identity, however, he must come to terms with his dual nature. There is perhaps no other Jewish-Latin American author who so programmatically incorporated Jewish identity and issues into his work (mostly novels and short stories), beginning with his first novel, *A guerra no Bom Fim* (*The War in Bom Fim*, 1972), and continuing on in such varied and original texts as *O ciclo das águas* (The Cycle of Water, 1976), *Cenas da vida minúscula* (Scenes of a Miniscule Life, 1991), and *A mulher que escreveu a Bíblia* (The Woman Who Wrote the Bible, 1999). Fellow writer Clarice Lispector became one of the most widely read and translated Brazilian authors of the twentieth century. Indeed, she may be considered one of, if not the, most influential and important Latin American women writers of the past century. However, there are only scant, mostly inferred references, to Jewishness in her writing. Critics point to the Jewish sensibility and worldview that permeate her literature, even while overt themes and topics may not (cf. Vieira; Lindstrom "Judaic Traces").

Isaac Goldemberg (1945–) is the literal embodiment of the *mestizaje* that Feierstein and Scliar fictionalize. He was born in Chepén, Peru, and raised by his Catholic mother until the age of eight, when he went to live with his Jewish father in Lima. A prolific poet and novelist, Goldemberg has lived in New York City since the mid-1960s where, in addition to writing, he holds an academic position. As a novelist he is known principally for *La vida a plazos de don Jacobo Lerner* (*The Fragmented Life of Don Jacobo Lerner*, 1978) and *Tiempo al tiempo* (*Play by Play*, 1984), both of which contain significant autobiographical material—the latter more closely follows Goldemberg's own life. In 2001, *The Fragmented Life* was named one of the one hundred most important works of global Jewish literature of the past 150 years. Curiously, the English version of this novel was published two years prior to its Spanish-language release in Lima. In 2001, Goldemberg published a much revised and expanded (almost doubling the original) version of *La vida a plazos* titled *En el nombre del padre* (In the Name of the Father). Both Goldemberg and his work are emblematic of Jewish-Latin American subjectivity.

The foregoing examples are meant to provide a basis for some of the primary themes, concerns, and authors from which later Jewish-Latin American novels emerge. By the 1970s and 1980s, Jewish-Latin American literature was becoming an identifiable socio-literary phenomenon and from the 1990s to the present, it has burgeoned into a vibrantly abundant body of work that expands across the Latin American continent. The novel has occupied a key position in the overall production of Jewish-Latin American writing. The remainder of this essay focuses on concentrated thematic clusters into which the Jewish-Latin American novel can be loosely grouped, not without significant overlapping in many cases.

REVISITING THE AGRICULTURAL PIONEER LEGACY

Returning to origins and rewriting the consecrated versions of the Jewish-Argentine past (such as *Los gauchos judíos*) is a project elaborated by several contemporary novelists. An early example is José Chudnovksy's (1915–1966) novel *Pueblo pan* (People of Bread, 1967), which carries an encomiastic prologue by Nobel laureate Miguel Angel Asturias (1899–1974). Unlike *Los gauchos judíos*, *Pueblo pan* contains a far more veracious account of life in an agricultural colony with its many hardships. While Chudnovksy is critical of the JCA he simultaneously values its role as a vehicle for Jewish progress. What he has in common with Gerchunoff is an ideological adherence to the ideals of the eighteenth-century intellectual Jewish enlightenment movement known as Haskalah and its emphasis on renewal through a physical and spiritual connection to the land.

One of the first and most parricidal (in the words of Edna Aizenberg, *Parricide on the Pampa*) instances of such a project can be found in the novels of Mario Szichman (1945–), who undertakes a four-volume caustic reexamination of the Argentine-Jewish past and present through his novelized saga of the Pechof clan that includes *Crónica falsa* (False Chronicle, 1969), *Los judíos del Mar Dulce* (The Jews of the Fresh-Water Sea, 1971), *La verdadera crónica falsa* (The True False Chronicle, 1972), and his culminating masterpiece *A las 20:25 la señora entró en la inmortalidad* (At 8:25 Evita Became Immortal, 1981). All the novels are based on the premise that official versions of history must be challenged and accepted norms questioned, particularly in the context of Jewish-Argentine history, which encapsulates the hard lessons learned by four generations of Pechofs. Less confrontational is Mario Gerardo Goloboff's (1939–) retelling of the agricultural experiments in his tetralogy comprised of *Criador de palomas* (The Pigeon Fancier, 1984), *La luna que cae* (The Setting Moon, 1989), *El soñador de Smith* (The Dreamer of Smith, 1990), and *Comuna verdad* (Truth Commune, 1995), published in English translation in a single volume under the title *The Algarrobos Quartet* (2002). The novels, which are highly lyrical in style, not only return the reader to the past of the Jewish colonies, but they also overtly deal with the repression of the 1976–1983 military dictatorship, particularly *Criador de palomas*. In a similar vein, Perla Suez's (1947–) trilogy of novels (*Letargo* [Lethargy, 2000], *El arresto* [The Arrest, 2001], *Complot* [Conspiracy, 2004]) recounts the protagonist's return to the Jewish colonies of Entre Ríos to explore her roots. These were also published collectively in English translation as *The Entre Ríos Trilogy* (2006). A curious connection to Gerchunoff's *Los gauchos judíos* can be found in Colombian Azriel Bibliowicz's (1949–) first novel, *El rumor del astracán* (The Rustle of Astrakhan, 1991), which narrates the Jewish immigrant experience in Bogotá in the 1930s. The intertextuality with *Los gauchos judíos* is found in the appearance of a character named Moisés Gerchunoff, an agricultural pioneer who settled in the colony of Moisés Ville, Argentina. He tells his Colombian counterparts tales of the Jewish gauchos on the Argentine pampas and the story of Baron Maurice de Hirsch. Through the character of Gerchunoff, Bibliowicz provides an overview of the Jewish presence in Colombia and Latin America.

The Historical Novel

The narration of history in a broader sense finds expression in a number of extraordinary novels that seek to vindicate Jews as integral to the historical development of Latin America and to legitimize their presence as a fundamental component of Latin American reality. This is achieved by creating narratives that hearken back to the colonial period, whether based on actual historical figures or fictional ones. The most strictly historical of these is *La gesta del marrano* (*Against the Inquisition*, 1991) by Argentine Marcos Aguinis (1935), which relates the real-life trials and tribulations of Francisco Maldonado da Silva, the sixteenth-century Jewish-Portuguese physician, and his son Diego Núñez da Silva. Other novels in this category take much more poetic license in their retelling of the Jewish past in Latin America. These would include Pedro Orgambide's (1929–2003) picaresque novelization of the figure of the wandering Jew in *Aventuras de Edmund Ziller en tierras del Nuevo Mundo* (Adventures of Edmund Ziller in the Lands of the New World, 1977); Moacyr Scliar's magical realist *A estranha nação de Rafael Mendes* (*The Strange Nation of Rafael Mendes*, 1983); and *Identidad* (Identity, 1980) by Argentine Antonio Elio Brailovsky (1946–), which blends past and present in narrating the story of a group of crypto-Jews who set sail for the New World in search of religious freedom. The novel was reissued with the title *Isaac Halevy, rey de los judíos* (Isaac Halevy, King of the Jews, 1997).

Venezuelan Alicia Freilich Segal's (1939–) clever *Colombina descubierta* (1991, Colombina Discovered) stands out as a novel published on the eve of the quincentennial of the encounter and inverts the story of Columbus by making him a woman, thus altering history by regendering it. Edna Aizenberg states: "Freilich constructs a restless text that combines the device of the lost manuscript with fragments of Columbian discourse, and the figure of the wise madwoman with elements of kabbalistic symbolism" (*Books and Bombs* 87). Mexican author Angelina Muñiz-Huberman (1936–)

has endeavored to rewrite the historic Luso- and Hispanic-Jewish past, mostly by fo-cusing on novelized life stories of individuals in such novels as *Morada interior* (Interior Dwelling, 1972), based on the life of Santa Teresa de Jesús, of *converso* background; *El mercader de Tudela* (The Merchant of Tudela, 1998), based on the life of the famous medieval Jewish traveler Benjamín de Tudela; *La burladora de Toledo* (The Seductress of Toledo, 2008), based on the sixteenth-century figure of Elena de Céspedes; and, most recently, in her novel about swashbuckling Jewish pirates *Los esperandos: piratas judeoportugueses. . . y yo* (The Esperandos: Judeo-Portuguese Pirates. . . and Me, 2017).

AUTO/BIOGRAPHY AND FAMILY HISTORIES

A common trend is the chronicling of family histories and auto/biographical narratives, which at first glance may read as personal stories but also serve to relate and preserve col-lective memory. A complete inventory is beyond the scope of the present account, but a brief register of essential texts would begin with Alicia Steimberg's (1933–2012) first novel *Músicos y relojeros* (*Musicians and Watchmakers*, 1971) and its continuation *Su espíritu inocente* (Her Innocent Spirit, 1981) that launched her career as one of the first Jewish women authors in Argentina to gain prominence as a writer. One of her later, and most critically acclaimed novels (recipient of the prestigious Planeta prize for novel) is the ex-perimental *Cuando digo Magdalena* (*Call me Magdalena*, 1992). *Cuando digo* reconnects with the above-mentioned two through the now adult narrator who continues her story under much different circumstances. Also from Argentina are the family histories *El libro de los recuerdos* (*The Book of Memories*, 1994) by Ana María Shua (1951), which recounts the history of her family in Argentina across three generations, and Manuela Fingueret's (1945–2013) endearing coming-of-age novel *Blues de la calle Leiva* (Leiva Street Blues, 1995). Mexican author Margo Glantz, the daughter of the renowned Yiddish poet Jacobo Glantz, is a major literary author and critic in Mexico. Among her many works, the one that most centers on Jewish identity is her 1981 auto/biographical *Las genealogías* (*The Family Tree*), in which she narrates many family anecdotes centered primarily on her father's deep involvement in the cultural and artistic environment of Mexico City. The text focuses on the process of acculturation and integration experi-enced by Jews in Mexico City between roughly 1920 and 1950. It is best characterized as a pseudo-novel for the way that it blends memoir, narration, extraliterary artefacts, and family photographs that lend a quality of documentary authenticity.

Sabina Berman (1954–), known primarily as a foremost contemporary dramatist in Mexico, is the author of *La bobe* (Bubbeh [Yiddish for grandmother], 1990). The novel is narrated by a young Mexican-Jewish girl who tells the story of her relationship with her grandmother, a Viennese aristocratic Jew who emigrated to Mexico. The novel is a lyrical evocation of Jewish identity from a specifically feminine perspective. Along the same lines, Marjorie Agosín's (1955) *Sagrada memoria: reminiscencias de una niña judía en Chile* (1994) offers an intimate look at the author's youth in her native Chile.

The book was translated into English as *A Cross and a Star: Memoirs of a Jewish Girl in Chile* (1995), and like Glantz's text, the English version contains a number of family photos. The novels in Susana Gertopan's family-saga trilogy, *Barrio Palestina* (Palestine Neighborhood, 1998), *El nombre prestado* (The Borrowed Name, 2000), and *El retorno de Eva* (Eve's Return, 2003), are noteworthy for being essentially the only novels that relate the Jewish-Paraguayan experience. Gertopan has since written nearly a dozen novels, the latest being *Todo pasó en septiembre* (It All Happened in September, 2019), which recounts the lives of three generations of Jewish women.

Autobiographical narratives by men include Argentine author Daniel Guebel's (1956–) confessional *El hijo judío* (The Jewish Son, 2018), and two novels by Jacobo Sefamí (1957–), whose roots are in the Mexican Shami community (Jews originating from Damascus), *Los dolientes* (Mourning for Papá, 2004) and *Por tierras extrañas* (Through Strange Lands, 2019). The former is an evocation of his father upon the occasion of his passing. The latter narrates his journey to his family's ancestral homelands of Turkey and Syria; *Bosque quemado* (Burned Forest, 2007) by Chilean Roberto Brodsky (1957–), which is as much a biography of his father as it is an autobiography of the narrator son (Brodsky himself); and finally, from Mexican Gerardo Kleinburg (1964) is *No honrarás a tu padre* (Thou Shalt Not Honor Thy Father, 2004), the plot of which centers on Alejandro Roth's reckoning with his own identity as the son of a Jewish father and his Catholic mistress. He declares from the beginning that he "self-identifies as a Jew, but it is his struggle for legitimacy within the Jewish community that marginalizes him as an outsider" (Lockhart, "Jewish (Men)ority Literature in Mexico" 259).

THE SEPHARDIC NOVEL

Novels by Sephardic authors are outnumbered by the Ashkenazic majority, though certainly there are important contributions. One of the foremost is Venezuelan Isaac Chocrón, whose many dramatic texts and novels incorporate Sephardic identity to one degree or another. He will be mentioned in the context of a different category below. Angelina Muñiz-Huberman has made a career of writing about Sephardim, both as a novelist and as an academic anthologist. In addition to her previously mentioned novels, is her memoir *El juego de escribir* (The Game of Writing, 1991), in which she details learning of her own Sephardic identity, a "secret" revealed to her by her mother— her parents were exiles of the Spanish Civil War. Another example is her novel *El sefardí romántico: la azarosa vida de Mateo Alemán II* (The Romantic Sephardi: The Ill-fated Life of Mateo Alemán II, 2005).

The Mexican writer Rosa Nissán (1939–) came to writing later in life upon completing a literary workshop with Elena Poniatowska. Her first novel, *Novia que te vea* (1992) was a major success in Mexico and was followed by a sequel *Hisho que te nazca* (1996). Both novels were published in English translation in a single volume titled *Like a Bride. Like a Mother* (2002). The film *Novia que te vea*, directed by Guita Schyfter, was released in

1994 to much acclaim. The novels tell the story of the young protagonist, Oshinica, as she navigates life torn between the strict traditions of her Sephardic family and the pull of mid-twentieth-century secular Mexican society. They also compare and contrast the Sephardic and Ashkenazic communities in Mexico City through her relationship with her best friend Rifka. *Novia* and *Hisho* were the first to incorporate significant portions of dialogue in Ladino. Unfortunately, in the English versions Ladino is entirely lost in the translation. In 2019, Nissán published the continuation of Oshinica Matarraso's story with the novel *Me viene un modo de tristeza* (Sadness Overcomes Me). Myriam Moscona (1955–), also from Mexico, is an accomplished poet who in 2012 published her first novel, *Tela de sevoya,* which has garnered much acclaim and has been translated into English as *Onioncloth* (2017). Like Nissan's novels, *Tela de sevoya* is also autobiographical. Structured in alternating discursive segments, the novel recounts Moscona's journey to Bulgaria to explore her family history and roots. *A chave de casa* (The House Key, 2007) by Brazilian Tatiana Salem Levy (1979–) can be added to this list as a novel that presents the protagonist's search for the Sephardic past.

THE HOLOCAUST NOVEL

As might be expected, the Holocaust had a profound impact on Latin America. Both first- and second-generation survivors of the Shoah, as well as other authors, have written novels that address the horrors perpetrated by the Nazi regime. Ana Benkel de Vinocur (1926–2006) was born in Poland and made her home in Uruguay following the liberation of Auschwitz. She is the author of the testimonial novel *Un libro sin título* (*A Book without a Title,* 1972), in which she narrates her experience in the infamous death camp. It stands as one of only a handful of first-person novelistic accounts written by Latin American Holocaust survivors.

José Rabinovich (1903–1978), who first began writing in Yiddish before transitioning into Spanish, became, much like Bernardo Verbitsky, a major figure in Jewish-Argentine literature. A prolific poet as well as a narrator, he is the author of two novels that deal more tangentially with the Holocaust. *El perro de Maidanek* (The Dog of Majdanek, 1968) is an allegorical narrative that equates Nazi brutality with canine ferocity. The second novel, *Campanas a media asta* (Bells at Half-mast, 1969) underscores the rift between Christians and Jews in the immediate post-Holocaust era. The plot revolves around a group of Holocaust survivors who are living in a village where a large church is planned to be built. The construction of the church brings to the fore fears of continued persecution. Neither novel has any Latin American content, but both are indicative of the author's desire to write about the psychological impact of the Shoah and are in keeping with his overall narrative worldview.

By contrast, Sergio Chejfec's (1956–) first novel, *Lenta biografía* (Slow Biography, 1990) brings the Holocaust directly to Argentina as the narrator son attempts to literally translate his survivor father's autobiography that was written in Yiddish, thus revealing not only the father's past but also revelations about his own present. In her analysis of the novel, Edna Aizenberg astutely concludes: "*Lenta biografía* brings together Judaism, Latin Americanness, and postcolonialism through shared ruptures and common hopes" (*Books and Bombs* 47). Two books by Brazilian authors address the Holocaust from an intergenerational perspective. Michel Laub's (1973–) *Diario da queda* (*Diary of the Fall*, 2011) weaves together the intersecting stories of a grandfather (a Holocaust survivor), father, and son, which constitute a profound meditation on Jewish identity, ethics, and memory. Likewise, Noemi Jaffe's (1962–) *O que os cegos estão sonhando?* (*What Are the Blind Men Dreaming?*, 2012) follows three generations of women in the same family who cope with the legacy of the horror of Auschwitz. Marco Schwartz (1956–) and Azriel Bibliowicz, both from Colombia, have written innovative novels that approach the topic of the Holocaust in distinctive ways. Schwartz's *El salmo de Kaplan* (*Kaplan's Psalm*, 2005) received the first prize for novel from the Norma publishing conglomerate. It is an entertaining story of a somewhat hapless would-be Nazi hunter who is convinced he is on the trail of the leader of a Nazi resurgence movement in a small town on the Caribbean coast. The novel was made into a film by Uruguayan director Álvaro Brechner as *Mr. Kaplan* (2014), with a change in locale to the Uruguayan coast. Azriel Bibliowicz's second novel, *Migas de pan* (Bread Crumbs, 2013), presents the kidnapping of Holocaust survivor Josué in Colombia and his family's desperate attempts to gain his freedom. Through the development of the plot, the author makes important connections between the violence of the Holocaust and that of the ongoing Colombian conflict.

A similar, and more direct comparison between the Holocaust and the Argentine military dictatorship can be found in Manuela Fingueret's novel *Hija del silencio* (*Daughter of Silence*, 1999). The novel narrates parallel tales of a mother and daughter who endure imprisonment and torture. The mother is a Holocaust survivor who was in both Terezin and Auschwitz before finding refuge in Argentina, and the daughter is a prisoner in a clandestine military detention center. It is only through her own confinement and mistreatment that the daughter finally comes to understand her mother's silence and distance. Comparably, the novel *Las cartas que no llegaron* (*The Letters that Never Came*, 2000) by Mauricio Rosencof juxtaposes the Holocaust and the Uruguayan military dictatorship through the stories of father and son.

THE GAY AND LESBIAN NOVEL

Gay and lesbian writing in Latin America is by now a thoroughly documented and inventoried body of literature. However, the contribution of Jewish-Latin American authors to such literature is only now becoming apparent, as an identifiable number of works have emerged. The first manifestation of a queer-Jewish novelistic enterprise is in the writing of Isaac Chocrón. Indeed, his 1972 novel *Pájaro de mar por tierra* (Landlocked Seagull) is a foundational work of Latin American gay literature. While this novel does not directly or in any meaningful way incorporate Jewish identity into the story, such is not the case in Chocrón's epistolary novel *Rómpase en caso de incendio* (Break Glass in Case of Fire, 1975), wherein the author overtly conjugates Sephardic and queer identities (a reflection of Chocrón himself). Sara Levi Calderón (pseudonym of Silvia Feldman 1942–) has the distinction of having written the second lesbian novel in Mexico, *Dos mujeres* (*The Two Mujeres*, 1990). In this autobiographical narrative, the author confronts the patriarchal constraints of Judaism in her effort to live a liberated life as a lesbian. Twenty-five years later, Levi Calderón published the tell-all sequel *Vida y peripecias de una buena hija de familia* (The Life and Travails of a Good Family Daughter, 2015). Cíntia Moscovich (1958–) penned the first Jewish-Brazilian lesbian novel with her *Duas iguais* (Two of the Same, 1998), which was published in Spanish translation as *Dos iguales* (2007) in the famous erotic literature series La Sonrisa Vertical of the Barcelona publishing house Tusquets. She has since become one of the major Jewish female voices in Brazil with several collections of short stories and another novel, *Por que sou gorda, mamãe?* (Mom, Why Am I Fat?, 2006).

Finally, the most comprehensive treatment of homosexuality as it relates to Judaism is *Uma leve simetría* (A Slight Symmetry, 2009) by Brazilian Rafael Bán Jacobsen (1981–). It is a coming-of-age love story between two adolescents in the hermetic Jewish neighborhood of Bom Fim in Porto Alegre, Brazil, made famous by the city's most renowned author, Moacyr Scliar. The story of Daniel and Pedro runs parallel to the retelling of the Jonathan and David biblical narrative. At the heart of the novel is the injunction from Leviticus 18:22, which prohibits a man to lie down with another as with a woman, thus establishing the crisis of the main character and narrator Daniel as he comes to terms with his love for his friend Pedro and struggles with his inner turmoil that pits his erotic desire against the Law.

OTHER AUTHORS AND NEW DIRECTIONS

There are a number of authors whose works are not easily categorized in any of the above groupings, but who have made important contributions to establishing the Jewish-Latin American novel as a viable narrative project. In Argentina these would include some well-established writers like Silvia Plager (1942–), Marcelo Birmajer (1966–), and María Inés Krímer (1951–). Plager is a prolific novelist whose works are generally on topics that captivate the reading public's imagination, Jewish and non-Jewish alike. Her 1994 *Como papas para varenikes* (Like Potatoes for Pierogi) is an ingenious parody of Laura Esquivel's (1950–) *Como agua para chocolate* (*Like Water for Chocolate*, 1989) set in contemporary Buenos Aires. It narrates the adventures and love life of Catalina Goldsmith, a middle-aged woman with a catering business, with a great deal of humor, eroticism, and, of course, Jewish recipes that unleash mayhem and hidden delights on those who partake of them. The novel has been a major success with multiple reprintings. The original was revised and reprinted in a new version with additions to the story in

2004. Equally successful, but with a much more serious tone is the novel *La rabina* (The Woman Rabbi, 2006), which narrates the process that protagonist Esther Fainberg goes through to become a rabbi. The novel takes place in Argentina, New York, and Israel. Plager's latest novel, *Pequeña Viena en Shanghái: la vida de una familia austríaca en el gueto judío de Hongkou* (Little Vienna in Shanghai: The Life of an Austrian Family in the Jewish Ghetto of Hongku, 2019) presents the little-known story of the Jewish community in China.

Marcelo Birmajer is principally known for his many volumes of short stories, though he has also written several noteworthy novels. *Tres mosqueteros* (*Three Musketeers*, 2001) directly links Argentine-Jewish identity to the period of the military dictatorship, while it also explores Jewishness on a global scale and the relationship that (many) Argentine Jews have with Israel. His novels are consistently inhabited by Jewish characters who become involved in all manner of intrigue as in the mystery/thriller novels *Las nieves del tiempo* (The Snows of Time, 2014) and *El rescate del Mesías* (The Rescue of the Messiah, 2018). María Inés Krimer introduces the reader to the first Jewish-Latin American female detective, Ruth Epelbaum, in her series of novels *Sangre kosher* (Kosher Blood, 2010), *Siliconas express* (Silicone Implants Express, 2013), and *Sangre fashion* (Haut Couture Blood, 2015). The novels are written in the best style of the Argentine *novela negra* (hard-boiled detective novel). One cannot overlook the work of Esther Seligson (1941–2010), one of the most productive and complex of Jewish-Mexican authors, especially her *La morada en el tiempo* (The Dwelling in Time, 1981). The novel is in a certain sense an attempt to rewrite the Torah, or at least engage with it as a master narrative that informs its structure, style, and tone. Seligson syncretizes Jewish and Mexican realities into one of the most outstanding and enduring novels in Mexican literature.

A key author from Uruguay is Teresa Porzecanski (1945) who, in addition to being a novelist and short-story writer, is trained as an anthropologist with significant publications in that field. Among her several novels are the early postmodern works *La invención de los soles* (1979) and *Mesías en Montevideo* (1989). These fragmented narratives are grounded in the identity and experience of their Jewish-Uruguayan characters, yet at the same time, they question national and global sociopolitical processes and challenge the patriarchal order that drives them. The novel *Perfumes de Cartago* (1994) narrates the Jewish experience in Montevideo in the 1930s, primarily from the perspective of Syrian-Jewish immigrants, while *La piel del alma* (1996) moves back and forth between the Uruguay of the 1950s and the convulsive history of Jews in fifteenth-century Spain.

In Brazil there is whole new generation of writers who are establishing themselves as the successors to such Jewish-Brazilian literary giants as Clarice Lispector, Moacyr Scliar, and Samuel Rawet (1929–1984). In addition to the previously mentioned Michel Laub, Noemi Jaffe, and Rafael Bán Jacobsen, this generation includes Julián Fuks (1981–), born in Brazil to Argentine exiles, with his novel *A resistência* (The Resistance, 2015); Flávio Izhaki (1979–), *Amanhã não tem ninguém* (Tomorrow Has No One, 2013); and Ronaldo Wrobel's (1968–) historical novel *Traduzindo Hannah* (Translating Hannah, 2010), which takes place in 1930s Rio de Janeiro during the Vargas regime. In the novel, filled with intrigue and suspense, the main character finds himself in a difficult position as a translator of Yiddish.

A writer who has made a sudden and productive impact is the Guatemalan-born Eduardo Halfon (1971–). His works include *El boxeador polaco*, which first appeared in 2008 and was later published in a revised and expanded edition in 2019 and in English translation as *The Polish Boxer*. It can be read as a novel or as a series on interconnected tales. The narrator's grandfather was a Holocaust survivor, who while mentioned in the text a few times really only participates in the chapter "El boxeador polaco," in which his story is told. The narrative thread of *El boxeador polaco* continues in *Monasterio* (*Monastery*, 2014) and *Signor Hoffman* (Mr. Hoffman, 2015).

There is little doubt that the Jewish-Latin American novel will continue to flourish in the twenty-first century, building on the strong foundation that has already been firmly established. Jewish-Latin American novelists have much to offer as they write about their intersecting identities. They will continue to challenge dominant modes of expression and simultaneously open new avenues of inquiry as they explore their roles within the diverse countries of Latin America. Furthermore, they will surely continue to turn their novelistic gaze inward to question established assumptions about what it means to be Jewish-Latin American.

Works Cited

Alperson, Mordejai. *Af Argentiner Erd*. G. Kaplansky, 1931.

Alperson, Mordejai. *Der Lindzshero*. Editorial Kaplansky, 1937.

Alperson, Mordejai. *El linyera*. Translated by Ethel Gater. Shalom Buenos Aires, 2012.

Agosín, Marjorie. *Sagrada memoria: reminiscencias de una niña judía en Chile*. Cuarto Propio, 1994. English version as *A Cross and a Star: Memoirs of a Jewish Girl in Chile*. Translated by Celeste Kostopulos-Cooperman. U of New Mexico P, 1995.

Aguinis, Marcos. *La gesta del marrano*. Planeta, 1991. English version as *Against the Inquisition*. Translated by Carolina de Robertis. Amazon Crossing, 2018.

Aizenberg, Edna. *Books and Bombs in Buenos Aires: Borges, Gerchunoff, and Argentine-Jewish Writing*. UP of New England, 2002.

Aizenberg, Edna. *Parricide on the Pampa? A New Study and Translation of Alberto Gerchunoff's* Los gauchos judíos. 2nd ed. Iberoamericana-Vervuert, 2015.

Berman, Sabina. *La bobe*. Planeta, 1991. English version as *Bubbeh*. Translated by Andrea G. Labinger. Latin American Literary Review Press, 1998.

Bibliowicz, Azriel. *Migas de pan*. Alfaguara, 2013.

Bibliowicz, Azriel. *El rumor del astracán*. Planeta, 1991.

Birmajer, Marcelo. *Las nieves del tiempo*. Sudamericana, 2014.

Birmajer, Marcelo. *El rescate del Mesías*. Sudamericana, 2018.

Birmajer, Marcelo. *Tres mosqueteros*. Debate, 2001. English version as *Three Musketeers*. Translated by Sharon Wood. The Toby Press, 2008.

Brailovksy, Antonio Elio. *Identidad*. Sudamericana, 1980. Reissued as *Isaac Halevy, rey de los judíos*. Tusquets, 2002.

Brodsky, Marcelo. *Bosque quemado*. Random House Mondadori, 2007.

Chejfec, Sergio. *Lenta biografía*. Puntosur, 1990.

Chocrón, Isaac. *Pájaro de mar por tierra*. Tiempo Nuevo, 1972.

Chocrón, Isaac. *Rómpase en caso de incendio*. Monte Ávila, 1975.

Chudnovsky, José. *Pueblo pan*. Losada, 1967.

Esquivel, Laura. *Como agua para chocolate*. Planeta, 1989. English version as *Like Water for Chocolate*. Translated by Carol and Thomas Christensen. Doubleday, 1992.

Feierstein, Ricardo. *Mestizo*. Milá, 1988. Rev. Edition, Planeta, 1994. English version as *Mestizo: A Novel*. Translated by Stephen A. Sadow. U of New Mexico P, 2000.

Fingueret, Manuela. *Blues de la calle Leiva*. Planeta, 1995.

Fingueret, Manuela. *Hija del silencio*. Planeta, 1999. English version as *Daughter of Silence*. Translated by Darrell B. Lockhart. Texas Tech UP, 2012.

Freilich Segal, Alicia. *Colombina descubierta*. Planeta, 1991.

Foster, David William. "The Formation of a Critical Argentine Consciousness in Bernardo Verbitsky's *En esos años.*" In *Social Realism in the Argentine Narrative* (North Carolina Studies in the Romance Languages and Literatures). U of North Carolina P, 1986, pp. 73–89.

Fuks, Julián. *A resistência*. Companhia das Letras, 2009.

Gerchunoff, Alberto. *Los gauchos judíos*. J. Sesé, 1910. Revised edition, Manuel Gleizer, 1936. English versions as *The Jewish Gauchos of the Pampas*. Translated by Prudencio de Pereda. Abelard Schuman, 1955. Aizenberg, in *Parricide on the Pampa*?

Gertopan, Susana. *Barrio Palestina*. 1998. 2nd ed. Servilibro, 2005.

Gertopan, Susana. *El nombre prestado*. 2000. 2nd ed. Servilibro, 2005.

Gertopan, Susana. *El retorno de Eva*. Arandurã, 2003.

Gertopan, Susana. *Todo pasó en septiembre*. Servilibro, 2019.

Glantz, Margo. *Las genealogías*. Martín Casillas, 1981. English version as *The Family Tree: An Illustrated Novel*. Translated by Susan Bassnett. Serpent's Tail, 1991.

Goldemberg, Isaac. *En el nombre del padre*. Alfaguara, 2001.

Goldemberg, Isaac. *Tiempo al tiempo*. Ediciones del Norte, 1992.

Goldemberg, Isaac. *La vida a plazos de don Jacobo Lerner*. Libre 1, 1978.

Goloboff, Gerardo Mario. *The Algarrobos Quartet*. Translated by Stephen A. Sadow. U of New Mexico P, 2002.

Goloboff, Gerardo Mario. *Comuna verdad*. Anaya and Mario Muchnik, 1995.

Goloboff, Gerardo Mario. *Criador de palomas*. Bruguera, 1984.

Goloboff, Gerardo Mario. *La luna que cae*. Muchnik, 1989.

Goloboff, Gerardo Mario. *El soñador de Smith*. Muchnik, 1990.

Grünberg, Carlos M. *Mester de judería*. Argirópolis, 1940.

Guebel, Daniel. *El hijo judío*. Random House, 2018.

Halfon, Eduardo. *El boxeador polaco*. Pre-Textos, 2008.

Halfon, Eduardo. *El boxeador polaco*. Rev. ed. Libros del Asteroide, 2019. English version as *The Polish Boxer*. Translated by Daniel Hahn, et al. Bellevue Literary Press, 2012.

Halfon, Eduardo. *Monasterio*. Libros del Asteroide, 2014. English version as *Monastery*. Translated by Lisa Dillman. Bellevue Literary Press, 2014.

Halfon, Eduardo. *Signor Hoffman*. Libros del Asteroide, 2015.

Iolovitch, Marcos. 1940. *Numa clara manhã de abril*. Preface by Moacyr Scliar. Movimento/ Instituto Cultural Judaico Marc Chagall, 1987. English version as *On a Clear April Morning*. Translated by Merrie Blocker. Academic Studies Press, 2020.

Isaacs, Jorge. *María*. Imprenta Gaitán, 1867.

Izhaki, Flávio. *Amanhã não tem ninguém*. Rocco, 2013.

Jacobsen, Rafael Bán. *Uma leve simetría*. Não Editora, 2009.

Jaffe, Noemi. *O que os cegos estão sonhando?* Editora 34, 2012. English version as *What Are the Blind Men Dreaming?* Translated by Julia Sanches and Ellen Elias-Bursac. Deep Vellum 2016.

Kleinburg, Gerardo. *No honrarás a tu padre*. Sudamericana, 2004.

Krimer, María Inés. *Sangre fashion*. Aquilina, 2015.

Krimer, María Inés. *Sangre kosher*. Aquilina, 2010.

Krimer, María Inés. *Siliconas express*. Aquilina, 2013.

Laub, Michel. *Diário da queda*. Companhia das Letras, 2011. English version as *Diary of the Fall*. Translated by M. J. Costa. Other Press, 2014.

Levi Calderón, Sara. *Dos mujeres*. Diana, 1990. English version as *The Two Mujeres*. Translated by Gina Kaufer. Aunt Lute Books, 1991.

Levi Calderón, Sara. *Vida y peripecias de una buena hija de familia*. Vocestinta, 2015.

Levy, Tatiana Salem. *A chave de casa*. Record, 2007.

Lindstrom, Naomi. *Jewish Issues in Argentine Literature: From Gerchunoff to Szichman*. U of Missouri P, 1989.

Lindstrom, Naomi. "Judaic Traces in the Narrative of Clarice Lispector: Identity Politics and Evidence." *Latin American Jewish Cultural Production*, edited by David William Foster. Vanderbilt UP, 2009, pp. 83–96.

Lindstrom, Naomi. "Shifting Critical Approaches to the Elusive Jewishness of *María* by Jorge Isaacs." *Decimonónica: Revista de producción cultural hispánica decimonónica*, vol 18, nos. 1–2, 2021, pp. 33–48.

Lockhart, Darrell B. "Grünberg, Carlos M." *Jewish Writers of Latin America: A Dictionary*, edited by Darrell B. Lockhart. Garland, 1997, pp. 243–46.

Lockhart, Darrell B. "Jewish (Men)ority Literature in Mexico." *Critical Approaches to Jewish-Mexican Literature / Aproximaciones críticas a la literatura judeomexicana*, edited by Darrell B. Lockhart, *Chasqui: revista de literatura latinoamericana* special issue #4, 2013, pp. 254–65.

Moscona, Myriam. *Tela de sevoya*. Lumen, 2012. English version as *Tela de sevoya / Onioncloth*. Translated by Jen Hoffer and John Plueker. Les Figues Press, 2017.

Moscovich, Cíntia. *Duas iguais*. L&PM, 1998. Spanish version as *Dos iguales*. Translated by L. G. Berlanga. Tusquets, 2007.

Moscovich, Cíntia. *Por que sou gorda, mamãe?* Record, 2006.

Muñiz-Huberman, Angelina. *La burladora de Toledo*. Planeta 2008.

Muñiz-Huberman, Angelina. *El juego de escribir*. Corunda, 1991.

Muñiz-Huberman, Angelina. *Los esperandos: Piratas judeoportugueses. . . y yo*. Sefarad, 2017.

Muñiz-Huberman, Angelina. *El mercader de Tudela*. Fondo de Cultura Económica, 1998.

Muñiz-Huberman, Angelina. *Morada interior*. Joaquín Mortiz, 1972.

Muñiz-Huberman, Angelina. *El sefardí romántico: la azarosa vida de Mateo Alemán II*. Plaza y Janés, 2005.

Nissán, Rosa. *Hisho que te nazca*. Plaza y Janés, 1996.

Nissán, Rosa. *Like a Bride. Like a Mother*. Translated by Dick Gerdes. U of New Mexico, P, 2002.

Nissán, Rosa. *Me viene un modo de tristeza*. Grijalbo, 2019.

Nissán, Rosa. *Novia que te vea*. Planeta, 1992.

Orgambide, Pedro. *Aventuras de Edmund Ziller en tierras del Nuevo Mundo*. Grijalbo, 1977.

Plager, Silvia. *Como papas para varenikes*. Beas Ediciones, 1994. Rev. ed. Vergara, 2004. Reissued with Planeta, 2010.

Plager, Silvia. *Pequeña Viena en Shanghái: la vida de una familia austríaca en el gueto judío de Hongkou*. Penguin Random House, 2019.

Plager, Silvia. *La rabina*. Planeta, 2006.

Porzecanksi, Teresa. *La invención de los soles*. Editorial M.Z., 1981.

Porzecanski, Teresa. *La piel del alma*. Seix Barral, 1996.

Porzecanski, Teresa. *Mesías en Montevideo*. Signos, 1989.

Porzecanski, Teresa. *Perfumes de Cartago*. Trilce, 1994.

Porzecanski, Teresa. *Sun Inventions. Perfumes of Carthage*. Translated by Johnny Payne and Phyllis Silverstein. U of New Mexico P, 2000.

Rabinovich, José. *Campanas a media asta*. Compañía General Fabril, 1969.

Rabinovich, José. *El perro de Maidanek*. Platense, 1968.

Rosencof, Mauricio. *Las cartas que no llegaron*. Santillana, 2000. English version as *The Letters That Never Came*. Translated by Louise Popkin. U of New Mexico P, 2004.

Schwartz, Marco. *El salmo de Kaplan*. Norma, 2005.

Scliar, Moacyr. *Cenas da vida minúscula*. L&PM Editores, 1991.

Scliar, Moacyr. *O centauro no jardim*. Nova Fronteira, 1980. English version as *The Centaur in the Garden*. Translated by Margaret A. Neves. Ballantine Books, 1984.

Scliar, Moacyr. *O ciclo das águas*. Globo, 1976.

Scliar, Moacyr. *A estranha nação de Rafael Mendes*. L&PM, 1983. English version as *The Strange Nation of Rafael Mendes*. Translated by Eloah F. Giacomelli. Ballantine Books, 1987.

Scliar, Moacyr. *A guerra no Bom Fim*. L&PM, 1972. English version as *The War in Bom Fim*. Translated by David William Foster. Texas Tech UP, 2010.

Scliar, Moacyr. *A mulher que escreveu a Bíblia*. Companhia das Letras, 1999.

Sefamí, Jacobo. *Los dolientes*. Plaza y Janés, 2004. English version as *Mourning for Papá*. Translated by K. S. García. Floricanto, 2011.

Sefamí, Jacobo. *Por tierras extrañas*. Universidad Nacional Autónoma de México, 2019.

Seligson, Esther. *La morada en el tiempo*. Artífice, 1981.

Shua, Ana María. *El libro de los recuerdos*. Sudamericana, 1994. English version *The Book of Memories*. Translated by Dick Gerdes. U of New Mexico P, 1998.

Sommer, Doris. "Isaacs, Jorge." *Jewish Writers of Latin America: A Dictionary*, edited by Darrell B. Lockhart, Garland, 1997, pp. 268–74.

Steimberg, Alicia. *Cuando digo Magdalena*. Planeta, 1992. English version as *Call me Magdalena*. Translated by Andrea G. Labinger. U of Nebraska P, 1992.

Steimberg, Alicia. *Músicos y relojeros*. Centro Editor de América Latina, 1971. English version as *Musicians and Watchmakers*. Translated by Andrea G. Labinger. Latin American Literary Review Press, 1998.

Steimberg, Alicia. *Su espíritu inocente*. Pomaire, 1981.

Suez, Perla. *El arresto*. Norma, 2001.

Suez, Perla. *Complot*. Norma, 2004.

Suez, Perla. *The Entre Ríos Trilogy*. Translated by Rhonda Dahl Buchanan. U of New Mexico P, 2006.

Suez, Perla. *Letargo*. Norma, 2000.

Szichman, Mario. *A las 20:25 la señora entró en la inmortalidad*. Ediciones del Norte, 1981. English version *At 8:25 Evita Became Immortal*. Translated by Roberto Picciotto. Ediciones del Norte, 1983.

Szichman, Mario. *Crónica falsa*. Jorge Alvarez, 1969.

Szichman, Mario. *Los judíos del Mar Dulce*. Galerna, 1971.

Szichman, Mario. *La verdadera crónica falsa*. Centro Editor de América Latina, 1972.

Szmulewicz, Efraín. *El hombre busca la tristeza*. Don Quijote, 1950.

Szmulewicz, Efraín. *Un niño nació judío*. Zig-Zag, 1940.

Verbitsky, Bernardo. *En esos años*. Futuro, 1947.

Verbitsky, Bernardo. *Es difícil empezar a vivir*. Losada, 1941.

Verbitsky, Bernardo. *Hermana y sombra*. Planeta, 1977.

Verbitsky, Bernardo. *Villa miseria también es América*. G. Kraft, 1957.

Vieira, Nelson. "Clarice Lispector: A Jewish Impulse and a Prophecy of Difference." *Jewish Voices in Brazilian Literature: A Prophetic Discourse of Alterity*. UP Florida, 1995, pp. 100–50.

Vinocur, Ana de. *Un libro sin título*. Juventa, 1972.

Wrobel, Ronaldo. *Traduzindo Hannah*. Record, 2010.

CHAPTER 19

....

THE ARAB NOVEL OF
LATIN AMERICA

....

CHRISTINA E. CIVANTOS AND TRACEY MAHER

ARAB immigrant literature in Latin America includes works in various genres and lan-guages, although most are in Arabic, Portuguese, or Spanish. Among literary genres, the novel is one of the primary forms in which Arab immigrants to the Americas and their descendants express their identity-construction processes and engage with the lit-erary traditions of their home region as well as their host country, including how the latter conceives of "Arabness." Arab Latin American novels need to be contextualized within both the cultural histories of the Arab world and Latin America, including at-tention to anti-immigrant and/or anti-Arab sentiment and orientalism. Latin America's ambiguous positioning within the category of "the West" and the legacy of al-Andalus (the Iberian Peninsula under Muslim rule) add further complexity to the social and historical context surrounding these novels. In what follows, we outline the prominent features of the novels of the Latin American *mahjar*, or place of exile and immigrant life.

Arabic-speaking immigrants arrived in Latin America as part of the immigra-tion wave from Europe and the Mediterranean to the Americas that started in the mid-nineteenth century. These Arabic speakers, who may or may not have identified as "Arabs," came from the province of Syria under Ottoman rule (present-day Syria, Lebanon, Israel, Palestine, and parts of Jordan) and were of various faiths (Muslims, Jews, and Christians), although most were of diverse Christian denominations. Since these immigrants traveled with Ottoman documents, they and their descendants are often still known as *turcos* (Turks) throughout Latin America. Additionally, viewed through a homogenizing orientalist lens, they have typically been associated with Islam, regardless of their religion. The so-called *turcos* mainly settled in Brazil and Argentina, with smaller numbers going to Chile, Mexico, Colombia, Central America, Venezuela, and the islands of the Caribbean. Later, the establishment of Israel in 1948 and the 1967 June War, as well as ensuing conflicts, led to an influx of Palestinians who chiefly settled in Chile, El Salvador, and Honduras. Then the Lebanese Civil War (1975–1990) produced a new wave of Lebanese immigrants, many of whom settled in the Triple Frontier area where Paraguay, Brazil, and Argentina meet.

The late nineteenth- and early twentieth-century immigrants typically worked as merchants of cloth, notions, and housewares, starting out as peddlers and then setting up shops. Their descendants and immigrants from the subsequent waves have primarily established themselves within the business-owning or professional classes of Latin America, with many becoming prominent in business, entertainment, and politics.[1] Though the first arrivals wrote poetry and experimented with narrative prose, primarily in Arabic, literary production in Spanish and Portuguese became the norm in subsequent generations.

Among the many significant differences between the regional and national contexts within which Arab immigrants found themselves is these immigrants' relationship to the "whiteness" to which *criollo* leaders aspired. In the Southern Cone, the massive influx of immigrants, most of whom were European, led to strong *criollista* movements, that is, efforts to establish the *criollo*—or inhabitant of Iberian descent associated with local traditions—as the legitimate national subject. The large population of European origin, together with the decimation of the indigenous population, led to discourses that categorize the non-European as other. Hence, Arab and Jewish immigrants, categorized as Semitic, initially faced hostility and are often still marked as non-European. In contrast, in regions with a high indigenous, *mestizo*, or Afro-descendant population, such as Mexico, Central America, the Caribbean, and Brazil, Arab immigrants aligned themselves more easily with the privileged classes within the pigmentocracies that prevailed despite the *mestizaje* rhetoric. This has led to a more pronounced concern with navigating discrimination and essentialist images of the *turco* in novels from countries such as Argentina and Chile, where overall the assertion of Arab identity is a more fraught issue. In both types of contexts, whether through efforts at self-positioning or happenstance, Arab immigrants have been active participants within national projects aimed at "whitening" the national body, or at least limiting the visibility of indigenous, African, and mixed-race constituents.

Given these dynamics, the intertwined pressure to assimilate to *criollo* culture (which was strongest through the mid-twentieth century), and personal preference, many authors of Arab descent do not overtly write as "Arabs" or "Syro-Lebanese" (the self-identification used in various countries). In a sense, any author with origins in the Arabic-speaking world is an Arab writer; nonetheless, only some of these writers involve Arabness in their literary work. As a result of the push and pull of the identity-construction process, many immigrant writers only use a persona rooted in their new culture.[2] Since trying to ferret out Arab traces within the work of an author from the second generation or beyond lends itself to the imposition of ethnicity markers, in this chapter we address works written by Arab immigrants themselves, regardless of themes, and works by descendants of Arab immigrants that address Arab immigration and Arab identity. Engagement with Arabness can take the form of different types of essentialism, including auto-orientalism, but can also take the form of a deep questioning of national and ethnic identities. Differences regarding the type of engagement with the Arab world and Arabness, and the resulting stances of the exile, the migrant, and the member of a diaspora, which often coincide with generational differences, are stronger than regional or national differences.

Arabic-Language Novels

Before 1930, the novel was not yet a dominant genre in Arabic letters. As a result, the number of Arabic-language novels written in Latin America is relatively small. Most of the extant novels in Arabic were written in the 1910s–1920s, and all tell stories about Arab characters, typically in an Arab setting. In contrast, most of the novels written in Spanish and Portuguese, and particularly those written in the 1910s–1930s, are set in either Europe or the Southern Cone of Latin America among non-Arabs.

Most Arabic-language novels produced in Argentina and Brazil can be categorized as "exile literature"; in other words, they are more concerned with the home culture than the immigrants' new surroundings. These novels address themes particularly salient in Arab societies, typically take place in the Levant or elsewhere in the Arab world, and are sometimes set in historical time periods. However, a few novels might be described as "migration literature" in that they focus on the experience of migrants, providing descriptions of their departures from the homeland, trans-continental journeys, and arrivals in the new country.

Exile Literature

A couple of novels written by immigrants to the Southern Cone seem to transfer their authors' transcontinental experiences to regional migration scenarios. Nasīb Isṭifān's novella *Daḥiyyat al-gharām* (Victim of Passion, 1925) portrays the return of an Emir's son to his native Lebanese village after living in Beirut for several years to complete his schooling. He falls in love with a young village girl, who has similarly returned from years in a convent, the Emir forbids this marriage with a commoner, and tragedy ensues. Thus, the novel touches upon issues of movement between village and city, focusing particularly on the return home, as well as themes of love across class boundaries and inter-generational struggles (Maher 2019, 130–146).

While *Daḥiyyat al-gharām* highlights the protagonist's return home, with virtually no depiction of his journey to or experiences in the city, Ilyās Qunṣul's *Fī mahabb al-rīḥ* (Exposed to the Winds, 1972) focuses on migration between village and city. It tells the story of a young man in the 1870s who is forced to leave his Syrian village and journey to Damascus, facing hardships and overcoming challenges before returning home. This emphasis on rural–urban movement allows Qunṣul to discuss issues of migration while remaining committed to the Arab setting, theme, and language. In further contrast to the protagonist of *Daḥiyyat al-gharām*, *Fī mahabb al-rīḥ*'s protagonist ultimately finds his home village to be the source of genuine happiness. This fairytale ending can be read as an indirect expression of its author's nostalgia and desire to remain connected to his Arab homeland. Having left Syria as a child in 1925, Qunṣul lived a few years in Brazil and almost his entire adult life in Argentina. Nevertheless, he chose to write this novel, like his poems and essays, in Arabic. This gesture is particularly notable given the limited number of Arabic speakers left in Argentina by the date of its publication (Civantos 2006, 201–2).

In contrast to the movement between village and city depicted in the novels of Isṭifān and Qunṣul, Muḥammad Shihāb al-Dīn Ḥammādī's Riwāyat ṭahārat al-ḥubb 'ind al-'arab (The Purity of Love among the Arabs, 1953) describes the nomadic movement of Bedouin Arab tribes between the deserts of eastern Syria and the Hejaz in the Arabian Peninsula in the early eighteenth century. The story begins with a conflict between two tribes that culminates in a violent battle. Decades later, the tribes' chiefs meet unexpectedly in an oasis where both are searching for fertile land. They agree to bring their families to live there for a few months in the hope of bringing about lasting peace between their tribes. The son and daughter of these chiefs fall in love and, after overcoming various obstacles, eventually marry and settle down in a new land located between their respective tribal homelands. A distinctive feature of the novel is various episodes in which characters cross-dress and role-play the opposite gender. At the same time, the novel consistently highlights the traditional virtues embodied by its main characters—courage, chastity, loyalty—explicitly associating them with the Arab people. This theme, reinforced by the novel's language, its nostalgic evocation of Bedouin traditions, and its message of reconciliation, suggests that the novel should be read politically as a call for Arab unity, an orientation that is made explicit in its dedication to King Saud.[3]

Political commitment to the Arab world is more explicit in works such as Anṭūn Sa'āda's Fāji'at ḥubb (Love Tragedy, 1931).[4] Set in an unnamed city in Greater Syria, despite brief references to the narrator having traveled to "America," the novel is exclusively concerned with exploring projects of artistic and political reform in the Levant. The main characters, a musician and an intellectual, are portrayed as eccentric, alienated from their contemporaries, and committed to the restoration of their country's past for the sake of its future after French colonial rule. This reflects Sa'āda's own political project: though he wrote Fāji'at ḥubb in Brazil (Beshara 2011, 10), it was published after his return to Lebanon, where he would establish the Syrian Social Nationalist Party (SSNP) in 1932. The SSNP opposed European colonialism and sought to form a Greater Syrian nation that would unify the countries of the Fertile Crescent.[5]

The SSNP's ideals also shape Nawwāf Ḥardān's Ḥafīd al-nusūr (The Grandson of Eagles, 1970), a historical novel set in Carthage during the Punic Wars that tells the story of a Carthaginian general who defends his city in its doomed struggle against the Roman Empire. As noted by Waïl Hassan, through Ḥafīd al-nusūr and other historical novels that Ḥardān published in Lebanon after returning from Argentina and Brazil, the author attempts to "demonstrate the common identity of the countries of the Fertile Crescent and to celebrate its heroic struggles against its enemies—mainly the Roman Empire, which stands for twentieth-century colonialism and imperialism in the region" (Hassan 547).

Some novels, though neither set in the Arab world nor featuring Arab characters, can nevertheless be read as addressing themes salient to Arab society. In addition to historical novels set in the Middle East, Naẓīr Zaytūn published *Dhunūb al-ābāʾ* (Sins of the Parents, 1932), which takes place in the city of Madrid and features Spanish characters. It tells the story of a doomed romance, with characters who fall victim to their society's transactional vision of marriage. Hassan argues that this can be read as an indirect critique of Arab or Brazilian societies (Hassan 547).

MIGRATION LITERATURE

Among the migration novels that describe the experience of Arabs in Latin America, there is a great deal of variation in terms of the importance of that setting for the story and the extent to which they explicitly discuss the migration journey. At one extreme, the main character in Anṭūn Anīs Shakūr's *Min al-laḥd ilā al-mahd* (From the Grave to the Cradle, 1940) notes a few times that he migrated to Brazil from Homs, but the novel is primarily centered on his dream journey to the afterlife and back. As Hassan notes, the novel is a "philosophical tale," and migration to Brazil "has no bearing whatsoever on the story" (546).

In contrast to Shakūr's novel, in which the Latin American setting plays no role in the story, Jūrj ʿAssāf's *Īmīlya* (Emilia, ca. 1925) straddles the boundary between both migration literature and exile literature.[6] In keeping with the migration genre, it depicts the journey between the Lebanese homeland and Argentina, including the main characters' departure from the port of Beirut, trans-Atlantic voyage (involving a shipwreck), arrival to Argentina, and settling in the new country. The novel centers on the relationship between its title character, a young woman named Emilia, and a young man who is drawn to her from the moment he sees her in the port of Beirut. Their love unfolds in parallel with their migration, such that love-as-journey is a theme that is played with throughout the novel.

Although various scenes take place in specific neighborhoods and landmarks in Buenos Aires, the novel is primarily concerned with the situation of women in Levantine societies. While most of the story is told by a male narrator who is a secondary character, the final chapter revisits the entire plot from the perspective of Emilia, when the narrator and the young man read her diary after her tragic death. The diary sheds light on various mysteries presented throughout the novel, and ultimately produces an emphatic condemnation of Levantine society's tendency to arrange marriages between young women and rich older men. This is a sensitive and potentially embarrassing topic for Arab migrants, but the Arabic language creates a space for open in-group conversation (both within the novel and extradiegetically). In this sense, the agency and critique of patriarchy expressed by Emilia remain accessible only to the Arabic-speaking community that constitutes its intended audience.

Perhaps the clearest example of a Latin American migration novel written in Arabic is Najīb Baʿqlīnī and Samʿān al-Ḥamātī's *Daʿās wa-Fadʿūs* (Daʿās and Fadʿūs, 1923).[7] This comical story focuses on a Lebanese Maronite man, Fadʿūs, who migrates from his village near Beirut to Buenos Aires, where he is eventually joined by his closest friend, Daʿās, and his fellow villagers. Much of the novel figuratively operates as a migrant's manual, relying on physical and linguistic humor to enliven its almost didactic descriptions of the possibilities and perils of migration. As a result, and unlike other Arabic-language novels produced in Latin America, *Daʿās wa-Fadʿūs* describes the entirety of the migration process in great detail.

The opening chapters are set in Lebanon and provide many critiques of its traditions and institutions, particularly the corrupt practices of the village priest, Būnā-Frām (Father Afrām). Through his interactions with Fadʿūs, the novel highlights the importance of being able to move between different roles and linguistic registers, presenting themes of performativity and power that recur throughout the novel. On the trans-Atlantic journey, Fadʿūs experiences discrimination, becomes the bumbling leader of a group of Arab migrants, fights against non-Arab migrants, takes on the role of middleman, and gradually shifts from seeing America as a nebulous continent of opportunity to understanding it as a set of concrete locations among which he must choose where to settle. The journey includes myriad adventures and misadventures, emphasizing that migration is not an easy or linear process.

Throughout, the novel emphasizes the challenges of being an immigrant while also pointing out the ways in which Arab migrants can both succeed economically and preserve their dignity and identity, if they maintain horizontal ties and solidarity with their fellow migrants. In the final chapters, the novel abandons its comic tone and becomes solemn and serious. As Fadʿūs welcomes Daʿās and other villagers to Argentina and helps them to avoid many of the pitfalls he himself experienced, he emerges as an authority figure. Yet this transition is also accompanied by his adoption of patronizing and judgmental views of the new migrants. The novel ends less on a triumphant tone than on a melancholic one, undermining the notion that migration and economic success are equivalent to moral progress.

The Arabic-language novels of the Latin American *mahjar* are primarily exile literature, set in the Arab world and with a focus on homeland issues. To a lesser degree, there are also examples of Arabic-language migration literature, set at least partially if not fully in Latin America and with a focus on Arab-world issues, the act of migration itself, and the process of settling into the receiving country.

Spanish- and Portuguese-Language Novels

The Spanish- and Portuguese-language novels of Arab immigrants and their descendants also lend themselves to categorization according to exile, migration, or diasporic orientations. While rare, there are works set entirely in the Arab world with Arab characters and addressing Arab themes. Yet because exile literature is oriented toward a homeland public, it is less likely to be written in languages unfamiliar to that audience. It is not surprising, then, that there are few novels written in Spanish or Portuguese that are set entirely in the Arab world with Arab characters and themes. Critically, when addressed to a Spanish- or Portuguese-speaking audience, an Arab-world setting can have dramatically different effects than those of exile literature written in Arabic. Jorge Elías Adoum's *Adonay, novela iniciática del colegio de los magos* (Adonai, Initiatory Novel of the School of Sorcerers, 1943), for example, relies on a Levantine setting to reinforce its esoteric and spiritual themes. Adoum also wrote books on the occult sciences and traveled around Latin America as a practicing hypnotist and expert in magnetism and suggestion. Thus, while Lebanon, Syria, and Palestine are familiar settings for Arabic-speaking audiences, they often operate as distant, exotic, and often spiritual or mystical reference points for Spanish- or Portuguese-speaking readers.

In contrast with the scarcity of exile literature, many of the Spanish- and Portuguese-language novels written by Arabs in Latin America can be categorized as migration literature in the sense that they focus on migrants' journeys and their experiences in the receiving country. Finally, there are works that may be considered diaspora novels: works set primarily in Latin America, in which migration narratives become family history or intergenerational lore, and the central focus is on the life of Arabs and their descendants in the new country. These novels often highlight relationships between generations, including language loss and retrieval, family traditions from the old world that mark differences from the dominant culture, experiences of bias and prejudice, struggles to retain some aspects of home culture while rejecting or adapting others, and the possibility of return, whether literal or figurative.

Migration Literature

Migration novels describe the challenges associated with departure, travel, and arrival in the Americas, which include prejudice against "turcos," linguistic and cultural barriers, and the economic hardships experienced by new migrants. Written for audiences that are often unfamiliar with the Arab world and its inhabitants, many also describe conditions in the homeland and attempt to challenge stereotypes about Arab migrants. The projects are often personal: most of these novels are either loosely autobiographical or based on the experiences of the author's parents or grandparents.[8]

Novels dealing with migration consistently emphasize the struggles of Arab migrants in Latin America and earlier examples highlight their successes. The earliest Portuguese-language novel depicting Arab migration to Brazil, according to Hassan, is Cecílio Carneiro's *A fogueira* (The Bonfire, 1942), which portrays the migration of a Lebanese man and his wife to São Paolo at the turn of the century (548). Though poor upon arrival, he ends up achieving great success in the booming coffee industry. The character, modeled on Carneiro's own father, is portrayed as someone driven by great ambition but also characterized by a rigorously honest disposition. In this sense, he is set apart from the stereotypical image of the dishonest *turco* in Brazil and comes to serve as a model of immigrant success (Hassan 548–49).

Later works do not shy away from portraying their main characters as flawed. Gilberto Abrão's *Mohamed, o latoeiro* (Muhammad the Tinker, 2009) is also a migration novel based on the experiences of the author's father, in this case a Syrian Alawite Muslim who settles in Paraná, Brazil. After a brief stint as a pack-peddler, the stereotypical profession of Arab migrants, he switches jobs and becomes a tinker. Hassan notes that the novel differs from others in the genre not only in terms of the religion and profession of the main character, but also in that he is portrayed as a trickster who "lives by his wits on the edge of respectability and the law" (Hassan 550). Moreover, the novel provides descriptions of life in Syria under Ottoman and then European control and of Islamic religious beliefs and practices (Hassan 550–51). In these ways, it adds new dimensions to portrayals of Arab migration to Latin America.[9]

Other works add to, or replace, the focus on an individual forebear with an emphasis on the receiving country. Salim Miguel's *Nur na escuridão* (Nur [Arabic for "Light"] in the Dark, 1999) is based on the diary of his father, who, along with the author's mother, migrated from Lebanon to Brazil (Hassan 550). The novel describes the choices made by migrants in determining where to migrate in the Americas, the experience of belonging to an immigrant community, and the discrimination faced by migrants in the receiving country. The novel mourns the loss of the Arabic language (and thus access to Arabic culture) across generations, as evidenced by the author's need for a translator to access his father's diary. It also devotes significant attention to the history and contemporary politics of Brazil (Hassan 550).

Edith Chahín's *Nahima* (2001) follows a similar pattern, but from a different gender perspective. It draws on the author's mother's experiences in Syria, her migration journey, and the challenges she faced in Latin America. El-Attar points out that this novel is also distinctive in its descriptions of "Arab women's resistance during these periods" (El-Attar 593). Chahín's work, which includes novels set in the homeland and featuring female characters, centers women and thus challenges male-dominated representations of Arab culture.[10]

Although the representation of receiving countries varies across texts, many novels explore the complex ties between migrants and their homelands, often relying on different literary devices to do so. One striking example is Emil Farhat's *Dinheiro na estrada: Uma saga de imigrantes* (Money on the Road: A Saga of Immigrants, 1987), which centers on a series of letters that a Lebanese mother writes to her son who has migrated to Brazil. Hassan notes that the novel is unique among Arab-Brazilian novels for its "depiction of life in Lebanon for family members who were left behind by the immigrants" (549). Through its epistolary structure, it addresses other issues relevant to life back in the homeland, such as corruption among members of the clergy and life under French colonial occupation. At the same time, the novel also addresses issues relevant to immigrant life in Brazil, from the immigrants' making a living as pack peddlers to immigrant involvement in a war between Brazil and Bolivia (Hassan 549).

Roberto Saráh's *Los turcos* (The Turks, 1961) contrasts the sacred quality of the Palestinian migrants' homeland—the Holy Land—with the profane, materialistic circumstances of their life in Chile. The novel opens in Bethlehem and follows three young Palestinians who emigrate to Chile. It is distinctive, according to El-Attar, in its "portrayal of the Bethlehem area and its Christian population, mostly peasantry, at the turn of the nineteenth century" (El-Attar 2017, 594). The migrants' sense of connection to the earliest Christian communities plays a central role in the migrants' experience, particularly as Chile is not what the young migrants imagined, and they face racial profiling and exclusion (El-Attar 2017, 593).

Other novels also emphasize the spiritual significance of the Palestinian homeland, using it to infuse their narratives with esoteric or otherworldly elements reminiscent of Adoum's *Adonay*. For instance, Jaime Hales Dib's *Peregrino de ojos brillantes* (A Pilgrim of Shining Eyes, 1995) is organized into chapters based on suits from the tarot deck and imbues the spatial journeys of migrants with divine purpose through a storyline involving reincarnation and a fortune teller. In doing so, it articulates a spiritual connection between Palestine and Chile.

A set of works that are *sui generis* are Emin Arslan's *Final de un idilio* (End of an Idyll, 1917), Juan Khury's *Ramsay* (1938), and Pablo Achem's *Bengala, fugaz en la noche negra* (A Flare, Fleeting in the Dark Night, 1931). Although Arslan was a Lebanese exile from the Ottoman Empire, Khury an immigrant from Syria, and Achem the descendant of Levantine immigrants, writing at a time of strong *criollista* and anti-immigrant sentiment in early twentieth-century Argentina, their narratives do not directly address the migration process nor the Levantine immigrant community. Nonetheless, these novels address the immigrant experience indirectly by addressing displacement and estrangement, as well as by participating in discourses that were dominant in the host country at the time during which they were written—the purported link between purity of speech and moral character—and raising doubts about discourses such as the ideal of a single national language and single national affiliation. These three authors used the paratextual spaces of prefaces and dedications, as well as other textual details, to insert the Syro-Lebanese community into Argentine culture amid the very discourses being used to exclude immigrants. Through prefaces and dedications that asserted their Syro-Lebanese identities and prose that demonstrated that even immigrants could write in proper Spanish, these texts counteracted the language-focused anti-immigrant rhetoric of their day.[11]

While the novels by Arslan, Khury, and Achem suggest a critique of the cultural politics of their host country, some novelists in other national contexts and later time periods have directly critiqued dominant (*criollo*) culture and its anti-Arab sentiment. Cánovas (2011) interprets the grotesque descriptions of Arabs in the novel by Saráh mentioned earlier as a way of criticizing the *criollo* perception of these migrants as repulsive (210–14, 222–23). In addition to the works by Abdala and Garib discussed below, there is the case of Luis Fayad's novel *Los parientes de Ester* (Esther's Relatives, 1978). Although *Los parientes de Ester* is mainly the story of a *criollo* Colombian family and life in Bogotá, through the main character's brother-in-law, Nomar Mahid, who is of Arab descent, the narrative criticizes *criollo* prejudice against *turcos*.

DIASPORA LITERATURE

In contrast with migration novels, other Spanish- and Portuguese-language novels are set primarily in Latin American countries and focus on the life of Arabs and their descendants in their new homes. These novels are diaspora novels insofar as they explore belonging and alienation, assimilation and resistance, and intergenerational fractures and connections between migrant (grand)parents and descendants born in the new country. These novels often address the distinctiveness of Arab identity and its place and relevance in Latin America, while also articulating engagement with Arab homelands in various ways. The novels may include stories-within-the-story describing life in the old country or migrants' first arrival in Latin America, which often play the role of family histories or founding myths. These stories often serve as foils or metaphors for the struggles and achievements of second- or third-generation descendants. Arab cultural markers, such as food, music, or religious traditions, preserve memories of historical dwelling places. Characters may dream of returning to a lost homeland, and some may even attempt some sort of actual return, thus setting the novel partially in Latin America and partially in the ancestral homeland.

As discussed by Hassan (551, 552–54), two novels by Milton Hatoum, one of Brazil's most prominent contemporary novelists, depict tense and even violent family dynamics, language loss, and a concern with what to do with the past. Hatoum's *Relato de um certo Oriente* (*Tale of a Certain Orient*, 1989) and *Dois irmãos* (Two Brothers, translated as *The Brothers*, 2000) both express a diasporic concern with reflecting upon the legacy of the emigres of the previous generation. Hassan suggests that *Relato de um certo Oriente* complicates conceptions of orientalism by multiplying the "orients" at hand and contends that the novels seek to evade exoticism and fixed identities (553–54).

Although Chilean Walter Garib's *El viajero de la alfombra mágica* (The Magic Carpet Traveler, 1991) focuses on the struggles of various generations, it is similar to Hatoum's novels in that it also portrays how subsequent generations relate to their immigrant past. The novel tells the multi-generational saga of the Magdala family, beginning with the patriarch, Aziz, and his journey from Palestine across South America to Chile. The title of the novel refers to Aziz's stories: he tells his children and grandchildren that he traveled to Chile on a magic carpet, establishing a connection to the Arab narrative tradition with an image from *The Thousand and One Nights* (popularized in English as *The Arabian Nights*). The practice of storytelling helps the novels' Arab characters deal with social rejection and other challenges, making it possible for the family to cope with, and indeed thrive in, a frequently difficult environment.

In contrast with Hatoum's works, Garib's novel adopts orientalist tropes in often problematic ways. Aziz takes on an indigenous mistress in Paraguay, with whom he lives in

Chile even after he marries a Palestinian woman, Afife. The latter accepts her husband's concubine and Aziz avoids thinking about how this situation affects Afife because he believes that she is "destined only to conceive kids and stimulate his erotic Palestinian voracity" (32).[12] The novel thus affirms orientalist visions of passive women, male chauvinism, and hypersexuality. These orientalist tropes are accompanied by other problematic essentializations. The indigenous concubine is referred to simply as "the Guarani Native" and never by her name, and is thus reduced to her ethnic identity. Moreover, as Afife grows to accept the concubine, she does so because she respects the Guarani Native's "primitive wisdom" (34), which is helpful in the domestic sphere.

In spite of these essentialisms, the novel goes on to describe how Aziz's descendants wrestle with the challenges of finding a place for themselves as Palestinians in Chile, often in the face of local prejudice, especially on the part of the Chilean upper class. In this way, the novel offers a dual critique of Chilean elites and the Arab migrants who seek their acceptance. While the third generation attempts to disown its Arab roots, El-Attar (2017) points out that the fourth generation re-establishes its connection to Palestine: one of them becomes active in pro-Palestinian causes, highlighting the ways in which many young Palestinian-Chileans remain committed to their evolving diasporic identity (599).[13]

Sharing characteristics with Garib's novel, the works of Arab Argentine Jorge Asís paint a vivid portrait of life in a multi-ethnic, working-class neighborhood in Buenos Aires, but reinscribe fixed identities instead of questioning them. In *Don Abdel Zalim, el burlador de Domínico* (Don Abdel Zalim, The Seducer of Domínico, 1972), the narrator and protagonist of the novel, Rodolfo Zalim, is an Arab-Argentinian, and the novel depicts the relationships among this titular character, his immigrant grandmother, and his first-generation parents. Rodolfo is surrounded by friends and neighbors who are also descendants of immigrants from across Europe and the Mediterranean. In this way, the novel emphasizes the ethnic diversity of Argentina's capital. Yet Asís's reliance on recognizable ethnic markers can reinforce orientalist stereotypes. Indeed, in a later trilogy of novels, he presents male Arab characters as inveterate seducers endowed with unquenchable sex drives and his female Arab characters as passive tolerators of male dominance.

Other diaspora novels focus on dismantling imposed essentialist identities. In the renowned Arab Argentine writer Juan José Saer's *La grande* (The Big One, translated as *La Grande*, 2005), one of the main characters, Nula, is a philosopher and wine dealer of Syrian descent. His heritage is discussed by the omniscient narrator through the story of his migrant grandfather's journey from Damascus and Nula's memories of this migrant's house in rural Argentina, with its distinctively Arab sounds, smells, and tastes. Through strategic uses of the term *turco*, the novel highlights how the term is used to mark certain immigrants as outsiders. In the process, the novel interrogates constructions of Arabness and ethnic identities in general.[14]

Other novels emphasize linguistic and cultural heterogeneity to question nationalist and immigrant identities. Durval Abdala's *El criado Braulio* (Braulio the Servant, 1962) is a social realist novel that depicts everyday life in Argentina's rural northwest provinces.

It highlights the diverse quality of this peripheral region by featuring characters from a range of ethnicities, including *criollo* and indigenous characters, reserving a prominent place for Arab immigrants. In this heterogeneous setting, linguistic diversity becomes an important theme, and the novel deploys a variety of languages, dialects, and registers in ways that challenge essentialist notions of Argentinian culture and identity.[15]

Héctor Azar's *Las tres primeras personas* (The Three First Persons, 1977), which straddles the distinction between migration and diaspora literature, uses linguistic multiplicity, together with a complex structure, to capture the intricacies of the migrant experience. This semi-autobiographical work tells the story of Lebanese migration to Mexico through a combination of polyphonic narratives, letters, photographs, historical citations, and a glossary. The novel relies on multilingual wordplay—in Spanish, Arabic, French, English, and Italian—as well as Mexican colloquialisms to reinforce the ambiguities and confusions that often characterize the process of migration. From its opening, which relies on the testimonies of three distinct members of the same family, to its conclusion, which tells of a third-generation migrant's enduring relationship with his deceased grandfather, the novel provides a purposefully fragmentary and rupture-filled account that resists simple interpretations of the Arab-Mexican experience.[16]

The linguistic and cultural richness of diaspora communities also features prominently in Jacobo Sefamí's *Los dolientes* (The Mourners, 2004). Set in Mexico City in 1996, it narrates the death of a Syrian Jewish father, and the seven-day period during which his family sits *shiva* and mourns him. As the family members share stories and reflect on the life of the deceased father, there are repeated references to Syrian Jewish religious and culinary traditions. The novel takes on an ethnographic quality as it describes the beliefs, customs, and dishes that characterize this diaspora community. Linguistic diversity plays a key role in this rich portrait that relies on a variety of languages, dialects, and registers, including standard Spanish, Mexican dialects, and both Hebrew and Arabic. The interplay of languages and registers enhances the novel's polyphonic quality and allows it to paint a multifaceted picture of the experience of grief, loss, and acceptance. Specific words and phrases—such as the Hebrew word for "father" and the Arabic word for "five" that refers to the protective symbol of the hand of Fatima—play a prominent part in the articulation and maintenance of group identity for this Jewish Syrian community.[17]

In other works, the theme of intergenerational relationships is tied to failure. Raduan Nassar's *Lavoura arcaica* (Ancient Tillage, 1975) describes the struggles of a Lebanese-Brazilian family living in isolation on a farm. The story focuses on the conflict between the second-generation father who wants to uphold a traditional patriarchal order, and the third-generation son, the narrator, who rebels against the stifling atmosphere of this authoritarian household. Hassan sees the novel as a "parable of the Prodigal Son," albeit one in which the return of the son leads to tragedy through the revelation of an incestuous love affair and the destruction of the family (Hassan, 551–52). Hassan points out that the novel can be interpreted "as a critique of certain immigrant tendencies toward isolationism and inflexible insistence on preserving the customs and traditions of the old country—that is, the resistance to *mistura* (mixture), which in the dominant discourse on national identity represents as the hallmark of Brazilianness" (Hassan 552).

The possibility of return to a lost Arab homeland is another theme found in Arab Latin American literature. In Gilberto Abrão's *O muçulmano e a judia* (The Muslim [Man] and the Jew[ish Woman], 2011), the return has tragic consequences. This novel tells the story of a doomed romance between a Muslim Palestinian-Brazilian man and a Jewish Egyptian-Brazilian woman. Despite their physical distance from the Israeli-Palestinian conflict, the couple's love is thwarted by their families, who cannot accept a relationship that defies diasporic loyalty to homeland causes. Both characters ultimately journey to Israel/Palestine, where the young man becomes a Palestinian freedom fighter and the young woman an Israeli soldier. The lives of the would-be lovers end tragically in a suicide bombing, leaving their families in Brazil to face this loss and achieve a sort of reconciliation. Hassan proposes that "the novel demonstrates the transnational dimensions of Brazilian identity and its sometimes irreconcilable allegiances, something that complicates the widespread idea of Brazil as a country where different cultures, races, and ethnicities mix harmoniously" (551).

Alberto Mussa's *O enigma de Qaf* (The Riddle of Qaf, 2004) presents another troubled return. The novel is narrated by a young Brazilian man of Lebanese descent who embarks on a complex journey to recover his Arab roots. Driven by his grandfather's stories of a pre-Islamic poet called al-Ghattash who belonged to the tribe to which he traces his ancestry, the narrator travels to Lebanon to pursue research at a local university. However, when he presents his findings, he is accused of forgery and forced to return to Brazil. The novel connects the main character's plot with the story of the legendary poet's journey to solve the mysterious "enigma of Qaf" and tales of pre-Islamic poets. For Hassan, this multi-layered effort "becomes a metaphor for the third-generation Arab Brazilians' attempt to rediscover – in fact, invent – their Arab roots" (Hassan 554).[18]

The theme of reinvention seen in Garib's novel is a main component of other works, such as Bárbara Jacob's *Las siete fugas de Saab, alias el Rizos* (The Seven Escapes of Saab, Alias Curly, 1992). The novel tells the story of a Mexican teenager of Arab descent, originally named Toribio after his father but nicknamed Saab by his family. His fraught relationship with both his father and his sister emphasizes inter- and intra-generational struggles that cause Saab to run away from home. He is eventually institutionalized, at which point the central narrative is largely replaced by other texts, including letters from Saab's sister, and a pair of stories penned by her and by Saab as a child. Saab's story, reminiscent in some ways of *The Thousand and One Nights*, features a fictional Arab hero named Saab who embarks on a journey in the 1800s to find the tomb of an Egyptian pharaoh, clashes with a sultan, and eventually manages to escape. This story-within-a-story blurs the border between fiction and reality: the nickname Saab was given to the main character of the frame narrative, the Arab-Mexican Saab, in reference to the protagonist of the short story that the Arab-Mexican Saab wrote. Additionally, the adventures described in that short story parallel the Arab-Mexican Saab's eventual break from his own father and his escape. Through this metafiction, Arab heritage is linked to creativity and resilience.[19]

CONCLUSION

The novels written by Arab migrants and their descendants in Latin America exhibit remarkable linguistic and thematic diversity. They range from Arabic-language works with an exilic focus on Levantine society, such as Isṭifān's *Daḥiyyat al-gharām* (Victim of Passion), to multilingual meditations on diasporic struggles over belonging and alienation, like Sefamí's *Los dolientes* (The Mourners). Many of them challenge prevalent linguistic and cultural ideologies, reworking established discourses and reinscribing them into new spaces within which they can craft statements about the Arab experience in Latin America.

The first Arab immigrants wrote in Arabic with Arab audiences in mind, but also crafted fascinating portraits of the migration experience. Later generations of Arab Latin American writers have often sought to reconstruct the image of their community for Spanish- and Portuguese-language readers, often through novels focused on the experience of Arab immigrants and their descendants. In doing so, they have validated these immigrant voices and asserted their ability to tell their own experiences. While some of these novelists, like Asís, rely on essentialist and self-orientalizing narratives, others, like Jacobs, challenge these frameworks by drawing on diasporic cultural repertoires to sustain creative resilience.

Arab Latin American writers developed a wide range of ways to address both Arabness and the identity discourses of their Latin American countries. In doing so, they opened new spaces for cultural agency and for varied performances of identity. Their texts combine moments of dislocation and relocation to produce new conceptions of place and belonging.

NOTES

1. On prominent figures of Arab descent in Latin American business, politics, and entertainment, see Alfaro-Velcamp (2007), Molina Guzmán and Valdivia (2010), Cepeda (2010), and Civantos (2012).
2. Some prominent writers of Arab descent whose novels refer in passing, if at all, to things Arab are Mexican Naief Yehya (1963–), Cuban Antón Arrufat (1935–), Chileans Guillermo Atías Martín (1917–1979) and Diamela Eltit (1949–), and Ecuadorean Jorge Enrique Adoum (1926–2009), son of previously mentioned Jorge Elías Adoum.
3. For more on Ḥammādī's novel, see Maher 2019, 90–129. The anonymous novel *Nuzhā'* (ca. 1925, Nuzha), named after its protagonist, is another Arab Latin American historical novel, this time set in nineteenth-century Greater Syria.
4. This novel was published together with *ʿĪd sayyidat Ṣaydnāya* (The Feast of the Lady of Saydnaya) under the title *Qiṣṣatān* (Two Stories). For more on Saʿādaʾs novel, see Maher 2019, 190–204.

5. Sa'āda was imprisoned several times for his political activity, returned to Brazil in 1938, lived in Argentina from 1939 until he returned to Lebanon in 1947, and was then executed there in 1949.

6. The novel was first published serially in *Jarīdat al-salām*, then in book form. For more on 'Assāf's novel, see Maher 2019, 149–190.

7. For more on al-Ḥāmātī and Ba'qlīnī's novel, see Civantos 2006, 202–12, and Maher 2019, 39–88.

8. Arab Latin Americans have also produced many overtly biographical or autobiographical texts, and the first of these are precursors to later novelistic narratives. For instance, the works of Syrian-Chilean Benedicto Chuaqui Kettlun and Lebanese-Mexican Dib Morillo. On Chuaqui see El-Attar 2017, 592.

9. One of Abrão's other novels, *O escriba de Granada* (The Scribe of Granada, 2014), demonstrates interest in the historical connection between Iberia and the Arabo-Muslim world via al-Andalus, as do other works by *mahjar* writers in other genres. On al-Andalus in Arab immigrant writings, see Civantos 2006, 62–68 and 199–200 and Civantos 2017, 129–30, 194–95, and 231–32.

10. Miguel Littín's *El viajero de las cuatro estaciones* (The Traveler of the Four Seasons/Stations, 1990) draws from the experiences of his Palestinian paternal grandfather and Greek maternal grandfather who emigrated to Chile (See El-Attar 2017, 595). Two works that draw from family and community narratives to portray the journey of Lebanese migrants to Colombia are Fayad's *La caída de los puntos cardinales* (The Fall of the Cardinal Points, 2000) and Juan Gossaín's *La balada de María Abdala* (The Ballad of María Abdala, 2003).

11. For more on Arslan, Khury, and Achem, see Civantos 2006, 164–87.

12. "Eludía pensar si ella se iba a sentir menoscabada por sus devaneos amorosos, destinada sólo a engendrar chiquillos y estimularle la glotonería de palestino sensual" (32).

13. For more on Garib's novel, see El-Attar 2017, 597–99, Civantos 2017, 514, and Samamé 2002. On Garib's novel, and others, as examples of transculturation, see Samamé (2003).

14. For more on Saer and Arabness, see Civantos ("On Becoming," 2019). On Saer and place, see Claesson (2013), Dolph (2014), Linenberg-Fressard (2007), and Monteleone (2006).

15. For more on Abdala's novel, including its use of Arabic as well as Quechua, see Civantos 2006, 189–94.

16. For more on Azar's novel, see Civantos 2017, 513.

17. For more on Sefamí's novel, see Civantos 2017, 511–13.

18. Another third-generation novel that narrates a reconnection with the past is Mexican Carlos Martínez Assad's *En el verano la tierra* (The Land in the Summer, 1994), which narrates a positive, though simplistic, experience of return through a Mexican-Lebanese man's voyage to the Middle East homeland of his forefathers.

19. For more on Jacobs's novel, see Civantos 2017, 514–15.

Works Cited

Abdala, Durval. *El criado Braulio*. Buenos Aires: Compañía Argentina de Editores, 1962.

Abrão, Gilberto. *Mohamed, o latoeiro*. São Paulo: Primavera, 2009.

Abrão, Gilberto. *O escriba de Granada*. São Paulo: Companhia Editora Nacional, 2014.

Achem, Pablo. *Bengala, fugaz en noche negra*. Santiago del Estero [Argentina]: Imprenta La Oriental, 1931.

Adoum, Jorge Elías. *Adonay, novela iniciática del colegio de los magos*. Quito: Imprenta Fernández, 1943.

Adoum, Jorge Enrique. *Los amores fugaces*. Quito: Seix Barral, 1997.

Alfaro-Velcamp, Theresa. *So Far from Allah, so Close to Mexico: Middle Eastern Immigrants in Modern Mexico*. Austin: University of Texas Press, 2007.

Arslan, Emin. *Final de un idilio*. Buenos Aires: Rodríguez Giles, 1917.

Asís, Jorge. *Don Abdel Zalim, el burlador de Domínico*. Buenos Aires: Corregidor, 1972.

Asís, Jorge. *Flores robadas en los jardines de Quilmes*. Buenos Aires: Losada, 1980.

'Assāf, Jūrj. *Imīlya*. Buenos Aires: Maṭba'at al-Salām, n.d. [ca. 1925].

Azar, Héctor. *Las tres primeras personas*. México: Grijalbo, 1977.

Ba'qlīnī, Najīb, and Sam'ān al-Ḥāmātī. *Da'ās wa-Fad'ūs*. Tucumán [Argentina]: Ṣada al-Sharq/El Eco de Oriente, 1923.

Beshara, Adel. *Qiṣṣatan: Two Novellas: Eid sayyidat Saydnaya and Faji'at Hubb*. Victoria: iPhoenix Publishing, 2011.

Cánovas, Rodrigo. *Literatura de inmigrantes árabes y judíos en Chile y México*. Madrid and Frankfurt: Iberoamericana/Vervuert, 2011.

Carneiro, Cecílio. *A fogueira*. Rio de Janeiro: J. Olympio, 1942.

Carneiro, Cecílio. *The Bonfire*. Translated by Dudley Poore. New York: Farrar & Reinhart, 1944.

Cepeda, María Elena. *Music ImagiNation: U.S.-Colombian Identity and the Latin Music Boom*. New York University Press, 2010.

Chahín Curí, Edith. *Nahima*. Barcelona: Debate, 2001.

Chahín Curí, Edith. *Fadua, la impetuosa doncella de Homs*. Madrid: Tabla Rasa, 2004.

Chahín Curí, Edith. *La trovadora de Jerusalén*. Madrid: Endymion, 2013.

Chuaqui, Benedicto. *Memorias de un emigrante*. Santiago de Chile: Orbe, 1942.

Chuaqui, Benedicto. *Memorias de un emigrante: Imágenes y confidencias*. Santiago: Nascimento, 1957.

Civantos, Christina. *Between Argentines and Arabs: Argentine Orientalism, Arab Immigrants, and the Writing of Identity*. Albany: State University of New York Press, 2006.

Civantos, Christina. *The Afterlife of Al-Andalus: Muslim Iberia in Contemporary Arab and Hispanic Narratives*. Albany: State University of New York Press, 2017.

Civantos, Christina. "Ali Bla Bla's Double-Edged Sword: Argentine President Carlos Menem and the Negotiation of Identity." *Between the Middle East and the Americas: The Cultural Politics of Diaspora*, edited by Evelyn Alsultany and Ella Shohat, Ann Arbor: University of Michigan Press, 2012, pp. 108–29.

Civantos, Christina. "Argentina and Hispano-America." *The Oxford Handbook of Arab Novelistic Traditions*, edited by Waïl S. Hassan, New York: Oxford University Press, 2017, pp. 501–22.

Civantos, Christina. "On Becoming an Arab Argentine Writer: Juan José Saer's *La grande*." *Review: Literature and Arts of the Americas*, vol. 52, no. 2, fall 2019, pp. 177–84.

Claesson, Christian. "La estela del traslado: lugar y recuerdo en *La mayor*." *Juan José Saer: La construcción de una obra*, edited by Ilse Logie. Sevilla: Universidad de Sevilla, 2013, pp. 107–22.

Dolph, Steve. "Juan José Saer: A Geographical Fiction, a Fictional Geography." *Frank Matter*, February 2, 2014.

El-Attar, Heba. "Chile." *The Oxford Handbook of Arab Novelistic Traditions*, edited by Waïl S. Hassan, New York: Oxford University Press, 2017, pp. 589–601.

Farhat, Emil. *Dinheiro na estrada: Uma saga de imigrantes*. São Paulo: T.A. Queiroz, 1987.

Fayad, Luis. *Los parientes de Ester*. Madrid: Alfaguara, 1978.

Fayad, Luis. *La caída de los puntos cardinales*. Bogotá: Planeta Colombia, 2000.

Garib, Walter. *El viajero de la alfombra mágica*. Santiago [Chile]: Fértil Provincia, 1991.

Gossaín, Juan. *La balada de María Abdala*. Bogotá: Planeta Colombiana, 2003.

Hales Dib, Jaime. *Peregrino de ojos brillantes*. Providencia [Santiago, Chile]: Casa Doce, 1995.

Ḥammādī, Muḥammad Shihāb al-Dīn. *Riwayat ṭahārat al-ḥubb ʿind al-ʿarab*. Buenos Aires: Maṭbaʿat Rustum Ikhwān, 1953.

Ḥardān, Nawwāf. *Ḥafid al-nusūr*. 2nd ed. Beirut: Dār al-Bāḥith, 1970.

Hassan, Waïl. "Brazil." *The Oxford Handbook of Arab Novelistic Traditions*, edited by Waïl S. Hassan. New York: Oxford University Press, 2017, pp. 543–66.

Hatoum, Milton. *Relato de um certo Oriente*. São Paulo: Companhia das Letras, 1989.

Hatoum, Milton. *Tale of a Certain Orient*. Translated by Ellen Watson. London: Bloomsbury, 2004.

Hatoum, Milton. *The Brothers*. Translated by John Gledson. New York: Farrar, Straus & Giroux, 2002.

Hatoum, Milton. *Shaqīqān*. Translated by Ṣafāʾ Abū Shahlā Jubrān. Beirut: Dār al-Fārābī, 2002.

Hatoum, Milton. *Dois irmãos*. São Paulo: Companhia das Letras, 2000.

Isṭifān, Nasīb. "Daḥiyyat al-gharām." *Dhuhūr wa-ashwāk*. Tucumán [Argentina]: n.p., 1925, pp. 64–106.

Jacobs, Bárbara. *Las siete fugas de Saab, alias el Rizos*. México, DF: Alfaguara and Consejo Nacional para la Cultura y las Artes, 1992.

Kabchi, Raymundo, ed. *El mundo árabe y América Latina*. Madrid: Ediciones UNESCO; Libertarias/Prodhufi, 1997.

Khury, Juan. *Ramsay*. Paraná: Juan Khury, 1938.

Linenberg-Fressard, Raquel. "La ciudad en el tiempo: *La grande* de Juan José Saer." *Les Villes et la fin du XXe siècle en Amérique Latine: littératures, cultures, représentations/Las ciudades y el fin del siglo XX en América Latina: literaturas, culturas, representaciones*, edited by Teresa Orecchia-Havas. Berlin: Peter Lang, 2007, pp. 357–67.

Littín, Miguel. *El viajero de las cuatro estaciones*. Madrid: Mondadori. 1990.

Macías, Sergio. *Presencia árabe en la literatura latinoamericana*. Santiago de Chile: Zona Azul, 1995.

Maher, Tracey. *Imagining Diaspora: Arabic Novels from Early Twentieth Century Latin America*. The University of Texas at Austin, PhD dissertation, 2019.

Martínez Assad, Carlos. *En el verano la tierra*. México, DF: Planeta, 1994.

Menéndez Paredes, Rigoberto. *Árabes de cuentos y novelas: el inmigrante árabe en el imaginario narrativo latinoamericano*. Madrid: Huerga y Fierro, 2011.

Miguel, Salim. *Nur na escuridão*. Rio de Janeiro: Topbooks, 2004.

Molina Guzmán, Isabel, and Angharad N. Valdivia. "Latinidad, Hybridized Bodies, and Transnational Identities: Disciplining the Ethnic Body." *Governing the Female Body: Gender, Health, and Networks of Power*, edited by Lori Reed and Paula Saukko. Albany: State University of New York Press, 2010, pp. 206–29.

Monteleone, Jorge. "Lo póstumo: Juan José Saer y *La grande*." *Insula: Revista de letras y ciencias humanas*, vol. 61, no. 711, 2006, pp. 14–17.

Mussa, Alberto. *O enigma de Qaf*. Rio de Janeiro: Record, 2004.

Mussa, Alberto. *Lughz al-qāf*. Translated by Waïl S. Hassan. Cairo: Al-Markaz al-Qawmī lil-Tarjama, 2015.

Mussa, Alberto. *The Riddle of Qaf*. Translated by Lennie Larkin. Laverstock: Aflame Books, 2008.

Nassar, Raduan. *Ancient Tillage*. Translated by K. C. S. Sotelino. New York: New Directions, 2017.

Nassar, Raduan. *Lavoura arcaica*. São Paulo: Companhia das Letras, 1975.

Noufouri, Hamurabi, Rita Veneroni, and Yusef Abboud, eds. *Sirios, libaneses y argentinos: fragmentos para una historia de la diversidad cultural argentina*. Buenos Aires: Fundación Los Cedros, 2004.

Nuzhā'. Buenos Aires: Maṭbaʻat al-Salām, n.d. [ca. 1925].

Qunṣul, Ilyās. *Fī mahabb al-rīḥ*. Buenos Aires: Ilyās Qunṣul, 1972.

Rafide, Matías. *Escritores chilenos de origen árabe: Ensayo y antología*. [Santiago, Chile]: Instituto Chileno-Árabe de Cultura, 1989.

Rebolledo Hernández, Antonia. "La "turcofobia': discriminación antiárabe en Chile, 1900–1950." *Historia*, vol. 28, 1994, pp. 249–72.

Rein, Raanan, ed. *Arabes y judíos en Iberoamérica: similitudes, diferencias y tensiones*. Sevilla: Fundación Tres Culturas del Mediterráneo, 2008.

Rein, Raanan, María José Cano, and Beatriz Molina Rueda, eds. *Más allá del Medio Oriente: las diásporas judía y árabe en América Latina*. Granada: Universidad de Granada, 2012.

Saʻāda, Anṭūn. "*Fāji'at ḥubb*". *Qiṣṣatān: ʻīd sayyidat Ṣaydnāyā wa-fāji'at ḥubb*. Cairo: Muʾassasat hindāwi, [1931] 2014, pp. 37–69.

Saer, Juan José. *La grande*. Buenos Aires: Planeta and Seix Barral, 2005.

Saer, Juan José. *La Grande*. Translated by Steve Dolph. Rochester, NY: Open Letter, 2014.

Said, Edward W. *Orientalism*. New York: Vintage Books, 1979.

Samamé, María Olga. "Aproximación a una novela de emigración árabe: *El viajero de la alfombra mágica* de Walter Garib." *Revista chilena de literatura*, no. 60, April 2002, pp. 23–54.

Samamé, María Olga. "Transculturación, identidad y alteridad en novelas de la inmigración árabe hacia Chile." *Revista signos*, vol. 36, no. 53, 2003, pp. 51–73.

Saráh Comandari, Roberto. *Los turcos*. Santiago de Chile: Editorial del Pacífico, 1961.

Sefamí, Jacobo. *Los dolientes*. México: Plaza Janés, 2004.

Shakūr, Anṭūn Anīs. *Min al-laḥd ilā al-mahd*. Rio de Janeiro: n.p., 1940.

Zaytūn, Naẓīr. *Dhunūb al-ābā'*. São Paulo: Maṭbaʻat Musāmarāt al-Muhājir, 1932.

CHAPTER 20

··

THE ASIAN-LATIN
AMERICAN NOVEL

··

IGNACIO LÓPEZ-CALVO

THERE is a rich, albeit mostly recent, cultural production by Latin American authors of
Asian ancestry that may help expose what is hidden in the official histories of nations
and, along the way, suggest alternative reconsiderations of national identities.[1] Although
the first Asian presence in the Americas is that of the Filipinos who came with the
Manila Galleon in the sixteenth century (they appear as characters in several early Latin
American novels), to my knowledge there are no significant novels published by Latin
Americans of Filipino heritage. The same can be said about novels by Latin American
authors of Korean background, even though there is indeed a small cultural production in other literary genres. And then, there are countries like Mexico (traditionally
with one of the richest literary productions in Latin America), which have a small cultural production in the fields of poetry, theater, memoirs, and essays but, surprisingly,
no significant novels by authors of Asian descent. This chapter, consequently, will concentrate on how the most representative Asian Latin American novels have recorded the
social history of Nikkei (overseas Japanese and their descendants) and Chinese-Latin
American/Tusán/*Huayi* 华裔 (overseas Chinese and their descendants) subject formation.[2] The increasing cultural production by Nikkei and Chinese-Latin American
writers in Latin America and the Caribbean in recent decades reflects the emergence of
two diasporic, minority discourses that are redefining national cultures by making them
more transnational and by calling into question the white-indigenous and white-black
dichotomies of the discourses of *mestizaje* and *mulataje*, respectively.

   Although over the last decade more critical attention has been paid to Asian Latin
American literature, there is still an unfortunate tendency to assume that if the author
is of Asian descent, there must necessarily be "Asian" traits in his or her writing; needless to say, it is not always the case. As will be seen, many Latin American authors of
Asian ancestry (most Chinese Panamanian authors, for example) do not address or reflect their ethnic background in their writings, and neither have many of them been
significantly influenced by Asian literatures and cultures. In the case of Nikkei literature,

the ideological discourse of *Nihonjinron*, a Japanese essentializing theory on the ontological principles of Japaneseness that was elaborated in contrast with the idea of an also essentialized "West," may have something to do with this problem. Perhaps because of Nihonjinron's self-orientalizing and static depiction of Japanese identity, critics sometimes overemphasize echoes of Japanese cultural heritage in Nikkei writing.

THE NIKKEI NOVEL

I begin this overview with the Japanese Brazilian novel, since Brazil easily boasts the largest Asian-Latin American production in the region. When addressing Nikkei issues and characters, the periods and events that are more often portrayed are the exploitation in coffee plantations during the inception of the immigration process, the oppression (including the epistemicidal measures imposed by Getúlio Vargas's [1882–1954] *Estado Novo* [New State; 1937–1945]) and forced relocation away from coastal areas during World War II, the fanatical reaction of Shindō Renmei immediately after the war, and the dekasegi phenomenon that sent 250,000 Nikkeijin "back" (for most it was their first time in the country) to Japan during the 1990s to work in factories. Other recurrent topics are racialization, miscegenation, cultural integration, and the quest for full citizenship. And many novels openly celebrate the many achievements of Nikkei communities and advocate for Nikkei cultural difference while, concomitantly, claiming their belonging to the nation.

Much of Japanese Brazilian literature conveniently avoids addressing the role of state-guided emigration in prewar imperial expansionism and postwar neocolonialism.[3] Yet a few texts do address migration-driven expansionism and imperialism, mostly when engaging Shindō Renmei, a Nikkei organization that, I would argue, could be considered the first terrorist organization in the Americas as well as the missing link between Japanese migration and imperialism. Brazilian Nikkei cultural production reflects the fact that many immigrants who claimed to have left the homeland out of patriotism (the emperor declared that it would be good for the national economy) were disappointed once they saw the appalling working and living conditions in coffee plantations; many, in fact, fled the plantations. Thus, in *Nihonjin* (2011), the first novel by the *Sansei* (third-generation) author Oscar Nakasato (1963–), a Japanese immigrant mentions: "these gaijin had told him that the emperor of Japan had deceived the poor farmers and the unemployed in the city, saying that they should emigrate because they could make money quickly in Brazil. But that, in fact, it was a project to expel the poor population, that were in excess in the country."[4] Not only did emigration companies take advantage of immigrants, but since government officials mandated them to succeed abroad, it would have been a dishonor to return without having met their economic goals. Thus, in *Nihonjin* one of the protagonists, Hideo, acknowledges that he "would not subject himself to the humiliation of returning to Japan in the same condition as when he left."[5] *Nihonjin* also denounces the oppression suffered by Nikkei during World War II: "One day, Ojiichan recalled, a Nihonjin from Araçatuba had been beaten to death because they suspected that he was a spy of the Japanese government. And when Japan won the battle against Singapore in 1942, and many thought the war was nearing its end, he and some friends had to celebrate in a low voice, as if they were all criminals."[6] Moreover, the novel's criticism of Japanese militaristic, imperial ideology is expanded through Hideo's membership in Shindō Renmei and his son Haruo's public rejection of it and simultaneous declaration of loyalty to Brazil.

Indeed, the Nikkei community was caught between two aggressive nationalist discourses: Japan's imperialism and Vargas's Estado Novo, which forbade Japanese-language schools, newspapers, and books, or even speaking Japanese in public, as denounced from the point of view of a young girl in Lúcia Hiratsuka's (1960–) novel *Os livros de Sayuri* (Sayuri's Books, 2008). The disgraceful episode of the fraudulent Shindō Renmei was, in part, an outcome of this predicament. It also exposes the long-range influence of imperial ideology and fascist indoctrination, which is taken up by Jorge J. Okubaro's (1937–) *O Súdito (Banzai, Massateru!)* (The Subject [Banzai, Massateru!], 2008), a 542-page blend of novel, historical, and sociological study, and journalism. Based on the biography of Okubaro's Okinawan father, Massateru Hokubaru, this is one of the works that openly links immigration with imperial expansionism: "Japanese emigration policy in the period before World War II had clearly become a means for Japanese territorial expansion."[7] Indeed, whether knowingly or not, and even if their primary motivation was to become wealthy in a short period of time, these immigrants became "brokers of Empire" (to use Jun Uchida's term), advancing, in their own way, Japan's commercial, political, and expansionist goals.

O Súdito is also one of the works that more visibly emphasizes the intra-ethnic divisions between Okinawans and Naichijin (mainland Japanese). Massateru and, by extension, all Okinawans are presented as victims of imperialist indoctrination first in Okinawan grade schools and later, in the case of those who migrated to Brazil, through the fascist literature received from Japan. This propaganda reinforces the protagonist's conviction about Japan's invincibility, the emperor's divine nature, and the need to patriotically give one's life for the fatherland, if necessary.

Japanese imperialism resurfaces in the *Nisei* (second generation) Júlio Miyazawa's (1948–) first novel, *Yawara! A Travessia Nihondin-Brasil* (Yawara! Crossing Nihondin-Brasil, 2006), where a character named Mariano condemns it, along with the Japanese state's negligence toward the Nikkei community when it ordered all its diplomats to leave Brazil after this country's declaration of war against the **Empire** of Japan: "It turns out that all of this is not going to change the minds of many Japanese descendants. That we were massacred here in Brazil and had to deal with it alone. That's what I'm trying to say the entire time: Japan abandoned us! Japan dumped us here so that we would handle it alone."[8] In these passages, Japanese Brazilian characters voice their progressive disassociation with the ancestral fatherland, which will ultimately result in their new national allegiance to Brazil.

State-organized emigration efforts resumed during the 1950s and 1960s, as the Japanese government believed it would help the postwar, resurging Japanese economy.

According to Sidney Lu, the decision was part of a neocolonial enterprise: "As Japan's overseas migration restarted at the beginning of the 1950s, South American countries that received most of the Japanese postwar emigrants were no longer portrayed as empty; nevertheless, they continued to be described as primitive but abundant in natural wealth, waiting for the civilized Japanese to explore and utilize" (16). This is reflected in *Yawara* when a character named Mariano states: "I made acid remarks about Japan, pointing out its colonialist stance, which was negotiating the acquisition of Brazilian land the size of a state, almost the size of Japan itself, for a soy plantation project that would demand the arrival of thousands of Japanese people."[9]

Imperial indoctrination is likewise indirectly condemned in Ryoki Inoue's (1946) *Saga. A História de Quatro Gerações de uma Família Japonesa no Brasil* (Saga. The History of Four Generations of a Japanese Family in Brazil, 2006) by displaying how characters have internalized imperialistic propaganda, including a sense of racial superiority. Thus, a character named Ryuiti Fukugawa exclaims: "We don't have to be considered equals, mainly because we're not equal. We are superior and that's what we need to show them!"[10] Later in the plot, parents demand from their children to be "superior" in school as well. Like previous novels, *Saga* associates immigration with expansionism in the context of empire by echoing Japanese state's efforts to preserve the loyalty of Nikkei communities in South America:

> One of the preponderant factors for this distortion of objectives was the strong presence of former military men among the Japanese expatriates who came to Brazil between 1928 and 1933. Many of them came here with the explicit mission of creating, in the countries where the Japanese community was beginning to be significant, both demographically and economically, nuclei of resistance to Western political and cultural domination. They became members of Shindō-Renmei and started to publicize the *yamato damashii*, literally imposing their ideas even if through violence. The leader of the association was Junji Kikawa, an ex-officer of the Japanese Imperial Army and a fanatical follower of the divinity represented by Emperor Hirohito.[11]

Further reflecting imperialist ideology, *Saga* also addresses the conflict between Naichijin and Okinawans when a sergeant of Okinawan ancestry complains: "When I have to talk with a Japanese, the expression on his face when I give my name is more than enough to show me that I'm not welcome."[12]

These novels historicize the evolution of Nikkei diasporic worldviews and politics from a mostly sojourner mentality as subjects of the Japanese empire to a progressive Brazilianization and disconnection with the ancestral homeland. Some reflect how this shift in national allegiance and identity formation, triggered by the destruction suffered by Japan during the war and the resulting impossibility of return, was a constant source of intergenerational conflict within Nikkei families. Overall, the Japanese Brazilian novel recovers a silenced past, combats the epistemic racism that peaked during the Estado Novo, and demands a place for Nikkei in the Brazilian national imaginary. It also records a history of active resistance to compulsory acculturation and portrays the existence of multiple, heterogeneous, and evolving identities and cultural practices, thus challenging Nihonjinron's essentialist idea of a static, fixed, and timeless Japanese identity.

I now turn to the Japanese Peruvian novel, since Peru has the second-largest Nikkei cultural production in the region. When addressing Nikkei issues, Japanese Peruvian cultural production tends to focus on major historical landmarks, including the inception of the immigration process and the suffering in plantations, the May 1940 lootings in Lima, the deportations to US internment camps during World War II, the victory of Alberto Fujimori in the 1990 presidential election, and the dekasegi diaspora. In consonance with Japanese Brazilian literature, Nikkei writing in Peru narrativizes the transition from a sojourner, insular mentality to a progressive cultural integration into mainstream society. These works often celebrate cross-cultural hybridization, with characters negotiating national allegiances or displaying multiple public and private identities; they also condemn nativism, Nipponophobia, and racism (including racism within the Nikkei community), particularly during World War II. And, as is typically the case of all Asian-Latin American writing, the Japanese Peruvian novel, which is for the most part quite recent, does not exhibit different formal characteristics from non-Asian Latin American cultural production.

Among the main representatives of the Peruvian Nikkei novel are Augusto Higa (1946–), with two short novels dealing with Nikkei issues and characters (*La iluminación de Katzuo Nakamatzu* [Katzuo Nakamatsu's Enlightenment, 2008] and *Gaijin* [2014]), and Fernando Iwasaki (1961–), whose novels are for the most part devoid of explicit references to a Nikkei identity. While still resorting to literature as a tool for empowerment, Iwasaki (like the short-story writer Carlos Yushimito [1977] and the Chinese Peruvians Julia Wong [1965] and Sui Yun [Kathie Wong Lo; 1955–]) claims a cosmopolitan, rather than national, belonging. Both Higa and Iwasaki, each with a few works that address Japaneseness but also writing about other issues, allow readers to appreciate Nikkei writing and self-representation in all its complexity, with a look at fluid, hybrid, and changing subjectivities.

Although his first publications dealt with the violence of the terrorist group Sendero Luminoso and of daily life in Lima's poor neighborhoods, more recently Higa has published *Japón no da dos oportunidades* (Japan Does Not Give Two Opportunities, 1994), a testimonial account about his experience as a dekasegi in Japan, two novels, and a short-story collection titled *Okinawa existe* (Okinawa Exists, 2013) and dealing with Nikkei characters and issues. The novel *La iluminación de Katzuo Nakamatsu* evidences, through its Nisei protagonist's psychological evolution, the processes of de-ethnification and re-ethnification that some Japanese Peruvians have undergone according to circumstances such as residence or sometimes also as a result of strategic essentialism. The alienated protagonist that appears in the title eventually finds his true identity through an epiphany or, in Japanese cultural terms, a *kensho* awakening.[13] A former college literature professor and frustrated writer, Katzuo Nakamatsu becomes suicidal after being fired because of his advanced age. Adding to the protagonist's existential angst is his disconnection with mainstream Peruvian society as well as his awareness of the historical discrimination suffered by his ethnic community. *La iluminación de Katzuo Nakamatsu* ultimately argues that, rather than a mere extension of Japan, Nikkei nowadays are undeniably Peruvian.

The protagonist of Higa's other novella dealing with Nikkei issues, *Gaijin*, is Setei Nakandakari, a greedy and contemptible Okinawan entrepreneur who arrives with no savings in Peru in 1923. After working in sugar plantations, he moves to Lima where he initially works as a street vendor in Jirón Ayacucho. Nakandakari overcomes widespread Nipponophobia in 1930s Peru by tolerating humiliations: as if enjoying confrontation or masochism, the protagonist keeps going to a coffee shop in Lima's Chinatown where he is often insulted. Eventually, he marries a *criollo* woman named Misha Arango in order to better integrate himself into Peruvian society. As a result, his bazaar is the only one that is not vandalized during a sacking of Nikkei shops in Lima. Even though he succeeds economically, Nakandakari's immorality (he later opens a brothel) challenges the cultural values and damages the reputation of Lima's Nikkei community. In consonance with the author's intention of mythologizing the character, Nakandakari remains contradictory, gloomy, and inscrutable; yet, unlike Katzuo Nakamatsu in Higa's previous novel, Nakandakari suffers no identitarian uncertainties: he feels fully Japanese and even shuts himself away at home during World War II. By the end of the novel, saddened by Japan's defeat, he will go insane (like Nakamatsu), hearing voices from the past, and will eventually die alone, despised by everyone around him.

For his part, Fernando Iwasaki (1961–) also has four works that deal with Japanese issues and characters: the historical study *Extremo Oriente y el Perú en el siglo XVI* (The Far East and Peru in the Sixteenth Century, 1992); the short story "La sombra del guerrero" (The Warrior's Shadow), included in the collection *Un milagro informal* (An Informal Miracle, 2003); the collection of essays *Mi poncho es un kimono flamenco* (My Poncho Is a Flamenco Kimono, 2005); and the novel (it could also be considered a short-story collection) *España, aparta de mí estos premios* (Spain, Take This Awards from Me, 2009). The humorous premise of this last work is that it promises to offer readers the perfect formula to win one of the many literary contests that proliferate all over Spain. Iwasaki then lightheartedly explores Japanese fascination with Spanish culture only to end up criticizing nationalist discourses in contemporary Spain, as well as the banalization of mass media (reality shows, clairvoyants, astrologists) and of life in general in Spain. Except for a female character in "La *geisha* cubista" ("The cubist *geisha*"), all the other stories include strange, male, caricaturized, Japanese characters, such as a Japanese Brigadist who has been hiding clandestinely in a cave for almost seventy years unaware of the end of the Spanish Civil War, or other Japanese characters who, determined to be Basque, Andalusian, or Catalan, have mastered the regional identity marks. In this case, therefore, the novel is not so much about the Japanese or Nikkei (after all, all of them are mere caricatures) as it is about the perception of the Japanese in Spain, as an excuse to sarcastically expose sociopolitical paradoxes mostly dealing with regional nationalisms in contemporary Spain.

Because Argentina has smaller Asian communities, Asian Argentinean cultural production is not as extensive as those in Brazil or Peru. But a notable novel is *Gaijin* (2003) by the Nisei Maximiliano Matayoshi (1979–), which addresses the creation of an immigrant, hybrid identity, all the while historicizing the Japanese and Nikkei experiences in Argentina. Using a first-person-narrative point of view, it tells the story of a Japanese immigrant called Kitaro and his adaptation to the host country. Working first in a dry cleaner, Kitaro later obtains a medical degree and then decides to return to his homeland after fourteen years in Argentina. Later, however, he misses Julieta, the daughter of one of his Japanese friends, and decides to return to Argentina, considering it now his new home. According to Koichi Hagimoto, "One of the values that Kitaro embraces is silence, which is described as an essential mode of communication for many Japanese immigrant characters in Gaijin" (91). The novel also denounces the racial discrimination suffered by Nikkei characters.

While there is a cultural production by Korean Chileans in the areas of poetry (Moisés Park [1982–]) and theater (Kyoung H. Park [1982–]), and by the Chinese Chilean poet (Luis Cruz-Villalobos [1976–]), the only two available Asian Chilean novels are *El nikkei—A la sombra del samurai* (The Nikkei—In the Shadow of the Samurai, 2013) and *El diario de Terry* (Terry's Dialogue, 2015) by the Nisei Ariel Takeda, a professor of Japanese history and culture. Whereas *El diario de Terry*, a novel written from the point of view of a Chilean Terrier, suggests that we must live in unity with the natural world and in brotherhood with other human beings, in *El nikkei—A la sombra del samurai* one finds a college student named Hiroshi ("Jiro"), the son of a Japanese immigrant, who is arrested, tortured, and imprisoned for a year during Augusto Pinochet's dictatorship. Although Jiro had planned to return to his former routine after being released from prison, his mother is suddenly assassinated by the dictator's goons, and his dying father, a descendant of samurai, commends him to fight for justice and for the family's honor. As a result, Jiro first trains firmly to transform himself into a samurai and a ninja, and then devotes himself to bravely fighting the dictatorship's crimes in Santiago. According to Maria Montt Strabucchi, "Orientalism seeps through the action novel and its multiple events, with the main character training to become a martial arts expert and described through traits belonging to an 'Oriental spirit.' When upset, Hiroshi remembers 'that lesson about the flexibility and stiffness of bamboo.' "14

THE CHINESE-LATIN AMERICAN NOVEL

The Chinese Peruvian novel shares common traits with much of Sino-Latin American writing. Texts dealing with Chinese or Chinese-Latin American characters and topics typically explore the motivations to emigrate from China, as well as the numerous obstacles on the path toward cultural integration, social agency, and full citizenship in the host country. With Chinatowns as the emblematic space of the Chinese diaspora, the shop counter often becomes the quintessential Chinese-Latin American chronotope and the symbolic borderline that separates the Chinese-Latin American world from mainstream society. It is also at the shop counter where transculturation processes take place; in fact, the depiction of these economic and sociocultural exchanges challenges stereotypes about Chinese insularity.

Although he has published novels unrelated to his Chinese origin, such as *La estatua en el jardín* (*The Statue in the Garden*, 2004) and *El furor de mis ardores* (*The Fury of My Ardors*, 2008), Siu Kam Wen (1951–) also finds inspiration in his experience as a Chinese-born young immigrant enduring racial discrimination and family self-exploitation in Lima's working-class neighborhood of Rímac. These traumatic memories, often dealing with language, place, and displacement, are collected in his novels *Viaje a Ítaca* (*A Journey to Ithaca*, 2004), *La vida no es una tómbola* (*This Sort of Life*, 2007), and *El verano largo* (The Long Summer, 2009). We learn, for instance, about the claustrophobia felt by younger generations of Tusanes in these ethnocultural enclaves that prevent them from properly adapting to mainstream society or even from pursuing their own professional dreams. Intergenerational conflicts dealing with the rejection of a shopkeeper's life and of Chinese traditional customs ultimately signal a prelude to the shift of allegiance from the ancestral fatherland to the host society.

Siu Kam Wen's young, autobiographical characters reject cultural practices like arranged marriage as well as their parents' extreme "work ethics," or their teachers' national or political affiliations. They are also more receptive toward miscegenation and the culture of the host country. His novel *La vida no es una tómbola* coincides with his short-story collection *El tramo final* in its denunciation of Chinese shopkeepers' exploitation of their families' and recent arrival's labor. It also offers a testimonial account of life in Lima's Chinese community during the 1960s, 1970s, and 1980s. This Bildungsroman explores the psychological evolution of the author's young alter ego, Héctor (Ah-Hung), who suffers from depression as a result of being forced to work twelve hours a day, including holidays, as a clerk in a family-owned grocery store in the neighborhood of Rímac. The Peruvianized Héctor's refusal to pursue a mediocre life as a shopkeeper clashes with his traditional father's Confucian expectation of filial piety and obedience. Other characters in the novel also express their rejection of the type of life chosen by Chinese shopkeepers obsessed with saving money while living in substandard dwellings. All in all, Siu Kam Wen's novels and short stories expose the fact that behind Chinese shopkeepers' economic success is not only an effective system of mutual economic support, but also their excessive frugality and self-sacrifice. In addition, *La vida no es una tómbola* reveals other practices, such as sending remittances to China, selling counterfeit birth certificates to unauthorized immigrants, and bribing immigration service employees. It also presents re-migration as a last-resort survival strategy, particularly after the radical populist Juan Velasco Alvarado rose to power.

The traumas of a Chinese upbringing and of intergenerational miscommunication between Chinese parents and their offspring reappear in *El verano largo*, another autobiographical novel. As in the previous work, the protagonist, Siu, laments having spent three years of his life without schooling because of his parents' indifference toward his education. His strict and unsympathetic upbringing will ultimately be the source of insecurities and traumas: "I had to build an armor of indifference and pride around my psyche. I learned to live without friendship or affection; I learned to live without female company. Therefore, when I enrolled in San Marcos, I did not feel, like other guys my age, the hormonal need to have a girlfriend."[15] Overcome by self-pity, Siu is also ashamed of the voluntary poverty chosen by stingy shopkeepers who blend living and working spaces, making him live in the messy and run-down backroom of a grocery store.

In turn, in *Viaje a Ítaca* the autobiographical narrator and protagonist returns to Lima in 1990 in pursuit of an arranged marriage that never materializes. Looking back, Siu resents the fact that the Peruvian government turned down his citizenship application after having lived in the country for over a quarter of a century, which prevented him from finding work in Peru and forced him to migrate to Hawaii. *Viaje a Ítaca* also includes a chapter titled "A Criminal Chronology of Peru" with an overview of historical Sinophobia, including a massacre of seventy or eighty Chinese indentured workers after the War of the Pacific in 1881 because of the support that approximately 1,500 of them provided for the invading Chilean troops, in revenge for the harsh mistreatment endured in Peruvian plantations; a massacre of about one thousand "coolies" at the hands of indigenous and black people in Cañete; and he also mentions Nipponophobia in the case of the negative reaction of the country's white elite to the victory of the Nikkei Alberto Fujimori during the 1990 presidential elections. The historical memory of the sustained oppression of Asians in Peru, therefore, is central to the creation of a Tusán discourse. Siu Kam Wen's works are not only a unique example of self-representation of the Chinese community but also represent a rewriting or counter-narrative of Peruvian history from a Chinese perspective.

Siu Kam Wen has also written two as yet unpublished novels. One is a 390-page historical novel about the Spanish conquest of Peru, titled "El mapa y la espada" (The Map and the Sword), subtitled "Una novela *wuxia* de la Conquista de Perú" ("A Wuxia Novel of the Conquest of Peru"; completed in 2013). As Siu explains in the novel's postscript, in the 1960s he read wuxia novels imported from China, Taiwan, and Hong Kong, which were literary versions of kung fu movies, with martial heroes and great love stories, and sometimes with the format of a Bildungsroman. This type of Chinese novel also influenced five of the stories in his collection *La primera espada del Imperio* (The First Sword of the Empire.) The map that appears in the title connects the conquest of Peru with a fugitive Chinese emperor and with the maritime explorations of the fleet of the Great Eunuch, the Chinese Admiral Zheng He, across the Indian Ocean and Africa.

His other unpublished novel is "El varón perfecto" (literally The Perfect Man but translated as "Murder in Eden," completed in 2017), which narrates, from different perspectives and with an analepsis, a love triangle between a Chinese poet named Jie Fang (Ray), who flees the political persecution after the student protests in Tiananmen Square, his wife Liu Bin (Flora) and his lover, Meng-er (Cindy). After a negative experience at a university in Utah, he and his wife move to Hawaii with their son, and are soon joined, in their humble shack, by the poet's mistress, whom he brings from China. His wife Liu Bin reluctantly accepts the fact that his lover is living under their same roof, but she resents even more the fact that her husband gave her child up for adoption to a Hawaiian couple. In the end, the mistress, whose real motivation was to flee China as soon as possible, leaves the poet Jie Fang to marry their neighbor, Bill Campbell (the novel's first narrator). Depressed and with a wounded ego, Jie Fang tries to fix his marriage, but it is too late: suddenly his wife announces her intention to divorce him because she is going to marry a Chinese exile whom they met during a stay at a French university. In the dramatic scenes that close the novel, the unfaithful poet cannot tolerate his wife leaving him for another man and ends up murdering her before committing suicide. Apart from this ménage à trois, "Murder in Eden" offers, through the narrator's and several characters' voices, an open criticism of the student revolts that ended with the massacre in Tiananmen Square, coupled with unconditional support for the Chinese government and the ruling Communist Party of China:

> Some, like Chai Ling, the diminutive and histrionic spokesperson for the most radical students, began to harbor the hope that "only when blood flowed in rivers through the square, would the country finally open its eyes." A massacre was expected, even desired.
> The troops trying to enter the capital to impose the curfew were prevented from doing so when the students and many common citizens, who had come massively to support the former, blocked their way with burnt vehicles of public transportation (more than two thousand of them), and other improvised barricades. The soldiers were told not to shoot and were unarmed, and when the students and the agitators realized that, they surrounded them, pulled them out of their trucks or armored vehicles, killed them with bricks, disemboweled them, tied them to a pole with their own intestines, and burned them with gasoline. (95)

While this interpretation of the Tiananmen Square massacre may be surprising to some readers, it is already present in the short story "El discurso" (The Speech), included in *El tramo final*, in which a teacher named Mr. Chen Hua, unaware that the boy admirers Mao Zedong, asks the thirteen-year-old Chiang Kei-Man to recite an anti-communist speech favoring the Kuomintang. Refusing to comply, Chiang Kei-Man pretends to be sick right before the ceremony and that night, he dreams of Tiananmen Square's red flags.

Julia Wong's (1965–) novellas *Bocetos para un cuadro de familia* (Sketches for a Family Portrait, 2006) and *Doble felicidad* (Double Happiness, 2012) also mobilize the cultural capital of an inherited ancestral culture to articulate social difference and denounce historical oppression. *Bocetos para un cuadro de familia* deals with the life of a (partly fictional) family of Chinese immigrants in the author's hometown of Chepén, who leave their farming life to become shopkeepers. In her insider's depiction of life within the Tusán community, Wong coincides with Siu Kam Wen in the presentation of Chinese shopkeepers' use of their living quarters as a warehouse: "a house was really nothing more than a storage room for oil cans, rice sacks and cinnamon bales, but one converted into a living space for a widower and his four children."[16] The first-person narrator is María Inés, a woman of both Chinese and Japanese ancestry who returns to Chepén after a twenty-year absence and celebrates her family's pride in their dual cultural heritages. Yet she also laments her grandfather's unwillingness to accept Peruvian culture, which was reflected in his obsession with watching Chinese films.

In a section titled "Brief historical review of Chinese immigration to Peru" included in another novella by Julia Wong, *Doble felicidad*, the semiautobiographical protagonist, Sofía Wu, reminds her readers about her community's historical plight. She mentions the high death rate in the ships that transported indentured workers, the restrictions on Chinese immigration, and the looting of Chinese businesses in Lima on May 9, 1909, blaming it all on "intolerance to and fear of different customs."[17] *Doble felicidad* narrates how at the age of four, Sofía was left behind with her father in Macau, after her Peruvian mother, unable to adapt to the new society, decided to return to Peru only with her other daughter, Mercedes. The suffering resulting from feeling abandoned by her mother will eventually lead to madness and suicide. The novel explores Sofía's strange relationship with her quiet father and her identitarian quandaries about Chineseness, sometimes falling into essentialist paragraphs where Chinese men are criticized for their proneness to gambling, opium consumption, and prostitution. Overall, Julia Wong's female, lyrical view of the inner life of the Chinese community provides a different but complimentary side of a world also pictured in Siu Kam Wen's oeuvre.

Moving away from Chinese topics, Mario Wong (1967–), a Tusán author who lives in France, explores the traumatic fear and psychological disorders caused by the 1980s political violence in Peru. His novel *El testamento de la tormenta* (Storm Testimony, 1997) and its rewriting, *Su majestad el terror* (His Majesty Terror, 2009), are characterized by the poetics of narrative fragmentation. Underscoring the ineffability of the existential angst and horror suffered by his generation as a result of the dirty war between the Peruvian government and the terrorist group Sendero Luminoso (as well as the MRTA [Túpac Amaru Revolutionary Movement]), the memory of terrorist attacks in both novels is fictionalized through a surrealistic and postmodern poetic prose that avoids realism.

Regarding the Chinese Cuban novel, the following are some of the key publications by Chinese and Chinese Cubans that constitute a type of ethnic minority discourse: Ch'en Lan Pin's *The Cuba Commission Report* (1877), a Chinese, official denunciation essay with depositions by Chinese indentured workers; Antonio Chuffat Latour's *Apunte histórico de los chinos en Cuba* (1927), an essay lauding the achievements of the Chinese community in Cuba (at times in detriment of the Afro-Cuban community); Regino Pedroso's identitarian poetry collections *Nosotros* (1933) and *El ciruelo de Yuan Pei Fu* (1955); Napoleón Seuc's *La colonia china de Cuba 1930–1960* (1998), a memoir and essay about the history of the Chinese Cuban community in Cuba and Miami; and Armando Choy's, Gustavo Chui's, and Moisés Sío Wong's *Our History is Still Being Written* (2005), a series of pro-Cuban Revolution interviews with Chinese Cuban generals who participated in Fidel Castro's internationalist missions, edited by Mary-Alice Waters. Yet none of these works can be considered novels.

In the case of Cuba, the novels dealing with Chinese and Chinese Cuban characters and issues were written by authors who do not identify as Chinese Cuban—even though several of them have some more or less remote Chinese ancestors, including José Lezama Lima (1910–1976), Guillermo Cabrera Infante (1929–2005), Severo Sarduy (1937–1993), and Zoé Valdés (1959–). Severo Sarduy, who had a Chinese ancestor with the surname

Macao, addresses Chinese and other Asian issues in his novels *Gestos* (Gestures, 1963), *De dónde son los cantantes* (*From Cuba with a Song*, 1967), *Cobra* (1972), *Maitreya* (1977), and *Colibrí* (Hummingbird, 1984). Even though the author claims to have adopted a parodical perspective, he still exhibits a tendency toward orientalist scenes of boundless cruelty and an orientalist libidination of Chineseness and Chinese Cuban women. In *De dónde son los cantantes*, for instance, an Asian tattoo artist punishes a man's voyeurism by pulling out one of his fingernails and then threatens him with further torture. And Chinese torture resurfaces in *Cobra* (1972), with conversations about "Leng T'che, the Chinese one-hundred-pieces torture" (57).[18]

In *Maitreya* (1977), Sarduy again falls into stereotypes of "Oriental sensuality." The connection of the Chinese world with desire, sensuality, and exotic splendor is found in the quasi-pornographic description of a *ménage à trois* that includes the Chinese Luis Leng and two Chinese lesbians in a New York Chinese restaurant. Chineseness is also linked to exoticized sexual desire in *De dónde son los cantantes*, where Mortal Pérez, a lecherous Spanish general, woos a Chinese transvestite called Lotus Flower, whom he confuses with a beautiful Chinese soprano and *vedette*. Overall, everything Asian in the novel seems to be a mere projection of Western Orientalist fantasies about "the Orient." In reality, Chinese characters and topics in Sarduy's oeuvre, as Roberto González Echevarría elucidates, do not respond to historical vindication or identitarian self-exploration; rather, they are part of his poetics: "it belongs to a moment of the development of his neo-Barroque aesthetics."[19] Another factor, according to González Echevarría, is "the surprising and fleeting fascination with Maoism of the Tel Quel group, the group of literary critics and theorists to which he was affiliated in Paris during the 1960s and 70s."[20] Finally, Julia Kushigian has pointed out "Sarduy's interest, in general terms, for everything Eastern, not only Chinese but also the Arab world and that of India and Japan."[21]

For her part, Zoé Valdés, who dedicates her novel *La eternidad del instante* (The Eternity of the Instant, 2004) to her Chinese grandfather Maximiliano Megía/Mo Ying, looks at Chineseness in Cuba through a benevolently orientalist lens that at times affects the verisimilitude of the plot. She exoticizes the oriental mystique by contrasting the sensuality and refinement of Chinese culture (although also pointing male chauvinism, and Chinese fondness for opium consumption, gambling and prostitution) with the perceived vulgarity of Cuban culture. *La eternidad del instante* praises the achievements of both mainland Chinese and the Chinese Cuban community, with the protagonist, Mo Ying/Maximiliano Megía, fondly reminiscing about Chinese Cuban ice-cream parlors, laundry rooms, hardware shops, and grocery stores. Other characters share the celebration of Sino-Cuban culture, mentioning the Chinese "saint" Sanfancón, the Shangai Theater, the *chiffá* (or Chinese charades), Chinese festivals, and the *chinita de la suerte* (good-luck little Chinese girl).[22] Surprisingly, her novel does not evince strong objections to the oppressive cultural practice of foot binding.

Unlike most other authors, Valdés adds a female perspective to the history of the Chinese in Cuba, underscoring the suffering of the wives and children whom indentured workers left behind in mainland China, often enduring long periods without contact with the migrating relative. Thus, a girl named Xue Ying criticizes the possible motives behind male emigration: "Instead of digging in with mom and us the children, he chose to simply say that he was going far away in search of wealth. You may have bought that, but I consider his decision only a poor excuse. He chose the easy way out: he reneged on the family and left mom with the weight of the world upon her shoulders."[23] These comments add alternative nuances to Chinese immigration, as if it were a way for Chinese men to prove their manliness. Yet, as is well-known, many Chinese indentured workers testified to have been deceived into emigrating or to have been abducted.

Another novel by Valdés, *Te di la vida entera* (I Gave You All I Had, 1996), plays with the character of the *china mulata* (mulatta Chinese), who appears as the object of desire in numerous Cuban narratives. The narrator lightheartedly describes the china mulata protagonist, Cuca Martínez: "She had a way of sashaying down a street, with a swish to the left and a swish to the right, of bobbing back and forth between Irish passion and Oriental patience, that could bring even the most languid penis to attention" (36).[24] Yet all this sex appeal will soon degenerate, as we learn that her life is nothing but an allegory of the progressive physical decay of Old Havana since 1959: "He was dying of love—for her and for his city. As if a city and a woman were one and the same, as if cities had a uterus" (54).[25]

As seen, these novels emphasize processes of transculturation and hybridity that have affected Chinese Cuban culture and that have contributed to the creation of diverse, evolving, and multifaceted identities. At the same time, they challenge binary notions of Cuba as a mulatto nation in which only the European and African ethnocultural components count; along the way, this processes of mestizaje, syncretism, and transculturation problematize the stereotype of Chinese insularity.

Reflecting the large population of Chinese ancestry in Panama, there are numerous Chinese Panamanian authors; yet not many of them have published novels. Among the most representative and prolific is Carlos Francisco Changmarín (he blended his two surnames, Chang and Marín, to express his mixed Chinese and criollo heritage; 1922–2012), whose works typically deal with ecological concerns, revolution, social justice, and class struggle. As Huei Lan Ye points out, "Changmarín recovers indigenous and peasant issues not only as a theme but also to demonstrate that underneath the coexistence of two cultural systems is the imposition of one world over the other, and that one culture's colonization of another produces an irremediable opposition."[26] Changmarín's interest in national sovereignty, anti-imperialism, and the recent history of Panama is reflected, for example, in the 1995 short-story collection *Nochebuena mala: invasión yanqui a Panamá, diciembre de 1989. Cuentos que no son cuentos* (Bad Christmas Eve: Yankee Invasion of Panama, December 1989. Short Stories that Are Not Short Stories). As is the case of most Chinese Panamanian authors, there are almost no references to his Chinese ethnic background in his oeuvre. One of the few exceptions is the poem "Porque yo vengo de tus viejas raíces ... " (Because I Come from Your Old Roots ... ") included in *Informe de amor a seis ciudades chinas* (Report of My Love for Six Chinese Cities), written in Beijing on October 23, 1959, when he was as part of a Latin American delegation that visited China.

Changmarín published two historical novels: *En este pueblo no mataban a nadie* (In This Town They Didn't Kill Anyone, 1992) and *El guerrillero transparente* (The Transparent Guerrilla Fighter, 1982). Whereas the former, based on two real-life crimes that took place in Santiago de Veraguas between 1938 and 1945, reflects how the construction of a Normal School is slowly bringing modernity to the sleepy town, *El guerrillero transparente* deals with the story of Victoriano Lorenzo, who fought in the Colombian civil war known as the War of the One Thousand Days (1899–1902), which led to Panama's independence. Changmarín also delivered his social message through children's literature, publishing the novels *El cholito que llegó a general* (The Little Indian Who Became a General, 1986) and the semiautobiographical *Las gracias y las desgracias de Chico Perico* (The Fortunes and Misfortunes of Chico Perico, 2005).

In turn, José Chen Barria (1945–) published the novel *En nombre de ellos* (In Their Name, 2007), dealing with a humble peasant girl named María who, following her teacher's advice, moves to the city to study while working as a domestic servant for an aristocratic family. In the end, María receives a college degree in economics, obtaining the best grades in the class, but the oligarchy's glass ceiling prevents her from obtaining her dream job.

Finally, the Chinese Costa Rican author and artist Otto Apui Sirias (1949–) has published numerous novels, including *El jinete con la herida en el pecho* (The Horseman with the Chest Wound, 2009), *Shi Pan y los huesos del dragón* (Shi Pan and the Dragon Bones, 2010), and *Viaje al remoto Puntalín* (Trip to the Remote Puntalín, 2016). This last novel, declared "of cultural interest" by the Costa Rican government in June 2015, deals with the author's Chinese ancestors and the history of Chinese immigration to Costa Rica. It is an epic account of Chinese immigrants who, not knowing quite well where they were travelling to, had to overcome uprootedness and loneliness in hopes of finding their "gold mountain" in California. The word Puntalín in the title refers to Puntarenas, which many Chinese immigrants thought referred to a country.

Conclusion

Overall, the Asian Latin American novel tends to celebrate the cultural identities and social achievements of Asian communities. It also condemns the racialization of their respective ethnic groups and, in some cases, the racism of their own community against the mainstream population. Asian-Latin American novelists often explore identitarian insecurities, including issues of self-image and cultural authenticity, as well as the aforementioned de-ethnification and re-ethnification processes. Characters may affiliate with either the sending/ancestral country or with the host society; or they may otherwise simply declare a transnational or cosmopolitan identity. Cultural translations and language borrowing are often used either to signal cultural difference or to invite readers to engage with Asian cultures and persons. This way, the Asian Latin American novel challenges Eurocentric discourses that essentialize their experience, often through

Orientalist stereotypes. Asian-Latin American authors resort to the epistemic privilege of their inherited millenary cultures to challenge the "Otherness" that their respective mainstream societies often assign to Asians and Asianness.

NOTES

1. For more information on these topics, see my articles "Latin America and the Caribbean in a Sinophone Studies Reader?" and "Asian-Peruvian Literature," as well as my books *Imaging the Chinese in Cuban Literature and Culture; The Affinity of the Eye: Writing Nikkei in Peru; Dragons in the Land of the Condor: Writing Tusán in Peru;* and *Japanese Brazilian Saudades: Diasporic Identities and Cultural Production.* Part of the information contained in this essay appears in the aforementioned publications.

2. The word *tusán,* used only in Peru, comes from the Chinese *Tusheng,* meaning "local born." Initially used to refer to Chinese descendants born in Peru, including those of mixed blood, today, as Rodrigo P. Campos explains on the website *Tusanaje,* the term is also used to refer to people of Chinese descent in other countries. *Huayi* 华裔 is the term in Mandarin for descendants of overseas Chinese

3. For more information, see my essay "Were Issei in Brazil imperialists? Migration-Driven Expansionism in Nikkei Literature."

4. "Esses gaijins lhe tinham dito que o imperador do Japão enganara os agricultores pobres e os desempregados da cidade, dizendo que deveriam emigrar porque poderiam ganhar dinheiro rapidamente no Brasil. Mas que, na verdade, era um projeto para expulsar a população pobre, que havia muitos excedentes no país" (72).

5. "Hideo não se submeteria à humilhação de voltar ao Japão na mesma condição em que saíra de lá" (110–11).

6. "Um dia, lembrou ojiichan, um nihonjin de Araçatuba fora espancado até a morte porque desconfiaram que era um espião de governo japonês. E quando o Japão venceu a batalha contra Cingapura, em 1942, e muitos pensavam que a guerra estava próxima do fim, ele e alguns amigos tiveram que comemorar em voz baixa, como se fossem todos criminosos" (92).

7. "A política emigratória japonesa na época anterior à Segunda Guerra Mundial tornou-se claramente um dos meios de expansão territorial japonesa" (124). The creation in 1923 of the Empire of Japan's *Takumushō* (Ministry of Colonial Affairs) was a key instrument in this process.

8. "Acontece que tudo isso não vai mudar a cabeça de muitos descendentes de japoneses. Que fomos massacrados aqui no Brasil e tivemos que virar sozinhos. E isso que estou tentando dizer o tempo todo: o Japão nos abandonou! O Japão nos largou aqui para nós nos virarmos souzinhos" (170).

9. "Eu fazia comentários ácidos sobre o Japão, falando sobre sua postura colonialista, que negociava a aquisição de terras brasileiras do tamanho de um estado, quase do tamanho do próprio Japão, num projeto de plantio de soja, que demandaria a vinda de milhares de japoneses" (170).

10. "—Não temos de ser considerados iguais, mesmo porque não somos iguais a eles. Nós somos superiores, e é isso que teremos que mostrar!" (79).

11. "Um dos fatores preponderantes para essa distorção de objetivos foi a forte presença de exmilitares japoneses entre os imigrantes nipônicos que vieram para o Brasil entre 1928

e 1933. Muitos deles vieram para cá tendo como missão exatamente criar nos países onde a colônia japonesa começava a ser significativa, tanto de ponto de vista demográfico como de económico, núcleos de resistência à dominação política e cultural do Ocidente. Tornaram-se membros da Shindô-Renmei e passaram a divulgar o *yamato damashii* literalmente impondo suas ideias ainda que de forma violenta. O líder da associação era Junji Kikawa, exoficial do Exército Imperial Nipônico e seguidor fanático da divindade representada pelo imperador Hirohito" (168).

12. "—Quando tenho de conversar com um japonês, a expressão de seu rosto no instante em que digo meu nome é mais do que suficiente para me mostrar que não estou sendo bem recebido" (225).

13. In the novel, Higa uses *kenshō* and *satori* as synonyms. However, while *satori* is considered a deep and lasting spiritual experience, a kenshō awakening refers to a brief glimpse at the true nature of existence.

14. "Aquella enseñanza sobre la flexibilidad y dureza del bambú" (n.p.).

15. "Tuve que construir una coraza de indiferencia y de orgullo alrededor de mi psique. Aprendí a vivir sin amistades ni afectos; aprendí a pasarme sin compañía femenina. Y por eso, cuando ingresé a San Marcos, yo no sentía como otros muchachos de mi edad el deseo hormonal de contar con una enamorada" (47).

16. "Casa que realmente era más un almacén de latas de aceite, sacos de arroz y fardos de canela, pero que se había convertido en un lugar habitable para un viudo y sus cuatro hijos" (12).

17. "La intolerancia y el miedo a las costumbres diferentes" (133).

18. "Leng T'che, la tortura china de los cien pedazos" (89).

19. "Pertenece a un momento del desarrollo de su estética neobarroca" (González Echevarría 288).

20. "La sorprensiva y fugaz fascinación por el maoísmo del grupo Tel Quel, el conjuno de críticos y teóricios de la literatura al que estuvo afiliado en París durante los años sesenta y setenta" (González Echevarría 288).

21. "Interés, en términos generales, por lo oriental, en Sarduy no solo de lo chino sino también del mundo árabe, la India, el Japón" (González Echevarría 288).

22. "The name Sanfancón, also San Fancon, San-Fan-Con, or San Fang Kong, represents a Western corruption of Cuan Yu, who, after his death, became the 'Venerated Ancestor Kuan Kong' and eventually the 'patron' of all Chinese immigrants to Cuba. Within the religious syncretism that took place in Cuba, San Fang Kong is identified with the Catholic Saint Barbara and the African Shango."

23. "En lugar de cerrar filas junto a mamá y sus hijos, prefirió argumentar que partiría lejos a buscar fortuna. Tal vez tú lo hayas creído, yo sólo considero su decisión un vulgar pretexto, eligió la vía más fácil. Zafarse del compromiso familiar y dejar a mamá con el peso de todo encima de sus espaldas" (92).

24. "Es que ella caminaba con un meneo, muy propio de su paciencia china y de su pasión dublinense contenida, que era un p'aquí, p'allá, de allá p'acá, que ponía duro al más blando" (62).

25. "En cada uno juró que se moría de amor por ella. Y por su ciudad. Como si mujer fuera sinónimo de ciudad. Y la ciudad tuviera útero" (90).

26. "Changmarín recupera lo indígena y lo campesino no sólo como tema, sino que también nos muestra que en la coexistencia de dos sistemas culturales subyace la imposición de un mundo sobre otro, y la colonización de una cultura sobre otra produce una oposición irremediable" (128).

Works Cited

Apui, Otto. *El jinete con la herida en el pecho*. Euned, 2010.

Apui, Otto. *Shi Pan y los huesos del dragón*. Andrómeda, 2010.

Apui, Otto. *Viaje al remoto Puntalín*. Euned, 2016.

Changmarín, Carlos Francisco. *El cholito que llegó a general: Victoriano Lorenzo*. Editorial Panamá, 1986.

Changmarín, Carlos Francisco. *En este pueblo no matan a nadie*. Ene, 1992.

Changmarín, Carlos Francisco. Las gracias y las desgracias de Chico Perico. Ene, 2005.

Changmarín, Carlos Francisco. *El guerrillero transparente*. Premio Ricardo Miró, 1985.

Changmarín, Carlos Francisco. *Nochebuena mala: invasión yanqui a Panamá, diciembre de 1989. Cuentos que no son cuentos*. Omar Torrijos Herrera, 1995.

Chen Barria, José. *En nombre de ellos*. Punto Gráfico, [2007] 2009.

Ch'en Lan Pin. *The Cuba Commission Report. A Hidden History of the Chinese in Cuba*. Introduction by Denise Helly. Johns Hopkins UP, 1993.

Choy, Armando, Gustavo Chui, and Moisés Sío Wong. *Our History Is Still Being Written: The Story of Three Chinese-Cuban Generals in the Cuban Revolution*. Edited by Mary-Alice Waters. Pathfinder, 2005.

Chuffat Latour, Antonio. *Apunte histórico de los chinos en Cuba*. Molina, 1927.

González Echevarría, Roberto. *Oye mi son: Ensayos y testimonios sobre literatura hispanoamericana*. Renacimiento, 2014.

Hagimoto, Koichi. "Beyond the Hyphen: Representation of Multicultural Japanese Identity in Maximiliano Matayoshi's *Gaijin* and Anna Kazumi Stahl's *Flores de un solo día*." *Transmodernity*, vol. 3, no. 2, spring 2014, pp. 83–108.

Higa, Augusto. *Gaijin*. Animal de invierno, 2014.

Higa, Augusto. *La iluminación de Katzuo Nakamatzu*. Asociación Peruano Japonesa, [2008] 2015.

Higa, Augusto. *Japón no da dos oportunidades*. Generación 94, 1994.

Higa, Augusto. *Okinawa existe*; Mesa Redonda, 2013.

Hiratsuka, Lúcia. *Os Livros de Sayuri*. Edições SM, 2008.

Huei Lan Yen. *Toma y daca: Transculturación y presencia de escritores chino-latinoamericanos*. Purdue UP, 2017

Inoue, Ryoki. *Saga. A História de Quatro Gerações de uma Família Japonesa no Brasil*. Globo S.A., 2006.

Iwasaki Cauti, Fernando. *España, aparta de mí estos premios*. Páginas de Espuma, 2009.

Iwasaki Cauti, Fernando. *Extremo Oriente y el Perú en el siglo XVI*. Pontificia Universidad Católica del Perú, 2005.

Iwasaki Cauti, Fernando. *Mi poncho es un kimono flamenco*. Sarita Cartonera, 2005.

Iwasaki Cauti, Fernando. "La sombra del guerrero." *Un milagro informal*. Punto de lectura, 2008, pp. 41–46.

López-Calvo, Ignacio. "Asian-Peruvian Literature." *Oxford Bibliographies in Latin American Studies*, edited by Ben Vinson, Oxford University Press, 2012.

López-Calvo, Ignacio. *The Affinity of the Eye: Writing Nikkei in Peru*. U of Arizona P, 2013.

López-Calvo, Ignacio. *Dragons in the Land of the Condor: Writing Tusán in Peru*. U of Arizona P, 2014.

López-Calvo, Ignacio. *Imaging the Chinese in Cuban Literature and Culture*. UP of Florida, 2008.

López-Calvo, Ignacio. *Japanese Brazilian Saudades: Diasporic Identities and Cultural Production.* UP of Colorado, 2019.

López-Calvo, Ignacio. "Latin America and the Caribbean in a Sinophone Studies Reader?" *Sinophone Studies: A Critical Reader*, edited by Shu-mei Shih, Chien-hsin Tsai, and Brian Bernards, Columbia UP, 2013, pp. 409–24.

López-Calvo, Ignacio. "Were Issei in Brazil imperialists? Migration-driven expansionism in Nikkei literature." *The Japanese Empire in Latin America*, edited by Sidney Lu and Pedro Iacobelli, Hawaii UP, forthcoming.

Lu, Sidney Xu. *The Making of Japanese Settler Colonialism: Malthusianism and Trans-Pacific Migration, 1868–1961.* Cambridge UP, 2019.

Montt Strabucchi, Maria. "Asian Chilean Writing and Film, and Chilean Orientalism." *The Cambridge History of Chilean Literature*, edited by Ignacio López-Calvo, Cambridge UP, 2021, 403–22.

Miyazawa, Júlio. *Yawara! A Travessia Nihondin-Brasil.* Edição do Autor, 2006.

Nakasato, Oscar. *Nihonjin.* Benvirá, 2011.

Okubaro, Jorge J. *O Súdito (Banzai, Massateru!)* Terceiro Nome, 2008.

Pedroso, Regino. *El ciruelo de Yuan Pei Fu. Poemas Chinos.* P. Fernández y compañía, 1955.

Pedroso, Regino. *Nosotros.* Letras Cubanas, 1984.

Sarduy, Severo. *Cobra.* Sudamericana, 1974.

Sarduy, Severo. *Colibrí.* Argos Vergara, 1984.

Sarduy, Severo. *De dónde son los cantantes.* Joaquín Mortiz, 1967.

Sarduy, Severo. *From Cuba with a Song.* Trans. Suzanne Jill Levine. Sun and Moon Press, 1994.

Sarduy, Severo. *Maitreya.* Translated by Suzanne Jill Levine. Ediciones del Norte, 1987.

Seuc, Napoleón. *La colonia china de Cuba 1930–1960. Antecedentes, memorias y vivencias.* Ahora Printing, 1998.

Siu Kam Wen. *La estatua en el jardín.* Diana, 2004.

Siu Kam Wen. *El furor de mis ardores.* Abajo el Puente, 2008.

Siu Kam Wen. *This Sort of Life.* Translated by Siu Kam-Wen. Introduction by Ignacio López-Calvo. Lulu, 2008.

Siu Kam Wen. *El tramo final.* Casatomada, 2009.

Siu Kam Wen. *El verano largo.* Abajo el Puente, 2009.

Siu Kam Wen. *Viaje a Ítaca.* Diana, 2004.

Siu Kam Wen. *La vida no es una tómbola.* Abajo el Puente, 2007.

Takeda, Ariel. *El diario de Terry.* Radio Universidad de Chile, 2015.

Takeda, Ariel. *El Nikkei: A la sombra del samurai.* Radio Universidad de Chile, 2013.

Uchida, Jun. *Brokers of Empire: Japanese Settler Colonialism in Korea, 1876–1945.* Harvard UP, 2014.

Valdés, Zoé. *La eternidad del instante.* Plaza & Janés, 2004.

Valdés, Zoé. *Te di la vida entera.* Planeta, 1996.

Wong Kcomt, Julia. *Bocetos para un cuadro de familia.* Borrador, 2008.

Wong Kcomt, Julia. *Doble felicidad.* Editatú, 2012.

Wong, Mario. *Su majestad el terror.* Pasacalle, 2009.

Wong, Mario. *El testamento de la tormenta.* Huerga y Fierro, 1997.

PART IV

GENDER AND
SEXUALITY

CHAPTER 21

NINETEENTH-CENTURY WOMEN WRITERS AND THE NATION

FRANCESCA DENEGRI

GENDER AND THE LITERARY FIELD

THE second half of the nineteenth century offered particularly fertile soil for the blossoming of literary women in Latin America following the romantics' adoption of the language of sentiment and the promotion of the notion of republican motherhood in the cultural and social fields of the new nations. However, as the entry of women in the literary field became increasingly visible, and their political agendas more audible, its disruptive dimensions to the established patriarchal order eventually set off the alarms.[1] This is exemplified most clearly by the fiction of Romantic Cuban writer Gertrudis Gómez de Avellaneda (Camagüey 1814–Madrid 1873), Argentine narrators Juana Manuela Gorriti (Rosario de la Frontera 1818–Buenos Aires 1892) and Eduarda Mansilla (Buenos Aires 1834–1892), Colombian Soledad Acosta de Samper (Bogotá 1833–1913), and especially by the first Peruvian *indigenista* Clorinda Matto de Turner (Cusco 1852–Buenos Aires 1909), whose work will be given attention here as they expose most clearly, through a combination of diverse aesthetic and ideological projects, the neocolonial logic of a discourse of modernization that demanded new forms of gender and racial violence in the name of progress and civilization.

The emerging female literary voices could be seen to coalesce with the master political male narratives, but mainly they undermined them, or openly dissented from them, most often combining all three modes of dialogue. As they entered cultural fields solidly dominated by men, they learned to device their own aesthetic strategies to find a place of enunciation that was subtle enough to ensure not only acceptance by their national interlocutors, but also celebration. Discerning, therefore, the heterogenous discursive positions of women writers within their own national fields is imperative in order to avoid the dubious assumption of unitary subjects imbued with innate rebellious qualities. Nineteenth-century Latin American intellectuals often expressed a high opinion and sometimes even unbridled enthusiasm for contemporary women writers, as evinced in Ricardo Rossel's presentation of Carolina Freire de Jaimes, the second woman, after Gorriti, to be honored with an invitation to join the prestigious "Club Literario de Lima" in 1875. Freire was an example of the modern, learned woman who combined the earthly, everyday concerns of a devoted mother and wife, with the "poetic" and "sublime" sentiments of the woman of letters, according to Rossel. Sitting next to her child's cot, he suggests, Freire writes "to the beat of her infant's rhythmic breathing . . . elevating her spirit to the remote regions of Truth and Beauty," upon completing her writing, he concludes, she would descend, "to her prosaic duties with her soul strengthened by faith and love"[2] (Rossel 18). As this arcadian but highly problematic image intended to suggest, the smooth, dutiful combination of domesticity, motherhood, and writing was to become the emerging, happy paradigm of the woman writer. Far from being a destabilizing figure in the patriarchal family of the new republics at a time of intense violence and continuous civil and international wars, her inclination to the world of "Truth" and "the poetic" was announced as instrumental in the formation of future learned, modern citizens. The fate of the emerging woman writer who had little cultural capital, will be henceforth shaped and mediated by this curious episteme of republican motherhood construed by male players in the field, their patrons in the national literary institutions, until they successfully found their own platforms.

The systematic representation of writing women as derivative from their position as angel of the house filtered through male, critical language in reviews, prologues, and anthologies. In his prologue to Gorriti's collection of short stories and novellas *Sueños y realidades*, Colombian writer José María Torres Caicedo wrote that her writing possessed "the sentiment of that which is good and beautiful"[3] (qtd. in Gorriti 1865, v-vi). Argentine Juan María Gutiérrez wrote of his admiration of the "incandescent vapours which, charged with love and tears, impregnates the episodes" of Gorriti's first novella, originally published in serialized form in Peruvian *El Comercio*, in 1845[4] (Gutiérrez 501). The celebrated "veladas literarias" in women's homes were an attempt to subtly permeate the feminine with the masculine, the domestic with the intellectual, the private with the public, and the sentimental with the political, thereby pushing the frontiers of what was generally expected to flow from their quills. They had the added effect of counterbalancing the dependency of women on male invitations to the tightly knitted "academias," "círculos," and "ateneos" that proliferated in the national period, "those illustrious corporations of men of letters, whose first and foremost title is that of growing a beard" as Gómez de Avellaneda wrote after her application for membership to the Real Academia Española was rejected in 1853 (Gómez de Avellaneda 1).[5] The practice of meeting at women's homes for domestic literary evenings was derivative of colonial "tertulias" (literary salons), held first in the salons of women of the Spanish and creole aristocracy, where guests recited panegyrics praising viceroys and high-ranking officials. Later, during the wars of independence, patriots like Mariquita Sánchez in Buenos Aires, Luisa Recabarren in Santiago, and Rosa Campusano, Manuela Sáenz, and Juana Manrique in Lima offered their homes as venues for political discussion on political and military strategies in the face of war against Spanish domination (Batticuore 2011; Contreras 2015).

In contrast to the more formal "tertulias," Gómez de Avellaneda, Gorriti, and Matto's "veladas" (soirées) provided an intimate and relaxed atmosphere where women of letters supported one another when reading their essays about topics of social relevance for them, including the education of women and their need to be included in the labor market. High-brow intellectual discussions on literature and culture were interspersed with piano recitals and charades where both the private language of affect and the public language of political power were interwoven and spoken together. Each velada followed a carefully designed program that hybridized the hierarchies of the high and the low, work and pleasure, thus undermining binary categories that underpinned the female/male tightly compartmentalized identities (Denegri 2018, 168–75). Gorriti's practice of inviting journalists of prestigious newspapers who then published the essays, poems, short narratives, and proceedings of the evening was crucial in making women's writing public and accessible to all corners of the nation (Batticuore 2000). An imagined community of both men and women of letters whose mission was to teach those in far-flung places about their shared territory and history was thus aptly mobilized (Anderson 1991) and later reproduced in Clorinda Matto's veladas of 1888. Matto elaborated on the figure of the journalist and writer as portable teachers in Arequipa's *La Bolsa* and later in her bi-weekly newspaper *Los Andes* (Miseres 2009–2010).

HYBRIDIZATION, HETEROGENEITY, AND THE CRITIQUE OF NATION

Gorriti was an early romantic writer who published short fiction, novels, and historical novellas when the figure of the woman writer was far from consolidated. Daughter of a distinguished family of politicians in Salta, Argentina, Gorriti married José Isidoro Belzú, who in 1848 became President of Bolivia, shortly before she fled from his side and settled in Lima, where she became a professional writer. An experienced and lone traveler across the Andes and the plains, her practice of deconstructing the increasingly unquestioned frontiers between barbarism and civilization, and the gendered private and public spaces, is taken to the very heart of her writing. In *Peregrinaciones de una alma triste* (Peregrinations of a Sorrowful Soul), first published in instalments in 1861 in *La Revista de Lima* and in book form in 1876, the stories of fellow countrymen and women who were being written out of history are told through the intimate dialogue between two childhood female friends. It opens when Laura appears at the doorsteps of the narrator's home—who like the author herself is a teacher, writer and literary hostess in Lima after a long journey on her own, and prepares to tell her stories, "as in the *Thousand and One Nights* . . . but with a difference: the offended Sultan is far away from his wife"[6] (Gorriti 1876, 19). Following a technique of multiple embedding, the American "Scherezade" unravels the thread of her oral narrative, structured around stories told in the first person by characters whom she has encountered in her travels across the South American continent, which are then registered by "Dinazarde." Laura's decentered narrative is constantly interrupted by her need for sleep, and by the domestic, literary, and pedagogical activities of her interlocutor; not least, by her own urge to leave the comforts of her friend's home and take to the road again, thus producing a hybridization of narrative time and real time. Laura's story is made up of recollections of South American landscapes, voices, and legends that she has collected from the Atacama desert, the Argentine pampas, the Paraguayan Chaco, and the Amazon jungle. What she brings into this private dialogue is a kaleidoscope of the folk stories of the Mocovi and Toba, the gothic imagination of the Cobija fishermen, the narratives of gauchos in the pampas, the sorrowful narrative of women in search of their dead husbands and children, the plight of slaves in Brazil, and the criminal complaint against state authorities in the Amazon basin. In letting each character speak, Gorriti challenged the notion of the homogenous national voice that reverberates in romantic novels such as Bartolomé Mitre's *Soledad* (1847), José Marmol's *Amalia* (1851), and Benjamín Cisneros's *Edgardo o un joven de mi generación* (*Edgardo or a Young Man from my Generation*, 1864).

One such character is "The captive of Humaitá." She is a Guaraní woman who narrates her kidnapping by a Brazilian army officer during the Paraguayan War (1865–1870). This "cautiva de Humaitá" interpolates Echeverría's "La cautiva" (The Captive, 1837), as she witnesses the massacre of her family and fights with a dagger to fend off her rapists, but unlike Echeverría's prisoner, she is not the victim of Pampa Indians, but of army officers who represent the forces of Christianity and civilization. In "Los bárbaros del siglo XIX" (The Barbarians of the Nineteenth Century), one of the final chapters of the novella, having arrived in Iquitos after a long journey along the Amazon river, Laura is harassed by a group of drunk government officials, who, having failed to rape her, vandalize her lodgings and murder her local steward. "There's two types of savage men," concludes the narrator, "those in the wild and those in civilization, the latter are the most menacing" (1876, 23).[7] The reworking of Sarmiento's well-rehearsed topic of civilization and barbarism was common practice amongst women writers of this century. Gertrudis Gómez de Avellaneda's earlier antislavery novel set on a Cuban sugar plantation, *Sab* (Madrid, 1841), which tells the story of the eponymous mulato slave, in love with his master's daughter Carlota, equally gives agency to a number of "other knowledges" ("saber del otro") represented in voices and oral traditions, including those of black and mulatto slaves, and of Guajiros marginalized by the narratives of civilization (Ibarra 2011). These "saberes del otro," unlike those represented in Facundo, included women of all social and ethnic groups (Davies 2003; Méndez 1998).

CIVILIZATION AND BARBARISM

Eduarda Mansilla (1834–1892), a contemporary of Gorriti's, was the niece of Argentine president Rosas, and sister of Lucio Mansilla, a prominent politician and writer of the generation of the 1880s. She devoted her life to travelling, music, and literature, turning her hand to various genres and languages, from romantic historical novels to modernista short stories, children literature, travel writing, theatre, and journalism. Of federalist background, she married Manuel Rafael García, a diplomat from a prominent unitarian family, thus bringing the national conflict right into the heart of her family life.[8] This situation nourished her writing and resulted in a questioning of Argentina's partisan politics and of the dichotomy between civilization and barbarism central to Argentine cultural debates. Two of her earlier novels, *El médico de San Luis* (The Doctor of San Luis, 1860) and *Pablo ou la vie dans les pampas* (Paul or Life in the Pampas, 1869), both written while she was living in Paris, attempted to translate this dichotomy for a European reading public whose sources of "other knowledges" was limited to European travelers' accounts. Her first novel tells the story of the virtuous doctor Wilson, who settles in the Argentine plains ("pampas"), far from the maddening crowd, with his pragmatic and devoted wife and their children, educated with strict reading material that he carefully filters and selects. It is through his friend, the omnivorous reader Armancio Ruiz, who longs for the attractions of the city, the buzz of literary life and the company of intellectuals, that the tension between city and countryside that pervades the master narrative of *Facundo* is explored. The doctor, who is suspicious of the "poison" of unsupervised reading, is at the end proven wrong when Ruiz is appointed to replace the local Judge, a man of little intellectual inclination and a poor record in meting out justice. With Ruiz's appointment, a future of accountable justice is predicted for San Luis.

It is, however, in her *Pablo ou la vie dans les pampas,* published originally in French, where the hegemonic discourse of "la ciudad letrada" (lettered city) is explored and questioned more fully (Rama, 1996). The novel's project is one of transatlantic cultural mediation, where the modern Argentine nation is represented from the anti-militarist perspective of a woman who lives in Paris and writes in French, for the benefit of a European public. Set also in the "pampas" but focusing on the "gaucho malo" (gaucho outlaw), Mansilla's text proposes a dialogue between her own *Pablo* and Sarmiento's classic essay, where she questions the arbitrary military conscription of the gaucho to fight in the war with Paraguay (Masiello 1997). The plot follows lovers Pablo and Dolores, both illiterate, who are forced into separation when he is recruited into the army despite producing his certification of employment ("conchabado"). As Pablo tries to desert the army, he is caught and imprisoned, the tragedy thickening when Dolores, from a federalist family, is killed in an Indian raid, and Pablo's mother Micaela, a unitarian, sets forth on a journey across the pampas and into Buenos Aires, searching for him. If she hopes to find justice and the rule of law in the modern city, all she will get is indifference, as she goes pleading from authority to authority and, having knocked at all doors, a journalist finally seems to take interest in her story. As her plight is thus made public and the identity of the colonel holding her son is revealed, she is issued a letter from the governor authorizing his release from prison, which, however, only precipitates his execution and plunges Micaela into madness. Female madness in the wake of violence and death permeates also Gorriti's "Argentine" stories, which are set in the war between unitarians and federalists. The closing images of madwomen walking around the forgotten battlefields of history through "streams of blood that the earth cannot absorb" searching, like Micaela, for their dead sons, fathers or brothers, is phantasmatically recurrent in Gorriti's "The black glove," "The deadman's bride" and "Spring's Star" (Denegri 1996).[9]

The conflict between civilization and barbarism that permeated the political debate in nineteenth-century Argentina is thus reformulated by both Mansilla and Gorriti as they denounce the double discourse of a progressive, urban lettered elite who uses the press and the centers of high learning to parade their defense of law and order but who, in their day-to-day practice, scoff at it and leave women to helplessly pick up the pieces. In Mansilla's novel, legal, and lettered mediums procured by Pablo and his family—the initial certificate of "conchabado," the intervention of the press in Buenos Aires, and the governor's letter—all fail to stop the final atrocity. In the final scene, reading and madness are bound together as an anonymous pedestrian cynically nudges his friend: "ask the mad woman to read to us the Governor's letter"[10] (Mansilla 1869, 318). If education is at the heart of Mitre's and Sarmiento's political program, the reading character as metonym of the educated citizen in Mansilla seems to only exacerbate barbarism, as Batticuore suggests (2005, 256). Gorriti's and Mansilla's madwomen resonate with full force with the more recent presence of dissidents during the Videla regime (1976–1983), the "Madwomen of the Plaza de Mayo" ("Locas de la plaza de Mayo"), known simply as "the madwomen" ("las locas"), who gathered regularly before the presidential palace in Mayo Square holding the photos of their loved ones and demanding "the Truth" about where they were. This is a truth, it goes without saying, into which the madwoman/ mother helplessly descends in a nation founded on power as violence, not a "Truth" to which she ascends, as Rossel's constructed image of learned mothers suggested in the introduction to this article.

Literature conceived as the appropriate space to explore and denounce national projects that systematically victimized women of subaltern groups is a common feature in the work of women writers of this century. If Gorriti's first novella, *La quena* ("The Quena," 1848), set at the time of the conquest, addressed the fictional nature of republican family life in a society founded on a colonial history of rape and exploitation, where the mestizo child is deprived of his identity, her short story "Si haces mal no esperes bien" ("If You Do Wrong, Expect No Good" 1861) transposes this endemic problem to a contemporary setting. In it, a young Andean woman is raped by an army colonel, and her daughter abducted five years later by her biological father, unaware that she is his own child. Cecilia is lost in the journey to Lima, where she was to be taken as a "present" to the Colonel's wife, and subsequently found wandering around by a French botanist who takes her to Paris and adopts her as a daughter. Twelve years later, following a plot rich in foreboding and hamartia (tragic flaw), seventeen-year-old Cecilia, unaware of her origins, marries Guillermo, the colonel's son. Upon returning to Lima from France with her husband, and on an outing in the Andean central valley, she accidentally meets a mad, disheveled shepherdess. After a scene of mutual recognition that follows the conventions of romantic narrative, the shepherdess recovers her sanity and launches into a soliloquy in which the nation's high brass, priests and landowners, are represented as evil rapists and abductors of children, and in which the so-called sacredness of the family during the republic is revealed to be a sham. "They say that our fathers ... reigned in this land that we have to pay so dearly for now, and that the whites came from a foreign land and stole their gold and their power" she cries out, "now that we are poor, now that we have nothing for them to take from us, they steal our children and make them slaves in their cities" (144).[11]

MISCEGENATION AND SEXUAL VIOLENCE

Clorinda Matto, a Quechua speaker and a close friend of Gorriti's, was a prolific writer known above all as the author of the first "indigenista," or Indian-based, novel, in Peru. Like her fellow writers, she experimented in various literary genres, from fiction, to theatre and autobiography, from *tradiciones*[12] to journalism and the essay, and founded literary journals, newspapers, and a printing press for women. The title of her first novel, *Aves sin nido* (*Torn from the Nest*, 1889), refers back to the conflict of mestizo children born out of rape whose search for identity is never solved as their white fathers disappear once they are conceived, literally becoming birds without a nest. In Matto's indigenista novel, set in the imaginary Andean town of Killac, Manuel and Margarita fall in love only to discover, like Cecilia and Guillermo before, that they are brother and sister, both children of the bishop of the Andean town of Killac. The trauma leaves Quechua Indian Marcela with a deep sense of shame as she leaves the vicarage, her head hanging, "looking down at the ground" (*Torn from the Nest* 11),[13] compounded with guilt as her husband threatens to commit suicide. The characters, like Gorriti's Cecilia, are victims of an established system that denies "the child of its father, the bird of its nest, the flower of its stem" (173).[14] The theme of abduction of Indian children is also woven into the plot of the novel as in the opening scene Marcela pleads to Lucia, wife of a businessman from Lima, to prevent her young daughter Rosalía from being taken away as domestic servant to the city of Arequipa. As Ana Peluffo argues, it is through the appropriation of indigenous voices that Matto managed to insert herself in the political field and condemn patriarchal and colonial violence (Peluffo 2005, 15).

Matto explores intersectional violence as the origin of a perverse process of miscegenation that destroys the project of national identity as it leaves the mestizo child wandering forever around in search of his elusive origin. In both Gorriti's and Matto's narratives, the rape of women of the subordinate class is a metaphor for the violence of a nation that, despite its rhetoric of patriarchal modernity, was still deeply enmeshed in colonial codes of social relations. In Matto's second novel, *Índole* (Matto, 1891), the victim of priestly sexual harassment is Eulalia López, a member of the petit bourgeoisie of Rosalina, whose confessor demands her sexual submission out of "compassion for his immense affection" (188).[15] Sexual violence in its most extreme form, feminicide, is the subject of some of Matto's "*Tradiciones Cusqueñas*" (Tradiciones from Cuzco), published in the periodical press in 1888. "Las dos partidas" (The Two Farewells), based on the real story of fourteen-year-old Angelita Barreda, killed in Cusco in 1836 by her confessor Eugenio Orós, "out of spite for unrequited love" is one of them (193).[16] The heinous crime however does not mobilize demands for justice from either family or community, as the narrator points out with certain ambivalence, finding consolation in the notion of women's self-sacrificial mission. Four years later, in "Lengua maprediciente" ("Cursed Tongue"), domestic violence is explored as Rafael justifies hitting his faithful wife Tomasa with the age-old argument of female infidelity. Likewise, in her last novel, *Herencia* (Inheritance, 1895), Aquilino Merlo brutally hits his pregnant wife Camila, accusing her of infidelity (Denegri 2019, 95–99). If sexual violence is clearly condemned by Matto, the belief that the victim's blood is needed to redeem the male criminal complicates the narratives and suggests unresolved ideological positions.

Aves sin nido was met with intense controversy following its successful publication in Buenos Aires and Lima in 1889, provoking a flood of critical reviews in the literary press. Liberal intellectuals praised it for its timely courage and progressive stance toward the Indians, but the general consensus was that the novel was offensive for its anti-Catholic spirit and defamatory intentions. Cusco's vicar Fernando Pacheco wrote to the author accusing her of having sown "the seed of war against Christ and his Church, against his dogmas and institutions" (letter dated October 21, 1890, quoted in Denegri 2019, 233). A year after its publication, the church banned *Aves sin nido*, and the prestigious weekly *El Perú Ilustrado*, where Matto was director, was temporarily closed down. Her apologists wrote from Buenos Aires, Santiago, Guayaquil, and Bogotá, paying tribute to the novel and lambasting the authorities for an act of censorship. An editorial of the Buenos Aires *El Diario* compared the novel to Harriet Beecher Stowe's 1852 bestseller *Uncle Tom's Cabin* for its expected impact on the abolition of the "brutal tyranny of the disinherited descendants of Rumiñahui"[17] and a letter from President Cáceres's of Peru was published in *El Perú Ilustrado*, declaring his support for the author and promising reforms with regards to the appointment of local authorities (Denegri 2018, 232). As the controversy raged on, the clamor of the Catholic lobby abated and gave way to a more personal form of aggression against Matto, targeting her gender and her Andean accent. For it was not only her anticlerical spirit that offended her foes, but a narrative voice that, apart from promoting Andean values and modes of social relations as alternatives to Lima-centered criollo culture, placed Andean women at the center of social and political reform in the country. For if in the novel Fernando Marín, the epitome of the modern, civilized man makes starchy "scientific" observations about the "degeneration of cerebral functions" in Indian brains due to a "absurd kind of vegetarian diet" (63), the narrator proceeds to emphasize the vigorous health, strategic intelligence, and robust canny of the Yupanquis and the Champis, the two Indian families exploited by the town's notables. If Margarita Yupanqui is not literate, she is shown to learn quickly, as she surprises Lucia, Fernando's wife, when in a matter of days she has mastered the art of reading. Likewise, if the authorities claim that "women should stay out of men's business and stick to their sewing, their knitting, and their kitchen" (31),[18] Lucía's successful displacement of political mobilization from the governor's office to her own house, suggests that it is in women's language and spaces that the power for social transformation lies.

The images evoked by the communities of Indian and mestizo characters in Killac and Rosalina contrast sharply to the Lima of Matto's third novel, *Herencia*, a city where social, cultural, and racial segregation gives way to yet another inversion of Sarmiento's dictum of civilization and barbarism. The "false" center occupied by Marín's positivist discourse in *Aves sin nido* crystallizes in one of the closing scenes representing a train accident, considered by many critics as "irrelevant" (Cornejo Polar, 9).[19] The scene opens as the locomotive looms up, provoking both jubilant remarks by Marin regarding technology and progress, and serious misgivings in Gabino, the Indian servant. On the train en route to Lima, Marin's eulogy of modernity goes on until it is abruptly halted when the train collides with a herd of cows and falls over a ravine, causing death and injuries, thus vindicating Gabino's apprehensions. A victim's bitter view of Peru as the only place where train accidents happen, epitomizes the unresolved conflict between a "traditionalist" or pastoral Andean discourse and the liberal, positivist ideology contained in Matto's perspective of national history.[20] If the modern characters in her three novels seem to propose Lima as the paradigm of civilization, the textual dissonances and subtexts found in the narratives suggest a more complex relation between history, ideology, and literary imagination.

SORORAL NETWORKS AND CRITIQUE OF MARRIAGE

Stories of women who, refusing to obey their husbands or brothers, follow their own convictions and successfully resist the mandates of patriarchy, abound in these gender narratives of the long "century of progress." Their power derives from an ability to appropriate the language of the subaltern and turn it into anti-patriarchal political projects. Refusal to obey male authority was also represented in women's travel narratives as primary motive to leave home and sally forth into the world, unaccompanied, though forever in fear of being caught, as in, among others, Gorriti's *Peregrinaciones de una alma triste*, where Laura flees from her domestic prison, and steps into the freedom of anonymity. Her journey around the vast continent is undertaken with resilience, always avoiding "the infinite difficulties that skirts provoke, especially in a journey" (Gorriti 228).[21] Matto, Gorriti, Gómez de Avellaneda, and fellow women writers before and after them, travelled extensively, mostly on their own, and wrote travel narratives where the narrators brave a hostile world single-handedly, discovering in the process a strong sense of mission reinforced by a well-earned independence. These writers, as many of their literary sisters, were far from embodying republican notions of ideal womanhood. Unmarried, separated from their husbands, widowed and single mothers, they were unswervingly determined to become independent professionals, not only earning their money through their work as writers, but also displacing their occupational and emotional center from home to the public realm, and from family to literary sororal networks.

Colombia's Soledad Acosta de Samper, an erudite and immensely prolific writer who wrote more than twenty novels, short stories, historical and scientific essays, translations, travel narratives, and plays, and who in 1878 founded the periodical *La Mujer*, where "only women will write," constructed a relatively more compliant, though tension-ridden, model of the woman of letters (Skinner 1999, 74).[22] Daughter of Colombian general Joaquín Acosta and wife of distinguished intellectual José María Samper, she was a tireless writer from an early age but was cautious, until late in her life, about entering the public domain. Doubts about her legitimacy as a woman of letters in a masculine literary field might explain her preference for using pseudonyms and for male narrators in her novels. Her first collection of fiction, all pieces previously published in instalments in the periodical press, was published in 1869. *Novelas y cuadros de la vida sur-americana* (*Novels and Tableaux of South American Life*) was preceded by a prologue, signed by her husband, in which the author's modesty was highlighted; so diffident was Acosta, Samper suggested, that had it not been for his insistence, she would not have published the book at all (Alzate 2015, 97). Acosta systematically made use of diverse narrative forms in her fiction, including letters, diaries and travel fragments, and relied often on more than one narrator—perhaps, again, as a strategy to avoid harsh judgment from her public—which somewhat hinders the critic's task of pinning down her political position. *Dolores*, the opening novel in the book, is the story of a young reader and writer who becomes ill and deformed with leprosy and is taken to a cave in the outskirts of the town to await her slow disintegration and solitary death. It has been suggested that Dolores's dreadful isolation is a mirror device used by the author to reflect on the situation of the contemporary woman writer in Colombia (González Stephan, 2005), an interesting interpretation that adds complexity to the panorama of sororal networking and support suggested in this article.

In *Teresa la limeña* (*Teresa from Lima*) the eponymous heroine and her French friend Lucila, both avid readers of romantic novels and classical literature, emulate the cultural models of womanhood offered in the novels that they read and dream of marrying men fashioned after Byron's *Manfred* and the like. The novel is a critique of the hegemonic notions of femininity promoted in romantic literature, and of the serious limitations they impose on women readers in their quest to become independent, self-reliant, and productive adults. The protagonists' identities, constructed from the material they can access in their libraries, will lead them to perish for unrequited love, unlike Rosita, a picaresque character who survives. *Laura*, published by instalments a year later, is the victim of an ill-conceived marriage; married to a French Don Juan, she falls into depression, giving birth to a stillborn, and ultimately dying of grief. Her next novel, *Constancia,* published two years later in 1872, is yet another story of doomed love, as the eponymous character marries a man she does not love and unlike her dutiful aunt, a traditional, Catholic housewife, Constancia does not conform to a life of suffering (Alzate 2013).

In *Una holandesa en América* (A Dutchwoman in America), published in instalments in 1876, we follow young Lucía, who meets Mercedes en route from Holland to Colombia, to meet her Irish father and siblings, her mother having died after an unhappy marriage. Lucía's image of Colombia, constructed from her Irish father's letters, is idyllic. Throughout the novel she will unlearn all lessons taught by correspondence and will likewise undo the civilization/barbarism dichotomy. She is also, like Teresa, Constancia, and Lucila, an educated and passionate reader of the romantics, but unlike them, she will learn to decodify, through experience and reflection, the plots that falsely prescribe love as a woman's one and only destiny. The novel follows her as she progresses into a self-reliant, hard-working farm manager, who educates her siblings, transforms her father's degraded "desert" into a prosperous plantation, and brings order to the community at large, all the while remaining resolutely single. In the meantime, Mercedes, despite being in appearance happily married, presents in her letters to her friend her own doubts as to whether marriage—an institution that by definition demands submission to husband—is a reasonable deal for women. Like Matto's Lucía and Gorriti's Laura, Acosta's Lucía gives a feminine twist to the notion of civilization, where the ethics of caring for the other extends from the family to the community at large, producing opportunities for new identities for women outside marriage.

If it is true that nineteenth-century women of letters constituted a culturally diverse and politically heterogenous group of writers who responded to the specific discursive demands of their national literary fields, it is also true, as Pura Fernández points out, that they remained articulated in extensive continental and transatlantic sororal networks (Fernández 2011). The permanent interconnection, interaction, and interlocution that they promoted in the domestic rituals enacted in veladas as well as in the spaces they offered one another to publish their work and to review one another's writings were all successful strategies to widen and strengthen their participation in public life. They also cultivated different forms of personal relations and friendships, both at home and abroad, going out of their way to welcome one another when travelling, dedicating their literary productions to each other, maintaining copious correspondence with one another, assembling genealogies of strong literary mothers, and even hiding together, as Gorriti and Peruvian novelist Mercedes Cabello did during the War of the Pacific, which pitted Chile against Peru and Bolivia (Cárdenas 2019).[23]

The weaving of national and international sororal networks that responded to a community of interests based on gender was, of course, paramount to ensure the survival of the nineteenth-century woman of letters in nations that felt a great ambivalence toward their increasing presence. Much as literary women were initially hailed by contemporary Latin American intellectuals as angels of the nations, modernistas at the end of the century hurried their dramatic demise by closing ranks and either ignoring or vilifying them. "I confess to not being fond of quilly women, that Safo and Corine are not pleasing to me," wrote Rubén Darío in his prologue to Zoila Aurora Cáceres Oasis de Arte (Art Oasis). "A Teresa de Jesús or a George Sand seem to me to be examples of moral teratology," he continues before asking the question as to why this "dislike of women of letters?" His answer was simple and brutal: "Possibly, or surely, because they are all, save certain exceptions, ugly" (Darío 1910, VII, VIII).[24] Strong and thriving as they were, sororal networks took on different forms as the nineteenth-century women of letters disappeared and the "new woman" in the twentieth century faced new challenges. During their lifetime, as I hope to have shown, the first generations of Latin American women writers from Gómez Avellaneda to Matto, managed to renegotiate, from a common perspective based on gender, their own positions within the existing literary institutions, and to redefine their identities in cultural fields overwhelmingly dominated by men. Though still not canonic, the corpus of nineteenth-century women's writing is proving to be an increasingly essential key for the analysis of modern Latin American cultural and literary history, as the fast-growing bibliography on the subject in both north and south suggests.

NOTES

1. "No decir pero saber, o decir que no sabe y saber, o decir lo contrario de lo que sabe" (Ludmer 48).
2. "Se sienta cerca de la cuna donde duerme el fruto de su amor y al compás de la suave respiración de su pecho infantil, deja correr la pluma empapada en santa inspiración . . . remonta su espíritu a las remotas regiones donde habitan la Verdad y la Belleza, y . . . vuelve a sus prosaicas tareas con el alma retemplada por la fe y el amor" (Rossel 1875–77, 18).
3. "El sentimiento de lo bueno y lo bello" (qtd. in Gorriti 1865, v).
4. "Emanaciones ardientes que cargadas de amor y de lagrimas se estiende [sic] sobre los cuadros y las escenas de La Quena" (Gutiérrez 1873, 501).
5. "Esas ilustres corporaciones de gentes de letras, cuyo primero y más importante título es el de tener barbas" (Gómez de Avellaneda 1871, 1).
6. "Como en 'Las Mil y una Noches' . . . aunque con una pequeña modificación, y es que el ofendido sultán está lejos de su enamorada sultana" (Gorriti 1876, 19).
7. "Hay dos clases de salvajes: los agrestes y los civilizados. Estos últimos son los mas temibles" (1876, 23).
8. The Federalist party, led by General Rosas and other caudillos such as Facundo Quiroga, defended the autonomy of provincial governments and the control of the Buenos Aires customs office. The federalist party fought a protracted civil war (1831–1852) against urban liberal forces known as the unitarians. National unification was however not achieved until General Roca, leader of the highly controversial "Conquest of the Desert," which defeated autonomous indigenous groups, acceded to power in 1880.
9. "Arroyos de sangre que la tierra no puede absorber" (Juana Manuela Gorriti, "El guante negro" in Sueños y realidades, Buenos Aires 1907, 99).

10. "Allons demander à la folle de nous lire la lettre du gouverner," Eduarda Mansilla, *Pablo ou la vie dans les pampas* (1869, 318).

11. "Dicen que nuestros padres, poderosos en otro tiempo, reinaron en este suelo que nosotros pagamos tan caro; y que los blancos viniendo de una tierra lejana, les robaron su oro y su poder. No sé si eso es cierto, pero ahora que somos pobres, ahora que nada pueden ya quitarnos, nos roban nuestros hijos para hacerlos, esclavos en sus ciudades" (Gorriti, "Si haces mal, no esperes bien" 170).

12. A short nineteenth-century Spanish American narrative fiction genre. The tradición fictionalized historical events, often set during colonial period. Created by Peruvian romantic writer Ricardo Palma, it quickly spread throughout the continent.

13. "Salir de la casa parroquial mirando al suelo" (Matto, *Aves sin nido* 13).

14. "Quitan el padre al hijo, el nido al ave, el tallo a la flor" (Matto, *Aves sin nido* 183).

15. "Lo que te exijo es simplemente compasion para un afecto inmenso, incommensurable (Matto, *Índole* 188).

16. "Ante el imposible de su correspondencia" (Matto, "Las dos partidas" 193).

17. "La brutal tiranía de los desheredados descendientes de Rumiñahui" (November 2, 1889. Reprinted in *El Perú Ilustrado*, 139, December 26, 1889, 1255).

18. "Las mujeres no deben mezclarse nunca en cosas de hombres, sino estar con la aguja, las calcetas y los tamalitos" (Matto, *Aves sin nido* 35).

19. "Sobrante" (Cornejo Polar 1977, 9).

20. "Estas cosas solo en el Perú pasan" (Matto 1984, 173).

21. "Evitando así las dificultades infinitas que las faldas encuentran en todo, especialmente en un viaje" (Gorriti, *Peregrinaciones de una alma triste* 228).

22. "No escribirán en La Mujer sino mujeres," (Skinner 74).

23. The War of the Pacific (1879–1883) began when Chile claimed nitrate rich Bolivian territory, which Peru, as Bolivia's ally, pledged to defend. After Bolivia's withdrawal from the dispute in 1880, Chile pushed into Peruvian territory on the pretence of a "civilizing mission," occupying Lima and neighboring Andean provinces. Chilean occupation lasted until the Treaty of Ancon was signed in 1883, whereupon Peru lost three large provinces in the south, and Bolivia became a landlocked country.

24. "Confieso ante todo que no soy partidiario de las plumíferas, que Safo y Corina me son muy poco gratas . . . Una Teresa de Jesús, o una George Sand, me parecen casos de teratología moral . . . ¿De dónde proviene mi poco apego a las mujeres de letras? Posiblemente, o seguramente, porque todas, con ciertas raras excepciones, han sido y son feas" (Darío VII).

Works Cited

Acosta de Samper, Soledad. *Novelas y cuadros de la vida suramericana*. Imprenta de Eug. Vanderhaeghen, 1869.

Acosta de Samper, Soledad. *Laura, constancia y una venganza. Tres novelas de Soledad Acosta de Samper*. Edited by Carolina Alzate. Instituto Caro y Cuervo/Ediciones Uniandes, 2013.

Acosta de Samper, Soledad. *Una holandesa en América*. Edited by Carolina Alzate. Ministerio de Cultura / Biblioteca Nacional de Colombia, 2015.

Alzate, Carolina. *Soledad Acosta de Samper y el discurso letrado de género, 1853–1881*. Iberoamericana, 2015.

Anderson, Benedict. *Imagined Communities. Reflections on the Origin and Spread of Nationalism*. Verso, 1991.

Alzate, Carolina. Laura, Constancia y Una venganza: tres novelas de Soledad Acosta de Samper / Edición, prólogo y notas de Carolina Alzate. Ediciones Uniandes; Instituto Caro y Cuervo, 2013.

Batticuore, Graciela. *El taller de la escritora. Veladas literarias de Juana Manuela Gorriti: Lima-Buenos Aires (1876–1877)*. Beatriz Viterbo, 2000.

Batticuore, Graciela. *La mujer romántica. Lectoras, autoras y escritoras en la. Argentina (1830–1870)*. Edhasa, 2005.

Batticuore, Graciela. *Mariquita Sánchez. Bajo el signo de la revolución*. Edhasa, 2011.

Cárdenas, Mónica. "Cocinando la paz. Afectos y sororidad en El mundo de los recuerdos de Juana Manuela Gorriti." *Ni amar ni odiar con firmeza. Cultura y emociones en el Perú pos-bélico (1885–1925)*, edited by Francesca Denegri, Fondo Editorial de la PUCP, 2019, pp. 153–70.

Cisneros, Luis Benjamín. *Edgardo o un joven de mi generación*. Librería de Rosa y Bouret, 1864.

Contreras Villalobos, Joyce. *Mercedes Marín del Solar (1804–1866). Obras reunidas*. Dirección de Bibliotecas, Archivos y Museos y Centro de Investigaciones Diego Barros Arana, 2015.

Cornejo Polar, Antonio. *La novela peruana*. Horizonte, 1977.

Darío, Rubén. "Prólogo." *Oasis de arte*, Zoila Aurora Cáceres. Hermanos Libreros Editores Garnier 1910, pp. vii–xi.

Davies, Catherine. "Founding-fathers and Domestic Genealogies: Situating Gertrudis Gómez de Avellaneda." *Bulletin of Latin American Research*, no. 22, 2003, pp. 423–44.

Denegri, Francesca. *El abanico y la cigarrera. La primera generación de mujeres ilustradas en el Perú (1876–1895)*. 1996.

Denegri, Francesca. *El abanico y la cigarrera. La primera generación de mujeres ilustradas en el Perú (1876-1895)*. Ceques, 2018, pp.168–175.

Denegri, Francesca. "Veladas con diferencia." *Ni amar ni odiar con firmeza. Cultura y emociones en el Perú pos-bélico (1885-1925)*, edited by Francesca Denegri, Fondo Editorial de la PUCP, 2019, pp 81–108.

Echeverría, Esteban. "La cautiva." *Rimas*, Imprenta Argentina, 1837, pp. 18–37.

Fernández, Pura. "Geografías culturales: Miradas, espacios y redes de las escritoras hispanoamericanas en el siglo XIX." *Miradas sobre España*, edited by Tomás Facundo et al. Anthropos, 2011, pp. 153–70.

Gómez de Avellaneda, Gertrudis. "La mujer considerada particularmente en su capacidad científica, artística y literaria." *Obras literarias de la señora doña Gertrudis Gómez de Avellaneda. Colección completa*, vol. 5, Imprenta y Estereotipia de M. Rivadeneyra, 1871, pp. 302–6.

González-Stephan, Beatriz. "La in-validez del cuerpo de la letrada: la metáfora Patológica." *Soledad Acosta de Samper. Escritura, género y nación en el siglo XIX*, edited by Carolina Alzate and Monserrat Ordóñez, Iberoamericana/Veurvert, 2005, pp. 361–80.

Gorriti, Juana Manuela. *Sueños y realidades*. Buenos Aires, Imprenta de Mayo de C. Casavalle (editor), 1865, pp. v–vi.

Gorriti, Juana Manuela. "If You Do Wrong, Expect No Good." *Dreams and Realities: Selected Fiction of Juana Manuela Gorriti*, translated by Sergio Waisman, Oxford UP, 2003, pp. 129–46.

Gorriti, Juana Manuela. *Peregrinaciones de una alma triste. Panoramas de la vida. Colección denovelas, fantasías, leyendas y descripciones americanas*. Casavalle, 1876.

Gorriti, Juana Manuela. "La Quena." *Sueños y realidades*, vol. 1. Biblioteca de la Nación, 1907, pp.23–82.

Gorriti, Juana Manuela. "The Quena." *Dreams and Realities: Selected Fiction of Juana Manuela Gorriti*, translated by Sergio Waisman, Oxford UP, 2003, pp. 1–40.

Gorriti, Juana Manuela. "Si haces mal no esperes bien." *Sueños y realidades*, vol. 2, Biblioteca de la Nación, [1861]1907 pp. 155–185.

Gutiérrez, Juan María. "La Leontina." *Revista del Río de la Plata*, no. 6, 1873, p. 501.

Ibarra, Rogelia Lily. "Gómez de Avellaneda's Sab: A Modernizing Project." *Hispania*, vol. 94, no. 3, September 2011, pp. 385–95.

Ludmer, Josefina. "Las tretas del débil." *La sartén por el mango. Encuentro de escritoras latinoamericanas*, edited by Patricia Elena González and Eliana Ortega, Huracán, 1984, p. 48.

Mansilla, Eduarda. *El médico de San Luis*. Eudeba, (1860) 1962.

Mansilla, Eduarda. *Pablo, ou la vie dans les Pampas*. E. Lachaud, digital version BNP. (1869), 2014.

Mármol, José. Amalia. Novela histórica americana. La Semana, *1851*.

Matto, Clorinda. *Aves sin nido*. Peisa, (1889) 1984.

Matto, Clorinda. *Torn from the Nest*. Translated by John R. Polt. Oxford UP, 1998.

Matto, Clorinda. *Indole*. Instituto Nacional de Cultura, (1891) 1974.

Matto, Clorinda. *Herencia*. Instituto Nacional de Cultura, (1895) 1974.

Matto, Clorinda. *Tradiciones cusqueñas*. Peisa, (1884) 1976.

Masiello, Francine. *Entre civilización y barbarie. Mujeres, nación y cultura literaria en la Argentina moderna*. Beatriz Viterbo, 1997.

Méndez Rodenas, Adriana. *Gender and Nationalism in Colonial Cuba: The Travels of Santa Cruz y Montalvo, Condesa de Merlin*. Vanderbilt UP, 1998.

Miseres, Vanesa. "De artesana de la palabra a obrera del pensamiento: Clorinda Matto de Turner y sus reflexiones en torno a la prensa en La Bolsa de Arequipa (1884)." *Boletín del Instituto Riva Agüero* (BIRA), no. 34, 2009–2010, pp. 171–88.

Mitre, Bartolomé. *Soledad. Novela original*. Imprenta de la Época, 1847.

Peluffo, Ana. *Lágrimas andinas: sentimentalismo, género y virtud republicana en Clorinda Matto de Turner*. Nuevo Siglo, 2005.

Rama, Ángel. *The Lettered City*. Translated by John Chasteen. Duke UP, 1996.

Rossel, Ricardo. "Discurso de presentación de Doña Carolina Freire de Jaimes." *Club Literario de Lima, Anales de la Sección de Literatura*. Imprenta del Universo de Carlos Prince, 1875–1877, p. 18.

Skinner, Lee. "Gender and History in Nineteenth-Century Latin America: The Didactic Discourses of Soledad Acosta de Samper," *INTI*, nos. 49/50, 1999, pp. 71–90.

CHAPTER 22

....

TWENTIETH-CENTURY WOMEN WRITERS AND THE FEMINIST NOVEL

....

MARÍA ROSA OLIVERA-WILLIAMS

THE twentieth century was the century of women and feminism. The history of Latin American women, who had occupied a secondary place, if not a non-place, in academic discourse was beginning to be rescued. It could not have been otherwise when the century opened with women's demands for equal rights. The magnitude of these claims was universal. And throughout the century, the concept of gender as a cultural construction developed with greater clarity, which helped make visible other cultural constructions of oppression in a modernity that had not completely shed its colonial heritage. Literature always reflects history—the period in which a literary work was written. Thus, when an important number of women entered the establishment of literature as novelists, a genre into which they had rarely ventured in the past (the nineteenth-century Peruvian authors Clorinda Matto de Turner and Mercedes Cabello de Carbonera, as well as the Argentine Juana Manuela Gorriti, are noteworthy exceptions), they demonstrated that the willingness to reclaim their place in history also prompted them to create long and complex works of narrative fiction—novels. This article focuses on the twentieth-century Latin American feminist novel and traces its course through the multiple positions that Latin American feminism took during that century. Many women writers, especially those of the first half of the twentieth century, opposed the adjective "feminist" for their novels and works. But activists and novelists alike focused on and confronted the forces that created a context of oppression and marginalization for women, in both politics and literature.

In Latin America, suffrage movements throughout the first four decades of the century made visible the need for women to be recognized as integral citizens of modern nations. Women fought for education and health rights; for social improvements that tackled endemic problems originating from colonialism and patriarchy, such as poverty, alcoholism, unemployment, prostitution, child abandonment, suicide, and venereal disease; for the political right to vote; and for equal civil rights. The processes of modernization that were changing the landscapes of Latin America launched women into the public arena. This is not to say that there were no women who fought for feminist ideals, even if they were not classified in this way, in previous centuries. It is enough to recall the masterful work of the seventeenth-century Mexican writer, poet, philosopher, composer, and Hieronymite nun Sor Juana Inés de la Cruz (1648?–1695). However, the changes produced by modernization made Latin American women struggle to occupy places in the world that was being created.

It seemed that passivity, immobility, and frailty, which were characteristics of the feminine ideal in nineteenth-century Western culture and components of what Sandra Gilbert and Susan Gubar called "the cult" of women as "death-angels" (Gilbert and Gubar 25), showed their falsehood. The voices and bodies of women crossed the threshold of the patriarchal house, understood as a place of protection and a prison at the same time, to claim their citizenship rights. This audacious movement implied freedom on the one hand, and on the other, the vulnerability of facing the outside as a metaphor for all the cultural constructs that made women invisible beyond the house. In this regard, the title of the book on prostitution by Uruguayan feminist leader Paulina Luisi (1875–1950), *Otra voz clamando en el desierto: proxenetismo y reglamentación* (Another Voice Clamoring in the Desert: Procuring and Regulation, 1948), is significant. Women from all backgrounds joined forces with other women: their fight for civil and political rights and especially for social and cultural changes was considered, from the perspective of women, universal. Feminist ideas from the early twentieth century were transnational.

In 1922, the Pan-American Conference of Women was held in Baltimore, Maryland, bringing representatives of twenty countries of the Americas. However, since 1910, women had come together in Latin America to fight for peace, education, and social participation, and in particular, against double standards for women and men (Gargallo 85). They created clubs and centers to discuss ways to make the twentieth century more equitable, and by the late 1940s, suffrage movements achieved their goal, with three exceptions—Nicaragua and Peru, where women won the right to vote in 1955, and Paraguay, which did so only in 1961.

In this effervescent moment for women, one wonders why Latin American women did not occupy a place as novelists in the establishment of literature until the 1950s. Although women had published novels in the 1920s (Venezuelan author Teresa de la Parra, 1889–1936, for example) and 1930s (Mexican and Chilean novelists Nellie Campobello, 1900–1986, and María Luisa Bombal, 1910–1980), respectively—their novels were considered brilliant exceptions and precursors of the feminist novel. Chilean sociologist and feminist Julieta Kirkwood (1936–1985) called the 1950s "the years of silence," for the Chilean case, but it extended to the rest of the Latin American countries (83). Already in 1929, Virginia Woolf (1881–1941), in her famous feminist manifesto *A Room of One's Own*, based on lectures she delivered in the two women's colleges of the Cambridge system—Girton and Newnham—a year before, addressed the impossibility of talking about novels penned by women. As Woolf explained, it was in part because women published so few novels, in part because women needed a place from which to observe the world and its inhabitants, and, above all, because women needed to have confidence in themselves, or in Woolf's words, to feel superior and to not just be the mirror in which man gains a strong image of himself (30). It would seem that women of the first half of the twentieth century certainly had confidence in themselves and in the legitimacy of their actions. However, the patriarchal ideology silenced female demands for the right to vote. For Kirkwood, this silencing in Chile manifested itself in the abandonment of publishing by women. She explained: "Women stop writing, they do not edit diaries, barely essays and novels, but a great amount of poetry, according to the critics, superfluous, neither creative nor brave (except for our Nobel Prize and 2 or 3 others)."[1]

In the 1980s, the Puerto Rican Rosario Ferré (1938–2016), one of the leading women authors in Latin America and a literary critic, focused on the topic of authenticity in an essay titled "La autenticidad de la mujer en el arte" ("Woman's Authenticity in Art"), included in Ferré's essay collection *Sitio a Eros* (34–39). Addressing young female readers and reflecting on Rainer Maria Rilke's assertion that the voice of a writer must be authentic, she wonders how a woman can be authentic if she does not know herself. Knowing herself means knowing her sexuality, her desires, and her evolving subjectivity, and in that process, discovering her own voice. Here, the concept of authenticity joins the concept of self-confidence referred to by Woolf in 1929. If writing is a journey of discovery, writing an authentic feminist novel is an aesthetic and ethical process to find a woman's own voice.

Several questions arise from what I have just said. What is a woman in a process that tries to break down the political, economic, social, racial, psychological, educational, legal, biological, medical, and philosophical barriers of patriarchy? What does it mean to be a Latin American woman in the twentieth century? Latin American women are and are not the same as women from the first world; the heritage of colonialism still weighs heavily on them in the twentieth century. For example, in "Toward a Decolonial Feminism," María Lugones (1944–2020), the Argentine feminist philosopher and US-based woman of color, as she identified herself, analyzes "the oppressive logic of colonial modernity" through the lenses of race and gender and the relation of each to normative sexuality (742). In doing so, she demonstrates that the modern sex/gender system has its roots in the colonial project that imposes a dimorphic sex/gender system framed through heteronormativity. Praised as the first scholar to articulate the concepts of coloniality of gender (Rivera Berruz), Lugones sees the status of white women alongside the status of white male colonizers, as both were committed to the reproduction of a racialized humanity and needed to defend their humanity against the concept of non-human that they invented for the racialized Other. Lugones argues that even when white women operated in a different nexus from the white male colonizer, gender played an important role in the human/non-human relationships of the colonized world. As Stephanie Rivera Berruz points out, "This critique problematizes any idea of shared gender in womanhood because it fails to account for the racial and class differences that cut across the formations of identities in the Americas" (n.p.).

Likewise, since Latin America is not a homogeneous continent, the writers' origins influence how their respective national histories enter in the creation of their fictional worlds. Furthermore, as Latin American feminist philosophers have pointed out, it is important to focus on intersectionality—the inter-relatedness of the concepts of gender, class, race/ethnicity, and religion, as these categories collectively shape the conditions of existence (Femenías 127–35). Therefore, Latin American feminist novels present different female voices. Authenticity and self-confidence do not imply the creation of a solid, unchangeable, and pure female self. There are many different women and histories in Latin America, and there are also, as Lugones demonstrated in "Playfulness, 'World'-Travelling, and Loving Perception" (1987) and "Purity, Impurity, and Separation" (1994), a plurality of selves in each person, which resists the oppressive logic of purity.

Finally, what is a feminist novel? I would define it as a work of fiction that portrays, from an evolving feminine point of view, a world deformed by cultural constructions that belittle the potential of individuals, especially women and all those who do not adhere to the patriarchal power system, which is heterosexual, white, and Eurocentric. The possibilities of this type of novel are many. On the one hand, a woman's voice emerges that reveals a world from an off-center position; on the other, it empowers that voice and that perspective by making it possible to imagine concrete changes beyond fiction.

How is the feminist novel in Latin America related to the history of Latin American feminism? The history of Latin American feminism presents three milestones. The first is marked by the women's movements that demanded political and civil equality at the beginning of the century and ended in the 1950s with "the years of silence," the term coined by Kirkwood. The second coincides with the violent history of dictatorships, civil wars, disappearances, torture, and deaths at the hands of repressive states, all of which moved women of all social and cultural levels to show how authoritarian regimes replicated patriarchal oppression and to oppose that oppression, challenging their historic exclusion from political life. This period spans the 1970s and 1980s. If in the 1970s women acted as militants, the 1980s are characterized by the expansive development of feminist theory and practice. The last decade of the century, which coincides with the third period of this history, is marked by the harmful effects of neoliberalism, which impacted women's activism and the development of feminist ideas. Economic policies especially harmed women in Latin America, who were forced to work under exploitative conditions in *maquiladoras* (sweatshops) or agricultural labor in the case of Mexico, as Gargallo explains (117), which led to the coining of the term "feminization of poverty." The individualization promoted by the ideology of the neoliberal market economy weakened feminist political activism. Governments and different agencies, such as NGOs, co-opted Latin American feminists, weakening the original oppositional power of the movement against state repression. Feminists had to abandon the investigation of the roots of inequality that affected local organizations and populations. In the 1990s, feminism entered university institutions. Women's studies programs were opened and served as spaces for counter-hegemonic resistance.

Some Latin American novelists were part of these movements. This is the case with Mexican writers Nellie Campobello, whose first novel, *Cartucho* (*Cartucho: Tales of the*

Struggle in Northern Mexico, 1931), presents the Mexican Revolution from the point of view of the author as a child and serves as a precursor to the feminist novel; Rosario Castellanos (1925–1974), considered the most important Mexican woman writer of the twentieth century, whose play *El eterno femenino* (*The Eternal Feminine*, 1975) is a brilliant feminist statement and the culmination of her groundbreaking 1950 master's thesis, *Sobre cultura femenina* (On Feminine Culture), as well as her novels *Balún Canán* (*Nine Stars*, 1957) and *Oficio de tinieblas* (*The Book of Lamentations*, 1962), in which the narrative, from a feminist perspective, shows a profound understanding of the ambiguities that underlie all struggles of power; and Elena Poniatowska (1932–), the author of novels that describe the situation of women from different social classes and occupations, such as *Hasta no verte Jesús mío* (*Here Is to You, Jesusa*, 1969) and *Tinísima* (1992), and the founder of *Fem*, a feminist magazine. Others include the Uruguayan Armonía Somers (1914–1994), whose pedagogical works paid attention to the situation of young women, and the Chilean Diamela Eltit (1947–), who in 1994 published *Crónica del sufragio femenino en Chile* (Chronicle of Women's Suffrage in Chile), in which she highlights the key role of the education of Chilean women in the first half of the twentieth century. Therefore, I propose to study the contributions of the twentieth-century Latin American feminist novel by following these three milestones of feminism.

REBELLIOUS DAUGHTERS IN THE PATRIARCHAL HOUSE

Beginning in the 1950s, greater numbers of Latin American women began to write novels, which were generally neglected, if not despised, by critics of their time. As we will see with the case of the novels by María Carolina Geel and Armonía Somers, there were exceptions to the scorn of the critics. It would seem paradoxical that in "the years of silence," women began to publish novels. However, within the framework of feminist movements, in which women sought to be recognized for their place in history, women novelists investigated through fiction their erotic impulses, those desires that had to be repressed to meet the demands created for the female gender. There were also novels that explored the feelings of vulnerability of the women who left the patriarchal house and lived in the non-place of the marginalized. This is the case with a novel published in 1940, a decade before the explosion of women novelists in Latin America, which demonstrates the importance of considering transitional works. In *Las que llegaron después* (Women Who Arrived Later), the Uruguayan author Paulina Medeiros (1905–1992), following the aesthetic parameters of social realism, populated the modern urban world of her fiction with a panoply of diverse female characters. The stories of these women converge in insecure transitional places, especially rented rooms. The vulnerability of these easily violated rented rooms parallels the vulnerability of the characters' sexualized bodies. From insecurity (real and symbolic), they claim their own place (stable and safe) in the world that they are helping to create. In 1940, Medeiros could only conceive of this place as a utopia: the perfect home of an ideal married couple, a home that ran the risk of becoming a cage for her if the harmony of powers between man and woman was broken. The female protagonist, Leila, reflects at the end of the novel on this possibility that would condemn her and women in general to loneliness and alienation. Invoking images from the poem "Hombre pequeñito" ("Little Man") by the Argentine modernist poet and feminist Alfonsina Storni (1892–1938), Leila thinks: "Alone in a golden cage where we are imprisoned to sing. Alone with our immense tenderness that children only seem to understand when they are young until they are older and leave" (326).[2]

The 1956 autobiographical novel *Cárcel de mujeres* (Women's Prison) by Chilean novelist and literary critic María Carolina Geel (1913–1996) also focuses on confined spaces: a women's prison. The novel is the fruit of the most sensationalized crime of its time—Geel's murder of the man she loved on April 14, 1955, in a distinguished meeting place of the Santiago bourgeoisie, the Hotel Crillón. As in Medeiros's *Las que llegaron después*, where the home is the space that shows the vulnerability of women who are in the open, in Geel's novel, the women's prison is the place where we can see how the system punishes and domesticates rebellious women. Prison allows us to read how gender is configured and how certain women rebel against this cultural construction. Geel, as the novel's first-person narrator, puts distance between herself and the other prisoners. From that perspective, the story underscores that while the narrator is out of place in the Casa Correccional de Mujeres del Buen Pastor (the Good Shepherd Women's Correctional Facility; the place where Georgina Silva Jiménez, Geel's legal name, served her 541-day sentence for the murder of Roberto Pumarino Valenzuela, her lover eleven years her junior), her case has similarities with those of the other women. Her status as a writer and her social class made Geel feel distant from the female prison population. In truth, she explains that she served her brief sentence in the correctional center more like a "convent pupil" than a prisoner. The other women were representations of a raw and savage femininity; she was, instead, suffering and processing the trauma of her female existence. The reality of her criminal act was impossible for her to accept, except as a rupture of her subjectivity. Before the judge of the First Criminal Court, the day after the murder, Geel stammered: "I don't know . . . the nerves . . . I loved him . . . it's life."[3] However, the fascination of the narrative of an "I" that is never confessional, does not talk of her crime, and tells the stories of the prisoners from the unique place of being inside the prison—but psychologically separated from and attracted by the feminine world that inhabits it—lies in the examination of femininity in crisis. This crisis is only captured through the plurality of stories that constitute *Cárcel de mujeres*.

Because of their crimes, the inmates at the Good Shepherd Women's Correctional Facility are cut off from society, and they must remain isolated until the system of disciplinary power decides that they are ready to reenter society. In *Discipline and Punish* (1975), Michel Foucault observes that the modern prison, with its *gentler* and *better* way of imprisoning criminals, has become the model for control of an entire society. The three main prison control techniques—hierarchical observation, normalizing judgment, and the examination—have become the norm of almost all modern institutions, factories, hospitals, and schools. The prison turns the women in the novel into criminals who need to be out of society. The women have broken the laws. However, the narrator who observes and examines them is someone who has also violated the law and, despite her hierarchical observation, questions the standardization of judgment through her writing, a hybrid aesthetic where autobiography, testimony, and fiction intertwine in a strange narrative that is fragmented into vignettes. By doing so, she also questions reality and the possibilities of the novel. As the Italian philosopher Gianni Vattimo proposes in *La società trasparente* (*The Transparent Society*, 1992), to experience ways of life different from our own opens up art to plural modes of existence, to forms of life ignored by hegemonic culture: "To live in this pluralistic world means to experience freedom as a continual oscillation between belonging and disorientation" (Vattimo 10). Disorientation, according to Vattimo, contributes to the "weakening" of the notion of "reality" and of "its persuasive force," promoting creative freedom (59). For the philosopher, "art is constituted as much by the experience of ambiguity as it is by oscillation and disorientation. . . . These are the only ways that art can (not *still*, but perhaps *finally*) take the form of creativity and freedom" (60).

Vattimo was thinking of the world of generalized internet communication that was clearly not the Chilean world of the 1950s. However, the journalistic sensationalism caused by Geel's crime, her prison experience, the activism of the institution of literature under the leadership of Alone (the pseudonym of Hernán Díaz Arrieta, the most powerful Chilean literary critic of the time) to prove the innocence of the author, and the book *Cárcel de mujeres*, written by Geel at the instigation of Alone, allow us to reflect on the experience of ambiguity, oscillation, and disorientation in this novel that creates a plural world of women within the limits of reality and reason. The multiple stories of the prisoners are projected as the multitude of subjects that inhabit the narrator in an ambiguous, oscillating, and disoriented way, and that only art can liberate.

In 2000, Chilean novelist Diamela Eltit helped get the novel republished. The new readers of *Cárcel de mujeres* belonged to the world described in Vattimo's *The Transparent Society*. However, Eltit's interest in the novel, as shown in her introduction, was not in the "creativity and freedom" of art, but rather in showing how the first-person narrative cannot be trusted as a voice of truth. In post-dictatorship Chile, when several testimonies by women, such as *El infierno* (*The Inferno*, 1993) by Luz Arce and *Mi verdad: "más allá del horror, yo acuso"* (My Truth: "Beyond Horror, I Accuse," 1993) by Marcia Alejandra Merino Vega, shocked readers and critics by revealing civic society's complicity with the Pinochet dictatorship, which I deal with in another work,[4] Eltit wanted to show the first-person narrator's manipulation to hide the truth of her crime—manipulations that weaken and blur the concept of reality. If *Alone* in 1956 tried to show the lack of guilt of a woman trapped in the world of fiction, Eltit intended to present Geel as a murderer precisely in the world of her novel. But the "I" that narrates gradually opens up to the stories of the other women, losing prominence. At the turn of the new millennium, the stories of female prisoners that Geel presents in *Cárcel de mujeres* make an impact by advancing ideas through fiction that Latin American feminisms and feminist philosophies will articulate decades later.

A novel that stands out for its focus on erotic desires and sexuality in creating modern female subjectivity is *La mujer desnuda* (*The Naked Woman*) by Armonía Somers. It was Somers's first novel, initially published in 1950 by the magazine *Clima* (nos. 2–3). In 1951, it was published as a book with the same text as the serialized novel, and in 1966, Somers published with Tauro a new version of the novel that she considered the definitive one. *La mujer desnuda* continued to be published. The 1990 (Arca) and 2009 (El cuenco de plata) editions reproduce the 1966 version with small changes in search of stylistic perfection. The multiple editions of this novel, which when it appeared in 1950 caused a revolution in local critical circles, attest to its relevance and interest.

The novel focuses on sex, eroticism, culture, society, limitations, and freedom in a modern world, and on life and death from the point of view of a woman who breaks free from the social norms of her class and embarks on a journey of self-discovery. These subjects, which were barely touched on in the 1950s, especially by women, were received differently in the 1960s in the context of the sexual revolution and the time when Somers produced the definitive version of the novel. In a 1990 interview, Somers said: "The writers . . . we tend to get ahead of things. Intuition, premonitions. This is what happened to *La mujer desnuda*. If I wrote it now, nothing would happen; it would read like a romance novel. At that moment the world was collapsing on us."[5] However, *La mujer desnuda* cannot be read as a romance novel; it does not have any of its characteristics. And it does have the characteristics of a feminist novel. There are three points in what Somers said that are key to reading her first novel: first, the characteristic of literature to get ahead of social mores and historical developments; second, the need for a socio-historical context conducive to articulating experiences and sensations, which explains the new version of the novel in the 1960s because a changing society requires new literary forms; and third, the need to approach it as a feminist statement, which she requested by means of the ironic mention that if she had written it in the 1990s, it would be read as a romance novel. This third point is important if we remember what the Argentine-Colombian novelist and art critic Marta Traba (1930–1983) said regarding the specificity of women's literature and the need to study it rigorously according to that specificity in "Hipótesis sobre una escritura diferente" (696–97).

The novel begins when its protagonist, Rebeca Linke, turns thirty, a significant age in the culture of the 1950s. If a woman was single, she risked being labeled a "spinster" and socially ostracized. Uruguayan women had won important legal battles—the right to vote in 1932, equal civil rights in 1946—but the civil code still considered her "incapacitated" to leave her parents' house before she was thirty if she had not married. On her thirtieth birthday, Rebeca Linke cuts all ties with the culturally European middle class to which she belongs. With a parodic gesture that replicates that of the femme fatale in film noir, she takes off a fur coat that covers her naked body and escapes to a country house that her social status and age allow her to have. There, outside urban life, Somers resorts to fantastic events to cleanse her protagonist of cultural limitations. Rebeca decapitates herself with a letter opener to empty her mind of the patriarchal ideology that produced the male gaze, a gaze by which a woman is converted into the universal Woman, erased of individuality (de Lauretis; Kaplan; Mulvey). Then, she puts the severed head on her shoulders as if the head were a helmet or an uncontaminated mind. After this ritual performance, Rebeca becomes "the naked woman" and is ready to start a journey of self-discovery. She will assume her own gaze and present the immediate social world, which is represented in the novel as a primitive village, through her eyes. The question is, was the world ready to see and accept "the naked woman" and share her gaze?

One of the most outstanding achievements of La mujer desnuda, which anticipates the anti-Oedipal theory of Deleuze and Guattari, is the representation of the family triad in the pre-symbolic state. On her journey through the woods, before reaching the village, "the naked woman" enters the humble cabin of a lumberjack named Nathaniel and his wife, Antonia. The older couple function as symbolic parents of "the naked woman," and her encounter with them as the last step in her cleansing of traditional social mores. Being naked allows her to discover her body, sensuality, and sexuality; being beheaded erases the male gaze that turns woman into the universal Woman; and entering Lacan's space of the Real—that maternal space that Julia Kristeva called "chora," where there are no boundaries (Kristeva 130) and which in the novel is represented by the couple's bed on which "the naked woman" climbs—allows her to enter the symbolic world, the village that awaits her, without preconceived concepts. The sleeping bodies of the lumberjack and his wife create a symphony of different sounds, which the naked woman complements with pleasure: "Every time he breathed in, sucking up almost all the air in the cabin, she accompanied the cyclone, struggling in the current like an insect caught in the plumbing.... This was a wonderful game ... She could have played it all night long or for the rest of her life"[6] (16). In the state of lethargy that precedes consciousness, the lumberjack attempts to control "the naked woman" by giving her the name of his wife, which she rejects, thus denying her entry into the world as an Oedipal daughter. "The naked woman" figuratively decapitates the father, preventing him from exercising the power to name, to impose his gaze and his law on the world and on her.

The arrival of "the naked woman" in the village causes chaos. Rumors of the existence of a new woman scare most of the inhabitants. However, her presence shows the concept of vulnerability that Judith Butler develops in Precarious Life: The Powers of Mourning and Violence (2004). The feminist philosopher conceives of vulnerability as an opening to the needs and claims of others. We all, in our everyday life, feel the vulnerability of being interpellated by the other. Butler adds that vulnerability "becomes highly exacerbated under certain social and political conditions, especially those in which violence is a way of life and the means of secure self-defense are limited" (29). In such situations, individuals can acknowledge a shared condition of vulnerability and act in solidarity with one another, or they can deny vulnerability "through a fantasy of mastery (an institutionalized fantasy of mastery)" that makes them believe that their lives and rights are more important than others (29). The culture of the 1950s that silenced women, and the culture of the 1960s, in which a new version of the novel was published, and which witnessed the younger generation's need to start changing norms that seemed naturalized in the ideology of the establishment, showed both versions of vulnerability.

There were those who opened themselves to the new in pursuit of a better humanity, which requires the ethic of a will "to become undone in relation to others" (Butler, *Giving an Account* 136), and those who fought to keep the status quo, believing that their ways of life and existence were the only ones worth saving. The novel reproduces this social and moral scenario and apparently ends with a failure, the dead body of "the naked woman" floating face down in the river, after the invulnerable villagers set their own village on fire, preferring to die rather than accept her gaze—a gaze that was changing the possibilities of power relations between certain people. There is a character, Juan, who falls in love with her new version of woman. Juan's wife can also articulate her lesbian desires due to the presence of "the naked woman." The village priest questions his authority because of her, and the children are eager to meet her.

In another work, I underscored that the plot's failure does not imply the novel's failure. Somers's novel is an example of "how women writers of the time used literature in revolutionary ways, privileging the vantage points of female characters or other marginalized figures, and at the same time appropriating and making canonical, avant-garde stylistic elements their own" (Olivera-Williams, "Boom, *Realismo mágico*" 287). This is true. However, the plot itself signals a certain degree of success in the revolutionary and surprising performance of "the naked woman." Nathaniel, the lumberjack and symbolic father, after the pre-symbolic encounter with "the naked woman," cannot return to his old routine and searches for her without knowing of her existence, only to discover—in a very lyric passage—that everything is inhabited by multitudes of beings. This opens the possibility of new ways of seeing the world without the limitations imposed by the patriarchal sex/gender system.

FROM A GENDER PERSPECTIVE

The 1970s was a decade of activism for women in Latin America. In the violent history of the period, women collectively participated in resistance to military state repression as well as in movements to engender human rights by seeking better access to education, healthcare, and urban services (Saporta Sternbach et al. 401). However, it was in the 1980s, and as a result of women's political activism during the previous decade, that Latin American feminist movements theorized about women's conditions in their respective countries of origin, taking into account the varied and specific oppressions against women because of their womanhood. The feminism of the decade was shaped by feminist magazines, films, and video collectives, centers for rape victims and abused women, feminist health collectives, lesbian groups, and feminist encounters that served as regional forums for debates about feminist politics and social justice in Latin America and the Caribbean (Saporta Sternbach et al. 404, 408).

During the 1980s Latin American women writers also produced numerous and important novels in which the world is seen from a gendered perspective. This means that they revisit Latin American history in their fiction from their off-center position as women; in other words, they show history through their gaze and in their words. These authors were closer to the development of the feminist movements than their predecessors. The explosion of the feminist novel was parodically labeled "boomito" (little Boom) by Rosario Ferré to draw a parallel to the Latin American Boom of the male novelists of the 1960s (Olivera-Williams, "Boom, *Realismo Mágico*" 280). The Latin American women writers of the 1980s had weight in the literary market, often exceeding the sales of their male colleagues. However, the spectacular production of Carmen Balcells, the Catalan literary agent who coined the term "Boom" to promote together with the poet-publisher Carlos Barral the cultural phenomenon of writers such as Julio Cortázar, José Donoso, Gabriel García Márquez, Carlos Fuentes, and Mario Vargas Llosa, did not happen with the women writers. The times were politically, economically, and culturally different. The cosmopolitan ambitions of the members of the Boom changed to the need to navigate in the maelstrom of globalization, governed by the movements of the neoliberal market and its violent consequences. Therefore, the female writers' boom did not make much noise in the cultural sphere. Ferré's parodic use of the diminutive could point to it being a sequel of the original Boom. The key to critically approach these feminist novels is to focus both on parody and on the experimental strategies they use to create textual bodies, which have the potential to be political and affect society because they are semiotically charged. The feminist novels of this period can be grouped into parodic and experimental.

In *Poetics of Postmodernism*, Linda Hutcheon focuses on the possibilities of parody to provide an independent voice through the texts that are parodied (130). Female authors embraced parody to gain space in the literary establishment through the legitimacy obtained by maintaining an explicit and implicit dialogue with the texts of their male Boom peers. Furthermore, this dialogue introduces a corrective mechanism that rewrites the male canonical texts in a decidedly feminine key. Hutcheon calls this type of parody trans-textual, explaining that this appropriation does not destroy the original text, but rather, recontextualizes it and plays with it (*A Theory of Parody* 6).

Chilean Isabel Allende (1942–) and Mexican Laura Esquivel (1950–) recur to this kind of parody in *La casa de los espíritus* (*The House of the Spirits*, 1982) and *Como agua para chocolate* (*Like Water for Chocolate*, 1989), respectively. Both authors, through the aesthetic of magical realism, parody Gabriel García Márquez's *Cien años de soledad* (*One Hundred Years of Solitude*, 1967). *Como agua para chocolate* and *La casa de los espíritus* were immediate commercial successes and made the authors two of the most widely read novelists in Spanish. However, early critics disparaged both novels as bad copies of the original. Their harsh criticism arose from a double problem. On the one hand, they did not see how parody was used to feminize the fictional world of the novels, making them independent from the original. The use of magical realism openly shows its debt to *Cien años de soledad*, but the objective of both novels is different from that of García Márquez's text. The Colombian author focuses on the broad history of Latin America to reexamine through fiction its violent foundation, including the violence of sexual domination, and to understand itself (González Echeverría 368). However, in the case of *Como agua para chocolate*, as Kristine Ibsen points out, the meaning of the novel does not depend on history, but "on the individual experience in relation to history" (112). On the other hand, the commercial success of women writers was a new phenomenon in Latin America that early critics were not ready to accept.

The Mexican Revolution gives a historical framework to the plot of *Como agua para chocolate*, even when the story moves beyond the revolution, since it is the story of the Garza family (the mother and her three daughters) told from the eyes of the protagonist, the youngest daughter, Tita. However, the revolution is felt and told as erotic passion. Esquivel does not re-create the history of the revolution as the myths of that historical event like García Márquez; on the contrary, history takes a back seat. Gertrudis, Tita's sister, joins the revolution out of an insatiable sexual awakening caused by a meal of quail in rose petal sauce flavored with Tita's blood and her erotic thoughts of Pedro, the man Tita loves. Gertrudis, inflamed with lust, runs naked through the fields and meets a *villista* who, without stopping his march, puts her onto the horse; in the saddle, they begin to make ravenous love. Gertrudis parodies and inverts the sexual prowess of García Márquez's male protagonists, as well as that of the traditional literary and cinematic representations of Mexican revolutionaries. Gertrudis cannot satisfy her sexual appetite with one man and has to go to a brothel to placate herself (*Like Water for Chocolate* 130). Then, she not only fights in the battlefield, but becomes a revolutionary general as well (180). This is the event that Tita records of the revolution. It is a personal event, which will not be part of the official history. However, it is this feminization of official history and canonical narrative that legitimizes the female world and its discourse.

The kitchen is a key place in the novel. It is a feminine space par excellence and a laboratory of knowledge closer to magic than to science, where cultures from different traditions merge. Therefore, cooking and the writing of recipes become ways of creating a feminine community. But Esquivel recurs to all the genres associated with the feminine—*novela rosa* (romance novel), feuilleton, and *telenovela* (soap opera)—to introduce to literature in a parodic way the female popular culture and practical knowledge from experience (the use of culinary metaphors to express Tita's emotional and physical state, for example). Esquivel not only uses trans-textual parody with García Márquez's novel, but she also parodies the genres of female popular culture to show and reject the ways in which they perpetuate stereotypical roles for women and men. The women in the novel are strong, generally stronger than the men, which is different from the traditional portrayal of women in popular culture. As Ibsen states, the women in the novel, through magical realism and the inversion of gender roles, show "the real experiences of women" (117), weakening, if not dissolving, "the textually mediated archetypes of Woman" (117) and the rigid dichotomies imposed by patriarchal thought.

Allende's *La casa de los espíritus* tells the saga of the del Valle/Trueba family from the early twentieth century to the military dictatorship of Pinochet in a way that is closer to *Cien años de soledad*. Magical realism, feminine popular genres (diaries, letters, embroidery, and romance novels, among others), and trans-textual parody feminize the narrative of contemporary Chilean history and of the Latin American novel. As in Esquivel's novel, the women here are stronger than the male characters. Their voices not only correct the narration of Esteban Trueba, the patriarch of the family, but are the ones who tell the story. It is an archive created by women from the materiality of their everyday world. However, the role reversal based on a parodic aesthetic in these novels leads one to wonder if the gender binary is reinforced or questioned.

In "Sociedad Anónima" (Corporation, 1999), Diamela Eltit reflects on the neoliberal market's strategies that transform the new versions of melodrama and the romantic feuilleton in a feminine key into a domesticated version of the gender question, thus intensifying "the social asymmetry between the cultural constructions assigned to the masculine and the feminine" (39). She sees in literature a powerful possibility of changing that social asymmetry because gender as a cultural construct is created through language. Literature, which does not follow "conservative" literary conventions, which can "decenter" the "centers," as Joyce did, can decolonize gender, race, class, and sex (Eltit, "Errante, errática" 23).

Novels such as Argentine Luisa Valenzuela's *Como en la guerra* (*He Who Searches*, 1977), Marta Traba's *Conversación al sur* (*Mothers and Shadows*, 1981), Eltit's *Lumpérica* (*E. Luminata*, 1983), and Uruguayan-Spanish Cristina Peri Rossi's *La nave de los locos* (*The Ship of Fools*, 1984) are some of the best examples of experimental styles that question hierarchical social structures from a feminist perspective. All these novels powerfully critique the Southern Cone dictatorships (Uruguay, 1973–1985; Chile, 1973–1990; and Argentina, 1976–1983) through in-depth examinations of patriarchal forms of social organization and the power structures that shape human sexuality and control gender relations. In these novels, gender—especially the feminine, but also the queer, as in the case of *La nave de los locos*—is especially charged with the weight and value of signs that allow for revolutionary readings and promote social transformations.

La nave de los locos's protagonist is a male not marked by patriarchal ideology; thus, his name is "Equis" ("X," Ecks). From exile he questions the entire range of hegemonic power in Western culture. Through exile he is born again. Consequently, he achieves an off-center look at that culture that ultimately excluded him and all those who opposed or questioned its power system from the known circle of the community. In addition, the novel creates a linguistic exile that forces readers to feel as though they are also expelled from familiar reading codes and need to learn how to read new signs, how to become "Ecks": "Foreigner. Ex. Banishment. Outside the womb of the earth. Uprooted: born again . . . You. You who are not. You know . . . How is the foreigner's soul" (10).[7] In *La nave de los locos*, love is an ethical pursuit toward the recognition of otherness.

THE FEMINIST NOVEL FACES NEOLIBERALISM

How does the feminist novel respond to the neoliberal economy's violence against women? How do the new feminist philosophies and the widely accepted use of the terms "gender" and "empowerment" affect the linguistic revolution of the feminist novel? As we have seen, literature always seems to be one step ahead of history. If gender and empowerment became part of the scholarly and everyday language in the 1990s, their concepts had already been developed in the fiction analyzed in this work. However, the violence of neoliberalism, excellently reproduced in the novel *Mano de obra* (*Labor Force*, 2002) by Diamela Eltit, seems to nullify the validity of questions about gender, race, or nationality. In the market economy, represented in the novel by the supermarket, the individual ceases to exist and becomes "a correct and necessary service part" (73),[8] whose initiative focuses on how to eliminate another *service part* in order to occupy that person's place and survive. In this bleak situation, history does not count. In fact, history is erased from the world governed by the supermarket's rules and only appears in the names of the workers' newspapers of the first two decades of the twentieth century. Nothing can connect the workers' movements of the past with this workforce that lacks history and group conscience. Men and women have become anonymous automatons at the service of the supermarket. Therefore, the concepts of home and family also disappear, and affective relationships are only a parody of a representation of humanity for show.

In this scenario, the phrase "feminization of poverty" is worth remembering. It is not that gender, race, and nationality do not matter but, rather, that in the maximum violence of late capitalism, these concepts reveal themselves as being created as means of domination. The novel creates that degree zero of time and history from which to think about new possibilities of gender, race, class, nationality—those categories that inform our individuality and subjectivity—and from where to write the new feminist novel for the twenty-first century.

NOTES

1. Translations are mine unless otherwise noted. "Las mujeres dejan de escribir, no editan diarios, apenas ensayos y novelas, pero sí gran cantidad de poesía, a decir de los críticos superflua, ni creativa ni valiente (salvo nuestra premio Nobel y 2 o 3 excepciones)" (Kirkwood 88). Gabriela Mistral won the Nobel Prize in 1945. Likewise, María Luisa Bombal's *La última niebla* (*House of Mist*, 1934) was a brilliant precursor to the Latin American Boom novels and the feminist novel.

2. "Solas en una jaula dorada, donde se nos aprisiona para el canto. Solas con nuestra inabordable ternura que solo parecen comprender los niños cuando pequeños hasta que son mayores y se van" (Medeiros 326).

3. "No sé . . . los nervios . . . lo quería . . . es la vida." "El crimen de María Carolina Geel en el Crillón, pasional . . . 'literariamente pasional'" (*La Segunda*, October 4, 1991, 4).

4. María Rosa Olivera-Williams, "Crimen, muerte y escritura: María Carolina Geel" (*El arte de crear lo femenino: ficción, género e historia del Cono Sur*, 2012, 131–56).

5. "Los escribidores . . . solemos adelantarnos a las cosas. Intuición, premoniciones. Es lo que pasó con *La mujer desnuda*. Si yo la escribiera ahora no pasaría nada, se leería como una novelita rosa. En aquel momento se venía el mundo encima." Carlos María Domínguez, "Charla en Montevideo con Armonía Somers" (*Clarín*, February 8, 1990).

6. "Cada vez que él aspiraba, vaciando casi el aire de la cabaña . . . íbase ella también en el torbellino, le entraba en su caudal, andando así semiahogada como un insecto de tuberías . . . . todo aquello . . . constituía un juego formidable en el que la mujer hubiese podido estarse la noche entera, la vida" (Somers 16).

7. "Extranjero. Ex. Extrañamiento. Fuera de las entrañas de la tierra. Desentrañado: vuelto a parir. . . . Vosotros. Los que no lo sois. Sabéis. . . . Cómo el alma del extranjero . . ." (Peri Rossi 10).

8. "Una correcta y necesaria pieza de servicio" (Eltit, *Mano de obra* 73).

WORKS CITED

Allende, Isabel. *La casa de los espíritus*. Plaza & Janés, 1982.

Allende, Isabel. *The House of the Spirits*. Translated by Magda Bogin. Knopf, 1985.

Arce, Luz. *El infierno*. Planeta, 1993.

Arce, Luz. *The Inferno: A Story of Terror and Survival in Chile*. Translated by Stacy Alba Skar. U of Wisconsin P, 2004.

Bombal, María Luisa. *La última niebla*. 1934. *Obras completas*. Introduction and compilation by Lucía Guerra. Editorial Andrés Bello, 1996, pp. 55–95.

Butler, Judith. *Giving an Account of Oneself*. Fordham UP, 2005.

Butler, Judith. *Precarious Life: The Powers of Mourning and Violence*. Verso, 2004.

Campobello, Nellie. *Cartucho*. E.D.I.A.P.S.A., 1940.

Castellanos, Rosario. *El eterno femenino: farsa*. Fondo de Cultura Económica, 1975.

Castellanos, Rosario. *Sobre cultura femenina*. Fondo de Cultura Económica, 2005.

Castellanos, Rosario. *Balún Canán*. Fondo de Cultura Económica, 1957.

Castellanos, Rosario. *Oficio de tinieblas*. J. Mortiz, 1962.

De Lauretis, Teresa. *Alice Doesn't: Feminism, Semiotics, Cinema*. Indiana UP, 1983.

Deleuze, Gill, and Felix Guattari. *Anti-Oedipus: Capitalism and Schizophrenia*. Translated by Robert Hurley, Mark Seem, and Helen R. Lane. U of Minnesota P, 1983.

Eltit, Diamela. "Errante, errática." *Una poética de literatura menor: la narrativa de Diamela Eltit*, edited by Juan Carlos Lértora, Cuarto Propio, 1993, pp. 17–26.

Eltit, Diamela. *Lumpérica*. 3rd ed., Seix Barral, 1998.

Eltit, Diamela. *Mano de obra*. Planeta, 2002.

Eltit, Diamela. "Sociedad Anónima." *Emergencias: escritos sobre literatura, arte y política*, edited by Leónidas Morales, Planeta/Ariel, 2000, pp. 28–40.

Eltit, Diamela. *Crónica del sufragio femenino en Chile*. SERNAM, 1994.

Esquivel, Laura. *Como agua para chocolate: novela de entrega mensuales con recetas, amores y remedios caseros*. Planeta Mexicana, 1989.

Esquivel, Laura. *Like Water for Chocolate: A Novel in Monthly Installments with Recipes, Romances, and Home Remedies*. Translated by Carol and Thomas Christensen. Doubleday, 1992.

Femenías, María Luisa. "The Challenge of Differences in Latin American Feminism." Translated by Amy A. Oliver. *Feminist Philosophy in Latin America and Spain*, edited by María Luisa Femenías and Amy A. Oliver, Brill/Rodopi, 2007, pp. 127–35. doi.org/10.1163/9789401204439

Ferré, Rosario. "La autenticidad de la mujer en el arte." *Sitio a Eros*, 2nd ed., Joaquín Mortiz, 1986, pp. 34–39.

Foucault, Michel. *Discipline and Punish*. Translated by Alan Sheridan. Pantheon, 1977.

Gargallo, Francesca. *Las ideas feministas latinoamericanas*. Universidad de la Ciudad de México, 2004.

Geel, María Carolina. *Cárcel de mujeres*. Edited and with a prologue by Diamela Eltit. Cuarto Propio, 2000.

Gilbert, Sandra, and Susan Gubar. *The Madwoman in the Attic: The Woman Writer and the Nineteenth-Century Literary Imagination*. Yale UP, 1979.

González Echeverría, Roberto. "Cien años de soledad: The Novel as Myth and Archive." *MLN*, vol. 99, no. 2, March 1984, pp. 358–80.

Hutcheon, Linda. *Poetics of Postmodernism: History, Theory, Fiction*. Routledge, 1988.

Hutcheon, Linda. *A Theory of Parody*. Methuen, 1985.

Ibsen, Kristine. "On Recipes, Reading and Revolution: Post-Boom Parody in *Como agua para chocolate*." *The Other Mirror: Women's Narrative in Mexico 1980–1995*, edited by Kristine Ibsen, Greenwood P, 1997, pp. 111–22.

Kaplan, E. Ann. "Is the Gaze Male?" *Powers of Desire: The Politics of Sexuality*, edited by Ann Snitow, Christine Stancell, and Sharon Thompson, Monthly Review P, 1983, pp. 309–27.

Kirkwood, Julieta. *Ser política en Chile: Los nudos de la sabiduría feminista*. CuartoPropio, 1990.

Kristeva, Julia. *Desire in Language: A Semiotic Approach to Literature and Art*. Translated by Thomas Gora, Alice Jarden, and Leon S. Roudiez. Columbia UP, 1980.

Lugones, María. "Toward a Decolonial Feminism." *Hypatia*, vol. 25, no. 4, fall 2010, pp. 742–59. *JSTOR*, www.jstor.org/stable/40928654

Lugones, María. "Playfulness, 'World'-Travelling, and Loving Perception." *Hypatia*, vol. 2, no. 2, summer 1987, pp. 3–19. *JSTOR*, www.jstor.org/stable/3810013

Lugones, María. "Purity, Impurity, and Separation." *Signs*, vol. 19, no. 2, winter 1994, pp. 458–79. *JSTOR*, www.jstor.org/stable/3174808

Luisi, Paulina. *Otra voz clamando en el desierto: proxenetismo y reglamentación*. Luisi, 1948.

Medeiros, Paulina. *Las que llegaron después*. Claridad, 1940.

Merino Vega, Marcia Alejandra. *Mi verdad: "más allá del horror, yo acuso*. M. Merino Vega, 1993.

Mulvey, Laura. "Visual Pleasure and Narrative Cinema." *Visual and Other Pleasures*, Indiana UP, 1989, pp. 14–28.

Olivera-Williams, María Rosa. *El arte de crear lo femenino*. Cuarto Propio, 2012.

Olivera-Williams, María Rosa. "Boom, *Realismo Mágico*—Boom and *Boomito*." *The Cambridge History of Latin American Women's Literature*, edited by Ileana Rodríguez and Mónica Szurmuk, Cambridge UP, 2016, pp. 278–95.

Peri Rossi, Cristina. *La nave de los locos*. Seix Barral, 1984.

Poniatowska, Elena. *Hasta no verte Jesús mío*. Era, 1969.

Poniatowska, Elena. *Tinísima*. Era, 1992.

Rivera Berruz, Stephanie. "Latin American Feminism." *The Stanford Encyclopedia of Philosophy* (fall 2020 edition), edited by N. Zalta. plato.stanford.edu/archives/fall2020/entries/feminism-latin-america/

Saporta Sternbach, Nancy, et. al. "Feminisms in Latin America: From Bogotá to San Bernardo." *Signs: Journal of Women in Culture and Society*, vol. 17, no. 2, winter 1992, pp. 393–434. https://www.journals.uchicago.edu/doi/10.1086/494735

Somers, Armonía. *La mujer desnuda*. 3rd. ed., no. 69, private and numbered edition, Tauro, 1967.

Somers, Armonía. *The Naked Woman*. Translated by Kit Maude. Feminist P, 2018.

Traba, Marta. *Conversación al sur*. 8th ed. Siglo Veintiuno, 1999.

Traba, Marta. "Hipótesis sobre una escritura diferente." *Lectura crítica de la literatura Americana: actualidades fundacionales*, edited by Saúl Sosnowski, Biblioteca Ayacucho, 1996, pp. 692–97.

Valenzuela, Luisa. *Como en la guerra*. 2nd ed. Casa de las Américas, 2001.

Vattimo, Gianni. *The Transparent Society*. Translated by David Webb. The Johns Hopkins UP, 1992.

Woolf, Virginia. *A Room of One's Own*, 1929. Feedbooks.

CHAPTER 23

FORM AND DIFFERENCE IN THE LATIN AMERICAN LGBTQ NOVEL

VINODH VENKATESH

THE presence of non-heteronormative novels in Latin America's literary genealogy can be traced to the fin-de-siècle period between the nineteenth and twentieth centuries, when authors such as Adolfo Caminha (Brazil 1867–1897, *Bom Crioulo* [*Bom-Crioulo: The Black Man and the Cabin Boy*], 1895), Raul Pompeia (Brazil 1863–1895, *O Ateneu* [*The Atheneaum: A Novel*], 1888), Carlos O. Bunge (Argentina 1875–1918, *La novela de la sangre* [The Novel of Blood], 1903), and Alfonso Hernández Catá (Cuba 1885–1940, *El ángel de Sodoma* [Sodom's Angel], 1928) published novels featuring male homosexual bodies and desires. These texts presented "the gay and lesbian as other, set in scenes dominated by discourses of the nation, science and law, often viewed through the lens of the 'decadence' of a social class or as a social or psychological pathology" (Balderston and Maristany 204). This is not surprising, given the nation-building ethos underlying these novels, as the queer, that is, all that stands opposed to the idealized paragon of the nation—typically the criollo male—was displayed as a perverse countertype not to be emulated.[1]

Indeed, Daniel Balderston and José J. Maristany argue that the representation of LGBTQ characters in the Latin American novel follows three broad stages, which are, of course, not discrete but rather have some level of thematic and tropic bleed at the margins. While the first stage is characterized by the novels mentioned above, the second follows a narrative "estheticizing of homosexuality," where the figure is seen as the "heir of the humanist tradition" (204). In this stage—featuring such writers as José Lezama Lima (Cuba 1910–1976), Virgilio Piñera (Cuba 1912–1979), Severo Sarduy (Cuba 1937–1993), Lúcio Cardoso (Brazil 1912–1968), and José Donoso (Chile 1924–1996)—the novelist and the novel subtly excise the figure from the broader body politic, focusing instead on building a deeper and more rounded representation. In the final stage, Balderston and Maristany point to Manuel Puig's (Argentina 1932–1990) canonical *El beso de la mujer araña* (*Kiss of the Spider Woman*, 1976) as a foundational text that allows the queer subject to bloom into a position of political action.

Working in tandem with these stages, the following pages forward an inquiry into the relationship between literary form and the writing of LGBTQ bodies, desires, and issues in the Latin American novel. Divided into two sections, the essay first provides the reader with a broad overview of the state of the Latin American LGBTQ novel, identifying key novelists and touchstone texts. Then, it proceeds to examine a wide assortment of novels through groupings of discrete criteria, including the confessional monologue, the musical novel, new historical fiction, and the neofantastic novel. In this second section, I am interested in teasing out connections between content and form, to provide a template for reading future LGBTQ production in the region.

Before proceeding, it behooves us to define the LGBTQ novel, a category—given the tacit relationship between the literary and the normative—that has historically been slippery.[2] For our purposes, I define the corpus as that formed by novels depicting LGBTQ bodies and desires in an intentional, holistic manner; often central to the development and denouement of the narrative, these LGBTQ themes and characters evolve as the reader progresses through the plot. In other words, LGBTQ characters are not secondary, flat points of reference to shore up the normativity of the protagonists, nor are the themes seen as perverse warnings of societal decline and depravity. The authorship of the LGBTQ novel also merits comment, as the author's sexuality and/or gender identity does not necessarily correlate with the libidinal flows extant in their texts. Other authors who are openly gay or lesbian may not write novels with LGBTQ content, thus leading us to not necessarily consider this dimension in the *poiesis* of the corpus. The bulk of LGBTQ novels are indeed lesbigay novels, that is, they portray and deploy lesbian and gay bodies and desires as succinct and discrete social categories. They are erected in opposition to analogous, hetero characters and behaviors; what differentiates them is their focus on same-sex love and sexual relations.

The LGBTQ novel may, in some cases, also be considered a queer literature, highlighting the Q in the acronym as a centripetal, deconstructive force that opens the text (and the reader) to an erotics of the horizon, that is, one not anchored in discrete categories, bodies, or even possibilities. By a queer literature, I am referring to a poetics that explores "everything that establishes a defiant stance to patriarchal heteronormativity . . . [and] can represent the legitimation of . . . a whole range of love practices between human beings" that disobey social norms and codes of the law (Foster 197).[3] Following this hermeneutic thread, Amy Kaminsky poses that queer studies or a queer literature, in opposition to gay and lesbian studies and literature, moves us "away from questions of identity . . . to questions of subjectivity . . .; away from community . . . to the relation of the queer subject to the body politic and to the nation; from representation of preexisting and retrievable gay themes to the performance of transgressive behavior as constitutive of categories like sexuality and gender" (210).[4] A queer gesture ultimately questions the structural and epistemological bases of heteronormativity; it is not simply a transgression, but rather, a perpetual (dis/re)configuration of social systems as they may be represented in a narrative world. This salient characteristic distinguishes queer literature from mimetic lesbigay texts that themselves do important work in terms of representation.⁵

Let us now turn to a chronology of LGBTQ novels in Latin America. Perhaps the first text to serve as a seed in this corpus is Caminha's *Bom Crioulo*. Transgressive not only due to its homoerotic themes, but also because it features an Afro-Brazilian protagonist (Amaro, a former enslaved man now a sailor) who is enthralled by a criollo teenager (Aleixo, also a sailor in the navy). What is striking about this novel, and what sets it apart from other texts that often depict gay men as depraved, infirm, or pederasts, is that the gay characters and their relationship are viewed "as something that is quite natural" (Foster 12). The novel, however, is quite different from modern LGBTQ texts that are invariably linked to social movements, in that it, quite contradictorily, also critiques their relationship as being unnatural (Howes 42). This ambiguity, that is, a representation of a sexuality that is first normalized and then also critiqued, in relation to male homosexuality opens seams propitious for queer readings. Also important—and this underlines its early position in our corpus—is that the novel is "neither a facile propagandistic work (that deploys homosexuality in axial and political terms) nor a work of despair but rather one of perplexity" (Howes 57).

Following the ethos of *Bom Crioulo*, the roadmap of LGBTQ novels in the first half of the twentieth century is punctuated by such authors and works as Hernández Catá, Bunge, Augusto D'Halmar's *Pasión y muerte del cura Deusto* (Chile 1880–1950; Passion and Death of Father Deusto, 1915), and Ofelia Rodríguez Acosta's *La vida manda* (Cuba 1902–1975; Life Demands, 1929). These novels are situated within the parameters of Balderston and Maristany's first stage, not yet fully exploring neither the queer subject nor its potential for radical politics and extra-literary action. Of interest in the Mexican context is *Los cuarenta y uno: novela crítico-social* (The Forty One: Critical-Social Novel, 1906) by Eduardo A. Castrejón (a pseudonym for an unknown author) that fictionalized the raiding of a party attended by cross-dressing and gay men in the capital city. The novel is at times dogmatic yet at others strangely transfixed by the imagined details of the party, allowing for the reader to land on either side of the dichotomy of acceptability.

The mid-century brings about a shift in the body of novels, as two authors of the Cuban neo-baroque, José Lezama Lima and Severo Sarduy, break new ground in the field. The former's masterpiece, *Paradiso* (1966), recounts the life of José Cemí, a character with clear autobiographical allusions to the author. Detailing his childhood illness, his love of literature, and a burgeoning homosexual drive, the novel attempts to rescue a gay ethos within the Western intellectual tradition. Perhaps the most important sections of the book are chapters 8 and 9: in the former, the narrator goes to great depths to describe non-heteronormative sex; in the latter, José furthers with his close friends an intellectual exploration of the moral legitimacy of homosexuality. Lezama Lima ultimately paid the price for the publication of this work, as he was functionally marginalized by the Castroist government from local intellectual and publishing circles. Perhaps seeing what had happened to Lezama Lima (among the broader anti-gay maneuvers engaged by the government), Sarduy published his novels in France, having first left to study there and then remaining after. With explicit camp and Baroque elements, Sarduy's novels are a kaleidoscope of images, textures, voices, and desires, often melded together in an exciting and excitable mélange that defies definition. Perhaps the most representative work is *Cobra* (1972), while *Pájaros de la playa* (*Beach Birds*, 1993) is valuable for its allegoric representation of the AIDS pandemic that ultimately took the author's life.

Published in 1966, José Donoso's *El lugar sin límites* (*Hell Has no Limits*) is an important text within the broader movement that is the Latin American Boom (though the author has also been associated with the post-Boom in posterior works). The text is centered on the life and tribulations of La Manuela, a trans madam of a brothel in a small town, El Olivo, that has fallen on hard times due to both changes in the region's economy and the stranglehold over its people by Don Alejo, a local landowner. The novel delves into the brothel's past, as it gives the reader a snapshot of the different characters that visit, including Pancho, a macho truckdriver who harbors an erotic fixation on La Manuela, a fixation that he cannot entirely embrace as it would dislocate him from the patriarchal gender system of the town. The novel ends with an episode of homosexual panic created by this anxiety, as Pancho and his brother-in-law, Octavio, harass and then beat the protagonist.

Important in Donoso's novel is the idea of *La loca*, a localized gender identity adopted by La Manuela that "describes homosexual people whose femininity crosses the boundaries of their assigned male gender because they wear makeup and/or accessories traditionally reserved for women" (González 123). La loca is not necessarily equated with transgendered identities, though it may be, but the reader must be careful in mobilizing terminologies borne in the Anglo context to a global scale. Indeed, this disjunction is at the core of Pedro Lemebel's discussions on homonormativity and how the hegemon of late capitalism may function in erasing regional gender expressions that are then moved to a double margin (Sifuentes Jáuregui 126–27).[6]

El lugar sin límites is a touchstone novel in its exploration of queer identities and homosexual panic. It also merits acclaim as it is one of the first Latin American LGBTQ novels to be adapted to the cinema; the homonym film by the Mexican Arturo Ripstein (1978) is a canonical entry in the genealogy of queer Latin American film, serving as a precursor to other successful adaptations from novels and short stories such as *Doña Herlinda y su hijo* (Doña Herlinda and Her Son; Jorge López Páez, Dir. Jaime Humberto Hermosillo, 1985), *El beso de la mujer araña* (Manuel Puig, Dir. Héctor Babenco, 1985), *No se lo digas a nadie* (Don't Tell Anyone; Jaime Bayly, Dir. Francisco Lombardi, 1998), *Antes que anochezca* (*Before Night Falls*; Reinaldo Arenas, Dir. Julian Schnabel, 2000); and *La virgen de los sicarios* (*Our Lady of Assassins*; Fernando Vallejo, Dir. Barbet Schroeder, 2000).

Manuel Puig's *El beso de la mujer araña* (1976), unlike its antecedents in this LGBTQ genealogy, places the queer subject within the crosshairs of the political and the national in an Argentina reeling from political violence and the rise of Jorge Rafael Videla immediately prior to the military coup of 1976. Written and published before the infamous coup, the novel takes place in the intimacy of a jail cell, in a space that puts two characters—Valentín (a political prisoner) and Molina (a queer man)—into a close physical, and emotional contact that they otherwise would not have had. Though published before the coup, it is important to note that the repression described in the novel continued, and even increased, after the coup. Through a series of conversations, references to popular films, and copious footnotes (wherein the author reflects on theories and constructs of sexuality and gender), the novel allows Valentín's leftist politics to mingle freely with Molina's worldview, thus engendering a critical reckoning of the role of sexual and gender liberation within the continent's leftist struggles at the height of the Cold War. The juxtaposition of the queer protagonist to the guerrilla fighter (an erotic strategy we will see later in Lemebel's *Tengo miedo torero* [*My Tender Matador*, 2001]) immediately sutures the libidinal under and overtones of the text with the violent reality faced by both men in and outside the prison walls.

The publication and popularity of *El beso de la mujer araña* opens the door for a bevy of other novels across Latin America, as a post-Stonewall social consciousness and rising feminist (and literary) movements increased the visibility of LGBTQ bodies and subjects in Latin America's novels (Williams 180). Sylvia Molloy's *En breve cárcel* (Argentina 1938–; *Certificate of Absence*, 1981) is an essential lesbian text that situates the reader in the intimate space of an apartment (and not the jail cell alluded to in the title), as a woman works through her sentimental past and present. In this sort of meta-writing, that is a writing about writing vis-à-vis sex, desire, and affection, the novel draws the reader in to the affective dimensions of queer love, breaking with fixed identitarian positions or gender roles.

Published a few years later, Rosa María Roffiel's *Amora* (Mexico 1945–; 1989) has been described as the first Mexican novel about lesbian love. Roffiel follows in the footsteps of such notable writers as Elena Garro (Mexico 1916–1998), Rosario Castellanos (Mexico 1925–1974), and Elena Poniatowska (Mexico 1932–) in imbuing Mexican letters with a potent feminist voice, but at the same time opens new venues by actively discussing lesbianism within feminism. That is not to say, however, that she has been as widely read as the previously mentioned authors; Roffiel's contemporary Ángeles Mastretta is perhaps better known due to the popularity of her 1985 classic *Arráncame la vida* (Mexico 1949–; *Mexican Bolero*). Like *Arráncame la vida*, *Amora* narrates the difficulties faced by women in everyday life in Mexico (though the former is historical in nature). But unlike Mastretta's piece, Roffiel's work delves into the amorous and physical relationships between women in a contemporary Mexico City; with autobiographical echoes, the novel is crucial in bringing to light lived lesbian experience within a cultural terrain that was ready for feminist and LGBTQ activism.

Amora is published when there were positive changes taking place in the Mexican literary field, as well as in society as a whole, that made it possible for LGBTQ characters and themes to be portrayed. Included in this genealogy are formative novels such as Miguel Barbachano Ponce's *El diario de José Toledo* (Mexico 1925–1994; *The Diary of José Toledo*, 1964), José Ceballos Maldonado's *Después de todo* (Mexico 1919–1995; *After All*, 1969), Luis Zapata's *El vampiro de la colonia Roma* (Mexico 1951–2020; *Adonis García: A Picaresque Novel*, 1979), and texts by such authors as José Joaquín Blanco (Mexico 1951–), Luis Montaño (Mexico 1955–1985), José Rafael Calva (Mexico 1953–1998), and Sara Levi Calderón (Mexico 1942–). Other authors not usually included within an LGBTQ genealogy will also write novels with favorable attitudes towards queer characters and themes, including Armando Ramírez in *Pu* (Mexico 1952–;1980).

The 1990s saw a boom of novels that built on the themes and literary techniques of their precursors. Of particular note in this period are novels by such authors as Reinaldo Arenas (Cuba 1943–1990), Antonio José Ponte (Cuba 1964–), Pedro Lemebel (Chile 1952–2015), Jaime Bayly (Peru 1965–), Fernando Vallejo (Colombia 1942–), Mario Bellatin (Peru-Mexico 1960–), Pablo Pérez (Argentina 1966–), and Cristina Rivera Garza (Mexico 1964–). This generation of writers—and I use the term generation very loosely here—bring LGBTQ characters and issues to a diversity of genres, including the autobiographical, the historical, the lyrical, and even the neofantastic. They deftly work with the conventions of specific types of the novel, all while exploring gay and lesbian themes and tropes. Importantly, these writers occupy a variety of positions within the field of Latin American literature, winning some of the most prestigious awards in hispanophone and world literature; some like Arenas, Bellatin, and Lemebel are the subjects of anthologies, monographs, and graduate dissertations; others such as Bayly are widely read as popular literature. The 2000s continued this centripetal trend in LGBTQ novels, featuring works by such authors as Mayra Santos Febres (Puerto Rico 1966–), Tryno Maldonado (Mexico 1977–), Ana Clavel (Mexico 1961–), Enrique Serna (Mexico 1959–), and Silvia Núñez del Arco (Peru 1988–).

It is at this juncture that I would like to turn our attention to the connection I alluded to above regarding literary form and the writing of difference in the Latin American novel. Specifically, I contend that the LGBTQ novel, at least in its most recent incarnations, may be categorized along the following discrete—although not comprehensive— criteria: the confessional monologue, where a first-person voice divulges the sexual and libidinal actions of the protagonist, at times outing themselves to the reader (following Anglo tropes of the closet) while at others evading completely a politics of liberation; the musical novel, where the rich lyrical heritage of the Latin American song is woven into the erotics of the novel, queering not only the characters and actions of the diegesis but also the broader extradiegetic cultural terrain; the new historical novel, where authors queer the past to disrupt the intimate relationship between the literary and the nation-building project; and the neofantastic novel, where lesbian, gay, bisexual, trans, and queer futures are reimagined along the lines of the surreal and the uncanny.

Let us turn to the first category. The confessional monologue is not unique to LGBTQ literature, but does allow for a close, dialogic relationship between the narrative voice and the reader. The direct nature of the voice, unmediated by the subjectivity of external observation and reporting, provides the reader with an intimate glance into the psyche of the narrator. It is in this linkage that the text is potentiated to generate an affective circulation; through thoughts, actions, and desires, the narrator may produce positive or negative affective intensities in the reader, thus orienting them toward or away (depending on their sensibilities) from the erotics of the text. The novel may thus build community through this circulation of affect, feelings, and emotion between the reader and the narrative voice, thus gesturing toward a community orientation towards LGBTQ bodies and issues in the social sphere.

We see this strategy play out in several novels in this genealogy, including Zapata's *El vampiro de la colonia Roma*. The novel is an oral text; there is scarce formal structure as we are to intuit that it is the transcription of an audio recording of the protagonist, Adonis García, recounting his lived experience as an attractive male prostitute. The language used is both fluid and hesitant, oscillating between the two as our normal speech patterns tend to do. It is the testimony of a young man submerged in the non-heteronormative habitus of Mexico City, and recounts his adventures and misadventures amongst a bevy of characters. While the protagonist's sexual practices are important in bringing non-heteronormative sex out of the darkness, the novel is also important in that it acknowledges a plurality of identities extant in Adonis's milieu: *bugas* (heterosexuals), *activos* (tops), *pasivos* (bottoms), *chichifos* (male sugar babies), *homosexuales*, and *locas* are all prevalent in the text, thus demythifying the notion of a homonormative, fixed identity.

The structure of the novel is significant in that its confessional substrate sutures the reader to the narrative voice. As Ariel Wind argues, "the stylistic choice to omit punctuation marks in the text serves to remind the reader that Adonis is orally relating his story, as well as serves as a reminder about socioeconomic class and profession" (581). It forces a reckoning of the positionality of the reader vis-à-vis the text before us; are we sociologists or anthropologists reviewing a testimony for scholarly insight? Perhaps the reader may even remove the technology of print, that is, read the text as oral lexemes as though we are listening directly to the protagonist in a more friendly and intimate conversation. Whatever argument is to be made, however, we arrive at the conclusion that the reader cannot adopt a disaffected stance in relation to the monologue, but must instead actively engage in a hermeneutics of listening/reading that implies an emotional, intellectual, or social investment in the erotics of the text.

The confessional monologue is a popular format in the Latin American LGBTQ novel; other examples include Vallejo's *La virgen de los sicarios* (*The Virgin of the Assassins*, 1994), where the narrative voice speaks directly to the reader (who appears in the third-person plural), making assumptions of our knowledge and thus situating us in temporal and spatial proximity to the narrator. With recognizable autobiographical tones, the novel relates the return of a writer, Fernando, to his hometown of Medellín, a city now overrun by the drug trade and its correlative violence. There he falls in love with a teenage prostitute and *sicario* (assassin), Alexis, who is gunned down in another example of the mayhem that is the urban jungle of the city. The narrator then begins a relationship with another young companion, Wilmar, who we discover later had shot Alexis dead. Just when Fernando seems to have gained some sense of closure and happiness in his relationship, the young sicario is also killed. There is no happy ending for the gay subject in *La virgen de los sicarios*, as the narrator's identity is subsumed by the asphyxiating violence of the city.

Vallejo's writings are characterized by their autobiographical character, as well as by their depiction of the death drive. These same traits are present in Arenas's *Antes que anochezca* (*Before Night Falls: A Memoir*, 1992). Arenas was a sexual and political dissident in Castro's Cuba, imprisoned multiple times for both reasons and denied the public accolades that a writer of his quality should have enjoyed. He was finally able to leave the island in the Mariel boatlift, and continued his resistance against the Cuban government abroad. The novel narrates Arenas's early life, his burgeoning skills at writing fiction, his contact with Lezama Lima and Piñera, his exile from Cuba, and finally the diagnosis of HIV/AIDS in the United States. The first-person, truth-telling nature of the memoir—like all testimonial novels—cannot leave the reader indifferent, as it captures the politico-somatic effects of the oppression of minority groups in the candid voice of a narrator that adopts the reader almost as a close friend or confidant.

While the confessional monologue sets the stage for an emotive tête-à-tête between the narrative voice and the reader, the musical novel, in turn, expands the possibilities of the LGBTQ novel beyond the printed surface of the page onto the ubiquitous plane of popular music. In these works, traditional musical genres, popular lyrics, and iconic superstars are erected and mobilized as paratextual referents to the libidinal development of the plot and its characters. In doing so, these novels may link the LGBTQ body to already established gay icons (such as Juan Gabriel), or queer what may be assumed to be heteronormative lyrics by decentering the lyrical voice from an inert, defined, cis and heterosexual position.[7]

Mayra Santos-Febres's *Sirena Selena vestida de pena* (*Sirena Selena: A Novel*, 2000) follows this narrative strategy. The novel describes the discovery of a young teenage hustler gifted with an incredible voice in the Santurce neighborhood of San Juan in the late 1990s, and their rise to stardom as a successful singer of boleros in Puerto Rico and the Dominican Republic. The transformation of the protagonist from derelict street urchin to glamorous drag starlet is at the center of the novel, as they captivate several men of power in the hotel and tourism industry, including Hugo Graubel, who cannot resist the charms of their voice.

Santos-Febres's novel expertly weaves together the vicissitudes of performance and the body with broader explorations of the socioeconomic realities of the Caribbean, all through the lyrical device of the bolero; that is, the singing and performance of its lyrics within the diegesis sets the stage for the narrative working through of the factors stated above. The bolero, after all, is propitious for such a move, as it is, as Iris Zavala notes, a hybrid genre embodying the heritage and history of Latin America (130). It is the bolero that allows for the protagonist's transformation into desired subject; it is the bolero that permits their migration to the idealized tourist imaginary of the Dominican Republic; it also the bolero that then allows a commentary on LGBTQ migrations and bodies in the Caribbean, as the novel explores identitarian and practical differences amongst men from the region, the United States, and Europe who visit the resorts as part of a global sex tourism. The novel, then, is a textual discovery of the linkage between performance, the body, and the sensual, but also a commentary on global queer migrations and cultures.

Published a year later, Lemebel's *Tengo miedo torero* is named after a homonym *pasodoble* sung in the novel by the titular character, La Loca del Frente, a working-class trans character who falls in love with Carlos, a young revolutionary, part of a guerrilla group staging a plot to assassinate the Chilean dictator Augusto Pinochet in 1986. The novel is scattered with boleros, tangos, and cuplés that highlight how the protagonist and Carlos become acquainted and then engage in a sentimental relationship. The novel rehearses the LGBTQ-revolutionary dialectic that was seen in *El beso de la mujer araña* and in vignettes of *Antes que anochezca*, conjugating sexual and political liberation through the dyad of lovers, although here the protagonist is nameless, only known by their identitarian position vis-à-vis their sociocultural milieu.

Regarding the titular lyrics, the song places La Loca in a submissive yet amorous position to the bullfighter, as he must protect them from some unseen and unnamed danger. The pasodoble, first composed by Augusto Algueró (and performed by such stars as Marifé de Triana, Lola Flores, Sara Montiel, and Carmen Sevilla), is, however, modified in the novel, as the words sang by La Loca "—Tengo miedo torero, tengo miedo que en la tarde tu risa flote!" ("I am afraid bullfighter, I am afraid that in the afternoon your laugh will float") (97)—do not quite line up with Algueró's lyrics.[8] This is of importance as it is the only song in the novel that is not accurately transposed, thus requesting that the reader take an active role in deciphering its triangulation with the two principal characters.[9] Perhaps the "fear" in the lyrics is related to the overbearing violence of patriarchy, or perhaps to the bloody suppression of dissident voices during Pinochet's regime. Another song of note that appears in the novel is "Fue tan poco tu cariño" ("Your love was not enough") the popular Juan Gabriel tune that is sung by La Loca as she ponders her one-sided relationship with Carlos. The song laments the loss of affection in a relationship as one lover leaves the other, though the lyrics appear prior to the one sexual scene between the two characters.

While the song is gendered, that is, the lyrical voice calls out to a feminine lover, its appearance in the novel draws the reader's attention to queer possibilities in the broader cultural terrain. Juan Gabriel, or Juanga as he was known by millions around the globe, was a pop icon in Mexico and the Spanish-speaking world, having conquered charts with his songs and stages with his flamboyant performances. While the singer never openly spoke about his sexuality, he is widely considered a gay icon. It is the juxtaposition of this song in the novel with other similarly gendered pieces that allows for a paratextual queering of the lyrical, encouraging the reader to read popular culture through a queer lens.[10]

Tengo miedo torero is, in addition to a text profoundly marked by an intertexual relationship with song lyrics, a new historical novel. This genre may be considered a subgenre or, equally, a mutation of the historical novel that aims to fictionalize the past (especially as how it may pertain to the construction of the modern nation-state). The new historical novel probes philosophical ideas instead of mimetically reproducing the past, distorts history through omissions and exaggerations, and fictionalizes historical figures. It, furthermore, amply refers to other intertexts in a palimpsestic fashion. Finally, the new historical novel is heteroglossic, parodic, and often carnivalesque (Menton 42–45). It is no surprise then that the qualities of the genre are especially propitious for a queer rewriting or imagination of the past.

This is evident in Lemebel's words, as the novel interpolates popular music, while focusing on the relationship between La Loca and the revolutionary (instead of what one would assume is of principal historical importance, that is, the assassination attempt on Pinochet). The dictator is also fictionalized, represented as a submissive husband to his wife's whims, and not the alpha-male persona that was adopted in public. The queer protagonist and, importantly, the queering of the Leftist revolutionary demythifies the hegemony of patriarchally gendered history, suggesting new practice of representation from the margins of the social body; the new historical novel is subjective and emphasizes the relativity of historiography (Pons 256).

Cristina Rivera Garza's *Nadie me verá llorar* (*No One Will See Me Cry*, 1999) is an important work in our survey, as it explores lesbian, bisexual, and trans tropes through a narrative situated in the final years of the government of Porfirio Díaz and the start of the Mexican Revolution at the beginning of the twentieth century. The protagonist, Matilda, leaves her native Veracruz to live with her uncle in the capital city. After a brief association with a group of anarchist revolutionaries (including Diamantina, with whom she falls madly in love), she leaves behind the comforts of city life for a nomadic existence. She becomes a prostitute in a brothel, La Modernidad, where she meets another lover, Ligia, who quickly becomes her partner in a stage performance for the locale's clients. Told through a poli-temporal framework, the scenes of her life as a prostitute are interlaced with her current situation as a patient in a psychiatric asylum, where she is interned after refusing the aggressive sexual propositions of a handful of soldiers.

Matilda is a transgressive character in all senses of the word. She eschews socioeconomic and gender expectations by leaving her uncle's house and by becoming a prostitute. She, furthermore, engages in lesbian and heterosexual relationships throughout the novel. The brothel is of particular importance, as it is owned by Madame Porfiria (also known as Santos Trujillo), a dolled-up, stocking-wearing trans rewriting of Porfirio Díaz as a loquacious and flamboyant madam who decorates the bordello in lavish paintings and extraordinary colors. The character is an acid critique of Díaz's government and how it left behind much of the population in the quest for a modernity enjoyed by the elites. Years after her stay in the brothel, and after the Mexican Revolution, the reader comes to learn that it is now known as El Progreso, thus suturing its carnivalesque space to the nation at large.

Matilda and Porfiria are queer characters erected by Rivera Garza in a narrative exploration of turn-of-the-century Mexico, engaging the reader in an imagination of history that deconstructs orthodox accounts of the period. While it does not directly represent contemporary LGBTQ communities or sociopolitical issues, the novel does, however, encourage a critical reexamination of history through the lens of contemporary understandings of gender. In doing so, the novel opens a door, guiding the reader through a metaliterary journey of the past that encourages multiple imaginaries for queer bodies and desires. A similar strategy is pursued in Herminio Martínez's *Diario maldito de Nuño de Guzmán* (Cursed Diary of Nuño de Guzmán, 1990) and *Invasores del paraíso* (Invaders of Paradise, 1998), where events of the Spanish conquest are given a homoerotic inflection, and Rafael Mellafe's *Tres caminos a Tacna* (Three Roads to Tacna, 2021), which chronicles the War of the Pacific between Chile and the Bolivian-Peruvian alliance in the late nineteenth century through the lives of two gay soldiers.

The final category in our survey through contemporary Latin American letters is the neofantastic novel. The fantastic novel was defined by Tzvetan Todorov in *The Fantastic: A Structural Approach to Literary Genre* (1973) as a text that confronts the reader to consider the ontology of the natural or supernatural in the diegesis; it "is that hesitation experienced by a person who knows only the laws of nature, confronting an apparently supernatural event" (25). While Todorov focused specifically on the narrative strategies of the genre, later critics have brought cultural studies, feminist, and even queer perspectives to the genre, suggesting that the fantastic is always written within a cultural horizon wherein the dialectic between the real and unreal exposes the epistemic limits of the present moment. The "neo" prefix follows Ana Rosa Domenella's observation that since the fantastic was at its peak in the nineteenth century, contemporary novels are instead written from a globalized, postmodern standpoint (373). The neofantastic is thus an update of the fantastic, parting from the notion that our contemporary reality is global and fragmented.

LGBTQ neofantastic novels situate LGBTQ bodies, desires, and identities within the narratological space of the fantastic, where elements of the real, the unreal, and the supernatural may be conjugated in a text and heuristic that decenters the reader from a position of static consumption, to a transformational dialectic that engenders critical self-reflection in regard to gender, sex, and identity. These are generally queer novels that, beyond representing lesbigay tropes, posit queer, reverse-palimpsestic gestures of de- and re-construction that perpetuate ad infinitum, even beyond the physical act of reading the text. I say a reverse-palimpsest because the text generates a centripetal force, moving outward as opposed to in, further and further away from a succinct, stable definition but instead towards queer multiplicities at a horizon point that escapes heteronormativity and a patriarchal order. The queer neofantastic novel embodies José Esteban Muñoz's notion of queerness as a "not yet here … an ideality" (1); it is a literature that encourages us to "think and feel a then and there" (1) of queer futurity, pushing past the frontiers of the extant cultural and libidinal horizon of the "here and now."

Ana Clavel's *Cuerpo náufrago* (Shipwrecked Body, 2005) follows the neofantastic aesthetic that was at the core of an earlier novel, *Los deseos y su sombra* (*Desires and Its Shadow*, 2000), a surreal text that follows a phantasmal protagonist as she meanders through Mexico City. Yet unlike *Los deseos*, *Cuerpo náufrago* is firmly centered on queer bodies and the possibilities of a "then and there"—both a temporal and spatial inversion and deconstruction—through its aesthetic and narrative development. The novel recounts the life of a woman, Antonia, who one day unexplainably wakes up in the body of a man, Antón. Clavel does not pause to ponder the why behind this change, or even suggest postulates for the reader to consider; instead, the transformation is taken as a fait accompli, as the novel jumps into Antón's negotiation of his body, gender, and desire in the streets of Mexico City.[11] The situating of the fantastic queer character within the city is central to the reading of the novel, as the move through the urban itinerary (and its social and cultural milieu) correlates with an identitarian and libidinal move in the protagonist as they negotiate their body, sex, and gender.

The movement of the character through the urban space is of interest, as Clavel shuns the ekphratic strategies that were deployed in *Los deseos* (and other novels featuring a literary flâneur) in favor of a virtualization of the city: the protagonist prefers riding the metro, the subterranean network of tunnels and passages that semantically and ideationally re-create the city above. The city thus becomes a virtual space, one we put together through the subway map as a topologic pastiche that defies spatio-temporal delimitations. In doing so, the novel portends a queer space, a hybrid of the physical city and imaginations of it, that, like the body of the protagonist, gestures toward Muñoz's futuristic "then and there."

Perhaps the best-known neofantastic queer novel coming from Latin America is Mario Bellatin's *Salón de belleza* (*Beauty Salon*, 1994). It is a short text rich in detail and elements of the fantastic that—though not anchored in a specific time and space like *Cuerpo náufrago*—moves the reader into an unfamiliar terrain, where the real and unreal fluidly meet in a lubricous chronotope that is very peculiar to the text. The narrative voice oscillates between the narrator's aquarium and descriptions of a beauty parlor where homosexual men infected by a mysterious disease (which we can infer is HIV-AIDS) are exiled to by society at large. Yet Bellatin's text does not talk of the aquarium and its inhabitants as a simple metaphor or symbol of the space of the beauty parlor; in identifying *Salón* as a fantastic novel, Ellen Lambrechts observes that "the narration does not explain why the course of the fish's lives run analogously to the narrator's life, . . . [evidencing] the lack of causal associations" (92). The resulting sensation of confusion in the reader is a definitive characteristic of the fantastic, as they experience an "incomprehensible, (con)fusion between the narrator and the fish, and between the parlor and the aquaria" (Lambrechts 92). Bellatin cultivates the fantastic through a sensuous and judicious use of language that, through carefully parsed images and strategic ambiguities, quite literally pulls the rug from under the reader, as they are left to decipher the real from the fantastic, the tangible from the ambiguous.

In creating this sense of uncertainty, the author situates the gay men, their mortality, and their rejection from society in a liminal space and time that escape mimetic and/or figurative readings. Their queer bodies engage in a dialectic with an also queered reader (by virtue of the fantastic), who is unable to locate themselves within the coordinates of a "here and now"—we are moved again to Muñoz's "then and there," in a hermeneutic that evades definition. Like Clavel's *Cuerpo náufrago* and Cristina Rivera Garza's *La cresta de Ilión* (*The Iliac Crest*, 2002), *Salón de belleza* is an exemplary novel of the queer, neofantastic genre.

This essay has attempted to provide the reader with an overview of the LGBTQ novel in Latin America, touching on some of the most important works and situating them within a cogent genealogy that is reflective of the social and cultural changes occurring outside the pages of the region's literature. While I have provided a broad (and definitely not exhaustive), "Latin American" scope to this outline, the reader may be interested in investigating national traditions; just as we have parsed together a history of the Latin American LGBTQ novel, one may find value in undertaking a similar journey through the Argentine, Cuban, or Mexican itineraries (to name just a few). All this being said, we can most definitively assert that while once located at the fringe of the literary body, these novels and their authors are now front and center of any serious conversation on Latin American literature.

NOTES

1. Regarding the case of Bunge, Joseph Pierce expertly demonstrates how the author modified the novel between editions to align the text and himself with a literary establishment bent on imagining the nation through fiction (55). The original version was more ambivalent toward difference, whereas the modified edition explicitly chastised the homosexual.
2. Balderston and Maristany rehearse this quandary at length (200–3).
3. "Todo aquello que instaura una postura desafiante a la heteronormatividad patriarcal . . . [y que] puede representar la legitimación de . . . toda una gama de prácticas del amor entre seres humanos" (Foster 197).
4. Kaminsky argues elsewhere that the queer is rooted in a postmodern practice that rejects the stability of the subject rooted in an essentialist ontology of identity (882).
5. Discussing the Argentine context in particular, Jorge Luis Peralta observes that there is a dichotomy between gay and queer literature, and that often queer studies/literature have been considered superior to the identitarian nature of a gay literature/studies, assuming the former is an evolution of the latter (180–81). Peralta, however, argues that this is not necessarily true, and that both literatures can exist in mutually exclusive circles.
6. We may include *La loca* within Jack Halberstam's schema of "trans*," which questions the fixedness of categories and positions (4).
7. A related set of novels follows the same strategy albeit through the cinema, that is, important films and movie stars are referenced in relation to LGBTQ characters and plot points. See, for example, *El beso de la mujer araña* or Luis Zapata's *La hermana secreta de Angélica María* (The Secret Sister of Ángelica María, 1989).
8. Augusto Alguero's original verse is: "Tengo miedo, torero de que el borde de la tarde, el temido grito flote" ("I am afraid bullfighter that at the start of the afternoon the feared scream will arise").
9. In an interview with Fernando Noy at the 2008 FILBA, Lemebel cheekily confessed that the lyrics of the song came from a conversation with a friend who performed Montiel pieces, and that the author only found out later that they were not accurate.
10. Though I have highlighted two LGBTQ novels that refer to popular music, there are several other works that feature LGBTQ characters and readings, though the novels themselves may not be considered within this genealogy. Here I am thinking of works by such authors as Franz Galich, Luis Rafael Sánchez, and Edgardo Rodríguez Juliá.
11. Jane Lavery adds that the pliability of the body and gender in Clavel's work "queers the more conventional narrative themes and genres associated with some of the more 'canonical' writers of the *boom femenino*" (1), and that Clavel is perhaps better described by her "queer aesthetics" (6) than her condition as a female novelist.

WORKS CITED

Alguero, Augusto. Lyrics to "Tengo miedo torero." *Lyrics Translate*, 2017, https://lyricstranslate.com/es/lola-flores-tengo-miedo-torero-lyrics.html

Arenas, Reinaldo. *Antes que anochezca*. Tusquets, 2010.

Arenas, Reinaldo. *Before Night Falls*. Translated by Dolores M. Koch. Viking, 1993.

Balderston, Daniel and José Maristany. "The Lesbian and Gay Novel in Latin America." *The Latin American Novel*, edited by Efraín Kristal, Cambridge UP, 2005, pp. 200–16.

Barbachano Ponce, Miguel. *El diario de José Toledo*. Madero, 1964.

Barbachano Ponce, Miguel. *The Diary of José Toledo*. Translated by Clairy Losel. UP of the South, 2001.

Bellatin, Mario. *Beauty Salon*. Translated by Kurt Hollander. City Lights Books, 2009.

Bellatin, Mario. *Salón de belleza*. Tusquets, 2013.

Bunge, Carlos. *La novela de la sangre*. Createspace, 2016.

Caminha, Adolfo. *Bom crioulo*. Todavia, 2019.

Caminha, Adolfo. *The Black Man and the Cabin Boy*. Translated by E. A. Lacey. Gay Sunshine, 1982.

Castrejón, Eudardo A. *Los cuarenta y uno. Novela crítico-social*. UNAM, 2013.

Ceballos Maldonado, José. *Después de todo*. Premiá, 1986.

Clavel, Ana. *Cuerpo náufrago*. Alfaguara, 2005.

Clavel, Ana. *Los deseos y su sombra*. Alfaguara, 2000. *Desires and Its Shadow*. Translated by Jay Miskowiec. Aliform, 2006.

Clavel, Ana. *Shipwrecked Body*. Translated by Jay Miskowiec. Aliform, 2008.

D'Halmar, Augusto. *Pasión y muerte del cura Deusto*. Instituto Internacional de Literatura Iberoamerican, 2019.

Domenella, Ana Rosa. "Tres cuentistas 'neofantásticas.'" *Cuento y figura (la ficción en México)*, edited by Alfredo Pavón, Universidad Autónoma de Tlaxcala, 1999, pp. 351–75.

Donoso, José. *El lugar sin límites*. J. Moritz, 1991.

Donoso, José. *Hell Has no Limits*. Green Integer, 1991.

Foster, David William. *Ensayos sobre culturas homoeróticas latinoamericanas*. Universidad Autónoma de Ciudad Juárez, 2009.

Foster, David William. *Gay and Lesbian Themes in Latin American Writing*. U of Texas P, 1991.

Halberstam, Jack. *Trans*. A Quick and Quirky Account of Gender Variability*. U of California P, 2018.

Hernández-Catá, Alfonso. *El angel de Sodoma*. Lingkua, 2014.

Howes, Robert. "Race and Transgressive Sexuality in Adolfo Caminha's *Bom-Crioulo*." *Luso-Brazilian Review*, vol. 38, no.1, 2001, pp. 41–62.

Kaminsky, Amy. "Hacia un verbo *queer*." *Revista Iberoamericana*, vol. 74, no. 225, 2008, pp. 879–95.

Kaminsky, Amy. "The Queering of Latin American Literary Studies." *Latin American Research Review*, vol. 36, no. 2, 2001, pp. 209–19.

Lambrechts, Ellen. "From Fantastic to Dystopian: The Transgressive Effect of Mario Bellatin's *Salón de belleza*." *Brumal: Research Journal on the Fantastic*, vol. 7, no. 2, 2019, pp. 91–110.

Lavery, Jane. *The Art of Ana Clavel: Ghosts, Urinals, Dolls, Shadows, and Outlaw Desires*. Legenda, 2015.

Lemebel, Pedro. *Tengo miedo torero*. Booket, 2019. *My Tender Matador*. Translated by Katherine Silver. Grover P, 2004.

Lezama Lima, José. *Paradiso*. Archivos, 1988. Translated by Gregory Rabassa. Dalkey AP, 2005

Marínez, Herminio. *Diario maldito de Nuño de* Guzmán. Diana, 1990.

Marínez, Herminio. *Invasores del paraíso*. Ediciones Castillo, 1998.

Mastretta, Angéles. *Arráncame la vida*. Cal y Arena, 1985.

Mastretta, Angéles. *Mexican Bolero*. Translated by Ann Wright. Viking, 1990

Mellafe, Rafael. *Tres caminos a Tacna*. Legatum, 2021.

Menton, Seymour. *Latin America's New Historical Novel*. U of Texas P, 1993.

Molloy, Sylvia. *Certificate of Absence*. Translated by Daniel Balderston and Sylvia Molloy. U of Texas P, 1989.

Molloy, Sylvia. *En breve cárcel*. Seix Barral, 1981.

Muñoz, José Esteban. *Cruising Utopia: The Then and There of Queer Futurity*. New York UP, 2009.

Peralta, Jorge Luis. "'Queer' y 'gay' como paradigmas críticos para la literatura argentina." *Chasqui*, vol. 49, no. 1, 2020, pp. 180–201.

Pierce, Joseph. "Regulating Queer Desire in Carlos O. Bunge's *La novela de la sangre*." *Revista Hispánica Moderna*, vol. 69, no. 1, 2016, pp. 55–71.

Pompeia, Raul. *O ateneu: crônica de saudade*. Ática, 1984.

Pompeia, Raul. *The Athenaeum: A Novel*. Translated by Renata Wasserman. Northwestern UP, 2015.

Puig, Manuel. *El beso de la mujer araña*. Seix Barral, 1976.

Puig, Manuel. *Kiss of the Spider Woman*. Translated by Thomas Colchie. Vintage, 1991.

Rivera Garza, Cristina. *La cresta de Ilión*. Tusquets, 2002.

Rivera Garza, Cristina. *The Iliac Crest*. Translated by Sarah Booker. The Feminist Press, 2017.

Rivera Garza, Cristina. *Nadie me verá llorar*. Tusquets, 1999.

Rivera Garza, Cristina. *No One Will See Me Cry*. Translated by Andrew Hurley. Curbstone, 2003.

Rodríguez Acosta, Ofelia. *La vida manda*. Stockcero, 2018.

Roffiel, Rosa María. *Amora*. Editorial Planeta, 1989.

Santos-Febres, Mayra. *Sirena Selena: A Novel*. Translated by Stephen Lytle. Picador, 2013.

Santos-Febres, Mayra. *Sirena Selena vestida de pena*. Planeta, 2016.

Sarduy, Severo. *Beach Birds*. Translated by Suzanne Jill Levine and Carol Maier. Otis Books, 2007.

Sarduy, Severo. *Cobra*. Edhasa, 1981.

Sarduy, Severo. *Cobra*. Translated by Suzanne Jill Levine. E. P. Dutton, 1975.

Sarduy, Severo. *Pájaros de la playa*. Tusquets, 1993.

Sifuentes Jáuregui, Ben. *The Avowal of Difference: Queer Latino American Narratives*. SUNY P, 2015.

Todorov, Tzvetan. *The Fantastic: A Structural Approach to a Literary Genre*. Cornell UP, 1975.

Vallejo, Fernando. *La virgen de los sicarios*. DeBolsillo, 2019.

Vallejo, Fernando. *Our Lady of the Assassins*. Translated by Paul Hammond. Serpents Tail, 2001.

Williams, Raymond. *The Twentieth-Century Spanish American Novel*. U of Texas P, 2003.

Wind, Ariel. "Mexico City and its Monsters: Queer Identity and Cultural Capitalism in Luis Zapata's *El vampiro de la colonia Roma*." *Revista Canadiense de Estudios Hispánicos*, vol. 38, no. 3, 2014, pp. 579–604.

Zavala, Iris. *Bolero: historia de un amor*. Celeste, 2000.

Zapata, Luis. *Adonis García: A Picaresque Novel*. Gay Sunshine P, 1981.

Zapata, Luis. *La hermana secreta de Ángelica María*. Cal y Arena, 1989.

Zapata, Luis. *El vampiro de la colonia Roma*. Random House Mondadori, 2004.

PART V

NARRATIVE TRENDS

CHAPTER 24

THE LATIN AMERICAN HISTORICAL NOVEL THROUGH THE LENS OF THE DICTATOR(SHIP) NOVEL

HELENE C. WELDT-BASSON

THE Latin American historical novel is defined by its constant intertwining of historical discourse and fiction. History is present in different forms, which makes it difficult to delimit what constitutes a historical novel in Latin America. Georg Lukács's classic definition was that the genre included the representation of a distant past, historical figures as minor rather than major characters, the hero as an average man who represented social trends and historical forces, and the general adherence to historical facts (21–61). Anyone familiar with the Latin American novel of the late twentieth and twenty-first centuries will immediately perceive that this definition has been outdated and subverted by postmodern literary trends. Seymour Menton (1993) defined new Latin American historical fiction following general postmodern lines. According to Menton, Latin American fiction is less focused on mimetically re-creating history and more on showing the impossibility of ascertaining the truth of any given historical account; history is not adhered to but distorted through omissions, anachronisms, and exaggerations. Menton also states that in the new historical novel, historical figures are no longer minor but rather major characters, and that these novels are characterized by metafiction, intertextuality, and dialogism as defining characteristics (22–25). María Cristina Pons (1996) makes the important point that the presence of history in a novel does not a historical novel make, but rather the purpose that history serves determines if a novel should be considered historical fiction. History must have more than a decorative function in a novel for it to be considered historical; the novel should make some point related to historical interpretation for it to truly be a historical novel (35).

The Latin American dictator novel and the dictatorship novel are a subgenre of Latin American historical fiction. Jorge Castellanos and Miguel A. Martínez (1981) distinguish between dictator novels and novels about dictatorship, clarifying that prior to the 1970s, only the latter existed. These focused on societal politics and social psychology under dictatorship, but not on the dictators themselves, who were only minor characters. In contrast, the 1970s brought novels in which the dictator is the protagonist, notably *Yo el Supremo* (*I The Supreme*, 1974) by Augusto Roa Bastos, *El recurso del método* (*Reasons of State*, 1975) by Alejo Carpentier, *El otoño del patriarca* (*The Autumn of the Patriarch*, 1975) by Gabriel García Márquez, and *Oficio de difuntos* (Office of the Dead, 1976) by Arturo Uslar Pietri. These novels were followed by many others, including *La novela de Perón* (*The Peron Novel*, 1985) by Tomás Eloy Martínez, *El general azul* (*The Blue General*, 1991) by Elizabeth Subercaseaux, *La fiesta del chivo* (*The Feast of the Goat*, 2000) by Mario Vargas Llosa, and *El chacal del general* (The Jackal of the General, 2007) by Mauro Zuñiga Araúz.

I will explore the intimate connection between the historical novel and its manifestations in the dictator(ship) novel by examining four pairs of novels (one dictator novel and one historical novel), each of which illustrates one of four general categories of the historical novel that I propose in *Redefining Latin American Historical Fiction* (2013): those that focus on national identity, magical realist novels, novels based on historical intertextuality, and historically symbolic novels (1–46). These four categories often overlap, as do dictator(ship) novels and non-dictator(ship) historical novels, so that this or any categorization is merely a tool for discussion.

National Identity

An example of the overlap between historical novel and dictator(ship) novel is *Amalia* by José Mármol, which is, coincidentally or not, Latin America's first historical novel as well as its first dictatorship novel. Published in serial form from 1851 to 1855, it focuses on the concept of national identity. *Amalia* portrays Juan Manuel Rosas, the governor of Buenos Aires from 1835 to 1852 and leader of the Federalist Party, which advocated for maintaining Argentina as a group of individually governed provinces, in opposition to the Unitarians, who wished to see the provinces united under a centralized government. *Amalia* is one of several Argentine works published during the mid-nineteenth century that establish the civilization versus barbarism dichotomy, associating civilization with Europe and barbarism with Rosas, the uneducated masses, and the Federalist Party.

Many critics believe that *Amalia* contains the fundamental elements of the nineteenth- and early twentieth-century dictator(ship) novels, principally that of political protest. Castellanos and Martínez describe Mármol's novel as a "simple Manichean war of light vs. dark" (79–80). Doris Sommer has shed new light on *Amalia* by seeing its protagonist, Daniel Bello, as embodying the desire of the writers of the Generation of 1837, who were mostly children of Unitarian families "to recognize the Federalist other in themselves, hoping they could produce a spark of reciprocity among the federalists in power . . . the youth from the Province of Tucumán stubbornly believed in the conciliation between the nation's intellectual center and the interior heartland" (87). Daniel Bello, who comes from a Federalist family but is ideologically a Unitarian, encapsulates this concept of conciliation. Similarly, Sommer points out that the love story between Eduardo Belgrano (from Buenos Aires) and Amalia (from the Tucuman province) ultimately symbolizes a "marriage" and thus a compromise, in the form of a national allegory, between the two groups (102). Whether the reader chooses to interpret *Amalia* as a political protest against the Rosas regime, or as a proposal for political conciliation, it is an excellent example of a dictatorship novel aimed at defining national identity.

The question of national identity is articulated within the pages of *Amalia* through the opposition between individualism versus association (which is essentially federalism versus centralism). The Unitarians were in favor of association or government centrality; the Federalists were against association of the provinces. However, the idea that Argentines inherently suffer from an excessive individualism, which is what stands in their way in the establishment of an effective government, is at the heart of this dichotomy, which loosely corresponds to civilization versus barbarism. Note the following montage of quotations:

> Without association . . . without the hope of being able to organize, overnight and without forethought, that lever of European progress that goes by the name of association, what can we count on for the work that we set ourselves? . . . My dear Belgrano has spoken for me on the subject of the spirit of individualism, that, to the misfortune of our country, has always characterized Argentines. (212–13)

> Individualism . . . is the cause of the failure of our compatriots to take action. Rosas did not find classes, he found only individuals when he set up his regime. (271)[1]

Beneath the dichotomy civilization-versus-barbarism lies another more deep-seated division: that of an intrinsic Argentine individualism opposed to political association. Mármol develops his novel around the effects of this essential individualism and attempts to define a new national character based on the concept of association.

Amalia, as a nineteenth-century dictatorship novel, is an early manifestation of the tendency to explore national identity through historical fiction in Latin America. More recently, Tomás Eloy Martínez's novel *Santa Evita* (1995) illustrates how the examination of national identity continues to be an important element in historical fiction by means of the representation of the historical figure of Eva Perón. In *Santa Evita*, Martínez traces the trajectory of Eva Perón's corpse. When Juan Perón was ousted from power in 1955, leaders of the coup took charge of Eva Perón's embalmed corpse and eventually sent the body to Italy to be buried, in this way avoiding the creation of a cult around her body and tomb by their political opponents. At the end of the novel, Martínez links his own identity to that of Eva Perón, connecting Evita with the essence of Argentina: "There was a moment when I told myself: If I don't write it, I'm going to suffocate. If I don't try to know her by writing her, I'm never going to know myself" (368).[2] This sentence is key to understanding *Santa Evita*, which traces the historical events surrounding Eva Perón's death and the destiny of her body. More importantly, it is an exploration of Argentine national identity through a historical icon.

Although the novel narrates events in the life of Eva Perón, the focus is on what happens to her body after her death. Martínez employs Evita's corpse to examine the necrophilous obsession that he sees as characterizing Argentine identity. Magdalena Perkowska views this obsession as a desire to recover the "Argentine other": the so-called "barbarism" of the masses, which has been rejected throughout Argentine history in favor of self-identification with European civilization (117–18). This is one possible interpretation of the metaphoric use of necrophilia in the novel. However, "necrophilous character" (as defined by Eric Fromm in *The Anatomy of Human Destructiveness*) may be a symbol of destructive politics, violence, and military power. It is one convinced that "the only way to solve a problem or conflict is by force or violence" (qtd. in Weldt-Basson, "Double Vision," 118).

In addition to the self-stated necrophilous obsession of the narrator (identified with Martínez himself) with Evita's corpse, the novel provides numerous examples of necrophilia. These include the implication that Eduardo Arancibia, who guarded Evita's body had sex with the corpse (251–52), Colonel Moori Koenig's longing for the corpse when it was taken from him and buried (236), and references to a body of Argentine literature focused on Evita's death. These works include Jorge Luis Borges's short story "El simulacro" ("The Simulacrum"), Rodolfo Walsh's short story "Esa mujer" (That Woman), and two works by Néstor Perlonger: his poem "El cadáver de la nación" (The Cadaver of the Nation) and the narrative text "Evita vive" (Evita Lives), which presents three vignettes about Evita's corpse. Of these texts, Walsh's story is particularly telling regarding the relationship between Argentine identity and Eva Perón's corpse. In "Esa mujer," the Colonel (a reference to Colonel Moori Koenig) states that he promised the Christian burial of Evita's corpse to her followers because "I am also Argentine," a sentiment echoed by the journalist who interviews the Colonel and who is identified with Walsh himself. This journalist/narrator states "Me too coronel, me too. We are all Argentines."[3] Through these multiple intertextual references, Martínez cements the idea that the search for Eva Perón's corpse and understanding of the figure of Evita, as well as the necrophilia implied therein, are essential for defining and comprehending Argentine identity.

Some other examples of historical fiction related to national identity are *The Death of Artemio Cruz* (*The Death of Artemio Cruz*, 1962) and *Terra Nostra* (1975) by Carlos Fuentes, *Cenizas de Izalco* (*Ashes of Izalco*, 1966) by Claribel Alegría, and the novels by Ana Teresa Torres *Doña Inés contra el olvido* (Doña Inés against Oblivion, 1992) and *El exilio del tiempo* (Exile in Time, 1990), and Laura Esquivel's *Malinche* (2006).

MAGICAL REALISM

The second category of historical fiction is that of magical realist novels. The term magical realism was coined by Franz Roh in his essay "Magical Realism: Post-Expressionism" (1925) and has been variably defined by numerous critics. In the most general terms, magical realism involves the incorporation of magical elements or a magical worldview into a background of (historical) reality. According to Lois Zamora and Wendy Faris, "Texts labeled magical realist draw upon cultural systems that are no less 'real' than those upon which traditional literary realism draws—often non-Western cultural systems that privilege mystery over empiricism . . . Their primary narrative investment may be in myths, legends, rituals" (3–4). Some contemporary historical and dictator(ship) novels fall within the category of magical realist texts. I focus here on *Cola de lagartija* (*The Lizard's Tail*, 1983) by Luisa Valenzuela and *Cien años de soledad* (*One Hundred Years of Solitude*, 1967) by Gabriel García Márquez. *The Lizard's Tail* centers on Juan Perón's minister of social welfare, José López Rega, who essentially became the dictator of Argentina after Perón's death in 1974. López Rega was the hidden power behind Isabel Perón, who became president upon her husband's death, but relied on López Rega for all her decision-making. López Rega is credited with having begun the Dirty War in Argentina through his terrorist group, the Triple A.

Magic fulfills two functions in *The Lizard's Tail*. First, López Rega employs magic to solidify his power. Second, his opposition also uses magical elements from the Umbanda religion to retaliate against him. The most interesting thing about Valenzuela's work is that although the entire novel seems like fantasy, a comparison to historical accounts of López Rega and his era suggests that much of the novel is in fact historical.

In the novel, the protagonist is never referred to as López Rega, but rather as El Brujo (the Sorcerer), which was historically his nickname. As we learn from Marcelo Larraquy's *López Rega: El peronismo y la triple A,* the real López Rega believed in the occult, engaged in magical Umbanda rites in Brazil, and believed himself to have magical powers (86–87.). There are parallels between what Larraquy and Valenzuela narrate. For example, Larraquy indicates that Ferrera, López Rega's good friend who introduced him to the Umbanda religion, had bought

> A piece of land outside of Porto Alegre . . . and he had donated it to the Umbanda priest . . . for his ceremonies. They called it the Temple of the Sun. . . . One sunset López went to the Temple of the Sun to participate in a purification ceremony that protected him from evil spirits. It was his initiation in the *candomble* ritual. . . . They sacrificed an ox with a blow to its neck. . . . Perón's majordomo, dressed in a white tunic, entered a circle painted white. The ox's blood fell on López Rega's bald spot. . . . According to the Afro-Brazilian rite . . . That magic had converted him into an all-powerful being.[4]

This description from Larroquy's historical account contains several elements that also appear in Valenzuela's novel, notably the Umbanda blood sacrifice performed by López dressed in a white robe. Compare Larroquy's words to the following passages from *The Lizard's Tail*:

> In the meantime, the drums are calling for a sacrifice and Estrella, so self-effacing, offers it herself. Her own menstrual blood, drop by drop, rhythmically, falling on the cloth of Oshalá which was so white before. (17)

The so-called Sorcerer . . . also dresses in white, and says he's religious. (69)

I know for sure that the wrath of the . . . self-called Lord of the Black Lagoon, made itself felt almost immediately. (161)[5]

Note that the "Kingdom of the Black Lagoon" in the novel is set up in direct opposition to "The Temple of the Sun," where the real López Rega received his initiation rites. The light/dark imagery symbolizes López Rega's descent into black magic, and his negative, violent use of the Umbanda rites. In contrast, the narrator (identified as Luisa Valenzuela) and her circle of friends who fight against López Rega and the subsequent military dictatorship also use Umbanda rites to counteract the "river of blood" caused by the torture mandated by López Rega and executed by the Triple A (referred to as the Triple E) in the novel: "They're getting ready for the Umbanda ceremony, all dressed in white, barefoot. With a certain degree of devotion, I stay in the back of the room, trying to retain what I see" (133).[6]

Another element that Valenzuela appropriates from the historical record is López Rega's use of perfume in his magical rites. Larroquy notes that "The secret—López knew it—was in the colors of his garments and the perfumes . . . López also searched for a planetary association for the utilization of perfumes, whose essences allowed the development of the spiritual potentialities of each planet!" (n.p.).[7] Similarly, Valenzuela writes, "That was how the initiation and the rituals began, along with the slow apprenticeship in recipes: the preparation of propitiatory perfumes, the soap of seven powers, talismans for and against the evil eye, herbs to make one fall in love, incense for cleansing, and its opposite, the pestilential unguent for revenge" (16).[8]

The use of Umbanda rites in the novel presents the "non-Western cultural system" of which Zamora and Faris speak. Although these rites may seem far-fetched to some, Larroquy confirms in his book that the Umbanda religion became quite popular among the Argentinean middle class during the 1960s and 1970s, thus illustrating how Valenzuela incorporates fact into her novel. Moreover, Valenzuela blends these magical elements with many historical facts about López Rega himself, such as his aforementioned paramilitary group (the Triple A), his involvement with the cocaine trade (for which he was subsequently prosecuted by the Argentine government), and his attempts to resurrect the deceased Juan and Eva Perón.[9]

Frequently in magical realist texts, the historical elements seem more fantastic than those invented. Such is the case in García Márquez's *One Hundred Years of Solitude*, which traces the life of the Buendía family from their founding of the town of Macondo to the family's ultimate destruction. The fight for independence from the Spanish Crown, the Colombian civil wars between liberals and conservatives, and the violent military repression of the striking banana workers are all documented occurrences that appear in the novel. Gene H. Bell-Villada points out that the character Apolinar Moscote "typifies the centralist tradition of old Spain" (104). One of the main protagonists, Colonel Aureliano Buendía, is engaged in the civil wars that continue throughout a good part of the novel. Finally, the banana strike of October 7, 1928, was followed by "military occupation of the entire area and assignment of strikebreaking troops to cut and ship banana bunches" (106).

Both Valenzuela's and García Márquez's novels illustrate how history can at times be more fantastic than fiction. Other major magical realist historical novels include such works as *El reino de este mundo* (*The Kingdom of this World*, 1949) and *El siglo de las luces* (*Explosion in the Cathedral*, 1962) by Alejo Carpentier, *La casa de los espíritus* (*The House of the Spirits*, 1982) by Isabel Allende, and *Vagos sin tierra* (Vagrants without Land, 1999) by Renée Ferrer.

HISTORICAL INTERTEXTUALITY

The third category of the historical novel that relies on historical intertextuality is well illustrated by the dictator novel *Yo el Supremo* (*I The Supreme* 1974) by Roa Bastos. It is based on the life of the dictator José Gaspar Rodríguez de Francia, who governed Paraguay from 1814 to 1840. The novel is highly dialogic and intertextual, citing (and altering) the travel diary *Letters on Paraguay* (1838) by John and William Robertson as well as *Ensayo histórico sobre la revolución del Paraguay y el gobierno dictatorial del Doctor Francia* (Historical Essay on the Paraguayan Revolution and the Dictatorial Government of Doctor Francia, 1828) by Johann Rengger and Marceline Longchamp, and Enrique Wisner's *El dictador del Paraguay Doctor José Gaspar Rodríguez de Francia* (The Dictator of Paraguay Doctor José Gaspar Rodríguez de Francia, 1923) (Weldt-Basson, *Augusto Roa Bastos's I The Supreme*, 110–70). These sources, largely from the nineteenth and early twentieth centuries, propagate a "black legend" about Francia that has subsequently been questioned by historians such as Julio César Chaves, whose book *El Supremo Dictador* (The Supreme Dictator, 1942) is also extensively cited in Roa Bastos's novel.

The extensive body of literary criticism on Roa Bastos's novel examines how it uses a variety of intertextual sources, largely concluding that the novel provides a postmodern view of the dictator in which the historical figure is humanized, with both a positive and negative side. The purpose of intertextuality in *I The Supreme* becomes clearer upon the subsequent publication in 1993 of the third book of Roa Bastos's trilogy on the "monotheism of power," the dictatorship novel *El fiscal* (*The Prosecutor*). *The Prosecutor* is based on Alfredo Stroessner, who governed Paraguay from 1954 to 1989. In contrast to *I The Supreme*, in which the dictator is the protagonist, Stroessner only appears once in *The Prosecutor*, and the novel largely revolves around the assassination attempt by the protagonist, Félix Moral.

In an interview with Rubén Bareiro Saguier, Roa Bastos indicated that he was obsessed with the idea of impossibility, a concept that informs his trilogy (135–36). Roa Bastos explains in the interview that the three "impossibilities" that characterize the novels of his trilogy are "the metaphysical paradise of a theology of salvation"[10] in the first novel of the trilogy, *Hijo de hombre* (*Son of Man*); "the obsessive impossibility of the absolute"[11] in *I The Supreme*; and "the impossibility of judging another" in *The Prosecutor* (136). In *The Prosecutor*, the question of the difficulty of judging centers around two characters:

Francisco Solano López, the president who led Paraguay into catastrophic Triple Alliance War against Uruguay, Argentina, and Brazil; and the protagonist Félix Moral, who dies during the assassination attempt. The novel posits, without answering, the question as to whether these figures are heroes or martyrs, leaving the reader with the postmodern idea of the "impossibility of judging another" person.[12] Although the impossibility of the absolute is represented in *I The Supreme* through the dictator's attempts to engender himself in a skull, thus becoming his own father and mother,[13] the concept of the impossibility of judging another proposed by the novel *The Prosecutor* resembles the intertextual vision of Dr. Francia found in *I The Supreme*.

One of the many types of discourses that compose the novel is the dictator's "Private Notebook." The compiler who organizes Dr. Francia's papers and other documents in the novel explains that the "Private Notebook" is a ledger book in which "El Supremo had set forth . . . events, ideas, reflections . . . those which in his opinion were positive in the Credit column; negative, in the Debit column" (17).[14] The book was destroyed in a fire a few days before El Supremo's death. Thus, the attempt to structure the novel as a potential judgment of the character (by himself) is subverted by the disappearance of the "proof" of the motivations for his actions. Posterity cannot judge El Supremo because the evidence of his actions and motives has been destroyed.

This idea is reinforced by frequent comments in *I The Supreme* regarding the falsity of writing. The relationship between writing and the impossibility of judging another can be seen in the following comment by the dictator: "If one wishes at all costs to speak of someone, one must not only put oneself in that someone's place: one must be that someone. Only like can write about like. Only the dead can write about the dead" (29).[15] In other words, an integral part of the process of judgment of a historical personage is reading books about the person. However, according to the dictator, there must be a total identification between the writer and his subject, for the book to be valid. Consequently, only El Supremo himself can write about and judge himself, as he attempts to do in his ledger book. Since posterity can only judge figures through books written by others, and these books are not reliable, judgment is impossible. Citing Pascal, the compiler first states that "all contemporary history is suspect" (287), while in his final note he indicates that "all non-contemporary history is suspect" (435).[16] If both contemporary and noncontemporary histories are unreliable, what does that leave the reader to use to judge the dictator and other historical figures? *I The Supreme* tells us, through intertextuality and dialogism, that Dr. Francia ultimately cannot be judged.

Historical intertextuality is also present in historical novels that do not deal with dictatorships, such as Gabriel García Márquez's *El general en su laberinto* (*The General in his Laybrinth*, 1989), based on the final days of Simón Bolívar. Bolívar has been idealized historically and celebrated as the father of Latin American independence. However, in *The General in his Labyrinth*, García Márquez humanizes him and shows some of his negative characteristics. In the "My Thanks" section at the end of the novel, García Márquez acknowledges Eugenio Gutiérrez Cely and Fabio Puyo Vasco, whose annotated collection of Bolívar's letters *Bolívar día a día* (Bolívar Day by Day, 1983) aided him in the construction of his novel:

> The Colombian historian Eugenio Gutiérrez Cely . . . prepared a card file for me that not only provided surprising information . . . but also gave me my first inkling of a method for investigating and ordering facts. Furthermore, his book *Bolívar día a día* (Bolívar Day by Day) . . . was a navigational chart while I was writing, which allowed me to move with ease through the periods in the character's life. (272)[17]

Although Cely is one of many people García Márquez thanks, a careful comparison between *The General in his Labyrinth* and *Bolívar día a día* reveals a highly intertextual connection in which the author has adopted the structure of Cely and Puyo's book in the construction of his novel. *Bolívar día a día* is presented as a travel diary that offers Bolívar's locations, voyages, fragments from his letters, and corresponding historical commentary for almost every day of his adult life. Similarly, García Márquez structures his novel as a series of locations and trips that Bolívar makes during his final days. Moreover, *The General in his Labyrinth* and the third volume of *Bolívar día a día* contain maps tracing Bolívar's travels that underscore the dialogue García Márquez creates with this source (Weldt-Basson, "The Purpose" 99–100).

Like *I The Supreme*, *The General in his Labyrinth*, in a postmodern fashion, is concerned with the question of the truth value of history. As critics have pointed out, García Márquez demystifies the heroic figure of Bolívar by humanizing him, thus presenting a "counter-history" to the official histories that have glorified Bolívar as a perfect hero (Bell-Villada 220). The vision of a dying Bolívar stands in stark contrast to the image most people hold in their minds. Equally significant to this demystification is García Márquez's muddling of the boundaries between fiction and history, confirming Roa Bastos's vision of the impossibility of knowing the truth and thus in judging the historical figure.

The "My Thanks" section illustrates how García Márquez conflates fiction and history. First, he claims that he "was not particularly troubled by the question of historical accuracy, since the last voyage along the river is the least documented period of Bolívar's life" (271).[18] Having denied the need for historical accuracy in a novel, the author then contradicts himself, stating that he spent two "long years sinking into the quicksand of voluminous, contradictory and often uncertain documentation . . . My absolute lack of experience and method in historical research made my days even more arduous" (272). These comments beg the question as to why such extensive research was even necessary when writing a work of fiction. Similarly, he thanks Aníbal Noguera Mendoza for proofreading the first version of the book manuscript where he discovered "half a dozen mortal fallacies and suicidal anachronisms that would have cast doubts on the exactitude of this novel" (273).[19] In addition to these suggestions of historical rigor, García Márquez concludes his work with a brief chronology of Bolívar's life, which allows the reader to cross-reference fictional events to historical ones to ascertain their truth value.

Why does García Márquez go to such lengths to emphasize the historical value of his novel? Showing the similarities between fiction and history is just another way of questioning the truth value of the historical record and illustrating its fictional nature. If a novel can be more historical than history books, then historiography can be more fictional than a novel. The author plays with these relationships by using and altering historical elements from Bolívar's letters for purely fictional purposes. Perhaps the best example of this is the small change the author makes in an excerpt from a letter Bolívar wrote to General Santander on August 4, 1823, which serves as the epigraph that introduces the novel. The excerpt reads: "It seems that the devil controls the business of *my* life"[20] (my emphasis). Bolívar originally wrote, "It seems that the devil controls the business of life."[21] The small addition "my" to the quotation changes the meaning entirely, focusing on the misfortunes of Bolívar's existence, as opposed to life in general. Small as the change is, it emphasizes the precedence of fiction over history and the way that what seems historical can be inaccurate or incomplete.

Other historical novels that rely heavily on intertextuality are the following: Fernando del Paso's *Noticias del imperio* (*News from the Empire*, 1989), Rosario Ferré's *El vuelo del cisne* (*The Flight of the Swan*, 2001), Antonio Benítez-Rojo's *Mujer en traje de batalla* (*Woman in Battle Dress*, 2001), Mario Vargas Llosa's *El paraíso en la otra esquina* (*The Way to Paradise*, 2006), and Nona Fernández's *La dimensión desconocida* (*The Twilight Zone*, 2016).

SYMBOLIC HISTORICAL FICTION

The final category of historical fiction is comprised by those novels where history is used symbolically. Often the history of one country is employed to evoke the history of another. This technique has been extensively used by Vargas Llosa. One of his most famous works is the novel *The Feast of the Goat*, which narrates the decline of Dominican dictator Rafael Leónidas Trujillo. The novel has three alternating sections: one about the dictator and his daily activities, another about the actions of his assassins, and a third one about Urania Cabral, the protagonist who was raped by Trujillo when she was fourteen, before leaving the country. Vargas Llosa interweaves purely fictional characters, such as Urania Cabral, with historical ones. The author undoubtedly used historical sources, such as *Trujillo: The Life and Times of a Caribbean Dictator* (1966) by Robert. D. Crassweller and *Trujillo: The Death of the Goat* by Bernard Diederich (1978), in the construction of his novel. Although Vargas Llosa humanizes Trujillo by showing his physical decay and his love for his mother, his portrayal is ultimately unsympathetic.

The structure of *The Feast of the Goat* is particularly interesting for its symbolic potential. Although all the events in the novel refer to the Dominican Republic, Vargas Llosa has cleverly slipped in a character from Peru:

> One historically based character, the minister Henry Chirinos, actually has nothing to do with the Trujillo dictatorship at all. Chirinos is based on a congressman during the Fujimori dictatorship in Peru (1990–2000) by the name of Enrique Chirinos Soto. According to Catherine M. Conaghan, the Peruvian Chirinos was "often

lampooned in the press for his weight and his drinking problem" (130) both of which are characteristics used to portray Henry Chirinos in *La fiesta del chivo*.

(Weldt-Basson, "Mario Vargas *Llosa's La fiesta del chivo*," 125)

Vargas Llosa undoubtedly uses this very minor character to suggest a parallel between the Trujillo dictatorship and the Fujimori government in Peru. Alberto Fujimori was elected president of Peru in 1990; his opponent in the election was Vargas Llosa himself. Fujimori, like Trujillo, relied on a corrupt and violent intelligence organization. In the Dominican Republic, Johnny Abbes García ran the SIM, while in Peru, Vladimiro Montesinos ran the SIN. Both governments controlled the presses of their respective countries and were guilty of human-rights violations. Vargas Llosa uses the elements of the Trujillo dictatorship to symbolically refer to political events in his own country.

Vargas Llosa's most recent novel, *Tiempos recios* (*Harsh Times*, 2019), is, like *Amalia*, both a historical and dictatorship novel. *Harsh Times* deals with the government of Jacobo Árbenz (1945–1951) in Guatemala and how its downfall was brought about by the United Fruit Company and the eventual intervention of the United States. Like *The Feast of the Goat*, it is a piece of symbolic historical fiction. Vargas Llosa uses events in Guatemala not only to illustrate Guatemalan politics, but also to point to the history of Cuba.

Harsh Times emphasizes the democratic nature of Árbenz's government. The United Fruit Company helped topple Árbenz by promoting newspaper articles supposedly showing his communist orientation, which in turn caught the attention of the United States and led to the eventual intervention of the United States and the CIA in Guatemala. The United States backed a successful coup led by the military officer Carlos Castillo Armas, who became the dictator of the country from 1954 to 1957. Castillo Armas's coup was supported by other dictators, such as Trujillo, and thus the novel also evolves into a dictatorship novel that focuses on these two figures. The association between Castillo Armas and Trujillo becomes a major focal point of the second half of the book, because despite his early support of the regime, Trujillo quickly evolves into Castillo Armas's enemy, when the latter does not fulfill the promises he had made to Trujillo. Trujillo sends his intelligence director, the ruthless Johnny Abbes García, to Guatemala to assassinate Castillo Armas. Vargas Llosa cleverly mixes historical and fictional elements using both historical and literary intertextuality.

Vargas Llosa links his novel to the history and trajectory of the dictator(ship) novel in Latin America through multiple allusions to *El señor presidente* (*The President*, 1946) by the Guatemalan writer Miguel Ángel Asturias. *The President* was written as an exposé of the dictatorship of Manuel Estrada Cabrera, who governed Guatemala from 1898 to 1920. The dictator appears in only a few scenes, but his presence is indelibly felt throughout all the action of the novel. It is considered a seminal work in the development of the genre, as it employs many new narrative techniques, including surrealist ones.

The first element that evokes *The President* is the kidnapping of Castillo Armas's mistress, Marta Borrero, which parallels the kidnapping of Camila Canales, daughter of General Canales, who falls out of favor with the dictator in *The President*. Angel Face (Cara de Ángel), the President's lackey, is attracted to Camila and thus decides to keep her for himself when General Canales is forced to flee. This is exactly what Johnny Abbes does in *Tiempos recios*.

A second allusion to *The President* is the nickname attributed to Castillo Armas. He is referred to as Cara de Hacha (Axe Face), which reminds one of Cara de Ángel (Angel Face). Moreover, Johnny Abbes tells his chauffeur that he has to be "at seven on the dot at the door of the Cathedral."[22] This also alludes to the beginning of *The President*, which takes place outside the cathedral. Finally, both books have a character by the name of Farfán. In *The President*, Major Farfán is the officer who arrests and betrays Angel Face, who had warned Farfán that the President was planning to kill him. In *Harsh Times*, Farfán is a speech writer and assistant to Castillo Armas, a historical personage rather than an invented character. Vargas Llosa uses these elements to signal a connection to the subgenre of the dictatorship novel and to pay homage to Asturias in the (literary) history of Guatemala.

Like many of Vargas Llosa's novels, *Harsh Times* is historical in nature. *La guerra del fin del mundo* (*The War at the End of the World*, 1981), *The Feast of the Goat* (2000), *The Way to Paradise* (2006), and *El sueño del celta* (*The Dream of the Celt*, 2010), just to name a few that are based on historical characters, significantly engage with historical intertexts and are all symbolic in nature. Toward the end of *Harsh Times*, the narrator specifically mentions one of the novel's historical sources: "Tony Raful knows everything about her [Marta Borrero] and has researched her past, and there is no doubt that much of what he's told me about her is true" (*Harsh Times*, 283).[23] The narrator then mentions the title of Raful's book, *La rapsodia del crimen* (*The Rhapsody of Crime*, 2017). A comparison between *Harsh Times* and Raful's book leaves no doubt that Vargas Llosa employed Raful's work in the construction of his novel.

By reading *La rapsodia del crimen*, the reader learns that the character Marta Borrero is based on Gloria Bolaños, the real name of Castillo Armas's mistress. Despite the name change, much of what *Harsh Times* narrates regarding Bolaños's relationship with Castillo Armas is historical, including her flight from Guatemala after his death, her relationship with Johnny Abbes García, her anti-communist commentary on the radio program *La Voz Dominicana* (The Dominican Voice), her possible association with the CIA, and her house in the United States. At the end of *Tiempos recios*, Vargas Llosa parodies Raful's text in the interview between Marta Borrero and a journalist named Mario Vargas Llosa. This interview mimics the one Raful conducts with Gloria Bolaños in his book. The description of Borrero's house in *Tiempos recios* resembles that of Bolaños's residence in Raful's book:

> No one can move through Marta's house without knocking down some object . . . . Statues, busts, and religious figurines . . . alternate with mummies and Egyptian catafalques, photos, paintings, and homages to Latin American dictators like Generalísimo Trujillo and Carlos Castillo Armas. The latter was *the great love of my life*, as she will confess to me momentarily, and she has dedicated an entire wall to him with a gigantic photo and a votive candle that flickers for him day and night.
>
> (*Harsh Times*, 276)[24]

Compare this passage to Raful's description of Bolaños's house:

> Her house seems surrounded by mystery, full of works of art, porcelain animals, cages ... gigantic photographs of world leaders ... Among the most striking is a photo of ... Trujillo ... the most impressive is a photo of ex-president Carlos Castillo Armas that covers the entire wall, under a votive flame that burns before his image .. . and for whom she expresses the greatest admiration and love.[25]

Vargas Llosa also copies Raful's use of nicknames in parentheses throughout his text:

> When Castillo Armas tried to name the station director, Broadfrost informed him that the CIA had already chosen one, a gringo by the name of David Atlee Phillips (the Invisible Man).... The colonel was further displeased to discover that one of the pilots hired to fly the Army of Liberation's planes was an adventurer and psychopath named Jerry Fred DeLarm (the Nutcase)
>
> (*Harsh Times*, 46–48).[26]

Note how the novel follows Raful's historical work:

> As Silfa recounts, security services in Costa Rica had protected the Cuban gangster Policarpo Soler ... [and] Jesús G. Cartas (The Strange One) ... Dr. Thomen ... was designated first-class secretary in the Dominican embassy in that country replacing Osvaldo Día Fernández (Bushy Eye-Brow), a sinister character. (my translation)[27]

Although all the historical material is about Guatemala, toward the end of the novel, the narrator slips in the following comment, pointing to the novel's symbolism:

> The three of us [Vargas Llosa, Tony Raful, Soledad Álvarez] are certain that the United States erred terribly in preparing a coup against Árbenz ... The victory was fleeting, pointless, and counterproductive. It helped foment anti-Americanism in Latin America all over again, and invigorated the Marxists, Trotskyites, and the Fidelists. ... The history of Cuba might have been different had the United States accepted the modernization and democratization of Guatemala that Arévalo and Árbenz attempted to carry out. Democratization and modernization were what Fidel Castro intended for Cuban society when he assaulted the Moncada Barracks on July 26, 1953, in Santiago de Cuba. At the time, he was far from the collectivist and dictatorial extremes that would leave Cuba petrified to this day in an anachronistic absolutism stripped of all semblance of liberty.
>
> (*Harsh Times*, 287–288)[28]

These final remarks cause the reader to rethink what they have read about Guatemalan history, in order to see the parallels with Cuban history. What might initially seem like a minor reflection recontextualizes the entire novel and creates a symbolic relationship between Guatemala and Cuba.

This chapter has merely touched the tip of the iceberg of Latin American historical fiction, and its subgenre, the dictator(ship) novel, which illustrates the characteristics of the larger genre. Although the heyday of Latin American dictatorships has ended and many countries now have democratically elected governments, the dictator(ship) novel subgenre continues through what are called (using a term coined by Marianne Hirsch), post-memory novels. These novels are written by second-generation writers who either were not born yet or were children during the dictatorship. They focus on how dictatorships are remembered and on how the lessons learned from them are passed down to subsequent generations that must learn to live with a past of violence. Countries like Chile and Argentina, which experienced brutal human-rights abuses during the 1970s and 1980s, have seen the publication of hundreds of novels that fit into this category, including such works as *La resta* (*The Remainder*, 2014) by Alia Trabucco Zerán, *La dimensión desconocida* (*The Twilight Zone*, 2016) by Nona Fernández, and *El fin de la historia* (*The End of the Story*, 1996) by Liliana Heker and *El espíritu de mis padres sigue subiendo en la lluvia* (*My Father's Ghost is Climbing in the Rain*, 2011) by Patricio Pron. Thus, history continues to be a major element in Latin American fiction.

NOTES

1. "Sin asociación . . . sin la esperanza de poder organizar, improvisadamente esa polanca de poder y de progreso europeo que se llama la asociación, ¿con qué contar para la obra que nos proponemos? . . . Mi querido Belgrano ha hablado por mí en cuanto *al espíritu de individualismo que por desgracia de nuestra patria ha caracterizado siempre a los argentinos*" (Mármol 227–330, my emphasis); "Rosas no encontró clases, *no halló sino individuos* cuando estableció su gobierno" (289, my emphasis); "Tales han sido los primeros medios empleados por él para debilitar la fuerza sintética del pueblo, cortando todos los lazos de la comunidad y *dejando una sociedad de individuos aislados* para ejercer sobre ellos su bárbaro poder" (311, my emphasis).
2. "Hubo un momento en que me dije: Si no la escribo, voy a asfixiarme. Si no trato de conocerla escribiéndola, jamás voy a conocerme yo" (Martínez 473).
3. "Yo también soy argentino. –Yo también, coronel, yo también. Somos todos argentinos" (Walsh 15).
4. "Un terreno en las afueras de Porto Alegre . . . y se lo había donado al pai Umbanda . . . para sus ceremonias. Lo llamaban el Templo del Sol . . . Un atardecer López fue al templo del Sol para participar de una ceremonia de purificación que protegía de los malos espíritus. Fue su iniciación en el ritual del candomble . . . sacrificaron a un buey de golpe en la nuca. Lo abrieron por el vientre y lo dejaron colgar atado de una soga. El mayordomo de Perón, vestido con una túnica blanca, entró en un círculo pintado de blanco . . . La sangre del buey cayó sobre la calva de López Rega. . . . Según la tradición en el rito afrobrasileño . . . La magia lo había convertido en un ser todopoderoso" (Larraquy, 203–204).
5. "Mientras tanto los tambores claman por un sacrificio y Estrella se los brinda . . . Es su propia sangre menstrual la que gota a gota, rítmicamente, sigue cayendo sobre el mantel de Oshalá que era tan blanco" (Valenzuela 26); "el brujo también se viste de blanco y dice que es religioso" (72); "Tengo entendido que las iras del señor de la Laguna Negra se hicieron sentir casi enseguida" (154).

6. "Se están preparando para empezar la ceremonia de Umbanda, todos vestidos de blanco, descalzos. Con cierta devoción me quedo en el fondo de la estancia, tratando de retener lo que estoy viendo, de incorporármelo" (Valenzuela, *Cola de lagartija* 132).

7. "El secreto—López lo sabía—estaba en los colores de sus prendas y los perfumes. . . . López también buscó una asociación planetaria para la utilización de perfumes, cuyas esencias permitieran desarrollar las potencialidades espirituales de cada planeta" (Larroquy, 153).

8. "Se inició así la iniciación y empezaron los rituales junto con el lento aprendizaje de recetas: la preparación de perfumes propiciatorios, el jabón de las siete potencias, los talismanes a favor y en contra del mal de ojo, las hierbas de enamorar, los inciensos para la limpia y su contracara, el pestilente ungüento para las salaciones" (Valenzuela, *Cola de lagartija* 25).

9. Larroquy (360) recounts the following attempt by López Rega to resuscitate Perón: "Cuando la muerte clínica ya era un hecho, intercedió López Rega: --El General ya murió en una ocasión y yo lo resucité—adivirtió. Lo tomó de los tobillos. Entrecerró los ojos y, con pronunciación monótona y ritmo constante, balbuceó unos mantras, en su intento de alcanzar armonía con lo Divino. Hasta que gritó: --¡No te vayas, Faraón!—al mismo tiempo que sacudía las piernas muertas del general. Al cabo de febriles intentos por volverlo a la vida, se resignó."

10. "La de hallar la bienaventuranza en el paraíso metafísico de la teología de la salvación" (Bareiro Saguier 136).

11. "La imposibilidad metafísica y obsesiva de lo absoluto" (Bareiro Saguier 136). By absolute, Roa Bastos is referring to something that is totally independent from external conditions or relations, complete within itself and thus unconditionally powerful.

12. "La imposibilidad de juzgar al otro" (Bareiro Saguier 136).

13. Note that this is very similar to the Sorcerer's attempt to engender a son with the male and female parts of his body, creating the "father-mother neuron" in *The Lizard's Tail* (Valenzuela 64).

14. "El Supremo había sentado . . . hechos, ideas, reflexiones . . . los que a su juicio eran positivos en la columna del Haber; los negativos en la columna del Debe..." (Roa Bastos, *Yo, el Supremo* 110).

15. "Si a toda costa se quiere hablar de alguien no solo tiene uno que ponerse en su lugar; Tiene que ser ese alguien. Únicamente el semejante puede escribir sobre el semejante. Únicamente los muertos podrán escribir sobre los muertos" (Roa Bastos, *Yo, el Supremo* 124).

16. "Toda historia contemporánea es sospechosa" (Roa Bastos, *Yo, el Supremo* 439–40); "toda historia no contemporánea es sospechosa" (609).

17. "El historiador colombiano Eugenio Gutiérrez Celys, en respuesta a un cuestionario de muchas páginas, elaboró para mí un archivo de tarjetas que no solo me aportó datos sorprendentes . . . sino que me dio las primeras luces para un método de pesquisa y ordenamiento de la información" (García Márquez, *El general* 272).

18. "Por otra parte, los fundamentos históricos me preocupaban poco, pues el último viaje por el río es el tiempo menos documentado de la vida de Bolívar" (García Márquez, *El general* 272).

19. "Mi viejo amigo Aníbal Noguera Mendoza . . . descubrió media docena de falacias mortales y anacronismos suicidas que habrían sembrado dudas sobre el rigor de esta novela" (García Márquez, *El general* 274).

20. "Parece que el demonio dirige las cosas de mi vida" (García Márquez, *El general* 9).

21. "Parece que el demonio dirige las cosas de la vida" (Gutiérrez Cely and Puyo Vasco 438).

22. "A las siete en punto en la puerta de la catedral" (Vargas Llosa, *Tiempos recios* 105).

23. "No hay duda de que muchas de las cosas que me ha dicho sobre ella Tony Raful que la conoce a fondo . . . deben ser verdad. . . . [en] *La rapsodia del crimen*" (Vargas Llosa, *Tiempos recios* 345).

24. Uno no puede moverse por la casa de Marta sin derribar algún objeto . . . Las estatuas, bustos y figuras religiosas . . . alternan con momias y catafalcos egipcios, fotos, cuadros y homenajes a dictadores latinoamericanos como el Generalísimo Trujillo o Carlos Castillo Armas. Este fue 'el gran amor de su vida', me confesará dentro de un momento y a él hay dedicada toda una pared con una fotografía gifante y una lámpara votiva en su homenaje que llamea día y noche (Vargas Llosa, *Tiempos recios* 336).

25. "Su casa parece envuelta en el misterio, llena de obras de arte, animales de porcelana, de jaulas, . . . de gigantescas fotografías de líderes mundiales . . . Entre las coas más llamativas está una foto de . . . Trujillo . . . la más impresionante . . . es una foto enorme del ex presidente Carlos Castillo Armas que cubre toda la pared, bajo una llama votivà de fuego que arde ante su imagen . . . y de quien ella expresa la más alta admiración y amor" (Raful, 151.)

26. "La CIA había ya designado a un gringo . . . David Atlee Phillips (El Invisible) para dirigirla . . . El coronel se llevó otro disgusto cuando supo que uno de los pilotos contratados para llevar los aviones del Ejército liberacionista era un psicópata aventurero, Jerry Fred DeLarm (El Loquito)" (Vargas Llosa, *Tiempos recios* 65–67).

27. Según relata Silfa, los servicios de seguridad de Costa Rica habían detectado al gángster cubano Policarpo Soler. . . [y] a Jesus G. Cartas (El Extraño) . . . el doctor Thomen . . . fue designado secretario de primera clase en la embajada dominicana a este país sustituyendo al señor Osvaldo Día Fernández (Cejijunto), personaje siniestro (Raful 144).

28. Los tres [Vargas Llosa, Tony Raful Soledad Álvarez] coincidimos en que fue una gran torpeza de Estados Unidos preparar ese golpe militar contra Árbenz . . . El triunfo que obtuvieron fue pasajero, inútil y contraproducente. Hizo recrudecer el antinorteamericanismo en toda América Latina y fortaleció a los partidos marxistas, trotskistas y fidelistas . . . Otra hubiera podido ser la historia de Cuba si los EEUU aceptaba la modernización y democratización de Guatemala que intentaron Arévalo y Árbenz. Esa democratización y modernización era lo que decía querer Fidel Castro para la sociedad cubana cuando el asalto al cuartel Moncada el 26 de julio de 1953 en Santiago de Cuba. Estaba lejos entonces de los extremos colectivistas y dictatoriales que petrificarían a Cuba hasta ahora en una dictadura anacrónica y soldada contra todo asomo de libertad" (Vargas Llosa, *Tiempos recios* 350–51).

Works Cited

Alegría, Claribel. *Ashes of Izalco*. Translated by Darwin J. Flakoll. Curbstone, 1989.

Alegría, Claribel. *Cenizas de Izalco*. 2nd ed. Educa, 1982.

Allende, Isabel. *La casa de los espíritus*. Bantam Books, 1993.

Allende, Isabel. *The House of the Spirits*. Translated by Magda Bogin. Simon and Schuster, 1985.

Asturias, Miguel Ángel. *The President*. Translated by Francis Partridge. Waveland Press, 1997.

Asturias, Miguel Ángel. *El señor presidente*. Losada, 1988.

Bareiro Saguier, Rubén. *Augusto Roa Bastos (caídas y resurrecciones de un pueblo)*. Trilce, 1989.

Bell-Villada, Gene H. *García Márquez: The Man and his Work*. U of North Carolina P, 2010.

Benítez-Rojo, Antonio. *Mujer en traje de batalla*. Alfaguara, 2001.

Benítez Rojo, Antonio. *Woman in Battle Dress*. Translated by Jessica Powell City Lights Books, 2015.

Borges, Jorge Luis. "El simulacro." *El hacedor. Obras completas*, Emecé, 1974, 789.

Carpentier, Alejo. *Explosion in the Cathedral*. Translated by John Sturrock. Little, Brown & Co., 1962.

Carpentier, Alejo. *The Kingdom of this World*. Translated by Lacy Lockert, Farrar, Straus, Giroux, 2017.

Carpentier, Alejo. *Reasons of State*. Translated by Francis Partridge. Writers and Readers Publishing Cooperative, 1977.

Carpentier, Alejo. *El recurso del método*. Plaza & Janes, 1987.

Carpentier, Alejo. *El reino de este mundo. Obras completas*, vol. 2, 4th edition. Siglo veintiuno, 1987.

Carpentier, Alejo. *El siglo de las luces*. Cátedra, 1985.

Castellanos, Jorge, and Miguel Á. Martínez. "El dictador hispanoamericano como personaje literario." *Latin American Research Review*, vol. 16, no .2, 1981, pp. 79–105.

Chaves, Julio César. *El Supremo Dictador*. 4th ed. Gráficas Yagües, 1964.

Crassweller, Robert D. *Trujillo: The Life and Times of a Caribbean Dictator*. Macmillan, 1966.

Del Paso, Fernando. *News from the Empire*. Translated by Alfonso González and Stella T. Clark. Dalkey Archive Press, 2009.

Del Paso, Fernando. *Noticias del imperio*. Fondo de Cultura Económica, 2012.

Diederich, Bernard. *Trujillo: The Death of the Goat*. The Bodley Head, 1978.

Esquivel, Laura. *Malinche*. Atria, 2006.

Esquivel, Laura. *Malinche*. Translated by Ernesto Mestra-Reed. Washington Square Press, 2006.

Fernández, Nona. *La dimensión desconocida*. Literatura Random House, 2017.

Fernández, Nona. *The Twilight Zone*. Translated by Natasha Wimmer. Graywolf Press, 2021.

Ferré, Rosario. *Flight of the Swan*. New York: Farrar, Straus, Giroux, 2001.

Ferré, Rosario. *El vuelo del cisne*. Vintage, 2002.

Ferrer, Renée. *Vagos sin tierra*. Servilibro, 2017.

Fromm, Eric. *The Anatomy of Human Destructiveness*. Holt, 1973.

Fuentes, Carlos. *The Death of Artemio Cruz*. Translated by Alfred Mac Adam Farrar, Straus, Giroux, 1991.

Fuentes, Carlos. *La muerte de Artemio Cruz*. Fondo de cultura económica, 1962.

Fuentes, Carlos. *Terra Nostra*. 7th ed. Joaquín Mortiz, 1992.

Fuentes, Carlos. *Terra Nostra*. Translated by Margaret Sayers Peden. Farrar, Straus, Giroux, 1976.

García Márquez, Gabriel. *The Autumn of the Patriarch*. Translated by Gregory Rabassa. Avon Books, 1977.

García Márquez, Gabriel. *Cien años de soledad*. 42nd ed. Sudamericana, 1972.

García Márquez, Gabriel. *El general en su laberinto*. 6th ed. Sudamericana, 1989.

García Márquez, Gabriel. *The General in His Labyrinth*. Translated by Edith Grossman. Penguin Books, 1990.

García Márquez, Gabriel. *One Hundred Years of Solitude*. Harper Perennial Classics, 2006.

García Márquez, Gabriel. *El otoño del patriarca*. Mondadori, 1987.

Gutiérrez Cely, Eugenio and Fabio Puyo Vasco. *Bolívar día a día*. 3 vols. Procultura, 1983.

Heker, Liliana. *The End of the Story*. Translated by Andrea G. Labinger. Biblioasis, 2012.

Heker, Liliana. *El fin de la historia*. Punto de lectura, 2004.

Hirsch, Marianne. *The Generation of Postmemory: Writing and Visual Culture After the Holocaust*. Columbia UP, 2012.

Larraquy, Marcelo. *López Rega, el peronismo, y la triple A*. Penguin Random House, 2018.

Lukács, Georg. *The Historical Novel*. Translated by Hannah and Stanley Mitchell. U of Nebraska P, 1962.

Mármol, Jorge. *Amalia*. Independently Published, 2020.

Mármol, Jorge. *Amalia*. Translated by Helen Lane. Oxford UP, 2001.

Martínez, Tomás Eloy. *La novela de Perón*. Vintage Press, 1985.

Martínez, Tomás Eloy. *The Perón Novel*. Translated by Asa Zatz. Pantheon Books, 1988.

Martínez, Tomás Eloy. *Santa Evita*. Punto de Lectura, 2006.

Martínez, Tomás Eloy. *Santa Evita*. Translated by Helen Lane. Vintage Books, 1997.

Menton, Seymour. *Latin America's New Historical Novel*. U of Texas P, 1993.

Parkinson Zamora, Lois, and Wendy B. Faris, eds. *Magical Realism: Theory, History, Community*. Duke UP, 1995.

Perkowska, Magdalena. *Historias híbridas: La nueva novela histórica latinoamericana (1985–2000) ante las teorías posmodernas de la historia*. Iberoamericana-Vervuert, 2008.

Perlongher, Néstor. "El cadáver de la nación." *Cadáveres*. Mate, 1997.

Perlongher, Néstor. *Evita Vive*. Sarita Cartonera, 2004.

Pons, María Cristina. *Memorias del olvido: La novela histórica de fines del siglo XX*. Siglo veintiuno, 1996.

Pron, Patricio. *El espíritu de mis padres sigue subiendo en la lluvia*. Vinatage Español, 2011.

Pron, Patricio. *My Father's Ghost Is Climbing in the Rain*. Translated by Mara Faye Lethem. Vintage, 2013.

Raful, Tony. *La rapsodia del crimen: Trujillo vs. Castillo Armas*. Penguin Random House, 2017.

Rengger, Johann, and Marceline Longchamp. *Ensayo histórico sobre la revolución del Paraguay y el gobierno dictatorio del Doctor Francia*. Translated by D.J.C. Pages. Imprenta de Moreau, 1828.

Roa Bastos, Augusto. *El fiscal*. Alfaguara, 1993.

Roa Bastos, Augusto. *I The Supreme*. Translated by Helen Lane. Alfred A. Knopf, 1986.

Roa Bastos, Augusto. *The Prosecutor*. Translated by Helene Carol Weldt-Basson. Farleigh Dickinson University Press, 2018.

Roa Bastos, Augusto. *Yo el Supremo*. 2nd. ed. Cátedra, 1987

Robertson, John Parish, and William Parish Robertson. *Letters on Paraguay: Comprising an Account of a Four Year's Residence in The Republic, under the Government of the Dictator Francia*. 3 vols. John Murray, 1839.

Sommer, Doris. *Foundational Fictions: The National Romances of Latin America*. U of California P, 1991.

Subercaseaux, Elizabeth. *El general azul*. Zeta, 1991.

Torres, Ana Teresa. *Doña Inés vs. Oblivion*. Translated by Gregory Rabassa. Grove Press, 2000.

Torres, Ana Teresa. *Doña Inés contra el olvido*. Monte Ávila, 1992.

Torres, Ana Teresa. *El exilio en el tiempo*. Monte Ávila, 1990.

Trabucco Zerán, Alia. *The Remainder*. Translated by Sophie Hughes. Coffee House Press, 2019.

Trabucco Zerán, Alia. *La resta*. Demipage, 2014.

Uslar Pietri, Arturo. *Oficio de difuntos*. Planeta, 1995.

Valenzuela, Luisa. *Cola de lagartija*. Planeta, 1983.

Valenzuela, Luisa. *The Lizard's Tail*. Translated by Gregory Rabassa. Farrar, Strauss, Giroux, 1983.

Vargas Llosa, Mario. *The Dream of the Celt*. Translated by Edith Grossman. Farrar, Straus, Giroux, 2012.

Vargas Llosa, Mario. *The Feast of the Goat*. Translated by Edith Grossman. Picador, 2001.

Vargas Llosa, Mario. *La fiesta del chivo*. Santillana, 2000.

Vargas Llosa, Mario. *La guerra del fin del mundo*. Seix Barral, 1981.

Vargas Llosa, Mario. *Harsh Times*. Translated by Adrian Nathan West. Farrar, Straus, Giroux, 2021.

Vargas Llosa, Mario. *El paraíso en la esquina*. Santillana, 2003.

Vargas Llosa, Mario. *El sueño del celta*. Santillana/Alfaguara, 2010.

Vargas Llosa, Mario. *Tiempos recios*. Alfaguara, 2019.

Vargas Llosa, Mario. *The War at the End of the World*. Translated by Helen R. Lane. Farrar, Straus, Girous, 1984.

Vargas Llosa, Mario. *The Way to Paradise*. Translated by Natasha Wimmer. Picador, 2003.

Walsh, Rodolfo. "Esa mujer." *Los oficios terrestres*. Ediciones de la flor, 1986.

Weldt-Basson, Helene Carol. *Augusto Roa Bastos's I The Supreme: A Dialogic Perspective*. University of Missouri Press, 1993.

Weldt-Basson, Helene C. "Double Vision: History and Politics in the Works of Augusto Roa Bastos and Tomás Eloy Martínez. *Chasqui*, vol. 41, no. 2, 2012, 107–123.

Weldt-Basson, Helene C. "Mario Vargas Llosa's *La fiesta del chivo*: History, Fiction or Social Psychology?" *Hispanófila*, no. 156, 2009, pp. 113–30.

Weldt-Basson, Helene C. "The Purpose of Historical Reference in Gabriel García Márquez's *El general en su laberinto*." *Revista Hispánica Moderna*, vol. 47, no.1, 1994, pp. 96–108.

Weldt-Basson, Helene Carol. *Redefining Latin American Historical Fiction: The Impact of Feminism and Postcolonialism*. Palgrave-Macmillan, 2013.

Wisner, Enrique. *El Dictador del Paraguay Doctor José Gaspar Rodríguez de Francia*. Concordia, 1923.

Zúñiga Araúz, Mauro. *El chacal del general*. Albacrome, S.A. 2011.

CHAPTER 25

....

MAGICAL REALISM AND THE MARVELOUS REAL IN THE NOVEL

....

AMARYLL CHANADY

FOR more than half a century, the Latin American novel has been widely associated with the literary mode of magical realism. Many Latin American critics, however, have questioned the theoretical usefulness of the term since the 1970s because of its vagueness and multiple origins, as well as its application to very different kinds of writing. Its lack of specificity is compounded by the general blurring of genres, whose distinctions are becoming even "fuzzier" in the global economy (Hart and Ouyang 20). According to Román de la Campa, magical realism has become a "buzzword" that is "loosely associated with an exotic and undifferentiated multiculturalist flavor" (10). Alberto Moreiras describes it as a "neocolonialist commercial mystification" since the publication of *El zorro de arriba y el zorro de abajo* (*The Fox from up above and the Fox from down below*), José María Arguedas's last novel in 1969, which "closes Latin American magical realism" (194). Likewise, in their anthology *McOndo* (1996), Alberto Fuguet and Sergio Gómez reject the relevance of magical realism today, since the world of Macondo, the mythical town in *Cien años de soledad* (*One Hundred Years of Solitude*, 1967) by the Nobelprize winner Gabriel García Márquez, has been replaced by McOndo, the world of MacDonald's, Macintoshes, and condominiums.

THE PROBLEM OF DEFINITION

....

Although publishers have undoubtedly found the term useful in their marketing strategy, the continued publication of academic studies on magical realism in the Latin American novel as well as in literature in other parts of the world suggests that the label is not merely a commercial buzzword. Critics do have a particular kind of fiction in mind, even if the meaning may be vague. Although it is impossible to agree on a definitive meaning, or to excavate a nucleus of essential signification in the history of critical discourse, it is important to discuss the most useful ways in which the term can be understood in order to discern the specificity of particular novels. Franz Roh's introduction of the term in art history in 1925 to describe post-expressionist painting, Ángel Flores's popularization of the term in Latin American literary criticism in 1955, and Luis Leal's divergent definition in 1967 (see the English translations in Zamora and Faris 15–31, 109–17, and 119–24) are important moments in literary history and have been widely analyzed in discussions of magical realism. However, post-expressionism in art, the new fiction that finally allows Latin America to enter the world literary stage with narrative innovation in the 1940s (Flores), and the representation of reality as a mystery (Leal) have very little in common with one another. Furthermore, both Flores and Leal refer to a wide variety of very diverse authors. The problem of definition is exacerbated by the invention of the term "real maravilloso" (marvelous real) by the Cuban Alejo Carpentier in the prologue to his 1949 novel *El reino de este mundo* (*The Kingdom of This World*), in which he insists that Latin American reality itself is marvelous. I will return to his understanding of the term and the debates it has led to in a subsequent section. Not only is the term marvelous real often used interchangeably with that of magical realism, but the Brazilian critic Irlemar Chiampi even coined a new term, marvelous realism (*realismo maravilhoso*), in her Portuguese-language study of magical realism (1980).

Despite the conflation of the two terms by Chiampi, her definition of marvelous realism (48–50) also suggests a possible way in which we can consider magical realism and the marvelous real as two different but related literary modes that, although often found together, can be differentiated in order to focus on different aspects of the novel today. Her reasons for preferring the term marvelous realism are threefold. Firstly, the Latin etymology of the term marvelous shows that one of its key meanings refers to the extraordinary, or something to be marveled at. As an example, she mentions Carpentier's novel *Los pasos perdidos* (*The Lost Steps*, 1953), in which there are no supernatural events, only an astounding nature. Secondly, the term refers to the supernatural, or what differs from our natural, empirical reality. Finally, the term marvelous refers to a well-known literary category, that is, fiction depicting supernatural events, as in the case of legends and fairy tales. The realism of the expression "marvelous realism," on the other hand, refers both to a literary style and to the belief in the specificity of Latin American reality, in which the marvelous is an important aspect. These characteristics of what Chiampi considers a single literary mode (and therefore marvelous *realism*, and not *real*) suggests a possible distinction we can make between the marvelous real (the more usual term, although it is, strictly speaking, an "ism" or mode of writing and not the real in itself) as a literary depiction of reality as extraordinary, on the one hand, and magical realism as the amalgamation of the natural, empirical world and the supernatural, on the other. In fact, magical realism is often considered in this way. A related definition involves the juxtaposition of realism and fantasy, in which both terms, however, are vague and can refer to several very different types of narrative, as in the case of Flores. If magical realism is to be considered a useful category of criticism, it is also important to distinguish it from well-known genres such as science fiction, fantasy literature that has little connection to reality, fairy tales, ghost stories, or legends. The "realism" indicates that it is concerned with social and historical reality and does not create escapist worlds removed from our own. These distinctions are of course only one way of talking meaningfully about magical realism since there has never been any consensus.

Ethnographic Fiction, Surrealism, and Primitivism

One of the debates around magical realism concerns the nature of the supernatural. Drawing on the emphasis of Flores on the influence of Kafka's fiction on the Argentine Jorge Luis Borges and other Latin American writers he considers as magical realists, many critics refer to the supernatural in magical realism in a very general sense. Other critics, however, associate the mode with the magical-mythical world view of premodern societies in which the supernatural is part of the normal way of apprehending reality. The Guatemalan writer and Nobel Prize winner Miguel Ángel Asturias explicitly associated his magical realism with the "original mentality" of the Mayan population of Guatemala as well as with "what the Surrealists around Breton wanted" ("Hearing the Scream" 58). Both he and Carpentier had spent several years in Paris and had connections with the surrealists. Asturias had also studied ethnography there and translated Mayan sacred texts into Spanish. As for Carpentier, he had conducted extensive ethnographical work on the Afro-Cuban population. These two central figures of magical realism, often considered its founders with their groundbreaking novels of 1949 (*Hombres de maíz* [*Men of Maize*] and *The Kingdom of This World*), can be linked to what the anthropologist James Clifford calls "ethnographic surrealism," defining the term surrealism (which he uses in a general sense) as "an aesthetic that values fragments, curious collections, unexpected juxtapositions–that works to provoke the manifestation of extraordinary realities drawn from the domain of the erotic, the exotic, and the unconscious" (118). Clifford explains the emergence of the French surrealist movement in the 1920s in the context of the aftermath of the horrors of the First World War and the development of modern ethnography with its interest in premodern or "primitive" mentalities. For Parisian surrealists, including artists close to André Breton as well as professional ethnographers who collaborated with the journal *Documents*, these belief systems provided "serious human alternatives" to Western modernity (120). For them, the "exotic was a primary court of appeal against the rational, the beautiful, the normal of the West" (127). He distinguishes between what he calls the "ethnographic surrealist attitude," which involves a critical contemplation of urban European society, and the superficial exoticism of the nineteenth century.

Clifford's emphasis on the surrealists' delight in unexpected juxtapositions, "cultural impurities and disturbing syncretisms" (131) points to obvious similarities with certain magico-realist techniques. The juxtaposition of the animal heads in a butcher's shop and the human heads in the barber's salon in Carpentier's *The Kingdom of This World* is a frequently analyzed example, even if the Cuban author explicitly rejected French surrealism as artificial in his prologue ("On the Marvelous Real in America," Zamora and Faris 85). At the end of his chapter on ethnographic surrealism, Clifford briefly discusses the importance of exotic artifacts for artists such as Picasso, who were not interested in other mentalities per se, but in the renewal of their artistic practice, which Clifford formulates as follows: "Something new was occurring in the presence of something exotic" (148). Likewise, we can consider magical realism, as it is manifested in the major novels of Asturias and Carpentier, as the emergence of new ways of writing fiction influenced not only by knowledge of avant-garde literary developments such as surrealism and expressionism, but also by contact with societies seen as Other. In a detailed analysis of what he considers the four main magico-realist novels (*The Kingdom of This World*, *Men of Maize*, Juan Rulfo's *Pedro Páramo*, and García Márquez's *One Hundred Years of Solitude*), as well as of the importance of modern ethnography and French surrealism, Erik Camayd-Freixas argues that what distinguishes magical realism is primitivism, or a new esthetic based on a "magical-primitive perspective" very different from traditional mimetic realism (11). In order to develop a uniquely American form of writing, Asturias, for example, takes inspiration from Mayan symbolism. At the same time, socio-historical reality is allegorized, as magic becomes a metaphorical presentation of the real. Primitivism, however, is not only the hallmark of novels based on indigenous or African perspectives, since Camayd-Freixas includes the rural, popular culture of García Márquez's Colombia and Rulfo's Mexico in his category of primitivism.

Cultural Heterogeneity and Empathic Fiction

I would like to return to one of the major differences between Asturias and Carpentier, on the one hand, and artists such as Picasso, on the other, who used exotic material as mere artistic stimulus. As ethnographers, both Latin American authors were deeply interested in other societies and their cultural specificity. At the same time, contrary to European ethnographers, they were interested in the diverse cultures of their own continent. As writers, their fictional representation of Mayan society, in the case of Asturias, and Afro-Cuban cultural practices, in the case of Carpentier, was not a mere ethnographic depiction of non-Western societies, but an extremely original creation of an empathic vision made possible not only by genuine interest in these societies, but also by narrative techniques that presented other worldviews from the inside. Contrary to indigenist fiction of earlier novelists who presented non-European cultures from an external point of view, both Carpentier and Asturias create narrators who identify with non-European characters. Empathic vision goes beyond the social criticism of the indigenists, whose external perspective transformed their characters into objects of pity, often presenting them as not quite human in their extreme misery and distancing them in a process of abjection.

As many critics have pointed out, the indigenous perspective re-created artistically in magico-realist novels often appears contradictory. A case in point is Carpentier's *The Kingdom of This World*, in which the description of Mackandal's burning at the stake is presented directly from the point of view of the black slaves, who believe that their revered leader escaped by transforming himself into an insect. This scene is followed by the explanation by the anonymous narrator that the slaves did not see that the white masters caught him and succeeded in executing him. Other scenes present a caricature of the white Lenormand de Mezy, or the in-between perspective of the protagonist Ti Noël, who contemplates supernatural events with wonder and surprise. Toward the end of the novel, Ti Noël's transformation into a goose is presented in a direct way, in a matter-of-fact juxtaposition of the natural and the supernatural: "Tired of risky transformations, Ti Noël used his extraordinary powers to change himself into a goose and thus live among the birds that had taken residence in his domain" (128).[1] Focalization moves between different figures of the novel in order to create various instances of empathic vision in a fictional world presented as heterogenous. In his landmark study of what he calls "narrative transculturation," Ángel Rama refers to the dual nature of the writing of Carpentier and Asturias, in which an internal reality (that of indigenous or black populations) is given a "significación externa" (external meaning [52]), or to that of José María Arguedas, whose "enfoque transculturante" (transculturating approach) involves assuming the values of indigenous cultures while writing for the dominant white culture (205). Transculturation involves moving between cultures, adopting elements from different worldviews, and creating new ways of writing. Although Rama sees Carpentier as an ambiguous figure, I would argue that the Cuban author's techniques of focalization enable him to arouse empathy for others in a heterogenous world. In *Men of Maize*, for example, differing explanations of supernatural events concern not only the alternative versions given by whites and Mayans, but also differences within Mayan and mestizo society itself. A case in point is the explanation that the magical connection between the curandero (healer) and a deer causes the healer's death when the deer is killed by a hunter, a supernatural explanation that is questioned by one of the indigenous Tecún brothers who suspects that the healer was killed by natural means in the armed indigenous uprising against the colonists. Even the German immigrant Don Deféric and his wife have very different attitudes to supernatural beliefs. Rather than delegitimize mythical-magical worldviews, these novels create plural narrative identifications.

AMERICANISM AND THE MARVELOUS REAL

In Carpentier's frequently quoted prologue to the novel *The Kingdom of This World*, he distinguishes between the artifices of French surrealism and his own writing, which presents Latin American reality itself as marvelous. He situates the authentic marvelous in the American continent, coining the expression *real maravilloso*, which implies the perception of the continent as marvelous or extraordinary, but above all the literary representation of the continent as such, since the marvelous real, despite its formulation, refers to a particular mode of writing and not to reality as such. Much has been written on the contradictions of this term, and especially on Carpentier's invocation of faith as an essential component (Carpentier, "On the Marvelous Real in America," Zamora and Faris 86). As critics have pointed out, Carpentier himself did not share the belief of Afro-Cubans in metempsychosis. Rather than constituting a contradiction, however, the reference to faith can be interpreted as the nexus between two different modes— magical realism that re-creates a magical-mythical worldview (pre-modern faith) from an internal narrative perspective, and the marvelous real that presents the New World, including the existence of pre-modern cultures, as astonishing (Carpentier's own belief in its extraordinary nature). Indeed, other passages of his prologue mention the importance of early Spanish chronicles that described the natural wonders, the presence of black and indigenous cultures, the mingling of architectural styles, and Carpentier's own astonishment when visiting the palatial ruins of Sans Souci, built by the first black king, Henri Christophe, at the beginning of the nineteenth century. The prologue is often considered as the expression of an external, European gaze, but one can argue that any description of parts of such a diverse continent by a Latin American author from a different milieu inevitably involves an outsider's gaze. More importantly, it illustrates a search for identity with its Americanist emphasis on the specificity of the continent, its cultural richness and beauty of nature, and its difference with Europe. In later writings, Carpentier preferred the term baroque to refer to a new form of literary expression for Latin America.

In *The Kingdom of this World*, Carpentier constantly evokes surprise and wonder, often through the eyes of the main character, the black slave Ti Noël, who is "surprised by the pomp of a Napoleonic style . . . never imagined" (77) and marvels "at the most unexpected and imposing spectacle he had seen in his long life" (78).[2] The incongruous syncretism of Sans Souci is a hallmark of what García Canclini called "hybrid cultures" (1989) in which modernity is combined with pre-modern artifacts, practices, and beliefs. Whereas the magical realism of the supernatural descriptions of metamorphosis coexists with the marvelous real expression of wonder in Carpentier's 1949 novel, his fictional account of a musicologist traveling to the Amazonian jungle in search of the origins of music (*Los pasos perdidos* [*The Lost Steps*], 1953) contains no supernatural events or development of a magical-mythical or magico-realist worldview. The urbanized first-person narrator marvels at the natural landscapes and indigenous cultures, a "world of wonder" full of "mystery" and "portents" (144), a "gateway of enchantment" (145)[3]. As he travels further into the jungle, he traverses different ages, arriving at the Paleolithic (181) and even the "darkest murk of the night of ages," where people are naked "like Adam and Eve before the Fall," fight with monkeys over palm hearts, and eat termites, lice, worms, and earth in the company of their "pre-dogs" (182).[4]

THE MARVELOUS REAL AFTER CARPENTIER

In light of the confusion surrounding the term magical realism and its frequent conflation with the equally confusing term marvelous real, it is interesting to consider an example of differentiation occurring forty years after Carpentier's prologue, in the twenty-fifth Spanish-language edition of Luis Sepúlveda's novel *Un viejo que leía novelas de amor* (*The Old Man Who Read Love Stories*, 1989). The plot of this novel, which won many prizes and has been translated into several languages, revolves around an old white or mestizo man who settles in a small village in the Ecuadorian jungle, partially assimilates the customs of the indigenous Shuar, and starts reading love stories as he witnesses with consternation the inroads of civilization and destruction of the environment. In the publisher's blurb on the book jacket, we are told that the novel is not magico-realist, but a revelation of the "la magia de la realidad" ("magic of reality"). Indeed, there are no unambiguously supernatural events, since the metamorphosis of elderly members of the Shuar tribe into fish, butterflies, and other animals is recounted from the point of view of the tribe's members and the assimilated protagonist under the influence of hallucinogenic drugs by the third-person narrator. In a later passage, another incident of metamorphosis is explicitly described by a member of the tribe as a story: "That's what they say happened" (*The Old Man* 118).[5]

This distinction between the magic of reality and magical realism echoes Carpentier's rejection of surrealism as artificial and opposed to the marvelous reality of the American continent. Like Carpentier, Sepúlveda had traveled to the Amazon Forest. What is meant by the expression "magic of reality" is partly indicated by the paintings reproduced on the covers of the novel. The twenty-fifth Spanish edition of 1995 gives us a primitivist depiction of the Amazonian jungle world with its iconic aras, iguanas, toucans, jaguars, and red frogs, painted by the German artist Wolfgang Rieder (*Regenwald*, or Rain Forest, 1991). The 1994 edition of the English translation shows the painting *Snake Charmer* (1907) of a lush tropical forest featuring a boa by the well-known primitivist Henri Rousseau, painted more than eighty years earlier. Both paintings illustrate a fascination with the jungle, suggesting either an exoticist flight from modern civilization or the love of a marvelous natural world increasingly threatened by development (the "unknown green world" mentioned in the first preface). However, the same preface also mentions the "magical storytelling" ("narraciones desbordantes de magia") of Sepúlveda's "distant friend" ("lejano amigo") Miguel Tzenke, an indigenous Shuar in the Amazon whom he credits for helping him create the novel. The expression "magical" can here be seen as a reference to the mystical-magical worldview of non-Western peoples, celebrated by the surrealists and Carpentier, and thus one of the meanings of magical realism. This worldview is not, however, developed from an internal point of view, as in Asturias's or Carpentier's 1949 novels in which numerous supernatural events are depicted directly. The reference to storytelling reveals the fascination with storytelling itself, as a way to live new experiences.

José María Arguedas: Magical Realism versus the Marvelous Real

Certain critics have disputed the status of the Peruvian author Arguedas as a magical realist, either because the more traditional writing in his best-known novel *Los ríos profundos* (*Deep Rivers*, 1958) is very different from the innovative style and narrative technique of Carpentier or Asturias, or because events are not presented as unambiguously supernatural. Julio Cortázar considered him as a folkloric and provincial writer, and linked his novels to indigenism, the literary mode of the first half of the twentieth century that focused on the injustices suffered by the indigenous populations of Latin America (43–55; discussed by Vargas Llosa 34–43). Like Carpentier and Asturias, Arguedas had studied ethnology. Unlike them, however, he was not influenced by surrealism and expressionism, was not linked with the writing of the Boom, and did not have the extensive European experience of his two fellow novelists. His knowledge of Quechua culture was acquired through ethnological research and his own personal childhood experience as a Quechua speaker. Camayd-Freixas explicitly refuses to consider the fiction of Arguedas as magical realism, considering it instead as an example of lyrical neo-indigenism (7). In his book-long study of Arguedas's life and "indigenist" fictions imbued by dreams of an archaic utopia, Mario Vargas Llosa describes him as a "cultural ecologist" (29) who rejects the emphasis of Marxist indigenists on progress and modernization as a means to greater justice for indigenous peoples, as this would entail the disappearance of their traditional culture, customs, and rituals.

Arguedas himself, however, used the term "magic" when he claimed to share the magico-mythical worldview of his Quechua countrymen (Vargas Llosa 30). In a 1965 interview with Tomás Escajadillo (22–23), Arguedas said his work was magical realist. He also used the term "cuentos mágico-realistas" ("magico-realist tales," Vargas Llosa 160) for a collection of ethnographic material he published as an ethnologist. But it is also in his fiction, including several short stories and his 1958 novel *Deep Rivers*, that Arguedas develops an animist view of nature, in which animals, plants, and rivers commune with humans through their shared spirituality. This is a world seen from within by his first-person narrator, and not from the point of view of an ethnographer describing an alien culture. In his fictional creation of a magical-mythical perspective in *Deep Rivers*, men may not be transformed into animals, as they are in Carpentier and Asturias. However, the empathic vision of the first-person narrator and protagonist Ernesto goes beyond a simply spiritual perception or lyrical description of nature. When he accompanies his father to Cuzco as a young boy, he tells him he sees the stones of the Inca wall moving and hears them talking (8).

Just as in Asturias and certain passages of Carpentier's *The Kingdom of this World*, an alternative rational explanation is sometimes provided. Ernesto's father, for example, tells him that he is confused and that the stones seem to be moving because of their asymmetrical lines. Later passages, however, are not accompanied by such questionings. Usually, the narrator's perspective is given without comment and thus maintains its centrality, even though it is focalized through a sensitive and subjective young boy. Ernesto tells us that when the bells ring, "bulls of fire, or of gold, emerge from the water dragging chains: they climb to the mountain peaks and bellow in the frost" (13).[6] He adds: "The carved serpents over the door of Huayna Capac's palace were writhing in the darkness.... They followed us, slithering, to the house" (13).[7] Nature is frequently animated, as in the case of the tree that "sings alone in a deep voice in which water, earth, and sky mingle" (24)[8]. The unmediated presentation of events that do not conform to a rational worldview resembles Asturias's and Carpentier's (1949) magico-realist technique of describing supernatural events by means of an internal focalizer, although the style is very different, and Arguedas expressed his reservations about the erudite writing of Carpentier in *El zorro de arriba y el zorro de abajo* (Vargas Llosa 38). Furthermore, as is the case of several other magico-realist novels, essential ethnographic information is provided to inform the non-native reader, as in the chapter "Zumbayllu," in which the author gives us detailed information about the meaning of the Quechua words *yllu* and *tankayllu* (64–65). In the transcultural fiction of Arguedas, heterogeneous points of view and discourses do not cancel the mythical-magical perspective created by the author, even if the events are described through the eyes of a narrator reminiscing about his past as a young boy instead of being presented by an anonymous narrator, as in Carpentier (1949) and Asturias. One major difference between Arguedas and Carpentier's 1953 novel is that nature is seen as familiar, nurturing, and intimately connected to his personal experience, and not as something extraordinary to be marveled at. Arguedas's magical realism thus involves a magical-mythical worldview, rather than the marvelous real, which often accompanies it.

POSTMODERNISM AND POSTCOLONIALISM

Many critics have associated magical realism with postmodernism. Wendy Faris, for example, situates it within the postmodern renewal of fiction with its emphasis on the art of storytelling, describing it as a "revitalizing force that comes often from the 'peripheral' regions of Western culture" (Zamora and Faris 165). According to Theo D'haen, magical realism is a "particular strain" of postmodernism from the margins (Zamora and Faris 194). The authors of the anthology *McOndo*, on the other hand, reject magical realism in favor of a literary "trend away from the exploration of national identities towards a new 'pop' conception of the local saturated by North American influence and the processes of globalization" (Swanson, "The Post-Boom Novel," Kristal 96). Although *McOndo* writing would be associated by most critics with postmodernism, it has no connection with key characteristics attributed to magical realism, such as the tensions between premodern magical worldviews and modern rationality or the juxtaposition of the natural and the supernatural. Furthermore, magical realist bestsellers such as Isabel Allende's

La casa de los espíritus (*The House of the Spirits*, 1982) are devalued by their accessibility and other features usually associated with postmodernism. Philip Swanson argues that this position regarding Allende illustrates the difficulty of "recognizing the genuinely popular and accessible dimension of Post-Boom writing and hints at a lingering hankering after the intellectual complexity or even elitism of the Boom" (Swanson, "The Post-Boom Novel," Kristal 94). The confusion is compounded by the relationship between the political discussion of postmodernity as a historical period with that of postmodernism as a literary style. In his study *Latin America Writes Back: Postmodernity in the Periphery*, Emil Volek, for example, calls the authoritarian regimes of Latin America the "curse of Macondo" in which "*Macondoamérica* has surpassed fiction" (xxiv–xxv). García Canclini is very critical of the "fundamentalism of *Macondismo*," a literary mode that depicts Latin America as a "premodern sanctuary," exalts irrationalism, and pitches "Latin America's heterogeneity in the marketplace of cultural globalization" (2001, 79–80; see also his discussion of postmodernism and hybridity in *Culturas híbridas*, 1989).

This is a very complex debate. However, it is important to question the conflation of postmodernism with magical realism. Whereas *One Hundred Years of Solitude* illustrates techniques generally associated with postmodernism (such as parody and metafiction, or the emphasis on writing and the fictionality of the text, as well as the inclusion of popular discourse), the two novels frequently considered as the first important illustration of magical realism in 1949 (*The Kingdom of this World* and *Men of Maize*) are much more difficult to classify as postmodernist, with the erudite, baroque style of Carpentier and the surrealist, expressionist writing of Asturias. As for Arguedas, his main novel, *Deep Rivers*, is very traditional in its narrative techniques. Postmodernism itself has been a hotly debated term since the 1970s and is often linked to the metafictional elements of much earlier writing, such as the novels of Laurence Sterne in the eighteenth century, and even Cervantes.

Magical realism has also been discussed as a form of postcolonialism (see, for example, Stephen Slemon in Zamora and Faris 407–26). Many elements identified by postcolonial theoreticians are very relevant to magical realist novels depicting cultural heterogeneity, colonization, racism, injustice, and resistance to the metropolitan center (I discuss this in detail in my chapter "The Latin American Postcolonialism debate in a Comparative Context," Mabel Moraña et al. 417–34). Major magico-realist novels criticize neo-colonial incursions from the north (García Márquez), as well as internal colonization of indigenous lands (Asturias). However, postcolonial theory in the English-speaking world in the aftermath of the independence of formerly colonized nations of the commonwealth since the 1960s generally ignores Latin America with its much earlier independence movements. An interesting new development is the general questioning of Western colonial paradigms and increasing global inequality linked to what Aníbal Quijano calls the "coloniality of power" (Moraña et al. 181–224). Cultural theorists such as Walter Mignolo advocate the necessity to "learn to unlearn" our hegemonic ways of thinking about the world in order to develop decolonial paradigms (Tlostanova and Mignolo 2012), while Boaventura de Sousa Santos advocates for "epistemologies of the South" (2014). In turn, Arturo Escobar (2018) makes an explicit connection between magical realism and newer ways of designing our lives which I will examine in more detail later.

REWRITING THE ARCHIVE AFTER THE BOOM: WOMEN'S WRITING

González Echevarría describes the archive as a "process of repeated combinations, of shufflings and reshufflings ruled by heterogeneity and difference" (24). Whereas González Echevarría concentrates on the written archive of the early Spanish chronicles, later non-fictional texts, and literary production, Rowe and Schelling underline the importance of the oral archive of indigenous, African, and popular European "colonial magic" that was "transmitted by women, in those spheres of life which most eluded the controls of the colonial institutions" (22–23). They describe it as an "alternative knowledge, from below," a "network of shared meanings," or a "vindication of pre-capitalist culture" (214). Magical realism after the Boom continues its renewal with new sources, written and oral, and contemporary preoccupations, such as women's place in society. An interesting example is Laura Esquivel's 1992 bestseller *Como agua para chocolate* (*Like Water for Chocolate*).

Many critics have been very dismissive of Esquivel as well as of the Chilean novelist Isabel Allende. Both, however, have rewritten the magico-realist archive in important ways. The Mexican Esquivel rewrites the figure of García Márquez's matriarch Úrsula, who becomes the authoritarian and sadistic Mamá Elena, owner of the ranch who terrorizes her daughters and employees, forcing her youngest daughter Tita to give up the love of her life, Pedro, to take care of her mother until her death. More importantly, Esquivel draws on different non-novelistic sources. Instead of using chronicles and ethnographic reports, her narrative uses recipes, not only as primary material for the emergence of the supernatural, but also to structure her novel about the De la Garza family living in turn-of-the-century Mexico. This feminine archive is transmitted to the youngest daughter Tita, the "last link in a chain of cooks who had been passing culinary secrets from generation to generation since ancient times" (*Like Water* 48)[9]. This translation, however, does not transmit the meaning of the Spanish original, in which the ancient times are explicitly specified as "la época prehispánica" (pre-Hispanic epoch, *Como agua* 46). Besides suggesting the predicament of many women in traditional families whose only power lies in domestic activities, the magical effects of the recipes that lie at the heart of every chapter emphasize the importance of the indigenous cultural legacy of Mexico. Contrary to the magico-realist novels of the 1940s, the native Other is no longer an icon of pre-modern mentality in a heterogenous and conflictual society, but an immanent part of contemporary society's culture and identity.

José Martí's distinction between mestizo America and North America in his well-known essay "Nuestra América" ("Our America"), first published in 1891, is also deconstructed in the novel. The character John Brown (who has the same name as the American abolitionist leader), the American doctor of the De la Garza family, lives north of the US border and has an indigenous Kikapu grandmother whose traditional cures he studies as part of his medical research. The porous border, traversed regularly by members of the family; the fact that Tita and Pedro speak excellent English; the fact that Mamá Elena's cousin lives in San Antonio, Texas, where she sends her second daughter Rosaura, now the wife of Pedro, to separate the two childhood sweethearts; and Gertrude's partly Black heritage traced back to a fugitive from the United States weave a complex web of transnational connections in an updating of discourses of identity based on differentiation with the proverbial neo-imperial north. Finally, the servant Chencha's supernatural stories about "La Llorona, the witch who sucks little children's blood, or the boogeyman" (*Like Water* 68)[10] are juxtaposed with reports of violence perpetrated by soldiers fighting for and against the Mexican Revolution. These "stories of hangings, shootings, dismemberments, decapitations, and even sacrifices in which the victim's heart was cut out" in an obvious reference to Aztec sacrifices (*Like Water* 68)[11] appear just as unbelievable to Tita as the fairytales, thus delegitimizing the truth of historical narratives. Not only does the novel develop the theme of the kitchen as a nurturing female space that is an originator of events, the site of new life (Tita is born on the kitchen table), and the catalyst for close relationships between classes (Tita and the servants) as well as between white and indigenous women (Tita's closeness to the cook Nacha and to the ghost of John Brown's Kikapu grandmother), but it also situates the female heterotopia with its spaces, texts, and discourses as equally valid as the male archive.

My second example of a female rewriting of the archive is Allende's best-selling novel *The House of the Spirits* (1982). Rather than a pale imitation of *One Hundred Years of Solitude* in which magical realism is trivialized by confining it mainly to a female world on the edges of historical change, we can see it as another updating of the magico-realist archive. Set in the Chilean capital Santiago and the ranch of Esteban Trueba, it recounts the vicissitudes of the Trueba family leading up to the violence surrounding the rise to power of Augusto Pinochet in 1973. The ghosts, premonitions, and telekinetic powers of the central figure, Clara, give way (although not entirely) toward the end of the novel to the description of the horrors of the political events, recounted by the last female member of the family, Alba, based on the notebooks of her grandmother Clara. The magico-mythic worldview of premodern societies in the Americas is replaced by the hermetic pursuits of modern city dwellers in a world that has lost other sources of the marvelous. While Clara and the three Mora sisters try to conjure up spirits with three-legged tables, her son goes to India in search of spiritualism and his friend Amanda imitates the style of French existentialists in the context of disenchantment and contestation of the "rationalization of modernity" (Beverley at al. 8). Carpentier's marvelous real is now located outside the continent. Furthermore, the heterogenous juxtapositions of *The Kingdom of This World* are parodied by the description of the furnishings of the French count Jean de Satigny, as the marvelous hybrid world of the black Henri Christophe is degraded to the bad taste of the count's collage of dyed ostrich feathers, Chinese vases, and turbaned statues.

FROM NATURE TO ECOLOGY

Nature has always been an important element in descriptions of the New World, from the Spanish chronicles and the more scientific reports of nineteenth-century botanical expeditions to the regionalist novel. Julia King and Stephen M. Hart describe the earth as a natural "archive . . . which the writers excavate with the tools of imagination and language" (Hart and Ouyang 55). They argue that the creation of a feminine archive by María Luisa Bombal and Teresa de la Parra "provide important insights into the pre-history of magical realism" (56) with their descriptions of the spiritual dimensions of nature. They also briefly discuss Miguel Asturias's novel *Men of Maize*, in which the magical beliefs of the Mayans are rooted in nature and inform the struggle of the indigenous population against the white and mestizo colonists. Nature is certainly central to the magical realism of Asturias's novel. Not only are characters transformed into their *naguals* or protective animals, as in the case of the shaman who becomes a deer or the mail carrier Nicho Aquino who turns into a coyote to travel faster, but nature is often humanized, with trees and shrubs described as eyelashes and eyelids. The intimate connection between maize and humans, based on Mayan sacred texts such as the *Popol Vuh*, which recounts the story of man's creation from maize, is the basis of the distinction between a natural form of life, in which maize is cultivated for food, and its cultivation for profit. The latter destroys the human soul, but also leaves the colonists themselves poor because the profits are reaped by landowners or other members of the wealthy classes. Much emphasis is placed on the destruction of nature by burning forests to clear land for farming. Furthermore, intensive farming destroys the richness of biological diversity, as sugarcane, cocoa and coffee shrubs, and almond trees disappear. Even though the ecological dimension is secondary to the destruction of the ways of life of the Mayan population, it becomes more central in later novels.

The ubiquitous theme of the "infierno verde" (green hell), a stock theme of earlier regionalist novels that represent nature as threatening and often fatal to humans who risk their lives in the name of progress, is taken up more recently by Sepúlveda (1989), who reframes the theme in the context of a pessimistic view of ecological destruction. He describes the ineffectual efforts of the poor colonizers of the Amazonian jungle who see the felled trees and destroyed vines grow back with unnatural vigor, the fruit of their labor washed away by the swollen river, and their companions die of disease, poisonous fruit, or the attack of man-eating boas as they battle the ravenous mosquitoes (31–32). Even if the indigenous Shuars teach them how to survive, the colonists continue to ignore the unsuitability of the environment for planting their crops and never learn how to adapt to a nature in which they, and not the forest, are the problem. The opposition between the malevolent green hell and the civilizing efforts of colonizers is inverted here, as whites and mestizos ignore the lessons of nature, central to the ways of life of the Shuar. The protagonist learns the language and hunting skills of the Shuar, but never becomes one of them, as he transgresses their rules of combat and is expelled from the group. Like the protagonist of Carpentier's *The Lost Steps*, the old man in the novel cannot enter the world of pre-modernity. Contrary to his literary predecessor, however, he has no modern world to go back to either and stays in his provincial backwater, reading love stories to alleviate his boredom and forget the ravages of civilization in the rain forest, illustrated by the powerful forces of progress that cut roads through the pristine jungle and force the Shuar and much wildlife to move away.

The centrality of this theme is emphasized by the main plot, which revolves around the attacks of a man-eating female ocelot originating in the senseless killing by a North American tourist of her five young cubs. It is the old man who must hunt down and kill the female ocelot to protect the lives of the settlers. The final pages provide a poignant contrast with Sarmiento's *Facundo*, one of the best-known texts of the nineteenth-century archive, in which the "tiger" hunts the caudillo and terrorizes him with a "fixed and bloodthirsty stare" (González Echevarría 120) after having killed and eaten eight men. Contrary to Sarmiento's protagonist, the old man in Sepúlveda's novel feels empathy for the ocelot (called *tigrillo* in the original Spanish) and caresses the head of the injured male, which he shoots out of mercy, then speaks to the female, caresses her dead body, and sheds tears for having to destroy a beautiful animal. Here, the myth of civilization and barbarism is inverted, as the old man reads love stories to escape from society, lamenting the "barbarity of man" (131; "la barbarie humana"; *El Viejo* 137). While Carpentier's protagonist leaves the idealized pre-modern world to write about it, Sepúlveda's disillusioned character tries to forget a jungle world on the brink of destruction, invaded by gold diggers, hunters, and colonists who worship the saint of money Onecén (One Cent, 80), through escapism provided by literature. In his two prefaces, Sepúlveda addresses his pessimistic rewriting of the archive to Chico Mendes, a well-known ecological leader who was murdered on behalf of progress, as well as to the Shuar union leader who gave him material for the novel.

FROM THE PLURIVERSE TO THE PLANETARY ECOLOGY OF OTHERS

The empathic representation of diverse worlds in magical realism intersects with several important issues, including genuine interest in other civilizations, a more heterogenous discourse of identity, a new way of writing fiction, and a critique of colonialism and neo-colonialism. On the other hand, many critics have insisted on the mainly literary interest of this writing (Vargas Llosa in his study of Arguedas), magical realism's irrelevance to Latin American contemporary reality (Fuguet and Gómez), its exoticism (de la Campa), its glorification of underdevelopment, and the perpetuation of the fetishism of a non-European Other. Very recently, however, cultural critics and other scholars have reread certain magico-realist novels in a new way. Arturo Escobar, an anthropologist who has conducted extensive fieldwork in the Cauca region of Colombia, turns to some key passages of *One Hundred Years of Solitude*, arguing that "highly accomplished literary works reveal essential aspects of human life and history with a sharpness and clarity that philosophy and the social sciences can hardly aspire to match" (27). He believes that the novel gives us important lessons about "technology and design in so-called traditional societies" (27), as it describes the introduction of modern inventions such as electricity and the cinema to Macondo, and especially the incursions of the North American banana company, which "represents the political economy of modern technology and design, the main driving engine of modernity" (29). The destruction at the end of the novel, we could add, suggests the impasse of the exclusive emphasis on modern, rational, design technology that Escobar criticizes in his book about the development of newer, more sustainable, forms of design and models of living. The central concept of his study is that of ontological design, which involves the "transition from the hegemony of modernity's one-world ontology to a pluriverse of socionatural configurations" and is a "tool for reimagining and reconstructing local worlds" (4). The new pluriverse is based on forms of communal collaboration and the struggle against pollution, impoverishment of workers, the ecological destruction caused by mining and intensive farming practices that deplete the soil.

Escobar's argument is not merely ecological, however. Toward the end of the book, he argues that the pluriverse will lead to the "generation of new imaginaries" and "acknowledge the multiple overlapping worlds and reals" (197). This brings us back to one of the central aspects of magical realism, so evident in the 1949 novels of Asturias and Carpentier. The conclusion of Escobar's study echoes another dimension often associated with magical realism, namely, a spiritual connection to nature. After quoting from a poem by Atahualpa Yupanqui about hearing stones talk, Escobar advocates for a "thinking-feeling with the Earth," which involves "the profound conviction of our indissoluble connection with the Earth and with everything that exists in the universe, the unity of all beings" (204). He refers to indigenous people who do not separate nature from humans and who defend mountains and lakes because they see them as "sentient beings" or "sacred entities" (217). This view of nature, echoing the indigenous worldviews depicted in the novels of Arguedas and Asturias, is here considered as an important tool for saving the planet.

In his study *The Ecology of Others* (2013), the French anthropologist Philippe Descola argues that the "relationship between humans and nature will, in all probability, be the most important question of the present century" (81) in the context of climate change, pollution, and the loss of biodiversity. He refers to the tropical geographer Pierre Gourou, according to whom we must study not only ecology, but "also how humans think about it" (84) in different societies and cultural traditions. I would add that the study of literature, in addition to anthropology and cultural geography, provides very important insights into the way we think about nature and our relationship to it. Many magico-realist novels give us an empathic understanding of other cultures, but also of what Descola calls "human and non-human" Others (87). More than eight decades since the surrealist critical questioning of modern society in the wake of the destruction of the First World War, these novels can be re-read as a prescient indication of our contemporary need for solutions to social injustice as well as planetary destruction.

NOTES

1. "Cansado de licantropías azarosas, Ti Noel hizo uso de sus extraordinarios poderes para transformarse en ganso y convivir con las aves que se habían instalado en sus dominios" (Carpentier, *El reino* 142).
2. "Ti Noel descubría de pronto, con asombro, las pompas de un estilo napoleónico . . . llevado a un grado de boato ignorado" (Carpentier, *El reino* 88); "por el espectáculo más inesperado, más imponente que hubiera visto en su larga existencia" (Carpentier, *El reino* 88–89).
3. "Lo maravilloso, anhelantes de mayores portentos" (Carpentier, *Los pasos*, 151), "una puerta de los prodigios" (Carpentier, *Los pasos* 153).
4. "Lo más tenebroso de la noche de las edades," "como Adán y Eva antes del pecado," "perros anteriores a los perros" (Carpentier, *Los pasos* 193).
5. "Así dicen que ha sido" (Sepúlveda, *Un viejo* 124).
6. "Salen del agua toros de fuego, o de oro, arrastrando cadenas: suben a las cumbres y mugen en la helada" (Arguedas, *Los ríos* 17).
7. "En la penumbra, las serpientes esculpidas sobre la puerta del palacio de Huayna Capac caminaban. . . . Nos siguieron, vibrando, hasta la casa" (Arguedas, *Los ríos* 18).
8. "que canta solo, con una voz profunda, en que los cielos, el agua y la tierra se confunden" (Esquivel, *Como agua* 29).
9. "Tita era el último eslabón de una cadena de cocineras que desde la época prehispánica se habían transmitido los secretos de la cocina de generación en generación" (Esquivel, *Como agua* 46).
10. "La llorona, la bruja que chupaba a los niños, el coco y demás horrores" (Esquivel, *Como agua* 68).
11. "Historias de colgados, fusilados, desmembrados, degollados e inclusive sacrificados a los que se les sacaba el corazón" (Esquivel, *Como agua* 68–69).

WORKS CITED

Allende, Isabel. *The House of the Spirits*. Translated by Magda Bogin. Atria Paperbacks, [1982] 2015.

Arguedas, José María. *Deep Rivers*. Translated by Frances Horning Barraclough. U of Texas P, [1958] 1978.

Arguedas, José María. *Los ríos profundos*. Alianza, [1958] 1987.

Asturias, Miguel Ángel. "Hearing the Scream: A Rare Interview with the Surprise Nobel Winner—Miguel Ángel Asturias." *Atlas*, vol. 14, no. 6, 1967, pp. 57–58.

Asturias, Miguel Ángel. *Men of Maize*. Translated by Gerald Martin. Verso, [1949] 1988.

Beverley, John, et al., eds. *The Postmodernism Debate in Latin America*. Duke UP, 1995.

Camay-Freixas, Erik. *Realismo mágico y primitivismo: Relecturas de Carpentier, Asturias, Rulfo y García Márquez*. UP of America, 1998.

Carpentier, Alejo. *The Kingdom of This World*. Translated by Pablo Medina. Farrar, Straus and Giroux, [1949] 2017.

Carpentier, Alejo. *The Lost Steps*. Translated by Harriet de Onís. U of Minnesota P, [1953; 1956 for first English translation] 2001.

Carpentier, Alejo. *Los pasos perdidos*. Penguin Books, [1953] 1998.

Carpentier, Alejo. *El reino de este mundo*. Seix Barral, [1949] 1976.

Chiampi, Irlemar. *O realismo maravilhoso: forma e ideologia no romance hispano-americano*. Perspectiva, 1980.

Clifford, James. *The Predicament of Culture: Twentieth-Century Ethnography, Literature, and Art*. Harvard UP, 1988.

Cortázar, Julio. "Julio Cortázar. Un gran escritor y su soledad." Interview. *Life en español*, vol. 33, no. 7, April 7, 1969, pp. 43–55.

De la Campa, Román. *Latin Americanism*. U of Minnesota P, 1999.

Descola, Philippe. *The Ecology of Others*. Translated by Geneviève Godbout and Benjamin P. Luley. Prickly Paradigm P, 2013.

Escajadillo, Tomás Gustavo. "Entrevista a José María Arguedas." *Cultura y Pueblo*, nos. 7–8, 1965, pp. 22–23.

Escobar, Arturo. *Designs for the Pluriverse: Radical Interdependence, Autonomy, and the Making of Worlds*. Duke UP, 2018.

Esquivel, Laura. *Como agua para chocolate. Novela de entregas mensuales con recetas, amores y remedios caseros*. Doubleday, [1989] 1992.

Esquivel, Laura. *Like Water for Chocolate: A Novel in Monthly Installments with Recipes, Romances and Home Remedies*. Translated by Carol Christensen and Thomas Christensen. Doubleday, [1989] 1992.

Fuguet, Alberto, and Sergio Gómez, editors. *McOndo*. Mondadori, 1996.

García Canclini, Néstor. *Consumers and Citizens: Globalization and Multicultural Conflicts*. Translated by George Yúdice. U of Minnesota P, [1995] 2001.

García Canclini, Néstor. *Culturas híbridas: Estrategias para entrar y salir de la modernidad*. Grijalbo, 1989.

García Márquez, Gabriel. *One Hundred Years of Solitude*. Translated by Gregory Rabassa. Avon Books, [1967; English translation 1970] 1971.

González Echevarría, Roberto. *Myth and Archive: A Theory of Latin American Narrative*. Cambridge UP, 1990.

Hart, Stephen M., and Ouyang, Wen-Chin, eds. *A Companion to Magical Realism*. Tamesis, 2005.

Kristal, Efraín, ed. *The Cambridge Companion to the Latin American Novel*. Cambridge UP, 2005.

Moraña, Mabel et al., eds. *Coloniality At Large: Latin America and the Postcolonial Debate*. Duke UP, 2008.

Moreiras, Alberto. *The Exhaustion of Difference: The Politics of Latin American Cultural Studies*. Duke UP, 2001.

Rama, Ángel. *Transculturación narrativa en América Latina*. Siglo XXI, 1982.

Rowe, William, and Schelling, Vivian. *Memory and Modernity: Popular Culture in Latin America*. Verso, 1991.

Santos, Boaventura de Sousa. *Epistemologies of the South: Justice against Epistemicide*. Routledge, [2014] 2016.

Sepúlveda, Luis. *The Old Man Who Read Love Stories*. Translated by Peter Bush. Harcourt Brace & Company, [1989] 1994.

Sepúlveda, Luis. *Un viejo que leía novelas de amor*. 25th ed. Tusquets, [1989] 1995.

Swanson, Philip. "The Post-Boom Novel." *Kristal*. Cambridge UP, 2005, pp. 81–101.

Tlostanova, Madina V., and Walter D. Mignolo. *Learning to Unlearn: Decolonial Reflections from Eurasia and the Americas*. Ohio State UP, 2012.

Vargas Llosa, Mario. *La utopía arcaica: José María Arguedas y las ficciones del indigenismo*. Fondo de Cultura Económica, 1996.

Volek, Emil, ed. *Latin America Writes Back: Postmodernity in the Periphery*. Routledge, 2002.

Zamora, Lois Parkinson, and Wendy B. Faris, eds. *Magical Realism: Theory, History, Community*. Duke UP, 1995.

CHAPTER 26

THE TESTIMONIAL NOVEL AND AUTOFICTION

CECILIA ESPARZA

THE *testimonio* emerged in Latin America during the 1960s as a genre situated between anthropology and literature, and it became widespread at a moment of great political polarization in the region. The first debates surrounding the testimonio called its literary status into question. However, in 1970, Cuba's Casa de las Américas (House of the Americas) included a category for testimonio in its prestigious annual literary prizes.

According to John Beverley's well-known definition, a testimonio is a narrative told in the first person by a narrator who was the protagonist or a real witness of the events in question: "The situation of narration of testimonio has to involve an urgency to communicate, a problem of repression, poverty, subalternity, imprisonment, struggle for survival, and so on, implicated in the act of narration itself" (26). The type of testimonio defined by Beverley emerges from the mediation of a lettered subject who encourages a marginal subject to produce the oral account of his or her life, which the interviewer transcribes, edits, and publishes. It is understood that the giver of testimonio speaks in the name of a community, as a case reflective of the situation of a certain social group (Beverley 27). The legitimacy and possibility of the subaltern's representation has been debated and criticized in stark terms by authors like Gayatri Spivak. For her part, Doris Sommer warns of the testimonio-giver's resistance to disclosing certain elements of his or her life that are untranslatable for lettered culture, thereby pointing out the impossibility of comprehensively interpreting minority narratives ("No Secrets").

The paradigmatic case of the mediated testimonio is *Me llamo Rigoberta Menchú y así me nació la consciencia* (*I, Rigoberta Menchú: An Indian Woman in Guatemala*, 1983), a book edited by Venezuelan anthropologist Elisabeth Burgos-Debray (1941–). Rigoberta Menchú (1959–) famously refused to reveal her Nahuatl name, and, in the book's final passage, she decides to keep certain secrets: "I'm still keeping my Indian identity a secret. I'm still keeping secret what I think no-one should know. Not even anthropologists or intellectuals, no matter how many books they have, can find out all our secrets" (Menchú 247).[1] Menchú, a K'iche' Maya leader from Guatemala, exposes the tortures and killings perpetrated against her community by the Guatemalan military dictatorship during the civil war (1960–1996). The book sparked controversy regarding the veracity and accuracy of certain facts, such as the circumstances surrounding the murder of one of Menchú's brothers. This controversy expanded into a questioning of the nature of testimonio itself as a genre that should be rigorously faithful to the facts it reports. At any rate, it is unquestionable that Menchú became a public voice in the international community as a result of her story's circulation, which transformed her into a defender of human rights and the first indigenous person to receive the Nobel Peace Prize, in 1992.

The testimonial novel is a genre that became popular in Latin America beginning in the 1960s, in parallel to the rise of the testimonio. Miguel Barnet puts forth the notion of the "testimony-novel" ("novela-testimonio") or "reality-novel" ("novela-realidad") (*La novela* 75–78) to define a genre whose value lies not only in its ethnographic character, but also in the way it re-creates facts central to a country's history or culture. Barnet explains that the testimony-novel is indeed a document, but one that simultaneously emphasizes the social facts narrated by its protagonists, which brings it closer to the aesthetic project of a national literature's canon.

Biografía de un cimarrón (*Biography of a Runaway Slave*, 1966) is the product of the testimonio of Esteban Montejo (1860–1973), collected by Miguel Barnet (1940–) in Cuba. The book has enjoyed critical acclaim and is considered the foundational text of the testimonial novel. In 1963, Barnet interviewed a 103-year-old man who had lived as an enslaved person in Cuba's sugar plantations and then as a runaway (known as a *cimarrón*) in the solitude of the forest, participated in one of the wars of independence, and lived through the United States' intervention in Cuba. In the introduction to the Spanish edition, Barnet indicates that his interest in Montejo's life was born of the sense of finding himself "before a legitimate participant in the Cuban historical process" (9),[2] able to narrate his own lived experience of key moments in the country's history. Although Barnet claims explicitly that his is a "truthful" text, he is aware of how close his work comes to literature.

Biografía de un cimarrón begins with the memory of a mythical time of freedom in Africa, where the ancestors lived safe from the white men's invasion. The story of Montejo's childhood is characterized by gaps and uncertainties surrounding the exact place of his birth, the identity of his parents, and the circumstances of his upbringing, which Montejo fills in with information he has been able to gather from his own inquiries. Lively indeed in this memoir is the recollection of intense labor, the strong urge to flee the plantation, and the punishment Montejo received as a chastening lesson.

Communal life in the so-called barracoons or slave quarters is presented as marked by deprivation and punishment, but not entirely lacking in countervailing moments behind the masters' backs: "Strange as it may seem, blacks had fun in the barracoons. They had their pastimes and their games" (26).[3] Esteban Montejo presents himself as having a rebellious character by nature: "I never liked to be near the masters. I was a *cimarrón* from birth" (22).[4] This character trait explains the long years Montejo spent as a runaway slave in the solitude of the forest, which he recalls as a happy time.

The abolition of slavery and the war of independence are recounted as festive moments, highlighting the bravery and revolutionary spirit of the black people who fought for the nation. The narrative emphasizes the repudiation of United States intervention in Cuba and the narrator's chagrin at the marginalization suffered by his black peers during this period. Thus, the text presents the image of a subject identified with history and national values, based on the opposition to any constraint on freedom and on the defense of autonomy against the rule of white slave owners or the US interests who dominated Cuba prior to the revolution of 1959.

The work of Gregorio Martínez (1942–2017) is dedicated to the representation of the Afro-Peruvian culture of Peru's southern coast, specifically in the Nazca region. His novels and short stories display the richness and worldview of a social group that suffered under slavery beginning in the colonial period, only to later toil under the *hacienda* system. *Canto de sirena* (Mermaid Song, 1977) is a work inspired by the *testimonio* of Candelario Navarro (1895–1985), an elderly Afro-Peruvian man. The novel has a complex structure that merges Candelario's life and beliefs with the region's history, from mythical times up to a present of poverty and neglect. Martínez succeeds in translating his character's "song" into writing with an extraordinary expressive richness: a product of his deep knowledge not only of vernacular speech, but also of the worldview the author shares as an Afro-Peruvian, likewise native to Nazca. Candelario is characterized by his irreverent humor and his great vitality, born of a sexuality that serves to organize not only bodies but also social life and his view of the cosmos itself. In the novel, carnivalesque laughter and grotesque realism are the instruments by which power hierarchies are symbolically inverted. Candelario shows off and boasts of his sexual prowess; he carries around a notebook titled "Travel Journal" in which he notes down the names and circumstances of his encounters with women: "I who take note of the pleasures of the flesh, a painstaking record of all the women who see fit to get into the mix and sleep with me, every single last one of them is right here in this notebook" (59).[5] He also recounts his gastronomic feats and his skill at devouring all sorts of animals—cats, dogs, snakes— which he knows how to prepare in exquisite recipes, following the culinary tradition passed down by his ancestors. The account of Candelario's sexual adventures is central to the text, expressing the pleasures of the working classes and a scatology that defies "white" social order.

Most critics have celebrated this novel's reclamation of bodily pleasure and popular cultural knowledge. However, as Margarita Saona points out, "from a gender studies perspective, an analysis of the celebration of the virility of subaltern groups is revealed as problematic" (105).[6] Candelario's sexual prowess can be interpreted "as a form of compensation, perhaps reifying the stereotype of black hypermasculinity without presenting a true subversion of the dominant order" (Saona 106).[7] Candelario possesses an acute awareness of injustice and of the arbitrary nature of the social order. His memories highlight campesinos' frustrated desire to reclaim the land they work, as well as their disillusionment with the Peruvian agrarian reform, which failed to improve land productivity and, therefore, brought no benefit to workers. The novel oscillates between passages narrating Candelario's life and moments of meditation and memory, at which the character proudly explains the knowledge and skills he has inherited from his ancestors. This is a case, as Carlo Ginzburg explains in *Il formaggio e i vermi* (*The Cheese and the Worms*, 1976), of the wisdom of the working class, based on experience and material knowledge of reality, which appears in union with a series of utopian aspirations for social renewal (9). *Canto de sirena* is also a novel that alludes to central texts of contemporary Latin American narrative. The imprint of *Pedro Páramo* is clear in the motif of the man who returns, hopeful, to his origins, only to find desolation and ruin. The echo of Rulfo's novel appears in many scenes that represent Coyungo's present; for example: "I had the sensation of having alit in a town of the dead, where the only living thing was the heat" (70).[8] Although the novel ends on a pessimistic note, with the image of Candelario mired in disenchantment and with Coyungo in ruins, *Canto de sirena* is a powerful affirmation of popular wisdom and black campesinos' desire for justice—a novel that, as James Higgins explains, "focuses in on Western culture from a relativistic perspective and repudiates the supposition that whiteness is the model other races should aspire to emulate" (365).[9]

Elena Poniatowska's *Hasta no verte Jesús mío* (*Here's to You, Jesusa!*, 1969) is a novel inspired by the testimonio of Josefina Bohórquez, a woman from Oaxaca who, at the author's request, told Poniatowska the story of her life, linked to central events in Mexican history. Based on successive interviews, Poniatowska creates the character of Jesusa Palancares, a woman of great strength who faces orphanhood and poverty from childhood, participates in the Mexican Revolution, and migrates to the capital to work as a laborer in various factories, a domestic worker, a laundress, and a dancer in bars located in Mexico City's slums. Poniatowska recognizes that the text is a testimonial novel, not an anthropological document: "I used the anecdotes, the ideas, and many idioms of Jesusa Palancares, but I could not claim that the text is a transcription of her life because she would reject that claim herself. I killed the excess characters, I eliminated as many sessions of spiritualism as I could, I elaborated where I saw fit, I pruned, I stitched, I mended, I invented" (qtd. in Lagos-Pope 10)[10].

According to Doris Sommer, one of the most interesting aspects of *Hasta no verte Jesús mío* is the perceptible tension between the interlocutor's desire to make Jesusa speak and the character's resistance to revealing her personal life—an aspect with which Poniatowska chooses to frame the novel, between its epigraph and the rebuff to the interviewer that closes the text: "Now fuck off! Go away and let me sleep" (303).[11] Sommer explains that, in this novel, unlike in other texts, there is a sensitivity toward difference, canceling out the common trope that presupposes an idealized rapport between the popular voice and the lettered interlocutor ("Taking a Life" 922). Critics have taken an interest in the way this character defies conventions surrounding the feminine in the Mexican literary and social traditions. Jesusa Palancares does not match the image of the heroine centered on "passivity, piety, submission, and patience" (Usandizaga 31).[12] On the contrary, this character's resilience, rebelliousness, pride, and self-sufficiency, along with her irreverence toward authority and her disillusionment with the Mexican Revolution's promises of social change, make Jesusa a transgressive character who learns to survive in a reality of extreme poverty and violence against women.

In the 1980s, a series of texts began to appear in Latin America that played with the limits between autobiographical and novelistic discourses. Some critics consider these texts as representative of a new literary genre, which they refer to as "autofiction," using the term coined by Serge Doubrovsky to describe his novel *Fils* (translatable as both "Threads" and "Son," 1977). Nonetheless, critics note that the creative, fictional dimension is already present in classical autobiographical texts, whose authors must undertake the same operations as the fiction writer: they must create a character, decide which events to include and which to omit, and consider the emphasis they will place on specific facts, the order or syntax of said facts, the meaning that will be retrospectively assigned to certain key moments (Gusdorf 28–48), and the final meaning they will impose upon the narrative, given that autobiography is generally written in order to make of oneself a character for posterity. The transparency of autobiographical writing has also been called into question by Paul de Man, for whom writing about one's own life implies a "disfigurement"—that is, the creation of a person or "mask," in the theatrical sense—and the subjugation of the written word, in his own terms, to the "technical demands of self-portraiture" (69).

Other critics consider autofiction not a genre, but rather what could be called a contemporary variant of autobiography, based on an awareness of the ever-present fictional dimension of self-representation, or a hybrid genre, establishing with the reader what Manuel Alberca calls an "ambiguous pact" of reading (12),[13] somewhere between the autobiographical pact (Lejeune 137) and the fictional pact. Such "hybrid" writing appears to differing degrees in recent literature, from texts based on the fusion of individual identity and national identity, as Sylvia Molloy explains (1–11), to radically experimental texts that take distance from realism and suggest a game to the reader, parodying the conventions of autobiographical writing.

The roots of autofiction can be traced back to the short stories of Jorge Luis Borges, some of which include a character who shares his name or whom we recognize as his avatar—"El Aleph" ("The Aleph") and "El Sur" ("The South") are representative examples—in fantastic accounts that call into question the truth of the autobiographical anecdote. The same can be said of the avant-garde work of Macedonio Fernández, which parodies the figurations of the first person: *Papeles de Recienvenido* (Newcomer's Papers, 1929) and *Continuación de la nada* (Continuation of Nothingness, 1944), for example. *El zorro de arriba y el zorro de abajo* (*The Fox from Up Above and the Fox from Down Below*, 1971) by José María Arguedas is a project centered instead on the connection between national and individual histories, and it can be read as autofiction *avant-la-lettre*. Arguedas amalgamates the diaries of his suicide with a novelistic plot, and a tale of pre-Hispanic myth. Set in Chimbote—a coastal city suffering the impact of foreign investment on the fishing industry and massive migration from other regions of Peru—the novel becomes a metaphor for the chaotic process of modernization the country underwent in the 1960s. Another interesting case is that of *La tía Julia y el escribidor* (*Aunt Julia and the Scriptwriter*, 1977) by Mario Vargas Llosa, a novel that alternates between autobiographical episodes from the author's youth—the character's name is Marito—and ever-more madcap radio serial scripts by the "scriptwriter" Pedro Camacho. The tone of the radio serial is carried over into the story of Marito's life, such that his love for Aunt Julia, an older relative of his, appears represented in the codes of melodrama, in a novel about literary vocation that explores the limits between high-brow literature and popular literature.

One way autofiction is practiced in Hispano-American literature is in the nostalgic search for family origins, attempting to secure within the text some past time now at risk of being forgotten and to explain the author's cultural identity. As Svetlana Boym explains, nostalgia in these texts "is a longing for a home that no longer exists or has never existed. Nostalgia is a sentiment of loss and displacement, but it is also a romance with one's own fantasy" (i). Such is the case of *Las genealogías* (*The Family Tree*, 1981)[14] by Mexican writer Margo Glantz, who sets about recording the memories of her parents, Russian Jews who emigrated to Mexico in the 1920s. At the same time, she reminisces about her own childhood and explores her identity as a woman who is both Mexican and Jewish. The text is made up of fragments of conversations with her parents, which the author recorded and edited. This record of her parents' life in Odessa and their early years in Mexico is filled in with metaliterary reflections on the writing of this autobiographical account, including an awareness of memory as a creative act: "Here, my memory comes in. It is a false memory. It comes from Babel. I often have to turn to certain authors in order to imagine what my parents remember" (43).[15] The text includes a series of old family photographs that reinforce the nostalgia for a time that can never be recovered.

According to Jorge Rufinelli, a fundamental motif stands out here: that of identification with the paternal figure (515). A fugitive from pogroms, an exile, a businessman, a dentist, a poet, a playwright, a visual artist, and a cultural organizer, Glantz's father is her role model: "I reincarnate into my father in his youth" (162),[16] she confesses when she recalls her visit to Russia. This identification leads her to explore the uprootedness both have experienced, and to celebrate cultural hybridity. The passage in which Glantz lists her belongings brings together objects passed down by her parents—"I have in my house a few inherited Jewish items, a shofar, the almost-mythic ram's horn trumpet, to stridently announce the fall of walls, a nine-armed candelabra"—in sequence with effigies of popular saints and replicas of pre-Hispanic idols: "And all this is mine and isn't mine, and I seem Jewish and I don't seem Jewish, and that's why I write—this— my family tree" (32).[17] The search for her origins and the narrative of her family diaspora are colored by the distinctive humor Glantz deploys in her literary work. Puns, misunderstandings arising from confusion between Russian, Yiddish, and Spanish; and irreverent jokes about traditions make of *Las genealogías* a narrative that affirms the vitality and richness of cultural hybridity.

The decision to track down "the plot of one's origins" is also the starting point for *Conjeturas sobre la memoria de mi tribu* (Conjectures on the Memory of My Tribe, 1996) by José Donoso. The Chilean writer sets out to write his family history, with a clear awareness that he is also undertaking an exercise in fabulation: "Now that I have turned seventy, and I have lilies and nostalgia to give and bequeath: I am sure the moment has come for me to revise and reexamine—reinventing it—the story of myself and mine, and to accept the extent to which it may be, and in fact is, 'tampered with'" (15).[18]

The book traces back the histories of the author's family, on the paternal and maternal sides: the Donoso family, established landowners in the provincial region of Talca, and the Yáñez family, prosperous members of the bourgeoisie. The text is imbued with nostalgia for a past that bears the prestige of tradition, in contrast to the superficial modernity of contemporary Chile, dominated by the prescriptions of neoliberal economics and eager to forget its history.

Donoso reconstructs and fabulates the story of his family, which is centered on his elderly great-aunts' house in Santiago and the colonial mansion in Talca, where the family lives with a legion of servants and illegitimate relatives or *guachos*, who evoke the atmosphere of *El obsceno pájaro de la noche* (*The Obscene Bird of Night*, 1970). The plots and motifs characteristic of Donoso's literary work are recognizable too in this text, which is genealogical and fictional at once: "These fantasies—what one has left of the past—are objects of 'tampered-with memory,' pure random conjecture; pure language" (99).[19]

Fernando Vallejo's *La virgen de los sicarios* (*Our Lady of the Assassins*, 1994) can also be read as both a nostalgic text and a critique of the present. This book represents an exploration of the violence that permeated Colombian society in the 1990s. The author creates an autofictional character called Fernando, who shares his social background, age, and place of birth, as well as his avowed homosexuality and his extremely critical attitude against religion, politics, and his country's traditional values. The novel explains the decay of the myth of the "South American Athens" to an interlocutor who knows little of Colombia's past and present, all in a cynical diatribe that also ravages the figure of the writer as representative of the lettered city and defender of the foundational liberal values of Latin American nations. Fernando, the novel's protagonist, is the opposite of the figure of the lettered intellectual: while he demonstrates his knowledge of the literary tradition through allusions to classic writers like Dante and Cervantes, he is an eccentric character, an expatriate, cut off from the circles of power and further marginalized by his homosexuality (Álvarez 27). Fernando returns to Medellín after thirty years of absence, only to find a city devastated by the violence of assassins and drug trafficking; a world he will traverse in the company of young lovers who work as hired killers. This quixotic couple, the intellectual and the hitman united by love, take justice into their own hands: following Fernando's order, Alexis, the sicario, shoots at passers-by who rub them the wrong way. The places Fernando remembers with nostalgia—his grandparents' estate where he spent his childhood, the town of Sabaneta—have now become communes for the poor, whom he despises as grotesque and ignorant. Vallejo thus critiques the clichés that emerge from certain interpretations of the Boom novels, in which Latin America is a mythical space where utopia is possible, to present instead a degraded and unsalvageable nation from the perspective of a narrator who expresses a visceral rejection, as violent as the reality he critiques, of the liberal values that have proven ineffective at confronting Latin America's contemporary problems.

Family history has also been explored from an intimist perspective in autofictional literature, primarily as a way to carry out the work of mourning the loss of loved ones. Such is the case of *El olvido que seremos* (*Oblivion: A Memoir*, 2005) by Héctor Abad Faciolince and *Lo que no tiene nombre* (That Which Has No Name, 2013) by Piedad Bonnett, both Colombian writers. Abad Faciolince tells the story of his father's 1987 murder, in the midst of political conflict and clashes with drug traffickers in Medellín. Dr. Abad, a progressive physician dedicated to social and political causes, is murdered by paramilitary forces, leaving his family embroiled in the disarray and pain that the text strives to process. In place of nostalgia for the family's past, *El olvido que seremos* is clearly a text that takes upon itself the work of mourning, in a personal and a national sense, and that turns to literature as a way to reckon with pain, in order to leave melancholy behind and imagine a future for Colombia. For her part, Piedad Bonnett writes a heartrending narrative about the suicide of her son, a young artist suffering a severe mental illness. *Lo que no tiene nombre* is centered on the story of the moment when the mother must face the terrible experience of burying her son. From the moment she receives word of her son's death, Bonnett takes note of her feelings, and of the impossibility of narrating that which evades any attempt at symbolic elaboration. With great bravery, Bonnett turns to literature in search of a language able to approach an experience at the limit—an experience understood, nonetheless, as part of her artistic body of work.

Also representative of the intimist perspective of autofiction are fictionalized diaries, the most important being *Los diarios de Emilio Renzi* (*The Diaries of Emilio Renzi*, 2019) by Ricardo Piglia. Written from his youth until his final years, when he faced serious illness, they were published in three separate volumes: *Años de formación* (*The Formative Years*, 2015), *Los años felices* (*The Happy Years*, 2016), and *Un día en la vida* (*A Day in the Life*, 2017). Piglia decides to use the first and third person to document the diary entries in the life of Emilio Renzi, an alter ego who also appears in his novels. In this way, his detour from fiction finds a place in the writing of the diary, which is reread and edited—the diaries take up 327 handwritten notebooks—before being published. The division of the "I" into the one who writes and the one who participates in the literary circuit of contests, prizes, conferences, and interviews is present from the "Author's Note" that opens the text: "He feels the strange sensation of having lived two lives. One written down in his notebooks and one in his memories" (*Formative Years*)[20]—an idea that is repeated throughout the diaries: "to . . . finally become a reader of myself, view myself as if I were someone else" (*A Day in the Life*),[21] he writes in an entry from 1976.

A central motif in Piglia's diaries is his experience of living clandestinely: in 1957, the year he started writing the diaries, his family was forced to leave Adrogué and move to La Plata in order to escape political persecution: "The move, in the middle of the night. We left at dawn, furtive, ashamed" (*Formative Years*).[22] The same sentiment is documented again years later, when he returns, after some time spent as a visiting professor in the United States, to a Buenos Aires in the hands of the military dictatorship. According to Graciela Montaldo, there is a nexus between underground living and simulation that Piglia explores in his diaries: "In *Los diarios* . . . we will find all that which he ended up developing in his fiction: the use of genres and possible blends between them, quotations, but also the emergence of 'life' as writing material and the problematization of the 'I,' all the grammatical shifts of fiction and the document, what Piglia would call 'the archive'" (Montaldo 4).[23] These subjects and traits of Piglia's work, along with his distrust of literary institutions, make of *Los diarios de Emilio Renzi* a text presenting an imposture that conceals a man who decided to be a writer before even having written a line.

In the 1980s, testimonios that included a fictional dimension were written by survivors of the military dictatorships of the Southern Cone. One example is *Recuerdo de la muerte* (Memory of Death, 1988) by Miguel Bonasso, who re-creates and re-elaborates Jaime Dri's testimonio by making use of the resources of the detective novel. A particularly interesting text, situated at the limit between the short story and the testimonio, is *The Little School* (1986) by Alicia Partnoy. This collection of short narratives was published in the United States, the country where the author went into exile, and appeared in Argentina in 2006. Partnoy, a survivor of detention and torture, decided to write a series of short stories—stories she presents as "true," despite the fact that, for example, she opts to recreate the voices of the *desaparecidos*, those "disappeared" by the dictatorship. Alicia Kozameh also wrote a short-story collection titled *Pasos bajo el agua* (*Steps under Water*, 1987), with a fictional character called Sara as protagonist, in order to narrate her own experience of kidnapping and captivity. Thus, in the three aforementioned texts, fiction broadens testimonio's range of expressive possibilities, such that, as Kozameh expresses, the text is able to represent not just individual experience but also the experience of the dictatorship's thousands of victims: "Either I myself or other *compañeras* lived it" (xvi).[24] These texts can be considered the antecedents of the testimonios of the generation of the children of the Southern Cone's disappeared, in which gaps in memory are filled by means of fiction, creating a narrative that declares itself "autofictional."

According to Ana Casas, this modality of autofiction intersects with testimonial narrative, since, although it may seem paradoxical, the resources of fiction collaborate in the construction of personal memory in relation to collective memory (11–13). Casas finds recurring traits in the works of young Southern Cone authors who belong to the so-called "generación de los hijos," or "generation of the children." In 1995, the collective H.I.J.O.S. (Hijos por la Identidad y la Justicia contra el Olvido y el Silencio, or Sons and Daughters for Identity and Justice against Forgetfulness and Silence) was formed in Argentina. This group follows the line of others, like the Madres y Abuelas de la Plaza de Mayo (Mothers and Grandmothers of the Plaza de Mayo), which gave new political meaning to family ties, with the end goal of opposing the policies of the governments that followed the military dictatorship, which sponsored a project of national reconciliation seeking to erase the violent past. Marianne Hirsch's notion of "mediated memory" or "postmemory" becomes useful in analyzing texts written by the generations that inherited the trauma caused by the violence of the military dictatorships. Gaps, contradictions, and ethical postures from inherited memory are articulated through autofiction by authors fully aware of using the possibilities of literature to approach the past's impact upon their identities, or to distance themselves from certain roles they might find uncomfortable or limiting. Family history is revised and partially transformed in fiction in the plots of books by Argentine authors such as *La casa de los conejos* (*The Rabbit House*, 2007) by Laura Alcoba, *Los topos* (The Moles, 2008) by Félix Bruzzone, *El espíritu de mis padres sigue subiendo en la lluvia* (*My Father's Ghost Is Climbing in the Rain*, 2011) by Patricio Pron, *Diario de una princesa montonera 110% verdad* (110% True Diary of a Montonera Princess, 2012) by Mariana Eva Pérez, and *Pequeños combatientes* (Little Combatants, 2013) by Raquel Robles. Examples from Chile include *Formas de volver a casa* (*Ways of Going Home*, 2011) by Alejandro Zambra and *La dimensión desconocida* (*The Twilight Zone*, 2016) by Nona Fernández.

One of the most interesting of these texts, thanks to the creativity deployed in its fictional references, is *Diario de una princesa montonera 110% verdad*. This book is characterized by its questioning of the official truths produced by the state, and also of human-rights movements that represented the disappeared as heroes or victims, obliging their children to assume an ethical and political posture that should, whether they wish it to or not, form the core of their identity. Pérez does not hesitate to criticize the "reality shows" that boast reunions of long-lost grandmothers and grandchildren; she mocks the homages and "reparations" organized by the state and other institutions; she makes use of family photographs and fiction in order to question the politically correct discourses of history. She assumes the identity of the "princess" in order to dismantle the possibility of idealized, fairy-tale narratives that always have a happy ending (75).

> The Montonera Princess followed protocol to the letter. In her girlhood, she revered the word of her noble absent parents, all the while intimately, guiltily fearing their return. In her adolescence, she cried over her wretched luck and hated the *milicos*. At twenty, she threw herself into the search for comrades in struggle, in captivity . . . She shed blood to identify her parents' remains. (28–29)[25]

The legacy of the past, the trauma of the disappeared, and contemporary discourse on memory are negotiated with great creativity in this text. As the narrator declares when she decides to use her mother's dress at her own wedding: "And that's what I do with all this. I take what I want and I turn it into something that's mine" (202)[26]—a declaration of freedom that testimonio would not allow her, made possible by autofiction.

La dimensión desconocida by Nona Fernández is important because it foregrounds an uncomfortable character for post-dictatorship narratives: the perpetrator of killings and torture. The author uses the title of the well-known television series *The Twilight Zone*, which was popular in Latin America in the 1970s, in order to map out the territory of violence: the detention centers and the torture and execution chambers in Santiago de Chile. The text is based on the testimonio of a historical character, police officer Andrés Valenzuela, referred to in the text as "the man who tortured people."[27] The most interesting part of Fernández's story is how she constructs this character, as "a normal, everyday man, like any other, not unusual at all"[28] who becomes, for her, "an obsession," "a ghost." Thus, "the man who tortured people" appears not as a monster or a soulless character; he is, instead, the embodiment of what Hannah Arendt called "the banality of evil": the protagonist of the "story that would open the door to the dark space, that final portal into evil and stupidity" (29).[29] Fernández looks at photographs of this character, films a documentary in which his statements appear, and projects his voice in passages that appear to be figments of her imagination, as well as others she writes in the form of poems. She compares the torturer—only eighteen years old when he joined the police—to her own teenage son, and even ends up identifying with him herself. The line between good and evil, between victims and perpetrators, is blurred in this text, which challenges official discourse on memory in Chile, as is evident in the scene of her visit to the Museo de la Memoria y los Derechos Humanos (Museum of Memory and Human Rights), where Fernández discovers a narrative that reworks the past, but that offers "happy slogans" (26)[30] with which to resolve historical trauma. "The man who tortured people" has no place in the archive of remembered images and characters: "The man I imagine lives in a more confusing place, somewhere more uncomfortable and harder to classify, and perhaps this is why he finds no space between these walls" (27).[31] Fiction, "what I imagine," is necessary in order to lend power to "what I read," "what I know" (phrases repeated throughout the text) in a story establishing an imaginary bond with a perpetrator of violence.

Finally, another form adopted by Latin American autofiction is that of the highly experimental narrative, in which the metafictional dimension and play with the tropes of self-representation are central to the text. Vincent Colonna calls this type of text "fantastic autofiction," as opposed to biographical or realist autofiction. These texts, as Pablo Decock explains, suggest a game with the fiction of the author or the figure of the author (42). This ludic approach to autofiction is practiced by Argentine writer César Aira and Peruvian-Mexican writer Mario Bellatin, two of its most recognized authors.

César Aira's is one of the most original and influential bodies of work in recent Latin American literature. According to Graciela Montaldo, in his short novels and ludicrous storylines, Aira places invention at the center of his conception of literature. In Aira's short novels, it is hard for the reader to understand what is being narrated, or to imagine how the story will end (Ladagga 43–46), in the face of the proliferation of his writing, the rupture of meaning, the loss of coherence, and the distraction and ramification of the plot, which is generally resolved through some avant-garde jest. In Aira's work, self-referential tropes appear continuously. As Decock explains, there is a paradox here: the centrality of the figure of the author stands in contrast to the ironic desacralization of said figure; for example, in the characterization of the child Aira as a character in *El tilo* (*The Linden Tree*, 2003) and *Cómo me reí* (*How I laughed*, 2005), or the little girl/boy called César Aira in *Cómo me hice monja* (*How I Became a Nun*, 1993), or the mad scientist in *El congreso de literatura* (*The Literary Conference*, 1997) and *Las curas milagrosas del doctor Aira* (*The Miracle Cures of Dr. Aira*, 1998) (43).

Although it is narrated in the third person, in *Las curas milagrosas del doctor Aira*, the informed reader will recognize the resemblance between author and character: the shared name, age, place of birth (the town of Coronel Pringles), and middle-class neighborhood (Flores) where Aira lives. The unhinged story of the doctor who performs miracle cures, pursued by Dr. Actyn—his archnemesis, straight from a comic book, who wants to make a mockery of him and prove he is a fraud—plus the description of his editorial project of publishing his miracle cures in installments, and the trick he falls for in attempting to cure a terminal patient who turns out to be none other than Dr. Actyn himself, is also a narrative that acts out the processes of fabulation. This novel refers to and condenses the work of Borges (Contreras 184): the miracle cure is the invention of a possible world, as Borges proposes in essays like "El arte narrativo y la magia" ("Narrative Art and Magic") and "La postulación de la realidad" ("The Postulation of Reality"). In this act, references to stories like "Funes el memorioso" ("Funes the Memorious"), "El Aleph," "El jardín de senderos que se bifurcan" ("The Garden of Forking Paths"), "Las ruinas circulares" ("The Circular Ruins"), "La biblioteca de Babel" ("The Library of Babel"), and "Tlön, Uqbar, Orbis Tertius," along with the Borgesian motifs of the universe, the labyrinth, the encyclopedia, parallel realities, confusion between dreams and wakefulness, artifice and reality, and literature as a rewriting of just a few metaphors or plots culminate in a riotous ending that celebrates and ridicules the figure of the author all at once: "And to think that this grotesque puppet was creating a New Universe!" (77)[32]

Mario Bellatin also writes brief novels that form a set, presenting recurring themes, one of the most important being reflection on writing itself. Several of his stories feature a protagonist who is a writer, sometimes identified directly as Mario Bellatin and sometimes a character who shares his ideas on writing or the circumstances of the author's life, such as missing an extremity or suffering a serious illness. Play with the possibilities of fiction, the relation between reality and fiction, and the privilege of writing and the creative act in the face of reality are topics of debate for Mario Bellatin and his double, called "¿Mi yo?" or "My I?" in *Disecado* (Sexto Piso, 2011). Bellatin and his double conclude that "words and authors find themselves each in different spaces: alternate and contemporary, but out of step with any union as others might perceive it" (20);[33] therefore, writing is a metafictional game that makes no guarantee of the truth of what is narrated. Hence, the purpose of the creative act is not the representation of a referent, but rather pure enjoyment: "writing only for the pleasure of seeing one word appear after another" (37).[34] *Flores* (*Flowers*, 2001) is a text made up of brief vignettes that can be read separately, "as if it dealt with the contemplation of a flower" (9),[35] the narrator says. For the reader unfamiliar with the details of Bellatin's life, the text is made up of narrative fragments characterized by cruelty, parents' disinterest in their children, biopolitics that classify bodies, and the dubious line separating the normal from the abnormal. Among Bellatin's autofictional texts, *Flores* stands out for the strange beauty of its exploration of the ambiguous and terrible emotions that dominate its characters.

The testimonio and the testimonial novel emerged in the 1960s, in a context of global political polarization, as a way to incorporate minorities into national and regional narratives. These texts represent an alternative to the novels of the so-called Latin American Boom, which sought to represent the region's reality as a totality. The testimonio and the testimonial novel instead tell the life stories of marginal subjects, mediated by the intervention of writers, journalists, or academics who speak out against injustice, violence, or the exercise of postcolonial power against the communities to which the givers of testimonio belong. For this reason, testimonio can also be seen as the direct account of individuals who lived through moments of crisis in Latin American history, as the result of revolutionary processes, military dictatorships, and armed conflicts. This is the case of the accounts of survivors of the Southern Cone dictatorships, the Peruvian internal conflict, and Colombian drug trafficking and paramilitary violence. While structuralism declared, in the voice of Roland Barthes, the "death of the author" in the academic world, in Latin America these genres—genres that establish an unbreakable relationship between the lives of individuals, marginal communities, and the historical circumstances of the present—took on tremendous importance.

At the end of the twentieth century and the beginning of the twenty-first, narratives began to appear that intentionally erased the limits between testimonio and fiction, and consciously incorporated the resources of the novel into autobiographical writing. "Autofiction" has been written in Latin America from a variety of enunciative positions: as an account revealing the author's genealogy, or rather as an intimist narrative examining personal processes. Autofiction also incorporates the testimonial account, in the writings of the second generation—the children of those disappeared by dictatorships and other violent processes—who intervene in the construction of the region's collective memory. Finally, this type of account has appeared as an experimental narrative, calling into question the very notion of the subject, reflecting on writing and the relationship between fiction and reality, and reworking the Latin American literary tradition.

Translated from Spanish by Arthur M. Dixon

Notes

1. "Todavía sigo ocultando mi identidad como indígena. Sigo ocultando lo que yo considero que nadie sabe, ni siquiera un antropólogo, ni un intelectual, por más que tenga muchos libros, no saben distinguir todos nuestros secretos" (Menchú 271).
2. "Frente a un legítimo actor del proceso histórico cubano" (Barnet 9).
3. "Aunque parezca raro, los negros se divertían en los barracones. Tenían su entretenimiento y sus juegos" (Barnet, *Biografía de un cimarrón* 34).
4. "A mí no me gustaba emparentarme con los amos. Yo era un cimarrón de nacimiento" (Barnet, *Biografía de un cimarrón* 28).
5. "Yo que llevo nota del goce carnal, un apunte minucioso de todas las mujeres que se avienen al entrevero y se acuestan conmigo, de esas todititas están aquí, en este cuaderno" (Martínez, 59).
6. "Desde los estudios de género, un análisis de la celebración de la virilidad de los grupos subalternos se nos revela problemática" (Saona 105).
7. "Como una forma de compensación que tal vez reifica el estereotipo de la hipermasculinidad negra sin presentar una verdadera subversión del orden dominante" (Saona 106).
8. "Tuve la sensación de haberme apeado en un pueblo de muertos donde lo único viviente era el calor" (Martínez 70).
9. "Enfoca la cultura occidental desde una perspectiva relativista y repudia el supuesto de que lo blanco es el modelo que otras razas deben aspirar a emular" (Higgins 365).

10. "Utilicé las anécdotas, las ideas y muchos modismos de Jesusa Palancares, pero no podría afirmar que el texto es una transcripción de su vida porque ella misma lo rechazaría. Maté a los personajes que me sobraban, eliminé cuanta sesión espiritista pude, elaboré donde me pareció necesario, podé, cosí, remendé, inventé" (qtd. in Lagos Pope 10).

11. "Ahora ya no chingue. Váyase. Déjeme dormir" (Poniatowska 318).

12. "Pasividad, piedad, sumisión y paciencia" (Usandizaga 31).

13. "Pacto ambiguo" (Alberca 12).

14. *Las genealogías* has been translated to English as *The Family Tree*. Margo Glantz. Susan Bassnett, trans., Serpent's Tail, 1991. However, the existing English text was inaccessible at the time of this article's translation.

15. "Aquí entra mi recuerdo, es un recuerdo falso. Es de Bábel. Muchas veces tengo que acudir a ciertos autores para imaginarme lo que mis padres recuerdan" (Glantz 43).

16. "Reencarno en mi padre joven" (Glantz 162).

17. "Yo tengo en mi casa algunas cosas judías heredadas, un *shofar*, trompeta de cuerno de carnero, casi mítica, para anunciar con estridencia las murallas caídas, un candelabro de nueve velas. . . Y todo es mío y no lo es y parezco judía y no lo parezco y por eso escribo-éstas–mis genealogías" (Glantz 32).

18. "Ahora que he cumplido los setenta años y cuento con lirios y nostalgia para dar y regalar: estoy seguro de que me ha llegado el momento de revisar y revalorar–reinventándola–mi propia historia y la de los míos, y aceptar todo lo que ella puede tener, y de hecho tiene, de 'trucado'" (Donoso 15).

19. "Estas fantasías –lo que a uno le queda del pasado– son objetos de la 'memoria trucada', pura conjetura azarosa; puro lenguaje" (Donoso 99).

20. "Tiene la sensación de haber vivido dos vidas. La que está escrita en sus cuadernos y la que está en sus recuerdos" (5).

21. "Convertirme por fin en el lector de mí mismo, verse como si uno fuera otro" (Location 302).

22. "La mudanza, en medio de la noche. Salimos a la madrugada, furtivos, avergonzados" (31).

23. "En *Los diarios* . . . vamos a encontrar todo aquello que él terminó desarrollando en su ficción: el uso de los géneros y sus posibles mezclas, las citas, pero también la emergencia de 'la vida' como material de la escritura y la problematización del 'yo', todos los desplazamientos gramaticales de la ficción y el documento, lo que Piglia llamará 'el archivo'" (Montaldo 4).

24. "Lo viví yo misma o lo vivieron otras compañeras" (Kozameh 9).

25. "La Princesa Montonera cumplió con todo lo que indica el protocolo. En la niñez reverenció de la palabra a sus nobles padres ausentes, mientras íntimamente y con culpa temía su regreso. En la adolescencia, lloró su suerte desdichada y odió a los milicos. A los veinte, se abocó a la búsqueda de compañeros de militancia, de cautiverio. . . Se sacó sangre para identificar los restos de sus padres" (Pérez 28–29).

26. "Y eso es lo que hago con todo esto. Tomo lo que quiero y lo convierto en algo mío" (202).

27. "El hombre que torturaba" (Fernández).

28. "Un hombre común y corriente, como cualquiera, sin nada particular" (7).

29. "Relato que abriría la puerta a la zona oscura, a ese portal definitivo del mal y la tontera" (Fernández 29).

30. "Felices consignas" (Fernández 26).

31. "El hombre que imagino habita un lugar más confuso, más incómodo y difícil de clasificar, y quizá por eso no encuentre espacio entre estas paredes" (Fernández 27).

32. "¡Y pensar que esa marioneta grotesca estaba creando un nuevo Universo!" (Aira 74).

33. "Las obras y los autores se encuentran situados cada uno en espacios diferentes: alternos y contemporáneos, pero desfasados de una unión tal como la podrían percibir los demás" (Bellatin, *Disecado* 20).

34. "Escribir solo por el gusto de ver aparecer una palabra detrás de la otra" (Bellatin, *Disecado* 20).

35. "Como si de la contemplación de una flor se tratara" (Bellatin, *Flores* 9).

WORKS CITED

Abad Faciolince, Héctor. *El olvido que seremos*. Planeta, 2005.

Abad Faciolince, Héctor. *Oblivion: A Memoir*. Translated by Anne McLean and Rosalind Harvey. Farrar, Straus & Giroux, 2006.

Aira, César. *Cómo me hice monja*. Beatriz Viterbo, 1993.

Aira, César. *Cómo me reí*. Beatriz Viterbo, 2005.

Aira, César. *El congreso de literatura*. Tusquets, 1999.

Aira, César. *Las curas milagrosas del doctor Aira*. Era, 2003.

Aira, César. *How I Became a Nun*. Translated by Chris Andrews. New Directions, 2007.

Aira, César. *The Linden Tree*. Translated by Chris Andrews. New Directions, 2018.

Aira, César. *The Literary Conference*. Translated by Katherine Silver. New Directions, 2010.

Aira, César. *The Miracle Cures of Dr. Aira*. Translated by Katherine Silver. New Directions, 2012.

Aira, César. *El tilo*. Penguin Random House, 2003.

Alberca, Manuel. *El pacto ambiguo. De la novela autobiográfica a la autoficción*. Biblioteca Nueva, 2007.

Alcoba, Laura. *La casa de los conejos*. Edhasa, 2007.

Álvarez, Moira. "El espacio acorralado: un estudio de *La virgen de los sicarios* de Fernando Vallejo y 'El gaucho insufrible' de Roberto Bolaño." *Chasqui. Revista de literatura latinoamericana*, no. 42, 2013, pp. 15–30.

Arendt, Hannah. *Eichmann in Jerusalem: A Report on the Banality of Evil*. Penguin, (1963) 1977.

Arguedas, José María. *The Fox from Up Above and the Fox from Down Below*. Translated by Frances Horning Barraclough. Pittsburgh, 2000.

Arguedas, José María. *El zorro de arriba y el zorro de abajo*. ALLCA XX, (1971) 1990.

Barnet, Miguel. *Biografía de un cimarrón*. Alfaguara, 1984.

Barnet, Miguel. *Biography of a Runaway Slave*. Translated by W. Nick Hill, Curbstone Press, 1994.

Barnet, Miguel. "La novela testimonio, alquimia de la memoria." *La palabra y el hombre*, no. 82, April–June 1992, pp. 75–78.

Bellatin, Mario. *Disecado*. Sexto piso, 2011.

Bellatin, Mario. *Flores*. Peisa, 2001.

Bellatin, Mario. *Flowers & Mishima's Illustrated Biography*. Translated by Kolin Jordan. 7 Vientos Press, 2014.

Beverley, John. "The margin at the center: on testimonio." *Modern Fiction Studies*, vol. 35, no. 1, Spring 1989, pp. 11–28.

Bonasso, Miguel. *Recuerdo de la muerte*. Punto Sur, 1988.

Bonnett, Piedad. *Lo que no tiene nombre*. Alfaguara, 2013.

Borges, Jorge Luis. *Obras completas*. Emecé, 1974.

Boym, Svetlana. *The Future of Nostalgia*. Basic Books, 2011.

Bruzzone, Félix. *Los topos*. Mondadori, 2008.

Casas, Ana. "El simulacro del yo: la autoficción en la narrativa actual." *La autoficción. Reflexiones teóricas*, edited by Ana Casas, Arco Libros, 2012, pp. 9–42.

Colonna, Vincent. *Autofiction et autres mythomanies littéraires*. Tristam, 2004.

Contreras, Sandra. "Aira con Borges." *La Biblioteca*, no. 13, spring 2013, pp. 184–98.

De Man, Paul. "Autobiography as de-facement." *The Rhetoric of Romanticism*, Columbia UP, 1984, pp. 67–81.

Donoso, José. *El obsceno pájaro de la noche*. Seix Barral, 1970.

Donoso, José. *Conjeturas sobre la memoria de mi tribu*. Alfaguara, 1996.

Doubrovsky. Serge. *Fils*. Galilée, 1977.

Fernández, Macedonio. *Papeles de recienvenido y Continuación de la nada*. Corregidor, 2004.

Fernández, Macedonio. *Obras completas*. Corregidor, 1974.

Fernández, Nona. *La dimensión desconocida*. Random House Mondadori, 2016.

Fernández, Nona. *The Twilight Zone: A Novel*. Translated by Natasha Wimmer. Graywolf, 2021.

Giordano, Alberto. *El giro autobiográfico en la literatura argentina actual*. Mansalva, 2008.

Ginzburg, Carlo. *El queso y los gusanos*. Muchnik, 1986.

Glantz, Margo. *Las genealogías*. Obras reunidas II. Fondo de Cultura Económica, (1981) 2008.

Gusdorf, Georges. "Conditions and Limits of Autobiography." *Autobiography: Essays Theoretical and Critical*, edited by James Olney, Princeton UP, 1980, pp. 28–48.

Higgins, James. *Historia de la literatura peruana*. Universidad Ricardo Palma, Editorial Universitaria, 2006.

Hirsch, Marianne. *The Generation of Postmemory. Writing and Visual Culture after the Holocaust*. Columbia University Press, 2012.

Kozameh, Alicia. *Pasos bajo el agua*. Contrapunto, 1987.

Kozameh, Alicia. *Steps under Water*. Translated by David E. Davis. U of California P, 1996.

Lagos-Poppe, María Inés. "El testimonio creativo de *Hasta no verte Jesús mío*." *Revista Iberoamericana*, no. 150, 1990, pp. 243–53.

Lejeune, Philippe. "Le pacte autobiographique." *Poétique*, no. 14, 1973, pp. 137–61.

Martínez, Gregorio. *Canto de sirena*. Mosca Azul, 1977.

Menchú, Rigoberta. *I, Rigoberta Menchú: An Indian Woman in Guatemala*. Edited by Elisabeth Burgos-Debray. Translated by Ann Wright. Verso, 1984.

Menchú, Rigoberta. *Me llamo Rigoberta Menchú y así me nació la conciencia*. Siglo XXI, 1983.

Molloy, Sylvia. *At Face Value. Autobiographical Writing in Spanish America*. Cambridge UP, 1991.

Montaldo, Graciela. "Complot y teoría: lo que vino después (sobre los diarios editados de Ricardo Piglia)." *Cuadernos Lírico* (online). Hors-série 2019. http://journals.openedition.org/lirico/7885; DOI: https://doi.org/10.4000/lirico.7885

Partnoy, Alicia. *The Little School: Tales of Disappearance and Survival*. Midnight Editions, 1986.

Pérez, Mariana Eva. *Diario de una princesa montonera -110% verdad*. Capital Intelectual, 2012.

Piglia, Ricardo. *The Diaries of Emilio Renzi: A Day in the Life*. Translated by Robert Croll. Restless Books, 2020. Kindle edition.

Piglia, Ricardo. *The Diaries of Emilio Renzi: The Formative Years*. Translated by Robert Croll. Restless Books, 2017. Kindle edition.

Piglia, Ricardo. *Los diarios de Emilio Renzi*. Debolsillo, Penguin Random House, 2019.

Poniatowska, Elena. *Hasta no verte Jesús mío*. Era, 1969.

Poniatowska, Elena. *Here's to You, Jesusa!* Translated by Deanna Heikkinen. Penguin Books, 2002.

Pron, Patricio. *El espíritu de mis padres sigue subiendo en la lluvia.* Random House Mondadori 2011.

Robles, Raquel. *Pequeños combatientes.* Alfaguara, 2013.

Rufinelli, Jorge. "Al margen de la ficción: autobiografía y literatura mexicana." *Hispania*, vol. 69, no. 3, September 1986, pp. 512–20.

Rulfo, Juan. *Pedro Páramo.* Fondo de Cultura Económica, 1955.

Saona, Margarita. "Las aventuras sexuales de don Candelario: las trampas de la masculinidad en *Canto de sirena* de Gregorio Martínez." *Poéticas de lo negro. Literatura y otros discursos acerca de lo afroperuano en el siglo XX*, edited by Richard Leonardo, Hipocampo, 2013, pp. 105–14.

Sommer, Doris. "Taking a Life: Hot Pursuit and Cold Rewards in a Mexican Testimonial Novel." *Signs. Journal of Women in Culture and Society*, vol. 20, no. 4, summer 1995, pp. 913–40.

Sommer, Doris. "No secrets." *The Real Thing: In Testimonial Discourse and Latin America*, edited by Georg M. Gugelberger, Duke UP, 1996, pp. 130–57.

Spivak, Gayatri. "Can the Subaltern Speak?" In *Marxism and the Interpretation of Culture*, edited by Cary Nelson and Lawrence Grossberg, U of Illinois P, 1988, pp. 271–313.

Usandizaga, Helena. "La reconstrucción del espacio marginal en *Hasta no verte Jesús mío* de Elena Poniatowska." *Lectora*, no. 1, 1995, pp. 25–34.

Vallejo, Fernando. *La virgen de los sicarios.* Alfaguara, 1994.

Vargas Llosa, Mario. *La tía Julia y el escribidor.* Seix Barral, 1977.

Zambra, Alejandro. *Formas de volver a casa.* Anagrama, 2011.

....

CHAPTER 27

POPULAR FICTIONS AND ARTISTIC NARRATIVE

Detective Fiction, Science Fiction, and Fantasy

....

PERSEPHONE BRAHAM

THIS article describes the development of genre fictions in Latin America and the Spanish-speaking Caribbean. While genres such as detective and science fiction are not native to Latin America, they have developed into important conduits for social and political criticism. The fantastic took root with the chronicles of conquest, and Latin American and Caribbean plantations stimulated the Gothic imagination. In contrast to most Anglophone genre fiction, Latin American genre fiction has never been intended as mere entertainment; rather, it has always engaged with systemic injustice, authoritarianism, and atavistic social mores.

Latin American writers and critics began to appreciate the critical potential of genre fictions in the early 1970s, despite a preoccupation with the valences attached to categories such as "popular" versus "literary" fiction. Historically, Latin America's literary elites have been skeptical about the existence of autochthonous "popular fictions," citing low levels of literacy and lack of discretionary buying power among the masses. Critics were concerned with delineating national and regional literatures from a somewhat self-imposed posture of cultural eccentricity that alternately privileged and rejected "universal" European models, and they considered genres like detective and science fiction escapist, inconsistent with Latin America's uneven modernity, and detrimental to the development of original narrative forms more attuned to Latin American difference.

However, critics do not necessarily decide what constitutes genre fiction. Genre fiction identifies itself through narrative conventions, unifying motifs (Leonardo Padura's *Las cuatro estaciones* ["Four Seasons," known in English as *Havana Quartet*] tetralogy), and character quirks—a penchant for cats or orange soda—that are familiar and gratifying to readers. Marketing is key: Mexico's Lectorum publishes *novela negra* under its Marea Alta imprint; Cuban detective novels carry a "Policiaca" or "Contraespionaje" logo; Paco Ignacio Taibo's books are labeled "una novela de Belascoarán." "Literary" writers may engage with genre without writing genre fiction: Gabriel García Márquez's *Crónica de una muerte anunciada* (*Chronicle of a Death Foretold*, 1981) depicts a crime, but is not about crime per se. Roberto Bolaño's *2666* (2004) brutally parodies the police procedural, highlighting the outlandish forensic performativity of a criminal state in service of a broader meditation on truth, narrative, and evil. Argentineans Juan José Saer and José Pablo Feinmann have written crime narratives, but Planeta, which publishes a vast catalog of genre fiction, markets them as "literary fiction." Conversely, some of the worst attempts at genre have been written by revered literary authors, for example, Carlos Fuentes's catastrophically banal *La cabeza de la hidra* (*The Hydra Head*, 1978) and *Vlad* (horror, 2010).

Genre parameters and taxonomy frequently inspire debate. Many authors write in more than one genre, or combine them, as did the great genre pioneers Edgar Allan Poe (1809–1849), Eduardo Ladislao Holmberg (1852–1937), and Arthur Conan Doyle (1859–1930). Some of the best Latin American genre writers never wrote novels (Horacio Quiroga [1878–1937], Jorge Luis Borges [1899–1986], Lino Novás Calvo [1903–1983]), and are not covered here. Space considerations also limit discussion to works that move the field in new aesthetic or thematic directions. The chapter is divided into three sections: Detective and Crime Fiction; Science Fiction, Fantasy, and Horror; and Genre Benders, which shows how recent generations enrich crime narrative with fantasy, horror, and science fiction.

DETECTIVE AND CRIME FICTION

It was recently suggested that we discard all crime-genre terminology in favor of "the novel of violence."[1] However, the rubric *novela negra* is widely accepted as describing a gamut of narratives centered on violence and criminal activity, even absent a hermeneutical agenda. *Novela negra* emerged in the second half of the twentieth century as a term of higher prestige than "mystery" or "detective novel," inspired by American hard-boiled stories by Raymond Chandler (1888–1959), James M. Cain (1892–1977), and Dashiell Hammett (1894–1961), rather than bourgeois whodunnits by Agatha Christie (1890–1976). The term derived cachet from the French *Série noire* imprint that published American hardboiled fiction.[2]

The earliest Latin American crime novels are Mexican dramatist Rodolfo Usigli's (1905–1979) *Ensayo de un crimen* (Rehearsal for a Crime,[3] 1944) about a neurotic would-be lady-killer, and Uruguayan Enrique Amorim's (1900–1960) *El asesino desvelado* (The Insomniac Assassin, 1945) published in Borges's *Séptimo círculo* detective series. Both explore the psychology of men obsessed with killing women, rather than detectives solving a mystery.

Mexico's first detective was Antonio Helú's (1900–1972) wily thief Carlos Miranda in the novella *La obligación de asesinar* (The Burden of Killing, 1947). María Elvira Bermúdez (1912–1988) followed with journalist Armando Zozaya in *Diferentes razones tiene la muerte* (Death Has Other Motives, 1953). Eschewing weighty themes of violence, atavism, and solitude ("the Great Death"[4]), these tales scrutinized rigid social mores, bureaucratic ineptitude, and petty vengeance. The detectives' effectiveness depended on their complete lack of social and symbolic consequence, and they resolved matters according to their own morality. Although they were sometimes disregarded by later generations (Taibo II 23), their disdain for law enforcement and institutions is fundamental to the novela negra.

Cuba's socialist detective novel is unique in Latin American crime fiction. Cuba's Ministry of the Interior launched the genre in 1972 to reinforce socialist authority, following a scandal involving poet Heberto Padilla (1932–2000), whose work criticized the Castro regime. About 20% of novels published in Cuba in the 1970s and 1980s were detective and spy stories. Cubans eschewed the solitary, cynical hard-boiled detective in favor of the police procedural; the new genre provided a vehicle for educating the populace, rebuking the previous generation's "difficult" literature, and modeling the unmasking of "antisocial" tendencies such as nonconformity and homosexuality. Better-known "counter-espionage" novels like Daniel Chavarría's (1933–2018) *Joy* (1977) and Luis Rogelio Nogueras's (1944–1985) *Y si muero mañana* (If I Die Tomorrow, 1978) experimented with documentary elements and innovative narrative strategies; Chavarría's *Allá ellos* (To Hell with Them, 1991) won the Dashiell Hammett prize. However, others were more heavy-handed, leading to an unfortunate preponderance of criminals of color, Jews, prostitutes, effeminate men, and people with physical deformities.[5] The onset of Cuba's profound economic crisis in the late 1980s halted most publishing and effectively shut down the genre.

Elsewhere in Latin America, the anti-authoritarian sentiment that marked 1968 unleashed a surge in genre production so proteic and prolonged that it has indelibly altered the literary landscape. Mexico's foundational novela negra, Rafael Bernal's (1915–1972) *El complot mongol* (*The Mongolian Conspiracy*, 1969) was published the year following the government's massacre of hundreds of demonstrators on October 2, 1968. Bernal inserted a hard-boiled policeman into an international spy story, where he was obliged to reflect on the homicidal ineptitude of Mexican authority, concluding that crime was no longer a discrete act of violence, but a systemic corporate and political assault on the public. Bernal's novel is cynical and humane, written in gritty, colloquial language that effectively naturalized the genre in Mexico. Jorge Ibargüengoitia's (1928–1983) *Las muertas* (*The Dead Girls*, 1977) lampooned the investigation of a series of murders around a brothel in Guanajuato. One of Latin America's first (albeit farcical) "true-crime" narratives, *Las muertas* projected Mexico's institutional complicity in mass murder, whether of students in Tlatelolco or Ayotzinapa or women in Ciudad Juárez, and has inspired generations of novela negra writers.

A tireless promotor of crime fiction in Spanish, Paco Ignacio Taibo II (1949–) coined the term *neopoliciaco* for his version of the novela negra. Neopoliciaco writers set themselves against elite literary culture, which they saw as reinforcing narratives of "the Great Death." The neopoliciaco features serial hard-boiled-style protagonists, foregrounds the futility of inquiry under criminal authoritarian regimes, and prioritizes symbolic counter-culturalism, such as driving a *vocho* (VW) in solidarity with auto workers' struggle against puppet unions. Taibo's *Días de combate* (Days of Combat, 1976) is the first of nine titles featuring Mexico City gumshoe Héctor Belascoarán Shayne; two others, *La vida misma* (*Life Itself*, 1987) and *La bicicleta de Leonardo* (*Leonardo's Bicycle*, 1993, both Hammett winners), feature writer José Daniel Fierro, who gets conscripted as a police chief in a northern town. Rafael Ramírez Heredia's (1942–2006) *Trampa de metal* (Metal Trap, 1979) is the first of three Ifigenio Clausel titles. Among Rolo Díez's (1940–) roughly fourteen crime novels, *Mato y Voy* (*Tequila Blue*, 1992), *La vida que me doy* (The Life I Live, 2001), and *Matamujeres* (Ladykiller, 2001) feature Mexico City policeman Carlos Hernández, whose investigations sometimes impinge on his own illegal activity, from pimping to arms dealing. All three deal with violence against women; the third involves the outrageous "serial killer" theory circulated around the murders of women in Ciudad Juárez.

The neopoliciaco mold—cynical but (generally) principled detective, New-Left politics, gritty but cherished urban setting, exposure of corrupt authority—proved useful in denouncing the crimes of US-backed dictatorships of the 1970s and 1980s, and the lackluster truth-seeking that followed.[6] In Chile, Ramón Díaz Eterovic's (1956–) first Heredia story, *La ciudad está triste* (The City is Sad, 1987), was published towards the end of Augusto Pinochet's rule. Sixteen others followed, all still in print by LOM with distinctive comics-style portraits of Heredia on their covers. Like fellow fictional detectives Belascoarán, Mario Conde, and el Zurdo Mendieta, Heredia maintains a metafictional dialogue with international crime writers, and his cat is named Simenon. Chilean exile Luis Sepúlveda (1949–2020), who was imprisoned by the Pinochet regime for over two years, presented ex-guerrilla Juan Belmonte in *Nombre de torero* (*The Name of a Bullfighter*, 1994) and *El fin de la historia* (The Purpose of History, 2017). Belmonte's cases connect Pinochet's henchmen with Cossack and Nazi atrocities. Roberto Ampuero (1953–), an anomaly in the traditionally leftist novela negra field, served in the government of conservative president Sebastián Piñera. Ampuero's *¿Quién mató a Cristián Kustermann?* (Who Killed Christian Kustermann?, 1993) is the first of seven titles featuring Cayetano Brulé, a Cuban-born private detective living in Valparaíso who interacts with bolero singers, Cuban dissidents, and Chile's great poet Pablo Neruda (1904–1973).

While Argentina's post-dictatorship novela negra did not generally follow the neopoliciaco mold, twenty-first-century writers have embraced it. Ernesto Mallo's (1948–) Inspector Lascano series (five novels published since 2011) is set in the late 1970s and early 1980s. "El Perro" Lascano is a member of the federal police investigating crimes that invariably intersect with the nefarious activities of Argentina's military *junta*, drug dealing, and human trafficking. Crime journalist Florencia Etcheves (1971–) also revisits past crimes: police detectives Francisco Juánez and Pipa Pelari investigate a girl murdered by her stalker in *La Virgen en tus ojos* (The Virgin in Your Eyes, 2012); a series of feminicides in Key West tied to a 1982 domestic murder in *La hija del campeón* (The Champion's Daughter, 2014); and the fourteen-year-old case of a disappeared girl in *Cornelia* (2016). The resonance of these cold cases in the present connects the Mothers of the Plaza de Mayo to the #NiUnaMenos movement, signaling that violence against women flourishes in same culture of impunity that protects the villains of history. Peru's Santiago Roncagliolo (1975–) likewise unearths suppressed history in *Abril rojo* (*Red April*, 2006), about official hypocrisy surrounding the long conflict between the Shining Path and the government, and *La pena máxima* (Maximum Penalty, 2014) about Peru's complicity with the Pinochet and Videla dictatorships. His detective, Assistant Prosecutor Félix Chacaltana Saldívar, is not driven by a moral agenda but by the overwhelming desire to accurately complete his paperwork.

Claudia Piñeiro's (1960–) "country" novels set in Buenos Aires's well-to-do gated communities—including *Las viudas de los jueves* (*Thursday Night Widows*, 2005), *Tuya* (*All Yours*, 2006), *Las grietas de Jara* (*A Crack in the Wall*, 2009), and *Betibú* (*Betty Boo*, 2011)—portray the moral erosions of Menemismo among a social class constituted by consumption, privatization, and exclusivity. Piñeiro has been compared to Alfred Hitchcock (Nelken); her books are bestsellers throughout Latin America, and she is the most widely translated Argentinean writer after Borges and Cortázar. Other of her narratives are more specifically political, such as *Las maldiciones* (The Curses, 2017), on Argentina's "nueva política," or politics sans ideological commitment, and *Catedrales* (Cathedrals, 2020) about a feminicide unpunished for thirty years.

In Cuba and Nicaragua, the neopoliciaco observes failed utopian projects. Leonardo Padura's "Four Seasons" tetralogy (*Havana Quartet*) brought Cuba's Special Period and the decline of the socialist apparatus to international readers thirsty for insight into Cuban life. Romantic, occasionally rum-soaked Havana policeman Mario Conde first appeared in *Pasado perfecto* (*Havana Blue*, 1991). Conde's investigations always shed light on cultural arcana, from gay authors silenced by the revolution to the vanishing Barrio Chino. Conde figures in nine books, including Hammett winners *Paisaje de otoño* (*Havana Black*, 1998) and *Neblina del ayer* (*Havana Fever*, 2005); the latest is *La transparencia del tiempo* (*The Transparency of Time*, 2018). Conde is loosely autobiographical: a would-be writer whose disillusion with the revolution is countered by his unshakable nostalgia for Havana, his people, and his youthful ideals.

Another semi-autobiographical detective, Sergio Ramírez's (1942–) Inspector Dolores Morales and his ex-Sandinista comrade Bert "Lord" Dixon are narcotics investigators in Managua's Sandinista Police. Ramírez was himself a guerrillero and later vice-president under an increasingly authoritarian Daniel Ortega. *El cielo llora por mí* (The Sky Cries for Me, 2008), nominally a thriller about drug-traffickers from Cali and Sinaloa, contains thinly veiled portraits of public figures. Morales, having literally given his leg for the Sandinista cause (he received a prosthetic in Cuba), is hopelessly outgunned by powerful enemies who have suborned the legal and judicial apparatus he serves. *Ya nadie llora por mí* (Now No One Cries for Me, 2017) has Morales working as a private detective on a case involving an oligarch's missing stepdaughter, alluding to accusations of sexual abuse levelled at Ortega by his stepdaughter in 1998. Ramírez received the Cervantes Prize in 2017 for his literary achievement.

Brazil's novela negra focuses on the psychological dimensions of crime and radical inequality. Rubem Fonseca (1925–2020) introduced the cultured, womanizing defense lawyer Mandrake in *A Grande Arte* (*High Art*, 1983), the first of several Mandrake stories. Mandrake lines his pockets providing special services for wealthy people. He is sympathetic to the plight of marginalized classes and deplores the fact of economic injustice, but opportunism and social advantage keep him from grand gestures toward denunciation or reform. A less cynical but also apolitical figure is Luiz Alfredo Garcia-Roza's (1936–2020) *carioca* detective inspector Espinosa. Garcia-Roza portrays crime as a matter of individual pathology rather than systemic corruption. A bibliophile like Mandrake, Espinosa appeared in twelve novels between 1996 and the author's death. The fast-paced stories depict the extreme wealth and abject poverty of a Rio de Janeiro occupied by homeless people, executives, professors, dentists, pimps, and policemen good and bad.

Patrícia Melo's (1962–) antihero Máiquel first appeared in *O matador* (*The Killer*, 1995), which recounts his transformation from used-car salesman to celebrated vigilante killer, followed by *Mundo perdido* (*Lost World*, 2006), in which he searches across Amazonia for his daughter, who is following the pastor of an evangelical mega-church. Melo, a screenwriter, has been compared to Quentin Tarantino (Cockrell). She presents crime as a common and expedient route to status and social mobility rather than a singularity. Máiquel serves the wealthy by killing poor people of color; only when he accidentally murders above his pay grade does he face real consequences. *Fogo-Fátuo* (Will-o'-the-wisp, 2014) introduces policewoman Azucena, navigating social media and politics as she investigates a celebrity murder. Melo's other novels include a bildungsroman about a favela drug-lord, a Hitchcockian, metaliterary critique of Brazil's publishing industry, and her most recent *Mulheres empilhadas* (Stacked-Up Women, 2019), about the ubiquitous problem of feminicide.

In the mid-1990s, Mexican writers turned from bankrupt nationalist mythologies to themes of narco-traffic and violence against women. The serial protagonist seemed on the verge of disappearing, along with the investigation of a criminal event as organizing principle. Díez's Hammett winner, *Luna de Escarlata* (Scarlett's Moon, 1994), portrays life in the capital as a series of grotesque aggressions inflicted by unwitting citizens upon each other. Juan Hernández Luna's (1962–2010) stories encompass multiple registers of criminality, from public groping to human trafficking, serial murder, and necrophilia; the fragmented perspective of his marginalized, displaced characters overtakes the unifying viewpoint of a detective. Two of his six crime novels, *Tabaco para el puma* (Tobacco for the Puma, 1996) and *Cadáver de ciudad* (Corpse City, 2007), won the Hammett. Gabriel Trujillo Muñoz (1958–) brings the novela negra to the US-Mexico border in eight tales featuring Mexicali-based human-rights investigator Miguel Ángel Morgado. Morgado deals with organ theft, migrant deaths, and fraught collaborations with US law enforcement, but his investigations are a background for Trujillo's devoted exploration of the history and everyday life of the cities of Baja California.

Violence skyrocketed in Mexico after the government declared war on cartels in 2006, accelerating the rise of the narcoliterature subgenre. Sinaloan Élmer Mendoza (1949–) observes *el narco* via his detective Edgar "El Zurdo" Mendieta—a member of the corrupt state police and possible drug addict. El Zurdo debuted in the Tusquets Prize-winning *Balas de plata* (*Silver Bullets*, 2008) and pursues justice within a decidedly relativistic moral scope, trading favors with narco-bosses to capture others. *La prueba del ácido* (*The Acid Test*, 2010) and *Nombre de perro* (*The Name of the Dog*, 2012) dialogue with the eponymous *Reina del Sur* (*The Queen of the South*, 2002), creation of Mendoza's friend, Spanish novelist Arturo Pérez Reverte (1951–). Mendoza's quick, colloquial prose does not exclude cultural allusion; *Cóbraselo caro* (Make Him Pay, 2005) lampoons narratives of the Great Death by representing a set of characters obsessed by *Pedro Páramo*.[7] *Asesinato en el parque de Sinaloa* (*Murder in Sinaloa Park*, 2017) inserts el Zurdo into el Chapo Guzmán's final escape before his extradition to the United States.

For twenty-first-century Mexican writers raised on Bernal, Ibargüengoitia, Mendoza, and Taibo, popularity and accessibility no longer carry the stigma imposed by previous generations of cultural stewardship. As Francisco G. Haghenbeck (1965–2021) stated: "For me, there are three important points in defining the success of a literary genera-tion: one, that they be universally translated, that they are followed by a good number of readers, as reflected in their book sales, and, of course, that they are recognized by national and international criticism" (276).[8] Haghenbeck's Sunny Pascal novels wander nostalgically through the 1960s in *Trago amargo* (*Bitter Drink*, 2007) and *El Caso Tequila* (The Tequila Case, 2010); Sunny is a half-Yankee beatnik working as a fixer for Hollywood studios; *Un puñado de balas* (A Fistful of Bullets, 2016) finds her on location in Spain with Luis Buñuel, trying to solve a murder from Spain's Civil War.

Martín Solares's (1970–) *Los minutos negros* (*The Black Minutes*, 2006) pays homage to Ibargüengoitia's *Las muertas* with a secondary plot involving the 1970s murders of several young schoolgirls in the fictional town of Paracuán (a portmanteau for ¿para cuándo? [when?]), alluding to Mexico's long-standing culture of impunity. Bernardo Fernández (BEF)'s (1972–) *Tiempo de alacranes* (Time of Scorpions, 2005) stars a re-bellious cartel hitman. In Grijalbo Award winner *Hielo negro* (Black Ice, 2011), the "psychonaut" Lizzy Subiaga is pursued by retired judicial police officer Andrea Mijangos, as she hunts for a super-drug that will erase all inhibitions, including the fear of death. *Hielo Negro* shows the integration of drug trafficking in the global finan-cial world, a plot that thickens in *Cuello blanco* (White Collar, 2013); in *Azul Cobalto* (Cobalt Blue, 2016) Subiaga turns her talents to the art market. Juan Pablo Villalobos's (1973–) *Fiesta en la madriguera* (*Down the Rabbit Hole*, 2010) presents the world of the narco through the eyes of a child, rendering it abstract, lyrical, and even humorous. Orfa Alarcón (1979–) focuses on the feminine experience in *Perra brava* (Mad Bitch, 2010), about a middle-class woman obsessed with the implications of her narco-trophy status, and *Loba* (She-Wolf, 2019), in which the spoiled daughter of a narcotrafficker struggles between fleeing his "pack" and fear of losing the privilege it offers.

A not-quite analogue to the Mexican narco-novela, the Colombian *novela sicaresca* depicts the world of drug traffickers and their hired assassins, or *sicarios*. Laura Restrepo's (1950) *Leopardo al sol* (*Leopard in the Sun*, 1993) received praise from García Márquez and is regarded as establishing the subgenre. Fernando Vallejo's (1942–) baroque, excoriating *La Virgen de los Sicarios* (*Our Lady of the Assassins*, 1999) and Jorge Franco's (1962–) bestselling *Rosario Tijeras* (1999) cemented the popularity of the novela sicaresca. The sicaresca is characterized by wildly variable configuration and quality. As

Margarita Jácome notes, Colombia's cultural custodians are unnerved by the genre's variability and success, owing to:

> A desire to establish at any cost the characteristics which, when employed repetitively by the authors, allow them to easily judge the quality of the works . . . [and] the high sales of books by little-known writers, that is, those not sanctioned by the intellectual circle in the country's capital and, with them, the entry of narconarratives into the category of bestsellers. (28)[9]

The worst of the sicaresca fetishizes women and glorifies a culture of mafia dons and fast money, which makes them highly adaptable as telenovelas. In a more philosophical vein, Guillermo Cardona's (1961–) *La bestia desatada* (The Beast Unleashed, 2007) and Juan Gabriel Vásquez's (1973–) *El ruido de las cosas al caer* (*The Sound of Things Falling*, 2011) show how narcotraffic corrodes and alienates Colombia's middle class, professionals, and future elites. In a way, such narratives demonstrate a tragic continuity with the perpetual, atavistic civil conflict represented in García Márquez's *Cien años de soledad* (*One Hundred Years of Solitude*, 1967).

SCIENCE FICTION, FANTASY, AND HORROR

Latin America has a long history of science fiction and fantastic literature.[10] Early science fiction in Latin America used space travel and spiritual displacement as commentary on contemporary debates or calls for reform. *Lima de aquí a cien años* (Lima One Hundred Years from Now, 1843) by Peruvian Julián M del Portillo (1818–1862) envisioned Peru in 1943 as a world center of invention and culture, free of internal conflicts. A common trope was a space voyage undertaken by the spirit of a dead protagonist. Puerto Rico's Alejandro Tapia y Rivera (1826–1882) wrote *Póstumo, el transmigrado* (Posthumous, the Transmigrated, 1872), in which a recently dead man ("muerto-vivo") flees his funeral vigil and travels to a moldering corner of the interplanetary spiritual bureaucracy to demand a new body. In a sequel, *Póstumo el envirginiado* (Posthumous the Invirginiated, 1882), the spirit-protagonist occupies the body of a woman, Virginia, who becomes a suffragist and dies in Spain's 1868 revolution. Cuba's Francisco Calcagno (1827–1903) wrote *Historia de un muerto* (Story of a Dead Man, 1875), narrating the process of decomposition from the cadaver's perspective. Holmberg's *Viaje maravilloso del señor Nic-Nac al planeta Marte* (The Marvelous Journey of Mr. Nic-Nac to the Planet Mars, 1876) unites the esoteric focus of *modernismo* and the scientific spirit of positivism, as the protagonist, Nic Nac, undertakes a spirit-journey to Mars, accompanied by a medium and a physician. They tour Theospholis, a city sharply divided into religious and (happier) scientific zones. *Querens* (1890) by Mexican Pedro Castera (1846–1906) mixed magnetism, hypnosis, and occult spiritualism in the story of an alchemist who animates an "idiot" girl with his own will and intellect.

Darwinism inspired *Desde Júpiter* (From Jupiter, 1878) by Chilean Francisco Miralles (aka. Saint Paul, 1837–1890), about a culture of Jovian scientists trying to gauge Chilean society's evolutionary and technological progress. In Calcagno's *En busca del eslabón: historia de monos* (In Pursuit of the Link: Story of Monkeys, 1888), the author debates scientists Don Sinónimo, Captain Thunderbolt, and "the false" Stanley, on the theories of Lamarck, Haeckel and Darwin, their application to race, and the evolutionary stages of life on other planets.

Between the late nineteenth century and the 1960s, respectable novels with a super-natural or scientific focus were generally treated as "fantastic" literature, a genre with more prestigious origins, while science fiction flourished in film, comics, and stories.[11] Mid-century science fiction writers include Mexicans Guillermo Zárraga (1892–1978) and Rafael Bernal, whose *Su nombre era muerte* (Its Name was Death, 1947) envisages intelligent mosquitos annihilating the human race. 1930s Chile saw several fantasies around a lost city of gold, and Hugo Correa's (1926–2008) anti-communist *Los altísimos* (The Highest Ones, 1959) inaugurated a "Golden Age" of science fiction lasting into the mid-1970s. At present, Latin American science fiction subgenres include cyberpunk, popular in Cuba; *ucronías* (alternate histories) popular in Brazil; apocalyptic futures dealing with the climate catastrophe, not surprisingly coming from the Caribbean; and *retrofuturismo* (steampunk) and *ciberchamanismo* (cyber-shamanism), mostly from Mexico and Chile. An important new variant is *Afrofuturismo*, also mostly from Brazil.

Post-revolutionary Cuba has a strong science fiction tradition, supported by the *David* prize and Cuban publishers *Dragón*, *Gente Nueva*, and *Letras cubanas*. Noted novels include Miguel Collazo's (1936–) *El viaje* (The Journey, 1968); the time-travelling *¿Dónde está mi Habana?* (Where is my Havana?, 1985), by F. Mond (1949–); and Daína Chaviano's (1960–) *Fábulas de una abuela extraterrestre* (Tales of an Extraterrestrial Grandmother, 1988). Agustín de Rojas (1949–2011) and Ángel Arango (1926–2013) are luminaries of Cuba's Soviet era: Rojas's trilogy portrays a perfect socialist utopia, and Arango's tetralogy a heroic quest for the ultimate human civilization. Yoss's (José Miguel Sánchez, 1969–) abundant production tends toward witty allegories of Cuba's recent history: sex tourism in *Se alquila una planeta* (A Planet for Rent, 2001), strategic sexual commerce with extragalactic species in *Condonautas* (*Condomnauts*, 2013), and medical diplomacy in *Súperextragrande* (Super Extra Grande, 2014). Cuba's cyberpunk commu-nity today includes Vladimir Hernández (1966–), Michel Encinosa (1974–), Alejandro Rojas Medina (1984–), Jorge Enrique Lage (1979–), and others.

Dystopian futures predominate in Mexican science fiction, like Mauricio Molina's (1959–) *Tiempo lunar* (Lunar Time, 1993). Gerardo Porcayo's (1966–) *La primera calle de la soledad* (The First Street of Solitude, 1993), considered the first Mexican cyber-punk novel, features hacker Zorro navigating corporate espionage and a holy war be-tween religious sects orchestrated by an AI. Trujillo Muñoz imagines a mutant bat/vampire army in *Espantapájaros* (Scarecrows, 1999), and a technology that "loses" trains carrying Jews to concentration camps during World War Two in *Trenes perdidos en la niebla* (Trains Lost in the Fog, 2010). Paulo César Ramírez (1974–) sets two steampunk novels in during World War One, including *El Escuadrón Cinco* (Squadron Five, 2018), in which Rasputin, Lawrence of Arabia, Mata Hari, General George Patton, and Pancho Villa combat a nefarious organization led by libertine occultist Aleister Crowley. Ramírez also wrote a pulp western and cowrote, with Guillermo Moreno and J. R. del Río, *Sangre y Jade: Las tierras salvajes* (Blood and Jade: The Savage Lands, 2021), an epic pre-Columbian tale in a nascent fantasy genre, "Macuahuitl y Náhuatl," that aligns with Neomexicanista movements in art and design.

In Chile, steampunk and techno-shamanism dominate the current landscape. Sergio Meier's (1965–2009) *La segunda enciclopedia de Tlön* (The Second Encyclopedia of Tlön, 2007) brings Sir Isaac Newton together with Borges. Jorge Baradit's (1969–) "cyber-shamanist" *Ygdrasil* (2005) is a mercenary tale of interconnective bio-spiritualism, while in *Synco* (2008), Salvador Allende defeats Augusto Pinochet and founds the world's first "cyberdemocracy."

Brazil's early forays into cyberpunk (sometimes called *tupinipunk*) include Alfredo Sirkis's (1950–2020) *Silicone XXI* (1985) and Fausto Fawcett's (1957–) *Santa Clara Poltergeist* (1991). As Elizabeth Ginway explains, Brazilian writers draw on the primitivism, violence, and eroticism of avant-garde movements like *antropofagia*, infusing their narratives with indigenous and Afro-Brazilian religious imagery. *Afrofuturismo* centers the Afro-Brazilian experience itself: Fábio Kabral's (1980–) science fiction novels take place in Ketu Three, a New World city of "melanized" men and women who were abducted from their home planet by aliens. The city's psychic phones, flying cars, and food supply are powered by Yoruba spirit magic. *O caçador cibernético da rua 13* (The Cybernetic Hunter of 13th Street, 2017) features a cybermutant spirit-hunter. *A cientista guerreira do facão furioso* (The Warrior Scientist of the Mad Machete, 2019) introduces young engineer Jamila Olabamiji, who becomes a target of corrupt corporate interests and joins a clandestine organization plotting to overthrow the city's psychic elite. Luiz Bras's (Nelson de Oliveira, 1966–) *Distrito federal* (Federal District, 2014) also envisions cybermutants wreaking vengeance on venal officials and businessmen. An anomalous precursor to Afrofuturismo might be Argentinean Angélica Gorodischer's (1928–) *Opus dos* (Opus Two, 1967), in which black Argentineans (a population elided in Argentinean identity narrative) rule a post-apocalyptic city like Buenos Aires.

Contemporary Caribbean science fiction critiques the destruction wrought by predatory capitalism and climate change. Erick Mota's (1975–) *Habana Underguater* (2010) envisions the city run by Lucumí brotherhoods in competition with evangelical and Catholic corporations. Orishas control cyberspace; a hurricane permanently submerged half the city due to a shoddy Soviet-engineered sea-wall. In Rita Indiana's (1977–) *La mucama de Omicumlé* (*Tentacle*, 2015), servant Acilde Figueroa undergoes a sex change via a drug called Rainbow Brite, and the last surviving sea-anemone is grafted to his head, launching him into 1991, where the President of the Republic informs him that he is the son of sea-deity Olokún and his destiny is to save the country by preventing the destruction of its coral reefs. Acilde's quest requires Taino, African, and European collaboration in multiple temporal spaces to prevent a catastrophic climate event.

GENRE BENDERS

The exercise of criminal investigation requires both empirical experimentation and metaphysical speculation; the grotesque nature of human violence invites forays into horror, while its ubiquity provokes conjecture about ultimate causes outside individual, human control. Latin American authors have always challenged genre, and genre-bending has reached critical mass in the twenty-first century.

Pedro Cabiya's (1971–) novels merge gothic, horror, science and detective fiction, and are replete with extraterrestrial invaders, global and celestial mafias, and technocrats in an epic battle for the future of the Caribbean. A zombie working for Big Pharma gets murdered in *Malas hierbas* (*Wicked Weeds*, 2011); aliens invade San Juan in *Trance* (2008), and no one notices. In *Tercer mundo* (Third World, 2019), the San Juan neighborhood of Santurce represents the birthplace, laboratory, and graveyard of global capitalism, the "umbilicus" of San Puerto Rico, the Caribbean, and the Global South, occupied and coveted by partisans of three "ontological domains": the First world (avatars of Western tradition); the Second (inhabited by orishas and indigenous deities); and the Third, where the humans or "*impermanentes*" live.

Two of Guillermo Saccomanno's (1948–) novels have won the Hammett Prize for crime fiction. However, the predominant characteristic of his work is horror. *77* (2008), set in that dark year of Argentina's military rule, portrays the nightmarish experience of a gay high-school teacher as his friends and students disappear. *Cámara Gesell* (*Gesell Dome*, 2012) portrays a Nazi-founded seaside resort. *El oficinista* (*The Clerk*, 2010), which won the Biblioteca Breve Award given by the Seix Barral publishing house, is a dystopian neo-noir set in a city ravaged by late capitalism's climate degradation, surveillance, mass shootings, and a rampaging virus.

Mexican writers increasingly combine crime fiction with horror, fantasy, and science fiction. Yuri Herrera's (1970–) *Trabajos del Reino* (*Kingdom Cons*, 2004), *Señales que precederán al fin del mundo* (*Signs Preceding the End of the World*, 2009), and *La transmigración de los cuerpos* (*The Transmigration of Bodies*, 2013) place noir elements in a post-apocalyptic, plague-ridden, unspecified Mexican border city. Heriberto Yépez (1974–) addresses the human cost of drug trafficking in *Al otro lado* (The Other Side, 2008), a work that, like Buñuel's *Los olvidados* (*The Young and the Dammed*, 1950), presents a story of children as a national allegory. The inhabitants of the symbolic City of Paso are "chiquinarcos" and thugs addicted to phoco, a symbolic amalgam of cocaine, rat poison, and dust from the cadaver dumping-grounds surrounding the city. Hilario Peña's (1979–) Malasuerte trilogy (*Bad Luck in Tijuana*, 2009; *La mujer de los hermanos Reyna* (The Reyna Brothers' Woman, 2011); and *Juan Tres Dieciséis* (John Three Sixteen, 2014) presents a kitschy, chaotic Tijuana where Detective Tomás Peralta (named Bad Luck for his unfortunate red hair) confronts local crime boss Sandkühlcaán, an ancient extraterrestrial who feeds on Tijuana's suffering, vice, and crime. Peña has also written a historical Western novel and a "narco-Western," billed in the cover blurb as "¡Vaqueros vs. narcos!" or "Cowboys vs. Narcos!"

Hyper-prolific novelist and lawyer Ricardo Guzmán Wolffer's (1966–) *Que Dios se apiade de todos nosotros* (May God Have Mercy on Us All, 1993) may be the first hard-boiled science fiction. Sepu, his journalist investigator, appears in numerous stories alongside vampires, werewolves, and his vigilante friend El Milanesas, fighting off zombies and extraterrestrial cabaret dancers in a mostly postapocalyptic Mexico City. Solares's *Catorce comillos* (Fourteen Fangs, 2018) and *Muerte en el jardín de la luna* (Death in the Moon Garden, 2020) feature detective Pierre Le Noir of the Parisian Nocturnal Brigade solving supernatural crimes while rubbing shoulders with famous Surrealists and occultists.

Bernardo Esquinca's (1972–) *Belleza roja* (Red Beauty, 2005), features a tabloid photographer (also named Esquinca) haunted by the desire to touch up the visual drama of violated corpses (alluding to Enrique Metinides [1934–], the famous photographer for *¡Alarma!* and *La Prensa*). Other novels feature Casasola, a cultural reporter obliged to report gruesome and bizarre events for the tabloid *Semanario Sensacional* (Sensational Weekly). In *Octava plaga* (The Eighth Plague, 2011), a scientist in the natural history museum discovers a new kind of insect as Casasola investigates a series of ritualistic murders, including of some of his colleagues. His ex-wife seems to be developing insect-like habits, along with the scientist. Casasola investigates human remains deposited at pre-Columbian sites in *Toda la sangre* (All the Blood, 2013); *Carne de ataúd* (Coffin Meat, 2016) presents Casasola's journalist grandfather in pre-revolutionary Mexico, chasing a serial killer of women, at the dawn of the *nota roja* genre. In *Inframundo* (Underworld, 2017) Casasola collaborates with the Council of Dead Tabloid Journalists[12] to prevent a powerful text from the conquest from materializing in the present. Thematizing Mexico's pre-Columbian past and the city's cultural and historical heritage, Esquinca dialogues with the literature of the Great Death without reifying it.

The *nota roja* motif that permeates Esquinca's oeuvre is not casual; Mexico has been described as "a crime-tabloid country" since at least 2010 (Hernández Navarro).[13] What Esquinca brings to the equation is an anti-realist principle that alienates continual, banal acts of violence (so tenaciously detailed in Bolaño's *2666*) and occasionally drives them into the realm of the Gothic. Casasola's abiding sense of disquiet, abject descriptions of deformed bodies that nobody notices, background noises of something scratching in the garbage, meta-literary and intertextual colloquy (from Sabato to Bolaño), collateral deaths of investigative journalists, and above all the *nota roja* headlines punctuating the novels—all point to a recapitulation of the novela negra's transformations, and the absorption of horror, fantasy, and science fiction gives it renewed relevance.

Notes

1. "La novela de la violencia" (Tavares-dos-Santos et al. 141).
2. In the inter-war and post-war periods, the disillusion with US institutions portrayed in the hard-boiled genre was intensely bound up with the vocabularies of American exceptionalism, the American Dream, consumer culture, and American masculinity. Starting in the 1940s, hard-boiled fiction drove an explosion in American mass-market

paperbacks, and the proliferation of "paperback original" imprints, often dedicated to genre fiction, including Ace (science fiction), Harlequin (romance), and Avon (romance, fantasy, detective fiction, science fiction) (Corlett n.p.).

3. Buñuel's 1955 film adaptation is known in English as *The Criminal Life of Archibaldo de la Cruz*; the novel has not been translated.

4. J. M. Servín argues that the Mexican literary establishment elides day-to-day violence, favoring grand discourses of "'the Great Death'—of the literature that wins prizes and prestige." ['"la Gran Muerte'—de la literatura que gana premios y prestigios"] (Servín 94).

5. See López-Calvo, "Cardi's El American Way of Death" on Cold War ideologies in Cuban socialist detective fiction.

6. Many neopoliciaco authors adapt the genre for historical investigation. Taibo and Padura revisit political crimes—the deaths of Leon Trotsky and Che Guevara—or historical events important to national culture. Nicaraguan writer Sergio Ramírez places poet Rubén Darío in the midst of a conspiracy against the tyrannical Somoza regime.

7. The *Pedro Páramo* gag pays homage to Bolaño's 2004 *2066*, in which, when someone attributes the Juárez murders to the supposed Mexican fascination with death, another retorts, "I'm sick of Mexicans who talk and act as if this is all *Pedro Páramo*" (624) ("Estoy harta de los mexicanos que hablan y se comportan como si todo esto fuera *Pedro Páramo*" [779]).

8. "Para mí, hay tres puntos importantes para definir el éxito de una generación de literatura: uno, que sean traducidos universalmente; dos, que sean seguidos por un buen número de lectores, reflejándose en ventas de los libros; tres, que sean reconocidos por la crítica nacional y, desde luego, internacional" (Haghenbeck 276).

9. " querer establecer a toda costa unas características que, empleadas por los autores de forma recurrente, permitan juzgar fácilmente la calidad de las obras . . . [y] Por último, a las altas ventas de obras de escritores poco conocidos, es decir, no sancionados por el círculo de intelectuales de la capital del país y, con ellas, la entrada de las narconarrativas en la categoría de las superventas" (Margarita Jácome 28).

10. See Rachel Haywood Ferreira's *The Emergence of Latin American Science Fiction*, Elizabeth Ginway's *Brazilian Science Fiction*, and Luis Cano's *Los espíritus de la ciencia ficción* (The Spirits of Science Fiction).

11. See Molina-Gavilán, et. al., "Chronology of Latin American Science Fiction,1775–2005" for a full chronology of Latin American science fiction.

12. El Consejo de Periodistas de Nota Roja Muertos.

13. "Un país de nota roja."

WORKS CITED

Alarcón, Orfa. *Loba*. Alfaguara, 2019.

Alarcón, Orfa. *Perra brava*. Planeta, 2010.

Amorim, Enrique. *El asesino desvelado*. Emecé, 1945.

Ampuero, Roberto. *¿Quién mató a Cristián Kustermann?* Debolsillo, 2019.

Baradit, Jorge. *Synco*. Plaza & Janes, 2018.

Baradit, Jorge. *Ygdrasil*. Ediciones B, 2007.

Bermúdez, María Elvira. *Diferentes razones tiene la muerte*. Talleres Gráficos de la Nación, 1953.

Bernal, Rafael. *El complot mongol*. J. Mortiz, 1969.

Bernal, Rafael. *The Mongolian Conspiracy*. Translated by Katherine Silver. New Directions, 2013.

Bernal, Rafael. *His Name Was Death*. Translated by Kit Schluter. New Directions, 2021.

Bernal, Rafael. *Su nombre era muerte*. Cumbre, 1956.

Bolaño, Roberto. *2666*. Anagrama, 2004.

Bolaño, Roberto. *2666*. Translated by Natasha Wimmer. Farrar, Straus and Giroux, 2008.

Bras, Luiz. *Distrito federal: rapsódia*. Patuá Editora Livros São Amuletos, 2014.

Cabiya, Pedro. *Malas hierbas*. Zemí Book, 2011.

Cabiya, Pedro. *Tercer Mundo*. Kindle, Zemí Book, 2019.

Cabiya, Pedro. *Trance*. Norma, 2008.

Cabiya, Pedro. *Wicked Weeds: A Novel*. Translated by Jessica Ernst Powell. Mandel Vilar, 2016.

Calcagno, Francisco. *En busca del eslabón*. Letras Cubanas, 1983.

Calcagno, Francisco. *Historia de un muerto y noticias del otro mundo*. imp. del Directorio, 1875.

Cano, Luis C. *Los espíritus de la ciencia ficción: espiritismo, periodismo y cultura popular en las novelas de Eduardo Holmberg, Francisco Miralles y Pedro Castera*. U.N.C. Department of Romance Studies, 2017.

Castera, Pedro. *Querens*. Talleres Linotipográficos "La Patria," 1923.

Chandler, Raymond. *The Long Goodbye*. Houghton Mifflin, 1954.

Chavarría, Daniel. *Allá ellos*. Letras Cubanas, 1991.

Chavarría, Daniel. *Joy*. Letras Cubanas, 1982.

Chaviano, Daína. *Fábulas de una abuela extraterrestre*. Océano, 2002.

Cockrell, Eddie. "The Man of the Year." *Variety*, February 25, 2003. https://variety.com/2003/film/reviews/the-man-of-the-year-1200543152/

Corlett, Oliver. "A Short History of Paperbacks – IOBA Standard." *The Journal of the Independent Online Booksellers Association*, vol. 2, no. 3, December 2001, p. 9

Collazo, Miguel. *The Journey*. Translated by David Frye. Restless Books, 2020.

Collazo, Miguel. *El Viaje*. Letras Cubanas, 1981.

Correa, Hugo. *Los altísimos*. Alfaguara, 2010.

Díaz Eterović, Ramón. *La ciudad está triste*. LOM, 2013.

Díez, Rolo *Luna de escarlata*. Roca, 1994.

Díez, Rolo *Matamujeres*. Resistencia, 2017.

Díez, Rolo *Mato y voy editado con Gatos de azotea*. Ediciones B, 1992.

Díez, Rolo *Tequila Blue*. Translated by Nick Caistor. Bitter Lemon, 2012.

Díez, Rolo. *La vida que me doy*. Conaculta-INBA, 2000.

Esquinca, Bernardo. *Belleza roja*. Fondo de Cultura Económica, 2013.

Esquinca, Bernardo. *Carne de ataúd*. Almadía, 2016.

Esquinca, Bernardo. *Inframundo*. Almadía, 2017.

Esquinca, Bernardo. *La octava plaga*. Almadía, 2011.

Esquinca, Bernardo. *Toda la sangre*. Almadía, 2013.

Etcheves, Florencia. *Cornelia*. Booket, 2019.

Etcheves, Florencia. *La hija del campeón*. Booket, 2019.

Etcheves, Florencia. *La virgen en tus ojos*. Planeta, 2020.

Fawcett, Fausto. *Santa Clara poltergeist*. Eco, 1991.

Fernández, Bernardo (BEF). *Azul cobalto*. Océano Exprés, 2016.

Fernández, Bernardo (BEF). *Cuello blanco*. Grijalbo, 2013.

Fernández, Bernardo (BEF). *Hielo negro*. Grijalbo, 2011.

Fernández, Bernardo (BEF). *Tiempo de alacranes*. J. Mortiz, 2005.

Fonseca, Rubem. *A grande arte*. Bertrand, 2013.

Fonseca, Rubem. *High Art*. Harper & Row, 1986.

Franco, Jorge. *Rosario Tijeras*. Mondadori, 2002.

Franco, Jorge. *Rosario Tijeras*. Translated by Gregory Rabassa. Seven Stories Press, 2005.

Fuentes, Carlos. *La cabeza de la hidra*. J. Mortiz, 1978.

Fuentes, Carlos. *The Hydra Head*. Translated by Margaret Sayers Peden. Farrar, Straus, Giroux, 1978.

García Márquez, Gabriel. *Chronicle of a Death Foretold*. Translated by Gregory Rabassa. Knopf, 1983.

García Márquez, Gabriel. *Cien años de soledad*. Sudamericana, 1967.

García Márquez, Gabriel. *Crónica de una muerte anunciada*. La Oveja Negra, 1981.

García Márquez, Gabriel. *One Hundred Years of Solitude*. Translated by Gregory Rabassa. Avon Books, 1971.

Ginway, Elizabeth. *Brazilian Science Fiction*. Bucknell, 2004.

Ginway, M. Elizabeth, and Andrew Brown. *Latin American Science Fiction: Theory and Practice*. Palgrave Macmillan, 2012.

Gorodischer, Angélica. *Opus dos*. Minotauro, 1967.

Guzmán Wolffer, Ricardo. *Que Dios se apiade de todos nosotros*. Consejo Nacional para la Cultura y las Artes, 1993.

Haghenbeck, F. G. *Bitter Drink*. Translated by Tanya Huntington Hyde, AmazonCrossing, 2012.

Haghenbeck, F. G. *El caso tequila*. Editorial Oceano de Mexico, 2016.

Haghenbeck, F. G. *Trago amargo*. Roca, 2009.

Haywood Ferreira, Rachel. *The Emergence of Latin American Science Fiction*. Wesleyan UP, 2011.

Helú, Antonio. *La obligación de asesinar*. Editorial Novaro-México, 1947.

Hernández Luna, Juan. *Cadáver de ciudad*. Zeta Bolsillo, 2008.

Hernández Luna, Juan. *Tabaco para el puma*. Roca, 1997.

Hernández Navarro, Luis. "País de nota roja." *La Jornada*, June 1, 2010. https://www.jornada.com.mx/2010/06/01/opinion/019a1pol

Herrera, Yuri. *Kingdom Cons*. Translated by Lisa Dillman. And Other Stories, 2017.

Herrera, Yuri. *Señales que precederán al fin del mundo*. Periférica, 2010.

Herrera, Yuri. *Signs Preceding the End of the World*. Translated by Lisa Dillman. And Other Stories, 2015.

Herrera, Yuri. *Trabajos del reino*. Periférica, 2004.

Herrera, Yuri. *La transmigración de los cuerpos*. Periférica, 2013.

Herrera, Yuri. *The Transmigration of Bodies*. Translated by Lisa Dillman. And Other Stories, 2016.

Holmberg, Eduardo Ladislao. *Viaje maravilloso del señor Nic-Nac al planeta Marte*. Biblioteca Nacional, 2007.

Ibargüengoitia, Jorge. *Las muertas*. J. Mortiz, 1977.

Ibargüengoitia, Jorge. *The Dead Girls*. Translated by Asa Zatz. Picador, 2020.

Indiana Hernández, Rita. *La mucama de Omicunlé*. Periférica, 2015.

Indiana Hernández, Rita. *Tentacle*. Translated by Achy Obejas. And Other Stories, 2018.

Jácome, Margarita. "¿Narco-novela o novela del narcotráfico? Apuntes sobre el caso colombiano." *Narcoficciones en México y Colombia*, edited by Marco Kunz and Brigitte Andriaenssen, Iberoamericana, 2016, pp. 27–52.

Kabral, Fábio. *A cientista guerreira do facão furioso*. Malê, 2019.

Kabral, Fábio. *O caçador cibernético da rua 13*. Malê, 2017.

López-Calvo, Ignacio. "Cardi's *El American Way of Death*: factography and the Cuban detective novel as Cold War ideology." *Global Cold War Literatures: Western, Eastern and Postcolonial Perspectives*, edited by Andrew N. Hammond, Routledge, 2012, pp. 30–42.

Meier Frei, Sergio. *La segunda enciclopedia de Tlön*. Puerto de Escape, 2007.

Melo, Patrícia. *Fogo-fátuo*. Rocco LTDA., 2014.

Melo, Patrícia. *The Killer*. Translated by Clifford E. Landers. Bloomsbury, 1998.

Melo, Patrícia. *Lost World*. Bloomsbury, 2010.

Melo, Patrícia. *O matador*. Rocco, 2009.

Melo, Patrícia. *Mulheres Empilhadas*. LeYa, 2019.

Melo, Patrícia. *Mundo perdido*. Rocco, 2010.

Mendoza, Élmer. *The Acid Test*. Translated by Mark Fried. MacLehose, 2017.

Mendoza, Élmer. *Asesinato en el Parque Sinaloa*. Random House, 2018.

Mendoza, Élmer. *El asesino solitario*. Tusquets, 1999.

Mendoza, Élmer. *Balas de plata*. Tusquets, 2008.

Mendoza, Élmer. *Cóbraselo caro*. Tusquets, 2005.

Mendoza, Élmer. *Efecto tequila*. Tusquets, 2004.

Mendoza, Élmer. *The Name of the Dog*. Translated by Mark Fried. MacLehose, 2019.

Mendoza, Élmer. *Nombre de perro*. Tusquets, 2012.

Mendoza, Élmer. *La prueba del ácido*. Tusquets, 2010.

Mendoza, Élmer. *Silver Bullets*. Translated by Mark Fried. MacLehose, 2016.

Miralles, Francisco. *Desde Júpiter. Curioso viaje de un santiaguino magnetizado*. Impr. Cervantes,1886.

Molina-Gavilán, Yolanda, et al. "Chronology of Latin American Science Fiction, 1775–2005." *Science Fiction Studies*, vol. 34, no. 3, 2007, pp. 369–431.

Mond, F. *¿Dónde está mi Habana?* Letras Cubanas, 1985.

Mota Pérez, Erick. J. *La Habana Underguater, Completa: Novela y Cuentos*. Atom, 2010.

Marga Nelken. "Argentinoir." *El Mundo*, January 19, 2012. https://www.elmundo.es/elmundo/2012/01/19/novelanegra/1326962848.html

Nogueras, Luis Rogelio. *Y si muero mañana*. Letras Cubanas, 2001.

Ortega, Gregorio. *Kappa 15*. Letras Cubanas, 1982.

Padura Fuentes, Leonardo. *Havana Black*. Translated by Peter R. Bush. Bitter Lemon, 2006.

Padura Fuentes, Leonardo. *Havana Blue*. Translated by Peter R. Bush. Bitter Lemon, 2006.

Padura Fuentes, Leonardo. *Havana Fever*. Translated by Peter R. Bush. Bitter Lemon, 2009.

Padura Fuentes, Leonardo. *La neblina del ayer*. Tusquets, 2005.

Padura Fuentes, Leonardo. *Paisaje de otoño*. Tusquets, 2016.

Padura Fuentes, Leonardo. *Pasado perfecto*. Tusquets, 2000.

Padura Fuentes, Leonardo. *La transparencia del tiempo*. Tusquets, 2018.

Padura Fuentes, Leonardo. *The Transparency of Time*. Translated by Anna Kushner. Farrar, Straus and Giroux, 2021.

Peña, Hilario. *Juan Tres Dieciséis*. Random House, 2014.

Peña, Hilario. *La mujer de los hermanos Reyna*. Mondadori, 2011.

Peña, Hilario. *Malasuerte en Tijuana*. Mondadori, 2009.

Pérez-Reverte, Arturo. *The Queen of the South*. Translated by Andrew Hurley. Penguin/Plume, 2005.

Pérez-Reverte, Arturo. *La reina del sur*. Alfaguara, 2002.

Piñeiro, Claudia. *All Yours*. Translated by Miranda France. Bitter Lemon, 2012.

Piñeiro, Claudia. *Betibú*. Alfaguara, 2011.

Piñeiro, Claudia. *Betty Boo*. Translated by Miranda France. Bitter Lemon, 2016.

Piñeiro, Claudia. *A Crack in the Wall*. Translated by Miranda France. Bitter Lemon, 2013.

Piñeiro, Claudia. *Catedrales*. Alfaguara, 2021.

Piñeiro, Claudia. *Las grietas de Jara*. Alfaguara, 2009.

Piñeiro, Claudia. *Las maldiciones*. Alfaguara, 2017.

Piñeiro, Claudia. *Thursday Night Widows*. Translated by Miranda France. Bitter Lemon, 2009.

Piñeiro, Claudia. *Tuya*. Alfaguara, 2008.

Piñeiro, Claudia. *Las viudas de los jueves*. Alfaguara, 2010.

Porcayo Villalobos, Gerardo. *La primera calle de la soledad*. Planeta, 2020.

Ramírez, Paulo César. *El Escuadrón Cinco: contra la terrible Orden de los Thelemitas*. Wave Books, 2018.

Ramírez, Sergio. *El cielo llora por mí*. Alfaguara, 2008.

Ramírez, Sergio. *Ya nadie llora por mí*. Alfaguara, 2017.

Ramírez Heredia, Rafael. *Trampa de metal*. Universo, 1979.

Restrepo, Laura. *Leopard in the Sun*. Translated by Stephen A. Lytle. HarperCollins, 2002.

Restrepo, Laura. *El leopardo al sol*. HarperCollins, 2005.

Río, J. R. del, Guillermo Moreno, and Paulo César Ramírez. *Sangre y jade: las tierras salvajes*, Tres Nahuales, 2021.

Roncagliolo, Santiago. *Abril rojo*. Alfaguara, 2006.

Roncagliolo, Santiago. *La pena máxima*. Alfaguara, 2014.

Roncagliolo, Santiago. *Red April*. Atlantic, 2018.

Rulfo, Juan. *Pedro Páramo*. Edited by José C. González Boixo. Cátedra, 1988.

Rulfo, Juan. *Pedro Páramo*. Translated by Margaret Sayers Peden. Grove Press, 1994.

Saccomanno, Guillermo. *77*. Planeta, 2008.

Saccomanno, Guillermo. *77*. Translated by Andrea G. Labinger. Open Letter, 2019.

Saccomanno, Guillermo. *Cámara Gesell*. Planeta, 2012.

Saccomanno, Guillermo. *Gesell Dome*. Translated by Andrea G. Labinger. Open Letter, 2016.

Sepúlveda, Luis. *El fin de la historia*. Tusquets, 2018.

Sepúlveda, Luis. *The Name of a Bullfighter*. Translated by Suzanne Ruta. Harcourt Brace, 1997.

Sepúlveda, Luis. *Nombre de torero*. Tusquets, 2017.

Servín, J. M. "¡Los alarmados de Alarma!" *Nexos*, vol. 35, 2013, p. 428.

Sirkis, Alfredo. *Silicone XXI*. Record, 1985.

Solares, Martín. *The Black Minutes*. Translated by Aura Estrada and John Pluecker. Black Cat, 2010.

Solares, Martín. *Catorce colmillos*. Random House, 2018.

Solares, Martín. *Los minutos negros*. Mondadori, 2006.

Solares, Martín. *Muerte en el jardín de la luna*. Random House, 2020.

Taibo II, Paco Ignacio. *La bicicleta de Leonardo*. Joaquín Mortiz, 1993.

Taibo II, Paco Ignacio. *Días de combate*. Planeta, 2004.

Taibo II, Paco Ignacio. *Leonardo's Bicycle*. Warner, 1996.

Taibo II, Paco Ignacio. *La vida misma*. Júcar, 1988.

Tapia y Rivera, Alejandro. *Póstumo el transmigrado: historia de un hombre que resucitó en el cuerpo de su enemigo, y su Segunda Parte, Póstumo el envirginiado: historia de un hombre que se coló en el cuerpo de una mujer*. Edited by Roberto Ramos-Perea. Publicaciones Gaviota, 2008.

Tavares-dos-Santos, José-Vicente, et al. "The Novel of Violence in Latin American Literature." *Globalization and the State in Contemporary Crime Fiction: A World of Crime*, edited by Andrew Pepper and David Schmid, Palgrave Macmillan UK, 2016, pp. 141–57.

Trujillo Muñoz, Gabriel. *Espantapájaros*. Lectorum, 1999.

Trujillo Muñoz, Gabriel. *Trenes perdidos en la niebla*. Jus, 2010.

Usigli, Rodolfo. *Ensayo de un crimen*. V. Siglos, 1980.

Vallejo, Fernando. *Our Lady of the Assassins*. Translated by Paul Hammond. Serpent's Tail, 2001.

Vallejo, Fernando. *La Virgen de los sicarios*. Pinto de Lectura, 2006.

Vásquez, Juan Gabriel. *El ruido de las cosas al caer*. Alfaguara, 2011.

Vásquez, Juan Gabriel. *The Sound of Things Falling*. Riverhead, 2013.

Villalobos, Juan Pablo. *Down the Rabbit Hole*. Translated by Adam Thirlwell. And Other Stories, 2013.

Villalobos, Juan Pablo. *Fiesta en la madriguera*. Anagrama, 2010.

Yépez, Heriberto. *Al otro lado*. Planeta, 2008.

Yoss. *A Planet for Rent*. Translated by David L. Frye. Restless Books, 2015.

Yoss. *Condomnauts*. Translated by David L. Frye. Restless Books, 2018.

Yoss. *Condonautas*. Abril, 2013.

Yoss. *Se alquila un planeta*. Restless Books, 2014.

Yoss. *Super Extra Grande*. Translated by David L. Frye. Restless Books, 2016.

Yoss. *Súper extra grande*. Apache, 2018.

CHAPTER 28

THE EXPERIMENTAL NOVEL IN LATIN AMERICA

ANDREAS KURZ

INTRODUCTION

THE past 150 years of literary development brought an impossible to encompass number of manifestoes, proposals, discussions, and polemics that tried to orient and sometimes fix the present and the future of how we write and read fiction. They also tried to find ways that would enable us to continue writing literary texts without actually knowing what literature is, to adapt the literary discourse to a rapidly developing social, ideological, and technical environment. In the twentieth century, literature is moving continually and there cannot exist a group of authors, a pre-formulated aesthetics, or a manifesto that did not instantly provoke a counter-reaction, counter-manifesto, or counter-aesthetics.

The Routledge Companion to Experimental Literature (2012) is an excellent survey of avant-garde tendencies in literature. It has a lot to say about the opening of tradition to something new. On the other hand, it rarely writes about the function of experiment in literature, nor does Julie Armstrong in her creative writing guide *Experimental Fiction* (2014). I am not criticizing. The terms experimental, avant-garde, modernist, and postmodernist literature have become close relatives, nearly synonyms. But what does experiment mean in literature? Does it have the same meaning in Latin America as in Europe and North America? Is there a specifically Latin American experimental novel? Are experiments in Latin American literature a transcultural phenomenon? Of course, I cannot answer these questions, but I will try to start a discussion and to analyze a few examples of what could be called Latin American experimental novels.

What Could Experiment Mean
in Literature?

Experiments are an essential part of the scientific world. In Karl Popper's epistemological system, they are an important element of the scientific World 3, the world that deals practically with abstract and always hypothetical theories. Yet, they are not the essence of science, nor is observation. Science and knowledge do not start with observation and experiment, but with a theory that has to be falsified by the aid of observation and experiment. In *Unended Quest* (1974), Popper states that his understanding of scientific work was changed by Einstein's approach to the functioning of experiment: "Einstein was looking for crucial experiments whose agreement with his predictions would by no means establish his theory; while a disagreement, as he was the first to stress, would show his theory to be untenable" (39). An experiment neither proves nor disapproves a theory: it only shows the need for an alternative theory, renowned observation, and modified experiments. In this sense, an experiment has no cognoscitive value at all, but shows the limits of our abilities to know and understand our world. Popper refers to crucial experiments theoretically established by Francis Bacon. This type of experiment permits an infinite number of inferences, deductions, and solutions (Ferrater Mora 1139), none of which can aspire to represent truth or solve tangible real-world problems, none of which encounters itself, at the same time, in direct contradiction to truth or is incapable to solve real-world problems. Could experiments based on the creative use of language in fiction be of this kind?

The scientific world of the Austrian-born philosopher reflects continuous movement, a highly dynamic and unstable development, whereas Thomas Kuhn's has stable phases, the accepted and working paradigms. However, Kuhn introduces the idea of revolution in science (6–8), a concept normally used to describe drastic political and social changes that may be based on scientific encounters, but that do not affect science itself as a system. Often motivated by sheer accident, experiments impulse changes in the reigning paradigm and are one of many potential starting points of a new paradigm that will establish itself in all existentially relevant fields, including art. Experiment, in this sense, would be a way to make visible a new paradigm, not objective reality. It would renew and define science, not the world. Bray, Gibbons, and McHale find the same self-referential process at work in experimental literature: "Experiment is one of the engines of literary change and renewal; it is literature's way of reinventing itself" (1). Could experiment based on the creative use of language in fiction also be of this kind?

I am aware of the differences between the scientific and literary discourses, but both are language-dependent and embedded in a specific historical and social environment. Their purpose is a refined knowledge of the world and the ontological position an individual occupies in it. This dependency is more visible in literature, where language is simultaneously the tool and the aim of experiment. However, as we will see later, Lyotard and others stress that it is also inherent to natural sciences, which need language to describe and communicate their work. As Popper stated in the frame of the "Positivismusstreit" (positivist dispute) of the 1960s, in this context, there cannot exist any differences between scientifical, social, or artistically oriented discourses.

What seems to be irrelevant to art and the creative work with language gains crucial importance in the history of Western literature, if we consider that the experimental character of poetry and narrative is often used as a qualitative criterion to measure the degree of innovation of a text. Nevertheless, there seems to be critical unanimity about the temporal limits of experiment in literature, about a spiral movement in which today's experiment is absorbed by tradition only to incite new experiments. This "tradition of rupture" simulates the process of Popper's epistemology. I cite a random definition included in the *Literary Dictionary* compiled by Gero von Wilpert, a highly popular critical tool for German students and scholars especially in the 1970s and 1980s, when experimental literature seems to reach a high point: "Experiment . . . in literature [means] the practical testing of new forms and manners of expression, and of content, testing their effectivity and possibilities as testimonies of a new human understanding." Literary experiments are always "provisional," but they will be "legitimized in and by established art as the vanguard of modern poetry" (Von Wilpert 254). Another labyrinthine definition that reformulates a commonplace: novel and pioneering tendencies sooner or later will be part of the tradition. "Today's most radical experiments often become tomorrow's conventions" (353) is the succinct formula found by Alber, Nielsen, and Richardson in 2012.

NINETEENTH-CENTURY EXPERIMENTATION AND LATIN AMERICAN FOUNDATIONAL NARRATIVES

The first writer to consciously introduce the term experimentation, borrowed from medical and natural sciences, in his creative literary work was Émile Zola, but he did not intend to write experimental novels. Zola published his essay "Le roman expérimental" (The Experimental Novel) in 1880. The beginnings of his naturalistic cycle about the Rougon-Macquart family date back over ten years. The findings and hypotheses of "The Experimental Novel" cannot be interpreted as the underlying principle that triggers and structures a literary text, as they are themselves the result of this text, of an ongoing experiment with language aiming to language. On the other hand, the out-comings can reshape Zola's approach to his creative work and modulate his use of language. The chronological order shows that experimentation is intrinsic to literary texts. Zola insists that an author observes and experiments consecutively: "we can easily say that the novelist is equally an observer and an experimentalist" (8). Observation gives him the facts, then he arranges his fictional characters in specific circumstances and introduces the experiment consisting of an unexpected and disturbing fact.

Of course, this is not the kind of experiment we use to have in mind when we talk about twentieth-century experimental literature, because Zola seems to be unaware of the fact that the final aim of his experiments is language, the text that he is writing. I insist: this type of experiment can be found in all literature. It can also be found in Latin American narrative since its very beginnings.

Nineteenth-century foundational narratives produced across the continent provide some illuminating examples. As Doris Sommer, in her groundbreaking study *Foundational Fictions* (1991), convincingly asserts, marriage and varying romantic constellations between potential couples represent political and economic options for the future of the developing Latin American nations. Sommer showed "an erotics of politics" that simultaneously generated and was generated by those texts. She proved "how a variety of novel national ideals are all ostensibly grounded in 'natural' heterosexual love and in the marriages that provided a figure for apparently nonviolent consolidation during internecine conflicts at midcentury" (6). Ignacio Manuel Altamirano's *Clemencia* (1869) offers different prospects between a female and a masculine pair: Clemencia and Isabel on the one hand, Valle and Flores on the other. Their possible marriages represent treason, patriotism, and Mexico's political and cultural dependency from France, England, Germany, or its political and cultural autonomy. The question is: what happens if? Ultimately, there are no marriages in *Clemencia*, only unfulfillable and counterproductive romantic dreams with violent outcomes. But in nineteenth-century Latin American foundational narrative, this is experiment: What happens if A and B, and sometimes C and D, are placed to act in a specific historical context? What happens if they come together, what if they repulse each other? As in Zola, the author does not control the experiment; he is, rather, the observer who describes the results. Most importantly, he is also the figure in the narrative that marks the experiment as being linguistic and literary, such is the case when Altamirano's omniscient narrator inserts direct references to the stories of E. Th. A. Hoffmann that construct Altamirano's novel (4).

What happens when a feminized slave called Sab imposes himself with his physical and moral strength on a male and Spanish dominated Cuban environment at the beginning of the nineteenth century? Whom could he marry, and which political outcomes could this marriage produce? This truly exceptional experiment proposed by Gertrudis Gómez de Avellaneda in her novel *Sab* (1841) cannot have any other outcome in the eyes of a nineteenth-century reader: Sab has to die before the experiment starts. The consequences only we, readers of the novel's future, can appreciate. In the described sense, Gómez de Avellaneda's work is experimental, but of course not consciously so, since it does not reveal or expose its experimental character, as the twentieth-century narrative will do; it only experiments.

Postmodernist Experiment in Latin America?

In his 1968 novel *62/Modelo para armar* (*62: A Model Kit*), Julio Cortázar draws on a playful example of this type of experiment: "Polanco dedicated himself to his scientific studies. He had submerged the electric shaver in a pot of porridge and studied the behavior of these heterogenous entities. Rumbling sounds could be heard and sometimes a portion of porridge flew through the air but did not adhere itself to the ceiling. Instead, it fell on the floor with a lugubrious snap. It was a chaste and enduring spectacle."[1] Cortázar's work is in itself an experimental novel. Understandably, he can see experiment as a chaste spectacle, as some kind of show without reference to the tangible world. Later in the novel, Polanco, Calac, and "my paredro," a strange non-existing but acting and talking figure, will repeat the experiment on a larger scale, where a lake will take the role of the porridge. The outcome will be the same: a spectacular movement in circles that leads to nowhere but is noisy, and dirty, and, in a literal sense, moving: a representation of the writing process that on the next level, the ontological one, could represent the process of living.

The experiment in Cortázar is not only a symbol, but also points to the creative process as such. The preromantic German philosopher Johann Georg Hamann cites, in his close-to-illegible *Aesthetica in nuce* (1762), the earl of Roscommon to underline his irrational understanding of an art that has to "shew(s) the stuff, but not the workman's skill" (69). Cortazar's experiments in *62: A Model Kit* brilliantly display the workman's skill, but they try to hide the *stuff* from the reader's eye. Cortázar experiments, as did Altamirano, Gómez de Avellaneda, and many others in the nineteenth century; however, he knows that he is doing so and that his experiments are targeting language and literature as autonomous and dynamic objects. Their structure and their specificities, which used to operate as an invisible engine of literary work, are now transferred to the surface and made visible. The inside-out movement I have just described and the development of literary experiment it triggered are possibly the most important feature of twentieth-century postmodernist writing, but I am convinced that they do not make Cortázar a Latin American postmodernist experimental writer who closely follows European models. However, he experiments.

By now the philosophical, scientific, and literary discussion of postmodernism is itself a tradition based on more than half a century of text production. A closer look at Jean François Lyotard's sharply written text *The Postmodern Condition: A Report on Knowledge* (1979) could be useful to explore the relationship between the shift from modernism to postmodernism in the philosophical worldview after World War II, as well as a possible analogous shift noticeable in the techniques and scope of creative literary production. The French philosopher sees postmodernism as a consequence of a loss of confidence in "metanarratives" originated by modern science and its demystifying and dehumanizing discoveries (XXIV). At the same time, science itself operates with metanarratives to legitimize its methods and results. That means there are two opposing kinds of knowledge: the scientific, based on provable facts, and the narration oriented, based on the vagueness, openness, and elasticity of language. Scientific knowledge is a denotative narrative—but still a narrative—that paradoxically excludes narrative knowledge based on connotation. Lyotard's definition is harsh: narrative knowledge has to include scientific knowledge but is devaluated as primitive and inaccurate by the latter (27) that, nonetheless, makes use of the former. He resumes the paradox: "Scientific knowledge cannot know and make known that it is the true knowledge without resorting to the other, narrative, kind of knowledge, which from its point of view is no knowledge at all" (29). The narrative that should legitimize science delegitimizes it because the basis of narrative knowledge is tautology and truism: something has to be science because a narrative that is not science says so (39). This represents an intriguing labyrinth that increases ontological, ideological, and epistemological uncertainties in many spheres of modern life, including literature.

In the "Appendix" to *The Postmodern Condition*, Lyotard deals directly with art and literature in a postmodern ontological context. He thinks that postmodernist writing abandons experiment because it wants to either restore a lost order of things or order the chaos left by the above-cited paradox. At first his judgment sounds devastating for postmodernist literature: "Artists and writers must be brought back into the bosom of the community, or at least, if the latter is considered to be ill, they must be assigned the task of healing it . . . for all those writers nothing is more urgent than to liquidate the heritage of the avant-garde" (73). However, at second reading experiment returns to postmodernism, because Lyotard admits that the artists "devote themselves to making an allusion to the unpresentable by means of visible presentations" (78). Modern science revealed things that cannot be represented anymore, and it made the representation of other metaphysical and unscientific things taboo. But, despite taboo, they want to be represented. It follows the need for a new use of language and narrative structure, of new experiments that make visible the invisible and unrepresentable. The laying open of the structure, the inside out movement we have seen in the example taken from Cortázar's *62: A Model Kit*, is one of those experiments, maybe the most significant one in postmodern literature worldwide.

Lyotard knows that this is a great opportunity for a narrative that could have been "lost" but survives as an ontological necessity (41). This reminds us immediately of the strange survival of religious thinking in modernist literature from Baudelaire onwards. In his essay on Baudelaire, Paul Bourget writes: "Whereas man no longer has the same intellectual need to believe, he has retained the need to feel as in the days when he believed."[2] A postmodernist paraphrase would read: if man has lost the intellectual need to understand his world, he has preserved the need of feeling as if he could still understand it. Literature and art could satisfy this need with their experiments. I am not sure if Lyotard would approve of my comparison with early modernist literature, but I think that his assertion that a "work can become modern only if it is first postmodern" (79) points in the same direction. Postmodernism comes not after modernism or modernity, on the contrary: it precedes them if we understand our immediate present as the modern. Postmodernism points to the future, as did Baudelaire's and Bourget's modernism because it is prior to something still unknown. This time paradox reveals what Matei Calinescu, in his *Five Faces of Modernity* (1977), describes as the transient character of all literature and art (66–67). They situate themselves in an area that refers to the past and the future at the same time, trying to identify and, in an ideal case, shape an intangible present, an area that Brian McHale names "the zone." Transience calls for experimentation. The ontological experimental character of literature cannot be altered; the form and directedness of experiments, nevertheless, changes from modernity to postmodernity.

In *Postmodernist Fiction* (1987), McHale finds clear criteria that enable us to distinguish between modernist and postmodernist literature. He does not highlight experiment as one of them, which is understandable because experiment is intrinsic to both ways of writing, as long as it aims to narrative, language, or, as Lyotard would put it, narrative-oriented knowledge. The main criterium that separates McHale's postmodernist from modernist fiction is philosophical. He resorts to Jakobson's concept of "dominants" and establishes epistemology as the dominant of modernist fiction, while ontology is that of postmodernism. Modernism questions and tries to transgress the boundaries of knowledge, while postmodernism does the same for the boundaries of being (9–10). McHale outlines the technique we called inside out as essential, if not generative, for postmodern literature. The structure that used to be invisible in the background of text now occupies its visible surface and, in this way, imitates "the complex ontological landscape of our experiences" (39). In this sense, postmodernism recuperates the long-lost value of mimesis for creative literature. A text is still able to imitate or analyze its real-world surroundings, but it does so not via description, but rather, by exposing its own skeleton and hoping that the total visibility of creation can bring some light into the complexity of a reality based on a series of logical, scientific, and political paradoxes. This form of writing is ontological because it reproduces world and life as such by questioning the sense, boundaries, and especially the tangibility and reality of both.

Brian McHale's analytic ideas work and can be tested on a vast number of European and North American literary texts. Nevertheless, their validity in Latin American literature is questionable. He himself uses Latin American works to illustrate his thesis: Jorge Luis Borges, and Carlos Fuentes's *Terra Nostra* as the prototype of postmodernist historic novel, and Cortázar's *Rayuela* (*Hopscotch*), *62: A Model Kit*, or Guillermo Cabrera Infante's *Tres tristes tigres* (*Three Trapped Tigers*). Despite the presence of Latin American postmodernist or experimental narrative in his study, McHale seems to incorporate it in a European- and North American-dominated critical discourse. Maybe he is right to do so, as some of the critical concepts produced in Latin America, such as "realismo mágico" (magical realism) and "lo real maravilloso" (the marvelous real), clearly address a European and North American readership. Yet I also think that trying to appreciate a separate Latin American path in postmodernist and experimental narrative could be useful.

Julio Cortázar's Experiments

McHale establishes the idea of a "zone," an elusive place in many postmodernist texts, existing and non-existing simultaneously, possibly the place where a book and its stories are actually created and develop. In Julio Cortázar's *62: A Model Kit*, there is, named as such, a zone. At the beginning of the novel Juan, or maybe "my paredros" or another narrator, reflects (or writes or says aloud): "in the zone one will have to start narrating, saying something because all of them are waiting for you to start narrating, the always restless and slightly hostile huddle at the beginning of a narrative. Somehow all of them are waiting for you to start narrating in the zone, anywhere in the zone, not knowing where because of so many places and nights and friends."[3] The zone is and is not a tangible place (a coffeehouse, a restaurant, a street corner), crowded or not, silent or noisy. It is as much the creative space, as the space where stories, lives, and characters are placed to act and react in different experimental constellations: what happens if . . . ? The zone's boundaries are not the pages or the covers of the book; they show the reality and tangibility of fiction and the fictionality and intangibility of reality. Three of Cortázar's four novels published in his lifetime form one zone, but the latter cannot be limited to the boundaries of three concrete books, because these are constantly removed, replaced, and rewritten by the readers who are, in postmodernist writing and criticism, the true center of literary production.

62: A Model Kit is the realization of Morelli's novelistic project in chapter 62 of *Rayuela*. Cortázar's Morelli plans a text that could imitate the work of neurotransmission that produces thought and feeling in our brains, a novel that would end with the "final mutation" of man who is seen only as an instrument of destiny that struggles to come to existence "in the midst of words and conduct and happiness sprinkled with blood and other kinds of rhetoric as this one."[4] The protagonists of the novel would not have the liberty of action or decision-making. Their author would be more an observer than a producer. He would place his figures in different environments, mostly unconnected: He would construct experimental constellations and watch their outcomes from a certain distance. *62: A Model Kit* works in this way. The novel unites and reunites a group of Argentine, French, and English protagonists in four cities: Paris, London, Vienna, and Buenos Aires. Temporal and spatial distance does not matter too much in this context. The figures rise out of the zone and return to it, they find themselves in a place somewhere between the actual settings of the story, if a story exists. Cortázar, in a short foreword, refers again to the intentions of Morelli in *Rayuela* when he writes: "aggression, regression and progression are also connatural to the intentions sketched out in the final paragraphs of chapter 62 of *Hopscotch*. They explain the title of this book and maybe will be carried out in its course."[5] It is necessary to highlight the word "maybe" in this sentence. Cortázar probably wrote the foreword after finishing the novel, but even then, he is not the master of his creatures, he is not an omniscient godlike writer as those of nineteenth-century narrative. It is destiny and chance that act in the novel and guide the figures, a procedure more alike to evolutionary bricolage than to neurotransmission.

Nevertheless, there are various interferences of a godlike author. Cortázar's protagonists call them "my paredros." The figure is an illusion, a fiction within the fiction, but it is an acting, guiding, and powerful illusion that seems to appear when the characters, especially "the tartars" Polanco and Calac, reach a narrative and ontological dead-end. "My paredros" is an author, but he/she/*they* are not the authors, nor the narrators, nor an alter ego of Cortázar. *They* could be a link between a tangible world and the intangible zone, one more element that reinforces the autonomous and self-developing plot of *62: A Model Kit*. What distinguishes Cortazar´s experiments from French-oriented postmodernist ones is that *they* could also be a narrative marker of the intromission of real-world problems and experience in the equally real fictitious world. The very ambiguous character of "my paredros" becomes clear when we pay attention to a seemingly inconsequential sentence taking place in a London restaurant: "My paredro paid, he divided the bill and relentlessly collected the share observing that he would pay the tip."[6] Only *they* could pay, because only *they* are still in touch with a world where paying a restaurant bill, dividing it, and calculating a tip has some importance.

There are other author figures in the novel: Calac who is a middle-aged Argentine writer and as such seems to stand quite close to Cortázar, an intrinsic narrator and even the name Julio Cortázar printed on the cover of the book have authorial functions, but none of them are the author or the narrator. They form and construct a linguistic jail, an independent-real, non-real world, yet offer the opportunity of escaping into another apparently more real-world, always conscious that there cannot be something *more* real.

Despite this intromission, Brian McHale's postmodern principle of ontologically independent fictional parallel universes seems to operate in the Argentine's novels, but there is another turning of the screw that could lead to a specific Latin American way of literary experimentation. For instance, if a reader follows the order of chapters given by Cortázar in his "Table of Instructions" to *Rayuela*, he would be lost forever in the loop constructed by the sequence 131-58-131 (11). However, this does not happen because the missing chapters are already read or will never be. There is an end to the reading process and consequentially to the universe *Rayuela*. If the reading includes chapter 62, the universe possibly continues or reaches new regions, this again depends on the concrete reader.

Most importantly, and unlike in some European postmodern tendencies, such as the French "nouveau roman" (new novel) or the constraint based Oulipian writing, Cortázar's narrative does not exclude real-world problems, pressing political and ideological conflicts, tangible violence or violation of civil rights, and so forth. Jèssica Pujol Duran informs that the Argentine writer refused a membership in the French dominated Oulipo group even though he esteemed it (124–25). The autoreferential and technical Oulipian approach to literature did not match his own ideas concerning the position of literature in society. Consequentially, *Rayuela* does not cut connections with the world outside the fictional text, nor does *62: A Model Kit*. In the latter, during the dinner paid by "my paredro," a half-comic, half-serious debate takes place between Austin and the Argentine "tartars" about the importance of revolutionary action. Austin, a young musician and later the possible murderer of Hélène, rejects the chaotic, playful, and seemingly senseless acting of Calac, Polanco, and Marrast: "Austin had confessed that, as a socialist, the activities of the group seemed to him at least useless, if not dangerous. Together with the conjugation of *jouir*, chosen especially following Polanco's council, Marrast had to support a plea in favor of mass-education and a fight against racism."[7] This is an ironic discussion that opposes the revolutionary value of play and laughter to concrete and often violent action. This scene where the actual political circumstances of the 1960s in France intrude in the fictional capsule will be a main preoccupation in Cortázar's last published novel in lifetime, the 1973 *Libro de Manuel* (*A Manual for Manuel*).

We should not forget that one of the possible endings of *62: A Model Kit* is a tragedy, the violent deaths of Hélène and Nicole, and that Austin, the revolutionary spokesman, could turn out to be a murderer. This possible tragedy becomes a real one in *Libro de Manuel*, where the intrusion of the revolutionary 1968 movements in the fictional world are the literary skeleton turned inside out. However, there is a turnaround in the novel, because now the same protagonists represent playful provocation, on the one hand, and risky action, on the other. The dichotomy between "tartars" and potential Austins is dissolved gradually in the plot, and plot now there is. Andrés, clearly an alter ego of Cortázar, oscillates between intellectual uncompromising happiness and his involvement in the revolutionary group "la Joda," led by Marcos. The group itself starts its activity with apparently senseless and funny performances, but it rapidly glides into much more dangerous and compromising plans, concretely the kidnapping of a leading political figure. Ludmilla, an actress, hesitates between Andrés and Marcos; she represents the difficult process of decision-making that Andrés undergoes, even though her own decision is clear when she turns definitively to Marcos. Andrés himself lives the process between the anarchic Ludmilla and the socially adapted and conformist Francine. Ludmilla, in a dialogue with Andrés, expresses her motives that outline the political potential of play and the inevitable commitment that literature and art have to accept: "-So, you will fill out your membership form -he said. // -Yes. The theater leaves a lot of time for different things, and in the last months I didn't have too much fun. // - I know, I know. I am neglecting you. I am roaming and I don't take you to see the bears. -You're not so important -said Ludmilla threatening one of my calves with the rather sharp heel of her shoe-. I know how to play alone, but now it's different, maybe a game that could be useful, one never knows" (*Libro de Manuel* 183).[8] The allusions are clear: they are games, but they could be useful games with social and political implications in a real-world scenario. In the end, Andrés takes his own decision. He will be part of "la Joda," he will act, but he will not give up the apparently senseless and vulgar pleasures of pure aesthetics that ultimately obtain their own revolutionary potential.

The novel's intention is a book prepared for baby Manuel, a collage consisting of all kinds of materials: newspaper reports about torture in Vietnam and Latin America; texts that illustrate the extreme superficiality of European and North American consumerism-oriented life; and others that simply reflect comic, grotesque, and ludic aspects of our existences. The novel's purpose and endpoint are the novel itself and its starting point, a novel written by many authors, told by many narrator figures who make their apparition in the text, act, suffer, love, reflect, and eventually die, who tell a story where, as Andrés states, "everything" fits (414).

As can be easily seen, the inclusion of a world outside literature, of concrete ideological and social problems, even the acceptance of a political commitment, does not exclude experimentation from writing. Not only does Cortázar apply the inside-out technique and construct an independent fictional universe, but he also operates with continuously changing narrative perspectives (a narrative "I" alternates with a "you" and a "*they*" in one paragraph or even in one sentence), with the discussion of literature and aesthetics as part of the diegesis, and so on. The objective of experiment is still the literary language itself, but it tries to prove that reconnection between literature and a world outside is possible and urgent.

Cortazar's novels show the Latin American way of experimenting. They show that Latin America is not a somehow fictional "zone" itself, as McHale insinuates but, rather, a historical environment that urges to be included in fiction as a concrete and only too tangible reality. Pujol Duran sees in this constellation "a will for formal experimentation with the political urgencies of the moment" (209) and qualifies Cortazar's writing as "experimentalism," meaning that experiment in Latin American literature is part of a very broad discourse that forms historical senses and changes from within, an experiment aiming language and literature. Yet this referent now includes concrete living, includes this area that connects the "zone" with the world outside it.

Even though Cortázar, especially via his debate with José María Arguedas, is considered by Mabel Moraña (2010) and other critics a cosmopolitan author opposing Latin American literature centered in regional tradition, his manner of literary experimentation demonstrates that Latin American narrative is capable of consciously applying the rules of transculturation that were defined by Fernando Ortiz and Ángel Rama, an application that guarantees the autonomy of the continent's writers and helps to break up the cultural hierarchy established between European literature and the one practiced in the former colonies. This interpretation also helps to recuperate transculturation as a concept that could face the dominance of European and North American discourse, instead of relegating it as an idea that has been absorbed by postcolonial mechanisms (Moraña 146–52). It is a long-lasting process that is far from being completed.

Ortiz coins the neologism "transculturación" in *Contrapunteo cubano del tabaco y el azúcar* (1940). He describes a very complex process leading from acculturation to deculturation to neoculturation and finally transculturation (96). The essence of the process is not a simple import/export of cultural features, but the loss, manipulation, and also enrichment of the imported in the hosting culture. New features arise that return to their origins where they again will be transformed and adapted, a never-ending and circular process without a pre-established hierarchy between donor and receiver.

Ángel Rama, in *Transculturación narrativa en América Latina* (1982), states that a transcultural mechanism has to work to guarantee the independence of Latin American literature, a literature that has to mold all kind of foreign influences, adapt them to its necessities, and be written for an incipient and to be educated or even created national or continental audience. Then it could restore the influences on their countries of origin where they have to be remolded and readapted (Rama passim). As I mentioned,

Rama does not include Cortázar in his list of transcultural writers. Nevertheless, the experimental character of the Argentine's novels allows us to state that his work follows the model because it takes into account concrete Latin American social and political circumstances that have to be interpreted as modulations of postmodernist culture as it has been described by Lyotard. They are modulations, not copies. This way, the original constellation can be modified or reshaped.

SALVADOR ELIZONDO WATCHING
HIMSELF WRITING

Even the most autoreferential and real-world independent postmodern experiment is put together in Latin America following a transcultural process. I refer to the writer-watches-writer-writing trope. In 2012, R. M. Berry cites William H. Gass, who, as early as 1970, classifies "those drearily predictable pieces about writers who are writing about what they are writing" (135) as a dead-end. Although Berry rescues the mimetic character of this kind of fiction because it includes a real reader and his/her real environment in the literary text (136–37), it is clear that the trope is dangerously close to a cliché.

The Mexican novelist Salvador Elizondo, a representative writer of a generation that started publishing in the 1950s, opens *El grafógrafo* (The Graphograph, 1972) with a fragment that reads like an apotheosis and a maybe involuntary parody of the technique: "I write. I write that I write. Mentally I can see myself writing that I write. I remember myself writing and also seeing myself writing."[9] Ten more lines of labyrinthine auto-observation follow. The trope is central in Elizondo's work, as it impulses three novels and all his short narrative. Nevertheless, *Elsinore: un cuaderno* (*Elsinore*), his last larger story, returns to seemingly nonexperimental realistic and mimetic tendencies that are also present in *Farabeuf* (1965), his most ambitious and celebrated novel.

El hipogeo secreto (1968, *The Secret Hypogeum*) seems to be the only work that could be catalogized as strictly autoreferential, Elizondo's attempt of creating a closed fictional universe without connection to the outer world. But even in *El hipogeo*, autoreferentiality is relative. In "La esfinge perpleja" (The Perplex Sphinx), one of the texts that form his critically oriented *Cuaderno de escritura* (Notebook of Writing), he states: "I would have conspired with myself to write a novel where there would not have been one sole order of reality not involved as a substance in the text. If I could write it, this would mean that the substance of the world are words . . . and that I would be, in some sense, the god."[10] This sounds like a postmodernist repetition of avant-garde poetics, like the Chilean Vicente Huidobro's "creacionismo" (creationism), César Vallejo's poetic projects, or the Brazilian movements grouped around the Andrade brothers. The old idea of a godlike author returns, but Elizondo knows that his verbal creations and linguistic experiments have to be contrasted with reality. Reality already has to be a part of the novel so that it can be (re)constructed or (re)invented with words.

Reality in many of his stories reveals itself through extremely violent acts, scenes, and images. At the same time, violence occurs in dreamlike, highly evasive, hieratic, and nebulous settings that include characters whose perspectives change continuously, whose gaze, much as in the French "new novel," is dominated by the observed objects, scenes, and images that become the true protagonists. Elizondo's fictional world is definitively one based on a language that tries to speak from within the objects and acts that a divine narrator places as experimental arrays.

Luzelena Gutiérrez de Velasco is right when she catalogues Elizondo's work as "novela de la escritura" (novel of writing), opposing it to the realistic narrative of Mexico's "La onda" (159). Even though the confessed influence of the "new novel" and James Joyce's linguistic experiments is unquestionable in Elizondo, and the ideas of a writer writing our existences or of a dreamer dreaming them are omnipresent in *Farabeuf*, *El hipogeo secreto*, and *Elsinore*, the tangible non-metaphysical reality finds a way to intrude and open the hermetic linguistic structure. Amadeo López is also right when he opines that *Farabeuf* can be characterized by "the continuous linguistic experimentation searching a writing that engenders itself in the instant of writing and suffices itself."[11] The novel moves in linguistic circles around a photograph taken in 1905 of a young Chinese man punished with the "torture of the hundred pieces." The text adapts the close-up cinematographic technique onto the image, but writing does not "suffice itself," as López states. The photograph is inserted into the novel (*Farabeuf* 122–23). With its physical presence, reality irrupts violently in the linguistic corpus of the text. Once again, its structure is turned inside out and shows the exceedingly tangible brutality that has become a part of our lives—that we have only too easily gotten used to. This means that the experiment practiced by him highlights a real problem, real pain, and real suffering. It shows a writer watching himself writing and observing the abnormality of violence emerging from the written words and sentences.

In "De la violencia" (On Violence), another text included in *Cuaderno de escritura*, Elizondo formulates his idea of violence as "the expression of a paralogical language through which violence manifests itself as a potentiality in all things of the world, creating a horribly necessary communication to all things through which the terror brawls trying to escape in a look, like a trapped beast, in the sense that has a cry or a laugh that say nothing."[12] Elizondo's statement resumes the transcultural process undertaken by experimental literature in Latin America. I tried to exemplify this with an overall analysis of his novels and with a more detailed exploration of the playful and ludic narratives written by Julio Cortázar. Although I would like to leave them as the final words of this contribution, I have to add some last sentences.

CONCLUSION

Experiment is a defining part of literature that works as does experimentation in physical sciences as described by Popper and other epistemologists. It shows us the limits of our capacity to know and understand our world; it proposes and samples, but it cannot prove nor verify. The conscious linguistic experiment in Latin American literature does not start with Cortázar or Elizondo. There are clear antecedents in the *modernismo* movement (Leopoldo Lugones in Argentine, Clemente Palma in Peru), the nineteenth-century novel, and authors like one of Borges's models, Macedonio Fernández, who experimented long before the rise of postmodernism and the existence of a theoretical discussion about experimental novels. Fernández, for instance, in his *Museo de la novela de la Eterna* (*The Museum of Eterna's Novel [The First Good Novel]*), a novel he initiated in 1925, occupies half of the text's complete volume with prologues. Agustín Yáñez's 1947 novel *Al filo del agua* (*The Edge of the Storm: A Novel*) could also be mentioned. In it, the Mexican author applies Joycean linguistic experimentation to clarify and outline social and religious conflicts originated by a clash between the progressiveness of the Mexican Revolution and the traditions of rural life.

Modernist and postmodernist literature in Europe and North America accentuated the importance of linguistic and structural experimentation in creative writing. Possibly due to the gap between these highly developed regions and Latin America, the correspondent literature of the latter includes acute ideological, social, and political conflicts as components of its experiments. As Salvador Elizondo implies, the threatening violent character of Latin American life could have been produced by an abuse of language, but linguistic-literary experimentation and the very analytic employment of language in the second half of twentieth century by the continent's writers, that we tried to exemplify with Cortázar and Elizondo, serve to make tangible those violent and suppressing phenomenon and, in an ideal and utopian scenario, contribute to its overcoming. Latin American experimental novel does not form itself a somehow fictional zone and playground for literature, but is an important protagonist in a transcultural process able to enrich postmodernist and contemporary writing in the cultural centers of Europe and North America.

Notes

1. "Polanco estaba entregado a sus estudios científicos, es decir que había sumergido la afeitadora eléctrica en una cacerola de porridge y estudiaba el comportamiento de esas entidades heterogéneas. Se oían como borborigmos y de cuando en cuando una porción de porridge saltaba por el aire pero no alcanzaba a pegarse al cielo raso y caía sobre el piso con un chasquido lúgubre. Era un espectáculo casto y duradero" (137).

2. "Si l'homme n'a plus le même besoin intellectuel de croire, il a conservé le besoin de sentir comme aux temps où il croyait" (8).

3. "En la zona . . . habrá que empezar a contar, habrá que decir algo porque todos ellos están esperando que te pongas a contar, el corro siempre inquieto y un poco hostil al comienzo de un relato, de alguna manera están todos allí esperando que empieces a contar en la zona, en cualquier parte de la zona, ya no se sabe dónde a fuerza de ser en tantas partes y tantas noches y tantos amigos" (11–12).

4. "manoteando entre palabras y conducta y alegría salpicada de sangre y otras retóricas como ésta" (476).

5. "Agresión, regresión y progresión son también connaturales a las intenciones esbozadas un día en los párrafos finales del capítulo 62 de *Rayuela*, que explican el título de este libro y quizá se realizan en su curso" (3).

6. "Mi paredro pagó, procedió a la división y recogió implacablemente las cuotas de todos, haciendo notar que la propina corría por su cuenta" (156).

7. "Austin había confesado a su profesor de francés y a Polanco que en su calidad de socialista las actividades del grupo le parecían por lo menos inútiles, por no decir peligrosas; junto con la conjugación de *jouir*, elegido especialmente por consejo de Polanco, Marrast había tenido que aguantarse un alegato en pro de la educación de las masas y de la lucha contra el racismo" (153).

8. "-Así que vas a llenar tu fichita de adhesión -le dije. / -Sí. El teatro me deja tiempo de sobra para otras cosas, y en estos últimos meses no me he divertido demasiado. / -Ya sé, polaquita, ya sé. Te descuido, me voy por ahí a vagar, no te llevo a ver los osos. / -No te des tanta importancia -dijo Ludmilla amenazándome una pantorrilla con el talón más bien filoso de un zapato-. Yo sé jugar sola pero ahora es otra cosa, un juego que a lo mejor puede servir para algo, nunca se sabe" (183).

9. "Escribo. Escribo que escribo. Mentalmente me veo escribir que escribo y también puedo verme ver que escribo. Me recuerdo escribiendo ya y también viéndome que escribía" (9).

10. "Me hubiera confabulado conmigo mismo para escribir una novela en la que no hubiera un solo orden de la realidad que no estuviera involucrado como substancia misma de ese texto. Si yo consiguiera escribirla, eso querría decir que la substancia del mundo son las palabras. . . y, en cierto modo, que yo soy el dios" (Kindle pos. 1510).

11. "La constante experimentación lingüística en pos de una escritura que se engendre en el instante y se baste a sí misma" (321).

12. "La expresión de un lenguaje paralógico mediante el que la posibilidad de violencia misma se manifiesta como potencia en todas las cosas del mundo, creando una comunicación aterradoramente necesaria a todas las cosas a través de las cuales el terror, como una fiera atrapada, en una mirada, en el sentido que tiene un grito o una carcajada que nada dicen, cabrestea, inútilmente, tratando de huir" (Kindle pos. 677–80).

WORKS CITED

Alber, Jan, and Henrik Skov Nielsen, and Brian Richardson. "Unnatural Voices, Minds, and Narration." *The Routledge Companion to Experimental Literature*, edited by Joe Bray, Alison Gibbons, and Brian McHale, 351–67. Routledge Taylor and Francis Group, 2012. Kindle edition.

Altamirano, Ignacio Manuel. *Clemencia. Cuentos de invierno*. 15th ed. Porrúa, 1991.

Armstrong, Julie. *Experimental Fiction. An Introduction for Readers and Writers*. Bloomsbury, 2014. ePDF.

Berry, R. M. "Metafiction". *The Routledge Companion to Experimental Literature*, edited by Joe Bray, Alison Gibbons, and Brian McHale, 128–41. Routledge Taylor and Francis Group, 2012. Kindle edition.

Bourget, Paul. *Essais de psychologie contemporaine*. Vol. 1. Librairie Plon, 1920.

Bray, Joe, and Alison Gibbons, and Brian McHale, eds. *The Routledge Companion to Experimental Literature*. Routledge Taylor and Francis Group, 2012. Kindle edition.

Bray, Joe, and Alison Gibbons, and Brian McHale. "Introduction." *The Routledge Companion to Experimental Literature*, edited by Joe Bray, Alison Gibbons, and Brian McHale, 1–3. Routledge Taylor and Francis Group, 2012. Kindle edition.

Calinescu, Matei. *Five Faces of Modernity*. Duke UP, 1987.

Cortázar, Julio. *Rayuela*. Punto de Lectura, 2006.

Cortázar, Julio. *Libro de Manuel*. Debolsillo, 2017.

Cortázar, Julio. *62/ Modelo para armar*. Alfaguara, 2016. EBook.

Elizondo, Salvador. *El grafógrafo*. Fondo de Cultura Económica, 2000.

Elizondo, Salvador. *Farabeuf*. Fondo de Cultura Económica, 2006.

Elizondo, Salvador. *Cuaderno de escritura*. 1st electronic ed. Fondo de Cultura Económica, 2012. Kindle edition.

Elizondo, Salvador. *El hipogeo secreto*. 1st electronic ed. Fondo de Cultura Económica, 2012. Kindle edition.

Fernández, Macedonio. *Museo de la Novela de la Eterna*. Cátedra, 1995.

Ferrater Mora, José. *Diccionario de filosofía*. Vol. 2. Ariel, 1994.

Gómez de Avellaneda, Gertrudis. *Sab*. 12th ed. Cátedra, 2017.

Gutiérrez de Velasco, Luzelena. "José Emilio Pacheco y el Nouveau Roman." *Reescritura en movimiento*, edited by Yvette Jiménez de Báez, El Colegio de México, 2014, 159–69.

Hamann, Johann Georg. "La Estética en una nuez (Aesthetica in nuce)." Edited and translated by Gerardo Rafael Pérez Anderson. Thesis Universidad Panamericana. Mexico City, 2014.

Kuhn, Thomas S. *The Structure of Scientific Revolutions*. 3rd ed. U of Chicago P, 1996.

López, Amadeo. "El universo novelesco de Salvador Elizondo." *Doscientos años de narrativa mexicana. Siglo XX*, edited by Rafael Olea Franco and Laura Angélica de la Torre, El Colegio de México, 2010, 321–44.

Lyotard, Jean-François. *The Postmodern Condition: A Report on Knowledge*. Translated by Geoff Bennington and Brian Massumi. Manchester University Press, 1984.

McHale, Brian. *Postmodernist Fiction*. Routledge, 2004. Adobe eReader Format.

Moraña, Mabel. *La escritura del límite*. Iberoamericana Vervuert, 2010.

Ortiz, Fernando. *Contrapunteo Cubano del tabaco y el azúcar*. Biblioteca Ayacucho, 1978.

Popper, Karl. *Unended Quest. An Intellectual Biography*. Routledge, 2005. Master e-book.

Pujol Duran, Jèssica. *From the Experimental to Experimentalism. Italo Calvino and Julio Cortázar in Paris (1963–1973)*. 2016. University College London, PhD dissertation.

Rama, Ángel. *Transculturación narrativa en América Latina*. 2nd ed. El Andariego, 2008.

Sommer, Doris. *Foundational Fictions: The National Romances of Latin America*. U of California P, 1991.

Von Wilpert, Gero. *Sachwörterbuch der Literatur*. 6th ed. Alfred Kröner, 1979.

Yáñez, Agustín. *Al filo del agua*. Editorial Porrúa, 1991.

Zola, Émile. *The Experimental Novel and Other Essays*. Translated by Belle M. Sherman. Haskell House, 1964.

CHAPTER 29

....

HISTORICAL, CRITICAL, AND THEORETICAL WORK ON THE LATIN AMERICAN NOVEL

....

JOSÉ EDUARDO GONZÁLEZ

IN 1986, enjoying the visibility that having published his groundbreaking *The Political Unconscious* only a few years earlier brought him, the Marxist critic Fredric Jameson (1934–) penned an essay that is still remembered today as one of the most controversial readings of the novel form: "Third-World Literature in the Era of Multinational Capitalism." What made other critics, especially those from the Global South, vehemently reject Jameson's essay was his unequivocal assertion that "all third-world texts are necessarily . . . allegorical, and in a very specific way: they are to be read as what I will call national allegories, even when, or perhaps I should say, particularly when their forms develop out of predominantly western machineries of representation, such as the novel" (69). The statement was rightfully attacked, among other things, for impoverishing the complex personal and historical stories told in "Third World" texts; for failing to recognize that contemporary "First World" writers, like Thomas Pynchon (1937–), also write national allegories; and for selectively treating the vast world literature that has not become part of the Anglo-European canon as if it were the Other (see Ahmad). But many also recognized that Jameson was correct in pointing out a connection among allegorical readings, the nation, and Third World novels.[1] Accepting that allegorical interpretation is an essential part of how the Latin American novel has been read compels us to search for the origin of this critical tradition. Do these national allegories exist, as Jameson argues, because of a relationship to an imperialist First World? As we look at the history of Latin American criticism of the novel in the next few pages, I will argue that the answer is not as simple. We will see that a series of factors has contributed to a specific way of reading the Latin American novel, among them the functions that have traditionally been assigned to this literary form in the region, the creation of a canon of narrations that lend themselves more easily to allegorical interpretation while ignoring alternative developments, and an indifference to the epistemological problems that for other critical traditions are essential to the emergence of this genre.

THE NOVEL AS NATIONAL ALLEGORY

In the late nineteenth century and early twentieth century, criticism of the novel in Latin America is mostly found in literary histories whose content reflects the deep ideological division between conservative and liberal intellectuals. The association of the novel genre with the life of the republic, as Beatriz González-Stephan reminds us, was initially a liberal strategy that took a literary composition considered dangerous and tied it to the "progress" of the Latin American countries, to the larger narrative of creating the "imaginary families" needed by modern nations. The strategy required attributing the novel an essential characteristic that has come to be an inherent part of how this genre has been read in our region: the power to shape society through its narrative rhetoric. For its part, conservative thought rejected the novel (and theater) as a waste of time or because these narrations supposedly warped people's view of reality. On the occasions they recognized the artistic qualities of the genre, conservative critics tended to disregard the social power that liberals attributed to fiction. For example, writing in the 1880s, the Chilean literary critic Pedro Nolasco Cruz, a longtime admirer of Émile Zola's (1840–1902) work, mounted a defense of the novel that was, in reality, a critique of the genre's alleged capacity to alter the life of its readers: "There can be no teaching without induction, without a clear and clean generalization, and it is the author's job to do that. If one simply gives readers teachings disguised as fiction and leave to readers or spectators themselves the task of discovering them, they will not bother to do so, and even if they do, they will never be sure that they are interpreting them correctly" (367).[2] In this ideological war, the liberal views imposed themselves and the consequences of the novel genre having been legitimized in connection a specific view of the nation-state would be felt for several decades in how literary critics in the region would read, historicize, and interpret the novel.

While theories of the novel that appeared in the early part of the twentieth century saw it as a form that grew out of the displacement from a previous form, such as the epic poem,[3] for Latin American critics, the shadow of a history that primarily assigns the novel a value in terms of the national discourse meant that other possibilities did not enter the critical conversation about the genre. For example, Ian Watt's well-known analysis of the rise of the novel suggests that it originally sought to distance itself from traditional, less realistic forms of storytelling. "From the Renaissance onwards," he explains, "there was a growing tendency for individual experience to replace collective tradition as the ultimate arbiter of reality" (9). Modern subjects replaced medieval faith with the belief in the possibility of apprehending reality through one's senses. The key element here is the relationship between an old-style narration, the romance, and a new realism emphasizing individual experience. Romance, a term that remains infrequently used among Latin American literary scholars, originally refers to the twelfth-century chivalric genre, often including adventurous and/or spiritual journeys, but not necessarily involving what today is known as a "romantic" story. In the theory of the novel, romance has come to refer to a premodern style of narration often set in "distant times," with traditional plots that make use of literary conventions involving an idealized view of reality, and characters who represent general human types as opposed to individuals. As mentioned above, the relationship between the modern novel and the romance can be described as one of displacement; that is, the novel becomes a representation of what happens when that ideal world of adventures and marvels is lost.[4] While the romance tended toward allegory, with black and white characters and simple plots, the novel focused on complex story lines about modern subjects. Latin American critics have yet to fully reflect on the relationship between the romance and the novel and how the question of "reality" at the center of the emergence of the Anglo-European novel developed differently in other regions.[5] For the moment, one can at least summarize that in the nineteenth century, the Latin American novel took at least two different directions, both partially influenced by the pre-realistic romance mode. On the one hand, a simpler Latin American world was invoked through an *indianista* genre that imagined a glorious native past, distant from the reality of contemporary indigenous populations; on the other, narrations that were more realistic became "allegorical" stories about the young republics and their bright future. In these allegories, the world of romance was projected toward a future in which cultural autonomy would become a reality and social struggles left in the past.[6]

VICTORY OF REALISM

At the turn of the twentieth century, as primitivist views of native cultures became untenable, indianista romance would disappear. But the association between the novel genre and the Latin American republics established in the nineteenth century continued to dominate readings of the genre in the region, leading critics to celebrate and canonize fictions that contributed to that association and ignore those works that deviated from it. What happens during the first quarter century with criticism of the Latin American novel can be best exemplified by briefly remembering how Mariano Azuela's (1873–1952) *Los de abajo* (*The Underdogs*, 1915) went from obscurity to being the prime example of the realist narrative of this period. In 1925, seeking to refute the idea that Mexican literature had become "effeminate," Francisco Monterde (1894–1985) brought to the attention of the Mexican public the "virile" qualities of Azuela's work and his portrayal of the revolutionary conflict (Ruffinelli 232). What was taking place, for the reading of the novel in the region, was the beginning of a critical process that systematically ignored the significant production of *modernista* and avant-garde novels written between the1890s and 1930s, because they did not meet the pattern of novel/ nation characteristic of works like those of the Mexican "novels of the revolution." No other Latin American style has produced more novels than *modernismo*. These fictions shared characteristics with modernista poetry, including a descriptive, meticulous, artistic style and the use of topics typical of the movement, such as the bourgeois interior, settings full of works of art and beautiful bric-à-brac, a view of women as femmes fatales but also as precious objects, and so on. But the modernista novel also departed from the novel/nation model that dominated Latin American fiction at the time in significant ways. Not only did it often employ cosmopolitan settings and themes, distrusting "the facile idealization of the countryside typical of most creolist fiction" (González Pérez 97), but it also focused on the individual rather than on the collective experience of modernity: "in nearly all modernist novels we find the figure of the artist-hero... who tries to desperately define his position and his role within the new Spanish American society" (González Pérez 97–98). A novel like Aurora Cáceres's (1877–1958) *La rosa muerta* (The Dead Rose, published in 1914, around the same time as Azuela's *Los de abajo*) in which the main character moves between Paris and Berlin, and includes no mention of or direct connection to Latin American culture, even though the characters are clearly Latin American, cannot be easily turned into a national allegory. This conflict between the novel as the narration of the nation and the elegant and self-involved *modernismo* is inscribed within the pages of many of Azuela's novels, sometimes openly, as attacks on modernista poets for being apolitical intellectuals, sometimes indirectly, through the rejection of modernista symbols.[7] It is vividly expressed in *Los de abajo* when Demetrio and his men, after the victory in Zacatecas, and encouraged by La Pintada, take possession of an elegant house instead of sleeping in a hotel. What is then described to the reader is the destruction of the modernista bourgeois interior: "[There were] books lying in piles on the floor, chairs and tables, the large mirrors thrown to the ground, smashed, the huge albums and the photographs torn into shreds, the furniture, objects d'art and bric-a-brac broken" (Azuela 111–12).[8]

As Andrés Bello (1781–1865) clearly saw when he evaluated the usefulness of this literary form for nineteenth-century Latin American culture, the novel can *only* fulfill its allegorical mission if the focus is shifted away from the individual:

> The novel, a composition that used to be frivolous, and which has in the past so eloquently portrayed great passions, has been recruited in the name of history. We have requested not that it tells us about the adventures of individuals, but that it shows us those individuals as true representatives of a country, of a period, of an opinion. We want to use it to get to know the private life of a nation. And do novels not always contain the secret memories of a nation's public life?
>
> (Andrés Bello, "Modo" 236)[9]

While, for many literary theorists, the origin of the novel form is seen as inseparable from the development of capitalism and the economic specialization that comes with it— the secularization of the state, the growth of a reading public, in essence, the rise of the middle-class—, in Latin America it became a literary form symbolizing the opposite of individualism. The novel genre became the form that represented not the anxieties of the middle-class modern subject, but the essential characteristics of the humans inhabiting the Latin American republics, an artistic product whose main objective was to search for the elements that make Latin American cultures unique, original, and describe them. In novels such as Azuela's *Las tribulaciones de una familia decente* (*The Trials of a Respectable Family*, 1918), the emerging middle class is portrayed not by a sole individual, but by a family, which since the nineteenth century was the favorite trope of national allegories. *Modernismo*, the movement generally associated with the emphasis on originality, with individualism and specialization and professionalization of writing, with the rise of the middle-class in Latin America, was necessarily reduced by critics to a revolution in poetic form.

A similar opposition between the novel as expression of the nation and alternative uses of the genre took place in the 1920s and 1930s as the avant-garde movements faced the hostility of the proponents of a realist, committed prose. For example, in Ecuador the first signs of an avant-garde literature in the local literary field occurred around 1922, with the poetry of Hugo Mayo (1895–1988), and very soon, the literary community witnessed the appearance of several short-lived periodicals that published manifestos and showcased the work of young writers affiliated to the movement. In a country where the novel genre was rarely practiced, a sudden flurry of narrative texts is published between the late 1920s and 1930s. But the avant-garde literary products would encounter opposition when a prominent intellectual of this period, Joaquín Gallegos Lara (1909–1947), criticized the novels of Humberto Salvador (1909–1982), like *En la ciudad he perdido un novela . . .* (In the City I Have Lost a Novel, 1930) (See Gallegos, "Pirandelismo"), and of Pablo Palacios (1982–), whose "intelligently subjective books" such as *Vida del ahorcado* (The Hanged Man's Life, 1932), he said, "possess a stingy, clowning and disoriented view of life, typical of the middle class" (Gallegos, "Hechos" 178–79).[10] To this type of prose, Gallegos Lara preferred novels like José de la Cuadra's (1903–1941) *Los Sangurimas* (1934), portraying life in the Ecuadorian east coast, or Jorge Icaza's (1906–1978) *Huasipungo* (*The Villagers* 1934), protesting injustices carried out by those in power against the indigenous population. In short, these were novels that sought to depict the realities of a sector of the nation that had been excluded from Ecuadorian literature and culture, but whose representation—as opposed to the subjective view of the middle-class individual in the "cosmopolitan" avant-garde novels—was key to achieving a clear view of the social situation of the country. In Gallegos Lara's case, his critical position reflected his Marxist beliefs, fueled by an early twentieth-century view of socialist realism as a superior narrative form. But this view of the novel as having the role of representing *all* the national reality, by casting light on social groups or problems usually ignored by local mainstream culture, eventually marginalized the avant-garde alternatives from the cultural scene. When Ángel Felicísimo Rojas (1909–2003) writes his richly crafted *La novela ecuatoriana* (The Ecuadorian Novel, 1948), considered one of the classics of modern literary criticism in Ecuador, this view of the genre has become consolidated and it drives his evaluation of the history of the novel in his country. For example, when describing Luis A. Martínez's (1869–1909) *A la costa* (To the Coast 1904), Rojas points out the relevance of this text as "the first novel, as far as we know, that inform us, through the narration of a fictional tale, about our most serious problems and reveal to us some of the fears and prejudices that existed in the mind of the middle-class sector at that time" (112).[11]

The victory of the novel as representation of the nation-state over competing uses of the genre repeated itself all over the region. It soon became the canonical interpretation of Latin American literature. In 1949 Pedro Henríquez Ureña (1884–1946) publishes *Las corrientes literarias en la América hispánica* (*Literary Currents in Hispanic America*), his assessment of the history of Latin American literature as a long search for self-expression. When he arrives at the section of contemporary literature (1920–1940), his description of the function of the Latin American novel has a familiar look: "A large part of the significant literature of Hispanic America today presents social problems, or at least describes social situations that contains the germs of problems. The novel is, normally, the form in which such aspects of society most frequently appear in modern times. In our literature they began to appear as soon as our novelists moved from romanticism to realism" (194). Needless to say, there are no modernista or avant-garde novelists in his account of this period. The combination of Latin America's self-expression and local social "problems"—to which Henríquez Ureña adds "nature"—became so normalized in the criticism of the novel that its origins, as well as other ways of understanding the genre, were rendered invisible.

THE BOOM AND THE CANON

The success of the Boom novelists—a group that includes Gabriel García Márquez (1927–2014), Mario Vargas Llosa (1936–), Carlos Fuentes (1928–2012), and Julio Cortázar (1914–1984)—will bring a slightly different interpretation of the novel. When, in 1953, a young journalist by the name of Gabriel García Márquez complains in an article about the "problems" of the novel in Colombia that "we have yet to have a novelist happily influenced by Faulkner, Joyce or Woolf" (116),[12] he is simply expressing a sentiment that is already clear for many authors of his generation: the idea of originality in the Latin American novel has changed and innovation in technique has moved to the center stage. This is an important development in the perception of the novel—by critics, readers, and authors—and it has nothing to do with the commercial success and book marketing strategies that are often associated with the Boom, but with relatively young authors measuring themselves and their practice of fiction writing against the history of the novel. They decide to use technique, experimentation, "language" as they sometimes call it, to free themselves from this history. When Boom authors take this generational step, what they have in mind as "history" is, logically, the canonized version of the novel as a miniature model of the nation, containing its geography, idiosyncrasies of its citizens, and social problems.

We can observe how much the role of the novelist has changed in Alejo Carpentier's (1904–1980) well-known article about the "problemática" (controversy) of the Latin American novel from 1964. Carpentier complains that for more than thirty years the Latin American novel "has given us a regional and picturesque fiction that in very few cases has explored the depths—the really transcendental aspect—of things" (10)[13] and argues that if Latin American authors want to write universal fiction, they should focus on portraying Latin American cities, like Joyce did with Dublin. However, his main concern is not really what kind of content is presented but, rather, finding an appropriate language to deliver it, moving the area of originality from content to style. And yet, when the Cuban author proposes the Baroque as the only style that makes sense for Latin Americans, the simple idea that there could be a single style that captures the essence of the region assumes a tradition of seeing the fusion of the novel form and the nation (or in this case, the region) that is decades old. Another prominent Boom writer, Carlos Fuentes, begins his study *La nueva novela hispanoamericana* (The New Latin American Novel, 1969), proposing an explanation for why in other regions of the planet literature focuses on the individual, whereas the Latin American novel does not: "In the fields of Haute-Savoie, in the Swiss snow-covered slopes, men learn about themselves when they enter in contact with nature. But in the Spanish American novel. . . nature is only an enemy that swallows, destroys human will. . . She is the protagonist, not the men eternally oppressed by her force" (10).[14] With a novelistic canon that appears to have come out of Henríquez Ureña's periodization, Fuentes asserts that the explanation for the "documentary and naturalist tendency" of Spanish American novel is that nature is the main character in these texts. Latin Americans, he says, achieved independence without being recognized as individuals because "Conquistadors came looking for natural treasures, not the personality of men" (11).[15] Against this flattened version of the history of the novel, Fuentes sees the rediscovery of "language" as that which frees the new novel from merely portraying a reality that immobilizes them: "if in Latin America literary works remained satisfied with reflecting or justifying the established order, they would be anachronistic, useless. Our works must possess disorder: that is to say, they must show another possible order, different from the current one" (31–32).[16] One could argue that in the Boom's emphasis on technique we are witnessing a return of the repressed, a return of the cosmopolitism of modernista and avant-garde novels. When Fuentes explains that authors are now aware that the novel is a linguistic construct, that "Latin Americans . . . are today contemporaries of all mankind. And they can, contradictorily, . . . be universal [authors] writing in the language of Peru, Argentina, or Mexico" (32),[17] his thinking exemplifies the approach to the novel that would dominate during this period, focused on experimental literary techniques as the locus of cultural autonomy, and as cultural and spiritual compensation for the "de-formation of our economy, our politics, our dependence, dis-unified, fragmented" (35).[18]

The same context helps us analyze one of the best-known reflections about the genre to come from Boom authors: Vargas Llosa's idea of the "total novel." Vargas Llosa's canon of the novel that came before the Boom, which he calls "primitive novel," is not different from Fuentes's and, like the Mexican author, he argues—quoting Rómulo Gallegos (1884–1969)—that nature is the real protagonist of pre-Boom novels. Latin American novelists before the Boom, he says, were not interested in creating something new but in merely reproducing reality; individuality disappeared from their pages, their "characters do not internalize dramatic events nor are their consciousness shaped by them, personal motives driving human conduct are absent" ("Novela primitiva" 30).[19] For Vargas Llosa, what changes with the novel of the Boom is that authors are not trying to portray reality objectively; instead, they want to describe their "personal" view of reality. No longer "slaves" to local reality, Latin American authors can create rigorous and coherent fictional worlds, using the entire arsenal of literary techniques available to them, freeing themselves from the realism that characterized the "primitive" novel. Vargas Llosa would develop these ideas further in his *García Márquez: Historia de un deicidio* (García Márquez: Story of a Deicide 1971), where he presents the concept of a "totalizing novel." In his study, the Peruvian novelist links together several ideas about fiction writing from a personal perspective, some of which have been criticized for being "romantic" views about literature that had been left behind by professional critics a long time ago.[20] For Vargas Llosa, novelists are consciously imitating (and, at the same time, replacing or rejecting) God when they decide to create their own reality in their works. "Each novel is a secret deicide," he explains, "a symbolic assassination of reality" (*García Márquez* 90).[21] A novel does not come from an author's contact with social reality, it is really based on topics that emerge from their personal obsessions, their "demons," which can only be "exorcised" through the act of artistic creation. The reality presented in a novel, if it wishes to compete with the "real reality," must seek to include "everything that exists both in life and in the imagination of men" (*García Márquez* 199–200).[22] In one of his chapters, Vargas Llosa complains that critics usually classify Spanish fiction as "rigorously realistic" and explains that this might be true for fiction after the Renaissance but not "for the fertile, multiple, daring pre-Cervantes narrative prose and, especially, that of the Novels of Chivalry. They are not 'unrealistic'; they are 'realistic' but their conception of reality is broader and more complex than the narrow view of reality that Renaissance rationalism established" (*García Márquez* 198).[23] What is interesting about Vargas Llosa's attempt at theorizing the novel is that the literature he is describing, and the characteristics he is emphasizing (the use of myths, legends, fantasy), are what we have previously described as romance. He is completely unaware of the historical work of Watt and other critics who locate the emergence of the modern novel genre as a rejection of the romance's unrealistic narrations. It is not surprising that Vargas Llosa has no problems arguing for a return to a pre-modern mode of writing because of the connection between romance and allegory. Despite his push for cosmopolitanism at the level of literary techniques and his critique of Latin American "primitive" fiction, Vargas Llosa is not opposed to the novel as an allegory of the nation: "the worlds [that authors] build with their fictions, and that are valuable in themselves, are also smaller versions, scale models, representations (psychological, fantastic or mythic) of Latin America" ("Novela primitiva" 31).[24]

TRANSCULTURATION AND THE NOVEL

Both Vargas Llosa and Fuentes are great examples of how a critical view that assigned the Latin American novel the role of representing the nation became such an accepted paradigm that its origin in interpretations made by earlier critics was forgotten. When critics begin to look for an explanation as to why the Latin American novel had "always" been realistic, focused on social problems and so on, or when authors begin to describe their own aesthetic projects as a fight against "essential" literary characteristics of the novel in the region, one can say that literary history has become second nature. It is not surprising that the work of one of the most important theorists of the novel genre in twentieth-century Latin America, Ángel Rama (1926--983), is rooted in a search for traditional "Latin American" social forces that somehow drive literary efforts to successfully represent Latin American culture. Avoiding the simplistic explanations based on an "untamed nature," Rama explains, at the beginning of *Transculturación narrativa en América Latina* (*Writing Across Cultures*, 1982), the historical beginnings of the three impulses that have molded Latin American literature: independence, originality, and representation. Rama argues that the persistent desire to develop a literature "autonomous" from Europe was the result of nineteenth-century *criollo* elites thinking that they were representing "national cultures," adding that the search for originality reflected the Romantic era in which this literature was born. The third element that has shaped Latin American literature is "representation." The only way to attain originality, according to Latin American Romantic writers, was "through literature's ability to represent the region that gave rise to it" (*Across* 5).[25] But if Rama clearly saw the historical conditions that created the literature that the Boom novel rejected, he was not yet ready to accept this tradition as a completely artificial selection of literary works, as a canon that could have easily included literary works that questioned any of those three claims, if different choices had been made. On the contrary, those nineteenth-century romantic gestures, while resulting from historical conditions, Rama insists, "mask another, more vigorous, more persistent source for Latin American writers: the distinctive cultural characteristics of the hinterlands of the Americas. In other words, the cultures that nourish Latin American literature are not the solitary work of a few literary elites but rather the massive efforts of vast societies to construct their symbolic languages" (*Across* 4).[26] For this reason, Rama's views on the Latin American novels often oscillate between his reconstruction of a historical process and a "feeling" that there is some kind of traditional, cultural "force" that manifests itself in literary creations. Rama's reading of the Latin American novel form in the twentieth century understands it as the outcome of a history of external modernizing "impulses" and the corresponding local and regional reactions or solutions. Each one of those impulses signified a greater integration into the world market. The first impulse occurs during the period we know as *modernismo* (1890–1920), and it forces Latin American writers to become more professional. They try to build a public for their writings, focus on aspects of an artistic product that would make it different from other works in the market, and pay attention to technique. Because Rama does not attribute much significance to the modernista novel, for him the second impulse, which occurs with the avant-garde of the 1920s, acquires relevance as the origin of twentieth-century fiction. An important element of Rama's view of the development of the Latin American novel is his reading of what happened during the 1920s, when, as mentioned above, a surge of realist writing focusing on local cultural concerns displaced the avant-garde movement. In the early 1970s, Rama proposed the idea that there were two avant-gardes emerging during the 1920s, one of them interested in cosmopolitan topics and experimentation with techniques of writing. The approach involved artists trying to insert themselves and their works as part of the European literary system. The other group of avant-garde writers were those, like César Vallejo (1892–1938), "whose works were created within a Latin American literary system. They drew from its structures and contributions, modifying and adapting them to new realities" ("Vanguardias" 63).[27] The second group comes from a first period when both the avant-garde and the regionalist/realist positions overlapped, before ideological clarifications forced them to take opposing views of the function of literature. This is the origin of Rama's best-known take on the Latin American novel, the theory of narrative transculturation.

Rama sees a third exterior impulse, consisting of an attempt to integrate Latin American society to the world market and modernize its culture, as taking place in the 1950s and 1960s. Its consequence, for the history of the novel, is the "invasion" (or "importation") of experimental narrative techniques. It parallels the market changes that occurred after the second world war and that brought industrial technology to Latin America in an effort to locally manufacture products that were previously imported. In other words, creating a Latin American experimental novel in the 1960s was, for Rama, somewhat like the literary equivalent of import substitution. What Fuentes, Carpentier, and Vargas Llosa saw as a new trend, their interest in a "language" or technique that allowed Latin American fiction authors to "free" themselves from the influence of the individuality-crushing "Nature" of the regionalist novel, acquires in Rama's hands a different meaning, as it signals the beginning of an era dangerously global. For Rama, not to recognize that narrative techniques were created in a specific cultural context, assuming that they could easily be imported to Latin America, was to run the risk of unwittingly transporting foreign values, turning Latin American content into "universal" content. In other words, it could mean creating novels that, in their artistic form, showed their disconnection from local culture. Rama sees the novels of some of the authors of this period, among them the aforementioned Fuentes and Vargas Llosa, as exhibiting a schism between form and content in their structure. He thus becomes interested in and praises the literary practice of a group of writers whose approach to literary creation he calls narrative transculturation.[28] According to Rama, transculturators do not use foreign narrative techniques to escape representing local context; instead, technique leads them to explore their cultural heritage. They respond to new cultural trends by looking for local equivalents, thus achieving the double task of modernizing local cultural products and protecting them from the de-culturation that might occur. They do not use technique to become cosmopolitan writers; they use it to defend local values, while at the same time recognizing that refusing to modernize only brings their cultures closer to obsolesce and extinction. Yet, they do not simply accept any foreign literary influence; they select those aspects of modern culture that they consider compatible with their regional cultures, while, at the same time, choosing from the local tradition those elements that can be updated, modernized. It is a double selection process that recognizes peripheral cultures as taking an active role in the act of forming their own cultural products and not passively accepting the impact of modernizing forces. Rama gives as an example the transculturators' response to the fragmentary "stream of consciousness" of the modern novel. They looked for "oral sources of popular narrative" and other "scattered discourses" such as "village gossip" as solutions that both recognized the value of local culture and allowed them to write using "modern" techniques (*Across* 26–27). Because much of Rama's theory of transculturation depends on privileging the figure of the Latin American intellectual, granting them the role of mediators, putting on their shoulders the responsibility for updating the local culture, the view of the novel form as representation of the nation resurfaces here with a new look. The *transcultured* novel becomes a model to follow for achieving cultural modernization. Rama uses José María Arguedas's (1911–1969) novel *Los ríos profundos* (*Deep Rivers* 1958) as an example of a text that borrows from modern culture while defending local traditions. Instead of using traditional indigenous forms of art, Arguedas employs a Western invention, the novel genre, which he modifies by inserting Quechua syntax and lyrics of Andean songs (*harawis* and *huaynos*) in the original language with a parallel Spanish translation. The result is a hybrid text that looks like avant-garde novels, but whose purpose is entirely different. By using the novel form, Rama argues, Arguedas is not looking to address the indigenous society, but the dominant culture in his nation and to insert, in that national culture, the elements he is borrowing from marginalized communities. The novel is thus assigned a new function: to solve in its form the conflicts that arise from a mixture of elements. "[Form] resolves, on the symbolic plane of artistic creativity, tensions engendered by contradictions [that express] real, objective cultural conflicts." Arguedas's text becomes "a scale model of the macro-structure that would be generated by full-scale transculturation" (*Across* 143).[29]

REPRESENTING HETEROGENEITY

One could argue that a paradigm shift takes place around the 1980s as new ways of reading the Latin American novel begin to appear. There are several developments that influenced this change, and it is difficult to give a complete summary of all of them in this brief essay, but one can safely point to the work of Antonio Cornejo Polar (1936–1997) as a transitional moment. His critical work presents a reading of the Latin American novel that begins to question the capacity of the genre to accomplish the task is being assigned to; that is, representing an *entire* nation. In a key essay, Cornejo Polar distances his theory of the irreducible heterogeneity of Latin American culture from Rama's transculturation concept because the latter implies "the construction of a syncretic plane that finally incorporates in a more or less unproblematic totality. . . two or more languages, two or more ethnic identities, two or more aesthetic codes and historical experiences" ("Mestizaje" 117).[30] In addition, the synthesis achieved by transculturation takes place "in the space of the hegemonic culture and literature," which is the traditional space of the national culture, thus leaving at the margins any discourses that have not influenced this "enlightened" literature (117).[31] From his first theorizations of the concept of heterogeneity, the novel occupied a privileged space in Cornejo Polar's thoughts on the old Latin American problem of representation. In his 1978 essay about the "double socio-cultural status" of indigenismo, he had already detected the first examples of unresolved textual tension in the colonial chronicles of Inca Garcilaso de la Vega (1539–1616) and Guamán Poma de Ayala (1535–1616), but it is the twentieth-century novel, especially Arguedas's work, that interests him the most. Reading the chronicles, he observed two models of what happens in literature when artistic form clashes with a heterogeneous content: 1) "the suppression of the referent because of external factors" or 2) "the capacity of the referent to modify. . . the official form" of the text. ("Indigenismo" 15).[32] In indigenista fiction, heterogeneity begins as "the fracture between the indigenous universe and its indigenista representation" ("Indigenismo" 17),[33] between an oral world and its written representation, both poles existing, not in a juxtaposed manner but in conflict with each other. Heterogeneity exists—either in the form of two incompatible structures, or with one of the poles being hegemonic and the other dependent. Cornejo Polar fully developed his ideas about heterogeneity and the trajectory of the novel in *Writing in the Air*, a book that has become one of the milestones of Latin American criticism. Following the architecture of his earlier approaches, though in a more detailed fashion, the Peruvian critic first unearths the origin of Latin American heterogeneity in the experience of colonization that the region underwent, but midway through his second chapter, he becomes interested in the novel as "one of the clear signs of nineteenth-century Latin American modernity" (*Writing* 82).[34] Cornejo Polar focuses on the use of the family as a micro-institution that lent itself to allegorizing the nation. He studies how in these national allegories the desire to achieve cultural homogeneity presents itself as attempting to create a linguistic space, a national literary language, in which all differences are smoothed over. However, in actuality, this discourse suppresses oral traditions and, with that, heterogeneity. Cornejo Polar then shifts his attention to the competing avant-garde and realist writing modes of the 1920s Ecuador, reading Palacio's urban fiction and Jorge Icaza's indigenista novels as two versions of the same desire to represent heterogeneity more accurately. Palacio rejects realism, Cornejo Polar explains, because he finds it to be a mere repetition of reality and thus incapable of capturing the meaning behind appearances. For his part, Icaza, by reproducing directly the everyday reality and speech in his novels, creates a text that legitimizes "the dialect of the middle and popular strata as a new norm for the national dialect, including his notorious interruptions in Quechua" (*Writing* 121).[35] In their efforts to include orality, however, there is still a homogenizing impulse, the only difference is that it now "aligns itself with the populace, in open conflict with the 'antinational' oligarchy" (*Writing* 123).[36]

In the pages that follow, Cornejo Polar studies the twentieth-century indigenista novel in Peru and begins to wonder if one can consider this genre as anything else than an Other of the indigenous world, an intrusion of modernity penetrating an archaic universe. In a manner reminiscent of Ian Watt's reflections of the epistemological problems at the heart of the birth of the modern novel, Cornejo Polar ponders the problem of having a non-indigenista author using this fictional form, speaking with a single voice, and trying to impose meaning: "The protagonists' words, as eloquent as they may be, are never heard: somehow they are always 'translated,' just as their world is constrained within a solid referential framework" (*Writing* 144).[37] Hence the importance that the critic attributes to Arguedas's work at the end of his study. Unlike Rama, Cornejo Polar is not interested in looking for the harmony of modern techniques and local cultural elements. Instead, he focuses on Arguedas's construction of "a plural subject experiencing discontinuous times and disparate cultures" (*Writing* 149–50).[38] Arguedas does this by creating a protagonist/narrator that "can only exist in dialogue with another, collective voice that defines its alterity in language" (*Writing* 149). Arguedas's *Los ríos profundos*, Cornejo Polar argues, is an "unstable" text, "a space disputed among several voices in a dialogue that is not always dialectic . . . since it can function without synthesis" (*Writing* 152).[39] While Cornejo Polar's views are still bound to the analysis of the novel in terms of the representation of the nation—in the end, *Los ríos profundos* is, as he says paraphrasing Arguedas himself, "the celebration of a homeland capable of joyfully taking in all homelands" (*Writing* 153)[40]—his theoretical work on the challenges that cultural heterogeneity brings to this paradigm, point to new directions for how to read the Latin American novel.

NOTES

1. Among those who agree to some extent with the applicability of Jameson's idea to Latin American literature are Antonio Cornejo Polar (*Writing* 83) and Doris Sommer (42).
2. "No puede haber enseñanza sin inducción, sin generalización clara y limpia, y al autor le toca hacerla. Si da simplemente la enseñanza envuelta en la ficción, y deja al lector o al espectador el trabajo de desentrañarla, éste no se lo tomará, y aun cuando se lo tome, nunca estará seguro de dar en lo cierto" (Nolasco 367).
3. See Michael McKeon's anthology, especially parts 2 and 3, in which the works of Lévi-Strauss, Frye, Freud, and Walter Benjamin are presented in the context of "the novel as displacement."
4. McKeon suggests that one could also read Lukács's theory of the novel in a similar way: as a displacement of the epic, the first nature, or the "parental home" (179).
5. Doris Sommer, while obviously aware of the importance of romance for the history of the novel, chooses to define "romance" in her study as "a cross between our contemporary use of the word as a love story and a nineteenth-century use that distinguishes the genre as more boldly allegorical than the novel" (5). In the present study, when I argue that a novel possesses elements of romance, I am not interested in the "romantic" aspects of the plot, but in romance understood as a mode of writing that favors the use of symbolic events, thus facilitating the possibility of reading a text as an allegory.
6. For the idea of seeing a historical future in terms of romance, see Jameson's *The Political Unconscious* (92–93).
7. For additional examples and an analysis of Azuela's representation of *modernismo* in his novels, see Ángel Rama's "Mariano Azuela."

8. "[Había] montones de libros sobre la alfombra, mesas y sillas, los espejos descolgados con sus vidrios rotos, grandes marcos de estampas y retratos destrozados, muebles y bibelots hechos pedazos" (Azuela, *Los de abajo* 151).

9. "La novela, composición antes frívola, a que la pintura de las grandes pasiones había dado tanta elocuencia, ha sido absorbida por el interés histórico. Se le ha pedido, no que nos cuente aventuras de individuos, sino que nos los muestre como testimonios verdaderos y animados de un país, de una época, de una opinión. Se ha querido que nos sirviese para conocer la vida privada de un pueblo; ¿y no forma ésta siempre las memorias secretas de su vida pública?" (Bello 247).

10. "Tiene un concepto mezquino, clownesco y desorientado de la vida, propia en general de las clases medias" (Gallegos, "Hechos, ideas" 178–79).

11. "La primera novela, a nuestro entender, que nos informe, a través de la narración de una historia fícticia, de nuestros problemas más agudos, y que nos revele algunas de las preocupaciones y prejuicios que latían en la conciencia de la clase media de esa época" (Rojas 112).

12. "Todavía no se ha escrito en Colombia la novela que esté indudable y afortunadamente influida por los Joyce, por Faulkner o por Virginia Woolf" (García Márquez 116).

13. "Nos ha dado una novelística regional y pintoresca que en muy pocos casos ha llegado a lo hondo—a lo realmente trascendental—de las cosas" (Carpentier 10).

14. "En los campos de la Alta Saboya, como en las pendientes nevadas de Suiza, los hombres se conocen a sí mismos en el contacto con la naturaleza. Pero en la novela hispanoamericana . . . la naturaleza es sólo la enemiga que traga, destruye voluntades, rebaja dignidades y conduce al aniquilamiento. Ella es la protagonista, no los hombres eternamente aplastados por su fuerza" (Fuentes 10).

15. "El conquistador llegó en busca de los tesoros de la naturaleza, no de la personalidad de los hombres" (Fuentes 11).

16. "Si en América Latina las obras literarias se contentasen con reflejar o justificar el orden establecido, serían anacrónicas: inútiles. Nuestras obras deben ser de desorden: es decir, de un orden posible, contrario al actual" (Fuentes 31–32).

17. "Los latinoamericanos . . . son hoy contemporáneos de todos los hombres. Y pueden, contradictoria, justa y hasta trágicamente, ser universales escribiendo con el lenguaje de los hombres de Perú, Argentina o México" (Fuentes 32).

18. "Las de-formas de nuestra economía, nuestra política, nuestra dependencia, separables, fragmentadas" (Fuentes 35).

19. "Los dramas no son interiorizados ni moldean las conciencias, no aparecen las motivaciones íntimas de la conducta humana" (Vargas Llosa 30).

20. A well-known debate between Ángel Rama and Mario Vargas Llosa that took place in the pages of *Marcha* (and other newspapers in the region) in 1972 started because of Rama's critique of Vargas Llosa's "outdated" critical approach to García Márquez in *Historia de un deicidio*. The entire debate has been collected in Ángel Rama and Mario Vargas Llosa's *García Márquez y la problemática de la novela* (Corregidor-Marcha, 1973).

21. "Cada novela es un deicidio secreto" "un asesinato simbólico de la realidad" (Vargas Llosa, *García Márquez* 90).

22. "Incorporar a la ficción cuanto existe en la vida y en la fantasía del hombre" (Vargas Llosa, *García Márquez* 199–200).

23. "Pero no lo es de la fecunda, múltiple, audaz narrativa precervantina, y, sobre todo, dentro de ella, de las novelas de caballerías. Estas no son 'irreales'; son 'realistas', pero su concepto

de realidad es más ancho y complejo que la ajustada noción de realidad que estableció el racionalismo renacentista" (Vargas Llosa, *García Márquez* 198).

24. "Los mundos que crean sus ficciones. Y que valen ante todo por sí solos, son, también, versiones, calas a diferentes niveles, representaciones (psicológicas, fantásticas o mítica) de América Latina" (Vargas Llosa, "Novela Primitiva" 36).

25. "Mediante la *representatividad* de la región en la cual surgía" (Rama, *Transculturación narrativa* 18).

26. "Enmascara otra más vigorosa y persistente fuente nutricia: la peculiaridad cultural desarrollada en el interior, la cual no ha sido obra única de sus élites literarias sino el esfuerzo ingente de vastas sociedades construyendo sus lenguajes simbólicos" (Rama, *Transculturación Narrativa* 17).

27. "Cuyas obras se construyeron dentro del sistema literario latinoamericano, apelando a sus estructuras y a sus contribuciones, tratando de transformarlo y adecuarlo a las nuevas realidades" (Rama, "Vanguardias" 63).

28. Rama borrows the term "transculturation" from the work of Cuban anthropologist Fernando Ortiz, though he had developed the concept before encountering Ortiz's work (see González 71).

29. "Resuelve sobre el plano simbólico de la creación artística las tensiones que han sido engendradas por contradicciones que . . . son manifestaciones expresas de una conflictualidad real y objetiva" "en la escala reducida . . . de la macroestructura que debía generarse en la operación transculturante" (Rama, *Transculturación narrativa* 236–37).

30. "La construcción de un nivel sincrético que finalmente insume en una unidad más o menos desproblematizada . . . dos o más lenguas, conciencias étnicas, códigos estéticos, experiencias históricas" (Cornejo Polar, "Mestizaje, transculturación, heterogeneidad" 369).

31. "El espacio donde se configuraria la síntesis es el de la cultura-literatura hegemónica"; "literatura ilustrada'" (Cornejo Polar, "Mestizaje, transculturación, heterogeneidad" 369).

32. "El sometimiento del referente por imperio de factores exógenos"; "la capacidad de ese mismo referente para modificar" (Cornejo Polar, "El indigenismo y las literaturas heterogéneas" 15).

33. "La fractura entre el universo indígena y su representación indigenista" (Cornejo Polar, "El indigenismo y las literaturas heterogéneas" 17).

34. "Uno de los signos mayores de la modernidad hispanoamericana en el XIX" (Cornejo Polar, *Escribir en el aire* 109).

35. "La lengua de los estratos medios y populares como nueva norma de la lengua nacional, incluyendo notorias interferencias quichuas" (Cornejo Polar, *Escribir en el aire* 155).

36. "Ese esfuerzo homogeneizador emplaza sus límites dentro de lo 'popular' y en abierta contienda con el espacio oligárquico, constantemente aludido como antinacional" (Cornejo Polar, *Escribir en el aire* 159).

37. "Los protagonistas, por más elocuentes que sean, en realidad nunca dejan oír su palabra verdadera: de una u otra manera son siempre 'traducidos', a la par que el mundo parece constreñido dentro de una sólida estructura referencial" (Cornejo Polar, *Escribir en el aire* 188).

38. "Un sujeto plural que asume experiencias distintas situadas en tiempos discontinuos y que remiten a culturas diversas" (Cornejo Polar, *Escribir en el aire* 197).

39. "un espacio disputado por varias voces a través de un diálogo que no siempre es dialéctico . . . puesto que bien puede prescindir de la síntesis superadora" (Cornejo Polar, *Escribir en el aire* 199).

40. "La celebración de una patria capaz de acoger, con gozo, a todas las patrias" (Cornejo Polar, *Escribir en el aire*, 200).

WORKS CITED

Ahmad, Aijaz, "Jameson's Rhetoric of Otherness and the 'National Alegory.'" In *Theory: Classes, Nations, Literatures*, Verso, 1992, pp. 95–122.

Arguedas, José María. *Los ríos profundos*. Cátedra, 2004.

Arguedas, José María. *Deep Rivers*. Waveland Press, 2002.

Azuela, Mariano. *Los de abajo*. Cátedra, 1989.

Azuela, Mariano. *The Underdogs*. Translated by E. Munguia, Jr. First World Library, 2004.

Azuela, Mariano. *Las tribulaciones de una familia decente*. Botas, 1938.

Bello, Andrés. "Modo de escribir la historia." *Obras Completas*, vol. 23, 1981, pp. 231–72.

Carpentier, Alejo. "Problemática de la actual novela latinoamericana." *Tientos y diferencias, Contemporáneos*, 1966, pp. 7–28.

Cornejo Polar, Antonio. "El indigenismo y las literaturas heterogéneas: su doble estatuto socio-cultural." *Revista de Crítica Literaria Latinoamericana*, vol. 4, nos. 7/8, 1978, pp. 7–21.

Cornejo Polar, Antonio. *Escribir en el aire. Ensayo sobre la heterogeneidad sociocultural en las literaturas andinas*. Latinoamericana Editores, 2003.

Cornejo Polar, Antonio. "Mestizaje, transculturación, heterogeneidad." *Revista de Crítica Literaria Latinoamericana*, vol. 20, no. 40, 1994, pp. 368–71.

Cornejo Polar, Antonio. "Mestizaje, Transculturation, Heterogeneity." Translated by Christopher Dennis. *The Latin American Cultural Studies Reader*, Duke UP, 2004, pp. 116–19.

Cornejo Polar, Antonio. *Writing in the Air: Heterogeneity and the Persistence of Oral Tradition in Andean Literatures*. Translated by Lynda J. Jentsch. Duke UP, 2013.

Cruz, Pedro Nolasco. *Pláticas literarias*. Imprenta Cervantes, 1889.

Fuentes, Carlos. *La nueva novela hispanoamericana*. Joaquín Mortiz, 1969.

Gallegos Lara, Joaquín. "El pirandelismo en el Ecuador." *La noción de la vanguardia en el Ecuador. Recepción, trayectoria, documentos (1918-1934)*, edited by Humberto Robles, Casa de la cultura ecuatoriana, 1989, pp. 143–46.

Gallegos Lara, Joaquín. "Hechos, ideas, palabras: *Vida del ahorcado*." *La noción de la vanguardia en el Ecuador. Recepción, trayectoria, documentos (1918-1934)*, edited by Humberto Robles, Casa de la cultura ecuatoriana, 1989, pp. 177–79.

García Gutiérrez, Rosa. *Contemporáneos: La otra novela de la Revolución Mexicana*. Universidad de Huelva, 2000.

García Márquez, Gabriel. "¿Problemas de la novela?" *Los novelistas como críticos*, edited by Norma Klahn and Wilfrido Corral, Fondo de Cultura económica, 1991, pp. 116–17.

González, José Eduardo. *Appropriating Theory: Ángel Rama's Critical Work*. U of Pittsburgh P, 2017.

González Pérez, Aníbal. "Modernist Prose." *The Cambridge History of Latin American Literature*, vol. 2, edited by Roberto González Echevarría and Enrique Pupo-Walker, Cambridge UP, 1996, pp. 69–113.

González-Stephan, Beatriz. *Fundaciones: canon, historia y cultura nacional, La historiografía literaria del liberalismo hispanoamericano del siglo XIX*. Iberoamericana Vervuert, 2002.

Heríquez Ureña, Pedro. *Las corrientes literarias en la América hispánica*. Fondo de cultura económica, 2004.

Heríquez Ureña, Pedro. *Literary Currents in Hispanic America*. Oxford University Press, 1945.

Icaza, Jorge. *Huasipungo*. Cátedra, 2005.

Jameson, Fredric. *The Political Unconscious*. Cornell University Press, 1981.

Jameson, Fredric. "Third-World Literature in the Era of Multinational Capitalism." *Social Text*, no. 15, 1986, pp. 65–88.

Martínez, Luis A. *A la costa*. Ministerio de Cultura, 2008.

McKeon, Michael, ed. *Theory of the Novel: A Historical Approach*. Johns Hopkins UP, 2000.

Rama, Ángel. "Las dos vanguardias latinoamericanas." *Moldoror, Revista de la ciudad de Montevideo*, no. 9, 1973, pp. 58–64.

Rama, Ángel. "Mariano Azuela: ambición y frustración de las clases medias." *Literatura y clase social*, Folios ediciones, 1983, pp. 144–83.

Rama, Ángel. *Transculturación narrativa en América Latina*. El Andariego, 2008.

Rama, Ángel. *Writing Across Cultures: Narrative Transculturation in Latin America*. Translated by David Frye. Duke UP, 2012.

Rama, Ángel and Mario Vargas Llosa. *García Márquez y la problemática de la novela*. Corregidor-Marcha, 1973.

Rojas, Ángel Felicísimo. *La novela ecuatoriana*. Fondo de Cultura económica, 1948.

Robles, Humberto. *La noción de la vanguardia en el Ecuador. Recepción, trayectoria, documentos (1918–1934)*. Casa de la cultura ecuatoriana, 1989.

Ruffinelli, Jorge, "La recepción crítica de *Los de abajo*." *Los de abajo*, edited by Jorge Ruffinelli, ALLCA XX, 1997, pp. 231–60.

Sommer, Doris. *Foundational Fictions: The National Romances of Latin America*. U of California P, 1991.

Vargas Llosa, Mario. *García Márquez: Historia de un deicidio*. Monte Ávila, 1971.

Vargas Llosa, Mario. "Novela primitiva y novela de creación en América Latina." *Revista de la universidad de México*, vol. 23, no. 10, June 1969, pp. 29–36.

Watt, Ian. *The Rise of the Novel. Studies in Defoe, Richardson and Fielding*. U of California P, 1957.

CHAPTER 30

....

THE LATIN AMERICAN NOVEL
AND NEW TECHNOLOGY

....

MELISSA A. FITCH

New technology has problematized the notion of literary genres and national identity like nothing that has come before. This chapter traces some of the challenges of this "new frontier" in literary creation, including the way in which concepts such as "novel," "author," "reader," or even national affiliation have become blurred within this radically different format. I argue that the only defining feature of the digital realm of literature is precisely the *fluidity* in almost all aspects. This article addresses some of the ethical concerns related to the creation of such texts as well as those that surround the production, consumption, and disposal of the technology used to access them. It provides brief references to a few of the forays into the genre before discussing at greater length critical analyses of two hypermedia texts, *Amor de Clarice* by Rui Torres (Portugal) and *Hotel Minotauro* by Doménico Chiappe (Peru-Venezuela-Spain).

When one begins to examine the work that has been done thus far, a fundamental question becomes apparent: is digital literature, in spite of some regional or national references, essentially "post"-national, in that it exists outside of national borders and is often the result of a confluence of people from myriad countries? Do those who create it have more in common with their colleagues around the world interested in the genre than with those who happen to reside within the same geographical boundaries? Is it even possible to distinguish between electronic literature produced in one country versus another, as Leonardo Flores provocatively asked in 2017? Can a prolific digital author, such as Peruvian-born Venezuelan Doménico Chiappe—someone who has lived for almost twenty years in Spain—be considered a "Peruvian," "Venezuelan," or even a "Latin American" writer? What about the case of other well-known digital authors from Latin America who moved to the United States long ago and, as a result, have a distinctly "Latinx" flavor to their writing, such as the US/Chilean writer Luis Correa-Díaz? One has to remember that the United States has the second-largest population of Spanish speakers in the world, just behind Mexico and ahead of Spain. The Latinx population is 18%, with a total of 60,600,000 people (Krogstad), making it larger than the populations of most Latin American countries. So, may we consider the United States a "Latin American" country?

Beyond that, does classifying digital narratives as "Latin American" mean that they must treat Latin American themes or take place in Latin American settings? As Taylor points out, intertext is one of the most common characteristics of new media creations (*Electronic Literature*, 261). Would *Amor de Clarice*, created by Portuguese artist Rui Torres and based on a story by Brazilian Clarice Lispector, be considered European or Latin American? The same goes for the other hypermedia narrative examined in this chapter, *Hotel Minotauro*, based on classical Greek and Roman mythology and related to artistic works from Spain, but created by a Latin American-born author. Is it a "Latin American" novel?

Beyond national identity, the notion of "novel" is also rendered problematic by digital narratives, in large part because new technology confuses our understanding of what generally constitutes the literary genre—namely that a work has a beginning, a middle, and an end, and that, one assumes, it follows a linear, or, at the very least a somewhat coherent, progression. This is not always the case for digital literature. Digital texts seem to have a greater kinship with the texture of poetry or video games than they do with narrative, and the reader/viewer must actively piece together the elements to derive meaning.

One of the challenges for scholars working in digital literary and cultural studies is that an analysis of the subject will often require additional expertise to grasp the technological, visual, and acoustic dimensions. It may also necessitate an examination of a text's online presence both pre- and post-production. Scholarly research may now include the online comments and conversations or posted video replies that the digital text may engender. It may include any resultant fan fiction, bringing up yet another ethical consideration. If there are one hundred writers involved in the creation of a digital novel, then who is the author? Is she or he simply the curator of the elements included in the final form of the text? Instead of an author, is this individual more of a gatekeeper?

One example of this is Chilean author Jorge Baradit's novel *SYNCO* (2008). The novel was created online on his social-media accounts by his many fans and collaborators, with segments seen on YouTube videos before the book ever came out in print. *SYNCO* was created collectively over social media, including the author's personal blog, a Facebook page, Twitter, and YouTube, where Baradit posted three trailers for the book. Before the print publication, readers had already become part of one or more of these social-media communities and had read each segment as Baradit wrote and posted them. They were able to listen to the soundtrack. They were able to read and critique the novel as it was written and engage with the author. They could even decide if they wanted to be a part of the narrative, appearing as characters. Thus, the novel was the result of a creative community. The readers' contributions changed the text. Baradit felt that the novel represented a collective intelligence instead of one imposed from the powerful author upon the powerless reader ("La última experiencia" n.p.). Of course, his name became the only one associated with it in the end. All of this underscores the ethical considerations at hand and demonstrates how the lines between producer and consumer have become blurred—everyone can be an author, photographer, filmmaker, or musician or, yes, cultural-studies critic, using the tools and apps available on our laptops, tablets, and cellphones.

As I have argued elsewhere, for literary scholars, the dilemma is that literature is authoritarian by definition, "author"-itarian (Fitch, "Fierce" n.p.). So is cultural criticism. Scholars impose order upon the text in an effort to derive meaning. David William Foster once defined our task in the humanities, as seeking "something meaningful to say that helps us better understand the world" (15). Digital literature, however, may expand outward in infinite ways. It may have no defined beginning or ending nor involve any fixed text at all. Our task as scholars has become less about understanding "the" story than it is about the multi-sensorial experience of interacting with the digital creation, something that can be a frustrating and ultimately disorienting task. An example of this is the work of early digital literature pioneer Carlos Labbé and his *Pentagonal: incluídos tú y yo* (*Pentagonal: You and I included*) from 2001.

Labbé is a Chilean writer, critic, screenwriter, and musician who lives in New York. His hypertext novel *Pentagonal: incluídos tú y yo* was his only work of digital narrative. It may be considered one of the country's foundational digital texts. The novel was created to be read on a screen and offers different paths for the reader to follow through hyperlinks, each of which leads to fragments that connect back to the opening image on the screen in which the reader sees a clipping from a newspaper that mentions an accident on a street in Santiago. Five words in the clipping have hyperlinks. When the reader clicks on them, the stories multiply out. We are led to emails, text messages, quotes, technical writings, and more. There is constant interaction with the text because we are "included," exactly as the title makes clear. Our action is required to create meaning. As I have mentioned elsewhere, *Pentagonal*, by the standards of technology today, feels like a relic from the distant past (Fitch, "Chilean" 999). It predates social media, and there is no sound or videos. Words reign supreme. Although the reader is active, he or she cannot change the text nor contribute to the creation of meaning in any sustained way beyond clicking on the links. The author has controlled all of our options. Perhaps, as a result, it is difficult for the reader to follow a narrative line or even sustain interest. Labbé has said that *Pentagonal* has exactly $307.010.375 \times 10234$ possible paths for the reader to follow ("El habla" n.p.). The hypertext thus becomes a puzzle, and there is no "correct" way to put the pieces together. While Nicolás Bourriaud has referred to "relational aesthetics" in digital literature, arguing that our participation becomes the source of pleasure, I argue that rather than pleasure, it creates a sense of vertigo and disorientation, hardly an enjoyable experience.

Unfortunately, the literary artistry of many of *Pentagonal*'s most exquisitely written passages is lost amid the labyrinth. It would seem that the author agrees, having not written any subsequent digital narratives. Indeed, he has said that people become so focused on the format that they are robbed of their critical capability to evaluate the writing itself. He is not interested in having "digital groupies" (Labbé, "El habla" n.p.); he wants a reader to be moved by his writing instead of becoming lost and dazzled by the technical aspects.

For some scholars within cultural and literary studies, the lack of clarity with regard to genres, authors, and readers has led to full-scale aversion in terms of addressing digital literature intellectually. How do we analyze something so fluid or, in some cases, unending? How do we begin to assess the impact of literary creations when each new day brings with it quite literally millions of new texts, in various forms? How can scholars approach the new genres that technology has created, and for which "literature" no longer seems an appropriate descriptive category? How do we handle authorship as a collaboration, not merely among writers of the text, but also among the teams of musicians, web designers, graphic designers, and programmers that may be involved in the final version? For researchers, all of these considerations can be exhausting to contemplate.

Claire Taylor, one of the genre's most important scholars, has argued that cultural-studies researchers must take three features into account when approaching a digital text: aesthetics, technologics, and ethics (*Electronic Literature* 263). This is the only way that one may grasp the complexity of the genre. Cultural and literary scholars are already accustomed to addressing the first. In digital texts, there are often multiple intertexts and from a range of artistic and literary sources. One can tease out these connections fairly easily. It is when we turn to the second point that things become a bit murky, because knowledge of technology—digital platforms and terminology—also becomes paramount to our understanding of a text. Digital creations are often self-referential, in that they include references to the process and context of their own making. Scholars would need to have some level of fluency in this language, not expertise, but at least a baseline recognition of many of the terms and platforms that are used.

Finally, there would have to be some acknowledgment of the ethics involved in all aspects of digital production—the large corporations that control digital platforms, the exploitation of the free labor of many individuals who contribute to the creation of a given text, the system of surveillance that is necessarily a part of using technology, in which one's clicks are generating profits for the corporations who will then sell that information to advertisers. While it appears to be "free" to use the platforms, someone is always making money, and it is rarely the authors. If there is no book being produced or sold, then how do authors make a living? Must they be independently wealthy to produce their works? Beyond that, if a digital text is a collective enterprise, how do the people who contribute get remunerated?

Although Taylor does not address it, I add to her third category of "ethics" the production, consumption, and disposal of the tablets, laptops, and cellphones that we must use to access digital creations, something I have discussed at length elsewhere (Fitch, "Fierce" n.p.). What are the working conditions in the factories, most of which are in developing regions? What happens to the used objects when, as a result of the intentional "planned obsolescence" corporations use to increase their profits, consumers must always buy the latest version of their phones and laptops? Their "old" objects are often shipped out of wealthy countries and deposited in toxic landfills in India or Africa, enormous dumps where people, often children, will scavenge through the highly toxic materials, searching for metals that may be salvaged and sold. As I have argued previously, cultural-studies scholars have always concerned themselves with the production and consumption of cultural narratives. Technology and digital creations, however, require that we consider the ethical consideration of disposal as well (Fitch, "Fierce" n.p.). All of this leads us to an inescapable question: to what degree are digital authors, and are we, as users/readers, complicit in this system of exploitation that exists on so many levels simply by virtue of accessing it? Then again, is "opting out" of technology even a possibility today, given that it predominates almost all aspects of our personal and professional life?

Moving beyond Taylor's formula, another area of concern for scholars in cultural studies and the humanities who may be interested in devoting their academic careers to digital texts is this: what happens when as a result, again, of the intentional "planned obsolescence" of technology, the platforms, and programs that house the digital work cease to function because they have become outdated and, as a result, the digital literary work disappears? What possible merit can be gleaned by analyzing a text, no matter how brilliantly crafted, if it no longer exists? In the case of *Amor de Clarice*, one of the digital creations examined below, it was created with Adobe Acrobat, which ceased to exist at the end of 2020 ("Adobe EOL"). Readers attempting to access digital texts done with the system are greeted with a rather stark "end of life" announcement.

To try to disseminate the wealth of electronic literature created around the world, a group of scholars formed the Electronic Literature Organization in 1999 and have worked diligently over the last twenty years to save and disseminate digital works from around the world, producing three (so far) volumes of electronic literature and also hosting international conferences on the topic. The texts are available online in multiple languages and are grouped by country. Each iteration has revealed the wealth of hypertexts being created. The work serves as an invaluable repository for scholars, and the organization enables them to connect with their colleagues on almost every continent. Many connected with ELO formed the *Red de Literatura Electrónica Latinoamericana*, litElat (Network of Latin American Electronic Literature), and, working together, in January of 2021, they released the first volume of electronic literature from Latin America and the Caribbean, a tome that includes eighty-one titles that were created in six languages and represents ten countries. The project was brought to life by some of the most important scholars in the genre—Claudia Kozak, Leonardo Flores, and Rodolfo Mata. While it is impossible for any such endeavor to include all of the digital creations that have been made within the Luso-Hispanic world, this initial volume, the first of what one hopes will be many more, gives the reader and new initiate to the genre a sense of the remarkable range of the digital texts available. The works are available for free for anyone with access to the internet, which again brings us to the topic of financing.

As mentioned previously, there is rarely any payment that goes to the authors who create digital narratives (nor the scholars who compile the texts for all to utilize). The bottom line is that writing literature online requires money from the author herself or himself or from an institution willing to fund the project and subsequently maintain a website in which it is housed. The lack of funds to maintain/update websites, platforms, and operating systems where the electronic literature is found has meant that in spite of the best efforts of those who seek to rescue such texts from obscurity, some of the creations have no doubt been lost. And there is one last consideration that must be taken into account. Even if a scholar has access to a digital work and elects to write about it, there is no guarantee that this research will be valued by their institution or count in any meaningful way toward their annual reviews. For scholars and/or administrators who have always worked exclusively within the realm of the printed text, there is often a fundamental lack of understanding or interest on the topic, and occasionally a refusal to acknowledge its importance for the purposes of promotion and tenure.

Despite the heroic efforts of global Latin Americanist scholars such as Flores, Kozak, Gainza, and many others to preserve and disseminate Latin American digital literature, there is no way to escape the fact that technology has increasingly become dominated by a few tech giants that we must rely on, most of which are in the United States, though increasingly they may originate in China, Korea, or Japan. Beyond that, it is important to remember that the digital divide continues to loom large, with 40% of the world's population without any internet at all (Kemp n.p.). New technology requires knowledge, time, and access. But who has access to the systems needed to read or produce digital literature? Generally speaking, the answer is those who have the most money and leisure time, neither of which are found in abundance in most of the world.

As I have argued elsewhere (Fitch, "Chilean" 996), Chilean scholar Carolina Gainza, one of the most important pioneers in the field of Luso-Hispanic digital cultural studies, acknowledges the dominance of US-based corporate entities behind much of internet content, including the "homemade" videos of YouTube influencers. Still, she argues that because people can produce digital texts collectively, this action undermines the individualism that neoliberalism is reliant upon. Readers can also find ways to destabilize meaning. For her, ideas about authorship in any traditional sense are thoroughly undermined by readers who can subvert meaning through the resignification of signs, in essence allowing them to revolt. The hackers become revolutionaries.

This was humorously illustrated when a new version of Jorge Luis Borges's short story "El Aleph" came out in 2009, written by Argentine Pablo Katchadjian. The author more than doubled the word count of Borges's work to write his "El Aleph Engordado" ("The Fattened Aleph"). He printed his work and distributed it to his friends as a Christmas gift. Subsequently, he was sued in 2011 by María Kodama, Borges's widow, who had the Intellectual Property Rights to the original story.

Many were outraged by the lawsuit. One, an Argentine writer/scholar who currently is at MIT, Milton Laüfer, decided to create his own digital versions of "El Aleph." The first was "El Aleph on a Diet," in which, when the reader accessed the text online, random words would automatically be edited out, creating, in the process, a much shorter version. Later, he created "El Aleph on AutoCorrect" in both Spanish and English versions, wherein the process of reading the text would change automatically to something incoherent, exactly as the autocorrect feature renders our writing incomprehensible. As a wink to the reader, Laüfer cheekily includes on the opening webpage of his new versions that the rights of the original belong exclusively to the María Kodama. No one can deny that Katchadjian and Laüfer created texts so complex and clever that the illustrious author himself would have no doubt derived great pleasure from them. We turn now to examining in greater depth two digital narratives, and in each case we focus on how a specific scholar has approached the work.

AMOR DE CLARICE

Amor de Clarice (2005) is a digital creation by Portuguese artist/writer Rui Torres. It is based on Brazilian writer Clarice Lispector's short story "Amor" ("Love," 1960). Lispector (1920–1977) was one of the country's most acclaimed writers. Readers are familiar with the existential themes in her work related to women's everyday life. Her stories and novels are often filled with the interior monologues and stream-of-conscious musings of protagonists who feel trapped and suffocated by their life circumstances. "Love" appeared in the collection *Family Ties* (*Laços de Família*, 1960). In it, we are privy to the fragmented, unhappy thoughts of Ana, as she rides a bus in Rio de Janeiro, thinking about her life as she visually takes in all that is around her. As stated, *Amor de Clarice*, the multimedia text based on the story, was created by Portuguese artist Rui Torres, a professor at the University Fernando Pessoa, Portugal. Torres teaches semiotics, literature, and hypermedia, and he directs the academic journal *Cibertextualidades*.

Brazilian literary critic Alckmar Luiz dos Santos argues that Torres's digital literary creation can be tied to Brazilian poet Oswald de Andrade's modernist masterpiece "Manifesto Antropófago" ("Anthropophagist Manifesto," 1928), in which he argued that colonized countries such as Brazil should ingest the culture of the colonizer in order to make it their own. The work, written in poetic prose, is considered among the most important in Brazilian literature, in part because it, in and of itself, provides examples of literary cannibalism, most famously in the case of Shakespeare's quote from Hamlet, playfully reworked as with "Tupi or not tupi, that is the question," referencing one of Brazil's most numerous indigenous peoples, a group that had been known in popular accounts of the day for their ritualistic cannibalistic practices. The critic argues that *Amor de Clarice* connects to Andrade's modernist notion in that identity is never fixed. It is always moving, never stable, because one is always in the process of devouring the Other (dos Santos 490). Torres turns Lispector's prose into fifty-two poems in which the author's words, like identity, are never fixed. They constantly interact with sounds and visual cues. Dos Santos argues that Torres's work, in and of itself, displays the anthropophagy of the printed word by the digital creation.

In Torres's digital work, fragments of Lispector's story move horizontally and vertically across the screen, and the reader may click on whatever she or he wants to hear. As dos Santos points out, the click is not instantaneous, so one is left looking at one's reflection while awaiting the program to upload. The sound of voices reciting the words begins to pile up, creating, as he poetically phrases it, "a rare and delicate crowd effect, a sort of prayer or collective ritual" (499). Torres produces a visual and auditory poem from Clarice's prose, finding the words' rhythm and place, incorporating the audio, verbal, or visual field.

Although the images on each page, the words, are the same for all readers/viewers, we are the ones who take control as we choreograph our reading. This serves to open up the work. It is like "reader response" criticism on steroids. The artist enables us to be privy to the protagonist's fragmentary thoughts. We feel her unhappiness in her marriage, and register what she sees on the trolley and out the window. But perhaps the most brilliant element of *Amor de Clarice* is that Torres includes the sound of deep breathing. As such, we, ourselves, are engaged in an act of anthropophagy, devouring and inhabiting the protagonist while reading and hearing her thoughts. But have we devoured her, or has she devoured us?

Dos Santos demonstrates how Rui's creation plays with the plurality of signifiers in utilizing the screen space. Some words of Lispector's text are in bold; others are more faded. The fragments of text move from the front to the back, from visible to invisible. We are watching and hearing them when we click on the words. I would argue that this collage of thoughts rings far truer to the protagonist's chaotic stream-of-consciousness thoughts than what is found in the story's original narrative form. The artist has cut up and reassembled Lispector's narrative prose to create a rhythm. But as dos Santos points out, Torres is not merely poeticizing the prose; he is introducing his own work of art into the original creation by inserting sounds and visual breaks, and through the selection of the words and sentence fragments he includes (492).

Dos Santos argues that Torres refuses to allow the continuity of the short story to dominate his creation. He ponders the best way for one to approach "reading" the multimedia version. Can it be done without knowing the original short story? Are the two works complementary, or are they confrontational? If one views the hypermedia, how can one make sense of the fragments and create any "story" around them? In the end, he argues that "What matters, in this case, are the new meanings he is capable of inventing from the fragments: as if every tiny fragment became a marker, a label, a reference pointing to an unrecoverable meaning and, at the same time, delimitating possibilities of signification in his [Torres's] reader's horizon of meanings" (494).

Although the fragments always carry a plurality of significations, the predominant sensation of engaging the online text is that of the protagonist's despair. We register the different images that she sees—the blind man, the dropped eggs, the branches of trees, bees, a cat, a sparrow, a garden, sensations of both delight and disgust, the strangeness of her own house, the evil of the world, the light of a candle, her children.

Ultimately, as dos Santos argues, Rui Torres's hypermedia creation brought Lispector's words to life like nothing else. It conveyed her protagonist's sense of detachment, the alienation from her own life that she was feeling. The critic is aware of how all of these elements of digital creation come into play to create meaning, "Clarice's short story, Rui's choices, constructions and interferences, my critical and theoretical perspectives; the always-relevant part of the programming and, by extension, of the programmers" (497). He concludes that "*Amor de Clarice* has made me hear, read and feel, in a very different way—I would even say closer—the writings of Clarice Lispector. Rather hidden elements of Clarice's writing are brought forth and presented in an attractive and original (why not say it?) form, beginning with the possibilities of seeing and listening, which in the written tradition stay hidden" (497). Indeed, *Amor de Clarice* underscores precisely what would be impossible to convey fully on a printed page. Thus, Rui Torres conveys Lispector's artistry in a way that surpasses that of the original.

HOTEL MINOTAURO

Hotel Minotauro (*Minotaur Hotel*, 2013–2015) is the hypermedia novel created by Doménico Chiappe, an author and journalist born in Peru. Chiappe lived his early life in Venezuela and has resided in Spain since 2002. He is widely known for the multimedia novel *Tierra de Extracción*, part of the second anthology of Electronic Literature Organization (Borrás et al. n.p.). Here we focus on his digital novel *Minotaur Hotel*, a project developed as part of the doctoral thesis at the Universidad Carlos III and available in Spanish, French, and English.

In the hypermedia novel Chiappe reworks the classical Minotaur myth. It has been a recurring motif in art and literature, particularly during the 1930s within avant-garde art and literature, used to convey the alienation of writers and artists at the time. As Claire Taylor argues, Chiappe draws a parallel between the Minotaur and the alienation of modern life of late capitalism. He is half-man, half-bull, and his mother, a human, is Pasiphae. Pasiphae has been punished by her husband Minos for her unrestrained sexuality—that which resulted in the Minotaur. She is condemned by her husband Minos to be trapped in a labyrinth forever, where her sexuality can be contained. In *Hotel Minotauro*, the labyrinth is, in fact, the hotel, in which the reader/player is in a hallway, and able to open two doors on the right and two on the left. We may elect to see what is behind each door in whatever order we like, although once we have clicked on all of the links contained within a "room," we are forced to return to the main hallway. We cannot exit the hotel or even leave the hallway. Behind each door, the possibilities of what we experience/see and read are finite. In this way, the author retains control.

We become characters in the story, centered in the hallway and making our choices. As Taylor points out, the third-person singular verb form is used in the instructions on the first page, and as such, it can refer to the Minotaur making his way through the hotel or it may be directed at us, using the formal address. The reader/player/Minotaur must decide which door to open. Throughout the novel, Chiappe references technology, making clear analogies between the labyrinth, described as a *red* or "net," and the internet experience; thus, we, like Pasiphae and the Minotaur, are also imprisoned in this labyrinth. However, as Taylor points out, it really is not a labyrinth at all. While it is true, we cannot escape, there is still a center, one to which we must return repeatedly. It is contained space, almost claustrophobic. A true labyrinth would be one that would multiply out in myriad ways. Similarly, it may not be considered nonhierarchic. The author is in control and we are forced to play by his rules. While the novel does not follow a fixed linear structure and we are allowed to make decisions, it does not feel "free" in any way. We are not forced to click on all of the doors, but we cannot escape. We are not allowed to roam through the hotel or go to the bar (although the ambient sounds in the initial image give one the impression that the bar or restaurant is nearby, perhaps we are just coming from it).

Taylor argues that the author may be pointing to precisely how our possibilities, the great utopian freedom that the internet initially had represented when it began in the 1990s, are, in fact, limited and constrained by the corporate entities that control it and, by extension, us: "Chiappe's playing with the rhizome metaphor thus brings us face to face with the realization that we cannot escape just as the minotaur of classical myth could not escape the labyrinth, so we are trapped within an increasingly corporate, enclosed spaces of the internet" (238).

The novel also offers a critique of social media and the commodification of self, specifically that of women. As Taylor points out, it is a critique of the need to create online social capital in a neoliberal world that is hyper-focused on competitive individualism. Chiappe is critiquing the system, and yet we, as readers/players, are placed in the uncomfortable position of being voyeurs and active participants. We are complicit.

We meet a young woman behind one of the doors, presumed to be Pasiphae, the Minotaur's mother. She is posting scantily clad, eroticized photos of herself to social media, and we see the number of "thumbs up" and "thumbs down" the photos have garnered, demonstrating "the ways in which women are compelled to self-present and self-regulate on social networking sites" (Taylor 239). Taylor points out that the image is blurry, grainy, deliberately seedy. It is, ultimately, grotesque. She argues that Chiappe uses the same abrasive aesthetic to critique late capitalism and the commodification and exploitation under the patriarchy of women's bodies on the internet.

While I understand Taylor's point, I find it too reductionist. It does not allow for a range of fluid desires that may not fit within the paradigm of compulsory heterosexuality or, for that matter, cis-gender categories. Perhaps the woman is putting herself on display, not for the male gaze but a lustful female gaze. Or perhaps she finds it titillating that anyone, regardless of gender identification, would desire her. Taylor states elsewhere in her essay that social media is used more by women than men, so is it not more likely that these hypersexualized images are not directed at men but rather at other women? She states, "Here, in Chiappe's updated version of the Minotaur myth, the content behind this door demonstrates how women's bodies and sexuality are yet again the subject of control, of censure, and in this case of voyeuristic pleasure (for an implied male gaze)" (243). But why deny the possibility that voyeur could be a woman, or it can be someone who does not identify along the gender binary at all? To say that any woman who elects to display her body is incapable of recognizing how the patriarchy manipulates her is reductionist. Perhaps she elects to do it because she feels fully sexual, sensual, powerful. This is not to deny the forces that exist and the connection between the cult of the individual and the values of neoliberalism, nor to deny the horrific reality of gender violence; it is to say that the topic is far more nuanced than the version presented, in which there is no acknowledgment of the spectrum of queer sexuality and gender identification.

What is clear is that Chiappe is making a critique of the so-called like economy connected to social media in which the experience of the self has become increasingly commodified. Self-worth is measured in "likes," laudatory words, or emojis that show "friends'" reactions. The critique continues when we open another door, behind which we find a writer and masked executioner having a conversation about capitalism, neoliberalism, and privatization. The executioner sentences the writer to death, and the sickle descends across the screen, cutting the words into fragments. During this entire sequence, there is guitar music and a voiceover reading of a short song about a corrupt, inept government filled with buffoons.

Behind this door, we also can read the first sentences of a series of emails, all of which seem to refer to the lustful "bad" woman in the other hotel room who got what she deserved. The email's sentences include crude references to her body. The sentences demonstrate the full force of the social-media lynch mob, intent on punishing the woman for her unrestrained lust. The connection with the original myth of Pasiphae is established in one of the email sentences when we read that the woman was from Colchis, the town on the Black Sea where Pasiphae was from. As Taylor argues,

> She represents all women who are compelled to present themselves online in the new regime of visibility. Thus, the story of the woman who is punished is not just an ancient myth whose barbarity we can easily distance ourselves from. Instead, we are implicated as participants within this new regime of visibility, and we, too, perpetuate the neoliberal conditions of the circulation of online social capital. We are part of this culture which simultaneously requires women to hypersexualize their bodies, present them for display, and then punishes them for doing so.
>
> (*Electronic Literature* 256)

Perhaps most importantly, Chiappe's *Minotaur Hotel* demands that the reader-voyeur interrogate his or her own complicity within this systemic violence of late capitalism.

If there is one certainty that the reader may take away from this brief examination into Latin American digital novels, it is that of the complex and fascinating challenge that awaits us as cultural-studies academics working within the digital realm. While the inclination of scholars might be to hide from the onslaught of sounds, texts, image, formats, storylines—to take refuge in the familiar experience of a printed book—it is my greatest hope that the exhilarating Mr.-Toad's-Wild-Ride experience of embarking upon analysis of Latin American digital texts will now be an attractive option. In this way, we will continue to open up new horizons for scholarly exploration that the artists, writers, and academic pioneers mentioned in this chapter have begun. This is the bright new world of "updated, revitalized cultural studies" that awaits us, as Taylor has phrased it (2019 265). Adventure beckons.

WORKS CITED

"Adobe Flash Player End of Life (EOL) General Information Page." *Adobe*, January 13, 2021. www.adobe.com/products/flashplayer/end-of-life.html

Andrade, Oswald de. "Anthropophagic Manifesto." *Revista de Antropofagia [Journal of Anthropophagy]*, São Paulo 1.1 (1928).

Baradit, Jorge. *SYNCO*. Ediciones B, 2008.

Baradit, Jorge. "La última experiencia inmersiva no va a tener que ver con que te cuenten sobre la batalla, te van a meter en ella." Interview by Carolina Gainza. *Cultura digital en Chile: literatura, música y cine*, May 2017. culturadigitalchile.cl/wp-content/uploads/2017/09/Jorge-Baradit.pdf

Borges, Jorge Luis. "El Aleph." *Obras Completas*, vol. 2, Emecé, 1989, pp. 617–28.

Borrás, Laura, et al. *Electronic Literature Collection*, vol. 2, edited by Leonardo Flores et al. February 2011. collection.eliterature.org/2/

Bourriaud, Nicolas. *Relational Aesthetics*. Translated by Simon Pleasance and Fronza Woods. Les presses du réel, 2002.

Chiappe, Doménico. "Hotel Minotauro." *Doménico Chiappe*, 2013–2015. www.domenicochiappe.com/hotel-minotauro

Dos Santos, Alckmar Luiz. "New Strategies of Anthropophagy in Brazilian/Portuguese Digital Literature." *Neohelicon*, vol. 36, no. 2, 2009, pp. 489–502.

Fitch, Melissa A. "Chilean Digital Literature." *The Cambridge History of Chilean Literature*, edited by Ignacio López-Calvo, Cambridge University Press, 2021. pp. 990–1022.

Fitch, Melissa A. "The Fierce Urgency of Now: Hispanic Studies, New Technology and the Future of the Profession." *Language, Image, Power: Luso-Hispanic Cultural Studies Theory and Practice*, edited by Susan Larson, Routledge, 2021. pp. 171–190.

Flores, Leonardo. "La literatura electrónica latinoamericana, caribeña y global: generaciones, fases y tradiciones." *Artelogie*, no. 11, 2017, n.p.

Foster, David William. "The Last Lecture." *El ambiente nuestro: Chicano/Latino Homoerotic Writing*, edited by N. Katherine Hayles; Nick Montfort; Scott Rettberg; Stephanie Strickland, Bilingual Press, 2005, p. 5.

Katchadjian, Pablo. *El aleph engordado*. Imprenta Argentina de Poesía, IAP, 2009.

Kemp, Simon. "Digital in 2020: Global Digital Overview." *Datareportal*. We Are Social, Hootsuite, January 30, 2020. datareportal.com/reports/digital-2020-global-digital-overview

Kozak, Claudia. "Esos raros poemas nuevos: Teoría y crítica de la poesía digital latinoamericana." *El jardín de los poetas: Revista de teoría y crítica de poesía latinoamericana*, Universidad Nacional Mar de Plata, June 2017, cajaderesonancia.com/index.php?mod=jardin&view=detalle&id=240

Krogstad, Jens Manuel. "Hispanics Have Accounted for More Than Half of Total U.S. Population Growth Since 2010." *Fact Tank: News in the Numbers*, Pew Research Center, July 10, 2020. https://www.pewresearch.org/fact-tank/2020/07/10/hispanics-have-accounted-for-more-than-half-of-total-u-s-population-growth-since-2010/

Labbé, Carlos. "El habla de lo digital no tiene que ver con la copia única, con el ejemplar, sino con la pulsión que se establece entre el usuario y lo que está ahí." Interview by Carolina Gaínza. *Cultura digital en Chile: literatura, música y cine*, July 2016, culturadigitalchile.cl/wp-content/uploads/2017/07/Carlos-Labbe%CC%81.pdf

Labbé, Carlos. *Pentagonal: incluidos tú y yo*. 2001. Universidad Complutense de Madrid, May 2016. www.ucm.es/info/especulo/hipertul/pentagonal/

Läufer, Milton. "*El Aleph a dieta*". *Milton Läufer*, August 14, 2015. www.miltonlaufer.com.ar/aleph/

Läufer, Milton. "El Aleph autocorregido." *Milton Läufer*, June 1, 2016. www.miltonlaufer.com.ar/alephautocorrect/

Lispector, Clarice. "Amor." *Laços de família*, Francisco Alves Editora, 1960, *Releituras*. www.rel
    eituras.com/clispector_amor.asp

Taylor, Claire. *Electronic Literature in Latin America: From Text to Hypertext*. Palgrave
    MacMillan, 2019.

Taylor, Claire. *Place and Politics in Latin American Digital Culture: Location and Latin
    American Net Art*. Routledge, 2014.

Torres, Rui. "Amor de Clarice." 2005. telepoesis.net/amorclarice/v2_js/index.html

PART VI

AUTHORS

CHAPTER 31

THE NEW FRONTIERS IN THE NARRATIVE OF MARÍA LUISA BOMBAL

ALEXIS CANDIA-CÁCERES

THE writing of María Luisa Bombal (1910–1980) is one of the most radical proposals in the Latin American literature of the early twentieth century. With three novels—*La última niebla* (*The Final Mist*, 1935), *La amortajada* (*The Shrouded Woman*, 1938) and *House of Mist* (1947); a handful of short stories—"Las islas nuevas" ("New Islands," 1939), "El árbol" ("The Tree," 1939), "Trenzas" ("Braids," 1940), "Lo secreto" ("The Unknown," 1944),[1] "La historia de María Griselda" ("The Story of María Griselda," 1946); and a few poetic chronicles—"Mar, cielo y tierra" ("Sea, Sky and Earth," 1940), "Washington, ciudad de las ardillas" ("Washington, City of Squirrels," 1940), and "La maja y el ruiseñor" ("The Maiden and the Nightingale," 1960)—she was able to chart new paths for narrative written in Spanish.

Analyzing the bulk of Bombal's literary productivity, it is striking that it is the result of efforts made during a limited period of time—with only twelve years between *The Final Mist* and *House of Mist*—and that it is, moreover, the product of young author: Bombal published her first text at the age of twenty-five and her last one at the age of thirty-seven.[2] Bombal thus emerges as a skilled, mature author, aware of her strengths and abilities, and of the risks she is willing to take with her first book.

Bombal was met with a mixed reception and appraisal in Chile. At first, her novels and short stories were reviewed and praised by the leading literary critics of the era. Thus, for example, literary critic Alone[3] argued with regard to *The Final Mist* that: "María Luisa Bombal writes from within and the words obey her. This is precious" (qtd. in Gligo 99).[4] Ricardo A. Latcham, meanwhile, asserts that "Ms. Bombal, with her short and concise story, has opened up a rupture in our dull landscape of novels" (qtd. in Gligo 99).[5] *The Shrouded Woman* won the Premio Municipal de Novela (Municipal Novel Prize) in 1942.

Nonetheless, and perhaps motivated by her lengthy stay in the United States and Argentina (1942–1973), a protracted silence hangs over her work, a silence that will reflect the fact that she did not win the Premio Nacional de Literatura (National Literature Prize), the highest institutional recognition for a writer in Chile. It is rumored that she did not win the prize because of her writer's block or because of her personal problems. In any case, the truth is that Bombal passed away in 1980 without ever having achieved a recognition that—as Alone mentions—needed Bombal much more than she needed the award.

In contrast to the lack of institutional recognition of her literary production, Bombal slowly earns the admiration of critics and writers both nationally and internationally. Amado Alonso's early review of *The Final Mist* in 1941 is followed by studies by such noted critics as Cedomil Goic, Hernán Vidal, Lucía Guerra, and Marjorie Agosín, among many others. For instance, novelist Manuel Rojas said about her fiction that it was: "Imprecise, surrealist, written like no woman and almost no man has written in Chile" (qtd. in Guerra, *Mujer* 42).[6] Jorge Luis Borges argued, in a review of *The Shrouded Woman*, that it is a "Book of sad magic, deliberately *suranée*, a book with a hidden structure, a book that our America will never forget" (81).[7] For his part, Juan Rulfo remarked about his relationship with writing and the figure of Bombal: "She gave me a copy of *La última niebla*, which I read in a single sitting. It was a marvellous novel, written with all the simplicity that one might desire . . . I told her that its pages had inspired several streets in Comala" (qtd. in Zuñiga 62).[8] Gabriel García Márquez, in turn, establishes a connection with his own writing project: "She is the forerunner of what has been called 'magical realism'" (qtd. in Zuñiga 63).[9]

That contention by the author of *Cien años de soledad* (*One Hundred Years of Solitude*, 1967) sheds light on one of the most remarkable characteristics of Bombal's writing: her ability to conquer new frontiers. For the purposes of this study, it is important to understand this concept through the proposal made by Joaquín Valhondo de la Luz, to the effect that, although there may be different types of frontiers, they all share a single element: "We are speaking about thousands of different frontiers, but with one thing in common by definition, namely, the boundary" (134).[10] Bombal was able to shift the boundaries of Latin American literature in the early twentieth century, thus conquering new "territories" that made it possible to incorporate and create aesthetic innovations and new modes of representation, to introduce better female voices and other erotic pleasures, and to capture different ways of experiencing and understanding religiosity. Although this is evidenced by her literature as a whole, this article will analyze her novels: *The Final Mist*, *The Shrouded Woman*, and *House of Mist*.

Bohemian Literature

María Luisa Bombal was part of the Chilean upper class. This is a defining element in her life history. First, because it gave her access to a privileged education in both Chile and France, which led to her admission to the School of Arts at the Sorbonne. There, she completed her studies in French literature with a thesis on Prosper Mérimée. Bombal undoubtedly had access to high culture and the arts. Second, belonging to her class implies restrictions related to a conservative ideology that sets strict rules regarding what a "well-educated girl," such as herself, can or cannot do. This is evident, for example, when considering that Bombal must return to Chile because of her other passion: theatre. Neither her family nor her social circle looks favorably on her joining the *l'Atelier* theatre in France: "María Luisa knows perfectly well that a woman performing on stage is frowned upon in her family and social environment" (Gligo 50).[11] Consequently, the patriarchal structure of her social class establishes the roles and duties that a woman "must" carry out, placing her, most often, in a secondary position in Chilean society: "During the 1930s, in Chile, the state and the nation were underpinned by a highly patriarchal structure, where the relationships between men and women were governed by patterns of domination and subordination" (Guerra, *Mujer* 15).[12]

Bombal returns to Chile in 1931. Following her return to the country, there are two events that will influence her literary trajectory. First, she becomes romantically involved with Eulogio Sánchez, a complex, difficult, and bitter relationship for the writer, which involves an attempted suicide and an attempted murder. Her relationship with Sánchez is significant because it influences, as Bombal herself acknowledges, the writing of *The Final Mist*:

> *La última niebla* is inspired by having had a lover I did not have . . . My first experience of love was quite frightening. I made him the husband; the novel has a rather tragic and unpleasant autobiographical basis . . . The sexual experience too; at that time, the rules were meant to be obeyed by the middle class . . . The novel is based on my first love, which ended in disaster.
>
> (*Obras* 340)[13]

Second, she was part of the national theatre and the bohemian scene of the 1930s. Returning to the dreams that had been dashed in France, she joined the Compañía Nacional de Dramas y Comedias (National Drama and Comedy Troupe), playing at least three different roles. She also comes into contact with a group of intellectuals and writers led by Pablo Neruda. This group met in Santiago's bars and cafés to discuss literary topics, in particular those associated with the new currents of the time. As Ágata Gligo notes: "Chilean poets and writers are steeped in avant-garde movements" (68).[14] The novelist Juan Uribe Echevarría describes Bombal's relationship with the group: "She was charming and very elegant at a time when we all dressed very badly" (qtd. n Gligo 69).[15] Uribe Echevarría gives an account of how a woman of the haute bourgeoisie becomes a member of a group, one from a different social class, but which shares the same interest in literature. Bombal demonstrates, in this regard, a broad and thorough knowledge of contemporary literature that allows her to be validated by Neruda himself. When considering these biographical elements, Bombal's contradiction between her life circumstances and aesthetics is understandable. Lucía Guerra addresses this ambivalence:

> her behavior and way of life were considered eccentric in the society of the era, while, paradoxically, she shared the hegemonic notion that the only aim and lot of women was love. Her life is thus woven into the fabric of the cultural imperatives imposed on women at the time and into her career as a writer, imperatives that were an essential factor.
>
> (*Mujer* 13–14)[16]

Following the rupture of her relationship with Sánchez, Bombal accepts an invitation from Neruda to go to Buenos Aires. There, she replaces the Chilean bohemia with the Argentine, immersing herself in the group that Neruda has established with Federico García Lorca and others. It is a period marked by her transformation into a writer. Indeed, two of the central works of Chilean literature will take shape in Neruda's flat: Bombal's *The Final Mist* and the Chilean poet's *Residencia en la tierra* (*Residence on Earth*). Bombal refers to the writing of her debut work as follows: "I must not be ungrateful for the mysterious influence I received from *Residencia en la tierra*, that book by Pablo Neruda which–with its metaphysical power–is, for me, the essence of his work. My first novel, *The Final Mist*, was born in the kitchen of his house. I was very young. I wrote at night" (*Obras* 355).[17]

During her time in Buenos Aires, Bombal also develops close ties with Jorge Luis Borges. This friendship was cemented by walks along the river, a love of cinema, and conversations about literature. Indeed, one of his dialogues addressed the composition of *The Shrouded Woman*. In the review he wrote of the novel, Borges notes the misgivings that he expressed to the Chilean writer:

> one, the obfuscation of the novel's human events by the great superhuman event of the sentient and meditative dead woman; the other, the obfuscation of that great event by the human events . . . she gave me the original manuscript of *La Amortajada* several months later. I read it in a single afternoon and I was able to see, with admiration, that in those pages, the disjunctive unerring risks I had foreseen were unerringly circumvented. (81)[18]

In Buenos Aires, working in a cultural environment in sync with the latest developments in European and world literature, she writes her most remarkable narrative works. She adopted a vision in which art is pursued and honed for the sake of art—literature for literature's sake—and in this sense, she took an innovative position toward naturalism, regionalism, or *mundonovismo*. Nonetheless, this does not imply, as we have seen above, that she was able to liberate herself from the class position that, in no small measure, determined the role of women in the early twentieth century. The author of *The Shrouded Woman* adopts, in this regard, a rebellion that cannot escape the "stigma of a conflict between the social and personal reality" (Gligo 69).[19]

No Place for Naturalism

The Final Mist and *The Shrouded Woman* shift the frontiers of Latin America narrative in the 1930s.[20] It is no coincidence that a number of literary critics, including Alonso (1941) and Goic (1968), have pointed to "strangeness" as a key characteristic defining Bombal's prose, a prose that, in the author's own perspective and in line with Blaise Pascal's reflection, is the conjunction of geometry, passion, and poetry. Indeed, Alonso and Goic's appraisals are interesting in terms that are connected to the central approach utilized by Harold Bloom to define the canonical condition of a text: "The answer, more often than not, has turned out to be strangeness, a mode of originality that either cannot be assimilated, or that so assimilates us that we cease to see it as strange" (3).

How, then, can Bombal's strangeness be understood and defined? First, Bombal constructs a world centered around women's experiences in which they have voice and begin thinking and speaking about themselves regarding their interpretations of reality, their romantic quandaries, social pressures, patriarchal norms, and the behavioral models established by the system of bourgeois control. She thus weaves female-centered storylines that run through her entire narrative production, from *The Final Mist* to "La historia de María Griselda." This type of writing was unusual in the 1930s, a period dominated by naturalism, *criollismo*, and socialist realism. Alonso[21] emphasizes, along these lines, that "Chilean novelists and short story writers, with surprising discipline, have applied and continue to apply themselves to achieving a naturalistic conception of the art of narration" (8).[22] This is relevant because, as Guerra suggests, it is a tendency that exacerbates "the values of the strong and vigorous masculinity of the peasant and the proletarian, following a much less strong literary perspective that attempted to utilize an equally virile style" (*Mujer* 163).[23]

Furthermore, *The Final Mist* blurs the boundaries between reality, dream, and reverie. Using the intimate narration of the protagonist, focused on her experiences, yearnings, and desires, a story is constructed that centers on the uncertainty about whether the sexual encounter with her lover was real or not. Throughout the novel, Bombal plays with the possibility of an event that, to a great extent, articulates the protagonist's life experience. Bombal's dilemma requires her to confront one of the key questions formulated by André Breton in the "First Surrealist Manifesto": "Why should I not expect from the sign of the dream more than I expect from a degree of consciousness which is daily more acute?" (12). Undoubtedly, the answer for Breton is negative. Moreover, in his theoretical proposal, it is essential to trace paths of connection between dream and wakefulness and, consequently, he expresses his belief in the "future resolution of these two states, dream and reality, which are seemingly so contradictory, into a kind of absolute reality, a surreality" (14).

The Shrouded Woman travels along a similar path, but in its case, the boundary that is blurred is the one that separates realism from the magical. In the case of this novel, the marvelous lies in the fact that the narration is based on the consciousness of a dead woman: Ana María. From her perspective, her story is told in relation to those (husband, children, daughter-in-law, sister, lover, priest) who attend her wake:

> As night beginning to fall, slowly her eyes opened. Oh, a little, just a little. It was as if, hidden behind her long lashes, she was trying to see.
>
> And in the glow of the tall candles, those who were keeping watch leaned forward to observe the clarity and transparency in that narrow fringe of pupil death had failed to dim. With wonder and reverence, they leaned forward, unaware that she could see them.
>
> For she was seeing, she was feeling.
>
> (*The Shrouded Woman* 157)

The harmonious fusion of the real and the marvelous reflects Bombal's avant-garde position. Indeed, the beginning of the novel is reminiscent of Kafka's statement about art, namely, that it is "a mirror which goes 'fast' like a watch" (qtd. in Deleuze and Guattari 28). More than a decade before the appearance of Alejo Carpentier's "marvelous real" and three decades before García Márquez's "magical realism," Bombal constructs a text that fuses different modes of representation.

When considering Bombal's contributions, it is clear that she is an avant-garde writer who, by all accounts, rejects the naturalism, mundonovismo, or criollismo that prevailed in the 1930s. Bombal charts out new paths, decisively, in the continent's literature, and, in these aspects, her attitude is connected to the assessment made by Ortega y Gasset in *La deshumanización del arte* (*The Dehumanisation of Art*, 1925). Ortega y Gasset argues that one line of action in the "modern art" is based on "curious iconoclastic urges"[24] that lead to "a sort of chemical reaction . . . set going by the clash between his individual sensibility and already existing art" (41, 43).[25] María Luisa Bombal clearly adopts a transgressive position vis-à-vis the established literature of the period.

Nonetheless, although the link that Bombal establishes with avant-garde movements and, particularly, with surrealism is evident, it is impossible to overlook the fact that the Chilean writer also has other influences. For Guerra, Bombal must be situated within "a broader aesthetic context, where the fantastic and the gothic of the nineteenth century, as well as the cinema, were important factors" (*Mujer* 33).[26] Furthermore, it is essential to mention that avant-garde movements, in Guerra's perspective, "despite their revolutionary character, produced a vision of 'the female' that was still anchored in phallogocentrism" (*Mujer* 33).[27]

From this perspective, it is impossible to overlook Bombal's place in contemporary Latin American narrative. In contrast to the position of Carlos Fuentes and Mario Vargas Llosa, who believe that the continent's new narrative begins with Juan Carlos Onetti, Vidal, without ignoring the importance of the author of *El pozo* (*The Well*, 1939), includes Bombal: "Rather, we are motivated by the desire to add her name to those of other pioneers, such as Arlt, Borges, Mallea and Bioy Casares" (41).[28] Bombal thus opens up new paths for the continent's literature.

BRAIDS AND "SHEETS OF FIRE"

Bombal's novels depict a bourgeois world marked by the gender divide. *The Shrouded Woman* illustrates this situation with a reflection—from the perspective of Ana María, the main character—on the aspirations of women and men: "Why, oh why must a woman's nature be such that a man has always to be the pivot of her life? Men succeed in directing their passion to other thing. But the fate of so many women seem to be to turn over and over in their heart some love sorrow while sitting in a neatly ordered house, facing an unfinished tapestry" (*The Shrouded Woman* 226). While men put their passion into "other things," which in the case of Bombal's world are associated with the handling of their haciendas and businesses and the sport of hunting, women are conditioned to gravitate toward sentimental attachments and the organization of domestic life.

In *Masculine Domination* (2000), Pierre Bourdieu addresses this division of roles, establishing that the social order "functions as an immense symbolic machine tending to ratify the masculine domination" (9), which is expressed, Bourdieu adds, in "the sexual division of labor, a very strict distribution of the activities assigned to each sex, of their place, time and instruments; it is the structure of space, with the opposition between the place of assembly or the market, reserved for men, and the house, reserved for women" (9). Undoubtedly, this situation was even more marked during the historical moment when Bombal's earliest novels were published. In Chile, women only obtained full political rights in 1949 and were able to vote in a presidential election for the first time in 1952. The Chilean female labor force in 1930, according to a study by Lucía Pardo, was only 19.2%.

Given this social landscape, the attitude adopted by Ana María in *The Shrouded Woman* is understandable, particularly when she has conflicts with her husband: "But she learned to find a refuge in family, in sorrow; she learned to overcome anxiety by surrounding herself with children, and with small duties" (*The Shrouded Woman* 225). A similar attitude is exhibited by the unnamed protagonist of *The Final Mist*, who, in a stark reflection, describes the expectations she has for her life: "Following him toward an infinity of insignificant tasks; toward a thousand trifling amusements; following him to live correctly—to cry from habit and smile out of duty" (*The Final Mist* 47). *House of Mist* situates the story's protagonist in a similar position. Deeply influenced by fairy tales, Helga's attitude is similar to that of Emma Bovary, in the sense that her reading conditions her way of understanding life. It is no coincidence that her subordinate position is described with a fantastical aura:

> And it all happened exactly as in my fairy tales. I became the lady of the manor, faithful wife of the absent warrior, doing her embroidery in the great hall of the castle, surrounded by her attendants; a solitary young noblewoman fighting her anguish and the long winter with the rhythm of a ballad and the devotion poured out on the roses her needle is shaping. (66)

Men have different ambitions and roles in Bombal's novels. Both Daniel (the husband has the same name in *The Final Mist* and *House of Mist*) and Antonio are landowners who are interested in investing in the public arena as a way to increase their fortunes and improve their social standing. In *House of Mist*, Bombal mentions a trait that serves to define Daniel and that can, incidentally, be extended to the rest of the husbands in her narrative he focuses "only saves to buy more and more land. They said that his woods, his lands, are like a mania with him" (17). For Guerra, they are subjects who act as "victors over nature and social environments, those who triumph both in the affairs of money and fame and in the adventures of war, love and knowledge" (*Mujer* 28).[29] This sense of victory is coupled with men's greater freedom to have multiple sexual partners—often simultaneously—throughout their lives.

The analysis of the abyss between women and men in Bombal's narrative can be supplemented by Vidal's assessment of the central theme of twentieth-century Latin American literature: "the crisis of the bourgeois social order" (41).[30] Faced with this crisis, Vidal argues that the most significant writers have taken a "subversive attitude towards the 'official' language of educational institutions and the media, which are used to train the minds of individuals, conditioning them to submit to the authorities, values, symbols and institutions of the bourgeoisie" (41).[31] This bourgeois order in Bombal's narrative is clearly represented by the male characters. Although Vidal accepts that they are predominantly "businessmen, landowners and lawyers, representatives of the established order, privileged" (94),[32] they are also "grey-haired, sagging and lifeless" (94).[33] Confronted by this class of subjects of power, women—"unable to discover an identity alongside them in the communion of fruitful love" (54)[34]—adopt a rebellious position that culminates, most often, in adultery, be it real or oneiric.

In *House of Mist* and *The Final Mist*, the Countess of Nevers and Regina are, respectively, unfaithful to their husbands. The Countess of Nevers betrays her husband with a bourgeois Don Juan at a party she organizes in her husband's absence. According to the aristocrat's account, it was merely a "slip." Regina, however, takes a more brazen attitude, reflecting her contempt for her marital life. She cheats on her husband—Daniel's brother—without no regard for appearances: "I enter the salon through a side door facing the rhododendrons. In the shadows two figures separate, disentangling so abruptly that Regina's tousled long hair catches on the stranger's coat button. Astonished, I can only stare" (*The Final Mist* 8). In response to marital apathy, Regina strives to live in excess, intensely enjoying the pleasures of life:

> Regina rises, crosses the room slowly, comes to my side, confronting me with her pale, defying face—a paleness due not to lack of color but rather to an intensity for life, violence smoldering just beneath the surface of her smile.
>   I feel as if I had fire in my veins.
>
> (*The Final Mist* 9)

Regina's attitude influences the erotic adventure—real or oneiric—of the protagonist of *The Final Mist*, infusing her with a desire for pleasure. After observing the scene described, she seeks out intimate contact with nature. First, by pressing her body against a tree, and then surrendering herself to the pond:

> Then I remove my clothes, my undergarments until my flesh glows with the same golden splendor afloat among the trees. And like this, naked and golden, I dive into the water.
>
> I had no idea that I was so white and beautiful. The water elongates my body so that it takes on unreal proportions. Before now, I never dared look at my breasts. Rounded and small, they seem like tiny blossoms suspended above the surface.
>
> I sink to my ankles in thick velvety sand. Warm currents caress and penetrate me. Like silky arms, aquatic plants embrace my body with their long tendrils. The fresh breeze kisses the nape of my neck, cools my feverish forehead.
>
> (*The Final Mist* 9–10)

The immersion in the pond represents an awareness of the body and its potential pleasures. Guerra adds that this episode also represents a submersion in sensuality: "an opening of the senses repressed by the patriarchal regime."[35] Both Regina's lover and the protagonist's lover in *The Final Mist* have the same physical traits. Regina's lover is described thus: "her companion, a tall, dark-haired boy" (*The Final Mist* 8) and the protagonist: "He has light-colored eyes set in a dark face" (*The Final Mist* 15). It is striking, in this sense, that the sexual desire of both women is focused on "brown" bodies, which, in contrast to the "paleness" of the bourgeois women, seems to be part of the pursuit of a vitality that has been lost by the individuals of their class. Although the class position of Regina's lover may be debatable, given the ties he maintains with a landowning family, in the case of the protagonist's lover, this is not the case, as she is led to a house on a "narrow street," which has an "abandoned garden," surrounded by a "rusty fence" and that, moreover, has no "furniture."

Bombal makes a transgressive gesture vis-à-vis the perspective of the Chilean elite in the early twentieth century, which, as Sonia Montecino suggests when examining the work of Francisco Encina and Jaime Eyzaguirre, defines itself as a white and Europeanizing class: "Reading the stories of Encina and Eyzaguirre weaves the threads of a 'Chileanness' that is seen as homogeneous. The prevalence of white over indigenous and black is the fundamental element of a mythology of origin" (119).[36] The protagonist of *The Final Mist* thus bypasses the "incestuous nature of bourgeois marriage"[37] and submerges herself in the "other" body from a different social class, which ultimately leads her to extreme pleasure:

> And then we roll entwined onto the center of the bed, his body covering mine like a huge hot wave that sets me afire with caresses until at last I feel him penetrating deep inside me and gathering me to him, and by then we are flowing together as on the silken crest of an endless wave that leaves me faint with rapture, surprised to hear a sob rising in my throat. And then for the first time I moan with pleasure and experience that sweet weariness produced by the precious weight of his body resting between my thighs.
>
> (*The Final Mist* 17–18)

According to Guerra, *The Final Mist* is the first Latin American novel that: "records the sexual Desire of the bourgeois woman, thus producing an unprecedented account of an orgasm experienced from a female perspective" (*La mujer* 67).[38]

The sexual desire of the bourgeois woman mentioned by Guerra extends to *The Shrouded Woman*. Both Ricardo and Ana María's features are interesting in this regard. Despite possessing the physical characteristics of his class—"clear eyes, your ruddy complexion tanned by the sun of the hacienda" (*The Shrouded Woman* 160)—Ricardo has a number of characteristics that are more similar to the protagonist's lover in *The Final Mist* than to the members of his own social class. There is an emphasis on his "wiry and nervous" (*The Shrouded Woman* 160) body, his strong, "burning" flesh. Ricardo has a brutal attitude that is attractive and seductive to Ana María. Far from the chastity demanded of the "angel of the hearth," Ana María adopts a rebellious and sexually open attitude from an early age, which is harshly described by the family priest: "I can still see you as a very young girl, violent and rebellious, giving yourself over to the demons of the flesh and of anger." (*The Shrouded Woman* 254–55). With this, the priest alludes to the active sexual life that the young woman leads with Ricardo:

> And then, remember? I clung to you desperately, murmuring, "Come," sighing: "Don't leave me," and the words "Always" and "Never." That night I surrendered to you, for no other reason than to feel your arm encircling my waist.
>   During three vacations, I was yours.
>
> (*The Shrouded Woman* 165)

Those summers end with Ricardo's departure and Ana María's pregnancy. Far from any kind of maternal feeling, Ana María only values the erotic component of it: "For many days, I lived stunned with happiness. You had marked me forever. Even though your repudiated it, you continued to possess my humiliated flesh, caressing it with your absent hand, altering it" (*The Shrouded Woman* 168–69). It is not insignificant, then that Ana María adopts an eroticism that ignores: "the harsh norms of her society, which have traditionally required unmarried women to have no sexual experience, symbolized by virginity."[39]

What the women in Bombal's novels have in common is that, although they participate in an economy of androcentric desire—in the words of Irigaray—they are also subjects who are open to erotic pleasure. This is the case of the Countess of Nevers, Regina and the protagonist of *The Final Mist* and Ana María. Despite the passion she felt for Ricardo, she finally experiences an orgasm with her husband:[40]

> It was as if from the very depth or her flesh a seething shiver was born which with each caress would begin to rise, to grow, to envelop her in rings up to the roots of her hair, until it clutched her by the throat, cut short her breathing and shook her, casting her finally, exhausted and sobered, upon the disordered bed.
>   Pleasure! So then, this pleasure!
>
> (*The Shrouded Woman* 218–19)

Bourgeois marriage clearly implies a social commitment that takes precedence over love or pleasure. *The Final Mist* and *House of Mist* tell the stories of women who accept marriage proposals that allow them to fulfil the demands of society, that is to say, to be mothers and wives. Consequently, the protagonist of *The Final Mist* and Helga are wed knowing that their husbands not only do not love them, but also that they are still attached to their dead wives and that they are, in this sense, playing the role of substitute lovers:

> What took place after that was unquestionably the most tragic experience any woman in love could have had to endure in all her life.
>
> No, I do not wish to describe that strange wedding night in which I came to know passion through the striving of a husband who sought in me the memory of another woman.
>
> (*House* 63)

Bombal's novels are, paradoxically, an opening and a closing. An opening because of the transgressive nature adopted by the women in the narratives but also a closing because of the impossibility of escaping the androcentric power rooted in marriage.

A DIFFERENT DEITY

Bombal's novels establish a distance from traditional religion and, in particular, from the Catholic Church. *The Shrouded Woman* is, in this regard, the text that most closely deals with the figure of God. According to the characteristics that Ana María attributes to the deity, it is clear that the image in question is, above all, the deity of the Old Testament. It is no coincidence that the woman refers at different times to the "terrible God" who seems "so remote, and so severe!" (*The Shrouded Woman* 179). Observing her sister, a fervent Catholic, from her deathbed, Ana María thinks that she is, instead, disintegrating "quite close to the earth." (*The Shrouded Woman* 178–79).

For Ana María, the problem is not religion itself, but rather its imposition through a site of power, which is, incidentally, an eminently male power, hence the open challenge she issues to the church. Ana María's behavior corresponds to a rebellion "against every limit that oppresses, and she only longs to let herself be carried away by her feelings, which are coordinated with the natural cycles" (Agosín 77).[41] It is precisely because of this attitude that she is constantly criticized by Father Carlos: "That same God, apart from Whom you so stubbornly tried to live!" (*The Shrouded Woman* 253) and, in particular, her questioning of the key aspects of faith: the existence of the soul—"I have no soul, Padre, I have no soul!" (*The Shrouded Woman* 253)—and the value of Heaven: "I said I did not care to go there because it sounds like such a boring place" (*The Shrouded Woman* 254). For this female character, Heaven can only have a value insofar as it satisfies her desires, and those desires involve a paradise similar to her hacienda—"I would like it to be the exactly as it is down here" (*The Shrouded Woman* 254)—but one that is open to the possibilities of erotic pleasure: "and also my cousin Ricardo always with me, and we be allowed sometimes to sleep on the moss in the evening, near the spring." (*The Shrouded Woman* 254).

Although Father Carlos connects Ana María's longing to a version of paradise on earth, the woman's longing seems to be connected to something else, namely, the desire to have a religious discourse and a ritual that corresponds to her life condition. She is thus, for example, open to the alternative of a different god:[42]

> a more secret and more compassionate God, the God who often caused me to sense Zoila . . .
> - Little girl, the new moon! Greet it three times and ask for three things that God will give you immediately . . . A spider scurrying across the roof at this hour! We will receive news . . . Jesus, you broke that mirror! If you don't break white glass, your luck will run out.
>
> (*La amortajada* 116)[43]

That folk religion, anchored in the earth, also appears in *The Final Mist* when the unnamed protagonist discovers a similar sign: "When my husband lit the lamp, a tiny spider on the ceiling, surprised in who knows what twilight dreams, scurried off to hide. 'A good omen,' I whispered, closing my eyes again" (*The Final Mist* 30). Like Ana María, she believes she sees small signs that reveal a transcendental reality, a kind of traces of a creator who, nonetheless, seems much more human.

From this perspective, Ana María feminizes "the notion of death by producing a counter-text to the biblical concept rooted in a patriarchal discourse" (Guerra, *Mujer* 174).[44] This counter-text has a crucial importance for understanding Bombal's reflection on the deity:

> And now she desires nothing more than to remain there *crucified to the earth*, suffering and enjoying in her flesh the ebb and flow of distant, far distant tides; feeling the grass grow, new islands emerge, and on some other continent, the unknown flower bursting open that blooms only on a day of eclipse.
>
> (*The Shrouded Woman* 259)

Crucifixion functions as a tortuous process that allows Christ to free Himself and ascend to heaven in order to sit at the right hand of God. Bombal denies this process and chooses, instead, to sink into the earth, to become part of nature, to merge with a larger space. Christ chooses to be reunited with the creator; Ana María with creation.

CONCLUSION

María Luisa Bombal conquer new borders in the contemporary Latin American literature. Following her return from France, she becomes part of the intellectual elite of

Chile and Argentina, developing—beginning in the mid-1930s—a literary proposal that was able to influence the trajectory of the continent's literature. Indeed, Carlos Fuentes argued that "María Luisa Bombal is the mother of us all" (Guerra, "María Luisa Bombal" 42).

In form because it introduced new modes of representation, anticipating, for example, "magical realism," utilizing ambiguity to dissolve the boundaries between reality and dream. To do this, she borrowed from avant-garde movements, combined them with other narratives in vogue in the 1930s, and passed them through her particular sieve to create an innovative literary project. She thus adopts an iconoclastic attitude toward the dominant movements of the period, namely, regionalism, mundonovism, and naturalism. In substance because she addressed the situation of women, advocating for a "rebellious" or "transgressive" attitude, particularly regarding erotism. She also questioned traditional religion, which led her to reflect on the possibility of accessing a different deity.

Bombal could not fully break free from the ideology of her social class. Accordingly, her writing tends to condemn and reveal the situation of bourgeois women, but, as in *The Final Mist* and *The Shrouded Woman*, her protagonists are unable to escape from male domination. Similarly, it is impossible to ignore that, first and foremost, Bombal depicts a bourgeois world, where there is a limited presence of characters from other social classes. Although this may be conditioned by her biography, it is also possible to conclude that, confronted by the preferences of naturalism, Bombal decided to look at a different reality, one that was more specific, personal, and intimate.

Bombal's writing is a brief, powerful, and decisive fiction event that building a strange and moving land for the Latin American literature.

Translated from the Spanish by Elsevier

NOTES

1. *The Final Mist*, "The Tree," "Braids," "New Islands," and "The Unknown" were published in *New Islands and Other Stories edition*, 1982.
2. "La maja y el ruiseñor" is the only exception in this regard.
3. "Hernán Díaz Arrieta, known as "Alone," is the best-known literary critic in Chile's history. For decades, he worked in different media outlets, wielding a power that influenced the recognition and obscurity of different national authors. Although his work was fundamentally expressed through journalism, books that contributed to the study of Chilean literature cannot be overlooked" (Candia-Cáceres 630).
4. "María Luisa Bombal escribe desde dentro y las palabras le obedecen. Esto es precioso" (Gligo 99).
5. "La señorita Bombal, con su breve y ceñido relato, ha abierto una brecha en nuestro aburrido campo novelesco" (Gligo 99).
6. "Imprecisas, surrealistas, escritas como ninguna mujer y casi ningún hombre ha escrito en Chile" (Guerra, *Mujer* 42).

7. "Libro de triste magia, deliberadamente *suranée*, libro de oculta organización eficaz, libro que no olvidará nuestra América" (Borges 81).

8. "Me regaló un ejemplar de *La última niebla* que leí de un tirón, me pareció una novela maravillosa, escrita con toda esa simplicidad que es deseable . . . le dije que sus páginas habían inspirado varias calles de Comala" (Zúñiga 62).

9. "Ella es la adelantada de lo que se ha dado en llamar "realismo mágico" (Zúñiga 63).

10. "Hablamos de miles de fronteras distintas, pero con un punto común por definición, esto es el límite" (134).

11. "María Luisa sabe perfectamente que la actuación de la mujer en las tablas es muy mal vista en su medio familiar y social" (Gligo 50).

12. "Durante la década de los treinta, en Chile, el Estado y la nación se fundamentaban en una estructura eminentemente patriarcal donde las relaciones entre hombre y mujer se regían por pautas de dominio y subordinación" (Guerra, *Mujer* 15).

13. *La última niebla* está inspirada en haber tenido un amante que no tuve . . . Mi primera experiencia amorosa fue bastante espantosa, yo lo puse a él como marido, la novela tiene una base autobiográfica bastante trágica y desagradable . . . La experiencia sexual también; en esa época, las regulaciones eran para que las obedecieran los de la clase media . . . La novela está basada en mi primer amor que terminó a balazo limpio (Bombal, *Obras* 340).

14. "Los poetas y los escritores chilenos están imbuidos en los movimientos vanguardistas" (Gligo 68).

15. "Era encantadora y muy elegante en una época en que todos nos vestíamos muy mal" (Gligo 69).

16. "Su conducta y modo de ser se consideraban excéntricos en la sociedad de la época mientras, de manera contradictoria, compartía la noción hegemónica de que la única meta y destino de la mujer era el amor. Por lo tanto, su vida se entreteje en la urdimbre de los imperativos culturales impuestos en ese entonces a la mujer y en su carrera de escritora, imperativos que constituyeron un factor esencial" (*Mujer* 13–14).

17. "No debo ser ingrata con el influjo misterioso que recibí de *Residencia en la tierra*, ese libro de Pablo Neruda que, con su poder metafísico, para mí es lo más hondo se su obra. En la cocina de su casa nació mi primera novela *La última niebla*. Yo era muy joven. Escribía de noche" (*Obras* 355).

18. "Uno, el oscurecimiento de los hechos humanos de la novela por el gran hecho sobrehumano de la muerta sensible y meditabunda; otro, el oscurecimiento de ese gran hecho por los hechos humanos . . . me dio unos meses después el manuscrito original de *La Amortajada*. Lo leí en una sola tarde y pude comprobar con admiración que en esas páginas estaban infaliblemente salvados los disyuntivos riesgos infalibles que yo preví" (81).

19. "Estigma de un conflicto entre la realidad social y personal" (Gligo 69).

20. *House of Mist* does not have the disruptive elements of the narrative texts published earlier. Although it is a novel based on *La última niebla*, it is impossible to ignore that it is an adaptation for a North American audience, and, in this sense, Bombal had to comply with a minimum number of pages and, above all, eliminate the novel's ambiguity.

21. Alonso situates Bombal very far from the naturalist concerns centered on "the rural areas and cities of their country, their coal mines, their fishermen, farmers and ranchers . . . their *rotos* (poor city-dwellers) and *huasos* (skilled horsemen). The more nationalist they are in their choice of materials, the more they follow the naturalist formula of the novel, not that of the sensitive and tormented Goncourt brothers, but rather the way it was made to

triumph by the powerful Zola for several decades" (8–9). Goic and Agosín take a similar approach to the link between Bombal, naturalism, and/or criollismo.

22. "Los novelistas y cuentistas chilenos, con sorprendente disciplina, se han aplicado y siguen aplicando a cumplir una concepción naturalista del arte de narrar" (8).

23. "Los valores de la masculinidad recia y vigorosa del campesino y el proletario, según una perspectiva letrada mucho menos recia que intentaba utilizar un estilo también viril" (Guerra, "Mujer" 163).

24. "Extraño sentimiento iconoclasta" (Ortega 82).

25. "Choque o reacción química entre su sensibilidad original . . . hallará en sí una espontánea, indefinible repugnancia a los artistas tradicionales, vigentes, gobernantes" (Ortega 83).

26. "Un contexto estético más amplio, donde lo fantástico y lo gótico del siglo XIX más el cine fueron factores relevantes" (Guerra, *Mujer* 33).

27. A ello, es necesario sumar que los movimientos de vanguardia, en la perspectiva de Guerra, "pese a su carácter revolucionario, produjeron una visión de "lo femenino" aún anclado en el falogocentrismo" (*Guerra, Mujer* 33).

28. "Más bien nos motiva el deseo de sumar su nombre a los de otros iniciadores tales como Arlt, Borges, Mallea y Bioy Casares" (Vidal 41).

29. "Los vencedores de la naturaleza y los entornos sociales, los que triunfan tanto en las empresas del dinero y de la fama como en las aventuras de la guerra, el amor y el conocimiento" (Guerra, *La mujer* 28).

30. "La crisis del orden social burgués" (41).

31. "Actitud subversiva dirigida contra el lenguaje 'oficial' de las instituciones educativas y de los medios de comunicación que sirven para el entrenamiento mental de los individuos, contribuyendo a su sometimiento a las autoridades, valores, símbolos e instituciones de la burguesía" (41).

32. "Hombres de negocios, latifundistas y abogados, representantes del orden establecido, aventajados" (94).

33. "Canosos, flácidos y desvitalizados" (94).

34. "Incapaces de encontrar junto a ellos identidad de tales en la comunión del amor fértil" (Vidal 54).

35. "Una apertura a los sentidos reprimidos por el régimen patriarcal" (81).

36. "La lectura de los relatos de Encina y de Eyzaguirre, teje los hilos de una "chilenidad" que se mira como homogénea. La prevalencia de lo blanco sobre lo indio y lo negro es el hito fundamental de una mitología de origen" (119).

37. "Naturaleza incestuosa del matrimonio burgués" (Vidal 107).

38. "Inscribe el Deseo sexual de la mujer burguesa produciendo, así, una inscripción inédita de la experiencia del orgasmo desde una perspectiva femenina" (*La mujer* 67).

39. "Las severas normas de su sociedad que tradicionalmente han requerido en la mujer soltera una inexperiencia sexual simbolizada por la virginidad" (Guerra, *La mujer* 84).

40. Antonio seems to be the exception to the lack of virility of the bourgeois man in Bombal's novels.

41. "Contra todo límite que oprima, y sólo añora dejarse llevar por sus sentimientos que se coordinan con los ciclos naturales" (Agosín 77).

42. This fragment only appears in the Spanish version of *The Shrouded Woman*.

43. "Un Dios más secreto y más comprensivo, el Dios que a menudo me hiciera presentir Zoila . . .

- Chiquilla, ¡la luna nueva! Salúdala tres veces y pide tres cosas que Dios te las dará en seguida. . . ¡una araña corriendo por el techo a estas horas! Novedad tendremos. . . ¡Jesús, quebraste ese espejo! Torcida va a andar tu suerte mientras no rompas vidrio blanco" (Bombal, *La amortajada* 116).

44. "La noción de la muerte produciendo un contratexto del concepto bíblico enraizado en un discurso patriarcal" (Guerra, *Mujer* 174).

Works Cited

Agosín, Marjorie. *Las desterradas del paraíso, protagonistas en la narrativa de María Luisa Bombal*. Senda nueva de ediciones, 1983.

Alonso, Amado. "Aparición de una novelista." *La última niebla*, María Luisa Bombal, Nascimento, 1941. 7–29.

Bloom, Harold. *The Western Canon: The Book and School of the Ages*. Harcourt Brace and Company, 1994.

Bombal, María Luisa. *La amortajada. La última niebla*. Seix Barral, 1994.

Bombal, María Luisa. *House of Mist*. Farrar Straus and Giroux, 2008.

Bombal, María Luisa. *Obras completas*. Edited by Lucía Guerra. Zig-Zag, 2011.

Bombal, María Luisa. *The Shrouded Woman. María Luisa Bombal: House of Mist and The Shrouded Woman*, U of Texas P, 1995. 157–259.

Bombal, María Luisa. *La última niebla. La amortajada*. Seix Barral, 1994.

Bombal, María Luisa. *The Final Mist. New Islands and Other Stories*. Translated by Richard and Lucía Cunningham. Cornell UP, 1988. 3–47.

Borges, Jorge Luis. "*La amortajada.*" *Sur* vol. 8, no. 47, 1938, pp. 80–81.

Bourdieu, Pierre. *Masculine Domination*. Translated by Richard Nice. Stanford UP, 2001.

Breton, André. *Manifestoes of Surrealism*. Translated by Richard Seaver and Helen R. Lane. U of Michigan P, 1969.

Candia-Cáceres, Alexis. "Detectives at the End of the World: Approaches in Twentieth-century Chilean Literary Critique." *A History of Chilean Literature*, edited by Ignacio López-Calvo, Cambridge UP, 2021. 627–647.

Deleuze, Gilles y Félix Guattari. *Kafka: Toward a Minor Literature*. Translated by Dana Polan. U of Minnesota P, 1986.

García Márquez, Gabriel. *Cien años de soledad*. Sudamericana, 1967.

Gligo, Agata. *María Luisa (biografía de María Luisa Bombal)*. Sudamericana, 1996.

Guerra, Lucía. *La mujer fragmentada: Historias de un signo*. Cuarto propio, 2006.

Guerra, Lucía. "María Luisa Bombal." *Spanish American Women Writers: A Bio-Bibliographical Source Book*, edited by Diane E. Marting, Greenwood, 1990. 41–52.

Guerra, Lucía. *Mujer, cuerpo y escritura en la narrativa de María Luisa Bombal*. Universidad Católica de Chile, 2012.

Montecino, Sonia. *Madres y huachos. Alegorías del mestizaje chileno*. Catatonia, 2010.

Onetti, Juan Carlos. *El pozo*. Signo, 1939.

Ortega y Gasset, José. *La deshumanización del arte y otros ensayos de estética*. Austral, 2016.

Ortega y Gasset, José. "The Dehumanization of Art." *The Dehumanization of Art and Other Essays on Art, Culture, and Literature*, Translated by Helene Weyl, Princeton UP, 1968, pp. 3–54.

Pardo, Lucía. "Una revisión histórica a la participación de la población en la fuerza de trabajo. Tendencias y características de la participación de la mujer." http://econ.uchile.cl/uploads/publicacion/3d9137ba-6367-48cf-b4ed-f739f2bbaa0f.pdf.

Valhondo de la Luz, Joaquín. "Reflexiones sobre el concepto de fronteras." *ETNICEX* no. 1, 2010, 133–45.

Vidal, Hernán. *María Luisa Bombal: La feminidad enajenada.* Hijos de José Bosch, 1976.

Zúñiga, Diego. *María Luisa Bombal, el teatro de los muertos.* Diego Portales, 2019.

CHAPTER 32

....

MAPPING JUAN RULFO

....

ANADELI BENCOMO

MANY generations of Latin American scholars have praised Juan Rulfo's works since the mid-1950s, when *Pedro Páramo* first dazzled readers. In 2017, in order to celebrate Rulfo's hundredth birthday, his literary legacy was extensively promoted by the publication of several essays that revisited his iconic texts. These recent readings are part of the interpretative framework in which we situate or "map" Rulfo within the literary geography of modern Mexican narrative. "Mapping Rulfo" has a double meaning: on the one hand, it addresses Rulfo's texts as objects to be mapped by literary critics; on the other, it refers to the notion that narratives function as cartographies for the real and imagined spaces of human experiences.[1]

BEYOND THE REGIONAL NOVEL

....

The initial mapping of Rulfo's short stories collected in *El llano en llamas* (*The Burning Plain*, 1953) located them in the dominion—thematically and stylistically—of literary regionalism. However, when *Pedro Páramo* was published in 1955, its narrative eccentricity did not conform to previous cartographies in twentieth-century Mexican narrative, such as the novel of the revolution or the lyric novel by the *Contemporáneos*. The novels of the revolution such as *Los de abajo* (*The Underdogs*, 1915) by Mariano Azuela (1873–1952) were written following the conventions of realistic fiction, while the short novels of the avant-garde writers in Mexico were exploring a style that combined poetic images and symbolist motifs as portrayed in *Novela como nube* (Novel like Air, 1926) by Gilberto Owen (1904–1952), or in *Margarita de niebla* (Misty Margarita, 1927) by Jaime Torres Bodet (1902–1974), and other fictions by the avant-garde writers known as the *Contemporáneos*. Prior to the publication of Rulfo's books, *El luto humano* (*Human Mourning*, 1943) by José Revueltas (1914–1976) and *Al filo del agua* (*The Edge of the Storm*, 1947) by Agustín Yañez (1904–1980), signaled a turning point in the regional novel, abandoning the representation of the Mexican Revolution as a national epic, and introducing inflections of realism that explored subjectivities and the emotional impact of external violence. Another important contribution of the post-revolutionary novel in Mexico was to position fiction as a critical discourse in contrast with upbeat versions of official history like the one depicted in the murals of Diego Rivera.

Latin American regionalism in the first half of the twentieth century had been the literary expression of a nationalist ideology. This ideology supported the notion of the country as a conglomerate of regional areas that participated symbolically in the collective movement through history, and toward the consolidation of a modern state. Although the setting of regionalist novels was rural, the conflicts displayed in their fictions reflected the impact of a centralized state that was in charge of the direction of the country. A national system of roads, for instance, is being built while Rulfo is driving his brand new car across the national territory as an advertisement man for the Goodrich tire company. As he scans withered villages during his road travels, he witnesses first-hand that mule drivers like Abundio in *Pedro Páramo* are becoming an anachronism in modern Mexico. In the mapping of the nation toward the projected future, some topography was harder to assimilate into that imagined community. At that point, one of the responsibilities of intellectuals and writers was to serve as promoters of a national imaginary where each element of the territory fulfills a specific role. The different spaces of the nation, the regional landscapes, are there to become meaningful sceneries through the interpretation of a clear-sighted intellectual. Thus the cartographic operation of transforming a space into a meaningful place begins with this discerning gaze.

In addition to mapping spaces, authors were invested with the social responsibility of recording (back) and imagining (forward) history in a swaying movement. The discourses of fiction were instrumental in calibrating the oscillation between national realities and the projections into a foreseeable future. In this context, different regions of the country were charged with specific values to contribute symbolically to the nation. The countryside, for example, was interpreted as a place linked to different categories of the picturesque and of authenticity that were successively translated into a specific set of literary topics and stylistic options. When Yañez and Rulfo introduced modern structures into the regional novel, they were violating the dictates of such distinctive ruralism. *Pedro Páramo*, as an epic of disaster where a moral of the defeated prevails (Monsiváis 257–58), clearly deviated from a nationalist paradigm and its hegemonic projections by bringing to the fore a history that could not be left behind. For Friedhelm Schmidt-Welle, this way of representing the rural context in tension with a national reality constitutes a sample of "non-nostalgic regionalism" that refers to local realities, without encapsulating them into a peripheral and idealized existence (282–84). Novels like *Pedro Páramo* were writing a version of regional narrative that did not obliterate the problems of rural areas, while also connecting their fate to national and international forces that were shaping their way of life. In an interview with Luis Harss, Rulfo specifically mentions his perception of the countryside as a reality that is not isolated from the rest of the country. He accuses the man of the city of ignoring that the problems of country people will eventually become his own "because, when the countryman moves to the city, there's a change. But to a certain extent he continues to be what he was. He brings the problem with him" (317).

In an opposite movement, Rulfo will incorporate the issues characteristic of metropolitan fiction into his version of the regional novel. As Mario Benedetti highlighted as early as in 1955, Rulfo works were distanced formally from traditional regionalism by their break with the notion of the anecdote as the key element of their stories, or by replacing the dominant narrator with colloquial dialogues, while highlighting the essential role of structure in the architecture of his texts. In addition, although his pages conveyed a truthful Mexican atmosphere, Rulfo did not charge his works with the lengthy depictions that were common in regionalist prose. Octavio Paz said the Rulfo was "our only novelist that offered an image—instead of a description—of Mexican landscape" (quoted by Adolfo Castañón 392).[2] His stark style and his narrative economy contribute to the elegiac effect of his writing: "Rulfo does not tell a story. He captures the essence of an experience" (Harss 313).

Pedro Páramo became an instant classic in Mexico, and it was soon recognized as a masterpiece of Latin American fiction. As Susan Sontag writes in her foreword to the translation by Margaret Sayers Peden, "*Pedro Páramo* is a classic in the truest sense. It is a book that seems, in retrospect, as if it has to be written" (ix). For Carlos Fuentes, *Pedro Páramo* constitutes the fullest expression of the novel in modern Mexico, an insuperable text that inaugurates a new period for Mexican narrative while simultaneously closing—by consecrating and assimilating—previous traditions. Gabriel García Márquez read the novel so many times that he knew it by heart, and Carlos Monsiváis wrote that only the poet Ramón López Velarde was comparable to Rulfo in the ability to re-create artistically a language that was exclusively Mexican, rooted in local traditions and in national history, conferring nationality to an artistic language.

CRITICAL APPROACHES TO RULFO'S WORKS

When mapping Rulfo, there are four main approaches to his works:

1. A perspective that focuses on narrative techniques, giving priority to language, style, and structure as markers of the modern writing of Rulfo (Luis Leal, Mariana Frenk, Joseph Sommers, Françoise Perus, Ángel Rama, Fabienne Bradu, José Ramón Ruisánchez, Bruno Bosteels, Anadeli Bencomo).
2. A mythical reading that identifies universal themes and archetypes in Rulfo's stories (Carlos Fuentes, Julio Ortega, Manuel Durán).
3. A sociocultural reading that inserts the fiction within its context of production (Carlos Blanco Aguinaga, Jean Franco, Margo Glantz, Joseph Sommers, Ariel Dorfman, Jorge Ruffinelli, Friedhelm Schmidt-Welle, Ignacio Sánchez Prado).
4. An inquiry about Rulfo, the author, the person behind the texts, his life as key to his fictions (Elena Poniatowska, Luis Harss, Reina Roffé, Nuria Amat, Juan Ascencio, Cristina Rivera Garza).

Recent essays like Cristina Rivera Garza's *Había mucha neblina o humo o no sé qué* (There Was a Lot of Mist or Smoke or Something, 2016) or Ignacio Sánchez Prado's "El clamor de la forma" (The Clamor of the Form, 2017) revisit Rulfo's work from a perspective that evaluates its place in a series of discourses about national modernization. In the midst of the euphoria of President Miguel Alemán's modernizing crusade (1946–1952), Rulfo decided to narrate the story of a deserted town in his native state of Jalisco as a tangible expression of the transformations of the countryside. The decadence of Comala, its imaginary existence in a suspended time, may be read as the other side of a nation marching toward modernization, urbanization, and industrialization. The irruption of the ideology of capitalist modernity clashed with the old rural structure of feudalism represented by Comala and its cacique, a dynamic succinctly explained by Jean Franco: "*Pedro Páramo* can be seen as a novel that reproduces not a coherent worldview but the actual fragmentation and breakdown of a social and moral order, the survival within a new social order of remnants of previous codes and the conflicts and confusions which arise from the mingling of the new and the old" (*Critical Passions* 441). When Rulfo writes about these adversarial forces, the narrative form evokes them through a fragmented structure, a plural set of voices that bring multiple perspectives, as well as a language that combines literary and colloquial prosodies.

When Rulfo goes to live and work in Mexico City, he becomes part of the migration that is transforming the communal life in villages across the country ("Luvina," "Comala"). By moving to the capital from Guadalajara, he faces a similar dislocation as to the one felt by avant-garde authors—Miguel Ángel Asturias, César Vallejo—who discovered their Latin American difference and heritage when they lived in Paris in the 1920s. In her insightful portrait of Rulfo, Rivera Garza invites us to re-read Rulfo as an urban writer—a person who, like many other people, migrated to the big city to work. When the eroded lands were unable to provide, thousands of peasants left their homes to venture into the cities. Rulfo joined the flow, and his condition of exile from Jalisco, made him more aware of other countrymen's desperate conditions. Years later, Harss will portray him as a man that still carried with him an intimate connection to his rural upbringing: "He is like his land: prematurely aged, deeply furrowed, careworn. . . . Rugged terrain fades into a hazy background" (295). Such a portrait invites the reader to anticipate the type of narrator that Rulfo would include in his fictions, one that would consubstantiate with the experience recounted.

THE NARRATIVE ROLE OF NATURE IN
PEDRO PÁRAMO

The literary narrator described by Walter Benjamin as the successor of the storyteller barely appears in *Pedro Páramo*, a textual feature that was already displayed in several of the short stories of *The Burning Plain* (Bosteels). In regionalist novels, it is common to find a lettered narrator that frequently judges the actions and thoughts of the fictional characters. This voice disappears in Rulfo's works, to be substituted by the dialogues or monologues of the peasants and villagers in charge of advancing the thin anecdote. Rulfo, in a conversation with Joseph Sommers, tells him that the real protagonist of *Pedro Páramo* is the town, not the *cacique* or another character in the novel. The statement is relevant because while the voices of the dead revisit the town's past throughout different passages in the novel, the natural forces above the ground represent an imperishable movement that inserts an uncanny dynamism in the spectral atmosphere. The sun, the moon, the rain, and the stars are humanized in several of the most memorable lines of the text, playing a decisive role in setting the narrative tone.[3] For example, the ancient earth moans every day, tired of its constant movement, the sad moon hides behind the mountains, the stars are fat from swallowing a long night. Instead of representing the action of natural elements as a framing device as commonly used in romanticism, they become active players in the unfolding of the story. The narrative conversion of nature from framing images into performative elements was present in some of the short stories of *The Burning Plain*, particularly in "Luvina," where the characterization of the wind is a crucial aspect of the storytelling.

> . . . that wind that blows over Luvina . . . takes hold of things as it was going to bite them . . . it takes the roofs off the houses as if they were hats, leaving the bare walls uncovered. Then it scratches like it had nails: you hear it morning and night, hour after hour without stopping, scraping the walls, tearing off strips of earth, digging with its sharp shovel under the doors, until you feel it boiling inside of you as if was going to remove the hinges of your very bones. (112)[4]

In *Pedro Páramo* the fragments describing the natural elements are poetically charged, revealing perhaps the gaze of Rulfo the photographer, who captured vivid outdoors images with vegetation in the foreground. In 1980, the Institute of Fine Arts of Mexico City published *Inframundo* (Underworld), a commemorative book showcasing some of Rulfo's most iconic photographs. The images captured by Rulfo's lens display a rare quality of animating nature, as we see in the trees portrayed from an angle that makes them taller, their trunks showing robustness, and their branches reaching to the sky. Another photograph reproduces cactuses aligned as troops ready for combat, and yet another shows the morning fog coming out of the vestiges of a house. In contrast, the images of people are still, like those of prehispanic sculptures and monuments. Likewise, his photographic gallery of ghost towns, deserted patios, and villages in ruins represents an atmosphere of desolation that reminds us of Comala, or Luvina.[5] Rereading *Pedro Páramo* with these photographic images in mind reinforces our perception of nature as a dynamic agent. The presence and agency of nature in the novel does not assume the role of antagonist usually assigned to it in the classic regional novel. Nature is not displayed to suggest resources ready for exploitation according to the capitalist logic of Western modernization.

As Françoise Perus has studied, the figure of the impersonal narrator within the fragmented structure of *Pedro Páramo* is the one in charge of describing natural elements. Although she does not pay much attention to these passages, I argue that they are crucial to introduce a third notion of time in the novel. Perus mentions two narrative times: a historical one linked to the story of Pedro Páramo's estate, the Media Luna; and a non-time that relates to Comala's voices, those of the buried bodies—Eduviges, Damiana, Dorotea (176). The impersonal narrator brings a third temporal notion while depicting non-human agents that follow a rhythm of existence outside human history, or human remembrances. It is as if the narrator were obliterated by the murmurs that do not require a voice to organize or analyze them. The narrator is confined to the margins of *history* and of *non-time,* displaced outside of the story and of the dialogues. The displacement turns the narrator into a sensitive observer of the exterior world, a textual presence auscultating a world that exists beyond the boundaries of history (Media Luna's story) and outside of the memories collected by the voices (Comala's stories). Therefore, nature introduces a time that transcends the stories: "The rain deadens sounds. *It continues to be heard even after everything,* flinging its icy drops, spinning the thread of life" (my translation, 88).[6] The significance of transcendental existence is made clear in the closing of the sentence that refers to the thread of life that continues *after everything.* The narrator stages in these brief and lyrical passages a setting that becomes a third plane: it is not the underground space filled with murmurs, nor is it the wasted land at the end of Pedro Paramo' life: "The sun was tumbling over things, giving them form once again. *The ruined, sterile earth lay before him*" (123).[7]

It is important to note the difference between the *non-time* of the subjectivist representation of the characters and that of the perpetual cycle of nature. Blanco Aguinaga made them synonyms in the fictional world of Rulfo, where he recognizes a common laconism in both, the internal thoughts, and the external flow of nature; a monotone rhythm of existence (95–96). This conception of a flattening force with similar effects internally and externally does not take into account that the natural elements in *Pedro Páramo* are not represented as passive entities annihilated by the fatalism of many of the characters to whom we listen in the novel. To a certain extent, I consider that the exterior world does not conform to historic time, without equating this transhistoricity to the *non-time* order of the murmuring voices. The sun, the sky, the wind, mark a distinctive course, cyclical, unstoppable: "Then the sky took over the night" (30).[8]

In this sentence where the sky takes over the night, the roles are reversed, suggesting that nature exists and acts upon the markers of time (day and night). A sky taking command of darkness violates the ineluctable fate of nocturnal pattern. The transposition of substantives that modify the conventional depiction (the night taking over the sky), enables an alternative image where the extension of the night—in space and time—may be altered, extended, or shortened, according to celestial forces. The prosopopoeia that characterizes many of the descriptions by the narrator transforms natural elements within the novel into natural *resources* used as active pieces of the narrative mechanism, pausing the brisk rhythm of memories and dialogues to introduce a different type of pulse to the prose, and to encourage an alternative expression of the course of time:

> the mantle of the night covering the earth (32)
> stars falling from heavens were reflected in the quiet eddies (69)
> As if the sky were raining fire (29)
> The moon had hung there a while, and then gone to hide behind the hills (105)
> the gray of a dismal, ashen sky seeping through (67)
> like a sturdy tree beginning to rot inside (108)
> a few clouds scattered by the wind that comes to carry off the day (54)
> the day turns, stopping and starting. (109)
> The rusty gears of the earth are almost audible (109)
> This ancient earth overturning darkness (109).[9]

In addition to the introduction of nature as an active presence in the discourse, what is striking in these lines is the use of a lyrical language and a poetic imagination associated with literary writing. Thus the pages of *Pedro Páramo* display a double materiality, a contrasting texture of the written words. On the one hand, there is an acoustic quality in the voices of the characters and their surroundings, and on the other, the prose of the narrator is highlighted as literary writing. Orality and writing as two different expressions of verbal language.

At first, the reader of Rulfo's novel starts following the tracks of the voices, gradually joining a verbal flow that breathes to its own rhythm, oblivious to the syntax of the written words. The effect of immersion into this oral universe suggests a possible way to reenact the act of reading *Pedro Páramo* through an art installation, where one would enter a set of connected dark chambers, guided by voices and sounds (rain, wind, birds) that would come from the walls, the floors and the ceiling ("you hear people talking and the voices seem to be coming through a crack, and yet so clear you can recognize who is speaking" [42])[10]—advancing through the rooms without a fixed order, while also experiencing tactile sensations, the texture of the walls, the strong heat in some of the passageways. People would follow the distinctive murmurs—some sounding closer than others—that would fill out the interconnected maze: "This town is filled with echoes. It's like they were trapped behind the walls, or beneath the cobblestones. When you walk you feel like someone's behind you ... you hear rustlings. And people laughing ... and voices worn away by the years" (41).[11]

Rulfo was aware of the acoustic materiality of the literary page read aloud, and as a result, in 1958 he created a collection of albums *Voz viva de México* (Living Voice of Mexico) in collaboration with the Universidad Nacional Autónoma de México (UNAM). Authors were recorded reading their literary works with the immediate goal of filing these records in the Spanish section at the Library of the Congress in Washington DC (Archive of Hispanic Literature on Tape). For this collection, Rulfo read and recorded his short stories, in what would become the first audio version of his works. Sixty years later, in 2020, *Pedro Páramo* would be recorded as an audiobook in a production by Jarpa Studio in Mexico. The book is narrated in a neutral Mexican Spanish by Mauricio

Carrera, and the result is somewhat similar to the original recording in Rulfo's voice. However, the stories of *The Burning Plain* and fragments of *Pedro Páramo* included in the recording of *Voz viva de México* are closer to the original texts, because the audio rendition in Rulfo's voice keeps alive the accent of people in Jalisco, where these stories take place. Unfortunately, in Carrera's rendition of the novel a good opportunity to perform the vocal materiality of *Pedro Páramo* was missed, since only one voice interpreted the text. A more convincing and effective reading for the audio format would have been one in which several readers/actors were in charge of bringing the prose to life. Mauricio Carrera narrates as if the entire novel were written in a single style, without modulating the diverse range of voices, intonations, or even volume of certain dialogues. There is not a noticeable vocal difference or change in cadence, for example, between the segments corresponding to the narrator and those of the characters speaking.

Readers of *Pedro Páramo* are exposed to a polyphonic prose, to a multitude of dialogues that distill the prosody of the colloquial language. Alongside the textual staging of orality, we recognize a speculative logic associated to gossiping as a communal practice in small towns. Instead of having a main narrator attesting to the facts, the novel displays ambiguous dialogues that propitiate a conjectural retrieval of the past. In other words, the accounts of the characters encountered by Juan Preciado in Comala relied mainly on perceptions and suppositions.

> "Who could he be?" the woman was asking.
> "Who knows?" the man replied.
> "I wonder what brought him here?"
> "Who knows?"
> "I think I heard him say something about his father."
> "I heard him say that, too."
> "You don't think he's lost? Remember when those people happened by who said they
>   were lost? . . ." (47–48)[12]

"Who knows?" is the key question to which the novel keeps coming back: Who knows about Juan Preciado's father? Who knows why the villagers abandoned Comala? Who knows the origin of this purgatory populated by voices? Instead of finding answers, the reader—alongside Juan Preciado—is thrown into a spectral realm that casts a shadow over the cartography of modernity in Mexico. When three years later Carlos Fuentes publishes *La región más transparente* (*Where the Air is Clear*, 1958), we are confronted with a literary response to the lingering questions of *Pedro Páramo*. Mexican fiction, like the promise of modernity, has moved to the urban confines, leaving behind a horizon populated with those still images captured by Rulfo's photographs. It is true, as Fuentes wrote in *La nueva novela hispanoamericana* (*The New Hispano-American Novel*, 1969), that *Pedro Páramo* closes a national narrative tradition, a way of mapping the country. Paradoxically, those open questions that linger throughout the novel grant the text its universality, a quality that transcends the documentary impulse of regionalism in Latin America.

LANDSCAPES OF MODERNITY

In the same year as *Pedro Páramo*, Miguel Otero Silva published his novel *Casas muertas* (Dead houses), a fictional account of the extinction of a rural town that is abandoned by people fleeing disease and poverty to chase opportunities in the booming oil industry in Venezuela. The settings of both novels are similar, a deserted town forgotten in the remapping traced by a modernization concentrated in specific locations, far away from the barren lands. Both, the Comala of *Pedro Páramo*, and the Ortiz of *Casas muertas*, are located outside the margins of Latin America's mid-century modernization. However, the narrative realism of *Casas muertas*, its chronological structure, and his traditional narrator situate this novel closer to regionalism than to the modernism of *Pedro Páramo*. It is also worth mentioning that *Mazamitla* (1955), a novel portraying the Mexican Revolution by Ricardo Garibay, is formally closer to *Pedro Páramo* since both experiment with narrating from multiple perspectives, breaking with lineal and chronological structures.

In the fifties, Rulfo was part of the Centro Mexicano de Escritores, where several authors were writing and reading one another's texts. Ricardo Garibay was one of those writers, and he is remembered as someone who vociferously belittled the drafts of *Pedro Páramo* that Rulfo read during the collective sessions. Both Rulfo and Garibay went on to publish their novels in the same year by prestigious presses, *Pedro Páramo* was included in the Fondo de Cultura Económica book series "Letras Mexicanas," and *Mazamitla* was published by Juan José Arreola in his Ediciones Los Presentes. Their stories take place in rural Jalisco, and both of them explore formal innovations. Juan Paredes, the brave revolutionary in *Mazamitla*, and Pedro Páramo are drawn through a combination of narrative conjecture, murmuring voices, and divergent accounts. Nevertheless, beyond these formal similarities, there is a very important distinction in regard to the projection of their fictions onto a national cartography and a historic imaginary. Garibay's novel looks retrospectively, reminiscent of the epic of the Mexican Revolution, while *Pedro Páramo* has no place for romantic heroism, either personal or collective.

Garibay did not anticipate the enormous interest generated by the publication of *Pedro Páramo*. It is then plausible that the unconventional style of Rulfo's writing triggered Garibay's bravado, because he recognized at the Centro Mexicano de Escritores that nobody else in that group was narrating in such a disturbing manner. Disturbing, unfamiliar, and confusing are the corresponding adjectives of a writing that does not conform to expectations. In this context, *Mazamitla* was destined to be the older and unattractive twin, given that its modernist twists did not upset the narrative realism characteristic of the discourses of Mexican regionalism. In contrast, *Pedro Páramo*'s conjunction of a rural setting and modernist style was puzzling, an attribute that manifests itself in every reading, revealing the quality of a literary classic.

Octavio Paz had published the influential essay *El laberinto de la soledad* (*The Labyrinth of Solitude*, 1950) some years before *Pedro Páramo*. Cristina Rivera Garza refers to them as "books *in situ*" (95) because they were produced in the midst of *alemanista* modernization, and they rapidly became the most emblematic texts of the fifties in Mexico.[13] *The Labyrinth of Solitude* is an essay that tries to defend an essence of Mexicaness that would resist the winds of secular modernity, while Rulfo's novel contemplates the consequences of this modernization. Although one may say that these books share a fatalist reading of contemporary Mexican history, their representations are guided by different perspectives. Rivera Garza highlights, for instance, the open references in Rulfo's novel to feminine sexuality (i.e., menstrual period, desire for a masculine body, incestuous relationships) as a suggestive way of reading the "body of the nation." Whereas Paz compares the homeland to the passive body of a raped woman—the *chingada*—in *Pedro Páramo* the feminine body is a desiring one. Women in the novel enjoy their sexuality, as shown by Susana San Juan's erotic reminiscence of her first husband, or by Eduviges Dyada, who eagerly goes to bed with the owner of Media Luna–"I crawled in bed with him. I was happy to. I wanted to" (18)[14]—pretending to be Dolores Preciado, who did not want to consummate her marriage during her menstrual period. In *The Decline and Fall of the Lettered City* (2002), Jean Franco also speaks of the role of women in terms of a crucial agency vis-à-vis a patriarchal state: "Rulfo establishes the feminine . . . as . . . a privileged arena on which to stage everyday acts of resistance . . . The feminine is transgressive of dominant codes whether of *caciquismo*, *bandolerismo*, the church, or the nation. Because it cannot speak directly through the dominant discourse, it must resort to inflection, irony, silence" (137).

Another indication of the subversive role of women in the novel is the scene included in the 45th segment, where a group of indigenous women descends into town to sell their herbs while radiating complicity, "telling jokes and laughing," wanting a "little pulque" to brighten the rainy day. The indigenous women gathered together contrast with the somber atmosphere of Comala, "the village seems uninhabited" (86),[15] with its silence, with its empty streets. Toward the end of the novel, there is another scene that could be interpreted as Susana San Juan's revenge against her confinement under Pedro Páramo's wishes. Her death unleashes one of the few episodes where the somber Comala comes to life, packed with people. When Susana San Juan dies, Pedro Páramo orders the ringing of the church bells to announce the passing of his beloved wife. The endless pealing that lasts for days attracts the people who arrive in great numbers, transforming the mourning ritual into a loud rural fair: "A circus showed up . . . And musicians . . . The bells felt silent, but the fiesta continued . . . There were cockfights and music, lotteries, and the howls of drunken men" (116).[16] The contrasting images of a glooming and quiet Media Luna and the bustling celebration communicate metaphorically the end of the rural regime that has died with Susana San Juan. A rancorous Pedro Páramo crosses his arms to signal his resistance to the future. His state will transform into a wasteland, while the vitality of the impromptu fair will transfer to other regions, generating an exodus of the locals: "everyone was leaving the village; all the people set out for somewhere else . . . " (61).[17] A few years later, this symbolic topic of the demise of the authoritarian landowner, accompanied by communal festivities, will become the subject theme of

Gabriel García Márquez's short story "Los Funerales de la Mamá Grande" ("Big Mama's Funeral," 1962).

It is not an exaggeration to declare that *Pedro Páramo* had a seismic effect in the field of Latin American fiction, and that its waves are still vibrating as gears of the literary earth. If initially the modernity of Rulfo's novel puzzled a few critics, as pointed out by Jorge Zepeda in *La recepción inicial de* Pedro Páramo (*The Initial Reception of* Pedro Páramo, 2005), its dimension as a literary classic of world literature was promptly accepted.

NOTES

1. As Robert T. Tally explains, the notion of literary cartographies involves the understanding of narratives as "mapping machines" (3).
2. "Es el único novelista mexicano que nos ha dado una imagen –no una descripción- de nuestro paisaje" (Octavio Paz qtd. In Castañón 392).
3. In 1954, when the first part of Rulfo's novel is published in the journal *Letras Patrias*, the title of the forthcoming novel was announced as *Una estrella junto a la luna* (*A star close to the moon*). This title reveals the importance of celestial elements in the setting of what would become *Pedro Páramo*.
4. "Ese viento . . . se planta en Luvina prendiéndose de las cosas como si las mordiera . . . se lleva el techo de las casas como si se llevara un sombrero de petate, dejando los paredones lisos, descobijados. Luego rasca como si tuviera uñas: uno lo oye a mañana y tarde, hora tras hora, sin descanso, raspando las paredes, arrancando tecatas de tierra, escarbando con su pala picuda debajo de las puertas, hasta sentirlo bullir dentro de uno como si se pusiera a remover los goznes de nuestros mismos huesos" (Rulfo, *Obra completa* 60–61).
5. In an insightful analysis, Enrique López Aguilar discusses the different approach in Rulfo's photographs to the human subjects (people and towns) and to the natural elements (149–52).
6. I use the italics to mark my own translation of these observations by the narrator because the Sayers Peden's translation misses the meaning of continuum carried by the phrase in Spanish: "La lluvia amortigua los ruidos. Se sigue oyendo aún después de todo, granizando sus gotas, hilvanando el hilo de la vida" (Rulfo, *Obra completa* 168).
7. Here again, Peden's translation does not convey the contrast between the perennial rhythm of nature (sunlight laying on things), and the measurable effect of human actions (Pedro Páramo refusal to work the lands of the Media Luna ranch). More accurate is the version by Lysander Kemp: "His ruined lands stretched out in front of him, empty" (123). "El sol se fue volteando sobre las cosas y les devolvió su forma. La tierra en ruinas estaba frente a él, vacía" (Rulfo, *Obra completa* 194).
8. "Entonces el cielo se adueñó de la noche" (Rulfo, *Obra completa* 128).
9. "la envoltura de la noche cubriendo la tierra (Rulfo, *Obra completa* 129)

> en los remansos el reflejo de las estrellas que se estaban cayendo del cielo (155)
> Como si el cielo estuviera lloviznando lumbre (127)
> La luna estuvo un rato allí y después fue a esconderse detrás de los cerros (180)
> traslucía el color gris de un cielo hecho de ceniza, triste, (153)
> como un tronco duro comenzando a desgajarse por dentro (183)
> unas cuantas nubes desmenuzadas por el viento que viene a llevarse el día (144)

el día va dándose vuelta, a pausas;
se oyen los goznes de la tierra que giran enmohecidos;
esta tierra vieja que vuelca su oscuridad"

(Rulfo, *Obra completa* 183).

10. "Oyes platicar a la gente, como si las voces salieran de alguna hendidura y, sin embargo, tan claras que las reconoces" (Rulfo, *Obra completa* 136).

11. "–Este pueblo está lleno de ecos. Tal parece que estuvieran encerrados en el hueco de las paredes o debajo de las piedras. Cuando caminas, sientes que te van pisando los pasos. Oyes crujidos. Risas. Unas risas ya desgastadas por el uso" (Rulfo, *Obra completa* 136).

12. "–¿ Quién será?–preguntaba la mujer.

> - Quién sabe–contestaba el hombre.
> - ¿Cómo vendría a dar aquí?
> - Quién sabe.
> - Como que le oí decir algo de su padre.
> - Yo también le oí decir eso
> - ¿No andará perdido? Acuérdate cuando cayeron por aquí aquellos que dijeron andar perdidos . . . "

(Rulfo, *Obra completa* 140).

13. These two titles, *Labyrinth of Solitude* and *Pedro Páramo*, became the two top sellers of the Fondo de Cultura Económica for many years.

14. "Me acosté con él, con gusto, con ganas" (Rulfo, *Obra completa* 119).

15. "se cuentan chistes y sueltan la risa"; "tantito pulque"; "El pueblo parece estar solo" (Rulfo, *Obra completa* 167).

16. "Llegó un circo, con volantines y sillas voladras. Músicos . . . Las campanas dejaron de tocar; pero la fiesta siguió . . . Se jugaba a los gallos, se oía la música; los gritos de los borrachos y de las loterías" (Rulfo, *Obra completa* 189).

17. "El pueblo se fue quedando solo; todos largaron camino para otros rumbos" (Rulfo, *Obra completa* 149).

Works Cited

Amat, Nuria. *Juan Rulfo, el arte del silencio*. Omega, 2003.

Ascencio, Juan. *Un extraño en la tierra. Biografía no autorizada de Juan Rulfo*. Debate, 2005.

Azuela, Mariano. *Los de abajo*. Fondo de Cultura Económica, 1990.

Bencomo, Anadeli, and Andrés Vázquez. "La hibridez narrativa en Juan Rulfo y Ricardo Garibay: 1945–1955." *Revista Lejana*, no. 10, 2017, pp. 1–11.

Benedetti, Mario. *Letras del continente mestizo*. Arca, 1972.

Blanco Aguinaga, Carlos. "Realidad y estilo de Juan Rulfo." *La narrativa de Juan Rulfo*, edited by Joseph Sommers, Sep/Setentas, 1974, pp. 88–116.

Bosteels, Bruno. "Reading Rulfo between Benjamin and Derrida." *Mexican Literature in Theory*, edited by Ignacio M. Sánchez Prado, Bloomsbury, 2018, pp. 111–38.

Castañón, Adolfo. *Arbitrario de literatura mexicana*. Lectorum, 2003.

Durán, Manuel. *Tríptico mexicano. Juan Rulfo, Carlos Fuentes, Salvador Elizondo*. SepSetentas, 1973.

Franco, Jean. *Critical Passions*. Duke UP, 1999.

Franco, Jean. *The Decline and Fall of the Lettered City*. Harvard UP, 2002.

Fuentes, Carlos. *La gran novela latinoamericana*. Alfaguara, 2011.

Fuentes, Carlos. *La nueva novela hispanoamericana*. Joaquín Mortiz, 1969.

Fuentes, Carlos. *La región más trnsparente*. Fondo de Cultura Económica, 1958.

Garibay, Ricardo. *Mazamitla*. Los presentes, 1955.

Harss, Luis. "Juan Rulfo: Contemporary Mexican Novelist." *New Mexico Quarterly*, vol. 35, no. 4, 1965, pp. 293–318.

Inframundo. El México de Juan Rulfo. Ediciones del Norte, 1983.

López Aguilar, Enrique. "La imagen desolada en la obra fotográfica de Juan Rulfo." *Revisión crítica de la obra de Juan Rulfo*, edited by Sergio López Mena, Praxis, 1998, pp. 137–53.

Monsiváis, Carlos. *Escribir, por ejemplo*. Fondo de Cultura Económica, 2008.

Otero Silva, Miguel. *Casas muertas*. Losada, 1955.

Owen, Gilberto. *Novela como nube*. UNAM, 2004.

Paz, Octavio. *El laberinto de la soledad*. Fondo de Cultura Económica, 1986.

Perus, Françoise. *Juan Rulfo. El arte de narrar*. UNAM-RM, 2012.

Poniatowska, Elena. *¡Ay, vida, no me mereces!* Joaquín Mortiz, 1993.

Revueltas, José. *El luto humano*. Era, 1980.

Rivera Garza, Cristina. *Había mucha neblina o humo o no sé qué*. Penguin Random House, 2016.

Roffé, Reina. *Juan Rulfo. Biografía no autorizada*. Fórcola, 2012.

Ruisánchez Serra, José Ramón. *Historias que regresan*. Fondo de Cultura Económica-Universidad Iberoamerica, 2012.

Rulfo, Juan. *El llano en llamas*. Read by Juan Rulfo. Voz Viva de México, vv-16, UNAM, 1963.

Rulfo, Juan. *Obra Completa*. Edited by Jorge Ruffinelli. Biblioteca Ayacucho 13, 1985.

Rulfo, Juan. *Pedro Páramo*. Translated by Lysander Kemp. Grove Press, 1959.

Rulfo, Juan. *Pedro Páramo*. Translated by Margaret Sayers Peden. Grove Press, 1994.

Rulfo, Juan. *Pedro Páramo*. Narrated by Mauricio Carrera. Storytel, 2020.

Sánchez Prado, Ignacio M. "Juan Rulfo: el clamor de la forma." *El Llano en llamas, Pedro Páramo y otras obras*, edited by Pedro Ángel Palou and Francisco Ramírez Santacruz, Iberoamericana-Vervuert, 2017, pp. 171–202.

Schmidt-Welle, Friedhelm. "Hacia un regionalismo literario no nostálgico: Juan Rulfo y Julio Llamazares." *El Llano en llamas, Pedro Páramo y otras obras*, edited by Pedro Ángel Palou and Francisco Ramírez Santacruz, Iberoamericana-Vervuert, 2017, pp. 281–300.

Sommers, Joseph. *Yañez, Rulfo, Fuentes. La novela mexicana moderna*. Monte Ávila, 1968.

Tally, Robert T. "Introduction: Mapping Narratives." *Literary Cartographies*, edited by Robert T. Tally Jr., Palgrave Macmillan, 2014, pp. 1–12.

Torres Bodet, Jaime. *Margarita de niebla*. UNAM, 2005.

Yañez, Agustín. *Al filo del agua*. Porrúa, 2008.

Zepeda, *La recepción inicial de Pedro Páramo (1955–1963)*. RM, 2005.

....

CHAPTER 33

JOSÉ MARÍA ARGUEDAS'S POETICS OF THE NOVEL

....

JAVIER GARCÍA LIENDO

THE novelist, poet, anthropologist, folklorist, teacher, and cultural promoter José María Arguedas was born October 18, 1911, in Andahuaylas, Apurímac province, in the southern Peruvian Andes. After his mother died in 1914, he spent most of his childhood among indigenous people, from whom he learned to speak Quechua and became familiarized with the hierarchical relationship between *indios* and *mistis*.[1] With his father, an itinerant lawyer, he visited several Andean cities and towns. He studied in a Catholic boarding school in Abancay (1924–1925) and continued his education in Huancayo (1928–1929) and Lima (1929–1930). Inspired by the indigenista movement of the 1920s and José Carlos Mariátegui and his famous *Amauta* journal (1926–1930), he started to write essays and literature while in Huancayo.[2] In 1931, Arguedas entered San Marcos University and, after various interruptions, graduated with a bachelor's degree in ethnology in 1950 and a PhD in the same discipline in 1963. Between 1937 and 1938, he was imprisoned in El Sexto penitentiary (Lima) because he participated in a student protest against a representative of Mussolini. From 1939 until his death, Arguedas taught in various schools and universities in the Andes and Lima. As an ethnographer and folklorist, he studied local cultures and capitalist modernization and advised and recorded migrant musicians in Lima. Arguedas also held public positions in folklore and cultural policy from which he sought to counter a homogenous understanding of Peruvian culture. He committed suicide on November 28, 1969, in Lima.

Arguedas's literary oeuvre garnered him national and international renown. His novels, short stories, and poems constitute one of the most complex works in Peruvian literature. They captured the multiple affective, epistemic, political, and cultural dimensions of a postcolonial country embroiled in an accelerating capitalist modernization, with a predominantly indigenous and rural population until the mid-1900s. From his vast intellectual production, Arguedas's novels are the best known and most studied. *Yawar Fiesta* (*Yawar Fiesta*, 1941) narrates the social and ideological tensions around a traditional Andean bullfight, in which a condor (representing indigenous people) is tied to the back of a bull (representing Spanish colonists), where it pecks at the animal as bullfighters fight it. *Diamantes y pedernales* (*Diamonds and Flints*, 1954) tells the story of a musician from the highlands who migrates to a socially stratified Andean town. For many, Arguedas's masterpiece, *Los ríos profundos* (*Deep Rivers*, 1958), is set in a big Andean city and explores the affective and epistemic tensions between Quechua cultures and the changing urban society through a child's lens. *El Sexto* (1961), based on the year Arguedas spent in jail, is the first of his novels set in a coastal city. *Todas las sangres* (*All the Bloodlines*, 1964) explores a Peru on the verge of historical implosion when the feudal-like system of the Andes collides with industrial mining, imperialist forces, and the possibility of peasant mobilization. *El zorro de arriba y el zorro de abajo* (*The Fox from Up Above and the Fox from Down Below*, published posthumously in 1971) narrates a small fishing cove's transformation into an industrial port that attracts impoverished migrants seeking the myth of progress. In the novel, the town's dramatic capitalist reorganization overlaps with the author's suicide plans, which eventually put an end to the writing of the novel.

Arguedas's novels have been at the center of foundational debates concerning Latin American literature and modernity. In Ángel Rama's theory of literary transculturation, *Los ríos profundos* plays a pivotal role in countering capitalist modernity's cultural homogenization. By introducing indigenous cultural forms, cosmovision, and language, Rama argues, Arguedas reformulates the genre of the novel and locates Latin American specificity within global modernity, overcoming the Eurocentric universality of the Western novel. Likewise, Arguedas's novels figure prominently in Antonio Cornejo Polar's theory of literary heterogeneity, which dismisses transculturation as a new form of *mestizaje* ("Mestizaje"). For Cornejo Polar, Arguedas's work critically opposes the assimilationist narratives of national culture that promote harmonious coexistence among different classes and ethnic groups. Instead, his novels reveal a postcolonial nation's conflicting historicity in which old and new power structures coexist. Finally, Alberto Moreiras considers Arguedas's posthumous novel a textual machine that produces radical heterogeneity and, therefore, brings to an end the ideology of transculturation and the quest for Latin American difference. While these represent only a small sample of the debates in which Arguedas's novels have prominently figured, they illustrate the vast theoretical and critical constellations that have emerged from them.[3]

This chapter will study Arguedas's novels centering on what I call his *poetics of the novel*, a term I borrow from Ricardo Piglia. Building on György Lukács's theory of the novel and Walter Benjamin's reflections on the figure of the narrator, Piglia defines an author's poetics not only as a function of multiple aesthetic decisions but also, fundamentally, as a novelist's formal response to productive and historical processes and contemporary discursive genres (e.g., oral communication, journalism, literature, scientific writing, media). In what follows, I will analyze Arguedas's poetics as a response to the challenge of narrating the epistemic, narrative, and affective dimensions of Peru's historical transformation during the twentieth century, particularly the clash between indigeneity, traditional social relations and structures, and capitalist modernization.

During Arguedas's life, Peru was profoundly altered by growing waves of capitalist modernization. At the beginning of the century, a system of domination over the indigenous population, based on servile relations and rigid social and cultural stratification, prevailed in the Andean region. However, this old order was entering a slow process of decomposition. On the one hand, the expansion of the hacienda system due to an increase in the export economy led to the arbitrary expropriation of indigenous lands, which triggered peasant rebellions during the first two decades of the twentieth century. On the other, the expansion of the Peruvian state and the indigenista policies of Augusto B. Leguía's Patria Nueva (1919–1930) ushered in a period of relative peace in rural regions that persisted until after the end of World War II. This period was also accompanied by the growth—extending from urban centers to the countryside—of industrial culture, capitalism, and state services. Peasants thus gained greater access to markets, nonfarm wage labor, schooling, modern politics, roads, and communications media. The image of two worlds "frozen" in place—indios and mistis—was rapidly disintegrating. Modernization impacted the indigenous communities and the traditionalist caste of mistis, who resisted the loss of their privileges. The resulting changes also stimulated migration from the rural Andean highlands to Andean cities and, in particular, to the coast and the Peruvian capital. Urbanization, social mobility, access to global culture, and new political identities drastically altered the national space and the historical trajectories of cultures that were transforming in unprecedented ways.[4]

Elsewhere I have argued that Arguedas was heavily engaged, through several different intellectual practices, in trying to understand these historical changes and assess the gains and losses they entailed for the indigenous population and Peru as a whole (*El Intelectual*). The possibility of overcoming the old order's brutal domination over indigenous groups was in tension with the certainty of irreparable cultural and epistemic loss. By the middle of the century, Arguedas's work—literary, ethnographic, folkloric, journalistic, and cultural—conveyed a sense of urgency and ambivalence about the direction taken by the changes and the intellectual and political stakes they entailed. Arguedas's incursion into the genre of the novel, I argue, was motivated by the need to narrate and make sense of these multidimensional historical transformations. One can discuss this poetics at various literary levels, such as language, characters, or plot. Here, I will principally focus on the formal aspects of his novels.

Focusing on *Yawar Fiesta*, *Los ríos profundos*, and *El zorro de arriba y el zorro de abajo*, I will discuss how Arguedas employs multiple discursive genres (fiction, biography, history, ethnography, folklore, sociology, mythology, dance, music) that deliberately resist merging into a single dominant narrative. I term this formal operation *antigenric coupling*. Some critical appreciations of Arguedas's novels as imperfect, naïve, or documentalist seem to respond to this characteristic (Vargas Llosa). From the perspective of the modern history of the novel, the antigenric coupling could be considered a novelistic flaw. Nevertheless, in Arguedas's case, it is a solution to his task as narrator. He positions himself against the regime of fictionality (Gallagher), thereby rejecting the notion of aesthetic autonomy. However, he does this not by ascribing to the narrative regime of realism and the principle of narration as correspondence; instead, his novels create a form that resists being read as *either* pure fiction *or* pure documentation. I contend that Arguedas's reason for writing against generic forms is that, in his view, no single discursive genre on its own can sufficiently narrate what was happening—not the novel (as received from tradition), indigenous myth or song, nor the social sciences.

YAWAR FIESTA (1941)

Arguedas's first novel was met with puzzlement by many readers. It appeared at a moment when the *novela indigenista* had consolidated as a genre, but *Yawar Fiesta* failed to conform to this genre's narrative and thematic conventions: namely, the use of realism and the explicit defense of the indigenous population (Kokotovic 39–40).[5] As Peter Elmore remarks, Ciro Alegría's *El mundo es ancho y ajeno* (*Broad and Alien Is the World*) was published the same year as *Yawar Fiesta*, and both were submitted to the same literary contest. While Alegría's novel was awarded first place, *Yawar Fiesta* barely received a lukewarm mention, likely because it did not recount the type of "archetypal story" that characterized *El mundo es ancho y ajeno*—or Jorge Icaza's novel *Huasipungo* (*The Villagers*, 1934)—that is, the story of a confrontation between an indigenous community and a landowner who holds the monopoly on violence (99).

   Yawar Fiesta's plot is set in Puquio, the small Andean capital of Lucanas province (Ayacucho).[6] The indio-landowner dichotomy does not adequately account for life in Puquio, which is marked by tensions and alliances between various ethnic groups. Moreover, this dichotomy also belies an incipient process of class differentiation within the local population and the economic and cultural influence of Puquio migrants residing in Lima. The events in the novel unfold in an urban space dominated by a colonial caste system whose influence is slowly being eroded by state expansion, commerce, population growth, and modern cultural forms (tango records, for example), as well as ideologies favoring modernization, indigenous rights, and socialism. In short, *Yawar Fiesta* explores the tension between Andean society and modernization. The dates indicated in the novel invite the reader to draw a connection with Patria Nueva's modernizing project (1919–1930) when the construction of highways—using forced indigenous labor—and the expansion of Peru's domestic market went hand in hand with a decrease in the expropriation of indigenous lands thanks to pro-indigenous legislation. The result was a period of relative peace in the Andes that would last until the 1950s (Remy).

   In *Yawar Fiesta*, a local tradition cornered by modernity epitomizes this historical transformation. The *Yawar* festival referenced in the title is organized by Puquio's indigenous population to commemorate Peru's independence and features a bull-fight (*turupukllay*). The novel's plot begins with the arrival of a state notice from Lima prohibiting the turupukllay under the pretext of protecting the "helpless native with his backward-oriented brain" (44).[7] This paternalistic *indigenista* intervention responds to the fact that the turupukllay always resulted in deaths and injuries among peasants who dared to confront the bull face to face and the eventual killing of the animal using dyna-mite. While Puquio migrants living in Lima offer to hire a Spanish bullfighter to con-tinue the tradition, the local priest and the majority of *mistis* in Puquio support the state order because they view the bullfight as a manifestation of sin and primitivism. Young *puquianos* going to college in Lima also intervene, but their views oscillate between defending indigenous traditions and condemning them as obstacles to the emergence of class consciousness among peasants. Therefore, the "subalternizing enlightenment view" (Kraniauskas 360) of the leftist youth leads them to adopt a tutelary position com-parable to that of the mistis and the church.[8] Andean society is not dichotomous, nor is modernization univocal in its actors, ideologies, and effects.

A key characteristic of *Yawar Fiesta* is that the story of the turupukllay does not un-fold linearly but rather is interspersed with various subplots and discourses that delay the progression of the storyline. This "aire un tanto caótico" [somewhat chaotic orga-nization] (Rodríguez-Luis 122) of the narrative has led some critics to fault Arguedas for having limited narrative ability. However, other critics have argued that the novel is, in fact, marked by intense formal experimentation (Elmore, Kokotovic, Portugal). Arguedas himself insisted numerous times on the importance of technique in his novel-istic work, observing on one occasion that "new techniques arise when there are worlds to reveal" (*Primer* 172).[9] He identified working with language as his greatest challenge, since he had to consider how to narrate a social world marked by diglossia between Spanish and Quechua.

Along with language, it is equally important to consider Arguedas's efforts to adapt the genre of the novel to the narrative needs of the moment. His genric manipulations show that the challenge of portraying the complex interplay between Andean society and modernization is resolved both at the story level and, fundamentally, on the level of narration. In its narrative dimension, *Yawar Fiesta* seeks to generate an effect of defamiliarization that prevents readers from accepting the novel's fictionality and leads them to problematize the limits of cultural representation.

These operations are exemplified in two of *Yawar Fiesta*'s formal features. First, the novel stresses that differing points of view may result in contrasting interpretations of the same facts. *Yawar Fiesta* opens with a panoramic survey of Puquio. The narrator, who is arriving from the coastal region, pauses at a mountain pass through which travelers arrive in the city. From there, as if looking through a camera lens, he offers the readers a wide shot of the city. Then, he zooms in on the main street, the mestizo neighborhood, and the *ayllus* (indigenous neighborhoods), describing the city's power relations, institutions, and customs. As these descriptions unfold, the exclamation "Indian town!" ("¡Pueblo indio!") is repeated several times. The phrase has at least two meanings. Voiced by the narrator, it conveys that, even though Puquio is a city, at its core, it is entirely dominated by the culture of the indios. In this sense, the phrase serves as a commentary—key to all of Arguedas's work—on the power of indigenous culture in the Andes, which "indianizes" many mistis even if they cannot recognize it. Nevertheless, when uttered by a coastal traveler arriving in Puquio, it conveys contempt, alluding to the grammar of racialization that depicts the indio as inferior and premodern. Thus, from the beginning of the novel, readers are confronted with two cultural focalizations, corresponding to an internal and an external gaze, which survey the same facts in antagonistic ways.

This double cultural focus appears numerous times in *Yawar Fiesta*, most notably in a scene in chapter 6 where the subprefect—a man of coastal origin who is the highest-ranking representative of the national government in the city—observes the indios gathering in the plaza from the ayllus to organize the turupukllay. The subprefect perceives the indios as a mass, a "dense drove" (49) without individual faces,[10] exclaiming: This is a theater! It's like a movie! (49),[11] and remarking "it's as if these towns were from another world" (50).[12] His gaze is that of the outsider who exclaimed "Indian Town!" in the first chapter. The subprefect's focalization in this scene juxtaposes that of the narrator, who in chapter 7 tells the story of the construction of the highway from Puquio to the coast, a project borne out of the initiative of the ayllus and communal labor. Here, too, the indios are presented as an anonymous mass, but this time, to highlight their communal identity and interest in modernization—which, according to the outside focalization, always comes from Lima.[13]

Another formal feature of *Yawar Fiesta* that exemplifies Arguedas's genric experimentation is what I have called antigenric coupling. The first two chapters of *Yawar Fiesta* consist of an ethnographic description of Puquio and the region's history of primitive accumulation (Beckman). Critics have viewed these chapters as auxiliary materials, or as an "explanatory prologue" ("prólogo explicativo") (Cornejo Polar, *Los Universos* 57), out of step with the story of the turupukllay. However, what seems like a defect from the perspective of the genre's fictionality is, for Arguedas, the only way to convey Puquio's social complexity to the reader. The novel assumes the task of recounting a local history that does not appear in history books. Critics have observed two other similar "interruptions" of the bullfight story: the recount of the history of local migration to Lima and the construction of the highway that appears in chapter 7, and the account of the mythical origins of Misitu—the wild bull captured by the indios in the heights of Puquio for the turupukllay—in chapter 8. In all cases, Arguedas stops the fictional narration to offer an ethnographic portrayal of ethnic and class changes generated by migration and a folkloric study of local culture.[14] The latter also relates to the insertion in the novel of songs in Quechua and Spanish—some of which were previously compiled and published by Arguedas—to create a sonic space and convey dimensions of Quechua culture that cannot be transmitted in other ways.[15] At times, the novel becomes a folklorist's notebook.

LOS RÍOS PROFUNDOS (1958)

Following *Yawar Fiesta*, Arguedas published the short novel *Diamantes y Pedernales* (1954). This is Arguedas's least studied novel, partly due to the enormous attention his next book, *Los ríos profundos*, received, which garnered Arguedas international recognition.

Los ríos profundos explores the social worlds of Abancay, a large city in the Andes, from the perspective of a boy, Ernesto, who serves as narrator and protagonist. Ernesto is a migrant who has spent his childhood traveling from town to town with his itinerant lawyer father.[16] He has arrived in Abancay to continue his education at a boarding school, where he comes into contact with children of different social classes and ethnicities and is confronted by frequent verbal and physical violence. The boarding school becomes a microcosm of Abancay's hierarchical society. Outside the school's walls, the city is surrounded by haciendas where indigenous serfdom, sadness, and defeatism predominate (199). However, later on, as Ernesto explores the city, he encounters urban indigenous groups who show a capacity for rebellion and self-organization. Ernesto contrasts these new worlds with his own childhood memories of nature, the solidarity intrinsic to rural life, and indigenous thinking. Individual memory, history, and Western and indigenous epistemologies interact in the novel to comprehend Andean society's social and cultural heterogeneity.[17]

Ángel Rama's analysis of *Los ríos profundos* (*Transculturación*) is, arguably, the most influential interpretation of the novel in the field of Latin American studies. *Los ríos profundos* plays a prominent role in Rama's critique of a particular reading of Latin American novels favored by the Boom, which tended to reinforce the opposition between a modern tradition of experimentation associated with authors such as Julio Cortázar and Mario Vargas Llosa, and a regionalist narrative tradition, oriented toward "ethnographic documentarism and the production of fictitious worlds related to folklore and *costumbrismo*" (Moraña 27).[18] Rama argues that, starting in the 1940s, writers like Juan Rulfo, João Guimarães Rosa, and Arguedas began experimenting with the formal conventions of the regionalist genre. Using techniques and languages borrowed from their countries' rural cultures, they produced a new type of regionalist novel.

Due to its composition from "humble materials" with little literary prestige, such as Quechua songs and myths, Rama considers *Los ríos profundos* a new artistic form hitherto unseen in Latin America. The importance of indigenous music and orality in *Los ríos profundos* leads him to read the work as a "novel-opera of the poor" ("novela-opera") (*Transculturación* 266), where music does not serve as a mere illustration of a premodern culture but instead ruptures the historical time of writing and therefore the genre of the novel itself. Music, he argues, introduces a different notion of temporality that opens new avenues for approaching indigenous culture (281–305). Similarly, Rama interprets Arguedas's decision to incorporate "mythical thought" in the novel as a gateway to indigenous epistemologies that reorganize the production of meaning in *Los ríos profundos*. Critics have pointed to the *zumbayllu* episode (chapter VI) and the scene where the Inca wall comes to life (chapter I) as clear examples of mythical thought in the novel.[19] Rama himself identifies three levels where myths appear in *Los ríos profundos*: as the worldview of certain characters, as autonomous pieces that serve as explanatory discourses, and as the author's cosmovision. According to Rama, the latter distinguishes *Los ríos profundos* from other contemporary poetic currents such as *lo real maravilloso*, which became practically synonymous with Latin American culture after the Boom. Rama observes that no reader of *El reino de este mundo* (*The Kingdom of this World*, 1949) believes that Alejo Carpentier shares his characters' mythical views, nor is the novel's narrativity put in question by myths (337). Arguedas, on the other hand, manipulates the novel form to such an extent in *Los ríos profundos* that, at times, it is difficult to separate the worldview of the narrator—or narrators—from that of the author.[20] Myths are not dissolved into *Los ríos profundos*'s narration but confronted from within, a good example of what I call antigenric coupling. The novel becomes a space where two discursive genres (novel and myth) are juxtaposed but retain their distinct cultural origins and logics for the production of meaning.

Another key theme in *Los ríos profundos* is the tension between peasant societies (haciendas and indigenous communities) and urban society in the Andes. The novel poses a question that neither the author nor the narrative resolve: will the feudal-like society of the Andes persist, or is it breaking down? Even though Ernesto's childhood memories offer a positive image of indigenous rural life, the novel tempers any idealization, underscoring the existence of violent relations of domination.[21] The stratified nature of Andean society is expressed in the novel both in the opening scenes set in Cusco and in the stories linked to the haciendas that dominate the social space of Abancay. The novel begins with Ernesto and his father's arrival at the home of El Viejo (The Old Man), a powerful hacienda owner and relative. The short visit confronts Ernesto with Andean landowners' absolute power and the melancholic resignation of the *pongos*—indigenous people who perform forced domestic service. The attitude of the pongos is then seen replicated among the *colonos*—tenant farmers in the *hacienda* system—when the narrator describes the physical punishments and the accompanying psychological and cultural abuse endured by the colonos of the Patibamba hacienda (198). When Ernesto tries to speak to a colona, she asks him not to address her. This leads him to conclude that the colonos "would no longer even listen to the language of the ayllus; they must have been compelled to forget it" (41).[22]

In sharp contrast with the horrors of the *haciendas* stands the neighborhood of Huanupata in Abancay, which Ernesto visits frequently. The landowners' power does not reach this neighborhood, whose inhabitants are mostly indigenous migrants who carry out commercial and service activities in the city. In Huanupata, there are also *chicherías*—popular restaurants serving food and *chicha* (fermented corn drink)—where migrant musicians play traditional instruments and songs from their hometowns. The most important characters in this city are the *cholas*, the owners of the chicherías, who represent the rebellious spirit and social empowerment of the urban migrants but who, at the same time, have not lost their indigenous culture.[23] The cholas, led by Doña Felipa, organize a subaltern revolt in response to the unjust hoarding of salt by the landowners (chapter VII). Ernesto accompanies the revolt, enthused by their capacity to organize and challenge the state-signorial power. Although the army's troops eventually put down the cholas' rebellion, the story signals a political agency in these women that could contribute to the old regime's dissolution. The final scenes of the rebellion are laden with mythical symbolism: pursued by the army, Doña Felipa—reminiscent of Juan Santos Atahualpa—hides in the jungle in hopes of one day returning to continue the fight. The novel seems to suggest a connection between Doña Felipa's story and the myth of the *inkarri* (the Inca that will return to restore the order that was lost during the conquest).[24]

The novel ends with a different rebellion: a typhus epidemic ravages the haciendas. The colonos of the Ninabamba hacienda demand that a priest is sent to celebrate a mass. In response to the landowner's refusal, the desperate colonos travel to Abancay, defying the police. Ernesto cannot believe his eyes: "Impossible. They couldn't do it. They couldn't. Didn't they get scared when they saw the *guardias*?" (225).[25] Despite his excitement, Ernesto is not sure how to interpret this display of rebellious spirit by the most abused group in the region. He harbors doubts because he suspects that the protestors lack the political consciousness of Doña Felipa and that the revolt will not result in significant changes to social structures. The novel's open and explicitly ambiguous ending confronts the readers with the various historical options at stake. These will be explored at a national level in *Todas las sangres* (1964), where US imperialism and political projects that seek to resurrect indigenous communitarianism as an alternative to the nation-state complicate the existing tensions between capitalist society and the old regime.[26]

EL ZORRO DE ARRIBA Y EL ZORRO DE ABAJO (1971)

In Arguedas's posthumous novel, *El zorro de arriba y el zorro de abajo* (hereafter referred to as *El Zorro*), the setting shifts from the Andes to the port city of Chimbote on the Peruvian coast. During the 1950s and 1960s, this small cove of artisanal fishermen, located north of Lima, became the most important fishing port in the world due to a boom in fishmeal and fish oil markets. The installation of a modern steel plant also transformed Chimbote into the most important steel producer in Peru. Economic growth attracted both foreign and domestic migrants, among them impoverished peasants and former mining workers from the Andes, who were obliged to overcome their fear of the sea upon arrival (Sulmont).[27] In 1967, Arguedas began to carry out ethnographic work in Chimbote to study cultural changes resulting from highland migration. He used tape recorders and photographic cameras to document and interview city residents and subsequently used this material in writing *El Zorro* (Bernabé).

El Zorro's Chimbote resembles the chicherías in *Los ríos profundos*, insofar as both are places that attract Andean migrants. *El Zorro* narrates scenes of contemporary life in Chimbote and the past lives of the migrants who arrive at the port, informing readers about rural ways of life on haciendas or Andean mines. Other stories recount the experiences of migrant Andean musicians who arrive in Lima. On the one hand, Arguedas is interested in contextualizing the more recent experiences of migration to Chimbote within the broader history of internal migration in Peru. On the other hand, readers of Arguedas's earlier novels will recognize in these stories another iteration of

Arguedas's desire to "transform" the novel into historiography or ethnography, as we saw in *Yawar Fiesta*.

Despite these correspondences with previous novels, Chimbote is unlike any other city or town in Arguedas's previous works. He describes Chimbote as a destructive space where social relationships are governed by money and by a myth of progress that leads people to forget their campesino ways of life and culture quickly. Subsumed in the city's production machinery, Andean migrants end up squandering their wages in canteens and brothels. As discussed before, Arguedas had explored in his earlier novels the historical transformation of Andean societies and Peru during the twentieth century, but Chimbote confronts him with something new. While working on *El Zorro*, Arguedas wrote to his psychiatrist: "I have truly—incredibly—passed from the age of myth and feudality syncretized with myth to [standing under] the fierce light of the twenty-first century" (Arredondo 283). Unlike Abancay in *Los ríos profundos*, Chimbote is a space without a colonial history, seemingly created out of nothing by capitalism. The ancient struggle between the two worlds of indios and mistis appears to have entered a radical reorganization, where those worlds and modernity itself—previously identified with Lima—have lost their recognizable forms.

In both form and content, the novel foregrounds the challenge of narrating this rapid historical transformation. One example is Arguedas's efforts to give voice in the novel to a variety of different subjects. The fishermen's obscene speech intersects with the language of a varied cast of other characters: North American priests, a popular prophet, industrialists, anti-capitalists, adventure-seeking foreigners, and Quechua speakers who are not fluent in Spanish but refuse to use their native tongue.[28] The reader is confronted with voices that collide, overlap, or ignore each other—voices that sometimes become unintelligible as if communication were impossible in the port city. The frustration or confusion resulting from this linguistic scenario signifies Arguedas's difficulties in accurately conveying the historical moment's conflicting complexities.

Arguedas's radical manipulation of the novelistic genre itself also evinces the narrative challenge posed by Chimbote's historical change. As I argued earlier, Arguedas's experimentation with the novel form is evident in his work, beginning with *Yawar Fiesta*. Nonetheless, in *El Zorro*, the parameters of the novel are pushed to their very limits. Readers are faced with a novel whose form dramatically thematizes its own conditions of possibility. Along with conventionally narrative sections, *El Zorro* includes diary entries, letters, and a speech entitled "No soy un aculturado" ("I Am Not an Acculturated Man") that Arguedas delivered in 1968 upon receiving a literary award. Also included is a theatrical dialogue between two foxes—referred to in the novel's title—that alludes directly to the *Huarochirí Manuscript* (circa 1598), originally written in Quechua and translated by Arguedas in 1966 under the title *Dioses y Hombres de Huarochirí*. The novel does not attempt to smooth over or obscure the differences between these multiple materials but instead obliges readers to confront a choppy, constantly interrupted text. In grappling with questions about how the work is to be read, one is forced to immediately discard the conventions of fictionality and the habits of the modern reader of literature.

The theatrical dialogue between the fox from above and the fox from below further challenges readers. As mentioned above, it interrupts the narration by inserting another discursive form and inviting readers to stop reading the novel and turn to *Dioses y hombres de Huarochirí*. The fox—split in *El Zorro* into two figures, one representing the Peruvian highlands, the other the coastal region—serves as an essential character in the Manuscript and the living oral tradition of the Andes, where it has four characteristics: it is *huaccha* (poor, orphaned), a migrant, a wise figure, and a musician (García Liendo "El Reflejo"). The fox's status as an orphan—lacking kinship relationships—allows it to be a great observer of life and historical changes in the Andes. Hence, the foxes' inclusion in the novel—in the story of their conversation in Chimbote and as individual characters in the main plot, seemingly engaged in a participant observation—draws a direct connection to indigenous epistemology. Lastly, the foxes' relation to *Dioses y hombres de Huarochirí* complicates *El Zorro*'s depiction of the ongoing historical transformation occurring in Chimbote, as an examination of *Dioses y hombres* demonstrates that indigenous societies have always migrated and undergone constant change. In this way, the foxes' dialogue underscores the complex dynamics of rupture and continuity that connect Chimbote with the pre-Hispanic and colonial past of Peru's indigenous societies.[29]

An examination of *El Zorro*'s early drafts reveals that the section published as "First Diary" was initially entitled "First Chapter."[30] The title change points to the formal decisions that Arguedas made in *El Zorro*, particularly concerning these "diary" sections, which insert the author into the novel, distinguishing him from the main narrator and inviting readers to follow autobiographical clues. The diaries constitute a writing genre that allows Arguedas to bring together biography and history, private and public life, projects, politics, and controversy. The psychological pain revealed in these sections intersects with the memory of a childhood spent among indigenous peoples, thereby privileging affect as a cognition system (Castro-Klarén). In these diaries, Arguedas also emphasizes his condition as a migrant who is knowledgeable about the cultures of the Andes and the coast. In addition, the diaries serve as a space for literary politics. Written at the height of the Boom of the Latin American novel—Gabriel García Márquez's *One Hundred Years of Solitude* was published in 1967—the novel thematizes the poetics of its author, asserting his affinities with Rulfo, García Márquez, and Guimarães Rosa as well as referring to Arguedas's controversy with Julio Cortázar, whom he sees as a professional writer guided by the demands of the world literary market. Arguedas also distances himself from the latter's formal experimentation, which he sees as influenced by narration modes taken from mass culture (Moraña 27). Finally, the diaries are also where the theme of suicide emerges, which is linked to the difficulty of narrating and finishing the novel.[31] Arguedas worked on *El Zorro* nearly until the day he decided to take his own life. In the final diary, he remarks on how he should have followed certain characters' stories, but the account is abruptly interrupted by final instructions to friends about his burial (245). The novel breaks all pretense of fiction with the reader and proposes possibly the most radical way of articulating literature and life by introducing the author's death into the novel.[32]

This diversity of materials in *El Zorro* has led some critics to consider it an unfinished work.[33] There are multiple signs of the novel's status as an incomplete work, particularly if we consider it was published posthumously. It also remains unclear how closely *El Zorro*'s publisher followed Arguedas's instructions and indications. However, it is also possible to interpret the work's incompleteness from the vantage point of Arguedas's poetics of the novel, which I have discussed in this chapter as antigenric coupling. It achieves its full expression in *El Zorro*, where Arguedas brings together literature, ethnography, history, mythology, biography, letters, music, dance, and folk tales without merging these components into a dominant narrative.

El Zorro allows us to perceive in Arguedas's novels a strategy of writing that works against genric forms. For him, the task of narrating what was happening in Peru exceeds the capacity of any given discursive genre on its own—whether the novel itself (as received from tradition), indigenous myth or song, or the social sciences. One could wonder why Arguedas ultimately chose the bourgeois genre of the novel rather than that of mythical sagas such as *Dioses y hombres de Huarochirí*. On the one hand, his choice reflected his desire to reach a broad and culturally heterogeneous audience, particularly Peruvian readers unaccustomed to academic writing conventions. On the other hand, his choice of form also responded to his conviction that the novel was capable of accommodating a variety of different epistemologies, modes of cognition, affects, and medialities (print, sound, visual), an accommodation that other discursive modes were incapable of due to their subjection to disciplinary rules. The novel, albeit only after undergoing a radical transformation, seems to be the only narrative form that allows him to bring together and record—in all their complexity—indigenous thought and ways of life, capitalist transformation, revolution, ethnic and class change, and local events ignored by history. As I mentioned above, in Arguedas's poetics, there is no attempt to merge this diversity of materials into a single narrative. Instead, they maintain their original markings and characteristics, thereby confronting readers with their limitations as well as with the importance of employing a variety of logics of sense-making for understanding indigenous cultures and historical change in twentieth-century Peru.

Arguedas's poetics is also reflected in his dissonance vis-à-vis the intellectual field of his time. By way of concluding this discussion, I would like to refer to two moments where this dissonance was particularly evident. During the Primer Encuentro de Escritores Peruanos (held in 1965), he engaged in a debate with his friend, the writer and literary critic Sebastián Salazar Bondy. The latter proposed defining literature as "a great lie, the most marvelous of lies" (Alegría et al. 104), which irritated Arguedas.[34] Salazar Bondy proceeded to clarify that he was referring to "verbal reality," as opposed to social reality, to which Arguedas responded ironically that such a distinction was only for academics: "it may be that verbal reality is a great truth in the study of literature, but verbal reality? It doesn't exist! The word is the name of things or . . . of what is thought about things; verbal reality is reality reality" (Alegría, et al. 140).[35] Although Arguedas's response raises a number of considerations, it nonetheless points to his divergence from established notions about fiction and the autonomy of the work of art.

That same year, Arguedas participated in a round-table discussion of *Todas las sangres*, where he reacted to the various academic assessments of his novel with a great sense of disappointment and alienation (Rochabrún). Several critics have addressed the intense emotional impact this round-table discussion had on Arguedas, with its effect on exacerbating the depression that led to his suicide. Another dimension of the discussion is helpful for elucidating his poetics. Arguedas's novel had found itself at the center of a disciplinary dispute between social science and literary studies scholars. On the one hand, the French sociologist Henri Favre accused Arguedas of creating a false representation of the Andes, arguing that the region no longer had a social caste system nor an indigenous society (ethnically defined) as Arguedas believed (39). On the other hand, critic Alberto Escobar, influenced by literary phenomenology, proposed a reading of the novel based on literary criticism's epistemological principles (34). Favre's and Escobar's critiques speak of a time when the social sciences and literary studies were undergoing a process of scientific specialization, as well as reflecting debates over artistic realism that had been reawakened in Latin America by the Cuban Revolution. Arguedas felt alienated from this disciplinary dispute and context. A study of his novels demonstrates that his position was defined, above all, by his commitment to a mode of writing that was in tension with the autonomization of literature and the specialization of intellectual work that had been prominent in Latin America since nineteenth-century *modernismo* (Ramos). However, Arguedas's position should not be seen as an anachronism but as his effort to politicize the literature of his era. Viewed from the present day, his poetics can be seen as an *avant-la-lettre* expression of what Josefina Ludmer would later term "postautonomous literatures"; that is, writings that do not seek to be read as literature and whose status as fiction is unknown and does not matter.

NOTES

1. In this chapter, I use the historical term *indio*, employed by Arguedas, to refer to indigenous populations from both peasant communities and haciendas. In Arguedas' oeuvre *mistis* refers principally to the class-ethnic group that concentrates power in Andean haciendas, towns, and cities. He defines it as follows: "'Mistis' are not white people. The term designates the masters (*señores*) of Western culture, or almost Western culture, who dominated the region politically, socially, and economically since colonial times. None of them are, of course, of pure white race or of pure Western culture" ("Puquio" 248). All translations from Spanish are mine.
2. In broad terms, indigenismo in Latin America refers to a wide array of discourses on the indio produced by non-indigenous intellectuals since colonial times. In the twentieth century (between 1920 and 1970), indigenista intellectuals were influenced by various systems of thought such as liberalism, anarchism, Marxism, nationalism, eugenics, and progressive education. In countries with a significant indigenous population, indigenismo is regarded as both a response to modernization and a political and cultural discourse that questioned the persistence of colonial structures and mentality. Peru's indigenismo had its defining moment in the past century during the 1920s. Championed by Andean intellectuals from Cusco and Puno especially, the movement took a regionalist stance defending the

importance of the Andes (historic center of the Inca empire) against Lima's dominance since the Hispanic colonization. Indigenista intellectuals denounced the indio's economic and political oppression and proposed a de-whitening process of national culture.

3. Ignacio Sánchez Prado has recently published a compelling examination of transculturation's role within debates and theories on the Latin American novel.

4. For a comprehensive overview of these historical changes, see Klarén.

5. On the indigenista novel, see Cornejo Polar (*Escribir; Literatura*) and Elmore.

6. In the novel, Puquio is described as a "town," a term that might lead the reader to imagine a social space closer to rural society than urban life. Nevertheless, as the province's capital, Puquio was a city with a political function and connection with the national state.

7. "indígena desvalido y de retrasado cerebro" (Arguedas, *Yawar Fiesta* 65).

8. Arguedas seems to comment here on the tensions among members of the Peruvian left after Mariátegui (1894–1930), particularly their difficulties with understanding *campesino* society and assessing culture's role in revolutionary politics in countries like Peru.

9. "Un nuevo estilo aparece porque hay un nuevo mundo que revelar" (Arguedas, *Primer* 172).

10. "Tropa cerrada" (Arguedas, *Yawar Fiesta* 71).

11. "¡Esto es un cinema! ¡Parece película!" (Arguedas, *Yawar Fiesta* 71).

12. "pueblos como de otro mundo" (Arguedas, *Yawar Fiesta* 72).

13. Likewise, this story questions the image of the *indio*—widespread in coastal cities—as melancholy, weak, and incapable of rebellion (Cornejo Polar, *Los universos* 54).

14. The history of the *chalos* (*cholos*) incorporated in Arguedas's novel predates by more than a decade the first studies on the formation of the *cholo* group—a new type of mestizo that became integrated into the capitalist urban economy without losing its Indian cultural matrix (Quijano).

15. The *huayno* that Arguedas reproduces in chapter 2 originally appeared in *Canto Kechwa* (1938). Music is a fundamental aspect of Arguedas's novels (Rama; Rowe *Ensayos*; Lienhard). Kraniauskas has characterized *Yawar Fiesta* as an "inter-medial" novel due to its combination of photography, writing, and sound (361).

16. Some critics have read *Los ríos profundos* as an autobiographical novel due to the similarities between Ernesto's itinerant life and family situation and Arguedas's.

17. See Escobar and Tarica for analysis of the important linguistic work Arguedas accomplishes in *Los ríos profundos*.

18. For this topic and the contextualization of the Arguedas-Cortázar debate within the Boom and the twentieth-first-century Latin American literary production see De Castro (*The Spaces*, chapter 6).

19. See A. Cornejo Polar's reading of the wall scene (*Escribir* 195–201) and Rowe's critique of this interpretation ("Sobre"). For a study of the mythical structure in the novel, see also Usandizaga.

20. It is impossible to discount that the proximity between Arguedas's childhood and Ernesto's story also plays a role in making it difficult to distinguish between the author's and the character's beliefs.

21. One perceives similar anguish in Arguedas's anthropological work. The dissolution of these relations of domination, which Arguedas urgently supported, also threatened the indigenous culture he so valued and that was formed within the framework of these relations of domination.

22. "ya no escuchaban el lenguaje de los ayllus; les habían hecho perder la memoria" (Arguedas, *Los ríos profundos* 200).

23. The *cholos* had already appeared in *Yawar Fiesta*. Here, the protagonist role is played by women, who are central characters in Arguedas's literature (Lambright). Anthropological studies on the *cholas* are quite useful for understanding this aspect of *Los ríos profundos*. See De la Cadena.

24. On the *inkarri* myth see Flores Galindo.

25. "¡Mentira! ¡Ellos no pueden! ¡No puede ser! ¿No se han espantado viendo a los guardias?" (Arguedas, *Los ríos profundos* 450).

26. For a study of *Todas las sangres* see Moore and Feldman.

27. The conflictive relationship of Andean migrants with the sea can be seen in the first chapter of the novel.

28. Lienhard published the transcription of recordings Arguedas made of Hilario M. (Hilario Caullama in the novel), a migrant from Puno who is proud of his Aymara culture, and of Esteban de la Cruz (identified by the same name in the novel), a former miner from Ancash (199–205).

29. For example, chapter 3 features a fox disguised as Don Diego, a visitor with animal features and dressed in archaic clothing (85). The scene of Don Diego and the machine is central to the analysis of capitalism and its social effects in the novel (Beasley-Murray).

30. I identified this change in an unpublished Arguedas manuscript, "El zorro de arriba y el zorro de abajo: Primera parte (Tercera corrección)," that is housed in the Arguedas archive at the Pontificia Universidad Católica del Perú. Consulted July 2007.

31. Letters are also included in this formal operation of the novel.

32. This is a paraphrase of Ricardo Piglia's hypothesis of reading as developed in one of his seminars, "Poéticas de la novela," which remains unpublished. On Arguedas's suicide and *EZ* see Rivera.

33. Lienhard comments on this situation in his important study of *EZ* (13).

34. "Una gran mentira, la más maravillosa de las mentiras" (Alegría et. al. 104).

35. "Puede que [la realidad verbal] sea una gran verdad [en] el estudio de la literatura, pero ¿realidad verbal? ¡No existe! La palabra es nombre de cosas o . . . de lo que se piensa sobre las cosas; lo que es realidad verbal es realidad realidad" (Alegría et. al. 140).

Works Cited

Alegría, Ciro et. al. *Primer Encuentro De Narradores Peruanos*. Latinoamericana, 1986.

Arguedas, José María. "Canto Kechwa." *Obra Antropológica*, vol. 1, Horizonte, 2012, pp. 146–85.

Arguedas, José María. *Diamantes y pedernales*. Lima: J. Mejía Baca, 1954.

Arguedas, José María. *Deep Rivers*. Translated by Frances Horning Barraclough. U of Texas P, 1978.

Arguedas, José María. *The Fox from Up Above and the Fox from Down Below*. Translated by Frances Horning Barraclough. U of Pittsburgh P, 2000.

Arguedas, José María. *El zorro de arriba y el zorro de abajo*. ALLCA XX, 1996.

Arguedas, José María. *Los ríos profundos*. 8th ed. Cátedra, 2005.

Arguedas, José María. "Puquio, una cultura en proceso de cambio." *Obra Antropológica*, vol. 4, Horizonte, 2012, pp. 245–91.

Arguedas, José María. *Todas las sangres*. Buenos Aires: Losada, 1964.

Arguedas, José María. *Yawar Fiesta*. Ediciones del Viento, 2006.

Arguedas, José María. *Yawar Fiesta*. Translated by Frances Horning Barraclough. Waveland, 2002.

Arredondo, Sybila. "El zorro de arriba y el zorro de abajo en la correspondencia de Arguedas." Arguedas, *El zorro de arriba y el zorro de abajo*, pp. 275–306.

Beasley-Murray, Jon. "Arguedasmachine: Modernity and Affect in the Andes." *Iberoamericana* 8.30 (2008): 113–28.

Beckman, Ericka. "The Historical Novel in Peru: José María Arguedas's *Yawar Fiesta*." *Mediations*, vol. 33, nos.1–2, 2020, pp. 69–84.

Bernabé, Mónica. "José María Arguedas, entre el campo y la ciudad." *Migración y frontera: Experiencias culturales en la literatura peruana del siglo XX*, edited by Javier García Liendo. Iberoamericana-Vervuert, 2017, pp. 199–223.

Carpentier, Alejo. *El reino de este mundo*. Mexico: Edición y Distribución Ibero Americana de Publicaciones, 1949.

Castro-Klarén, Sara. "'Like a Pig, When He's Thinkin': Arguedas on Affect and on Becoming an Animal." *José María Arguedas. The Fox from up above and the Fox from Down Below*, edited by Julio Ortega, University of Pittsburgh Press, 2000, pp. 307–23.

Cornejo Polar, Antonio. *Escribir en el aire: Ensayo sobre la heterogeneidad sociocultural en las literaturas andinas*. CELACP, 2003.

Cornejo Polar, Antonio. *Literatura y sociedad en el Perú: La novela indigenista*. Lasontay, 1980.

Cornejo Polar, Antonio. *Los universos narrativos de José María Arguedas*. Horizonte, 1997.

Cornejo Polar, Antonio. "Mestizaje, Transculturación, Heterogeneidad." *Revista de Crítica Literaria Latinoamericana*, vol. 20, no. 40, 1994, pp. 368–71.

De Castro, Juan E. *The Spaces of Latin American Literature: Tradition, Globalization, and Cultural Production*. Palgrave Macmillan, 2008.

De la Cadena, Marisol. *Indigenous Mestizos*. Duke UP, 2000.

Elmore, Peter. *Los muros invisibles: Lima y la modernidad en la novela del siglo XX*. Mosca Azul, 1993.

Feldman, Irina. *Rethinking Community from Peru: The Political Philosophy of José María Arguedas*. U of Pittsburgh P, 2014.

Flores Galindo, Alberto. *Buscando un inca: Identidad y utopía en los Andes*. Horizonte, 1988.

García Liendo, Javier. *El intelectual y la cultura de masas: Argumentos latinoamricanos en torno a Ángel Rama y José María Arguedas*. Purdue UP, 2017.

García Liendo, Javier. "El reflejo y la memoria: Los zorros en la última novela de Arguedas." *Palimpsestos de la antigua palabra*, edited by Helena Usandizaga< Peter Lang, 2013. Pp. 137–71.

Klarén, Peter. *Peru: Society and Nationhood in the Andes*. Oxford UP, 2000.

Kokotovic, Misha. "Transculturación Narrativa Y Modernidad Andina: Nueva Lectura De *Yawar Fiesta*." *José María Arguedas: hacia una poética migrante*, edited by Sergio R. Franco, Instituto Internacional de Literatura Iberoamericana, 2006, pp. 39–60.

Kraniauskas, John. "A Short Andean History of Photography: Yawar Fiesta." *Journal of Latin American Cultural Studies*, vol. 21, no. 3, 2012, pp. 359–78.

Lambright, Anne. *Creating the Hybrid Intellectual Subject, Space and the Feminine in the Narrative of José María Arguedas*. Bucknell UP, 2007.

Lienhard, Martin. *Cultura popular andina y forma novelesca: zorros y danzantes en la última novela de Arguedas*. Horizonte, 1990.

Ludmer, Josefina. "Literaturas Postautónomas 2.0." *Propuesta Educativa*, vol. 32, 2009, pp. 41–45.

Moore, Melisa. *En la encrucijada: Las ciencias sociales y la novela en el Perú.* Universidad Nacional Mayor de San Marcos, 2003.

Moraña, Mabel. *Arguedas/Vargas Llosa: Dilemmas and Assemblages.* Translated by Andrew Ascherl. Palgrave Macmillan, 2016.

Moreiras, Alberto. "The End of Magical Realism: José María Argueda's Passionate Signifier." *The Exhaustion of Difference: Politics of Latin American Cultural Studies,* Duke UP, 2001, pp. 184–207.

Piglia, Ricardo. *Las tres vanguardias: Saer, Puig, Walsh.* Eterna Cadencia, 2016.

Portugal, José Alberto. *Las novelas de José María Arguedas: Una incursión en lo inarticulado.* Pontificia Universidad Católica del Perú, 2011.

Quijano, Aníbal. *Dominación y cultura, lo cholo y el conflicto cultural en el Perú.* Mosca Azul, 1980.

Rama, Ángel. *Transculturación narrativa en América Latina.* El Andariego, 2008.

Ramos, Julio. *Divergent Modernities: Culture and Politics in Nineteenth-Century Latin America.* Translated by José Saldívar. Duke UP, 2001.

Remy, María Isabel. *Historia de las comunidades indígenas y campesinas del Perú.* Instituto de Estudios Peruanos, 2013.

Rivera, Fernando. *Dar la Palabra: Ética, política y poética de la escritura en Arguedas.* Iberoamericana-Vervuert, 2011.

Rochabrún, Guillermo, ed. *La mesa redonda sobre* Todas Las Sangres. Instituto de Estudios Peruanos, 2000.

Rodríguez-Luis, Julio. *Hermenéutica y praxis del indigenismo.* Fondo de Cultura Económica, 1980.

Rowe, William. *Ensayos arguedianos.* SUR, 1996.

Rowe, William. "Sobre la heterogeneidad de la letra en *Los ríos profundos*: Una crítica a la oposición polar escritura/oralidad." *Heterogeneidad y literatura en el Perú,* edited by James Higgins, CELACP, 2003, pp. 225–49.

Sánchez Prado, Ignacio. "The Persistence of the Transcultural: A Latin American Theory of the Novel from the National-Popular to the Global." *New Literary History,* vol. 51, no. 2, 2020, pp. 347–74.

Sulmont, Denis. "El Boom De Chimbote." *Academia.edu.* 2006.

Usandizaga, Helena. "Amaru, Winku, Lay'ka, Supay o Demonio: Las fuerzas del mundo de abajo en *Los ríos profundos*." *José María Arguedas: Hacia una poética migrante,* edited by Sergio R. Franco, Instituto Internacional de Literatura Iberoamericana, 2006, pp. 227–46.

Vargas Llosa, Mario. *La utopía arcaica: José María Arguedas y las ficciones del indigenismo.* Fondo de Cultura Económica, 1997.

CHAPTER 34

....

THE STAR OF THE HOUR

One Hundred Years of Clarice Lispector

....

CLAIRE WILLIAMS

CLARICE THE CULTURAL ICON
....

ALTHOUGH it will be mainly remembered for the challenges and crises caused by the Coronavirus pandemic, the year 2020 was one of celebration for readers of the Brazilian writer Clarice Lispector, for it marked the centenary of her birth. One hundred years since she was born in a tiny village in the Ukraine, Lispector and her work have achieved canonical status, not only in Brazil, where she lived most of her life, becoming a naturalized citizen in 1943, but around the world. Her books have been translated into dozens of languages, from Catalan to Chinese, and the most recent set of translations into English, published by major publishing houses New Directions in the United States and Penguin in the United Kingdom, has undoubtedly boosted her popularity in the Anglophone world, gaining her new and vocal supporters, including influential names such as Jhumpa Lahiri, Ali Smith, and Colm Tóibín.

Despite the challenges it posed organizers, directors, editors, and publishers, 2020 still saw the fruition of a large number of commemorative initiatives, such as the reissuing by Rocco, Lispector's Brazilian publishers, of her complete literary works, with bold, bright covers, designed by Victor Burton using details from Lispector's own paintings, and the publication of *Todas as cartas* (All the Letters, 2020), part of a series grouping "all" her works, including her journalism, according to genre. Her Parisian publishing house, Éditions des femmes, brought out a "Coffret Anniversaire" (Anniversary Chest), and literary magazines and academic journals celebrated the anniversary with special issues. The Instituto Moreira Salles (IMS), a cultural center that houses the bulk of Lispector's archive, launched a section of their website devoted exclusively to her, making available digitalized photos and scans of documents, manuscripts, audio recordings, and videos, including lectures on her work, with material in English as well as Portuguese (*Clarice*

Lispector).[1] Academic conferences organized around the world (for example, São Paulo and Macau), brought together both scholars and enthusiasts—journalists, novelists, artists, musicians, filmmakers, friends—to discuss the author's work and to pay tribute to her achievements. Even her son, Paulo Gurgel Valente, emerged from a discreet silence to contribute an afterword (2020) to the centennial edition of the most recent English translation of probably her best-known book, *A hora da estrela* (*The Hour of the Star*, 1977), participate in a Webinar organized by Princeton University, and be interviewed for Argentinian daily *Clarín* (Abdala 2020).[2]

The pandemic adversely affected many events, which had to be postponed, like the planned exhibition at the IMS of women artists "Constelação Clarice" (Constellation Clarice) (curated by Verónica Stigger and Eucanaã Ferraz), or the distribution to cinemas of the feature films *A Paixão segundo G.H.* (*The Passion according to G.H.*, adapted from the homonymous book published in 1964), directed by Luiz Fernando Carvalho, and *O Livro dos Prazeres* (*The Book of Pleasures*, an adaptation of *Uma aprendizagem ou o livro dos prazeres* [*An Apprenticeship or the Book of Pleasures*, 1969]), directed by Marcela Lordy. Other initiatives simply moved online, which at least had the advantage of making them accessible to a wider audience worldwide.

Such a wide and varied amount of activities to celebrate one author, in the midst of a global pandemic, speaks to the undeniability of Lispector's place as a cultural figure of international importance as well as to the depth of her writing's impact on her passionate readers. She is a writer who inspires real hero-worship now, and whose fame has spread beyond the borders of her country, but her critical fortunes ebbed and flowed during her lifetime. Her first novel, *Perto do coração selvagem* (*Near to the Wild Heart*, 1943), was unlike anything readers had come across before, particularly in comparison to the socio-realist, regionalist novels in vogue in Brazil at the time. The story of a young woman's intellectual, psychological, emotional, linguistic, moral, and social development in a stiffly patriarchal world was greeted with such wonder and enthusiasm that at least one review or article about it came out every month in the year following its publication (Sousa 69). The writing was strange, not always strictly grammatical—the protagonist was impulsive, twisted, lacking social filters. The long streams of consciousness, shifts from first to third-person narrative, and linguistic experiments prompted comparisons with modernism; the reflections on being, bad faith, and the absurdity of life evoked existential philosophy. In 1944, Antonio Candido, renowned literary critic, hailed the novel as a new dawn ("raiar") for Brazilian literature, claiming that its young author pushed Portuguese to places where no one had gone before (Candido 127).

After such acclaim and applause, Lispector was under pressure to write a follow-up that matched the introspective explosiveness of her debut novel. This would be a difficult task in any circumstances, but the year after *Perto do coração selvagem* was published, she left Brazil to accompany her diplomat husband on postings to Europe and the United States, and lived abroad, except for short holiday periods back home, for the next sixteen years. During this time, she did publish two novels and drafted another, but she also became a mother, endured the tedium of carrying out the duties of a diplomat's wife, and kept up a lively correspondence with her literary and journalist friends back in Rio, as well as with her beloved sisters (Lispector, *Todas as cartas*). She was able to maintain a presence in the literary and publishing worlds by contributing short stories and *crônicas*[3] to newspapers and literary magazines, but upon separation from her husband and a return to Rio in 1955, she needed to reassert herself as a serious writer. This she did with the publication in 1960 of a book of short stories, *Laços de família* (*Family Ties*), and the weighty, existentialist *A maça no escuro* (*The Apple in the Dark*, 1961). While raising her two sons, she continued to write powerful fiction, as well as supplementing her income with less prestigious work: translations of foreign blockbusters and classics into Portuguese, story books for children, interviews with celebrities in the popular magazines *Manchete* (1968–1969) and *Fatos e Fotos: Gente* (1976–1977), and what became a much-loved Saturday column in the daily newspaper *Jornal do Brasil* (1967–1973), via which she gained a wider audience.[4]

All in all, Lispector published eight novels, five short-story collections, three children's books, a book of interviews, and two books of crônicas before her death in 1977. In the seven years immediately following her death, another novel, another book of unpublished short stories, two collections of crônicas, and another children's book came out. Since then, almost all these texts have been republished, the stories widely anthologized or gathered in new thematic collections, and all manner of unpublished material collected into volumes or digitalized by the IMS: correspondence, writing for women's pages, essays, notebooks. Her work is available in many formats and editions, studied at Brazilian secondary schools and, in fragmented form, scattered over the internet and social media (Athayde and Rocha; Mota).

LISPECTOR'S IDIOSYNCRATIC STYLE AND APPEAL

The capacity to surprise and wrongfoot readers at the levels of syntax, metaphor, content, and plot that had so impressed the readers of her first novel became characteristic of Lispector's idiosyncratic writing, which changes from story to story and book to book, and, importantly, stands out distinctly from her contemporaries' work. Her translators have commented on the considerable challenge of maintaining the strangeness of her expression and not falling into the trap of domesticating or correcting it. Her metaphors and similes bring together apparently disparate elements, inviting reinterpretations of reality, questioning what we take for granted. For example, in a pair of crônicas about the experience of visiting the custom-built, recently inaugurated (1960) capital city of Brasília, she wrote:

> Brasília is the landscape of insomnia. . . . Brasília is a tennis court. . . . Brasília smells like toothpaste. . . . Brasília is pure protein. . . . Brasília is slim. And utterly elegant. It wears a wig and false eyelashes. . . . Brasília is a mass suicide. . . . Brasília is a pair of

stainless-steel scissors. . . . Brasília is the sound of ice cubes in a glass of whiskey, at six in the evening, the hour of nobody.

(Lispector, *Complete Stories* 574, 576, 578, 581, 584, 589, 593)[5]

The multi-sensory comparisons listed in the crônicas, based on visits to Brasília in 1962 and 1974, evoke the impact of the modernist architecture, foregrounding corporeal reactions to the energy and elegance of the city, but amid the comedy and chaos are unsettling images of violence and death, perhaps alluding to the turbulent times of the military dictatorship (1964–1985). In a similar way, the mismatch between lovers is manifested in the imagery in this passage from *Perto do coração selvagem*:

"Otávio," she'd suddenly say to him, "has it ever occurred to you that a dot, a single dot without dimensions, is the utmost solitude?" . . . As if she had tossed a hot coal at her husband, the phrase flipped about, wriggling through his hands until he rid himself of it with another phrase, cold like gray, gray to cover the interval: it's raining, I'm hungry, it's a beautiful day.

(*Near to the Wild Heart* 25)[6]

This passage vividly illustrates Joana's interest in physics and metaphysics, and Otávio's incapacity to connect with her on an intellectual level. Her burning words turn to ash (here translated as "gray," the word "cinza" also means "ash") in his hands, and her bright thought is dimmed by his banal statements. It also directly contrasts a female and a male mode of expression, as if exemplifying Hélène Cixous's feminist concept of *écriture feminine*.[7] Indeed, Lispector's writing consistently questions rigid categories of all sorts, including gender and the formation of the traditional family unit, which prove so hard to perform and uphold, as evidenced in the stories of *Laços de família*. Likewise, imagery of crumbling, ruins, cracks, hard surfaces, and carapaces barely containing the messy chaos within are strewn throughout *A paixão segundo G.H.*, a novel about reconstructing identity and/through language.

In her pioneering study, the first monograph on Lispector in English, *Passionate Fictions: Gender, Narrative, and Violence in Clarice Lispector* (1994), Marta Peixoto describes the author's practice as aggressive not only in physical terms but also at a textual level, particularly directed toward patriarchal structures (xiv). Rather than representing "the literal, political violence of war and torture, or other overt forms of state brutality, which are all too prevalent in Latin America and indeed the world. There are crimes in Lispector, but they are used mainly for their symbolic value, as vehicles and correlatives of guilt and inner conflicts" (101–2). Despite what is often a minimal plot or storyline (a woman decides to clean a room, two teenagers see a "haunted" house, a chicken escapes), her fiction has great psychological intensity and lyrical beauty. Acts committed are not crimes in a legal or political sense, or sins in a religious sense, but they still condemn the perpetrators to soul-searching, guilt, and shame and, rarely, though occasionally, pride and joy. Characters may be faced with a dilemma or choice (Jolley), or forced to deal with strange encounters with people or things radically different from themselves and the lives they take for granted (Sá; Williams). The narrative accompanies them attempting to process their sensations and impressions, turning them into words, and trying to interact with the confusing, restricting world around them. Frequently structured around an epiphany, or moment of revelation, the texts twist in unexpected directions, ending ambiguously and always surprisingly: "Life just is for me, and I don't understand what I'm saying," *The Passion according to G.H.* (183);[8] "Don't forget that for now it's strawberry season. Yes," *The Hour of the Star* (77).[9]

This disruption of expectations is also what Peixoto describes as the "undermin[ing of] the authority of reason," or the privileging of "the intuitive and the improvisatory, which she associates with the feminine" over the standard, canonical, masculine "rational construction and logical progression" (xiv). This gendered conflict is exemplified in the relationship between male narrators and female characters in her last two novels, *A hora da estrela* (1977) and *Um sopro de vida* (*A Breath of Life*, 1978), which also satirize male dominance and arrogance in the literary world. In fact, a surprisingly wide range of embodied female experience, from childhood to old age, is played out in the stories and novels, inspiring one enthusiastic reader to pronounce that "the work of Lispector, as a whole, is the *Moby-Dick* of a certain kind of femininity: the female relationship to the female body" (Daniels 2017, n.p.).

It is feelings and impressions in all their messiness that the characters are trying to process but cannot stifle. Lispector declared: "Fortunately for me, my books are not overloaded with facts but the repercussion of facts on individuals" (Borelli, 70).[10] This shift of emphasis from rationality to affect is encapsulated in the statements from the first page of *A hora da estrela*: "Thinking is an act. Feeling is a fact" (*The Hour of the Star* 3).[11] Lispector avoids answers, definitions, and facts (so important to the self-proclaimed narrator of that novel, Rodrigo SM) but revels instead in ambiguity and potential, her intention being not "writing in order to respond, but in order to stretch the question to its furthest point, where no response could ever be anything but a compromise" (Borelli 77).[12]

Some readers are fans of Lispector's longer fiction, others prefer her short stories or newspaper crônicas, though genre is not a category that she allowed to restrict her, famously, and casually saying, in *Água viva* (*Água Viva*, 1973), a particularly slippery text, "No use trying to pin me down: I simply slip away and won't allow it, no label will stick" (7).[13] A look at the descriptive subtitles she occasionally used suggests Lispector wanted to create new genres evoking physical sensations, such as "impressões leves" (brief impressions) for the collection of crônicas and fragments *Visão do esplendor* (Vision of Splendor, 1975) or "pulsações" (pulsations) for *Um sopro de vida* (*A Breath of Life*, 1978).[14] Moreover, this spirit of invention and creation is patent in her constant reflections on the act of writing and other forms of artistic creation in her crônicas, and can be seen in her insistence on practice and technique when interviewing celebrities writer/artist characters, but it is also expressed by her characters:

> Then she made up what she should say. Eyes closed, surrendered, she softly spoke words born in that instant, never before heard by anyone, still tender from their

creation—fragile, new shoots. They were less than words, just loose, meaningless syllables that flowed and merged, were fertilized and reborn in a single being only to break apart immediately afterwards, breathing, breathing. . .

(*Near to the Wild Heart* 129)[15]

This story will be made of words that will gather in sentences and from these a secret meaning emanates that goes beyond words and sentences. Naturally, like every writer I'm tempted to use succulent terms: I know splendid adjectives, meaty nouns, and verbs so slender that they travel sharp through the air about to go into action, since words are actions, don't you agree? . . . Words are sounds transfused with unequal shadows that intersect, stalactites, lace, transfigured organ music.

(*The Hour of the Star* 6–7, 8)[16]

Perhaps it is the impressionistic nature of Lispector's prose, or its openness to multiple readings that has attracted devotees, because so many readers feel a very visceral connection. Upon reading her for the first time, Hélène Cixous famously felt an immediate affinity, wondering "Who are you who are so strangely me?" (169). Her texts can be enjoyed and studied from a plethora of different critical standpoints. For example, *A paixão segundo G.H.* has been read with a focus on ecofeminism and zen (Owen), "nonmodernity" (Paulson), motherhood (Hedrick), mysticism (Krabbenhoft), avant-garde Brazilian sculpture (Anitagrace), the sense of touch (Goh), or the use of "Holy Land imagery" (Hornike), and neurologists have gone so far as to diagnose G.H. with "temporal lobe epilepsy" (Deo and Charlier).

Lispector's works have left a considerable impact on her readers; many enthusiasts speak of falling in love with her or claim that her writing has changed their lives. Indeed, her own life story sometimes seems more like fiction. When she was just an infant, her family fled Stalin's brutal pogroms in search of a better life in South America. She grew up in the Jewish community in Recife, a city in northeastern Brazil, and the family moved to Rio when she was fifteen (in 1935). In life as in literature, Lispector did things differently from most people. She studied law and became one of Brazil's first woman journalists. She wrote from a young age, publishing her first short story in a literary magazine in 1940. On her return to Rio from Washington DC in 1959, she lived as a divorcée and single mother in a conservative, largely Catholic society. She was never able to make a living from literature in her lifetime, and she worked in a male-dominated field; nonetheless, her reputation as a distinguished writer grew throughout her lifetime, and she was awarded a number of prizes.

This life of exception and trailblazing has inspired a number of biographies in different languages and formats, including a cartoon book for children, *Clarice Lispector para meninas e meninos* (Clarice Lispector for Girls and Boys, Fink and Sáa), and a guide to Rio de Janeiro focusing on neighborhoods and sites significant in her life, based on tours run by the author (and biographer) Teresa Montero: *O Rio de Clarice: Passeio afetivo pela cidade* (Clarice's Rio: A Personal Tour around the City).[17] She is also one of the few Brazilian authors to have warranted a literary afterlife—several of them, in fact: she has been fictionalized by writers from around the world in numerous works of poetry and prose.[18] She appears as a character within the fiction, sometimes named, always recognizable to readers already acquainted with the details of her life. For the rest of this chapter, I will engage briefly with some of these incarnations of Lispector to explore the aspects of her life and works that are manifested most frequently and forcefully in other authors' texts.

"CLARICE" THE CHARACTER

Retired academic and prize-winning author Vilma Arêas is fiercely protective of Lispector's life and work, fearful that the real person and, more importantly, the originality of the work are lost amid the sheer volume of critical readings and growing number of biographical accounts. In the mid-1970s she and Lispector attended group therapy sessions and became friends ("Entrevista"). Her short story "Sobre os Espelhos" (On Mirrors) describes Lispector's bearing and presence with some unexpected metaphors and emphasizes the discomforting impact of meeting and knowing her (17–20):[19]

> Clarice is a pale nail, a thorn in the sole of your foot. I've never walked upright since I saw Clarice. She passed by and–too late!–my heart had rolled over. But I've never looked back, not once. I meet Clarice and start speaking nonsense. Because when she wants, she can be a flower, but also a rough woman with rings of sweat under her arms, chewing the fat thigh of a chicken while swigging mouthfuls of beer. It's no secret that she would eat human flesh if she had to.[20]

And yet, for all the pain and panic she causes the narrator, "Clarice" also inspires loyalty and devotion. The relationship portrayed by Arêas evokes the intimacy between them through images and anecdotes, the older woman offering advice, always conscious of a woman's looks, the younger woman only too aware of her imperfections. Their friendship is close; so close that the narrator is overwhelmed by Clarice even as the latter is dying: "I looked in the mirror. But instead of my own, I saw her face tied down by threads on the pillow" (20).[21] Arêas's tender, frank, iconoclastic story emphasizes the physicality of the female body and playful friendship (empathy represented through the mirroring effect), rather than describing her subject's intangible intellectual or mystical qualities, which is what many interviewers and critics have done (and still do).

There is no doubt that personal acquaintance with Lispector gives even a fictional portrait of her, like this one, extra credibility. Other authors who did not have the privilege of meeting or knowing her have had to rely on biographical material and have been obliged to use her writing (fiction and non-fiction) as a primary source. Building on the received knowledge to fill gaps and solve mysteries has often inspired authors to produce literature that can be categorized as, for example, "historiographic metafiction" (Hutcheon) or "postmodernist biofiction" (Layne). The works created might range from speculating about unknown elements or "missing" events in writers' lives, or rewriting those lives: imagining what might have happened if they had made other choices, or had alternative opportunities, and encountered different people and places.

Literature and life interweave closely in *Clarice Lispector: o tesouro de minha cidade* (Clarice Lispector: The Treasure of my City) by Ana Miranda, a well-known author of historical fiction and bio-fiction. In order to maintain a close intertextual relationship, Miranda decided:

> I would only read what Clarice had written, nothing that other people had written about her, so as to give my reading purity and avoid interferences, and that's what I did: I read all Clarice's books in the order in which they were written and published, as if I were reading an autobiography, hers, and mine. I read her letters. At the end, when the book was ready, I did manage to read the biography by Nádia Battella Gotlib, and used it to complement what I knew about Clarice. I looked at the photos, saw Clarice in sandals and a fur coat and thought: that was me . . .
>
> (Possani, "Anexo" 134–35)[22]

The novella takes the form of short fragmentary texts, told in the third person, or by a first-person narrator, with titles as enigmatic as "Secreta certeza" (Secret Certainty) and as specific as "Clarice continua a andar nas ruas do Rio de Janeiro" (Clarice Carries on Walking the Streets of Rio de Janeiro) (Miranda, *Clarice Lispector* 46, 36–37). As the latter title suggests, there is a focus on the female body travelling across the city, and even one fragment ("Uma cartografia" [A Cartography]) that simply lists street names mentioned in Lispector's works (38). The protagonist, "Clarice," has the freedom to roam and observe, but she is also a lonely, melancholy figure who rarely interacts with anyone else, apart from observing them from afar. She is not homeless; indeed, her apartment is described in great detail, but she is restless and rootless, always searching: "Clarice feels her heart racing. In the streets she searches for the peace she has not found inside herself" (92).[23] The narrative creates atmosphere and affect through adjectives, the occasional use of free indirect speech, and, rarely, direct speech. Clarice does not even need to be physically present in the action. Outside her apartment building: "There is no plaque, but there is the presence of Clarice. She comes in the sea breeze, the light, the air, the leaves blown by the wind, the moonlight. Clarice lives in ethereal things. Her plaque is made of clouds and salty waves and sand" (20).[24] This ghostly Clarice is a distillation of elements recurring in Lispector's fiction, but she is curiously insubstantial, lacking the warmth and humor that biographers describe, as well as the network of friendships and family that clearly supported the "real" Lispector. Miranda's work blurs the distinction between biography, autobiography, and fiction, with the potentially misleading effect of conflating Lispector the author (and Ana Miranda the author) with Clarice the character, and also with Lispector's fictional characters like G.H. (from *A paixão segundo G.H.*), who gazes across the city from her penthouse, or the young Joana (from *Perto do coração selvagem*) playing with language. Miranda recognized this overlap, describing her novella as "a conversation between two writers, Clarice and I, imagined by me, using her words as a starting point."[25]

Another way of "knowing" Lispector without having met her is through the intense and long-term study of her life and works, as what Matt Hills calls the "scholar-fan." Lucilene Machado and Edgar Cézar Nolasco are academics who have published literary critical research on Lispector (Machado "Entre abanicos e castanholas"; Nolasco *Clarice Lispector, Restos de ficção*). They have also taken their relationship with the author one step further by writing their own stories and crônicas, gathered in a collection entitled *Claricianas* (2006), which is a self-declared homage to Lispector, to mark the thirtieth anniversary of her death.[26] Their short texts, which they term "minibiografias ficcionais" (fictional minibiographies), constitute attempts to re-create the "fantasmático e espectral" (phantasmatic and spectral) side to her literature by jogging the (informed) reader's memory through well-placed allusions to aspects of her life and works (7).

This sort of fiction functions on several layers, with different reverberations in the reader, depending on how well they know Lispector's life and works. Nolasco and Machado have created an elaborate game of "spot the reference" that appeals especially to connoisseurs, though it does not exclude the uninitiated. The first-person narrator of Machado's twenty-six fragments is a woman reflecting on how to live, love, and write. Some of her sentences *almost* quote Lispector. For example, "Nasci para três coisas: amar, amar e amar" (There are three things for which I was born: to love, to love, and to love, 25) closely resembles lines from the crônica "As três experiências" (The Three Experiences): "There are three things for which I was born and for which I am prepared to give my life" (Lispector, *Discovering the World* 134–35).[27]

Nolasco goes further and creates a protagonist who behaves much like the version of herself Lispector portrayed in her crônicas, and similar to some of her characters. His unnamed female character stands at the window of her apartment, gazing at the sea, smoking. She visits a fortune teller, argues with her maid, and suffers from insomnia. Furthermore, Nolasco's Clarice is an author with grand literary pretensions, who wants to write like "Shakespeare, Homer and Virgil, Dante, Kafka, Machado, Woolf, Lispector, or even Borges himself" (64).[28] This direct reference to Lispector and her inclusion in a list of canonical writers reminds the reader of the fictional nature of what they are reading: although the character is *a* "Clarice," she is not *the* Clarice. This is reinforced by circumstantial details such as the character writing on a computer, or, more obviously, the dating of one section to November 16, 2005 (*Claricianas* 52).

More, slightly longer "minibiografias ficcionais" follow in Nolasco's 2014 collection *Quem tem medo de Clarice Lispector?* (Who's Afraid of Clarice Lispector?). Different facets of the character constructed in *Claricianas* are revealed, many based on facts about Lispector's life (hosting a dinner party for Brazilian diplomats in Washington, smoking "Hollywood" brand cigarettes, going to a conference on witchcraft). However, Nolasco also invents transgressive new personae, named in the titles, such as "A anfitriã falida" (The Failed Hostess), "A pornográfica" (The Pornographic Woman), or "A criminosa assumida" (The Self-Declared Criminal), thereby inventing elements that *might* have been part of Lispector's personality or behavior that she suppressed or fantasized about.

Furthermore, he fictionalizes potential encounters, such as conversations with Borges and Paulo Coelho, and goes so far as to imagine his protagonist visiting the multi-media exhibition celebrating Lispector that took place at the Museu da Língua Portuguesa in São Paulo in 2007. In this way, he invites readers to consider how Lispector would have reacted to the twenty-first-century world and the commemoration of her life and work, if she were still alive.

Lispector is a writer who inspires feelings of empathy and empowerment but also awe and a kind of worship and sense of unworthiness that might prevent her readers from writing about or like her. One way to sidestep that issue has been to hide her behind a many-layered disguise. For the poet Idra Novey, the process of translating *A paixão segundo G.H.* into English was overwhelmingly intense, "scrambl[ing] the syntax" of her daily life and leaving her "stunned alive" (*The Visitor* 5). After completing the translation, she wrote a series of poems entitled *The Visitor* (2014), as a way of processing the experience. She also published a comic novel entitled *Ways to Disappear* (2016), which, like the poems, deals closely with the relationship between a translator and an author. The disguise means that readers who have no knowledge of Lispector's life and literature can enjoy the novel on its own terms, whereas aficionados can smile at the ways the caricature distorts the original.

Novey's author character is named Beatriz Yagoda, and her family did migrate to Brazil, but from South Africa, not Eastern Europe. Like Lispector, she is green eyed and writes avant-garde prose. However, unlike the elegant, reserved Lispector known from the biographies, or the melancholy wanderer evoked by Ana Miranda, Yagoda has a rich and varied sex life, a gambling problem, a wicked sense of humor, and a Jabuti prize,[29] and she smokes cigars.

Ways to Disappear is most revealing when it describes the relationship between author and translator. Emma, the translator, feels duty and commitment toward Yagoda, as well as a fascination with the writer's daily life. Novey vividly conveys the "splendor" of translation and the translator's privileged access to "their" writer, coming to know them in intimate ways through their use of language (132). Emma is the only one who can decode the clues hidden in the text and solve the mystery of Yagoda's disappearance. The novel is also a satire of the publishing industry; academics' appropriation of writers and their works, the difficulty of marketing translated fiction in the Anglophone market, the media's use of scandal to sell books, and the dangers of being in the public eye. And yet, although there are echoes and likenesses in their stories, Beatriz Yagoda is definitively not Lispector.

More similar, although also disguised, is Vera Sigall, a secondary, though pivotal, character in Chilean author Carla Guelfenbein's novel *Contigo en la distancia* (*In the Distance with You*, 2015). At the end of the book, a polyphonic literary whodunnit with a murder and a lost manuscript, Guelfenbein explains that Lispector's life is "interwoven with Vera Sigall's and my own," and acknowledges having used Benjamin Moser's biography as part of her source material (407). The Jewish migrant background shared by Vera and Lispector (and the author herself) enables Guelfenbein to introduce episodes that show anti-Semitism among the Santiago elite, as well as the rootlessness felt by characters caught between different cultures. Like Novey's novel, it portrays the literary and publishing worlds, this time mid-twentieth-century, and the difficulties, particularly for women, to establish a literary career. Guelfenbein also grants Vera a healthy and active old age into the twenty-first century, grandchildren, a great inspirational love affair, and the opportunity to reap the benefits of her literary success in a democratic country: none of which Lispector, who died aged fifty-six, while Brazil was still under military dictatorship, was able to enjoy.

In one last example, Afro-Brazilian author Conceição Evaristo has created a poetic diptych from an imagined encounter between Lispector and Carolina Maria de Jesus, whose diary of *favela* life, published as *Quarto de Despejo* (The Junk Room), propelled her to fame upon its publication in 1960. They shared the same publisher, Francisco Alves, and there is a famous newspaper photo of them together at a book-signing event where Lispector was promoting *Laços de família* and de Jesus her diary. Evaristo's poems "Clarice no quarto de despejo" (Clarice in the Junk Room) and "Carolina na hora da estrela" (Carolina in the Hour of the Star), from the collection *Poemas da recordação e outros movimentos* (Poems of Remembrance and Other Movements, 2017), weave together both authors, titles, and well-known episodes from their books. In "Clarice no quarto de despejo," a dialogue is established which acknowledges the class and race differences between the two women. "Clarice" peers into the junk room and puts on fine white gloves ("luvas claríssimas") to pick through imaginary litter (97), whereas Carolina lived in the junk room (the metaphor she developed in her diary to denote the slums, where society dumps its rejects) and picked rubbish for a living.

Despite the social divide, Clarice listens to Carolina and, even more importantly, reads beyond her words, to see the person behind them: "Nobody reads me, Clarice, / Nobody can decode / the only lack I don't suffer from / loneliness" (97).[30] *A hora da estrela* is Lispector's demonstration of the difficulties of writing about poverty in a meaningful way, and, though playful and metafictional as well, it can be seen as a response to Carolina's stark representation of the facts of life in a favela and a provocation to readers to see and listen to those less fortunate than themselves. Evaristo's poems and "Macabéa, Flor de Mulungu" (Macabéa, Mulungu Flower, 2012), her reinterpretation of the story of the poor northeastern migrant girl, from *A hora da estrela*, highlight Lispector's social engagement as well as foregrounding the importance of female collaboration and complicity.

The authors I have mentioned above use a range of styles to vividly convey their own Lispectors: realist (Arêas), impressionist, or even Cubist, for the fragments and unusual angles (Nolasco, Miranda), caricature (Novey, Guelfenbein), and montage (Evaristo). Their Clarices are a blend of fact, fiction, admiration, and imagination, the result of a relationship derived from reading and a deeply felt empathy with the deceased author. One hundred years since her birth, Lispector is still very much alive through her questioning texts and also through her literary afterlives. The process of channeling or resurrecting her mirrors what literary critic and lecturer Affonso Romano de Sant'anna wrote about Lispector's own practice: "My friend was very special. She was mixed in magically and seductively with the characters she created. Literature was her flesh and blood" (72).[31]

NOTES

1. Some archive material, including correspondence and personal documents, can also be found in the AMLB at the Fundação-Casa Rui Barbosa in Rio de Janeiro.
2. He also contributed a moving tribute to his father, the diplomat Maury Gurgel Valente, in the literary magazine *Quatro Cinco Um* (2020).
3. The crônica is a journalistic genre popular in Latin America similar to an op-ed article, or regular column. The *cronista*, or columnist, reflects on current events from a personal perspective, often developing an idiosyncratic style and wide readership.
4. Most of the interviews have been collected in *Entrevistas* (2007) and the crônicas in *Todas as crônicas* (2018).
5. "Brasília é a paisagem da insônia . . . Brasília é uma quadra de tênis. . . . Brasília tem cheiro de pasta de dentes. . . . Brasília é proteína pura. . . . Brasília é magra. E toda elegante. Usa peruca, e cílios postiços. . . .Brasília é um suicídio em massa. . . .Brasília é uma tesoura de aço ouro. . . . Brasília é barulho de gelinho no copo de *whisky*, às seis horas da tarde. Hora de ninguém." Clarice Lispector, "Brasília," in *Para não esquecer* (1992), pp. 76, 78, 86.
6. "Otávio–dizia-lhe ela de repente–, você já pensou que um ponto, um único ponto sem dimensões, é o máximo de solidão? . . ." "Como se ela tivesse jogado uma brasa ao marido, a frase pulava de um lado para outro, escapulia-lhe das mãos até que ele se livrasse dela com outra frase, fria como cinza, cinza para cobrir o intervalo: está chovendo, estou com fome, o dia está belo" (Lispector, *Perto do coração selvagem* 42–43).
7. Hélène Cixous's passionate pronouncements about Lispector's works, from 1979 onward, were instrumental in the Brazilian writer becoming better known in Europe, and particularly by readers interested in feminism. See, for example, *L'heure de Clarice Lispector* (1989) and *Reading with Clarice Lispector* (1990).
8. "A vida se me é, e eu não entendo o que digo. E então adoro. ————" (Lispector, *A paixão segundo G.H.* 183). The last line of *A paixão* has a particular challenge for the translator because it turns the intransitive verb "ser" (to be) into a transitive, reflexive verb: literally, "life is itself to me." Chris Daniels has suggested the radical solution of creating a new verb in English, translating the phrase as "life itselfs me," (2006, np).
9. "Não esquecer que por enquanto é tempo de morangos. Sim" (Lispector, *A hora da estrela* 106).
10. "Meus livros felizmente para mim não são superlotados de fatos, e sim da repercussão dos fatos nos indivíduos" (Borelli, *Clarice Lispector* 70); unless otherwise attributed, all translations into English are mine.
11. "Pensar é um fato. Sentir é um ato" (Lispector, *A hora da estrela* 25).
12. "Escrever não para responder, mas para levar a pergunta a seu ponto mais agudo, onde toda resposta não seria mais que acomodação" (Borelli, *Clarice Lispector* 77).
13. "Inútil querer me classificar: eu simplesmente escapulo. Gênero não me pega mais" (Lispector, *Água viva*, 13).
14. Much of the material from *Visão do Esplendor* is yet to be translated, but the crônica "Brasília" does appear in *The Complete Stories* (2015). *A Breath of Life* has been translated by Johnny Lorenz (2012).

15. "Então ela inventou o que deveria dizer. Os olhos fechados, entregue, disse baixinho palavras nascidas naquele instante, nunca antes ouvidas por alguém, ainda tenras da criação – brotos novos e frágeis. Eram menos que palavras, apenas sílabas soltas, sem sentido, mornas, que fluíam e se entrecruzavam, fecundavam-se, renasciam num só ser para desmembrarem-se em seguida, respirando, respirando . . . " (Lispector, *Perto do coração selvagem* 155).

16. "Esta história será feita de palavras que se agrupam em frases e destas se evola um sentido secreto que ultrapassa palavras e frases. É claro que, como todo escritor, tenho a tentação de usar termos suculentos: conheço adjetivos esplendorosos, carnudos substantivos e verbos tão esguios que atravessam agudos o ar em vias de ação, já que palavra é ação, concordais? . . .As palavras são sons transfundidos de sombras que se entrecruzam desiguais, estalactites, renda, música transfigurada de órgão" (Lispector, *A hora da estrela* 29, 31).

17. In Brazil, there are far fewer biographies of women than men, and literary biographies are also a niche genre, so Lispector continues to be a trailblazer even after her death.

18. Many actresses have also played Lispector on stage and on film, including Aracy Balabanian, Rita Elmor, and Beth Goulart. *De Corpo Inteiro* (2009), directed by Lispector's great-niece Nicole Algranti, is an adaptation of Lispector's interviews with celebrities for popular magazines. In the film, eight different actresses (including the three mentioned above) portray the writer.

19. The title of the collection, which won the Jabuti prize for short stories in 1992, is a clear reference to the section about a third leg or tripod in Lispector's *A paixão segundo G.H.*

20. "Clarice é uma unha clara, espinho na planta do pé. Nunca mais andei direito desde que vi Clarice. Ela passou e—tarde demais!—meu coração rolou. Mas não olhei para trás nem uma vez. . . . / Encontro Clarice e digo coisas sem nexo. / Porque ela pode ser uma flor quando quer, mas também uma mulher bruta com rodelas de suor debaixo do braço, mastigando a coxa gorda de uma galinha aos golinhos de chope. / Não é nenhum segredo que comeria carne humana se necessário" (Arêas, "Sobre os espelhos" 17–18).

21. "Olhei [no espelho]. Mas em vez do meu vi seu rosto amarrado de fios sobre o travesseiro" (Arêas, "Sobre os espelhos" 20). This moment might remind readers of the interchangeable reflections of the protagonist Macabéa and the narrator Rodrigo S.M. in *A hora da estrela*.

22. "Eu só ia ler o que a Clarice tinha escrito, nada do que outras pessoas escreveram sobre ela, para fazer uma leitura com pureza e sem interferências, e foi assim, li os livros todos da Clarice na ordem como foram escritos e publicados, como se lesse uma autobiografia, dela, e minha. Li as cartas. No final, com o livro pronto, ainda li a biografia escrita pela Nádia Battella Gotlib, e complementei meu conhecimento sobre a Clarice, vi fotos, e percebi, a Clarice de sandália e casaco de pele, isso era eu . . . " (Possani, "Anexo" 134–35).

23. "Clarice sente o coração batendo descompassado. Ela procura, nas ruas, a paz não encontrada dentro de si" (92).

24. "Não há nenhuma placa, mas há a presença de Clarice. Vem pela maresia, pela luz, pelo ar, pelas folhas à brisa, pelo raio de luar. Clarice vive nas coisas etéreas. Sua placa é feita de nuvens e ondas salgadas e areia" (Miranda, *Clarice Lispector* 20). Since Miranda's novella was published, a commemorative plaque has been attached to the apartment building at no. 88 Rua Gustavo Sampaio, where Lispector resided from 1966 to 1977.

25. "Uma conversa entre duas escritoras, eu e a Clarice imaginada por mim a partir de suas palavras" (Possani, "Anexo" 135).
26. As in English the Portuguese suffix "-ana" can be added to Christian names to create a mass noun or adjective: hence Clariciana or Lispectoriana. Here the authors indicate the plurality of their literary tributes by adding an "s."
27. "Há três coisas para as quais eu nasci e para as quais eu dou a minha vida" (Clarice Lispector, *A descoberta do mundo* 99–100).
28. "Shakespeare, Homero e Virgílio, Dante, Kafka, Machado, Virgínia, Clarice, ou até mesmo Borges" (64).
29. The Jabuti is Brazil's most prestigious literary prize.
30. "Ninguém me lê, Clarice, / Ninguém decifra em mim / a única escassez da qual não padeço, / a solidão" (Evaristo, *Poemas da recordação*, 97).
31. "Minha amiga era muito especial. Se misturava mágica e sedutoramente às figuras que criava. A literatura era sua carne e osso" (Sant'anna, "Sete anos sem Clarice" 172).

WORKS CITED

Abdala, Verónica. "Paulo Valente, hijo de Clarice Lispector: 'Algunos tienen una sensibilidad superior, eso les da placeres y sufrimiento." *Clarín*, August 7, 2020. https://www.clarin.com/cultura/paulo-valente-hijo-clarice-lispector-sensibilidad-superior-da-placeres-sufrimiento-_o_odORtYnAW.html.

Anitagrace, Joyce. "The Writer as Visual Artist: Clarice Lispector's *A Paixão segundo G.H.* in Dialogue with the Neo-Concrete Art Movement." *Luso-Brazilian Review*, vol. 51, no. 2, 2014, pp. 31–67.

Arêas, Vilma. "Entrevista com Vilma Arêas." Interview for SESC São Paulo, February 10, 2020. https://www.sescsp.org.br/online/artigo/13990_ENTREVISTA+COM+VILMA+AREAS

Arêas, Vilma. "Sobre os espelhos." *A terceira perna*, Brasiliense, 1992, pp. 17–20.

Athayde, Manaíra Aires, and Rejane Cristina Rocha. "A circulação da literatura no mundo on-line: os casos de Clarice Lispector e de Caio Fernando Abreu." *Estudos de Literatura Brasileira Contemporânea*, vol. 59, 2020, pp. 1–25.

Borelli, Olga. *Clarice Lispector: Esboço para um possível retrato*. Nova Fronteira, 1978.

Candido, Antonio. "No Raiar de Clarice Lispector." *Vários Escritos*, Duas Cidades, 1970, pp. 125–31.

Cixous, Hélène. *"Coming" to Writing and Other Essays*. Translated by Sarah Cornell, Deborah Jensen, Ann Liddle, and Susan Sellers. Harvard UP, 1991.

Cixous, Hélène. *L'heure de Clarice Lispector*. des femmes, 1989.

Cixous, Hélène. *Reading with Clarice Lispector*. Edited and translated by Verena Andermatt Conley. U of Minnesota P, 1990.

Daniels, Chris. "My Motto Is: 'Translation Fights Cultural Narcissism.'" Interview by Kent Johnson, *Jacket*, vol. 29, April 2006. http://jacketmagazine.com/29/kent-iv-daniels.html

Daniels, J. D. "Rules for Consciousness in Mammals." *The Paris Review*, May 26, 2017. https://www.theparisreview.org/blog/2017/05/26/rules-for-consciousness-in-mammals/

De Corpo Inteiro. Directed by Nicole Algranti, Tabocca Filmes, 2009.

Deo, Saudamini, and Philippe Charlier. "Temporal Lobe Epilepsy in *The Passion According to GH*." *The Lancet*, vol. 17, no. 3, 2018, p. 210.

Evaristo, Conceição. "Macabéa, flor de mulungu." *Clarice Lispector: Personagens reescritos*, edited by Mayara R. Guimarães and Luis Maffei, Oficina Raquel, 2012, pp. 15–21.

Evaristo, Conceição. *Poemas da recordação e outros movimentos*. Malê, 2017.

Fink, Nadia, and Pitu Saá. *Clarice Lispector para meninas e meninos*. Sur, 2016.

Goh, Irving. "Le Toucher, le cafard, or, On Touching-the Cockroach in Clarice Lispector's *Passion according to G.H.*" *MLN*, vol. 131, no. 2, 2016, pp. 461–80.

Gotlib, Nádia Battella. *Clarice: Uma vida que se conta*. Ática, 1995.

Guelfenbein, Carla. *Contigo en la distancia*. Alfaguara, 2015.

Guelfenbein, Carla. *In the Distance with You*. Translated by John Cullen. Other Press, 2018.

Hedrick, Tace. "Mother, Blessed Be You Among Cockroaches: Essentialism, Fecundity, and Death in Clarice Lispector." *Luso-Brazilian Review*, vol. 34. no. 2, 1997, pp. 41–58.

Hills, Matt. *Fan Cultures*. Routledge, 2002.

Hornike, Dafna. "Bridging the Imaginary Gap between Distant Cartographies—the Visit that Never Was." *After Clarice: Reading Lispector in the Twenty-First Century*, edited by Adriana X. Jacobs and Claire Williams, Legenda, 2022.

Hutcheon, Linda. *A Poetics of Postmodernism: History, Theory, Fiction*. Routledge, 1988.

Jesus, Carolina Maria de. *Quarto de Despejo: Diário de uma favelada*. 1960. Ática, 2001.

Jolley, Jason R. "'Preciso cuidar mais de mim'; Intrapersonal Ethics in *Laços de família*." *La palabra según Clarice Lispector: aproximaciones crít*, edited by Luciana Namorato and César Ferreira, Universidad Nacional Mayor de San Marcos, 2011, pp. 153–66.

Krabbenhoft, Kenneth. "From Mysticism to Sacrament in *A Paixão segundo G.H.*" *Luso Brazilian Review*, vol. 32, no. 1, 1995, pp. 51–60.

Layne, Bethany. *(Post)modernist Biofictions: The Literary Afterlives of Henry James, Virginia Woolf, and Sylvia Plath*. 2013. University of Leeds, PhD dissertation. https://etheses.whiterose.ac.uk/6523/

Lispector, Clarice. *Água viva*. 1973. Francisco Alves, 1990.

Lispector, Clarice. *Água Viva*. Translated by Stefan Tobler. Penguin, 2012.

Lispector, Clarice. *An Apprenticeship or the Book of Pleasures*. Translated by Stefan Tobler. New Directions, 2021.

Lispector, Clarice. *Uma aprendizagem ou o livro dos prazeres*. 1969. Francisco Alves, 1994.

Lispector, Clarice. *A Breath of Life*. Translated by Johnny Lorenz. New Directions, 2012.

Lispector, Clarice. *Complete Stories*. Translated by Katrina Dodson. Penguin, 2015.

Lispector, Clarice. *A descoberta do mundo*. 1984. Francisco Alves, 1994.

Lispector, Clarice. *Discovering the World*. Translated by Giovanni Pontiero. Carcanet, 1992.

Lispector, Clarice. *Entrevistas*. Rocco, 2007.

Lispector, Clarice. *A hora da estrela*. 1977. Francisco Alves, 1992.

Lispector, Clarice. *The Hour of the Star: Centennial Edition*. Translated by Benjamin Moser. New Directions, 2020.

Lispector, Clarice. *A maça no escuro*. 1961. Francisco Alves, 1992.

Lispector, Clarice. *Near to the Wild Heart*. Translated by Alison Entrekin. New Directions, 2012.

Lispector, Clarice. *A paixão segundo G.H.* 1964. Francisco Alves, 1991.

Lispector, Clarice. *Para não esquecer*. 1978. Siciliano, 1992.

Lispector, Clarice. *The Passion According to G.H.* Translated by Idra Novey. New Directions, 2012.

Lispector, Clarice. *Perto do coração selvagem*. 1943. Francisco Alves, 1994.

Lispector, Clarice. *Um sopro de vida*. 1978. Francisco Alves, 1991.

Lispector, Clarice. *Todas as cartas*. Rocco, 2019.

Lispector, Clarice. *Todas as crônicas*. Rocco, 2018.

Machado, Lucilene. "Entre abanicos e castanholas: recepção de Clarice Lispector na Espanha." 2013. UNESP-Rio Preto, PhD dissertation. https://repositorio.unesp.br/bitstream/handle/11449/106333/arf_lmg_dr_sjrp.pdf?sequence=1&isAllowed=y

Miranda, Ana. *Clarice Lispector: o tesouro de minha cidade*. Relume Dumará, 1996.

Montero, Teresa. *O Rio de Clarice: Passeio afetivo pela cidade*. Autêntica, 2018.

Mota, Karyn. "Clarice Lispector na Era Digital: 'Em todas as frases um clímax.'" *100 años de Clarice Lispector*, edited by Mariela Méndez, Claudia Darrigrandi, and Macarena Mallea, Corregidor, 2021, pp. 43–66.

Nolasco, Edgar Cézar. *Clarice Lispector: Nas entrelinhas da escritura*. Annablume, 2001.

Nolasco, Edgar Cézar. *Restos de ficção: A criação biográfico-literária de Clarice Lispector*. Annablume, 2004.

Nolasco, Edgar Cézar, and Lucilene Machado. *Claricianas*. 7 Letras, 2006.

Nolasco, Edgar Cézar, and Lucilene Machado. *Quem tem medo de Clarice Lispector?* Intermeios, 2014.

Novey, Idra. *Clarice: The Visitor*. Sylph, 2014.

Novey, Idra. *Ways to Disappear*. Little, Brown, 2016.

Owen, Hilary. "Clarice Lispector Beyond Cixous: Ecofeminism and Zen in *A paixão Segundo G.H.*" *Gender, Ethnicity, and Class in Modern Portuguese-speaking Culture*, edited by Hilary Owen, Edwin Mellen Press, 1996, pp. 161–84.

Paulson, William. "The Invention of a Non-Modern World." *Closer to the Wild Heart: Essays on Clarice Lispector*, edited by Cláudia Pazos Alonso and Claire Williams, Legenda, 2002, pp. 198–212.

Peixoto, Marta. *Passionate Fictions: Gender, Narrative and Violence in Clarice Lispector*. U of Minnesota P, 1994.

Possani, Taíse N. "Anexo: Um Diálogo com Ana Miranda." "Ana Miranda, Leitora de Clarice Lispector." 2009. Universidade Federal de Rio Grande, MA Thesis. http://repositorio.furg.br/bitstream/handle/1/2685/taisepossani.pdf?sequence=1

Sá, Olga de. *Clarice Lispector: A travessia do oposto*. Annablume, 2004.

Sant'anna, Affonso Romano de. "Sete anos sem Clarice." *Com Clarice*, edited by Affonso Romano de Sant'anna and Marina Colasanti, UNESP, 2013, pp. 169–72.

Sousa, Carlos Mendes de. *Clarice Lispector: Figuras da Escrita*. Centro de Estudos Humanísticos, Universidade do Minho, 2000.

Valente, Paulo Gurgel. "My Mother, Between Reality and Fiction." *The Hour of the Star, Centennial Edition*, by Clarice Lispector, New Directions, 2020, pp. 81–89.

Valente, Paulo Gurgel. "Um homem luz." *Quatro Cinco Um*, vol. 37, September 2020. https://www.quatrocincoum.com.br/br/artigos/memoria/um-homem-luz

Williams Claire. *The Encounter between Opposites in the Works of Clarice Lispector*. HiPLA, 2006.

CHAPTER 35

CARLOS FUENTES'S NARRATIVE UNIVERSE

MAARTEN VAN DELDEN

INTRODUCTION

CARLOS Fuentes (1928–2012) was among the most prominent and prolific Latin American novelists of the twentieth- and early twenty-first centuries. In the course of a career that spanned over sixty years, he produced a vast oeuvre of novels, short stories, essays, newspaper articles, plays, and screenplays. Fuentes's narrative works were characterized both by the search for formal innovation and by a concern with social and political content. He was intensely preoccupied with the history and culture of his home country, while at the same time expressing an expansive cosmopolitan outlook. His work is filled with references to writers from the world of Hispanic letters—from Miguel de Cervantes and Bernal Díaz del Castillo to Jorge Luis Borges, Pablo Neruda, and Octavio Paz—but it also engages in a sustained dialogue with writers belonging to the broader Western tradition—from Erasmus and Denis Diderot to William Faulkner, Franz Kafka, and Marcel Proust. He wrote with stunning stylistic verve and literary inventiveness, and produced some of the most memorable novels of his generation, most notably his early novels, *La región más transparente* (*Where the Air is Clear*, 1958; henceforth *La región*) and *La muerte de Artemio Cruz* (*The Death of Artemio Cruz*, 1962; henceforth *Artemio Cruz*). Fuentes was one of the four key members—along with Julio Cortázar, Gabriel García Márquez, and Mario Vargas Llosa—of the Boom of the Latin American novel. Indeed, it is sometimes argued that the Boom owed a great deal to his networking and promotional skills (Ayén 599; Fiddian 97). Still, his critical reputation has not equaled that of García Márquez and Vargas Llosa, both of whom won the Nobel Prize for Literature, and have enjoyed greater critical attention than Fuentes. Especially noteworthy is the paucity of interest in Fuentes's late work, that is, of the last decade or so of his life. Nevertheless, Fuentes remains a central figure in the history of the Latin American novel.

SELF AND OTHER

Fuentes began his career as a writer in the 1950s, in the shadow of international modernism (Williams 98), which dominated the Western literary scene of the first half of the twentieth century, and of French existentialism (Van Delden, *Carlos Fuentes* 11–26), which shaped the cultural and political debates of the post-war years. From the former he absorbed important lessons about narrative form and about how to make the novel more responsive to the subjective dimension of life. The latter drew his attention to questions of freedom and responsibility and to the role of the committed intellectual in a turbulent and changing world. At the same time, Fuentes was profoundly influenced by his local context. In the wake of the Mexican Revolution, the country had experienced a pronounced nationalist cultural awakening. Fuentes was both a critic of this movement and a participant in it. He mocked and attacked the political regimes, as well as the social and cultural customs, that emerged from the revolution. And yet, there was never any doubt about his allegiance to Mexico, as a focal point of his work, and as a key cultural and political cause he deeply cared about. In short, throughout his career, Fuentes balanced a fascination with individuality with a commitment to community.

La región registers the impact of modernist precursors such as Faulkner, James Joyce, and Virginia Woolf in the extensive use of the technique of the interior monologue as well as the conspicuous rejection of linear narrative. The novel also shares with modernist (as well as existentialist) writing a concern with the isolated individual trying to create a meaning for their life, free of social and cultural impositions and expectations. Still, the emphasis on subjectivity stands in counterpoint to an equally strong preoccupation with the individual's relationship to the other or to the group to which he or she belongs. Consider, to begin with, the unorthodox use Fuentes makes of the interior monologue in his novel. Whereas some sections of *La región* use the technique of the interior monologue in a conventional sense, others appear to mimic the device while subtly departing from it. Typically, an interior monologue registers a character's thoughts as they stream through his or her mind. In Fuentes's first novel, passages of this kind are combined with passages in which a character appears to be engaged in an interior monologue, but is in fact speaking to another character. The other character in question is usually the mysterious Ixca Cienfuegos, a man of indigenous descent who somehow has access to the entire range of the novel's characters, and succeeds in getting many of them to embark on long, introspective speeches. Yet the presence of an interlocutor gives these passages a mixed character, as monologues that are nevertheless part of a dialogue.

A similar tension to the one between the monological and the dialogical in the presentation of the characters' speech emerges from one of the novel's central conflicts, the one that pits Cienfuegos against Rodrigo Pola. Insofar as he is an aspiring poet, Pola is a typically modern character. Furthermore, his concern with self-creation and individual freedom connects him to a long line of modernist and existentialist literary figures. Ixca, by contrast, represents an entirely different set of values: spurred on by his mother, an indigenous woman named Teódula Moctezuma, Cienfuegos wants to precipitate a return to the communal values that reigned at the time of the Aztecs. The conflict between Pola and Cienfuegos, between the ancient and modern worlds, between the individual and the community, remains unresolved at the end of *La región* (Van Delden, *Carlos Fuentes* 26). However, the presence of this conflict in Fuentes's novelistic universe at this early stage of his career points to a central preoccupation of his work.

Fuentes's second major novel, *Artemio Cruz*, provides an even purer example of the modernist tradition of literary introspection (Fiddian 100). He goes further in *Artemio Cruz* than in *La región* in exploring the flow of a character's thoughts, and in breaking with conventional narrative structure. Long sections of the novel capture the contents of Artemio's consciousness, as he prepares for his death, thinks back on his life, and interacts with the family members and friends who gather by his bed in the hospital. The text jumps between sharply divergent observations, memories, and sensations, in a way that is often difficult for the reader to follow, while offering a lifelike and intimate portrait of the final days of Artemio's life. At the same time, the novel implicitly views Artemio from a judgmental perspective that is generally absent from representations of the isolated subject among Fuentes's modernist and existentialist precursors. In Joyce's *A Portrait of the Artist as a Young Man* (1916) and Jean-Paul Sartre's *La Nausée* (*Nausea*, 1938), to give two examples of this tendency in twentieth-century literature, being cut off from one's fellow human beings is, on one level at least, a sign of one's authenticity. In *Artemio Cruz*, it comes across as a punishment for having led a self-centered life without consideration for others.

The condemnation of Artemio's excessive individualism is complemented in the novel by the inclusion of a series of motifs that evoke the themes of human contact and communion, experiences the protagonist lacks and longs for. Consider, for example, the frequent references to the act of touching or caressing another person (Van Delden, "Hands-on Modernism"). In developing this motif, Fuentes is building on "the trope of two hands desiring contact" that he had already explored in *La región* (Long 42). Unfortunately, the caresses that should matter the most to Artemio as he confronts his imminent death, those of his wife Catalina, fail to overcome the deep gulf separating them after a decades-long unhappy marriage. "What a useless caress" (6)[1] is a central refrain in the novel, as Artemio reflects on his inability to establish a connection with his wife. Or consider, on a sociopolitical level, the novel's evocation of the Mexican Revolution as a kind of all-encompassing embrace of the Mexican people with each other, an embrace from which Artemio feels excluded, indeed by which he feels threatened (276). In sum, the novel employs innovative literary techniques in order to explore the depths of an individual's consciousness; at the same time, it gestures repeatedly toward the need to overcome the individual's isolation and to advance the values of community and solidarity.

The tension between the demands of individual autonomy, on the one hand, and commitment to one's fellow human beings, on the other, is explored again in a late novel by Fuentes, *Los años con Laura Díaz* (*The Years with Laura Díaz*, 1999; henceforth *Laura Díaz*), a kind of complement and counterpoint to *Artemio Cruz*. By this time, Fuentes has turned away from the eye-catching experimentalism of his early novels, although he retains their broad historical sweep, for *Laura Díaz*, like *Artemio Cruz*, seeks to sum up twentieth-century Mexican history, now with the life of a woman instead of that of a man serving as a vehicle for this exploration. Laura Díaz grows up in the port city of Veracruz and on her family's coffee plantation in the interior of the state. She eventually marries a labor leader, moves to Mexico City, and has two sons. Late in life, after the death of her husband, she embarks on a career as a photographer. Her life intersects with a number of major events in twentieth-century history, including the Mexican Revolution, the Spanish Civil War, the Holocaust, McCarthyism, and the 1968 Tlatelolco massacre in Mexico City. A central thread running through the story of Laura's life is her desire to live an autonomous and independent existence. When her marriage begins to falter, and her love for her husband evaporates, she leaves him, in search of a deeper personal fulfilment, something she finds with a series of lovers. When, in her late fifties, she takes up photography, her art turns out to be a form of self-discovery, even as she seeks to capture the reality of the world around her: "she found herself in the very act of photographing something totally alien to her own life" (440).[2] Although the recognition she receives for her work is surely of great significance to Laura, the fact that she has found a "room of one's own," as Virginia Woolf called it, or what the narrator defines as "a sovereign island of her own" (453),[3] is surely just as important to her.

Still, the emphasis on freedom and independence is balanced by an equally strong stress on Laura's connectedness to others. When the *Porfiristas* execute her half-brother in the early days of the Mexican Revolution, the young Laura is left with a profound sense of obligation toward her deceased sibling: "I am going to be faithful to you," she says, "by always imagining you, living in your name, doing what you did not do" (58).[4] Later in life, she develops a symbiotic relationship with her son Santiago. At one point in the narrative, Laura realizes that her life has meaning "only if I dedicate it to the life of someone who needs me" (408).[5] In sum, the novel is simultaneously the story of Laura's difficult struggle to forge an independent path through life *and* the story of her discovery of the need to assume responsibility for others.

Fuentes further explored the idea of one's responsibility toward others through the motif of the abandoned, dead, or missing child, which appears repeatedly in his work. Consider the following examples. In "Malintzin de las maquilas" ("Malintzin of the Maquilas"), a story from *La frontera de cristal* (*The Crystal Frontier*, 1995, henceforth, *La frontera*), a single mother named Dinorah, who works in a *maquiladora* (assembly plant) in Ciudad Juárez, cannot afford child care for her young son and, as a result, is forced to leave him alone at home when she goes to work. In order to prevent him from leaving the house, she ties him to a table with a rope. One day, she comes home only to discover that her son has tried to untie himself from the table to which he is attached, but has managed instead to strangle himself. The story is not a condemnation of the mother, for the reader feels compassion for Dinorah; instead, it draws attention to the plight of low-wage workers in a society without adequate social services. The fact that a child is the principal victim of this social drama makes the situation depicted by Fuentes all the more haunting.

Other narratives with the same motif focus on the question of personal responsibility rather than societal failure. In *La silla del águila* (*The Eagle's Throne*, 2002; henceforth *La silla*) we see not one, but two abandoned children. The novel explores the world of politics in Mexico and the naked struggle for power that characterizes it, but it does so against the backdrop of the personal lives of the novel's protagonists. Two of the main characters, María del Rosario Galván and Bernal Herrera, enjoy a passionate love affair, but when the fruit of their relationship turns out to be a child with Down syndrome, they decide to put their political ambitions first. Instead of devoting themselves to the care of their child, something that would demand a sacrifice on their part, they place him in an asylum where over time they visit him more and more sporadically. The importance of the motif of the abandoned child to *La silla* is reflected in the fact that the narrative concludes with an interior monologue in which the child reflects on his painful sense of solitude. In counterpoint to the story of María del Rosario and Bernal's child stands that of Nicolás Valdivia, an ambitious young politician who, by the end of the novel, has become the nation's interim president. Valdivia, too, had been abandoned as a child. His mother is from a wealthy family from the US-Mexico border region; when she becomes pregnant by a man from a humble background, her family dispatches her to Barcelona to give birth to the child, who is placed in the care of a Catalan working-class family. Both narratives stress how concerns about social standing and political ambition override the need to care even for one's own child. Other works by Fuentes in which the motif of the missing or abandoned child appears include *Cambio de piel* (*A Change of Skin*, 1967), *Agua quemada* (*Burnt Water*, 1981), *La campaña* (*The Campaign*, 1990), and *La voluntad y la fortuna* (*Destiny and Desire*, 2008; henceforth *La voluntad*). The repeated presence of this motif reveals something highly significant about Fuentes's literary art: even though he wrote novels and short stories of great formal complexity and dazzling erudition, he returned repeatedly to a very simple message about our obligation to care for others.

GEOGRAPHY OF THE NOVEL

Alongside a profound sense of the significance of time in human life and society, Fuentes also displayed a powerful spatial imagination. One observes this in the frequent appearance of maps in his work, his penchant for offering panoramic views of the geography of his country, his fondness for landscape description, and his intense sense of place, among other aspects of his writing. Mexico stands at the center of his novelistic universe, with the country's capital, Mexico City, capturing the most attention. Although Fuentes's focus on the nation was a hallmark of his work, he never saw Mexico as a unified entity, nor did he regard it as existing in isolation from the rest of the world. On the contrary, he was deeply interested in the border region between Mexico and the United States, as a space where Mexican identity was reaffirmed in the face of a frequently hostile other, but also as the place where one observed a dilution of the country's national character and its merging with foreign elements. Fuentes lived in Washington DC as a child and remained fascinated by the United States for the rest of his life, as we can see from the frequency with which he located his narratives (or parts of his narratives) in the neighboring country, not only along the border, but also in cities such as Los Angeles, Chicago, and New York, and even in a small town in Iowa. Still, it was clear that Fuentes preferred Europe, specifically western Europe, over the United States, as a cultural pole-star and political guide. Fuentes was trained as a young man at the UNAM by a group of Spanish academics who had sought refuge in Mexico after the Spanish Civil War, an experience that fostered in the Mexican author a powerful and lasting attachment to Spanish culture (Fuentes, *Nuevo tiempo mexicano* 177–86). This attachment inspired him to meditate in both fictional and non-fictional texts on Mexico's deep ties to Spain. Equally strong as Fuentes's Hispanophilia was his Francophilia. He lived in Paris on dif-ferent occasions, served as Mexico's ambassador to France from 1975 to 1977, and was buried in Paris's Montparnasse cemetery. Parts of several novels he wrote are set in Paris, and many characters from other novels he authored spend time in the French capital. And, of course, Fuentes's narrative works are replete with references to French literature, including the writers of the Enlightenment (Reid), Proust (Ruffinelli 114), and Gérard de Nerval and other nineteenth-century poets (Díaz 187–88). Although France and Spain were the European countries to which Fuentes felt most attracted, his literary universe includes references to England, Germany, Czechoslovakia, Greece, the Dalmatian coast, and other locations.

In their groundbreaking article on Fuentes's "literary maps,"[6] Alejandro Lámbarry and Julia Isabel Eissa Osorio point out that Mexico City is the most frequently used location in Fuentes's narrative world. They also note that Fuentes has a preference for setting his novels in certain neighborhoods, such as the Centro Histórico, Colonia Roma, Juárez, Hipódromo-Condesa, Polanco, and Las Lomas de Chapultepec, areas of great historical importance, in which cultural, economic, and political capital are concentrated (180). This spatial focus reflects Fuentes's interest in portraying Mexico's elites, especially its ec-onomic elites, as we see in characters such as the tycoons Federico Robles and Artemio Cruz from Fuentes's early novels *La región* and *Artemio Cruz* and the entrepreneurs of his late novels, such as Maximiliano Monroy in *La voluntad* and Adán Gorozpe in *Adán en Edén* (*Adam in Eden*, 2009). But Lámbarry and Eissa Osorio overstate their case when they suggest that Fuentes was *exclusively* concerned with the city's dominant neighborhoods and that "the cities of misery, the favelas, and the poverty belts are left out of the representation of Mexican identity."[7] Consider the following examples from different stages of Fuentes's career. *La región* includes a set of working-class characters whom we often see in their homes in the city's poorer neighborhoods, or in the places where they work or seek entertainment. The protagonist of "El hijo de Andrés Aparicio" ("The son of Andrés Aparicio"), the closing narrative of *Agua quemada*, lives in an area of the city so marginal that it does not even have a name. The settings of the interlinked stories of *Todas las familias felices* (*Happy Families*, 2006; henceforth *Todas las familias*) include the presidential mansion and the luxurious apartment of a wealthy gay couple; however, in counterpoint to the focus on elite spaces, the volume repeatedly evokes the city's streets, filled with tens of thousands of abandoned children who live "alone and without any family."[8] Note that Fuentes's representations of Mexico City also reveal his interest in floating spaces, such as the Bulevar in *Cristóbal Nonato* (*Christopher Unborn* 1987), an enigmatic gathering place for the city's inhabitants defined by the fact that it is a constantly mutating space without a fixed location (326); and subterranean spaces, images of which are widespread in contemporary Mexican literature (François), and which, in Fuentes, include the basement in "Chac Mool" (1954), where pre-Columbian gods hide; the tunnels underneath the pyramid in *Cambio de piel*; and the underground prison in *La voluntad* (119–20). There is no doubt that Fuentes was especially fascinated by urban locations linked to the nation's elite; however, alongside this interest there was an enduring concern with employing fictional space to offer as complete as possible a depiction of the country's capital.

In evoking Mexico as a whole, Fuentes revealed a similarly encompassing ambition. Nevertheless, it is equally clear that he emphasized certain regions over others. Particularly noteworthy is the frequency with which his novels—or parts of his novels—are set in the state of Veracruz and the city of Acapulco. Artemio Cruz's birth takes place in Veracruz, as does that of Laura Díaz. Veracruz also plays an important role in *Cambio de piel*, where it is the never-attained destination of the road trip on which the four main characters embark, and in *La campaña*, in which the protagonist's journey through a war-torn continent during the struggle for independence from Spain culminates in Veracruz, where he meets a priest named Quintana, known to all as "the last defender of an egalitarian revolution in Northern America."[9] In *Cristóbal Nonato*, Veracruz has been invaded by US marines, an echo of the occupation of the city by the United States during the Mexican Revolution. Acapulco plays a perhaps even more significant role in Fuentes's geographic imagination. Key scenes in *La región* and *Artemio Cruz* take place in Acapulco, and the coastal city is central to *Cristóbal Nonato*, with long sections set there, including the scene in which the narrator is conceived by his parents. The narrator of *La voluntad* is a decapitated head lying on an Acapulco beach. The two places—Veracruz and Acapulco—are in some ways complementary, with the former reminding us of the country's past and Acapulco representing the future (Lámbarry and Eissa Osorio 178). Veracruz, the first city established by the Spaniards in Mexico, harks back to the conquest, whereas Acapulco, focused on the tourism industry, and offering a hedonistic lifestyle, showcases the country's modernization, without omitting some of its devastating consequences, including social and economic inequality and environmental degradation. Both locations also point toward worlds that lie beyond Mexico. In *Artemio Cruz*, Fuentes connects Veracruz to Cuba and the Mediterranean, whereas in *Cristóbal Nonato* Acapulco is linked to the rising economies of East Asia.

As stated, another important space where Mexico's ties with the outside world come into view is the US-Mexico border, which becomes an especially prominent location in Fuentes's narrative world in the 1980s and 1990s, culminating in the publication of *La frontera*, in which the majority of the interlinked stories composing the volume are set in the border region. For the Mexican characters in *La frontera*, the United States embodies the promise of prosperity, as well as the threat of discrimination, exploitation, and outright violence. Fuentes includes characters who are seduced by the United States and others who forge new hybrid identities, combining elements from both sides of the border. However, the most common response is that of a reinforcement of Mexican identity in the face of the United States "other," a dynamic represented with special force in "Malintzin de las maquilas." In *Gringo viejo* (*The Old Gringo*, 1985), a novel set during the Mexican Revolution, with two American characters in leading roles, Fuentes underlines the profound differences between the two countries and appeals to Mexico's northern neighbors to make a greater effort to recognize their Mexican "others" (Van Delden, "Íntimos enemigos" 165–70). The topic of US ethnocentricity appears in other works from this period, such as *Diana, o la cazadora solitaria* (*Diana: The Goddess Who Hunts Alone*, 1994), an autobiographical novel based on the author's 1970 affair with the actress Jean Seberg, which culminates in a visit on the part of the narrator to the small Midwestern town where his former lover had grown up. The town is bathed in a false innocence rooted in the utter lack of interest of its inhabitants in what is happening outside their own small world. Still, Fuentes's depiction of the United States was not uniformly negative. *Laura Díaz*, for example, concludes with a chapter set in Los Angeles, described in the novel as a multicultural city where Mexican immigrants feel at home and thrive.

Lámbarry and Eissa Osorio note that Europe occupies an even more important role in Fuentes's geographic imagination than the United States, and they draw attention to the relative lack of interest in South America (176). However, by focusing only on the spaces occupied by the protagonists of Fuentes's novels and the places where they reside (174), the two critics end up offering too restricted a perspective on the spaces encompassed by Fuentes's narrative, which include a long and haunting scene set in Buenos Aires in *Cambio de piel*, a key thematic thread in *Una familia lejana* (*Distant Relations*, 1980; henceforth *Una familia*) concerned with a group of River Plate authors who emigrated to France, and a series of references to the Central American wars of the 1980s in *Todas las familias*, none of which are reflected in the critics' map. And while Lámbarry and Eissa Osorio rightly emphasize that the Europe of Fuentes's imagination is primarily western Europe (192), they overlook the fact that key scenes in *Cambio de piel* are set in Prague and the Greek islands, while the Dalmatian coast appears in *Cumpleaños* (*Birthday*, 1969) and in *Todas las familias*. Still, it is true that Europe was central to Fuentes's geographic imagination, Spain and France in particular. What, then, do these two countries represent for the Mexican novelist?

In examining Spain's place in Fuentes's narrative universe, one immediately grasps how space and time are interlinked, for Spain is primarily connected to the past. This is clear from the inclusion of episodes from the conquest of Mexico in *Cambio de piel*, *Terra nostra* (1975) and *El naranjo* (*The Orange Tree*, 1993), from the vast and meticulous reconstruction of sixteenth-century Spain in *Terra nostra*, and from Fuentes's persistent interest in the Spanish Civil War—which is briefly evoked in *La región*, has a chapter devoted to it in *Artemio Cruz*, and plays a key role in *Laura Díaz*. Although there are occasional references to modern-day Spain in Fuentes's work, as in the evocation of "a rich, European, progressive, Spain" (169) of the 1980s at the beginning of "Viva mi fama" ("*Viva mi fama*"),[10] one of the narratives included in *Constancia, y otras novelas para vírgenes* (*Constancia and Other Stories for Virgins*, 1990), the overall emphasis of his work is firmly on how the history of Spain has shaped the course of Mexican history (as a result of the conquest) or helps clarify key twentieth-century ideological and political conflicts (as in the Spanish Civil War).

France, too, matters in Fuentes's work in large part insofar as it is connected to Mexico and Latin America. Fuentes published two novels in which French settings play a central role, *Terra nostra* and *Una familia*. In the former novel, Paris provides the setting for the opening and closing chapters; in the latter, Paris and its environs are the novel's primary setting. What is striking, however, about the French setting of *Una familia* is how stripped bare it is. The novel presents two key settings: the dining room of the Automobile Club de France, empty save for two characters, an elderly Frenchman named Branly and the narrator, and a villa in the Parisian suburb of Enghien-les-Bains, inhabited solely by a man named Victor Heredia and his son. The novel is utterly lacking in the social density of Fuentes's Mexican novels. The denuded quality of the setting has a clear purpose: it sets the stage for a series of hidden links to Mexico, Latin America, and the Caribbean to rise to the surface. In short, Fuentes sets his novel in France, but only in order to trace a path back to the Americas. The Parisian chapters of *Terra nostra* offer a striking contrast to *Una familia*, for they are as crowded and multitudinous as the latter novel is hauntingly empty. Still, Fuentes's aim in setting these chapters in Paris is not so much to evoke a specifically French space; on the contrary, the Paris of *Terra nostra* is both a passageway taking the reader back to Spain and Mexico and a place of reunion for the novel's Latin American characters. Paris matters insofar as it is connected to the Spanish-speaking world.

If there was ever a Latin American writer who fully participated in world literature, it was surely Carlos Fuentes. But what does this survey of the role of geographic space in his writings reveal about the manner in which the Mexican novelist claimed a place for himself in the world republic of letters? Theorists of world literature have depicted an opposition between a local, particularistic, and nationalist pole and a universal and cosmopolitan one. Pascale Casanova speaks of a periphery where a functionalist aesthetic reigns and a center (located in Paris) where the cause of aesthetic autonomy prevails, while Mariano Siskind posits a contrast between a nation-bound and identity-driven form of writing, on the one hand, and an expansive, cosmopolitan tradition, on the other. Fuentes's career complicates these oppositions, for his work is deeply cosmopolitan while never abandoning its focus on nation and identity. The double orientation of Fuentes's narrative shows that the two poles are far more difficult to disentangle than is often acknowledged. As Reindert Dhondt argues, rather than seeing Fuentes as either a nationalist or a post-national author, it makes more sense to see him as a "transnational" writer, someone who goes beyond the nation, without, however, rejecting it.

PAZ AND NERUDA

In 1985, when Fuentes was teaching a course at Harvard University, his head teaching assistant, Verónica Cortínez, suggested that perhaps the first lecture of the semester had been too difficult for his undergraduate students to comprehend. Fuentes brushed the TA's concern aside. "My audience," he said, "is Octavio Paz" (Cortínez). It would be hard to think of a more vivid expression of Paz's intellectual ascendancy over his younger colleague. Fuentes had first met Paz in Paris in 1950 and had been deeply impressed by the Mexican poet and essayist, who had just published two of the most important books of his career, *El laberinto de la soledad* (*The Labyrinth of Solitude*, 1950) and *Libertad bajo palabra* (*Freedom through the Word*, 1949). Years later, Fuentes vividly evoked the impact of Paz's writings: "My friends and I had read those books aloud in Mexico, dazzled by a poetics that managed simultaneously to renew our language from within and connect it to the language of the world" (Fuentes, "How" 22). The meeting in Paris marked the beginning of a long friendship that finally foundered when the Mexican historian Enrique Krauze published "La comedia mexicana de Carlos Fuentes" ("The Guerrilla Dandy"), a fierce and unforgiving attack on Fuentes's work, in the journal *Vuelta*, of which Paz was the founder and general editor (Aguilar Rivera 105–42; Flores 493–539). Paz defended the decision to publish Krauze's essay stating an unwillingness to censor a close collaborator. Fuentes felt betrayed and the two men never repaired their friendship. Still, the break-up toward the end of Paz's life cannot disguise the fact that Fuentes's work is permeated with Paz's presence, and that it is especially indebted to the Mexican poet's ideas about Mexico.

Fuentes's conception of Mexican history was profoundly shaped by his reading of *El laberinto* and other works by Paz. Consider the Mexican poet's interpretation of the contemporary Mexican psyche as still bearing the imprint of the Spanish conquest. In Paz's view, the Mexican's sense of solitude was a direct result of the trauma of the conquest. The Mexican viewed the conquest as a rape of the indigenous woman by the Spanish male conquistador; consequently, he repudiated both the father-figure, for being a rapist, and the mother-figure, for having been raped. In short, Mexicans saw themselves as the product of a violation, one that deeply undermined their sense of identity. For Paz, the widespread use of the verb "chingar" and its variants in contemporary Mexican speech was a sign that the past lived on in the present. Fuentes was obviously captivated by these ideas, for he included a long meditation on the word "chingar" in *Artemio Cruz*. Furthermore, he placed the notion of violation at the heart of the plot of the novel, for the protagonist turns out to be the product of the rape of an Afro-Mexican woman by a *criollo* landowner. In short, parts of *Artemio Cruz* could be seen as an attempt to illustrate Paz's ideas about Mexican identity.

Fuentes also drew on Paz in approaching the Mexican Revolution. Paz interpreted the Mexican Revolution as an act of self-discovery on the part of the Mexican people. Fuentes echoed this idea in various works over the course of his career. One of the main characters of *La región* is an intellectual named Manuel Zamacona, clearly based on Paz, in spite of Fuentes's disavowals ("South of the Border"). Zamacona devotes much time and effort to meditating on questions related to Mexican culture, history, and identity, and some of his ideas sound distinctly Pazian. Among them is the notion that the Mexican Revolution was first and foremost a revelation of the nation's identity. Fuentes returns to this idea in *Gringo viejo* in a scene in which a band of revolutionaries enter the ballroom of a hacienda they have occupied and for the first time in their lives see their own reflections in the mirrors lining the room. The metaphor is clear: thanks to the revolution, these men and women are discovering who they truly are. It is important to add, though, that whereas Fuentes was following in Paz's footsteps in his reading of the psycho-cultural dimension of the Mexican Revolution, he added some significant ingredients of his own to the interpretation of this central episode of twentieth-century Mexican history. While Paz had depicted the Mexican Revolution as an immersion of the nation in its own being, Fuentes emphasized the plurality of cultural elements that came to light during the revolution. As Zamacona put it in *La región*, "every person who has existed in the course of Mexican history came alive during the Revolution, bearing the burden of their problems."[11] What Fuentes offered, in effect, was an elaboration of the interpretation put forward by Paz (Rojas 140).

Whereas Paz provided Fuentes with tools with which to think about Mexican history and culture, Neruda gave him a model for reflecting on the relationship between the writer and his world. Fuentes first met Neruda at a writers' conference held in Concepción, Chile, in January 1962, as he explains in an essay about his friendship with the Chilean poet. What is most noteworthy about how the Mexican novelist introduces Neruda in this essay is his emphasis on the poet's voice: "I heard Pablo Neruda before I met him," he writes (Fuentes, "Neruda").[12] The poet is giving a reading by the ocean; Fuentes has arrived a little late and hears Neruda's voice before the man himself comes into view. But the voice's priority in time is a way of signaling the priority of the voice in Fuentes's conception of Neruda as a poet. And what does this voice express? As the scene by the side of the ocean in Concepción unfolds, Fuentes observes how the poet's voice seems to mingle with the sound of the ocean, as if Neruda had become one with his surroundings (129). In Fuentes's presentation, Neruda embodies the romantic vision of the poet as a mouthpiece of the natural world. Later, in a brief anecdote about an encounter with a group of workers in Concepción, Fuentes expands on this idea by depicting Neruda as the voice not only of nature, but of the Chilean people as well. Fuentes is strolling along the banks of the river Bío Bío, when he comes across a group of men playing the guitar and singing Neruda's verses. When Fuentes points out that Neruda would be delighted to know that his poetry was being put to music, the men have no idea what he is talking about. They have never heard of Pablo Neruda. For Fuentes, this is a sign that Neruda had become one with his people. "Neruda," he proposes, "had become part of the anonymous word, of the voice of all."[13]

The idea of the Latin American writer as someone who does not simply write about himself, or about his personal concerns, but who instead strives to recover and express the overlooked dimensions of his culture, was key to Fuentes's thinking. He developed the idea most fully in the essays of *Valiente mundo nuevo* (Brave New World, 1990), where he refers repeatedly to the writer's obligation to give "a name and a voice" to his continent.[14] The emphasis on witnessing and naming may have seemed somewhat at odds with Fuentes's avant-gardist stress on the subversive role of literature, in relation both to traditional social norms and conventional ideas surrounding the referential dimension of the novel (Fuentes, *La nueva novela*). The idea of the writer as the voice of his culture surely gained strength in Fuentes's thinking with the rise in the 1980s of Latin American testimonial literature, with which he may have felt himself to be in competition. But it was clearly a part of his aesthetic throughout his career, as we can see from the frequent inclusion in his novels of characters who represent the people, from Beto and Gladys in *La región* to Marina the *maquiladora* worker in *La frontera*. Another character belonging to this category is Bernabé Aparicio, whose story Fuentes narrates with the help of a series of Nerudian echoes in "El hijo de Andrés Aparicio," a story dedicated, not coincidentally, to the Chilean poet.

Agua quemada combines elements of two different genres: the short-story collection and the novel. The four narratives can be read separately, like short stories, but they are at the same time interlinked not just thematically, but also through certain characters who recur in different narratives, resulting in the creation of interconnected plots. The effect is to combine the compression of the short story with the more expansive vision of the novel. Fuentes was to use the form again in *La frontera* and *Todas las familias*. "El hijo de Andrés Aparicio" tells the story of Bernabé Aparicio, who lives in poverty with his mother in a nameless shantytown on Mexico City's outskirts. He struggles in school and is frustrated in his love life, but eventually finds a kind of substitute home when he is recruited into a rightist paramilitary gang known as the *gavilanes*. After killing a student, Bernabé ends up in prison, but the leader of the gang arranges his release. At the end of the story, we see Bernabé committed to a life of crime. Neruda, who had already been a strong presence in earlier novels by Fuentes, especially *La región* (Boldy, *Narrative* 25), is a key point of reference in this story too. Fuentes establishes a link with the Chilean poet through the theme of the voice, and the idea of community. As a child, Bernabé had struggled with an inability to speak or express himself, a kind of loss of voice that echoes his lost state within Mexican society. When a character named Ureña reads the famous lines from Neruda's 1947 poem "Alturas de Macchu Picchu" ("The Heights of Macchu Picchu"), which evokes his anguish about the lack of meaning in his life, the reader realizes that Bernabé struggles to understand Neruda's words, while at the same time seeing his own experience reflected in them. "*You were also the broken fragment of an unfinished man*,"[15] Ureña recites, capturing Bernabé's state of mind with the help of Neruda's words. Later, in prison, Bernabé has a dream that draws on the exalted vision of community and harmony with which "Alturas" concludes: "He dreamed without being able to separate his dream from a vague but impetuous desire that all that exists be for all the earth, for all of us together, water, air, gardens, stone, time."[16] But Bernabé's subsequent pursuit of a life of crime and material gain shows that the Nerudian dream of redemption is just that: a dream. In sum, by giving a voice to a marginal character, Fuentes follows Neruda's idea of the writer as the voice of the people. At the same time, he distances himself from the Chilean poet's transcendent hopefulness, offering a much darker view of the paths that are open to ordinary people in 1970s Mexico.

An optimistic and affirmative stance runs through Fuentes's writings. One sees this in elements of his work ranging from the celebratory perspective on the Mexican Revolution to the detailed and loving re-creation of different aspects of Mexican life and culture. It also emerges from his views on the role of literary and cultural production, which he often regarded as having redemptive powers (Fuentes, *The Buried Mirror* 338–39). It is worth noting, however, that Fuentes expressed his positive outlook on topics such as the Hispanic tradition, Latin American literature, and Mexican culture in a more unadulterated form in his essays than in his fiction. His narrative works combine elements of joy and optimism with an often fierce pessimism. In his fiction, he sets out not only to affirm and build up, but also to criticize, attack, and dismantle. As Steven Boldy observes, Fuentes's work becomes noticeably darker—more cynical and angry—toward the end of his career (Boldy, "De la afrenta"). What might account for the fractured quality of Fuentes's vision of the world? By way of an answer, one might simply note that Fuentes had a complex mind, which led him to look at reality not from a single perspective, but from varying points of view. However, this feature of Fuentes's work can also be connected to his mixed literary and cultural inheritance: he drew both on the traditional Latin American intellectual's sense of responsibility toward their community, which they feel they must help strengthen and build up, *and* on the unremittingly skeptical and subversive strain in modernist literature, according to which the writer must always remain an outsider, committed to the tasks of criticism and demystification (Van Delden, *Carlos Fuentes* 168).

Notes

1. "Qué inútil caricia" (11). All English translations are my own.
2. "Se encontró a sí misma en el acto mismo de fotografiar lo más ajeno a su propia vida" (513).
3. "La isla de su soberanía" (527).
4. "Voy a serte fiel . . . imaginándote siempre, viviendo en tu nombre, haciendo lo que tú no hiciste" (74).
5. "Sólo . . . si la dedico a la vida de alguien que me necesita" (476).
6. "Mapas literarios" (177).
7. "Las ciudades-miseria, las favelas o los cinturones de pobreza quedan fuera de la representación identitaria del mexicano" (183).
8. "Solos sin familia" (258).
9. "Último defensor de una revolución igualitaria en la América septentrional" (213).
10. "La España rica, europea, progresista" (192).
11. "En la Revolución aparecieron, vivos y con el fardo de sus problemas, todos los hombres de la historia de México" (281).
12. "Escuché a Pablo Neruda antes de conocerlo" (129).
13. "Había regresado a la palabra anónima, a la voz de todos" (131).
14. "Nombre y voz" (202).
15. *"Fuiste también el pedacito roto de hombre inconcluso"* (126).

16. "Soñó sin poder separar su sueño de un deseo vago pero impetuoso de que cuanto existió fue para la tierra, para todos unidos, el agua, el aire, los jardines, la piedra, el tiempo" (136).

WORKS CITED

Aguilar Rivera, José Antonio. *La sombra de Ulises: Ensayos sobre intelectuales mexicanos y norteamericanos*. Centro de Investigación y Docencia Económicas / Miguel Ángel Porrúa, 1998.

Ayén, Xavi. *Aquellos años del boom: García Márquez, Vargas Llosa y el grupo de amigos que lo cambiaron todo*. RBA, 2014.

Boldy, Steven, ed. *Carlos Fuentes y el Reino Unido*. Fondo de Cultura Económica, 2017.

Boldy, Steven. "De la afrenta al melodrama: La familia, la violencia y el crimen en las últimas obras de Carlos Fuentes." *Mexican Studies / Estudios Mexicanos*, vol. 28, no. 2, summer 2012, pp. 243–63.

Boldy, Steven. *The Narrative of Carlos Fuentes: Family, Text, Nation*. U of Durham P, 2002.

Casanova, Pascale. *The World Republic of Letters*. Translated by E. B. DeBevoise. Harvard UP, 2005.

Cortínez, Verónica. Personal interview. October 15, 2020.

Dhondt, Reindert. "'I Move, Therefore I Am': Carlos Fuentes's Transnational Mexicanness." *Literary Transnationalism(s)*, edited by Theo D'haen and Dagmar Vandebosch, Brill / Rodopi, 2018, pp. 205–20.

Díaz, Roberto Ignacio. *Unhomely Rooms: Foreign Tongues and Spanish American Literature*. Bucknell UP, 2002.

Fiddian, Robin. "Carlos Fuentes: *La muerte de Artemio Cruz*." *Landmarks of Latin American Fiction*, edited by Philip Swanson, Routledge, 1990, pp. 96–117.

Flores, Malva. *Estrella de dos puntas. Octavio Paz y Carlos Fuentes: Crónica de una amistad*. Ariel, 2020.

François, Liesbeth. *Subterranean Space in Mexico City Literature: Imagining the Megalopolis from Below*. Palgrave, 2021.

Fuentes, Carlos. *Adán en Edén*. Alfaguara, 2009.

Fuentes, Carlos. *Adam in Eden*. Translated by E. Shaskan Bumas and Alejandro Branger. Dalkey Archive Press, 2012.

Fuentes, Carlos. *Agua quemada: cuarteto narrativo*. Fondo de Cultura Económica, 1981.

Fuentes, Carlos. *Los años con Laura Díaz*. Alfaguara, 1999.

Fuentes, Carlos. *The Buried Mirror: Reflections on Spain and the New World*. Houghton Mifflin, 1992.

Fuentes, Carlos. *Burnt Water: Stories*. Translated by Margaret Sayers Peden. Farrar, Straus & Giroux, 1986.

Fuentes, Carlos. *Cambio de piel*. Joaquín Mortiz, 1967.

Fuentes, Carlos. *La campaña*. Fondo de Cultura Económica, 1990.

Fuentes, Carlos. "Chac mool." *Los días enmascarados*, pp. 9–27.

Fuentes, Carlos. *Change of Skin*. Translated by Sam Hileman. Farrar, Straus & Giroux, 1968.

Fuentes, Carlos. *Christopher Unborn*. Translated by Alfred MacAdam. Farrar, Straus & Giroux, 1989.

Fuentes, Carlos. *Constancia and Other Stories for Virgins*. Translated by Thomas Christensen. Farrar, Straus & Giroux, 1990.

Fuentes, Carlos. *Constancia y otras novelas para vírgenes.* Fondo de Cultura Económica, 1990.

Fuentes, Carlos. *Cristóbal Nonato.* Fondo de Cultura Económica, 1987.

Fuentes, Carlos. *The Crystal Frontier: A Novel in Nine Stories.* Translated by Alfred MacAdam. Farrar, Straus & Giroux, 1997.

Fuentes, Carlos. *Cumpleaños.* Joaquín Mortiz, 1969.

Fuentes, Carlos. *The Death of Artemio Cruz.* Translated by Alfred MacAdam. Farrar, Straus & Giroux, 1991.

Fuentes, Carlos. *Diana, o la cazadora solitaria.* Alfaguara, 1994.

Fuentes, Carlos. *Diana: The Goddess Who Hunts Alone.* Translated by Alfred MacAdam. Farrar, Straus & Giroux, 1995.

Fuentes, Carlos. *Los días enmascarados.* Era, 1982.

Fuentes, Carlos. *Distant Relations.* Translated by Margaret Sayers Peden. Farrar, Straus & Giroux, 1982.

Fuentes, Carlos. *The Eagle's Throne.* Translated by Kristina Cordero. Random House, 2007.

Fuentes, Carlos. *Una familia lejana.* Era, 1980.

Fuentes, Carlos. *La frontera de cristal: una novela en nueve cuentos.* Alfaguara, 1995.

Fuentes, Carlos. *Gringo viejo.* Fondo de Cultura Económica, 1985.

Fuentes, Carlos. *Happy Families: Stories.* Translated by Edith Grossman. Random House, 2008.

Fuentes, Carlos. "El hijo de Andrés Aparicio." *Agua quemada,* pp. 95–139.

Fuentes, Carlos. "How I Started to Write." *Myself With Others,* pp. 3–27.

Fuentes, Carlos. *Holy Place and Birthday: Two Novellas.* Translated by Suzanne Jill Levine and Margaret Sayers Peden. Farrar, Straus & Giroux, 1988.

Fuentes, Carlos. "Malintzin de las maquilas." *La frontera de cristal,* pp. 129–60.

Fuentes, Carlos. *La muerte de Artemio Cruz.* Fondo de Cultura Económica, 1962.

Fuentes, Carlos. *Myself With Others.* Farrar, Straus & Giroux, 1988.

Fuentes, Carlos. *El naranjo, o los círculos del tiempo.* Alfaguara, 1993.

Fuentes, Carlos. *La nueva novela hispanoamericana.* Joaquín Mortiz, 1969.

Fuentes, Carlos. *Nuevo tiempo mexicano.* Aguilar, 1995.

Fuentes, Carlos. *The Old Gringo.* Translated by Margaret Sayers Peden. Farrar, Straus & Giroux, 2007.

Fuentes, Carlos. *The Orange Tree.* Translated by Alfred MacAdam. Farrar, Straus & Giroux, 1994.

Fuentes, Carlos. *La región más transparente.* 2nd ed. Fondo de Cultura Económica, 1972.

Fuentes, Carlos. *La silla del águila.* Alfaguara, 2002.

Fuentes, Carlos. *La voluntad y la fortuna.* Alfaguara, 2008.

Fuentes, Carlos. "Pablo Neruda." *Personas.* Alfaguara, 2012, pp. 129–44.

Fuentes, Carlos. "The Son of Andrés Aparicio." *Burnt Water,* pp. 188–231.

Fuentes, Carlos. "South of the Border." *Saturday Review,* December 17, 1960, p. 27.

Fuentes, Carlos. *Terra nostra.* Seix Barral, 1975.

Fuentes, Carlos. *Terra Nostra.* Translated by Margaret Sayers Peden. Farrar, Straus & Giroux, 2013.

Fuentes, Carlos. *Todas las familias felices.* Alfaguara, 2006.

Fuentes, Carlos. *Valiente mundo nuevo: Épica, utopía y mito en la novela hispanoamericana.* Fondo de Cultura Económica, 1990.

Fuentes, Carlos. "Viva mi fama." *Constancia y otras novelas para vírgenes,* pp. 181–279.

Fuentes, Carlos. *Where the Air Is Clear.* Translated by Sam Hileman. Farrar, Straus & Giroux, 1960.

Fuentes, Carlos. *The Years with Laura Díaz*. Translated by Alfred MacAdam. Harcourt, 2000.

Joyce, James. *A Portrait of the Artist as a Young Man*. Viking Press & B.W. Huebsch, 1916.

Krauze, Enrique. "La comedia mexicana de Carlos Fuentes." *Vuelta*, no. 139, June 1988, pp. 15–27.

Krauze, Enrique. "The Guerrilla Dandy: The Literary and Political Illusions of Carlos Fuentes, Everybody's Favorite Mexican." *The New Republic*, June 27, 1988, pp. 28–38.

Lámbarry, Alejandro, and Julia Isabel Eissa Osorio. "Mapas literarios en la narrativa completa de Carlos Fuentes: construcción de una identidad cultural mexicana y escritura de una obra desde la periferia." *Revista de Estudios Hispánicos*, vol. 52, no. 1, March 2018, pp. 171–98.

Long, Ryan. *Fictions of Totality: The Mexican Novel, 1968, and the National-Popular State*. Purdue UP, 2008.

Paz, Octavio. *El laberinto de la soledad*. Fondo de Cultura Económica, 1950.

Paz, Octavio. *Libertad bajo palabra*. Tezontle, 1949.

Reid, Marc Olivier. "Carlos Fuentes, Reader of the Enlightenment." *Revista de Estudios Hispánicos*, vol. 47, no. 2, June 2013, pp. 223–48.

Rojas, Rafael. "Fuentes entre dos revoluciones." Boldy, *Carlos Fuentes y el Reino Unido*, pp. 139–58.

Ruffinelli, Jorge. "Las ciudades perdidas de Carlos Fuentes." *Texto Crítico: Revista del Centro de Investigaciones Lingüístico-Literarias de la Universidad Veracruzana*, vol. 10, no. 28, January–April 1984, pp. 114–21.

Sartre, Jean-Paul. *La nausée*. Gallimard, 1938.

Siskind, Mariano. *Cosmopolitan Desires: Global Modernity and World Literature in Latin America*. Northwestern UP, 2014.

Van Delden, Maarten. *Carlos Fuentes, Mexico, and Modernity*. Vanderbilt UP, 1998.

Van Delden, Maarten. "Hands-on Modernism: Touch and Gesture in Carlos Fuentes's *La muerte de Artemio Cruz*." *The Reptant Eagle: Essays on Carlos Fuentes and the Art of the Novel*, edited by Roberto Cantú, Cambridge Scholars Publishing, 2015, pp. 36–50.

Van Delden, Maarten. "Íntimos Enemigos: Carlos Fuentes y los Estados Unidos." Boldy, *Carlos Fuentes y el Reino Unido*, pp. 159–75.

Williams, Raymond Leslie. *The Writings of Carlos Fuentes*. U of Texas P, 1996.

....

CHAPTER 36

MARIO VARGAS LLOSA BETWEEN LITERATURE AND POLITICS

....

SABINE KÖLLMANN

PROLIFIC writer and public intellectual, the Peruvian author and Nobel Laureate Mario Vargas Llosa is one of the most important, influential, but also controversial figures in Latin American literature, with a career that spans more than sixty years and includes nineteen novels to date. Narrative fiction is at the core of a wide-ranging body of work that comprises plays, memoirs, essays, literary criticism, and journalism. In all of these genres his passion for storytelling comes to the fore. Vargas Llosa's contribution to Latin American and world fiction earned him the 2010 Nobel Prize in Literature "for his cartography of structures of power and his trenchant images of the individual's resistance, revolt, and defeat."[1] The political dimension emphasized by the Swedish Academy is only one of many different facets of a novelistic oeuvre that encompasses everything from social criticism to melodrama, dictatorship novels to playful social satire, historical fiction to erotic novels, and crime fiction to novels about art and literature itself. Vargas Llosa often combines contrasting elements within a single novel. The unifying factor in his writing is his dual interest in the effects of politics on the individual and the role of fiction and the writer in society. His novels are concerned with the reality of lives shaped by social and political factors such as violence and social injustice, on the one hand, and by private passions and obsessions, on the other. The search for truth—about a crime, a historical occurrence, a disappearance, or a protagonist's true identity or character—is the overarching theme in his fiction. At the same time, he explores the particular kind of truth that literature is able to tell, "the truth of lies."[2] Based on reality and reflecting it, but free to add, modify, or leave out facts, fiction creates an imaginary world made of words that provides the opportunity to dream and to be free, while at the same time telling the truth about human desires, aspirations, and fears. Literature not only compensates for life's shortcomings, it also questions the world as it is by confronting it with a counterworld of the imagination, creating a tension that reveals the need for change. Vargas Llosa introduces a number of writer-protagonists who reflect on the ambiguous nature of fiction and on the process of turning reality into fiction.

Born on March 28, 1936, in Arequipa, Peru, Vargas Llosa spent his childhood with his mother in the Bolivian town of Cochabamba, where he developed an early passion for reading, encouraged in his interest for literature by his supportive maternal family. At the age of eleven, back in Peru and attending school in Piura, his mother revealed to him that his father, whom he had believed to be dead, was in fact alive and was going to live with them in Lima. In his Nobel Lecture Vargas Llosa describes how, at that point, literature became a necessity for escaping the oppressive presence of an authoritarian father by "taking refuge in those worlds where life was glorious, intense, one adventure after another, where I could feel free and be happy again . . . It became a way of resisting adversity, protesting, rebelling, escaping the intolerable."[3] This experience shaped his life-long understanding of reading and writing as subversive activities that challenge the status quo. His reaction to the trauma of his father disrupting his happy life was "writing, in secret, like someone giving himself up to an unspeakable vice."[4] Since these formative years, he sees literature as a way of transforming a hostile, unhappy, or restrictive reality into fiction by turning what he calls his demons into language and literary form. These demons can be experiences in his personal life (the theme of the father recurs throughout his work), they can be rooted in history (the 1950s Latin American dictatorships reappear in several key novels), or derive from culture, such as his invention of erotic scenarios inspired by works of art. The act of writing, understood in this way, demands an author's total dedication.

His father sent fourteen-year-old Mario to the Leoncio Prado Military Academy in Lima in the hope of suppressing his passion for literature—without success: his two years in that institution provided Vargas Llosa with the experiences on which he based his first novel. Back in Piura in 1952, he wrote the unpublished play "La huida del Inca" ("The Flight of the Inca") and directed it himself at the local theatre. He rejected his father's plan to enrol him at the conservative Catholic University in Lima to study law. Instead, he studied literature as well as law at the National University of San Marcos, where he joined a clandestine Marxist group while also working as a journalist, both experiences that would later inform his fiction. In a further act of rebellion, the nineteen-year-old married his aunt-in-law Julia Urquidi, ten years his senior and divorced. With her he moved to Europe on a scholarship to study for a doctorate in literature at the Universidad Complutense in Madrid. By the late 1950s his short stories had gained some recognition in France and in Spain. Vargas Llosa moved to Paris with his wife in pursuit of his dream to become a professional writer. Paris was the city of Jean-Paul Sartre and Albert Camus, whose ideas about *littérature engagée* (literature of commitment) influenced him greatly. Juggling various jobs in teaching and journalism, he finished his first novel, which won him the Biblioteca Breve Prize by the Spanish publishing house Seix Barral in 1962 and was published a year later under its final title *La ciudad y los perros* (*The Time of the Hero*, 1963). His marriage to Julia Urquidi ended in 1964; he fictionalized their love story in his 1977 novel *La tía Julia y el escribidor* (*Aunt*

Julia and the Scriptwriter). In 1965 he married his first cousin Patricia Llosa, a marriage that lasted until 2015; they have three children.

The first Biblioteca Breve Prize awarded to a Latin American writer drew attention to a new kind of literature coming from Latin American authors whose first successes launched the so-called Boom in Latin American literature, seeing their works published and widely read across Europe and beyond. During the 1960s the authors associated with the Boom were united in their enthusiastic support for the Cuban Revolution. Vargas Llosa became associated with the country's cultural institute *Casa de las Américas*, serving on the board of its journal and acting as a juror for its literary prize. The Cuban connection firmly established the link between literature and politics in the reception of Latin American fiction in general and of Vargas Llosa's work in particular. The widespread view of his narrative of the 1960s as representing a socialist phase in his writing was promoted not least by his 1967 acceptance speech for the Rómulo Gallegos Prize in Caracas, "La literatura es fuego" ("Literature is Fire"), which became notorious for its firebrand rhetoric, linking fiction to revolutionary politics. Under the surface, however, the speech lays out his view, consistent throughout his career, that literature is always rebellious and in opposition to the existing reality, under whatever regime, a statement that Vargas Llosa has repeated many times since, most prominently in his Nobel Lecture of 2010. He began to notice worrying signs of repressive tendencies in Cuba, but did not speak out until the eruption of the Padilla affair in 1971, which marked the end of the Boom writers' unity. The humiliating treatment of Cuban poet Heberto Padilla, who had defied government restrictions, led to international protests, in which Vargas Llosa assumed a lead role. Disillusioned with a political system that punished dissent and shunned open discussion—Vargas Llosa has always relished controversial disputes and is no stranger to polemical exchanges—he became one of the most vociferous critics of Fidel Castro and a passionate defender of freedom of speech, a cause he pursued as president of PEN International from 1976 to 1979. Widely read, translated, and internationally recognized with awards for his literature, he became notorious for what was perceived as an ideological about-face from the left to the right of the political spectrum.

Back in Lima in the 1980s, Vargas Llosa became increasingly involved in Peruvian politics. Asked to participate in a commission sent to the Andes to investigate the massacre of eight journalists in the context of the Maoist terrorism of Sendero Luminoso (Shining Path), he drafted the final report, whose findings were disputed by the political left. Concerned with questions of freedom and an open, democratic society as the way to pursue social justice, Vargas Llosa had studied liberal thinkers such as Isaiah Berlin, Karl Popper, Jean-François Revel, and Raymond Aron, and the free-market economists Friedrich Hayek and Ludwig von Mises, which had turned him into an ardent supporter of free-market liberalism. When in 1987 Peruvian president Alan García planned to nationalize the banking system, Vargas Llosa headed a political movement against these plans. Carried by a wave of enthusiasm from his supporters and led by his liberal convictions, he decided to run for the presidency of Peru in the 1990 election. His inexperience as a politician—he insisted on telling the truth about planned austerity measures—and the alliance his movement entered into with established conservative parties lost him the trust of the public. He was beaten in the second round of the election by the relatively unknown Alberto Fujimori (who implemented many of the measures proposed by his opponent) and left Peru for Europe, where he continued his fight against the increasingly authoritarian Fujimori by pressing for sanctions against his native country. Fujimori threatened to strip him of his citizenship, at which point Vargas Llosa was granted Spanish nationality. He still holds dual citizenship and is based in Madrid, from where he continues to comment on worldwide issues. Despite his statements in favor of freedom, democracy, and human rights, he remains a highly controversial figure. In recent years, his interventions in Latin American election campaigns in support of hard-right candidates have caused consternation amongst friends and foes alike.

After his interlude as a politician, Vargas Llosa resumed his life of travelling the world to teach university courses, undertake research for his novels, and to accept a multitude of literary awards, honorary doctorates, and state honors from all over the globe. Widely respected in his dual role as writer and public intellectual, the 2010 Nobel Prize in Literature was the crowning glory of a long and illustrious career. The excitement around his person following the announcement only briefly interrupted his life of writing.

Vargas Llosa's first novels introduce thematic, structural, and narrative features that characterize his work throughout his career. The world of the military, the brothel, the neighborhood, and the family, especially the father-son relationship, are the subject matter of many of his works. They are first depicted in his debut novel *La ciudad y los perros* (*The Time of the Hero*, 1963), together with the recurring themes of machismo, violence, corruption, and—particularly important in view of his most recent work—the manipulation of the truth. The novel gained its author a certain notoriety due to the unflinching depiction of the activities of a group of military cadets in the Leoncio Prado Military Academy in Lima that appears under its real name: submitted to humiliating initiation rituals, the "dogs," as the first-year students are called, organize themselves under the leadership of the ruthless Jaguar and subvert the strict military order by all sorts of illegal activities, sexual depravities, and the attempted theft of exam papers. A cadet's betrayal of the perpetrator of the break-in leads to the traitor's death during a field exercise, a fatal incident that the military leaders cover up to preserve the school's reputation. The novel caused outrage at Leoncio Prado, where, legend has it, a thousand copies of the book were burned—but the notorious book-burning episode has been shown to be just that, a legend, born out of a series of rumors, exaggerations, and incendiary metaphors used to describe the work and its context (King 517–37).

The title *La ciudad y los perros* (literally "The City and the Dogs") indicates its dual structure, a compositional device that Vargas Llosa reworks in numerous variations in later novels, where two apparently opposing realms reveal similarities or contaminate each other. The cadets move between the closed world of the military school with its own code of conduct and the open city outside the barracks, the world of the students' families, their neighborhood, and their girlfriends. But behavior from outside the military school spills over into life in the barracks and vice versa: the boy Ricardo, who seeks safety in the school from his father's brutality, is branded The Slave by his peers, bullied, and dies under suspicious circumstances. The Jaguar, who used to be a petty criminal, organizes the illegal activities in the barracks. The class and racial prejudices that dominate Peruvian society are perpetuated inside the microcosm of the military academy. Likewise, the machismo that reigns inside the barracks is at once a reflection of the value system that rules society outside and reproduces it. The dualism of the two narrative centers uncovers the problem of authenticity and roleplay, another recurring theme in Vargas Llosa's work. In contrast to their civil identities, cadets know each other and their superiors by nicknames that assign them a role within the dog-eat-dog mentality of the military academy, where you have to "be real tough, to have guts . . . Screw them first before they screw you" (*The Time of the Hero* 23).[5] The character Alberto, known as the Poet, is the first example of an autobiographically inspired writer-protagonist in Vargas Llosa's work. He finds his niche in the brutal world of the academy by providing his peers with pornographic stories for their entertainment, creating sexual fantasies as a counterworld to the military. But his gift with words is just an opportunistic way to survive the law of the jungle in the barracks. His one authentic act of taking a moral stand and telling his lieutenant the identity of The Slave's killer is undermined by the superior officers whose priority is not justice. The truth about the shooting of The Slave, the central event that divides the novel into two parts, remains ambiguous until the epilogue of the novel—and even then, doubts remain about the Jaguar's confession. Life continues after Leoncio Prado, which was nothing but a "three-year parenthesis"[6] (391) that did not alter the status quo.

La ciudad y los perros received much praise for its young author's assured use of narrative techniques such as shifting narrative voices and perspectives, and the distorted time sequence with frequent flashbacks. Temporal fragmentation allows for revealing juxtapositions in the manner of cinematic montage. Alberto has some interior monologues, while the cadet Boa's non-coherent stream of consciousness is a technique reminiscent of Faulkner. A first-person narrator in some of the flashback segments is not identifiable until the epilogue, where he turns out to be identical with the Jaguar, a surprising "hidden fact," as Vargas Llosa later calls this narrative device.[7] *La ciudad y los perros* also contains the beginning of another of the author's major narrative techniques, the "communicating vessels,"[8] where events or dialogues on different levels of time or between different people are intermingled without explanation. This happens in Alberto's telephone conversation with his superior, where his dramatic revelations about the killer of The Slave are interspersed with the background conversations in the bar from where he is calling, a technique derived from Flaubert. The French author is also the model for Vargas Llosa's frequent use of free indirect style to approach a protagonist's interior point of view.

La casa verde (*The Green House*, 1966) advances these literary devices and introduces two other narrative techniques used to transform reality into fiction: the "Chinese box"-technique[9] of nestling stories within stories, and the "qualitative leap,"[10] where a shift in the level of reality changes the quality of a narrated event, for example from a realistic account to a mythical one. This happens with the Green House of the title, a brothel in the sandy surroundings of Piura, which exists in two incarnations: the one founded by the mysterious Don Anselmo and burnt down by a mob whipped up by the town's priest exists in the collective memory of the inhabitants of Piura, but nobody is sure any more whether its story is real or a legend, while the second Green House exists on the same level of time and reality as the people discussing the legendary first brothel from sixty years earlier. The novel's fragmented narration creates a simultaneity that uncovers hidden links between events and people across time and space. The spatial organization of *La casa verde* relies once again on a dual structure with two geographical centers, the town of Piura in the desert region of northern Peru and the Amazon jungle. The contrasting settings become intertwined by protagonists from one area who unexpectedly appear in the other, such as the indigenous girl Bonifacia, forcibly removed from her family and her tribe in the jungle by soldiers acting on behalf of the nuns in a Catholic mission, who ends up in Piura's Green House as the prostitute La Selvática (the jungle girl). Color symbolism contributes to the work's strong visual, cinematic quality that helps the reader through a highly complex novel of seventy-two non-linear narrative sequences, where time and space seem to dissolve. The broad panorama of landscapes, people, and stories is Vargas Llosa's first attempt at the "total novel," able to encompass a complex world in all its diverse aspects (geographical, social, psychological, religious, cultural, mythical), reflecting a wide range of human experiences. A number of the novel's protagonists, above all the policeman Lituma, reappear in later works, a feature modelled on Balzac's vast fictional universe with its "integrating vision"[11] of human existence in all its shades.

In *Conversación en La Catedral* (*Conversation in the Cathedral*, 1969), Vargas Llosa's virtuoso handling of narrative technique, structure, and language reaches its greatest complexity. The monumental, multi-faceted work is at once a murder mystery, a novel about political corruption, and a *Bildungsroman* that traces a young writer-protagonist's aspirations, failures, and final resignation. In a labyrinth of stories, voices, places, and time levels, which are intricately linked, the novel renders a bleak portrayal of life in Lima around the time of Manuel Odría's military dictatorship in the 1950s, the period when Vargas Llosa was growing up. The protagonist Santiago Zavala's experiences as a student and Marxist conspirator at San Marcos National University, and as a crime journalist at a local newspaper, echo the author's biography. But Zavalita ends in mediocrity in a climate of general moral decay and political corruption. The novel's leitmotif, established in the first few sentences, draws a parallel between society and the individual: "At what precise moment had Peru fucked itself up? . . . He was like Peru, Zavalita . . . he'd fucked himself up somewhere along the line. He thinks: when? . . . He thinks: there's no solution" (3).[12] The complex narrative evolves out of a conversation that Santiago has in a dilapidated bar with Ambrosio, his father's former chauffeur, now down on his luck. Out of this four-hour conversation grow all the other conversations and events in the past, partly in the form of "telescopic dialogues" (Oviedo, "diálogos telescópicos" 252) that zoom in from one level of narration to another, and partly reflected in Santiago's and Ambrosio's minds in the shape of two parallel streams of consciousness. The mysterious question that hangs over this conversation only becomes clear toward the end: Santiago is tortured by his doubts of whether it was his father who ordered Ambrosio to murder the prostitute La Musa, because she was blackmailing Fermín Zavala with knowledge of his sexual relationship with his chauffeur. At the end of the novel, after four hours' talking, Santiago leaves without an answer to his question. The truth remains hidden. The ending of the novel is as bleak as its beginning, echoed in the excrement-colored visual impressions, the disturbing sounds, and disgusting smells of the city under its gray, drizzly skies.

Despite the novel's bitter social criticism that is in tune with Vargas Llosa's affiliation with socialism at the time, the episodes involving the students' communist cell reveal his skepticism about a commitment that is guided by ideology and requires an uncritical belief in an absolute truth. Santiago's romantic idea about radical politics becomes another of his lost illusions. Underneath the surface of a novel that denounces political authoritarianism and corruption in the strongest terms, there are nevertheless the first signs of its author's disillusionment with left-wing politics. The hopelessness of his portrayal of Peruvian politics and its devastating effect on the individual, but also the degree of structural complexity, reach a peak in *Conversación en La Catedral*. In the following novel, Vargas Llosa continues his criticism of militarism, machismo, and religion with a new twist: introducing humor, irony, and farce.

The two opposing poles of the military and the brothel, present in all three novels of the 1960s, take center stage in *Pantaleón y las visitadoras* (*Captain Pantoja and the Special Service*, 1973) and become intertwined in a comical way. With a fanatical sense of duty Captain Pantoja follows orders to set up a secret special force of prostitutes to service the military in the Amazon jungle—and makes it the most efficient unit in the armed forces. The novel also introduces a religious fanatic, Brother Francisco, who is as zealous as his antagonist, Pantoja. A parallel crescendo of fanatical behavior drives both military special service and religious movement to a cataclysmic end. The novel's innovative features include parodies of different sorts of text such as letters, military reports, Freudian dream analyses, and sensational journalism in print as well as in radio broadcasts.

The world of popular radio then becomes the focus of the metafictional self-parody *La tía Julia y el escribidor* (*Aunt Julia and the Scriptwriter*, 1977). As in the previous novel, its humor derives from the clash of two completely incongruous worlds that become entangled. The story of a radio station that employs both Varguitas, an aspiring highbrow writer with the name Mario Vargas, and Pedro Camacho, a prolific scriptwriter of serialized melodramas, alternates with chapters containing the fictional episodes of different radiodramas. The two levels contaminate each other, when Varguitas and his aunt Julia's wedding begins to resemble a soap opera, while the melodramas become mixed up—misinterpreted by some listeners as a postmodern stroke of genius—because Camacho is no longer able to keep his different storylines apart. In the end the serious writer has to take over and adopt the practice of popular fiction writing.

The fusion of sophisticated literary craft and captivating storytelling characterizes what is one of the key works of Vargas Llosa's oeuvre, *La guerra del fin del mundo* (*The War of the End of the World*, 1981). The historical novel about a violent clash of religious and nationalistic fanatics in nineteenth-century Brazil combines the social concerns of his earlier novels with the anti-ideological stance that he adopted in the 1970s. The work comes closest to his ideal of the "total novel," bringing together a multitude of storylines, characters, and realms of human experience in an action-driven narrative that is carefully constructed to establish a symmetry on the formal level, corresponding to the symmetry of fanatical behavior on the level of plot.[13] Two ideological and geographical poles, the millenarian movement in Brazil's poor northeast and the state capital Bahía representing the newly established republic, come into conflict because they completely misinterpret the motivations of the other side. The republic sends troops to suppress what they understand to be a reactionary, monarchist conspiracy. They encounter powerful resistance from the socio-religious movement, which rejects the introduction of civil marriage and opposes other modernizing measures as the work of the Anti-Christ. The two sides confront each other in four bloody military campaigns, until Canudos, the settlement of the rebellious movement under its charismatic leader, Antônio Conselheiro, is razed to the ground. Confronting the religious leader is an equally charismatic military leader, Moreira César, whose fanatical patriotism makes him similarly blind to the truth about his opponent. The role of the press in distorting the truth about the millenarian movement is highlighted by a writer-protagonist, a short-sighted journalist who changes his preconceived opinions when he ends up inside Canudos and experiences the solidarity of the millenarian movement firsthand. After the war he is determined to clear up the mutual misunderstandings that escalated the conflict by writing the true story of Canudos. Vargas Llosa raises the question of historical truth using multiple perspectives that allow the reader to see the historical events from different angles (sometimes literally, when episodes are told twice from different points of view). He invents a whole narrative layer that is absent from historiography, the point of view of the *jagunços*, the motley crew of followers of the Counselor, some of whom are given an interior perspective by the otherwise omniscient narrator to reveal their beliefs and motivations.

This procedure of adding invented elements to the known historical facts to create a fictional truth becomes the main subject matter of the following novel, *Historia de Mayta* (*The Real Life of Alejandro Mayta*, 1984), in which a writer-protagonist tries to reconstruct a futile and misguided Trotskyist rebellion in the Andean city of Jauja in order to create a novel about the events. The writer-character, an avatar of Vargas Llosa himself in an invented not-too-far future, explains that he bases his novel on extensive research so as "to lie knowing what I lie about."[14] The Spanish phrase has become Vargas Llosa's oft-repeated definition of his method of transforming historical reality into fiction: only by knowing the historically documented facts, interviewing witnesses, and visiting the locations of a historical occurrence is he free to imagine his own, fictional, version of events that has its own "truth," that is, an order and a coherence that might be absent from an opaque reality. The novel reveals the process of creating this kind of fictional truth by ascribing characteristics to the fictional Mayta that the "real" Mayta, who appears at the end, does not have. There are also two layers of "reality," an apocalyptic present of Peru in a civil war, in which the writer-protagonist does his research, and the "real" present of the writer's interview with Mayta himself, of course another construct by the extra-fictional author. Hidden behind this multi-layered metafictional game with different versions of "truth" is Vargas Llosa's own construction of the truth: his political criticism of left-wing idealists whose readiness in the past to pursue their goals with violence was a precursor of terrorist extremism and chaos in the present.

In the shorter novels that follow, Vargas Llosa experiments with different genres, while continuing the theme of fact and fiction. The search for the truth about a gruesome murder is at the center of the crime novel *¿Quién mató a Palomino Molero?* (*Who killed Palomino Molero?*, 1986). The investigating policemen identify the murderer and his motive, but the public is more inclined to believe rumors and conspiracy theories. It appears that the sober facts have less appeal than exciting fictional stories. This is also what the writer-protagonist of *El hablador* (*The Storyteller*, 1987), closely resembling Vargas Llosa, finds, when he imagines that the photograph he sees in an exhibition of an indigenous storyteller in the Peruvian jungle is an old friend from university, who was obsessed with the fate of indigenous communities. The writer makes up a scenario in which this friend had joined the remote community of the Machiguengas and become one of their ambulant storytellers, whose crucial function in their dispersed society he compares to the importance of modern creators of stories like himself. Every second chapter renders the imagined discourse of such a Machiguenga storyteller (who is, however, an outsider and retells Kafka's *Metamorphosis* and episodes from the Bible). The metafictional level of the novel is highly complex and intriguing, but Vargas Llosa's representation of the indigenous question has attracted much criticism.

The same can be said about his portrayal of the Andean world in *Lituma en los Andes* (*Death in the Andes*, 1993), whose nature and inhabitants, seen through the perspective of the policeman Lituma, seem hostile and inscrutable. The detective novel is set in the 1990s climate of violence and fear caused by Sendero Luminoso's terrorism. Alternate segments deal with the brutal arbitrary killings of innocent people by the terrorists, and the search for the truth about the disappearance of three construction workers, who turn out to be the victims of archaic rituals of sacrifice to Andean deities. Irrational violence dominates both levels of the plot. By contrast, one of the policemen tells his colleague a story of romantic love and desire, creating a counterworld that enables the two outsiders to survive the lonely nights in these hostile surroundings. In the end, what seemed too unreal to be true turns out to be the truth in both narrative strands.

Imagined erotic scenarios and their contamination of reality are the subject matter of two erotic novels, *Elogio de la madrastra* (*In Praise of the Stepmother*, 1988) and *Los cuadernos de Don Rigoberto* (*The Notebooks of Don Rigoberto*, 1997), where Vargas Llosa introduces a new element: art as inspiration for erotic roleplay. Don Rigoberto's private fantasies, inspired by his collection of erotic art, dominate his sex life with his second wife, Lucrecia, while she gets entangled in a very real transgressive game with her stepson. When Fonchito, an angelic-looking, manipulative teen, reveals his affair with his stepmother, Rigoberto suffers the sudden collapse of his carefully erected nocturnal counterworld of dreams and transgressive desires. Alternate chapters of *Elogio de la madrastra* present a highly original form of *ekphrasis*, the description of art in words.

Following on from the reproduction of paintings reaching from Titian to Francis Bacon and Fernando de Szyszlo to Fra Angelico, a narrative voice from inside each painting fantasizes about the situation they find themselves in. *Los cuadernos de Don Rigoberto* picks up the story of the now separated couple. This time it is the stepson who has become obsessed with art. He seduces his stepmother into imitating poses from Egon Schiele's erotic paintings, while back at home his father dreams up elaborate erotic encounters of his estranged wife with other men and women. In the end, the family reunites due to more clever scheming by the son, a Lucifer-like manipulator who will continue to be a source of concern for his parents in Vargas Llosa's 2013 novel *El héroe discreto* (*The Discreet Hero*), alarming them with the shifting borders between fantasy and reality.

The theme of roleplay and manipulation continues in *Travesuras de la niña mala* (*The Bad Girl*, 2006), an episodic love story with a female protagonist who appears in many different incarnations, but is never quite what she seems. The aspiring writer and romantic Ricardo falls in love with her in Lima when they are both young, but she disappears—until he happens to come across her again in different parts of the world, under different guises. The truth about her real identity remains hidden until the end, when Ricardo nurses her through her terminal illness after her abusive affair with the Japanese Fukuda (the associative link between this unpleasant character and Vargas Llosa's nemesis Fujimori is perhaps not accidental). Sex, rebellion, violence, and melodrama, the ingredients Vargas Llosa once defined as necessary for a good read (*La orgía perpetua* 713; *The Perpetual Orgy* 11–12), link this novel to the already mentioned detective novel *El héroe discreto* (*The Discreet Hero*, 2013), a story of fathers and sons, and of standing up to intimidation and corruption, and to *Cinco esquinas* (*The Neighborhood*, 2016), with its steamy lesbian affair played out against the background of the ruthless, corrupt regime of Fujimori and his head of the National Intelligence Service, Vladimiro Montesinos, who manipulate the truth with the help of the gutter press.

Standing out from these miscellaneous works are four major novels of the new millennium that represent a renewal of Vargas Llosa's totalizing ambition, following on from the grand designs of *La casa verde*, *Conversación en la catedral*, and *La guerra del fin del mundo*. Two of these novels follow their protagonists in their fanatical pursuit of an ideal that cannot be achieved, while the other two are historical novels uncovering the truth and lies of power. *El Paraíso en la otra esquina* (*The Way to Paradise*, 2003) and *El sueño del celta* (*The Dream of the Celt*, 2010) have historical protagonists: Flora Tristán, Peruvian-French writer, feminist, and socialist activist, and her grandson, the painter Paul Gauguin, both dedicate their lives to an elusive ideal, which they chase in their travels around the world, while Roger Casement, the Celt of the 2010 novel, a British diplomat honored for exposing human-rights abuses in the Congo and in Peru, becomes an Irish nationalist and follows his dream of Irish independence by treason and collusion with Germany during the First World War. Tristán and Casement pursue a political ideal, while Gauguin's dream is an artistic one: he aims to liberate himself from social and moral constraints to find a more authentic form of art. All three protagonists leave behind a secure bourgeois existence to chase their utopian ideal, and all three lives end in failure (Gauguin's role in revolutionizing art was only recognized after his death).

El Paraíso en la otra esquina follows the model of parallel lives. Chapters alternate between Flora Tristán and Gauguin toward the end of their lives, remembering their struggles to achieve their respective ideals: social justice and gender equality in the political activist's case, a radical renewal of art in the painter's. Vargas Llosa uses an ambiguous second-person narrator to maintain a dialogue with his protagonists' motivations, obsessions, and doubts. The two main figures, whose lives do not touch, are driven by a rebellious spirit, born in Tristán's case out of the trauma of abuse in her marriage, in Gauguin's case out of his passions and instincts that are linked to his creative impulse. The two lifelong concerns of Vargas Llosa, politics and the creative process, are embodied in these two very different utopian dreamers searching for an alternative, better world against all odds. Vargas Llosa continues his experiments with *ekphrasis* by not only describing Gauguin's paintings but also inventing a backstory to their genesis (that reflects above all his own creative process). The themes of illness, pain, physical decay, and death that are present in Vargas Llosa's later works play an important part in this novel with its moving narrations of both protagonists' end of life from their interior perspective.

Even more ambitious in scope, content, and form than the 2003 novel of parallel lives is *El sueño del celta* of 2010. It concentrates on one protagonist, a very complex, contradictory character who moves from hero to anti-hero in the course of his eventful life that plays out on three continents. The many unresolved questions about the historical Roger Casement's life give Vargas Llosa ample room for invention. The author explores Casement's possible motives for turning from British consul and human-rights champion to fanatical nationalist, convinced that Ireland must liberate itself from British rule by armed rebellion. This leads him to the gallows for treason, a verdict influenced by the so-called Black Diaries recording his secret homosexual life. The diaries' authenticity has never been established without doubt, but Vargas Llosa finds an answer that fits into his own literary convictions: that Casement did indeed write the diaries, but their content was a mixture of fact and fiction, written as an act of catharsis in response to the atrocities that he witnessed and recorded in great detail in his official reports. Casement represents many of Vargas Llosa's recurring themes: youthful idealism and disillusionment, religious fervor, nationalism, and the turn to fanaticism and armed revolt. The Catholic theme of original sin runs through a work that shows how greatness and weakness, angels and demons exist side by side in one personality. *El sueño del celta* explores the dark side of human nature on various levels: the contrast between Casement's impeccable official correctness and his forbidden private passions, the inconceivable brutality with which indigenous populations are exploited in the colonies, and the depth of depravity that human beings can sink to if the circumstances allow them to exert their unbridled power over others. The novel's complexity on the level of content is reflected in its intricate structure: running across the three main geographically defined parts is a dual partition with chapters alternating between Casement's last weeks in prison from his own point of view, and his past life, narrated by a variety of voices using many of the complex narrative techniques known from Vargas Llosa's previous works. This multifaceted "total novel" ends with an epilogue in which the author clearly steps out of the narrative world and comments on his literary construct, a feature that will recur in the most recent novel. *La fiesta del Chivo* (*The Feast of the Goat*, 2000), one of the most important works in Vargas Llosa's oeuvre, and *Tiempos recios* (*Harsh Times*, 2019), his most recent novel, return to the main subject matter of his early novels: politics, authoritarianism, and the distortion of truth. In both historical novels the murder of a dictator takes center stage and is narrated twice, from two different perspectives: that of the assassins and that of the dictator. The first half of both narratives devotes alternate chapters to the assassins' tense wait to execute their killing, which happens in the middle of the novel, an event that is only much later narrated from the murder victims' perspective.

In *La fiesta del Chivo* Vargas Llosa invents a network of relations between historical and fictional protagonists that lends his historical fiction coherence and verisimilitude, but leaves it open to accusations of historical falsification. The novel fictionalizes the violent end to the thirty-one-year dictatorship of Rafael Leónidas Trujillo in the Dominican Republic in 1961. It follows the documented course of events in the country before and after the despot's assassination. But, in addition, it imagines the inner voices of the assassins, ascribing to each of them a different motive for taking part in the murder, thus exposing the system of absolute control that the dictator exerts not only over the state but also over every individual. Vargas Llosa also gives the dictator himself an inner voice: he takes the known facts about Trujillo's cruelty and vanity, his charisma and powers of manipulation, and lets the dictator reveal his abuses of power and his hubris in his own words. This narrative strategy goes further than a denunciation of the structures of power of his evil regime. It exposes the dark side of a human being allowed to exert total control over his country.

The abuse of whichever woman takes Trujillo's fancy, including the wives and daughters of his ministers, becomes the pivot of Vargas Llosa's novel with its protagonist Urania, who returns to the country to reveal the truth about her own father offering his virgin daughter to Trujillo as a gift to remain in his favors. The abuse of paternal power, one of Vargas Llosa's recurring themes, is combined here with the theme of machismo and sexual abuse by the "Father of the New Fatherland." The profusion of pompous titles and panegyrics bestowed on the dictator by the country's intellectuals is shown to play an important part in distorting the truth about "The Benefactor" Trujillo. Complementing the manipulations of public opinion is the systematic violation of human rights, personified in the historical protagonist Johnny Abbes García, the head of Trujillo's Military Intelligence Service, who organizes the rule of terror that keeps Trujillo in power.

Johnny Abbes reappears in a crucial role in *Tiempos recios*, set in Guatemala in the 1950s at the time of the military dictatorship of Carlos Castillo Armas, who led the 1954 coup against the elected president Jacobo Árbenz and his agrarian reform project, a coup that was orchestrated by the United States to secure the interests of the United Fruit Company. Castillo Armas, hated for his brutal repression and persecution of large parts of the population, was assassinated three years later under circumstances that were never satisfactorily explained. This is where Vargas Llosa finds room for invention for his political novel that is also a murder mystery, imagining in great detail the role that Johnny Abbes and Trujillo play in the assassination of Castillo Armas. The colorful protagonist Marta Borrero Parra, real-life mistress of the dictator, turned lover of his murderer Johnny Abbes, is the subject of one of several alternating narrative strands. The novel's time structure is fragmented, the different time levels and plot lines of Marta and the assassins briefly converging in the aftermath of the murder in the middle of the novel. The shady role of Trujillo is highlighted in a chapter in which Vargas Llosa uses his technique of telescopic dialogues, intermingling conversations on different time planes to illustrate cause and effect: the meeting in 1957 in which Trujillo orders Johnny Abbes to eliminate the hated Guatemalan dictator repeatedly zooms in on the conversation between Trujillo and Castillo Armas in 1954, when the latter came to seek his support for the imminent coup and made promises to Trujillo that he never kept, hurting the Dominican dictator's pride and vanity.

The discontinuous time structure of the thirty-two numbered chapters is framed by two sections titled "Before" and "After" that are semi-journalistic in character. In the part preceding the main narrative, Vargas Llosa exposes the systematic spreading of lies about Jacobo Árbenz's political aims, a misinformation campaign to maintain the United Fruit Company's unbridled exploitation of the country. Vargas Llosa explains how the distortion of the truth by manipulating the press in the United States and further afield was orchestrated by the father of public relations and propaganda, Edward L. Bernays, who convinced the Western world that Árbenz was a communist, and that Guatemala was in danger of becoming a Soviet satellite, threatening the whole of Central America and the Panama Canal. This lie about an idealistic president, who actually stood for social justice and democratic structures modelled on the United States, Vargas Llosa explains, was spread so efficiently that it took hold in world opinion and paved the way for US intervention against a democratic reformer in order to safeguard its own economic interests.

The final section ("After") reinforces Vargas Llosa's strong message about this destructive meddling in Latin American affairs during the Cold War. The author steps out of his fictional world, reporting his visit in the present to the real Marta Borrero Parras in Washington DC to find an answer to two open questions: Was she working for the CIA? And was Johnny Abbes really murdered in Haiti (as he narrates in his final chapter)? Vargas Llosa receives no answer to the first question from the octogenarian, but Marta assures him that Abbes García, notorious torturer and murderer, was helped to escape to the United States by the CIA and given a new identity. Vargas Llosa is undecided whether to believe her. But he is more than clear about the conclusion he wants the reader to draw from his novel: the brutal suppression of democracy and social justice in Guatemala is to blame for the rise of radical left-wing sympathies among Latin American youth (including himself), which in turn led to polarization and extremism.

The outspoken denunciation of the harmful influence of the United States in Latin America in the 2019 novel is surprising, coming from an author who abandoned his left-wing rhetoric fifty years earlier. It proves that Vargas Llosa's work eludes categorization:

themes and techniques from a presumed socialist phase continue in what is sometimes called a postmodern phase of parody and pastiche; metafiction and the game with writer-protagonists or author-characters pervade the whole oeuvre; anti-ideological ideas can be found throughout; social justice never ceased to be a topic; and the ingredients of sex, melodrama, and violence, dominant in some less ambitious works, also pervade the "total novels." While Vargas Llosa's post-1969 novels have become more accessible, he continues to use the narrative devices developed in his early work to great effect. The manipulation of the truth, a central theme already present in his first novel, is later combined with the question of journalism's role in distorting reality. *Tiempos recios*, it can be argued, contains the answer to the question dominating *Conversación en la cathedral* (where it was still limited to Peru):[15] When did it all go wrong for Latin America? In his 2019 novel Vargas Llosa has found a possible answer in the deliberate distortion of the truth about Guatemalan democratic reforms during the Cold War, "the lie that passed for the truth and changed the destiny of Latin America."[16]

NOTES

1. "The Nobel Prize in Literature 2010," www.nobelprize.org/prizes/literature/2010/summary/.
2. See Vargas Llosa's essay "La verdad de las mentiras."
3. "Refugiarme en esos mundos donde vivir era exaltante, intenso, una aventura tras otra, donde podía sentirme libre y volvía a ser feliz. . . . Se volvió una manera de resistir la adversidad, de protestar, de rebelarme, de escapar a lo intolerable." ("Discurso Nobel" n.p.) www.nobelprize.org/prizes/literature/2010/vargas_llosa/25185-mario-vargas-llosa-discurso-nobel/.
4. "Y fue escribir, a escondidas, como quien se entrega a un vicio inconfesable, a una pasión prohibida" ("Discurso Nobel" n.p.) www.nobelprize.org/prizes/literature/2010/vargas_llosa/25185-mario-vargas-llosa-discurso-nobel/.
5. "Es ser bien macho, tener unos huevos de acero . . . O comes o te comen" (26).
6. "El oscuro paréntesis de tres años" (378).
7. "El dato escondido" (see "El dato escondido" in *Cartas a un joven novelista* 1372–1380).
8. "Los vasos comunicantes" (see "Los vasos comunicantes" in *Cartas a un joven novelista* 1381–1387).
9. "La caja china" (see "La caja china" in *Cartas a un joven novelista* 1366–1371).
10. "El salto cualitativo" (see "Las mudas y el salto cualitativo" in *Cartas a un joven novelista* 1357–1365).
11. "Esa vision integradora" ("Un mundo" 39).
12. "¿En qué momento se había jodido el Perú? . . . Él era como el Perú, Zavalita, se había jodido en algún momento. Piensa: ¿en cual? . . . Piensa: no hay solución" (9).
13. For a visual representation of the novel's symmetry, see Köllmann 157.
14. "Mentir con conocimiento de la causa" (77).
15. "At what precise moment had Peru fucked itself up?" (3). "¿En qué momento se había jodido el Perú?" (9).
16. "Una mentira que pasó por verdad y cambió el devenir de América Latina." Quoted from the publisher's blurb.

Works Cited

King, John. "Una ficción incendiaria: Reflexiones sobre la recepción de *La ciudad y los perros* en Estados Unidos y el Reino Unido." *La ciudad y los perros*, edited by Real Academia Española, Alfaguara, 2012, pp. 517–37.

Köllmann, Sabine. *Vargas Llosa's Fiction and the Demons of Politics*. Peter Lang, 2002.

"The Nobel Prize in Literature 2010." www.nobelprize.org/prizes/literature/2010/summary/

Oviedo, José Miguel. *Mario Vargas Llosa: la invención de una realidad*. Seix Barral, 1982.

Vargas Llosa, Mario. *Aunt Julia and the Scriptwriter*. Translated by Helen R. Lane. Farrar, Straus and Giroux, 1982.

Vargas Llosa, Mario. *The Bad Girl*. Translated by Edith Grossman. Farrar, Straus and Giroux, 2007.

Vargas Llosa, Mario. *Captain Pantoja and the Special Service*. Translated by Ronald Christ and Gregory Kolovakos. Harper & Row, 1978.

Vargas Llosa, Mario. *Cartas a un joven novelista*. In *Ensayos literarios I*. Círculo de Lectores/ Galaxia Gutenberg, 2006. 1292–1389.

Vargas Llosa, Mario. *La casa verde*. Seix Barral, 1966.

Vargas Llosa, Mario. *Cinco esquinas*. Alfaguara, 2016.

Vargas Llosa, Mario. *La ciudad y los perros*. Seix Barral, 1963.

Vargas Llosa, Mario. *Conversación en La Catedral*. Seix Barral, 1969.

Vargas Llosa, Mario. *Conversation in the Cathedral*. Translated by Gregory Rabassa. HarperCollins, 2005.

Vargas Llosa, Mario. *Los cuadernos de Don Rigoberto*. Alfaguara, 1997.

Vargas Llosa, Mario. *Death in the Andes*. Translated by Edith Grossman. Farrar, Straus and Giroux, 1996.

Vargas Llosa, Mario. *The Discreet Hero*. Translated by Edith Grossman. Farrar, Straus and Giroux, 2015.

Vargas Llosa, Mario. "Discurso Nobel." www.nobelprize.org/prizes/literature/2010/vargas_ll osa/25185-mario-vargas-llosa-discurso-nobel/

Vargas Llosa, Mario. *The Dream of the Celt*. Translated by Edith Grossman. Farrar, Straus and Giroux, 2012.

Vargas Llosa, Mario. *Elogio de la madrastra*. Tusquets, 1988.

Vargas Llosa, Mario. *The Feast of the Goat*. Translated by Edith Grossman. Farrar, Straus and Giroux, 2001.

Vargas Llosa, Mario. *La fiesta del Chivo*. Alfaguara, 2000.

Vargas Llosa, Mario. *The Green House*. Translated by Gregory Rabassa. Harper & Row, 1968.

Vargas Llosa, Mario. *La guerra del fin del mundo*. Seix Barral, 1981.

Vargas Llosa, Mario. *El hablador*. Seix Barral, 1987.

Vargas Llosa, Mario. *Harsh Times*. Translated by Adrian Nathan West. Macmillan, 2021.

Vargas Llosa, Mario. *El héroe discreto*. Alfaguara, 2013.

Vargas Llosa, Mario. *Historia de Mayta*. Seix Barral, 1984.

Vargas Llosa, Mario. "La literatura es fuego." *Contra viento y marea I (1962–1972)*, Seix Barral, 1983, pp. 176–81.

Vargas Llosa, Mario. *Lituma en los Andes*. Planeta, 1993.

Vargas Llosa, Mario. "Un mundo sin novelas." *Letras Libres*, no. 2, 2000, pp. 38–44.

Vargas Llosa, Mario. *The Neighborhood*. Translated by Edith Grossman. Farrar, Straus and Giroux, 2018.

Vargas Llosa, Mario. *The Notebooks of Don Rigoberto*. Translated by Edith Grossman. Farrar, Straus and Giroux, 1998.

Vargas Llosa, Mario. "La orgía perpetua. Flaubert y Madame Bovary." *Ensayos literarios I*, Círculo de Lectores/Galaxia Gutenberg, 2006, pp. 699–909.

Vargas Llosa, Mario. *Pantaleón y las visitadoras*. Seix Barral, 1973.

Vargas Llosa, Mario. *El Paraíso en la otra esquina*. Alfaguara, 2003.

Vargas Llosa, Mario. *The Perpetual Orgy: Flaubert and Madame Bovary*. Translated by Helen Lane. Farrar, Straus and Giroux, 1986.

Vargas Llosa, Mario. *In Praise of the Stepmother*. Translated by Helen Lane. Farrar, Straus and Giroux, 1990.

Vargas Llosa, Mario. *The Real Life of Alejandro Mayta*. Translated by Alfred MacAdam. Farrar, Straus and Giroux, 1986.

Vargas Llosa, Mario. *The Storyteller*. Translated by Helen Lane. Farrar, Straus and Giroux, 1989.

Vargas Llosa, Mario. *El sueño del celta*. Alfaguara, 2010.

Vargas Llosa, Mario. *¿Quién mató a Palomino Molero?* Seix Barral, 1986.

Vargas Llosa, Mario. *Tiempos recios*. Alfaguara, 2019.

Vargas Llosa, Mario. *La tía Julia y el escribidor*. Seix Barral, 1977.

Vargas Llosa, Mario. *The Time of the Hero*. Translated by Lysander Kemp. Farrar, Straus, and Giroux, 1966.

Vargas Llosa, Mario. *Travesuras de la niña mala*. Alfaguara, 2006.

Vargas Llosa, Mario. "La verdad de las mentiras." *La verdad de las mentiras. Ensayos sobre literatura*, Seix Barral, 1990, pp. 5–20.

Vargas Llosa, Mario. *The War of the End of the World*. Translated by Helen Lane. Farrar, Straus and Giroux, 1984.

Vargas Llosa, Mario. *The Way to Paradise*. Translated by Natasha Wimmer. Farrar, Straus and Giroux, 2003.

Vargas Llosa, Mario. *Who Killed Palomino Molero?* Translated by Alfred MacAdam. Farrar, Straus and Giroux, 1987.

CHAPTER 37

···

ALL THE NOVELS,
THE NOVEL

Cortázar's Relentless Search for Aesthetic Freedom

···

CAROLINA ORLOFF

It was November 1983 and Julio Cortázar stopped in New York, where also novelist Luisa Valenzuela lived, on his way back home to Paris. He already suspected that he was ill but was determined to fulfill his political obligations that, in the following months, would take him to Nicaragua, Cuba, and Argentina. Cortázar and Valenzuela spent the entire day talking; Cortázar even asked her to go with him to the airport. According to Valenzuela, it was on their way to take his plane that he mentioned that he planned to take a month off to write a new novel, the first one in a decade. "I owe it to myself," Cortázar said; "so often I put off the need to write fiction. I owe it to literature, which has helped me so much. I repeatedly get asked to write short stories and, instead of short stories, I deliver essays on Central America" (qtd. in Valenzuela 14).[1]

When Valenzuela asked Cortázar about the new novel he had in mind, he replied that he did not have any clear storyline in his head and that, in any case, even if he had one, he was not keen to share it because, like García Márquez, he felt that: "If I explain something about the story I am writing, I destroy it *ab ovo*. If I do as much as to insinuate it before it is written, I am tearing it to shreds" (qtd. in Valenzuela 14).[2]

This makes me wonder not just about this novel's storyline, contents, and characters, but also about its form, because Cortázar was an insatiable explorer and innovator of forms. Indeed, he had become more so with every novel he wrote and—I believe—the more politically engaged he became through his writing career. In the words of Saúl Sosnowski, "One of the defining features in the works of Cortázar is the crisscrossing of genres, the bringing into question of all kinds of limitations, and the efficient nurturing of a single literary expression" (9–10).[3] I would add that this crisscrossing became key for Cortázar beginning with *Rayuela* (*Hopscotch*). Up to that point, his conception of the novel as a literary expression had been certainly playful in content, but somewhat conservative when it came to form; with the publication of *Rayuela* in 1963, that changed completely.

Sosnowski continues: "Cortázar's *oeuvre* provokes a state of readiness. To go through it in any of its aspects, is to admit that at any point, and from any sentence, the turn can emerge for once and for all, the turn that will disrupt anything that had been foreseen. Many of his texts point towards recondite spaces which are subjected to the unexpected, to the rationally unprecedented; they settle down in the act of questioning and challenging of all things conventional" (9–10).[4] Anyone who has read Cortázar's narrative, and this is most apparent in the short stories, will know that the element of the unexpected, the rationally inconceivable, is always present. It is what marks Cortázar's conception of the fantastic as "the sudden indication that on the fringes of the Aristotelian laws and of our own reasoning mind, there are perfectly valid mechanisms . . . that our logical brain does not accept" (González Bermejo 78).[5] Or, as he would put it later, "the fantastic is something that presents itself without being summoned. For me, it is always an 'irruption' . . . a break in causality or temporality, a break in the physical and psychological laws. 'Everything was going smoothly and then, suddenly'" (Cortázar Papers).[6] Bearing Cortázar's own ideas regarding the fantastic, as well as Sosnowki's reflection, there are two notions that are central to understanding Cortázar's novelistic aesthetic project: a state of readiness (on the part of the reader) and the questioning and challenging of conventional form.

This is perhaps the core difference between Cortázar's novels and those of his contemporaries. The fact that Cortázar was constantly looking for something else, not just in terms of content, but also in terms of form; to experiment with the conventional limitations of what the novel was supposed to be set Cortázar apart from his peers. For unlike Mario Vargas Llosa, Carlos Fuentes, Gabriel García Márquez, and many others, Cortázar relentlessly questioned and problematized the form of the novel in a way that went beyond aesthetics. For him, it was an ontological, even political endeavor inasmuch as his "transgression" of convention had a correlation in the political sphere. Let's remember that during his lifetime, Cortázar would publish four novels: *Los premios* (*The Winners* 1960), *Rayuela*, *62/modelo para armar* (*62: A Model Kit*, 1968), and *Libro de Manuel* (*A Manual for Manuel*, 1973).

However, Cortázar also wrote three short novels that would remain unpublished before his death in 1984. Taking these into account, Cortázar's novelistic corpus consists of: *Divertimento* (written in 1949, published in Spanish in 1986); *El examen* (written in 1950, published in 1986; *Final Exam*, 2000); *Diarios de Andrés Fava* (written in 1951, published in 1995; *Diary of Andrés Fava*, 2005); and *Los premios*, *Rayuela*, *62/Modelo para armar*, and *Libro de Manuel*. In the decade that followed the publication of what would be Cortázar's final novel, *Libro de Manuel*, and until his death, he wrote his best-known short story collections and collaborative works. During this period Cortázar also published most of his more experimental books, developing his collage books *La vuelta al día en ochenta mundos* (*Around the Day in Eighty Worlds*, 1967) and *Último Round* (*Final Round*), but, now also including other media such as the comic, poetry, photographic art, and travel journal. This makes the opening anecdote even more poignant:

Cortázar's desire to return to the novel undoubtedly implied a reappraisal of his own relationship to fiction.

Jaime Alazraki writes that the ideas that Cortázar had of the novel were influenced by three aesthetic and philosophical movements: romanticism, existentialism, and surrealism (11). Even his impertinent attitude toward the restrictions of the conventional novel had its roots in Cortázar's formal reflections and preoccupations in relation to the novel per se. Indeed, before publishing *Los premios*, Cortázar wrote two essays, "Notas sobre la novela contemporánea" (Notes on the Contemporary Novel, 1948) and "Situación de la novela" (The Situation of the Novel, 1950), which reveal his profound examination of the genre and his conscience of the limits and possibilities of the novel as a form (Alazraki 10): "They also show that long before Morelli's notebooks included in *Rayuela*, for Cortázar to write novels and theorize on this expressive instrument as such, constituted the heads and tails of one single operation" (Alazraki 10–11).[7]

Cortázar evolved ideologically from anti-Peronist to socialist. However, despite his own contradictions, he always believed that no one, let alone a political ideology or a government, should force a writer to follow imposed rigid formulas.[8] Intellectual restrictions were as intolerable as political ones. When his literature reflected this belief, emphasizing, for instance, the central need for humor and playfulness as part of a political revolution, left-wing intellectuals accused him of not taking politics seriously enough or of not being sufficiently committed to the revolutionary cause. In effect, the more Cortázar got involved in actual political struggles outside his world of fiction, the more emphatic his fear would become regarding the increasing rigidity of revolutionary processes. Consequently, toward the end of his life, indeed around the time when he met Valenzuela, Cortázar felt that his understanding of politics and the role of it in his writings was certainly different and distanced him from many of the active revolutionaries. According to Peter Standish, it is true that Cortázar's literature, and his novels in particular, lends itself to multiple interpretations because it is not a kind of literature proposing "unique and absolute truths" (469).

For this reason, the political dimension of his writings also varies in manifestation and meaning. However, this is not only because Cortázar disagreed with aesthetic dogmas, but also because his own understanding of political revolution was constant and all-embracing: "The contribution of a great kind of literature is crucial for a political revolution to be able to move from its prior steps and its material victories, to a revolution which is all-encompassing" ("Literatura en la revolución" 68).[9] Hence, for Cortázar, a revolutionary novel is not one that necessarily has a "revolutionary content," but rather one that "aims to revolutionize the novel itself" (73).[10] This observation leads to the conclusion that almost everything written by Cortázar, insofar as he tried to question received aesthetic—and political—norms and categories, tried to be revolutionary and, generally speaking, also political. This is what differentiated his novels not only from those of his peers of the Boom, but also from those written by a generation of Latin American novelists. It is also why it is impossible to talk about Cortázar's novelistic project without talking about politics.

In "Notas" (1948), Cortázar states that: "the novel is one of those monsters that man accepts, encourages and keeps by his side; a mixture of heterogeneities, a griffin turned into a domestic animal" (193).[11] Cortázar continues this imagery in another early article, "Situación" (1950), where the novel is described as "the impure thing, the monster of multiple legs and multiple eyes" (307).[12] Cortázar further claims the novel is needed "to know himself and know the world" ("Situación" 300).[13] He argues that since the beginning of the twentieth century, the novel as a genre has moved progressively toward an "immediate reality," so that by 1950 what inspires novelists to write is that "visible desire to establish direct contact with the current quandaries of man, in the sphere of historical facts, and also of participation and of immediate life" ("Situación" 315–16).[14] For Cortázar, the novel is, therefore, the literary genre that should allow a person to know the world and, in particular, to know the history and his own position in it. He affirms that the novel's basic aim should be "to manage to comprehend and contain the totality of a person," and that, in effect, novels are written either "to escape reality or stand in opposition to it, showing it just as it is or should be" ("Situación" 315).[15]

These first texts make clear that Cortázar aimed to provide his readers with a universe that would allow them to think about themselves, while at the same time establishing a direct, immediate link with their historical present. For him, within the context of modern reality, characters have an uneasy proximity to the readers: "there are no longer *characters* in the contemporary novel. There are just accomplices. Our accomplices who are also witnesses getting on the stand to declare things which almost always condemn us . . ., helping [us] to understand more clearly the precise nature of the human situation of our time" ("Situación 302–03).[16]

El examen follows a group of five friends for one day and one night prior to a final university examination that two of them have to take. It is set against the surreal backdrop of a sinking Buenos Aires, invaded by a steadily thickening fog, bizarre flying mushrooms, and choking fluff floating in the air. The gradual physical disintegration of the urban landscape is never explained in the plot; moreover, the characters do not find it particularly odd or threatening. In terms of form, it is a conventional novel, indeed with a quasi-Aristotelian classic unity of time and space. As in *Los premios*, the fantastical elements coexist with and are interwoven into the reality that the characters inhabit.

In a note to *El examen*, written more than thirty years after the novel had been completed, Cortázar mentions the supposed premonition that the text manifests with regard to events that took place in Argentina between 1952 and 1953. Namely, the death of Eva Perón and the state funeral witnessed by more than two million people (Luna, 56). *El examen*, narrated in the present, foreshadows a future that, according to Cortázar, is bound to be the repetition of that present. So much so that in the note, he concludes that the novel remains pertinent because "the nightmare from which it was born remains" (5).[17] Importantly, Cortázar then stresses the need for *El examen* to be published, given its "free language, its fable without morale, its Buenos Aires melancholy" (5).[18] It is tempting to read this solemn statement as somewhat ironic, based on the fact that the novel suffered from indirect political censorship. Cortázar wrote in a letter to Fredi Guthman: "[*El examen*] won't be published due to issues with its plot, but it has been useful for me to finally write the way I like to write: in total freedo" (*Cartas I*, 263)[19] However, the book was rejected, by the then editor of Losada, allegedly because of the use of profanity. In any case, it is important to underline that what defines the essence of one of Cortázar's the first novels remains at the core of all his novelistic corpus: the search for aesthetic freedom.

Preoccupation with the negative effects of Peronism on culture and education is expressed unambiguously in *El examen*, *Divertimento* and *Diario de Andrés Fava*. *Divertimento* was Cortázar's first novel, completed in February 1949. Like *El examen*, and indeed all of Cortázar's novels, the protagonists are a group of friends, called "Vive como puedas" ("Live as you can"), that very much foreshadows *Rayuela's* "Club de la Serpiente" ("Serpent Club"), and like all of these early novels up until and partly including *Rayuela*, the location is Buenos Aires. It is conventional in form, but interwoven with pretentious conversations on art, poetry, music, and politics, irrupts an early manifestation of Cortázar's fantastic element: the ghost of Argentinian historical figure Facundo Quiroga's wife. In turn, *Diario de Andrés Fava* was part of *El examen* but was then excluded. As the title implies, it is written in the form of a diary. Although it is a diary without dates, it keeps the genre's philosophical and introspective content. Andrés Fava, the sole character in this book, is one of the protagonists of *El examen*. He was Cortázar's first *alter ego* and, even though he allegedly commits suicide at the end of *El examen*, his namesake reappears in *Libro de Manuel* representing—like Oliveira in *Rayuela*—the *petit-bourgeois* intellectual. Andrés, in this early novel, lives in a world of ambivalences and contradictions (and in that sense, he seems to be a genesis of Oliveira), and the text somehow reflects this in its chaotic lack of linearity. Reading *Diario* along with along with *El examen* enables the reader to get to know, as it were, this character in an unconventional and playful way. Unconventionality and playfulness would remain at the center of Cortázar's conception of the novel as a literary form of expression.

Another of Cortázar's central themes prior to his departure for Paris in 1951 is the sense of entrapment and hopelessness about the future. For example, Andrés Fava states: "Later nothing [. . .]. Please forget about that word for a while" (*EX* 216).[20] For Andrés, the future is so bleak that it is futile even to use the word "later." In addition, when talking to his former lover Clara, Andrés sees "Clara's skull underneath her face and her hair. . . . The skull could speak. Future death inhabited under this fog, under the stench of the city" (197–98).[21] In his analysis of the "Buenos Aires melancholy" of *El examen*, Patrick O'Connor defines the metaphor of the skull as a metonymy for the novel's mood (O'Connor 11). While anticipating the hopelessness of the characters' fate, this image, besides summarizing the novel's mood, emphasizes Andrés's understanding of the city's physical decomposition as a sign of their lifeless, hopeless future.

Towards the end of *Divertimento*, ironically as he proposes a toast, one of the main characters, el Insecto, announces: "Tomorrow, which is the big word, the great dispenser of postponement . . . Tomorrow, repeated Marta. How could she even imagine such a word? *Demain, mañana*, tomorrow. What horror" (139).[22] If there is no tomorrow, and history has become, as the narrator in *El examen* says, "a single moment, a single miserable word" (97) the protagonists are faced with a single dilemma or, according to Clara, "an ontological *cachet*," namely: "*To leave or to stay / The game of being / It hardly is – later – the time before*" (224).[23] Given the consequences of Peronism, the characters feel that to live immersed in such falsity is immoral and that the only solution is to escape. Thus, Juan and Clara leave physically on a boat that sails out into the Río de la Plata, while Andrés, who states "I am also leaving,"[24] kills himself and also takes the life of his immaterial double Abel, in a kind of atavistic duel. In turn, Stella seems to escape intellectually, prioritizing trivia such as providing food and water for the canary over the pressing circumstances. Finally, the fifth member of the group, "el cronista," instead of reporting on the crumbling of Buenos Aires, sleeps soundly. Possibly commenting on the "dormant" state of serious journalism during Peronism, "el cronista" is thus left to his own parallel, dream-like reality as the novel concludes.

And it is not just the characters who go into exile. Cortázar's anti-Peronism would admittedly be the main factor behind his leaving the country for Paris in 1951, never to return to live in Argentina. Within a generalized alienation of the intellectuals from the Peronist regime, Cortázar's self-imposed exile could be said to be intrinsically linked to the deterioration of culture under Perón: "I didn't come to Paris to sanctify anything but rather because I was drowning inside a Peronism that I was unable to understand in 1951 when a loudspeaker in the corner of my house prevented me from listening to Bela Bartok's quartets" ("Carta a Saúl Sosnowski" 78).[25]

Somewhat ignored by critics, *Los premios*, Cortázar's first published novel, shows "his early preoccupation with the destiny of his fellow men, his personal way of experiencing reality and his capacity for an aesthetic organization" (Maturo 87).[26] The novel tells the story the winners of a state-run lottery, all from Buenos Aires. They represent different sectors of Argentinian society: from the *petit-bourgeois* couple, Lucio and Nora, to the very humble Presutti family. When they are all summoned to the London bar in downtown Buenos Aires, however, they are told that their prize is a cruise on the *Malcolm*. The cruise will last three or four months, but the destination remains a mystery. Once onboard, what is also kept undisclosed is why the passengers are not allowed access to the stern of the boat. This is where the novel's monstrous element tacitly resides. As the passengers insist on being told why they cannot breach the stern, the myth and fear of a monstrous presence increases. This brings about such a crisis that the journey eventually has to be truncated, and after only three days, the *Malcolm* is back in Buenos Aires, after a bizarre and intense journey to nowhere.

Even though never depicted, the idea that a monster is onboard affects the passengers. Their reactions and interactions are dictated by their fear of the unknown, but also by the threat that the unknown might take over the ship. The intrusion of the monstrous, like the gradual sinking of the city in *El examen*, introduces a fantastic element into the text, following Cortázar's notions of the fantastic as an irruption to the logically expected. As readers, we know that it is illogical for there to be flying mushrooms and for no one to perceive that as abnormal; likewise, we deem it irrational for there to be an invisible monster on a boat and for that to be ultimately the cause of someone's death (Medrano is killed as he tries to discover what is on the stern). Central to this fantastic dimension is the idea, in both *El examen* and *Los premios*, of an intangible yet ubiquitous presence that grows and takes over the space, be it physically or psychologically. Cortázar uses the fantastic to highlight specific aspects of the given logical reality from which the fantastic element emerges. In this reading, these aspects, through the use of allegory, are political, notwithstanding the inherent ambivalence of Cortázar's use of the fantastic. In turn, this ambivalence will become more acute through Cortázar's aesthetic and political evolution.

In describing his own uncertainty regarding the monstrous element in *Los premios*, Cortázar places himself in the same position as his characters: "I was in the same position as López, Medrano, or Raúl. . . I didn't know what was happening astern either" (qtd. in Harss et al. 225). Keeping the monstrous—that which is fantastic, but also allegorical—undefined calls to mind several other instances when Cortázar, looking back on the inspiration for his own writings, chooses to retain the vagueness of central elements, apparently to avoid falling into categorical notions that would, in turn, restrict the artistic freedom that he deemed paramount.

Likewise, in the introductory note that he appended to *Los premios*, he clarifies: "I would like to clarify to you [to you, reader] . . . that I was *not* moved by allegorical intentions, let alone ethical ones" (440).[27] From very early on, Cortázar would find it essential to include explanatory notes in his novels, expressing a need to define his ideological position in relation to his fictions, so as to leave no room for aesthetic or indeed political (mis)understandings. It would appear that at this early stage, Cortázar opts to hold the explicitly political at arm's length, in his understanding that if a novel is too political, it may lose aesthetic value. In other words, at this point, he attempts to keep the explicitly political and the literary separate, even though his writings contradict that. The vexed issue of politics versus aesthetics preoccupies Cortázar from the beginning of his writing career right up to his final days, with *Libro de Manuel* being probably the most controversial and in terms of its reception, the most problematic of his creative outcomes.

Much has been written about Cortázar's best-known novel. Yet, in keeping with the logic of this article, I will look at it in terms of Cortázar's political ideas. At the time of writing *Rayuela* in the early 1960s, he had not yet openly identified with any political ideology, though he was growing closer to the left. This began to be articulated in *Los premios* with the characters' expressions of solidarity and the possibility of a "new man" embodied in Medrano. So, while writing *Rayuela*, Cortázar was searching for a political ideology, and this search is at the core of this novel. It is this search, this permanent state of questioning which in turn made *Rayuela* one of the most important expressions of Latin American modernity for, in the novel, as Carlos Fuentes claimed, "we see better than ever before our doubts, our debts, our possibilities" (42).[28] It is through that incessant questioning that Oliveira, *Rayuela*'s main character and Cortázar's alter ego, reveals his incapacity, and at times reluctance, to commit himself to any form of action. Cortázar does not aim to impose a political stance upon the reader. Still, through Oliveira's unwillingness to take a political position, he presents a crucial dilemma central to the political processes of the 1960s, and that remains equally significant for the reader. In many respects, the kind of questioning prevalent in *Rayuela* would gradually acquire a more explicitly political tone over the course of Cortázar's evolution as a novelist.

After traveling to Cuba in 1963 and openly converting to socialism, it would appear that Cortázar's ideological quandary had been solved. However, this is a simplification of his position regarding artistic creation. For Oliveira, however, the dilemma remains openly unresolved. He will not engage in any form of political struggle, yet he is still pulled toward some kind of collective solidarity. With hindsight, for Cortázar, it was a sort of sporadic reflection that contained the most explicit political meaning of the novel. He declares so to González Bermejo: "Without everything that is translated in *Rayuela*, I wouldn't have been able to take this step which abruptly took me to discover Latin America, by means of the Cuban Revolution... Don't Oliveira and Morelli already say it? 'My salvation... also has to be the salvation for everybody'" (78).[29] Yet, although concerned for the collective, this assertion remains within the protagonist's fundamental unresolved dilemma. Beyond Cortázar's somewhat selective view of Oliveira, it is Oliveira's reluctance to commit himself that is key to the political dimension of the novel. In that reluctance, there is a will to remain outside politics. Nevertheless, despite his ideological immobility, his "moderate ataraxia," as the narrator calls it (*Hopscotch* 18),[30] Oliveira is not by any means an apolitical being. The unresolved action/inaction dilemma, and the intellectual as well as emotional paralysis that this provokes in him, allows Oliveira—indeed, it almost obliges him—to stand back and observe both sides. And although he is politically passive, it is through that detachment that Oliveira feels that he can truly observe the world (and believe in bad faith that he is not part of it). This correlates to what Cortázar was feeling at the time in relation to his own position in the world and, in particular, when it came to justifying his "being" Argentinian and getting involved with Argentinian as well as Latin American political issues without giving up his Parisian life. For Cortázar, this refusal to commit allowed him to achieve greater insight into the issues in question. In turn, by means of the attitudes that resulted from Oliveira's observations, the novel transmits, perhaps, a will to rebel against that acquiescence. Although *Rayuela* does not contain an explicit political message, it does convey a spirit of rupture beyond its unconventional aesthetics. Presenting us with a protagonist who chooses to remain disengaged from his socio-political context can, in itself, be read as a provocation within the ideological "subversion" that *Rayuela* came to represent.

Indeed, remarkably on the back cover of the first edition of the novel, iconic editor Francisco Porrúa described the novel as "the construction of a counter-novel in literary terms and of a denunciation in ideological ones; . . . an exasperated complain against the inauthenticity of human life and of aesthetic and psychological literature" (qtd. in Montaldo 603).[31] With its ground-breaking "instruction manual," *Rayuela* is written for a reader who not only is expected to be "active" in leaping between chapters and not following a conventional order, but also in allowing for the possibility of a process of questioning.

In terms of form, *Rayuela* is undoubtedly the most successful representation of that which Sosnowski identified as bringing into question all kinds of limitations. The fact that the author from the onset tells us readers directly how to read the novel, and provides us with instructions, not only was revolutionary in many ways, but it was also playful, controversial, alive. In other words, the explosion that *Rayuela* brought about in terms of the concept of the novel was the very essence of Cortázar's ambition as a novelist and as an intellectual. Cortázar tells González Bermejo: "*Rayuela* is a sort of demand for total authenticity in a man; a request for the reader to do some self-criticism and merciless revisioning, so that all the pre-received ideas, all the cultural inheritance can be criticized" (72).[32] In *Rayuela*, this is spelled out by Morelli, a radical fictional writer and theorist who reflects on the art of fiction, playfully alluding back to the book we are reading. In Morelli's schema it is the knowing—as opposed to Oliveira's observing—that has to be active, in order to change something in the ideological structure that society imposes upon us. It is there that the "merciless revisioning" that Cortázar calls for takes place. It is an act of revision that admittedly is not exclusively political but that, nonetheless, necessarily engages with politics: "to use the novel . . . just as one uses a revolver to keep the peace, changing its symbol" (396).[33]

Whether following the active or passive reading of *Rayuela*, only a few chapters into the novel, Oliveira displays his unresolved dilemmas between aesthetics and political engagement and action or inaction (chapter 3). *Rayuela* thus presents political elements that, although they do not transform it into a political novel, nevertheless give rise to uncomfortable ethical as well as political questions that readers cannot avoid, and which could challenge their political ideology. The novel does not aim for catharsis; rather, it seeks to instill in the reader a degree of estrangement that allows them to carry out a renewed reading of their own principles and of those of the socio-political space that they inhabit. Thus, as Morelli would argue, the novel is a dynamic bridge that does not carry a specific message or a political slogan, but rather aims to function as a coagulant, merging all the different factors that should trigger readers to reflect upon their own ideology, as well society and their position in it.

The implicit political dimension of *Rayuela* lies in the capacity of the book to make the reader think not only about the revolution of aesthetic conventions and narrative traditions, but also about the implications of a renewed political consciousness. It is not in vain that, when it was published, *Rayuela* was understood by the intelligentsia of the Argentinian left to be a model of ideological questioning. In this sense, whereas in *El examen* and *Los premios* the political dimension remained within the confine of allegory, in *Rayuela* the political is implicit and to an extent utopian, in that it relates to a necessity of questioning thought and behavior, responsibility and awareness, outside the realm of the fictional text. This explains in part the novel's positive reception among the left since, as Omar Prego Gadea elucidates, *Rayuela* "coincides with an era of radical questioning among the Latin American youth, an era of deep historical shake-ups" (114). In response to the reading of *Rayuela* as a "revolutionary" novel, Cortázar claimed: "The notion of *Rayuela* as a revolutionary novel . . . is one that I share. And it's not just me, but also the most lucid of critics who have underlined that a book that does not contain a single word of politics . . . does contain at the same time a series of explosive elements that must be considered revolutionary" (qtd. in Prego 188).[34]

Five years later, Cortázar published *62/modelo para armar*. Although *62* stands on its own ground, it is supplemented by Cortázar's two "collage books," *La vuelta al día en ochenta mundos* (*Around the Day in 80 Worlds*, 1967) and *Último Round* (Last Round,

1969). The possibility of fundamental social and political change signaled by the triumph of the Cuban Revolution in 1959 was accompanied by a shift in the conception of the role of the artist and intellectual in Latin American society. As a prime example of this, the Boom was said to have its main foundation in political changes on the continent. Cortázar was, to this extent, not exceptional in being inspired by the social utopia that the revolution represented; at least temporarily, many of the best-known figures of Latin American literature showed their support for the Cuban cause. García Márquez, Vargas Llosa, Fuentes would all at some point believe that they could inspire radical political change through their literature. Yet, it was apparent that some writers' support for Cuba depended upon factors that little had to do with political ideology. This was not the case for Cortázar; for him, unlike many or most of his peers who believed in Cuba as part of some kind of temporary or opportunistic ideological affair, Cuba became, in his words, his own "Road to Damascus" (*Cartas 2* 1225).[35]

In 1969 David Viñas published an article that seemed to go against the dominant trends in literary criticism of that time. One year after the publication of *62*, Viñas issued a warning regarding what he called the "dangers" of Cortázar's increasing influence upon new writers. Fascination with the formal experimentation embodied by *62*—Viñas claimed—would lead to nothing but the characteristics that he associated with Cortázar, namely, "increasing marginalization," "abdication from any modifying project," "lack of interest," and "total isolation" (73).[36] For Viñas, *62* represented part of a process of depoliticization that could only lead to isolation from socio-political realities and to political impotence. Óscar Collazos, likewise, argued that novels like *62* were turning their back on the political concerns of Latin America in defense of their avant-garde aesthetic exploration (29). In the face of such criticism, Cortázar felt moved to defend the literary experimentation of his novel, claiming that he had to write *62* as "un experimento de la experimentación" (an experiment on experimentation) in an attempt to continue to explore uncharted aesthetic territories (*Último round 1* 260), irrespective of what political ideologies dictated. Aware of the reactions that *62* would spark, even before it was published, Cortázar wrote in a letter to Martiniquais writer Jean Bernabé: "It is almost amusing to tell you . . . that I am about to correct. . . a novel that is going to spark fury in all of my 'engaged' friends because they will surely find it *insolently literary*. I still believe that man's freedom can be achieved through many paths, even when we think of the new man as envisaged by Che" (*Cartas 2* 1222).[37]

It is due to its "insolent literariness" that *62* could be said to represent one of the two paths in Cortázar's writing after Cuba. Indeed, given its hermeticism, *62* exemplifies the path of "pure fiction." Due to its content and its formal complexity, *62* has largely been considered an ahistorical and explicitly non-political novel; for critics such as Jason Weiss, this was only natural, for Cortázar had always insisted that his artistic freedom was not to be compromised to serve any purpose other than its own (91). For other critics and fellow Latin American writers, *62* was simply unacceptable if Cortázar were to be taken "seriously" as a committed socialist writer. Yet it is clear that "seriousness" was never at the center of Cortázar's concerns, even less so when it came to politics and his novels. On the contrary, he will insist on the urgent need for humor within the somewhat rigid political revolution. So, although the novel is not explicitly political, it is permeated with the ideas that Cortázar was dealing with at the time.

Like the "Club de la Serpiente" in *Rayuela*, in *62* there is also a "revolutionary" group, yet this is a group based upon a seemingly utopian point of view; the more avant-garde aim of wanting to break with the tradition of a pre-established order. Unlike "La Joda" of *Libro de Manuel* and their *microagitaciones*, the groups in *Rayuela* as in *62* present themselves as bourgeois, aloof, and decentered, yet there is certainly a presence of a group concept somewhat unified by one common drive in *62* (Franco 115).

62 begins with an introductory note that explains that the novel stems from chapter 62 of *Rayuela* in which Morelli describes his ideal novel as "everything would be a kind of disquiet, a continuous uprooting, a territory where psychological causality would yield disconcertedly . . . " (*Hopscotch* 363).[38] Following Morelli's principles, *62* is a novel that defies standard notions of fixity in the reading experience, while challenging conventional formulations of linearity, characterization and narrative. *62* has no thematic center; ultimately, its very a-centeredness must be understood paradoxically as the novel's unifying trait. It could be argued that *62* is that Flaubertian "novel about nothing," which, more than a decade earlier, even before Morelli, Andrés Fava aimed to write (*Diario* 112).

62 is made up of unconnected fragments that, given its subtitle, the reader will hope to assemble somehow. In the introductory note, Cortázar mockingly warns his readers that the assemblage that the novel requires will not be intra-textual, as it was in *Rayuela*, but rather, arguably as part of the book's "transgressions of literary convention" (*62* 7),[39] the montage will be made by the reader, a posteriori and outside the text. Cortázar explains that this montage should be "like a decant process happening after reading whereby the reader must choose what counts and what ultimately can give sense to so much biased stupidity" (*Cartas 3* 1333).[40] Furthermore, the search for rational sense within "so much biased stupidity" needs not to be restricted to the aesthetic realm of the novel, but could effectively be extended to the day-to-day world of the reader. This in turn relates to the understanding that Cortázar had of literature as a means to opening oneself to different views of reality.

Libro de Manuel describes the day-to-day reality of a group of friends, "La Joda," mostly Argentinian exiles, living in Paris. Simultaneously with the "political" activities they carry out within the group, such as planning how to raise money for revolution through extorsive kidnappings, they all contribute to the writing of a book for baby Manuel, the son of two of the novel's protagonists, Susana and Patricio. The material that the characters put together for his scrapbook ranges from newspaper articles and advertisements to official government reports, and even the typed minutes of a meeting between a journalist and Fidel Castro (*Libro* 273–79). The prologue to the book explains that these newspaper articles, which are reproduced in their original French, Spanish, Italian, or English, were the actual articles that Cortázar read, cut out and kept as he was writing *Libro de Manuel*: "One should not be surprised by the frequent inclusion of news stories that were being read as the book was taking shape . . . the Monday and Thursday news that became of momentary interest to the characters was incorporated into the course of my work on Monday and Thursday" (*Manual for Manuel* 3).[41] As Cortázar fur-ther clarifies in his "Corrección de pruebas," this had to be done in an attempt to "[tell] a story that pretends to reflect also our own History of this very morning," since in effect, "the book's intention of immediacy is the only reason why it was written" (27).[42]

The documents are inserted in the text to bring to the fore a reality for the reader to see and act upon. With time, the action implied in such witnessing seems to be the prevention of historical amnesia. Cortázar alludes to this in his note with regard to the news of the killing of Israeli athletes in Munich and the total lack of journalistic coverage of the events happening at the same time in the Patagonian city of Trelew (*Libro* 9),[43] where sixteen members of left-wing Peronist movements (including ERP, Montoneros, and FAR) were executed after they tried to escape from prison. This view of the press as arbitrary truth-pickers is repeated in the novel through some of the comments that the characters make about the manipulation of information, as they read out the clippings.

Libro de Manuel's collage format brought Cortázar closer to his ambition to awaken the reader through the insertion of political facts that Cortázar considered important and wanted to put forward in testimonial form. More directly than in conventional prose, the constant visual interruptions caused by the reproduction of newspaper arti-cles, in their original format, create an alienating effect that has to do precisely with their testimonial nature. The clippings, thus, represent the reality of the non-fictional world during the actual writing of the novel, while they also constitute a non-fictional frame for the fiction. This double reality in the form of the novel becomes testimony to histor-ical events but also of an aesthetic experiment.

Cortázar would have it that the "rule of the game" is that these clippings represent, but also *are*, reality so that when combined with the absurd and humoristic elements of the novel, that "reality" becomes more realistic: "The 'real' thing: the clippings. The 'absurd': details such as the use of the penguin to carry fake dollars. The convergence of these two makes reality more real."[44] It could be said, though, that the insertions in fact under-line the "authenticity" of the fictional storyline with which they are linked. However, Cortázar's introductory note, telling us about the origins of the newspaper articles in the authoritative voice of Cortázar the author, provides a testimonial dimension to the insertions that the reader cannot then assume to be fictional. This quality is enhanced by the seemingly unaltered typographical reproduction of the insertions.

Even though readers might decide to visually skip the extra-textual insertions in their avidness to continue with the flow of the fictional plot, the contents of the fragments are nevertheless incorporated into the novel's narrative thread. Therefore, even if the reader chooses not to scrutinize the insertions, they will be "forced" to read about them through the narrative. This emphasizes the irony behind Cortázar's assertion that "those who don't want to see it [the evidence], won't" ("Mi ametralladora" 12),[45] for eve-rything that is laid out typographically on what Parkinson Zamora calls the "verbal surface of the narrative," is also explained within the prose (60). *Libro de Manuel* thus challenges the reader by combining revolutionary didacticism with avantgarde stylistic techniques. These techniques are introduced with the aim of conveying political signifi-cance through the alienation produced by the "authenticity" and contents of the articles enclosed. Although it may be argued that newspaper articles are familiar, when inserted within the fictional narrative they hinder the reader from fully surrendering to a fictional realm and, thereby, have a disrupting, alienating effect on the reading experience.

By means of this collage technique, Manuel's book is being created as the narrative progresses. The reader is effectively in baby Manuel's place, reading the book. The lack of explicit connection among the narrative sections emphasizes the idea that, more than in any of Cortázar's previous novels, the reader has to be an active participant in connecting and understanding the text as a unit. In this sense, the structure of the text aims to make the reader aware of the political reality presented through the inserted newspaper clippings. Each inserted fragment represents a halt, not only in the visual flow of the narrative but also, crucially, in the continuity of the story. Consequently, through the collage technique, the reader is expected to be emotionally drawn to the plot's action, while at the same time alienated from it by the challenge implied in the novel's form and content. However, this inevitably ceases to surprise the reader as they work through the entire length of the novel; so that in the very repetition of the technique, the shocking effect that succeeds in the stories, in *Libro de Manuel* loses impact as the insertions gain predictability.

The novelistic project of Julio Cortázar was a process of relentless exploration that began with the more formally conventional early novels, *El examen*, *Divertimento*, and *Los premios*, moved on to break many aesthetic norms with *Rayuela*, concerned itself with metaphysical experimentation in *62*, and with playful combinations of formats in the fragmentary *La vuelta* and *Ultimo Round*, to arrive at *Libro de Manuel*, where many of the elements explored in all the previous writings are combined, with the additional historical urgency and a desire for politically "useful" effects. It could be argued that, given the negative reception, and even rejection, of *Libro de Manuel* at the time, Cortázar finally decided to separate his longer fiction from his active political life. Politics would remain at the core of some of his most celebrated later short stories, yet would be absent from his other books, such as *Territorios* or *Autonautas de la cosmopista*. Cortázar would, however, also carry on exploring other aesthetic media in order to better communicate the political message he believed in. Yet, he would never return to the genre of the novel, although, thanks to Valenzuela, we now know he had intended to.

In a 1980 interview, Cortázar claimed, "The novel is truly the open order. [. . .] since it's open, you can take a leap of faith, and the characters even begin to live their lives almost on their own. [. . .] the novel gives you the compensation of improvisation, of freedom" (Naper et al.).[46] In that relentless exploration of the freedom that the novel as a form provides, Cortázar found a new way of narrating experience. Anything that is avant-garde, novels that are "insolently literary" will always be political in the sense that they purposefully go against orthodoxia, they rebel against the official model, the official version. Cortázar's novels, certainly after *Los premios*, conspire against all things orthodox in more radical ways, and perhaps more genuine, than any other writers of the Boom, and indeed, of any other Latin American novelist of the twentieth century. This avidness to explore the novel as a form, to break the conventions of his own prose even when it had been successful, undoubtedly distinguished Cortázar from the writers of his generation. It is impossible to know or even get close to guessing what that other novel he had in mind and did *not* tell Valenzuela about was going to be like but, without a doubt, it would have been yet another innovative explosion of the novel as a form; perhaps an endless kind of novel that renews itself, like Morelli would have it.

Notes

1. "Me lo debo . . . Tantas veces postergando la necesidad de escribir ficción. Se lo debo a la literatura que tanto me ha ayudado. Me piden cuentos, y yo les digo sí, claro, y en lugar de cuentos les hago llegar un texto sobre América Central" (qtd. in Valenzuela 13–14).
2. "Si explico algo que estoy escribiendo lo destruyo *ab ovo,* si se dice así, lo hago polvo si solamente lo insinúo antes" (qtd. in Valenzuela, 14).
3. "Uno de los rasgos definitorios de la obra de Cortázar es el cruce de géneros, el cuestionamiento de toda frontera y el cultivo eficaz de una única expresión literaria" (Sosnowski 9–10).
4. "La obra de Cortázar incita a un estado de disponibilidad. Recorrerla en cualquiera de sus tramos es admitir que en cualquier momento y desde cualquier renglón puede surgir la vuelta que por una vez y ya para siempre, trastocará lo anticipado. Muchos de tus textos apuntan hacia espacios recónditos que son sometidos a lo inesperado, a lo racionalmente inaudito; se instalan en el cuestionamiento e impugnación de lo convencional" (Sosnowski 9–10).
5. "La indicación súbita de que al margen de las leyes aristotélicas y de nuestra mente razonante, existen mecanismos perfectamente válidos . . . que nuestro cerebro lógico no acepta" (González Bermejo 98).
6. "Lo fantástico es algo que se presenta sin ser llamado. Para mí ha sido siempre una 'irrupción' . . . una ruptura de la causalidad o la temporalidad, de las leyes físicas y psíquicas. 'Todo iba bien, y justo entonces'" (Cortázar Papers).
7. "Demuestran también, mucho antes de los *Cuadernos* de Morelli incluidos en *Rayuela,* que para Cortázar novelar y teorizar sobre el instrumento expresivo constituían el anverso y reverso de una misma operación" (Alazraki 10–11).
8. On the political and aesthetic evolution in Cortázar's fiction, see my *The Representation of the Political Element in Selected Writings of Julio Cortázar.*
9. "El aporte de una gran literatura es fundamental para que una revolución política pase de sus etapas previas y de su triunfo material, a la revolución total" (Cortázar, "Literatura en la revolución" 68).
10. "revolucionar la novela misma" (Cortázar "Literatura en la revolución" 73).
11. "La novela es uno de esos monstruos que el hombre acepta, alienta, mantiene a su lado; mezcla de heterogeneidades, grifo convertido en animal doméstico" (Cortázar, *Obra Crítica* 2 193).
12. "La cosa impura, el monstruo de muchas patas y muchos ojos" (Cortázar, *Obra Crítica* 2 307).
13. "Para conocerse y conocer" (Cortázar, *Obra Crítica* 2 300).
14. " el deseo visible de establecer contacto directo con la problemática actual del hombre en un plano de hechos, de participación y vida inmediata" (Cortázar, *Obra Crítica* 2 315–16).
15. "Para escapar de cierta realidad, o para oponerse a ella, mostrándola tal como es o debería ser" (Cortázar, *Obra Crítica* 2 315).

16. "Ya no hay *personajes* en la novela moderna; hay solo cómplices. Cómplices nuestros, que son también testigos y suben a un estrado para declarar cosas que, casi siempre, nos condenan . . . ayud[ándonos] a comprender con más claridad la exacta naturaleza de la situación humana de nuestro tiempo" (Cortázar, *Obra Crítica* 2 302–3).

17. "La pesadilla de donde nació sigue despierta" (Cotázar, *El examan* 5).

18. "Su libre lenguaje, su fábula sin moraleja, su melancolía porteña" (Cortázar, *El examen* 15).

19. " . . . no se podrá publicar por razones de tema, pero me ha servido para escribir por fin como a mí me gusta, en plena libertad"(*Cartas/1*. 253).

20. "Después nada . . . Olvidate de esa palabra por un rato" (Cortázar, *El examen* 216).

21. "el cráneo de Clara bajo su rostro y su pelo. . . . El cráneo hablaba. La muerte futura vivía bajo este humo, este hedor de la ciudad" (*EX*, 197–98).

22. "Mañana, que es la gran palabra, la gran dispensadora del aplazamiento . . . . Mañana – repitió Marta. ¿Cómo pudo imaginarse siquiera la palabra? Demain, tomorrow, mañana, qué horror" (Cortázar, *Divertimento* 139).

23. "un momento, una mísera palabra" (Examen 97; "resuena altisonante y almafuerte" (*Examen*, 97); "un *cachet* ontológico'" (*Examen*, 223); "*Irse, quedarse / Juego del ser / Apenas es - después - el antes*" (*Examen* 224, 224).

24. "Yo también me voy" (*Examen*, 241).

25. "No me vine a París para santificar nada, sino porque me ahogaba dentro de un peronismo que era incapaz de comprender en 1951, cuando un altoparlante en la esquina de mi casa me impedía escuchar los cuartetos de Bela Bartok" (Cortázar, *Cartas* 3 78).

26. " . . . su temprana preocupación por el destino de los suyos, su personal manera de sentir la realidad y su capacidad de organización estética" (Maturo 87).

27. "Quisiera decirle [a usted, lector] . . . que *no* me movieron intenciones alegóricas y mucho menos éticas" (*Pre* 440).

28. "en él vemos, mejor que nunca, nuestras dudas, nuestras deudas, nuestras posibilidades." (Fuentes, 157).

29. "Sin todo lo que traduce *Rayuela* yo no habría podido dar este paso que me llevó bruscamente a descubrir, a través de la Revolución Cubana, una América Latina . . . ¿No dicen ya Oliveira y Morelli en *Rayuela*: 'mi salvación . . . tiene que ser también la salvación de todos, hasta el último de los hombres?" (González Bermejo 78).

30. "ataraxia moderada" (Cortázar, *Rayuela* 32).

31. "a construcción de una contranovela en lo literario y de una denuncia en cuanto a lo ideológico. . . exasperada denuncia de la inautenticidad de la vida humana y de la literatura estética y psicológica . . . *Rayuela* es un texto que vuelve obligadamente cómplice al lector, que busca una apertura", Francisco Porrúa qtd. in Graciela Montaldo, 'Destinos y recepción', in Cortázar, *Rayuela*, ed. Ortega and Yurkievich, pp. 597–612, at p. 603.

32. "La idea de *Rayuela* es una especie de petición de autenticidad total del hombre; que deje caer, por un mecanismo de autocrítica y de revisión despiadada, todas las ideas recibidas, toda la herencia cultural, pero no para prescindir de ellas sino para criticarlas".

33. "Usar la novela como se usa un revólver para defender la paz, cambiando su signo" (*Rayuela* 45253).

34. "La noción de *Rayuela* como novela revolucionaria . . . es la que tengo yo también. Y no solo yo, sino la crítica más lúcida acerca de *Rayuela* . . . que ha hecho hincapié en que un libro que no dice ni una sola palabra de política . . . contiene al mismo tiempo una serie de elementos explosivos que hay que considerar como revolucionarios" (Prego Gadea 188).

35. Cortázar to Jean Thiercelin, 2 February 1968, *Cartas/2* 1225.

36. "Arrinconamiento creciente," "abdicación de todo proyecto modificador," "desinterés," "enclaustramiento y encierro total" (Viñas, "Después de Cortázar" 73) 8.

37. "Es casi *divertido* decirle que . . . me dispongo a corregir . . . una novela que encolerizará a todos mis amigos "comprometidos" puesto que la encontrarán *insolentemente "literaria"*; yo sigo creyendo que por muchos caminos se va a la libertad del hombre e incluso al hombre nuevo que buscaba y quería el Che" (Cortázar to J. Bernabé, 30 January 1968, *Cartas/2* 1222.)

38. "Todo sería como una inquietud, un desasosiego, un desarraigo continuo, un territorio donde la causalidad psicológica cedería desconcertada, y esos fantoches [los personajes] se destrozarían o se amarían o se reconocerían sin sospechar demasiado que la vida trata de cambiar la clave en y a través y por ellos" (Cortázar, *Rayuela* 417).

39. "Diversas transgresiones a la convención literaria" (Cortázar, *62* 7).

40. " . . . como una decantación posterior a la lectura, en la que el lector debe escoger lo que cuenta y lo que finalmente puede dar un sentido a tanta insensatez parcial". Cortázar to Graciela Maturo, *Cartas/3* 1333.

41. "No sorprenderá la frecuente incorporación de noticias de la prensa, leídas a medida que el libro se iba haciendo . . . las noticias del lunes o del jueves que entraban en los intereses momentáneos de los personajes fueron incorporadas en el curso de mi trabajo del lunes o del jueves" (Cortázar, *Libro de Manuel* 7–8).

42. "una historia que pretende reflejar también nuestra Historia de esta misma mañana (porque) la intención de inmediatez del libro [es la] única razón de su escritura" (Cortázar, "Corrección de pruebas" 27.).

43. The note regarding the massacre in Patagonia is not included in the English translation.

44. Julio Cortázar Papers, Series 1C, Box 2, Folder 43. "Lo 'real': los recortes. Lo 'absurdo': cosas como el pingüino para traer dólares falsos. La convergencia de eso vuelve más real la realidad."

45. "El que quiera las verá, y el que no quiera verlas no las verá" (Cortázar "Mi ametralladora" 22).

46. "La novela es realmente el orden abierto. . . siendo abierta, tú te lanzas. Y los personajes empiezan a vivir un poco por su cuenta. . . la novela te da la compensación de la improvisación, de la libertad" (Namer et al.).

Works Cited.

Alazraki, Jaime. "Prólogo." *Obra crítica/2*, edited by Jaime Alazraki, Alfaguara, 1994, pp. 9–14.

Collazos, Óscar. "Encruzijada del lenguaje." *Literatura en la revolución, revolución en laliteratura. Polémica*, Óscar Collazos et.al. Siglo XXI, 1970, pp. 7–37.

Cortázar, Julio. *Around the Day in Eighty Worlds*. Translated by Thomas Christensen. North Point P, 1986.

Cortázar, Julio. *Cartas/1 1937–1963*. Edited by Aurora Bernárdez. Alfaguara, 2000.

Cortázar, Julio. *Cartas/2 1964–1968*, Edited by Aurora Bernárdez. Alfaguara, 2000.

Cortázar, Julio. *Cartas/3 1969–1983*. Edited by Aurora Bernárdez. Alfaguara, 2000.

Cortázar, Julio. "Corrección de pruebas en Alta Provenza." *Convergencias/divergencias/incidencias*, edited by Julio Ortega, Tusquets, 1973, pp. 13–36.

Cortázar, Julio. *Diario de Andrés Fava*. Alfaguara, 1995.

Cortázar, Julio. *Diary of Andrés Fava*. Translated by Anne McLean. Archipelago, 2005.

Cortázar, Julio. *Divertimento*. Sudamericana, 1986.

Cortázar, Julio. *El examen*. Sudamericana, 1986.

Cortázar, Julio. *Final Exam*. Translated by Alfred MacAdam. New Directions, 2000.

Cortázar, Julio. *Hopscotch*. Translated by Gregory Rabassa. Pantheon, 1966.

Cortázar, Julio. *La vuelta al día en ochenta mundos*. Siglo XXI, 1967.

Cortázar, Julio. *Libro de Manuel*. Sudamericana, 1973.

Cortázar, Julio. "Literatura en la revolución, revolución en la literatura: algunos malentendidos a liquidar." *Literatura en la revolución, revolución en la literatura. Polémica*, Óscar Collazos et.al. Siglo XXI, 1970, pp. 38–77.

Cortázar, Julio. *Los premios*. Santillana, 1960.

Cortázar, Julio. *Manual for Manuel*. Translated by Gregory Rabassa. Pantheon, 1978.

Cortázar, Julio. "Notas sobre la novela contemporánea." *Obra Crítica/2*. Alfaguara, 2004, pp. 191–204.

Cortázar, Julio. *Obra crítica/2*. Edited by Jaime Alazraki. Alfaguara, 1994.

Cortázar, Julio. *Rayuela*. Edhasa/Sudamericana, 1977.

Cortázar, Julio. *62: A Model Kit*. Translated by Gregory Rabassa. Pantheon, 1972.

Cortázar, Julio. *62/modelo para armar*. Sudamericana, 1968.

Cortázar, Julio. *Territorios*. Siglo XXI, 1978.

Cortázar, Julio. *Último Round*. Siglo XXI, 1969.

Cortázar, Julio. *The Winners*. Translated by Elaine Kerrigan. Pantheon, 1965.

Cortázar, Julio. Julio Cortázar Papers, Princeton University Library, Manuscripts Division, Series 1C, Box 2, Folders 42, 43.

Cortázar, Julio, and Carol Dunlop. *Autonauts of the Cosmoroute*. Translated by Anne McLean. Archipelago, 2007.

Cortázar, Julio, and Carol Dunlop. *Los autonautas de la cosmopista*. Carol Dunlop. Alfaguara, 1983

Franco, Jean. "Julio Cortázar: Utopia and Everyday Life." *Inti* nos. 10–11, 1979–80, pp. 108–18.

Fuentes, Carlos. "Julio Cortázar." *Personas*, Alfaguara, 2012, pp. 145–58.

González Bermejo, Ernesto. *Revelaciones de un cronopio: conversaciones con Cortázar*. Edhasa, 1978.

Harss, Luis, and Barbara Dohmann. *Into the Mainstream: Conversations with Latin American Writers*. Harper & Row, 1967.

Luna, Félix. *La comunidad organizada*. Sudamericana, 1985.

Maturo, Graciela, *Julio Cortázar y el hombre nuevo*. Sudamericana, 1968.

Namer, Claude, et. al. *Topografía de una mirada*. Films for the Humanities, 1988.

O'Connor, Patrick. "Melancholia porteña and Survivor's Guilt." *Latin American Literary Review*, vol. 23, no. 46, 1995, pp. 5–32.

Orloff, Carolina. *The Representation of the Political Element in Selected Writings of Julio Cortázar*. Tamesis, 2013.

Parkinson Zamora, Lois. "Movement and Stasis, Film and Photo: Temporal Structures in the Recent Fiction of Julio Cortázar." *Review of Contemporary Fiction*, vol. 3, no. 3, 1983, pp. 51–65.

Prego Gadea, Omar. *La fascinación de las palabras*. Aguilar, 1984.

Sosnowski, Saúl. "Julio Cortázar ante la literatura y la historia." *Obra crítica/3*. JulioCortázar, Alfaguara, 2004, pp 9–31.

Standish, Peter. "Los compromisos de Julio Cortázar." *Hispania* vol. 80, no. 3, September 1997, 465–71.

Valenzuela Luisa. "Julio Cortázar más allá de la vigilia." *Julio Cortázar desde tres perspectivas*. *Julio Cortázar desde tres perspectivas*, Luisa Valenzuela et. al. Fondo de Cultura Económica, 2002, pp. 13–29.

Viñas, David. "Después de Cortázar: historia y privatización." *Cuadernos hispanoamericanos*, no. 234, June 1969, pp. 734–39.

Weiss, Jason. "Interstitial spaces (Julio Cortázar)." *The Lights of Home: A Century of Latin American Writers in Paris*, Routledge, 2003, pp. 81–93.

CHAPTER 38

....

GABRIEL GARCÍA MÁRQUEZ AS LOCAL AND UNIVERSALIST, TRADITIONAL CUM MODERNIST STORYTELLER

....

GENE H. BELL-VILLADA

"*EL Boom de la novela.*" Such was the shorthand term applied from early on to the sudden flowering of Latin American prose fiction during the second half of the twentieth century. The locution further conveyed the twin facts of international critical acclaim and hefty sales. The trajectory of Colombia's Gabriel García Márquez (1927–2014) is emblematic of this moment in literary history. And his *Cien años de soledad* (*One Hundred Years of Solitude*, 1967) symbolizes that development as no other work does.

In that book, and in subsequent fictions short and long, García Márquez expanded the reach of narrative, broadening our sense of what storytelling could do. First and foremost among his innovations was the fusion of magical with real events—for example, a priest who levitates to gather church funds, a beautiful girl who rises to heaven as she waves good-bye, an auto mechanic who always arrives surrounded by swarming yellow butterflies. There was also *One Hundred Years*'s widened human and experiential range, depicting labor strikes and military repression without the heavy hand of socialist realism; public events like civil strife and war without scanting private realms like love, sex, family life, and personal loneliness; tragic losses and multiple deaths yet without forgetting that life can be very funny, too. It was, in the words of fellow novelist Mario Vargas Llosa, a "total novel" that takes on as many aspects of reality as is possible within its pages.

From its initial publication in Buenos Aires, sales of *One Hundred Years* grew dizzyingly into a Latin America–wide event. In the translations soon following, the book metamorphosed into an international phenomenon, winning the Prix du Meilleur Livre Étranger in France and the Chianciano Prize in Italy. Today, it stands as a worldwide

classic with sales in the tens of millions, and with countless admirers and literary disciples across the globe.

In his subsequent work, García Márquez exhibited an uncanny knack for reinventing
himself. In *El otoño del patriarca* (*The Autumn of the Patriarch*, 1975) he produced a
magisterial portrait of a Caribbean dictator and—with its six chapter-length paragraphs
of poetic prose, and its ever-shifting chronology and countless points of view—
reconceived the very shape of the novelistic genre. In several later books he gave flight
to his gifts as a uniquely original novelist of romantic love. And there is his shorter fiction: even before *One Hundred Years* the Colombian had penned a set of tales that would
in time become standard anthology favorites; and two later volumes featured further
instances of his "magical-realist" and multicultural side both. Finally, there is his life-
long career in print journalism, a profession that he started practicing at age twenty,
honing his skills as investigative reporter and opinion columnist, as humorist as well as
muckraker, and often defending Latin America in the face of imperial power.[1] So well
regarded was he among the broader Spanish-speaking reading public that in his lifetime
he often was—and still is—referred to simply via his adult nickname "Gabo."

LIFE AND WORKS

García Márquez was born on March 6, 1927, in the impoverished, sweltering, inland village of Aracataca, located in the Department of Magdalena, in Colombia's Caribbean region.[2] His first ten years were spent being raised by his maternal grandparents, Colonel
Nicolás Márquez and Tranquilina Iguarán, who had only reluctantly accepted their
rebellious daughter Luisa's marriage to his Conservative father-to-be Gabriel Eligio.
Grandpa encouraged the boy's bookish and storytelling bent, and shared with him his
experiences of past civil wars. From numerous female kin and indigenous household
servants, in turn, the boy absorbed local folklore. Grown-up Gabo would later recall
those childhood years as the most crucially formative of his entire life.

In the wake of the colonel's illness and death in 1937, little Gabito moved in with his
birth parents, who were constantly shifting dwellings between Sincé and Sucre (two
other inland small towns) and coastal Barranquilla, where he continued his studies, later
transferring as a boarding student, on scholarship, to the prestigious Liceo Nacional in
Zipaquirá, near highland Bogotá. In all, it was the beginning of a peripatetic, unsettled
existence.

At this point something must be said about the overall map of García Márquez's
world. His fiction is mostly set in northern Colombia's coastal zone, with its tropical
heat and ethnic-African demographic presence. Its denizens refer to themselves as
costeños ("coastals"), in contradistinction with residents of the more prestigious, prosperous Andean highland of Bogotá, known as *cachacos* (untranslatable, though roughly
analogous to "Yankees" within the United States). The coastal region encompasses,
as one goes from west to east, the colonial-architectural beauties of Cartagena; the

commercial-industrial port of Barranquilla (renowned for its carnival); Santa Marta, where Simón Bolívar breathed his last; the Sierra Nevada, a compact, snowcapped mountain range; and the Guajira peninsula, the desert habitat of the indigenous Wayúu (known as *guajiros*), with its largest town Riohacha.

The area is traversed south to north by the Magdalena River. Also worth mention are assorted inland settlements such as Sucre (with its river port), Ciénaga, and Aracataca. The latter two were among several small towns amid which, in the early twentieth century, the Boston-based United Fruit Co. set up growing, harvesting, and transport operations, with harsh labor conditions that ultimately sparked the workers' strike and massacre of 1928. These localities and events serve as overall setting for García Márquez's major narratives, though he only seldom refers to them specifically. (The one major exception is "Macondo," the name of a former banana plantation near his hometown.) He has thus made coastal Colombia his universe, giving it a literary profile, a mythic existence, much as Joyce did with Dublin and Faulkner with rural Mississippi (Bell-Villada 2010, 15–21).

On high school graduation in 1946, Gabo enrolled as a law student at the Universidad Nacional in Bogotá—mostly to please his parents. Since his early teens, however, he had been composing practice pieces as part of his dream of becoming a writer, and now had the good fortune to place a couple of beginner's fictions in a national daily's cultural supplement. Then, in 1948, everything changed: the brutal assassination of Jorge Eliecer Gaitán, a highly popular Liberal politician, sparked massive riots in the capital—and the lockdown of the university.

Gabo now transferred to law school in more tranquil, coastal Cartagena; he also took on a job as daily columnist for *El Universal*, a local daily. During free time and years on he worked on an abortive manuscript novel, an autobiographical family chronicle called "La casa." Meanwhile he abandoned his law studies while further eking out a trickle of apprentice tales for the national press. Morbidly introspective, these exercises in narrative deal mostly with the insides of characters' heads. Presumably inspired by Kafka—whom the Colombian had recently discovered—they are steeped in the Czech-German's angst and loneliness without his whimsical fabulism or fanciful humor. Years hence Gabo had them gathered in a volume entitled, after one of its pieces, *Ojos de perro azul* (1974; the "Eyes of a Blue Dog" section in *Innocent Eréndira* and *Collected Stories*), with a view to sweeping aside a spate of pirated editions. Its contents, juvenilia of interest to scholars only, are by no means the García Márquez the world now knows and admires.

El Universal was the start of a restless Gabo's fifteen-some years' drifting precariously in journalism as he held successive jobs, or freelanced it, in Barranquilla, Bogotá, Europe, Caracas, Havana, New York, and Mexico City up through 1964. The author's talent for ruffling officialdom's feathers became manifest in his 1955 series of interviews—conducted for Bogotá's *El Espectador*—with the shipwrecked survivor of a Colombian Navy destroyer that, as it turned out, had been transporting contraband and was under-equipped for safety. The newspaper was threatened by the then-military dictatorship and was eventually shut down for several months; the maritime account itself would later appear as a short book called *Relato de un náufrago* (*The Story of a Shipwrecked Sailor*, 1970) and sell ten million copies.

Even as he moved around over this decade and a half, García Márquez was conscientiously devouring literature from the Greek tragedians on through the twentieth-century avant-garde, working steadily on his apprentice and journeyman writer's craft, and staking out his themes, territory, and tone. The resulting, now-familiar entity stands out as a unique grand synthesis of personal recollection, regional folklore, real-life history, and the technical advances of modernism. Many of the best-known private episodes and facts and even individual names in his fiction are taken directly from his own family or from town anecdotes. As a single instance, his grandmother Tranquilina and the materfamilias Úrsula in *One Hundred Years* share the maiden name "Iguarán." Similarly, folk tales from various locales and ethnicities pepper García Márquez's art (e.g., the recurring story of the young girl changed into a spider for disobeying her parents). And the spirit of *vallenato* musical ballads and other popular songs infuses much of his writing, with specific allusions to legendary figures such as Francisco el Hombre and composer Rafael Escalona.[3] Regarding history, the country's numerous civil wars, the decades of United Fruit control in Colombia, the documented behavior of Latin American despots, and the acknowledged abuses or political complicity of the Catholic Church all play key roles in select García Márquez narratives. The pirate raid on Riohacha by Francis Drake, which opens chapter two of *One Hundred Years*, is factual, from 1596. (The Colombian author, incidentally, liked playing wryly with the English buccaneer's name, inserting it gratuitously—as well as that of the Duke of Marlborough—here and there in several of his works.)

García Márquez fuses all this traditional material with the experimental devices of twentieth-century modernism.[4] His most celebrated advance, of course, concerns the seamless interweaving of magical with ordinary, plausibly realistic situations. He reportedly first learned of the approach from reading Franz Kafka's account of traveling salesman Gregor Samsa's morning "metamorphosis" into a man-sized bug—who nevertheless tries to continue with family life and even ready himself for work.[5] A later such magical model came from Mexican writer Juan Rulfo's novel *Pedro Páramo* (1955), about a desert town populated largely by ghosts who dialogue regularly amongst themselves and with living souls.[6] Although García Márquez did not invent magic-cum-realism, it was he who elevated it into a consistent procedure, a workable mode, a believable, long-term technique all its own. A couple of ghosts put in memorable repeat appearances on the pages of *One Hundred Years*.

From Faulkner in particular, the Colombian assimilated the use of non-linear time, whereby past, present, and future occurrences are scrambled and co-exist via flashbacks and flash-forwards, with systematic switching from one chronological frame to another. (Rulfo himself had organized his *Pedro Páramo* plot along "Faulknerian" lines.) From Joyce, Dos Passos, and Virginia Woolf as well as Faulkner, Gabo further picked up the device of more or less unreliable, perhaps shifting narrators who tell events from their specific, personally skewed points of view.[7] Related to this approach is the direct, seemingly unmediated depiction of a character's innermost thoughts, the technique known as "stream-of-consciousness." Finally, from these committed experimentalists the Colombian disciple learned of the uses of overall design and, as it were, literary architecture. Modernist innovators, in breaking from the serial schemata of nineteenth-century fiction, in its stead arranged their narrations almost as if they were simultaneous shapes on a tapestry or canvas—in what Princeton scholar Joseph Frank called "the spatialization of form."[8] All of the above modernist features make up García Márquez's uniquely, meticulously structured novel *The Autumn of the Patriarch*, with its ever-fluctuating narrators and time-frames, and its correspondences and repetitions that play off each other across beginning, middle, and end (Bell-Villada 2010, 81–86).

Mention must also be made of Hemingway, whom the Colombian often acknowledged as a model for his own short fictions.[9] The larger-than-life American Nobel's short-story art is known for its crisp understatement, its hinting at larger unseen realities via minimal verbal material—as per his "iceberg" theory whereby a mere seventh of the total plot is visible to the readerly eye. Some of Gabo's greatest stories—"Tuesday Siesta," "Artificial Roses," "One of These Days," "The Handsomest Drowned Man in the World"—exemplify to perfection his "Hemingwayesque" approach to the genre.

When all is said, García Márquez cannot be easily characterized as an "autobiographical," or a "folk" or "regional," or a "satirical," or a "historical" novelist. Nor, despite these clear influences from the modernists, can he be regarded primarily as an "avant-garde" writer—even though most all of his mature fictions qualify as experiments in form and content. His total vision and practice absorb and meld all of the above features into an encompassing whole far too complex to be reduced to a single, simplifying label.

In 1955, during his employ at *El Espectador*, García Márquez saw his first book, *La hojarasca* (*Leaf Storm*), issued by a small, fly-by-night Bogotá outfit called SLB. (Having initially worked on the manuscript in 1950–1951, he had then faced some difficulty placing it with a reputable publisher.) The novel stands also as Gabo's very first in-depth depiction of the layered world of Macondo, with its banana-company backdrop, small-town tensions, and tropical heat. Set mostly on a stifling afternoon in September 1928, it is organized around a controversial upcoming burial and is told mostly by three different voices: an aging colonel, his thirtyish daughter Isabel, and her nameless little boy, each of them recalling past histories via flashbacks. With its multiple points of view and ever-present coffin, the novel is clearly shaped by the guiding example of *As I Lay Dying* by Faulkner. *Leaf Storm* demonstrates all the marks of an evolving journeyman's authentic novelistic début, with a strong sense of place and its deployment of key narrative techniques, while yet lacking in the author's wryly comical, ironically smiling touch.

At the time that *Leaf Storm* appeared, García Márquez was something of a star reporter in Colombia. With a view to shielding him from government reprisal for his shipwrecked-sailor series, *El Espectador* now shipped him off to Europe to serve as their foreign correspondent. The job initially went well as he wrote and filed dispatches from across the Old World, and also briefly pursued studies at a prestigious film school in Rome. Unfortunately, on arrival in Paris in early 1956 he found out that the daily had been shut down by the dictatorship. Though they graciously sent him money for return air fare, Gabo chose rather to cash it in, remaining in Europe to write full-time. A glamorous period it was not; for a year or so he was literally the starving artist, huddled in a proverbial unheated garret, getting by on precarious freelancing assignments as well as return-bottle deposits. *La Bohème* without the music, it was.

And yet, there amid such deprivation Gabo produced his first small masterpieces and composed a distinctive geography and a melody of his own. From that Paris attic came forth the novella *El coronel no tiene quien le escriba* (*No One Writes to the Colonel*, 1961). Its elderly, unnamed protagonist lives with his spouse in hunger and destitution as he waits in vain for a military pension. The dictatorship having recently killed their son who had been supporting them, the surviving couple's sole hope for possible income is the colonel's beloved fighting cock.

And a year hence, in a London hotel room, the author (nominally in town to learn the language) started crafting the bulk of the stories that would make up the collection *Los funerales de la Mamá Grande* (1962; "Big Mama's Funeral" section in *Collected Stories*). Both volumes—set either in Macondo or in the anonymous river port (modelled after Sucre) that is the colonel's home and would later serve as the locality for *Chronicle*—evoke the subtle, everyday conflicts that can well up between ordinary folk and small-town authority figures (e.g., a priest, a mayor, a local oligarch, a money lender). In each of these works we experience Gabo's now-familiar narrative voice—a spare irony mingled with empathic compassion, along with moments of outrageous, ribald humor. In addition, the "Big Mama" tale first fully articulates Gabo's gift for exuberant hyperbole in the service of mocking satire while offering a more mythologized history of Macondo. Each of these works drew sparse if admiring attention when first issued by small presses. In the wake of *One Hundred Years* they became classics.

The writer's wanderings continued when, in December 1957, he moved to Caracas to take on employment at a couple of Venezuelan glossies (marrying his childhood sweetheart Mercedes Barcha a few months later)—following which, in his enthusiasm for the budding Cuban Revolution, he came aboard as a staffer for its press agency Prensa Latina first in Bogotá, then Havana, and finally New York from 1959 to 1961; he settled next in Mexico City, where he was variously engaged by local pulps and US advertising firms, in addition to writing film scripts on the side (the latter are largely forgotten today). During these drifting years and previously, he was laboring long term on *La mala hora* (*In Evil Hour*, 1962), a manuscript political novel from which the *Colonel* and *Big Mama* narratives were fortunate spin-offs.

The novel itself is a broad depiction of a town (again based on Sucre) where ongoing military rule is disrupted by the mysterious postings of anonymous printed lampoons onto people's front doors. The presence of the leaflets, which simply state unsavory truths known to all, can only be characterized as a "magical" trait. Organized in the form of recurring fragments à la John Dos Passos's *Manhattan Transfer* (Janes 1981, 35), it is the García Márquez opus that comes closest to protest literature—perhaps one reason why the author once described it in an interview as his weakest novel (Monsalve 4). The manuscript nonetheless won the Esso Prize in 1962, the same year it was first issued in Spain by a high-handed publisher that had had its prose corrected to "proper" Castilian. The book did not see acceptable print form until 1966.

From 1961 to 1965, García Márquez suffered a severe case of writer's block, coming up solely with false starts and the occasional film scenario. The situation was partly aggravated by combined work, family responsibilities, and his having to adapt to the complex, multilayered world of Mexico's cultural milieu. And then, in mid-1965, there came the now-legendary flash of inspiration: while steering his Opel for vacation in Acapulco with wife Mercedes and their two young boys, in his mind Gabo could hear vividly the opening and imagine the rest of the novel that he had been struggling to write since his teens. Turning the car around and heading back to the capital city, he asked his spouse to handle the family finances for the time being, and eventually resigned from his ad-agency job as he went on to hole up inside his study for more than a year, drafting and typing eight hours a day even as the foursome barely survived with Mercedes pawning this and that and everything, and back rents piling up, and friends providing generous loans.

The outcome of this prolonged siege in a room, as we know, was *One Hundred Years of Solitude*. Issued in May 1967 by Editorial Sudamericana in Argentina, the novel quickly became a sensation throughout the Hispanic world, and eventually grew into an international literary phenomenon as well. Its 350 pages chronicled seven generations of a fictive Buendía clan intermingled with the history of their village, Macondo, and told of sectional conflicts and ideological wars along with disquieting accounts of banana-company imperialism and repression and local decline. Contents further comprised a cast of characters ranging over every sort of human type and conveyed a full spectrum of human emotions, with tragedy and comedy and love stories in equal measure. Formally, there was the book's biblical breadth and design, with a genesis, an exodus, scripture, plagues, a deluge, numerous begats, and a final apocalypse. And there was its Faulknerian, to-and-fro structuring of time (with three different moments encapsulated in its very opening lines) yet subtly, imperceptibly so. And, it goes without saying, its masterful interweaving of magic and realism helped fashion an entire narrative subgenre for generations to come.

The dizzying best-sellerdom and critical success of *One Hundred Years* transformed Gabo's life beyond recognition, from roving journalist and obscure if respected *littérateur* to publicly renowned artist-personality. Overwhelmed by media attention and other such perquisites of fame, later in 1967 with his nuclear family he shipped off and moved to Barcelona, then an enclave of relative freedom within Generalissimo Franco's fraying dictatorship. The city was also home to a lively publishing sector (including Carmen Balcells, his literary agent) and to a growing number of well-regarded Spanish-language authors.

The Colombian would spend seven years there. His great novel may have put "Macondo" on the map, enshrining it as a kind of shorthand term for Latin America, but its maker was now putting that mythic, inland realm behind him, physically for the while, and literarily for good. While settled in Barcelona, García Márquez published his next story collection, bearing the mock-tragic, mock-overstated title, *La increíble y triste historia de la cándida Eréndira y de su abuela desalmada* (*The Incredible and Sad Tale of Innocent Eréndira and Her Heartless Grandmother*, 1972), customarily abbreviated as

Innocent Eréndira. Its seven fictions all take place in villages on Colombia's northern littoral. Tellingly, each and all of Gabo's subsequent novels were to feature Atlantic-coastal towns as their chief setting.

The title novella, spun off from a script for a film later to be directed by Brazilian cineaste Ruy Guerra, relates—via a parodic fairytale-and-love-story—the wrenching account of an early teen forced into sex work by her evil-grandmother-cum-wicked-stepmother, and is also a subtle study in power. It shares with the shorter stories the tender, understated, playfully sympathetic yet unsentimental irony previously given voice to by Gabo in his *Big Mama* collection. A couple of the other stories—"A Very Old Man with Enormous Wings" (about a possible angel, fallen into a rural couple's chicken coop) and "The Handsomest Drowned Man in the World" (about a mysterious, redemptive cadaver that washes up on a village shore)—have become classroom favorites and anthology classics. A more openly experimental fable—"The Last Voyage of the Ghost Ship" (a lonely young man's monologue about his fantastical, recurring oceanic vision)—consists of a seven-page-long paragraph and is thus a harbinger of García Márquez's next "big" novel.

That novel, *El otoño del patriarca* (*The Autumn of the Patriarch*, 1975), finished in 1974, portrays the life cycle of a Caribbean dictator, and, in doing so, proves to be even more far-reaching and original than was *Solitude*. The history of an anonymous tyrant who rules over his nameless tropical republic, it unfolds via six chapters, each one a single paragraph in length, the sixth of these, in turn, being one, single, fifty-plus-page sentence. The narrative point of view is multiple, often unidentified, and constantly shifting, as are the time frames that spread over at least a century. The author's bent for hyperbole is taken to inordinate extremes with the despot's mythical lifespan of somewhere between 107 and 232 years, and with the book's climax, the removal of the Caribbean by the colonial "gringo" masters who transport the seawaters in numbered boxes off to Arizona. And yet, despite all this literary artifice, the novel has as its raw-materials basis the real-life histories of notorious, twentieth-century strongmen such as Venezuela's Gómez, the three Nicaraguan Somozas, and the Dominican Trujillo, these further elaborated on by the accounts of ancient Roman historians like Suetonius.

The book immediately sold a half-million copies. Readers and reviewers who had expected a Macondo sequel, however, were soon disappointed, and many found its formal and stylistic intricacies daunting. Critical and popular responses have remained divided to this day. Meanwhile García Márquez emerged from his isolation, eventually returned to Mexico, and began assuming a more public and political profile—his first such article in years being a protest against the overthrow of Chile's democratically elected socialist president Salvador Allende by military dictator general Augusto Pinochet. With his own money Gabo now helped launch a biweekly, left-wing magazine in Bogotá called *Alternativa* that would survive—following much government harassment and even a mysterious bomb in its offices—until 1980.[10]

More notably, Gabo became an ardent advocate of the Cuban Revolution and a friend of Fidel Castro's, but also wrote in favor of reformist, left-leaning governments in Portugal and Peru; defended Panamanian president Omar Torrijos's campaign to nationalize the Canal; and celebrated the Sandinista guerrillas' struggle and victory over the fifty-year Somoza regime. This "advocacy journalism" remained with him over the rest of his writing life. In addition, he cultivated friendly ties with European social democrats such as Spain's Felipe González and France's François Mitterrand, and with Liberal and Conservative presidents of Colombia, too. (Whole books could be written about Gabo's ties with the powerful.) And, in an unusual gesture, shortly around the publication of *Patriarch*, he declared himself "on strike," vowing to publish no more fiction until the fall of Chile's Pinochet.

García Márquez's writer's strike would last half-a-dozen years, he breaking it voluntarily with the wildly heralded *Crónica de una muerte anunciada* (*Chronicle of a Death Foretold*, 1981). This relatively short novel brings together two intertwined, atavistic, Iberian folk-cults: premarital female chastity and family-motivated honor killing. Set in the 1920s in a river settlement resembling Sucre (with an imaginary Caribbean coast added), its central, gruesome plot could not be simpler: a local bride is forcibly returned home by her glamorous, rich, out-of-town groom on their wedding night because she is not virginal, and in response her twin brothers end up brutally murdering the young man who, she says, had deflowered her (though indirect evidence suggests his "innocence"). The story itself is loosely based on a shocking, real-life incident that occurred in Sucre in 1951, the then-young author having been personally acquainted with each one of those involved.[11]

Once again, however, the narrative design is vastly complex, with its five chapters shifting about both in chronology and on the character(s) being spotlighted, and also with constant, metafictional focus on the piecing-together (hence, the "chronicle" of the title) of the total tale. Moreover, from all this intrigue there will emerge a love story, a lovers' reunion-in-the-making that deftly spoofs the familiar array of love-story commonplaces.

Indeed, of the four more novels García Márquez would still write, three of them concentrate specifically on male-female romance of some unusual sort. The author's daily writing habits were dramatically interrupted, however, when his fame achieved a sudden new peak: the granting of the 1982 Nobel Prize for Literature, he being the youngest such recipient since Camus in 1957. Throughout the Hispanic world the award became cause for clamorous celebration. The Nobel Committee's official statement in early fall singled out his wide popularity, his "wild imagination," and (of course) his mixture of the fantastical and realistic. In Stockholm, the December ceremony was the most festive in memory, with accompaniment by Latin music ensembles featuring sixty-some performers, and with Gabo himself sporting not a European coat and tie but the traditional, white-linen, *liqui-liqui* suit of Colombia's Caribbean. His acceptance speech defended a Latin America historically beset by foreign imperialisms.

Once the shouting had stopped, García Márquez returned to his novel-in-progress, now being crafted on a personal computer: *El amor en los tiempos del cólera* (*Love in the Time of Cholera*, 1985). At its core, it is an account, first, of a three-year-long, adolescent boy-girl amour, cut short by the girl's upwardly mobile father; girl eventually weds a physician and civic leader of old-patrician stock, who implements anti-cholera sanitation measures; boy in turn stays single, rises in his river-navigation career, and, although sexually active, remains true to his first love; and at long last the couple—in the wake of girl's widowhood fifty years hence—reunite and they consummate their relationship aboard a river cruiser.

Set largely in a town resembling Cartagena roughly between 1875 and 1935, *Love* is the author's lengthiest and—a flashback of five decades aside—his most traditional narrative opus. Consciously modeled after nineteenth-century realist fiction, it comes chock-filled with period detail as well as all sorts of love-ties and love references. On the other hand, it goes beyond that traditional genre in showing erotic romance triumphant in old age, as well as in its frank portrayals, throughout, of sex. Presumably for this set of reasons, *Love* is Gabo's most accessible work, its popularity second only to that of *One Hundred Years*.

International success and authorial wealth had not blunted his creativity, García Márquez continued to demonstrate. The Colombian's next venture, *El general en su laberinto* (*The General in His Labyrinth*, 1989), constitutes, within his total oeuvre, a bit of an anomaly, a novel focused explicitly on a widely known, real-life figure: Simón Bolívar (1783–1830), leader of the forces that had freed the territory of six Latin American republics-to-be from Spain's three-centuries-old imperial rule. It depicts the Liberator in his last few months of life—now weary, defeated, and ground-down by post-independence rivalries and factionalism—as he sails with his retinue down the Magdalena River, purportedly headed toward exile in Europe, though, as it actually will turn out, to his melancholy death in the port city of Santa Marta. Also portrayed from up close is Bolívar's legendary relationship with his lover and intimate confidante, the remarkable Manuela Sáenz (1797–1856), who more than once saved the man's life.

As in other previous novels by García Márquez, Bolívar's dying "present" alternates with extended flashbacks into the paladin's early growth, development, and military-political career, as well as into his intimate personal life. Some major biographical lacunae are filled in via fictive past love affairs, all of which help further vary and spice up the plot. Owing to the intrinsic limits posed by the historical subject matter, the book has none of the author's signature traits of exaggeration or magic, and precious little of his humor. Still, one must admire the literary master for bringing Latin America's most venerated hero down to human scale, for showing him with certain personal flaws and on occasion literally naked—an overall approach for which the novelist was subjected to harsh criticism by historians and other selected public keepers of the Liberator's flame.

The dozen stories gathered in *Doce cuentos peregrinos* (*Strange Pilgrims*, 1992) share in common the experiences and ambivalences lived by Latin Americans who, for some reason or other, happen to be residing in or passing through Old Europe, in localities ranging from Oporto to Vienna. Here, the long-standing contrasts and traditional dichotomies between a "civilized" Europe and a "barbaric" Latin America find themselves repeatedly, subtly, and slyly reversed. (Perhaps it is more than accidental that the volume was issued in the year of the Columbus quincentennial.) Several of the pieces—"Light is Like Water," "The Saint"—continue with García Márquez's magical-realist side.

They and others—for example, "Maria dos Prazeres," "The Trace of Your Blood in the Snow"—are as excellent and moving as any of the author's previous short fictions.

In *Del amor y otros demonios* (*Of Love and Other Demons*, 1994), García Márquez returned to his eponymous subject of male-female attraction, though again with a startling difference. With eighteenth-century Cartagena as its setting, it tells of a chaste, consensual, truly yet tragically loving bond that develops between a thirty-six-year-old librarian-priest of Peninsular origin and a white, upper-class, twelve-year-old girl who has been informally raised by the slave community. The choice of time and place allows the author occasion to portray, vividly and skillfully, such familiar Colonial ills as idle aristocracy, narrow church dogmas and Inquisition controls (as well as some subtle challenges to that hegemony), and Black slavery. Concerning the latter, *Of Love* is the only novel of Gabo's that offers a close look at the daily cultural life and religious world-view of Colombia's (Nueva Granada's in this case) Afro-Hispanics.

Brevity notwithstanding—just under two hundred pages—the book is unusually complex, with an imbedded prologue, several subplots, movements back-and-forth in time, and magical-realist touches, and moreover comes populated by a wide cast of characters representing various aspects of the era. Filled with allusions to courtly love and Renaissance love-poetry traditions, *Del amor* is among Gabo's artistically and culturally richest single works.

Owing to his frank left-wing views and Cuban connections, García Márquez since the 1960s had found himself on the US Immigration "blacklist," allowed entrance into the country only under restricted conditions—this even though US editions of his books sold widely and, in 1978–1982, his son Rodrigo García was attending Harvard College. In September 1994, however, President Bill Clinton (whose favorite novel was reportedly *One Hundred Years*) met with García Márquez as a guest at Martha's Vineyard, together with fellow novelists William Styron and Carlos Fuentes. As a result of that legendary encounter, the travel ban was rescinded, and Gabo gained easy visa access to el Norte, where son Rodrigo was being launched as a filmmaker in Hollywood.

Around this time, the author was returning to his original roots as a journalist, working on what would be entitled *Noticia de un secuestro* (*News of a Kidnapping*, 1996). His most lengthy volume of dedicated reportage, in its structuring it is every bit as artful as his fiction. Set in Bogotá in 1991, at the height of Colombia's infamous "drug war," it narrates—based on material gathered from many hours of interviews—the forced abduction and months-long captivity of ten media or political figures by youthful thugs employed by Pablo Escobar, the notorious narcotrafficker.

The fear-filled, claustrophobic ordeal of the captives and their eventual release, told in the odd-numbered chapters, alternate with the even-numbered chapters that focus in turn on the more "normal" world outside—the victims' relatives and their emotional sufferings, along with the slow, mostly ineffectual maneuvers of the central government. In the course of his initial investigations García Márquez had hoped to interview Escobar while in detention; that prospect, however, was overtaken by events: the last few pages give readers a close if second-hand look at the drug capo himself, his charisma, his strange authority—plus his dramatic escape and final execution by the security forces (to the detriment, alas, of the author's plans). Incidentally, with its extensive Bogotá setting, *News* is Gabo's only *cachaco* book, as biographer Gerald Martin notes (522–23).

The Colombian author's hundred-page swansong of a novel, *Memoria de mis putas tristes* (*Memories of My Melancholy Whores*; 2004) is, like previous works of his, a love story with an odd twist, something like an offbeat fairytale. Provocative title notwithstanding, the book features no consummated sex, its remembrances of prostitutes being made up of conversations at a local bordello plus of ongoing friendships with paid partners past. The nameless bachelor-narrator for his ninetieth birthday asks to bed down with a virgin, which the owner willingly obliges. He will now spend a years' worth of evenings at the brothel, lying unclothed next to a fourteen-year-old factory seamstress-cum-novice hooker—who will remain both sound asleep and naked throughout the plot—while he does no more than gently stroke and kiss her brown-colored skin as well as leave her small gifts in the mornings. By the story's halfway point, the nonagenarian has fallen joyfully, passionately, publicly in love—his very first time ever—with his coy mistress. And on the last page, a laughing madam informs the old codger that the girl, now fifteen and fully filled out, is madly in love with him, too. A blissful and open ending, then; what is to follow, the reader may decide.

Despite its brevity and seeming slightness, *Memories* demonstrates a complexity akin to that of other García Márquez books. At least half of the text consists of flashbacks, as rendered by its unreliable raconteur. Its literate narrator being a music critic for a local daily and also an erstwhile Latin teacher, it features a fair number of passing allusions to dictionaries, folklore, current art and letters, and music both classical and popular. Its disturbing subject matter and its form are modelled after a Japanese novel, *House of the Sleeping Beauties*, by Nobel laureate Yasunari Kawabata, quoted from in the epigraph to *Memories*. Its setting is Barranquilla (a coastal city for which the author always felt much affection) without ever specifying so, even as some of the town's cultural personalities and landmark locations are invoked by name. The work thus tellingly represents Gabo's signature fusion of local with cosmopolitan, universalist ingredients.

Other than *Vivir para contarla* (*Living to Tell the Tale*, 2002), a moving 577-page memoir of his initial three decades, the author was to publish no more new narrative books in his lifetime. However, he did leave behind an enigmatic short story, "En agosto nos vemos" ("We'll See Each Other in August"), that may or may not have been intended as part of a novel. Appearing in the Barcelona newspaper *La Vanguardia* weeks after his death in 2014, it tells of a happily married fifty-two-year-old woman, Ana Magdalena Bach (her father is a conservatory director), who, following a visit alone to her mother's grave on an unnamed tropical island, seduces a stranger in her hotel room (a highly erotic episode, even for García Márquez)—with a disquieting, surprise ending. The manuscript, otherwise unpublished, now forms part of the vast collection of Gabo papers (over 27,000 items) housed in the Harry Ransom Center at the University of Texas-Austin, inaugurated in 2020.

During his last eight years García Márquez experienced severe memory loss, was scarcely able to recognize his friends—a sad and ironic fate for a literary master whose life's work had been premised on recapturing and reinventing the past. Still, public observance of his accomplishments continued in his homeland and elsewhere, especially in 2007, on the occasion of his eightieth birthday.

On March 17, 2014, he died at age eighty-seven from pneumonia. A month hence, Colombian head of state Juan Manuel Santos declared three days of national mourning, with flags at half-mast. A memorial service at Mexico City's Palacio de Bellas Artes on April 21 was officiated by the presidents of both Colombia and Mexico; thousands of ordinary admirers stood outside, queuing up to attend the event. Newspapers from across the Spanish-speaking world gave the farewell front-page coverage.

WORLD LEGACY

One Hundred Years of Solitude is "probably the most influential novel of the last third of the twentieth century." So adjudged Michael Denning, a professor of American Studies at Yale, in 2006 (703). His statement might well be further expanded to characterize the book's creator as the most influential *novelist* from that time-period. Gabo's mark can be seen even at the level of the everyday press. The very titles of the Colombian's books now serve as templates for catchy newspaper headlines on the order of "Chronicle of an X Foretold," "Love [or X] in the Time of X," "The Autumn of the Patriarch [or of X]," and of course "X Years of Solitude [or of X]." In a striking detail, two managers of the "Modern Love" feature for the Sunday *New York Times* reported in an "Inside the *Times*" column on May 3, 2020, at the height of the COVID-19 pandemic, that during the month of March alone they had received a total of seventy-eight manuscript submissions entitled. . . "Love in the Time of the Coronavirus" (Jones and Lee, 2)!

Similarly, in the Spanish-speaking world, news reporters casually allude or draw comparisons to characters and episodes from García Márquez, much as is done with past classic authors or the Bible. More specifically, the word "Macondo" is now an occasional, shorthand referent in its own right for Latin America, and it has been further appropriated for the names of hotels, pharmacies, bookstores, and other businesses, and even (irony of ironies) for the BP oil rig that blew up and wrought destruction on the Louisiana coast in 2010. On a more relevant instance, in September 2019 in Nairobi, Kenya, the first annual Macondo Literary Festival was inaugurated, with attendance by Anglophone and Lusophone literati from across the sub-Saharan continent.

The narrative trait that has most contributed to Gabo's world prominence, of course, is his fabled "magical realism." Though he did not pioneer it, he did expand the subgenre and its techniques into an entire approach to storytelling, with a full repertory of procedures all its own (as Wendy Faris notes in depth), in the process offering an alternative to established realisms, whether the bourgeois, social, or socialist variety. The "realism" part of the term, it bears emphasizing, is as important as the "magical," and novelists can and do now mingle the everyday with elements unreal or supernatural, sans devolving either into escapist fantasy or didactic allegory. In our time, a publishing season hardly goes by without a new work of fiction being linked in passing to magical realism or compared by reviewers to the Colombian's foundational text.

Within American letters, Nobel laureate Toni Morrison oftentimes acknowledged her indebtedness to García Márquez, a literary kinship observable, for instance, in the eponymous ghost that haunts the pages of her masterpiece *Beloved*, as also in such phantom apparitions as found in William Kennedy's *Ironweed* and in John Nichols's *The Milagro Beanfield War*. US Latino writers like Rudolfo Anaya, Cristina García, and Junot Díaz similarly incorporate magic into their narratives. Conversely, in the nineteenth-century antebellum world conjured up by Colson Whitehead in *The Underground Railroad* (Pulitzer Prize, 2017), that metaphorically named escape route is imaginatively transformed into an actual, subterranean, steam-powered, metal rolling stock for fugitive slaves.

In the region now increasingly known as the Global South, "Magical Realism. . . becomes the literary language of the emergent post-colonial world," the Indian-English theorist Homi Bhabha has remarked (6–7). In that vast, post-imperial area (and in modernized Japan as well), magical realism serves as a vital means for breaking away from imported European models and, in replacement, for exhuming non-realist, fantastical traditions from their own respective pasts and adapting such ancestral narrative praxes to their current writing needs, thereby turning the local into the universal. Mozambican writer Mia Couto notes, "Africa is full of Macondos . . . In Mozambique it isn't magical realism we live. It's real realism." Or, along the same lines, Ugandan novelist Moses Isegawa (who signals *One Hundred Years* as inspiration for his *Abyssinian Chronicles* [2000]) once observed, "In Uganda you hear stories as fantastic as those García Márquez tells. In fact, your live them daily" (both cited in Janes 2022, 216).

This South-to-South influence takes on many and varied forms. In the case of South Asia, *One Hundred Years* has been widely translated into and commented on in several of the region's vernacular languages, and into English as well. The Colombian's work has achieved an especially successful following in the Malayalam-speaking state and adjoining regions of Kerala, where some critics go so far as to hail García Márquez as a Malayalam writer (Gupta and Naved). In another, more individual literary kinship, Sri Lankan-Canadian novelist Michael Ondaatje (author of *The English Patient*) in the late 1970s actually went on a personal pilgrimage to Aracataca and then wrote an imaginative essay about the experience, in which he extols *One Hundred Years* as "the bible of the twentieth century" (21).

The best-known instance of magical realism impacting South Asian letters is, of course, the Pakistani-English novelist Salman Rushdie, whose widely acclaimed *Midnight's Children* (1981) interweaves the conflicted history of post-Independence India with the telepathic powers of its protagonist Saleem Sinai and of his exact contemporaries. In response to the death of García Márquez, Rushdie wrote a moving tribute to his fellow novelist, praising him for breathing literary life into "a reality I knew from my own experience in India and Pakistan . . . This world was mine, translated into Spanish" (n.p.).

In China, amid the relative normalcy that followed the turmoil of the cultural revolution, García Márquez would become "an inspirational figure." His 1982 Nobel award served as proof that Third World literature could command worldwide attention and prestige. A high point of this Gabo presence in East Asia is Mo Yan, "the true disciple of magical realism" (Teng), author of the 1986 *Red Sorghum* novel series (made into an internationally released film in 1987) and the 2012 Nobel laureate for literature. The prize committee in their statement singled out Mo's "hallucinatory realism [that] merges folk tale, history and the contemporary."

The extent and specificity of García Márquez's sway in non-Western letters is at times astounding. African writing now has its dictator novels and its equivalents to Macondo history, both of them present in, for example, *The Laughing Cry* (1982) by Congolese Francophone writer Henri Lopès (Armillas-Tiseyra 65). In the Arabic-speaking world, it has been said that the death of Gabo received more public attention than did the passing of Egypt's Naguib Mahfuz in 2006 (El Attar). More concretely, Lebanese author Elias Khoury reportedly constructed his work of fiction *Majma 'al-Asrar* (Junction of Secrets, 1994) around an intertextual reimagining of *Chronicle of a Death Foretold* and of its characters of Arab origin (Civantos cited in El Attar 238–39).

In Japan, Konzaburō Ōe (Nobel, 1994) frankly acknowledged the influence of *One Hundred Years* on his own writing; his novel *The Game of Contemporaneity* (1979; as yet untranslated) uses a remote town as a pretext to explain modern Japanese history and also to contest the official version of that past (Robledo 280–81). The most widely renowned novel by Haruki Murakami, *1Q84*, has numerous flashes of alternate, parallel realities that manifest themselves in its 1984 Tokyo setting. More broadly, Murakami uses magical realism as a means of exploring Japan's identity issues (Robledo). And, in 2017, a fifty-four-year old Yuki Ishii published her very first novel, with the telling title *A Hundred Years of Mud* (Robledo).

These are but glimpses of the myriad of ways in which the writings of García Márquez have become a world presence and, in turn, encouraged and helped writers across the world to reshape writing—in the Global South, in East Asia, and in the United States, particularly in the latter's Third-World inflected portions. The Boom of the Novel in Latin America was and is a special moment in the history of literary art, comparable to the emergence of Russian narrative in the nineteenth century. And García Márquez's supremely artful fictions represent that creativity at its utmost.

Notes

1. Regarding the author's political stances, see Ignacio López-Calvo, "Coloniality and Solitude in García Márquez's Public Speeches and Newspaper Articles."
2. The most thorough biography of the novelist to date is Gerald Martin's *Gabriel García Márquez: A Life* (2008). See also Dasso Saldívar, *García Márquez: El viaje a la semilla: La biografía* (1997), which focuses more specifically on the years up to 1967.
3. Regarding *vallenato*, see Bell-Villada and Katz Montiel, "Music as Formal and Signifying Feature in García Márquez's Mature Fiction."

4. See Juan De Castro, "Gabriel García Márquez and the Remaking of the World Canon," for the connection to the modernists. As early as 1950, the author in his journalism was frankly advocating for the writing of Colombian novels influenced by Joyce, Faulkner, and Virginia Woolf (*Obra periodística*, vol. 1, p. 269). And in a 1951 column, he stated that his favorite authors were Faulkner, Kafka, and Virginia Woolf, and that it was his hope to write like them (ibid., p. 581).

5. His moment of discovery is recounted in the interview with *El Manifiesto*, "Journey back to the Source," pp. 81–82.

6. For Rulfo's influence, see Saldívar's biography, pp. 410–12.

7. See Oberhelman, *The Presence of Faulkner in the Writings of García Márquez*, passim.

8. Frank, "Spatial Form in Modern Literature," passim. See also Bell-Villada, *García Márquez* (2010), pp. 81–87.

9. In a 1981 column for *El País* entitled "Mi Hemingway personal," García Márquez rendered special tribute to the American author's short-story art and acknowledged Hemingway's influence on his own craft.

10. For this side of the author, see Bell-Villada, "García Márquez as Public Intellectual."

11. For an in-depth look at this background, see Eligio García, *La tercera muerte de Santiago Nasar*.

WORKS CITED

Bell-Villada, Gene H. "García Márquez as Public Intellectual." *A History of Colombian Literature*, edited by Raymond Leslie Williams, Cambridge University Press, 2016, pp. 311–21.

Bell-Villada, Gene H. *García Márquez: The Man and His Work*. 2nd ed, revised and expanded. U of North Carolina P, 2010.

Bell-Villada, Gene H., and Ignacio López-Calvo, eds. *The Oxford Handbook of Gabriel García Márquez*. Oxford UP, 2022.

Bell-Villada, Gene H., and Marco Katz Montiel. "Music as Formal and Signifying Feature in García Márquez's Mature Fiction." *The Oxford Handbook of Gabriel García Márquez*, edited by Bell-Villada and López-Calvo. Oxford UP, 2022, pp. 413–38.

Bhabha, Homi K. Introduction. *Nation and Narration*, edited by Homi K. Bhabha, Routledge, 1990, pp. 1–9.

Civantos, Cristina. "Orientalism and the Narration of Violence in the Mediterranean Atlantic: Gabriel García Márquez and Elias Khoury." *The Global South Atlantic*, edited by Kerry Bystrom and Joseph R. Slaughter, Fordham UP, 2018, pp. 165–85.

De Castro, Juan. "Gabriel García Márquez and the Remaking of the World Canon." *The Oxford Handbook of Gabriel García Márquez*, edited by Bell-Villada and López-Calvo. Oxford UP, 2022, pp. 96–109.

Denning, Michael. "The Novelists' International." *The Novel*, vol. 1: *History, Geography, and Culture*, edited by Franco Moretti, Princeton UP, 2006, pp. 703–25.

El Attar, Hebat-Allah A. "The Arabs and Gabriel García Márquez." *The Oxford Handbook of Gabriel García Márquez*, edited by Bell-Villada and López-Calvo. Oxford UP, 2022, pp. 232–45.

Faris, Wendy. "García Márquez and Magical Realism." *The Oxford Handbook of Gabriel García Márquez*, edited by Bell-Villada and López-Calvo. Oxford UP, 2022, pp. 31–49.

Faulkner, William. *As I Lay Dying*. Random House, 1966.

Frank, Joseph. "Spatial Form in Modern Literature." *The Widening Gyre: Crisis and Mastery in Modern Literature*, Rutgers University Press, 1963, pp. 3–62.

García, Eligio. *La tercera muerte de Santiago Nasar. Crónica de la crónica*. Mondadori, 1987.

García Márquez, Gabriel. *El amor en los tiempos del cólera*. Bruguera, 1985.

García Márquez, Gabriel. *The Autumn of the Patriarch*. Translated by Gregory Rabassa. Harper & Row, 1976.

García Márquez, Gabriel. *Chronicle of a Death Foretold*. Translated by Gregory Rabassa. Knopf, 1982.

García Márquez, Gabriel. *Cien años de soledad*. Sudamericana, 1967.

García Márquez, Gabriel. *Collected Stories*. Translated by Gregory Rabassa and J. S. Bernstein. Harper & Row, 1984.

García Márquez, Gabriel. *El coronel no tiene quien le escriba*. Aguirre Editorial, 1961.

García Márquez, Gabriel. *Crónica de una muerte anunciada*. Sudamericana, 1981.

García Márquez, Gabriel. *Del amor y otros demonios*. Mondadori, 1994.

García Márquez, Gabriel. *Doce cuentos peregrinos*. Sudamericana, 1992.

García Márquez, Gabriel. *Los funerales de la Mamá Grande*. Sudamericana, 1972.

García Márquez, Gabriel. *El general en su laberinto*. Oveja Negra, 1989.

García Márquez, Gabriel. *The General in His Labyrinth*. Translated by Edith Grossman. Knopf, 1990.

García Márquez, Gabriel. *La hojarasca*. Sudamericana, 1972.

García Márquez, Gabriel. *La increíble y triste historia de la cándida Eréndira y de su abuela desalmada*. Barral, 1972.

García Márquez, Gabriel. *In Evil Hour*. Translated by Gregory Rabassa. Harper & Row, 1979.

García Márquez, Gabriel. *Innocent Eréndira and Other Stories*. Translated by Gregory Rabassa. Harper & Row, 1978.

García Márquez, Gabriel. *Leaf Storm and Other Stories*. Translated by Gregory Rabassa. Harper & Row, 1972.

García Márquez, Gabriel. *Living to Tell the Tale*. Translated by Edith Grossman. Knopf, 2003.

García Márquez, Gabriel. *Love in the Time of Cholera*. Translated by Edith Grossman. Knopf, 1988.

García Márquez, Gabriel. *La mala hora*. Sudamericana, 1972.

García Márquez, Gabriel. *Memoria de mis putas tristes*. Vintage Español, Random House, 2004.

García Márquez, Gabriel. *Memories of My Melancholy Whores*. Translated by Edith Grossman. Knopf, 2005.

García Márquez, Gabriel. "Mi Hemingway personal." *El País* (Madrid), July 28, 1981. https://elpais.com/diario/1981/07/29/opinion/365205612_850215.html

García Márquez, Gabriel. *News of a Kidnapping*. Translated by Edith Grossman. Knopf, 1997.

García Márquez, Gabriel. *No One Writes to the Colonel and Other Stories*. Translated by J. S. Bernstein. Harper & Row, 1968.

García Márquez, Gabriel. *Noticia de un secuestro*. Mondadori, 1996.

García Márquez, Gabriel. "La obra inacabada de García Márquez: 'En agosto nos vemos.'" https://www.lavanguardia.com/cultura/20140420/54405144781/gabo-en-agosto-nos-vemos.html

García Márquez, Gabriel. *Obra periodística I. Textos costeños*. Edited with an Introduction by Jacques Gilard. Bruguera, 1981.

García Márquez, Gabriel. *Of Love and Other Demons*. Translated by Edith Grossman. Penguin, 1995.

García Márquez, Gabriel. *Ojos de perro azul*. Plaza y Janés, 1979.

García Márquez, Gabriel. *One Hundred Years of Solitude*. Translated by Gregory Rabassa. Harper & Row, 1970.

García Márquez, Gabriel. *El otoño del patriarca*. Sudamericana, 1975.

García Márquez, Gabriel. *Relato de un náufrago*. Tusquets, 1970.

García Márquez, Gabriel. *The Story of a Shipwrecked Sailor*. Translated by Randoph Hogan. Knopf, 1986.

García Márquez, Gabriel. *Strange Pilgrims*. Translated by Edith Grossman. Knopf, 1993.

García Márquez, Gabriel. *Vivir para contarla*. Norma, 2002.

Gupta, Sonya Surabhi, and Shad Naved. "South Asian Readings of Gabriel García Márquez." *The Oxford Handbook of Gabriel García Márquez*, edited by Bell-Villada and López-Calvo, 2022, pp. 264–76.

Janes, Regina. *Gabriel García Márquez: Revolutions in Wonderland*. U of Missouri P, 1981.

Janes, Regina. "García Márquez in Africa." *The Oxford Handbook of Gabriel García Márquez*, edited by Bell-Villada and López Calvo, 2022, pp. 209–31.

Jones, Daniel, and Miya Lee. "What's Modern Love in a Pandemic?" *The New York Times*, May 3, 2020, p. 2. https://www.nytimes.com/2020/05/01/reader-center/modern-love-coronavirus.html

Kafka, Franz. *Selected Short Stories*. Translated by Willa and Edwin Muir. Random House, 1952.

Kennedy, William. *Ironweed*. Viking, 1983.

Khoury, Elias. *Majma' al-Asrar*. Dar al-Adab, 1994.

Lop`es, Henri. *The Laughing Cry: An African Cock and Bull Story*. Translated by Gerald Moore. Readers International, 1987.

López-Calvo, Ignacio. "Coloniality and Solitude in García Márquez's Public Speeches and Newspaper Articles." *The Oxford Handbook of Gabriel García Márquez*, edited by Bell-Villada and López-Calvo, 2022, pp. 439–54.

El Manifiesto. "Journey back to the Source." Interview. *Conversations with Gabriel García Márquez*, edited by Gene H. Bell-Villada, UP of Mississippi, 2006, pp. 78–92.

Martin, Gerald. *Gabriel García Márquez: A Life*. Viking Canada, 2008.

Monsalve, Alfonso. "Una entrevista con García Márquez: La novela, anuncio de grandes transformaciones." *Lecturas Dominicales* in El Tiempo (Bogotá), January 14, 1968, p. 4.

Morrison, Toni. *Beloved*. Knopf, 1987.

Mo, Yan. *Red Sorghum: A Novel of China*. Translated by Howard Goldblatt. Viking, 1993.

Murakami, Haruki. *1Q84*. Translated by Jay Rubin and Philip Gabriel. Knopf, 2011.

Nichols, John. *The Milagro Beanfield War*. Ballantine, 1976.

Ondaatje, Michael. "García Márquez and the Bus to Aracataca." *Figures in a Ground: Canadian Essays on Modern Literature Collected in Honor of Sheila Watson*, edited by Diane Bessai and David Jackel, Western Producer Prairie Books, 1978, pp. 19–31.

Robledo, Gonzalo. "*One Hundred Years of Solitude* and Its Influence in Japan." *The Oxford Handbook of Gabriel García Márquez*, edited by Bell-Villada and López-Calvo. Oxford UP, 2022, pp. 277–91.

Rulfo, Juan. *Pedro Páramo*. Fondo de Cultura Económica, 1955.

Rulfo, Juan. *Pedro Páramo*. Translated by Margaret Sayers Peden. Grove Press, 1994.

Rushdie, Salman. "Magic in Service of Truth." *The New York Times Book Review*, April 21, 2014. https://www.nytimes.com/2014/04/21/books/review/gabriel-garcia-marquezs-work-was-rooted-in-the-real.html

Rushdie, Salman. *Midnight's Children*. Knopf, 1981.

Saldívar, Dasso. *García Márquez: El viaje a la semilla: La biografía*. Alfaguara, 1997.

Teng, Wei. "Gabriel García Márquez in China." *The Oxford Handbook of Gabriel García Márquez*, edited by Bell-Villada and López-Calvo, 2022, pp. 246–63.

Whitehead, Colson. *The Underground Railroad*. Doubleday, 2016.

CHAPTER 39

REPORTAGE, TESTIMONY, AND BIOGRAPHY IN THE NOVELS OF ELENA PONIATOWSKA

MICHAEL K. SCHUESSLER

ELENA Poniatowska is the author of more than fifty books that encompass almost every literary genre, including the novel and its various forms: semi-autobiographical, biographical, epistolary, and testimonial. Despite her wide-ranging literary production, Poniatowska is best known for the journalistic genres she reinvented in Mexico, in particular, the chronicle and the group testimonial, which is most closely related to the New Journalism of the 1960s as developed and practiced in the United States by such writers as Tom Wolfe and Joan Didion. An outstanding example of the latter, *La noche de Tlatelolco* (*Massacre in Mexico*, 1971), first published in English in 1975, is a collective account of the 1968 assault on students by government forces in Mexico City's Plaza de las Tres Culturas, where dozens, and perhaps as many as several hundred, demonstrators were killed by members of a paramilitary group known as the Olimpia Battalion.

Although Poniatowska—who in 2013 was awarded the prestigious Cervantes Prize—has enjoyed enormous success as a writer and journalist, for many years she was somewhat excluded from Mexican literary circles. Because she was reporting as a journalist day and night, she rarely found time to participate in the social activities of Mexico's literary society. Moreover, she was still rather young when she became convinced that the only books worth writing were useful ones, books meaningful to her country. This attitude regarding the themes of her growing body of fiction was what led Poniatowska to write what many critics consider her most significant novel, *Hasta no verte Jesús mío* (*Here's to You, Jesusa!*, 1969), first published in English in 2001.

For Poniatowska, the price of chiles and tomatoes, reports of evictions and land invasions, were much more meaningful than the often-fleeting notions of the contemporary literary vanguard. Far from belonging to Mexico's underclass, Poniatowska is descended from the last king of Poland, Stanislas Augusto Poniatowski, and from the marshal of Napoleonic France, Prince Josef Ciolek Poniatowski. Her family includes among its illustrious ancestors an archbishop, a composer, an astronomer, and several writers, including her aunt Pita—Guadalupe Amor—the mystical poet who, in an interview with her young niece, proclaimed herself to be "the absolute queen of hell." Given Poniatowska's royal pedigree and strong left-wing inclinations, which were in opposition to what she calls her "absurd nobility," in Europe some people still refer to her as "La Princesse Rouge" (Poniatowska, Personal interview).

Poniatowska was born in Paris in 1932 and immigrated to Mexico when she was ten years old, along with her mother and sister Kitzia, who were fleeing the perils of western Europe, which was at that time in the throes of the Second World War. Her mother, Paula Amor de Ferreira Iturbe, was a Mexican born in Paris whose ancestors had left Mexico with Porfirio Díaz and other prominent "porfirista" families. Doña Paulette met her future husband, Prince Jean E. Poniatowski Sperry, during a ball held at the Rothschild's family home on the Place de la Concorde in Paris, and they married shortly after, in 1931. The couple had three children: Elena, Kitzia and Jan, the youngest, who died in an automobile accident in 1968, when he was only twenty-two years old. Poniatowska began her education in France, where her grandfather gave her her first lessons in French and mathematics. Upon her arrival in Mexico City, she continued her elementary schooling at the British "Windsor School" and concluded her formal education at the Convent of the Sacred Heart (Eden Hall) in Torresdale, near Philadelphia, Pennsylvania. There she completed a program of academic classes: four years of general studies, as well as lessons in dance, religion, and etiquette. Although her teachers advised her to continue her studies in Manhattanville College, a sudden devaluation of Mexico's currency left her parents unable to finance her university education and Elena returned to Mexico.

Once in Mexico, Poniatowska studied shorthand and planned to find work as a bilingual secretary, but she never pursued a bachelor's degree. According to her, she "never even came close to a university, not even by night" (Schuessler XIII), although she has been awarded several *honoris causa* degrees by universities in Mexico and abroad. While Poniatowska is the first to point out that her higher education was less than conventional, the subjects of her copious interviews, which included Alfonso Reyes, Luis Buñuel, Octavio Paz, Diego Rivera, Juan Rulfo, André Malraux, and Rosario Castellanos, among many others, became the generous teachers of a young woman who was always curious and occasionally impertinent.

Lilus Kikus (1954), Poniatowska's first serious attempt at creative writing, was published in the collection "Los Presentes" (Those Present), directed by writer Juan José Arreola. It is a series of interwoven texts that may be read both as a collection of short stories or, as some readers and critics have chosen to do, a semi-autobiographical *novella*. As to the book's enigmatic title—also the name of its young protagonist and alter ego—the author explains that "it was an invention, because there was a childish riddle that went something like 'Matakikus'" (qtd. in Schuessler, *Elena Poniatowska* 76).[1] Indeed, what some consider to be Poniatowska's first attempt at the novelistic genre could also be classified as young adult fiction, due both to the age of its protagonist as well as the situations she encounters and the way in which they are construed. As her mother recalled it, in the pages of her first book Poniatowska included one or two of her friends and she also appears as a character, although only indirectly: "There is a bit of autobiography towards the end of *Lilus Kikus*, but not much. *Lilus Kikus* was an apprenticeship. She had already taken lessons in order to improve her written Spanish, because at school she had only studied English" (qtd. in Schuessler, *Elena Poniatowska* 76).

For a first book, *Lilus Kikus* sold well and received positive reviews, although only five hundred copies were printed for the first edition. In his review, Ermilo Abreu Gómez, an eminent critic of twentieth century Mexican literature, declared: "This is an astonishing book. No one writes this way in Mexico today. Elena Poniatowska, as very few current writers, has what is called a 'feeling for language' " (qtd. in Schuessler, *Elena Poniatowska* 76).[2] In an allusion to the precocious childhood of Sor Juana Inés de la Cruz of whose poetry Abreu Gómez was an early scholar and promoter, he concludes his text with an implicit comparison to the Hieronymite nun, who also surprised her superiors with great acumen at an early age: "I can hardly comprehend how someone so young has managed to achieve such mastery in her writing style," he concludes (qtd. in Schuessler, *Elena Poniatowska* 76).[3]

One of the first to review Poniatowska's first book was Carlos Fuentes, at that time the aspiring author of *Los días enmascarados* (The Masked Days, 1954), also published in the collection "Los Presentes." The title of his dialogical review, "Elena Poniatowska, *Lilus Kikus*," published in the *Revista de la Universidad de México* in 1954, alludes to the curious—and inferred—relationship between Elena the writer and the little girl, Lilus Kikus, which, according to him, was both an alter ego and pseudonym. At the same time, Fuentes explores the possible precursors of Poniatowska's book, which include Daisy Ashford, author of *The Young Visiters*, which she allegedly wrote at the age of nine while revealing "the same natural astonishment, that perverse ingenuity, of *Lilus Kikus*."[4] Another work, *Tiko*, by Consuelo Pani, is also mentioned by Fuentes due to the fact that in it, like in Poniatowska's first work, "reality is seen sort of sideways, as if from an obelisk in the air, or under the minimal abundance of foliage among the weeds" (Fuentes 30).[5]

Another commentator of Poniatowska's first book was Emmanuel Carballo, at that time already a respected literary critic and author of many essays on Mexican literature, whose review appeared in the pages of "México en la Cultura," cultural supplement of the newspaper *Novedades*, on November 7, 1954. For Carballo, one of the most interesting aspects of *Lilus Kikus* is precisely its literary pedigree, as, according to his reading, the book seems to cross genres:

> *Lilus Kikus* strongly resists being included in the usual categories employed by literary critics. Strictly speaking, it is not a short story, nor is it a novel. To be a short story, it lacks being linked to an anecdote; to be a novel, it would have to build up a plot, an argument, to develop its characters. The common thread that links the twelve short and lovely chapters is this little girl, apparently an ingénue, this astonished girl for whom life may be understood through hieroglyphs, signs, symbols . . .
>
> (Carballo qtd. in Schuessler, *Elena Poniatowska* 79–80)[6]

Although Carballo hits the mark with respect to the book's complex and innovative structure, it was the prophetic article published by Artemio Garfias under the ominous title "Lilus Kikus en peligro y sin salvación" (Lilus Kikus in Danger and without Salvation), which best foresaw the impact that Poniatowska's literary oeuvre would have upon the Mexican literary community during the second half of the twentieth century.[7] Garfias underlines the talent for observation possessed by the young writer, a talent that will serve her well during her entire career since her descriptions, reflections, and analysis of Mexican reality are the rudiments that, years later, will make her worthy of journalistic and literary fame based on her unappeasable curiosity regarding what goes on in the streets, in the markets, in the poorest neighborhoods:

> *Lilus Kikus* . . . is in certain danger of becoming the great writer her book heralds or, to the contrary. . . .turning into the inefficient housewife of a family whose best memories will remain sealed in the letters that she will have written to two or three intelligent friends . . . The news is bad, very bad, for our society; it is very good, on the other hand, for Mexico. It is not always that a first book appears in Mexico, or in any other country, carries with it the certainty that its author is a great writer. Lilus Kikus has launched her challenge, and she has done so with an outsized audacity.
>
> (qtd. in Schuessler, Elena Poniatowska 80–81)[8]

Many years passed until Poniatowska published another semi-autobiographical novel along the lines of *Lilus Kikus*, most notably *La "Flor de Lis"* (The "Fleur-de-Lis") in 1988, whose title is inspired by the name of a traditional tamale shop located in the Condesa neighborhood in Mexico City. In this work the author similarly draws upon her own childhood experiences to create her protagonist, a French girl named Mariana who arrives in Mexico with her younger sister, Sofía, and their lovely mother, Luz, after the Second World War. Upon their arrival from France, they discover their own Mexican identity, long forgotten amidst their European genealogy. Up to here, *La "Flor de Lis"* may be considered an autobiographical novel or even a memoir. However, the author later introduces characters and situations that do not correspond to her life as an adolescent, as in the case of the peculiar priest Teufel, whose name means devil in German. According to Poniatowska, she was inspired to invent this character by the *prêtres-ouvriers* (worker-priests) of France, who abandoned the clergy after coming into contact with the working classes. Furthermore, Father Teufel becomes an indispensable tool in terms of the narrative, as he permits the author to stand away from her own subjectivity in order to observe, document, and comment on the life of the protagonist.

In the text written for the presentation of *La "Flor de Lis"* and published in the Mexican daily *La Jornada* on April 30, 1988, Antonio Lazcano Araujo considers the presence of the author in this novel. Her role, apparently as the protagonist, dissolves into a universe of literary characters that emerge from other, earlier, short stories and who come to life and inhabit their own narrative space after passing through the sieve of Poniatowska's literary imagination to then be combined with autobiographical features:

La "Flor de Lis" is not a book of memoirs, but it is not difficult to see in Mariana the same *rétroussé* nose, the sky-blue eyes with the same expression of candor, the same innocence combined with a devilish curiosity and an acute intelligence we see in Elena Poniatowska . . . Where did La "Flor de Lis" spring from? Every book hides autobiographical elements among metaphors and paraphrases. . . . These are characters that Elena Poniatowska has been weaving with the invisible darning thread of her writing in order to form a novel, to invent a life for Mariana, to relate part of her autobiography, and to explore the Federal District of the fifties, where it was still possible to meet a young white-gloved duchess in a red Colonia del Valle Coyoacán public bus.

(Lazcano 7)[9]

Recalling the enthusiasm provoked by the publication of *Hasta no verte Jesús mío* almost two decades prior, several critics discover new qualities in La "Flor de Lis" that are only revealed when the literary fiction is separated from the life of the author: a difficult feat for the writer and for many critics, who insist on pointing out what is essentially biographical, or at least self-referential, in nearly all feminine artistic expressions. From the baroque sonnets of Sor Juana Inés de la Cruz to Frida Kahlo's painful self-portraits, these representations may indeed be considered as confessional to a certain degree, but that does not diminish their inventive quality. In this case, Poniatowska's work showcases virtues that merit critical attention and thwart any attempt to define her as simply a weaver of intimist texts. Moreover, one of the most significant innovations to be discovered in La "Flor de Lis" is that of the creation of a feminine literary universe, one inhabited by three females in particular: Mariana, Sofía, and their mother. In this way, the book fills an important gap in the history and tradition of the Mexican novel, especially because this particular work is not a testimony of poverty and hopelessness nor that of a disinherited female revolutionary, or *soldadera*, but that of a privileged society in full decadence, one that continues a literary tradition begun by her aunt, Guadalupe Amor, whose autobiographical novel *Yo soy mi casa* (I am My House) was published three decades earlier, in 1957.

Critic and novelist José Joaquín Blanco confirms the observation made by Lazcano Araujo in his aforementioned text:

The concept of the "feminine" novel on the other hand, is closer to La "Flor de Lis," in the sense that it is not only a novel by a woman about other women, but it is also about the long life *in gineco*, (among females) . . . The fact that it joyously assumes a closed world that women make to protect themselves, love themselves, enjoy themselves and learn from one another is a great contribution, as it frequently remains an "age of shadows" in feminine biographies that only illuminates their contacts with men.

(Blanco 374)[10]

In 1964 Poniatowska met the person who would make the greatest impact upon her personal, professional, and spiritual development: an elderly washerwoman from the southern state of Oaxaca whose name was Josefina Bórquez.[11] The writer discovered Josefina one day when she heard her shouting at the top of her lungs from the roof of the building where she worked washing overalls and other workmen's garb. Only a year before, in 1963, Poniatowska had published an illustrated chronicle of the Sunday activities of Mexico's lower classes: *Todo empezó el domingo* (Everything Began on Sunday), an ethnographic adventure that, as she insists, led her down a path that was quite different from the road she was apparently destined to follow, one lined with cocktail parties, baby showers, wedding receptions, and other activities of Mexico's upper classes. Included in her book *Luz y luna, las lunitas* (Light and Moon, the Little Moons, 1994), a collection of essays including photographs by Graciela Iturbide, Rosa Nissán, Paula Haro, and Héctor García (her newspaper photographer of many years), is a chronicle aptly entitled "Vida y muerte de Jesusa" (Life and Death of Jesusa),[12] in which Poniatowska pays homage to her "Mexican Virgil," the individual who uncovered for her the mysteries of Mexico City's urban underworld: one ignored by a revolution that, according to Jesusa, never gave anything to anybody, except to the new political bosses who now occupied the place of those aristocratic Mexican families—like Poniatowska's—who escaped to France during the twilight of Porfirio Díaz's ostensibly interminable presidency. In this *memento mori*, originally composed by the journalist in 1978, the year of Josefina's death, Poniatowska relates how, little by little, she entered Josefina's world, and provides the information necessary for a better understanding of this unusual friendship that, five years after meeting for the first time, would come to fruition in a prodigious novel: *Hasta no verte Jesús mío* (*Here's to You, Jesusa!*), originally published in Spanish in 1969 and in English in 2001.

The first times that Elena visited Jesusa in her home, her hostess was not the least bit welcoming; on the contrary, she was scornful of her curious visitor:

— What do you want? What business do you have with me?
— I want to talk to you.
— To me? Listen I work. If I don't work, I don't eat. I don't have time to hang around chatting. ("Introduction" viii)[13]

Jesusa never ceased greeting Poniatowska with a sullen attitude and mocking demeanor, not willing to show affection for that spoiled little Mexican girl who, to Jesusa, was the symbol of utter uselessness and a constant reminder of the social injustice put on display by her abject poverty. And thus, week after week, Poniatowska would enter a world of overflowing toilets and no running water, dirty toilet paper scattered on the floor, and the smell of urine that permeated the tenement's patio. After spending several weeks with Jesusa, Poniatowska got up the nerve to ask her about her life: her wretched present and adventurous past, her dreams and her disappointments born with the advent of Porfirio Díaz and, later, her participation in a revolution designed to overthrow him, but which did not live up to its lofty promises.

Evidently, Jesusa pretended not to find this weekly waste of her time interesting at all, but little by little she began to give in to her young disciple's entreaties, always under the condition that Poniatowska, who knew nothing about manual labor, would help her with her many chores, which never seemed to fit into the two hours that Jesusa had available for her young acquaintance. Poniatowska began to visit Jesusa once a week, often taking with her an enormous old-fashioned tape recorder that somebody had lent her. As Poniatowska did not know how to use the contraption, sometimes it did not record and she had to repeat the same questions she had asked the time before. Jesusa's reaction was always that of annoyed disdain that gradually became entwined with an almost imperceptible affection. Throughout all the interviews, which normally lasted two to three hours, Jesusa initiated her candid pupil into another Mexico, one full of suffering, hunger, ugliness, and misery. But little by little, amidst scolding and ridiculing, Poniatowska extracted from Jesusa a personal odyssey. In this formidable Mexican woman, she was to discover an inner force of her own, an incredulous attitude towards life that coincided with her own personal bewilderment.

Little by little, a sisterhood was born between the two women, something which Jesusa called "la querencia," a personal bond that, although never mentioned out loud, sometimes became palpable in the melancholy room inhabited by Jesusa, her chickens, and her recollections. According to Poniatowska, her debt to Jesusa is enormous:

> Never has one human being done so much for another as Jesusa has for me. And I knew she was going to die, as she wished; that is why every Wednesday my heart tightened when I thought that she might not be there. "Some day when you come, you won't find me, you'll just find air."
>
> ("Introduction xv)[14]

One of the critical observations often made regarding *Hasta no verte Jesús mío*, an extraordinary testimonial, a product of many hours of dialogue with the woman who would become its protagonist, is encapsulated in the question: Who does the book belong to? Is it the work of Elena Poniatowska or Josefina Bórquez? At one point in her long requiem, Poniatowska confesses that, like Oscar Lewis, the author of *The Children of Sánchez*, which caused an enormous scandal upon its publication in Mexico, she did not improve the conditions in which Jesusa lived either:

> Neither the doctor of anthropology, Oscar Lewis, nor I, lived the lives of the others . . . For Oscar Lewis, the Sánchez family became splendid protagonists of the so-called anthropology of poverty. For me, Jesusa was a true character, the best of all. Jesusa was right: I profited from her, I took advantage of her, just like Lewis profited from the Sánchez family . . . Lewis and I made money on our books about Mexicans who live in tenements [and] I continued to be, more than anything else, a woman in front of a typewriter.
>
> (Poniatowska, *Luz y luna* 51)[15]

In novelistic terms, some critics underscore the roguish nature of her novel, which reinaugurates a literary sub-genre that had been absent from Mexico since the time of Joaquín Fernández de Lizardi, whose *El periquillo sarniento* (*The Mangy Parrot*, 1831), translated into English by Katherine Anne Porter, describes the vicissitudes of his anti-hero of the same name. This picaresque novel, written as a vehicle to criticize the political and social institutions of New Spain at the dawn of Mexico's Independence, is also considered by many critics to be the fledgling nation's first modern novel. A century and a half later, *Here's to You, Jesusa!* came to represent a true landmark of twentieth-century Mexican narrative and, as such, has had various sequels, among which the most extraordinary is undoubtedly *El vampiro de la colonia Roma* (*Adonis García* 1979), a neo-picaresque novel written by Luis Zapata. His book was published ten years after Poniatowska's and relates the adventures, dreams, and disappointments of a young male prostitute of Mexico City, who, as a new Lazarillo de Tormes, goes from master to master, always attempting to improve his lot in life within the strict hierarchy of his society and times.

In her aforementioned essay "Vida y muerte de Jesusa" (Life and Death of Jesusa), Poniatowska reconstructs the process of writing the novel and the manner in which it was finally composed, pointing out that each meeting with Jesusa was a long interview that the author would transcribe day after day, until she had managed to accumulate nearly a thousand typewritten pages. Notwithstanding the amount of information gathered, the author confesses that in her novel she was unable to make visible what was essential in Jesusa, incapable of re-creating the profound nature of her protagonist. By accumulating adventures, moving from one anecdote to another, Poniatowska was guided by her subject's fascinating life as a nomad, a life that encompassed a revolution, many loves, quarrels, disillusionment, and a newfound religious zeal instilled in her through the miraculous healer, "Roque Rojas," and his histrionic spiritualism. Jesusa's vital and spiritual experiences are firmly inscribed in the first sentences of Poniatowska's novel: "This is my third time back on Earth, but I've never suffered as much as I have now. I was a queen in my last incarnation, I know, because I saw my train during a revelation" (Poniatowska, *Here's to you Jesusa!* 3).[16]

Among the works Poniatowska has penned throughout a literary career spanning over half a century, one stands out due to its structural uniqueness and emotional power. It is also an homage to her gender and a veiled reference to her own feminine condition: *Querido Diego, te abraza Quiela* (1976) translated in 1986 as *Dear Diego*. This epistolary novella comprises a series of letters that are at the same time heartrending and affectionate, whose recipient, the famous artist Diego Rivera, never responds to their author, the Russian painter and mother of his only son, Angelina Beloff. At the same time, this short work of fiction reflects Poniatowska's own suffering at that time, for her marriage to the Mexican astrophysicist Guillermo Haro had not provided the loving support that she yearned for:

> Carmen Gaitán of Editorial Océano asked me to write a preface for the two novels by Lupe Marín: *La única* (The One and Only), and *Un día patrio* (A Patriotic Day). To learn more about Marín, I read the English biography of Diego Rivera by Bertram Wolfe: *The Fabulous Life of Diego Rivera*. There I discovered Angelina Beloff, Rivera's first wife and the mother of his only son, who died in Paris of meningitis. Instead of

writing the preface, I began to write the letters that I thought Angelina Beloff would have written to Diego Rivera. It surprised me that years later she had come all the way to Mexico to find him. She went to Bellas Artes looking for him, and he passed right by Beloff without even recognizing her. In reality, I think I was writing to Guillermo, disguising myself as Angelina Beloff, because he was completely absorbed by his astronomy, and I felt very alone.

(qtd. in Schuessler, *Elena Poniatowska* 175)[17]

On July 12, 1978, Carlos Monsiváis, longtime friend and guardian angel of Poniatowska's since the 1968 student massacre, and a familiar presence in Mexican culture of the latter half of the twentieth century, published a review of his friend's book in the pages of *Siempre!*. The article, entitled "In the Studio, Everything Has Remained the Same," ("En el estudio, todo ha quedado igual") evokes the first sentence of Poniatowska's epistolary novella and, upon closer inspection, is in reality much more than an unpretentious literary review. In his text, Monsiváis also offers a critical assessment of Poniatowska's literary oeuvre as well as her intellectual trajectory, from the publication of *Lilus Kikus* in 1954 to the present. With regard to Poniatowska's latest work, his opinion is encouraging:

> The voice of those ostensibly vanquished; the mothers of those students who simply disappeared, the beast of burden known as Jesusa Palancares in *Here's to You, Jesusa!*, the anachronistic creature who, when writing to Diego, expresses femininity as the sum of all defeats. But in these narratives of struggles and sufferings, Elena Poniatowska finds an optimal vehicle to widen the space of understanding of lives and dramatic personal experiences.
>
> (Monsiváis, n.p.)[18]

Although it may be argued that *Hasta no verte Jesús mío* may rightly be considered Poniatowska's first biographical novel, what sets it apart from all the others she would eventually publish is the fact that the young journalist had direct, personal access to her subject, whose real name was Josefina Bórquez and who, as we have seen, Poniatowska subjected to many hours of extensive interviews. For this reason alone, I am inclined to consider the former as an exceptional example of the "testimonial novel," where, by definition, the author designs a work of creative fiction anchored in the life experiences of her subject, whom he or she may interview and question. Thus, *Hasta no verte Jesús mío* is at once analogous yet dissimilar from Poniatowska's other testimonial works not considered in this essay, such as *La noche de Tlatelolco* (1971) and *Nada, nadie. Las voces del temblor* (*Nothing, Nobody: Voices of the Mexico City Earthquake*, 1988), which, as pointed out at the beginning of this essay, are more akin—due to their technique and structure—to the book-length works of New Journalism, for example those published by US journalists such as Truman Capote (*In Cold Blood*, 1966).

Furthermore, all of Poniatowska's subsequent works of biographical fiction were motivated, as she has pointed out on numerous occasions, by her own research as well as information gleaned from interviews with individuals familiar with the subject of the novel, such as in the case of her most widely celebrated work of biographical fiction,

Tinísima (1992), published in English as *Tinísima* in 1996. Over a period of more than twenty years, Poniatowska would publish five more novels of this kind: *Paseo de la Reforma* (1996), *La piel del cielo* (*The Skin of the Sky*, 2001), *El tren pasa primero* (The Train Goes First, 2005), *Leonora* (2011), and *Dos veces única* (Twice Unique, 2015), the latter inspired by Guadalupe Marín, the charismatic wife of Diego Rivera and mother of two of his three daughters. Given the limited scope of this essay, and because it is the first of her biographical fictions translated into English, in what follows, I will concentrate on *Tinísima*, Poniatowska's intimate novel of epic proportions, at once literary biography and the history of an exceptional period in the history of Mexico and the world, beginning after the fall of Porfirio Díaz in Mexico (1911) and continuing through the major political upheavals of early-twentieth-century Europe, in particular the birth of the Soviet Union (1922) and the outbreak of the Spanish Civil War (1936–1939).

In a roundabout way during the early 1980s, Poniatowska discovered an extraordinary woman who, like herself, was a Mexican at heart, and whose artistic and political contribution to post-revolutionary Mexico is an impressive example of cultural militancy. In a curious case of parallel lives, Tina Modotti also emigrated with her family to America, albeit under very different circumstances. While Poniatowska, her sister Kitzia, and their mother came to Mexico City in 1942, fleeing the war in Europe, Modotti and her family moved to San Francisco, California, from Udine, Italy, around the turn of the twentieth century, in search of the American dream. As an indirect result of her participation in Italian-language plays in San Francisco, Modotti found work as an actress in the silent movies that were then being made in Hollywood, where she was inevitably typecast in stereotypical roles such as the tiger-eyed Latin vamp with a menacing scowl and a dagger held between her teeth. In Los Angeles, she met the photographer Edward Weston, with whom she traveled to Mexico in 1923. They arrived in a country euphoric at the triumph of the Revolution, and where local artists were employed by the government under the patronage of José Vasconcelos, Secretary of Public Education. In an atmosphere full of great expectations and encouraged by her new partner, Cuban revolutionary Julio Antonio Mella (1903–1929), Modotti discovered her true calling: that of militant photographer devoted to the international communist party.

Because of her activities and attitudes, Modotti revealed herself to be the individual who helped Poniatowska better understand her own role in the world at large. As with Josefina Bórquez and Angelina Beloff, chance led her to Tina when the Mexican cinematographer Gabriel Figueroa commissioned Poniatowska to write a script for a movie about Modotti's life. The film was never made, but Poniatowska had already invested a great deal of time and energy in the project by the time she learned that it had been abandoned. At the same time, she realized that through her numerous interviews with central figures of the period, including Manuel Álvarez Bravo, Vittorio Vidali, Pablo O'Higgins, Guadalupe Marín, Yolanda Modotti, and others, she had accumulated an enormous amount of material for a literary project that would eventually become a sweeping portrait of post-revolutionary Mexico and postwar Europe, comparable in scope to the imposing imagery of Rivera, Orozco, and Siqueiros, and an homage to an era in Mexico that, according to Poniatowska, was unrivaled in the twentieth century.

The novel, baptized as *Tinísima* in honor of the superlative dimensions of its subject and her times, is a true epic of culture and politics as they developed in the first three decades of the twentieth century. The story follows the unswerving trajectory of the protagonist, and travels through the bourgeois bohemia of Los Angeles, Mexico City, the Russia of Stalin, Lenin, and Trotsky, and civil-war-torn Spain, where Modotti fought alongside "Commander Carlos," whose real name was Vittorio Vidali.

In an interview with Javier Molina, published in *La Jornada* on 20 September 1992, Poniatowska feels compelled to contemplate the generic nature of *Tinísima*, as many critics still insisted at the time that her narrative was merely journalistic while ignoring its undeniable literary qualities:

— Do you consider [*Tinísima*] a historical novel?
— I don't know how to establish such categories. Fernando del Paso says that his book *Noticias del imperio* (*News from the Empire*) is a historical novel, but I don't want to make the same mistake as the national textbooks that want to turn the current presidency into national history.
— [The book] may be historical, political, social, a chronicle of the culture of the era but, above all, it is a novel; it is literature. Can you please comment on this?
— It is a novel in which I tried to turn exposition—words taken from my interviews—as well as what I read in the newspapers, into literature. If the book's language echoes old-fashioned Spanish, that is because as the years went by, I began to internalize my subject, Tina Modotti, and I brought her forth with the greatest of ease. She made me grow and through this novel I learned a lot. ("*Tinísima*" 22)[19]

In her review of *Tinísima*, published in *Excélsior* on December 16, 1992, the Mexican poet and essayist Ethel Krauze discovers the "intimate mirror" that Poniatowska's novel provides: it is the manifestation of personal and political convictions, of the carnal and humanistic desires of its protagonist and, to a certain point, of its author. Although Krauze does not recognize the importance of the personal—intimate—link to be found between Poniatowska and her subject, she sees in the novel a history of women in the collective sense:

> *Tinísima* is much more than the biography of Tina Modotti—the Italian photographer who lived in our country and became the scandal of the era: a liberated woman, a professional, and a militant communist. It is the intimate reflection of a woman who struggles with her social ideals and her need for individual expression, her importance and her courage, her love for men, and her love for others, her austere discipline and her wish for aesthetic contemplation. It is the timely journey of any woman who discovers her own intelligence and searches for her identity in order to make sense of her own existence.
>
> (Krauze, qtd. in Schuessler, *Elena Poniatowska* 215–16)[20]

Tinísima earned Poniatowska the Mazatlán Prize for the second time (she had already received the award in 1971 for *Here's to You, Jesusa!*). Due to this critical attention, *Tinísima* received enough acclaim and editorial success to interest the New York-based Farrar, Straus, and Giroux publishing house, which, in 1997, launched a (greatly abridged) English translation of the novel prepared by Katherine Silver.

In 2019, sixty-five years after the publication of her first work of fiction, *Lilus Kikus*, the anecdotes of a precocious girl who at times appears to be analogous to their creator, and who speculates about the rights of lizards on a windowsill, Poniatowska returned to her family roots in an extensive autobiographical novel that, when completed, will comprise two volumes: *El amante polaco* (The Polish Lover).[21] In the first volume, the only one published as of yet, Poniatowska delves into her paternal lineage, that of Stanislaus II Augustus, the last king of Poland, lover of Catherine the Great: a cultured and enlightened man of his times who spoke numerous languages. In the novel she intertwines historical fiction with her own personal memories as a little girl growing up in Mexico and, perhaps most poignantly, with episodes of her life as an aspiring young writer. Not surprisingly, in the year of the #Me Too movement in Latin America, it is in this brief section that the scant criticism of the novel has focused, because in one of these segments Poniatowska—without ever revealing his name—recounts the afternoon in December when she was sexually assaulted by her teacher and literary mentor, Juan José Arreola, whose child she would bear nine months later:

> I am young and am always smiling. I laugh easily. One afternoon, in the middle of class, the Maestro rises, scrawny, his hair standing on end, a rod growing inside his trousers. "You are a peacock who has come to parade around in a chicken coop," he tells me . . . I head towards the door. "Ah, no, it's not so easy," he warns. And I pay the price for having gone up the stairs so hastily; I pay the price for Vivaldi's "The Four Seasons," which spin now in their winter so as to shroud me; I pay the price for the rooftop and for each stair that I now descend quickly towards the exit. In the street I don't understand, I only know that, just like him, the rooftop with its spread sheet has given me a wallop.
>
> (Poniatowska, *El amante* 332–33)[22]

Unsurprisingly, this slightly veiled accusation caused an uproar in Mexico's literary and academic communities: most members coming to Poniatowska's defense, while others, including members of Arreola's family, rushed to their relative's defense and, in an attempt to demonstrate his innocence, published fragments of the letters sent by Poniatowska to her erstwhile maestro and father of her newborn son. In an article entitled "El maestro y la esritora" (The Maestro and the Writer), written by Mexican feminist Marta Lamas and published in the weekly *Proceso*, (#2251 December 22, 2019), she questions what constitutes rape:

> What is rape? According to the *Real Academia* (Spanish Royal Academy), it is defined by having sexual relations with women through the use of force. While rape

may be committed by an unknown man, the vast majority of this kind of sexual assault is committed in "safe" surroundings (one's home, school or at work) and by men who are acquaintances or even friends. I read [Poniatowska's] lines and I imagine a Maestro who is weary of the innocence and ingenuity of this young woman, who would go upstairs and visit him to discuss literature; a Maestro who is a dyed-in-the-wool macho, sure of himself, of his powers of seduction, for whom nothing could be more "normal" than to turn his female students into lovers. And as Elena, the upper-class princess, the cheerful blonde, doesn't give in like the rest, he takes her by force.

(Lamas 45)[23]

It remains to be seen if Poniatowska chooses to elaborate upon this challenging moment in her personal life within the pages of the second volume of her expansive genealogical novel, or if she will simply move on, working with a discipline and talent that has defined herself and her work for almost seventy years of uninterrupted creation.

NOTES

1. "Fue un invento porque había una adivinanza que decía algo así como 'Matakikus'" (Poniatowska, qtd. in Schuessler, *Elenísima* 128–29).
2. "Se trata de un libro insólito. Así no se escribe en nuestro México actual. Elena Poniatowska, como muy pocos escritores de hoy, tiene lo que se dice el sentido del idioma" (Abreu, qtd. in Schuessler, *Elenísima* 129).
3. "Casi no entiendo que una persona tan joven haya logrado tal dominio en su manera de escribir" (Abreu, qtd. in Schuessler, *Elenísima* 129).
4. "Ese mismo asombro natural, esa misma ingenuidad perversa de *Lilus Kikus*" (Fuentes 30).
5. "La realidad está vista, como de costado, o desde un obelisco en el aire, o desde la minima frondosidad de las hierbas" (Fuentes 30).
6. "*Lilus Kikus* se resiste a entrar fácilmente en los habituales casilleros de la crítica. Estrictamente no es un cuento, tampoco una novela. Para ser cuento le falta circumscribirse a una anécdota; para ser novela, plantear un conflicto, desarrollar los caracteres. El hilo de unión entre sus doce pequeños y hermosos capítulos es esta niña aparentemente ingenua, esta joven asombrada para quien la vida se entiende a base de jeroglíficos; los signos, los símbolos" (Carballo, qtd. in Schuessler, *Elenísima* 132).
7. Although the brief note is signed only with the initial letters A. G., the full name of the mysterious critic, already somewhat blurred, appears jotted down in Poniatowska's own hand in one of her many newspaper scrapbooks.
8. "*Lilus Kikus*, apenas asomada a la literatura, está en el inevitable peligro de ser la gran escritora que anuncia su libro o, por el contrario, si otras circunstancias son más poderosas, la ineficiente madre de familia cuyo mayor recuerdo quedará en las cartas que haya escrito a dos o tres amigas inteligentes . . . La noticia es mala, muy mala, para la sociedad; muy buena en cambio para México. No siempre que aparece un primer libro puede tener México, o cualquier otro país la certeza de un gran escritor. *Lilus Kikus* ha lanzado su reto, y con bien desmedida audacia" (qtd. in Schuessler, *Elenísima* 133–34).
9. "La '*Flor de Lis*' no es un libro de memorias, pero no es difícil adivinar en Mariana la misma nariz respingada y fruncida, los ojos con la misma candorosa mirada de panóptico azul

cielo, la misma inocencia mezclada con la curiosidad endiablada y la aguda inteligencia a la que Elena Poniatowska nos tiene acostumbrados. . . ¿De dónde brotó *La 'Flor de Lis'*? Todo libro esconde, entre la metáfora y la paráfrasis, elementos autobiográficos, y en este nuevo libro confluyen y reencarnan personajes prefigurados en cuentos de años atrás, 'Castillo en Francia', 'De Gaulle en Minería', 'El inventario', personajes que Elena Poniatowska ha ido hilvanando con los zurcidos invisibles de su escritura para escribir una novela, inventarle la vida a Mariana, relatar parte de su autobiografía y describir al Distrito Federal de los años cincuenta, cuando todavía era posible encontrarse con una duquesita de guantes blancos trepada a bordo de un camión colonia Del Valle-Coyoacán" (Lazcano Araujo, 7).

10. "El concepto de 'novela femenina', en cambio, sí está más próximo a *La 'Flor de Lis'*, en el sentido de que no es sólo una novela de una mujer sobre otras mujeres, sino sobre la larga vida *en gineco*, en feminidad. . . en realidad, constituye una gran aportación el hecho de asumir, y jubilosamente, el mundo cerrado que en buena parte de sus vidas hacen las mujeres para protegerse, quererse, divertirse, aprender unas de otras, y que frecuentemente queda como una "edad de tinieblas" de biografías femeninas que sólo iluminan sus contactos con los hombres" (Blanco 374).

11. Although her real name was Josefina Bórquez, Poniatowska almost always refers to her novel's protagonist as "Jesusa," even when she is referring to the person who inspired the work. I am conscious of this fact and have followed suit: the protagonist of her novel and the person who inspired it will be referred to as Jesusa from here on.

12. An abridged version of "Vida y muerte de Jesusa" is included as the "Introduction" to *Here's to You, Jesusa*, the English-language translation of *Hasta no verte Jesús mío*.

13. "—¿Qué se trae? ¿Qué trae conmigo?—Quiero platicar con usted.
—¿Conmigo? Mire, yo trabajo. Si no trabajo, no como. No tengo campo de andar platicando" (Poniatowska, *Luz y luna*, 38).

14. " —Nunca, ningún ser humano hizo tanto por otro como Jesusa hizo por mí. Y se va a morir, como ella lo desea, por eso cada miércoles se me cierra el corazón de pensar que podría no estar. "Algún día que venga, ya no me va a encontrar, se topará nomás con el puro aire" (Poniatowska, *Luz y luna* 44).

15. "Ni el doctor en antropología Oscar Lewis, ni yo asumimos la vida ajena. . . Para Oscar Lewis, los Sánchez se convirtieron en espléndidos protagonistas de la llamada antropología de la pobreza. Para mí Jesusa fue un personaje, el mejor de todos. Jesusa tenía razón. Yo a ella le saqué raja, como Lewis se la sacó a los Sánchez. La vida de los Sánchez no cambió para nada; no les fue mejor ni peor. Lewis y yo ganamos dinero con nuestros libros sobre los mexicanos que viven en vecindades. . . Seguí siendo ante todo, una mujer frente a una máquina de escribir." (Poniatowska, *Luz y luna* 51) (This passage is not included in the English versión included as the introduction to *Here's to You, Jesusa*).

16. "Ésta es la tercera vez que regreso a la tierra, pero nunca había sufrido tanto como en esta reencarnación ya que en la anterior fui reina. Lo sé porque en una videncia que tuve me vi la cola" (Poniatowska, *Hasta no verte Jesús mío* 9).

17. Carmen Gaitán de la editorial Océano me pidió que hiciera un prólogo para las dos novelas de Lupe Marín: *La única* y *Un día patrio*. Para saber más de Lupe Marín leí la biografía en inglés de Bertram Wolfe: *The Fabulous Life of Diego Rivera*. Ahí encontré a Angelina Beloff, su primera mujer y madre de su único hijo que murió de meningitis en París.

En vez de hacer el prólogo me puse a escribir las cartas que pensé que Angelina Beloff hubiera podido escribirle a Diego Rivera. Me llamó mucho la atención que ella viniera a México siguiendo a Rivera. Lo fue a buscar a Bellas Artes y él pasó a su lado sin siquiera reconocerla. En realidad siento que estaba escribiéndole a Guillermo disfrazándome de Angelina Beloff, porque él estaba metido en su astronomía, y me sentía muy sola" (qtd. in Schuessler, *Elenísima* 139).

18. "La voz de los vencidos ostensibles: las madres de los estudiantes desaparecidos, la bestia de carga conocida como Jesusa Palancares en *Hasta no verte Jesús mío*, la criatura anacrónica que al escribirle a Diego expresa la feminidad como suma de derrotas. Pero en estos relatos de empeños y sufrimientos, Elena Poniatowska halla una vía óptima para ampliar el espacio de comprensión de vidas o vivencias dramáticas. Al iluminar la identidad y las mentalidades de las víctimas, las acerca y las despoja de su inefable carácter remoto y vagaroso" (Monsiváis, n.p.).

19. "—¿Considera usted que [*Tinísima*] se trata de una novela histórica?

—No sé poner categorías. Fernando del Paso dice que su libro *Noticias del imperio* es una novela histórica, pero yo no quisiera cometer el mismo error de los libros de texto que quieren hacer pasar el sexenio actual a la historia.

—Puede ser histórica, política, social, el testimonio de la cultura de una época, pero, antes que todo, es una novela: literatura. Háblenos de ello, por favor.

—Es una novela en la que intenté pasar a la literatura testimonios, palabras de entrevistas, y también lo que yo leía en los periódicos. Si parece un español antigüito es sobre todo por eso. Ahora, a medida que pasaron los años se fue internando Tina Modotti, y ya la eché para afuera con mayor facilidad. Me hizo crecer, aprendí mucho con esta novela" (Poniatowska, "*Tinísima*" 22).

20. "Tinísima es mucho más que la biografía de Tina Modotti, la fotógrafa italiana que vivió en nuestro país para escándalo de la época: mujer liberada, profesional, comunista militante. Es el espejo íntimo de una mujer que lucha entre sus ideales sociales y su necesidad de expresión individual, su importancia y su temple, su amor al hombre y su amor a los demás, su austera disciplina y su gana de contemplación estética; en fin, el actualísimo itinerario de toda mujer que emerge a la inteligencia, a la búsqueda de su identidad para encontrar el sentido de la propia existencia" (Krauze qtd. in *Elenísima* 288).

21. The second volume (libro dos) appeared in 2021.

22. "Soy joven, sonrío a todas horas, río con facilidad. Una tarde, a media clase, el Maestro se yergue amenazante, flaco, los cabellos parados, un palo también dentro de su pantalón. 'Usted es un pavorreal que ha venido a pavonearse a un gallinero', me espeta. . . . Me acerco a la puerta. 'Ah; no, no es tan fácil', amenaza. Y pago por subir las escaleras con tanta premura, pago por *Las cuatro estaciones* de Vivaldi, que giran ahora su invierno para amortajarme, pago por la azotea y por cada escalón por el que ahora desciendo a toda velocidad hacia la puerta de salida y ya en la calle no entiendo, sólo sé que, así como él, la azotea con su sábana tendida me ha dado una bofetada" (Poniatowska, *El amante* 332–33).

23. "¿Qué es una violación? Según el Diccionario de la Real Academia es tener acceso carnal con una mujer por fuerza. Existen las violaciones por hombres desconocidos, pero en su gran mayoría ocurren en ámbitos seguros (la propia casa, la escuela, el trabajo) y por varones cercanos o conocidos. Leo esas líneas e imagino a un Maestro harto de la candidez de esa jovencita ingenua, que subía a verlo y a platicar con él de literatura; un Maestro

troquelado por el machismo, seguro de sí mismo, de su poder de seducción, para quien lo "normal" era convertir a sus alumnas en amantes. Y como Elena, la princesa fifí, la güerita sonriente, no se comporta como las demás, la toma a la fuerza" (Lamas 45).

Works Cited

Blanco, José Joaquín. "Elena Poniatowska: píntame angelitos güeros." *Crónica literaria: un siglo de escritores mexicanos*. Cal y Arena, 1996, pp. 373–76.

Fernández de Lizardi, José Joaquín. *El periquillo sarniento*. Porrúa, 1949.

Fuentes, Carlos. "Elena Poniatowska, Lilus Kikus." *Revista de la Universidad de México*, vol. 9, nos. 1–2, September–October 1954, p. 30.

Fuentes, Carlos. *Los días enmascarados*. Los Presentes, 1954.

Lamas, Marta. "El maestro y la escritora." *Proceso*, December 22, 2019, p. 45.

Lazcano Araujo, Antonio. "La flor más bella, sus pétalos de hoja de tamal." *La Jornada de los Libros*, April 30, 1988, p. 7.

Monsiváis, Carlos. "En el estudio todo ha quedado igual." *Aproximaciones y reintegros*, edited by Carlos Mapes, Ediciones Trilce, Kindle edition, 2020.

Poniatowska, Elena. *El amante polaco*. Seix Barral, 2019.

Poniatowska, Elena. *Dear Diego*. Translated by Katherine Silver. Pantheon Books, 1986.

Poniatowska, Elena. *Dos veces única*. Seix Barral, 2015.

Poniatowska, Elena. *Hasta no verte Jesús mío*. Era, 1969.

Poniatowska, Elena. *Here's to You, Jesusa!* Translated by Deanna Heikkinen. Penguin, 2001.

Poniatowska, Elena. "Introduction." *Here's to You, Jesusa*. Farrar, Strauss, and Giroux, 2002, pp. vii–xxx.

Poniatowska, Elena. *La "Flor de Lis."* Era, 1988.

Poniatowska, Elena. *La noche de Tlatelolco. Testimonios de historia oral*. Era, 1971.

Poniatowska, Elena. *Massacre in Mexico*. Translated by Helen R. Lane. Viking Press, 1975.

Poniatowska, Elena. *Leonora*. Planeta, 2011.

Poniatowska, Elena. *Lilus Kikus*. Los Presentes, 1954.

Poniatowska, Elena. *Lilus Kikus and Other Stories*. Translated by Elizabeth C. Martínez. University of New Mexico Press, 2005.

Poniatowska, Elena. *Luz y luna, las lunitas*. Era, 1994.

Poniatowska, Elena. *Nada, nadie: las voces del temblor*. Era, 1988.

Poniatowska, Elena. *Paseo de la Reforma*. Joaquín Mortiz, 1996.

Poniatowska, Elena. Personal Interview. September 12, 2004.

Poniatowska, Elena. *La piel del cielo*. Alfaguara, 2001.

Poniatowska, Elena. *The Skin of the Sky*. Translated by Deanna Heikkinen. Farrar, Straus & Giroux, 2004.

Poniatowska, Elena. *Querido Diego, te abraza Quiela*. Era, 1976. Alianza, 1978.

Poniatowska, Elena. *Tinísima*. Era, 1992.

Poniatowska, Elena. *Tinisima*. Translated by Katherine Silver. Farrar, Straus & Giroux, 1996.

Poniatowska, Elena. "*Tinísima*, literatura en una sucesión de atmósferas deslumbrantes." Interview with Javier Molina. *La Jornada*, September 20, 1992, p. 22.

Poniatowska, Elena. *Todo empezó el domingo*. Illustrated by Antonio Beltrán. Fondo de Cultura Económica, 1963.

Poniatowska, Elena. *El tren pasa primero*. Alfaguara, 2005.

Schuessler, Michael K. *Elena Poniatowska: An Intimate Biography*. University of Arizona Press, 2007.

Schuessler, Michael K. *Elenísima: Ingenio y figura de Elena Poniatowska*. Booket, 2013.

Zapata, Luis. *Las aventuras, desventuras y sueños de Adonis García, vampiro de la colonia Roma*. Grijalbo, 1979.

Zapata, Luis. *Adonis García: A Picaresque Novel*. Translated by Edward A. Lacey. Gay Sunshine Press, 1981.

CHAPTER 40

RITA INDIANA'S TENTACLED NOVELS

RITA DE MAESENEER

RITA Indiana (1977–) is a highly elusive figure, a nomadic and androgynous persona. She writes novels, poems, short stories, and columns, as well as (screen)plays for television and theatre. She is also a visual artist, a successful singer-songwriter, and performer. Her music videos are mostly produced by her Puerto Rican partner, video artist Noelia Quintero Herencia. As is the case with many Caribbean islanders, Indiana's trajectory is characterized by multiple displacements. She was born and raised by her mother and other, mostly female, relatives in Santo Domingo, where she attended a Catholic school. After studying art history for a year, she enrolled in the Altos de Chavón School of Design. She frequently visited her father in the United States, who, like many other Dominicans, had started a "business" there. In 1989, he was killed in the Bronx. Indiana has lived in Spain and the United States. She resided many years with her partner and their children in San Juan, Puerto Rico. She recently moved to New York. Indiana's nomadism thus fits into the tradition of the Caribbean Intellectual diaspora.

Her ungraspable, liquid identity is also apparent from her name. Until 2005, she signed her books as Rita Indiana Hernández, omitting Sánchez, her second last name. The decision to be called Rita Indiana is highly significant from a gender and racial point of view. As an out and proud lesbian, the elimination of her father's last name (Hernández) could be related to her questioning of patriarchal filiation and structures (Bustamante, "Expresar" 819–20). She was baptized Rita Indiana in honor of her great-grandmother Rita Indiana del Castillo y Rodríguez-Objío, whose husband added Indiana because of her dark skin. In a Dominican context, *Indiana* recalls *indio*, which describes the complexion of people of mixed ancestry. The term *indio* is preferred to mulatto or black because it is devoid of any semantic allusion to the African heritage, which, in the Dominican imaginary, is associated with Haitians, the "other primitive" (Torres-Saillant; Valerio-Holguín). This anti-Haitianist ideology found its cruelest expression in the 1937 Massacre of Haitians on the Haitian-Dominican border, a genocide ordered by dictator Rafael Trujillo (1930-1961). Through her name, Rita Indiana, who is light-skinned, claims her ancestry's non-whiteness, playfully alluding to the Puerto Rican expression to indicate black roots "¿Dónde está tu abuela?" (Where is your grandmother?). Her chameleonic way of presenting herself is also concretized in her music videos, where she appears as a person with a hundred faces, from drag king to mulatto Virgin. It is not a coincidence that her musical moniker is La Montra, a Dominicanized way of pronouncing the non-existing feminine form of *el monstruo* (the monster), which emphasizes her being out of order and out of "normality."

In "Como un dragón" ("Like a Dragon"), the apocalyptic lead song of her new album "Mandinga Times," which was released in September 2020, La Montra refers explicitly to her literary endeavors, criticizing other rappers' "shitty" lyrics. The English translation reads as follows: "Don't worry about the lyrics, I am my own teacher. In the time that you made a chorus, I wrote five novels."[1] Although her musical and literary expressions are intrinsically intertwined on a thematic and stylistic level, this article will focus on her five, relatively short, novels. In her overview of the critical production on Rita Indiana's work, Feliciano-Arroyo distinguished three thematic nuclei: "the rendering visible of nonheteronormative genders and sexualities; the questioning of the Dominican racial imaginary, particularly in its exclusion of blackness; and the creation of transnational imaginaries of identification and belonging, including the incorporation of migrant and diasporic experiences" ("Indiana" n.p.). It is undeniable that issues concerning queer and/or racialized bodies in a globalized and multi-ethnic world are central to the work (and life) of this postmodern author, who comes from a country where whiteness, patriarchy, Hispanophile culture, and Catholicism prevail(ed).

However, this essay will insist less on the racial and queer aspects that lie at the heart of many articles (e.g., Palacios, Vera Rojas, Bustamante, "Rita Indiana Hernández," Jaime). Instead, it will explore how these texts spread their tentacles to a number of relevant tendencies in contemporary literature, and specifically in Latin American prose, without neglecting the vernacular and specific traits of her poetics. In this way, Rita Indiana epitomizes the peripheral writer in the twenty-first century, who is at the same time local and global. More precisely, the following topics will be discussed: the urban youth culture novel for *La estrategia de Chochueca* (Chochueca's Strategy, 2000); the dictator novel and the Latinx novel for *Papi* (*Papi: A Novel*, 2005), translated into English in 2016; the foundational tropes of literacy/orality and civilization/barbarism in Latin American literature for *Nombres y animales* (Names and Animals, 2013); science fiction and the ecocritical novel for *La mucama de Omicunlé* (Omicunlé's Maid, 2015), translated as *Tentacle* (2018); and the novels of political disenchantment for *Hecho en Saturno* (*Made in Saturn*, 2018).

In order to grasp the originality of Indiana's narrative, the Dominican literary context has to be taken into account. The political circumstances of the twentieth century did not facilitate the development of a flourishing literary scene. Instead, it was marked by marginalization and insularism. During Trujillo's dictatorship, many authors, like short-story writer Juan Bosch (1909–2001), had been forced into exile. Other writers, mostly poets, tried to cope with the limited freedom of expression by producing hermetic texts, as was the case of the *Poesía sorprendida* (Surprised Poetry) Movement of the 1940s, which was inspired by surrealism. The neo-Trujillist Joaquín Balaguer administration (1966–1978; 1986–1996) did not stimulate literary activity either. Whereas the Boom authors in the 1960s explored more universal ways of writing novels and implemented modernist techniques, Dominican narrative was still rather regionalist and traditional. Nevertheless, some experimental techniques were used by the acclaimed writer and polygraph Marcio Veloz Maggiolo (1936–2021), and by René del Risco Bermúdez (1937–1972), whose undeniable influence on Indiana and other contemporary Dominican writers has yet to receive scholarly attention. Since the eighties, women writers, such as Chiqui Vicioso (1948–), Ángela Hernández (1954–), or Aurora Arias (1962–), have tried to make their way through the *machista* literary scene. At the same time, there was a renewed interest in the country's African cultural roots from writers such as Manuel Rueda (1921–1999) or Aída Cartagena Portalatín (1918–1994). On the musical scene, José Duluc (1958–) and the non-conformist Luis Días (1952–2009), nicknamed Terror, recovered traditional African rhythms, mixing them with other beats. Terror's repertoire exerted a powerful influence on many contemporary Dominican writers such as Aurora Arias and Rita Indiana (Maguire; Morales 319–20). During the nineties, the production of historical novels on the Trujillato, predominantly seen from the victims' point of view, increased substantially. The so-called dictator novel was popular on the island, but it scarcely entered into a dialogue with (post)Boom innovations (Gallego Cuiñas, *Trujillo*; De Maeseneer, *Encuentro* 39–49; *Seis ensayos* 19–49). Paradoxically, the most successful novels that dealt with the Trujillo dictatorship were written abroad: *In the Time of the Butterflies* (1994) by Dominican-American Julia Álvarez, and *The Feast of the Goat* (2000) by Hispano-Peruvian Boom writer Mario Vargas Llosa. Indiana's texts represent a poignant rupture with what she once called, the "diarrhea of the Trujillo novels" (in De Maeseneer, *Seis ensayos* 182 n. 62).[2]

La estrategia de Chochueca is a semiautobiographical coming-of-age novel that concentrated on space and relegated history to a secondary role (De Maeseneer, "Rita Indiana Hernández" 156). Indiana foregrounds a group of adolescents of different races, classes, backgrounds, and sexual preferences at the end of the 1990s. Starting with the mission to return a stolen sound system to its owners, the seventeen-years-old, white, bisexual narrator Silvia presents snapshots of her nocturnal wanderings (*flâneries*) in underground Santo Domingo and her interactions with her friends: Octaviano, the author of the theft; Tony, a weird cybernerd; Bernardo, an ex-member of the group who became an Evangelical and works at a Wendy's; Salim, a brown male sex worker (a *sankypanky* in Dominican Spanish); Amanda, a bisexual Norwegian exchange-student; and the older homosexual Franco. The group's behavior is modeled on Chochueca's strategy. This bizarre person, inspired by an existing character in urban mythology, disregarded established norms. He wandered through the streets like a zombie, wearing the used clothes of deceased people that he begged of their relatives after the funeral. Thus, he made "the shoes of a dead man walk" (Hernández 49).[3] Similarly, at the end of the novel, Silvia visits Franco in the hospital, because he has almost been beaten to death as a result of a homophobic aggression. When he is asleep, she puts on his trousers, thus performing Chochueca with a queer twist. The focus is on the "subversive cartography of the Dominican identitarian topography" (Rodríguez 95).[4] These hedonist youth tribes (in Maffesoli's sense) and the subcultures of drugs, sexual explorations, and "coolishness" (Strobel) are reminiscent of novels such as the Colombian cult novel ¡Que viva la música! (Liveforever, 1977) by Andrés Caicedo, and many texts of the McOndo-generation (De Maeseneer, "Pos-McOndo" 128–29).

In La estrategia de Chochueca Indiana lays the foundations of her characteristic style. The direct and crude tone, the humor, the irreverence, the orality, Dominican speech peppered with English words, the musical allusions that add a sonic texture to the text (Maillo Pozo), and the references to popular culture as well as to high culture were substantially different from the coetaneous Dominican literary production. For example, in the fifth chapter, preceded by the quote, " . . . because the violin leaps like an eye . . . " (Hernández 57),[5] extracted from José Lezama Lima's poem "Thoughts in Havana," the narrator describes the youngsters' cocaine-induced hallucinations. The ecstatic exclamation "¡queea biieeeanmng!" is followed by a two-page-long enumeration of affirmations, the rhythm of which is marked by the obsessive repetition of yo in each sentence (Hernández 57, 58–59). The text also contains interesting examples of what can be considered another stylistic hallmark, namely her use of metaphors and similes. The apocalyptic city is compared to a "labyrinth of dust" and tourists are described in a comical way, with their "bodies made of marshmallow" (Hernández 18, 62–63).[6] By featuring young urban characters in this particular style, this frenetic novella constituted an important turning point in the Dominican literary landscape.

Situated in the late eighties, Indiana's second novel, Papi, is told in the first person by an eight-year-old girl, who is desperately waiting for her father's visits in Santo Domingo. In her mind, her adored father is an all-powerful businessman in the United States, while in reality, he is involved in drug dealing and other illegal transactions. Like many migrants, he returns to the island to show off his new riches, and like other Dominican men, he is the typical macho and a super-tíguere (a Dominican term for a street thug). When her unreliable father finally shows up, he is only present by means of his numerous gifts of consumer goods, because she has to share him with his family, girlfriends, and business associates. The narrative, imbued with the girl's fantasies, intertwines ingenuity with satire, horror, and science-fiction scenes. She behaves like the innocent child. For example, when her father promises to take her to the Walt Disney World Resort during her (imaginary) visit in the United States, she is naïvely overexcited. However, in other fragments, she exemplifies the evil child. For example, when papi and his daughter are trying to flee in a flying car from a group of girlfriends who are chasing them, she attacks them with a lollypop, for lack of another weapon (Bustamante, A ritmo desenfadado 151–55). This performance resembles a horror scene, and the flying car is reminiscent of the television series Knight Rider, alluded to in the book's epigraph. Tellingly, this dizzying array of words and images, narrated at hip-hop speed, also ends in a hospital. In the last chapter, the narrative shifts when the girl visits her mother, who has never been privileged by papi. The daughter moves away from her paternal fixation, as she is confronted with the harsh reality of her vulnerable mother, who is recovering from uterine and breast cancer. Despite the mutilation of these female parts of her body, she represents the potential of another form of mother-hood (Vera Rojas 204).

Many critics have read *Papi* as a variation on the dictator novel, in which the patriarchal power relations are transposed to the private sphere (Duchesne Winter "*Papi*"; De Maeseneer, *Seis ensayos* 170–82; Díaz-Zambrana; Horn 116–22). The novel consequently evokes the cult of personality, clientelism, massive building projects, exaggerated virility, and US imperialism, here concretized in consumer goods and advancing anglicization. Papi is associated either with God and the devil, or in this case with the movie monster, Jason from *Friday the 13th*. As happens with the dictator in *The Autumn of the Patriarch* by García Márquez, who is mentioned as the author of papi's eulogy, the first pages already suggest that the father could be dead. After he is shot under obscure circumstances, he survives in a kind of cyber body. Aside from patriarchal power relations, other authoritarian structures are tackled, such as the hierarchy on a gender level, for example, when the narrator insists on papi's feminine looks as a child, or when she cross-dresses as papi and tries to seduce her Cuban stepmother with a musical performance. Concerning religion, the sect that is created to honor the dead father with his daughter as a prophet is criticized for its fanatism and lucrative goals. From an economic perspective, the tyranny of our consumer society, characterized by accumulation and ephemerality, is denounced through spectacularization (Duchesne Winter "*Papi*").

In addition, as contemporary Dominican literature is considered postnational and postmonolingual (De Maeseneer "Los escritores"), *Papi* can be read in light of the stories written by Latinx writers. The typical plot of the Latinx coming-of-age novels, such as *How the García Girls Lost their Accent* (1991) by Julia Álvarez, consists in opposing a nostalgic idealization of life back home to the harsh life of the central characters in the United States and the difficulties of integration. Indiana distances herself from the conventional migrant narrative. She rather presents the other side of the diaspora, shifting from problems related to growing up as a migrant in the United States to the life of the abandoned and/or waiting family in the homeland. A comparison could be drawn with Dominican-American writer Junot Díaz's short story "Aguantando," included in *Drown* (1996). Yunior, nine years old, depicts his life in poverty with his brother Rafa and his mother, who works many hours at a chocolate factory for an exploitative wage in Santo Domingo. His father left for the United States and broke his promise to send money. They are holding on (aguantando), waiting for his return and to go to the United States together. Whereas Yunior describes the situation in his homeland as non-Edenic, insisting on the socioracial hardships, and considers his father's absence mostly with an ironic detachment, Indiana's narrator exaggerates her father's achievements in a grotesque way and satirizes the dictatorial Dominican political context. Both texts shed a new and more complex light on the unfulfilled dreams of migration.

Nombres y animales revolves around a fourteen-year-old, white, middle-class girl, who has a summer job as a receptionist in the veterinary clinic of her uncle, Fin Brea, while her parents go to the Expo in Sevilla in 1992. In this fragmented, hallucinatory, and often comical novel situated in Santo Domingo, different members of the (extended) family are presented in brief sketches. Her aunt, Celia Prieto, runs construction sites and, according to the narrator, she has neon signs in her head. The grandparents' servant, Armenia, has special gifts as a clairvoyant. The grandmother invents different stories of the same event, such as the encounter with the transgender character Ramona, who asked for a job as servant. The narrator's brother Mandy is in a hospital recovering from a fight with his girlfriend's jealous lover. Uncle Fin is more interested in Buddhism than in his job. He has an illegitimate son, Uriel Peña, who ends up being accepted by the family. This mosaic of stories is presented through the lens of the unnamed protagonist, who is obsessed with finding a name for a stray cat while struggling with her own identity, her relation to the other, and her budding lesbian sexuality. The few chapters that concentrate on her life recall *La estrategia de Chochueca*. She goes to rave parties with her friends, such as the Italian Vita and her cousin Claudia, with whom she falls in love. They are joined by the Haitian construction worker Radamés, mostly called Rada. He is employed at the clinic to wash and brush the animals, and will end up arrested for being undocumented. Together, they attend concerts in which an explicit homage is paid to Luis Días and the African substratum, since his performance during a concert in defense of *gagá* is described, a Dominican genre of music inspired by the Haitian voodoo related *rara* and brought to the country by migrant workers.

The historical setting in 1992 and the allusion to the Expo in Sevilla invites the reader to consider the book as a reflection on Latin America's foundational tropes that date back to the colonization of the New World in 1492 and permeate its literature. The colonial endeavors could only function by adopting binary structures. One of the strategies to subjugate the natives was to treat them as non-human, and thus animalizing them; they were even accused of cannibalism. This way, barbarism was opposed to civilization, to say it with Sarmiento's words. In *The Lettered City*, Ángel Rama explored another strategy of domination, namely literacy. The colonizers considered their literacy superior to the alleged orality of the New World. Thus, they imposed written laws and appropriated the power of naming, which is supposed to be an expression of human behavior, a civilizing act (Aillón Valverde 73–74), an entry into the Lacanian symbolic order of language, so to speak.

Nombres y animales points to these two colonial binaries. Firstly, on a diegetic level, the connecting thread is the protagonist's quest for a name (for the cat). She writes down lists of fanciful possibilities in a notebook, but fails to dominate and domesticate the cat. The illiterate Radamés hides her notebook and after his detention, the narrator retrieves it and tries to put together the shredded and damaged pages. Rada does not share her belief in the power of the written word and naming, as he has more affective and effective forms of approaching an animal. Giving a name also implies determining a sexual identity. It is thus not coincidental that the protagonist remains unnamed, because she has not yet come to terms with her sexuality. Hence, this novel represents a questioning of the lettered city and the power of naming.

Secondly, the animalization of the other as a strategy of violent subjugation is represented in the Haitian Radamés. A shopkeeper calls him ape, and when he is arrested together with other Haitians, they are transported as "cows to the slaughter-house" (Indiana, *Nombres* 195).[7] Paradoxically, the distinction between men and pets, often humanized by their owners, is mostly blurred by Rada. Uncle Fin is surprised by Rada's skills as an animal hairdresser, cutting a poodle's hair who sits on his lap "as a girl." Radamés explains that he used to cut his sisters' hair in Haiti. The uncle's reaction that Rada's "sisters were not animals" is not devoid of racist undertones (Indiana, *Nombres* 51, 53).[8] The narrator is also struggling with the dehumanizing prejudices against Haitians that she has internalized. For example, at first she is worried that her classmates could see her with a Haitian in a restaurant, but little by little, her attitude changes. At the end of the novel, she is determined to save Radamés. Beyond the strategy of animalizing the other, the novel calls for a reconsideration of the dichotomy between animals and men. This is also questioned by other authors, such as Cuban Ronaldo Menéndez in *Las Bestias* (The Beasts, 2006), and this approach fits into the context of contemporary animal studies, as inspired by Agamben or Giorgi.

These concerns related to animalization and naming resonate in the epigraphs in English that precede each of the twenty chapters, and in the general epigraph, "Are we not men?," repeated in chapter 17. Unrelated to the plot, these quotes address the fluid borders between animals and men. The importance of voice as a distinctive marker of humanity, for example, is referred to in the following sentences: "He says nothing, said the Satyr. Men have voices" (Indiana, *Nombres* 32). "Say the words" (Indiana, *Nombres* 190) alludes to language that expresses laws, as a means of domination. The epigraphs are citations from H. G. Wells's science fiction and horror novel *The Island of Doctor Moreau* (1896). This book, written in response to Darwin's evolutionary theory, concentrates on the failed experiment by Doctor Moreau and his assistant Montgomery to create humanized animals by means of vivisection. The Beast People cannot be subjugated and they return to their animal state, even though they had recited the Law imposed by their human creator. For example, they are prohibited to eat fresh meat, which has "the taste of blood," the last chapter's epigraph (Indiana, *Nombres* 198). Wells's book also has been read as an allegory of the colonial situation. Thus, the only possibility for the colonized subaltern consists of returning to the savage animal condition when s/he is deprived of Western civilizing influence (Duchesne Winter, "La isla" 182–85). As opposed to Wells's colonial ideology, Indiana defends a more nuanced approach to binaries.

The next step in Indiana's trajectory is *La mucama de Omicunlé*, an eco-futurist, queer, time-travel novel, translated as *Tentacle* (2018). It constitutes a shift from the first person to the third person, presenting snapshots of various characters. The narration jumps back and forth between the future of the twenty-first century (2024/2027/2037), the end of the millennium (1991/2001), and the seventeenth century after 1606. *Tentacle* opens in a post-apocalyptic Santo Domingo in 2027, an age of environmental collapse and hypercapitalism, when successive ecological disasters (a seaquake, the spilling of biochemical weapons) have turned the sea into a chocolate-colored sludge, devoid of life. Racial and gender elements are revisited in this futuristic context. Acilde Figueroa, a former sex worker, is employed as the maid of dictator Said Bona's religious counselor, Esther Escudero. In the opening scene, Acilde activates a security device that automatically exterminates a Haitian, infected with an epidemic virus. Acilde's only dream is to gather money for a gender-reassignment drug that does not require surgery. It is ironically called Rainbow Bright (in the Spanish text), as a double reference to the colors of the LGTBQ + flag and to the girl of the children's television series *Rainbow Brite* (as written in the English translation). Acilde places her/his individual satisfaction above the collective good. S/he is not aware that s/he is the elected successor of Esther Escudero, a priestess in the *santería* religion, named Omicunlé, which means the cloak that covers the sea. Omicunlé is at the service of Olokun, the deity of the bottom of the sea. Olokun is distinguished by sexual fluidity, as explained by Rita Indiana's source, the Cuban anthropologist Lydia Cabrera (Rogers). Acilde, the new incarnation of Olokun, is tasked with saving the country by preventing the disasters that threaten Santo Domingo and the marine environment. To do so, s/he has the power to return in time. Acilde's main avatar in the past is the Italian Giorgio Menicucci. This art lover and cook arrived in 1991 at Sosúa, on the northern coast of the Dominican Republic. He organized a fundraising event in 2001, selling art to save the Sosúa's coral reef, which was the dream of his Jewish partner Linda Goldman. Nonetheless, Acilde/Giorgio does not accomplish her/his mission to prevent disasters. Another character with time-traveling powers in this labyrinthine novel is Argenis Luna. This would-be painter, who works as Psychic Goya in a tarot call-center, is given the opportunity to participate in Giorgio's art project. He reincarnates in the seventeenth century in Côte de Fer as a castaway hosted by an all-male buccaneers' band under the lead of the attractive Roque, another avatar of Acilde/Giorgio. Argenis makes strange buccaneer engravings with cow blood, which leads him to a total psychic breakdown.

The plot's partial setting in Sosúa on the northern coast is relevant in this novel. After the *Devastaciones* in 1606, an attempt by Spanish governor Osorio to depopulate the northern region of the island in order to prevent illicit trade with Protestant colonies and smugglers, only adventurous castaways, buccaneers, and maroons continued to live in that region. They formed a kind of multi-cultural and violent free state. For a living, they exchanged the skins (cueros) of savage cows for other goods and used them even to "pay" for whores (which is why in Dominican Spanish *cuero* is still a disdainful way to refer to a female sex worker). Since the nineties, Sosúa has become one of the multiple destinations for sex tourism (with *cueros* and *sanky-pankies*) and there are also some transgender-friendly places. Finally, the real foundation of Sosúa is linked to the Jewish diaspora, as represented by its descendant, Linda Goldman, whose last name recalls one of the most powerful investment banks, Goldman Sachs. As alluded to in the novel, Trujillo invited Jews to settle in Sosúa after 1940, in order to please the United States and meanwhile perhaps whiten the race. This initiative turned out to be unsuccessful because very few Jews arrived in the Dominican Republic, and they did not intermingle with the local population in Sosúa. Instead, they created their own orderly, agricultural community as well as a flourishing meat and dairy industry.

The time-travel technique, the futurist setting, and the belief in hyper technology make the novel one of the multiple examples of science fiction or, more generally, the speculative genre. This is very successful in recent Latin American literature, for example in Argentinean Pola Oloixarac's *Las constelaciones oscuras* (*Dark Constellations*, 2015). Furthermore, the simultaneity of different lives can be related to the fantastic, which has gained renewed visibility in contemporary Latin American literature, often with a gothic twist, for example, in Argentinean writer Samantha Schweblin's *Distancia de rescate* (*Fever Dream* 2014).

In the translation into English (and other languages) the novel is entitled *Tentacle*, as a metonymic reference to the sea anemone. In the plot, this polyp is the connecting element between the different time periods. In 2027 Acilde kills Esther, the guardian of the world's last magic sea anemone. Selling this valuable animal allows her to buy the gender-transformation injection. After her/his transformation, Acilde is crowned with the tentacles of the anemone to make her/him a saint, referring to the Olokun "*kari osha* crowning ceremony" (Herrero-Martín 58). Acilde Figueroa/Giorgio Menicucci is then rescued by descendants of the indigenous Tainos, who took care of the coral reef of Sosúa in 1991. In 2001, Argenis is stung by a sea anemone and, in a delirium caused by his allergic reaction, experiences a parallel life in the seventeenth century. Moreover, the motif of the tentacle is highly significant in relation to the novel's ecocritical purposes. Like many other ecocritics, Donna Haraway considers the disappearing coral reefs, the sea anemones' habitat, as emblematic of the transformative effects of human activities on earth, the Anthropocene, and of the exploitation of the earth and the sea, or the Capitalocene, based on colonial relations. Haraway pleads for a tentacular thinking in the Chthulucene, where humans live interconnected with chtonic elements under the earth and under the sea, such as spiders, corals, or octopuses. The term Chthulucene derives from the *Pimoa Cthulhu* spider. Haraway insists that it is not named after "The Call of Cthulhu" (1928), "H.P. Lovecraft's misogynist racial-nightmare monster Cthulhu (note spelling difference), but rather after the diverse earthwide tentacular powers" (101). Instead of Haraway's spider, Indiana opts for the hermaphrodite sea anemone and she highlights the spiritual dimension of the debate, because the anemone is "invested with the spirituality of Afro-Caribbean and Taino belief systems, endowed with the powers of marine orishas and linked to Taino myths about the sea" (Deckard and Oloff 10). In this way, she rewrites "The Call of Cthulhu," the ecophobic and racist Lovecraftian story about the monster with an octopus-like head that could destroy the world and is worshipped by diabolical African voodooists and demonic indigenous tribes.

Tentacle is not only an intertextual play on Lovecraft's weird ocean fiction, but Indiana is also profoundly indebted to Cuban writer Alejo Carpentier (1904–1980). She builds on his neo-baroque techniques and on his "war on time," to say it with the title of his short stories (Pelage 150–59). She enters into a dialogue with Carpentier's ideas concerning Caribbean islanders as people of the sea, that were revisited by Antonio Benítez-Rojo in *La isla que se repite* (*The Repeating Island* 1989). She defends the co-existence of real and marvelous elements, as explained in Carpentier's famous prologue to *El reino de este mundo* (*The Kingdom of this World* 1949). This marvelous real is often confounded with magical realism, particularly in its European reception, which tries to connect Indiana's work with and at the same time distance it from this Latin American selling marker par excellence (De Maeseneer "La recepción" 379). More particularly, the omnipresence of Goya, the father of modern art, inevitably recalls Carpentier's *El siglo de las luces* (*Explosion in a Cathedral* 1962) and its epigraphs of Goya's etchings, *Disasters of War*

Even in very specific scenes, parallelisms can be drawn. For example, both authors describe the life of the pirates by alluding to physician Alexander Esquemeling's memoirs, *The Buccaneers of America*, originally published in Dutch in 1678 as *De Americaenshe Zee-Rovers*. Moreover, Carpentier's reflections on the disenchantment with revolutionary ideas in *El siglo de las luces* bring us to Indiana's last novel to date, *Made in Saturn*.

Although the transnational scope has been apparent since Indiana's first novel, which features people and cultures of different countries, the Dominican Republic (and in particular, its capital) has always played a central role. Instead, *Hecho en Saturno*, previously announced as *Los trajes* (*The Suits*), is partially set in Havana. In 2004, the wannabe-painter Argenis has messed up his life again. He is sent to a clinic in Cuba to follow a heroin detox program. His therapy fails because he is exploited as a health tourist by the Cuban doctor Bengoa. The rehab was paid for by his father. He is a decorated revolutionary hero who opposed Balaguer in the seventies. He is now an important politician in the Dominican Republic whose drug addicted son had to be banned from his entourage. The linear narrative evokes the conflict-ridden relation between Argenis and his family. A traumatic turning point was his father's betrayal during his childhood. Argenis had been promised a pair of sneakers for Christmas, but his father preferred to use the money for his own profit. He asked the black tailor Loudón to make a suit that would dress him for success, giving him the appropriate outfit to move up the ranks in the Party for Dominican Liberation. Indiana criticizes the fact that former left-wing political forces are bribed through clientelist positions and now tied to the state apparatus they once resisted. When Argenis is back in Santo Domingo, he asks Loudón to make a suit in an attempt at reconciliation, transforming himself into a copy of his father. During a luxury dinner, paid for by his father, he meets Giorgio Menicucci and Linda Goldman (the characters from *Tentacle*). They offer him a significant sum of money for his engravings of the Sosúa-project, which they still keep in their basement. After an emotional encounter with his old blind Maestro Céspedes, who painted a Goyaesque Saturn devouring his son, and who gives Argenis, his "heir," the brush that he bought in Italy in 1976, Argenis decides to leave for Cuba. At the airport's passenger control, dressed in his new suit, he is determined to walk, the novel's final word. This puzzling and ambiguous end does not make clear if he did "find his way home." The reference to a blues song about drug problems, or (wrong) decisions in general, functions as the novel's epigraph. Ironically, it was originally performed by a music band called Blind Faith.

Hecho en Saturno is based on the idea that the revolution, like Saturn, devoured its children. It expresses disenchantment with the left-wing revolutionary dreams, guided by the polar star of the Cuban Revolution in Latin America. When Argenis sees a poster "on which Castro stood gesticulating on a podium, over the phrase 'Patria o muerte, ¡venceremos!,'" he thinks: "Eighties sneakers had aged better than these slogans" (Indiana, *Made in Saturn* 69).[9] On the one hand, Indiana's poignant picture of the current Cuban system, a "socialist ideal turned into merchandise" (Indiana, *Made in Saturn* 29),[10] ties in with the satirical approach to the ruins of the Revolution by Cuban writers, such as Ena Lucía Portela's *La sombra del caminante* (The Walker's Shadow, 2001). On the other hand, the text addresses parents' ideological passions at the expense of their commitment to their children. This conflict is at the core of the so-called literature of the children of Argentina and Chile. It is also featured in *El nervio principal* (*Ramifications*, 2018) by Mexican Daniel Saldaña, who focuses on the distress of a child whose mother disappeared to join the Zapatista movement in Chiapas.

In retrospect, Indiana has called her first three novels the "trilogy of the unbearable/crazy girls," pointing to the underlying personal experiences that fueled these texts. Her underground life in Santo Domingo as a teenager, the traumatic loss of her murdered father at the age of twelve, her work in a veterinary hospital, together with a Haitian boy whom she did not really get to know, have inspired the different novels. In this way, the three texts can be considered as partly autofictional, a tendency that permeates contemporary fiction (Corral 375–463). It is present in texts from Mexico (e.g., Guadalupe Nettel's *El cuerpo en que nací*; *The Body where I was Born*, 2011) to Chile (e.g., Alejandro Zambra's *Formas de Volver a casa*; *Ways of Going* Home, 2011). Indiana's last two novels are connected by the character of Argenis. *Made in Saturn* comprises explicit summaries of Argenis's life, as described in *Tentacle*. Argenis Luna's experiences are based on Indiana's own during her unfinished arts studies. In *Tentacle*, the encoded references to the Caribbean art scene can be easily traced back. For example, the instrumentalization and commodification of the artistic expressions of the South are satirized in the figure of the Cuban art curator Iván de la Barra, an allusion to Cuban essayist and curator Iván de la Nuez (Garrido 355, n. 3). In recent interviews, Indiana declared that it was not improbable that Argenis would appear again in her next novel, which would then complete her second trilogy.

In this era of hyper mediality and the absorption of book publishing into a global entertainment and information industry, writers participate actively in the promotion of their work and often become celebrities (Moran). Whereas today, many Latin American writers, such as Bolivian Edmundo Paz Soldán, Mexican Yuri Herrera, or Chilean Lina Meruane, rely on their intellectual capital and combine an academic career in the United States with creative writing, Indiana's way of consolidating her authorial figure (Meizoz) in the cultural field has been slightly different, although she was recently hired to teach creative writing at NYU (fall 2022). It started with what Feliciano-Arroyo calls self-management (*autogestión*). Indiana auto-published her first texts, a recurring method in the Dominican Republic due to the editorial void, and distributed them in underground circuits. Her novels were subsequently noticed by small-press publishing houses in Puerto Rico. Her next achievement was her contract in 2011 with the independent publishing house Periférica, based in Cáceres, Spain, an influential gatekeeper between Latin America and Spain (Gallego Cuiñas, "Independent publishers"). In 2011, following her contributions to *El País* as a columnist and her musical success, she was nominated by the Spanish newspaper as one of the hundred most influential Latinx personalities. She garnered a series of awards and nominations, among which finalist for the II Biennial Award for the Novel Mario Vargas Llosa in 2015 with *Tentacle*. Regarding translations, the English version of *Papi* was published by University of Chicago Press. Her last two works were released in Britain by a small publisher, based on a subscription model, "And other stories," which also promotes the work of Mexican writers Juan Pablo Villalobos and Yuri Herrera. The fact that Cuban American writer

Achy Obejas was hired to translate *Papi* and *Tentacle* is remarkable, because she is an important gatekeeper for the Hispanic Caribbean: she translates both into and from Spanish, for example, Junot Díaz (into Spanish) and Cuban authors Wendy Guerra and Ena Lucía Portela (into English). Indiana's success is legitimized by renowned writers, such as Junot Díaz, who can be considered the ambassador for Dominican writing (De Maeseneer, "Los escritores" 26). The increasing weight of publishing houses and awards, and the growing number of translations into different languages (English, Italian, German, Norwegian, French) contributed to consolidate her authorial self in the international literary field. The same evolution can be observed with regard to her musical achievements. Whereas her previous music recordings with bands such as Miti Miti in the nineties were very much underground, her latest album "Mandinga Times" (2020), was produced by Puerto Rican Eduardo Cabra, nicknamed Visitante, the former musical brain of Calle 13, one of Latin America's most famous bands.

Indiana epitomizes the precarious position that contemporary artists, originating from a Latin American peripheral area, adopt in the twenty-first century. Her novels are local and global at the same time. Their "tentacles" reach a wide public and touch upon many of the dominant issues facing humanity today: climate change, colonial legacies and violence, and the function of the arts, identity, race, and gender. In all this, Indiana maintains her profoundly personal touch, which takes root(s) and routes in and from the Caribbean. At a linguistic level, she defends her writing in Dominican in the following way: "To write in Dominican means that they are going to ask you to add a glossary to your novels, to write in a more convenient and nicer language. It means that you will receive letters of refusal from editors and agents in which they explain that the universal language is the generic one and yours is orality" (Indiana, "Escribir" n.p.).[11] By claiming orality, this quintessential expression of Caribbeanness, she builds clearly on her literary forebears, Guillermo Cabrera Infante and Luis Rafael Sánchez, who pleaded to write, respectively, in Cuban and in Puerto Rican.

Although it is difficult to evaluate a writer whose work is still in progress and to a certain extent unpredictable, it is probable that Indiana will continue to challenge the literary (and musical) scene. When I asked her for an appropriate picture to illustrate one of my articles on Dominican literature, she sent me a photograph in which she is sitting next to a Games of Thrones–like sword. This can be seen as a symbol of her provocative attitude. She laughs at too much seriousness by using a popular-culture reference. At the same time, she plays with the phallic pen-sword symbol that so many politically committed Latin American male Boom writers referred to. However, this attitude does not undermine a thorough commitment to her Caribbean context.

Notes

1. "Por la letra no te preocupe / Que yo soy mi propia escuela / En lo que tú sacate un coro / Yo escribí cinco novelas." All English-language translations are mine, except for Indiana's *Papi*, *Tentacle* and *Made in Saturn*.

2. "Diarrea novelera trujillista" (De Maeseneer, *Seis ensayos* 182, n. 62).

3. "Hacer caminar los zapatos de un muerto" (Hernández 49).

4. "Cartografía subversiva de la topografía identitaria dominicana" (Rodríguez 95).

5. *"Porque el violín salta como un ojo"* (Hernández 57).

6. "Laberinto de pelusas;" "sus cuerpos de *marshmallow"* (Hernández 18, 62–63).

7. "Vacas pal matadero" (Indiana *Nombres* 195).

8. "Como a una niña;" "sus hermanitas no eran animales" (Indiana *Nombres* 51, 53).

9. "En él [afiche] Castro gesticulaba en un podio sobre la frase "Patria o muerte, ¡Venceremos!" Los tenis de los ochenta han envejecido mejor que estas consignas" (Indiana, *Hecho en Saturno* 81).

10. "El ideal socialista convertido en mercancía" (Indiana, *Hecho en Saturno* 33).

11. "Escribir en dominicano significa que te pedirán que añadas un glosario a tus novelas, que escribas en un lenguaje más cómodo, más amable. Que recibirás cartas de rechazo de editores y agentes en las que te explican que lo universal es lo genérico y lo tuyo es la oralidad" (Indiana, "Escribir" n.p.).

Works Cited

Agamben, Giorgio. *The Open. Man and Animal*. Stanford UP, 2004.

Aillón Valverde, Miguel. "Relatos salvajes: animalidad y migrancia en *Nombres y animales* de Rita Indiana." *Kipus: Revista andina de Letras y estudios culturales*, no. 44, 2018, pp. 65–80. doi.org/10.32719/13900102.2018.44.4

Benítez-Rojo, Antonio. *The Repeating Island: The Caribbean and the Postmodern Perspective*. Duke UP, 1997.

Bustamante, Fernanda. *A ritmo desenfadado*. Cuarto Propio-Cielonaranja, 2014.

Bustamante, Fernanda. "Rita Indiana Hernández: una escritura que retuerce los márgenes y los paradigmas de representación identitaria." *Rita Indiana. Archivos*, edited by Fernanda Bustamante, Cielonaranja, 2017, pp. 259–89.

Bustamante, Fernanda. "Expresar un posicionamiento, exponer la intimidad: la imagen de autora en Rita Indiana y su 'yo' autorial." *Revista Iberoamericana*, vol. LXXX, no. 268, July–September 2019, pp. 813–37. doi.org/10.5195/reviberoamer.2019.7809

Carpentier, Alejo. *El siglo de las luces*. Siglo XXI Editores, 1984.

Carpentier, Alejo. *El reino de este mundo*. Siglo XXI Editores, 1991.

Carpentier, Alejo. El siglo de las luces. Compañía General de Ediciones, 1962.

Corral, Wilfrido H. *Discípulos y maestros 2.0. Novela hispanoamericana hoy*. Iberoamericana-Vervuert, 2019.

Deckard, Sharae, and Oloff, Kerstin. "'The One Who Comes from the Sea' Marine Crisis and the New Oceanic Weird in Rita Indiana's *La mucama de Omicunlé* (2015)." *Humanities*, vol. 9, no. 3, 2020, pp. 1–14. doi.org/10.3390/h9030086

De Maeseneer, Rita. *Encuentro con la narrativa dominicana contemporánea*. Iberoamericana-Vervuert, 2006.

De Maeseneer, Rita. "Los escritores de origen dominicano en los Estados Unidos y la condición postmonolingüe." *Ínsula*, no. 885, September 2020, pp. 26–29.

De Maeseneer, Rita. "¿Pos-*McOndo*? La narrativa hispanocaribeña del siglo XXI." *McCrack: McOndo, el Crack y los destinos de la literatura latinoamericana*, edited by Pablo Brescia and Oswaldo Estrada, Albatros, 2018, pp. 123–35.

De Maeseneer, Rita. "La recepción de la literatura dominicana en algunos países europeos (2000–2018), un estudio de caso de una literatura 'periférica.'" *Romance Notes*, vol. 59, no. 2, 2019, pp. 371–82.

De Maeseneer, Rita. "Rita Indiana Hernández." *The Contemporary Spanish-American Novel*.

De Maeseneer, Rita. *Seis ensayos sobre narrativa dominicana contemporánea*. Editorial del Banco Central, 2011.

Bolaño and After, edited by Will H. Corral et al., Bloomsbury, 2013, pp.156–59.

Díaz, Junot. "Aguantando." *Drown*, Faber and Faber, 1996, pp. 53–69.

Díaz-Zambrana, Rosana. "¿Una alternativa a la novela del dictador? Paternalismo, nación y posmodernidad en *Papi* de Rita Indiana Hernández." *Sargasso*, no. 2, 2008-2009, pp. 83–92.

Duchesne Winter, Juan. "*Papi*, la profecía, espectáculo e interrupción en Rita Indiana Hernández." *Revista de Crítica Literaria Latinoamericana*, vol. XXXIV, no. 67, 2008, pp. 289–309.

Duchesne Winter, Juan. "La isla de Rita Indiana. Animación del lenguaje en *Nombres y animales*." *Rita Indiana. Archivos*, edited by Fernanda Bustamante, Cielonaranja, 2017, pp. 197–205.

Feliciano-Arroyo, Selma. *Autogestión: Reconfiguring the Spaces of Cultural Production in Latin America*. 2011. U Pennsylvania, dissertation. *ProQuest*, https://repository.upenn.edu/disser tations/AAI3500228

Feliciano-Arroyo, Selma. "Indiana Hernández, Rita." *Oxford Research Encyclopedia of Literature*. September 26, 2018, Oxford UP, n.p. doi.org/10.1093/acrefore/ 9780190201098.013.402

Gallego Cuiñas, Ana. *Trujillo: el fantasma y sus escritores. Historia de la novela del trujillato*. Mare & Martin, 2006.

Gallego Cuiñas, Ana et al. "Independent publishers and social networks in the 21st century: the balance of power in the transatlantic Spanish-language book market." *Online Information Review*, vol. 44, no.7, 2020, pp.1387–1402, https://doi.org/10.1108/OIR-10-2019-0342

Garrido Castellano, Carlos. "'La elocuencia que su entrenamiento como artista plástico le permitía.' Subalternidad, cultura e instituciones en *La Mucama de Omicunlé* de Rita Indiana Hernández." *Hispanic Research Journal*, vol.18, no. 4, July 2017, pp. 352–64. *Taylor and Francis Online*, doi.org/10.1080/14682737.2017.1337845

Giorgi, Gabriel. *Formas comunes. Animalidad, cultura, biopolítica*. Eterna Cadencia, 2014.

Haraway, Donna. *Staying with the Trouble. Making Kin in the Chthulucene*. Duke UP, 2018.

Hernández, Rita Indiana. *La estrategia de Chochueca*. Isla Negra, 2003.

Herrero-Martín, Rosana. "Olokun or the Caribbean Quantum Mind: An Analysis of Transcultural Metaphysical Elements within Rita Indiana's Novel *Tentacle*." *Journal of West Indian Literature*, vol. 27, no. 2, November 2019, pp. 52–67.

Horn, Maja. *Masculinity after Trujillo. The Politics of Gender in Dominican Literature*. UP Florida, 2014.

Indiana, Rita. *Papi*. Vértigo, 2005.

Indiana, Rita. *Papi*. U Chicago P, 2016.

Indiana, Rita. *Nombres y animales*. Periférica, 2013.

Indiana, Rita. *La mucama de Omicunlé*. Periférica, 2015.

Indiana, Rita. *Tentacle*. And Other Stories, 2018.

Indiana, Rita. *Hecho en Saturno*. Periférica, 2018.

Indiana, Rita. *Made in Saturn*. And Other Stories, 2020.

Indiana, Rita. "Escribir en dominicano." *El País*, June 3, 2019. https://elpais.com/cultura/2019/05/31/babelia/1559316070_072959.html

Jaime, Karen. "'Da pa' lo' do'": Rita Indiana's Queer, Racialized Dominicanness." *Small Axe*, vol. 19, no. 2, July 2015, pp. 85–93. doi.org/10.1215/07990537-3139394

Maguire, Emily A. "'Hace[r] encantadora la idea del desencanto': Luis 'Terror' Días en los cuentos de Aurora Arias." *El sonido de la música en la narrativa dominicana. Ensayos sobre identidad, nación y performance*, edited by Médar Serrata, Instituto de Estudios Caribeños, 2012, pp. 147–66.

Maillo Pozo, Sharina. "La comunión entre música y literatura en *La estrategia de Chochueca*. En busca de la heterogeneidad perdida." *El sonido de la música en la narrativa dominicana. Ensayos sobre identidad, nación y performance*, edited by Médar Serrata, Instituto de Estudios Caribeños, 2012, pp. 217–34.

Meizoz, Jérôme. *Postures littéraires. Mises en scène modernes de l'auteur*. Slatkine, 2007.

Moran, Joe. *Star Authors. Literary Celebrities in America*. Pluto Press, 2000.

Morales, Ed. "No la llamen Lady Gagá." *El sonido de la música en la narrativa dominicana. Ensayos sobre identidad, nación y performance*, edited by Médar Serrata, Instituto de Estudios Caribeños, 2012, pp. 317–26.

Nettel, Guadalupe. *El cuerpo en que nací*. Anagrama, 2011.

Palacios, Rita M. "Actos peatonales, actos de consumo: La queerificación del espacio en *La estrategia de Chochueca*." *Hispania*, vol. 97, no. 4, Dec. 2014, pp. 566–77. *Project MUSE*, https://doi.org/10.1353/hpn.2014.0108

Pelage, Cathérine. *Littératures dominicaines en mouvement. Les performances littéraires de Rita Indiana et Rey Andújar*. PU de Rennes, 2020.

Rama, Ángel. *The Lettered City*. Duke UP, 1996.

Rodríguez, Néstor. *Escrituras de desencuentro en la República Dominicana*. Siglo XXI Editores, 2005.

Rogers, Charlotte. "Rita Indiana's Queer Interspecies Caribbean and the Hispanic Literary Tradition." *Small Axe Project, sx salon*, vol. 34, June 2020, n.p. http://smallaxe.net/sxsalon/discussions/rita-indianas-queer-interspecies-caribbean-and-hispanic-literary-tradition

Strobel, Leah. "The Cool, the Quick, and the Erotic: Outrunning Identity in Rita Indiana Hernández's *La estrategia de Chochueca*." *New Readings in Latin American and Spanish Literary and Cultural Studies*, edited by Laura M. Martins, Cambridge Scholars Publishing, 2014, pp. 121–33.

Torres-Saillant, Silvio. "The Tribulations of Blackness: Stages in Dominican Racial Identity." *Callaloo*, vol. 23, no.3, 2000, pp. 1086–1111. *Project MUSE*, https://doi.org/10.1353/cal.2000.0173

Valerio-Holguín, Fernando. "Primitive Borders. Cultural Identity and Ethnic Cleansing in the Dominican Republic." *Primitivism and Identity in Latin America. Essays on Art, Literature, and Culture*, edited by Erik Camayd-Freixas and José Eduardo González, U of Arizona P, 2000, pp. 75–88.

Vera Rojas, María Teresa. "¡Se armó el juidero! Cartografías imprecisas, cuerpos disidentes, sexualidades transgresoras: hacia una lectura queer de Rita Indiana Hernández." *Prosopopeya*, 7, 2011–2012, pp. 185–205.

Zambra, Alejandro. *Formas de volver a casa*. Anagrama, 2011.

CHAPTER 41

....

TRANSNATIONAL, INTERMEDIAL PRESSURES IN ROBERTO BOLAÑO'S PROSE POEM NOVELS

....

JONATHAN B. MONROE

WHILE the Chilean-born Roberto Bolaño's posthumously published *La Universidad Desconocida* (*The Unknown University*) and *Cuentos completos* (Complete Short Stories, 2010) consolidate his prodigious achievements in both poetry (in verse and prose) and short fiction, it is above all his twelve published novels (and a thirteenth, co-authored with A. G. Porta, *Consejos de un discípulo de Morrison a un fanático de Joyce* (Advice from a Morrison Disciple to a Joyce Fanatic, 1984) that have established him as the most consequential writer of his generation from Latin America and as the region's most influential novelist since Gabriel García Márquez. From his first two published novels in the early 1980s, *Amberes* (*Antwerp*, 2002/1980) and *Monsieur Pain* (1999 / 1981–1982; as *La senda de los elefantes* [The Path of the Elephants, 1984]); to the five he would publish between 1996 and 2000, *La literatura Nazi en América* (*Nazi Literature in the Americas*, 1996), *Estrella distante* (*Distant Star*, 1996), *Los detectives salvajes* (*The Savage* Detectives, 1998), *Amuleto* (*Amulet*, 1999), and *Nocturno de Chile* (*By Night in Chile*, 2000); to three posthumously published between 2004 and 2012, *2666* (2004), *El Tercer Reich* (*The Third Reich* 2010; written 1989), and *Los sinsabores del verdadero policía* (*Woes of the True Policeman*, 2011), Bolaño demonstrated an acute sense of the intermedial, transnational pressures facing the novel in the last quarter of the twentieth century and first few years of the twenty-first.

Strikingly manifest in the trajectory the following will trace between Bolaño's two remaining, bookend novels—El *espíritu de la ciencia-ficción* (*The Spirit of Science Fiction*, 2016), his first yet most recent to appear, dating from the same period as *Antwerp, Monsieur Pain*, and *Consejos* (1980–1984); and *Una novelita lumpen* (*A Little Lumpen Novelita*, 2002), the last to appear before his death in 2003—are the transnational and intermedial pressures that would prove an enduring concern throughout his career.

Hailed by Juan E. De Castro as "the most admired Latin American writer of the last decades, not only in the region but throughout the world" (134), by Ignacio López-Calvo as "the most influential writer of his generation and the only Latin American author in the last twenty-five years to have become canonical in the United States and to have achieved world literary status" ("World Literature" 30), Bolaño is a writer whose "planetary consciousness" extends, as López-Calvo puts it, "beyond national projects" (35). Confirming these assessments, Héctor Hoyos observes that among writers of the "Global Latin American Novel," Bolaño is the only one to have gained "a critical mass of transnational readership. . . . In Spanish, and in Chile in particular, Bolaño became Bolaño only after his international canonization" (4–5). In the last decade, Bolaño's increasingly global influence has continued to register in such titles as Sarah Pollack's "After Bolaño: Rethinking the Politics of Latin American Literature in Translation" (2013); *The Contemporary Spanish-American Novel: Bolaño and After* (Will H. Corral, Nicholas Birns, and De Castro 2013); Hoyos's *Beyond Bolaño: The Global Latin American Novel* (2015), the edited volumes *Roberto Bolaño, a Less Distant Star* (López-Calvo 2015) and *Roberto Bolaño as World Literature* (Birns and De Castro 2017); Jeffrey Lawrence's *Anxieties of Experience: The Literatures of the Americas from Whitman to Bolaño* (2018); and De Castro's *Writing Revolution in Latin America: From Martí to García Márquez to Bolaño* (2019); as well as my *Framing Roberto Bolaño: Poetry, Fiction, Literary History, Politics* (2019) and forthcoming edited volume *Roberto Bolaño in Context* (2022). As these publications attest, and as Andrews rightly predicted, "All indications are that Bolaño's work is being taken up and integrated into traditions of literary and popular culture, and that coming years will see it monumentalized and officialized" (204). Referring in 2018 to both a "post-Bolaño era" and a "Bolañian Turn in Contemporary Latin/o Fiction," Lawrence characterizes Bolaño, similarly, as not only "the most important literary model for Latin American writers," but also "one of the most important contemporary literary models for writers in both the English- and Spanish-speaking worlds," a writer who has "forced US and Latin American writers to confront the cultural expectations of their literary practices" (27).

Affirming the transnational character of Bolaño's literary interests and formation, in his 2002 interview with Carmen Boullosa "Reading is Always More Important than Writing," one of the last before his death the following year, Bolaño remarked: "Needless to say, I'm not one of those nationalist monsters who only reads what his native country produces. I'm interested in French literature . . . in American literature of the 1880s . . . . As a teenager, I went through a phase when I only read Poe. Basically, I'm interested in Western literature, and I'm fairly familiar with all of it."[1] As this self-representation and Bolaño's entire body of work make clear, including numerous essays and interviews, hybrid fictional/non-fictional prose, his literary, cultural, social, and political worlds were shaped not only by Chile (1954–1968), Mexico (1968–1977), and Spain (1977–2003), the three principal locations of his life and work, but also by the Americas, and by Europe, more inclusively. Bolaño's indebtedness in particular to Poe's dismantling of the equation of poetry with verse, in *The Philosophy of Composition* (1846) and *The Poetic Principle* (1850), and to the prose poems of Charles Baudelaire and Arthur Rimbaud,[2] becomes clear from the outset in *Antwerp*, the only "novel" Bolaño maintained did not "embarrass" him.[3] Foundational and enduring in the development of what I have called elsewhere his prose poem novels (or "poemas-novela"),"[4] their combined influence is equally clear, and remarkably consistent, in both *The Spirit of Science Fiction* (196 pages, 206 in the original) and *A Little Lumpen Novelita* (109 and 112 pages), the former composed of thirty-six unnumbered, untitled sections (twenty-eight in Part I, eight in Part II), all but four an average prose poem length of one to five pages, the latter of sixteen numbered, untitled sections between three and five-and-a-half.

Without naming the novel as such, but with unmistakable implication, in the 1862 sales-pitch of a letter to Arsène Houssaye, literary editor of *La Presse*, that would become the Preface to *Le Spleen de Paris*, Baudelaire positions his invention of the prose poem as a challenge to the ascendancy of the novel, and its increasing hegemony over poetry, in the mid-nineteenth century. In their deep indebtedness to Baudelaire's and Rimbaud's prose poems, Bolaño's prose poem novels attest to his understanding of the prose poem as foundational not only for modern poetry but for modern literature itself—arguably more profoundly transformative over time, as has become increasingly clear over the past two decades in such works as Claudia Rankine's *Don't Let Me Be Lonely: An American Lyric* (2004), *Citizen: An American Lyric* (2014), and *Just Us: An American Conversation* (2020), than even the free verse of Walt Whitman's *Leaves of Grass (1855)*, or the alexandrines of *Les Fleurs du Mal* (*The Flowers of Evil*, *1857*).

Questioning the systems, hierarchies, and limits of genre, of poetry and the novel, of the "poetic" and the "prosaic," the "literary" and "non-literary," the prose poem's oxymoronic challenge to both verse poetry's receding, "residual" status and the novel's "emergent," soon-to-be "dominant" prestige (in Raymond Williams's apt terms) finds deep resonance, as Bolaño understood, in the increasingly intermedial, transnational challenges facing the late-twentieth, early twenty-first-century novel.[5] Responding to the symbiotic "new medium" and ascendant genre of the mid-nineteenth century, the commercial newspaper and the serial novel (the "binge TV" of its time), Baudelaire's prose poems sought to be at once convenient and commodifiable (Baudelaire's "commode"; "À Arsène Houssaye" 275). With *Le Spleen de Paris'* (*Paris Spleen*) fifty numbered, titled *petits poèmes en prose* (Little Poems in Prose) as template, each an average half-page to three pages, similarly, *Antwerp*'s fifty-six numbered, titled prose poems reclaim, reinvent, and repurpose the prose poem's cross-genre legacy in the form of his first published, thoroughly disjunctive, prose poem "novel."

Anticipating and sharing with *Antwerp* the acute interest in questions of genre and media that would remain a consistent feature of Bolaño's mature style, *The Spirit of Science Fiction* deploys a distinctive combination of narrative strategies and formal and thematic preoccupations. In some respects a mystery, given the novel's inherent interest and quality, the decision to withhold its publication during Bolaño's lifetime makes perfect sense in light of the extent to which it served, as Bolaño must have been keenly aware, as a rich seed bed and source book, a site of "drafts and embryos" (López-Calvo,

Critical Essays 39). To have published it sooner would have risked preempting novels yet to come, in some respects more accomplished, polished, fully realized—*Monsieur Pain, The Third Reich, Nazi Literature of the Americas, Distant Star, The Savage Detectives, Amulet, 2666,* most notably—making significant parts of their material appear anticlimactic and/or derivative. Yet where *Antwerp*'s negotiations of these concerns move most decisively in the direction of detective fiction, the genre at once "literary" and "popular" that would remain Bolaño's signature investment—albeit with gestures toward science-fiction film plots in its two brief concluding texts—Bolaño's first, prior novel, for the remainder of his life still unpublished, offers the most explicit exploration of his initial, youthful sense of science fiction's potential as an alternative path to the same "cross-over" goal. For the most part abandoned thereafter, that potential still resonates, however obliquely, in such later novels as *The Third Reich, Amulet,* and *2666.*

The relation between poetry and the novel, the novel and the prose poem in particular, registers in *Antwerp* almost exclusively as matter of form, not as so often in Bolaño's later work through poets and other characters identified with poetry, but through its disjunctively Rimbaldian, meta-textual, linguistic and narrative self-reflexivity. In its opening, prose poem length, one-and-a-half page text, by contrast, a Tequila- and Vodka-fueled dialogue/interview between an unnamed reporter and young writer said to have won an also unidentified prize, *The Spirit of Science Fiction* establishes a dialectic between prose poem and novel it will pursue throughout both formally and thematically. Its next brief text, a two-page first-person account by a second narrator-character as yet unnamed, introduces the young writer by his first name only, "Jan" (5, 21). Its third, a one-and-a-half page letter-as-sales-pitch—recalling Baudelaire's prose poem preface to Arsène Houssaye—to Alice Sheldon, the first of nine to U.S-North American science fiction writers, reveals his full name, "Jan Schrella" (8, 24). Only some 170 pages later, in the last of the novel's nine letters, to Phillip José Farmer, does it disclose his full identity as "Jan Schrella, / alias Roberto Bolaño" (178, 204), a seventeen-year-old poet and aspiring science fiction writer.

Interweaving the Chilean-born Jan's nine letters with the narratives of the novel's other central figures (both also alter-egos of Bolaño), "Remo"—Jan's Chilean friend and roommate in a rooftop apartment in Mexico City, revealed clearly by name as the narrator of the novel's second brief text, its most frequent kind, only some eighty-seven pages in—and their mutual friend, José Arco, the novel prefigures the intricacy with which *The Savage Detectives* interweaves Juan García Madero's first-person, epistolary prose poems with the narratives of his two slightly older mutual friends and mentors, Arturo Belano and Ulises Lima. Alternating systematically, in its triangulated narratives of Jan, Remo, and José Arco, among five different genre types, *The Spirit of Science Fiction*'s complex novelistic structure develops as follows, from most to least frequent[6]: 1) fifteen first-person accounts by Remo about himself and his friends in Mexico City; 2) nine letters from Jan to US science-fiction writers; 3) six first-person sketches by Jan of a science-fiction novel set incongruously at a "Potato Academy" ("la Academía de la Papa o de la Patata"; 9; *Espíritu* 25) in Chile adjoining various (especially English, French, German, Russian) World War battle theaters; 4) five dialogues, between Jan and Remo, brainstorming Jan's prospective Potato Field Academy/World War II/science fiction narrative; and finally 5) four interviews with Jan about his award-winning poetry and science-fiction novel in progress.

Beginning with the first of Jan's four interviews and concluding with the last of his nine letters, the novel is divided into two main parts, comprising 181 of its 196 pages (112 and 59 pages, respectively), with the following patterns of repetition and variation:

Part I:

    1) Jan interview, Remo narrative, Jan letter;
    2) interview, Remo, Jan/Remo, Remo
    3) letter, Remo, Jan/Remo
    4) letter, Remo, Remo, Jan/Remo, Jan/Remo, Remo
    5) letter, Jan, Remo
    6) letter, interview, Remo
    7) letter, Jan, Remo,
    8) interview, letter, Remo

Part II:

    9) Jan/Remo, Remo, Remo
   10) letter, Remo, Remo, letter

Mexican Manifesto (Remo and Laura)

Of the novel's thirty-seven discrete sections, the first ten of twelve from one-and-a-half to three pages, thirty-two are of prose poem length. The five remaining, at seven, ten, ten, fourteen, and seventeen pages, all first-person narratives in the voice of Remo, including the concluding "Mexican Manifesto" ("Manifiesto mexicano"),[7] fall within the more expansive range of a short story. Reconstructing his life in Mexico City as a "fairly pretentious recent arrival" from Chile and "clumsy" poet ("Un recién llegado bastante pretencioso y un torpe poeta," 38, 42)—like Bolaño, and like Jan, Remo's friend and roommate, but four years older, at twenty-one the same age as their mutual friend José Arco—Remo's narratives offer early examples of what will prove to be among Bolaño's most characteristic concerns: poetic apprenticeships and poetry workshops, friends and rivals, teachers and mentors, fellow poets and first loves. In their supporting cast, including "Jeremías Moreno" and "Marino Pérez . . . Jeremías's buddy and the co-coordinator of the other workshop, the official Faculty of Literature workshop" (9),[8] Dr. Huachofeo, Dr. Ireneo Carvajal and Don Ubaldo, Estrellita, José Arco; the Torrente sisters, Angélica, Teresa, and Lola, they establish a template for a wide range of characters in such later novels as *Distant Star*—Arturo Belano and Bibiano O'Ryan; Alberto Ruiz-Tagle/Carlos Wieder; Juan Stein and Diego Soto; the Garmendia twins, Angélica and Verónica—*The Savage Detectives* (Juan García Moreno, Arturo Belano and Ulises Lima; Auxilio Lacouture Amadeo Salvatierra) and *Amulet* (Auxilio Lacouture, Arturo B., Leonara Carrington, Remedios Varo).

With all these interconnections, what is perhaps most striking about the frames of reference that emerge in *The Spirit of Science Fiction*, as the first novel of an aspiring young

Latin American, to that point Chilean-Mexican (not yet Spanish-European) writer, in the mid-to-late 1970s, is the extent to which they are shaped and informed as much by the US-European-Soviet hegemony of the post-World War II, Cold War period, as by specifically Latin American concerns from which that hegemony proved inseparable. In the end both unsurprising and predictable, from a historical and literary-historical perspective, these contextual frames deeply inform the thinly displaced, fictional-autobiographical reconstruction of Bolaño's first two years in Mexico City, after his family's move there from Chile in 1968, that lies at the heart of his first novel. Set "near the Andes in the south of Chile, . . . nothing like these charming Mexican villages," in a "nightmarish, hellish Santa Bárbara," Jan's sketches of a science fiction story begin at the Potato Academy he describes as "one of the many secret faculties of the Unknown University that are scattered around the world" (9).[9] Recalling the uncanny adjacencies and spatial displacements of a boarding house, a bank, law offices, and tenements in Franz Kafka's *The Trial*, the novel's Borgesian, Escheresque, Möbius-strip fluidity intermingles contexts and sources at once literary and cultural, economic and techno-logical, social and political, as intermedial, drawing on stock footage from countless World War II movies, as they are intertextual.

Intertextually, the novel establishes from the outset and throughout—from its first explicit literary references, to Dostoevsky's *The Idiot* ("El Príncipe Idiota," 5, 21) and a "Conrad story" ("Un cuento de Conrad!," 18, 34) to Remo's late advice to Jan to "read other Russian writers, other writers in general," among them Tolstoy and Bulgakov: "You can't spend your life reading stories about spaceships and extraterrestrials" (120)[10]—Bolaño's characteristically capacious literary-historical range, and novelistic imagination, encompassing both Europe and the Americas. While Latin American authors make their appearances ("the new Peruvian poetry, the Hora Zero group . . . young Mexican poets" [81]),[11] their prestige tends to be subordinated to that of especially Anglo-American (Conrad, Fitzgerald, Vachel Lindsay, Frost, Eliot, Melville, Emerson, Lewis Carroll, Milton) and French authors (Mallarmé, Chateaubriand, de Vigny, Verlaine, Perec, Sartre, Camus, Simone de Beauvoir, Proust, the Goncourt Brothers). Similarly, while Jan spends his days reading "cartloads" of science fiction books José Arco steals for him "from specialty English bookstores . . . few and far between in Mexico City" (127),[12] José Arco tells Remo, in response to a story about Georges Perec ("one of the best" ["uno de los mejores"]; 165, 190), that in contrast to " 'the jackasses . . . lining up for Octavio Paz's lectures'"—'Fucking Latin America and its fucking young intellectuals!' "—he spends "hours digging around" the "Librería Francesa" (162–63).[13]

Accompanying these Anglo-American and French preferences, later shared by Juan García Madero, Arturo Belano, and Ulises Lima in *The Savage Detectives,* is the sense Jan conveys in the second of his nine letters, to James Hauer, of Latin America's "alien" situation. Recalling the dream of a lost "science fiction story . . . about interplanetary travel" he discussed with a "never too-esteemed . . . oft-remembered teacher" who "died just a few months later," a story to be set in "1928 France . . . 1939 France" (the latter the setting for *Monsieur Pain*) with Russian characters, Jan asks Hauer if he thinks Latin Americans have "any hope of writing good science fiction," if his committee might award "grants—Hugo grants, Nebula grants—*to the Third World natives* who do the best job describing robots," maybe "testify on our behalf—in solidarity . . . on the political stage" (21–22).[14] Reiterating the Latin American writer's "Third World" status and disadvantaged position in his seventh letter, the second of two to Ursula Le Guin, Jan writes: "I try to learn, study, observe, but I always come to the same conclusion: it's not easy, and I'm in Latin America . . . I'm Latin American . . . and to add insult to injury, I was born in Chile . . ." (111).[15]

Acutely aware of what he understands to be the Latin American writer's peripheral position, a position at once geopolitical and literary, he addresses all his letters to science fiction writers in the United States, "writers who might reasonably be supposed to be alive and whom I like: James Tiptree Jr., Theodore Sturgeon, Ray Bradbury, R. A. Lafferty, Fritz Leiber, Alfred Bester (If only I could communicate with the dead, I would write to Philip K. Dick)" (111–12).[16] While his transnational, "interplanetary" sketches and letters to seven American writers—Alice Sheldon, James Hauer, Forrest J Ackerman, Robert Silverberg, Fritz Leiber, Ursula Le Guin (2 consecutive), James Tiptree, Jr. (Alice Sheldon's pseudonym), Philip José Farmer—establish science fiction as Bolaño's initial choice for a cross-over genre, at once "literary" and popular, with transnational resonances encompassing Europe and the Americas, that choice would soon give way in his next two novels, *Antwerp* and *Monsieur Pain*, even more definitively in such later novels as *Distant Star*, *The Savage Detectives*, *2666*, and *Woes of the True Policeman*, to his much greater investment in detective fiction, the genre with which his work remains most strongly identified.

If the detective is "a street form of the intellectual," Christopher Domínguez Michael remarks in his prologue to *The Spirit of Science Fiction*, "the practice of video games is a rudiment of universal history, a projection that breaks the linearity of time" (my translation; 16).[17] At the core of both detective and science fiction, alongside questions of history and literary value, is a sustained interest in the integral shaping role, increasingly transnational and global, of media and popular culture. Thus affirming, in the novel's fourth and final interview with Jan Schrella ("alias Roberto Bolaño"), the extent to which Bolaño's novelistic imagination already extended, even before his departure from Mexico for Spain, beyond Latin America to Europe and the Americas, the reporter asks: "'Why are your stories always set in Europe? Don't you know that true universality lies in the particular, the local?'" Replying that "'The truth is . . . no part of [his] humble first work is set in Europe,'" yet acknowledging that his imagination has been shaped by "books read in childhood," and by magazines with names he can't recall, "*U-2, Commando, Spitfire*" (108–9),[18] Jan attests to the role of reading in his formation, but also to the increasingly global, intermedial impact of popular culture during the post-World War II, Cold War era. "Back then for reasons unknown," according to his friend Remo, "writing workshops (talleres literarios) were blossoming in Mexico City as never before," the number of poetry journals said to have increased in just two years from 32 to 125 to 661" (50).[19] Yet while poetry, fiction, literary history, and politics remain, as I have argued elsewhere, the four cornerstone concerns of Bolaño's work throughout his career, *The Spirit of Science Fiction* establishes from the outset as well, in its saturation of proper names and images from popular culture, a keen awareness of the intermedial challenges confronting the novel, and literature generally, in the final two decades of the twentieth century and first few years of the twenty-first.

The uneasy cohabitation of literature, media, and popular culture surfaces in Remo's description of the room he shares with Jan—"Scattered papers, newspaper clippings, science fiction books, maps, and dictionaries that were piled around his mattress like a kind of library dump" (94)[20]—and in Jan's self-description in the third of his four interviews: " 'I'm not here for my magnificent poems. . . . I've squandered my adolescence in seedy movie theaters and pestilent libraries. . . . Who the hell do you think I am, Sid Vicious?" (76–78).[21] Invoking such familiar images as "Yuri Gragarin and his space suit" ("en su traje espacial"; 15, 65) and "an atomic bomb" ("una bomba atómica"; 64, 88), the novel suggests the extent to which Bolaño's sense of the possibilities of science fiction was shaped, even as an "alien" Chilean, Mexican, Latin American writer, by the space and arms race between the United States and the Soviet Union. With its frequent references to movie stars and tv shows, Disney cartoons, animated films, and popular music—including Marlene Dietrich and Bob Dylan (45, 66); Rin-Tin-Tin (64, 88); Spiderman (105, 137); Fred Astaire (126, 150); Speedy Gonzalez and Johnny Hallyday (161, 187–88); Mary Poppins (165, 190); and Hopalong Cassidy (171, 197)—*The Spirit of Science Fiction* attests to the global domination of a media-saturated culture industry. From the Lindbergh kidnapping (18–19, 34) and Yankees games (146, 171) to the John Birch society (143, 168), US popular culture and media, in particular, permeate Bolaño's novelistic imagination, establishing in the process a sense of the increasingly transnational, intermedial pressures, in Latin America as elsewhere, of the post-World War II, Cold War era.

Among the many precursors of such Latin American literary mentors in Bolaño's later novels as *Distant Star*'s Diego Soto and Juan Stein, *The Savage Detectives*' Amadeo Salvatierra, and *By Night in Chile*'s Farewell, *The Spirit of Science Fiction* includes Pedro Huachofeo, author of *The Paradoxical History of Latin America*, a "five-hundred-page tome . . . full of stories half of which don't take place in Latin America" (34);[22] Don Ubaldo Sánchez, the "old poet and Michoacán politico," creator, and editor of the journal, *My Enchanted Garden*;[23] and his friend Dr. Ireneo Carvajal, publisher of *Mexico and Its Arts* and *Poetry Bulletin of Mexico City* and a self-described "cinema-club neorealist" ("un neorrealista de cineclub"; 140, 165). Taken together, these characters figure a continual questioning of literature's cultural value and currency, of "renowned intellectuals and men of letters (God shit on them)" and the "Republic of Letters" (75–76),[24] of how we "define literature"[25]—"Literature. According to me, yes, according to Octavio Paz, for example, no"—of what counts, and what doesn't, as "outside the realm of literary history" (132).[26]

Processing Carvajal's remarks that while in Mexico City "we seek out the cheapest and most pathetic drug or hobby: poetry, poetry magazines," in London teenagers "play for a few months at being pop stars," and in the United States, "they're getting into video," Remo speaks of his belief that "Latin America's greatest literary successes came in verse form," in the poetry, in particular, of César Vallejo, Gabriela Mistral, and Vicente

Huidobro. Yet while affirming what he calls the "poetry of our poor countries," he anticipates the challenges posed to literature's cultural currency and prestige by increasingly transnational, intermedial pressures: "I don't think that video is the Americans' drug, though actually I don't know whether you're talking about video games or making movies. But I can tell you that a new hobby is gaining ground: war-gaming" (140–41).[27]

Positioned as it is before his exchange with Remo and José Arco about the rise of video games and the war-gaming industry in the United States, Carvajal's narrative offers a parable of sorts of US hegemony and its imperialist impact on literature and culture in Latin America and beyond. Imagining in Part II's concluding text, Jan's final letter to an American science fiction (Philip José Farmer), an anthology of science fiction stories called "something like *American Orgasms in Space* or *A Radiant Future*," Jan advocates for "a camaraderie between Latin Americans and North Americans," for "orgies that future citizens of Latin America and the U.S. can take part in ... at the very least ... a cease in hostilities ... peace" (176–77).[28]

Announcing in the letter's final sentence—preceding the signature in which he reveals himself to be "alias Roberto Bolaño"—that he is "seventeen" and "A week ago ... lost [his] virginity" (178),[29] Jan sets the stage for Remo's erotic, nostalgic first-person remembrances in the novel's concluding "Mexican Manifesto." Recalling Remo's introduction to "the world of public bathhouses" by Laura, his first love, a story that mentions "the best ... Gimnasio Moctezuma," in its lobby the "mural of the Aztec emperor" by an "unknown artist" (181), and "the worst, a place in Casas Alemán, fittingly called the Wandering Dutchman" (196),[30] "Mexican Manifesto" tellingly references neither literature nor media and popular culture. A story in this sense of pure "experience," it carves out and affirms a space apart, a more personal space resisting, if not altogether escaping, both U.S. hegemony and the geopolitical binaries, conflicts, and impasses—American-Soviet, Latin American-North American, North-South—of the post-World War II, Cold War period.[31]

Strikingly manifest from the beginning, as we have seen, in *The Spirit of Science Fiction* and *Antwerp*, transnational, intermedial pressures continue to shape Bolaño's work throughout his career—in the pivotal role of the film *Actualité* in *Monsieur Pain*; *The Third Reich*'s war-gaming; the sky-writing poet Carlos Wieder's turn to photography and pornographic film in *Distant Star*; *2666*'s teenage Rosa Amalfitano, who "stopped reading books and later became a video addict" ("dejó de leer libros y se hizo videoadicta"; 185, 133) and her older boyfriend "Charly Cruz, the video king" ("el rey de los videos"; 391, 309), and the TV celebrity Reinaldo's show "*An Hour with Reinaldo*" ("*Una hora con Reinaldo*"; 458, 574). In *A Little Lumpen Novelita*, the last of Bolaño's novels published during his lifetime, two years into the twenty-first century and a year before his death in 2003, these pressures reach a fitting culmination.

Divided, like *The Spirit of Science Fiction* into a series of brief, discrete texts, at 109 pages comparable in length to *Antwerp* and *Le Spleen de Paris*, *A Little Lumpen Novelita* is composed of sixteen untitled, yet numbered sections. Set in Rome and narrated in the first-person voice of "Bianca," a "mother and a married woman" who "not long ago ... led a life of crime" (3), the novel announces early on that "TV and videos play an important role in its story" (6).[32] Recently orphaned, during the past of the story's narration, Bianca works at a hair salon and lives in an apartment with her brother. High-school dropouts—"Gradually we gave up on getting an education . . . books and notebooks from which we would learn nothing"—the two of them spend their days and nights watching TV, "first the talk shows, then cartoons, and finally the morning shows with interviews and news about famous people." Dreaming of "a better future," a word Bianca says she "didn't care about"—though she "had ideas," they "never extended into the future"—her brother is initially presented, in the novel's opening section, as aspiring to be "Mr. Rome and then Mr. Italy or Master of the Universe" (6–7).[33]

Expanding the shaping role of media and popular culture, the novel's second section moves beyond TV, "an American series" and "a game show," to Bianca's brother's growing interest in "dirty movies," their habit of visiting video stores, renting X-rated movies, sometimes two movies at once, with stars like "Sean Rob Wayne" and "Tonya Waters," and Bianca's own "omnivorous" tastes including "romance, . . . classic horror, gore, psychological horror, crime horror, military horror" (11–13).[34] Economically precarious and politically detached— "My father read *Il Messagiero*. My brother and I didn't read anything (it was a luxury we couldn't afford). I don't know which papers are right-wing and which are left-wing" (21)[35]—Bianca finds herself feeling increasingly "consumed" by a "lumpen" life in watching TV figures centrally (27).[36] Seeing "the negative of passionate moments whose point of reference was always a TV series or the whispering of girls now forgotten" (29),[37] even as she enters into sexual relationships with her brother's two "friends"—unsure which one, she thinks the Bolognan—she reflects on her life and prospects, reading a questionnaire in *Donna Moderna*, a magazine she reads at the salon, through comparisons to such celebrities as Brad Pitt, Edward Norton, Robert De Niro, Maria Grazia Cucinotta, "Audrey Hepburn and Henry Fonda," the latter the novel's only occasion for a literary reference, to *War and Peace*, not the novel but the film of the novel, which she saw "a while ago on TV" (43).[38]

Increasingly unhappy—Saturdays and Sundays "the worst," her brother's friends staying up "all hours watching TV"—Bianca soon turns to that most enduring of TV series plots, "a life of crime" (47).[39] Afraid of "becoming a prostitute," but sensing that "it was all a matter of getting used to it" and "gradually losing interest in the shows" she used to see (51),[40] she allows the Bolognan and the Libyan to draw her into a scheme targeting an Arnold Schwarzenegger prototype, a former bodybuilder and retired movie star in Rome whose movies were seen "all over the world"—"real name . . . Giovanni Dellacroce . . . stage name . . . Franco Bruno"—whom people called "Mr. Universe," after the title he had won "twice in the early sixties, or Maciste . . . the character he played in four or maybe five movies, all huge hits in Italy and around the world" (59).[41] A synecdochic, faded figure of global media and celebrity, pop-cultural success, said to have been born in Pescara, to have lived since he was fifteen in Rome, Maciste himself, now blind, has ceased being either a subject or object of media consumption, having seen his last movie "fifteen years ago" (72).[42]

Most strikingly, given the deeply integral, informing role of literary history throughout Bolaño's other novels, from which *A Little Lumpen Novelita* marks such a pronounced departure, Maciste's house contains, next to its gym, a "reading room or library (that's what he called it)" without "a single book." (74).[43] Suggesting Bolaño's growing sense of the late twentieth- and early twenty-first-century's emptying out of high literary culture in the age of media ("electronic," "digital," "social," "new"), Maciste's bookless library stands in stark contrast to the elegant library near the beginning of Part V of *2666*. Filled with works of German Romanticism in particular, the latter provides the foundation for the young Hans Reiter's eventual transformation into the German novelist Benno von Archimboldi. As Bianca spends increasing time with Maciste, falling in love with him even as she continues to look for a safe that is nowhere to be seen, she comes to think of her own apartment as "smaller every day . . . with the echoes of thousands of hours of television . . . just an apartment . . . dead," of Maciste's house, by contrast, as both "a promise" and "a disease" (91).[44] When certainty that there is no safe leads her to know "for sure" that she isn't "in love with him"—"Everything seemed as clear as could be and as entertaining as a TV show and still I was close to tears" (101)[45]— and she returns to her own apartment to find her brother, the Bolognan and the Libyan all as usual watching TV, she gives them time only to "watch the end of the show" before they must "pack their suitcases and get out." Only after watching the show "all the way through, not even missing the commercial breaks," does she finally turn off the TV (108).[46]

Remembering thereafter, in the novel's concluding paragraph, something of a minimal return to reading, still constrained by economic precarity—buying a "paper (not every day, because we didn't have enough money to buy the paper every day)" (109)—Bianca nonetheless figures in the end, even as she affirms her resolve for self-determination, challenges the novel itself continue to face, challenges *A Little Lumpen Novelita* helps us understand and process, some two decades since, not least with its concluding, conjoined inflections toward both detective and science fiction, in the era of digital platforms and social media:

> I watched TV, I listened to the news on the radio at the salon, afraid of coming across a final shot of Maciste sprawled on the ground, in a pool of blood (his cold blood), and alongside it ID photos of the Bolognan and the Libyan, staring at me nostalgically from the page or from the screen of our TV set (which was really ours now, not our dead parents), as if these pictures—of killers and victim killer and victims—were evidence that outside the storm still raged, a storm not located in the skies of Rome, but in the European night or the space between planets, a noiseless, eyeless storm from another world, a world that not even the satellites in orbit around the Earth could capture, a world where there was a place that was my place, a shadow that was my shadow. (109)[47]

While *The Spirit of Science Fiction*'s opening epigraph from Antonin Artaud tells us that "All writing is garbage. . . . All writers are pigs. Especially writers today" (13),[48] the sense of urgency and persistent inquiry throughout Bolaño's writing says otherwise. Speaking to us from opposite ends of his career, the continuing investments and enduring commitments of *The Spirit of Science Fiction* and *A Little Lumpen Novelita* invite us to reclaim and repurpose, now twenty-two years into the twenty-first century, questions of value not only for the novel, or for literature, but also for what counts as culture, as civilization itself, in an alien, Anthropocene age.

NOTES

1. "Por supuesto, no soy de esos monstruos nacionalistas que sólo leen lo que produce el terruño. Me interesa la literatura francesa.... la literatura norteamericana del ochocientos... Cuando era adolescente hubo una época en que sólo leía a Poe. En fin, me interesa y creo que conozco un poco de toda la literatura occidental" (63).
2. Hence Bolaño's most frequent narrator, "Arturo Belano." As for Rimbaud, Baudelaire remains for Bolaño, as he puts it in his pivotal late essay "Literature + Illness = Illness" ("Literatura + enfermedad = enfermedad") "father of them all" ("el padre de todos"; 133; *Cuentos* 524).
3. "The Last Interview," with Mónica Maristain. "La única novela de la que no me avergüenzo es *Amberes*, tal vez porque sigue siendo ininteligible" (117).
4. On Bolaño's use of the term "poemas-novela" in *Los detectives salvajes* (151) and his development of the prose poem novel throughout *The Savage Detectives* in particular, see my *Framing Roberto Bolaño*, chapter 6, "Dismantling Narrative Drive" (106–29).
5. See Monroe, *A Poverty of Objects*; Mikhail Bakhtin, *The Dialogic Imagination*; and Williams, *Marxism and Literature* (108–14, 115–20, and 121–28).
6. I use the term "novelistic" in the Bakhtinian sense of a dialogical, polyphonic, heteroglossic prose interweaving multiple genres of speech and writing. Novelistic in precisely this sense in a characteristically brief, intense space, the prose poem remains for Bolaño an integral structural principle throughout his career. Embracing this principle even in such works of monumental length as *The Savage Detectives* and *2666*, his prose poem novels challenge and complicate more traditional expectations that the novel will offer narratives of "longue durée." Like *Antwerp*, but in a more familiar if no less complex narrative mode, *The Spirit of Science Fiction*'s intricate pattern of alternating genres of speech and writing, each the length of an average prose poem, establishes an enduring, remarkably varied, continually evolving template, as Bolaño's career would subsequently prove, for prose poems "writ large," expansive and expandable, neither "poem" nor "prose" alone, nor reducible to the prose poem itself as "not novel," but a third term, a "genreless genre" with endless cross-, multi-, intergenre possibilities. Tellingly, *The Spirit of Science Fiction*'s first literary reference is to Dostoevsky, Bakhtin's novelistic hero par excellence.
7. Placed by Bolaño at the end of the novel, where it functions in effect more as coda than conclusion, only in 1984, "Mexican Manifesto" also concludes Part II of the collected poems Bolaño assembled (in both verse and prose) for *The Unknown University*. Composed almost entirely of poems in prose (only six in verse), in contrast to Parts I and III (both all verse), Part II reprints and repurposes as well, as the collection's literal and figural centerpiece, under the title "Gente que se aleja" ("People Walking Away"), Bolaño's first published prose poem novel, *Amberes* (*Antwerp*). On Bolaño's "farewell" to poetry in and as verse in *The Unknown University*, and the prose poem's pivotal legacy, see my *Framing Roberto Bolaño*, chapter 4, "Poetry at the Ends of Its Lines" (65–85).

8. "El compadre de Jeremías y el coordinador de otro taller, el taller official, de la facultad" (Bolaño, *El espíritu* 25).

9. "Cerca de los Andes, en el sur de Chile. Es un pueblo espantoso . . . nada parecido a estos hermosos pueblitos mexicanos . . . esa Santa Bárbara de las pesadillas o de las rayas . . . una de las tantas facultades esparcidas por el mundo de la Universidad Desconocida" (Bolaño, *El espíritu* 25).

10. " 'Tendrías que leer a otros autores rusos; en general a otro tipo de escritores. No te vas a pasar la vida leyendo historias de naves espaciales y extraterrestres' " (Bolaño, *El espíritu* 144).

11. " 'La nueva poesía peruana, el grupo Hora Zero, la navaja de plata de . . . los jóvenes poetas mexicanos' " (Bolaño, *El espíritu* 105).

12. "A carretadas . . . de librerías especializadas en literatura de lengua inglesa, poco abundantes in el DF" (Bolaño, *El espíritu* 151).

13. " 'Joder con los jóvenes intelectuales de Latinoamérica! . . . / . . . —Yo voy a la Librería Francesa! Mientras los pendejos hacen cola en las conferencias de Octavio Paz yo me paso horas escarbando por ahí!' " (Bolaño, *El espíritu* 187–88).

14. "Un cuento de ciencia-ficción . . . sobre viajes interplanetarios. . . Nuestro sueño, refunfuñó mi nunca demasiado alabado professor, debe ser la Francia de 1928. . . . la Francia de 1939 . . . Mi siempre recordado maestro murió tan sólo unos meses después. Cree usted, ahora, que podemos escribir buena literatura de ciencia-ficción? . . . becas—becas Hugo, becas Nébula—a los nativos del Tercer Mundo que mejor describan un robot? . . . acaso . . . dar un apoyo testimonial —solidario . . . en el plano politico?" (Bolaño, *El espíritu* 38–39).

15. "Intento aprender, estudiar, observar, pero siempre vuelvo al punto de partida: es duro y estoy en Latinoamérica, es duro y soy latinoamericano, es duro y para terminarla de amolar nací en Chile . . ." (Bolaño, *El espíritu* 136);

16. "En lo que respecta a las cartas todas están dirigidas a escritores de ciencia-ficción de Estados Unidos; escritores a los que razonablemente supongo vivos y que me gustan, como James Tiptree Jr., Theodore Sturgeon, Ray Bradbury, R. A. Lafferty, Fritz Leiber, Alfred Bester. (Ay, si pudiera communicarme con los muertos le escribriría a Philip K. Dick.)" (Bolaño, *El espíritu* 136).

17. "Si el detective . . . es una forma callejera del intellectual, la práctica de los videojuegos es un rudimento de la historia universal, una projección que rompe la linealidad del tiempo" (Bolaño, *El espíritu* 16).

18. " 'Por qué tantos escenarios europeos? Acaso no sabe que la auténtica universalidad está en lo particular, en la provincia?' 'En realidad . . . no hay escenarios europeos en mi humilde ópera prima'; "lecturas infantiles . . . Revistas cuyos nombres no recuerdo: U-2, Comando, Spitfire" (Bolaño, *El espíritu* 133).

19. "En aquel tiempo, ignoro por qué razón . . . los talleres literarios florecieron en el Distrito Federal como nunca antes" (Bolaño, *El espíritu* 73).

20. "Recortes de periódicos, libros de ciencia-ficción, mapas y diccionarios que conformaban una especie de biblioteca-basurero que crecía alrededor de su cochón" (Bolaño, *El espíritu* 119).

21. "Es evidente que no estoy aquí por mis "magníficos" versos. . . . he gastado mi adolescencia en cines malsanos y bibliotecas infectas. . . . Quién demonios cree que soy yo? Sid Vicious?" (Bolaño, *El espíritu* 100–1).

22. "La *Historia paradójica de la Latinoamérica* . . . Un mamotreto de quinientas páginas . . . en donde se narran infinidad de anécdotas, la mitad de las cuales no suceden en Latinoamérica" (Bolaño, *El espíritu* 53–54).

23. "El Viejo poeta y politico michoacano Ubaldo Sánchez . . . Mi Pensil" (Bolaño, *El espíritu* 73).

24. "Unos intelectuales y hombres de letras tan renombrados (Dios se cague en ellos) . . . la República de las Letras" (Bolaño, *El espíritu* 99).

25. "Depende . . . de lo que consideremos literatura" (Bolaño, *El espíritu* 156).

26. "Literatura? Sí, para mí sí; para Octavio Paz, por poner un ejemplo, no) . . . una cierta ahistoricidad literaria" (Bolaño, *El espíritu* 132).

27. "Buscamos la droga o el hobby más barato y más patético: la poesía, las revistas de poesía . . . juegan durante algunos meses a ser estrellas de la cancion . . . les está dando por el video . . . la disciplina literaria con mayores logros en América Latina . . . La poesía de nuestros pobres países . . . —No creo que sea el video la droga de los norteamericanos, aunque la verdad no sé si usted se refería a los videojuegos o a filmar sus propias películas. Pero puedo asegurarle que un nuevo hobby está ganando terreno: los juegos de Guerra" (Bolaño, *El espíritu* 165–66).

28. "Podría titularse *Orgasmos americanos en el espacio* o *Un futuro radiante* . . . camaradería) entre latinoamericanos y norteamericanos . . . las orgías que pueden practicar . . . los futuros ciudadanos de Latinoamericana y de Estados Unidos" (Bolaño, *El espíritu* 204).

29. "Tengo diecisiete años y . . . Hace una semana dejé de ser virgen" (Bolaño, *El espíritu* 204).

30. "El mundo de los baños públicos . . . El primero . . . Gimnasio Moctezuma . . . algún artista desconocido . . . un mural en donde se veía al emperador Azteca" (Bolaño, *El espíritu* 207); "El peor, un local de Casas Alemán llamado convenientemente El Holandés Errante" (223).

31. On questions of experience in Bolaño, and in North and South American literature generally from the mid-nineteenth century to the present, see Jeffrey Lawrence's *Anxieties of Experience,* in particular his "Epilogue: After Bolaño: Toward a Contemporary Literature of the Americas" (206–41).

32. "Ahora soy una madre y también una mujer casada, pero no hace mucho fui una delincuente" (Bolaño, *Una novelita* 3); "La tele y el vídeo ocupan un lugar importante en esta historia" (6).

33. "Paulatinamente fuimos dejando de lado los estudios . . . los libros y cuadernos en donde nada íbamos aprender"; "Matábamos el tiempo viendo la tele, primero las entrevistas, después los dibujos animados, finalmente los programas matinales con entrevistas y conversaciones y noticias de los famosos"; "un futuro mejor. . . . que a mí el futuro no me importaba, que se me ocurrían ideas, pero que esas ideas . . . nunca se proyectaban hacia el futuro" (Bolaño, *Una novelita* 6–7).

34. "Una serie americana y luego un concurso . . . películas cochinas . . . escapadas por los videoclubs . . . dos películas a la vez . . . Sean Rob Wayne . . . Tonya Waters . . . Era omnívora . . . las películas de amor . . . las de terror clásico, el cine gore, las de terror psicológico, las de terror policial, las de terror bélico" (Bolaño, *Una novelita* 11–13).

35. "Mi padre compraba Il Messaggero. Mi hermano y yo no compramos periódicos (es un lujo que no nos podemos permitir). Yo no sé qué periódoco es de derechas o de izquierdas" (Bolaño, *Una novelita* 21).

36. "Me consumía . . . veíamos la tele . . ." (Bolaño, *Una novelita* 27).

37. "Veía negativos de experiencia pasionales cuyo punto de referencia siempre era una serie de television o el murmullo ha olvidado de unas niñas" (Bolaño, *Una novelita* 29).

38. "*Guerra y paz*, con Audrey Hepburn y Henry Fonda. La vi hace poco en la tele" (Bolaño, *Una novelita* 43).

39. "Los sábados y domingos eran los peores días . . . (ellos seguían viendo la tele hasta la madrugada) . . . una delincuente" (Bolaño, *Una novelita* 47).

40. "Una puta . . . intuía que todo era cuestión de acostumbrarse. . . . mi interés por los programas que antes solía ver comenzó a decaer de forma paulatina" (Bolaño, *Una novelita* 51).

41. "Su nombre real era Giovanni Dellacroce. . . . Su nombre artístico era Franco Bruno. La gente lo llamaba Mister Universe, pues había obtenido este título dos veces, ambas al principio de la década de los sesenta, o Maciste, que fue el personaje que interpretó en cuatro, tal vez cinco, películas, todas de gran éxito, tanto en Italia como en el resto del mundo" (Bolaño, *Una novelita* 59).

42. "La última película que él había visto fue hacía quince años" (Bolaño, *Una novelita* 72).

43. "La sala de lecturas o biblioteca (así la llamaba él), donde no había ni un solo libro" (Bolaño, *Una novelita* 74).

44. "Cada día más pequeño . . . con los ecos de miles de horas de televisión . . . una promesa y una enfermedad" (Bolaño, *Una novelita* 91).

45. "Supe sin ninguna que no estaba enamorada de él . . . Todo me pareció claro . . . como un programa de television y, sin embargo, poco me faltó para que me pusiera a llorar allí mismo" (Bolaño, *Una novelita* 101).

46. "El boloñes y el libio estaban viendo la tele . . . Que vieran el programa hasta el final y que luego hicieran las maletas y se fueran. . . . Y cuando acabó el programa, que vi íntegro, sin perderme ni siquiera los espacios comerciales . . . apagué la tele" (Bolaño, *Una novelita* 108).

47. "Leía la prensa (no todos los días porque no teníamos dinero para comprar el periódoco a diario), veía la tele, escuchaba las noticias de la radio en la peluquería, temerosa de encontrar la figura final de Maciste tirado en el suelo, en medio de un charco de sangre (su sangre fría), y junto a él las fotos tipo carnet del boloñés y del libio, mirándome con nostalgia desde una página o desde la pantalla de nuestra tele que ya era realmente nuestra y no de nuestros padres Muertos, como si las fotos de ellos, los asesinos y las víctimas, fueran la señal de que en el exterior aún persistía la tormenta, una tormenta que no estaba localizada sobre el cielo de Roma, sino en la noche de Europa o en el espacio que media entre planeta y planeta, una tormenta sin ruido y sin ojos que venía de otro mundo, un mundo que ni los satélites que giran alrededor de la Tierra pueden captar, y donde existía un hueco que era mi hueco, una sombra que era mi sombra" (Bolaño, *Una novelita* 109–10).

48. "Toda escritura es una marranada. . . . Todos los escritores son unos cerdos. Especialmente los de ahora" (Bolaño, *Una novelita* 13).

Works Cited

Andrews, Chris. *Roberto Bolaño's Fiction: An Expanding Universe.* Columbia UP, 2014.

Bakhtin, Mikhail. *The Dialogic Imagination: Four Essays.* Translated and edited by Caryl Emerson and Michael Holquist. University of Texas Press, 1981.

Baudelaire, Charles. "À Arsène Houssaye." *Oeuvres completes.* Edited by Claude Pichois, vol. 1. Gallimard, 1976, pp. 275–76.

Baudelaire, Charles. *Le Spleen de Paris. Oeuvres complètes.* Edited by Claude Pichois, vol. 1. Gallimard, 1976.

Baudelaire, Charles. *Les Fleurs du Mal. Oeuvres complètes.* Edited by Claude Pichois, vol. 1. Gallimard, 1976.

Birns, Nicholas, and De Castro, Juan E., editors. *Roberto Bolaño as World Literature.* Bloomsbury, 2017.

Bolaño, Roberto. *Amberes.* Anagrama, 2002.

Bolaño, Roberto. *Antwerp.* Translated by Natascha Wimmer, New Directions, 2012.

Bolaño, Roberto. *By Night in Chile.* Translated by Chris Andrews, New Directions, 2003.

Bolaño, Roberto. *Cuentos completos: Llamadas telefónicas / Putas asesinas / El gaucho insufrible.* Anagrama, 2013.

Bolaño, Roberto. *Los detectives salvajes.* Anagrama, 1998.

Bolaño, Roberto. *Distant Star.* Translated by Chris Andrews, New Directions, 2004.

Bolaño, Roberto. *El espíritu de la ciencia-ficción.* Alfaguara, 2016.

Bolaño, Roberto. *Estrella distante.* Anagrama, 1996.

Bolaño, Roberto. *A Little Lumpen Novelita.* Translated by Natasha Wimmer, New Directions, 2014.

Bolaño, Roberto. *La literatura nazi en América.* Seix Barral, 1996.

Bolaño, Roberto. "Literatura + enfermedad = enfermedad." *Cuentos completos.* Anagrama, 2013, pp. 515–33; "Literature + Illness = Illness." *The Insufferable Gaucho.* Anagrama, 2013, pp. 123–46.

Bolaño, Roberto. *Monsieur Pain.* [Original title *La senda de los elefantes* (The Path of the Elephants), 1984. Ayuntamiento de Toledo, Concejalía del Area de Cultura, 1993]. Anagrama, 1999.

Bolaño, Roberto. *Monsieur Pain.* Translated by Chris Andrews. New Directions, 2010.

Bolaño, Roberto. *Nazi Literature in the Americas.* Translated by Chris Andrews. New Directions, 2008.

Bolaño, Roberto. *Nocturno de Chile.* Anagrama, 2000.

Bolaño, Roberto. *Una novelita lumpen.* Anagrama, 2002.

Bolaño, Roberto. *The Savage Detectives.* Translated by Natasha Wimmer. Farrar, Straus, & Giroux, 2007.

Bolaño, Roberto. *Los sinsabores del verdadero policía.* Anagrama, 2011.

Bolaño, Roberto. *The Spirit of Science Fiction.* Translated by Natasha Wimmer. New Directions, 2019.

Bolaño, Roberto. *El Tercer Reich.* Anagrama, 2010.

Bolaño, Roberto. *The Third Reich.* Translated by Natasha Wimmer. Farrar, Straus, & Giroux, 2011.

Bolaño, Roberto. *2666.* Anagrama, 2004.

Bolaño, Roberto. *2666.* Translated by Natasha Wimmer. Farrar, Straus, & Giroux, 2008.

Bolaño, Roberto. *La Universidad Desconocida.* Anagrama, 2007.

Bolaño, Roberto. *The Unknown University.* Translated by Laura Healy. New Directions, 2012.

Bolaño, Roberto. *Woes of the True Policeman.* Translated by Natasha Wimmer. Farrar, Straus, & Giroux, 2012.

Bolaño, Roberto and A.G. Porta. *Consejos de un discípulo de Morrison a un fanático de Joyce.* Anthropos, 2006.

Boullosa, Carmen. "Reading Is Always More Important than Writing." Interview by Carmen Boullosa. Translated by Margaret Carson. *The Last Interview and Other Conversations,* Melville House, 2009, pp. 53–68.

Corral, Will H., Birns, Nicholas, and De Castro, Juan E., editors. *The Contemporary Spanish-American Novel: Bolaño and After.* Bloomsbury, 2013.

De Castro, Juan E. *Writing Revolution in Latin America: From Martí to García Márquez to Bolaño*. Vanderbilt UP, 2019.

Domínguez, Christopher Michael. "El arcón de Roberto Bolaño. *Prólogo*." Roberto Bolaño, *El espíritu de la ciencia-ficción*. Alfaguara, 2016, pp. 9–16.

Dostoevsky, Fyodor. *The Idiot*. Translated by David McDuff. Penguin, 2004.

Hoyos, Héctor. *Beyond Bolaño: The Global Latin American Novel*. Columbia UP, 2015.

Lawrence, Jeffrey. *Anxieties of Experience: The Literatures of the Americas from Whitman to Bolaño*. Oxford UP, 2018.

López-Calvo, Ignacio, editor. *Roberto Bolaño, a Less Distant Star: Critical Essays*. Palgrave Macmillan, 2015.

López-Calvo, Ignacio, editor. "World Literature and the Marketing of Roberto Bolaño's Posthumous Works." *Critical Insights: Contemporary Latin American Fiction*, edited byIgnacio López-Calvo. Salem Press, 2017, pp. 26–41.

Maristain, Mónica. "The Last Interview." *Roberto Bolaño: The Last Interview and Other Conversations*. Edited by Sybil Perez, Melville House Publications, 2009, pp. 93–123.

Monroe, Jonathan B. *A Poverty of Objects: The Prose Poem and the Politics of Genre*. Cornell UP, 1987.

Monroe, Jonathan B. *Framing Roberto Bolaño: Poetry, Fiction, Literary History, Politics*. Cambridge UP, 2019.

Monroe, Jonathan B. "Mapping Bolaño's Worlds." *Roberto Bolaño in Context*. Edited by Jonathan B. Monroe, Cambridge UP, forthcoming 2022.

Monroe, Jonathan B., editor. *Roberto Bolaño in Context*. Cambridge UP, forthcoming 2022.

Poe, Edgar Allan. "The Philosophy of Composition." *The Raven: Poems and Essays on Poetry*, edited by C. H. Sisson, Carcanet, 2012, pp. 138–50.

Poe, Edgar Allan. "The Poetic Principle." *Poems and Essays on Poetry*, edited by C. H. Sisson, Carcanet, 2012, pp. 88–95.

Pollack, Sarah. "After Bolaño: Rethinking the Politics of Latin American Literature in Translation," *PMLA*, vol. 128, no. 3, 2013, pp. 660–67.

Rankine, Claudia. *Citizen: An American Lyric*. Graywolf, 2014.

Rankine, Claudia. *Don't Let Me Be Lonely: An American Lyric*. Graywolf, 2004.

Rankine, Claudia. *Just Us: An American Conversation*. Graywolf, 2020.

Whitman, Walt. *Leaves of Grass. Poetry and Prose*. Library of America, 1996.

Williams, Raymond. *Marxism and Literature*. Oxford UP, 1977.

CHAPTER 42

....

MANUEL PUIG

Between Pop-Art and Psychoanalysis

....

JORGELINA CORBATTA

THE work of Manuel Puig (1932–1990), considered by some critics as part of the Latin American post-Boom, distinguishes itself by being highly experimental and-at the same time, for being able to reach a very vast audience. In his writing Puig had the ability to combine the seduction of popular culture (especially the movies he loved so much but also song lyrics, soap-opera, and detective fiction) and the in-depth knowledge of the human mind and motivations provided, mainly, by psychoanalysis. Puig's inclusion in his writing of elements considered as low culture, together with his embrace of *kitsch* and *camp* have misled many critical approaches of his work—considered as merely entertaining and quite superficial. Mario Vargas Llosa's opinion of Puig's narrative as "an undemanding, pleasing literature that has no other purpose than to entertain" is well known (n.p.). My contention is that Puig's work is a serious attempt to use not only a post-Freudian vision of human beings but, also, to give a new look at socio-cultural and political aspects of Argentina, Latin America, and even the United States.

This study of Puig's work is modelled upon a critical frame composed by two axes. The first one is the notion of *mythe personnel* (Charles Mauron's *psychocritique*)—together with some of Freud's, Otto Rank's, and Lacan's writings, as instruments to explore Puig's recurrent obsessions that texture the autobiographical substratum of his fictions. The second axis is the notion of *collective myths* that permeates the collective unconscious—coming from popular culture and mass-media (Claude Levi Strauss's "bricolage," Susan Sontag's "kitsch" and "camp," Umberto Eco's "popular culture and mass communications," and that were masterfully manipulated by Puig in the construction of his narrative).

Puig's novels, based on their geographical location in strict correlation to his personal itinerary around the world, can be classified in three cycles. The cycle of Coronel Vallejos, which includes *Betrayed by Rita Hayworth*, and *Heartbreak Tango*; the next two novels, *The Buenos Aires Affair* and *Kiss of the Spider Woman*, constitute the Buenos Aires cycle; and his other four novels, *Angelical Pubis, Eternal Curse to the Reader of*

These Pages, Blood of Requited Love, and *Tropical Night Falling* are part of the Americas cycle with their locations—respectively, in Mexico, United States, and Brazil. All the novels show a recurrent structure: they are divided into two parts with six or eight chapters each (except *Eternal Curse to the Reader of These Pages*).

Puig was born in 1932 in a little Argentine town in las pampas, General Villegas (fictionalized as Coronel Vallejos), where his two first novels take place. *La traición de Rita Hayworth* (*Betrayed by Rita Hayworth*, 1968)—according to Puig, 95 percent autobiographical, is centered in Toto's childhood, going almost daily to the movies with his mother, escaping from his father, his community, even his own physical reality. Although the novel opens with a "gallery of voices" (as Emir Rodríguez Monegal has called it [*La traición de Rita Hayworth*, 376]), in which is difficult to distinguish who is talking, about what and to whom, its main narrative strategy is based on internal monologues (or stream-of-consciousness), plus a school composition, one-sided dialogue, pages of diaries, an anonymous communication, and a never-sent letter that closes the novel. This letter, written by Toto's father, gives him a voice—for the first and only time, allowing the reader to learn first-hand about a character to which we have had access only through the perspective of the others. The first part of the novel presents Toto (Puig's *alter ego*) as a boy in Coronel Vallejos, in interaction with his parents, cousins, neighbors, friends, and schoolmates; in the second one, Toto is in a boarding school in Buenos Aires, searching for his sexual identity while dealing with socio-cultural and political conflicts. Sexuality, money, religion, social class, and politics are leitmotivs woven into a background canvas in which Toto moves and develops, always nurtured and alienated by the movies he watches. During his whole life and work, Puig rejected violence and power games by replacing them with a mythic world full of beauty, kindness, and sensibility inspired in Hollywood. Those movies offered him respite from an authoritarian, repressive, and *machista* culture that rejects weakness and sensitivity. All the themes that appeared in his work are different versions of his recurrent preoccupation with power struggles based on exploitation and domination, and the roles that society imposes on individuals, starting with the roles imposed on men and women because, as he often said, "sexual oppression is the school of all the other oppressions" (Bacarisse 219).

Puig's second novel, *Boquitas pintadas. Folletín* (*Heartbreak Tango: A Serial*, 1969), is somehow an easier novel to read, structured as a soap opera in which each chapter, called *entregas* (meaning both installment and surrender), opens with an epigraph reproducing fragments of familiar tango lyrics. The narrative strategy is mainly what Claude Lévi-Strauss defined, in *La Pensée Sauvage* (*The Savage Mind*, trans. 1966), as "bricolage," a skill of using things that are at hand and recombining them to create something new. In this novel it takes the form of a combination of letters and exchanges, a photo album, newspaper clippings, diary entries, tarot readings, medical and police reports, phone conversations, (Catholic) confessions, a radio soap opera (an example of a text inside the text or *mise en abyme* [Dällenbach], as in *Hamlet*, Cervantes, or Borges). The protagonist is Juan Carlos, a *macho* type with whom several women are in love (a widow, a schoolteacher, an ex-beauty queen), and who dies of tuberculosis.

All the characters are consumed by passion, as in soap operas (the *folletín* of the subtitle) but, in opposition to the traditional soap opera's happy ending (with the reward of the good people and the punishment of the bad ones), *Heartbreak Tango* is the narrative of the frustrations and failures of all those-in Puig's words "who had believed in the canons of their time, who had accepted the rules of the game and who had ended in a very bad shape" (Sosnowski 74).[1] In these two novels, we can notice Puig's preoccupation, or rather obsession, with the idea that the domination of women by men is at the origin of all other forms of domination; that is: employer/worker; government/masses; reason/feeling; conscious/unconscious; good taste/bad taste; high culture/low culture; criticism/creativity (Hegel's parable of master/slave rewritten by Marx and Engels). These pairs of opposite elements are part of Puig's *personal myth* (submissive mother/dominant father) that, in the social order, adopt the form of *collective myths* that rule the collective unconscious and the characters' behavior, all of whom build their identities by imitation, acting like characters in a melodrama, speaking the language of bolero and tango lyrics, radio plays and sentimental movies.

Puig's third novel, *The Buenos Aires' Affair. Novela policial* (*The Buenos Aires' Affair: A Detective Novel*, 1973), inaugurates the Buenos Aires cycle. Its subtitle, detective novel (as *Heartbreak Tango's* subtitle *A Serial*) states the generic status in which the text is inscribed, which, as in the previous case, is completely subverted in a combination of adhesion/perversion or, as Severo Sarduy wrote "an apotheosis that is also a mockery" (626).[2] *The Buenos Aires Affair* narrates a violent story—apparently following the conventions of the genre (murder, investigation, final resolution)—but, in a complete subversion of its rules, the novel turns out to be a psychological and sociological exploration of the Argentine reality from 1930 to the 1960s. As Puig states in my interview ("Brief Encounter: An Interview with Manuel Puig"), *The Buenos Aires Affair* is "an investigation of the Argentine mistake: political and sexual mistake" (170).[3] The two main characters are an art critic, Leo and Gladys, a plastic artist, involved in a sadomasochist relationship that takes to its extreme the power struggles of Puig's first two novels while presenting, at the same time, his personal reaction to the negative critical appreciation of his own work. Puig identifies himself with Gladys, and her *ars poetica*—with her taste for bricolage and castoff materials in opposition to another female plastic artist, conservative and respectful of the canon. As in the two previous novels, the plot must be reconstructed like a puzzle, and each chapter has an epigraph reproducing scenes from Hollywood movies played by the female film stars Puig loved. The epigraphs are in dialogical interaction with the text they precede, and synthesize, in an idealized dimension, its emotional content. In addition, there are footnotes that contain detailed references to Glady's masturbatory acts. Other forms of bricolage/intertextuality include police reports, newspapers' political headlines, romantic poems (Glady's mother recites them while looking for her missed daughter) and classical romantic music, operas, comic magazines, psychoanalytic sessions, and an interview with Gladys supposedly published in *Harper's Bazaar*. This interview, which is titled "The Buenos Aires Affair," functions like a microcosm inside of the novel—another example of *mise en abyme* (example the radio soap opera in *Heartbreak Tango*), and not only does it provide the key to read it but it is also Puig's own ars poetica.

El beso de la mujer araña (*Kiss of the Spider Woman*, 1976) is Puig's best-known and most popular novel. There is no doubt that the play, the Oscar-nominated film and the glamorous Broadway musical based on the novel, have contributed to its popularity. It is also true that the novel is, as his first one, clearly autobiographical in Puig's identification with Molina, one of the two characters, and in his devotion to movies. As was the case in *The Buenos Aires Affair*, *Kiss of the Spider Woman* again makes use of footnotes. It is also important to mention that the progressive reduction in the number of characters, already initiated in the previous novel, confronts us here with only two protagonists: Molina, the homosexual window dresser, and Valentín, the intellectual guerrilla fighter. They are confined in a prison in Buenos Aires, accused of sexual and political subversive acts, respectively, against the socio-political and moral order. They interact with each other mainly through the movies that Molina narrates to Valentín. As Puig has explained, "They can't face certain subjects directly. Slowly, and unconsciously, they reveal themselves [through the movies Molina tells the other]" (Ronald Christ 572). While Molina identifies himself with heroines of movies from the 40s (subdued women vs dominant men), Valentín identifies, rather ambivalently, with the revolutionary type represented by the iconic figure of Che Guevara. During the period they are in prison together, Molina and Valentín, in an interaction resembling the dialogical dyad of analyst/analysand (with exchangeable roles), start to change. Valentín becomes more in contact with his own emotions and feelings, while Molina begins to develop a different perception of himself in relationship to the other, and to society in general. The footnotes, for their part, play a didactical function by instructing the reader about different theoretical approaches to the subject of homosexuality. In Puig's words, "I said to myself: well, the information has been violently denied, so I will violently incorporate it into the narration, it will be there as an explanation, a footnote" (Christ 573). An important aspect in Puig's narrative strategy is evident here: his total rejection of the third person narration (that he sees as another form of power exercise) in favor of using mostly dialogues and interior monologues as tools for characters' self-presentation and action development. In this, as in many other occasions, Puig makes a good use of Borges's advice, who, in his prologue to *Martín Fierro*, writes "In my brief experience as a narrator I have verified that to know how a character talks, is to know how that character is."[4] Puig's resistance to using the third person (except in some passages in which its exaggeration becomes parodic) is shown here in all its purity. His desire to *disappear* behind his characters, in clear opposition to a device that he conceives as authoritarian and repressive, is in consonance with Umberto Eco's notions of *opera aperta* and an active participant reader. Rather ironically, one of the multiple meanings of *Kiss of the Spider Woman* consists in postulating freedom inside a prison cell where two men are incarcerated, by using fantasy and imagination. In this way, Puig turns the prison into an island of freedom inside a society ruled by authoritarianism, repression, censorship and self-censorship. A place *out of the world* ("anywhere out of the world" as in Baudelaire) or, as we read in the novel's last line, "this dream is short but this dream is happy" (281).[5]

Pubis Angelical (1979), the first novel of the American cycle, is situated in Mexico City and, like the former one, takes place entirely inside a closed room. In this case, it is a hospital room where Ana, a divorced Argentinian woman close to thirty and very beautiful (everyone says she looks like Heddy Lamarr), is treated for cancer. There she is visited by Beatriz (a Mexican feminist lawyer) and Pozzi, her ex-lover, a left-wing Peronist lawyer and defender of political prisoners, who has come from Argentina to convince her to collaborate in the kidnapping of Alejandro, a wealthy ranch owner, right-wing Peronist, nationalist, and puritan with whom Ana was engaged to be married before leaving the country. During the day Ana talks to her visitors and writes in her diary; through those conversations and from her diary, we penetrate her conscience and become aware of her past. During the night, Ana has elaborated dreams in which she doubles herself into two other women: an actress of 1930 also called *Ama* (Mistress) or "the Beauty" in the first part of the novel; and into a sexual social worker identified as W218, who lives in a totalitarian society of the future, in the second part. While the first part uses the devices of fantastic literature, the second one adopts those of science fiction. In Ana's dreams, elements of her daily life constantly reappear, and some of them repeat themselves throughout the three stories (Ana/Ama/W218), revealing Ana's unconscious conflicts. There are, then, two axes: one is synchronic (day at the hospital/night dreams); the other is diachronic (Vienna/Hollywood/Mexico/Urbis Aquarius/Urbis Eternal Ice). This novel, like the previous four, takes elements from popular culture—mainly movies but also bolero lyrics—and is very invested in psychoanalysis (dreams, doubles, the uncanny), while investigating, at the same time, Argentina's political history with the presentation of the different factions of Peronism, Socialism, and leftist subversive movements. During the three months in the hospital Ana experiences changes. Her interaction with Beatriz's feminist ideas, and with Pozzi's political ideas, together with the writing of her diary and the transmutation of her daily experiences into dreams, constitute a process of self-reflection. This is a process that helps her think over her past life and to be ready for a transformation towards maturity as a daughter, a mother, a friend, and a lover.

Maldición eterna al que lea estas páginas (*Eternal Curse to the Reader of These Pages*, Puig 1980) takes place in 1978 in New York and, like the other novels, has a two-part structure but instead of eight chapters each, there are twelve and eleven chapters respectively. Its plot develops only through dialogues and split-monologues (except for the last chapter, which includes five letters, a job application, and a testament), and evolves mainly around two characters. One is Ramírez, a seventy-four-year-old Argentinian political activist who, after being imprisoned and tortured, is left paralyzed and amnesic. He is brought to the United States by the Human Rights Commission and lodged in a nursing home. The other character is Larry, a thirty-six-year-old American of Italian descent who, although having a degree in history, has quit teaching and makes a living doing minor jobs. He is hired by an agency to push Ramírez's wheelchair around Greenwich Village. Through dialogues, real or imagined (kind of hallucinations or two-folded monologues on Ramírez's side), both men present themselves in their current circumstances, remember their pasts and also start experimenting some changes because of their mutual interaction. At the beginning Ramírez appears as helpless and defenseless because of his age/exile and suffering in Argentina before his departure, in open contrast with the hardness of Larry, who refuses any human contact with him. But Ramírez is determined to prevail in his new world by decodifying its language, history, and cultural patterns. To do so, he takes notes, reads history books, and consults encyclopedias, while trying to extract—as in a sort of vampirism—as much information as possible from Larry. The narration turns into a form of psychodrama in which Ramírez/Larry play different roles (native/foreigner, father/son, therapist/patient, oppressor/oppressed). In that interaction, Ramírez not only recovers his own past, and his relationship with his family and his country, but also puts in motion repressed feelings and memories in Larry, who is thus forced to face and express them in a new way, free of clichés and stereotypes. Again, as in the previous pairing of Gladys/Leo, Molina/Valentín, Ana/Pozzi, and now Ramírez/Larry, there is a recurrent structure that mimes the dyad analyst/analysand and their mutual interaction. Vietnam, Marxism, Oedipus complex, mother/father/son relationship, leftist movements in Argentina, marriage and sexual encounters, and social classes are recurrent topics of discussion that go from the general to the personal in acts of self-exploration, defense, transference, and eventual changes. If in the first part of the novel, it is Ramírez who stages the dialogues and interrogates Larry most of the time, sucking information like a vampire, in the second part the power game is inverted when a package of three French novels arrives. While in prison in Argentina, in order to avoid censorship, Ramírez had written in a ciphered code, on the margins of those novels, a diary about his political activity. Larry, by decodifying those messages, is able to learn not only about Ramírez's past life but also to get in contact with important documentation about his political activism, an aspect that interests him as a historian, and could help his career. It is important to add that this novel was initially written in English, with a native speaker as "informant" (as they are called in anthropology), and was later translated into Spanish. Puig has explained that he sat with this man three times a week, for two hours in paid sessions, asked him questions (or put him "in staged situations"—as Ramírez does with Larry—in the fictional version of it), and typed the answers that became the dialogues in the novel. In my interview ("Brief Encounter"), Puig clarifies, "I wrote some two hundred pages of notes in English. As you know, until then Spanish had been my psychological and linguistic vehicle, a language of which I have all the keys; now I have all the information in a language of which I don't have the keys" (175–76).[6] An interesting phenomenon starts to take place with this novel, one of self-translation and trans-lingualism, which will continue in the next two "Brazilian" novels.

Sangre de amor correspondido (*Blood of Requited Love*, 1982) follows the same procedure of the previous novel in the sense that Puig wrote it with an *informant*—in this case a bricklayer who came to his apartment to do some repair work. Puig, fascinated by his use of the Portuguese language and his way of telling stories, sat with him (as with the fictional Larry—and before that with Pozzi's informant) three times a week in paid sessions which he now was allowed to tape. The result of re-writing those notes are two novels, one in Spanish and the other in Portuguese, that appeared at the same time. The already mentioned progressive reduction in the number of characters ending in two in the three previous novels, turns here into only one, Josemar, in whose head multiple voices tell the same story over and over again, with multiple versions, contradictions, and repetitions. The presence of contradictory versions of the same situation recurrently repeated and modified recalls, according to Rodríguez Monegal ("*Sangre de amor correspondido*"), Akira Kurosawa's 1950 film *Rashomon*. In this case, for the character's interior monologues, traditionally in first person, Puig uses a third person through which the character projects an idealized version of himself while fighting with other voices that intend to make him face the reality of his own situation. Josemar is a small-town Brazilian soccer player and a sort of re-edition of Juan Carlos (*Heartbreak Tango*)—or Héctor (Toto's cousin in *Betrayed by Rita Hayworth*)—at least in his fantasies, which are nurtured, mostly, in revenge and resentment. His most frequent antagonist is Maria da Gloria whom, it seems, he brutally deflowered when she was fifteen years old. She was then abandoned by him and lost her mind. In this narrative Josemar is, at the same time, *metteur en scene*, actor and author of a recurrent obsession, the deflowering of Maria da Gloria, an act inspired less by love than as a vindication for his economic and socio-cultural inferiority. Social class and ethnic differences, together with economic deprivation, could be thus compensated by sexual possession inside of a community in which virginity still has a priority value in relationship to women. But, as we continue reading, we start wondering whether the deflowering really took place or is the protagonist's fantasy, an illusion created to palliate the harshness of his own life. In a story told over and over again, contradicted by the chaos of voices in Josemar's head (the feminine voices of the mother, his lovers and the "mother of his sons," his black half-brother, his real father, and the adoptive one) we progressively become aware of his mental illness.

Cae la noche tropical (*Tropical Night Falling*, 1988) is Puig's last novel. It takes place again in Brazil, more exactly in Rio de Janeiro, and is centered around three Argentinian women: two are old women, the sisters Nidia and Luci, and the third one is Silvia, a younger psychologist who lives in the same apartment building. The novel is divided into two parts, with six chapters each. The first seven chapters consist mainly of dialogues between the two sisters who are mostly confined in their apartment, occasionally walking to the beach. During those dialogues they remember their past and their losses (both have lost their husbands and Nidia, also her daughter), as well as the good times together. As is usual in Puig, they watch old movies on which they project their own fantasies and ghosts. Most of the films they watch, or remember, have to do with suffering women (Vivian Leigh, Barbara Stanwick), and there are also references to romantic narrative (Bronte sisters) and poetry, but their recurrent and almost obsessive topic of conversation is Silvia's life, especially her love life. Nidia, like Molina did with Valentin, narrates Silvia's life to her sister in a way that could be totally fantasized, based upon her own life and personality, prejudices, and needs. In chapter four, Puig goes back to his technique of bricolage by introducing a newspaper dominical supplement that Luci reads before going to bed. In a fragmentary way (that mimes Luci's half awaken attention and reading), we read about an old colonial palace in ruins invaded by homeless people; notions like *performance, post-modern, clean* and *dark* together with Marshall Berman's *All That is Solid Melts into the Air* ("a book that deserves more than any other to be the *must* of the summer" 53) ("el *must* del Verano" 59); an enumeration of rock groups as part of Brazilian popular music; a laudatory article on the Italian writer and Puig's friend Leonardo Sciascia (*Tropical Night Falling* 54–56; *Cae la noche tropical* 60–62); bikinis; and the description of the Bay of 365 islands (that will reappear in Nidia's narration of her own trip there with Silvia, and also in Silvia's trip with her lover). Chapter seven opens with a letter from Silvia to Luci, before attempting suicide, in which she tries to understand her sentimental failures by debating (like Ana in her diary) between being a traditional woman and a modern one. The following chapters include several letters from Nidia to Luci (who dies soon after her arrival to Switzerland to see her son) in which she recounts her relationship with Ronaldo (a doorman in Silvia's building) and his wife Wilma, whom she plans to help financially. This immersion of Nidia in a subculture of poverty and marginalization, with which she is completely unfamiliar, will later complicate her life both emotionally and legally. She also continues her relationship with Silvia, in a less intense way than Luci. Other textual materials are letter exchanges between the different characters, and official documents as police reports of Ronaldo's rape of a minor. Many subplots are intertwined here dealing with exile—voluntary in the case of the two sisters versus Silvia obliged to flee Argentina during the military rule. The topics of migration and marginalization -based upon social deprivation and political turmoil (that started with *Pubis*) are explored here again, with the addition of the marginalization of elderly people. In Puig's words, "[The novel] takes place in contemporary Rio and everything is seen through old people's eyes: Argentinian old women living here. And he adds, 'The old people can see the problems of the young. They discuss them all the time . . . comparing different epochs . . . and trying to play a part in the story' " (Bacarisse 218).

Puig did not tire of repeating that the "modern novel begins with Freud," and, as we have already seen, throughout his writing he deals extensively with both the collective unconscious and his own and non-transferable unconscious. Psychoanalysis, for Puig, was a tool not only to create his characters and their interaction but also for self-analysis. In my interview he says ("Brief Encounter"), "I write novels because there is something I don't understand. What I do is locate that special problem in a character and then try to understand it. That's the genesis of all my work." And he explains, "Because of my unconscious defenses, I am incapable of facing the problem directly. There are obstacles that prevent me from doing so. Yet I can do it through a literary character. It's easier! And since all my problems are rather complicated, I need an entire novel to deal with them." And he concludes, "It's like a personal therapy" (171).[7] In addition to the use of psychoanalysis to create characters and as a personal therapy, Puig adopts the "talking cure" as a way of structuring his novels. The reduction from a great number of characters, in his two first novels, to only two (or even one in the case of Josemar), constitutes a manner of reproducing the dyad analyst/analysand engaged in dialogues, inner monologues, and even shared silence.

Faithful to this practice, in his novels Puig uses different psychoanalytic lenses. *In Betrayed by Rita Hayworth* Toto's situation is presented as a classic oedipal one: the son attached to his mother with whom he shares movies, sensitivity, and intellectual curiosity in opposition to an authoritarian father seen as violent and threatening. This basic triangle, with its power struggles and well-defined roles (*macho* husband vs submissive wife), is presented from the point of view of the son (Puig's *mythe personnel*) and is reproduced in all socio-cultural and economic levels. Toto (Puig's alter ego) liberates himself by escaping to the movies and later on by becoming a writer. In *Heartbreak Tango* the power games continue across the different social classes, masked under the sentimentalism of tango lyrics. "The ideology of the great passion, according to Puig, with its vehicle of "lo cursi" or "kitsch" playing the double function of expressing emotions, and escaping mediocrity and pain. In turn, the collective myths, forged by films, song lyrics, detective fiction, soap operas, and romantic writing, provide identity to the characters, and constitute a possibility for personal improvement (more beautiful, richer, more educated and successful, etc.). Regarding this, in my interview Puig states, "I always talk about my preoccupations with the contents of the collective unconscious . . . And if I can locate those contents and write about them, I will be able to capture the reader's attention because we will share the same commonalities" ("Brief Encounter" 169).[8]

In *The Buenos Aires Affair* Puig adopts the Freudian technique of writing "case histories" (that, in Freud's were read as "short stories") in order to describe Gladys and Leo. In both cases, sexuality and politics are entangled together, as well as art. Masturbation, in both characters, or violent sexual acts are common practices accompanied by sublimation through artistic creativity on the part of Gladys, and through artistic contemplation in Leo as an art critic. They also operate as doubles that oppose, and complement, each other. The aforementioned interview with Gladys (where Puig states his own ars poetica) is complemented by one of Leo's analytic sessions in which many of the usual psychoanalytic techniques are introduced: free association, identification with the analyst, transference, and dreams. In this "text inside the text" (another example of *mise en abyme*), Leo is able to express his psychic fears and fantasies: his guilt feeling of *having killed* his mother (who died after his birth), his recurrent sexual problems, and his ambivalent political, aesthetic, and ethical choices. For example, Leo's debate and final decision to choose María Esther, instead of Gladys, to represent the country in the San Pablo exhibit. Leo and Gladys represent not only the complementary roles of critic and creator but also the two opposite and complementary psychic attitudes of sadism/masochism. What is more, Gladys/María Esther would conform to another pair of opposites in the area of creation. Gladys, with her taste for bricolage and castoff material is Puig's alter ego whereas María Esther represents the conservative artist with her reactionary views about divorce and abortion and with a rationally structured art plan. In the end, Puig applies some kind of "poetic justice" by killing Leo in a car accident, and "rescuing" Gladys through a fortunate encounter with a neighbor, a young married wife and mother who invites her in and saves Gladys from jumping off the balcony. The detective novel, as before the folletín, has been once again perverted (à la Hitchcock) and utilized as a frame for a psychoanalytic study of two very sick characters, in a sadomasochist relationship entangled with the sublimation of art. It also brings a hidden autobiographical reference of an author (Puig identified with Gladys) injured by a conventional critic as another form of a sado-masochist relationship. But back to the detective novel, as the literary critic Peter Brooks has reminded us,

Freud "was a student of Sherlock Holmes who perceived the close analogies between psychoanalysis and detective work" (48). Puig, then, only had to follow that path in this novel.

In *Kiss of the Spider Woman* Puig comes back to Hollywood B movies of the 1940s, retold by Molina to Valentín and through which we learn about their identities, feelings, political views, and values. In an interview in *The Paris Review*, Puig refers to those movies as "dreams, totally stylized—the perfect stuff of films because dreams allow you the possibility of a synthetic approach" (260). And he adds, "I learned certain rules of storytelling from [them]. But what interests me more about those films is examining the effect they had on people" (261). Molina, as a spider woman weaving her web (like Scheherazade's storytelling), entertains and seduces Valentin. And the movies, as the dreams in Freud's theory, are the vehicle and projection of the wishes and fears of the two protagonists who, along with their verbal exchanges (similar to the psychoanalytic dyad), are able not only to express and explore them but also to experience a process of mutual transformation. As was already stated, Valentín becomes aware of his feminine side, and Molina starts to respect himself as a human being, free of stereotypes and clichés. In the footnotes (another of the many traces of Borges in Puig), the reader gets access to a vast information about homosexuality from a psychoanalytic point of view. It is important to mention that in the last quotation, attributed to a fictional Danish Doctor Anneli Taube, we can detect once again Borges's influence.

In *Pubis angelical* psychoanalysis returns through what Freud called "the royal road to unconscious," that is, dreams. In this case Puig combines them with two low-culture popular genres, fantastic literature in the first part and science fiction in the second. He also uses other psychoanalytic lenses: Otto Rank's double, Freud's the uncanny, and Jacques Lacan's *stade du miroir* (mirror stage) and "archive."[9] Lacan is also introduced as a topic of discussion between Ana and Pozzi and, as so often in Puig, this is also a clue given to the reader for the analysis of the text. As already seen, Ana, the protagonist, splits in her nocturnal dreams (there are also daydreams) into both an actress from the thirties who can easily be identified with Hedy Lamar and an entity called W218 in the Ice Age. The presence of a multiplicity of doubles (whether oneiric, phantasmagoric, filmic, or speculative) reveals once again the fantasies and terrors of the protagonist since this novel, like all those by Puig, is structured on the idea of exposing a conflict and the process leading to its resolution. By expressing her fears and fantasies through her oneiric doubles and her daily exchanges with Pozzi (and Beatriz), Ana tries to liberate herself from the repressions imposed by social patterns and slowly starts to change.

Eternal Curse to the Reader of These Pages is again structured around the interaction between two characters (like Gladys/Leo, Molina/Valentín and Ana/Pozzi) but, this time, with big differences in age (Ramírez is seventy-four, and Larry is thirty-six), language (Spanish vs English), national origin (Argentina vs United States), and culture. During their dialogues, and nocturnal hallucinations on the part of Ramírez, there are various versions of the Oedipal triangle (old man/young man/woman), adopting the roles of father/son or unlawful authority figure and submissive subject. An instance of this is Ramírez's last hallucination (in the penultimate chapter of the novel) about Larry asking for his help while exposed to the stare of a man who watches him. This man stirs up all the violence, unpredictability, and destructiveness of the father figure (Larry's father and Ramírez as his actual substitute) but also all of Puig's father figures from Berto on. At the same time, these figures represent, in a broader sense, authority: God, the Argentine military, the boss in the factory, and capitalism. Regarding the recurring use of the Freudian uncanny, Puig's entire oeuvre is an obsessive search for the forgotten, a patient weaving of "the return of the repressed." Or, what I called his mythe personnel, constituted by the repetition of Puig's personal obsessions under recurrent versions of the same. In addition, the theme of exile, which started with Ana in Mexico, returns here together with references to Argentina's politics under military rule.

Blood of Requited Love reduces the preceding so-called analytic dyads to the monologue, in third person, of only one character, Josemar, who is constantly arguing with several voices (corresponding to Maria da Gloria, other lovers, his sons' mother, his own mother, his father and step father, his half black brother) about the truth, or not, of memories concerning mainly and obsessively to his defloration of Maria da Gloria, but also about his job, his financial situation, and socio-cultural and ethnic status. In my interview ("Brief Encounter"), Puig explains that he used the third person for Josemar talking about himself because, in his own words, "he is unable to assume himself as a character, he is unable to accept himself as he is, always attempting to live in a constant fantasy."[10] Josemar rejects his real self and projects himself like an ideal one, the super macho, the football star, while denying the other voices in the first person that keep asking questions, confronting, and accusing him. Those voices represent the reality principle colliding with the fantasy self that he is working so hard to present and preserve. Moreover, these dialogic voices in the protagonist's head could suggest that he may suffer from a sort of multiple-personality syndrome bordering on psychosis. His discourse turns around sexual/imagined practices, the antagonism between men and women, and the obligation to be a *macho* when, in reality, Josemar is an underdeveloped being in terrible need of his mother and in constant conflict because of the loss of a father. More than ever before, Puig constructs the text with free associations, metaphors, and symbols. The sequence of the associations usually represents reactions to Josemar's fears: the recurrent reference to his extreme virility, for example, is nothing but his fear of his own aggressive manliness while aroused by the color red associated with blood, with snakes, with birds locked inside.

In his last novel, *Tropical Night Falling*, Puig chooses again to build his narration around two characters: two older sisters from Argentina living in a kind of chosen exile in Brazil, plus another Argentinean, Silvia, a younger psychologist neighbor to whom the reader has access mainly through the vicarious narrative of the two others. For the first time in Puig's work, we deal not with patients in analysis (Leo) or with people discussing psychoanalysis (Valentín, Ana and Pozzi, Larry), or with Puig providing the reader psychoanalytic information (notes to *Kiss of the Spider Woman*), but rather with a psychologist/psychoanalyst (the distinction is not very clear according to Luci's information) as a character. It is an innovation and a puzzle because apparently Silvia is not able to deal with her sentimental life better than the other characters.

In the aforementioned interview with Pamela Bacarisse, Puig clarifies: "The novel is mainly about the need for affective projections," and he adds "it's mainly about the human need to be attached" (218). These are very precise words that have to do with psychoanalytic theories, in particular with developmental and relational ones that run from Freud and Winnicott on. If, as John Bowlby asserts, "the attachment experience is from the cradle to the grave" (218), in retrospection we can trace Toto's close attachment to his mother Mita, transposed all along Puig's work up to this novel in which his mother is fictionalized as Luci. Other forms of attachments are those of Nidia and her dead daughter, which she will later replace with the Brazilian young people (mainly Wilma); Silvia's attachment to Luci and, at the end, her recovered relationship with her own son. If we talk about attachments, we are also talking about separation, losses, and mourning together with memory, forgetfulness, and melancholy. The three Argentine women have a lot to mourn-loss of country, of language, separation from loved ones and their death. The cases of the migrant and deprived Brazilian youngsters, and of the widow with whom Silvia gets involved, are similar. The disruption of human attachment is indirectly presented in the reference to a visit of the sisters to the Brontë museum, and in the mention of *Wuthering Heights*, where an orphan, Heathcliff, falls in love with the daughter of the landowner who adopts him. Although she marries someone else and dies in childbirth, he is obsessed by her memory until his death, twenty years later. In spite of all this darkness, *Tropical Night Falling* is one of the most optimistic of Puig's novels and love, with its multiple variations, is a recurrent topic in it. Mainly, maternal love in the strict sense of mother/son and mother/daughter but is also an important component in the peculiar love relationship of Silvia in which there is a combination of lust, helplessness and manipulation, surrender and resistance. Silvia, as other women in Puig's fiction (Mita, Gladys, Ana), is also a woman looking for her own identity, her sexuality, and her maternal role. Fortunately, she seems satisfied with her profession. In addition, it is important to note that in Puig's novels many male characters die: the seducer Juan Carlos and his low-class double Pancho, the sadistic art critic Leo, the idealists Molina and Pozzi, the political activist Ramírez. Women, instead, survive: starting with Mita, continuing with Gladys, Ana, Silvia and Nidia, most of them mothers who have the ability of giving "unconditional love" as a final and probably only redemption. In my book *Manuel Puig: Mito personal, Historia y Ficción* (Manuel Puig: Personal Myth, History, and Fiction, 2009), I compare him with Spanish filmmaker Pedro Almodóvar in a chapter titled "Ambos amamos tanto a las mujeres que quisiéramos ser una de ellas: Manuel Puig/Pedro Almodóvar" ("We both love women so much that we would like to be one of them"). Manuel loved his mother in particular and women in general and his work is, among many other things, a beautiful homage to women and the feminine.

A final note regarding Puig's literary models. In my interview he confesses ("Brief Encounter"), "I don't have traceable literary models because I haven't had great literary influences in my life. Instead, that space has been occupied by cinematographic influences" (167). As an example, he mentions Ernst Lubitsch, Josef von Sternberg (specially *Dishonored*), Hitchcock (there is a long reference to his potential use of a scene of *Psycho* in *The Buenos Aires Affair*), and also Roman Polanski (*Chinatown*). Through

Puig's letters, though, we become aware of his vast literary knowledge and his acquaint-ance with Borges's work with whom, according to Suzanne Jill Levine, he had studied in Buenos Aires (80). We can then argue that his alluded literary ignorance was more a glamorous posture than a real fact. Puig knew the writing of his contemporaries very well, the same as Borges from whom he copied many of his literary strategies (use of parody and footnotes, intertextuality, humor, and genre transgressions) as well as their shared fondness for "los géneros menores" (minor genres), the detective novel and serials, the fantastic, science-fiction, and Hollywood movies and directors. Therefore, the real lineage is Borges/Puig, and not Puig/Cortázar/Arlt as some critics have tried to establish.[11] No space to debate this here. Only a final digression in order to recon-cile Puig's declaration of literary ignorance as well as succinctly explain his position re-garding fiction and his way to approach reality. In my interview ("Brief Encounter"), Puig only mentioned two writers, William Faulkner and Franz Kafka. "I like the beauty of Faulkner's poetry" (167) and, regarding Kafka, he said: "I think he truly illustrates the way the environment oppresses the individual. Also, he shows how the uncon-scious control our lives. And he talks about the internal prisons we carry inside" (168).[12] These prisons that he, for sure, carried inside gave us one of the most lucid and human narratives of the twentieth century.

Notes

1. "Esa gente que había creído en los cánones de una época, que habían aceptado las reglas del juego y les había ido, por lo general, muy mal" (74).
2. In the original text in Spanish we read: "*Boquitas pintadas* es la trasgresión paródica, el doble irrisorio del folletín" ("Encuentros con Manuel Puig" 557).
3. This is Ilan Stavan's translation in his abbreviated rendition of my original interview in Spanish. There we read: "Una línea de investigación en el error argentino. . . . Error politico, error sexual" ("Encuentros con Manuel Puig" 594).
4. "En mi corta experiencia de narrador he comprobado que saber cómo habla un personaje es saber quién es" (11).
5. "Este sueño es corto pero es feliz" (287).
6. "Tomé como doscientas páginas de notas en inglés . . . Antes, el lenguaje era vehículo de psicología y de caracteres, un lenguaje del que tengo todas las claves; ahora tengo todos los datos en un idioma del que no tengo las claves" ("Encuentros con Manuel Puig" 620).
7. "Escribo novelas porque hay algo que no comprendo, un problema muy especial y entonces se lo achaco a un personaje, a un tercero y, de ese modo, a través de ese personaje trato de aclararlo. La genesis de tod a mi obra ha sido ésta: no me atrevo a enfrentar el problema directamente porque sé que hay defensas inconscientes, hay frenos que no me dejan llegar a ciertos enfrentamientos dolorosos. En cambio, a través de un personaje es mucho más fácil, todo se puede ver con mayor facilidad, y como todos mi problemas son bastante complicados, siempre se me ha hecho necesaria toda una novela para desarrollar un problema . . . Entonces, la elección de la novela no es deliberada, sino que es una forma que se presta al desarrollo de una actividad mía, casi de terapia personal" (("Encuentros con Manuel Puig" 605).

8. "Yo siempre hablo de mi preocupación por los contenidos del inconsciente colectivo . . . y en la medida en que dé con estos contenidos voy a poder interesar al lector, porque van a ser elementos comunes a los dos" ("Encuentros con Manuel Puig" 600).

9. In the already mentioned interview with Christ, Puig says: "I find the new French school of psychoanalysis very interesting. Very hard to follow, but interesting. Lacan and his disciples" (577). In a special way, the notion of 'mirroring,' "I have the impression that there's definitely something there" (577). ("Encuentros con Manuel Puig")

10. "Él no se asume como personaje . . ., no se acepta como es y trata de vivir una fantasía constante" (274).

11. See Corbatta, Jorgelina, "Puig y sus precursores o hacia un nuevo canon (Borges/Puig)."

12. "Bueno, creo que él [Kakfa] es el que mejor ilustra toda esa cuestión que a mí me interesa tanto: la opresión del medio ambiente sobre el individuo, la cuestion inconsciente, el mundo de cárceles internas que llevamos sin saberlo. Esa red que tenemos cada uno de represiones construida adentro. Pero a mí me interesa referirlo todo siempre directamente a la realidad. Kafka se deja llevar por la fantasia; a mí me interesa localizarlo de algún modo" ("Encuentros con Manuel Puig" 596–97).

WORKS CITED

Bacarisse, Pamela. "An Interview with Manuel Puig." *Carnal Knowledge: Essays on the Flesh, Sex and Sexuality in Hispanic Letters and Film*. Edited by Pamela Bacarisse, U of Pittsburgh, 1991, pp. 217–23.

Bowlby, John. *Attachment and Loss*, vol. 1: *Attachment*. Basic Books, 1969/1982.

Borges, Jorge Luis. *El "Martín Fierro."* Columba, 1960.

Brooks, Peter. *Psychoanalysis and Storytelling*. Blackwell, 1994.

Christ, Ronald. "A Last Interview with Manuel Puig." *World Literature Today*, vol. 65, no. 4, Autumn 1991, pp. 571–78.

Corbatta, Jorgelina. "Brief Encounter: An Interview with Manuel Puig." Translated and adapted by Ilan Stavans. *William H. Gass. Manuel Puig Number*, edited by Arthur M. Saltzman (Gass) and Ilan Stavans (Puig). *The Review of Contemporary Fiction*, vol. 11, no. 3, fall 1991, pp. 165–176.

Corbatta, Jorgelina. "Encuentros con Manuel Puig." *Revista Iberoamericana* nos. 123–24 (April-Sept. 1983). pp. 591–620.

Corbatta, Jorgelina. *Manuel Puig: Mito personal, historia y ficción*. Corregidor, 2009.

Corbatta, Jorgelina. "Puig y sus precursors o hacia un nuevo canon (Borges/Puig)." *Revista Iberoamericana*, no. 241, 2012, 965–82.

Dällenbach, Lucien. *Le récit spéculaire. Essai sur la mise en abyme*. Editions Du Seuil, 1977.

Eco, Umberto. *Apocalypse Postponed*. Indiana U.P., 1994.

Eco, Umberto. *The Open Work*. Harvard UP, 1989.

Freud, Sigmund. *The Standard Edition of the Complete Psychological Works of Sigmund Freud*. Edited by James Strachey in collaboration with Anna Freud. The Hogarth Press, 1968.

Lacan, Jacques. *Ecrits. A Selection*. Norton, 1977.

Levine, Suzanne Jill. *Manuel Puig and the Spider Woman. His Life and Fictions*. Farrar, Straus Giorux, 2000.

Levi-Strauss, *The Savage Mind*. U of Chicago P, 1966.

Mauron, Charles. *Des métaphores obsédantes au mythe personnel. Introduction a la psychocritique.* José Corti, 1966.

Puig, Manuel. *El beso de la mujer araña.* Seix Barral, 1976.

Puig, Manuel. *Betrayed by Rita Hayworth.* Translated by Suzanne Jill Levine. E.P. Dutton, 1971.

Puig, Manuel. *Blood of Requited Love.* Translated by Jan L. Grayson. U of Minessota P, 1999.

Puig, Manuel. *Boquitas pintadas. Folletín.* Sudamericana, 1969.

Puig, Manuel. *The Buenos Aires Affair. Novela Policial.* Sudamericana. 1973.

Puig, Manuel. *The Buenos Aires Affair: A Detective Novel.* Translated by Suzanne Jill Levine. E.P. Dutton, 1976.

Puig, Manuel. *Cae la noche tropical.* Seix Barral, 1988.

Puig, Manuel. *Eternal Curse to the Reader of These Pages.* Random House, 1982.

Puig, Manuel. *Heartbreak Tango: A Serial.* Translated by Suzanne Jill Levine. E.P.Dutton, 1987.

Puig, Manuel. *Kiss of the Spider Woman.* Translated by Thomas Colchie. Vintage, 1991.

Puig, Manuel. *Maldición eterna a quien lea estas páginas.* Seix Barral, 1980.

Puig, Manuel. *Pubis angelical.* Seix Barral, l979.

Puig, Manuel. *Pubis Angelical.* Translated by Elena Brunet. U of Minnesota P, 2000.

Puig, Manuel. *Sangre de amor correspondido.* Seix Barral, 1982.

Puig, Manuel. *La traición de Rita Hayworth.* Jorge Álvarez, 1968.

Puig, Manuel. *Tropical Night Falling.* Translated by Suzanne Jill Levine. Simon & Schuster, 1988.

Rank, Otto. *The Double. A Psychoanalytic Study.* University of North Carolina Press, 1971.

Rodriguez Monegal, Emir. "*La traición de Rita Hayworth.* Una tarea de desmitificación." *Narradores de esta América* II, AlfaArgentina, 1974, pp. 365–80.

Rodriguez Monegal, Emir. "*Sangre de amor correspondido.* " *Vuelta,* no. 72, November 1982, pp. 34–35.

Sarduy, Severo. "Note to the Notes to the Notes. . . A Propos of Manuel Puig." *World Literature Today,* vol. 65, no. 4, autumn 1991, pp. 625–30.

Sontag, Susan. *Against Interpretation and Other Essays.* MacMillan, 1966.

Sosnowski, Saul. "Entrevista con Manuel Puig." *Hispamérica,* vol. 1, no. 3, 1973, pp. 70–80.

Vargas Llosa, Mario. "Saved by Rita Hayworth." *The New York Times,* August 13, 2000. https://archive.nytimes.com/www.nytimes.com/books/00/08/13/reviews/000813.13vargast.html

Wheaton, Kathleen. "Manuel Puig." *Latin American Writers at Work. The Paris Review,* edited by George Plimpton, The Modern Library, 2003, pp. 256–73.

PART VII

RECEPTION

CHAPTER 43

....

THE LATIN AMERICAN NOVEL
IN ENGLISH AND FRENCH

....

ROBERTO IGNACIO DÍAZ

SINCE the mid-nineteenth century, authors biographically related to Latin America have often written novels in languages regarded as foreign to the region, most prominently English and French. The choice of these other tongues over Spanish and Portuguese, or the Amerindian languages, is typically linked with various forms of migration. A person born in Latin America who settles in another part of the world may easily adopt the tongue spoken and written in that new location. Likewise, a descendant of English- or French-speaking migrants to the region may opt to write in her ancestors' language and, not infrequently, may also reside in a place where it is spoken. Whether any novel written in any language by any author with ties to the region may in fact be read as a Latin American work remains an open question; this is, after all, a heterogeneous, shapeshifting corpus. But, as this chapter seeks to show, this critical endeavor to find and highlight textual bonds is not a matter of taxonomy or literary history alone, but an attempt at reading new meanings concealed by the *idées reçues* of linguistic determinism, or the belief that one shared tongue ought to be the touchstone of national literatures. When some English- and French-language novels are read alongside, or within, the traditional corpus of Latin American fiction, important meanings may surface that would otherwise remain concealed. While these affinities may complicate the well-guarded limits of the region's national literatures, often predicated upon the purported virtues of monolingual expression, opening up the concept of the Latin American novel to include these other texts highlights the long reach of the region's literary systems and the complexity of its cultural history. Idiosyncratically, some of these works with dual literary-historical legacies and loyalties are privileged spaces for analyzing the hybrid nature of much writing in Latin America, or the contacts between the region and other parts of the world. Further, some of these novels are distinctively crafted works that bespeak a sense of the extraterritorial, as George Steiner would have it,[1] or explicitly or implicitly mediate between cultures and literary traditions.

The body of Francophone novels by Latin American authors, or authors who may be regarded as such, includes works written as early as the Romantic period. A germinal figure is María de las Mercedes Santa Cruz y Montalvo (1789–1852), better known as the Comtesse Merlin or Condesa de Merlín; born in Havana, she was a longtime resident of Paris and wrote exclusively in French. But she is hardly alone. Ramón Emeterio Betances (1827–1898), born in Cabo Rojo, Puerto Rico, and Eduarda Mansilla de García (1834–1892), a native of Buenos Aires, also lived in France and wrote fiction in French. Jules Supervielle (1884–1960), one of the three illustrious Francophone poets of French descent born in Montevideo (Isidore Ducasse and Jules Laforgue are the other two), wrote three novels in that language. From the mid-twentieth century to the present, the ranks of Latin Americans writing novels, often autofiction, in French include Eduardo Manet (1930), born in Cuba, plus Silvia Baron Supervielle (1934), Copi (born René Damonte Botana, 1939–1987), Santiago Amigorena (1962), and Laura Alcoba (1968), all natives of Argentina. Most prominent among these authors is Héctor Bianciotti (1930–2012), also an Argentine by birth, and—along with José-Maria de Heredia, the Parnassian poet born near Santiago de Cuba—the only member of the Académie française to have come from Latin America until the election of Mario Vargas Llosa in 2021. Like a few of the aforementioned writers, Bianciotti was a translingual author who switched from Spanish to French in mid-career, or wrote in both languages. While these novelists are not as well-known as the Latin American poets who wrote at least partly in French, such as Chile's Vicente Huidobro and Peru's César Moro, they make up what might cautiously be read as a Latin American chapter of the global Francophone tradition.

The English-language corpus of Latin American novels is even richer. An emblematic author is W. H. Hudson (1841–1922), the son of immigrants from Massachusetts in Argentina, where he is known as Guillermo Enrique Hudson; a migrant himself, he spent almost fifty years in Britain. But the bulk of English-speaking novels relatable to Latin America has been written in the United States. Much of this body, as one might expect, is connected with journeys of migration to the north. The earliest such author is María Amparo Ruiz de Burton (1832–1895). Born in Baja California, she is credited for being the first Mexican-American author to write novels in English and, therefore, an unwitting founder of Latino literature. Given that the study of Latino authors is solidly anchored in the established discussion about cultural production in the United States, the critical gesture of bringing their novels into other critical configurations may appear at first as a kind of abduction, yet the fact remains that many of these works resound, at least partly and often powerfully, with some of the salient themes and forms of Latin American literature. Novelists such as John Rechy (1931), Rudolfo Anaya (1937–2020), Julia Alvarez (1950), Oscar Hijuelos (1951–2013), Judith Ortiz Cofer (1952-2016), Sandra Cisneros (1954), Cristina Garcia (1958), and Junot Díaz (1968), while firmly situated in US American literary culture, often create characters and craft plotlines that concern Latin America—both its nations and its diasporas. A closely related group is that of translingual novelists living in the United States who, like Bianciotti with Spanish and French, adopted English only after writing and publishing in their native Spanish in their home countries. These authors include María Luisa Bombal (1910–1980) and Ariel

Dorfman (1942), from Chile; Rosario Ferré (1938–2016) and Giannina Braschi (1953), from Puerto Rico; and Valeria Luiselli (1983), from Mexico. Yet another group of authors writing in English is even more assertively cosmopolitan: Elena Castedo (1937), born in Spain and a resident of Chile before settling in the United States, wrote in English and translated her own work into Spanish; and Chloe Aridjis (1971), born in New York City to an American mother and a Mexican father and a resident of Mexico and the Netherlands, writes exclusively in English.

But what are these novels like? What kind of argument can be crafted so that at least some of these authors' texts can be productively read as Latin American novels? And if they can, what might be gained or lost? An initial approach to these questions may be to focus on themes and plots as well as on readers—real-world persons or textual constructs—to view how these novels acquire new meanings when read in the context of Latin American literature or its various national configurations. Consider, for instance, the Comtesse Merlin, whom Gastón Baquero dismissed as a "cubana escritora" (a Cuban who writes) who did not rise to the level of an "escritora cubana" (8; a Cuban author). Based at least partly on Merlin's French, Baquero's exclusionary stance is now dismissed as overly rigid. As critics have shown, Merlin's works—especially *Mes douze premières années* (My First Twelve Years, 1831), her childhood memories of Cuba, and *La Havane* (Havana, 1844), a richly textured travel narrative—can in fact be read appropriately as richly Cuban and Latin American works. An early narrative, *Histoire de la sœur Inès* (The Story of Sister Ines, 1832) is a Romantic tale of patriarchal authority and doomed love set in slaveholding Havana and surroundings – arguably the earliest novel by a Cuban author. Merlin's other fictional works, though, are more challenging to connect with either the author's birthplace or Cuban literature. *Les Lionnes de Paris* (The Lionesses of Paris, 1842), for one, contains references to slavery and abolition that may resound obliquely with political discussions in Cuba, but the plot concerns the fashionable world of the French capital with French readers exclusively in mind. Elsewhere in the Caribbean, Ramón E. Betances's *Les deux Indiens* (The Two Indians, 1857) is set in Puerto Rico at the time of the Spanish conquest and has been critically analyzed as part of the author's project to create an Antillean federation. While Merlin's and Betances's French-language texts may appear as eccentric vis-à-vis the larger bodies of Cuban and Puerto Rican literatures, their Francophone nature is less remarkable if read within the multilingual bodies of Caribbean literary systems, which include not only French and English, but other languages as well.

The best-known nineteenth-century novel by a Latin American author written in French is surely Eduarda Mansilla de García's *Pablo ou la vie dans les pampas* (Pablo or Life in the Pampas, 1869), the story of a young gaucho who, like José Hernández's *Martín Fierro*, is conscripted against his will into the Argentine army. In several ways, Mansilla de García's novel exemplifies some of the traits that can be found in a good number of Latin American-affiliated fictional works written in French or English since then. For one, its first edition opens with a letter addressed to the author by Édouard Laboulaye, the French jurist, whose words denote an archetypal foreign reader enthusiastically seeking the thrills of literary exoticism:

Your *Pablo* has given me one of the most vivid pleasures a book can offer. It has made me live in a country that I have never seen and probably never will. It has made me understand feelings and passions that lack the same ardor or form in our cold climate. . . . In it you see the Pampa, its inexorable serenity during the day, its animation at night. One becomes interested in Pablo, in his beloved, in his mother. One lives with the *gaucho malo*, one is removed from ordinary life, from the boredom of daily life. (1–2)[2]

As if to assert her authority on local matters, Mansilla de García's narrator speaks as part of a group labelled as "us Argentines," which occasionally explicitly invokes a "European reader"[3] for whom the novel appears to be written. The narrator knowledgeably underscores, for instance, the vastness of the country in which the story is set, a place where one estancia can be three times as large as a German principality. Likewise, the text contains numerous italicized Spanish words that refer to Argentina's cultural and material specificity even as they capture its foreignness: *yerba*, defined in a footnote as "a kind of indigenous tea" (57); *ombu* [sic], "a tree of the pampas" (61); or *fortin* [sic], "a detachment of troops protecting the frontiers" (94).[4] Not unexpectedly, the human body emerges as a visible site of the exotic. Characters and fashions are outlandishly magnetic; guitar-playing Pablo wears a *chiripá*, and Dolores, the sixteen-year old mestiza whom he loves, has thick black tresses that almost reach to the ground. A group of soldiers, too, is distinctly non-European, for it includes Blacks and mixed-race men, which the narrator underscores as a sign of difference from European armies. As in much of Argentine literature of the nineteenth-century, Buenos Aires is alluded to as the site of European civilization, while the indigenous people, by contrast, are described, as an "infernal avalanche" (270)[5] bent on destruction, as the narrator's account of an attack on the town of Rojas seeks to demonstrate: "After choosing first to ransack the shops, the savages killed a good number of people, not counting the women whom they had abducted or murdered, after having satisfied their ferocious appetites in them" (270).[6]

Indeed, *Pablo* also spoke clearly to Argentine readers. In 1870, a year after its publication in Paris, the novel was serialized in Buenos Aires' *La Tribuna*, translated into Spanish by Lucio V. Mansilla, the author's brother. The periodical praised Mansilla de García for "her love of her Fatherland" and excused her foreign tongue: "Eduarda writes in French a purely Argentine novel" (Mansilla de García).[7] Indeed, despite its language, reading *Pablo* within the nation's literary corpus made sense. As Francine Masiello observes, the novel "was designed as a commentary on the modern Argentine nation," inserting itself into political debates on the conscription of gauchos, which, in Mansilla de García's plot, triggers a series of events that end tragically for the female characters. Ironically, even as Lucio V. Mansilla rendered his sister's words in Spanish, he actively undermined her authority on lexical and other matters: "The author describes 'chañar' as a small thorny tree. She is wrong; the 'chañar' is a corpulent tree, lasting for centuries" (qtd. by Masiello n.p.). *Pablo* nonetheless remains persuasive as a national work, and that it does so in perfect French signals, as Alejandra Laera notes, Mansilla de García's emergence as "cultural mediator between Argentina and Europe."[8]

Victor Hugo, for one, loved *Pablo*, as he confesses in a letter to the author, still living in Paris: "Madam, your book has captivated me. . . . You have shown me an undiscovered world" (qtd. in Alvarado-Larroucau 24).[9] But yet another author, the Argentine novelist Gabriela Cabezón Cámara, has words that capture the relevance of *Pablo* for discussions of history and culture in the nation, and of the magnetism of the text for any reader. Writing the introduction for a new Spanish-language edition of the novel by Penguin Clásicos, she views in Micaela's search for Pablo, her conscripted son, a prefiguration of the Madres de la Plaza de Mayo, and suggests a powerful connection between Dolores's tresses, which cannot be destroyed, and such issues as the tensions between class and ethnicity in Argentina. With an eye to hyperbolic depictions of violence, she deems the text's most interesting scene—"worthy of Quentin Tarantino, worthy of a twentieth-century comic book"[10] —to be when Rosa, a Black woman cuts off a native cacique's arm, then the other, to protect Dolores.

The River Plate region—specifically, Uruguay—is also the setting of W. H. Hudson's *The Purple Land* (1885). Like *Pablo*, Hudson's first fictional work highlights the peculiarities of the land for the foreign reader—a British audience that can feel at home in the author's Anglophone practices and might even sympathize with the text's original title: *The Purple Land that England Lost*. Jean Franco dismisses Hudson as "the English writer whose youth was spent in Argentina" (39). Indeed, the protagonist, Richard Lamb, is a European young man who sees the South American republic with fresh eyes. As the first-person narrator, he conveys exoticism, often, again, by means of an italicized lexicon or a focus on peculiar bodies clad in outlandish fashions. Describing a scene at a *pulpería*, defined as "store and public-house all in one" (21) for the sake of the British reader, Lamb relishes the sight of an old man who has "a dry skin, though his hair and mustache were black as jet [and] was dressed in shabby gaucho habiliments–cotton shirt, short jacket, wide cotton drawers and *chiripá*, a shawl-like garment fastened at the waist with a sash, and reaching down half-way between the knees and ankles" (22). The landscape too is remarkable. Early on, Lamb climbs Montevideo's Cerro and, like Columbus or Darwin, surveys the splendors of nature newly revealed to him: "Whichever way I turn, . . . I see before me one of the fairest habitations God has made for man: great plains smiling with everlasting spring; ancient woods; swift beautiful rivers; ranges of blue hills stretching away to the dim horizon" (12). Mesmerized by this Arcadian splendor against a predictable background of political instability, he invokes "a thousand young men of Devon and Somerset" and "British bayonets"—a military intervention that will rescue the land from political turmoil and deliver a happy ending: "And afterwards there would be peace, and the grass would be greener and the flowers brighter for that crimson shower" (13).

Yet, for all his exoticist proclivities and imperialist imaginings, Lamb is the textual creation of an Anglo-Argentine writer, an author known in his native country as Guillermo Enrique Hudson. The author may have taken permanent residence in England, but the novel, though written in English, bears the signs of River Plate literary practices. A naturalist who would soon go on to publish books with such titles as *Argentine Ornithology* (1888) and *Idle Days in Patagonia* (1893), Hudson displays his familiarity with gaucho storytelling and poetry in several passages of *The Purple Land*. At the pulpería, Lamb listens to and reports on the old man's disquisition on fate and free will with gusto: "so vivid and minute were his descriptions—sparkling with passion, satire, humor, pathos—and so dramatic his action, while wonderful story followed story, that I was fairly astonished, and pronounced the old *pulpería* orator a born genius" (22, italics in the original). Lamb's admirative stance signals the passage of gauchos from silent exotic figures to voices whose cultural productions animate the text. Most remarkable, as I have argued elsewhere, is Lamb's—or Hudson's—attempt to integrate Spanish-language poetical forms into the English prose; after listening to a gaucho sing a ballad, Lamb renders it English, regretting that his version cannot reproduce the musical notes—which, after all, literary texts cannot do—and that the words are "translated almost literally, therefore without rhymes" (28).[11] Despite these linguistic shortcomings, Jorge Luis Borges notes what he perceives as Lamb's process of acculturation.[12]

Hudson's complete works were published in London in the 1920s, and each volume bears an inscription marking his double habitation in two different parts of the world: "W. H. Hudson / Born on the South American Pampas / Natus Circa 1846–Obiit London 1922" (n.p.). To link the author's birth with nature would surely have pleased the naturalist, whose books repeatedly returned to the South American landmass. One of them is *Green Mansions: A Romance of the Tropical Forest* (1904), which Luis Leal described as a "jungle novel"—a precursor to José Eustasio Rivera's *La vorágine* (*The Vortex*, 1924) and Alejo Carpentier's *Los pasos perdidos* (*The Lost Steps*, 1953).

Published in 1885, the same year as *The Purple Land*, María Amparo Ruiz de Burton's *The Squatter and the Don* is broadly regarded as a groundbreaking work in what we now know as Mexican-American literature. As if Ruiz de Burton intuited the eventual rise of such a corpus, the novel does not spend much time looking back nostalgically on old Mexico, her birthplace, but instead projects itself dynamically into the future, a time in which citizens of Mexican descent—the "orphaned Spano-Americans" (103), as one character describes them—will be treated fairly. Set in the 1870s, more than two decades after the Treaty of Guadalupe-Hidalgo, Ruiz de Burton's novel is very much a tale of the law, or, more specifically, the new laws of the United States that allow newly arrived "squatters," such as the enterprising William Darrow and others, to settle in lands that belong to people who had been there since before the Mexican-American War. Among the latter is Don Mariano Alamar, who recalls "the good old times of yore" (123) even as he fights to firm up the legal claims to his land near San Diego. A passage early in the novel quotes the letter of the law—the Land Act of 1851: "No. 189. *An Act to ascertain and settle the private land claims in the State of California*, says the book" (88, italics in the original). But the narrator offers a sardonic interpretation of it: "An Act to *unsettle* land titles, and to upset the rights of the Spanish population of the State of California" (88, italics in the original). Written in idiomatic, dialogue-rich English prose, only occasionally does *The Squatter and the Don* text slip into Spanish—"vaquero" (94)—or, rather ironically, into the interlingual: "vaquering" (95). Rather than branding itself as a purveyor of the exotic, the text asserts its own status linguistically and thematically as a US American novel. When Clarence Darrell and Mercedes Alamar, the romantic couple at the heart of the plot, sail north to San Francisco (eventually reaching New York and Washington DC), the narrator focuses on the view of San Diego's shore from deck, "to be merged into the blue hills of Mexico beyond, as if obeying the immutable law which says that all things must revert to their original source" (123). That wistful moment is virtually the only textual glimpse of the old country or suggestion that California might become again part of Mexico.

Readers seeking a work of Latin American literature in *The Squatter and the Don* may feel that the novel, intent on exploring connections with the United States, does not speak to them at all. But if Ruiz de Burton's old-fashioned romance of injustices and expectations is read from the viewpoint of many works of Latino literature, often intertwined with the affairs of Latin American countries and diasporas, it acquires new resonances that may yet retrieve it for the other side of the literary border—which is, of course, a culturally permeable divide. In recent years, both *The Squatter and the Don* and *Who Would Have Thought It?* (1872), Ruiz de Burton's first novel, have been republished by Modern Library and Penguin Classics respectively, signaling her rising status as an author worth reading for her literary and historical insights into issues of justice and ethnicity in the United States. That her works have not been translated into Spanish suggests that she has not reached readers in Latin America in any great numbers—but that too may change.

The conjoined issues of translation and readership have come to the fore recently in relation to *L'Homme de la pampa* (The Man of the Pampas, 1923), the first of three novels in French by Jules Supervielle. As Sylvia Molloy recounts, a new Spanish-language version of the novel, by Damián Tabarovsky, was a resounding success in Argentina, which, as she notes, shares "an imaginary" ("Traffic in Translation" 273) with the author's native Uruguay. If reading the novel in the French context appears, for Molloy, to be "an exercise in surrealist dream logic" or "an experiment in magic realism *avant la lettre*" (277), to read it in the River Plate context can be "a salutary counterpart, an antidote of sorts" (280) to such classic regionalist texts as Ricardo Güiraldes's *Raucho* (1920) and *Don Segundo Sombra* (1926). But what, exactly, does Supervielle's novel say about the subject of its title? The narrator of Mansilla de García's *Pablo*, in what sounds like an ethnological approach, compares "the man of the pampas" with sailors, whose capacity for long distance vision gauchos purportedly share. As if looking back to Mansilla de García's text yet regarding it with irony, Supervielle's *L'Homme de la pampa* is the absurd story of Fernández y Guanamiru, a wealthy Uruguayan who builds an artificial volcano on his estancia, which he then seeks to transport by ship to France. If volcanoes are emblems of the exotic—a magnificent one erupts at the end of "Les Incas du Pérou" (The Incas of Peru) in Jean-Philippe Rameau's *Les Indes galantes* (The Amorous Indies, 1735)—the object crafted by Guanamiru is, by contrast, a spectacular parody, as if the exotic had reached its limits and could only be reproduced artificially and had to be exported for others to admire. After many twists and turns, the plot leads to Bordeaux and Paris; at the Place de la Concorde, the Egyptian obelisk metamorphoses into an ombu even as Guanamiru literally explodes in "eruptive megalomania" (187),[13] among clouds of lava and ash. Focusing on the text's impossible geographical dislocations—including, for instance, a ride on the Paris metro in which the Mexican border lies right after the Palais-Royal station—Mariano Siskind reaches the conclusion that the novel is "resistant to the fetishization of cultural difference, including that which is built upon Latin American difference" (14). Indeed, if anything, Supervielle's impossible tale exposes the pleasures and claims of exoticism as hyperbolic fabrications; his man of the pampas will remain free to do as he pleases, even if that means bursting the literary expectations of such readers as Laboulaye or Hugo.

A more nuanced, if still ironic, vision of transatlantic cultural relations is at play in *Le Voleur d'enfants* (*The Colonel's Children*, 1926), the tale of a South American colonel named Bigua who lives in Paris and, as the French title reveals, is in the habit of kidnapping children, whom he and his wife, Desposoria, then lovingly raise as their own. While there are no fantastic explosions in this rather urbane tale, Bigua is nonetheless a disquieting foreign presence in Paris. The novel's theatrical first scene takes place in a busy street just outside the Galleries Lafayette, where a little boy is snatched by the mysterious colonel, who moves around the city with an insider's familiarity. Unbelievably, the children dwelling in the Biguas's well-appointed flat appear to be content, but an erotic tale of dangerous liaisons soon emerges with the arrival of Marcelle, the only girl. Words in Spanish occasionally appear, a few denoting Supervielle's River Plate connections–"matés" (44, *sic*), "estancias" (56)—but their exotic qualities are ironically qualified. As the novel comes to an end, all characters are to be found on a ship crossing the Atlantic Ocean; its sequel, *Le Survivant* (*The Survivor*, 1928), has them landing in Montevideo, where new adventures ensue. On the last page of *Le Voleur d'enfants*, Supervielle inscribes the places where the novel was written: "Paris, Océan Atlantique, Uruguay" (158). The route of textual composition appears to mark the author's literal and literary in-betweenness.

Despite their linguistic difference and implied penchant for non-local readers, Mansilla de García, Hudson, Ruiz de Burton, and Supervielle wrote novels that can be critically connected to Latin American practices of writing and reading. The corpus of English- and French-language novels becomes more complex from the second half of the twentieth century; if nothing else, there are simply more works to consider, and authors appear to cross linguistic borders more flexibly than in earlier periods. Nonetheless, it is possible to recognize two main modalities. First, as in the texts seen so far, multiple novels by all kinds of authors develop themes or plots that function as links with Latin America or its nations. Some of these works, in a self-reflexive mode, include the adoption of a new language as a plot element, which makes them especially interesting sites for viewing the twists and turns of linguistic permutation. Second, despite authorial connections to the region, a few novels lack any obvious textual bonds with Latin American literature, which arguably makes their inclusion here more of a challenge for readers and critics.

Consider, for instance, the large corpus of Latino novels in the United States, most of which focus on characters of Latin American descent and their enduring family stories. Such is the case of John Rechy's first novel, *City of Night* (1963), whose narrator describes his Mexican lineage early on, even though the novel is not about his parents:

"that man who alternatively claimed French, English, Scottish descent–depending on his imaginative moods—that strange man who had traveled from Mexico to California spreading his seed—that turbulent man, married and divorced, who then married my Mother, a beautiful Mexican woman who loves me fiercely and never once understood about the terror between me and my father" (21). In *Bless Me, Ultima* (1972), the classic Chicano novel by Rudolfo Anaya, Spanish tinges an ancestral story in a land where it preceded English: "My father had been a vaquero all his life, a calling as ancient as the coming of the Spaniard to Nuevo Méjico" (2). While its setting is Chicago, far from the border, Sandra Cisneros's famous *The House on Mango Street* (1989) also focuses on the legacies of family, culture, and language: "In English my name means hope. It means sadness, it means waiting. It is like the number nine. A muddy color. It is the Mexican records my father plays on Sunday mornings when he is shaving, songs like sobbing" (10). Awarded the Pulitzer Prize, Oscar Hijuelos's *The Mambo Kings Play Songs of Love* (1989) is a tale of the cultural bonds between Cuba and the United States, forged through music and television, as the narrator establishes at the novel's onset: "When I heard the opening strains of the *I Love Lucy* show I got excited because I knew she was referring to an item of eternity, that episode in which my dead father and my Uncle Cesar had appeared, playing Ricky Ricardo's singing cousins fresh off the farm in Oriente Province, Cuba, and north in New York for an engagement at Ricky's nightclub, the Tropicana" (3). Physical and linguistic migration—from the Dominican Republic to New York, and from English to Spanish—lies also at the heart of Julia Alvarez's *How the García Girls Lost Their Accents* (1991): "As the only immigrant in my class, I was put in a special seat in the first row by the window, apart from the other children so that Sister Zoe could tutor me without disturbing them. Slowly, she enunciated the new words I was to repeat: *laundromat, corn flakes, subway, snow*" (166; her italics). But migration is also linked to unlearning a language, as in Cristina Garcia's *Dreaming in Cuban* (1992): "Pilar, her first grandchild, writes to her from Brooklyn in a Spanish that is no longer hers" (7).[14] Also a Pulitzer recipient, Junot Díaz's *The Brief Wondrous Life of Oscar Wao* (2007) is not a tale of characters learning a new tongue or forgetting an old one, but rather a novel very much at home in the peculiar form of Spanish-blotted English in which it is written. If anything, it is monolingual readers of English who must learn new words and concepts, such as *fukú*, the curse imported from the old country, which plays a role not only in the protagonist's family chronicle, but in American history itself: "For what Kennedy's intelligence experts failed to tell him was what every single Dominican, from the richest jabao in Mao to the poorest güey in El Buey, from the oldest anciano sanmacorisano to the littlest carajito in San Francisco knew: that whoever killed Trujillo, their family would suffer a fukú so dreadful it would make the one that attached itself to the Admiral jojote in comparison" (3). It is unlikely that all readers understand the items in every rhyming couplet deployed by the author, yet it is safe to assume that they keep reading.

Confidently, Díaz interfuses an unitalicized Dominican-inflected Spanish lexicon in his English language novel—all part and parcel of the unapologetic hybridity Michiko Kakutani remarked on in an early review in which she described the text as "a wondrous, not-so-brief first novel that is so original it can only be described as Mario

Vargas Llosa meets 'Star Trek' meets David Foster Wallace meets Kanye West" (n.p.). Yet, while it might still be easier to place Díaz's book in the shelves of U.S. American literature, one can imagine a richer life for the novel if also read, for instance, within the systems of Dominican and Latin American literatures, where at least some readers will be able to decipher its foreign words with utmost certainty and, furthermore, connect the compelling story to other tales of regional and national life. This is, after all, a novel about Dominican immigrants in the United States as well as a novel about the Dominican Republic itself, whose citizens often emigrate to the north because of the political failures chronicled in the text. Indeed, many of Díaz's readers may actually express themselves in what Nuria Barrios, in a review of the novel's Spanish translation, calls "a new language to express a new lifestyle." Unlike Supervielle's *L'Homme de la pampa*, say, which can be read differently in the French and River Plate contexts, Díaz's novel emerges, arguably, as an uncanny text in which languages and cultures are fearlessly and inseparably conjoined.

The coexistence of languages is also one of the themes of Valeria Luiselli's *Lost Children Archive* (2019), the chronicle of a New York family as well as a story of Latin American migrant children at the U.S.-Mexico border. Since Luiselli had written two previous novels in Spanish, her status as a Mexican author is linguistically indisputable, which grants her a measure of freedom when it comes to shifting to a new tongue. Indeed, the novel is very much an apology for the public coexistence of a plurality of languages. The narrator, who reveals early on that her grandmother "was Hñähñu and spoke Otomí" (16), is working, along with her husband, on a project to record the city's multilingual soundscape: "There were eight hundred languages in New York City, and after four years of work, we had sampled almost all of them" (19). She also provides legal translations to an acquaintance whose children have been detained for crossing the border. Like Ruiz de Burton's *The Squatter and the Don*, Luiselli's sprawling novel is a tale of the law and how it protects, or not, persons of Latin American descent in the United States. Indeed, in its denunciation of a present-day injustice, *Lost Children Archive* may serve as a steppingstone for reconsidering the legal issues expounded in that novel as an enduring theme in English-language works by authors from Latin America. Likewise, Luiselli's own translingualism after writing in Spanish is also a good prism for assessing María Luisa Bombal's *House of Mist* (1947), an English-language reworking of *La última niebla* with an eye to a Hollywood film; Ariel Dorfman's *Konfidenz* (1995), which retakes the some of the political questions of his previous work; Rosario Ferré's *The House on the Lagoon* (1995), published two years before *La casa de la laguna*, translated by Ferré herself; or Giannina Braschi's *Yo-Yo Boing!* (1998) and *United States of Banana* (2011), written in Spanglish and English, respectively.

Like their English-language counterparts, Francophone authors have also frequently written works connected with their native countries. Eduardo Manet's *Rhapsodie cubaine* (Cuban Rhapsody, 1996), for instance, focuses on Cuban emigrants, such as the Harvard-educated young man, who decries the nationalist nostalgia of exiles in Miami, always talking about "Cuba. Missing Cuba. Returning to Cuba. Fidel's death or fall" (63–64). Politics is also one of the subjects in Laura Alcoba's works. Her first novel, *Manèges*:

Petite histoire argentine (*The Rabbit House*, 2007) is an autofiction about her childhood in Argentina at the onset of the military regime in the late 1970s. Again, as we saw in other authors, Alcoba's tidy French prose occasionally cites Spanish words, consistently placed in italics and at times redolent of her native country, as in such gastronomical terms as *dulce de leche* (92) and *matambre* (95). But the Spanish word most often used in the text is *embute*, a peculiar, rough-sounding noun derived from *embutir* ("to stuff") that refers to a room in the narrator's house where her mother and other fellow militants set up a clandestine printing press. The word is placed at the center of the narrator's recollections; not finding it in any dictionary, she, now a woman living in France, writes to the Real Academia de la Lengua Española in search of a definition, only to conclude that *embute* was a jargon term used by Argentine revolutionaries.[15] As she reflects on these linguistic matters, Alcoba obliquely underscores how her adoption of French as a literary tongue serves as a refuge from the harsh history of her native land, where her father is in prison. In *Le Bleu des abeilles* (The Blue Color of Bees, 2013), which focuses on her new life in an inelegant suburb of Paris, little Laura learns to feel at home in France and in French, the language in which she will compose her memories of a Spanish-language childhood. As the text ends, the girl suddenly speaks in French to her mother, who is surprised and replies, in Spanish, "You spoke in French!" (134).[16] While *Le Bleu des abeilles* is the latter work, one may think of it as a precursor to *Manèges*, which could not have been written had Alcoba not learned French first.

In her study of French and self-translation, Sara Kippur devotes a chapter to Héctor Bianciotti, whom she describes as an author "deeply invested in distancing himself from his Latin American roots and in cultivating a French audience, even a French aesthetic" (*Writing It Twice* 108). For Bianciotti, an early form of detachment was to ensure that French translations of his works were published before the Spanish-language originals; yet another, more extreme, milestone was to abandon Spanish altogether and adopt French as his sole literary tongue. Oddly, as Kippur points out, Bianciotti penned four rather long autofictions—one in Spanish and three in French—where he painstakingly examines his daily life in Argentina, Italy and Spain, and chronicles a return trip to Argentina, but hardly devotes any attention to the decades he spends as a Francophone author in France, which culminated in his elevation to the Académie française. In the third volume, *Le Pas si lent de l'amour* (The Slow Pace of Love, 1995), the first-person narrator recounts his first years in Europe—the arrival by ship in Naples, followed by a sojourn in Rome and five years in Madrid—and does so without using any words in Italian or more than a handful in Spanish. In the last chapter, he examines his literary passage into French—the language of his text—and concludes: "And so with French. I would never know whether it has truly accepted me, but that, like the ivy that wraps itself around a tree, it has dried up the Spanish in me, of that I am convinced" (330).[17] It might be easy to read the death of the Spanish-language author as the Argentine writer's epitaph, but one may also read Bianciotti's existence in French as an afterlife from which Latin American literature, or at least its remains, can be contemplated from a new vantage point. Ultimate distance from Argentina is signaled by the rather sumptuous French in which Bianciotti writes, yet the emerging gap between his birthplace and his adopted tongue is as much about Argentina as it is about anything else.

As if proclaiming absolute literary detachment, other French- and English-language authors broaden the gap between their native country and fictional works by deleting virtually all references that might be construed as connections with the corpus of Latin American literature. Consider the three novels by Chloe Aridjis, all written in English. The first, *Book of Clouds* (2009), is the story of a Mexican woman set in post-reunification Berlin, while the third, *Sea Monsters* (2019), unfolds mostly in a beach town in Oaxaca. But the second novel, *Asunder* (2013), focuses on a character, Marie, who works as a guard at London's National Gallery, with virtually no references to Latin America. Consider as well the works of Silvia Baron Supervielle, written almost exclusively in French. Her first novel, *L'Or de l'incertitude* (The Gold of Uncertainty, 1990) follows Italian scholar and explorer Antonio Pigafetta as he reconstructs, under Ferdinand Magellan's command, the voyage of the *Victoria* along the South American coast, while *La Rive orientale* (The East Shore, 2001), to cite just another example in a vast body of work, takes place, as the title suggests, in Uruguay. But then there is *La Frontière* (The Border, 1995), the poetical tale of a young boy dancing alone on a beach who is watched by a woman, and then he goes into a forest—and Latin America, or Argentina, is nowhere to be seen. Once asked whether she saw herself as a Latin American writer, Baron Supervielle replied, "What I know is that I do not write like the French. . . . Once someone told me: really, you're a foreigner on both sides" (Weiss).[18] Or, as Kippur explains, her texts "acutely insist upon the *non*-national, the transnational, the space between nations, languages, or shores? ("Pour ou contre une littérature-monde?" 216). Toward the end of Baron Supervielle's *Le Regard inconnu* (The Unknown Glance, 2020), an enigmatic story that can be read both as a long prose poem and a short novel, the speaker or narrator, situated in a nameless place, suddenly invokes the Seine, in the north, and the River Plate, in the south, imagining both as one and the same river connected by the Atlantic Ocean: "It is my abandoned country and faces. It is an absolute view of the boreal continent descending into the sea and resurfacing between two cities, Buenos Aires and Montevideo, of the austral continent" (101).[19] In these translingual passages from France to Argentina, or from Mexico or Cuba to the United States, what matters is fluidity, the state of unsettledness, and the possibility of transports. Like rivers or oceans, novels get written, flow endlessly through all kinds of places, and shift forms with absolute freedom as they move from one reader to another.

NOTES

1. In *Extraterritorial,* Steiner focuses on the "linguistic unhousedness" of Beckett and Nabokov, who wrote in languages not their own, and that of Borges, whose writings are bound with literatures in many tongues.
2. "Votre *Pablo* m'a donné une des plus vives jouissances qu'un livre puisse procurer; il m'a fait vivre dans un pays que je n'ai jamais vu et que probablement je ne verrai jamais; il m'a fait comprendre des sentiments et des passions qui n'ont ni la même ardeur ni le même

aspect sous notre froid climat; . . . on y voit la Pampa, son inexorable sérénité durant le jour, son animation durant la nuit; on s'intéresse à Pablo, à sa bien-aimée, à sa mère; on vit avec le *gaucho malo,* on est tiré de la vie commune, de l'ennui de tous les jours" (Mansilla de García 1–2).

3. "Nous autres Argentins" (18); "lecteur européen" (30–31).

4. "Espèce de thé indigène" (57); "arbre des pampas" (61); "détachement des troupes qui garnit les frontières" (94).

5. "Infernale avalanche" (270).

6. "Après avoir pillé de préférence les boutiques, les sauvages avaient tué pas mal du monde, sans compter les femmes qu'ils avaient enlevées ou assassinées, après avoir satisfait sur elles leurs appétits féroces" (270).

7. "Su amor a su patria"; "Eduarda escribe en francés una novela puramente argentina."

8. "Mediadora cultural entre la Argentina y Europa."

9. "Madame: Votre livre m'a captivé. . . . Vous m'avez montré un monde inconnu" (qtd. by Alvarado-Larroucau 24).

10. "Digna de Quentin Tarantino, digna de un cómic del siglo XX" (Cabezón Cámara).

11. See Díaz, *Unhomely Rooms* 134–40. Cf. Molloy, who notes how translations of Hudson in Argentina resort to "an aggressively local Spanish" (*Vivir entre lenguas 54,* "un español agresivamente local") that mimics the speech of Gauchos and exceeds the nativist strains of much writing in the country.

12. Borges describes it as "venturoso acriollamiento" (210, fortunate Creolization).

13. "Mégalomanie eruptive" (Supervielle, *L'Homme de la pampa* 187).

14. On the absence of Spanish or interlingual forms thereof, see Gustavo Pérez Firmat, who points to the gap between an author's language and that of the represented world: "Even the English of Latino writers, with some exceptions, bears little resemblance to the hybrid sounds and rhythms of the barrios where many of them grew up. What happened to the Garcia girls has also happened to the writers: they have lost their accents. For every Latino writer like Gloria Anzaldúa and Roberto Fernández, who endeavor to reproduce the actual speech, the *idioma,* of a particular group of Latinos, there are several like Cristina Garcia and Julia Alvarez, who translate it into something like George Santayana's Received Standard English" (139, italics in the original).

15. See Duarte dos Santos and Gasparini, who examine "embute" as a kind of ruin or relic ("ruina o reliquia" 281) of Alcoba's spatially and temporally remote pre-French world.

16. *"¡Hablaste en francés!"* (134, Alcoba's italics).

17. "Ainsi du français. Jamais je ne saurais s'il m'a accepté, mais que tel que la lierre qui s'enroule autour d'un arbre il a desséché en moi l'espagnol, de cela je suis convaincu" (Bianciotti 330).

18. In an essay, Baron Supervielle broaches the subject of taxonomy with a measure of skepticism: "My writing is in harmony with the French language, but not because I employ that language am I a French writer. . . . Classification by language is a functional solution, but it eludes something essential, which is proper to the writer and inherent to creation" ("Mon écriture s'harmonise avec la langue française, mais ce n'est pas parce que je me sers de cette langue que je suis un écrivain français. . . . La classification par langues est une solution fonctionnelle, mais elle élude quelque chose d'essentiel, qui est propre à l'écrivain, et inhérent à la création" (*L'Alphabet du feu* 124).

19. "Il est mon pays et mon visage abandonnés. Il est une vue absolue du continent boréal qui descend dans la mer et resurgit entre deux villes, Buenos Aires et Montevideo, du continent austral" (Baron Supervielle 101).

WORKS CITED

Alcoba, Laura. *Le Bleu des abeilles*. Gallimard, 2013.

Alcoba, Laura. *Manèges: Petite histoire argentine*. Gallimard, 2007.

Alvarado-Larroucau, Carlos. "Eduardo Mansilla y Victor Hugo: un breve intercambio epistolar marcando los inicios de la literatura francófona de Argentina." *Çedille: Revista de Estudios Franceses*, no. 10, 2014, pp. 21–33.

Alvarez, Julia. *How the García Girls Lost Their Accents*. Plume Book, 1992.

Anaya, Rudolfo. *Bless Me, Ultima*. Warner Books, 1994.

Baquero, Gastón. "Introducción a la novela." *La Enciclopedia de Cuba*. Playor, 1975. 10 vols. 3:1–21.

Baron Supervielle, Silvia. *L'Alphabet du feu: Petites études sur la langue*. Gallimard, 2007.

Baron Supervielle, Silvia. *La Frontière*. Corti, 1995.

Baron Supervielle, Silvia. *L'Or de l'incertitude*. Corti, 1990.

Baron Supervielle, Silvia. *Le Regard inconnu*. Gallimard, 2020.

Baron Supervielle, Silvia. *La Rive orientale*. Seuil, 2001.

Barrios, Nuria. "Un lenguaje nuevo." Rev. of *The Brief Wondrous Life of Oscar Wao*, by Junot Díaz. *El País*, 6 June 2008. https://elpais.com/diario/2008/06/07/babelia/1212795556_850215.html

Bianciotti, Héctor. *Le Pas si lent de l'amour*. Bernard Grasset, 1995.

Borges, Jorge Luis. "Sobre *The Purple Land*." *Otras inquisiciones*. Alianza, 1976. 138–42.

Braschi, Giannina. *United States of Banana: A Graphic Novel*. Amazon Crossing, 2011.

Braschi, Giannina. *Yo-Yo Boing!* Amazon Crossing, 2011.

Cabezón Cámara, Gabriela. "Nota preliminar." Eduarda Mansilla de García, *Pablo o la vida en las pampas*, edited by Alejandra Laera. Kindle, 2019.

Carpentier, Alejo. *Los pasos perdidos*. Editorial de Arte y Literatura, 1976.

Cisneros, Sandra. *The House on Mango Street*. Vintage, 1991.

Díaz, Junot. *The Brief Wondrous Life of Oscar Wao*. Riverhead Books, 2007.

Díaz, Roberto Ignacio. *Unhomely Rooms: Foreign Tongues and Spanish American Literature*. Bucknell UP, 2002.

Dorfman, Ariel. *Konfidenz*. Farrar, Straus & Giroux, 1994.

Ferré, Rosario. *The House on the Lagoon*. Farrar, Straus & Giroux, 1995.

Franco, Jean. *Spanish American Literature since Independence*. Ernest Benn, 1973.

Garcia, Cristina. *Dreaming in Cuban*. Alfred A. Knopf, 1992.

Güiraldes, Ricardo. *Don Segundo Sombra*. Editorial Losada, 1975.

Güiraldes, Ricardo. *Raucho*. Centro Editor de América Latina, 1968.

Hijuelos, Oscar. *The Mambo Kings Play Songs of Love*. Farrar Straus Giroux, 1989.

Hudson, W.H. *The Purple Land*. AMS Press, 1968.

Kakutani, Michiko. "Travails of an Outcast." Rev. of *The Brief Wondrous Life of Oscar Wao*, by Junot Diaz. *The New York Times*, September 4, 2007. https://www.nytimes.com/2007/09/04/books/04diaz.html

Kippur, Sara. "Pour ou contre une littérature-monde?: Héctor Bianciotti, Silvia Baron Supervielle, and the Case of Argentina." *Contemporary French and Francophone Studies*, vol. 13, no. 2, 2009, pp. 211–22.

Kippur, Sara. *Writing It Twice: Self-Translation and the Making of a World Literature in French.* Northwestern UP, 2015.

Laera, Alejandra. "Nota preliminar." Eduarda Mansilla de García, *Pablo o la vida en las pampas*, edited by Alejandra Laera. Kindle, 2019.

Luiselli, Valeria. *Lost Children Archive.* Vintage, 2019.

Manet, Eduardo. *Rhapsodie cubaine.* Bernard Grasset, 1996.

Mansilla de García, Eduarda. *Pablo o la vida en las pampas.* Penguin Clásicos, 2019. Kindle.

Mansilla de García, Eduarda. *Pablo ou la vie dans les pampas avec une lettre de M. E. Laboulaye (Éd. 1869).* Hachette Livre-BNF, 2018.

Masiello, Francine. "Lost in Translation: Eduarda Mansilla de García on Politics, Gender, and War." Biblioteca Virtual Miguel de Cervantes, 2012. http://www.cervantesvirtual.com/obra/lost-in-translation-eduarda-mansilla-de-garcia-on-politics-gender-and-war/

Merlin, María de las Mercedes Santa Cruz y Montalvo, comtesse. *Histoire de la sœur Inès.* Imprimerie de P. Dupont et Laguionie, 1832.

Merlin, María de las Mercedes Santa Cruz y Montalvo, comtesse. *Les Lionnes de Paris.* Librairie d'Amyot, 1845. 2 vols.

Merlin, María de las Mercedes Santa Cruz y Montalvo, comtesse. *Mes douze premières années.* Imprimerie de Gaultier-Laguionie, 1831.

Molloy, Silvia. "Traffic in Translation: Rereading Supervielle." *French Global: A New Approach to Literary History*, edited by Christie McDonald and Susan Rubin Suleiman, Columbia UP, 2010, 273–81.

Molloy, Silvia. *Vivir entre lenguas.* Eterna Cadencia, 2016.

Pérez Firmat, Gustavo. *Tongue Ties: Logo-Eroticism in Anglo-Hispanic Literature.* Palgrave Macmillan, 2003.

Rameau, Jean-Philippe. *Les Indes galantes.* Harmonia Mundi, 2019.

Rechy, John. *City of Night.* Grove Press, 2013.

Rivera, José Eustasio. *La vorágine.* Biblioteca Ayacucho, 1976.

Ruiz de Burton, María Amparo. *The Squatter and the Don.* Arte Público, 1992.

Santos, Debora Duarte dos, and Pablo Gasparini. "En el embute del francés: Sobre *Manèges / La casa de los conejos* de Laura Alcoba." *Alea: Estudos Neolatinos*, vol. 17, no. 2, 2015, pp. 277–90.

Siskind, Mariano. "Modernismo global y literatura mundial: Reflexiones sobre las dislocaciones cosmopolitas del significante francés." *Revista Chilena de Literatura*, no. 96, November 2017, pp. 13–28.

Steiner, George. *Extraterritorial: Papers on Literature and the Language Revolution.* Atheneum, 1976.

Supervielle, Jules. *L'Homme de la pampa.* Gallimard, 1988.

Supervielle, Jules. *Le Survivant.* Gallimard, 1981.

Supervielle, Jules. *Le Voleur d'enfants.* Gallimard, 1987.

Weiss, Jason. "Silvia Baron Supervielle." *Itineraries of a Hummingbird* (blog). https://www.itinerariesofahummingbird.com/silvia-baron-supervielle.html

CHAPTER 44

THE WORLDWIDE INFLUENCE OF THE LATIN AMERICAN NOVEL

NICHOLAS BIRNS

BEGINNINGS TO 1950

THE growth of colonial literatures to world status is often represented as a shift from the provincial to the emergent to the cosmopolitan. Doris Sommer attributes this envisioned trajectory to the Latin American Boom writers who she says claimed that "only now" was "the continent gaining cultural independence, by Calibanizing the range of European traditions" (Sommer 1). Though Sommer understands that contours of this model are understandable, her work has done much to disprove it, and point out that there were compelling novels in Latin American before the Boom. The "growth" model of colonial literatures furthermore neglects the fact that colonialism is always worldly, as Srinivas Aravamudan argued in *Tropicopolitans* (1999), and that "inhabitants of the torrid zones that were the object of Europe's colonial ambition" (Aravamudan 6) carried with them their own worldliness. The oppression and marginalization of the colonized, and the mechanisms of colonial governance, are not confinable to a determinate space. Given that the worlding of the indigenous peoples of the Americas after 1492, and more operatively in 1519 and 1532, was involuntary, Latin American literature from the beginning was worlded by its colonial status. The Aztec empire, called by its rulers the *Ēxcān Tlahtōlōyān*, and the Incan realm of Tahuantinsuyo had not registered globally before their respective Spanish conquests. These realms were not only impressive politically but also contained a deep cultural history whose resonance was still felt still after the conquest. Yet we should remember that, in the words of Aníbal Quijano, colonialism constituted an order dependent on "the social classification of the world's population around the idea of race" (533). Latin American ideologies and practice of mestizaje and transculturation undermine the hierarchies critiqued by Quijano, making the expression of literary narrative an agent in this process of cultural decolonization.

Miguel de Cervantes's short story "El celoso extremeño" sees "the Indies" as a place of embarrassment and exile, and it must not be forgotten that denunciations of the colonial as lesser and provincial still presume a global world. Such writers as Sor Juana Inés de la Cruz in New Spain, Juan de Espinosa Medrano ("Lunarejo") in Peru, and Cláudio Manuel da Costa (Glauceste Satúrnio) in Brazil wrote for metropolitan audiences in Spain and Portugal as much as for people in their home country. Both the Spanish and Portuguese colonial empires had access to the Atlantic and Pacific. meaning colonial South American writers could be read in Timor, Goa, or the Philippines as well as their home countries. Indeed, in the colonial era the empires of the two Iberian nations constituted a significant part of the globe, encompassing the Atlantic, Pacific, and Indian oceans, and including many areas that were later dominated by other languages. The Franciscan chronicler Luis Jerónimo de Oré, writing circa 1617, wrote of the Spanish explorations of the North Atlantic seaboard. Oré spoke of a "big river, fed with fresh water" (de Oré 101) that the expedition named the San Pedro. That this river would become more famous as the Potomac makes us see the iconicity and ecology of lands now paradigmatically *norteamericanas* through a Spanish-speaking lens. To know that the Potomac, the river on which the US government sits, had a Spanish name before an English (appropriated from the Algonquin) one lends not just a frisson of cognitive estrangement but also a lesson that cosmopolitanism was a property always possessed by the Spanish Americas. This was so even if the Anglosphere tried to deny it to them.

The independence of Latin American countries in the 1810s and early 1820s was enfranchising in political terms. It was a global event in that it was intricately bound up with the Napoleonic Wars and the establishment of the United States as a permanent power. Certainly, independence leaders such as the Venezuelan Francisco de Miranda sought—in the terms of the Indo-Trinidadian writer V. S. Naipaul's memorable essayistic portrait of him—"a way in the world" (Naipaul 1994). National independence offered the new countries of Latin America access to the world that their colonial relation to Spain had inhibited.

But in literary terms, the era of national independence was provincializing. After attempts for regional or Pan-American unity failed, writers of each region became inevitably engaged in conducting their own national institutions. Sommer has termed these "foundational fictions," which neither sought nor received transnational acclaim. As Sommer shows, the writers of nineteenth-century national romances received international influences from writers as disparate as Stendhal and Fenimore Cooper. But their work in turn acquired little valence outside of the region. Indeed, it showed little interest in doing so. One of the few to be translated in this era was the Brazilian romancer José de Alencar, whose *O Guaraní* (1857) was translated by James W. Hawes as *The Guarani* for the California-based magazine *Overland Monthly* in 1893. The Peruvian novelist Clorinda Matto de Turner, who had married an Englishman, saw her 1889 novel *Aves sin nido* (*Birds Without Wings* (1904) translated into English and published in London by a firm that largely published Christian books, Charles J. Thynne. Even a writer of extraordinary subtlety and agility as the Peruvian Ricardo Palma, although perhaps avoiding *costumbrismo* in the narrowest sense in his *Tradiciones peruanas,* was resolutely local in his approach. Palma did not presume a readership outside Peru and certainly the Americas. In this, he was typical of nineteenth-century Latin American prose writers. Indeed, poets of the late nineteenth century, such as the Nicaraguan Rubén Darío gained more global renown than any novelist of the time. The romantic Colombian novelist Jorge Isaacs gained some canonicity in the wider world perhaps because his novel *María* (1867), being called by *The New York Times,* on April 28, 1918, an "undisputed position in the front ranks of the world literatures" (72). Isaacs's work at least partially navigated, as Ericka Beckman puts it, "the space-time of global capitalism" (Beckman 539).

Latin America was best known in languages other than Spanish or Portuguese through representations of it in novels by outsiders, whether by the Englishmen W. H. Hudson and R. B. Cunningham Grahame, who epitomized the cultural aspects of what Jessie Reeder has termed the British "informal empire" in South America, especially Argentina in the late nineteenth century, or by the transnational writer Joseph Conrad, who was a fierce critic of the US-sponsored Panamanian revolt against Colombia in 1903. Conrad's portrayal of the fictional republic of Costaguana in *Nostromo* (1904) is, in some sense, a thematic ancestor of Gabriel García Márquez's *Cien años de soledad* (*One Hundred Years of Solitude,* 1967), particularly if one considers the title of the fictional internal history written by Don José Avellanos, *Fifty Years of Misrule.* Even in Spain, it took until the end of the nineteenth century for such critics as Juan Valera and Marcelino Menéndez y Pelayo to take account of writers of the Western Hemisphere.

Latin America did not participate much in either the First or even the Second World Wars, but both conflicts were internationalizing events that led cognoscenti in the metropolitan enclaves of the Global North to take more notice of the entire world. Alfred Coester published *The Literary History of Spanish America* in New York in 1916. The *Times*'s mention of Jorge Isaacs as the undisputed master occurred just as the US was most involved militarily in the First World War. Isaac Goldberg established himself as the chief explainer of South America to the North in the 1910s and 1920s. In "As Latin America Sees Us," published by H. L. Mencken's *American Mercury,* Goldberg wrote on the Uruguayan essayist José Enrique Rodó's *Ariel* and made his readers face the fact that South Americans generally viewed their Northern counterparts as avatars of "gross materialism." In 1923, Alfred A. Knopf published Goldberg's anthology *Brazilian Literature,* which included the work of Joaquim María Machado de Assis, now considered incontestably the greatest Brazilian writer of the late nineteenth century, and Euclides da Cunha, the nation's extraordinary chronicler of social upheaval in the backlands. But Thomas Walsh's review in *The New York Times* spotlighted the poetry of Olavo Bilac and the cultural history of Manoel de Oliveira Lima as the truly salient names in Brazilian intellectual life. In general, before 1960, and contrary to claims about the hegemony of the novel made by postcolonial critics such as Homi Bhabha and Timothy Brennan, the Latin American novel was not in the forefront of the region's literary reception worldwide. North American critics like Waldo Frank and, later, Selden Rodman were as interested in poetry as in fiction, and were looking for generalizations about the region, such as that it was an alternative to North American materialism, and that (somewhat by extrapolation from Spanish neutrality in the First World War) it had achieved a happier, less competitive social fabric. This led to Frank being in contact with the Peruvian thinker José Carlos Mariátegui and his journal *Amauta*. But Frank emphasized more the artistic potential of the continent than the achievement of individual writers. The Mexican Revolution—object of both left-wing adulation and right-wing paranoia in the Northern Hemisphere—did occasion some literary interest. Mariano Azuela's *Los de abajo* (1920) was translated as *The Underdogs* by Enrique Munguia Jr. in 1929, and published by Brentano's, a bookstore chain that also had a publishing imprint. But it was less Mexican writers that had world influence at this time. Rather, it was Mexico itself, cast as an exotic, politically and aesthetical innovative backdrop. This avatar of Mexico influenced the fiction of writers such as the British novelists Graham Greene and Malcolm Lowry and the short fiction of the British-born, Mexican-residing expatriate Leonora Carrington, more famous as a painter.

The Second World War era also saw Latin America receive more notice abroad. The Peruvian novelist Ciro Alegría received the Pan American Award in 1941. This included publication by the ancestor firm of today's Farrar, Straus, and Giroux (later to publish Roberto Bolaño's *2666*), and possible (seemingly never realized) serialization in *Redbook*. If this was basically the echo of a larger orientation towards global literature, Latin America did at least gain from this echo. In general, 1940s discourse about Latin America in the US was dominated by "explainers" such as Samuel Putnam. Putnam translated Euclides da Cunha's *Os Sertões* (1902) as *Rebellion in the Backlands* in 1943. Waldo Frank introduced Helen Caldwell's translation of Machado de Assis's *Dom Casmurro* in 1953. But by saying that the author's Afro-Brazilian racial background evidenced precisely "nothing" (Machado de Assis 13) about his genius, Frank made Machado's novel safe for still-existing racial segregation in the US and made its aesthetic impact only a quirky one. The Venezuelan writer Rómulo Gallegos, renowned as both novelist and statesman, produced in *Doña Barbara* (1929), a novel that was translated worldwide, in the general spirit of internationalism fostered by the war. Robert Malloy translated it into English in 1948, and René L. F. Durand rendered it into French in 1951. *Doña Barbara* was translated into German and published in Zürich in 1952 by the anti-Nazi German diplomat and literary scholar Werner Peiser. This act underscored the way translations of Gallegos functioned as a sort of diplomatic outreach, and that their cultural capital was more in the realm of international relations than in the literary field. It was because of this climate that, in the 1950s and early 1960s, Colombian intellectuals Germán Arciniegas or Eliseo Vivas were better known than any Latin American novelist. So, after a point, were the poets Pablo Neruda and César Vallejo. The first Latin American writer to win a Nobel Prize for Literature was the poet Gabriela Mistral of Chile in 1945. With some other literatures the genius of individual writers was spotlighted and then led to a reading of the soul of the nation or region. But, before the emergence of Jorge Luis Borges and Gabriel García Márquez, the global consensus was content to proceed to that sort of cultural reading without any substantive novelistic intermediary. Sommer points out that the post-1960 Boom writers acted like they were the only Latin American novelists worth reading, and that this led to: "disingenuous dismissal" (1) of the great novels of the nineteenth and early twentieth centuries. Part of the reason they could do this, though, is that these novels, though they had travelled to some extent globally, did not fully circulate worldwide.

1950 TO 1973

This changed for long-term and immediate reasons. The long-term reason has to do with the Cuban Revolution, the most convulsive event in Latin America in all of the twentieth century. But, even before the impact of that event had been fully felt, the definitive act of global reception had already occurred in an unlikely country and with respect to a most atypical writer. French literature had been as much a model for Latin American writers as Spanish. The abortive French imperial engagement in Mexico under Napoleon III had been partially responsible for the emergence of "Latin America" as umbrella term to describe most of the of non-English-speaking regions of the Western Hemisphere. Yet Latin American literature had never received much notice in France. This changed with the Second World War. This conflict saw some French intellectuals take refuge in South America. Roger Caillois spent the war years in Argentina, where he became familiar with Argentine writers such as Victoria Ocampo and Jorge Luis Borges. Caillois edited a book series, *La Croix du Sud* (Southern Cross), for the influential French publisher Gallimard. Caillois included the early novels of the Cuban Alejo Carpentier and the fiction of the future Guatemalan Nobel winner Miguel Ángel Asturias. But Jorge Luis Borges was his biggest "discovery."

That Caillois himself became famous as a theorist of play and that he introduced the idea of the "ludic" into global intellectual terminology, fortified his ability to cast Borges as a playful yet profound sage whose fictions were conceptual parables that were diverting, speculative, and disruptive of received paradigms. Borges won the Prix Formentor (along with Samuel Beckett, who with Borges and Nabokov made up the trinity of canonical late modern writers) in 1961. This facilitated his entry into the pantheon of contemporary writing. Borges was published in the United States by Grove Press and New Directions. These were two paperback presses associated with cutting-edge literature that published work that was socially dissident and thematically risqué. That the two publishers issued separate, slightly overlapping collections of Borges's work in short order—*Ficciones* (retaining the Spanish original) by Grove Press in 1962 and *Labyrinths* (using the title form the French translation supervised by Caillois, and not a title originally used by Borges himself) by New Directions, also in 1962.

Caillois had real knowledge and life experience of Latin America. Yet his writings on Borges, and the publicity about Borges Caillois fostered, saw Borges's Argentine origins as only an accident. This tendency was followed by his Anglo-American interpreters, including Ronald Christ and Norman Thomas di Giovanni. Christ's *The Narrow Act:*

Borges and the Art of Allusion (1969) saw Borges as a philosopher of literature who alluded to past works in a way not derivative but profoundly creative, distilling a new analytic of truth out of sifting through the past. The sense of self-conscious literariness here resembled the North American practice of metafiction and the Franco-American textual practice of deconstruction. Borges was indeed praised by John Barth and Paul de Man, respectively the leading representatives of each current. Yet there was always something determinate or even, to cite Christ's title, narrow, about the way Borges was read in the 1960s that mitigated excessive textual multiplicity. De Man captured the problem with the standard reception of Borges by stating that other critics depicted Borges as a "moralist." This sort of rigid interpretation makes into an epistemic prompt what Borges, in stories such as "El Aleph" ("The Aleph"), sees as something rare and ineffable. That the Aleph exists, in Borges's world, does not mean it is on every street-corner. Nor can it be distilled into a sort of literary-philosophical cracker-barrel wisdom.

Any sense that Borges's own stories had multiple possibilities was squelched. So were any more material substrates to Borges's fiction. His Argentine context was neglected, but so were other aspects of Borges. His fiction, for instance, is steeped in references to the lore of Judaism and Islam. This is something with a profound meaning in a Latin America whose colonization was concomitant with the culmination of the *Reconquista* and the rhetoric of *limpieza de sangre*. There was something commodified and restricted about the 1960s reception of Borges in both France and the Anglo-American world. But this reception was truly significant because it marked the first time a Latin American fiction writer became famous outside the region not as a sociological symptom.

Borges became an international celebrity. That celebrity had the effect of making the literary field responsive to Latin American inflections. Borges introduced high literariness into the global idea of Latin American literature, which remained even after the popularity of middlebrow writers such as Isabel Allende or Paolo Coelho. Borges's influence indeed quickly moved into popular culture, such as the Ellery Queen mystery novel *The Player on The Other Side* (1963, in fact authored by Theodore Sturgeon from an outline by Ellery Queen). This book transplants and rewrites Borges's theological mystery tale "Death and the Compass," with its emphasis on the four letters of the ineffable name of God. But Borges's work was seen as an intellectual achievement, not a political or anthropological one. Borges, though thoroughly and comfortably rooted in Argentina, came through France. The literariness of Borges inflected the reception of later writers even though both their manifest politics and their foregrounding of the political were very different than his; it kept Latin American literature, no matter how politically torqued, on a literary plane.

Just as Borges was reaching the apogee of his world fame, Latin America was making news in far more politically concrete ways. The Cuban Revolution and the emergence of Fidel Castro as the leader of Cuba placed a revolutionary, pro-Soviet government ninety miles away from the United States, and signaled to the world that Latin America was no longer a backwater. That the Cuban Revolution was concurrent with the decolonization of Africa and Asia and the emergence of a bloc of non-Western nations at the 1955 Bandung Conference led to the idea of the "Third World," which united the continents of Asia, Africa, and the region of Latin America as underprivileged and emerging, even though the cultural heritages of the three continents were, in general, quite divergent. Indeed, what the three continents had most in common, aside from underdevelopment, was being contested regions in the Cold War. The timing of the independence of most African states, the onset of the Civil Rights movement in the United States, and the Cuban Revolution made international readers particularly on the alert for new literatures of Latin America that would speak to the region's changing social conditions.

This gap was ripe for filling by a new generation of Latin American writers called "The Boom." Although the Boom included older writers such as the Argentine Julio Cortázar, a core member of the Boom, and, far more peripherally, Alejo Carpentier, the group of writers who became most famous worldwide were born in the late 1920s or 1930s: Gabriel García Márquez, Carlos Fuentes, and Mario Vargas Llosa. The Boom writers were from disparate countries—Argentina, Cuba, Colombia, Mexico, and Peru in the case of the five above, and mostly did not emerge from the national culture industries of their home countries but through a transnational network of awards, agents, and publishers. The Spanish agent Carmen Balcells was crucial to the success of most of them, as were Spanish publishers such as Seix Barral (publisher of Vargas Llosa) and Alfaguara (publisher of Fuentes and the Chilean José Donoso). This was paradoxical in that the right-wing regime of Generalissimo Francisco Franco was in power in Spain until 1975 and the Boom writers were all (even true of the younger Vargas Llosa) various stripes of radical leftists.

These writers all had fifty-year careers under the transnational gaze. The Boom writers came up when young, and, especially, Fuentes and Vargas Llosa could be translated in English over a fifty-year period and write into their own reception worldwide. Translation of their work was not just ransacking the backlist, as, ironically, became the case for the tragically short-lived Roberto Bolaño. Moreover, their translation was a vitally political act. Although, as with Russian literature, the metropole, as Pascale Casanova argues, inevitably saw in Latin American literature its own attitudinal gratifications and needs, the generally *mestizo* character of Latin American culture meant that, unlike in the Russian case, the distant culture to which it permitted entrance was not just an alternate form of whiteness. (Argentina was of course an exception here). Carpentier's *El siglo de las luces* (1962) was translated almost instantly into English (from the French version) by John Sturrock as *Explosion in the Cathedral* in 1963. It was an overtly political book dealing with decolonization and Enlightenment in the Caribbean. On the other hand, Cortázar's *Rayuela* (1963), translated into English as *Hopscotch* in 1966, with its aleatory, out-of-order storytelling, seemed a purely metafictive and technical achievement, yet Carpentier's book has many non-realistic moments, and Cortázar's an implied critique of institutional power. The Boom writers were translated into an Anglophone world in the throes of aesthetic as well as political change. In turn, they contributed to both.

Carlos Fuentes's *La región más transparente* (1958) was translated as *Where the Air Is Clear* by the painter Sam Hileman in 1960 and published by the small firm of Ivan Obolensky). Mario Vargas Llosa's *La ciudad y los perros* (1963) was translated into

English by Lysander Kemp in 1966 as *The Time of The Hero* and published by Grove Press, one of Borges's publishers. These books launched those writers' long careers in the Anglosphere, where they became comfortable as academics and lecturers. But the central book of the Boom, and of all Latin American literature, was Gabriel García Márquez's *Cien años de soledad* (1967). It was translated into English by Gregory Rabassa and published as *One Hundred Years of Solitude* in 1971. Even well before publication, the book was heralded in the English-speaking world. In *The New York Times* of April 15, 1969, Henry Raymont wrote that "Harper & Row believes it has a best-seller on its winter list" with the translation. This article, entitled "Latin Writers Stirring Up US Publishers' Interest," signaled a growing receptivity in the United States to Latin American fiction. Despite their manifest differences, the article mentioned Borges along with the "intellectual revolutionaries" García Márquez, Vargas Llosa, and Fuentes, as well as *Paradiso* by the Cuban writer José Lezama Lima. Another sign of a growing global interest in Latin American literature was the founding of the journal *Review* by Ronald Christ and Emir Rodríguez Monegal in 1968 under the auspices of the Center for Inter-American Relations. *Review* started out inconspicuously as a place to consolidate the English-language reviews of translated Latin American writers. Yet the journal quickly began to publish critical articles, original reviews, and fiction. It became both a publicity vehicle for the highbrow dissemination of the literature and a discursive frame to assess its import. Importantly, *Review* provided a vehicle that was not narrowly academic but was yet specialized and non-journalistic, influencing a readership that could be at once highbrow without having to read in Spanish or master the literary field in a strictly scholarly sense. This meant that, as opposed to the era of Samuel Putnam or Waldo Frank, the general reader was less at the mercy of the "explainers."

The Boom writers were thus part of a cultural opening in the Western world. But they were so in a different way in what was then the Soviet bloc. Irina Hostova has recorded the translations into Slovak of Spanish American literature from 1945 onward. After the inevitable *Doña Barbara*, translated into Slovak in 1961, and novels by the Argentine Ernesto Sabato and the Ecuadorian Jorge Icaza, writers of a generation older than the Boom but whose rejection of bourgeois realism and whose leftist politics were of a similar mien. In the early 1970s, Cortázar, Carpentier, and García Márquez were rapidly translated. The books that were translated into Slovak show some traces of a leftist bias. Two books by the Peruvian *indigenista* writer Manuel Scorza were included. But writers far from leftist such as the Argentine Ricardo Güiraldes were also translated, as he had been in the West when *Don Segundo Sombra* appeared in English in 1945. Asturias, whose Nobel win came right as the Boom was cresting in world renown, was older and more directly political than the Boom. But his work also found welcome in the East Bloc. These translated writers, though mostly left-wing in personal conviction, were not rigidly Socialist Realist in aesthetic terms. Their translation in the East Bloc betokened a freer and more creative range of expression that, without violating the totalitarian constraints of the Communist Soviet satellite government of Czechoslovakia, showed writers in the East Bloc that there was a way to write outside state guidance. García Márquez, of a stature to be interviewed by Soviet leader Mikhail Gorbachev in *Soviet*

Life in 1987, was sympathetic to Cuba and, to a degree, to Soviet Power, while making clear he was unenthusiastic about hard-Stalinist terror. This stance made his work, and that of the Boom writers in general, acceptable to official taste while going beyond official aesthetics, in a way that was, in actual circulation, dissident.

1973 TO 1995

The 1970s and early 1980s saw the translation of works by the major boom writers continue unabated. The success of the Avon trade paperback of *One Hundred Years of Solitude*—a book that in packaging resembled a fantasy or science-fiction novel—opened up a broad, crossover readership that saw in Latin American fiction a robustness lacking in traditional literary fare. As with Scorza in the East Bloc, writers of a more *indigenista* inclination, such as José María Arguedas, were auxiliary beneficiaries of the translation boom, although indicatively Arguedas's *Los ríos profundos* (*Deep Rivers*) appeared translated by Frances Horning Barraclough from University of Texas Press, not a commercial publisher. There also developed an interest in what might be termed a *segundo equipo* of Boom writers. This tendency emphasized those from countries that were objectively important or in the news but whose writers were not included at the top of the Boom. Ecuador, for instance, offered only Icaza, who was too old and too regional to be a part of the Boom, and Demetrio Aguilera Malta, who was only slightly younger and too much of a social realist. Icaza's *indigenista* novel *Huasipungo* (1934) was translated in 1964 by Southern Illinois University Press. Aguilera Malta's *Siete lunas y siete serpientes* was translated as *Seven Serpents and Seven Moons* by University of Texas Press in 1979. But neither made any sort of broad impact. Attention to Cuban writers was divided between Lezama Lima, Guillermo Cabrera Infante (championed by Susan Sontag) and Severo Sarduy (lauded by Roberto González Echevarría of Yale) in a way that, combined with the reluctance of some on the Left to read anything anti-Castro, fractured attention to the island's literature. José Donoso, a Chilean writer, playfully invented a fictional Ecuadorian writer, Marcelo Chiriboga, as their peer (one imagines Borges writing a coy *conte* indicating that Chiriboga was the only member of the younger generation he would compare to himself). Donoso. partially as a consequence of his self-appointment as a Boom writer in *Historia personal del Boom* (1972; translated as *The Boom in Spanish American Literature: A Personal History* [1977]), adduced as a supplementary member of the Boom, especially after the violent military overthrow of Salvador Allende in 1973.

The overthrow of Allende at once underscores the urgency of the Boom writers and pointed to what became a certain deficiency in them as politics changed in the 1970s. The Boom writers had criticized the rulers of their home countries, but only as a stagnant barrier to the region becoming like the rest of the world (as Vargas Llosa had done with the Odría regime in 1969's *Conversación en La Catedral* (translated as *Conversation in the Cathedral*. 1974), a temporal retardant much like the endemic jungle of Macondo in *One Hundred Years of Solitude*. That the Chilean regime, far from being a clumsily paternalistic *junta*, was a hyper-modern autocracy manifesting a tendency that Alfred Stepan called "bureaucratic authoritarianism." Indeed, the Pinochet government pioneered economic policies later known worldwide as neoliberalism. This disconnect meant that books like García Márquez's *El otoño del Patriarca.* 1975 (*The Autumn of the Patriarch*, 1976), where a dying dictator is treated with some slight degree of affection, seemed behind the times, and not an advance over Asturias's *El Señor Presidente*. Even the Boom-era book most specifically dedicated to continuing the *novela del dictador* subgenre, the Paraguayan Augusto Roa Bastos's 1974 *Yo El Supremo* (translated into English as *I, the Supreme* in 1986, although allegorically commenting on the present, now the face of it was about only, arguably, the third worst dictator in Paraguayan history, José Rodríguez de Francia, who most likely trailed both Francisco Solano López and the then-incumbent, Alfredo Stroessner, in horribleness. Vargas Llosa's great historical novel *La Guerra del fin del mundo* (1981), translated as *The War of the End of the World*, in 1984, by Helen Lane, rewrote da Cunha's account of the Brazilian backlands in the 1890s. It seemed to be as much a warning against millenarian Marxism as against rightist dictatorships. This was indicated in the *New York Times* review by novelist Robert Stone in July 1984, giving early insight into Vargas Llosa's drift to the Right. The Boom novelists continued to receive acclaim, but they did so in a different world than the heady years immediately following the Cuban Revolution.

García Márquez recognized this gap in "The Solitude of Latin America," his Nobel Prize speech of 1982. Here, he thanked the Swedish Academy for welcoming his continent into literature (the same way they had with the Australian Patrick White nine years before). But the Colombian writer devoted most of his speech to excoriating US support for Latin American dictators. He even indicated the United States had a role in two recent plane crashes that had killed leaders more sympathetic to the Left.[1] When juxtaposed to Vargas Llosa's and Fuentes's open break with Fidel Castro in 1971 after the latter's imprisonment of the dissident Heberto Padilla, the cracks in the Boom consensus were evident.

In this period, Brazilian literature's worldwide fame was dominated by one individual. This was Jorge Amado, who made a considerable impact in the US after his Penn State lectures of 1971. Amado's *Dona Flor and Her Two Husbands* (*Dona Flor e Seus Dois Maridos*, 1966) was translated into English in 1969 and adapted into an internationally successful film in 1976. A short-lived Broadway musical adapting the work, *Sarava*, premiered, and flopped, in 1979. Amado's work was more popular than literary. Yet a world readership understood it as magical realism and, in its portrait of the Afro-Brazilian community in Brazil, addressing racial issues more directly than any of the Boom writers. Minority writers became more translated in the early 1980s. These included the Jewish-Brazilian writer Moacyr Scliar and his Jewish-Argentine counterpart Mario Szichman. The gay male Argentine writer Manuel Puig saw his *El beso de la mujer araña* (1976; translated as *Kiss of the Spider Woman* in 1979) become popular as a book, a film, and a musical—the latter far more successful than *Sarava*.

In May 1985, Juan Goytisolo published an article, "Captives of Our 'Classics,'" in *The New York Times*. This great Spanish writer might have seemed, from the title, to be criticizing excessive reverence for Cervantes or Calderón; instead, the classics meant were the Latin American Boom writers, who Goytisolo accused of "very limited field of images already familiar to the reader: those of an oppressed continent taking up arms in revolt" (Goytisolo 1). The civil conflicts in Left-dominated Nicaragua and right-dominated El Salvador seemed to be offering new material for these scenarios. Writers like Salman Rushdie (*Midnight's Children*, 1981), Joyce Carol Oates (*Bellefleur*, 1980), the later John Barth (*The Tidewater Tales*, 1987), and Graham Swift (*Waterland*, 1983) had brought Latin American influences to represent national aspiration and regional distinction in the Anglophone world. Despite all this, writers in Spanish themselves seemed to be finding the Boom image that had been so commercially successful aesthetically constraining. Yet sometimes only by traversing through and transcending a stereotypical impression can a world reader find the truth of a particular literature. The India-based scholar Minni Sawhney wrote of her initial discovery of Latin American literature, which she saw at first through media images of revolution, than as analogies to her own situation, and finally in its own right. Even as its appeal to privileged high-literary readers began to fade, the literature of the Boom sparked exciting discoveries in parts of the world that a generation before might have only known of Latin America as countries on a map.

1996 TO PRESENT

By 1996, Latin America was no longer in the news worldwide. The end of the Cold War had stoked out the Nicaraguan and El Salvador conflicts (media images of which very generally tended to foster a Boom view of what Latin American society was). Latin American literature's global image was ripe for a generational turnover. Two manifesto-wielding groups, Crack in Mexico led by Jorge Volpi and McOndo in Chile led by Alberto Fuguet, stepped into the breach. These groups presented literary agendas very different from what the aging Boom, and a readership used to the Boom as representative of Latin America, would wish. McOndo, called by a French commentary a "surprising title,"[2] was of particular shock in altering the name of García Márquez's territory to evocations of McDonalds and MacIntosh that measured "a certain modernity"[3] in the region. The end of the Cold War ended the era of Latin American asymmetry as perceived by the world market. The emphasis shifted from books describing how Latin America was different from the developed world to books emphasizing how Latin America particularly evidenced questions and modes of affect articulated worldwide. Yet, as Wilfrido Corral points out, the Crack and McOndo writers, though receiving worldwide publicity, was more an inter-generational gesture than a true literary innovation, never really made an impact on the literary field at a world level. The neoliberal consensus of the 1990s did not really need affirmation from the Global South, and the emergence of Latinx writing in the US publishing sphere attracted more notice than new voices from below the Rio Grande. It was an older writer, who also first became known in 1996, who provided the true step beyond the Boom in the world influence of Latin American literature. This was Roberto Bolaño. A Chilean-born writer who had spent his formative years in Mexico and lived as an adult in Spain, Bolaño had the transnational and cosmopolitan background that fit well into the globalizing preoccupations of the 1990s and then the curiosity about a post-9/11 world. Yet Bolaño was also more successful worldwide than the Crack or McOndo because his books directly incorporated traumatic political events, from the Pinochet coup to the 1968 student revolt in Mexico to the femicides in Ciudad Juárez. For all of Bolaño's deep reading and arch literary playfulness, there was also an element of *testimonio* in his work that reached readers looking for books with political awareness that were not weighted down by the orotund sensibilities of the twentieth-century leftism that, as Bolaño pointed out in his Caracas speech accepting the Premio Romúlo Gallegos in 1999, was now discredited. Bolaño's largest works, *The Savage Detectives* and *2666*, combined the social breadth and formal interest typical of the total novels of the Boom writers with the allusiveness and literary gamesmanship of Borges (one of whose publishers, New Directions, launched Bolaño in the United States). The unfolding of Bolaño's reputation in many ways paralleled that of Borges. Although Bolaño's manifest political content was part of his appeal, he was surrounded with a more purely literary aura than the Boom writers. Younger American writers like Rachel Kushner, Ben Lerner and Jenny Zhang were attracted by Bolaño's arid and irreverent sensibility, but also to the way he was able to embed personal and political experience within a literary field. In other words, Bolaño's success built upon a literary field already established by previous writers, as Teng Wei has pointed out with respect to Bolaño's reception in China. Thus what was in Latin American terms a distinct division between the generation influenced by the Boom writers and Bolaño was less determinate outside Latin America. The emergence of the Russian novel, to a smaller extent the Japanese novel, and the Latin American were the three biggest contributors to the establishment of a conceptual bridge between European and world fiction that enabled anything like an idea of *Weltliteratur* to emerge. The inspiration of these three literatures to non-Western writing meant that their reception had a different temporality than they did in the West. Russian writing, for instance, was given a new life by Soviet influence in the Third World, and in these regions magical realism was seen as a successor to socialist realism the way it was seen more as a successor to modernism in the Western world. African, Asian, and South Pacific authors like Kojo Laing of Ghana, Emi Kurniawan of Indonesia, and Epeli Hau'ofa of Tonga—writers of different backgrounds, modes, and generations—were influenced by magical realism.

Thus, in the world influence of the Latin American novel, magical realism or García Márquez were not as periodized as they were within the region, and splayed and folded into the reception post-Boom writing. Even after the political solidarity of the Third World had long evaporated, non-Western countries looked to Latin America as a bridge between underdevelopment and world literary markets. This was also true of Indigenous writers in Australia such as Alexis Wright in *Carpentaria* (2006) and

New Zealand—*Potiki* (1986) by Patricia Grace. These writers saw in Latin American approaches both the totalizing cultural awareness of the Boom writers and the lucid political witness of the post-Boom, validations of the literary visibility of their experiences of peripheral and subaltern identities. Beyond these specifics, the very potential visibility of literature from anywhere in the world marketplace, and the understanding of analogies of oppression and cultural subordination across contexts, was something fostered by the success of the Boom. Much of the influence of the Boom novel was in the forms of magical realism, not just as a mode of representation but also as a kind of quirky regionalism that would permit hidden concerns of metropolitan nations to resonate in literary terms in the way that García Márquez's Macondo had. This was reliant on a version of what James Buzard has called "autoethnography."

As Juan E. de Castro pointed out, the internet and the emergence of democracy in Spain paradoxically (considering the rhetoric of anti-colonialism in Third World literary discourses) and the 1990s economic prosperity of Spain made Spain more of a center for its ex-colonial literatures. The internet multiplied the effect of geographically distant speakers of the same language and thus made the Hispanosphere and the Lusosphere, as wholes, more cognitively available to the Anglosphere and to other markets like the German and Scandinavian often influenced by Anglophone taste. The Internet also rendered those languages spoken in disparate places worldwide more important. It was after 1989 that Spanish definitively surpassed French as a global language, and that the independence of Timor Leste from Indonesia underscored the fact that Lusophone literature did not belong to a small country on the periphery of Europe but to a populous group of countries in four different continents.

The García Márquez contention that Latin America was out of synch with the rest of the world was no longer de rigueur in a Latin America swept by neoliberal capitalism and participating in global popular culture. By the time the Generation X writers of the Crack and McOndo groups entered their fifties, though, it was looking less that the mistake had been García Márquez's in casting Latin America as backward. The Global North may, instead, have erred in assuming it had conclusively surpassed the political malevolence and social absurdity that troubled Macondo. If the McOndo writers cast themselves as primarily repudiating the Boom, that motion inevitably had less staying power than the original motion. Indeed, the Borges of "Pierre Menard" might observe that all the reactions against the Boom were, in how they continued to evoke the Boom even as an antagonistic reference point, the most profound testimony to its achievement.

Yet Bolaño's popularity led to the wide translation of other offbeat, highbrow Latin American writers such as the Mexican Daniel Sada and the Argentines César Aira (championed by the American musician and memoirist Patti Smith), Ricardo Piglia (whose faux diaries as "Emilio Renzi" played into the global trend of autofiction), and Juan José Saer, as well as the reclamation of deceased writers such as the Colombian Álvaro Mutis and the Argentine Roberto Arlt. These writers were unmistakably Latin American in background. But they were citizens of the republic of letters first, before any reducible national feeling. The Boom writers had tended, in their reception, to resolve into Sommer's "foundational fictions" in conveying a sense of nationally defined meaning. In export, they became as formulaic in their national determination as the nineteenth-century imitations of James Fenimore Cooper ever had been. Conversely, the twenty-first century model of Latin American literary identity was more literary than national. A case in point is the surge of interest in the mid-twentieth-century Brazilian novelist Clarice Lispector. Lispector had been known in England and France since the 1980s and had been the object of Feminist scholarship by Hélène Cixous and thorough close reading by Nelson Vieira. But she did not become really known until a biography by Benjamin Moser and a series of new translations appeared in English in the 2010s.

Machado de Assis was the object of periodic discoveries in the English-speaking world. The most recent was in 2020 when two prestigious firms (Penguin and Liveright) published rival translations of his novel *Bras Cubas*. The "discoveries" paralleled the times: Waldo Frank's 1953 introduction stressing his novelistic craft over his racial background, the 2020 one stressing his Blackness as a key component of his imaginative genius. But there was never a discovery of Brazilian literature as a body, the way that first Borges and then García Márquez unquestionably led to the discovery of Latin American literature as a body that could then include writers of different generations, backgrounds, styles, and orientations. Correspondingly, the Latin American Boom writers lacked a single "discoverer." Although translators like Gregory Rabassa were influential, there was no one "Svengali" who was behind the rise of the Boom writers the way Caillois sponsored Borges in the France of the 1960s or Moser sponsored Lispector in the global space of the 2010s. Though, as with all literary movements, the worldwide canonicity of the Boom was mediated by publishers, reviewers, and bookstores, it had a notably broad base, and registered a genuine literary enthusiasm and not just the passing vogue of a coterie. The post-Boom writers sometimes seemed more at the mercy of commercialized and commodified mechanisms such as *Granta* magazine's *Bogota39* lists of the best Spanish American writers, issued in 2007 and 2017, which provided good publicity but little analytical insight. Even though many of the global reviews of these writers avoided the sentimental anthropology that had characterized liberal metropolitan reactions to the Boom, they often veered excessively in the opposite direction. Their reshuffling of highbrow praise without any underlying contact with the culture from which the books came seemed merely a culturally prestigious mode of positive publicity.

If the world recognized Latin American literature as a commercially viable high literature, though, it still valued it as a high literature for the oppressed. The two younger writers who gained the most international renown in the first two decades of the twenty-first century were Juan Gabriel Vásquez and Alejandro Zambra. The Colombian Vásquez attracted notice for his chronicling of the Colombian drug wars in *El ruido de las cosas al caer* (*The Sound of Things Falling*, 2011) and his rewriting of Joseph Conrad (and tacitly of García Márquez) in *Historia secreta de Costaguana* (*The Secret History of Costaguana*, 2007). The Chilean Zambra's pellucid *récits* reflect obliquely back on his childhood in the Pinochet dictatorship, as in *Formas de volver a casa* (2011) translated into English as *Ways of Going Home* (2013). Zambra's peripheral and ironic stance towards the traumatic experience, as the Belgian critic Bieke Willem suggests, is a model for writers in similar positions in very different cultures. Willem's phrase, "a suburban revision of nostalgia," indicates how Zambra's effect can be both specific to his own natal and cultural conditions and yet semantically available for export to other situations.

The global publishing category these books inhabit was enabled by the emergence of a body of Latin American fiction that extended the Western tradition towards people victimized, sidelined, or excluded by the West. This continuing link can be seen in Valeria Luiselli's *Lost Children Archive* (2019). Luiselli is a younger Mexican writer who is well established in the contemporary Mexican canon. But she chose to write this book in English. Far from being a sellout to the language of global hegemony, Luiselli's skillful use of documentary self-awareness, a steeping in European philosophy and aesthetics, and a radical openness to the suffering of migrants and displaced people, is a deep challenge to continuing hegemonic assumptions. Luiselli turns the English language inward, to undermine and subvert its hierarchal assumptions. The world influence of the Latin American novel has, although mediated by institutions and particular critical desires, persistently drawn attention to perspectives and experiences that otherwise would not have been heard.

Notes

1. The two political leaders are Ecuadorian President Jaime Roldós, killed in an airplane crash on May 24, 1981, and Omar Torrijos, Panamanian military leader and key figure in the negotiations with the United States regarding the handover of the Canal Zone to his country, who died in a crash on July 31, 1981.
2. "Titre surprenant" (Decante 150).
3. "Une certaine 'modernité'" (Decante 150).

Works Cited

Amado, Jorge. *Doña Flor and Her Two Husbands*, tr. Harriet de Onís, Avon, 1969.

Aravamudan, Srinivas. *Tropicopolitans: Colonialism and Agency*. Duke UP, 1999.

Azuela, Mariano. *The Underdogs*, tr. Enrique Mangula, Jr., Brentano's, 1929.

Barth, John. *The Tidewater Tales*. New York: Putnam, 1987.

Beckman, Ericka. "Jorge Isaacs's *María* and the Space-Time of Global Capitalism." *SEL Studies in English Literature 1500–1900*, vol. 56, no. 3, 2016, pp. 539–59.

Buzard, James. *Disorienting Fiction: The Autoethnographic Work of 19th-Century British Novels*. Princeton UP, 2005.

Carpentier, Alejo, *Explosion in a Cathedral*, tr. John Sturrock, Gollancz, 1963.

Casanova, Pascale. *The World Republic of Letters*. Translated by M. B. DeBevoise. Harvard UP, 2004.

Christ, Ronald. *The Narrow Act: Borges's Art of Allusion*. New York UP, 1969.

Conrad, Joseph. *Nostromo: A Tale of the Seaboard*. Harper, 1904.

Cortázar, Julio, *Hopscotch*, tr. Gregory Rabassa, New York: Pantheon, 1967.

Corral, Wilfrido. with Juan E. De Castro and Nicholas Birns. *The Contemporary Spanish American Novel*. Bloomsbury, 2013.

Decante, Stephanie. "Réalisme virtuel contre réalisme magique: préface et Nouvelles de *McOndo.*" *América, cahiers de CRICCAL*, vol. 2, 2000, pp. 105–14.

De Castro, Juan E. *The Spaces of Latin American Literature*. Palgrave, 2008.

De Man, Paul. "A Modern Master." *The New York Review of Books*, November 19, 1964. https://www.nybooks.com/articles/1964/11/19/a-modern-master/

Donoso, José. *The Boom in Spanish-American Literature: A Personal History*. Columbia UP, 1977.

Fuentes, Carlos, *Where The Air Is Clear*. Tr. SamHileman, Obolensky, 1960.

García Márquez, Gabriel. "The Solitude of Latin America." https://www.nobelprize.org/prizes/literature/1982/marquez/lecture/1982

de Oré, Luis Jerónimo. *Accounts of The Martyrs*. Edited and translated by Raquel Chang-Rodríguez. U of New Mexico P, 2017.

García Márquez, Gabriel. *The Autumn of the Patriarch*, tr. Gregory Rabassa, Harper, 1976.

García Márquez, Gabriel. *One Hundred Years of Solitude*, tr. Gregory Rabassa, Harper and Row, 1970.

Goytisolo, Juan. "Captives of Our 'Classics.'" *New York Times Book Review*, May 26, 1985, p. 1.

Grace, Patricia. *PotikI*. Penguin New Zealand, 1986.

Hostova, Ivana. *Identity and Translation Trouble*. Cambridge Scholars, 2017.

Luiselli, Valeria. *Lost Children Archive*. Knopf, 2019.

Machado de Assis, Joaquim Maria. *Dom Casmurro*. Translated by Helen Caldwell, introduction by Waldo Frank. Noonday Press, 1953.

Naipaul, V. S. *A Way in The World*. Knopf, 1994.

Oates, Joyce Carol. *Bellefleur*. Dutton, 1980.

Puig, Manuel, IKiss of the Spider WomanI. Tr. Thomas Colchie, New York: Random House, 1979.

Quijano, Aníbal. "Coloniality of Power: Eurocentrism and Latin America." Translated by Michael Ennis. *Nepantla: Views from South*, vol. 1, no. 3, 2000, pp. 533–80.

Raymont, Henry. "Latin Writers Stirring Up New York Publishers' Interest," *The New York Times*, April 15, 1969, p. 41.

Reeder, Jessie. *The Forms of Informal Empire*. Johns Hopkins UP, 2020.

Roa Bastos, Augusto, *I. The Supreme*, tr Helen R. Lane. Knopf, 1986.

Rushdie, Salman. *Midnight's Children*. Jonathan Cape, 1981.

Sawhney, Minni. "Latin American Studies in the Indian Classroom," *LASA Forum*, fall 2014, Web. https://forum.lasaweb.org/files/vol45-issue4/Dossier-2.pdf

Sommer, Doris. *Foundational Fictions: The National Romances of Latin America*. U of California P, 1993.

Stepan, Alfred. *Rethinking Military Politics: Brazil and the Southern Cone*. Princeton UP, 1988.

Stone, Robert. "Revolution as Ritual." Review of *The War of the End of the World* by Mario

Swift, Graham. *Waterland*. Heinemann, 1983.

Vargas Llosa, Mario, *Conversation in the CathedraI*. Tr. Gregory Rabassa, New York: Harper and Row, 1974.

Vargas Llosa, *New York Times*, August 12, 1984. https://archive.nytimes.com/www.nytimes.com/books/98/06/28/specials/llosa-war.html

Vargas Llosa, Mario, *The Time of The Hero*, tr. Lysander kemp, Grove, 1963.

Vargas Llosa, Mario, *The War Of The End of The World*, tr. Helen R. Lane, Farrar, Straus, and Giroux, 1984.

Vásquez, Juan Gabriel, *The Secret History of Costaguana*, Ir. Anne McLean, New York: Riverhead Books, 2012.

Vásquez, Juan Gabriel, *The Sound of Things Falling*, tr. Anne McLean, Riverhead, 2013.

Walsh, Thomas. "Brazil's Literary Figures." *The New York Times Book Review*, February 18, 1923, p. 8.

Wei, Teng, "On Depoliticized Politics: Roberto Bolaño's Reception in China," *Roberto Bolaño as World Literature*, edited by Juan E. De Castro and Nicholas Birns, Bloomsbury, 2017. pp. 167–82.

Willem, Bieke. "A Suburban Revision of Nostalgia: The Case of Alejandro Zambra's *Ways of Going Home*," *Literature and the Peripheral City*, edited by Lieven Ameel, Palgrave Macmillan, 2015,pp. 184–97, pp. 167–82.

Wright, Alexis. *Carpentaria*. Giramondo, 2006.

Zambra, Alejandro. *Ways of Going Home*, tr. Megan McDowell, Farrar, Straus, and Giroux, 2013.

CHAPTER 45

THE LATIN AMERICAN NOVEL AS WORLD LITERATURE

BENJAMIN LOY

LATIN American literature's location within the global literary field has been strongly debated in the numerous theorizations presented within the world literature paradigm as the idea rose to new prominence over the past twenty-five years. These debates have focused on two closely related aspects in particular: the question on how to situate Latin America with regard to an assumed "Western" center; and the theoretical and methodological premises on which these mappings to be based. Two of the most discussed approaches are Pascale Casanova's and Franco Moretti's respectively. Both share a clear spatial distinction between center and periphery within the "World Republic of Letters," which is to be conceived of as exclusively within the one-dimensional logic of Western modernity. This kind of spatialized history, however, is ultimately justified by what Casanova calls the "temporal law of the world of letters," which means needing "to be old in order to have any chance of being modern or of decreeing what is modern" (89). According to this point of view, criticized by Latin American scholars as "hegelianismo superficial" ("superficial Hegelianism") (Sánchez Prado, "Hijos" 28), Latin American literatures can never aspire to be more than recipients, or imitators of the center's innovative forms. This notion of hierarchy in both cases is closely related to the methodological and epistemological premises of Casanova and Moretti that, instead of case studies or close readings that might alter and relativize their concepts, look to field theory (Casanova) and *distant reading* (Moretti) to create their positivist models of global literary evolution.

Without denying the fact that the global literary system is "simultaneously one, and unequal" (Moretti 46), numerous scholars of Latin American literature have questioned this sort of literary determinism by offering alternative readings centering on the complexity and non-linearity of processes of circulation and translation, as well as on the Eurocentric notions of spatiality and temporality.[1] The theoretical and methodological bases to these approaches tend mostly to emphasize the sociological, material, and economical dimensions of world literature on a concrete scale, as well as the value of close reading and the literary text itself as genuine spaces of "worlding" (Cheah). While the first tendency has been recently explored by a new wave of publications centered on processes of translation and global book markets,[2] the latter is the point of departure of Héctor Hoyos's exemplary study on the *Global Latin American Novel*. It focuses on the ability of certain novels to articulate forms of "world consciousness" and "to preserve, not resolve, tensions between particularism and generalization, vernacular and widely understood linguistic practices, high-prestige and low-prestige denominations, cultural essentials and relativism, 'parochial' and 'world-class' aesthetic values, and locally embedded and abstractly detached art forms" (22–23). One of the innovative points in Hoyos's book is that it brings out global dimensions of Latin American novels that had been read mostly from local perspectives (such as Diamela Eltit's *Mano de obra* [*Labor Force*, 2002]). However, this specific notion of the global Latin American novel raises two questions that will be of importance as we continue to approach this subject:

1. If global, according to Hoyos, "is nothing more and nothing less than a metaphor that operates according to the paradoxical logic of *multum in parvo*" (5)—would it then not be ultimately possible to read almost every novel as a sort of "global novel," considering that every "local" narrative scenario in one way or another can be opened up into a wider global "embeddedness"? As the boundaries of this category of "worldliness" are necessarily unstable, it seems more convenient to conceive it as a scale. In other words: the dimension of the "global" can be more or less explicit in a novel, ranging from genuine cosmopolitan aesthetics to rather encrypted forms of "worldliness."[3]

2. Is it truly possible to speak about a novel as world literature without taking into account the question of a text's effective circulation on an international scale (or lack thereof)? To provide an example: despite her wide recognition in Chile and Latin America, Diamela Eltit (1949–) has had little reception and circulation by the global literary market. Thus labelling her work as world literature would be anything but self-evident. It is obvious that dimensions like circulation or sales numbers will never fully determine the belonging of a work to the category of world literature. However, to leave them out and to ignore that world literature is something that only exists and, to use David Damrosch's notorious expression, "gains in translation" (289), has the effect of transforming the label into a rather arbitrary concept without any "real-world" anchoring.

In view of these introductory remarks, this article aims to give an overview of the history of the Latin American novel as world literature between modernity and the present by focusing on the changing material and aesthetic conditions of its production. For the sake of greater analytical coherence, we will consider as "global' " novels in a stricter sense texts that, on the one hand, exhibit (more or less explicitly) forms of "worldliness" and cosmopolitanism and, on the other hand, novels that have (at least to some degree) acquired international visibility and circulation. Building upon the broad and recent research on Latin American world literature, the structure of this text is threefold: my point of departure is modernist cosmopolitan "world consciousness" and the early forms of global circulation of Latin American novels (1880–1960); then, I briefly treat the well-researched global dimension of the Boom and post-Boom novels as world literature between 1960 and 1990; finally, and more in detail, I will examine the fundamental changes in the Latin American and global book markets after 1990, and how new material and aesthetic constellations have shaped the contemporary Latin American novel in and as world literature.

Global Consciousness, (Mostly) Local Novels (1880–1960)

Latin America's entry to world literature began at the end of the nineteenth century with the rise of *modernismo*—not so much in the sense of an effective presence of works in the European literary centers of Paris and London but in the creation of what Mariano Siskind famously calls "cosmopolitan desires." The post colonial constellation of Latin America and the changing material conditions of global modernity enabled a new group of authors to transform the world of letters into "a blank screen for the projection of their modern hopes. It is a discursive attempt to posit a literature outside Latin American literature, one that they imagine as a universal repository of modernist aesthetics where marginal cosmopolitans find the bits and pieces they can put together to articulate a nonparticularistic cultural modernization" (Siskind, *Cosmopolitan Desires* 104). This cosmopolitan discourse, which goes hand in hand with the search for a continental identity, is articulated by authors such as José Martí (1853–1895), Rubén Darío (1867–1916), and José Enrique Rodó (1871–1917). The latter, for example, notes in a programmatic text entitled "La novela nueva" ("The New Novel," 1896), which seems to anticipate Borges's famous essay "El escritor argentino y la tradición" ("The Argentine Writer and Tradition," 1951), that it is "necessary to convince that the ideal image for thought is not in the roots that burrow but in the tops of the tree splayed in the air and that the borders on maps are not the geography of the spirit and that one's intellectual homeland is not one's country."[4]

However, this new consciousness of the world hardly found a material equivalent as Latin America did not register as an engine of cultural exports. Indeed, up until World War I, the region's literature was made for internal consumption. Given the enormous geographic spread and the limited means of book production, literary distribution was penurious across the continent, which meant that national literatures were defined by the local and almost entirely self-contained. (Stavans 292)

If short forms, such as *crónicas* and poetry, had a certain international circulation thanks to modernist magazines and newspapers, this hardly applied to Latin American novels which—notwithstanding their aesthetic quality—fit mostly into what Moretti describes as the "compromise between a western formal influence (usually French or English) and local materials" (50). However, this sort of "compromise" would soon turn out to be a distinctive mark of modern Latin American literature and its cosmopolitan aesthetics: not being bound to vernacular traditions, Latin American writers—and novelists in particular—were free to be "lectores salvajes" ("wild readers"), to use a term coined by Alberto Julián Pérez. Their literary production was based on innovative readings and a detached recombination of European modernism and Spanish (neo)baroque forms, intermixed with elements of local and indigenist traditions, or as Mexican writer Alfonso Reyes (1889–1959) stated in 1942, "Tradition has weighed less, and this explains their boldness" (120).[5]

In a way, this model also turned out to be accurate in describing the creation of what would later be Latin America's most famous contribution to world literature: magical realism. In their novels, writers such as Miguel Ángel Asturias (1899–1974) and Alejo Carpentier (1904–1980) marked the beginnings of this internationally oriented aesthetics with continental identitarian ends. Other writers, such as Adolfo Bioy Casares (1914–1999) and Juan Rulfo (1917–1986), would contribute to the development of new narrative forms with novels such as *La invención de Morel* (*The Invention of Morel*, 1940) and *Pedro Páramo* (1955). The dominant literary forms of the time, however, were shorter narrative (and poetic) forms. This had much to do with the precarious state of the Latin American publishing industry in the first half of the twentieth century. The lack of a professional publishing infrastructure hindered the transnational circulation of books within Latin America (and beyond). Full-time writers were an exception and print runs hardly ever exceeded a few thousand copies. However cosmopolitan the aesthetics of these Latin American authors may have been and even when their work was translated relatively quickly after first publication (as in the case of Rulfo, for example)— the material conditions and the scarce circulation make it difficult to speak of a truly global Latin American novel before 1960.

THE RISE AND FALL OF THE NEW LATIN AMERICAN NOVEL: BOOM AND POST-BOOM (1960–1990)

The 1960s saw the rise of a set of decisive conditions that would transform the Latin American novel into what Mads Rosendahl Thomsen calls a "temporal sub-center" (35) in world literature. These conditions were both aesthetic and material: the first step, as William Marling and Álvaro Santana-Acuña point out in their groundbreaking studies on Gabriel García Márquez, consisted in the creation of a common label, the New Latin American Novel, and a region-spanning form of literary standardization (Santana 41). In a new and highly collaborative manner, writers such as Mario Vargas Llosa (1936), Gabriel García Márquez (1927–2014), Carlos Fuentes (1928–2012), and Julio Cortázar (1914–1984) shaped a new form of Latin American novel-writing that combined the narrative innovation of modernist European and American novels and representations of Latin American history suitable for export and an international readership. At the same time, the enhancement of the material conditions for these processes of literary circulation was of decisive importance: a new network of transregional Latin American publishers and literary magazines allowed the authors' idea of an overarching Latin American type of writing and identity to find a larger non-national readership. Gatekeepers, agents, and literary prizes contributed in establishing Boom authors on the transatlantic publishing circuit. Barcelona became the new hub for their burgeoning worldwide circulation. Translations and new series dedicated to Latin American novels (such as the "Croix du Sud" series at Gallimard or the "Lateinamerika-Programm" at Suhrkamp) provided not only the Boom authors but also their precursors a fixed place in the contemporary canon of world literature. Political factors played a role as well: the Cuban Revolution shifted the attention of Western readers to Latin American culture and politics, while the ideologically driven sponsoring of translations by East and West also pushed their politically "preferred" literary visions of Latin America.[6] Considering the amount and importance of material factors here, the Boom authors are proof of my initial thesis that a discussion of world literature only makes sense if we take into account the concrete circulation of books and recognize the vital dimension of the literary market. To cite Santana's observation on García Márquez: "Counterfactually, if *One Hundred Years of Solitude* had been published in the 1920 and 1930s, if would have passed as work of *regionalista* literature" (38).

As for the "worldliness" and "global" aesthetics of the New Latin American Novel, the international success enjoyed by the emerging Latin American world literature seems somewhat paradoxical: the narrative spaces of novels such as García Márquez's *Cien años de soledad* (*One Hundred Years of Solitude*, 1967), Vargas Llosa's *La casa verde* (*The Green House*, 1966), and Fuentes's *La muerte de Artemio Cruz* (*The Death of Artemio Cruz*, 1962) are mostly limited to local backdrops and stories. However, it was precisely this kind of locally-grounded "exoticism" that appealed—in combination with the Boom's intertextual and formal references to a modernist canon—to the Western reading public. This was especially the case for the novelistic subgenre of magical realism. Nevertheless, in other regions of the world, and particularly in the Global South, the Boom was read in a completely different, postcolonial way. Works like *One Hundred Years of Solitude* rendered visible "the relation between the universality of (colonial, postcolonial, capitalistic) modern history, and the particularity of local forms of oppression" (Siskind, "Magical Realism" 855). In this sense, the "worldliness" of the New Latin American Novel can be read as grounded in the representativity and assimilability of its local contexts for different readerships across the globe. The merit of the Boom novels, as stated earlier, was not only their anchoring of Latin American literature on the map of world literature but their inauguration of a process of global commodification of a "unified [Latin American] identity from sports to music that was easy to export" (299), as Stavans notes on the effects of the Boom in the 1980s. However, it is worth noting once and again that this "representativity" of the Boom novels in world literature was in reality confined to the work of a small group of white, middle-class, male writers that in its success overshadowed alternative forms of novelistic production, notably that of female and indigenous writers.

By the late 1980s the once-innovative genre of the New Latin American Novel, and magical realism in particular, had begun to fade along with the Boom as a whole. This had to do with both political and material conditions: the revolutionary hopes and the idea of the engaged novelist as an agent of social change had been swept away by the wave of dictatorial regimes coming to power in the region and their shutting down of the cultural freedom and exchange of the previous decades. The collapse of the Latin American publishing industry contributed to this notion of exhaustion that found its aesthetic counterpart in the commodification of magical realism by so-called post-Boom authors like Isabel Allende (1942–), who transformed the genre into a "pure aesthetic form disengaged from the traumatic historical displacement that had constituted its context of emergence at the height of its cultural-political power" (Siskind, *Cosmopolitan Desires* 95). At the end of the Cold War, and in the context of the epochal change of 1989, the Latin American novel had reached a turning point that prefigured the new literary aesthetics and fundamental changes to come within the global book markets in the 1990s.

Changing Logics in a Multipolar World: The Global Latin American Novel (1990–2020)

The dissolution of the world's bipolar structure following 1989 was progressively mirrored in the field of world literature by the differentiation and inclusion of "new players" in the global literary market. The growing interest of Western publishers in writers and works from Eastern Europe, Africa, and Asia led to fundamental changes in the structure of global publishing and shifts in readers' attention to these "emergent" regions in world literature. This affected Latin American literature(s) and their formulas for world literary success from prior decades. The established topics of Latin American exoticism and exceptionalism—important factors in the Boom authors' reception—began to fade in view of a growing normalization of the region's political and economic realities. This does not mean that the García Márquez & Co. Generation disappeared overnight;[7] rather, as Gustavo Guerrero points out, the 1990s are marked by an intergenerational struggle, in the sense of a "pronounced gap between the anachronism of the former, who still lay claim to a progressively more questioned representativity, and the difficulty of the latter, who search for means to establish their distance from the former and establish a different identity" (153).[8]

At the same time, Latin American publishing industries came almost completely under the control of international conglomerates, an effect of an "aggressive policy of acquisition on the part of Spanish enterprises" (Yúdice 651).[9] These processes of concentration of market power led, as Jorge Locane argues, to a two-fold logic in the production of Latin American literatures and novels in particular with on the one hand a type of literature published by internationally operating publishers, labelled "literatura latinoamericana" ("Latin American literature"), and tailored to international circulation and readership; and on the other hand, a different form of local literature, "a Latin American literature produced in conditions of material precarity that, despite or precisely for this reason, favor the development of dissident and alternative aesthetic forms" (Locane, *De la literatura latinoamericana* 48).[10] Though this separation, in view of some writers that publish with both local and international publishing houses, turns out to be slightly more complex, the basic dichotomy between authors/works circulating on an international scale and others that, for different reasons, never transcend their regional or national realm, is accurate.

However, the novels that are part of this Latin American world literature at the turn of the millennium are not characterized by a common unity of literary form. Rather, what they have in common is that from the start of their production they are usually embedded in clear-cut networks and processes of selection, promotion, and circulation on an international scale. The same goes for the new generation of authors trying to undermine the traditional and over-politized author-images of their Boom-precursors through alternative forms of authorship such as the "joven escritor" ("young writer") (Guerrero 156) and the "escritor apátrida" ("stateless writer") (Volpi 193). However, they ultimately all have one thing in common: their international circulation depends essentially on the decisions of internationally operating Spanish publishing houses and literary prizes. Other factors that have intensified the production of Latin American novels for a global audience are the growing professionalization and differentiation of the business of literary agents and translators, the creation of national translation programs as part of new foreign cultural politics (particularly in Argentina, Brazil, and Chile), as well as the increased importance of international bookfairs (Frankfurt, Guadalajara, etc.) and literary festivals (Bogotá 39, Hay Festival, etc.) as spaces for the trading of book rights and for granting visibility to specific authors within a new and global "economy of prestige," to use a term coined by James English.

Nevertheless, the literary aesthetics and authorial strategies within the field of the Latin American novel oriented toward world literature between 1990 and the present exhibit a vast diversity. The first and most prominent phenomena in this respect can be seen in two collective manifestos. *McOndo* was the title of an anthology published by the Chileans Alberto Fuguet (1963–) and Sergio Gómez (1962–) in 1996. It incorporated some of the later most renowned authors of their generation like Rodrigo Fresán (1963–) and Edmundo Paz Soldán (1967–), even if the majority of them, including Fuguet and Gómez, did not have lasting literary success. The second was the manifesto published in 1996 by the Mexican group *Crack* (its members were Jorge Volpi (1968–), Ignacio Padilla (1968–2016), Eloy Urroz (1967–), Pedro Ángel Palou (1966–), Vicente Herrasti (1967–), and Ricardo Chávez-Castañeda (1961–)). Without going into detail with regard to these exhaustively studied movements, we can state retrospectively that their impact must be localized on the meta-level of debating the conditions of production of Latin American literature from the perspective of the global book market, rather than on the level of literary content and quality itself. While *McOndo* focused on a critique of the petrification of Latin American literature and culture(s) through the paradigm of magical realism and posited a new (self-)image based on buzzwords such as "lo bastardo, lo híbrido" ("what is bastard, what is hybrid" (Fuguet/Gómez 15)), the *Crack* members gravitated around a new "estética de dislocación" ("aesthetics of dislocation") as essential part of a cosmopolitan critique against the magical realist imperative (see Sánchez Prado, *Strategic Occidentalism* 77).[11] If *McOndo* argued for a renewed image of Latin America that, nevertheless, maintained the continental perspective of its precursors, the *Crack* manifesto erased any vernacular dimension, instead basing its aesthetic program for the groups' coming novels on the essence of a Western modernist canon (see Palou's "first commandment" in the manifesto: "You will love Proust over all the others"—"Amarás a Proust sobre todos los otros") (Volpi et al.). However, the effective presence of these authors within world literature was ultimately scarce, despite a certain visibility and several prizes and translations of Volpi and Padilla's novels. The strategy of a new Latin American literary aesthetic that would either assimilate the image of the continent into global urban realities (*McOndo*) in a sort of "estilo internacional" ("international style") (Echevarría, *Desvíos* 175), or purge almost any trace of local specificity (*Crack*) did not seem to appeal to the global book market and its readers.

It can thus be said that in the late 1990s, "U.S. publishers, critics, and readers seemed to be awaiting the appearance of the successor to García Márquez, a new author-figure around whose persona and work the terms of a new breed of Latin American fiction [could] be fixed" (Pollack 353). Here the rise of Roberto Bolaño (1953–2003) as the new global paradigm of the Latin American novel occurred. The reasons for Bolaño's success have been widely discussed and all of them played their part. As an author-figure, Bolaño combined several ingredients that made him suitable for the creation of a new Latin American myth. For one, his early death at the age of fifty, which preceded his canonization in world literature, allowed for unchallenged projections onto his persona. These included his imprisonment under Pinochet (true but over-emphasized, as testimonies have proven), his alleged drug addiction (false), and his supposedly "savage" life as an outlaw poet (truest of his younger years in Mexico but definitely false for the rest of his life in Spain). The principal reason for his success, however, must be seen in Bolaño's "ability to connect with readers of all stripes" (Echevarría, "Bolaño internacional" 176). This is especially pronounced in his novels and concerns not only their "readability" and detective plots but also the possibility of establishing intertextual connectivity for readers from the most heterogeneous cultural and literary contexts (Loy, "Mocking World Literature"). In addition to this, Bolaño's novels, such as *Los detectives salvajes* (*The Savage Detectives*, 1998) and *2666* (2004), are characterized by their world consciousness, even if their "globality" in a stricter sense is limited to a European-American narrative space (Africa or Asia, except for a few scattered episodes, do not form part of Bolaño's world).

Bolaño, as Nicholas Birns observes, reminds "the reader that Latin America is not just a surreal world on its own, like a science-fiction locale, but a part of the world. . . . Whereas the Boom writers might have seen Latin America as a catastrophic special case . . . Bolaño links issues in the political life of Mexico and Chile with the effect and aftermath of global totalitarianisms of both right and left" (59). This is also the reason why

Bolaño can be considered as the point of departure of a new form of the contemporary Global Latin American novel, one "that embodies the intensification of cultural inter-dependence in the post-1989 period, conceiving totalities from its own historical coordinates" (Hoyos 191). Thus, Bolaño combines the two factors we initially fixed as basic conditions to classify a work and author as world literature: an effective global reception and a literary "worldliness" that is all the more pronounced in Bolaño's novels, as they "unite three diverse strands of world-literary criticism which often remain separate within academia: the materialist study of reception, production, and dissemination in the market; the study of the evolution of the aesthetics and form in order to represent the new 'global' content; and the study of the politics and aesthetics of translation" (Deckard 205–6).

It is obvious that Bolaño's global success has, in much the same manner as the Boom authors before him, overshadowed the work of most of his fellow writers, transforming him into a "synecdochal figure . . . who in many circles has come to represent the en-tirety of contemporary Latin American literature" (Hoyos 7). However, the main difference between Bolaño and his contemporaries, as well as the following generation of authors born in the 1960s, 1970s, and 1980s, lies in the fact that virtually none of them created a comparable and internationally recognizable aesthetics of a *Latin American novel*—that is, an iconic vision of continental dimensions that was also read as such outside of the Spanish-speaking world. Instead of this, the post-Bolaño generation[12] departs from a different perspective that is not (or at least not primarily) centered on the history and reality of Latin America as a whole, even if this does not mean that "Latin America has disappeared as the principal location or center of interest, but that it begins to be perceived as having a postnational character, lacking a fixed identity" (Volpi 176).[13] This "lack of identity" has certainly changed the conditions of the international reception of the Latin American novel: although the models embodied by the Boom authors and Bolaño are still important reference points for publishers, critics, and readers, contemporary writers and their works can hardly be categorized in the same way as their precursors. As welcome as this fact may be in terms of providing for a greater diversity of styles and a more differentiated, less clichéd notion of Latin America, it definitely has complicated the task of placing Latin American authors on the global book market.[14]

Consequently, an appraisal of the contemporary Global Latin American Novel must be centered on certain subgenres and individual authors rather than on a comprehensive aesthetics (as in the case of the Boom authors, even if their works were far more diverse than the unifying, market-oriented label of the Boom suggests). For example, this holds true for the probably most-renowned contemporary Latin American author, whose broader global reception started somewhat belatedly after 2010, despite his being a contemporary of Bolaño's: César Aira (1949–). His work stands, like that of Mario Bellatin (1960–), for an experimental strain in Latin American literature that in the international reception has tended to be read through its affinity to (post)modernist world literature rather than to questions of Latin American history and identity in a stricter sense.

As for the popular subgenres of the contemporary Latin American novel in world literature, there is the broad corpus of Latin American novels dedicated to Nazism and the Latin American entanglements with the historical movement and its aftermath. This relates to a specific global constellation of memory-literature and can be considered a "displaced figure of globalization" (Hoyos 26). Latin American Nazi-novels range from *Crack* member Jorge Volpi's *En busca de Klingsor* (*In Search of Klingsor*, 1999) and Ignacio Padilla's *Amphitryon* (*Shadow Without a Name*, 2000) to more recent novels such as Edgardo Cozarinsky's (1939–) *Lejos de dónde* (Far from Where, 2009), Eduardo Halfon's (1971–) *El boxeador polaco* (*The Polish Boxer*, 2008), Lucía Puenzo's (1976–) *Wakolda* (*The German Doctor*, 2011), and Rodrigo Hasbún's (1981–) *Los afectos* (*Affections*, 2015).

The memory of Latin America's political violence of the second half of the twentieth century, already a keystone in some of the Boom authors' and Bolaño's works, has kept appealing to a global audience and has been present throughout contemporary Latin American novels in world literature. This holds particularly true for a set of post-memory-novels written by a younger generation of writers. Some examples in this extensive corpus with international circulation are works such as Alejandro Zambra's (1975–) *Formas de volver a casa* (*Ways of Going Home*, 2011), Patricio Pron's (1975–) *El espíritu de mis padres sigue subiendo en la lluvia* (*My Father's Ghost is Climbing in the Rain*, 2011), Alia Trabucco Zéran's (1983–) *La resta* (*The Remainder*, 2015), and Nona Fernández's (1971–) *Chilean Electric* (2015), with all of these authors hailing from the Southern Cone. In Brazil there is Julián Fuks's (1981–) *A resistência* (*Resistance*, 2015); in Colombia, Héctor Abad Faciolince's (1958–) *El olvido que seremos* (*Oblivion*, 2005) and Juan Gabriel Vásquez's (1973–) *El ruido de las cosas al caer* (*The Sound of Things Falling*, 2011); in Peru, Claudia Salazar's (1976–) *La sangre de la Aurora* (*Blood of the Dawn*, 2013) and Diego Trelles Paz's (1977–) *La procesión infinita* (*The Endless Procession*, 2017); and in El Salvador Claudia Hernández's (1975–) *Roza, tumba, quema* (*Slash and Burn*, 2017), to name just a few examples.

Another perspective on specific forms of "worldliness" in contemporary Latin American novels is to be found in an equally extensive corpus about different forms of migration and global entanglements between Latin America and other regions of the world. Examples would be novels about relationships between Latin America and Asia, such as José Manuel Prieto's (1962–) "Russian novels" like *Rex* (2007), Ariel Magnus's (1975–) *Un chino en bicicleta* (*A Chinese Man on a Bike*, 2007), Santiago Gamboa's (1965–) *Hotel Pekín* (2008), and Julián Herbert's (1971–) *La casa del dolor ajeno* (*The House of the Pain of Others*, 2015); on African and Arab dimensions, there is Rodrigo Rey Rosa's (1958–) *La orilla africana* (*The African Shore*, 1999) and Lina Meruane's (1970–) (rather essayistic) *Volverse Palestina* (*Become Palestinian*, 2014); and on Latin American migration to the United States, particularly in the works of internationally-acclaimed Mexican authors, such as Yuri Herrera's (1970–) *Señales que precederán al fin del mundo* (*Signs Preceding the End of the World*, 2009), Antonio Ortuño's (1976–) *La fila india* (*The Indian Queue*, 2013), Aura Xilonen's (1995–) *Campeón Gabacho* (*The Gringo Champion*, 2015), and Valeria Luiselli's (1983–) *Lost Children Archive* (2019).

Xilonen's and Luiselli's books would also be examples of another recent trend in Latin American novel production: writing in other languages than Spanish and Portuguese. Besides Xilonen's Spanglish, a linguistic phenomenon present in the works of many

Latinx authors, other writers such as Peruvian Daniel Alarcón (1977–) in *Lost City Radio* (2007), Dominican Junot Díaz (1968–) in *The Brief Wondrous Life of Oscar Wao* (2007), and Luiselli in the mentioned novel written in English. Yet other authors, such as Argentines Laura Alcoba (1968–) (*Manège*, 2007) and María Cecilia Barbetta (1972–) (*Nachtleuchten*, 2018), publish acclaimed novels in French and German. Beyond this, the question of a specific language and style of Latin American novels written for a global market has been discussed with regard to Rebecca Walkowitz's influential book *Born translated*, particularly with regard to the works of authors like Valeria Luiselli (see Logie) and Guadalupe Nettel (see Locane, *De la literatura latinoamericana* 143).

However, the most remarkable tendency of the contemporary Latin American novel in world literature is probably a new predominance of female writers from the whole continent, in contrast to the male-dominated reception of the twentieth century. Their massive presence on the (Latin) American and international scale has led critics to proclaim a new "Boom femenino," which proves once more the longevity of this pattern of reading for international readers of Latin American literature. Regardless of the label, the observation that the contemporary Latin American novel in world literature is dominated by women (see Gallego Cuiñas, "Feminismo y literatura (argentina) mundial") is uncontested. So is the fact that many of these novels allow for readings as "global novels" in the sense of a genuinely globalist aesthetics. A prime example of this would be the work of Samanta Schweblin (1978–). In her short novel *Distancia de rescate* (*Fever Dream*, 2014), she combines the principles of fantastic narration with a critique of the global soy industry and its agrobusiness in Argentina, while in *Kentukis* (*Little Eyes*, 2018), a novel about the issues of planetary digital communication, she creates a truly global setting with locales from Hong Kong to Lima. All of Schweblin's texts play with elements of horror, which has become, in different forms, one of the preferred subgenres of a new generations of female writers in Latin America with international visibility. Novels such as Agustina Bazterrica's (1974–) *Cadaver exquisito* (*Tender is the Flesh*, 2017), Mónica Ojeda's (1988–) *Mandíbula* (*Jaw*, 2018), and Mariana Enríquez's (1973–) *Nuestra parte de noche* (*Our Part of the Night*, 2019) are proof of this.

The rise of this new generation of female writers has gone hand in hand with substantial changes in the publishing world and the Latin American and global book market. In Latin America (and Spain), the overwhelming market power of multinational conglomerates has been countered in the past two decades by a growing network of new independent publishers that have been vital for the publication and distribution of many Latin American authors on their way into world literature (Becerra; Gallego Cuiñas, "Bibliodiversidad"). The same goes for recent trends in the United States and the United Kingdom where new editorial projects such as Coffee House Press, Graywolf, Deep Vellum, And Other Stories, and Charco Press have been the hubs of this new generation of writers in English translation. New success stories of Latin American female writing like Valeria Luiselli (Sánchez Prado, "El efecto Luiselli") and the re-discovering and (re-)translation of other twentieth-century key figures like Clarice Lispector (1920–1977) (spurred by Benjamin Moser's biography) have been important within these processes of circulation too.

One of the most telling examples of this fundamental change might be the International Booker Prize. While the Latin American nominees in the first three rounds from 2005 to 2009 were García Márquez, Fuentes, and Vargas Llosa, the candidates on the long and short-lists between 2015 and 2020 were César Aira, Raduan Nassar (1935–), Juan Gabriel Vásquez, Samanta Schweblin (twice), Ariana Harwicz (1977–), Alia Trabucco Zerán, and Gabriela Cabezón Cámara (1968–). These new networks inside and outside Latin America have also enabled a new visibility for writers from Latin American and Caribbean countries traditionally underrepresented on the global book market, as proven recently by Dominican Rita Indiana (1977–), Ecuadorian María Fernanda Ampuero (1976–), and Bolivian Liliana Colanzi (1981–).

CONCLUSION

Recent research on Latin American literature in and as world literature has emphasized the necessity of alternative and specialized readings as counterparts to generalist mappings of the global literary field. Instead of the Hegelian and, as in the case of Casanova, visibly melancholic attempts to read and order the world from the point of view of the European center (for one last time), an adequate history of world literature in modernity is only conceivable as the always-elusive history of heterogenous developments. This does not mean that power relations and center-periphery aspects do not matter. The opposite is true, as we have seen—global literary spaces essentially depend on materialist categories that are determined by relations of economic inequality, as we define them through categories of production, selection, translation, and circulation. However, the global literary space is criss-crossed by trails beside the main roads of market-driven publishers' politics. Even peripheral literatures—and Latin America offers a strong tradition of examples ranging from Borges to Bolaño—are capable of intervening directly with the aesthetic principles of the center (Sánchez Prado, "Hijos" 29). In the global literary field, material shortcomings do not coincide with a boundedness of ideas.

The history of the Latin American novel in world literature unfolds within these dialectics of the imaginary and the material. Its modernist writers think globally but lack the means to be at the same level as their peers from the center. During the glory years of the Boom, we saw the coincidence of both factors, imaginary and material. The present, however, is characterized by new complexities that may ultimately end up dissolving the category of "Latin American" literature to give way to new constellations beyond geographical labels and literary genres. So even if the contemporary Latin American novel in world literature has already (perhaps irrevocably) lost much of its historic specificity, we still seem far away from Erich Auerbach's pessimistic stance that the globalization of literature might result in a "single literary culture, only a few literary languages, and perhaps even a single literary language. And herewith the notion of *Weltliteratur* would be at once realized and destroyed" (3).

Notes

1. See for example the contributions in Sánchez Prado, *América Latina*; Müller and Gras, and Guerrero et al., as well as the books by Siskind, Hoyos, and Locane. On alternative spatializations and temporalities of world literature within programmatic essays by Latin American writers, see Loy, "La (in)soportable levedad."

2. See Guerrero et al. 2021, *World Editors*.

3. The question of when the term "global" applies to transnational constellations (or does not) is seldom discussed and cannot be treated extensively here. However, it is remarkable that the labels "globality" and "world" seem to be employed particularly for relations between Latin American and Western literatures, while in the case of exchanges between "peripheral" areas alternative labels and concepts such as "Orientalism," "Global South" or "South-South" prevail (see for example Müller et al.; López-Calvo, *Alternative Orientalisms*; Klengel and Ortiz Wallner; Gasquet and Majstorovic).

4. "Necesario convencer de que la imagen ideal del pensamiento no está en la raíz que se soterra sino en la copa desplegada a los aires, y de que las fronteras del mapa no son las de la geografía del espíritu, y de que la patria intelectual no es el terruño" (Rodó).

5. "La tradición ha pesado menos, y esto explica la audacia" (Reyes 120).

6. On this point, see for example María Mudrovcic's article on the importance of the Center for Inter-American Relations "in producing what is now–rightly or wrongly, accurately or not–called 'Latin American literature' in the United States" (142); the circulation of Latin American literature with global communist and fascist contexts are discussed by Locane, "Literatura comunista," and Loy, "Fascist World Literature." For the relation between Revolution and the Novel in Latin America see De Castro.

7. On these generational struggles see for example Corral 99–199.

8. "Pronunciado desfase generacional entre el anacronismo de los unos, que siguen arrogándose una representatividad cada vez más cuestionada, y la dificultad de los otros, que buscan la manera de marcar su distancia y de construirse una identidad diferente" (Guerrero 153).

9. "Agresiva política de adquisición por parte de las empresas españolas" (Yúdice 651). On the radical changes in the global publishing industry after 1990 see the seminal studies by Schiffrin and Thompson.

10. "Una literatura latinoamericana producida en condiciones de precariedad material relativa que, no obstante o justamente por ello, favorecen el desarrollo de formas estéticas disidentes y alternativas" (Locane, *De la literatura latinoamericana* 48).

11. Ignacio López-Calvo aptly observes on the ongoing *ex negativo* significance of magical realism for new generations: "Although magical realism is no longer a major frame of reference for many contemporary Latin American authors, the fact that they consider it an influence to avoid is still significant" (López-Calvo xxiii).

12. For an overview of this generation see for example Corral, Birns, and De Castro.

13. "América Latina haya desaparecido como escenario o centro de interés, pero sí que empieza a ser percibida con un carácter posnacional, desprovisto de una identidad fija" (Volpi 176).

14. On these challenges see the transcription of two roundtables on Latin American and global book markets in Guerrero et al., *World Editors* 419–40.

Works Cited

Abad Faciolince, Héctor. *El olvido que seremos*. Alfaguara, 2005.

Alarcón, Daniel. *Lost City Radio*. Harper, 2007.

Auerbach, Erich. "Philology and 'Weltliteratur.'" *The Centennial Review*, vol. 13, no. 1, winter 1969, pp. 1–17.

Barbetta, María Cecilia. *Nachtleuchten*. Fischer, 2018.

Bazterrica, Agustina. *Cadaver exquisito*. Alfaguara, 2017.

Becerra, Eduardo. "Apuntes sobre políticas editoriales en (y sobre) América Latina en el marco de la literatura mundial: el caso de la narrativa en el cambio de siglo." *World Editors*, edited by Guerrero et al., De Gruyter, 2021, pp. 63–70.

Birns, Nicholas. "The Part about the Critics: The World Reception of Roberto Bolaño." *Critical Insights: Roberto Bolaño*, edited by Ignacio López-Calvo, Salem Press, 2015, pp. 50–64.

Birns, Nicholas, and Juan E. De Castro, editors. *Roberto Bolaño as World Literature*. Bloomsbury, 2017.

Bioy Casares, Adolfo. *La invención de Morel*. Losada, 1940.

Bolaño, Roberto. *Los detectives salvajes*. Anagrama, 1998.

Borges, Jorge Luis. "El escritor argentino y la tradición." *Jorge Luis Borges: Obras Completas I. (1923–1949)*, edited by Rolando Costa Picazo and Irma Zangara, Emecé, 2009, pp. 438–444.

Casanova, Pascale. *The World Republic of Letters*. Harvard UP, 2004.

Cheah, Pheng. *What Is a World? On Postcolonial Literature as World Literature*. Duke UP, 2016.

Corral, Wilfrido. *Discípulos y maestros 2.0.: novela hispanoamericana hoy*. Vervuert-Iberoamericana, 2019.

Corral, Wilfrido, Juan E. De Castro, and Nicholas Birns, editors. *The Contemporary Spanish-American Novel: Bolaño and After*. Bloomsbury, 2013.

Cozarinsky, Edgardo. *Lejos de dónde*. Tusquets, 2009.

Damrosch, David. *What Is World Literature?* Princeton UP, 2003.

De Castro, Juan E. *Writing Revolution in Latin America: From Martí to García Márquez to Bolaño*. Vanderbilt UP, 2019.

Deckard, Sharae. "Roberto Bolaño and the Remapping of World Literature". *Roberto Bolaño as World Literature*, edited by Burns and De Castro, Bloomsbury, 2017, pp. 203–21.

Díaz, Junot. *The Brief Wondrous Life of Oscar Wao*. Faber and Faber, 2007.

Echevarría, Ignacio. *Desvíos: un recorrido crítico por la reciente narrativa latinoamericana*. Universidad Diego Portales, 2007.

Echevarría, Ignacio. "Bolaño internacional: algunas reflexiones en torno al éxito internacional de Roberto Bolaño." *Estudios Públicos*, no. 130, 2013, pp. 175–202.

Eltit, Diamela. *Mano de obra*. Planeta, 2002.

English, James. *The Economy of Prestige. Prizes, Awards, and the Circulation of Cultural Value*. Harvard UP, 2005.

Enríquez, Mariana. *Nuestra parte de noche*. Anagrama, 2019.

Fernández, Nona. *Chilean Electric*. Alquimia, 2015.

Fuentes, Carlos. *La muerte de Artemio Cruz*. Fondo de Cultura Económica, 1962.

Fuguet, Alberto, and Sergio Gómez. "Presentación." *McOndo*, edited by Alberto Fuguet and Sergio Gómez, Mondadori, 1996, pp. 9–22.

Fuks, Julián. *A resistência*. Companhia das Letras, 2015.

Gallego Cuiñas, Ana. "Feminismo y literatura (argentina) mundial: Selva Almada, Mariana Enríquez y Samanta Schweblin." *Literatura latinoamericana mundial*, edited by Guerrero et al., De Gruyter, 2020, pp. 71–96.

Gallego Cuiñas, Ana. "Bibliodiversidad y contracultura material: un análisis cualitativo y cuantitativo de la edición independiente en lengua castellana." *World Editors*, edited by Guerrero et al., De Gruyter, 2021, pp. 71–94.

Gamboa, Santiago. *Hotel Pekín*. Seix Barral, 2008.

García Márquez, Gabriel. *Cien años de soledad*. Editorial Sudamericana, 1967.

Gasquet, Axel, and Gorica Majstorovic, editors. *Cultural and Literary Dialogues Between Asia and Latin America*. Palgrave, 2021.

Guerrero, Gustavo. *Paisajes en movimiento. Literatura y cambio cultural entre dos siglos*. Eterna Cadencia, 2018.

Guerrero, Gustavo, Jorge J. Locane, Benjamin Loy, and Gesine Müller, editors. *Literatura latinoamericana mundial. Dispositivos y deslindes*, De Gruyter, 2020.

Guerrero, Gustavo, Benjamin Loy, and Gesine Müller, editors. *World Editors: Dynamics of Global Publishing and the Latin American Case between the Archive and the Digital Age*. De Gruyter, 2021.

Halfon, Eduardo. *El boxeador polaco*. Pre-textos, 2008.

Hasbún, Rodrigo. *Los afectos*. Random House, 2015.

Herbert, Julián. *La casa del dolor ajeno*. Random House, 2015.

Herrera, Yuri. *Señales que precederán al fin del mundo*. Editorial Periférica, 2009.

Hernández, Claudia. *Roza, tumba, quema*. Laguna Libros, 2017.

Hoyos, Héctor. *Beyond Bolaño: The Global Latin American Novel*. Columbia UP, 2015.

Klengel, Susanne, and Alexandra Ortíz Wallner, editors. *Sur/South. Poetics and Politics of Thinking Latin America/India*. Vervuert-Iberoamericana, 2016.

Locane, Jorge J. *De la literatura latinoamericana a la literatura (latinoamericana) mundial. Condiciones materiales, procesos y actores*. De Gruyter, 2019.

Locane, Jorge J. "Literatura comunista mundial: Jorge Amado en la República Democrática Alemana y China." *World Editors*, edited by Guerrero et al., De Gruyter, 2021, pp. 191–208.

Logie, Ilse. "¿Escritores en la traducción y para la traducción? Dos ejemplos: Valeria Luiselli y Mario Bellatin." *Literatura latinoamericana mundial*, edited by Guerrero et al., De Gruyter, 2020, pp. 207–22.

López-Calvo, Ignacio. "On Magical Realism as an International Phenomenon in the Twenty-First Century." *Critical Insights: Magical Realism*, edited by Ignacio López-Calvo, Salem Press, 2014, pp. xvi–xxxi.

López-Calvo, Ignacio, editor. *Alternative Orientalisms in Latin America and Beyond*. Cambridge Scholars, 2007.

Loy, Benjamin. "La (in)soportable levedad de la tradición: hacia una lectura latinoamericana de la literatura mundial." *Inti: Revista de literatura hispánica*, vols. 85–86, 2017, pp. 36–52.

Loy, Benjamin. "Mocking World Literature and Canon Parodies in Roberto Bolaño's Fiction". *Roberto Bolaño as World Literature*, edited by Burns and De Castro, Bloomsbury, 2017, pp. 153–66.

Loy, Benjamin. "Fascist World Literature from Latin America: The Case of Miguel Serrano." *World Editors*, edited by Guerrero et al., De Gruyter, 2021, pp. 209–28.

Luiselli, Valeria. *Lost Children Archive*. Vintage, 2019.

Magnus, Ariel. *Un chino en bicicleta*. La otra orilla, 2007.

Marling, William. *Gatekeepers. The Emergence of World Literature and the 1960s.* Oxford UP, 2016.

Meruane, Lina. *Volverse Palestina.* Random House, 2014.

Moretti Franco. "Conjectures on World Literature." *Distant Reading,* edited by Franco Moretti, Verso, 2013, pp. 43–62.

Mudrovcic, María Eugenia. "Políticas culturales en los procesos de integración regional: el sector editorial en el Mercosur." *Revista Iberoamericana,* vol. LXVII, no. 197, 2001, pp. 755–66.

Müller, Gesine, and Dunia Gras Miravet, editors. *América Latina y la literatura mundial: mercado editorial, redes globales y la invención de un continente.* Iberoamericana-Vervuert, 2015.

Müller, Gesine, Jorge J. Locane, and Benjamin Loy, editors. *Re-mapping World Literature: Writing, Book Markets and Epistemologies between Latin America and the Global South.* De Gruyter, 2018.

Müller, Gesine, and Mariano Siskind, editors. *World Literature, Cosmopolitanism, Globality: Beyond, Against, Post, Otherwise.* De Gruyter, 2019.

Ojeda, Mónica. *Mandíbula.* Candaya, 2018.

Ortuño, Antonio. *La fila india.* Seix Barral, 2013.

Padilla, Ignacio. *Amphitryon.* Espasa-Calpe, 2000.

Pérez, Alberto Julián. "La enciclopedia poética de Rubén Darío." *Revista Iberoamericana,* vols. CXLVI–CXLVII, 1989, 329–38.

Pollack, Sarah. "Latin America Translated (Again): Roberto Bolaño's *The Savage Detectives* in the United States." *Comparative Literature,* vol. 61, no. 3, 2009, pp. 346–65.

Prieto, José Manuel. *Rex.* Anagrama, 2007.

Pron, Patricio. *El espiritú de mis padres sigue subiendo en la lluvia.* Random House, 2011.

Puenzo, Lucía. *Wakolda.* Emecé, 2011.

Rey Rosa, Rodrigo. *La orilla africana.* Seix Barral, 1999.

Reyes, Alfonso. "La inteligencia americana." *América en el pensamiento de Alfonso Reyes,* edited by José Luis Martínez, Fondo de Cultura Económica, 2012, pp. 119–29.

Rodó, José Enrique. "La nueva novela." *Cervantes virtual,* 2011. http://www.cervantesvirtual. com/obra-visor/la-novela-nueva/html/de690840-7a44-11e1-b1fb-00163ebf5e63_2.html

Rosendahl Thomsen, Mads. *Mapping World Literature: International Canonization and Transnational Literatures.* Continuum, 2008.

Rulfo, Juan. *Pedro Páramo.* Fondo de Cultura Económica, 1955.

Salazar, Claudia. *La sangre de la Aurora.* Malas Tierras, 2013.

Sánchez-Prado, Ignacio M. "'Hijos de Metapa': un recorrido conceptual de la literatura mundial (a manera de introducción)." *América Latina en la "literatura mundial,"* edited by Ignacio M. Sánchez Prado, Instituto Internacional de Literatura Iberoamericana, 2006, pp. 7–46.

Sánchez-Prado, Ignacio M. *Strategic Occidentalism: On Mexican Fiction, the Neoliberal Book Market, and the Question of World Literature.* Northwestern UP, 2018.

Sánchez-Prado, Ignacio M. "El efecto Luiselli: notas sobre la nueva literatura mexicana y la lengua inglesa." Guerrero et al., *World Editors,* De Gruyter, 2021, pp. 95–108.

Santana-Acuña, Álvaro. *Ascent to Glory: How One Hundred Years of Solitude Was Written and Became a Global Classic.* Columbia UP, 2020.

Schiffrin, André. *The Business of Books: How International Conglomerates Took Over Publishing and Changed the Way We Read.* Verso, 2000.

Schweblin, Samanta. *Distancia de rescate.* Random House, 2014.

Schweblin, Samanta. *Kentukis*. Random House, 2018.

Siskind, Mariano. "Magical Realism." *The Cambridge History of Postcolonial Literature*, edited by Ato Quayson, vol. 2, Cambridge UP, 2012, pp. 833–68.

Siskind, Mariano. *Cosmopolitan Desires. Global Modernity and World Literature in Latin America*. Northwestern UP, 2014.

Stavans, Ilan. "The Latin American Novel as International Merchandise." *Global Latin America*, edited by Matthew C. Gutmann and Jeffrey Lesser, U of California P, 2016, pp. 291–301.

Thompson, John B. *Merchants of Culture. The Publishing Business in the Twenty-First Century*. Plume, 2012.

Trabucco Zerán, Alia. *La resta*. Demipage, 2015.

Trelles Paz, Diego. *La procesión infinita*. Anagrama, 2017.

Vargas Llosa, Mario. *La casa verde*. Seix Barral, 1966.

Vásquez, Juan Gabriel. *El ruido de las cosas al caer*. Alfaguara, 2011.

Volpi, Jorge. *En busca de Klingsor*. Seix Barral, 1999.

Volpi, Jorge. *El insomnio de Bolivar. Cuatro consideraciones intempestivas sobre América Latina en el siglo XXI*. Debate, 2009.

Volpi, Jorge, and others. "Manifiesto Crack." *Revista de Cultura Lateral*, vol. 70, 2000. http://cir culolateral.com/tema/070manifiestocrack.htm

Walkowitz, Rebecca. *Born Translated: The Contemporary Novel in an Age of World Literature*. Columbia UP, 2015.

Yúdice, George. "La reconfiguración de políticas culturales y mercados culturales en los noventa y siglo XXI en América Latina." *Revista Iberoamericana*, vol. LXVII, no. 197, fall 2001, pp. 639–59.

Xilonen, Aura. *Campeón Gabacho*. Random House, 2015.

Zambra, Alejandro. *Formas de volver a casa*. Anagrama, 2011.

Index

Harmada (Hatoum), 287
Harman, Graham, 166
Haro, Guillermo, 190, 696
Haro, Paula, 694
Harss, Luis, 125
Hart, Stephen M., 468
Harwicz, Ariana, 166, 268, 798
Hasbún, Rodrigo, 165, 796
Haskalah movement, 335
Hassan, Ihab, 146, 148
Hassan, Waïl, 351–52, 354–55, 357, 359–60
Hasta no verte Jesús mío (Here's to You, Jesusa,
    Poniatowska), 132, 190, 406, 477, 689,
    693–97
Hatoum, Milton, 287–88, 357
Hau'ofa, Epeli, 781
La Havane (Havana, Merlin), 757
Havilio, Iosi, 167
Hayek, Friedrich, 638
Hay Festival, 170, 171, 173, 793
Hecho en Saturno (Made in Saturn, Indiana),
    707, 715–16
Hegel, G.W.F., 50, 740
Heker, Liliana, 271
Helena (Machado de Assis), 66
Helú, Antonio, 492
Hembros: asedios a lo Post Humano (Fe/males:
    Sieges of the Posthuman, Prado), 270
Hemingway, Ernest, 674
Henríquez Ureña, Pedro, 530–31
Herbert, Julián, 166, 174, 194, 796
Heredia, José-Maria de, 756
Herencia (Inheritance, Matto), 394–95
Heringer, Victor, 288
La hermana menor: un retrato de Silvina
    Ocampo (The Little Sister: A Portrait of
    Silvina Ocampo, Enríquez), 269
Hermana y sombra (Sister and Shadow,
    Verbitsky), 333
Hermano mestizo (Mestizo brother, Larreal),
    302
Hernández, Ángela, 233, 708
Hernández, Claudia, 213, 796
Hernández, Felisberto, 121n10
Hernández, Vladimir, 499
Hernández Catá, Alfonso, 419, 421
Hernández Luna, Juan, 496

Hernández Martínez, Maximiliano, 203
El héroe discreto (The Discreet Hero, Vargas
    Llosa), 645
La heroína mexicana (The Mexican Heroine), 34
Herrasti, Vicente, 793
Herrera, Priscila, 297
Herrera, Yuri, 166, 172, 194, 501, 716, 796
heterogeneity
    Arguedas and, 588
    Cornejo Polar and, 219–20, 231, 243, 535–38,
        588
    magical realism and, 459–60
    postmodernism and, 148
    Wayuu society and, 300
He visto la noche (I Have Seen the Night,
    Zapata Olivella), 228
Hielo Negro (Black Ice, Fernández), 497
Higa, Augusto, 370–71
Higgins, James, 477
La hija del adelantado (The Governor's
    Daughter, Milla), 201
La hija del campeón (The Champion's Daughter,
    Etcheves), 494
Hija del silencio (Daughter of Silence,
    Fingueret), 340
La hija de Marx (Marx's Daughter, Obligado),
    266
La hija única (Only Child, Nettel), 194
"El hijo de Andrés Aparicio" ("The Son of
    Andrés Aparicio," Fuentes), 625, 631
Hijo de hombre (Son of Man, Roa Bastos), 443
Hijo de ladrón (Thief's Son, Rojas), 263
El hijo judío (The Jewish Son, Guebel), 267, 338
H.I.J.O.S. (Hijos por la Identidad y la Justicia
    contra el Olvido y el Silencio, or Sons and
    Daughters for Identity and Justice against
    Forgetfulness and Silence), 482
Hijuelos, Oscar, 756, 763
Hilda Furacão (Hilda Hurricane: A Novel,
    Drummond), 287
Hills, Matt, 612
El hipogeo secreto (The Secret Crypt, Elizondo),
    153, 520–21
Hiratsuka, Lúcia, 368
Hirsch, Marianne, 450, 482
Hirsch, Maurice de, 330, 336
Hisho que te nazca (Nissán), 338–39